THE LONDON DIARIES OF WILLIAM NICOLSON, BISHOP OF CARLISLE
1702–1718

William Nicolson, bishop of Carlisle from 1702 to 1718 and later bishop of Derry and archbishop of Cashel, was in the tradition of great post-Revolution churchmen who were also first-rate scholars and active politicians—men of the stamp of Burnet, Wake, Atterbury, and Gibson. Unlike these famous contemporaries, however (Wake excepted), Nicolson for most of his career as a bishop kept a daily diary, and for many years an extremely detailed one. Of its London sections, covering thirteen of the bishop's fourteen visits to the capital from Carlisle and running to nearly 130,000 words, only a few fragments have ever been printed. Yet the diaries form a unique record of political, social, and intellectual activity in the metropolis during the reigns of Queen Anne and George I.

This definitive scholarly edition presents the complete surviving text of the London diaries, with extensive commentaries by the editors; through it emerges an invaluable picture of the extra-diocesan life of a man of manifold interests, avid curiosity, and tireless energy. Nicolson was on close terms with most of the dominant figures in the Whig party, with virtually all the leading Low Church divines, and with a wide circle of scholars, collectors, and *virtuosi*. Above all the early volumes of his diaries constitute easily the best private source extant for the debates and work of the House of Lords at a time when it was at the apogee of its prestige and political influence. Publication of the entire London diaries here greatly enriches the store of source material available in print for the study of England's Augustan age.

Clyve Jones is Assistant Librarian, Institute of Historical Research. Geoffrey Holmes is Professor of History, University of Lancaster.

Queen Anne in the House of Lords, by Peter Tillemeans.
(Reproduced by kind permission of Her Majesty the Queen.)

The London Diaries
of William Nicolson
Bishop of Carlisle
1702–1718

Edited by
Clyve Jones
and
Geoffrey Holmes

CLARENDON PRESS · OXFORD
1985

Oxford University Press, Walton Street, Oxford OX2 6DP
London New York Toronto
Delhi Bombay Calcutta Madras Karachi
Kuala Lumpur Singapore Hong Kong Tokyo
Nairobi Dar es Salaam Cape Town
Melbourne Auckland
and associated companies in
Beirut Berlin Ibadan Mexico City Nicosia

Oxford is a trade mark of Oxford University Press

Published in the United States
by Oxford University Press, New York

British Library Cataloguing in Publication Data
Nicolson, William
The London diaries of William Nicolson,
Bishop of Carlisle 1702–1718.
1. Nicolson, William   2. Church of England—
Bishops—Biography   3. Bishops—England—
Biography
I. Title   II. Jones, Clyve   III. Holmes,
Geoffrey
283'.092'4   BX5199.N/
ISBN 0–19–822404–4

Library of Congress Cataloging in Publication Data
Nicolson, William, 1655–1727.
The London diaries of William Nicolson, Bishop of
Carlisle, 1702–1718.
Includes index.
1. Nicolson, William, 1655–1727.   2. Great Britain—
Politics and government—1702–1714.   3. Great Britain—
Politics and government—1714–1727.   4. Great Britain.
Parliament. House of Lords—History—18th century.
5. London (England)—Intellectual life—18th century.
6. London (England)—Social life and customs—18th
century.   7. Politicians—Great Britain—Biography.
8. Church of England—England—Bishops—Biography.
I. Jones, Clyve, 1944-   .   II. Holmes, Geoffrey S.,
1928-   .   III. Title.
DA497.N5A34   1983   941.06'9'0924 [B]   83–5339
ISBN 0–19–822404–4

Typeset by Joshua Associates, Oxford
Printed in Great Britain
at the University Press, Oxford
by David Stanford
Printer to the University

For my mother
and to the memory of my
father

C. J.

The Twenty-Seven Foundation and the late Miss Isobel Thornley's Bequest to the University of London have generously supported the cost of publication of this volume.

Preface

William Nicolson (1655–1727), the one-time Fellow of Queen's College, Oxford, who became Archdeacon of Carlisle and later, successively, Bishop of Carlisle, Bishop of Derry, and Archbishop of Cashel, was more than just a prominent ecclesiastic of his day. He was an active figure in central and local politics, deeply committed during the last twenty years of his life to the Whig cause and to 'Revolution principles'. In addition, he was a much-respected scholar and antiquarian and a bibliographer of renown. That he should also have been the most assiduous and, over a prolonged period, the most informative diarist of the early eighteenth century is thus a singular stroke of good fortune. We can be virtually certain that during the whole period of Nicolson's tenancy of the see of Carlisle, from 1702 to 1718, he kept a daily record of his activities: in so doing he was following a habit begun spasmodically in the late 1670s and in 1690, and resumed in earnest in 1701. A substantial part of this record relates to time spent in London. In his sixteen years as an English bishop Nicolson attended thirteen parliamentary sessions. There were only two, those of 1703–4 and 1709–10, from which he absented himself entirely; although, because of the Jacobite rebellion and its northern aftermath, he did miss about two-thirds of the freakishly long session of March 1715–June 1716. This conscientious (and financially embarrassing) discharge of his duties as a member of the House of Lords involved residence in London for just over a quarter of his episcopal time—for some fifty months altogether. And for all but seven of these months his diaries have survived, either in his own original manuscript volumes with their green or ivory covers, or in the form of accurate nineteenth-century copies.

Into these London diaries the Bishop packed about 130,000 words of richly varied information about his life, work, and leisure in the capital of Queen Anne and George I. As a parliamentary diarist, especially up to 1706, while he was still captivated by the novelty of Westminster politics, he provides a unique day-to-day record of the proceedings and procedure of the late Stuart and early Georgian House of Lords. Indeed his are, amazingly, the only parliamentary diaries of any scale to survive for the reign of Queen Anne, and by the happiest of chances they coincide with a period when the talents and political importance of the Lords have rarely, if ever, been surpassed. But outside parliament, too, Nicolson was generally at pains to put on paper a record both of his personal involvement in, and his observation of, political activity in London during his many visits; above all when that activity impinged—as so often it did at this period—on Church affairs in general, and on his own, sometimes stormy, diocesan concerns in particular. While in London he met most of the leading Anglican divines of the day and heard many of the Church's most distinguished preachers. He also kept in close touch, not only by correspondence but also through the medium of his fellow-Cumbrians in London (including an endless stream of visitors), with the state of his diocese, as he did with all manner of local concerns. So, despite his absence from Convocation Nicolson's London diaries are a source of obvious value for studying the troubled history of the Church in the eighteenth century's first two decades. Not least, they represent from start to finish a seam of social documentation that is of the first importance. Convivial of spirit and robust of constitution, the Bishop crammed into his London winters and springs, in addition to a full programme of business, a social round that would have daunted the most insatiable clubman. Among many different circles of friends and acquaintances Nicolson moved with ease; but nowhere more spontaneously, nor with greater stimulus and delight to himself, than in the cultivated society of fellow scholars, antiquaries, and collectors, the *virtuosi* of Augustan London. In this elite, if sometimes eccentric, company the bishop was himself a leading light. Thus a highly distinctive, and too often neglected, part of the intellectual history of his day is vividly illuminated by scores of pages of his London diaries.

On each of these accounts individually the case for publishing the diaries is very strong. Collectively, it is overwhelming. And it is indeed ironic that although substantial extracts from the voluminous local sections of Nicolson's diary have been in print for many years only a tiny proportion of the London matter has ever been printed.

It was our original intention to make certain limited excisions from the text of the diaries in the interests of economy. The Delegates of the Oxford University Press, in the best traditions of that house, were apprehensive about the wisdom of this policy; and the further we progressed with our work the more convinced we became that their reservations were justified. What follows is, therefore, the entire surviving text of what William Nicolson wrote in his diaries during his thirteen visits to London between November 1702 and March 1718. Although only four of these visits are wholly recorded, and two more partly recorded, in the Bishop's own surviving manuscript volumes, the late nineteenth-century 'Ware transcripts' of the remaining, now untraceable, volumes maintain such high standards of accuracy (on this point see below, pp. 106–8) that we have felt fully justified in making use of them to produce a complete edition.

Acknowledgements

During our eleven years' work on this volume we have incurred many obligations which we readily and gratefully acknowledge. The Corporation of Carlisle, the Librarian and staff of Tullie House, Carlisle, and Professor Nicholas Mansergh, Master of St John's College, Cambridge, kindly gave us access to and permission to publish the manuscript volumes of Nicolson's diaries in their possession. The following private owners of manuscripts allowed us to consult and publish materials in their collections, and so contributed much to the enrichment of the editorial matter: the Duke of Atholl (Atholl MSS at Blair Atholl), the Duke of Beaufort (Beaufort MSS at Badminton), the Duke of Buccleuch (Drumlanrig MSS at Drumlanrig Castle), the Marquess of Downshire (Trumbull MSS at the Berkshire Record Office), Lord Binning (Mellerstain Papers at Mellerstain), Lady Ravensdale (Panshanger MSS at the Hertfordshire Record Office), Lady Anne Bentinck (Portland MSS at the British Library and Nottingham University Library), Sir John Clerk of Penicuik, Bt (Clerk of Penicuik Papers), Mrs O. R. Bagot (Levens Hall MSS), Mr George Howard (Castle Howard Archive), and the late Miss Olive Lloyd-Baker (Lloyd-Baker MSS at the Gloucester Record Office). The archivists, librarians, and staff of the following institutions greatly facilitated the use of the manuscripts and printed materials in their care: Bedfordshire Record Office; Berkshire Record Office; Bodleian Library; Borthwick Institute, York; British Library; Cambridge County Record Office at Huntingdon; Cambridge University Library; Cheshire Record Office; Christ Church Library, Oxford; Church Commissioners; Codrington Library, Oxford; Corporation of London Record Office; Corpus Christi College, Cambridge; Cumbria County Record Office at Carlisle and Kendal; Dean and Chapter Library, Carlisle; Devon Record Office; Fitzwilliam Museum, Cambridge; Gloucestershire Record Office; Guildhall Library, London; Hampshire Record Office; Hereford Record Office; Hertfordshire Record Office; History of Parliament Trust; House of Lords Record Office; Huntington Library, California; Institute of Historical Research, London; Kent County Archives Office; Lambeth Palace Library; Leicestershire Record Office; London University Library; Public Record Office; National Library of Ireland; National Library of Scotland; National Library of Wales; National Register of Archives (Scotland); Northamptonshire Record Office; Northumberland Record Office; Nottingham University Library; Queen's College,

ACKNOWLEDGEMENTS

Oxford; St Andrews University Library; Scottish Record Office; Staffordshire Record Office; Surrey Record Office; Trinity College, Dublin; Warwick County Record Office; Westminster Abbey Muniments Room and Library; Westminster City Library; Worcester Record Office; and York Minster Library.

The following individuals have given generously of their expert knowledge to help illuminate the many recondite areas to be found in Nicolson's diaries: Dr John Beckett, Dr Eveline Cruickshanks, Dr D. J. Dickson, Professor Elizabeth Foster, Mr Stephen Green, Dr Diana Greenway, Mr G. Milwyn Griffiths, Dr David Hayton, Dr Hans-Christoph Junge, Dr John Kent, Sir Oliver Millar, Mr William O'Sullivan, Dr R. Page, Mr John Sainty, Mr John Sims, Mr H. J. R. Wing, Dr Ian Wood, and Mrs Susan Youngs. Our greatest debt of gratitude is owed to Professor Joseph Levine whose far-ranging knowlege of the history of eighteenth-century antiquarianism and the lives of the *virtuosi*, among whom Nicolson spent so much of his time, was cheerfully and unstintingly put at our disposal. His contribution to this edition is second only to that of the editors and pp. 11–17 of the Introduction are his work. Generous grants from The Twenty-Seven Foundation and the University of London Central Research Fund Committee greatly helped to ease the financial burden of the research and the preparation of the typescript. Thanks are due to our typists Mrs P. Hepburn and Mrs K. R. White who gallantly coped with what was at times an exceedingly messy typescript, and to Mr Alasdair Hawkyard who helped to produce the index. Finally, we wish to thank our two respective families who throughout the prolonged gestation of this edition gave much-needed encouragement. Ella Holmes actively engaged in the work as transcriber and secretary, while Ernest and Constance Jones during these long years continued (though not without the occasional falter) to believe that their son would eventually finish the project.

London and
Burton-in-Lonsdale

C.J.
G.S.H.

Contents

xiii

CONTENTS

Illustrations

Tables

Abbreviations

Acts Parl. Scot.	*The Acts of the Parliament of Scotland* (12 vols., Edinburgh, 1814–75).
Add.	Additional.
Addison Letters	*The Letters of Joseph Addison* (ed. W. Graham, Oxford, 1941).
Armorial	R. S. Boumphrey, C. R. Huddleston, and J. Hughes, *An Armorial for Westmorland and Lonsdale* (Cumberland & Westmorland Antiquarian & Archaeological Society, Extra Series xxi [1975]).
Atterbury Epist. Corr.	*The Epistolary Correspondence, Visitation Charges, Speeches, and Miscellanies of Francis Atterbury* [by J. Nichols] (5 vols., 1783–90).
Bennett, *Tory Crisis*	G. V. Bennett, *The Tory Crisis in Church and State, 1688–1730. The Career of Francis Atterbury, Bishop of Rochester* (Oxford, 1975).
Bennett, *White Kennett*	G. V. Bennett, *White Kennett, 1660–1728, Bishop of Peterborough* (1957).
BIHR	*Bulletin of the Institute of Historical Research.*
BL	British Library.
Bodl.	Bodleian Library.
Burnet, *History*	G. Burnet, *A History of My Own Time* [ed. M. J. Routh] (6 vols., Oxford, 1833).
Chamberlayne, *Present State*	E. Chamberlayne, *Angliae Notitia, or the Present State of England* [up to 1707], and J. Chamberlayne, *Magnae Britanniae Notitia, or the Present State of Great Britain* [from 1708].
CJ	*Journals of the House of Commons.*
Coxe, *Marlborough*	W. Coxe, *Memoirs of John, Duke of Marlborough, with his Original Correspondence* (ed. J. Wade, 3 vols., Bohn edn., 1847–8).
CSPD	*Calendar of State Papers Domestic.*
CTB	*Calendar of Treasury Books.*
Cumberland Families	C. R. Hudleston and R. S. Boumphrey, *Cumberland Families and Heraldry* (Cumberland & Westmorland Antiquarian & Archaeological Society, Extra Series xxiii [1978]).
CW	*Transactions of the Cumberland & Westmorland Antiquarian & Archaeological Society.*

Dalton	*English Army Lists and Commission Registers, 1661–1714* (ed. C. Dalton, 6 vols., 1892-1904).
Dalton, *George I*	C. Dalton, *George the First's Army, 1714-1727* (2 vols., 1910-12).
Defoe, *Tour*	D. Defoe, *A Tour through England and Wales* (2 vols., Everyman edn., 1928).
Diary	Nicolson's MS Diaries, Tullie House Library, Carlisle.
Diary of Earl Cowper	*The Private Diary of William, First Earl Cowper, 1705-1714* (ed. E. C. Hawtrey, Roxburghe Club, Eton, 1833).
DNB	*Dictionary of National Biography.*
EcHR	*Economic History Review.*
EHR	*English Historical Review.*
Ferguson, *Cumberland and Westmorland MP's*	R. S. Ferguson, *Cumberland and Westmorland MP's from the Restoration to the Reform Bill of 1867* (Carlisle, 1871).
GEC *Barts.*	*The Complete Baronetage* (ed. G. E. C[okayne], 5 vols., Exeter, 19 .
GEC *Peerage*	G. E. C[okayne], ... *...lete Peerage* (ed. V. Gibbs, 13 vols., 2nd edn., 1910-59).
Hearne, *Collections*	*Remarks and Collections of Thomas Hearne* (11 vols., Oxford, 1885-1907).
HJ	*Historical Journal.*
HLRO	House of Lords Record Office.
HMC	Historical Manuscripts Commission.
HMC *Lords MSS*	Historical Manuscripts Commission, *Manuscripts of the House of Lords,* New Series (12 vols., 1900-77).
Holmes, *British Politics*	G. Holmes, *British Politics in the Age of Anne* (1967).
Holmes, *Sacheverell*	G. Holmes, *The Trial of Doctor Sacheverell* (1973).
Hopkinson	R. Hopkinson, 'Parliamentary Elections in Westmorland and Cumberland in the late 17th and early 18th Centuries' (unpublished Newcastle Ph.D., 1973).
James	F. G. James, *North Country Bishop: A Biography of William Nicolson* (New Haven, 1956).
Jerviswood Correspondence	*Correspondence of George Baillie of Jerviswood* (Bannatyne Club, Edinburgh, 1842).
Journal to Stella	J. Swift, *Journal to Stella* (ed. H. Williams, 2 vols., Oxford, 1974).
Lathbury, *Convocation*	T. Lathbury, *A History of the Convocation of the Church of England* (1842).

LJ	*Journals of the House of Lords.*
Luttrell	N. Luttrell, *A Brief Historical Relation of State Affairs* (6 vols., Oxford, 1857).
Marlborough–Godolphin Corr.	*The Marlborough-Godolphin Correspondence* (ed. H. L. Snyder, 3 vols., Oxford, 1975).
Musgrave, *Obituary*	W. Musgrave, *Obituary prior to 1800* (ed. G. J. Armytage, Harleian Society, 6 vols., 1899–1901).
N.	Nicolson.
N & Q	*Notes and Queries.*
Nicolson and Burn	J. Nicolson and R. Burn, *The History and Antiquities of the Counties of Westmorland and Cumberland* (2 vols., 1777).
Nicolson Epist. Corr.	*Letters on Various Subjects, Literary, Political and Ecclesiastical, to and from W. Nicolson* (ed. J. Nicols, 2 vols., 1809).
Nicolson, *Miscellany*	W. Nicolson, *Miscellany Accounts of the Diocese of Carlisle* (ed. R. S. Ferguson, Cumberland & Westmorland Antiquarian & Archaeological Society, Extra Series i [Carlisle, 1877]).
NLS	National Library of Scotland.
NLW	National Library of Wales.
Parl. Hist.	W. Cobbett, *The Parliamentary History of England* (36 vols., 1806–20).
PRO	Public Record Office.
RO	Record Office.
Rogers, *Protests*	J. E. T. Rogers, *A Complete Collection of the Protests of the Lords* (3 vols., Oxford, 1875).
Sedgwick	*The House of Commons, 1715–1754* (ed. R. Sedgwick, 2 vols., 1970).
SHR	*Scottish Historical Review.*
Speculum Dioeceseos Linc.	*Speculum Dioeceseos Lincolniensis sub Episcopis Gul. Wake et Edm. Gibson, A.D. 1705-1723,* pt. i, Archdeaconries of Lincoln and Stow (ed. R. E. G. Cole, Lincoln Record Society, iv [1913]).
SRO	Scottish Record Office.
Statutes of the Realm	*The Statutes of the Realm* (10 vols., 1810–28).
Swift Corr.	*The Correspondence of Jonathan Swift* (ed. H. Williams, 5 vols., Oxford, 1963).
Sykes, *Gibson*	N. Sykes, *Edmund Gibson, Bishop of London, 1669-1748* (1926).

ABBREVIATIONS

Sykes, *Wake*	N. Sykes, *William Wake, Archbishop of Canterbury, 1657–1737* (2 vols., Cambridge, 1957).
TCD	Trinity College, Dublin.
Thoresby, *Letters*	*Letters of Eminent Men, Addressed to Ralph Thoresby, FRS* (2 vols., 1832).
Thoresby, *Diary*	*The Diary of Ralph Thoresby, FRS, Author of the Topography of Leeds (1677–1724)* (ed. J. Hunter, 2 vols., 1830).
Trevelyan, *Queen Anne*	G. M. Trevelyan, *England under Queen Anne* (3 vols., 1930–4).
TRHS	*Transactions of the Royal Historical Society.*
UL	University Library.
ULC	University Library, Cambridge.
Vernon Corr.	*Letters Illustrative of the Reign of William III from 1696 to 1708. Addressed to the Duke of Shrewsbury by James Vernon, Esq., Secretary of State* (ed. G. P. R. James, 3 vols., 1841).
Ware transcripts	Transcripts of Nicolson's MS diaries made under the supervision of Mrs H. Ware, now in Tullie House Library, Carlisle.
Wentworth Papers	*The Wentworth Papers, 1705–1739* (ed. J. J. Cartwright, 1883).

Editorial Note

The guiding principle of this edition has been to preserve the original, while presenting a text that makes the diaries convenient to the reader and intelligible without frequent recourse to the footnotes. The following rules have therefore been adopted.

Spelling. The original spelling has been preserved. If Nicolson's spelling of proper names differs from the modern one, the latter has been supplied in square brackets when the name first occurs in the text.

Punctuation. The original has been retained, except where facility of reading and understanding required some addition or correction to conform with modern usage. Nicolson's use of the hyphen in proper names has been retained (e.g. the Black-Swan).

Contractions. All Nicolson's standard contractions (including ampersands, but excepting those such as Mr, Dr, &c. for etc.) have been expanded without the use of square brackets, e.g. wch becomes which, yt becomes that, AB becomes Archbishop, D. of Devonshire becomes Duke of Devonshire. Square brackets have, however, been used for the expansion of all proper names, e.g. D. Devon becomes Duke [of] Devon[shire], D.K. becomes Dean K[ennett]. Christian name initials have been expanded in square brackets on the first occurrence only, e.g. 'Sir C[hristopher] M[usgrave]' thereafter 'Sir C. M[usgrave]'. Nicolson frequently employed an apostrophe in place of an *e* in forming plurals and past participles. These have been changed to an *e*.

Capitalisation. The original has been followed, except that proper nouns and words beginning new sentences have been capitalised.

Paragraphs. Nicolson's use of paragraphs has been generally, though not invariably, retained. Nicolson also used long dashes to indicate a natural break in the sense. Some of these have been converted into paragraphs.

Errors in text. Minor ones have been silently corrected, while others have been indicated in the notes by the abbreviation Repl., for replaced.

Underlining. Nicolson invariably underlined proper nouns, direct quotations, and titles of books, pamphlets, etc. In this edition italics have been used only for quotations, titles of books, names of taverns, and the words *Content* and *Not Content* in the recording of a division in the House of Lords.

Square brackets. All editorial insertions are in square brackets. Persons identified by Nicolson only by their official title have been named in square brackets the first time they appear in each parliamentary session, e.g. 'Archbishop of Canterbury [Wake]'. However, Nicolson himself occasionally used square brackets to enclose material in the text. These have been retained with a note indicating that they are 'Nicolson's brackets' or 'Brackets in MS'.

Note on dates. All dates are given in the Old Style of the Julian Calendar, but it is assumed that each new year begins on 1 January. Both Old and New Style dates are given for the occasional reference to documents written from the Continent or by Continental envoys or agents in London.

Place of publication. London is the place of publication unless otherwise stated.

Introduction

The London Life and Circles of William Nicolson (1655–1727)

EARLY LIFE AND CAREER, 1655–1702

When William Nicolson was nominated to the diocese of Carlisle on 8 May 1702 he was following a trend, set by his predecessors, for the northern marcher see to be occupied by local men. This tradition of native bishops,[1] perhaps unique among English bishoprics, is largely explained by the diocese's geographical position adjacent to Scotland with the consequent need for a strong influential bishop: within the society of the far north-west, with its highly distinctive brand of provincialism, a man with local connections was best able to exert such influence; Nicolson's local background told heavily with the Musgrave family, who with the Lowthers controlled the nerve centre of political power in the two border counties of Cumberland and Westmorland, and it was the Musgraves who were largely responsible for gaining the diocese for Nicolson.[2]

Although born and bred in Cumberland, the eldest son of Joseph Nicolson, Rector of Plumbland, Cumberland, Nicolson was no provincial when he succeeded to the bishop's mitre. Having been educated at a local school, he went up to Queen's College, Oxford (the college for Cumbrian scholars previously attended by his father), graduating BA in 1676 at the age of twenty-one and MA in 1679. While occupying a fellowship at Queen's from 1679 to 1682 Nicolson quickly established a reputation as a leading Anglo-Saxon scholar, and came under the patronage of another Cumbrian, the then Secretary of State, Sir Joseph Williamson. Williamson sent Nicolson to Leipzig in 1678, where the future bishop learnt German, an asset which was to stand him in some stead thirty-six years later on the accession of George I.

While at Oxford, besides displaying great intellectual industry and curiosity (characteristics which, the diary amply illustrates, remained with him throughout his mature years), Nicolson acquired the reputation 'of a drinking fellow and boon companion'.[3] This

---

[1] Between 1598 and 1747 the diocese was occupied by native bishops for 88 years. James, p. 3. This brief biographical introduction is largely based on James, chapters 1–4 and on the *DNB*.

[2] The only other serious candidate for the see, the incumbent dean, William Grahme, also came from a local family.

[3] Hearne, *Collections*, i. 187.

love of good company and good ale Nicolson never lost, as frequent trips to *The Dog* and other London taverns testify.

Though carrying on his learned interests and publications,[4] Nicolson's Oxford career was terminated by his acceptance of the vicarage of Torpenhow, Cumberland, in 1681 (which he held until he exchanged it with his brother-in-law in 1699 for the living of Addingham, Cumberland). In 1682 Nicolson was appointed Archdeacon of Carlisle (the only archdeaconry in the diocese) and to the rectory of Great Salkeld. He eventually became Bishop Smith's right-hand man, and as his diocesan grew more infirm and Dean William Grahme's sojourns in London grew longer, Nicolson found himself effectively running the diocese.

His political interests, always strong and at this stage Tory and committed to the Musgraves, found an outlet in the parliamentary elections in the two north-western counties. Always an enthusiast for everything he did, Nicolson trod on many toes, and at one point, it was rumoured, he came near to being arrested for treasonable involvement with the Grahme family.[5]

By the time of Bishop Smith's death in 1702, however, Nicolson had sufficiently established his position in north-western society to hope for promotion to the deanery of Carlisle, fully expecting Dean Grahme to succeed as bishop. In the event—and despite his later protests and calumny aimed at Nicolson—Grahme appears to have refused the bishopric on financial grounds.[6] Sir Christopher Musgrave with the aid of Nicolson's friend, Archbishop Sharp of York,[7] was able to ensure that Queen Anne's first episcopal appointment went to the 'Northern Bear', as Thomas Hearne, the Oxford antiquary, with some justification dubbed the Archdeacon of Carlisle. William Nicolson was consecrated at Lambeth on 14 June 1702, where another friend, Edmund Gibson, later Bishop of Lincoln and London, preached the sermon.

The parliamentary duties of an early-eighteenth-century bishop were linked in many cases with a firm sense of party responsibility. Vitally important in this respect was the acrimonious 'Convocation Controversy' of 1697–1701 and the turbulent first session of the re-called Convocation of Canterbury in 1701, which completed the schism of the post-Revolutionary Church into 'High' and 'Low' parties and made inescapable the fusion of these parties with the Tory and Whig parties in the State. Although Nicolson, as the holder of one of

---

[4] See below pp. 11–17, 'Nicolson as a Virtuoso'.

[5] See HMC *10th Report, Appendix iv* [Bagot MSS], pp. 332–6.

[6] See below p. 55.

[7] See the correspondence between them before 1702 in Gloucestershire RO Lloyd-Baker (Sharp) MSS.

the four English bishoprics within the Province of York,[8] was spared direct involvement in the Convocation battles of 1702 to 1717, he proved himself from the start a dedicated parliamentarian. During his tenure of Carlisle a total of more than four years out of slightly less than sixteen were given over to his political duties, and winter after winter (in later years it was the springs and summers) found him installed in lodgings convenient for the House of Lords, usually in the Old Palace Yard, Westminster, or in Manchester Court. How, therefore, did he spend his time in London, and in what circles did he move?

NICOLSON'S LONDON CIRCLES

William Nicolson was a vigorous, impulsive, and gregarious man of strong interests and commitments. Though a fine scholar he was the very reverse of the scholar-recluse, and his innate sociability, combined with powerful family, local, religious, and political loyalties—and not least with his consuming passion for the history and relics of the past—made his social life in London a whirl of activity in four (sometimes overlapping) circles. Regularly and, it would seem with equal facility, he moved among northerners (notably Cumbrians and Scots) and his own numerous kin, among the leading antiquaries of the day, among divines, and among peers and politicians.

Northerners and Relatives

Local patriotism was far stronger in the early eighteenth century than it is today. A man of any standing from Nicolson's own 'country', that is from Cumberland or Westmorland, could naturally expect when in London to have some association with a prelate who was both a Cumbrian born and bred himself and, as the diocesan of Carlisle, *ipso facto* one of the 'great men' of the north-west. Clannishness was by no means the preserve of the north-westerner. There are many other instances of similar groups from other parts of Britain preserving their local identity in the metropolis; indeed some of them, particularly those embracing peers and politicians, were formally organised into clubs, which tended to appropriate particular London taverns.[9] The sense of common identity experienced by men from the same county or region was one of the few bridges which by Anne's reign could still span the social as well

---

[8] The other three were Chester, Durham, and York. While the bishopric of Sodor and Man was technically part of the Province of York its occupation did not carry with it membership of the House of Lords.

[9] See, for example, Holmes, *British Politics*, p. 301 for the Suffolk Club and Cornwall, and J. H. Plumb, *The Growth of Political Stability in England 1675-1725* (1967), p. 33 and n. 2 for Herefordshire, Cornwall, and Lancashire.

as the political chasm between Whig and Tory; and we can see this reflected in bipartisan action on local matters in parliament.[10]

It is hardly surprising, therefore, to find evidence in abundance throughout Nicolson's London diaries of the strength of these common local interests or to find the bishop himself, almost from the start of his parliamentary career, very close to the heart of this social web. We shall see later,[11] in examining Nicolson's circle of aristocratic friends, that whereas his social contacts with Lords Carlisle, Wharton, and the 2nd Viscount Lonsdale—all prominent landowners in the north-west—were soon cemented by shared political views, his friendship with the Earl of Thanet, the main Tory landowner in Westmorland (albeit an absentee), survived for some five years their political disagreements. Many of Nicolson's closest social contacts among the divines and members of the House of Commons also had north-western backgrounds or connections.

A Cumbrian did not have to be a peer, a politician, or a divine, however, to find a welcome in the bishop's London lodgings, to sup with him at a tavern or at his brother's house in Salisbury Court, or to be invited to the 'Club of Northern friends, at the *Globe*' patronised by Philip Tullie and the other brothers of Nicolson's Chancellor and Vice-Dean, Thomas Tullie.[12] On 13 December 1705 Major John Orfeur, later to be an unsuccessful parliamentary candidate for Cockermouth, was one of Nicolson's early morning visitors, and being 'newly returned from Barcelona [he gave the bishop] a sorry Account of the Rashness, &c. of the Earl of Peterborough'. He had been preceded at the bishop's lodgings by Colonel Eliakim Studholme, also later to be an unsuccessful parliamentary candidate, this time for Carlisle. Earlier in the session Studholme and Nicolson had spent a convivial evening discussing book-collecting while Orfeur, later in December 1705, kept Nicolson so long one morning that he had to be sent for by the House to read prayers.[13] Lesser fry were not turned away, even when they interrupted the bishop's evening chore of letter writing, as did his tenant and neighbour from Rose, Robert Thomlinson.[14]

Many of Nicolson's visitors were not of a purely social character. As a lord of parliament and a frequenter of the circles in which politicians and government officers moved, Nicolson was bound to be sought out by the needy and greedy as a channel for office, money or other forms of patronage. Until he became Lord Almoner

[10] For examples see Holmes, *British Politics*, p. 46 n.; *The Parliamentary Diary of Narcissus Luttrell 1691–1693*, ed. H. Horwitz (Oxford, 1972) on the Land Tax and other fiscal debates.   [11] Below pp. 21–4.

[12] Nicolson spent a convivial evening with this Club in Dec. 1705.

[13] See below pp. 296, 328, 333.   [14] See below p. 361 and also p. 301.

in 1716, the bishop had little or no patronage of his own outside his diocese. As Almoner Nicolson did dispense royal charity, but as the funds were limited he could do very little, and his cherished aim to found lectureships in Anglo-Saxon at Oxford and Cambridge failed. He did, however, manage to assist a few young scholars, both before and after becoming Almoner.[15]

The diary reveals that a steady stream of patronage seekers found their way to his lodgings. Many were men and women from Cumberland and Westmorland, for the simple reason that the bishop was one of but a handful of north-western peers and MPs in London with the key to the doors of the powerful.[16] A not untypical day was New Year's Day 1706 when two of Nicolson's six visitors at his levee were 'private petitioners'. The case of the murdered customs official, William Churdon, is a good example of Nicolson soliciting patronage for a local suppliant. Churdon's widow seems to have applied to Nicolson for help in getting a pension, and the bishop went straight to the top, successfully presenting the case to Lord Treasurer Godolphin.[17]

Many of the 'beggars', as Nicolson often called his visitors in search of patronage, belonged to Nicolson's own family. Fetherston Nicolson, son of the bishop's cousin James Nicolson, an attorney of Penrith, obtained a post in the customs in 1706 and advancement in 1711 through Nicolson's offices.[18] Other examples are fairly numerous, yet the bishop could hardly be accused of abusing his position to push the interests of his family. Of the bishop's 'extended family', as defined by his loose use of the term 'cousin', only a small proportion gained positions, advancement, or pensions through his efforts. Not until he had at his disposal the resources of the rich see of Derry, to which he was translated in 1718, does Nicolson seem to have laid himself open to a direct charge of nepotism.[19] According to Archbishop King of Dublin, by this time not on good terms with Nicolson, 'the Bishop of Derry since his translation to that Sea has given about 2000 *ll* in benefices to his English friends and relations'.[20] In London, however, he was more restrained in his use

[15] For the personal patronage dispensed by Nicolson see James, pp. 225-7. For Nicolson as Lord Almoner see below pp. 58-9.

[16] Nicolson was sometimes merely used as an introduction to a particular peer rather than to government patronage, e.g. below pp. 549-50. This seems to be the only case recorded in the diary of Nicolson being rewarded for his services by a successful supplicant—with six bottles of sack.

[17] Below pp. 230, 254, 345.   [18] See below pp. 220-1, 530.

[19] See James, p. 266. He was, however, accused by Hugh Todd of favouring his family at Carlisle. See York Minster Library, Hailstone Collection QQ 2.7., p. 29: Todd's 'Representation of the Grievances of the Diocese of Carlisle', 16 Oct. 1706.

[20] National Library of Ireland MS 2056 (unfoliated): King to Southwell, 29 Dec. 1725.

of patronage, striving on behalf of a worthy case, such as 'Admiral Nicols',[21] but sometimes refusing to see a begging visitor. Occasionally the almost incessant stream to his door seemed to overwhelm him and the relief of someone calling on 'a pure visit' is evident in the diary.

The heart of Bishop Nicolson's social life in London was undoubtedly his immediate family, which, besides his children who were infrequently to be found in the capital, consisted of his younger brother and sister, Joseph and Frances (his wife, Elizabeth, never visited London while Nicolson was bishop). Joseph Nicolson was an apothecary, who became Master of the Apothecaries' Society in 1721 and died in 1724, and lived at Salisbury Court off Fleet Street. Several times a week, on average, the bishop was to be found in the evenings at his brother's house. More infrequently Joseph and his family dined with the bishop, or they joined him in one of his sightseeing tours of the capital, possibly being joined by one of the bishop's numerous 'cousins'.[22] Frances Nicolson, the bishop's sister, called 'Sister Rothery' in the diary since her marriage to Edward Rothery, apparently lived in Dorset and looked after the children of the Hon. Henry Thynne, son of Viscount Weymouth. Thynne, as MP for Weymouth and Melcombe Regis from 1702 until his death in December 1708, must have had long periods of residence in London as did Bishop Nicolson. He obviously brought his children with him for Sister Rothery, sometimes together with her son Joseph and daughter Mary ('Mal'), is to be found visiting her brother on many occasions.[23]

Beyond his immediate family, the bishop was often socially involved with his enormous 'extended family'. His use of the term 'cousin' was so all-embracing, as was common, as to catch within its net any distant relation of his father's or his mother's family. The latter, the Briscoes of Crofton, Cumberland, appear many times in the diary. The Briscoes had married into many other local families besides the Nicolsons, and thus brought influential local men into the bishop's large family orbit: men such as William Gilpin, principal legal adviser to the Lowthers of Whitehaven, and George Langstaff, Deputy Chapter Clerk and Receiver and Treasurer to Carlisle Chapter. Other men influential at a local or national level who were related to the bishop included the brothers Thomas and William Pearson. Thomas was Rector of Nether Denton, Cumberland, and Principal of St Edmund's Hall, Oxford, while William was

---

[21] See below pp. 369, 373, 384, and Appendix D, below p. 711.
[22] See p. 9 for a genealogical table of Nicolson's immediate family.
[23] For Sister Rothery see *CW* iii (1903), 2 n.

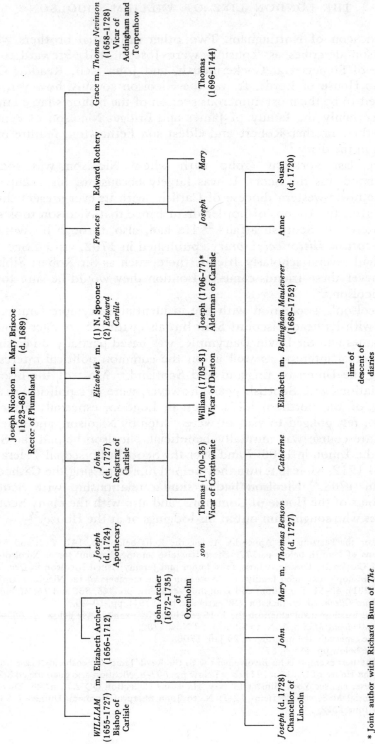

Bishop Nicolson's Immediate Family

Joseph Nicolson m. Mary Briscoe
(1623–86)   (d. 1689)
Rector of Plumbland

WILLIAM m. Elizabeth Archer
(1655–1727)   (1656–1712)
Bishop of
Carlisle

Joseph (d. 1724) Apothecary

John (d. 1727) Registrar of Carlisle

Elizabeth m. (1) N. Spooner
(2) Edward Cartile

Frances m. Edward Rothery

Grace m. *Thomas Nevinson*
(1658–1728)
Vicar of Addingham and
Torpenhow

Thomas
(1696–1744)

John Archer
(1672–1735)
of Oxenholm

son

Thomas (1700–35)
Vicar of Crosthwaite

William (1703–31)
Vicar of Dalston

Joseph (1706–77)*
Alderman of Carlisle

Joseph

Mary

Anne

Susan
(d. 1720)

Joseph (d. 1728)
Chancellor of
Lincoln

John

Mary m. *Thomas Benson*
(d. 1727)

Catherine

Elizabeth m. *Bellingham Mauleverer*
(1689–1752)

line of
descent of
diaries

* Joint author with Richard Burn of *The History and Antiquities of the Counties of Westmorland and Cumberland*.

Names in italic are mentioned in the diaries.

Archdeacon of Nottingham. Two other influential brothers whom Nicolson describes as 'cousins' were Joseph Relf, Steward to the Duke of Somerset at Cockermouth, and John Relf, Reading Clerk to the House of Lords. It was the Nicolson cousins, however, who seemed to be the most numerous section of the bishop's large family, and certainly the family of James and Bridget Nicolson of Penrith, with their brother Robert and eldest son Fetherston, feature many times in the diary.[24]

The last northern group with whom Nicolson was socially associated was the Scots. It was largely because of his occupation of the north-western diocese of Carlisle, with its ever present threat, even after the Union, of border disturbance that Nicolson took such an interest in Scottish affairs.[25] He had, also, through his work on the *Scottish Historical Library*, published in 1702, visited Scotland and had several scholarly friends there, such as Sir Robert Sibbald. Whenever these friends came to London they would be sure to call on Nicolson.[26]

Nicolson's association with the influential Dalrymple family, not only with its head Viscount Stair but also with the younger brothers Sir James and Sir David Dalrymple, was based partially on common intellectual interests as well as on the common political interest of seeing the Union of England and Scotland.[27] Most of the bishop's associations with Scottish peers, however, were of a political nature. Many of the northern lords when in London, especially after the Union, felt obliged to visit or were visited by Nicolson, and much of this intercourse was mutually beneficial. Nicolson helped the Scots over the Union in 1706–7 and over the Scottish Episcopal Toleration Bill of 1712, while in return they helped him in passing the Cathedrals Bill in 1708.[28] Nicolson had a similar relationship with Scottish members of the House of Commons, and also with the many Scottish divines who sought him out at his lodgings or at the House.[29]

[24] For the Pearsons see Appendix A; for the Relfs below pp. 147, 240; and for the Nicolsons of Penrith below p. 172. There was also another 'cousin' James Nicolson, this time of Castlegate, Carlisle, whose sons James and Jeremy visited Nicolson in Dec. 1710. For the bishop's 'extended family' see 'Notes on some members of the Nicolson family' in *CW* i (1901), 48–51. For Gilpin and Langstaff see below pp. 345, 366 and *The Memoirs of Dr Richard Gilpin*, ed. W. Jackson (*CW* extra ser. ii [1879]), pp. 10–40.

[25] For his close involvement in the 1715 rebellion, for example, see below pp. 635–6.

[26] HMC *Laing MSS* ii, 5: N. to Sibbald, 28 Nov. 1702.

[27] See especially the meeting on 29 Jan. 1703.

[28] See below pp. 453–5, 572–5.

[29] The best example is his involvement with the Revd. James Greenshields's case brought before the House of Lords in 1711. See below pp. 507–8. Nicolson also encouraged Scots in his diocese, e.g. see York Minster Library, Hailstone Collection QQ 2.7., p. 28; Buccleuch (Drumlanrig) MSS, vol. ci, items 72–7: N. to John Sharp of Hodham, Dumfries, 23 Oct. 1703–5 June 1712.

Nicolson as a Virtuoso
by Joseph M. Levine

When in 1694 Ralph Thoresby came at last from Leeds to Salkeld to visit his friend William Nicolson, Archdeacon of Carlisle, he was entranced. Although the two men had corresponded for several years, they had somehow never met. Now, after the usual pleasantries, they retired from the company to look at Nicolson's museum. Thoresby was delighted with his friend's, 'delicate collection of natural curiosities . . . coins and medals . . . and many choice authors in print'. He was especially pleased with the archdeacon's manuscript collections, particularly the materials assembled for the projected *History of the Kingdom of Northumberland*. And, after supper, he remembered, 'he shewed us several remarkable sea-plants, and obliged us with most excellent discourse, that I almost grudged my sleeping time'.[30]

The friendship was inevitable. Apart from the coincidence that each kept a diary and that each was embarked upon a local history, the two northerners were typical Augustan 'virtuosi' and shared a common passion for all that passed then for 'modern' learning. As Nicolson's collections suggest and as Thoresby's own museum demonstrates, there was not much in either natural or human history that escaped their interest. Especially, perhaps, they were drawn to antiquities, to the remains of Celtic, Roman, and Saxon Britain. But they did not overlook the Danes or Normans either, nor, for that matter, the Elizabethans or Augustans; and the wide world of nature was never far behind. Both men eventually became members of the Royal Society, contributed to its *Philosophical Transactions*, and joined in its great fellow work of discovery and description. With so many common interests it was natural for them to seek each other out, even as all men of the Baconian persuasion seem then to have sought each other out, for the advancement of knowledge. The idea of a community of the learned, of a formal society or an informal correspondence, was always paramount among the virtuosi. As Nicolson remarked to his friend in 1694, 'All the great improvements in learning are carried on in France and Italy by societies of persons proper for such undertakings. I know no reason why history and antiquities should not be this way cultivated.' When some years later an informal 'club of antiquaries' began to meet in London Nicolson was soon invited to attend.[31]

[30] Thoresby, *Diary*, i, 275; D. H. Atkinson, *Ralph Thoresby the Topographer* (Leeds, 1895), i, 322-3.
[31] Thoresby, *Letters*, i, 162: N. to Thoresby, 7 May, 1694. For the invitation to Nicolson see his diary for 27 Apr. 1709; for Thoresby's museum, see the appendix to his *Ducatus Leodiensis* (Leeds, 1715).

Nicolson's interests had developed early. While still a student at Oxford, he caught a glimpse of the new field of Saxon studies and this may have inspired his tour through Germany in 1678 under the patronage of Sir Joseph Williamson. When, upon his return, Williamson founded a Saxon lectureship at Queen's College, the young scholar became the first incumbent, lecturing for the next three years every Wednesday in term time. Bishop Fell asked him to complete Francis Junius's Anglo-Saxon dictionary and he seems to have begun the work but his preferment as archdeacon in 1682 aborted the project and closed his professional career as a scholar, although, to be sure, Anglo-Saxon remained an abiding interest and Nicolson an acknowledged master.[32] At Leipzig he had already displayed his interest in natural history, translating into Latin an essay by Robert Hooke on the motion of the earth, while the fruits of his journey abroad were recorded in the *Atlas* of Moses Pitt, much of which was written by Nicolson (1680-2).[33] His scholarship won him preferment in a Church of England particularly sensible of the value of learning. But in Carlisle he was a long way from London and the virtuosi. To some extent he was thrown back upon his own local resources but he kept up a diligent correspondence with his old friends at Queen's and his new ones in the north country and he purchased large numbers of books. He was not to return to London for eighteen years.

It is tempting to treat Nicolson's learning as amateur and indeed there was often something of the dilettante behind the virtuoso. But to leave it at that would be a serious mistake. The real advancement of learning, as Bacon correctly foresaw, lay as much with the virtuosi as with the professional scholars and academics. With his new appointment, Nicolson thrust himself passionately into the service of Church and State but he salvaged every minute he could for pursuits he thought equally important and valuable. 'I am abundantly convinced that, if ancient history were more heeded, and better understood, we would be much more at quiet than we are.'[34] What a blessing it would be if true learning would replace 'the many rascally disputes about the matters of religion which are now in fashion!' But if disputes could not always be ignored—as in the case of the Convocation Controversy—then historical research could discover the truth and win the battle.[35] Thus Nicolson's desire

---

[32] Nicolson had met Junius at Oxford; his transcription of the dictionary is in Bodl. MS Fell 8-18; see James, p. 16 n.

[33] Nicolson's contribution to the *Atlas* is described in a letter to Thoresby, 6 Mar. 1692, Thoresby, *Letters,* i, 120-2.

[34] Thoresby, *Letters,* i, 299-301: N. to Thoresby, 9 Aug. 1697.

[35] Among other things Nicolson furnished ammunition for William Wake in his quarrel

to discover the past existed sometimes for its practical value but even more for its own sake and it was disinterested enough to lead him to assist even in the researches of his religious enemies, the Catholic, Obadiah Walker, the non-juror, George Hickes, and the non-conformist, Thoresby.

Of course Nicolson was not equally proficient in nor equally committed to the whole range of 'modern' learning. He took sides with William Wotton in the quarrel between the ancients and the moderns (Swift's battle of the books) and accepted Wotton's arguments that the 'modern' disciplines were all those that had been either unknown or underdeveloped in Antiquity, and that they surpassed the ancients because they were by their nature cumulative.[36] Of these subjects Nicolson particularly valued the new historical disciplines of philology and antiquities, and the advancing scientific disciplines of botany and geology. He seems to have understood from his days at Queen's that the techniques of classical linguistic and archaeological study could equally well be applied to the civilisations of the Celts and Saxons and Danes. And he understood too the value of the monuments, the non-literary remains, for the study of the past. At once he took advantage of his new opportunities in the north. He sought out the ancient runes at Bewcastle and Bridekirk and sent off notices to the *Philosophical Transactions*; he collected old words from the local dialect, some of which were printed by John Ray as a *Glossarium Northanhymbricum*;[37] he kept track of every ancient medal and monument discovered there. And he soon hatched a plan to further all these studies with a work of his own, a volume that came to be known as the *English Historical Library*.

What was needed urgently, Nicolson believed, before further advance could be made in recovering English history, was a critical survey of what had so far been accomplished. 'A General *Examen*, a sort of an Universal *Index Expurgatorius*, that points out the mistakes and errors of every page in our several Historians, is what we chiefly want.' But that would require, 'the joynt Labours of a Society of English Antiquaries and Historians'; it might be enough,

with Atterbury and engaged in a long controversy over his visitation rights with Hugh Todd within his diocese, in both cases drawing freely on his researches in old manuscripts.

[36] *Nicolson Epist. Corr.* i, 71–4: N. to Wotton, 11 Sept. 1697. Nicolson also assured Wotton that he had the support of two others of his scholar-friends, Thomas Tanner and White Kennett (BL Add. MS 34265, f. 38). In general, for background, see J. M. Levine 'Ancients, Moderns and History', in *Studies in Change and Revolution*, ed. P. Korshin (1972), pp. 43–75.

[37] *Philosophical Transactions*, xv (1685), 1287–95; the *Glossarium* was printed in John Ray, *Collection of English Words*, 2nd edn. (1691), pp. 139–52.

he thought, 'for a Man that lives in such an obscure corner of the Earth,' to describe in general and necessarily imperfect terms the achievement of the English historians.[38] This he set out to do, including in time not only the narrative writers from the Romans on but the records also of ecclesiastical and legal history as well as a chapter on English coins. He received help from many of his friends, including Thoresby and Wotton. The work appeared in three parts between 1696 and 1699; on the whole it was well received although it provoked some bitter controversy. At once Nicolson began a *Scottish Library* and later still an Irish one. For a long while the three works (republished together in 1736 and 1776) provided a standard and essential bibliographical reference for the aspiring British historian.[39]

While this was Nicolson's chief undertaking of the 1690s, he did not abandon his scientific interests, although he was more conscious here of his amateur status. He spent his summers, especially, rambling and 'simpling' with his nephew, John Archer, assiduously collecting plants, rocks, and fossils and exchanging them with others. His interest as a cleric was particularly provoked by the geological controversies that marked the decade. Here in a succession of works by Burnet, Hooke, Woodward, Whiston, and others, there appeared a series of efforts to explain the history of the world from Creation, relying both upon the narrative account in Genesis and upon the evidences of nature then beginning to accumulate so abundantly in the cabinets of the learned, and especially upon the fossils and rock formations which had so recently become the object of serious and systematic study.[40] Here was a problem not unlike that posed by ancient history: how to reconcile the literary sources with the evidence of coins and monuments, and Nicolson looked on with consuming interest. He was bemused by the bitter controversies that developed between the rival theorists and was unable to choose among them although the arguments of Dr Woodward in favour of Noah's flood and the dissolution of the earth appealed to him the most. Somehow he managed to remain on good terms with all the

[38] *The English Historical Library or a Short View and Character of most of the Writers now extant either in Print or Manuscript which may be serviceable to the Undertaking of a General History of the Kingdom* (1696). The difficulty of one man attempting the task is set out in the preface and in a letter to Thoresby, 29 Oct. 1696, Thoresby, *Letters*, i, 257–58.

[39] Nicolson provoked at least two bitter critics, Simon Lowth and Francis Atterbury. He answered the latter at length in an open letter to White Kennett published in the *Scottish Historical Library* (1702). The *Irish Historical Library* was completed after Nicolson had been translated to the bishopric of Derry and appeared in 1722.

[40] See, for example, Martin Rudwick, *The Meaning of Fossils* (1972), and J. M. Levine, *Dr. Woodward's Shield: History, Science and Satire in Augustan England* (Berkeley, 1977).

contestants, no easy achievement when to side with one meant the bitter enmity of the rest. 'I am clearly for encouraging the ingenious inventors of all new systems,' he wrote to Woodward's bitter enemy, Edward Lhwyd, 'and giving them leave to enjoy the honour as well as the inward satisfaction of all their pretty opinions.'[41] He was more tolerant than many of his fellow divines who saw danger in the new philosophical speculation and the proliferation of so many theories about the meaning of the Mosaic revelation. He sent his advice and criticism, as well as rocks and fossils, indiscriminately to the different parties, with a polite scepticism and good humour that kept him on good terms with everyone. He might 'think more like a Divine than a Philosopher',[42] but it was obvious that he was really very adept at identifying and classifying the fossil and mineral evidence and quite sophisticated in comparing the different theories. He was rewarded by being elected to the Royal Society on 5 December 1705 on the nomination of Dr Woodward.

Meanwhile Nicolson was being sought out for each of the great co-operative historical projects of his time. When the young Edmund Gibson was given the responsibility of translating and re-enlarging William Camden's *Britannia*, he turned to Nicolson (among many others) for help with the northern counties. Their friendship had begun earlier when Gibson began to edit the *Anglo-Saxon Chronicle*, a work that had once tempted Nicolson. Immediately he promised his aid which was gratefully acknowledged when the work appeared in 1695.[43] Again, when George Hickes turned to Nicolson for help he too received it gratefully. Hickes was not only a considerable scholar but a talented leader and organiser and as his work grew in size and ambition, he drew within his circle a whole network of Saxon scholars, young men such as Humfrey Wanley and Edmund Thwaites, William Elstob and the medallist, Sir Andrew Fountaine. All contributed substantially to the collaborative enterprise that appeared a little belatedly in 1703–5 as the *Thesaurus of Northern Languages*.[44]

[41] *Nicolson Epist. Corr.* i, 103–5: N. to Lhwyd, 31 Jan. 1698; for a detailed criticism of Woodward's theories which were published in his *Essay towards a Natural History of the Earth* (1695), see *Nicolson Epist. Corr.* i, 83–6: N. to Woodward, 28 Oct. 1697.

[42] Ibid., pp. 29–31, 100–1: N. to Lhwyd, 26 May 1692, and N. to Woodward, 13 Jan. 1698.

[43] Thoresby, *Letters*, i, 124–7: N. to Thoresby, 25 June 1693. John Mill had asked Nicolson to edit the *Anglo-Saxon Chronicle* in 1686; Nicolson's notes for the *Britannia* are in Bodl. MS Top. gen. C 27, ff. 1–2. He also helped Gibson with the second edition which appeared very belatedly in 1722.

[44] *Linguarum Vett. Septentrionalium Thesaurus* (2 vols., Oxford, 1703–5). Hickes's gratitude to Nicolson is expressed in the preface, I, p. iv, and in a letter, 25 Apr. 1699, *Nicolson Epist. Corr.* i, 119–21.

Nicolson came to know all these men, contributed in one way or another to their various activities, and, most helpfully, sold a lot of subscriptions to what was an expensive and somewhat recondite enterprise. Along the way he also contributed support to the compilers' individual efforts, especially perhaps to Thwaites's Saxon Pentateuch. After he became bishop he appointed two of them, Elstob and Thomas Benson, as his chaplains. Finally, when Edward Lhwyd, the Oxford scholar, determined to do for the Celts what Hickes had done for the Saxons, namely to recover the whole of their ancient language and culture, he too turned to Nicolson who promptly furnished him information, encouragement, and more subscriptions.[45] Hickes's tribute on another occasion shows something of the esteem in which he was held as a scholar. Nicolson had written an introduction to a book in which the Lord's Prayer was given in one hundred different languages. It shows him, Hickes wrote to the editor, 'to be a very great man, and to have a most exact Judgement . . . I know not what is most to be admired in it, the vast variety of Reading, or the putting all his Observations together in so short, clear, and easy, a Discourse.'[46]

Thus, when Nicolson returned at last to London in 1701, for the first of a succession of visits, he was recognised by everyone as an accomplished scholar. He was accepted equally by the antiquaries and the natural philosophers, and their society and their cabinets were thrown open wide to receive him. He sought out especially the collectors of 'curiosities' and 'rarities' who like himself, but often on a much grander scale, tried to assemble the evidence of natural and human history in their museums. In those days almost all the important collections were still in private hands, but the community of the virtuosi made them easily accessible to visitors and the diary entries of Nicolson as he made his rounds may be checked against those of others such as Thoresby (who indeed continued to share his pleasures with Nicolson by mail), or Humfrey Wanley, or foreigners such as Christopher Erndtel or Z. C. von Uffenbach.[47] Nicolson does not seem to have missed much: wherever

---

[45] Lhwyd's work was known as the *Archaeologia Britannica* (Oxford, 1707). Only one volume appeared dealing with the ancient Celtic languages; Lhwyd's death in 1709 halted the project.

[46] Bodl. MS Top. gen. C 27/1, ff. 52–3: Hickes to John Chamberlayne, 26 May 1713. The work was entitled *Oratio Dominica in diversas omnium fere gentium linguas versa* (1715) with Nicolson's contribution as an appendix.

[47] Thoresby, *Diary*, i, 335–9; Bodl. MS Ballard 13, f. 91: Wanley to Charlett, 19 Dec. 1700. Erndtel published his account as *De Itinere suo Anglicano et Batavo* (Amsterdam, 1711), translated into English in the same year; there is a translation of Uffenbach by W. H. Quarrell and Margaret Mare, *London in 1710 from the Travels of Z. C. von Uffenbach* (1934).

there were coins or manuscripts, inscriptions or old books, fossils or other natural remains, there he might be found taking notes, interrogating the owners, and enjoying the camaraderie of shared pursuits.[48] He sought out the great collectors such as Pembroke and Harley, his fellow scholar-bishops, Lloyd, Moore, and Gibson, the astonishing physician-naturalists, Dr Woodward and Dr Sloane, and those lesser lights, with their most extraordinary museums, Parson Stonestreet, Mr Charleton, and Mr Kemp. He dined with Dr Woodward and his friends at Gresham College, with Gibson, Richard Bentley, and Gilbert Burnet at Lambeth Palace, and on another occasion with those old friends and distinguished virtuosi, Samuel Pepys and John Evelyn. And he looked over the collections of the botanists, Leonard Plukenet, Samuel Doody, Adam Buddle, and James Petiver. He also visited the institutions, the Royal Society which still met at Gresham College, the library at Cotton House, the richest in the kingdom for old manuscripts, the Royal Library, the College of Arms, and so on. (In the second edition of the *English Historical Library* he reported on their contents.) Each visit to London was filled with a double exhilaration, high politics on the one hand, intense intellectual discovery on the other.

How did he pack it all in, the clerical career, politics, family and friends, and the amazingly broad intellectual concerns and contributions?[49] Obviously, Nicolson was a man of uncommon energy and forceful personality. (He walked or rode, we are told, between 2,500 and 3,000 miles a year.) At the same time he was, in most respects, a perfect representative of his kind—the Augustan virtuoso. Like Wotton and Woodward, Hickes and Lhwyd, and so many others, he reminds us of a time, before all learning was specialised and academic, when it was still possible, even desirable, to combine activity in the world, political skill and ambition, with a broad intellectual culture profound enough to make a real contribution to the advancement of learning.

Divines

During his sixteen years in parliament Nicolson had social commerce with most of the bishops who were in London during the sessions. Yet his circle of regular friends on the bench was small and close-knit:

---

[48] For example see Appendix B below, pp. 698–703.

[49] There were other scholarly activities as for example his *Leges Marchiarum* (1705), a collection of the border laws, and the dissertation on Saxon law that he contributed to David Wilkins's *Leges Anglo-Saxonicae* (1721). Under the circumstances it is not surprising perhaps that he never finished his Northumberland history which remained *rudis indigestaque moles*. Its ambitious design is laid out for Thoresby, 23 Sept. 1691, Thoresby, *Letters*, i, 116–17.

never more than six at any one time, and (including Gibson, who was not elevated until 1716) only seven in all throughout the sixteen years—Tenison, Sharp, Wake, Evans, Gibson, Trimnell, and Dawes. The five Whigs (Sharp and Dawes being Tories) account for nearly half of all Nicolson's meetings with bishops. Outside this small inner group lay an outer circle comprising prelates whom Nicolson saw regularly, though less frequently: Bishops Burnet, Moore, Hough, Tyler, Talbot, and Wynne.[50] The other twenty-five bishops whom Nicolson met in London outside the House took up slightly less than a quarter of the time he spent in social contact with his episcopal brethren.

In striking contrast to his relations with temporal lords and politicians Nicolson from the start preferred the company of the Low Church group of bishops. The repercussions of his involvement in the bitter Convocation Controversy of 1697–1701[51] profoundly influenced his ecclesiastical friendships from then onwards. In his first session in parliament, of the fourteen bishops whom Nicolson met socially only four were Tories (and three of these he met only once each). In his second session of 1704–5 he widened his circle of acquaintances, most of his new social contacts among the bishops being Tories (though socially he met few of these again). From 1705–6 until 1718 Nicolson made social contact with ten new Whig bishops ard nine new Tories. This seeming parity is deceptive, however, as few of the new Tory acquaintances were renewed in subsequent sessions. Dawes and Robinson are exceptions to this, but even here contact was not very frequent. All the new Whig contacts, however, with the exception of Hoadly, were renewed again and again.

Until his death in 1715 it was Archbishop Tenison whose society Nicolson sought and enjoyed most frequently and regularly. This was only natural for Tenison was not only his Primate but also the effective head (even when incapacitated by illness) of that group of Whig bishops with whom Nicolson was associated from the first in ecclesiastical matters and later in politics too. Wake, who in 1715 succeeded Tenison, regarded Nicolson as his right hand in 1718;[52] Tenison in 1714 could have claimed the same. From 1704 onwards Nicolson was invariably called to meetings of Whig bishops at Lambeth, social in guise but designed to co-ordinate political actions.[53] After the establishment of Harley's ministry, Nicolson's position in the Whig clerical circle was acknowledged by his closest fellow-

---

[50] They accounted for a further 13% of all Nicolson's episcopal meetings.
[51] For the Controversy see Bennett, *White Kennett*, pp. 26–55; Bennett, *Tory Crisis*, pp. 44–63; Sykes, *Wake*, i, 80–116.
[52] See below p. 681.   [53] e.g. see below pp. 148, 152–3.

traveller on the road to Church Whiggery, Bishop Trelawney of Winchester, at a dinner attended by Bishop Trimnell, Deans Black-burne and Kennett, and Archdeacon Gibson, where the company was 'nobly entertained as friends to the old Establishment and Ministry'.[54]

In some respects intellectual pursuits played rather less part than one might have imagined in the episcopal company Nicolson chose to keep. Only his meetings with Bishop Humphries of Hereford (who was Nicolson's most frequent social associate in the 1702–3 session but because of his absence from London was not seen again until the 1705–6 session) seems to have been prompted almost exclusively by historical and linguistic interests. On the other hand such interests clearly enriched enormously his relations with other leading divines (Gibson and Burnet, to mention but two), while his clerical friendships in general also brought him into contact with some of the most brilliant and enquiring minds of his age, quite apart from his fellow antiquaries. Within one week in November 1705, at Tenison's table and Sharp's, he met Newton once and Bentley twice.[55]

Only in two cases did northern neighbourliness mean very much in Nicolson's choice of episcopal friends. He did see much of Arch-bishop Sharp of York in London. Their friendship before Nicolson's elevation to the episcopacy, Sharp's help in gaining the diocese of Carlisle for Nicolson, and most of all, the archbishop's position as Nicolson's Metropolitan and immediate ecclesiastical superior are the reasons for their many social contacts.[56] Nicolson's friendship with Sharp survived until the latter's death in 1714 despite political differences such as Sharp's opposition to Nicolson's Cathedrals Bill in 1708. The close relationship between Nicolson and his Metro-politan was carried over to Sharp's successor, Archbishop Dawes;[57] though how far true friendship dictated it must be doubtful. Nicolson mentions meeting Dawes but once before the latter's eleva-tion to the bishopric of Chester in 1708, and rarely after that; it was only upon Dawes's translation to York that he became one of Nicolson's more frequent social contacts in the years 1714 to 1718. Nicolson had very little to do socially with either Dawes's predecessor or his successor at Chester, and appears to have been on no more

[54] Below p. 566. A similar dinner took place at Trelawney's house in Chelsea in 1712, attended by Burnet, Hough, Moore, Talbot, Evans, Trimnell and Nicolson. See below, p. 576.

[55] See below pp. 298, 301.

[56] Sharp was often the first or one of the first bishops Nicolson contacted on his arrival in London. Nicolson also paid his New Year respects to Sharp before any one else.

[57] Dawes was after 1714 one of the first bishops to be visited by Nicolson upon his arrival in London.

than the most formal terms with Bishop Crew of Durham.[58] They were all Tories.

In the later years from 1712 to 1718 Nicolson was rarely in the company of Tory bishops and, despite differences over the Schism Act and the later attempts to repeal both this and the Occasional Conformity Act, his social life at the higher ecclesiastical level was largely dominated by a small group of Whig bishops—Tenison, Evans (translated to Meath in 1716), Gibson, Wake, and Trimnell.

Nicolson's London circles naturally included a very large number of divines, a few of whom—notably his most constant companion, Edmund Gibson—themselves achieved bishoprics towards the end of his career at Carlisle. Yet as with the bishops, and (as will appear) with peers and politicians, his regular intimates were few. A small inner group, consisting of Gibson, William Lancaster, John Waugh, White Kennett, Edward Gee, and Dean Grahme, accounted for nearly three-quarters of Nicolson's recorded meetings with divines outside the bench. Of this group only Grahme was a Tory; Lancaster had High Tory leanings, but in politics was 'the very epitome of a trimmer, usually subservient to the Government of the day';[59] but the rest were Whig. There were three other clerics of whom Nicolson from time to time saw a good deal in London: John Grandorge, Francis Atterbury, and the non-juror George Hickes.[60] Though politics was of some importance in all these relationships, three other factors, mentioned earlier, were of equal if not greater significance: mutual intellectual interests, an Oxford and preferably a Queen's College connection, and Lakeland associations.

All the nine clerics just referred to, except Gee, were Oxford educated; and Lancaster as Provost, and Waugh and Gibson as Fellows, were connected with Queen's College. It was Lancaster's position at Queen's that ensured his continued friendship with Nicolson, who retained a keen interest in what went on in his old college. Many of Nicolson's casual social acquaintances were from Queen's, and to have been at the college was sufficient to gain entry into the bishop's wider social circle.

Five of the bishop's closer clerical associates had north-western connections: Gibson, Waugh, and Grahme were either born there or came from local families; Grahme, as sometime Dean of Carlisle, had a double connection with the two counties, and this, along with the bishop's long association with the family, kept Dean Grahme

[58] Nicolson met Stratford three times, Gastrell twice, and Crew, in sixteen years, a mere five times.

[59] Bennett, *Tory Crisis*, p. 149.

[60] These two groups, comprising four Whigs, four Tories, and one trimmer, accounted for 80% or so of Nicolson's meetings with clerics.

20

on Nicolson's visiting list long after his move to Wells, and despite the dean's occasional tetchy antipathy to Nicolson. Atterbury's position as Dean of Carlisle was the sole reason for his London meetings with Nicolson, and neither of these two old adversaries can have derived much social satisfaction from them, though the bishop acknowledged being 'treated . . . very decently at Dinner' in Atterbury's 'pretty box' of a house in Chelsea in December 1705.[61] They only met, however, between 1704 and 1711 when Atterbury was dean. While Atterbury was Dean of Christ Church (1711–13) contact was nil, and Nicolson only saw him a couple of times after his elevation to Rochester in 1713. Grandorge's local connection is the most tenuous of the group; he was chaplain to Lord Thanet, and appears to have broken social contact with the bishop at much the same time as his employer, that is, after the 1709/10 session.

Common intellectual interests did much to enrich Nicolson's close friendships with Gibson and with Kennett, and they were the sole reason for his relationship with Hickes.[62]

Edmund Gibson's remarkable position of dominance within Nicolson's clerical circle (he accounts for very nearly a quarter of all the bishop's meetings with divines and other bishops) is probably explained by the fact that he alone appears to fulfil all the four main criteria by which Nicolson chose his friends: he was a local Cumberland man, a fellow Queen's man, a fellow antiquary, and a Whig. Beyond doubt his ever-strengthening ties with clerics of the stamp of Gibson and Kennett helped to stimulate Nicolson's interest in reforming activities with which Low Churchmen were especially associated, such as the work of the SPCK and the Charity School Movement.

Peers and Politicians

On the evidence of his diaries Nicolson associated socially and on private business with about forty peers. Of these a smaller inner circle of ten peers with whom he met frequently can be regarded as his social and political friends among the temporal lords. These ten peers, eight of them Whigs, ranked in order of the number of meetings outside the House each had with Nicolson, were Carlisle, Halifax, the 2nd Viscount Lonsdale, Somers, Wharton, Thanet, Sunderland, Cowper, Pembroke, and Townshend. Meetings with these ten accounted for over three-quarters of Nicolson's recorded meetings with peers.

[61] See below p. 331.

[62] A good example of Nicolson's relationship with Hickes is seen on 21 Jan. 1706 when the bishop takes Hickes with him to see Bishop Humphries, where the evening is spent discussing Saxon linguistics.

The bishop's social contacts with Lord Pembroke were based on their mutual interests in antiquities, and the occasions on which they met were always taken up with discussions on antiquarian matters or with the viewing of Pembroke's collection.[63] Nicolson's friendship with Halifax also developed out of mutual learned interests,[64] but this association became more of a political one as Nicolson moved socially and politically into the ambit of the Junto.

The four Junto peers, Halifax, Somers, Wharton, and Sunderland, accounted for well over a third of Nicolson's social meetings in his circle of peers, and Somers and Halifax particularly occupied a good deal of the bishop's time. Two of the other Whig peers with whom Nicolson was in frequent social contact were a close Junto associate Lord Carlisle (with whom Nicolson had more contact than with any other single peer)[65] and Lord Lonsdale. They (along with Lord Wharton) had strong local connections with Cumberland and Westmorland, and the bishop's meetings with all three were largely concerned with local political issues or issues of patronage within the two Lakeland counties.

Lord Thanet, the one other Tory peer (apart from Pembroke) with whom Nicolson maintained a steady intimacy (and this appears to end after the 1709–10 session) was a careful, though absentee, landlord in Westmorland and a conscientious Anglican patron, with the best interests of the Church very much at heart.[66]

It is a common aphorism that a man is known by the company he keeps, and from 1705 to 1706 Nicolson's social connections clearly mark him out as a 'State' if not a 'Church' Whig. After that session the bishop only had about twenty private meetings with Tory peers in London over the next twelve years. The contrast with his first session in parliament could hardly be more striking. In the winter of 1702–3, Nicolson met only two Whig peers socially, his regular contacts being with such 'Church party' stalwarts as Nottingham, Longueville, Weymouth, Godolphin, Rochester, and Thanet. In his second session, that of 1704–5, Nottingham and Thanet remained in his circle, but into it now, for the first time, came Somers, Wharton and Halifax. From the start of the next parliament these contacts are increased and the young Lord Lonsdale appears in London. By the time Nicolson adds Carlisle to his circle in 1706–7, his social round among the Whig peerage is firmly established.

Nicolson's relations with politicians (other than peers) shows the

---

[63] See below pp. 502, 554.
[64] See below pp. 380, 446.
[65] About a quarter of the bishop's meetings with peers.
[66] See Gloucestershire RO Lloyd-Baker MSS Box 4, Bundle A52: Thanet to Sharp, 13 Dec. 1698 (printed in A. T. Hart, *The Life and Times of John Sharp, Archbishop of York* [1949], pp. 158-9).

same structural pattern as his other social circles. Over many winters and springs, he saw a large number of MPs of varying political hues, but most of them he saw only once or twice, and very rarely in more than one session. His core of close political friends in St Stephen's Chapel was surprisingly small. Only five MPs were members of his close circle, and all five were representatives of Cumberland or Westmorland seats: Christopher Musgrave, Sir James Montagu, James Lowther, James Grahme, and Gilfred Lawson. Among them, they account for nearly 60 per cent of the meetings with members of the House of Commons which the bishop noted in his London diaries.

Nicolson saw, visited, and entertained Christopher Musgrave (MP for Carlisle 1702-5) in every single session up to 1715. Among the lay politicians he remained Nicolson's most constant political companion down to 1710-11 when he was, to some extent, displaced by Sir James Montagu and by James Lowther of Whitehaven. That the head of the Musgrave family should hold this position in the bishop's circle of London friends can be no surprise. It has already been observed that Christopher's father, Sir Christopher Musgrave, 4th Baronet (MP for Westmorland 1702-4), had long been a political associate of Nicolson's, and had in 1702 been largely responsible for gaining Nicolson his bishopric. He became Nicolson's political mentor during his first session in Parliament.[67] Christopher Musgrave junior did not inherit this mantle on his father's death, but Nicolson's strong sense of loyalty to the family clearly and understandably persisted. Despite the steady shift of his political allegiance beginning in the session of 1704-5, Nicolson remained on the warmest terms not only with Christopher Musgrave, but with his brothers, particularly Joseph (MP for Cockermouth 1713-15), and his nephew Sir Christopher Musgrave, 5th Baronet (MP for Carlisle 1713-15).[68] Christopher, or a member of his family, was always among the very first people Nicolson visited on his arrival in London. He was frequently called upon to dine at Christopher's house in Swallow Street, Westminster, along with other Tory politicians; and around this partisan table important local and national issues were regularly discussed, for example, Occasional Conformity and the 'Tack' (upon which Nicolson differed from most of the company). Although the special relationship with the Musgraves lasted well beyond Nicolson's conversion to Whiggery, it began to decline from 1712 onwards.

This same decline also appeared in Nicolson's relationship with the

[67] See below p. 126.
[68] The Musgrave family accounted for nearly 40% of Nicolson's meetings with politicians (Christopher himself accounted for 20%).

Grahme family. Colonel James Grahme of Levens (MP for Appleby 1702-8, and for Westmorland 1708-27) had, like Sir Christopher Musgrave, also been a political ally in the north before Nicolson's elevation to .the bench, and their friendship survived at least until 1715, although their meetings after 1710 were infrequent. Perhaps things were not quite the same again between the two men after Grahme's indifference if not opposition in the Commons to Nicolson's 1708 Cathedrals Bill.

Nicolson's relations with Gilfred Lawson—long-serving knight of the shire for Cumberland (1701, 1702-5, 1708-34) and the other Tory in his inner political circle—also survived his conversion, even to the extent that Lawson supported Nicolson in the Commons in 1711 when he was censured for helping Halifax's brother, Sir James Montagu, in the Carlisle election of 1710.[69] Meetings with Lawson took place regularly up to at least 1717.

Although the centre of Nicolson's inner political circle of peers and Commoners moved after his conversion to Whiggery away from his Tory friends, especially after the Tories' opposition to his Cathedrals Bill in 1708, he never lost contact with the Musgraves, Lawson, or James Grahme as he did with Nottingham and, later, even with Thanet. In 1711 Nicolson's 'good friends' in the House of Commons over the Carlisle case were both Whigs and Tories.[70] Neighbourliness, old obligations, and local patriotism still held some sway over his political friendships, even when Montagu and Lowther came to usurp the place of the old favourites later in Anne's reign.[71]

NICOLSON AS POLITICIAN AND PARLIAMENTARIAN

Political Allegiance

When Nicolson entered the House of Lords towards the end of 1702, he did so as a confirmed moderate Tory under the patronage of, and under a financial obligation to, the Musgrave family, and with the help and friendship of Archbishop Sharp, also a Tory and a moderate High Churchman.[72] His political activities as Archdeacon of Carlisle had certainly not been those of an unthinking partisan. He had, for example, tried to heal the breach between the leading Tory and Whig families of Cumberland, the Musgraves and the Lowthers, in order

[69] See below pp. 559-60. Col. Grahme also supported Nicolson on this occasion.
[70] See below p. 561.
[71] Of all Nicolson's close political circle who had received a university education (and only Christopher Musgrave had not) only Montagu was not an Oxford man, while James Lowther, Gilfred Lawson, and Richard Musgrave were Queen's College men.
[72] See *CW* ii (1902), 160; below p. 126; Cumbria (Carlisle) RO Lonsdale MSS: James Lowther to Sir John Lowther of Whitehaven, 5 May 1702.

to 'restore Peace to the Neighbourhood';[73] and despite accusations of his being implicated with the Jacobite Grahme family in the 1690s[74] he was wholehearted in supporting the Revolution and the Williamite government, believing that

Whoever represents you in Parliament must take the Oath of Allegiance, and Subscribe the Association. These are all the Securities required by the Government: And (give me leave to say it) I can hardly think that man to be a good Christian, or a Loyal Subject, that expects any farther Satisfaction on this Head. [He had, as he told Henry Fleming in 1700] An Earnest desire to see You all Unanimous in the true Interests of the Established Church and State Government . . .[75]

In his first two sessions in the House, Nicolson was to pursue a moderate Tory line, but in the following few years he was to change to the position of what may be best termed a 'State Whig'. He was a supporter of the Whigs in secular matters while retaining a moderate Tory position over Church affairs. Nicolson's dislike of Dissenters was more acute than that of the genuine Low Church divines, and this led him to support the Occasional Conformity bills of 1702–4; but, significantly, not the 'Tack' of November 1704 which he believed would lead parliament and the nation 'into any sort of Confusion'.[76] Although, years later, he was to approve both the revived Occasional Conformity Act of 1711 and the more malicious Schism Act, and vigorously oppose their attempted repeal, these were, by him, relatively isolated departures from an otherwise fairly straight Whig path.

The death of Sir Christopher Musgrave in July 1704 was an important landmark along Nicolson's political path. His political ties with the family gradually loosened, until by 1708 he was refusing to support the Musgrave and Grahme families in the county elections for Cumberland and Westmorland, and backing Sir James Montagu (the brother of the Junto Whig Lord Halifax) at Carlisle.[77] In Parliament Nicolson's new Whig allegiance had been manifest since, at least, 1705.

Perhaps the most important single cause of Nicolson's breach with his political past was his conflict with his *bête noire*, the High Tory Dean Francis Atterbury, who was dispatched to Carlisle through the influence of Godolphin and Harley in the autumn of 1704. Relations between them were disastrous from the start and Nicolson soon found himself opposing the virulent Tory-supported 'Church in

[73] Cumbria (Kendal) RO Rydal MS 5253: N. to [Sir Daniel Fleming?], 27 Apr. 1698.

[74] Levens Hall MSS: T. Banks to James Grahme, 1 Nov. 1695; see also HMC *Bagot MSS*, p. 332; *CSPD 1695*, p. 119.

[75] Cumbria (Kendal) RO Rydal MS 5568: N. to Fleming, 15 Oct. 1700.

[76] See below p. 238; see also p. 236.

[77] *CW* ii (1902), 201–2; Levens Hall MSS D/M: Christopher Musgrave to James Grahme, 27 May 1708; below p. 468. The change in Nicolson's political allegiance has been traced in James, pp. 170–97.

Danger' campaign of 1705-6, with which Atterbury was so prominently associated. The dean's opposition to Nicolson in the Chapter at Carlisle eventually developed into a national issue; and Nicolson found so little sympathy in his plight from Tory politicians or even from his old friend, Sharp, that his alliance with the Whig bishops and peers was inevitably cemented. They it was who supported him over the Cathedrals Bill of 1708 designed to restore the legal basis of episcopal power at Carlisle and the other threatened cathedrals of the 'new foundation'.[78] Opposition to this bill, or at best neutralism, by former Tory associates in both Houses[79] merely served to complete Nicolson's disenchantment with his old party.

Other personal factors played their part. With the Whig leaders, Halifax and Somers, Nicolson worked closely in the Committee on Records, and formed friendships based on mutual respect for learning and scholarship. With the more down to earth Lord Wharton he seems to have developed a close working relationship both in the House of Lords and at a local level.[80] And all this time his attachment to the Low Church bishops was growing. Nicolson had been associated with Whig clerics, particularly Gibson and Wake, from the early days of the Convocation Controversy. Atterbury again proved to be the catalyst which fused Nicolson to his moderate Whig episcopal colleagues during the Carlisle Cathedral Controversy. Nicolson came to regard Archbishop Tenison of Canterbury, that epitome of moderate Low Churchmanship, as 'a rock, and the centre of unity in the English Church'.[81] Gibson and Wake came to have great influence on Nicolson, and while he was away from the centre of politics in his northern diocese he relied heavily on these two divines for information and direction.[82] His friendship with Gibson was even to withstand the severe strains put upon it by their differences over the proposed repeal of the Occasional Conformity and Schism Acts.[83] Gibson's wish upon Nicolson's translation to Derry in 1718

[78] See below, pp. 428-33; *Vernon Corr.* iii, 357-8; *Addison Letters*, pp. 92, 96-7; BL Add. MS 6116, f. 8.

[79] e.g. Col. Grahme. See Levens Hall MSS D/M: Christopher Musgrave to Grahme, 15 May 1708.

[80] Particularly over the Parton Harbour Bill in Feb. 1706 where they worked together in support of the Lowthers of Whitehaven against the Duke of Somerset. See below pp. 369, 380, 383, 385; Cumbria (Carlisle) RO Lonsdale MSS D/Lons/W bundle 27: Thomas Littleton to [James Lowther], 2 Mar. 1706. For an example of their co-operation locally, see *Nicolson Epist. Corr.* ii, 402-4: N. to Wharton, 29 Dec. 1709.

[81] *Nicolson Epist. Corr.* ii, 467: N. to Gibson, 28 Nov. 1717.

[82] See Gibson's letters to Nicolson, 1702-4 and 1712-14, in Bodl. MS Add. A269, and Nicolson's extensive correspondence with Wake in Christ Church, Wake MSS (copies of part of this correspondence are in BL Add. MS 6116).

[83] See below p. 668; *Nicolson Epist. Corr.* ii, 466-8, 472-3: N. to Gibson, 28 Nov., 9 and 14 Dec. 1717.

'that the old correspondence, which is now near 30 years standing may never fail till death us doe part'[84] was realised.

Issues, however, were of great importance too: Nicolson became a more enthusiastic supporter than most Tories of the War of the Spanish Succession and its conduct, while the steady slide of the more extreme Tories and High Church clergy towards Jacobitism, culminating in the Succession crisis of 1713–14 only served to confirm Nicolson in his support for the Whig constitution.[85]

Attendance in Parliament

From the first winter to the last of his tenure of the see of Carlisle Nicolson was a conscientious attender of parliament. During his sixteen years as bishop he only missed two parliamentary sessions, 1703/4 and 1709/10, both winters in which he was preoccupied with visitations of his diocese. In most of the fourteen sessions he attended he appears to have been a regular and active member of the House.

Table 1
Nicolson's attendance at the House of Lords

	a	b	c	d	e	f
1702/3	84	63	61	75%	73%	97%
1704/5	99	90	83	91%	84%	92%
1705/6	95	82	76	86%	80%	93%
1706/7	86	73	66	85%	77%	90%
1707/8	105	67	66	64%	63%	99%
1708/9	91	57	57	63%	63%	100%
1710/11	109	67	63	61%	58%	94%
1711/12	107	57	53	53%	50%	93%
1713	65	22	15	39%	23%	68%
1714	75	43	40	57%	53%	93%
1715	110	97	89	88%	81%	92%
1716	104	70	62	67%	60%	89%
1717	75	75	59	100%	79%	79%
1717/18	70	55	46	79%	66%	84%
Total	1275	918	836	72%	66%	91%

a = Days in the session. (Figures from the *Lords' Journals*.)

b = Days in Nicolson's residence in London. (Figures from the *Lords' Journals*.)

c = Days on which Nicolson attended. (Figures obtained by subtracting the 'absence' figure from *b*. The 'absence' figure is from either the diary or the MSS minutes column of the table in note 87, giving preference to the diary column if available.)

d = Possible % attendance of Nicolson. (Figures express *b* as a % of *a*. They show the % of the parliamentary session Nicolson actually resided in London.)

e = % attendance of Nicolson in whole session. (Figures express *c* as a % of *a*.)

f = % attendance of Nicolson in his period of London residence. (Figures express *c* as a % of *b*. % figures are taken to the nearest whole number.)

[84] Bodl. MS Add. A269, p. 77: Gibson to N., 29 July 1718.
[85] Cumbria (Carlisle) RO Lonsdale MSS D/Lons/W bundle 32: N. to James Lowther,

The evidence for his, or any other member's, attendance at this time, however, is by no means as straightforward as is commonly assumed. The *Lords' Journals* print a list of those peers present at the beginning of each day's meeting. This list is an amended form of the list compiled by the Clerk Assistant of the House in the manuscript minutes he kept of the Lords' proceedings. There are minor differences in the names of the peers who appear in the printed and in the manuscript versions of the list. The latter is, generally speaking, the fuller of the two and can be regarded as the more reliable record of who attended the House on a particular day. But even this list is far from being completely accurate[86] as a comparison with Nicolson's own record of his attendance shows.[87] Nicolson is normally consistent in noting his own attendance. On 12 March 1707, for instance, he carefully records that this was the first day he had missed going to the House in the 1706/7 session; yet both the *Journals* and the manuscript minutes had recorded his absence on eight occasions before that day.[88] A collation of the official printed version with Nicolson's own record reveals that he was absent on

7 Feb. 1715. Nicolson continued to actively support the Whigs in Cumberland even after his translation to Derry in 1718 (Castle Howard Archives, Correspondence of 3rd Earl of Carlisle 13/3: James Lowther to Carlisle, 23 Mar. 1720).

[86] See C. Jones, 'Seating problems in the House of Lords in the early eighteenth century: the evidence of the manuscript minutes', *BIHR* li (1978), 139–42.

[87] *Nicolson's absences from the House:*

	LJ	MSS Minutes	Diary
1702/3	5	4	2
1704/5	4(+5)[1]	4(+5)	2
1705/6	11	9	6
1706/7	15	15	7
1707/8	4	3	1
1708/9	2	1	0
1710/11	10	8	4
1711/12	5	4	4
1713	9	7	− (No diary)
1714[2]	4	4	− (Incomplete diary)
1715	9	9	8
1716	8	8	− (No diary)
1717	17	17	16
1717/18[3]	9	9	− (Incomplete diary)

[1] Figures in brackets are absences recorded after 15 Jan. 1705, for which there is no diary.
[2] The incomplete diary records attendance on one day when *LJ* and MSS minutes record absence.
[3] The incomplete diary records attendance on two days when *LJ* and MSS minutes record absence.

[88] See *LJ* xvii, 178, 192, 199, 206, 221, 226, 235, 262. These days included proceedings on the Scottish Union and on the bill on the security of the Church of England, two areas in which Nicolson had strong interests. For each day there is a diary entry affirming his presence.

only about half the number of occasions the *Journals* would have us believe. This is a most significant difference; and it underlines the fallibility of any work on the House of Lords which is based on the printed presence lists. Unfortunately it also undermines any comparison between Nicolson's parliamentary zeal and that of his episcopal colleagues. For lacking, as we do, any other parliamentary diaries[89] we can only base our assessment on the official printed lists.

Only once, in 1717, was Nicolson in London for the whole of the parliamentary working days of the session. For the rest his periods of residence in the capital ranged from the untypically low 39 per cent of the 1713 session to 91 per cent of that of 1704–5, with an overall average of just under three-quarters of the working duration of all the sessions he attended.

It was common form among both spiritual and lay lords, even among the most politically committed, to absent themselves from London for some part, at least, of parliamentary sessions. The early weeks were especially unpopular. Nicolson does not seem, at first, to have shared this view. His late arrival for his first session (1702/3) was caused by diocesan problems. For his next three sessions he was present on the opening day (or arrived only a day or so late). For his fourth, fifth, and sixth sessions, however, he came up late; was on time for the next two; and thereafter was late for four of the last five (1717 being the exception). Although he stayed to the end of four of the nine sessions at which his attendance was delayed, towards the end of his career (doubtless learning from experience) Nicolson shared the general 'objection to an early appearance in parliament . . . [because of] their late entring upon Bussiness of consequence'.[90] On the other hand, prompt arrival usually served as justification for early departure.[91] The most remarkable instance took place in June 1714, when he left for Rose the day before the final vote on the violently controversial Schism Act, which he supported, leaving his proxy with Bishop Wake of Lincoln. Wake opposed the act but nevertheless appears to have cast Nicolson's proxy vote for it in opposition to his own.[92] So long as Nicolson was in town, however, he was an ultra-conscientious attender at

[89] Bishop Wake's diary (Lambeth Palace MS 1770), covering 1705 to 1725, is the only other major bishop's diary contemporary with Nicolson's, but Wake is far less consistent in noting his attendance at the House. For his first session from Nov. 1705 to Mar. 1706, for example, the *LJ* records his attendance at 67 sittings (out of a possible 95), whereas his diary explicitly records attendance on 24 occasions (two of which were on days when the *LJ* records his absence).

[90] Bodl. MS Add. A269, p. 47: Gibson to N., 29 Nov. 1715.

[91] The sole exception was the session of 1717.

[92] See below p. 607.

Westminster: on average he missed only one day in every ten on which Parliament sat. It was a good record by any standard.

It was certainly very good by episcopal standard. In the twelve parliamentary sessions during Queen Anne's reign the average daily attendance of bishops, as recorded in the *Journals*, was ten,[93] so that each day when Nicolson attended sixteen of his colleagues, on average, were absent. On 16 March 1705, two days after the end of the parliamentary session, Gibson described Bishop Cumberland of Peterborough (then aged 74) as 'a constant attendant at the Lords'.[94] For the session 1704–5, though he was in London for the whole session (whereas Nicolson missed a tenth of it), Cumberland only attended 66 per cent of the possible days he could have sat, compared with Nicolson's attendance record of 92 per cent.[95] One further example of Nicolson's attendance record is illuminating. Regular formal days of thanksgiving—30 January, 29 May, 5 November—when after prayers the House adjourned to hear a commemorative sermon in Westminster Abbey were badly attended, not only by peers, but also by the bishops. Characteristically, Nicolson missed only three such occasions out of the fourteen which occurred during his sojourns in London.[96]

The pattern of Nicolson's day-to-day attendance in the House is also interesting. It was the duty of the most junior bishop in the Lords to read prayers before the proceedings of the day began. This Nicolson performed for the first time on 20 November 1702. He appears, at first, to have found the task of getting to the House in time for prayers onerous. 'They keep me close confined, as chaplain to the Upper House. They will, I hope, shortly set me and others at liberty', he wrote on 28 November 1702.[97] None the less, he performed this duty well. He was recorded first on the bishops' bench by the Clerk on 47 per cent of his attendance days and was one of the first three bishops to arrive for 89 per cent of his attendances during the 1702–3 session.[98]

By the time Nicolson attended his second session of 1704–5, there were two bishops junior to him on the bench: Beveridge of St Asaph and Hooper of Bath and Wells. Yet Nicolson was still

---

[93] *English Historical Documents, 1660–1714*, ed. A. Browning (1953), p. 957.

[94] Bodl. MS Add. A269, p. 7: Gibson to N., 16 Mar. 1705.

[95] Figures based on *LJ* xvii, 154–319.

[96] The three occasions were towards the end of his career on 29 May 1716 and 1717, and 30 Jan. 1718. There is some indication that by the early Hanoverian period few Whigs cared to appear on such public days (Bodl. MS Add. A269, p. 59: Gibson to N., 1 Jan. 1717).

[97] HMC *Laing MSS* ii, 5: N. to Sir Robert Sibbald, 28 Nov. 1702.

[98] This analysis is based on the 'presence lists' in the HLRO Manuscript minutes. For the validity of this source as an indicator of seating, see C. Jones, 'Seating problems in the House of Lords', *BIHR* li (1978), 139–45.

sometimes called upon to read prayers, either because he was the most junior bishop present, or to oblige a colleague; and he continued to do so—at least once because he was the only bishop in the House[99]—until 1714 when the last recorded instance appears in his diary.[100]

It was doubtless a tribute to the regularity of his early attendance that when the House decided to start work an hour earlier than usual, to get through a finance bill, it was the Bishop of Carlisle who was called on for prayers.[101] For even in 1704–5 and 1705–6 he continued, four days out of five, to occupy one of the first three places on the bench.[102] Between 1706–7 and 1713 he grew tardier; but thereafter recovered his reputation for being an early bird until a final relapse in 1718.[103]

Nicolson's habit of arriving earlier than most of his brethren does not necessarily mean that he spent more time than them on parliamentary business. He was not above leaving before the end of a debate, as he notes several times, to take a meal with a colleague or friend.[104] He was also capable of leaving shortly after prayers, and of just calling at the House and not attending the proceedings because they failed to interest him. But these few lapses in his record are outnumbered by the many references in the diary to his attending early, staying late through a long debate, attending when few fellow-members of the House bothered to turn up, including occasions when he was the only bishop present, and attending when he was ill.

Private and money bills were notorious deterrents both to attendance and to participation. Such proceedings often degenerated into social events. But not for Nicolson.

The Money-Bill [was] read a second time [he records on 21 December 1702], and Committed to a Committee of the whole House; wherein 'twas read again (paragraph by paragraph) and piece-meal assented to. The Chairman (Lord Longvil) putting the Question and I only answering; for no other Lord in the House regarded what was doeing, this being onely (*pro forma*) to preserve a seeming Right to dissent from or amend, any part of a Money-Bill as well as others.

Nicolson's zeal on this occasion may be attributed to his interest in procedure (which is evident from the diary) and the novelty of the

---

[99] Below p. 490.   [100] 12 May 1714.
[101] See below p. 333.
[102] In 1704/5 he was first in 55% of his attendances and in the first three in 83%, and in 1705/6 32% and 80% respectively.
[103] The low point was reached in 1713 when he was in first place in 7% of his attendances and in the first three in 21%. In 1716 he was 31% and 66% and in 1718 9% and 30%.
[104] See below pp. 140, 318, 532.

occasion, coming, as it did, just over a month after he first took his seat in the House. On 16 April 1709, however, five days from the end of the session and the day on which he had booked his seat home in the York coach, six and a half years after he first sat in the Lords, Nicolson was 'in the House, till after Three, attending on Private (and Money) Bills; in pure Duty'.

Nicolson's use of his Proxy Vote

The privilege a member of the House of Lords had of leaving his proxy vote with a fellow-member[105] had its limitations. Proxies could not be used in committees or in judicial causes. Nicolson was fully aware of these limitations: he had left his proxy with Bishop Wake during the crucial session of 1709–10 when Sacheverell was impeached, and because his 'Voice cannot be given by Proxy, in matters of Judicature', Nicolson told Gibson and Wake, 'that my Horses were ready for Saddling on an Hours warning, and that on a Lawful Call, I should not be backward in venturing my Carcass'.[106] Although the proxy system was useful in enabling a conscientious peer in his absence to carry out his parliamentary duty in a limited way, Nicolson, as his attendance record shows, needed no reminding by Tenison, that there was 'a good deal of difference between your Lordship's person and Proxy'.[107]

Was Nicolson as conscientious in using his proxy as he was in his personal attendance? Three features emerge from an analysis of the available evidence.[108] First, when he missed two parliamentary sessions in 1703–4 and 1709–10, Nicolson ensured that his proxy was given to a trusted colleague, probably to cover the whole session. Second, when he expected to be late in attending a session, Nicolson again ensured that his proxy was available in time to cover most of the period for which he would be absent. Even in session nine when

[105] See Holmes, *British Politics*, pp. 307–8, 398; and below p. 137 for the working of the proxy system.

[106] BL Add. MS 6116, f. 19: N. to Wake, 2 Feb. 1710.

[107] Bodl. MS Add. A269, p. 19: Gibson to N., 30 Nov. 1712.

[108] The proxy books in which a lord's proxy was entered by a clerk of the House are not complete for the period of Nicolson's diary. Volume vii of the HLRO Proxy Books covers 1685–1733, but there are no records for the following periods (contemporary with Nicolson's diary): Nov. 1702–Oct. 1704, Mar. 1707–Nov. 1710, June 1712–Apr. 1715. The last lacuna is partially filled by vol. viii which runs from Feb. to Aug. 1714. Thus for sessions 1, 5, and 6 of the diary, and the two sessions when Nicolson was absent—1703–4 and 1709–10—there is no official record of whether Nicolson exercised his proxy right. Fortunately there is some unofficial evidence which fills some of the gaps, but there is still no full information for sessions 5, 6, and 9 (see Table 2). The proxy books seem to have been made up at a latter stage from loose sheaves of proxy lists sewn together and bound. They list the proxy holder, the proxy held, date of entry, and (when applicable) date of vacating and reason.

he arrived on 14 March 1713, well before the opening sitting on
9 April, Nicolson had sent his proxy to Wake in January of that
year.[109] In January 1716, even though Archbishop Wake had a valid
proxy from Nicolson entered at the end of the previous session on
7 September 1715, which was to remain valid until vacated by
Nicolson's reappearance in the House on 2 March 1716, Nicolson
sent, at Wake's request, another proxy 'to remove all Scruple'.[110]
It seems, therefore, reasonable to assume that in sessions five and six,
for which we have no proxy evidence, Nicolson probably made his
proxy available for the early parts of the sessions which he missed.

Third, when he left early before the end of a session, Nicolson
usually left his proxy (he did not in sessions two to five). Though he
stayed to the end of session six, earlier he had thought that there
might 'be Room enough for a longer Stay than perhaps I shall be
well able to make' and he had hinted that he would be leaving his
proxy with Wake.[111] In 1717, though he again stayed in London
until the end of the session on the 15 July, Nicolson last attended
the House on 6 July and on 11 July Bishop Blackburne entered
Nicolson's proxy to cover the last four days of the session.[112] All this
confirms the impression of conscientiousness gained from the bishop's
attendance record.

Comparisons with other bishops is difficult as no work has been
done on the proxies for this period. There is evidence, however, that
some of Nicolson's colleagues on the episcopal bench were not so
regular in providing proxies. For example, in the important debates
on the Schism Bill in June 1714 the Archbishop of Canterbury and
the Bishops of Gloucester and Worcester were absent from the House
for the whole of the session and yet failed to provide proxies.[113]
Worcester and Gloucester were also the only two bishops absent
from the 1710–11 session and they failed to provide proxies, as
did St Davids and Winchester in 1705–6. In 1711–12 two of the

[109] This was undoubtedly in response to a call from Tenison for 'all the Bishops to be at
the opening of the Parliament', which he thought would be in early Jan. 1713 (Bodl. MS
Add. A269, p. 19: Gibson to N., 30 Nov. 1712).

[110] Wake had asked for a new proxy because he had been translated from Lincoln to
Canterbury since he had received Nicolson's last one. Nicolson, however, thought his earlier
proxy 'stands good; provided it was in the Clerk's hands, and entered in the Book before the
last Adjournment' (BL Add. MS 6116, f. 35: N. to Wake, 9 Jan. 1716).

[111] Ibid., f. 10: same to same, 4 Dec. 1708.

[112] It seems fair, therefore, to assume Nicolson probably did the same at the end of
session 9.

[113] See below p. 606; and Bodl. MS fol. θ 666, f. 68^V, for the two votes of 11 and
14 June when the three bishops were noted as absent. Nor were these taken into account
in Nottingham's forecast of the vote on the 14th, see Leicestershire RO Finch MSS Political
Papers 161. There are no proxies recorded for them in HLRO Proxy Book viii (complete
for this session).

Table 2:
Nicolson's proxies

Session	Proxy holder and dates	Sittings before WN's arrival	Dates of WN's residence in London	Sittings after WN left London	Proxy holder and dates
1		15	14 Nov. 1702–22 Feb. 1703	6	Abp Sharp of York: 21 Feb. 1703– [1]
1703/ 1704	Abp Sharp of York[2]	Absent			
2		1	24 Oct. 1704–4 Mar. 1705	9	No proxy entered[3]
3		1	26 Oct. 1705–5 Mar. 1706	12	No proxy entered[4]
4		0	20 Nov. 1706–24 Mar. 1707	13	No proxy entered[5]
5		38	24 Dec. 1707–5 Apr. 1708	0	Nicolson contemplated leaving proxy with Bp Wake of Lincoln[6]
6		34	5 Feb. 1709–29 Apr. 1709	0	
1709/ 1710	Bp Wake of Lincoln[7]		Absent		
7		6	8 Dec. 1710–5 Apr. 1711	36	Bp Evans of Bangor: 4 April 1711– [8]
8		0	Nov. 1712–2 Apr. 1712	50	Bp Evans of Bangor: 31 Mar. 1712– [9]
9	Bp Wake of Lincoln: Jan. 1713[10]	0	14 Mar. 1713–May 1713	43	

		Period	No.	Diocesan / Metropolitan	No.
10		31 Mar. 1714–14 June 1714	10	Bp Wake of Lincoln: 12 June 1714–[11]	22
11		25 Mar. 1715–9 Sept. 1715	4	Bp Wake of Lincoln: 7 Sept. 1715– 2 Mar. 1716.[12]	9
1716	Abp Wake of Canterbury: 7 Sept. 1715–2 Mar. 1716[13]	2 Mar. 1716–26 June 1716	34		0
12		19 Feb. 1717–22 July 1717	0	Bp Blackburne of Exeter: 11 July 1717–[14]	0
13	Abp Wake of Canterbury: 16 Nov. 1717–16 Jan. 1718[15]	11 Jan. 1718–17 Mar. 1718	15		0

[1] Diary, 21 Feb. 1703 (below p. 207).
[2] BL Blenheim MS DII-10: List of proxies in Lord Sunderland's hand dated, by internal evidence, to the 1703/4 parliamentary session. Dean and Chapter Library, Carlisle, Nicolson's Collection, iii, 195, gives the date the proxy was sent to Archbishop Sharp as 25 Oct. 1703. None the less Sharp, who first attended the session on 11 Nov. 1703, did not register Nicolson's proxy until after prayers on the morning of 14 Dec. 1703. Thus it was 'too late' to be used in the important vote on the 2nd Occasional Conformity Bill (Lancashire RO DD Ke 82; LJ xvii, 334).
[3] HLRO Proxy Book vol. vii.
[4] Ibid.
[5] Ibid.
[6] BL Add. MS 6116, f. 10: N. to Wake, 4 Dec. 1708.
[7] Ibid, ff, 17 and 19: N. to Wake, 15 Dec. 1709 and 2 Feb. 1710. Dean and Chapter Library, Carlisle, Nicolson's Collection, iii, 195, gives the date the proxy was sent to Bishop Wake as 26 Nov. 1709.
[8] HLRO Proxy Book vol. vii.
[9] Ibid.
[10] Bodl. MS Add. A269, p. 20: Gibson to N., 23 Jan. 1713.
[11] HLRO Proxy Book vol. viii.
[12] Ibid, vol. vii.
[13] Ibid.
[14] Ibid.
[15] Ibid.; BL Add. MS 6116, f. 60: N. to Wake, 28 Nov. 1717.

five absent bishops failed to provide their proxies, including
Bishop Robinson of Bristol who held the office of Lord Privy Seal.
Generally speaking, when a large number of bishops were absent
for the whole session, the majority did ensure that their proxies
were available.[114] But many of those who provided proxies were
not so prompt as Nicolson in providing them. The session of 1711–12,
when there was anxiety and excitement about the peace negotiations and the terms of the Anglo-French preliminaries, was an
exception in that all the proxies were registered on or before the
first day of the session. Usually they were late, often up to a month
after the session opened, and in 1706–7 two proxies were later
still. On 21 January 1707 (the session having opened on 3 December
1706) Bishop Hall of Bristol, after making a lame excuse for not
attending, confessed

I have not sent my Proxy, becaus I was told with great assurance there was no
use of it. But on Saturday night the Bishop of Worcester told me 'twas needful
to send it speedily upon account of some motion made in the Hous by the Earl
of Nottingham. Therefore I do it by this first opportunity . . .[115]

He proved, however, not to be the last to register, for the Bishop of
Ely's proxy did not reach the book until 18 February. For Nicolson
—as for his friend Wake[116]—such negligence would have been
unthinkable.[117]

---

[114] In 1704–5, for example, all eight bishops absent (not including the vacant St Davids)
provided proxies. In 1706–7 of the five absent (excluding the vacant Winchester) only
Gloucester (the same Bishop Fowler who failed to register his proxy in 1710–11 and 1714)
did not enter a proxy.

[115] Surrey RO Somers MS D10: Hall to Somers, 21 Jan. 1706[/7].

[116] Of the eight occasions when Wake records his absence from the House between 1705
and 1717 (which coincide with the survival of the proxy records) he only failed twice to
cover his absence, and both occasions were the fag end of sessions. See Lambeth Palace
MS 1770: Wake's diary, *passim*.

[117] Nicolson also seems to have been assiduous in the collection and use of the proxies of
fellow bishops (though the evidence for the early part of Nicolson's career is again scanty).
In his first session, Nicolson was given Sharp's proxy and that of the moderate Whig Bishop
Kidder of Bath and Wells (both on 11 Jan. 1703), though Kidder soon thought better of it,
due to Nicolson's use of it on 11 Jan., and on 16 Jan. vacated it by appearing in the House
(see below pp. 00–00). From 1714 to 1718 Nicolson received the following proxies from
several Whig bishops:
  Wake of Lincoln, 10 Mar.–9 April 1714
  Cumberland of Peterborough, 8 May–14 June 1714
  Cumberland, 27 May 1715–22 Feb. 1716
  Talbot of Salisbury, 3 Mar.–6 Mar. 1716
  Fleetwood of Ely, 9 Apr. 1716–(vacating not recorded)
  Wake of Canterbury, 12 June 1716–(vacating not recorded)
  Wake, 31 Jan.–11 Mar. 1718
  (Source: HLRO Proxy Books vii and viii).

The Committee Man

(i) *General committee work and the Journal Committee*   Committee work formed an important part of the legislative, judicial, and inquisitorial work of the House of Lords. Unfortunately the formal records of the House tell us relatively little about the proceedings of committees, beyond the bare outline, and virtually nothing about their *working* membership.[118] The practice was to constitute a committee of all those present in the House on the day of its appointment; and this *full* membership was recorded in the *Journals*.[119] But obviously only a small section of those nominated and entitled to sit bothered to attend at all, and of those a still smaller proportion attended regularly.[120] For example, during the first month and a half of his sitting in the Lords (23 November to 29 December 1702) Nicolson was appointed to thirteen committees, while his diary records his attending only four.[121] As a conscientious attender of Lords' sittings, he automatically attended many meetings of Committees of the Whole House.[122] But he only occupied the chair of such a committee three times: on 22 March 1709 on the Mutiny Bill, on 31 January 1711 on the Malt Bill, and on 5 September 1715 on the Palatines Bill.[123]

During Nicolson's sixteen years in the House only one bishop, Burnet, was called on with any regularity to be chairman of the Committee of the Whole House. He took the chair twenty-one times from 1703 to 1711, though this pales beside the record of some of the peers, notably the 3rd Earl of Clarendon's 124 contributions in the years 1710-18.[124]

[118] The records of the meetings of 'select' or private committees are to be found in the HLRO Minutes of Committees: vols vi (1698-1704), vii (1704-10), and viii (1710-20) cover the period of the diary. Between 1702 and 1718 these minutes list only twice the members attending specific meetings: the committee enquiring into the Commissioners of Accounts, 28 Mar. 1704 (HLRO Minutes of Committees, vi, 450), and the committee on the Public Records, 15 Nov. 1704 (ibid., vii, 2). The records of the Committee of the Whole House are in the HLRO Manuscript Minutes of the House. Neither of these two types of records are printed in the *LJ*, though limited selections from the Minutes of Committees appear in HMC *Lords MSS*.

[119] See J. C. Sainty, *The Origin of the Office of Chairman of Committees in the House of Lords* (HLRO Memorandum no. 52 [1974]), p. 2.

[120] An attendance of 'no less than 26' was correctly considered a 'verie full Committee'. SRO Montrose MSS, GD220/5/826: Montrose to Mungo Graham, 11 Dec. 1718.

[121] *LJ* xvii, 171-202 *passim*; below pp. 151, 154-5.

[122] For the function and membership of these 'Grand Committees', see below p. 91.

[123] *LJ* xviii, 676; xix, 207; xx, 223. Nicolson makes no mention of his chairing the Committee on the Palatines in the diary. See also Sainty, *Chairman of Committees*, and his notes upon which this publication is based, now HLRO Hist. Coll. No. 181.

[124] The other two most prominent peers as chairman were the 1st Lord Herbert with sixty-eight contributions and the 2nd Earl of Stamford with fifty-seven. Besides Nicolson and Burnet only eight other bishops chaired the Committee of the Whole House, and only

As for the 'select' or private committees of the House Nicolson notes his attendance at a great many, concerned both with public and private matters. In the former category we find committees on addresses of the House to the Queen, inquiring into deficiencies in the law, on the conduct of the war (particularly on the navy), on trade, on public bills such as the Scottish Episcopal Toleration Bill and the Sheriffs Bill, and finally on the condition of the public records.[125] His private committees were usually concerned with estate bills, with bills connected with particular bishops or churches, and with the naturalisation of aliens.[126] Finally he participated in the business committees of the House: the Committee for Privileges (though Nicolson only once records his attending it, on 31 March 1708), a committee on the standing orders of the House, and the Committee for inspecting the *Journals*.[127]

Yet despite the impression gained from the diary of a fairly assiduous committee man, Nicolson was not chosen as the chairman of a select committee until 1711,[128] and he only officiated four times thereafter.[129]

Despite the fact that bishops often formed a high proportion of the members attending the House, particularly on important occasions, they were not chosen chairman of select committees as often as their attendance record would seem to warrant.[130] It should be added that none of the great public questions of the day were given to select committees chaired by bishops. Their expertise was usually reserved for Church matters (both public and private bills) and social questions,[131] and they also did their share of routine work on private estate and naturalisation bills.

two of these, Dawes and Robinson, chaired more committees than Nicolson. HLRO Hist. Coll. No. 181; Sainty, *Chairman of Committees*, pp. 17–20.

[125] See below pp. 302 (for addresses); 350 (for law); 188 (for war and navy); 446 (for trade); 586, 596 (for Toleration and Sheriffs Bills); for a discussion of the Public Records Committee, see below pp. 40–4.

[126] See below pp. 157 (for estates); 381 (for bishops and churches); 351 (for naturalisation).

[127] See below p. 617 for the Standing Orders' Committee.

[128] Below p. 567.

[129] In 1715 Nicolson chaired two committees, one on a bill for All Souls College, Oxford, and one on a private estate bill, while in 1716 and 1717 he chaired a further two committees, one of which was on a naturalisation bill. HLRO Minutes of Committees, viii, 120, 133, 148, 170. None of these occasions is mentioned in the surviving diary.

[130] Between 1702 and 1718 only six bishops chaired more than two committees in any one session. Burnet was the most active bishop, chairing eighteen committees between these years. Nicolson was fourth, ranked behind Talbot and Dawes (with twelve each) and Trelawney and Compton (with five each) (Sainty, *Chairman of Committees*, pp. 17–20).

[131] e.g. the Bishop of Lichfield's struggle to augment the number of canons (below p. 372), the mortuaries in the diocese of St Asaph (below p. 608), workhouses and vagrants, and the poor in Bristol.

It is strange, nevertheless, that Nicolson, so regular an attender of the House and of committees, should not have been chosen chairman of select committees more often and not until he had been in the House for nine years. Seniority may have played some part in the choice,[132] and by the time Nicolson reached a senior position on the bench the practice of employing bishops as chairmen was on the wane.[133]

Two of Nicolson's committees deserve special mention. One was an internal 'business' committee, the Journal Committee, in whose work he played a useful part from 1709 to 1716. This committee was established at the beginning of each session and was responsible for reading the manuscript journals of the House and for certifying that they were correct.[134] Nicolson first mentions attending the committee on 27 April 1709, and from then until 25 January 1716 he is recorded as signing the *Journal* nineteen times. His diary, however, reveals that the committee met more often than the number of signings in the *Journal* would indicate. For example on 24 March 1711 Nicolson notes: 'The Bishop of Peterborough, Bishop of Landaff and I, went over the Journals of this Session (in a Committee) as far as the end of January; to Mr Johnson's great satisfaction.' The *Journal* shows that the three bishops signed their examination at meetings on 3 and 4 April 1711 (the period of the *Journal* covered was 18 April 1710 to 28 March 1711). On 4 April Nicolson records that he was chairman of the committee, the only time he appears to have held this post.[135]

The bishops seem to have been regular attenders at the Journal Committee, often forming the majority and sometimes the whole of its membership. Nicolson, with his particular interest in the records of Parliament, was the most active bishop on the committee, and was an important figure in this small corner of parliamentary activity.

Of much wider importance, however, was his work on the Public Records Committee.

[132] Of the bishops who chaired committees between 1702 and 1718, more than half were raised to the episcopate between 1674 and 1699, and these appear more frequently as chairmen than those raised to the episcopate after 1702. Bishop Evans of Bangor, for example, consecrated in 1702 and a regular attender, only chaired two select committees. Seniority did not seem to figure in choosing chairmen of the Committee of the Whole House. Political reliability seems to be the criterion here: Burnet chaired it more frequently in the years of Whig ascendancy and the same is true for Robinson and Dawes in the years of Tory control.

[133] The major exception was the Bishop of Bangor in 1790–4. See Sainty, *Chairman of Committees*, pp. 20–33.

[134] The committee, which was technically a sub-committee of the Committee for Privileges, met several times a session to read and sign the Journal. The names of those who signed, the date of their signing, and the dates covered by the Journal examined, are printed in the *LJ*.

[135] *LJ* xix, 239, 269.

(ii) *The Committee on the Public Records*   Nicolson arrived in London in November 1702 with a scholarly reputation as Anglo-Saxonist and bibliographer undamaged by the recent controversy with Atterbury, and with the substantial achievement of the volumes of the *English Historical Library* and the *Scottish Historical Library* to his name. Only eight days after his arrival he learned, in the course of dinner with Burnet, that the 'Records in the Tower [were] confused'.[136] Nicolson was no stranger to the records of Chancery stored in the Tower of London, having first used them in 1678 at the behest of Thomas Machell, then a Fellow of Queen's College.[137] On 11 December Nicolson made his first visit to the Parliament Office—the repository of parliamentary records housed in the Jewel Tower near the House of Lords. Twelve days later he was at the Office again along with the members of a committee—prompted by inter-House disputes over the Occasional Conformity Bill—charged with examining precedents of bills carrying financial penalties which had been initiated in the Lords. The peers who met at the Parliament Office on 23 December, Lords Sunderland, Manchester, Anglesey, Herbert, and Somers, were (with the exception of Herbert) some of the men Nicolson was to work with on the Committee for Public Records in the next few years.

This select Committee for the records was established during Nicolson's absence from the 1703–4 session under the chairmanship of Lord Halifax. Halifax, who shared the bishop's antiquarian interests and was to become his friend, was the man behind a project of 'beginning a vast Design in Collecting the publick Records'.[138] The committee met four times during the 1703–4 session, receiving reports on conditions in the Tower of London and in the Treasury Office in the Exchequer. The following November, after the government had been asked to consider remedies, a second committee was appointed to further inspect the records. Meanwhile a sub-committee, headed by Sir Christopher Wren, had reported on the conditions in the Tower.[139]

Nicolson was made a member of this second committee, appointed on 11 November 1704, and was present at its opening meeting on the following day, when Halifax was again chosen chairman. Indeed,

[136] See below p. 131.
[137] Nicolson described this work in the Tower as 'this drudgery . . . I was unwillingly putt upon.' See R. S. Ferguson, 'Wills relating to the Dean and Chapter Library at Carlisle . . .', *CW* 1st ser. iv (1880), 2.
[138] See below p. 231.
[139] See below p. 223. For the meeting and proceedings of the 'first' select committee, see HLRO Minutes of Committees, vi, 347, 349, 357; HMC *Lords MSS* vi, 36–8. See PRO SP 45/21; T1/89; T1/92 for documents on the committee's investigations into the State Paper Office and the Tower.

Halifax was to chair all but two of the fifty meetings of the select committees on various types of records which were held between 20 December 1703 and 11 July 1713.[140] At the first meeting of the second committee Nicolson and Bishop Williams of Chichester were deputed to inspect what had been done at the Tower since the previous winter. This they did on 13 November. As a noted antiquarian Nicolson was undoubtedly the most expert member of the committee, although Lord Somers had an unrivalled expertise in the field of legal records.[141] On 16 November 1704 Nicolson viewed the Remembrancers' and the Augmentation Offices, and the next day descended early on the Tower with Bishop Williams. They were joined there by some other members of the committee and viewed the improvements being carried out by the clerks. Nicolson's private interests undoubtedly coincided with his public work, which enabled him to devote more time to working on the records than was warranted or required by the committee. This interest not only led to Nicolson appointing one of his servants to copy out for his own use a report by Peter Le Neve, on the condition of the records in the Treasury Office given to the committee on 28 December 1705,[142] but it also led him to establish close connections, which often bloomed into friendships, with the men responsible for looking after the records, for example George Holmes.[143] As a consequence Nicolson became the unofficial channel of communication between these men 'in the field' and the committee. This channel was established quite early,[144] and proved mutually beneficial to all concerned.

In the 1705-6 session the committee was not revived until mid-December; but meanwhile Nicolson occupied himself with quizzing Lord Somers about Chancery and Paper Office records and with solo tours of inspection of the Tower and of the Parliament Office. After a discussion with Nicolson, Halifax proposed to the House that the committee be revived on 15 December, and it was the bishop who was responsible for widening the committee's brief into a consideration of the future of the Cotton Library.[145]

---

[140] HLRO Minutes of Committees, vi, 347–viii, 50 *passim*.

[141] For Somers's activities with the records, see W. L. Sachse, *Lord Somers* (Manchester, 1975), pp. 242–3.

[142] The copy is still among the Nicolson MSS in the Dean and Chapter Library, Carlisle (Nicolson MSS iii, pp. 317–25). Nicolson also partially copied, and his servant completed, other reports brought in to the committee (ibid., pp. 329–39, 341–7).

[143] See below p. 229 for Holmes.

[144] On 1 Dec. 1704. There were three more meetings of this committee in this session, resulting in a report which was presented to the House on 31 Jan. Unfortunately we cannot be sure whether Nicolson attended these meetings as his diary is missing for the period after 15 Jan. 1705.

[145] Below p. 329.

The committee's first working meeting took place on 22 December under Halifax, where the bishop's pet topic of the Cotton Library was raised, along with the Paper Office and the records in the keeping of the Master of the Rolls.[146] Before the next meeting on 28 December, Nicolson had discussed the committee's work with the clerks responsible for looking after the records and had been informed of various other collections of records which had not yet fallen within the purview of the committee. He was also told that the committee was causing 'much alarm' among certain record keepers.[147] Nicolson, with Halifax, Somers, and Rochester, attended the next meeting, where the Keeper of the Paper Office and the deputies to the Chamberlains of the Exchequer were interviewed on the condition of their records, and Lord Keeper Cowper and Lord Chief Justice Holt acquainted the committee with the state of the Cotton Library.[148] Nicolson, however, despite his interest was not above being tempted away by Archbishop Sharp to dinner.[149]

On 7 January 1706 Nicolson made another visit to the Tower, but seems to have missed the next committee meeting on 14 January, possibly because he was engaged in a long committee on naval affairs. Nor did he attend on 16 January, when the Master of the Rolls reported on his office.[150] He did hear, however, Halifax's report to the House on 17 January on the deficiencies in the Paper Office, and on the following day was at the well-attended committee. This committee, which received a catalogue of the Paper Office and then adjourned to the Westminster Chapter House to inspect the fabric and the records of the Chamberlains of the Exchequer, may have been so well attended because of Halifax's report which revealed neglect of the records in the Paper Office by several Secretaries of State.[151]

Two of the next three meetings were adjourned for want of a quorum, Nicolson being among those absent; but he acceded to a specific request from Halifax on 13 February and attended with other members of the committee an inspection of the Paper Office

---

[146] HMC *Lords MSS* vi, 37; vii, 57.

[147] Below p. 336. Later at least one of the Six Clerks in Chancery approved of the work of the committee and, despite the inconvenience of being 'tied by the Legg this short Vacation to attend and watch their Lordships Motions in relation to our Office', he feared 'noe harm from them soe am very Easy, [and] I rather hope for Good' (Hereford County RO Brydges MSS A81/23a: William to Francis Brydges, 13 and 22 Mar. 1710).

[148] Below p. 338; HMC *Lords MSS* vi, 37–8; vii, 57.

[149] Below p. 338.   [150] HMC *Lords MSS* vi, 38.

[151] *LJ* xvii, 69; HMC *Lords MSS* vi, 38. At this meeting Nicolson had intended to acquaint the committee with the records in the Fishmongers' keeping and of the books belonging to the old Court of Requests. According to the minutes, the committee does not appear to have considered the records of the Court of Wards in Fish Yard until Feb. 1709 (HMC *Lords MSS* viii, 27).

on the following day. Thereafter the bishop missed three committee meetings in February and March, including that held on 4 March, the day before he left for the North, at which its members agreed to an address which was reported to the House the same day and agreed to.[152] A further six meetings concerned with the Cotton Library were held after Nicolson's departure from London.[153]

After the active session of 1705-6, the Committee on the Public Records entered a period of quiescence for nearly three years (though a committee for the Cotton Library was established in 1707, the result of which was a bill enabling the Crown to purchase the library).[154]

The revived Committee on Records, appointed on 27 January 1709, met formally for the first time on 4 February, the day before Nicolson's arrival in London.[155] Between then and his first recorded attendance on 23 March, the committee sat eight times.[156] It seems inconceivable that Nicolson did not attend some of these meetings. He certainly attended an inspection by the Committee of the Records in the Queen's Bench and the Court of Wards on 12 April and paid private visits to the latter on 13 April and to the Tower on 15 April. The final meeting of the session saw Nicolson making amendments to Halifax's report from the committee, which was then put before the House and agreed to on 20 April.[157]

From the spring of 1709 the committee lay becalmed until March 1711.[158] Earlier in the 1710–11 session, Nicolson had seen Le Neve and had been informed of the likely conflict between the latter and Halifax over keys to the records of the Treasury, and had made his usual private visit to the Tower and the Remembrancer's Office. Further private visits to these two repositories and to the Rolls Chapel, the Parliament Office, and Lambeth Palace Library followed during the session,[159] while the committee concerned itself with the records of the Queen's Bench, the Cotton Library, the records of the Court of Wards kept in Fish Yard, and the Rolls Chapel.[160] The final meeting took place on 31 May 1711, after Nicolson had left for his diocese.[161]

The session of 1711-12 sees Nicolson's last recorded entries in

[152] HMC *Lords MSS* vi, 38; *LJ* xviii, 135-6.

[153] HLRO Minutes of Committees, vii, 186, 190, 192-3, 195; HMC *Lords MSS* vii, 57-8.

[154] See HMC *Lords MSS* vii, 58-9. For the Cotton Library Committee see ibid. vi, 38. Nicolson had heard of its impending revival on 9 Jan. 1707.

[155] HLRO Minutes of Committees, vii 334; HMC *Lords MSS* viii, 27.

[156] HLRO Minutes of Committees, vii, 339-48. For its proceedings, see HMC *Lords MSS* viii, 27-8.   [157] Below pp. 497-8; *LJ* xvii, 715-17.

[158] See *LJ* xix, 19, 247; below pp. 556, 562.

[159] Below pp. 527, 564.   [160] HMC *Lords MSS* viii, 28-9.

[161] For its report to the House, see *LJ* xix, 314.

his diary concerning the committee. On 26 February 1712 Nicolson saw Halifax and discussed his wish to remove the Rolls Chapel records to the Tower; and on 12 March he acted as a channel for a petition from Thomas Madox, a Clerk of the Augmentations Office, to the committee.[162]

The last select Committee on Public Records in Queen Anne's reign was appointed in June 1713 to inquire into the state and condition of the Queen's Remembrancer's Books and the Port Books belonging to the Commissioners of the Customs. The committee, chaired again by Halifax, met seven times, producing a report on 11 July 1713.[163] But Halifax's chief coadjutor over the past eight and a half years had this time no part in its compilation. The needs of his diocese had called him north by the end of May.

The result of all this work on the public records was the publication in 1719 of the parliamentary report which formed the basis for future work on the public records in general and on state papers in particular.[164] The pity of it was that of the three leading members of the committee, two—Lords Halifax and Somers—were dead by the time of publication, while the third—Bishop Nicolson—was in political exile in Ireland.[165]

The Prelate-Politician in action: Lobbying, Whipping, and Party Organisation

The political importance of the bishops in the Court and party struggle for control of the House of Lords has been discussed elsewhere,[166] but little has been said of their role in the day-to-day

[162] The committee met only once during this session, on 16 May 1712, six weeks after Nicolson had left London (HMC *Lords MSS* viii, 29).

[163] *LJ* xix, 606–7; see HMC *Lords MSS* viii, 29–30 for its proceedings. William Lowndes's report to Lord Oxford on the location and state of the public financial records in 1713 can be found in BL Loan 29/45B/12/268–71.

[164] *The Report of the Lords Committees Appointed by the House of Lords to View and Consider the Public Records*. For a discussion of some aspects of the committee's work see E. M. Hallam, 'The Tower of London as a Record Office', *Archives*, xiv (1979), 3–10; 'Problems with Record Keeping in early eighteenth-century London: Some Pictorial Representations of the State Paper Office, 1705–6', *Journal of the Society of Archivists*, vi. no. 4 (1979), 219–26.

[165] Because of the variable nature of Nicolson's private record in his diary as to whether he attended committees, there are only two sessions—1705–6 and 1710–11—where there is a full record of his attendance at this committee. In the first session he attended five of the eight meetings which were held during the period of his London residence. In 1711 he attended all three. A comparison with other members of the committee is impossible as we only know the names of those who attended four of the committees (HMC *Lords MSS* vi, 36–7; below pp. 338, 356), and two inspection tours (below pp. 228, 377). Halifax, whose attendance as chairman is known, was certainly the most active member, and it seems safe to assume Somers (with his legal expertise) and Nicolson (with his bibliographical expertise) were not far behind.

[166] Holmes, *British Politics*, pp. 398–400.

politics both inside and outside the House. Nicolson's diary gives a rare insight not only into his own activities but into those of some of his colleagues on the bench.

For one thing there are many instances in the diary of Nicolson being lobbied by outside interests and used as a channel by which to push a bill through the House. We have already seen how Nicolson supported the Lowthers of Whitehaven over the Parton Harbour Bill; and he continued subsequently to help James Lowther in the House.[167]

One of the first occasions which the diary reveals of Nicolson being lobbied over a private bill (though one in which he was intimately concerned as Bishop of Carlisle) was in November 1704. It was then that Thomas Coke of Melbourne, Derbyshire, Vice-Chamberlain of the Queen's Household, saw him about bringing in a bill to confirm the agreement made between Coke and Bishop Smith, Nicolson's predecessor, concerning the rectory of Melbourne. Before Nicolson's elevation to the bishopric, Coke had used him as a go-between with other bishops in an unsuccessful attempt to pass a similar bill.[168] Now Nicolson was in a position to give direct help and with this help Coke's second attempt succeeded, his bill receiving the royal assent in March 1705.[169]

Nicolson was also lobbied over private petitions concerning judicial causes before the Lords. The success of the suppliants in persuading the bishop to attend was mixed. Mary Lamplugh was successful in getting the bishop to attend her cause, while Dr Woodroffe had his petition promptly returned.[170] As one would expect Nicolson was lobbied by a large number of clerics (e.g. Dean Binckes of Lichfield over his bill before the House),[171] and by members of the Commons.[172]

Nicolson, however, was well able to reverse the process and turn lobbyist himself, particularly when he was closely concerned in some piece of legislation or in a judicial cause. Two case histories, one from 1707–8, the other from 1711, will serve to illustrate his skill and persistence in lobbying and exploring all channels open to the experienced politician which the Bishop of Carlisle had by then become.

Nicolson arrived in London for the 1707–8 session with the

---

[167] See above p. 26 for the Parton Harbour Bill; and Cumbria (Carlisle) RO Lonsdale MSS D/Lons/W, bundle 12: Lowther to [Gilpin], 25 Aug. 1715, for an example of later co-operation.

[168] See CW i (1901), 41.   [169] See below pp. 218–19; HMC Lords MSS vi, 227–8.

[170] See below pp. 328, 358, 361.   [171] Below p. 372.

[172] As stated above, the lobbying by both sides over the Parton Harbour Bills was the most important instance.

prospect of facing the case of Hugh Todd in the Court of Common
Pleas. The bishop had recently excommunicated Todd, a Canon
and Prebendary of Carlisle, for his part in the controversy over the
validity of Nicolson's right to act as Visitor to the Cathedral
Chapter.[173] Todd had appealed and Nicolson had to show cause why
a prohibition should not be awarded. The bishop soon learned from
his lawyers that his case in law was uncertain. It is not clear from the
diary whether Nicolson on his arrival in London had already begun
to think about legislation as the answer to his problem of how to
restore his *ante bellum* position in the Chapter at Carlisle; that is,
to regain his right as Visitor, which had been brought into question
by Dean Atterbury's challenge to the validity of the foundation
statutes of the Cathedral.

At first Nicolson appears to have put all his effort into a campaign
to muster support on behalf of his case in the Court of Common
Pleas. He received much encouragement from the bishops assembled
at the traditional Boxing Day dinner at Lambeth, from the two archbishops individually, and from the influential Junto peers, Sunderland,
Halifax, and Somers, at his first attendance at the House on 7 January
1708. He had also begun work, with Gibson, on his printed *Case*, which
was to prove his main weapon in the propaganda war that was soon
to develop with Atterbury over the Cathedrals Bill. Not all his early
lobbying was successful. He met with some opposition, or at best
coolness towards his case, some of it close to home. His former dean,
William Grahme, was unimpressed; and so, more significantly, was the
latter's brother, Colonel James Grahme, MP for Appleby.

It was on 12 January that Lord Somers first indicated that he was
prepared to introduce a bill in the House to validate the statutes of
Carlisle, and similar cathedrals of a Henrician foundation. Within
three days Nicolson, who had the full encouragement of Archbishop
Tenison, was in a position to present him with a draft bill. Meanwhile
Todd's case in the Court of Common Pleas was going badly for the
bishop. Eventually, despite Nicolson employing the legal services
of Serjt. Chesshyre and Sir Joseph Jekyll, one of the ablest Whig
lawyer-politicians, Todd successfully procured a final writ of prohibition against the episcopal sentence. Nicolson, after procrastination which at one stage threatened to turn support away from the
bill, was forced to absolve Todd. The result could be interpreted as a
judicial bolstering of Atterbury's position. It became all the more
imperative to get the bill through parliament.

---

[173] For the background to this controversy, see James, pp. 163-9; Bennett, *Tory Crisis*,
pp. 90-7; and below pp. 428-30. The following paragraphs are based on Nicolson's diary
and on Lambeth Palace MS 1770, ff. 56ᵛ-58ʳ: Wake's diary.

By the end of January 1708 Somers had converted Nicolson's draft into a bill and it received Tenison's seal of approval. The archbishop threw his weight publicly behind the bill with a circular letter to the bishops of his province urging their support. The bill was introduced into the Lords on 3 February by Somers 'with a pathetic speech', and a second reading was ordered for 7 February. Although prospects in the Upper House, with its now firm Whig-Court majority, seemed good, Nicolson was not betrayed into complacency. He was beginning to turn his attention towards the House of Commons where the bill would go after it had passed the Lords, and where the outcome seemed rather less secure. Work continued with Gibson on his *Case*, with the swaying of opinion in the Commons now specifically in mind. Sir Joseph Jekyll, as MP for Eye, promised Nicolson his support for the bill in the Commons, as he already had done to his brother-in-law, Somers. The second reading of the bill went off quietly and it was committed for a week later.

On 13 February, a Friday as it happened, Nicolson received the bad news from Lord Chancellor Cowper that the Queen opposed the bill. It seemed she had been influenced by Archbishop Sharp informing her that the judges of the Common Pleas had condemned the statutes of Carlisle Cathedral. Nicolson, fully aware of the importance of the Queen's support, especially if she were to attend the debates on the bill,[174] hurried off to present Sharp with his *Case*, and the archbishop promised 'to set Her Right'.[175] Nicolson continued to brood over his fellow bishops, informing Wake of Lincoln on 14 February, that the Committee of the Whole House had been postponed until 19 February and that he need not attend the House until then. The postponement had been engineered by Godolphin, Somers, and Cowper as 'the best way to set the Queen at Rights, and to prevail for a ready Dispatch in the House of Commons', for all the judges were ordered to be present in the Lords and the Queen's attendance was predicted. The prediction was confirmed a few days later.

On 16 February Nicolson took his *Case* to the printers, collecting the final copies at 3 o'clock the following afternoon. He immediately delivered the first copy to Sharp, only to be told by his Metropolitan that he had opposed the bill because of Nicolson's refusal to obey the decision of the Court of Common Pleas. Next day, on the eve of the resumed debate on the bill, Nicolson, armed with his

---

[174] For the political importance of the Queen's presence at debates, see Holmes, *British Politics*, pp. 390-1.

[175] Sharp himself was finally to oppose the bill, as was his son, John Sharp, MP for Ripon, in the Commons.

newly printed *Case* and using a coach borrowed from Bishop Wake, started to lobby his fellow members of the Lords in earnest, reaching thirteen lords that morning, both Whigs and Tories, bishops and peers, and significantly six of the leading Scottish peers. Having learned, from Jekyll, that the judges would unanimously declare for him on the following day, Nicolson continued his canvassing in the afternoon, reaching three more Scottish peers, three judges, and three bishops. Nicolson's lobbying continued until the last minute. 'The Bishop of Car[lisle] did not give his printed case to the Bishop of Win[chester] till he came to the house [on 19 February] when her Majesty was there.'[176]

The events of 19 February repaid all his efforts and those of his allies. Sharp objected to the bill as touching the Queen's prerogative, but this ploy to use the Queen's presence against the bill was effectively countered by Somers, Halifax, and Townshend. 'And the Bill', writes Nicolson, 'was agreed to, on the Question, by such an Irresistable Majority, that no Lord had the Hardyness to call for a Division.' The bill passed its third reading, only three voices dissenting, and was sent to the Commons on 24 February.

Armed with Archbishop Tenison's permission to use his circular letter in lobbying the Commons, Nicolson had begun his preparations there in earnest on 21 February, seeing the influential Sir Richard Onslow, a future Speaker, and James Lowther. Canvassing of members continued steadily for the next few days, Nicolson again paying particular attention to the Scots who were 'most zealously and unanimously my friends'.

Atterbury, who believed that the bill would founder in the Commons,[177] now launched his counter-attack in the paper war in the form of a broadsheet. Nicolson, ever ready, replied with a broadsheet of his own the day after Atterbury's appeared! But he was chastened to learn from Somers and the Duke of Devonshire that there were some Whig opponents in the Commons, among them the brilliant barrister, Sir Thomas Parker, MP for Derby, who could only be pacified if Nicolson bowed to the Court of Common Pleas and granted Todd his absolution. This the bishop finally and reluctantly agreed to. The bill passed the Commons' second reading on 28 February by the small majority of twenty-eight. 'All agreed', wrote Nicolson, 'we must be more diligent against Thursday [the committee stage].'

On 1 March began the critical week for the bill, and Nicolson pulled out all stops. On that day, having previously armed himself with the statutes of the cathedrals of the Henrician foundation from

---

[176] Bodl. MS Ballard 39, f. 33: James Harris to [Charlett], 24 [Feb.] 1708.
[177] *Atterbury Epist. Corr.* iii, 285: Atterbury to Trelawney, 6 Feb. 1708.

Lambeth and having visited Wake who described him as 'full of preparing for his bill', Nicolson and a small group of five friends devised the final tactics at *The Dog* tavern, dividing the lobbying of the still unconvinced members between them. The plan was put into operation throughout the 2, 3, and 4 March. Nicolson's new *Case* and a copy of the statutes were distributed to as many MPs as was physically possible, and fellow bishops were recruited in the conversion drive. Even when the committee stage was delayed for five days by the unexpected news of the attempted invasion by the Pretender, the campaign continued though at a reduced rate. On 9 March a now confident bishop saw the bill pass the committee with ease, two motions against it having been defeated by majorities of forty-three and fifty. Nicolson's hard work had paid off handsomely, and he celebrated in typical style with some of his lieutenants.

A last minute attempt to sabotage the bill on 18 March by John Sharp, MP, was foiled. The Lords agreed to the Common's amendments to the bill on 19 March and it received the royal assent on the following day. Nicolson received the grateful thanks of Archbishop Tenison.

The same lobbying skills Nicolson again used to good effect over the case of James Greenshields, a Scottish Episcopalian minister, persecuted by the Kirk, who was preparing to bring his appeal to the House of Lords early in 1711.[178] Here Nicolson was in the thick of a *milieu* in which he evidently felt at home—the emigré Scots in London.[179] This is probably why he was chosen by Greenshields as the man to give him the entrée into English parliamentary circles. Greenshields brought his case to Nicolson on 27 December 1710, and on the same day he was touring with Nicolson the houses and lodgings of the Scottish peers and members of the Commons. Since the 1710 election there had been an episcopalian majority among the forty-five Scottish Commoners and the sixteen representative peers in the Westminster Parliament, so that there was a solid basis of support for the cause.[180]

Using the good offices of Gibson, Nicolson secured for Greenshields

[178] The following paragraphs are based on the diary and on Lambeth Palace MS 1770, f. 105[V]: Wake's diary.

[179] See above p. 10.

[180] Richard Dungworth, one of Greenshields's associates, classified the sixteen representative peers in Nov. 1710 as seven Episcopal Tories, eight Court Tories, and one Presbyterian Court Tory. He classified the Scottish MPs as twenty-five Episcopal Tories, fourteen Court Tories, and seven Whigs. In Jan. 1711 he further classified the peers as forty-seven Professed Episcopalians, and eighteen Not Disaffected (to the episcopal persuasion). Christ Church, Wake MS 17, ff. 268–9; 5, f. 13: Dungworth to Wake, 11 Nov. 1710, 14 Jan. 1711. The Nov. 1710 list has been printed in D. Szechi, 'Some insights on the Scottish MPs and peers returned in the 1710 election', *SHR* lx (1981), 61–75.

an audience with Tenison. On this occasion when Nicolson was fighting for the toleration of the Episcopal Church in North Britain, he found the Tories standing with him, including his erstwhile opponent over the Cathedrals Bill, Archbishop Sharp. All was not plain sailing, however, and the Presbyterian Duke of Argyll, an ally of the Tory ministry, made his opposition plain.

Nicolson began lobbying in early January 1711, concentrating on the Scottish peers, members of the Junto, and the bishops. At the same time he was kept in touch with Scottish episcopal feeling by the frequent visits he received from Scottish divines and associates of Greenshields. On 19 February the appeal was introduced into the Lords by Lord North to be heard on 1 March. Just before the hearing, Nicolson arranged a meeting in his lodgings to plan the approach in parliament. Present were Lords Somers and Cowper (probably the two best legal brains in the House) and the Bishops of Bangor, Lincoln, and Norwich—all moderate Whigs. It was decided to restrain Greenshields's appeal 'to the Civil part, without touching on the Authority of the Kirk'. This wise strategy aimed at avoiding conflict between Whig and Tory, English and Scot, worked and on 1 March the sentence of the Edinburgh magistrates and the Scottish Lords of Sessions was unanimously reversed with 'little or no Debate on the main Subject'. The whole of the bench of twenty bishops present agreed in their desire to uphold Greenshields. The successful conclusion to the case led the following session to the introduction by the Harley ministry of a bill for the toleration of episcopacy in Scotland.[181]

As we shall see later[182] the Archbishop of Canterbury presided from Lambeth over a stringent whipping system, designed to secure the maximum attendance at Westminster of all bishops of a Low Church or 'moderate' persuasion. Once in London and attending Parliament the discipline organised by Tenison and his lieutenants continued. The traditional large gathering at Lambeth for dinner on Boxing Day of all the bishops present in London, though largely a social occasion, was used to discuss pressing religious and political problems.[183] Smaller, and usually party biased groups met frequently at Lambeth and in the houses and lodgings of other bishops to discuss and organise. Nicolson's diary is a major source for revealing this organisation in action. A good example is the meeting on 3 December 1705 at Lambeth, three days before the 'Church in Danger' debate, where it was decided 'that every Bishop say something,

[181] See below pp. 531–53.   [182] Below p. 604.
[183] e.g. below pp. 437, 525; and Lambeth Palace MS 1770, f. 72^V: Wake's diary, 26 Dec. 1708.

of the State of his own Diocese, on Thursday'. Tenison clearly expected his party to stand up and be counted.

Upon Nicolson's arrival in London from Carlisle his first visitors usually included a Whig bishop or Gibson, acting as Tenison's envoy, who briefed Nicolson on the situation in parliament and on the general state of politics. Nicolson himself, during the course of a session, often acted as the carrier of news to Lambeth which kept the frequently disabled Tenison informed of proceedings in the House, and in later years he performed the same service for Wake.[184] On important occasions Tenison would summon the bishops to attend on a particular bill or debate.[185] Whipping, however, was not exclusively the province of the Archbishop, and on one occasion at least Nicolson was 'hauled' to the House by an MP to attend on a bill which had suddenly been returned from the Commons.[186] This particular bill, which was designed to give toleration to Episcopalians in Scotland, was close to Nicolson's heart. It provides, therefore, a rare insight into the exercise of political pressure on the Whig bishops.

The bill as introduced was generally approved of, but it contained certain oaths to which the Scottish Episcopalians objected.[187] The Lords, however, amended the bill, including the oaths. The Commons approved the Lords' amendments, except the altering of the oaths and they restored the oath of abjuration as it was taken in England. On the vote in the Lords on whether to pass the bill with the Commons' amendments, the bishops split on party lines, the Whigs against the bill, the Tories for it. Nicolson, though a State Whig, could have been expected to support the bill, as he supported toleration in Scotland. He had also been partly responsible for its emergence by his strong advocacy of James Greenshields's case the previous year. The bill was designed to prevent the recurrence of such a case. From Greenshields's report of the vote on 26 February 1712, it appears that Nicolson was leaving the chamber to vote with his Tory colleagues on the bench in support of the bill when he was stopped by two Whig bishops, Wake of Lincoln and Evans of Bangor, who successfully cajoled him to staying and voting against the bill. Political allegiance and the pressure of a party machine can be seen here triumphing over personal and clerical predilections, although the manœuvring over the oaths, especially over the form of abjuration, doubtless helped to salve Nicolson's conscience.

[184] e.g. below pp. 529, 590 for Tenison; and pp. 674–81 for Wake.
[185] e.g. when Nicolson was summoned to attend the Schism Bill in 1714, below p. 611.
[186] Below p. 589.
[187] The manœuvrings over and the debates on this bill are discussed in detail below pp. 572-5.

NICOLSON'S FINANCES AND HIS TRANSLATION
TO DERRY

Hugh Todd commented in his history of the diocese of Carlisle that

some of our Bishops have never seen their Diocese; Others have never visited there; Some have never or very seldome, confirmed the younger Sort of their People; Others, as of late have procured commenddary Livings in London, where they Reside, and came down, Once in Two or three years . . . the Reason They allege for this Extraordinary Conduct, is the Remoteness and Poverty of the Bishoprick.[188]

The diocese was indeed 'small, unpeopled' and poor, the richest living being the vicarage of Torpenhow worth £140 a year.[189] Nicolson's successor, Samuel Bradford, who was bishop from 1718 to 1723, was given the prebendary of Westminster, 'to encourage his going into a remote and cold Country', and also held the vicarage of St Mary le Bow in London *in commendam* with the bishopric, which he considered no more than his due.[190] John Waugh, Bradford's successor as Bishop of Carlisle (1723–34), and a native of the diocese, soon came to regret the 'folly of quitting Hamme his home as Dean of Gloucester, with an income of "a good £300 a year" for Rose Castle'.[191] How much, then, was the see of Carlisle worth to William Nicolson, who held no living *in commendam* with his bishopric?[192]

It is difficult to establish the exact value of a bishopric in early eighteenth-century Britain. Little, if any, contemporary evidence is available and what does exist may be contradictory. For Carlisle, the lowest valuation recorded is the official one of £531 for first fruits, which is based on the 1534 values,[193] while the highest is

[188] Bodl. MS St Edmund Hall 7/2, p. 191.

[189] Bodl. MS Ballard 4, f. 14: N. to Charlett, 24 Sept. 1702; BL Add. MS 6116, f. 15: N. to Wake, 13 Oct. 1709; Gloucestershire RO Lloyd-Baker MSS Box 4, L90: N. to Sharp, 26 May 1702. The best livings in the gift of the bishop outside the diocese were Newcastle-upon-Tyne worth about £250, and Rothbury, Northumb., worth 'about the same'. The prebendaries of the diocese were worth about £50 and the archdeaconry, which Nicolson had held for twenty years, a mere £60 a year (Diary, vol. 1b: 25 May 1702). While holding the archdeaconry, Nicolson also held the living of Addingham (from 1699) which was worth about £90 which was 'better than either the archdeaconry or the prebend of Carlisle' (*CSPD 1702-3*, p. 103: Sharp to Nottingham, 4 June 1702). In 1707 there were thirty-seven livings in the diocese with values not exceeding £50 a year, the lowest, Shap, was worth £6 (Cumbria [Carlisle] RO DRC/1/6, pp. 155–6: Carlisle Diocesan Register, 1702–34).

[190] BL Lansdowne MS 1013, f. 238: Kennett to Blackwell, 6 Apr. 1718; Christ Church, Wake MS 21, f. 135: Bradford to Wake, 22 June 1719.

[191] Bodl. MS Add. A269, pp. 90, 104: Gibson to N., 16 Aug. 1720, 12 Apr. 1724.

[192] For a contemporary view of bishoprics and commendams see Christ Church, Wake MS 18, ff. 393–4: Wake to ?, n.d. (but before 1708). The most notorious bishop for pluralism was Hooper (*Atterbury Epist. Corr.* iii, 171–3; W. M. Marshall, *George Hooper, 1640-1727, Bishop of Bath and Wells* [Sherborne, 1976], pp. 91–7, 100–2).

[193] J. Ecton, *Liber Valorem* (1711). Todd in his history of Carlisle diocese gives the 1534 values of the 'Spiritualities' at £308, those of the 'Temporalities' at £268, giving a

£1,300, a figure given in 1762 by which time episcopal incomes had risen since the early years of the century, especially since the 1740s and the rapid recovery in agrarian prosperity after 1750.[194] The real revenue during Nicolson's occupation of the diocese is likely to lie somewhere between these two figures. Fortunately three contemporary *estimates* exist for Carlisle: Nicolson's own upon his entry into the diocese was around £775 per annum, while Bishop Wake valued Carlisle at £800, and Todd in his history of the diocese arrived at a figure of £900.[195]

Like that of most bishoprics the income of Carlisle varied from year to year with the fluctuations of its landed rents and the vagaries of agriculture. Adding up the rents of the see as recorded in Nicolson's undated rent book[196] gives a total of £455 in cash, plus payments in kind including corn, oats, rye, malt, and salmon. The regular payment of rent in cash and kind, as well as the value of the yields of the bishop's own lands, varied from year to year, largely depending upon the weather. In 1706, for example, Nicolson reported that his 'rents were very well paid';[197] while 1708 was 'generally speaking the most plentiful with me, of any, since I came to Rose'.[198] The year 1714, on the other hand, proved 'droughty' and the 'scarcest' he had known to that date: his own hay yield was down to 120 cart-loads from the 326 of 1708.[199] Consequently, Nicolson's income often did not rise to the level of his expectations. For example his visitation fees in 1704 '(deducting Expences in Bills and my private pocket-Charges) hardly amounted to 10 *ll* Clear. Many of the Clergy are in Arrears for their Procurations.'[200] In 1709

gross value of £577, 'but after deducting necessary Payments, the clear value was reduced to £531 4 11 at which Sum, it is this Day, without any Diminution charged for First Fruits and Tenths' (Bodl. MS St Edmund Hall 7/2, pp. 188–9).

[194] *The Correspondence of George III*, ed. J. Fortescue (1927), i, 35.

[195] N. Sykes, *Church and State in England in the Eighteenth Century* (1934), p. 150; Christ Church Wake MS 18, f. 393; Bodl. MS St. Edmund Hall 7/2, p. 191. See also D. R. Hirschberg, 'Episcopal Incomes and Expenses, 1660–c. 1760', in *Princes and Paupers in the English Church 1500–1800*, ed. F. Heal and R. O'Day (Leicester, 1981), p. 214.

[196] Dean and Chapter Library, Carlisle, Nicolson's MSS Collection, iv, pp. 284–462. The only complete account book of Nicolson during his tenure of the see of Carlisle known to have survived shows that in 1706 he received £451 in cash (Tullie House Library, Carlisle: Bishop Nicolson's Account Book for 1706, printed below as Appendix D).

[197] Levens Hall MSS D/M: C. Musgrave to J. Grahme, 20 Apr. 1706.

[198] This is in marked contrast to the hard times generally found in Cumbria at this time, the years 1707 to 1709 being the worst of all, when it was 'rare to meet with [a farmer] who pays his rent punctually' (Cumbria [Kendal] RO WD/TE, ix, 145: B. Browne to Lady Otway, 13 Mar. 1708, quoted in J. V. Beckett, 'English Landownership in the later seventeenth and eighteenth Centuries: The Debate and the Problems', *EcHR* xxx [1977], 574).

[199] Ware transcripts, xxx, 2. For details of the hay yield in 1706, a better than average year, see below Appendix D.

[200] *CW* i (1901), 122.

Nicolson's half year's accounts (including arrears of tenths for 1708) amounted to only £117. 16s. 9d.[201] In a good year, 1708 for example, he calculated his 'whole rental' at £775, whereof only £390 seems to have been met, to which was added £105 in arrears from 1707, giving the bishop a sum of £495. He had also £347 in 'disbursements and money in hand' and £147 of rents in arrears.[202]

If a gross revenue of around £800 in a good year is accepted it places Carlisle among the poorest of English and Welsh bishoprics: much better off than, say, Llandaff, 'one of the poorest bishopricks in Christendom' as Bishop Tyler described it,[203] with around £300 a year,[204] but running far below the 'big three' of Winchester, Durham, and Canterbury with values in the mid-eighteenth century of between £5,000 and £7,000.[205] Whatever the accurate figure may have been, tenure of the see of Carlisle must have unquestionably placed a great financial strain upon its bishop. 'No bishoprics', thought Burnet, 'can be, in any good degree, served under 1000 *l* a year at least.'[206] Unfortunate bishops such as Nicolson still had to meet the many diocesan obligations and duties out of their meagre revenue. This made it difficult for a bishop to support a family and the status involved in holding a bishopric, particularly if he was resolved to be an active and resident bishop. In addition the duty of parliamentary attendance, a heavy enough charge even on the richer bishops, was 'intolerable to the poorer'.[207] It was magnified in the case of Carlisle by the diocese's remoteness from London, and what Bradford described as 'the extraordinary expence which I find attends one at so great a distance'.[208] It was the expenditure involved in holding so unremunerative a bishopric which had led Dean

---

[201] *CW* xxxv (1935), 116.   [202] Ware transcripts, xxvi, 2-4.
[203] NLW Plas yn Cefn MS 2788: Tyler to Humphries, 23 Sept. 1706.
[204] Wake's valuation in Christ Church, Wake MS 18, f. 393. Bishop Beaw's estimate in 1699 was £230 (Lambeth Palace MS 930, f. 49: Beaw to Tenison, 21 Aug. 1699), while Lord Sunderland's was £400 (below p. 364). A modern estimation has arrived at a figure of £500, while noting that Beaw's income, resulting from holding two rectories and a vicarage *in commendam*, was around £1,000 a year (J. R. Guy, 'William Beaw: bishop and secret agent', *History Today*, xxvi (1976), 801).
[205] *Correspondence of George III*, i, 33, 36, 41. Again allowances must be made for the mid-century inflation of rents. The only valuations contemporary with Nicolson for the richer sees to have so far come to light are £2,500 in rents (plus other sources of revenue, e.g. timber pales, tithes, ecclesiastical fees) for Winchester (Hampshire RO Farnham Castle MSS E/B18: Thomas Crawley to Bishop Trelawney, 17 Feb. 1713); £2,400 for Salisbury (Staffordshire RO Paget MSS D603 Correspondence Box xvi c.: R. Acherley to Lord Paget; Wake MS 18, ff. 393-4); and £2,282 for York (Borthwick Institute Sharp MSS ii, 1: Sharp's valuation of rents of estates belonging to diocese, 1693/4). See also Hirschberg, 'Episcopal Incomes and Expenses', pp. 213, 215-16.
[206] Burnet, *History*, vi, 237.   [207] Ibid., p. 228.
[208] Christ Church Wake MS 21, f. 135: Bradford to Wake, 22 June 1719. Bradford only visited his diocese twice—in 1719 and 1721.

Grahme of Carlisle to refuse it when offered in 1702, claiming that the income would beggar him if he accepted. Grahme was in the fortunate position of already holding a prebend's stall at Durham worth £800 a year, and since he would have had to give up his prebendary as well as the deanery on accepting the bishopric, he would assuredly have been the loser by the change.[209]

Nicolson's expenses are a little easier to pin down accurately than the revenue he received. The evidence surviving in his various almanacs bears on three areas of expenditure: family, diocesan, and parliamentary.

Nicolson had children to support, a 'Cargoe of Seven Children' he once described them,[210] five of whom were daughters for whom husbands had to be found and settlements made. By 1717 with four still unmarried (Mary, his eldest, had married the bishop's chaplain, Thomas Benson, in 1714, possibly with a settlement of £300),[211] Nicolson complained that he was unable to 'furnish out Proportions proper for their respective Settlements'.[212] But by far the most expensive single item in the bishop's family expenditure was the education of his two sons, Joseph and John, at Oxford, and the subsequent installation of Joseph into a living in Lincolnshire. Nicolson lists in detail[213] what Joseph cost him at Queen's College, Oxford, from 1707 to 1712: a total of £446. Joseph's preferment to Mareham-on-the-Hill in 1714 cost a further £49, and in March 1715 the bishop gave his son £20 to help rebuild a barn. In eight years Joseph had cost his father at least £515, more than the net annual income from the bishopric in a good year. The bishop evidently rated the education of his sons high in his priorities and must have made sacrifices to that end. In December 1707 he wrote to his son's tutor at Queen's, telling him that he had 'so many Irons in the Fire this winter' that he doubted whether he could support a visit of his son to London in 1708, but at all cost his son's fees and expenses would be paid (£76 was paid out in 1708). The bishop must have relented for he records £13. 15s. 0d. as the cost of Joseph's

[209] Dean Grahme's mercenary refusal of Carlisle did not prevent his grousing about how badly he had been treated by the Musgraves whom he held responsible for getting the bishopric for Nicolson. For the evidence for Grahme's refusal see HMC 6th Report, Appendix, p. 340: J. Yonge to R. Graham, 4 May 1702. For his unjustified disappointment at not getting the bishopric and his refusal to return to the diocese, even though he remained dean until 1704, see his letters to his brother in Levens Hall MSS C/G1.

[210] BL Add. MS 6116, f. 54: N. to Wake, 31 Jan. 1717.

[211] Ware transcripts, xxx, 6.

[212] BL Add. MS 6116, ff. 54, 58: N. to Wake, 31 Jan., 21 Oct. 1717.

[213] Ware transcripts, xxix, 2-3.

stay in London in 1708 (including a new suit).[214] By 1714 Nicolson had his second son at Queen's College.[215]

The major expense for any bishop arising from his diocesan duties came with his first assumption of a new bishopric. Nicolson laid out over £500 within two months. Such expense was crippling and the bishop had to resort to his two brothers for loans of £286 and £220. His expenditure for the first year of his episcopacy was a staggering £905.[216] The debts arising from his first year were to burden him for several years. Not until March 1704 did he clear with his brother John (his financial adviser in the diocese) 'the summs laid out for me upon my confirmation, Consecration, etc., with the greatest part of my First Fruits',[217] and not until 1709 did he clear himself of his financial obligation to the Musgrave family entered into before he became Bishop of Carlisle.[218]

By far the largest drain on Nicolson's purse was the regular attendance expected at the winter's parliamentary sessions in London.[219] In the winter of 1707–8 he calculated that

my attendance in Parliament . . . ammounted to about 170 *l.* in four months; whereof 70 *l.* may be struck off for the expences (extraordinary) of Law-suits [against Dr Todd] and Mr Benson. The Least I can propose to spend on that occasion makeing the like stay will be 100 *l.* without purchaseing of Cloathes.[220]

This figure seems to have been on the low side. Nicolson's Account Book has survived for 1706 and in it he recorded all his expenditure for the whole year.[221] It is possible therefore to calculate exact totals

[214] Bodl. MS Eng. lett. c.130, ff. 8–9: N. to John Hill, 8 Dec. 1707; Ware transcripts, xxix, 2.

[215] BL Add. MS 6116, f. 34: N. to Wake, 1 Nov. 1714.

[216] James, p. 95, quoting Ware transcripts, v, 2; xv, 1–3. Nicolson had been warned in May 1702 by Archbishop Sharp of the likely expense on entry into a see. Nicolson 'waited on the Archbishop who shewed his Accounts (double to a Bishop's) for coming into his See; twixt 6 and 700 *ll.*' (Diary, vol. 1b: 25 May 1702). In 1705 Wake calculated his fees upon his promotion to Lincoln to be £598 (Huntington Library HEH Bishop Gibson's Collection, bound vol. of letters, p. 50).

[217] *CW* xlvi (1946), 218: Diary, 3 Mar. 1704. Nicolson's financial plight did not stop him being up to date with his payments of Tenths. In July 1706 he had paid up to Christmas 1704. No bishop was more current in his payments than Nicolson and some had not paid since 1673! (PRO T1/99, f. 72: 'Accounts of Auditors of Her Magesties Imprest Accounts', 15 July 1706). Nicolson records paying out £160 in 1706/7 for 'Tenths and Fees'. See below Appendix D.

[218] See below p. 482. Nicolson paid £85 on 27 Feb. 1706 to Christopher Musgrave for his 'Account and Inter[es]t' (below Appendix D).

[219] Even Archbishop Sharp of York, with a see worth around £2,300 a year, complained of 'the expences these [parliamentary] journeys put me to which I can very ill bear' (Leicestershire RO Finch MSS Letters & Papers Gen. Ser., Bundle 22: Sharp to Nottingham, 31 Mar. 1702).

[220] Ware transcripts, xxv, 10, printed in *CW* iv (1904), 46.

[221] Printed below as Appendix D.

of the bishop's expenditure during the parts of the two parliamentary sessions which fell in the year 1706 (the last half of session 3 and the first third of session 4). From 1 January to 5 March 1706 Nicolson spent £190. Even allowing for the extraordinary expense of repaying part of his loan from the Musgraves, this leaves a total expenditure of £105 for just over two months. If one adds to this the expenses Nicolson incurred from 21 November to 31 December 1706 while in London, the total expenditure for the three and a half months while attending parliament comes to £229 (or £144 if one ignores the £85 repaid to Christopher Musgrave).[222]

Nicolson's expenditure involved in attending parliament probably continued to run at a higher rate than his own comment about his expenses in 1707-8 would seem to indicate. In the three-month parliamentary session of 1714 his expenses were £222 (whereof £98 was for 'extraordinaries' such as books, a gown and fees for his son Joseph, coffee and tea (£3), a new periwig and clothes, and a horse).[223] Yet there is no evidence in the diary to suggest that Nicolson entertained on the scale that bishops were expected to.[224] Nor did the Bishops of Carlisle have their own house or palace in London, unlike some of their brethren, for Carlisle House in Lambeth was in Nicolson's day leased out as a pottery. Nicolson, therefore, had to take lodgings in and around Palace Yard, Westminster.[225]

Swelling the bishop's parliamentary expenses was the cost of his travelling between Rose and the capital. In October 1701 he went to London for the publication of the *Scottish Historical Library*.[226] His journey cost him £7. 1s. 7d. while his return journey in February and March 1702 cost £9. 16s. 6d.,[227] a total of £16. 18s. 1d. The

[222] For another miscalculation of parliamentary expenses see the estimate of John Clerk's (Commissioner for the Union, 1706, and MP for Scotland, 1707-8) of £120 (plus extraordinary expenses of £70 on cloaths, etc.). In 1707-8 he admitted that 'as for the expences of a parliament man tis true they will bee 200 lib. a year' (SRO Clerk of Penicuik MSS GD18/3131/21-22: Clerk to Sir John Clerk of Penicuik, his father, 12 Mar. [1706]; GD18/3140/22: same to same, 4 Mar. [1708]).

[223] Ware transcripts, xxx, 2-3. The year's expenses for 1714 were £872, including £300 to his new son-in-law, probably as the marriage settlement, and £93 for his son Joseph's preferment (ibid., pp. 5-6).

[224] Wake once advised the augmentation of the poorer bishoprics in order partly to help 'towards the Keeping a private table, as they usually do here' (Christ Church Wake MS 18, f. 393). Bishop Talbot (no doubt on a private income, as Oxford was reputed to be worth only £600 a year) spent around £80 on wines and spirits in 1707 (Worcestershire RO Pakington MS 705:349/5117/3). For the modest scale on which Nicolson entertained, see below Appendix D.

[225] In 1706 these cost him 16s. a week (below Appendix D).

[226] See *CW* i (1901), 37-43.

[227] Diary 1a. His whole stay in London for five months in 1701-2, including travelling, cost him £51. 15s. 1d.

expense of a London journey by 1706 had more than trebled to a cost of £27. 15s. 6d. for the single journey south (£50 for the round trip).[228] With an annual expenditure in attending parliament of between £100 and £200 out of a gross income of around £800 (net income of around £500) in a good year, it is not surprising that after sixteen years at Carlisle he was looking for a lucrative translation.

Even by 1710 Nicolson was complaining that 'I have been so far from grasping at Wealth, that (should I dy to morrow) my wife and Children would not find their Condition bettered to the value of one hundred pounds for every year that I have been a Bishop'.[229] On the accession of King George I Gibson hinted that Nicolson might expect a lucrative recognition for his hard-working loyalty to the Protestant Succession. Although Gibson's suggestion of Durham[230] did not materialise, since Lord Crew resolutely refused to die (he survived until 1721 having occupied the see for forty-seven years!), Nicolson was appointed Lord Almoner to the King, an office formerly held by Lloyd and Sharp, and more recently by Smalridge and Wake. The appointment was delayed, however, until April 1716, and Gibson hastened to assure him that it was merely 'a preparation to marks of favour somewhat more substantial'.[231]

The office of Lord Almoner carried prestige and influence from the patronage the holder was capable of bestowing from public funds. Financially, however, it brought no relief to a poor bishop, for the office carried no fee. It also entailed a good many duties which probably involved Nicolson in longer residences in London and therefore in greater expense.[232] After his translation to Derry,

[228] See Appendix D. In some years travelling was cheaper: in 1718 the journey south only cost £19. 8s. 6d. (Ware transcripts, xxxii, 39–40). The cost of travel depended largely on the tastes of the traveller. John Clerk (see above, note 222) estimated that the return trip from Edinburgh to London in 1706 could be done for £19: £7 single fare on the coach, provided the hire charge was spread over six passengers, while 'the expense of Living on the road for 12 days coming and 12 days going, is about a crown a day for a man and his servant which is 5 pounds Sterling [sic]' (SRO Clerk of Penicuik MS GD18/3131/21). Archbishop King of Dublin, on the other hand, spent £137. 19s. 9d. on a trip to Bath from Dublin in Oct. 1722 (TCD MS 1995, no. 2008a), while Lord Yester spent £61. 7s. 0d. on his trip to London from Edinburgh in Oct. 1708 and this only paid for the hire of the coach and servants, the maintenance of the coach and horses, the carriage of his trunk, and the cost of posting letters on the road (NLS MS 14655, 'Horse bills', etc.).

[229] Bodl. MS Add. C. 217, f. 43: N. to Sharp, 1 Jan. 1710.

[230] Bodl. MS Add. A269, pp. 33–4: Gibson to N., 10 Aug. 1714.

[231] Ibid., p. 60; same to same, 28 Feb. 1716; for the date of Nicolson's appointment to the office of Almoner see BL Add. MS 38889, f. 98: Townshend to the Clerk of the Signet, 27 Apr. 1716.

[232] The office was particularly arduous around Easter, not only because of the work associated with Maundy Thursday, but also because the Almoner was pestered by the poor, gentry, and nobility alike (St Andrews UL Gibson MS 5181: Carteret to Gibson, 19 Sept. 1723).

Nicolson confessed that 'Had I continued in the Almoners office, without some better Support than the Bishoprick of Carlisle, I must have starved myself, and left my Children upon the Parish'.[233] Unfortunately for him the 'marks of favour' which Gibson had led him to expect had still not materialised eighteen months later. Nicolson's actions in organising opposition to the proposed repeal of the Occasional Conformity Act early in the session of 1717 and his later opposition to Benjamin Hoadly, a favourite of the Court, in May to July 1717 probably alienated the King and threatened to blight the bishop's prospects. Bishop Evans, recently translated from Bangor to Meath in Ireland, had written to Nicolson on the death of Bishop Hartstonge of Derry in January 1717 hoping that he (Nicolson) would be translated there. Derry had a rental of £2,400 a year plus fines, and Nicolson confessed to 'dreaming of such a Land of Havilah . . . But, where's that gracious hand that will reach out to use these Apples of Gold!' Though his family circumstances, he realised, called loudly for such a translation, he was 'not very fond of being transplanted at the Age of 62 years, into the Kingdom of Ireland'. Nicolson still hoped for either a remove 'into a Warmer Habitation, or allowed to keep within Doors where I am'.[234]

By the early winter of 1717–18 Nicolson saw the prospects of a comfortable old age receding. His family, particularly his four unmarried daughters, were an increasing burden, and he was becoming manifestly discontented.

I have attended my Duty in Parliament for fifteen years [he wrote to Wake], as constantly as any of my Brethren. I have not one Senior on the Bench (the Bishop of Peterborough only excepted) who has not been translated; and very few Juniors who do not hold Commendams. I live at the greatest Distance, and (considering the forementioned Charge [his family]) am the least able to continue in the Service, I have also the Mortification to know (not withstanding Lord S[underland's] gracious Professions) that everything that is worth my Acceptance, is previously designed for other Persons. That one side of the Court is very favourable to me, I am most thankfully sensible. But, this is so far from raising my Hopes of having the Condition of my Fortunes in the World bettered, that (I think) I have rather Cause to suspect that it may Occasion a new Obstruction.[235]

[233] BL Add. MS 6116, f. 69: N. to Wake, 23 Aug. 1718.
[234] Ibid., f. 54: same to same, 31 Jan. 1717. Hartstonge was succeeded by St George Ashe, Bishop of Cloger, Archbishop King's candidate, but he survived for only a year. Wake was reported as opposing Nicolson's translation to Ireland (Bodl. MS Add. A269, p. 68: Gibson to N., 5 Feb. 1717). Gibson estimated Derry's value at £2,500: it was the second richest see in Ireland after the Primate's see of Armagh (Lambeth Palace MS 2168, ff. 127-8).
[235] BL Add. MS 6116, f. 58: N. to Wake, 21 Oct. 1717. Nicolson's reference to 'one side of the Court is very favourable to me', meaning the family of the Prince of Wales, with whom he was on terms of some intimacy (see below p. 644), would not have been lost

Nevertheless, Nicolson's friends continued to try to promote 'his Retirement to more wealth and Ease',[236] and in the spring of 1718 (despite a last minute stand in the Lords against the government which he thought had cost him the prize)[237] he was offered translation to Derry. He readily accepted, though he was to be jolted by the King's insistence that he reside in his new diocese. The government, realising Nicolson's continuing vocal opposition on religious affairs, may have wanted to remove him in preparation for the coming attempt at repealing the Occasional Conformity and Schism Acts.[238]

On his return to England, however, from his primary visitation of Derry, all Nicolson's qualms had been allayed by the discovery that Derry had already wrought a financial miracle. 'The Rents of the See of Derry for Six Months (without one shilling in Fines) have brought me £1213 Out of which I have cleared all the Expences on my Translation, and laid by more Money than I could have saved out of This [Carlisle] in Seven Years'.[239] What a contrast with his financial position upon his elevation in 1702! His sudden access to prosperity in Ireland can be seen in the proportionately rapid rise in his annual expenses. Those recorded for 1719 and 1721-5 ranged from £1,023 in 1721 to £1,521 in 1723 (which included his last visit to London in 1722-3).[240] Yet in his last years Nicolson was, on average, only spending half his rental income. Long delayed though it had been by rough weather, his ship had at last come in. Derry had indeed brought him 'comfort in both pockets'.[241]

THE LAST YEARS, 1718–1727

Nicolson had been translated to Derry on 21 April 1718 (letters patent issued on 2 May) and by 3 June he was in Dublin on the way to his first visit to his new diocese. He was enthroned at Londonderry on 22 June. There followed a triennial visitation from his

on Wake. He was to be banned the Court after the quarrel between the King and his son because he refused to stop seeing the Princess of Wales.

[236] BL Lansdowne MS 1013, f. 238: Kennett to Blackwell, 6 April 1718.
[237] See below p. 680.
[238] His replacement at Carlisle, Samuel Bradford, voted for repeal in Dec. 1718. It was not unknown for Irish bishops to spend a good deal of time in England: Charles Hickman, Bishop of Derry, even took a house in Fulham (Berkshire RO Trumbull Add. MS 134: R. Bridges to Sir W. Trumbull, 18 July 1712); while Thomas Hacket, Bishop of Down (1672-94), because of his persistent absenteeism, earned the sobriquet 'Bishop of Hammersmith' (W. E. H. Lecky, *History of Ireland in the Eighteenth century* (5 vols, 1913), i, 204-5).
[239] BL Add. MS 6116, ff. 68-9: N. to Wake, 23 Aug. 1718.
[240] Ware transcripts, xxxiv, 5; xxxvi, 10-23, xxxviii, 4; xxxix, 26-7; xl, 2; xli, 3.
[241] Bodl. MS Add. A269, p. 78: Gibson to N., 23 Aug. 1718.

Metropolitan, Archbishop Lindsay of Armagh, the Irish Primate, in early August. By 17 August Nicolson was back at Rose to spend the autumn and winter winding up his affairs at Carlisle. He returned finally to Ireland in early May 1719, where he was to remain until his death, except for a six months visit to Cumberland and London in 1722-3.

Despite his age, increasing infirmity, and bitterness at what proved to be a political and intellectual exile, Nicolson characteristically threw himself into his new duties, both in his diocese and in the Irish House of Lords in Dublin.[242] His appointment to Derry had been vigorously opposed by Archbishop King of Dublin, leader of the native Anglo-Irish faction in the episcopacy. Consequently, Nicolson found himself forced politically into the 'English party' at Dublin which fully supported the English government in Ireland. He was, however, not appointed to the Privy Council until 1726. Yet despite his alien minority position, Nicolson proved to be an active attender of the Irish Parliament, maintaining his excellent record established at Westminster.[243]

On the death of Archbishop Lindsay in 1724, Nicolson was mentioned as a possible successor, but he wrote to Wake saying he wished to end his days comfortably at Londonderry.[244] This he managed to do despite his nomination to the archbishopric of Cashel on 10 January 1727 (letters patent dated 28 January). The honour, which in fact meant a financial loss for Nicolson's family, came because of his support of Primate Boulter's scheme for the augmentation of the poorer Irish livings. Nicolson accepted the honour so that the friend of his declining years, Bishop Downes of Meath, might be translated to the richer see of Derry,[245] whose resources he needed to support his family, just as Nicolson had in 1718. Nicolson, however, was spared the ordeal of another move. On 14 February 1727, in his seventy-second year, he suffered a stroke at his study desk in Derry and died. He was buried, no monument being erected, in Derry cathedral.[246]

[242] For a description of Nicolson's Irish years, see James, chapters 11-12.
[243] See James, pp. 250-1.   [244] Ibid., pp. 262-4.
[245] Derry was worth £500 a year more than Meath, while Cashel was worth £1,700 (Lambeth Palace MS 2168, ff. 127-8), a loss to Nicolson of £700 a year. Boulter, however, estimated the loss to Nicolson's family at £500 (Ware transcripts, xli, 34: Boulter to Carteret, 18 Feb. 1726/7 [copy]).
[246] James, p. 280.

2

The House of Lords in the
Early Eighteenth Century

THE HOUSE OF LORDS IN EARLY
EIGHTEENTH-CENTURY POLITICS

When William Nicolson was consecrated Bishop of Carlisle in June 1702 the House of Lords had recently embarked on what was to prove the most stirring and influential two decades in its history. The impeachments of 'the Whig lords' in the spring and summer of 1701 staked out for the Upper House a place squarely in the forefront of the fierce party struggles of the early eighteenth century. It still held that place in July 1717 when it acquitted the late Prime Minister, the Earl of Oxford, on a charge of high crimes and misdemeanours brought by the Commons (and did so, it is worth noting, amid one more in the succession of quarrels between the two Houses that marked a period when tensions, friction, and deadlock between them often seemed commoner than harmonious cooperation). The high feeling aroused by Sunderland's Peerage Bill when it was twice brought into parliament in 1719 undoubtedly reflected the concern of many commoners lest the balance of the constitution between King, Lords, and Commons, already tilted too far, in many eyes, in favour of the Lords, might become permanently upset. The defeat of the second bill in December 1719, after a great debate in the Commons and the most devastating speech of Walpole's career, can now be seen to have heralded the approaching end of a unique period of parliamentary history. By February 1724—the close of an extraordinary phase during which half the entire collection of episcopal sees changed hands in the space of twenty-eight months,[1] making the Lords as safe for the government of the day as it was to remain, by and large, for the rest of the century—a very different political world was in being from the one Nicolson had inhabited during his sixteen years at Westminster.

It is thus a most fortunate coincidence that the best of the parlia-

[1] From Nov. 1721, reliable Court supporters were installed in Durham, Gloucester, Bangor (twice), and Chichester; in London, Lichfield, Carlisle, Rochester, Norwich, Ely, Salisbury, and Winchester (the last eight, plus Bangor for the second time, all being filled in 1723); and Hereford and St David's (these two in February 1724). After that, the installation of Bradshaw and Weston at Bristol and Exeter later in 1724, and the nomination of Clavering to Llandaff, merely gilded the lily.

mentary diaries to survive from the first two decades of the eighteenth century was kept by a spiritual lord at a time when the House of Lords was at the very peak of its prestige and influence. The reasons for. this golden period were various. The sharply bipartisan nature of the political system throughout virtually the whole period from 1701 to 1717 obviously played a very important part, for it neutralised the strongest political characteristic which had stamped the Lords since the Reformation (except during fleeting interludes, such as the years 1546–7 and 1640–1)—namely, its loyal support for the Crown and the King's ministers. Although there was always a squadron of Court peers in the Lords in every early-eighteenth-century parliament, it never constituted anywhere near a majority in itself. Most of those who shared the benches of the House with Nicolson between 1702 and 1718 voted on political issues, in general, as their party loyalties disposed them: and none more boldly so than the bishops, though their successors in the age of Walpole and the Pelhams were to become epitomes of the House's pliancy in support of the Whig oligarchy.

In consequence, despite a number of ministerial measures which threatened briefly to bring the House of Lords to heel,[2] there were many intervals when it proved vexatious to the ministry of the day, when its behaviour was difficult to predict or control, and when it certainly could not be relied upon to chime in harmony with the Commons. The Tory ministers and the Commons' measures of 1701 and of 1702–4 had many a rough ride in the second chamber. It embarrassed the Marlborough–Godolphin duumvirate and the 'Treasurer's Whigs' in the session of 1707–8 and still further discomfited the Godolphin-Junto coalition in March 1710. It threatened to topple the Oxford administration in December 1711 and exerted great pressure on the same ministry in the session of 1713 and, even more so, in that of 1714. As late as 1717, as we saw, it was capable of following its own determinedly individual course. Nevertheless, the Lords still played a key role in government parliamentary strategy on a number of occasions, usually as a counterweight to extremism in the Commons. This is how Godolphin tried to use it in 1703 (a session Nicolson did not attend) and in 1704, and how Harley deployed it against the excesses of the October Club in 1710–11.

Another, and obviously associated, reason for the exceptional

[2] Notably, the establishment of firm government control over the election of the sixteen Scottish representative peers from 1710 onwards; the block creation of Lord Oxford's 'dozen' peers in Dec. 1711; and the more systematic use of pensions and offices by the Whigs after 1714 to appease aristocratic supporters of the second and third rank (for examples of these see below, 25 Feb. 1718).

political prominence of the Lords during the period of Nicolson's diary was the calibre of its membership. Between 1702 and 1718 there were only three politicians of the very front rank, Sir Edward Seymour, William Bromley, and Robert Walpole, who did not spend at least some time in the House of Lords. During the last years of William III's reign and for over half of Queen Anne's the Whig party was frequently outgunned, and sometimes close to demoralization in the Commons. All the major Whig campaigns of that period were directed from the Upper House, where all five of the lords of the Whig Junto—Somers, Halifax, Orford, Wharton, and the third Earl of Sunderland—sat by the end of 1702; and in many of those campaigns it was there that the most crucial battles, by design, were fought. Some of the Junto's most talented or active lieutenants, men such as Townshend, Bolton, and (from 1706-7) Cowper and Devonshire, were also peers. The two dominant figures among the High Tories between 1702 and 1711, Rochester and Nottingham, were also two of the Olympian figures in the Lords throughout that time, as Nicolson's accounts of debates clearly show. The three leading 'managers' of Queen Anne's administrations between 1702 and 1714, Godolphin, Marlborough, and Robert Harley, Earl of Oxford, operated in that capacity from the Lords, except for the short interlude from August 1710 to May 1711, when Harley was still in the Commons as Chancellor of the Exchequer. By 1716 Rochester, Godolphin, Wharton, Halifax, and Somers were dead, while Marlborough, disabled by illness, had ceased to play any role in politics. But with James Stanhope raised to the peerage in the following year, three of the four leading Whigs of the younger generation who contested the inheritance of the Junto sat in the Upper House.

It has often been said that the eighteenth-century Whigs were an 'aristocratic' party. The label is a hopelessly simplistic one: Whiggery had significant support from every major order of society and from every major occupational group during Anne's reign and in the early years of George I, and the peerage of 1702-14 was remarkably evenly divided in its party affiliations. But it was unquestionably of immense importance in the history of post-Revolution Whiggery, and probably crucial to the ultimate achievement of the long Whig oligarchy after 1714, that in the period from 1698 to 1714, when the natural bias of the electorate was heavily pro-Tory (the Whigs decisively won only one of the eight General Elections fought during those sixteen years), the party could muster such an exceptional array of talent in the Lords. It is at least doubtful whether in 1700-1, 1702-4, and 1710-14, years when the tide was flowing so remorselessly against them and they faced an implacable enemy bent on achieving a lasting supremacy, the Whigs could have avoided the fate that subsequently overtook their opponents without the rallying-ground and the base for counter-attack which the Lords provided for them.

In the first five or six years of Queen Anne's reign, and especially down to 1706, Nicolson's accounts of proceedings in the Lords are often full enough to convey something of the high quality which the political debate there at this time was capable of achieving.[3] Men of outstanding parliamentary ability were involved. On the Whig side, Somers, Halifax, and, later, Cowper were parliamentary orators of the first order; Sunderland was a fiercely combative, if not always controlled, speaker; Wharton—rumbustious, provocative, resilient, and witty—was as devastating an exponent of the verbal duel as he was of swordplay; and Halifax, too, though it was said of him that there was 'not a man in our house that speaks more handsomely nor that understands trade, taxes and all things concerning the public revenue better',[4] was as much a master of the sharp debating cut-and-thrust as he was of more orthodox, closely informed speechmaking. Wharton and Halifax, in fact, were largely responsible after 1700 for a minor revolution in the debating style of the Lords, hitherto ponderous and formalized, shaped in the main by the House's penchant for the elaborate set-piece. As Lord Dartmouth, a Secretary of State and Lord Privy Seal in the Tory administration of 1710-14, was to write many years later, they 'brought up a familiar style with them from the House of Commons, that has been too much practised in the House of Lords ever since, where everything formerly was managed with great decency and good manners'.[5] The Commons, wrote a Scots peer in Queen Anne's reign, was 'a House that loves free speaking';[6] and the House of Lords in Nicolson's time was slowly adjusting itself to the notion that in a party-ridden age the old conventions were no longer invariably appropriate, although both sides made some effort to preserve them when the Queen was present *incognito* at their debates.

For the High Tories in the first half of Queen Anne's reign, the Earl of Rochester, whom Lord Balmerino was later to find (after his first taste of Westminster) the soul of 'probity and firmness . . . excellent versed in the minutest forms [of procedure], anc excellent charming speaker',[7] showed himself quite capable of matching the Junto in

---

[3] This is not to say, of course, that every peer was capable of sustaining a uniformly high standard of debate. On this point, see below, pp. 95–8.

[4] SRO GD 45/14/352/10 (Dalhousie MSS): [Lord Balmerino] to [Harry Maule of Kellie], 2 June [1711].　　　　　　　　　　　　　　　　[5] Burnet, *History*, v, 234 n.

[6] SRO GD 45/14/352/3: Balmerino to Maule, 30 Jan. [1711].

[7] SRO GD 45/14/352/2: Balmerino to Maule, 16 Jan. [1711].

debate on their own terms. So too was the 'silver-tongued' Lord Guernsey, formerly a barrister of distinction and one of the two sons of the former Lord Chancellor, Nottingham, to grace the early eighteenth-century peerage. Guernsey's brother Daniel, the second Earl of Nottingham, remained, on the other hand, deeply attached to the lengthy set speech that had been the vogue in the seventeenth century, earning a dubious immortality as Swift's 'Orator Dismal';[8] and the 'great guns' of Lord Haversham,[9] the other leading spokesman for the High Tories at this period (though he was a renegade Whig), also needed a long range to be fully effective.

There were exceptional talents, therefore, brought to bear in the political debates of the House of Lords in the early eighteenth century; and it is sad that, because Nicolson's reporting became so perfunctory in the later years of his diary, we have scarcely anything from his pen to illumine the parliamentary skills of those who blossomed politically during the second half of Anne's reign or who only appeared on the Lords' scene after 1707. Among the sufferers are Townshend, Devonshire, Argyll, and Oxford; also the fifth Earl of Anglesey—the former Arthur Annesley, MP—and Henry St John, Viscount Bolingbroke (both of whom favoured 'the Commons' style' when they moved to the Lords) and Lords Carteret and Stanhope. It is also our misfortune that Nicolson was either absent during (or left no surviving account of) some of the major political battles in the Lords—over the second Occasional Conformity Bill in 1703, for example, over the 'Scotch Plot' in 1703–4, over the Aylesbury men in 1705, over the Sacheverell impeachment in 1710, over the great offensive against the Tory peace policy in December 1711, and over the 'Succession in danger' issue in 1714. About the passing of the Schism Bill in the latter session, also, he has left us all too little. Nevertheless, almost all the great party issues of the day, except the 'conflict of interests' between the landed gentry and the 'monied men', are paraded at some stage in Nicolson's pages.

Foremost among these issues is religion. The extent of the religious toleration that was enjoyed, or ought to have been enjoyed by the Protestant dissenters under the umbrella of the Act of Indulgence of May 1689 became a matter of acute controversy in Queen Anne's first parliament. The first Occasional Conformity Bill dominates the parliamentary sections of Nicolson's diary in his first session at

[8] 'Nottingham spoke excellently against the [Schism] Bill', wrote George Baillie, a Scottish MP, 'and I am told never better than upon this occasion'. Mellerstain Letters, vi: Baillie to his wife [5 June 1714], fragment.

[9] BL Loan 29/237, f. 115: Godolphin to Newcastle, 13 Nov. [1705]. For Haversham, see also below, pp. 95–6.

Westminster (1702-3) and the fate of the third bill, bringing on its projected 'tack' to a money bill, is anxiously recorded in 1704-5. The advance of nonconformity under 'the Toleration' was also one of the main complaints of the High Tories during the full-dress Lords' debate on 'the Church in danger' issue (December 1705), of which Nicolson left a fine account; and the Cathedrals Bill (1708), promoted by Somers and Archbishop Tenison from the House of Lords in order to uphold the authority of bishops over their chapters, was of particular concern to Nicolson, whose struggle with the unmanageable Dean Francis Atterbury at Carlisle (symbolising all that was unhappiest in the distraction of the post-Revolution Church of England by both ecclesiastical and political parties) made such a measure, in the eyes of Whigs and Low Churchmen, urgently necessary. When the Whigs were securely entrenched in power after 1716, toleration for dissenters became a major political issue again, for the last time in Nicolson's lifetime; and now divisions among the Whigs themselves, and not least among Church Whigs, were revealed which earlier had been very much muted. The matter did not finally come to a vote in the Lords until December 1718, after Nicolson had gone to Ireland. But as a leading conservative among the Whig bishops he was involved in the important preliminary skirmishes of 1717-18 (sessions twelve, thirteen, below) and records some of these in his pages.

The opposing religious philosophies of Whigs and Tories and their conflicting attitudes to the question of the relations of Anglicans with non-Anglicans provide one of the main explanations of their failure to see eye to eye over the parliamentary and 'incorporating' Union of England and Scotland, ultimately forged in 1707: for after 1689 it was abundantly clear that one *sina qua non* of such a Union must be the recognition by England of the Presbyterian Kirk as the established church in Scotland. Nicolson, holding a border see and counting many Scots among his friends, was more than commonly concerned with the amicable and peaceful resolution of the various problems outstanding between the two nations; and the long haul towards the passing of the Acts of Union by the Westminster and Edinburgh parliaments, in which the House of Lords played a key part, figures prominently in his diary entries for the sessions of 1702-3, 1704-5, 1705-6, and 1706-7. The Upper House was likewise closely involved in the consequences of a whole series of taxing issues which the growing pains of the new Union precipitated at Westminster during the years 1708-12. The fate of the Scottish Privy Council (1708), the Treason Bill (1709), the Greenshields and Hamilton cases (1710-11 and 1711-12), and the passing of the Act for the Toleration of Episcopacy in Scotland (1712) all, at some stage, became political issues, and three at least became sharp 'party matters'. The diary touches on all of them and on some it provides valuable fresh insights.

The chief justification of the Treaty of Union from the Whig point of view was its seeming the only certain means of safeguarding the Protestant Succession in Scotland (the Scots, having declined to associate themselves with the English Act of Settlement of 1701, later went on to aggravate the situation further by passing a highly vexatious 'Act of Security' through their own parliament).[10] Support for the legal right of the House of Hanover to succeed to the throne after Queen Anne's death and unqualified opposition to the claims of the Stuart Pretender united all Whigs, in and out of parliament, and in Lords and Commons alike after 1701. By the last years of William III's reign the Tories seemed to have almost resolved the ideological dilemma in which the events of 1688-9, and especially the precipitate flight of James II, had involved them, and except for a small minority they appeared to have renounced the Jacobite path. But before the next reign was many years advanced the old uneasiness and equivocation on the score of the succession, which was in the end to lead to the paralysing crisis of the party in 1714, began to reassert itself; and in the diary we see this emerging in the Lords' debates on the State of the Nation in December 1705 and in the subsequent protracted proceedings on the Junto's Regency Bill in 1705-6.

So long as the Spanish Succession War of 1702-13 lasted, and the Bourbon enemies of the Grand Alliance continued to shelter James II's son, Prince James Francis Edward Stuart, recognise him as James III of England, and offer the likeliest source of foreign aid to any attempted invasion of the British Isles by the Pretender, Tory Jacobitism was bound to smack to some extent of treason in Whig eyes. The weakest card in an otherwise strong Tory hand with the electorate was the party's suspect position on the succession issue. On the other hand, their general attitude to the war itself and to war strategy—based on a profound distrust of too close a commitment to Continental allies, a particular suspicion of England's old commercial rivals, the Dutch, and above all an opposition to an over-heavy involvement in land warfare in the Low Countries—was often a popular suit for them, except during the middle years of Queen Anne's reign, 1704-8, when the Duke of Marlborough's popularity with his countrymen was high. Marlborough was by now no favourite with his old friends the Tories, and in all Nicolson's references

[10] See Introduction to Session 2, below, pp. 210-12.

to Lord's proceedings in connection with the Spanish Succession War (in the sessions of 1702-3, 1705-6, 1707-8, 1710-11, and 1711-12) there are strong whiffs of party opportunism and the pursuit of vendettas against Marlborough and his favoured Whig generals. This is true even of the fullscale House of Lords inquiry into the disastrous state of the war in Spain (January 1711), even though Spain was the one land theatre for which the Tory party's leaders did profess some enthusiasm. The party men of the Commons were certainly not alone in relishing the attempted vilification or even destruction of opponents by parliamentary investigation or attack. And Nicolson's accounts of some of the manœuvres of both parties in the Lords in the sessions of 1702-3, 1707-8, 1710-11, 1715, and 1717 all serve to illustrate, while chronicling events of this nature, that issues alone were not the only elements in aristocratic politics in the early eighteenth century—even when enmeshed with the contest for office. The noble lords were not, like their counterparts in St Stephen's Chapel, dependent on the favours and antipathies of a volatile electorate, and they were certainly less bitterly vindictive over personalities than were the Commons. But neither were they always able to attain in their 'golden period' that lofty altruism which, to lords with both a strong sense of tradition and a firm concept of Christian duty, was a proper aspiration for the members of the 'grand council' of the kingdom.

THE TOPOGRAPHY OF THE HOUSE

The External Setting

The Palace of Westminster (see fig. 1), which housed the parliamentary buildings and three law courts—Chancery, Queen's Bench, and Common Pleas—was, by eighteenth-century standards, a vast complex. The buildings, huddled together on the low-lying banks of the Thames,[11] were largely medieval, and formed the basic components of the kingdom's main royal residence in the capital before the Court moved to Whitehall in 1529.

The Palace buildings, though they were to survive well into the nineteenth century (and Westminster Hall, the Jewel Tower, and the crypt of St Stephen's Chapel still survive today), were in varying states of decay.[12] The Commons, for example, had been quite extensively altered in 1692 by Sir Chrispher Wren, who had removed

[11] The Palace was still subject to flooding in Nicolson's time, see below, p. 326.

[12] The decayed fabric of the Palace was the reason why Surveyor General William Benson drew up his plan of 1719 upon which fig. 1 is based. For the whole incident which led to Benson's dismissal see *The History of the King's Works*, ed. H. M. Colvin (6 vols., 1963-82), v, 392-7.

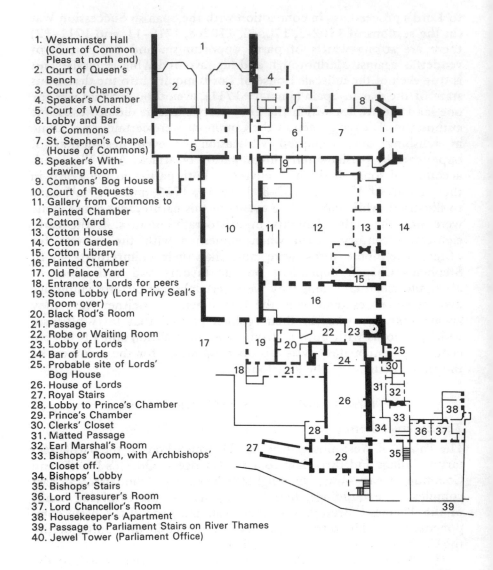

1. Westminster Hall
   (Court of Common
   Pleas at north end)
2. Court of Queen's
   Bench
3. Court of Chancery
4. Speaker's Chamber
5. Court of Wards
6. Lobby and Bar
   of Commons
7. St. Stephen's Chapel
   (House of Commons)
8. Speaker's With-
   drawing Room
9. Commons' Bog House
10. Court of Requests
11. Gallery from Commons to
    Painted Chamber
12. Cotton Yard
13. Cotton House
14. Cotton Garden
15. Cotton Library
16. Painted Chamber
17. Old Palace Yard
18. Entrance to Lords for peers
19. Stone Lobby (Lord Privy Seal's
    Room over)
20. Black Rod's Room
21. Passage
22. Robe or Waiting Room
23. Lobby of Lords
24. Bar of Lords
25. Probable site of Lords'
    Bog House
26. House of Lords
27. Royal Stairs
28. Lobby to Prince's Chamber
29. Prince's Chamber
30. Clerks' Closet
31. Matted Passage
32. Earl Marshal's Room
33. Bishops' Room, with Archbishops'
    Closet off.
34. Bishops' Lobby
35. Bishops' Stairs
36. Lord Treasurer's Room
37. Lord Chancellor's Room
38. Housekeeper's Apartment
39. Passage to Parliament Stairs on River Thames
40. Jewel Tower (Parliament Office)

N

Fig. 1. The Parliamentary Buildings in the Early Eighteenth Century

70

the roof and clerestory of St Stephen's Chapel and had put in a new ceiling at a much lower level, while constructing members' galleries on the north and south side. This work, designed to improve the comfort of the members, had partly been necessitated by the decayed fabric of the building: 'the House [of Commons] where they now sit is much decayed and in danger of falling', and 'it being now so crazy that it will hardly keep up this sessions'.[13] The whole Palace presented externally a picture of a mass of squalid and undistinguished buildings (Westminster Hall excepted), which retained a patina of medieval charm despite centuries of tinkering and alterations to convert them to functions for which they had not been designed and to which they were ill suited.[14]

Westminster Hall (1)[15] had been built in the reign of William II and was the most public building at Westminster. Its walls were lined, until the reign of George III, with the stalls and counters of book and printsellers, mathematical instrument makers, sempstresses, haberdashers, and other tradespeople, and it must frequently have taken on the atmosphere of an undercover market. By 1708 it also contained a coffee house. The Warden of the Fleet, in his capacity as *ex officio* Keeper of the Palace, leased out these stalls for his own profit.[16]

Despite the obvious noise and lack of privacy, the upper, or southern, end of the Hall was the site of two important law courts —Chancery and Queen's Bench (2, 3). These two courts were housed in makeshift wooden enclosures which provided a draughty and uncomfortable home.[17] The Court of Common Pleas in its enclosure at the northern end of the Hall, was even more inconveniently situated. Not until 1739 did the wooden enclosures make way for more substantial and elegant constructions. But even these buildings, on the same site as the older structures, had no ceilings and were open to the Hall, thus the old problems of 'the inclemency of very cold, damp air' continued. The courts apparently had no form of heating or artificial lighting capable of counteracting the gloom of the Hall.[18]

The Hall was only occasionally used for parliamentary purposes.

[13] HMC *Hastings MSS* ii, 336–7: newsletters, 9 and 12 Jan. 1692. For details of the alterations see *History of the King's Works*, v, 401–4.

[14] Engravings in J. T. Smith, *The Antiquities of Westminster* (1807) give a good idea of the external appearance of the Palace.

[15] Numbers in brackets indicate the building on fig. 1.

[16] *History of the King's Works*, v, 388; Mellerstain Letters, iii: George Baillie to his wife, 16 Dec. 1708.

[17] *History of the King's Works*, v, 389. For an illustration of the courts in the late seventeenth century see ibid., plate 55B.

[18] Ibid., p. 390.

During the time of Nicolson's diaries, two great state trials—those of Sacheverell (1710) and Rober Harley, Earl of Oxford (1715-17) —took place in Westminster Hall. The House of Lords before which they were impeached was too small to accommodate the crowds which both trials were expected to (and indeed did) generate.[19] The Hall also provided a temporary home for the Lords in 1719, when extensive repair work necessitated their moving.[20]

The Hall was on occasions used for great ceremonials. On 3 January 1705, for example, the banners captured at Blenheim (previously displayed in the Tower of London) were transferred with great pomp to Westminster Hall.

St Stephen's Chapel (House of Commons) (7) had been built in the fourteenth century as the main chapel to the royal palace. It was first used by the Commons in the parliament of 1547, and it remained their regular venue until its destruction by fire in 1834. Though its internal arrangement is not of direct interest to the readers of Nicolson's diaries, a few observations may be useful as Nicolson may well have attended some debates, and during the Carlisle election dispute of 1710, in which the bishop was implicated, he was called to the House, where a seat was provided for him. The seating of members basically consisted of four rows of benches set out in a near horseshoe-shaped arrangement, with the Speaker's chair at the east end and the bar at the west end of the chamber.[21] By the time Nicolson's diaries begin there were three galleries running around the north, west, and south walls of the House at first-floor level. The first to be constructed in 1621 was for 'strangers' at the west end. It was reached by a new set of stairs constructed in 1670 in the south-east corner of the Lobby (6).[22] The north and south galleries, designed to carry extra seating for members (the chamber could not seat the 513 MPs entitled to sit even with these two galleries) were the ones built in 1692, and were reached by stairs built in the north-east and south-east turrets of the Chapel; these in turn were approached by a passage built out from the east wall of the Chapel and entered through a door knocked through

[19] See Holmes, *Sacheverell*, pp. 109-13.

[20] *History of the King's Works*, v, 394-5.

[21] For a plan of the House and its seating arrangements see *A Register of Parliamentary Lists, 1660-1761*, ed. D. Hayton and C. Jones (Leicester, 1979), plan 3.

[22] E. R. Foster, 'Staging a Parliament in Early Stuart England', in *The English Commonwealth 1547-1640: Essays in Politics and Society Presented to Joel Hurstfield*, ed. P. Clark, A. G. R. Smith, and N. Tyacke (Leicester, 1979), pp. 132, 241 n. 21; *History of the King's Works*, v, 400. The siting of the stairs is conjectural, but is based on Sir Christopher Wren's 'Plan of the Houses of Lords and Commons with the Benches of Accomodation', *c*.1710 (Westminster City Library, Extra-illustrated copy of T. Pennant, *Some Account of London*, iii (1825), f. 105).

the old east wall behind the Speaker's chair. These two galleries, which had originally contained only one row of benches each, were widened to hold two rows in 1707 to accommodate the extra forty-five MPs admitted at the Union with Scotland.[23]

Like the Lords, the Commons had control over who was admitted to hear debates, and on occasions members of the Lords were excluded.[24] When they were allowed in they could either sit in the strangers' gallery (as did the Dukes of Argyll, Montrose, and Roxburghe during the debates on the abolition of the Scottish Privy Council in December 1707),[25] or on four rows of benches along the west wall of the chamber at ground level which were below the bar and were, therefore, not officially part of the House.[26] By the mid-eighteenth century these seats 'below the bar', as they were known, were the recognised accommodation for the lords.[27] On occasions, however, this arrangement caused ill-feelings among MPs as the Lords did not reciprocate with official seats for the Commons in their House. MPs could either stand below the bar or sit in the gallery during the time of its existence (1704–11).[28]

The Court of Requests (10) was a large barn-like structure, with internal dimensions of about 100 ft. by 40 ft., and had been built in the twelfth century, when it was known as the White Hall. It had been used by the Lords as their meeting place in the early fifteenth century. Adapted for use as the Court of Requests (a name by which it was to be known until its conversion into the House of Lords in

[23] *History of the King's Works*, v, 400–4. The Lords made no such alterations to accommodate the extra sixteen Scottish representative peers.

[24] 'Since the commons turn'd out the lords in Steell's business, the lords, to be even with them, have turn'd them out' (*Wentworth Papers*, p. 365: [P. Wentworth] to [Lord Strafford], 6 Apr. 1714).

[25] Atholl MSS (Blair Castle, Blair Atholl, Perthshire), 45/7/190: Lord James Murray to [Atholl], 5 Dec. 1707. We should like to thank the Duke of Atholl for allowing us to use and quote his family papers. One piece of evidence suggests that the galleries may not have been regarded as the correct place for peers to sit in the Commons in the reign of Queen Anne: 'Sir Edward Seymor who perceiving My Lord Wharton *incognito* in one of the Galleries said there was a Noble Lord there (nodding towards the place where he was) who could give them the best account of the Misterie of proceedings in Scotland if he pleased' (SRO GD124/5/259/3 (Mar and Kellie MSS): William Cleland to James [Erskine], 6 Dec. 1705). Our italics.

[26] Neither were the north and south galleries, consequently members wishing to vote had to descend on to the floor of the chamber: 'several other Scots people, who had been resolved to be against me, could not prevail with themselves to go to the lenth to vote against me, so they went up to the Gallerys and Skulkt their, as did a good many other of the English' (SRO GD 220/5/808/18b (Montrose MSS): [Mungo Graham] to Montrose, 13 Feb. 1711).

[27] See P. D. G. Thomas, *The House of Commons in the Eighteenth Century* (Oxford, 1971), p. 150.

[28] On 9 Jan. 1711 many peers were of the opinion that the affair of Lords Gallway and Tyrawley was of such public concern that any MP 'ought not to be refused going into the Gallery' (*Wentworth Papers*, p. 170: Wentworth to [Lord Raby], 9 Jan. 1711).

1801),[29] it had ceased to be used as such for some time before the Court's abolition during the Civil War. At the Restoration this abolition was confirmed, but the building was not put to any specific new use, unlike its fellow court abolished at the same time—the Court of Wards (5). This had been converted into several rooms, including an auction room and a coffee house.

By the early eighteenth century the Court of Requests' main function was as an informal meeting place where the public could mingle with members of parliament, both lords and Commoners, and the latter with each other, and as an informal adjunct to the law courts. 'Tewesday last being the day that the House of Lords had the Scotsh affairs before them', wrote Lord James Murray to his father, the Duke of Atholl, 'I waited att the Court of requests all that day, and spoke to those that got the memoriall'.[30] 'I have made several visits to my friends', wrote the Scottish MP George Baillie to his wife, 'and had the honour this day to be saluted by my Lord Duplin in the Court of Requests with whom I talked a pretty while.'[31] Many a peer was lobbied or accosted there. Lord Wharton, on his way to the House in March 1714, had a pamphlet thrust into his hand in the Court of Requests, which later the same day formed the basis of an attack by the Whigs on the government.[32] At times of political crisis the large dimensions of the building enabled it to hold enormous crowds who, in modern parlance, gathered to heckle as well as observe parliamentary proceedings, and who at times were there to remind members of the presence of the mob. On 14 December 1709, when Dr Sacheverell first went to the Commons to be impeached, 'over a hundred other clergymen thronged the court, some there out of curiosity but most of them— those who "thought themselves attacked in the person of their brother"—to lend moral suport'. Later during his trial the doctor 'held court like a great minister at his *levee*' in the Court of Requests.[33] The Court may also have been an unofficial 'waiting-room' for the Lords when the House was, particularly on formal occasions such as the opening of a session, so full with strangers that members were unable to get in: 'I stood in the court of requests till the Queens Speech was over', admitted Lord Balmerino, 'and to

---

[29] The influx of Irish representative peers and bishops at the Union with Ireland in 1800 finally convinced the Lords that they urgently needed more space. The Court was also used as a temporary home for the Commons in 1692 when Wren was engaged in alterations to their Chamber (*History of the King's Works*, v, 403).

[30] Atholl MSS 45/8/37: 3 Mar. 1708/9.

[31] Mellerstain Letters, vi: 18 Feb. 1714.

[32] *Wentworth Papers*, p. 359: [Wentworth] to [Strafford], 5 Mar. 1714.

[33] Holmes, *Sacheverell*, pp. 90, 108–9.

morrow we are to consider it in a committee'.[34] The Court acted as
the central public meeting place for those concerned with parliamentary affairs, much more so than Westminster Hall.

The Painted Chamber (16) had been built in the thirteenth
century as part of the expansion of the Palace by Henry III. It had
been used by the Lords in the reign of Henry VII as their regular
meeting place.[35] After the Lords in the following reign had moved
into the former Queen's Chamber (26), also built by Henry III as
a private appartment for his consort, the Painted Chamber developed
by the seventeenth century into the regular venue for joint conferences between the two Houses of Parliament, and occasionally it
was used by the Committee of Petitions.

The circuitous route the Commons had to take to the Painted
Chamber on such occasions, through the Court of Requests, led
to the construction by Wren in 1678–9 of the gallery running down
the east side of the Court of Requests (11). It was a timbered structure, 8 ft. wide, resting on timber posts and with a tiled roof. It
was to be replaced by a brick gallery of more generous dimensions
in 1722-5.[36]

The Painted Chamber, a large room 80 ft. by 26 ft.,[37] was
under-used even when housing joint conferences, as only a small
proportion of the membership of each House was usually nominated
to attend.[38] The formal procedure of such a conference was well
established by the middle of the seventeenth century. At the east
end of the Chamber, by the windows overlooking the Cotton Garden
(14), were arranged three benches, running north to south across
the room parallel to the east wall. Then came a long table and finally
another bench similarly arranged. This *ensemble* occupied only that
part of the Chamber between the east wall and the door on the south
wall which led into the Lords' Lobby (23).[39] The Lords' representatives sat on these forms while the Commons stood bare-headed
beyond them in the body of the Chamber.[40] The rules of procedure

[34] SRO GD45/14/352/12: to H. Maule, 15 Jan. [1712].

[35] J. E. Powell and K. Wallis, *The House of Lords in the Middle Ages* (1968), pp. 530, 548, 574.

[36] *History of the King's Works*, v, 400.

[37] The exact dimensions come from Wren's 'Plan for a Room at the House of Lords for the Cotton Library, 1703', *Wren Society*, xi (1934), plate xxx.

[38] Sometimes the Commons attended *en masse* (*Proceedings of the Short Parliament of 1640*, ed. E. S. Cope and W. H. Coates Camden 4th series xix (1977), p. 201).

[39] See *Wren Society*, xi, plate xxxii: a 'Site Plan from Westminster Hall to Parliament Stairs' (undated, but certainly the reign of Queen Anne), which shows the distribution of furniture as described above, which must be regarded as accurate as the seating lay-out of the House of Lords is correctly shown.

[40] 'And in ye painted chamber A table was placed and double formes around it. Without these formes we all stood bare headed. The Lords after we had attended some time, came

forbade the Commons to cross into the areas of the benches reserved for the Upper House.[41] Often the conference was simply a formal exchange of information, representatives of each body speaking and replying for their colleagues present at the meeting. The Lord Chancellor or Keeper often spoke for the Lords.[42] In times of political crisis, however, the conference could abandon much of the formal constraints. At such times the meetings were often conducted by a small but important group of managers who dominated their colleagues.[43] Formal restraints were, however, never totally abandoned and the Lords' precedence over the Commons was always enforced.

The Prince's Chamber (29) was also built by Henry III and served as the Queen's Chapel. Approximately 48 ft. by 20 ft., it had become by the late seventeenth century the regular meeting place for private or select committees of the Lords (see below p. 132: 23 Nov. 1702). It also had a secondary function as the royal robing room when the monarch attended parliament on formal occasions such as the opening or the giving of royal assent to bills. The Chamber was also used by the monarch as a private room when attending debates incognito, as Charles II, James II, William III, and Anne were wont to do. During long debates the monarch probably withdrew to the Prince's Chamber for refreshment. Charles II, who regularly attended debates, on occasions had his meals brought into the Chamber. It was possibly here that Queen Anne dined with Lord Halifax during Sacheverell's trial.[44]

The royal entrance to the Palace (27) was from Old Palace Yard up a flight of stairs into the Prince's Chamber.[45] The entry into the

and sate within ye formes . . . It was said by ye Lord Chamberlaine, That their Lops ought to sit, as they did in Parliament [i.e. by precedence], but they did not' (*Short Parliament*, p. 201).

[41] In a dispute between the two Irish Houses of Parliament in 1737 over the Commons going 'within the bar', which separated the two Houses at conferences, the Lords (under the influence of the English peers) deliberately followed English procedure rather than Irish, which did allow the Commons within the bar (BL Add. MS 47008A, ff. 12-13: William Taylor to Lord Perceval, 17 Dec. 1737). We should like to thank David Hayton for this reference.

[42] e.g. *Short Parliament*, pp. 201-3.

[43] e.g. the conference of 6 Feb. 1689, which lasted three to four hours, was principally managed for the Lords by four peers and a bishop. See E. Cruickshanks, D. Hayton, and C. Jones, 'Divisions in the House of Lords on the Transfer of the Crown and Other Issues, 1689-94: Ten New Lists', *BIHR* liii (1980), 61.

[44] K. H. D. Haley, *The First Earl of Shaftesbury* (Oxford, 1968), p. 601; Holmes, *Sacheverell*, p. 116. The Queen certainly withdrew from Westminster Hall during the trial to dine 'in a little room by the House of Lords' (Badminton House, Beaufort Papers 509.101.3: Lord Suffolk to his sister, 2 Mar. 1709/10).

[45] Benson's plan of 1719 (Sir John Soane Museum: 35.5.25) indicates that the royal entrance, or 'King's Stairs' were on the south-east corner of the Prince's Chamber (see *History of the King's Works*, v, 398). The plan does not show the stairs at the west end of the

Chamber for the Lords was through a small lobby (28), and it was the collapse of this lobby's ceiling in the winter of 1718-19 that led the then Surveyor-General, William Benson, to draw up the plan of the Palace of Westminster upon which fig. 1 is based.[46] The resulting survey found that the roof of the Prince's Chamber was giving way under the weight of a great quantity of documents stored there. These were the records of the Court of Requests and Wards put there in 1711.[47]

The House of Lords was surrounded on the north and east sides by a series of rooms and offices.[48] The peers' official entrance was through the Stone Lobby (18, 19), over which an office for the Lord Privy Seal had been constructed in 1677. A passage (21), 7 ft. 6 in. wide, ran from the Stone Lobby to the House of Lords, so that peers could proceed directly to the House without passing through their own Lobby (23) a room 12 ft. by 11 ft. Another route took the peers past the Black Rod's Room (20)[49] into the Robe or Waiting Room (22), a room 23 ft. 10 in. by 11 ft. and then into the Lobby. Even this small room was often full of those seeking patronage. Ralph Bridges sought preferment from Bishop Compton, his employer, 'And this I begged of the Bishop whom I found in a crowd at the Lords Lobby'.[50]

The bishops had their own entrance and stairs (35), which led off the passage leading from Old Palace Yard down to Parliament Stairs (39), where it was possible to catch a boat for Lambeth (as Nicolson often must have done on his way to visit Archbishops Tenison and Wake) or Fulham, the London home of the Bishop of London. The bishops' stairs led directly into an irregular L-shaped block of buildings running north along the east side of the House and east towards the river. These buildings contained the rooms of some of the great officers of state, the Earl Marshal (32), the Lord Treasurer (36), and the Lord Chancellor (37). The other rooms were offices for the clerks of the House (30), a room for the bishops (33), with dimensions of about 15 ft. by 13 ft., which had a closet (constructed by Wren in 1695) for the use of the two archbishops.

Chamber leading into Old Palace Yard. These are, however, shown on Wren's plan of c.1710 (see note 22, above). An external view of these stairs can be seen in Smith, *Antiquities of Westminster*, p. 38.

[46] See above, note 12.

[47] *History of the King's Works*, v, 392.

[48] Exact dimensions for these rooms come from two Wren plans: 'New Rooms at Westminster for the Bishops, April, 1695', and the plan mentioned in note 37 above, *Wren Society*, xi, plate xxx.

[49] It was over this room that Wren in 1703 intended to put the Cotton Library (see below, pp. 80-1).

[50] Berkshire RO Trumbull MS 55: Bridges to Sir W. Trumbull, 11 June 1714.

The sanitary arrangements of the Palace were primitive. In the first half of the seventeenth century and at the Restoration, the Wardrobe department of the King's Household was responsible for regularly supplying 'pewter chamber pots and "necessary" or "close" stools with pans' for the Palace.[51] All this equipment was housed in two separate 'bogg houses', one each for the Lords and Commons (9, 25).[52] Without main drainage, it was necessary to employ 'porters and labourers who made "all clean and carried out the soil" ',[53] no doubt to dump it straight into the Thames.[54] This system of sanitation, scarcely changed since the Middle Ages, was undoubtedly persisted with well into the eighteenth century.

The Jewel Tower (40), built in the fourteenth century as part of the fortifications of the Palace, had been used by the Wardrobe department of the medieval Royal Household to store the King's jewels and robes. From 1621 it became the permanent home of the 'Parliament Office', when the first floor was set aside for the storing of the official records of the Lords. Parliamentary records, as distinct from government records, had been kept since 1497, but up until 1621 they had, for all practical purposes, been part of the personal luggage of the clerks.[55] The Commons records, unlike those of the Lords, were stored in a room above the ceiling of the House constructed in 1692. Consequently they perished in the 1834 fire.

The tower was in need of repair by the early eighteenth century,

---

[51] Foster, 'Staging a Parliament', pp. 135, 242.

[52] 'Bogg House' is the term used by Benson on his 1719 plan. He clearly marks the Commons' one, but that for the Lords remains unmarked, though listed in the legend to the plan. No. 25 on fig. 1 is its conjectured position, being near the House and having an outside wall for ventilation. A Wren plan (see above, note 39) shows a medieval guarderobe at this point. Nicolson, who never mentions the Lords' bog, does note a visit to the Commons', largely because of the entertaining graffiti he finds there (21 Jan. 1703). He uses the term 'House of Office'. The Commons' bog played a not insignificant role in the defeat of a government bill in 1714 because William Lowndes, Secretary to the Treasury, who had 'been obliged to goe to the house of office' was locked out of the Commons at the time of the vote, though 'he ran with his breeches in his hand' (*Wentworth Papers*, p. 372: newsletter, 20 Apr. 1714).

[53] Foster, 'Staging a Parliament', pp. 137, 243.

[54] This was one of the reasons why the Thames stank so much, particularly in summer. As a consequence the atmosphere of both the Lords and Commons could become oppressive. When 400 members were crammed into St Stephen's Chapel on 18 Mar. 1714 for the debate on the expulsion of Richard Steel, the galleries were cleared of 'strangers' after three hours; and Baron Schütz, the Hannoverian special envoy, had to confess to his masters that 'indeed, the heat in the chamber had become so terrible that it was almost unbearable, and I myself withdrew at this time'. BL Stowe MS 226, ff. 306-7: Schütz to Bothmar, 19 Mar. 1714 (translation).

[55] M. F. Bond, 'The Formation of the Archives of Parliament, 1497-1691', *Journal of the Society of Archivists*, i (1955-9), 156.

and was reconstructed from 1717 to 1728 to accommodate an already vast and still increasing body of documents.[56]

The Palace of Westminster remained technically a royal residence after the departure of the Court to Whitehall, and it and its immediate precincts came under the control of the Lord Great Chamberlain and the Office of Works. The jurisdiction of the two Houses under the Lord Great Chamberlain, however, was not precisely laid down and this remained an area of contention and doubt.[57]

The day-to-day running of the House of Lords and the buildings under its jurisdiction was the responsibility of the Lords' Housekeeper, whose apartments were situated towards the river (38). In 1705 the accommodation consisted of two small rooms and a small cellar under the Lord Treasurer and the Lord Chancellor's rooms. There were also two other small cellars with a yard, washhouse, passage, and conveniences, and a garden 48 ft. by 38 ft. occupied by the Housekeepers. In the garden they had lately erected a small room or closet at their own expense. All these buildings were 'in such decay that they are in danger of falling down in a short time'. The accommodation was not large enough for the Housekeeper's family, particularly during the time of frequent parliaments, and they had to rent adjoining rooms on an annual basis.[58]

The office[59] which bore this particular title—Housekeeper to the House of Lords—dated from 1509. The office had become virtually hereditary in the family of Wynyard since 1573, and for the period of Nicolson's diaries, Anne Incledon, née Wynyard, and her husband, John (he alone after Anne's death in 1705), were responsible for the daily running of the House.

The building known as Cotton House (13) had been part of the college or free chapel royal of St Stephen's, which had been dissolved at the Reformation. Alienated from the Crown in 1552,[60] it had several owners before it passed into the hands of Sir Robert Cotton,

[56] See *History of the King's Works*, v, 410-11.

[57] For example, see the dispute between the clerks of the two Houses over the gallery (11), Devon RO 63/2/11/1/12 (Ley MSS): J. Ley to J. Hatsell, 31 Oct. 1769. For a further conflict of opinion over jurisdiction see an incident concerned with the demolition of a wooden shed in the Palace precincts which involved the Lord Great Chamberlain, the Lord Chamberlain of the Household, the Warden of the Fleet (*ex officio* Keeper of the Palace), the Surveyor General, and the Clerk of the Parliaments (Huntingdonshire RO DDM32/5/1756 (Manchester MSS): undated, but late seventeenth century).

[58] *CTB 1705*, p. 406.

[59] The following information on the office and its holders comes from an unpublished paper, 'The Office of the Housekeeper of the House of Lords, 1509–1847', by J. C. Sainty. We are very grateful to John Sainty for allowing us to use this material.

[60] *Calendar of Patent Rolls, Edward VI*, iv, 325.

the great antiquarian', by 1586.[61] It was he who established the great library, which along with the house passed in direct descent to his grandson, Sir John Cotton, who by act of Parliament in 1700 (12 & 13 Will 3, c. 7), vested the library in trustees for the public benefit.

The house, a four storey building of twenty-one rooms and four garrets, sat inconveniently between the House of Commons and the Painted Chamber.[62] Access to Cotton Yard was by way of a passage under the Court of Requests. A garden, 160 ft. by 171 ft., running from the house down to the river also belonged to the family.[63] The continuing inconveninece of this private patrimony within the precincts of the Palace, combined with the Lords' concern over the library, led the House of Lords in 1705 to establish a committee to inspect the library. It sent for the trustees and found that nothing had been done to implement the 1702 act: no way of passage to the library had been made, and no library-keeper had been appointed to replace the blind Togry Smith. The Lords then addressed the Queen in 1705 to ask the Cotton family to name a price for its purchase. Wren had previously valued the property at £4,000. Sir John Cotton countered with an offer of £5,000, which Wren considered an over-valuation, pointing out that at least £200 would have to be spent immediately to stave off the decay to the buildings. In 1706 the property was sold by Sir John at the compromise price of £4,800.[64]

The great library of books and manuscripts was housed in a 'narrow little Room, damp and improper for preserving the Books and Papers'.[65] This room, 38 ft. long but only 6 ft. wide, was on the second floor of the house,[66] and abutted directly on to the north wall of the Painted Chamber (15). Elizabeth Read Foster has shown that the library was one of the main sources used by Members of Parliament in the early seventeenth century for historical and parliamentary precedents and information.[67] The collection thus soon came to be regarded as the unofficial library for parliament, so that the non-accessibility of the material in the early years of Anne's reign, was one of the main concerns which had roused the Lords.

[61] E. R. Foster, 'A Library for Parliament in the Early Seventeenth Century', *The Library Chronicle*, xl (1976), 208.

[62] For Wren's description of the House, see *Wren Society*, xi, 120. It was written on his plan of the building of 1706, see ibid., plate xxxix.

[63] Dimensions from ibid., plate xxxii.

[64] For a summary, with accompanying documents, of the trunsactions leading to the library and house passing to the nation see *Wren Society*, xi, pp. 48–59.

[65] These were the words of the Lords' committee established in 1705 to inspect the library. Ibid., p. 54.

[66] Ibid., p. 120.

[67] Foster, 'A Library for Parliament', pp. 208–9.

Nicolson's diaries suggest that the library of Robert Harley, later Earl of Oxford, may have played a similar role to the Cotton Library in the early eighteenth century. Kept by Humphrey Wanley, it was available to interested scholars, and it may have been used by certain members of parliament. Harley's residence in York Buildings, a river-front block, at the south-west corner of Buckingham Street (the Whitehall end of the Strand), was certainly not as convenient as the Cotton Library, but Harley was prepared to lend material from his collection to selected individuals, including Nicolson. Harley lived in York Buildings from 1701 to 1714. The manuscripts in the library were moved to his son's house in Dover Street in 1717, while the bulk of the printed material was moved to Edward Harley's country home, Wimpole Hall in Cambridgeshire.[68]

It had been the intention of the donor of the Cotton Library that it should be kept in the house which bore its collector's name, and an act of 1706 provided for a convenient room on or near the Cotton Garden,[69] but no new accommodation was built. The house was shored up to prevent its collapse, and the library continued to be housed there until 1721.[70]

The Internal Arrangement of the Building

The House of Lords was comparatively small,[71] being internally about 70 ft. long by 27 ft. wide.[72] The 'debating floor' of the House, that part between the south (or throne) wall of the House and the bar, where the lords sat, was only 54 ft. long (see fig. 2). The benches upon which the lords sat were arranged as follows: on the west side there were two rows of benches running north from the door in the south-west corner, which led to the Prince's Chamber, down to the bar of the House, a distance of about 45 ft. There were four benches of unequal length in each row. These were where the peers sat. The front row of benches (known as the earls' bench) was where the peers of the rank of earl and above (plus the great officers of state) were supposed to sit. The back row was the barons' bench. On the

[68] C. E. Wright, 'Humphrey Wanley: Saxonist and Library-Keeper', *Proceedings of the British Academy*, xlvi (1960), 110-13.

[69] *Statutes of the Realm*, viii, 625-6 (6 Anne c. 30).

[70] For its later history, see *History of the King's Works*, v, 418.

[71] Of the major buildings on the site only the Prince's Chamber was smaller. The first part of this section is based on C. Jones, 'Seating Problems in the House of Lords in the Early Eighteenth Century: the Evidence of the Manuscript Minutes', *BIHR* li (1978), 132-6. We are grateful to the editor for allowing us to reproduce part of this article.

[72] The following description is based on the work of Wren and Sir John Soane, who demolished the old House of Lords in 1823. Wren's dimensions were 69′ 7″ × 26′ 6″ given in the plan of *c.*1710 (see note 22, above). But see his plans in *Wren Society*, xi, plates xxxvii and xxxviii (plans date 1704-5) where the width is given as 25′ 6″. Soane's dimensions are 70′ 6″ × 27′ (Westminster City Library, Box 56, no. 22, a plan of 1823).

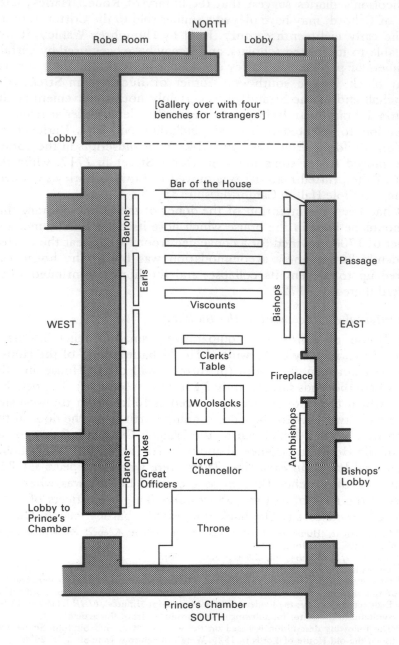

NORTH

Robe Room

Lobby

[Gallery over with four
benches for 'strangers']

Lobby

Bar of the House

Barons

Earls

Viscounts

Bishops

WEST

EAST

Clerks'
Table

Fireplace

Woolsacks

Archbishops

Barons

Dukes

Lord
Chancellor

Great
Officers

Bishops'
Lobby

Lobby to
Prince's
Chamber

Throne

Passage

Prince's Chamber
SOUTH

Fig. 2. The House of Lords in the Early Eighteenth Century

82

opposite side of the House sat the spiritual lords, divided into two groups by the fireplace; the archbishops south of the fireplace on one 7 ft. bench, and the twenty-four bishops north of the fireplace on two rows of benches about 20 ft. long. The remaining benches ran east to west across the room between the clerks at their table and the bar. There were seven of these cross benches, each 14 ft. long. The front cross bench was reserved for the viscounts and the other six were for the 'overspill' from the barons' bench (and if necessary from the earls' bench).[73] The rest of the seating in the House consisted of a bench for the clerks, the throne, the wool-sacks for the Lord Chancellor (or Keeper) and the legal officers of the Crown, and finally a seat for the Black Rod below the bar, next to the northern end of the earls' and barons' benches.

Because one can calculate the dimensions of the benches in the House, it is possible to work out the actual seating capacity of the chamber with a good degree of accuracy.[74] The two rows of temporal benches contained about 45 ft. of seating space each, while the seven crossbenches gave another 101 ft. Thus the peers had a total of about 190 ft. of seating. Allowing a meagre 18 in. per person, the House could seat about 125 peers.[75] The same calculations applied to the spiritual benches indicates that they could easily hold the maximum attendance. Thus the House could in theory hold around 151 lords.

The House, however, was not large enough to hold its total theoretical membership during the early eighteenth century. In 1703 there were 161 peers (excluding females, exiled peers, Catholics, and minors), a total House with the bishops of 187. By the end of Queen Anne's reign, with new creations and the sixteen Scottish representative peers admitted in 1707, the peers totalled 179 (a House of 205 with the bishops).[76] It is quite obvious, however, that the full membership was never expected to attend. During Queen Anne's reign an attendance of over seventy was common only during important debates. There were ninety-one present at the division on the 'Church in danger' on 6 December 1705, and in March 1710 at the impeachment of Dr Sacheverell 121 lords voted. The same figure

[73] The precise seating arrangements had been laid down by the 1539 act (31 Hen. VIII, c. 10), and the arrangement was still accepted as the legal basis of seating in the eighteenth century. For details see Jones, 'Seating Problems', p. 134 n. 5.

[74] The following calculations are based on Soane's plan (see note 72, above) and Wren's in *Wren Society*, xi, plates xxx, xxxii, xxxvii, xxxviii, xl.

[75] This calculation is based on the allowance given in the only eighteenth-century computation of the seating capacity of the Commons by Temple Luttrell in 1777 (J. Almon, *Parliamentary Register* (17 vols., 1775–80), vii, 143–4).

[76] *Parl. Hist.* vi, 146, 1243–6.

was reached on the second reading of the Septennial Act in April 1716, while the exceptional attendance of 151 was recorded on 27 June 1717 at the acquittal of the Earl of Oxford.[77]

Contemporaries certainly regarded a big attendance on such important occasions to be around one hundred.[78] On 26 November 1702 Nicolson attended 'A full House. 20 Bishops; all the great Ministers; &c.' The actual attendance on that day was eighty-one, not an unusually high figure. Peter Wentworth noted on 14 January 1712 that 'the house of lords was very full, and there was great expectations to hear what the Queen wou'd say'. The numbers present that day were 121.[79] On 12 January 1720 an attendance of 121 lords was thought to constitute a 'very full' House. George Douglas, MP for Linlithgow Burghs, however, thought that ninety-eight lords constituted 'a foul house'.[80] So despite the fact that in theory the House could hold 150 or so lords, and therefore ought to have easily held any normal attendance, contemporaries often regarded the cramped conditions on such occasions as decidedly uncomfortable.[81]

The House was certainly too small to put into operation the seating arrangements laid down by the 1539 Act. The result was that the lords tended to sit by rank, though this was not always the case and sometimes the peers were to be found on the bishops' benches and *vice versa*, but within ranks there was no attempt to sit by precedence. Latecomers to the House had to make the best of it and sat in any available space. Usually the lords sat in small party groupings,[82] while the Scottish peers, after 1707, sometimes sat in national groups which ignored rank and party.[83]

From 1704 to 1711 there was a 'strangers" gallery in the Lords. Nicolson's diary records in considerable detail the reasons for its construction. It was designed to 'prevent these Confusions in the House which had been common of late when the Queen appeared on the Throne', and was to be used by 'Foreign Ministers and other strangers' and the ladies of the Court on formal occasions.[84]

The Palace of Westminster, as described above, was open to the

[77] See C. Jones, 'The Impeachment of the Earl of Oxford and the Whig Schism of 1717: four new Lords' lists', *BIHR* lv (1982), 66–87.

[78] See Lord Poulett's comment, 8 Nov. 1704.

[79] *Wentworth Papers*, p. 251: Wentworth to [Strafford], 14 Jan. 1712; *LJ*. xxi, 191–2.

[80] Cheshire RO Cholmondeley MS DCH/X/8: Newburgh to Cholmondeley, 12 Jan. [1720]; SRO GD150/346/9 (Morton MS): Douglas to Morton, 23 June 1713.

[81] See Leicestershire RO Finch Papers, Letters and Papers Gen. Ser. Bundle 22: Sharp to Nottingham, 31 Mar. 1702.

[82] For details see Jones, 'Seating Problems', *BIHR* li, 136–45.

[83] SRO GD45/14/352/24: Balmerino to H. Maule, 9 June [1713].

[84] See 15 Nov. 1704; Luttrell, v, 484. It was objected to by several peers, and by 21 Dec. more peers disliked it for it made the House dark. It was saved by only a majority of nine.

public, and standing orders which forbade all but peers, bishops, and the necessary attendants of the House from entering the chamber, the lobbies and the committee chamber, were continually being broken. George Baillie recorded that public advertisements were 'dropt' in the Lords.[85] Indeed it was not unknown for the environs of the House to be so crowded that it caused an interruption to business.[86] Nicolson does not record a wholesale invasion of the House by strangers (except on ceremonial occasions, see below 23 Dec. 1702), which was not unknown later in the century.[87] Nor, indeed, does he record the penetration of the chamber by uninvited strangers, though there is evidence that this did take place, despite door-keepers (who, for added security, were placed outside the doors when the House was in debate by a standing order of 1707).[88] Such an intruder was a Norfolk squire up in town on holiday in 1714 who

had the good luck without any assistance to place himself so well at the dore of the house of Lords, that when the Usher of the black rod came with Sir Thomas Hanmer [Speaker of the Commons] to the dore, he clapt in before all the members at Sir Thomas's Back, and with him to the Barr of the Lords, and stood behind him wilst he made his speech to the Lord Chancellor.[89]

The gallery by its very existence encouraged strangers to attend sittings of the House. Though on some occasions the House excluded all strangers, including MPs,[90] usually they were able to get in, and were even encouraged to attend at times.[91] George Baillie recorded that 'I stood about eight hours in the house of Lords hearing their debate upon the triall [of Sacheverell] but that was not all for I had a multitude of people on my back the whole day'.[92] Thus the House

It was designed to seat one hundred (see *Wren Society*, xi, plates 36 and 37: the first design was adopted as it did not involve any radical alterations to the building and was consequently cheaper).

[85] Mellerstain Letters, iv: to Montrose, 3 Jan. 1711 [/12].

[86] 16 Jan. 1703.

[87] On 16 Jan. 1741 Archbishop Potter was unable to speak because he was 'quite hid by persons standing before him. At length with very great difficulty the House was intirely cleared' (BL Add. MS 6043, f. 53).

[88] No incident seems to have occurred such as the comical one in the Commons in 1694 when 'a Frenchman got privately into the House of Commons and sat down some time before he was discovered'. As the House was receiving a report from Lord Nottingham concerning intelligence on the Brest Fleet, it is not surprising that the man was arrested. Folger Shakespeare Library, Washington, Newdigate newsletters, 14 Feb. 1694 (microfilm in Bodl.); *CJ* xi, 88. We owe this reference to Eveline Cruickshanks.

[89] W. B. Gurdon, 'The Gurdon Papers. No. xi', *The East Anglian*, new ser. v (1893–4), 145. We are grateful to David Hayton for this reference.

[90] e.g. in chagrin at the Lords being excluded from the Commons during the debates on Richard Steele's expulsion. See *Wentworth Papers*, p. 365. Mungo Graham was also excluded from the Lords because they 'turned out all persons' (SRO GD220/5/808/3a: [Graham] to Montrose, 6 Jan. 1711), but was allowed in on the following day.

[91] *Wentworth Papers*, p. 170: 9 Jan. 1711.

[92] Mellerstain Letters, iii: Baillie to his wife, 14 Mar. 1709 [/10].

ought not to have been surprised that journalists began to take advantage. Finally one of them, the distinguished Huguenot writer Abel Boyer,[93] went too far and published in his *The Political State of Great Britain* a full account of debates in the House in January 1711, based on notes taken in the gallery, on the rather sensitive subject of the conduct of the war in Spain. He and his printer, John Baker, were hauled before the House and censured. As a result, on 5 March 1711, the 'Lord Great Chamberlain was ordered to pull down the Gallery'. The disappearance of the gallery did not prevent all strangers from entering the House, but as they now certainly needed more influence to do so, they were probably more acceptable to the House.[94]

The problem of accommodating distinguished visitors, however, remained. In 1737 another gallery was erected, again following the 1704 design, but this also proved unsatisfactory and it was pulled down in 1740. George III complained several times of the lack of this facility and other galleries were considered, but the problem was not solved until the removal of the House to the Court of Requests in 1801.[95]

We are fortunate in having a fine painting of the interior of the House of Lords during the early eighteenth century. By Peter Tillemans (1684-1734), a native of Antwerp, who came to England in June 1708 and made his reputation as a topographical, landscape, and sporting painter,[96] it is entitled 'Queen Anne in the House of Lords'[97] and shows the House during a formal sitting, probably at the opening of parliament, with the Queen on the throne and the peers in their parliamentary robes,[98] with the members of the Commons stood without the bar of the House (see frontispiece). The Queen is surrounded by her ladies-in-waiting and courtiers. To her right stand

[93] For Boyer see G. C. Gibbs, 'Abel Boyer Gallo-Anglus Glossographus et Historicus, 1667-1729: his early life 1667-1689', *Proceedings of the Huguenot Society of London*, xxiii, no. 2 (1978), 87-98.

[94] Wentworth, brother to Lord Strafford, continued to record debates after the gallery's disappearance, while in 1717 great ladies attended the trial of Lord Oxford at the bar of the House (Badminton House, Beaufort Papers, drawer 26: R. Price to [Lady Coventry], 27 June 1717).

[95] *History of the King's Works*, v, 392.

[96] He appears to have been patronized by members of both parties. See J. Harris, *The Artist and the Country House* (1979), pp. 224-5, 232-8; R. Raines, 'Peter Tillemans, Life and Work, with a List of Representative Paintings', *Walpole Society*, for 1978-80, xlvii (1980), 21-59.

[97] For a description see O. Millar, *The Tudor, Stuart and Early Georgian Pictures in the Collection of Her Majesty the Queen* (2 vols., 1963), i, 167.

[98] Peers only wore their robes at state openings, at royal assent to bills (though this was not always the case, 23 Dec. 1702), and upon their introduction to the House. Bishops normally wore Convocation dress (black gown with white lawn sleeves) for both formal and every-day sittings.

two peers, one holding the sword of state and one behind with the cap of maintenance. On her left·stand the four great officers of state: the Lord Chancellor (who, as Speaker of the House, would normally have sat on the woolsack immediately in front of the throne), the Lord Treasurer, the Lord President of the Council, and the Lord Privy Seal. These last three would sit on the upper part of the front bench on the temporal side of the House in a normal sitting. The second rank of great officers (the Lord Great Chamberlain, the Earl Marshal, the Lord Admiral, the Lord Steward, and the Lord Chamberlain of the Household) would occupy the middle section of the earls' bench on such a formal occasion, and indeed the fifth peer from the upper end of the bench is holding a white staff of office.

Immediately in front of the Queen stand heralds. In front of them on the two facing woolsacks sit the Lord Chief Justice, three other judges, and four Masters in Chancery. Between them and the cross-benches can be seen the clerks' table, covered with books and papers, with four clerks with their backs to the viewers, and one at each end of the table.[99]

The Armada tapestries lining the walls of the House can be clearly seen. They record the victory over the Spanish flcct, and were commissioned by the Earl of Nottingham, Lord High Admiral and commander of the English fleet in 1588. They cost £1,628, and were later sold to James I. They were not set up in the House until the early 1640s.[100]

The ceiling, erected in 1623–4 by Inigo Jones, concealed the high pitched roof. The plaster barrel vault is painted with imitation coffering in a *trompe-l'œil* effect. Designed to enable the chamber to be lit from above by dormer windows, it was a larger version of the ceiling at the Queen's Chapel which Jones was building at the same time.[101] Another source of light was a large medieval window at the north end of the House. It overlooked the roof of the Lobby, and in consequence it seems fair to assume that the interior of the chamber on all but the most sunny day must have been gloomy if not dark.[102]

The clock, next to the fireplace, was installed by James East in 1673, replacing an earlier clock which dated from the Restoration.[103]

[99] These would be the Clerk of the Parliaments, the Clerk Assistant, the Reading Clerk, the Copying Clerk, plus two clerks.

[100] T. Pennant, *Some Account of London* (3rd edn., 1793), p. 91. Engravings of the tapestries are to be found in J. Pine, *The Tapestry Hangings of the House of Lords* (1739).

[101] J. Harris, S. Orgel, and R. Strong, *The King's Arcadia: Inigo Jones and the Stuart Court* (1973), p. 125.

[102] See *History of the King's Works*, v, plate 52; and *Wren Society*, xi, plate 36.

[103] *History of the King's Works*, v, 400.

The fireplace itself, which failed effectively to warm the House in winter,[104] received its ornamentation in 1713, Wren having received instructions from the Lord Great Chamberlain to provide 'an Adornment of wainscot over the Chimney piece in the House of Lords'.[105] This feature helps to date the picture to 1713 or 1714, assuming that it was painted during the Queen's lifetime.[106]

THE ORGANISATION AND CONDUCT OF BUSINESS

The organisation of the House and the conduct of its business were controlled by a set of self-made rules known as standing orders and resolutions.[107] But as we have seen with seating arrangements, where the daily facts bore little or no resemblance to the principles which were supposed to regulate seating, so the day-by-day pattern of activity within the House often ignored or contravened the rules. Nicolson records an incident on 16 January 1703 where the resolution regarding the registering of proxies after prayers was broken. But while on the one hand the House has rules which at any time it may be found tacitly ignoring, on the other hand the lack of a standing order bearing on a particular aspect of its activity does not mean that at this very time there is not an accepted practice or convention in operation —a procedure which later will come to be enshrined in a standing order. The practice of the Contents going below the bar in a division illustrates this point: not formalised into a standing order until 1691, it was first recorded as taking place in 1675, when because of poor light those 'who gave their Contents withdrew below the bar for the easier counting of the House'.[108] Thus the pinning down of the procedure followed by the House at any given time is difficult: the standing orders form only a loose framework within which the House operates and experiments, a framework which might be and was sometimes forgotten. Only in the area of its appeal work does the House appear to have scrupulously followed its standing orders.[109] Since little work has been done on the development of procedure in the early

---

[104] See *History of the King's Works*, v, 405, n. 1.

[105] Quoted in ibid., p. 391.

[106] Millar (*Tudor, Stuart and Early Georgian Pictures*, i, 167) is unable to date the picture more precisely than 1708-14. He thinks Tillemans may have drawn on Kneller's seated state portrait for his image of the Queen, thus the picture may post-date Anne's death. Raines dates the picture as ?c.1709 ('Peter Tillemans', p. 58).

[107] For a full list of the standing orders up to 1714 see HMC *Lords MSS* x, 1-27; see also ibid., xii, 1-27.

[108] Quoted from the Manuscript Minutes by J. C. Sainty and D. Dewar, *Divisions in the House of Lords: An Analytical List 1686 to 1857*, HLRO Occasional Publications No. 2 (1976), pp. 8-9.

[109] See HMC *Lords MSS* xii, p. xxxv.

eighteenth century[110] this section of the introduction does no more than tentatively sketch in the outlines of the organisation of the House and convey some impression of how it functioned on a day-to-day basis.

One thing that is certain is that each day was different, not only in what happened, or in what business came before the House, but also in the daily timetable. However, certain broad areas of business can be established which impinged upon the House on the majority of its working days, and it is possible to distinguish the elements that went into the making of the daily timetable.

The House normally began its day's work at 11 o'clock in the morning (see below 25 Nov. 1702).[111] Attendance at the beginning of the day's proceedings, which started with prayers conducted by the junior bishop present, was poor and the numbers built up as the day went on.[112] The House normally sat until dinner time, which in the early eighteenth century was around 1.00 or 2.00 in the afternoon.[113] Thus the House normally sat about three hours each day. Towards the end of a day's sitting, numbers attending declined as peers and bishops drifted off to dinner. This decline was probably more pronounced on days when appeal cases ended the proceedings. Nicolson recorded on 9 February 1703 that five bishops and three peers heard such cases in the afternoon, whereas sixty-three lords are recorded as attending that day.[114] Often the standard sitting of three to four hours was not long enough for all the business before the House, and if this was sufficiently pressing, important, or interesting, it was quite common for the sitting to last into the late afternoon and, on very exceptional occasions, late into the night. Sometimes such business detained the bulk of the membership

---

[110] The work that has been published is largely by John Sainty: on divisions (above, n. 108); on the development of the office of Chairman of the Committees (see above, pp. 37–44: 'The Committee Man'); and on the leadership of the House (J. C. Sainty, 'The Origin of the Leadership of the House of Lords', *BIHR* xlvii [1974], 53–73). Elizabeth Read Foster is working on a book on the procedure of the Lords, 1603–60, and her interim conclusions are published in 'Procedure in the House of Lords during the early Stuart period', *Journal of British Studies*, v. no. 2 (1966), 56–73.

[111] In the early seventeenth century it normally began at 9.00 a.m. (Foster, 'Procedure', p. 62), and went on until midday. Although the normal time for the start of the daily sitting during the time of Nicolson's diaries was 11.00 a.m., the House sometimes started earlier, at 10.00 a.m., or during periods of increased activity, such as in late Feb. and early Mar. 1710 during Sacheverell's trial, earlier still at 9.00 a.m. Occasionally the House would not sit until midday (16 Jan. 1703; *LJ* xvii, 172, 197, 199, 376, 691; xix, 82–96, 108).

[112] Nicolson sometimes arrived late, e.g. at noon on 2 Jan. 1705. Lord Balmerino records arriving at 1.00 p.m. (SRO GD45/14/352/10: to Harry Maule, 2 June [1711]). Even on momentous days such as 16 Mar. 1710 when 122 voted on the first article of Sacheverell's impeachment, only eighty were present by about 11.00 a.m. (*LJ* xix, 108–9).

[113] M. Girouard, *Life in the English Country House* (1978), p. 147.

[114] *LJ* xvii, 274. For appeal cases see below, pp. 100–5.

until the end. On one occasion the Earl of Portland felt obliged to postpone the magnificent dinner he was giving to Prince Eugene of Savoy until 'about Six a clock the house of Lords haveing by chance that day debated on important affairs'.[115]

In the early seventeenth century private or select committees met at either 8.00 a.m. or 2.00 p.m., before or after the House itself had sat. By the Restoration these times had changed to 9.00 a.m. or 3.00 or 4.00 p.m., but by Queen Anne's reign, the time had become standardised at 10.00 a.m.[116] After prayers, the House got down to business. This was laid before them each day in the order for that day. No deviation from the pre-determined order of business was permitted. In the 'Church in danger' debate on 6 December 1705 Archbishop Sharp concluded his speech 'with a Motion for asking the Opinion of the Judges how the Laws stand as to Schools and seminaries of Dissenters'. This was seconded by the Bishop of Norwich. Later in the debate Lord Anglesey called for Sharp's question to be put, but Lord Godolphin corrected him, saying 'The Order of the Day determines what is the main Question and that is to take place of any incidental Question. The main Question is whether the Church be in danger from her Majesties Administration.'[117]

The humdrum business of the day usually followed: appeal cases, the receipt of addresses and petitions, first readings of bills, etc. Sometimes, of course, this kind of business would occupy the whole day. If, however, there was an important piece of business in the timetable, this would follow upon the routine business and would invariably occupy most of the Lords' time.[118]

The House was under the general direction of the Lord Chancellor (usually a peer) or the Lord Keeper (usually a commoner) who was *ex officio* Speaker of the House. During the period covered by Nicolson's diaries three men held the office of Lord Keeper or Chancellor: Sir Nathan Wright (1700–Oct. 1705), William Cowper,

[115] Nottingham UL Portland MS PwB/79b: -?- to -?-, [1711]. Lord Coventry recorded sitting until after 9.00 p.m. on 7 Dec. 1702 (Badminton House, Beaufort Papers, drawer 23: to his wife. Printed in HMC *12th Report, Appx 9*, p. 96). The debate on Sacheverell's impeachment on 16 Mar. 1710 lasted twelve hours until 11.00 p.m. (C. Jones, 'Debates in the House of Lords on "The Church in Danger", 1705, and on Dr Sacheverell's Impeachment, 1710', *HJ* xix [1976], 763).

[116] Foster, 'Procedure', p. 66; *LJ* xiii, 137, 151, 166. The change to a standard 10.00 a.m. meeting for all committees seems to have taken place during the mid-1690s. Along with a standardisation of time there occurred a standardisation of venue, with all committees normally meeting in the Prince's Chamber.

[117] Jones, 'Debates in the House of Lords', pp. 763, 766, 768.

[118] Even before the longest debate in contemporary memory, that on 16 Mar. 1710 on Sacheverell's impeachment, the day began with an hour's general business (Jones, 'Debates in the House of Lords', p. 763; *LJ* xix, 108–9).

later Lord Cowper (1705–Sept. 1710, and Sept. 1714–May 1718), and Simon Harcourt, later Lord Harcourt (Oct. 1710–1714). If the Speaker was a commoner, he was not a member of the House and had no right to speak or vote in debates. When the House went into a Committee of the Whole House,[119] a chairman was chosen by the House who sat on a chair by the clerks' table,[120] and the Lord Keeper, if he were a commoner, had then to leave the House; but the Lord Chancellor (or Lord Keeper if he were a peer) simply vacated the woolsack and took his place on the earls' bench where he could speak and vote as an ordinary member of the committee.[121] While acting as Speaker he could also, by leaving the woolsack, speak in debates as a peer.[122]

The most important job of the Lord Chancellor or Lord Keeper in debates was the putting of the question to the House, and deciding upon the result of the 'collective voice' vote.[123] If a division was called for, he read the results to the House. Unlike his namesake in the Commons, he had little but persuasive power to keep order. The House kept its own order, deciding, for instance, who should speak if two lords rose together. The House also appointed the tellers at a division.[124] Unlike his counterpart in the Commons, the Speaker of the Lords had no casting vote in a tie— in the Lords tied votes were by convention carried in the negative.[125] A strong-minded Lord Chancellor could, however, do a great deal through his force of personality and knowledge of the rules of the House to steer the House in the direction he wanted. A peer probably carried more weight on the woolsack than a commoner, and, if a respected man of the law, he could do a great deal beyond his role as laid down in standing orders. Harcourt once added words to a motion, which were objected to by many in the House, but the Chancellor 'said he want itt so' and carried the House with him.[126] He often intervened in

[119] Designed to give the House the same freedom of debate as was usual in select committees. It is first mentioned in the *Journals* in 1606 (Foster, 'Procedure', pp. 67–8).

[120] Sainty, *Chairman of Committees*, p. 2.

[121] George Baillie recorded on one occasion that the Chancellor in a Committee of the Whole House cast the decisive vote (Mellerstain Letters, iii; to his wife, 26 Mar. 1709).

[122] Foster, 'Procedure', p. 59.

[123] See below, pp. 93–4 for procedure on divisions.

[124] There were certain peers in the House who were recognised as having a good knowledge of procedure, for example, Lord Rochester who was described as 'excellently versed in the minutest forms', and Lord Ferrers 'who knows the forms of our house exactly' (SRO GD45/14/352/2: Balmerino to Maule, 16 Jan. [1711]). A small group of such men, especially if they held high office, together with a forceful Chancellor could probably control the proceedings of the House under normal circumstances.

[125] e.g. 11 and 16 Jan. 1703.

[126] *Wentworth Papers*, p. 364: [Bathurst] to [Strafford], 6 Apr. 1714. See also ibid., p. 403, where Cowper, an ex-Lord Chancellor, intervened to prevent a tedious reading of all the papers presented to the House.

debates, as did his precursor Cowper, to bring the House back to the point in question when it had drifted off into irrelevances, as it often did.[127] The Chancellor could also bring debates to an end by calling for the question to be put, as Harcourt is reported as doing during a tedious debate when he 'clos'd in with the Motion'.[128]

When the monarch attended formally the Chancellor stood next to her on the steps of the throne. More important politically, however, were the informal appearances of the sovereign in the Lords, a frequent occurrence between the Restoration and 1714. There is no record of George I attending incognito, though he assiduously attended the House on all formal occasions.[129] Queen Anne's first such attendance was on 29 November 1704.[130] The length of time the Queen stayed in the House varied. She did occasionally sit through a whole debate, eleven hours on 16 March 1710 and five hours on 16 December 1704.[131] The latter was probably more typical of her staying-power. Her poor health prevented many marathon sittings (indeed towards the end of her life it drastically reduced the number of times she attended incognito), and her endurance could be sorely tried by rambling or boring speeches, and she was not above leaving a debate in the middle of a speech if her interest flagged.[132] Fairly typical, especially of her later years, was her attendance at the debate on the 'affair of Spain' on 9 January 1711. The debate started at 11.00 a.m. and the division at the close, according to Nicolson took place at 10.00 p.m., but, as Mungo Graham reported, 'the Queen was their 3 or 4 hours and left them'.[133]

---

[127] See, e.g., Cowper's intervention on 16 Mar. 1710 (Jones, 'Debates in the House of Lords', p. 771).

[128] *Wentworth Papers*, p. 363. For an outline of the history of the office see M. Bond and D. Beamish, *The Lord Chancellor*, House of Lords Information Office Publications Series No. 2 (1977).

[129] J. C. Sainty, *Parliamentary Functions of the Sovereign since 1509*, HLRO Memorandum, no. 64 (1980), p. 5. The monarch sometimes attended informally private bills or causes, e.g. the Duke of Norfolk's Divorce Bill in 1693 (Cruickshanks, Hayton, and Jones, 'Divisions in the House of Lords', p. 74 n. 121).

[130] For the convention of the monarch attending incognito see Holmes, *British Politics*, pp. 390-1. Though on such occasions her attendance was not officially recognised by the House, it was noted in the *Journals*. Her presence sometimes caused a debate to be much longer than it need to have been as arguments already used were rehearsed again for her benefit (15 Dec. 1704).

[131] Jones, 'Debates in the House of Lords', p. 763; HMC *Ormonde MSS* new ser. viii, 125: Coningsby to Ormond, 16 Dec. 1704.

[132] For the two occasions, on successive days, when the Queen embarrassed the two Finch brothers, Nottingham and Guernsey, by leaving during their speeches, see Holmes, *Sacheverell*, pp. 214, 220.

[133] SRO GD220/5/808/4: Graham to [Montrose], 9 Jan. 1711; *LJ* xix, 187.

Divisions

The only area of procedure which needs to be laid out in detail for the readers of Nicolson's diaries is the methods of voting in the Lords.[134] There were three. First, the formal voting by 'individual voice', whereby each peer stood in turn, in reverse order of precedence, and declared Content or Not Content. This was cumbersome and rarely used, the best documented instance in the early eighteenth century being at the trial of Dr Sacheverell.[135] The breakdown of seating arrangements in the House led gradually to the method of individual voices being replaced by that of 'collective voice', whereby the House shouted aye or no and the volume of sound on each side determined the question. It is clear from a comparison of the number of recorded divisions with the number of questions decided, that it was the one most commonly used in the House. A third method developed, however, to determine questions when the collective voice did not produce a clear-cut majority acceptable to both sides. The earliest description of this method dates from 1610, when the lords were counted in two groups, the Contents standing and the Not Contents seated. A later refinement, to facilitate counting, was for the Contents to withdraw below the bar of the House. They were then counted by a teller as they passed back through the bar, the other side having been counted where they sat in the chamber. This refinement originated in 1675 and was enshrined in a standing order of 1691. The only way to abstain was to withdraw from the chamber before the question was put.

The Lord Chancellor, as we have seen, decided when the collective voice should be called for; in Committees of the Whole House, the chairman undertook that function. If the collective voice seemed not to have produced a definite majority, or when one side was dissatisfied, a lord might call for a division, and provided that the request were seconded a division had to be taken. The procedure is described in the following account by Lord Balmerino of a debate on Scottish and Irish trade:

now it being put to the vote tho I saw the contents had it, I said the not contents had it (or should have it) upon which Lord Conway and I were appointed tellers and we were 21 they 34 (which is a pritty full house after 6 months sitting).[136]

[134] For a longer treatment of this subject see Sainty and Dewar, *Divisions in the House of Lords*; and *A Register of Parliamentary Lists, 1660–1761*, pp. 7–10.

[135] See Holmes, *Sacheverell*, pp. 223–4.

[136] SRO GD45/14/352/10: [Balmerino] to [Maule], 2 June [1711]. For another illustration which also reveals a piece of neat parliamentary footwork by Wharton, see Kent Archives Office U1590/C474/10: enclosure in Addison to H. Walpole, 18 Feb. 1706/7, quoted below, pp. 394–5.

The actual counting of the votes in a division was the job of the tellers, except on the rare occasions when the individual voice method was used, when the clerks reckoned the votes. Two tellers, one from each side of the question (usually, and after 1712 invariably, of the same quality in the peerage),[137] were named by the Lord Chancellor or the chairman of the Committee of the Whole House, and the tellers were themselves included in the voting numbers, contrary to the practice in the Commons. On judicial questions all the members could vote, though it was a convention that the bishops did not do so in any case involving the death penalty.[138] The Lords had one privilege denied to members of the Commons, that of voting by proxy. An absent lord could, if he wished, leave his proxy with a colleague to cast on his behalf. Several restrictions had been placed on their use by Nicolson's time, the most important being that they could not be used in select committees nor in the Committee of the Whole House.[139]

Many questions, of course, never got as far as a division. If the matter were uncontroversial; if one side were so greatly outnumbered that they realised that a division would be futile and would only serve to 'show the Thinnesse of their Party';[140] if the vote on the main question had been decisive and everything else were let go by default;[141] or if one side had wearied of the struggle,[142] then the question would be decided *nemine contradicente*.[143]

Business

The two broad areas of business in which the House concerned itself were legislation and the hearing of appeal cases from the lower courts. But beyond these two functions, the House also acted as the forum (as did the Commons) for the great debates on the state of the nation, which might arise from legislation under consideration

[137] For the last occasion on which tellers of different degree officiated on 6 May 1712 see the division listed in Sainty and Dewar, *Divisions in the House of Lords*. John Relf, Reading Clerk 1664–1711, certainly regarded it as proper that tellers should be 'of the same quality' (HLRO Relf's Book of Orders, p. 683, quoted in ibid., p. 9).

[138] This was decided by the House in 1679, see *A Register of Parliamentary Lists, 1660–1761*, p. 34. Also a lord did not vote in a case or any motion directly involving him, though this did not prevent a peer doing so if he insisted, such as the unsavory Lord Mohun during the Duke of Hamilton's privilege case on 8 Feb. 1712 (HMC *Lords MSS* ix, 189). As Lord Ferrers explained, 'except a man be impeached they [the House] never hinder him to vote tho a discreet and modest man will abstain from it, thus the Earl of Peterburrow might vote his own narrative [about the war in Spain] just and honourable, and carry it by his single vote, against his enemies . . .' (SRO GD45/14/352/2: Balmerino to [Maule], 16 Jan. 1711).

[139] For a full discussion of proxies, see above, pp. 32–6: 'Nicolson's use of his proxy'.

[140] See Kent Archives Office, U1590/C474/10, referred to above, note 136.

[141] See 2 Dec. 1702.

[142] *Jerviswood Correspondence*, p. 17, quoted below, 6 Dec. 1704.

[143] e.g. see 25 Oct. 1704.

(such as the debates on the Occasional Conformity Bill), or from the inquisitorial role the House might play from time to time (as over the conduct of the war in Spain). At other times a great debate might equally be fired by the call by an individual peer for an inquiry into a particular aspect of the conduct of the nation's business. Perhaps the most famous cases of such initiatives are the calls by Lord Haversham for debates on whatever issue of the hour particularly interested him or seemed likely to embarrass the ministry. Haversham's demands developed into annual events which usually came early in the parliamentary session and they continued until his death in November 1710. He printed his own speeches on these occasions, and these were often eagerly awaited by the public, both as serious probes into the nation's ills and as entertaining reading. When Lord Suffolk came up to London from Audley End especially to hear Haversham deliver one of his celebrated harangues, only to find Haversham too ill to deliver it, his disappointment was tempered by the knowledge that 'in a little time after, he will oblige us all in the printing of it, which if I be in Town, when it comes out, I will be sure to send it to your Lordship'.[144] When it finally appeared, Lord Yester, sending it to his father, considered it 'the best he ever made'.[145]

Since the full-dress debate, including set-pieces of the Haversham type, was still very common during the time Nicolson sat in the House, some attempt to capture the atmosphere of the House on such occasions is called for.

These debates often had an air of theatre about them, and the Lords usually had ample warning of when the next performance was due. Lord Haversham, for instance, in mid-December 1709, asked 'that a day be appointed to consider of the State of the Nation, and he humbly proposed it might be the next day after the Recess', that is nearly a month ahead. He went on to request a call of the House to ensure that 'there might be a full House'.[146] The advance notice was not always as long as this: the 'Church in danger' debate of 6 December 1705 had its origins in a motion of Lord Halifax, seconded by Lord Rochester, made on 30 November.[147]

[144] Badminton House, Beaufort Papers, drawer 18: Suffolk to [?Coventry], 12 Jan. 1709[/10]. See also Berkshire RO Trumbull MS 53: J. Bridges to Trumbull, 10 Jan. 1709/10.

[145] NLS Yester Papers 7021, f. 147v: Yester to Tweeddale, 18 Jan. 1709[/10]. Haversham's speech of the previous year, however, was sent to Sir William Trumbull merely to 'give you a quarter of an hour's Entertainment' (Berkshire RO Trumbull Add. MS 132: J. Tucker to Trumbull, 21 Jan. 1708/9).

[146] BL Blenheim Papers E26: Mainwaring to Duchess of Marlborough, 'Thursday Evening' [15 Dec. 1709]; Beaufort Papers, drawer 18: Suffolk to [?Coventry], 12 Jan. 1709 [/10].

[147] Jones, 'Debates in the House of Lords', p. 760.

Time was usually sufficient, however, for both sides and all partici-
pants to prepare themselves well in advance. Consequently spectators
were sometimes conscious of a lack of spontaneity about the
speeches and debates.[148] 'All the great men spoke prepared', wrote
William Cleland of the seven-hour long debate on the 'Church in
danger',[149] and Nicolson described Bishop Hooper's contribution to
it as 'a Rambling (but elaborate and sett) Discourse' (below 6 Dec.
1705). On an earlier occasion, Nicolson had prepared a written
speech on Occasional Conformity, which in the event he was unable
to deliver (below, pp. 137-8). On 16 March 1710 Burnet 'made a
very long and learnedly historical account of the Doctrine of Passive
Obedience'[150] which was probably delivered from notes. In contrast
to the early seventeenth century when a peer apologised for using
notes,[151] they appear to have been regularly used in Nicolson's time.[152]
Lord Nottingham was observed taking notes in a debate in July
1714, a practice, which to judge from the survival of such notes in
his papers from other debates,[153] was common on his part. Lengthy
pauses between speeches, especially at the start of a debate, were
apparently a feature of the Lords.[154] It is possible that some of the
notes which we know were often used to frame a reply to a previous
speech were jotted down during these silences.

The more 'familiar style' which seasoned Commons' debaters
such as Thomas Wharton, Charles Montagu, and Arthur Annesley
brought up with them to the Lords had, therefore, a strong tradition
to break down. The iconoclasts were helped to some extent by the
influx of Scottish peers after 1707, for they seem to have favoured
a more direct and uninhibited method than many of their English
counterparts, those that is who chose to speak at all. The Viscount
of Kilsyth sat for two and a half years before making his maiden
speech, which when delivered consisted of some forty words. None
the less it was described by his colleague Balmerino as full of 'honesty
and good sence',[155] which was in strong contrast (in its brevity as
well as its content) to many a speech from the English peers. The
Duke of Argyll shared something of Wharton's reputation for direct,

[148] This is in contrast to the early seventeenth century, see Foster, 'Procedure',
p. 70.
[149] SRO GD124/5/259/3: Cleland to James [Erskine], 6 Dec. 1705.
[150] Jones, 'Debates in the House of Lords', p. 770.
[151] Foster, 'Procedure', p. 70.
[152] e.g. Wentworth Papers, p. 393.
[153] Ibid., p. 404; Jones, 'Debates in the House of Lords', pp. 762 n. 14, 764 n. 28.
[154] See, e.g., BL Add. MS 28252, f. 82, quoted in Jones, 'Debates in the House of Lords',
p. 765; BL Blenheim Papers E26: Mainwaring to Duchess of Marlborough, 15 Dec. 1709;
below, 24 Nov. 1704.
[155] SRO GD45/14/352/24: [Balmerino] to [Maule], 9 June [1713].

no-nonsense speaking, if not for his wit. On 16 March 1710 he 'spoke very severely against the Church men's medling with Politicks, and of their insolent expectations . . .',[156] while on 6 April 1714 he was described as 'very smart, which was to be expected from him'.[157] Though the Scots revealed a lack of knowledge of procedure to begin with, relying for guidance upon English colleagues such as Lord Ferrers, they provided some good debaters, particularly Mar, Ilay, and Loudoun, and also (if his own reports are to be believed) Balmerino.[158] Ilay and Loudoun, as we shall see, were particularly impressive in Scottish legal appeals.

It is clear that there was a small core of active peers and bishops who regularly took the lead in debates, though others were by no means excluded. Many of them were mentioned earlier,[159] and a few others, such as Buckingham and Burnet should be added to the list.

It should be said that the quality of debate was not uniformly high, despite an impressive array of front-line talent. Some peers could be guaranteed to drone on at length, boring their listeners in the process. The House was usually fairly tolerant, but some speakers went too far:

The *Marquess of Caermarthen* in a tediously long speech . . . which could hardly be heard by any, harangued the House. He was a little interrupted by the *Duke of Richmond's* calling it a long story, but he said it was Reason to him and he'd goe on with it if he kept them to the morning.[160]

Over three years later the same peer, having meanwhile succeeded his father as Duke of Leeds, 'made long speeches full of nonsense'.[161] The debate on the first article of the impeachment of Dr Sacheverell on 16 March 1710 was unusual on two counts: it was, as we have seen, one of the longest in living memory and over thirty peers and bishops are known to have spoken (a record for any debate in Anne's reign), some of whom hardly ever spoke at other times.[162] To judge by the length of their printed speeches Lord Haversham and Bishops Talbot and Burnet must by themselves have occupied the House for at least two and a half hours. They at least were worth

---

[156] Jones, 'Debates in the House of Lords', pp. 769-70.

[157] *Wentworth Papers*, p. 366. On 2 June 1713 Argyll was described as speaking 'very handsomely, long, & violently for us which disposed the whigs much to incline to us'. SRO GD45/14/352/19: [Balmerino] to [Maule].

[158] SRO GD45/14/352/2, 13: [Balmerino] to [Maule], 16 Jan. [1711], 24 Jan. 1712.

[159] See above, pp. 63-6.

[160] Jones, 'Debates in the House of Lords', p. 771. For a joint gaffe by Carmarthen and his father, the Duke of Leeds, see ibid., p. 768.

[161] SRO GD45/14/352/24: [Balmerino] to [Maule], 9 June [1713].

[162] See Holmes, *Sacheverell*, pp. 215-20. This underlines the point that a very small active core of lords ran debates.

listening to,[163] but the calibre of many other contributors was to say the least variable, and Lord Cowper, towards the end of the debate, complained of their lordships' irrelevances,[164] taking 'notice how wide some of 'em spoke, and told 'em what the strict Question was'.[165]

The recorder of Carmarthen's tedious speech on this occasion who was almost certainly in the gallery, also complained of the inaudibility of other speakers:

My *Lord Anglesey* and my *Lord Nottingham* both spoke long[166] but so low that I could know little more than their general Votes for the Dr . . . My *Lord Sunderland* spoke but not to be heard . . . My *Lord Seafield* spoke very much and earnestly but the tone made it not intelligible to me.[167]

The barrel-vaulted ceiling and the walls hung with heavy tapestries could hardly have been conducive to good accoustics. Many peers may well have had difficulty in hearing, particularly if the speaker had his back to the listener and there happened to be a good deal of background hum. On one occasion the problem was so severe that the Lord Chancellor could not hear the King's own words, even though he was standing next to him on the steps of the throne!

Not having yet received a copy of the king's speech [he later wrote] I desire you to send me one . . . the noise in the house and my being behind the king's back making it impossible for me to hear the words from his Majesty's mouth in the house.[168]

It would seem that Queen Anne (who in any case was noted for her clear enunciation) was accorded more courtesy than was George I.

I got him [Lord Dundonald] in to the house of Lords [wrote Lord Tullibardine] where wee heard the Speach, which I thinke was a very smooth one, and nothing that can be excepted against. The fine way of delivery made it no less agreeable, for the Queen spoke so distincktly and with such an easy pronounciation that would have made any thing pass, tho it had not been so well composed, and I belive there was very few there but what heard perfectly well. . . .[169]

---

[163] Jones, 'Debates in the House of Lords', pp. 769, 770.
[164] Often a well argued speech would be followed by a series of irrelevant ones in which the debate drifted off the point. See, e.g., *Wentworth Papers*, p. 364: [Bathurst] to [Strafford], 6 Apr. 1714, where Bolingbroke was followed by a series of such speeches and the situation had to be saved by Ferrers proposing a question.
[165] Jones, 'Debates in the House of Lords', p. 771.
[166] For Nottingham's reputation for being long-winded and repetitious see J. A. Downie, 'Swift's Dismal', *N & Q* ccxxiii (1978), 43; and C. Jones 'Swift's Dismal defended', *N & Q* ccxxviii (1983), 30-1.
[167] Jones, 'Debates in the House of Lords', pp. 770-1.
[168] PRO SP35/24/21: Lord Chancellor Parker to -?-, 8 Dec. 1720.
[169] Atholl MSS 45/3/148: to Duchess of Atholl, 3 Nov. 1703.

Legislation

Parliamentary bills could originate either in the Lords or in the Commons, except for money bills which, by convention, started in the Commons[170] and which the Lords had no power to amend: they could only accept or reject them. All bills irrespective of their origin went through the same stages. There was a first reading, which was not the formal stage it has since become (for example the Exclusion Bill of 1680 was rejected by the Lords on its first reading).[171] At the second reading it was decided whether to commit or not. It was at the third stage, the committee stage, that a detailed consideration of legislation took place and that amendments were made. Public bills were normally committed to the Committee of the Whole House, while private or select committees dealt with local and private bills—highways, estate, and naturalisation bills among others.[172] The chairman of the committee reported on the bill to the House, which then voted on whether to accept or reject the amendments. The third reading then followed, and if passed the bill went on to receive the royal assent after it had been passed by the other House. If the bill had originated in the Lords, it was sent down to the Commons after the third reading, and would often return with amendments which the Lords had to accept or reject and then return to the Commons for confirmation. A contentious piece of legislation often shuttled back and forth several times until one House gave way to the demands of the other.[173] Conferences between the two Houses were, however, used in attempts to reach a compromise over such legislation—the first Occasional Conformity Bill is a case in point.[174] It was not unknown for a bill to be lost because it had not completed the necessary stages by the time of a prorogation or dissolution of parliament; and some measures, like the Scottish Linen Bill of 1711, were deliberately delayed in the hope that they would lapse with the end of the session.[175] The likely length of the sitting consequently became a prime consideration for anyone contemplating the introduction of a piece of private legislation, and a gamble often had to be taken on whether a bill would complete all its stages in time.

[170] See 22 Dec. 1702.
[171] See HMC *Ormonde MSS* new ser. v, 490: Longford to Ormond, 16 Nov. 1680.
[172] Sainty, *Chairman of Committees*, p. 2.
[173] See, e.g., the case of the Treason (Scotland) Bill in 1709, where the Commons, realising that the bill would not pass the Lords with their revised amendments, dropped their insistence upon them in order to get the bill through the Upper House (below, pp. 473–5).
[174] See below, pp. 146, 160–1, 168, 174–5, 191.
[175] SRO GD45/14/352/10: [Balmerino] to [Maule], 2 June [1711].

Appeals

Besides public legislation, the House spent much time on appeals: in fact judicial business probably took up as much as two-thirds of the timetable of the Lords.[176] Yet historians have shown remarkably little interest in this aspect of parliamentary work.[177] It undoubtedly lacks the immediate attraction of political events, but it was a most important function of the Lords and, if Nicolson's attitude was at all typical, members of the House were prepared to devote considerable time to the hearing of legal cases.[178]

The idea of a final appeal from a lower court to the Court of Parliament was established by the fourteenth century. Chancery was the court from which most appeals came, and the Lords had only acquired the right to hear equity appeals in 1675. Appeals from Chancery or any other English court came by way of a writ of error from the House to the lower court. Thus they did not require a re-hearing and normally were not very time consuming.[179] There was a steady flow of appeals in the early eighteenth century. During 1712-14, for example, fifty-eight separate proceedings came before the Upper House: two from Exchequer Chamber (the court of appeal from the Queen's Bench for certain specified types of actions), twenty-one from Chancery, six from Exchequer, two from Queen's Bench, and the rest from Scottish and Irish courts.[180] After the 1707 Union, the bulk of appeals which came before the House were Scottish. These were not treated as hearings by way of a writ of error; consequently they had to be heard *de novo* and did import a heavy burden upon the House.[181] By an order of 19 April 1709, Scottish appeals to the Lords gave automatic stays of execution and the Scots were not slow to take advantage of this. Thus by the time

[176] The number of references in *LJ* gives some indication of the proportion of time taken up by appeal cases, and for the period 1712-14 the 'records of appeals comprise the largest class of records surviving' (HMC *Lords MSS* xii, p. xxxiii).

[177] The exceptions are Robert Stevens in *Law and Politics: The House of Lords as a Judicial Body, 1800-1976* (Chapel Hill, 1978), and David Johnson in HMC *Lords MSS* xii, pp. xxxiii-xxxix.

[178] Many a peer or bishop could have echoed Balmerino's comment: 'we have nothing . . . to do, but private causes In which I have hitherto taken more part then well fell to my share' (SRO GD45/14/352/8: [to Maule], 1 May [1711]). For the details of procedure governing appeals see HMC *Lords MSS* xii, p. xxxv.

[179] Stevens, *Law and Politics*, pp. 6-10. They probably took up no more than three or four hours each, see 15 Jan. 1703.

[180] HMC *Lords MSS* x, p. xxxvii. For the courts of equity from which appeals could go to the Lords, see M. F. Bond, *Guide to the Records of Parliament* (1971) p. 114.

[181] Appeals were so costly that a threat of one was often enough to produce a settlement. Sir Edward Blackett reckoned that if he took a case in which he was involved as far as the Lords, which he threatened to do, it would cost his opponent twenty times the value of the disputed case (Northumberland RO ZBL 189 [Blackett (Matfen) MSS], Sir Edward's Letterbook: to Mr Ward, 18 May [1710]).

Nicolson left the Lords in 1718, such business had reached alarming proportions.[182] The question of Irish appeal cases was to be settled by the act of 1720 (6 Geo. I, c. 5), a direct result of the *Annesley* v. *Sherlock* case,[183] which denied the Irish House of Lords the right to hear appeals from Irish courts.

During the period covered by Nicolson's diaries, all members of the House were entitled to sit in judgment on appeal cases. There was no concept of such cases only being heard by 'law lords', though the judges and those peers with past experience as barristers or judges, or of acknowledged legal acumen had great influence on the House. 'Dry fare' they may have been to some,[184] but many peers—to whom, naturally, matters of property, inheritance, and marriage were of more than common importance—were prepared actively to involve themselves in such proceedings, and even more were prepared to attend hearings and if necessary vote. A not un-typical day was 11 June 1713 when five appeals were heard by a House consisting of the Lord Chancellor, six bishops, and fifty-five peers.[185] Lord Coventry reported attending 'the tedious examination of evidence, on behalf of Lord Anglesey in a case now depending before us upon an appeal of his Lady . . . [which] kept me in the house, fasting 'till 4 in the afternoon'. No doubt the tedium was partly relieved by Lady Anglesey's evidence of the 'barbarous usage, and beating she received'.[186] The large numbers sometimes recorded as being present at some appeals may be explained by special reasons: a particular case may have been followed that very day by an important and interesting piece of legislation, or even by one of the House's great debates;[187] some cases had direct or indirect political implications or involved party ties; while others had clear constitutional importance.[188] However, large numbers of lords were also recorded as attending cases when the issues seem to have been exclusively legal. Between 1714 and 1718 there were several legal votes in which between forty and fifty-two lords were engaged.[189]

We are fortunate that a collection of letters has survived which illustrate how an appeal case proceeded in the Lords, as well as

[182] This was the judgment of Sir John Lauder of Fountainhall, quoted in Stevens, *Law and Politics*, p. 9.

[183] See below, p. 671; HMC *Lords MSS* xii, pp. xxxviii–xxxix, 376–87.

[184] Stevens's opinion, *Law and Politics*, p. 7.

[185] HMC *Lords MSS* x, p. vii.

[186] Beaufort Papers, drawer 23: to his wife, 26 Mar. 1700.

[187] e.g. the debate on 17 Mar. 1710 on Sacheverell's impeachment was preceded by business including an appeal (*LJ* xix, 111).

[188] e.g. *Annesley* v. *Sherlock*.

[189] See HMC *Lords MSS* xii, p. xxxvi.

the numbers and names of lords who were prepared to give their time to such business. And since the letters concern Scottish cases, they illuminate the peculiarities associated with the new kind of appeal. The letters were written in 1720 by Duncan Forbes, at this time Deputy-Advocate and later to become one of Scotland's most eminent lawyers, to Lord Grange, Lord Justice Clerk and brother to the exiled Earl of Mar. They cover the period 12 January to 12 May 1720.[190]

Taking two days which figure prominently in the correspondence —25 and 30 March—a total of eighty-one peers attended on both days. Of these only three could be described in modern terminology as 'law lords': the current Lord Chancellor (Lord Parker) and two former Lord Chancellors, Cowper and Harcourt. A further twenty-five held, or had held legal office of some kind, many of these were Scottish offices. The most prominent example of the latter was the Earl of Ilay, an Extraordinary Lord of the Sessions from 1708 and Lord Justice General from 1710, both offices held until his death in 1761.[191] Such an eminent Scottish lawyer was invaluable when the House was involved in Scottish cases originating within a legal system alien to English peers and lawyers, as were other Scots versed in the law. Outside this group of 'qualified' peers was a further group who had some form of legal qualification, even of the most flimsy or technical sort. The best example, for he involved himself a good deal in legal appeals, is the Earl of Sunderland, described by Forbes— perhaps ironically—as 'that Eminent Lawier', who could boast no more than an honorary LL D from Cambridge and who was Recorder of Coventry from 1710 to his death in 1722.[192] This group of 'pseudo-qualified' peers together with the 'qualified' made up a total of thirty-five peers present on the two days under consideration. There were thus present forty-six peers who had no form of legal qualification at all.

In the cases reported by Forbes between January and May 1720, fourteen peers are named by him as speakers. Six of these were Scottish and may well have involved themselves only in Scottish cases. Of these six, two (Roxburghe and Rothes) had no qualifications, while of the rest, two (Ilay and Loudoun) held Scottish legal offices, and two had at some time held such offices. Of the eight English peers named, four held or had held high legal office,[193] while

[190] SRO GD124/15/1197.

[191] Details concerning offices, etc., come from *GEC Peerage*.

[192] SRO GD124/15/1197/33: [Forbes] to [Grange], [1 Apr. 1720]. Lord Rochester (d. 1711) was, as we have seen, described by Balmerino as well versed in the law (see above, p. 65). He had been a student at the Middle Temple in 1660, Recorder of Salisbury in 1685, and held an honorary DCL from Oxford (1700).

[193] Parker, Cowper, Harcourt, and Trevor.

two were without any qualifications.[194] The other two, who were partially qualified, were Lords Sunderland and Coningsby, the latter having been Custos Rotulorum for Hereford and Radnor since 1714. Of these fourteen, the most active were Argyll (an Extraordinary Lord of Session, 1704–8), Harcourt, Sunderland, and North and Grey. Did the fact that unqualified peers actively took part in cases mean that the course of justice was adversely affected? It would seem that, as a general rule, after listening to the case under consideration from the lawyers on both sides and after listening to the advice of the judges,[195] the House was guided by the opinions of those lords in the House with acknowledged legal training. Forbes makes the point graphically in the following letter:

I might tell You a tale that hapened friday Last. One Monsieur Pleineouf, a foreign Minister was Brought into the house of Lords whilest a Cause was a trying to satisfy his Curiosity. Lord Sunderland Made up to him and asked how he liked the place? Pray says Pleineouf what are these Gentlemen with Gowns and Bands at the Bar? Why says My Lord they are lawiers: And what are they a Doing? My Lord answered they were arguing a Cause. Pray My Lord Where are the judges?, why says My Lord we the peers are the judges. Hela! Mon Dieu. Cries the Frenchman. You the judges! there is not one Lord in the House that Minds the Least Morsell of the Cause. You are all a talking to one another or to me:[196] Its no matter for that Answers the peer. There are three or four Lords on the House who understand the Laws very weel, and give attention; and the house Always Gives in to their opinion. Very weel says Pleineouf than You [and] the Rest of the Lords take it upon your Conscience and honour, Not that the Cause is just or Unjust. But that the Lords who Listen are Good Lawiers and just judges:[197] But pray My Lord. Do these Lawier Lords Never Differ in opinion? how Does the House Govern its self in a Case of that Kind. why say my Lord — But here his Lordship was Luckily Interrupted By somebody who had a word for his private Ear and so the Conversation Ended.[198]

Forbes was well aware of the importance of the opinion of the legally qualified peers, but equally aware that the opinion was not always given from strictly judicial motives:

Nothing could have given us a Chance of Success in any of our Cases but the appearance of all the Lawiers of the house on our Side, and if the Conjecture that I have mentioned Concerning H[arcour]t be true [that he was under the Court's influence and had thus spoken for reversal, contrary to expectations], here is our End of any faint hopes we had Left.[199]

[194] Newcastle and North and Grey.
[195] For the judges giving advice, see 15 and 22 Jan. 1703, and HMC *Lords MSS* xii, 315, 369. For the judges generally see Foster, 'Procedure', p. 61.
[196] Cf. the House being reprimanded by the Duke of Leeds for not taking notice of a cause in progress, 15 Jan. 1703.
[197] See 5 Feb. 1703, for Nicolson taking an opposite view to the House on a case.
[198] SRO GD124/15/1197/33: [Forbes] to [Grange], [1 Apr. 1720].
[199] GD124/15/1197/11: [to Grange], 11 Feb. 1720.

At this point we can see politics interfering in judicial causes, and this was not uncommon. Earlier, on 23 January, Forbes had reported an issue where the Court and the Tory opposition lined up on opposite sides:

Yesterday when the house was pretty thin it was moved by Lord North and Gray that . . . the first vacant Days Might be appointed for hearing these Causes. The Motion was seconded by Lord Trevor and by Lord Harcourt but by this Last in a Manner not so firm as we had reason to Expect it was opposed with Great Vigour by so many of the C[our]t as were present in so much that the Duke of Newcastle as weel as the Chancellor Made Speeches.[200]

However, the contrary was also true: politics could be overridden by the justice of the case, as Lord Wharton found on 12 February 1703 when in a private case his Whig colleagues Lord Halifax and Bishop Burnet voted against him. But even in cases where politics were not responsible for a difference of opinion, conflict could easily happen if a peer was determined enough to try to sway the House. Lord Sunderland was on one occasion able to nullify the opinions expressed by Ilay and Loudoun, and to throw his weight on the side of the Lord Chancellor Parker and Lord Cowper, even 'tho he Owned he Did not very weel understand the Law of Scotland in that Behalf'.[201] But while the non-professional could, at times, exert an influence on the judicial decisions, the professional lawyers in the House could often with a single speech decide the fate of a case:

My Lord Clarendon read the Ladys petition. My Lord [Chancellor] Parker stood and oposed it and concluded after his reasons It should be rejected upon which all the house nemine Contradicente Cry'd reject it![202]

As we have seen unanimity, even amongst the professional legal peers, was not always the case, so that even if as a rule the House followed the opinions of such men, we come to the question posed by the French visitor to the House: what did the House do when there was a disagreement amongst the lawyer peers or even between them and the non-professionals? A comparison of the number of appeals heard with the number of divisions on such cases shows that

[200] GD124/15/1197/6: [to Grange].

[201] Ibid./33: [Forbes] to [Grange], [1 Apr. 1720]. Sunderland was so persuasive on one occasion that he 'convinced Lord Harcourt, and the Bishops to a Man to follow their Leader' (ibid./39: [same] to [same], 12 May [1720]). The Scots suffered, to begin with, from their ignorance of the Lords' procedure (NLS MS 6416, f. 111: Lovat to Forbes, 8 May 1718), and sometimes they were not understood by the English: Robert Dundas 'spoke More Quick than they use to speak here, and as his language was less Understood than could be Wished for, several of the Lords Ceased to Listen With that aplication that became a Decent audience' (GD124/15/1197/9: [Forbes] to [Grange], 4 Feb. 1720).

[202] NLS MS 6416 (Halkett of Pitfirrane MSS), f. 98: Lovat to Forbes, 8 Mar. 1718.

104

most were decided without proceeding to a division.[203] Even when there was strong disagreement over a case, a unanimous decision could be reached without a vote (see below 15 Jan. 1703). Strong party issues involved in a case could, however, force the House to a division (below 22 Jan. 1703), and when the judges called into a case gave conflicting legal interpretations, the House invariably went to a division.[204] It was disagreements among the professionals which created the possibility of injustice being done, for the bulk of the voters in the resulting division would in most cases be the professionally unqualified. Party loyalty, personal friendships, private animosities—all could sway them. Yet the unqualified were not totally ignorant of the issues at stake in a case. Since the 1690s those bringing appeals had had to produce enough printed cases outlining their arguments for each lord to have his own copy,[205] and it is clear that a good deal of lobbying went on.

Although, as we have said, there was no such thing as a typical day in the life of the House of Lords, a perfectly normal day in the early eighteenth century would consist of four or five hours of unglamorous, and quite often tedious, work concerned with bills and legal appeal cases. Occasionally a long and more interesting debate would arise out of this daily routine to enliven their lordships' work and perhaps rouse their passions, but the really grand debates in which oratorical talents could be flourished to the full were fairly rare events. Though Nicolson's diaries may seem at times to belie this, we must remember that, while he is obviously interested in all aspects of the work of the House, it was the great moments in the House under Queen Anne which excited the mind and stirred the blood of this godly but politically conscious prelate, so that the routine nature of so much of the proceedings in the Lords is not often (and how grateful we should be for this!) fairly reflected in his pages. None the less there is much in the bishop's diaries to help the historian to a clear understanding of how the House of Lords functioned in the first two decades of the eighteenth century, and there are pages here which recall, as few other contemporary documents have the power to do, the distinctive bouquet of its vintage years.

---

[203] Of the 296 divisions between 1702/3 and 1717/18, only thirty-nine (13%) were on appeal cases.

[204] See, e.g., *Roper* v. *Hewet* (HMC *Lords MSS* x, pp. xxxvii, 148–50). This was one of only two appeal cases (out of fifty-eight) decided by a division between 1712 and 1714.

[205] Stevens, *Law and Politics*, p. 12.

The Diaries:
History, Provenance, and Composition

HISTORY AND PROVENANCE

The original diaries, as left by Nicolson, descended to the Lindesay family of Loughry, Co. Tyrone, through Nicolson's third daughter Elizabeth who married the Revd Bellingham Mauleverer, Rector of Maghera, Co. Derry.[1] Their third daughter, another Elizabeth, married John Lindesay of Loughry in 1743. By 1888, when the diaries were entrusted to Bishop Harvey Goodwin with the prospect of publishing them, the diaries formed part of a collection of forty odd volumes of Nicolson manuscript materials, containing, besides the diaries proper, several volumes of almanacs, accounts and theological, archaeological, and other scholarly notes. The 'Lindesay diaries' seem to have covered the years 1684-5, 1690, 1701-9, 1711-15, and 1717-25. There were some gaps, the most noticeable being 25 March 1703-4 July 1704, 16 January-25 March 1705, 9 November-31 December 1711, and 17 March-7 July 1713.

The diaries, along with some other of the manuscript material, were transcribed under the supervision of Bishop Goodwin's daughter, Mrs H. Ware, in preparation for publication. For the most part the diaries from 1684 to 1714 were transcribed in full. From 1714 to 1725 the text appears to have been edited by Mrs Ware by leaving out 'the entries of no interest'.[2] This regrettable practice seems to have coincided with the decline in Nicolson's interest in keeping a diary,[3] so that after 1714 the diaries consist sometimes of little more than lists of visitors and of visits made by Nicolson.

After the transcription was completed the diaries were presumably returned to the Lindesay family in Ireland. Between the date of their return and the 1940s many of the original volumes of the diaries were lost. When the surviving volumes were presented to the Tullie House Library in Carlisle by Mrs Gabbett of Ballaghtobin, Callan, Co. Kilkenny, a descendant of Bishop Nicolson, only nine volumes of the diaries and four volumes of almanacs were known to exist.

---

[1] The next few paragraphs are based on the history of the diary in *CW* i (1901), 1; xxxv (1935), 80-1; xlvi (1946), 191.

[2] See Ware transcript, xxx, 6 (below, p. 607).

[3] See ibid., xxviii, 141 (below, pp. 607-67).

These nine volumes contained one (covering 25 March 1703–4 July 1704) which Mrs Ware had not seen. The originals as they now exist at Tullie House are:

1a (1 Jan.–13 Mar. 1701/2)
1b (13 May–31 Dec. 1702)
2   (1 Jan.–24 Mar. 1702/3)
3   (25 Mar. 1703–4 July 1704)
4   (5 July–23 Nov. 1704)
5   (24 Nov. 1704–15 Jan. 1704/5)
6   (25 Mar.–30 Dec. 1705)
7   (1 Jan.–24 Mar. 1705/6)
8   (25 Mar. 1706–3 Apr. 1707)

Tullie House Library also possesses the 'Ware transcripts' which cover the same dates as the original volumes (with the exception of volume 3) and these transcripts also cover the now missing original volumes up to 1725.

One other original volume of the diaries is known to exist (and was not seen by Mrs Ware). This covers the dates 25 March 1709–31 December 1710. It belongs to Professor P. N. S. Mansergh, Master of St John's College, Cambridge.[4]

Thus the only major gaps now left in the diaries, taking the surviving original volumes and the Ware transcripts together are 16 January–25 March 1705, 9 November–31 December 1711, 17 March–7 July 1713, and the year 1716. It is probable that there was a volume covering the first of these gaps which is now lost. The 1711 missing section was written by Nicolson in his 1711 almanac, while the 1713 section was in a 'Journal in separate sticked Leaves'.[5] Both of these were lost before the Ware transcription was made. There may never have been a diary for 1716, but if there was it is also now lost.

Bishop Goodwin's project of printing the diaries *in extenso* was not carried out, but Mrs Ware's husband, the Bishop of Barrow-in-Furness and the then president of the Cumberland and Westmorland Antiquarian and Archaeological Society, published large extracts from his wife's transcriptions. These extracts appeared in the Society's *Transactions* between 1901 and 1905, and were almost exclusively concerned with the local activities of Nicolson in his diocese; only

---

[4] Throughout this edition it will be referred to as the 'Mansergh volume'. It was found by Mrs E. M. O. L. Mansergh in about 1935 among documents at Fairfield House, Tipperary.
[5] See below, p. 602.

a very small proportion of the London sections of the diaries was published. Since 1905 the two volumes that the Wares did not see (covering 1703-4 and 1709-10) have been published almost in full. But again the 1703-4 diary is entirely concerned with Nicolson in the Carlisle diocese, as is most of that of 1709-10. The following is a detailed list of the sections of the diaries which have appeared in print in the Society's *Transactions*:

1 Jan. 1684-20 July 1685 (printed in full)	
3 June 1690-31 Dec. 1690 (extracts)	*CW* i (1901), 6-48
29 Nov. 1701-13 Mar. 1702 (extracts)	
13 May 1702-24 Mar. 1703 (extracts)	*CW* ii (1902), 156-94
25 Mar. 1703-4 Apr. 1704 (printed in full)	*CW* xlvi (1946), 192-222
5 Apr. 1704-4 July 1704 (printed in full)	*CW* l (1950), 114-29
5 July 1704-15 Jan. 1705 (extracts)	*CW* ii (1902), 195-230
26 Mar. 1705-3 Apr. 1707 (extracts)	*CW* iii (1903), 1-58
6 Apr. 1707-21 Mar. 1709 (extracts)	*CW* iv (1904), 1-46
25 Mar. 1709-31 Dec. 1710 (printed almost in full)	*CW* xxxv (1935), 80-145
1 Jan. 1711-7 Nov. 1711; 1 Jan. 1712-16 Mar. 1713; 7 July 1713-2 Mar. 1714 (extracts)	*CW* iv (1904), 47-70
24 May 1714-17 Dec. 1715; 11 Jan. 1717-30 Dec. 1717; 18 Jan. 1718-22 Mar. 1718; 2 July 1718-18 Aug. 1718; 22 Mar. 1719-28 Nov. 1725 (extracts)	*CW* v (1905), 1-31

THE LONDON DIARIES

This edition of the London sections of Bishop Nicolson's diaries prints the full text that has survived, in either the original volumes or in the Ware transcripts.[6] The following table sets out the sections of the text published in this edition with the sources from which they come:

[6] A comparison of the Ware transcription with the original diaries shows that the transcribers employed by Mrs Ware were very accurate. The editors of this edition have, therefore, been able to place great trust on the Ware transcripts for the years for which the originals have been lost. Any obvious mistakes in transcription have been corrected.

Session	Dates	Source
1	14 Nov. 1702–22 Feb. 1703	Original vols. 1b & 2
2	24 Oct. 1704–15 Jan. 1705	Original vols. 4 & 5
3	26 Oct. 1705–5 Mar. 1706	Original vols. 6 & 7
4	20 Nov. 1706–24 Mar. 1707	Original vol. 8
5	24 Dec. 1707–5 Apr. 1708	Ware trans. vols. 23 & 24
6	5 Feb. 1709–29 Apr. 1709	Ware trans. vol. 24 & Mansergh vol.
7	8 Dec. 1710–5 Apr. 1711	Mansergh vol. & Ware trans. vol. 26.
8	1 Jan. 1712–2 Apr. 1712	Ware trans. vol. 28
9	14 Mar.–16 Mar. 1713	Ware trans. vol. 28
10	31 Mar. 1714–14 June 1714	Ware trans. vol. 30
11	25 Mar. 1715–9 Sept. 1715	Ware trans. vol. 31
12	19 Feb. 1717–22 July 1717	Ware trans. vols. 33 (Text A) & 32 (Text B)
13	11 Jan. 1718–17 Mar. 1718	Ware trans. vol. 32

The three gaps in an otherwise complete record of William Nicolson's thirteen visits to London as Bishop of Carlisle are as follows:

Session	Dates
2	16 Jan.–25 Mar. 1705
8	?13 Nov.[7]–31 Dec. 1711
9	17 Mar.–14 June 1713

THE COMPOSITION OF THE DIARIES

Although Bishop Nicolson carefully noted in his diaries the evenings on which he wrote letters,[8] nowhere does he state how (or why) he kept the records which form the basis of the diaries, nor is there any mention of how he wrote it into the original small, leather-bound manuscript volumes. This is in contrast to Samuel Pepys, who makes several references to his methods, so that along with an analysis of the text and the volumes of his diary it has been possible to establish Pepys's methods of construction.[9] With Nicolson's diaries, textual

[7] See below for the uncertainty about the date of his arrival in London in 1711.

[8] He was a fairly prolific letter writer. Between 1 Jan. and 5 Mar., and 11 Nov. and 31 Dec. 1706 he records writing 296 letters (Tullie House, Carlisle: Nicolson's Account Book, 1706).

[9] See The Diary of Samuel Pepys, ed. R. Latham and W. Matthews (11 vols., 1970–83), i, pp. xliii–xlv, xcvii–ciii. Cf. Sir Edward Dering's methods of composition, The Diaries

analysis is the only way of trying to establish how the original diary volumes were written.

Such an analysis would seem to indicate that a similar method to that used by Pepys, though perhaps slightly less complicated, was used by Nicolson. That is, the diaries as they have come down to us were probably written into the volumes from rough notes and memory at various intervals, which varied from probably the evening of the day described to at least a couple of weeks later.

The overall neatness of the diary with very few crossings out or erasures, the total lack of marginal notes or other interjections beyond the occasional word, suggest that the text of the diaries was not composed directly into the volumes but was copied from rough notes.[10] No rough notes have been found by the editors in any collection of Nicolson manuscripts that have survived (excepting some far from 'rough' antiquarian notes referred to below). None the less there are indications that Nicolson used other materials in composing the diary. The entries for 11 and 13 January 1703 both contain long quotations from documents (a parliamentary proxy in Latin and an address from the Lords to the Queen) on which he must have taken notes for incorporation into the diary. On 10 December 1702 the bishop wrote to his friend Ralph Thoresby concerning, among other things, the quarrel between Lords Halifax and Osborne which had occurred in the Lords that day.[11] The account in the letter is slightly fuller and has more immediacy about its style than the diary entry for that day. Nicolson could well have used the letter as a source for his diary entry; or, alternatively, he may have drawn on notes for writing both the letter and the account in his diary.

There are two volumes of notes, largely antiquarian in character, one of which contains diary-like entries for Nicolson's visits to antiquaries on 4 and 19 January and 5 and 12 February 1712.[12] These notes, written in a neat hand, may well have been intended by Nicolson for inclusion in his final draft of the diary. They were certainly written before the relevant sections of the diary were composed for Nicolson refers to the more detailed account of his visits in his diary entries.[13]

and Papers of Sir Edward Dering Second Baronet, 1644 to 1684, ed. M. F. Bond (1976), pp. 16–17.

[10] The evidence of neatness is perhaps not so conclusive as it may at first seem. Nicolson was very neat in the writing of his draft letters as those in Bodl. MS Add. C217 reveal. There are, however, sufficient alterations in these letters to show that they are drafts despite their fluency of style.

[11] See Fitzwilliam Museum, Cambridge, Spencer Perceval Bequest, Packet B: N. to Thoresby, 10 Dec. 1702.

[12] Bodl. MS Gen. Top. c.27/1, ff. 4–11, printed as Appendix B, below, pp. 698–703.

[13] See below, p. 576.

Nicolson records in his entry for 4 January 1705, after a visit to a tavern in Fleet Street where he witnessed 'wondrous feats' by an armless German who wrote with his mouth and feet, that 'Samples of these [writings] are in the cover of this book'. It is highly unlikely, however, that the bishop carried his diary around with him during the day. Since these particular samples no longer survive, it is likely that the German did not write directly into the volume, but that the samples were written on loose pieces of paper which were later inserted into the 'pockets', between the outer leather cover and the boards, at the end of the volume. Most of the original volumes of Nicolson's diaries have this feature, and some contain original notes, largely of a literary character.

It is a reasonable assumption that many entries, though not necessarily a majority of them, were very promptly written up. One which bears every mark of immediacy is that which reports the stabbing of Harley on 8 March 1711. Nicolson adds at the end of his account that 'my Information [is] as yet Imperfect'. In his entry for 9 March the bishop records a report from Atterbury that Harley was in no danger, thus indicating that the account for 8 March was written before that for 9 March and certainly before Atterbury's information reached Nicolson.

There are, however, just enough examples of factual error and mistaken dating in the diaries to suggest—though not conclusively —that the recording of events on the day they happened was not Nicolson's habitual method. The reporting to the Lords of the Committee on Records' report which took place on 20 April 1709 is entered by Nicolson at the end of his entry for 19 April. In his entry for 1 March 1709, the bishop notes the agreement for the Commons to a Lords' address to the Queen, although in fact it was voted on 2 March. Neither of these errors would presumably have been made if the entry in question had not been made some days after the event.

It is possible that delays in writing up his notes were longer than usual at the fag-end of parliamentary sessions, when Nicolson was preparing for his journeys back to Carlisle. For example, on 16 February 1703 he records that a bill was adjourned to 22 February, upon which day it was rejected. As he was on the road home on the latter date and would probably not have heard of the rejection until much later, probably after his arrival home on 2 March, it is likely that this entry for 15 February was not composed until four to five weeks later.

There are two examples of unusual entries in the diaries which throw further light on composition methods. Under 11 November

1704 Nicolson repeats (with slight variations) his account of his meeting in the evening with Archbishop Sharp. His first account of the meeting ends at the bottom of the recto side of the page of the diary. Immediately on turning that page over, at the top of the verso side, a second account of the meeting begins. Presumably the second account results from Nicolson forgetting that he had already recorded this meeting. If this is so, it is clear proof that Nicolson did not necessarily complete a day's entry each time he took up his diary, and that sometimes he broke off writing in mid-entry if it was late, or in other respects convenient or necessary for him to do so.

Nicolson's entry for 11 December 1704 is particularly interesting. It begins on the top of the left-hand page and continues to the bottom of that page. There then follows a blank right-hand page, and the entry starts anew with the date on turning over this blank page, that is, overleaf at the top of the next left-hand page. In the first entry for 11 December the bishop describes the opening of the debate in the House, after noting that the Queen was present, by stating that Lord Somers began the debate. The second account is virtually the same until the first speaker, who is now Lord Wharton, is mentioned. Wharton's speech is different from that of Somers in the first account, while Somers does not speak at all in the second account of the debate. Nicolson appears to have made a mistake in writing up the beginning of the entry for 11 December. The speech attributed to Somers in the first version of the debate is exactly the same in content as that made by Somers in Nicolson's entry for 6 December 1704. It is significant that his account of both debates on 6 and 11 December (both on the state of Scotland) begin in exactly the same way: after some private business, the Queen enters the chamber and the order of the day is read. It seems clear that Nicolson was writing up the section of the diary containing both debates at some later date, and appears to have got his notes for the 6 and 11 December muddled and to have realised his mistake only after he had written a page of his mistaken account for 11 December.

A close examination of the penmanship and changes in ink in the nine volumes of the original diaries lends weight to the above hypothesis on their composition. In general it is not possible to detect significant changes in ink or penmanship in most of the diaries, but there are some detectable differences in volumes 1b, 2, and 6. These differences indicate that small blocs of daily entries were probably written up at the same time. For example, 6 to 11 June and 11 to 17 June (in vol. 1b) differ from each other and from those entries on either side in ink and penmanship. Similarly the entries in the second half of November 1705 (in vol. 6) can be divided into separately written sections as follows: 15-22 November, 23 November, 24-5 November, 26-7 November, end of entry for 27 November, and 28-30 November. There are other indications that, as for the entry for 27 November 1705, an entry for one day might have been written up on two separate occasions: the end of the entry for 29 June 1702 (vol. 1b) differs in the type of ink used from the beginning of the entry; and the ink and penmanship change halfway through the entry for 12 February 1703 (vol. 2). One can deduce, therefore, that at certain times the diaries were written up in small groups of daily entries, though single days and even parts of days might be entered into the diaries separately.

For all these occasional anomalies and errors, and the clear evidence that there was often a time-lag between the compilation of the original notes or memoranda on a day's London doings and the completion of the final record, the overwhelming impression which the diaries convey is one of precision and almost invariable certainty on points of detail. Nicolson is concerned throughout predominantly with his own direct experiences. Where he does record at second-hand (e.g. news of proceedings in the Commons) he often reports his source.

THE REASONS FOR KEEPING THE DIARIES

As noted above, Nicolson nowhere in his surviving diaries explains why he kept such an extensive and detailed record of his life. We do not know whether the 'Lindesay' diaries as they existed in 1888 were the complete surviving diaries or whether even by that stage large sections of the diary had been lost.[14] The subsequent finding of two volumes of diaries not transcribed or seen by the Wares together with the loss of several volumes between their transcription by the Wares and the final deposit of the surviving originals in Tullie House lends credence to the possibility that Nicolson had kept a continuous (or fairly continuous) diary from the early 1680s.

Between 16 July 1678 and 24 March 1679, Nicolson was journeying through Holland and Germany. During his tour he kept a diary of what he saw and did.[15] In style and content it is not too dissimilar from the diaries of his London sojourns as Bishop of Carlisle. His keen interest in all he saw is there; detailed descriptions of towns visited and buildings seen; transcriptions of monumental inscriptions; descriptions of libraries visited and catalogues transcribed (he seems to have transcribed the manuscript catalogues of

[14] See above, p. 106.
[15] Called 'Inter Hollandicum. Inter Germanicum', it is now Queen's College (Oxford) MS 68.

all the libraries he visited); and, not forgetting one particular pleasure of the flesh, an expert's opinion of the local brews encountered, particularly mum, a speciality of Brunswick.[16] Nicolson undertook the trip at the prompting of his Oxford mentor, Sir Joseph Williamson, and it was for his eyes that this diary was kept.[17] Could it be that this early attempt at diary-keeping ignited a passion in Nicolson for keeping a record of his daily life and that he continued to keep a diary, though in his later years his interest faded somewhat?[18]

Of the three commonly accepted reasons for the keeping of diaries in seventeenth-century England—economic (diaries better described as account books), personal and political (aid to memory), and religious (desire to examine one's soul)[19]—only the second really applies to Nicolson. Nowhere, except perhaps upon the death of his wife in late 1712 (*CW* iv [1904], 60), does Nicolson go in for introspection. Also his economic activities were charted in separate account books and rarely enter the diaries proper. Undoubtedly the diaries, whose contents, particularly during his London trips, are crammed with political and social news and events, were used by Nicolson as an aid to the memory. Perhaps he used them in letter writing; perhaps he read them to his family during the long summer evenings in the diocese? But are these sufficient reasons for expending so much time and energy on keeping such a monumental record? Surely in Nicolson's undoubted colossal energy (coupled with his insatiable interest in an astounding range of subjects) lies at least a partial answer to why he kept the diaries. They were kept for enjoyment, and they formed a record as well as a part of his many-faceted life. Despite the cursory nature of the entries in the last few sessions (only partly attributable to the depredations of Mrs Ware), they are a truly remarkable document.

[16] See ibid., entry for 5 Sept. 1678.

[17] See ibid., the dedication and the last page.

[18] His interest picked up again upon his translation to Derry, and the diaries continued up to at least 1725 (though due to Mrs Ware's 'editing' it is difficult to tell how full they originally were).

[19] See A. Macfarlaine, *The Family Life of Ralph Josselin, a Seventeenth-Century Clergyman* (Cambridge, 1970), pp. 3-15.

The Diaries

Session 1

14 November 1702–22 February 1703

Nicolson missed the opening weeks of Queen Anne's first parliament, that of 1702-5. His election as Bishop of Carlisle on 13 May 1702 had been followed by a short visit to London, from 9 to 24 June, for the purposes of his consecration.[1] While in the south he had also received the degree of Doctor of Divinity from both Cambridge and Oxford, although in Oxford's case he had first to suffer an unseemly rebuff which he attributed, with some justice,[2] to the machinations of Francis Atterbury and the High Church fellows of Christ Church.[3] The rest of the summer and early autumn, however, he spent in Cumberland: part of the time repairing his predecessor's negligence in the matter of confirmations, the rest at Salkeld rectory, recouping his resources after the inevitable heavy outlay of his early days in office.[4]

On 4 November he set out for London via York, where on 6 November he heard that the Scottish commissioners for the union, who had earlier passed through the city, were 'all averse from entring upon the point of Church-Government, some out of Love (and others fear) of Presbytery'. Nicolson left York on 9 November, travelling south by coach. One of his fellow passengers, a Mr Bell who was a customs officer at Newcastle, told him that Lord Stair (with whom he had conversed) 'seemed not to have considered the Trade and Debts of England; nor that Scotland (in case of an Union) ought not to come in as contributors to pay off our Arrears'. Nicolson was petitioned by two other fellow passengers over a case 'now depending in Chancery; and like to come before the House of Lords'. The journey took him through Newark, Stilton ('famous for good cheese'), Huntingdon, and on 'to Stephenage, by the way of Bugden [where the Bishop of Lincoln had a palace] and Bigglesworth, 23 long and bad miles', during which part of the journey the

[1] Diary, vol. 1b (unpaginated). The consecration took place at Lambeth on Sunday, 14 June (*CW* ii (1902), 156, 160-7).

[2] *Atterbury Epist. Corr.* iii, 246: Atterbury to Bishop Trelawney, 11 Sept. 1704. See also below, 25 Nov. 1702.

[3] For the affair of the degrees, which involved Edmund Gibson as well as Nicolson, see Diary, vol. 1b; *CW* ii (1902), 161-8; *Atterbury Epist. Corr.*, pp. 263-4.

[4] He spent over £500 in two months, much of it on necessary entertainments, and postponed until the following year the removal of himself and his family to the bishop's residence at Rose Castle (James, p. 95). For Nicolson's feat in confirming 5,500 persons in 1702, ibid., p. 138.

coach encountered four men 'pretending to be Sportsmen; but supposed to be Highwaymen. Mr Bell in a fright.' London was finally reached on 14 November.[5]

The general election held in July and August 1702 had produced 'a Church of England Parliament' to gladden the hearts of the Tories. Their party had the largest majority seen in the House of Commons since 1685. At the same time, the House of Lords was evenly balanced; and the Queen, acting on the advice of the Duke of Marlborough (her Captain-General) and his friend Godolphin, Lord High Treasurer, had remodelled almost out of recognition the ministry she had inherited from William III. Her 'Cabinet Council' now included such High Tory stalwarts as Rochester, Nottingham, Seymour, Jersey, Buckingham, and Wright, while its Whiggish component had shrunk effectively to two.[6] The Cabinet thus contained a powerful element responsive to the demands of the new House of Commons for strongly Tory religious policies: policies hostile to Protestant Dissent, for instance, and accommodating to the militant High Church postures being struck by the representatives of the lower clergy in Convocation. Destined to be equally controversial was the undisguised preference of the same group of ministers and their parliamentary followers for the pursuit of a limited strategy, primarily maritime and colonial in emphasis, in the war with France—the new war, which England had entered, as a member of the Grand Alliance, in May 1702. This was a preference emphatically not shared either by Marlborough and Godolphin or by the Whigs, although some common ground did exist (between Marlborough and Nottingham, for example) on the necessity for a strategy that would embrace the Mediterranean, if not Flanders and Germany.

Religion and the conduct of the war were to be two of the most prominent issues of Nicolson's first parliamentary session in London; indeed religion, in one way or another, cast its shadow over almost all the rest. The session had begun on Tuesday, 20 October. This was just over four weeks before Nicolson took his seat in the chamber of the House of Lords at Westminster,[7] duly forewarned by his Cumbrian neighbour, Sir Christopher Musgrave—a Tory whose parliamentary service went back almost to the Restoration— 'of the eyes that were, and would be, upon my behaviour and voteing . . .'

On 4 November the Commons had given leave to William Bromley,

[5] *CW* ii (1902), 184–6.

[6] The Duke of Devonshire (Lord Steward) and the Duke of Somerset (Master of the Horse), both moderates. Thomas Tenison, Archbishop of Canterbury, also had a seat in the Cabinet, but he was a sleeping-partner for the most part.

[7] On 18 Nov. below.

one of the members for the High Anglican stronghold of Oxford University, to bring in a bill to prevent 'Occasional Conformity'. This was a practice which had become increasingly prevalent since the middle years of the previous reign. Protestant nonconformists who wished to circumvent the bars against their holding municipal and state office, while still complying with the letter of the Corporation Act and the Test Act, found they could do so, if their consciences permitted, by taking the Anglican sacrament with studied infrequency, as a matter of form: usually this meant taking communion in the parish church no more than once a year. Largely because of the electoral influence of these so-called 'Occasional men', and especially the Presbyterians, in the many parliamentary boroughs where the franchise was vested in the corporation or in the freemen, this practice had become by 1702 as obnoxious to the lay Tories on political grounds as it was to their High Church clerical allies on religious grounds. The clergy were in a state of high alarm about the real and imagined advance of Dissent since the 1689 Toleration Act, and they looked to their Tory allies to buttress one of the remaining 'fences' protecting their preserves, the legal monopoly of office by Anglicans, by sponsoring a bill designed to stamp out Occasional Conformity by savage fines.[8]

Such was the bill which was making its way through the lower house of parliament, contested fiercely but unavailingly by the Whigs, at the time of Nicolson's arrival in London. It was sent up to the Lords on 2 December, where at once it ran into a storm raised by Wharton, Somers, and other leading Whigs.[9] Nicolson himself approved of it and drafted an undelivered speech expressing his conviction that the occasional communicant 'eats and drinks his own damnation'.[10] But the issue split both the bishops' bench and the lay peers into two almost equal camps; and the long, bitter struggle that ensued, culminating in a deadlock between the two houses of parliament which threatened to wreck the whole session, may have been the first step in converting the Bishop of Carlisle to the view that what was desirable in principle might be inexpedient in practice.[11]

[8] The fines proposed in, and agreed by, the Commons were: £100 for attending a Nonconformist meeting while holding office, under the Crown or in a corporation; £5 a day for every day an incumbent continued in such an office after attending a meeting.

[9] Below, 2, 3, Dec.   [10] Below, 3 Dec.

[11] Nicolson has very valuable entries tracing the progress and abortion of the bill, from 2 Dec. 1702 onwards, on the following days: 2, 3, and 4 Dec.; 7 Dec. (the day of the 'grand debate' on the penalties clause—a triumph for Somers and the turning-point in the bill's fortunes); 9 Dec.; 17 Dec. (the date of the first conference between the two Houses); 18 Dec.; 22, 23 Dec.; 8 Jan. 1703 (when the bill's opponents in the Lords made the definitive statement of the reasons for their stand); 13 Jan.; 16 Jan. (the day of the great 'open'

In the early stages of this struggle, on 9 December, when the Lords apprehended a move by a now angry House of Commons to 'tack' the Occasional Conformity Bill to a money bill, they passed a historic motion condemning 'tacking' as unconstitutional. This motion—surprisingly opposed by Nicolson—was promptly embodied in standing orders where it was to take on a critical significance in November 1704 when the High Tory commoners went beyond mere threats and actually attempted this desperate tactic. But well before that it had become the source of some argument during the latter half of the session of 1702-3. The argument developed during the debates on a bill, dear to the Queen's heart, settling a new revenue on her consort Prince George; for the whiff of a 'tack' in this bill smelt very much like a rat to the Whigs.[12] Indeed, Lord Rivers, speaking in the Upper House on 11 January 1703, virtually accused the Commons of using it to prepare the way for a much more serious atrocity over Occasional Conformity. Putting the argument in its broader context, however, it must be said that relations between the two Houses were uncommonly touchy throughout this whole parliament, and that in the opening session they began as they meant to go on. The dismissal of one of the lords spiritual from office at the behest of the Commons[13] introduced a sour spirit almost from the start. At one point the petulance of the hotter Tory members even led to their refusing, briefly, to send up to the Lords the Malt Tax Bill, the government's second most important source of supply. 'When (at this rate)', wrote the bewildered and increasingly impatient Nicolson, 'will this session be brought to a conclusion?'[14]

Although Occasional Conformity was the most controversial question in politics during the winter of 1702-3, it was not the only source of grave division among churchmen, nor the only issue which tended to push some clerics of moderate Tory views into closer association with the Whigs. There was also much bad blood between the two houses of Convocation, the representative synod of the Church of England clergy. Since its recall in February 1701, after an intermission of more than eleven years, the Convocation of Canterbury had enjoyed the right, claimed for it by High Church

conference in the Painted Chamber and of the most crucial of the Lords' votes); and 29 Jan. (when the Tory peers secured a major, but as it happened unavailing, concession from the opposition in a thinly attended House).

[12] For the Diary's various references to this bill, see below, 11-19 Jan. 1703.

[13] The Bishop of Worcester was removed from his post as Lord Almoner to the Queen, see below, 20 Nov.

[14] Diary, 15 Jan. 1703. Cf. 'the sharp votes against the Commons' passed by the Lords on 18 Feb.

champions during the furious 'Convocation Controversy' of 1697–1701, of sitting coincidentally with parliament. During the polemical battles which had followed the publication of Atterbury's *Letter to a Convocation Man* in 1697[15] Archdeacon Nicolson had lent his scholarly aid to the more Erastian, Low Church view of Convocation's rights and powers, as propounded by White Kennett, William Wake, and Edmund Gibson. In 1702, when he became Bishop of Carlisle, with no seat in the Convocation of Canterbury, Nicolson found himself an involved spectator of a heated extension of the previous engagement—an extension which was to last, except in years of prorogation, until the Assembly received its *coup de grâce* in 1717.

The bishops, constituting the Upper House, supported by a small though able minority of moderates in the other chamber, found themselves seriously embroiled session after session with the Lower House's rampant High Church majority. In 1702 their wrangles were less concerned than in the previous year with matters of dogma and Church policy. In 1701 it had been heretical writings and the interpretation of the Anglican Articles which had aroused so much feeling and caused so much disorder. Now it was the status and powers of the Lower House itself which had become the centre of controversy. Atterbury had claimed for the Lower House a virtual independence of the Archbishop of Canterbury's presidential authority, not least the right to sit and do business in defiance of the Primate's prorogation orders; and in the 1702–3 session the High Churchmen signalled their bellicose intentions on the very first day of meeting, 20 October, by electing the uncompromising Dean of Christ Church, Dr Aldrich, as Prolocutor instead of the more moderate and politically uninvolved William Beveridge.[16]

In the weeks that followed the Highflying party, or 'Atterburian faction',[17] continued along this collision course. First it rejected a compromise proposal from the bishops which would have given the Prolocutor limited discretionary powers and the Lower House the right to have their *committees* meeting, preparing business, while the Upper House stood prorogued.[18] Next it picked what Nicolson considered to be an 'insolent' quarrel with the Bishop of Bangor.[19] Then from late November to late January it engaged in a devious manœuvre to entrap the bishops into endorsing a vote that episcopacy was 'of divine apostolical institution' and thus, in effect, promulgating

---

[15] Atterbury was the main, though not the sole, author of this widely read pamphlet.
[16] Luttrell, v, 227.
[17] Nicolson's phrase, Diary, 16 Dec. 1702.
[18] For the outcome, see Diary, 25 Nov.
[19] For the occasion, see Diary, 15, 20 Nov. 1702.

a new canon without the royal licence required since the time of Henry VIII.[20] Finally it attempted, without conspicuous success, to enlist the support of the Queen, the law officers of the Crown, and the Tory House of Commons for its pretensions.[21] Little wonder Bishop Burnet wrote at the end of this session in February 1703 of 'the two houses being fixed in an opposition to one another'.[22]

Fear of 'Presbytery', the fear which fuelled the agitation against Occasional Conformity and lent extra animus to the parish clergy's hostility towards Whiggish bishops, had a decisive bearing on another important event of William Nicolson's first winter in parliament. This was the opening of negotiations for a treaty of union between Scotland and England. A period of serious strain in Anglo-Scottish relations since the early 1690s had prompted William III's last message to parliament, dispatched from his sick bed on 28 February 1702, in which he recommended 'a firm and intire union' between the two countries and proposed 'that a treaty for that purpose might be set on foot'. In March, shortly after Queen Anne's accession, a bill authorising the Crown to nominate commissioners to negotiate with the Scots was carried through parliament; although, significantly, the High Tories in the Commons forced a division and recorded 119 votes against it, marshalled by Sir Edward Seymour who was on the brink of re-entering the Cabinet.[23] The commissioners had already begun to meet their Scottish counterparts in the Cockpit in Whitehall shortly before Nicolson arrived in London, and they continued their discussions throughout November, December, and January.[24] Being on close terms with many prominent Scots Nicolson had a particular interest in the outcome: and he was personally well disposed to the idea of a union.[25]

In some areas—over a common parliament and over free trade, for example—the commissioners made good progress. On 15 December Nicolson found the Archbishop of Canterbury still 'in good hopes of the Union'.[26] Religious differences and suspicions, however, proved a major stumbling block, notably the question of whether the Scottish Episcopalians should be re-established, granted a 'Toleration', or left unprotected, entirely dependent on the charity of the

[20] Nicolson refers to this ploy in an entry on 15 Dec.

[21] Ibid. See also Diary, 1, 6 Jan. 1703; and for earlier encouragement given by the Commons, 21 Nov. 1702.

[22] Burnet, *History*, v, 70.

[23] Ibid., v, 13; BL Add. MS 17677 YY, f. 202.

[24] For the negotiations of 1702-3 see P. W. J. Riley, 'The Union of 1707 as an Episode in English Politics', *EHR* lxxxiv (1969), 499-504. The proceedings of the commissioners, 10 Nov. 1702 to 3 Feb. 1703, are printed in *Acts Parl. Scot.* xi, App., 145-61.

[25] HMC *Laing MSS* ii, 5.

[26] Below, 15 Dec., though cf. Diary, 21, 26 Dec.

markedly uncharitable Presbyterian Kirk.[27] As the mood of the Tories in parliament and in the government changed in consequence, first from wariness to apathy, then from apathy to distaste, so the chance of the commissioners completing their work before the end of the session dwindled away. And the complacent view taken by some Scots, such as Stair and Sir David Dalrymple[28] could not disguise the fact that the commissioners' unfinished task rendered negligible the possibility that they would ever reassemble once they were adjourned by the Queen on 3 February 1703. In fact, both the incentive and the will that eventually brought the Union to pass in 1706-7 were missing in 1702-3. So was the presence in strength on the English commission of the Whigs; and, cautious though their support for the negotiations was, in their understandably defensive mood of 1702 (indeed, it was withdrawn altogether in 1703), the Whigs' principles and priorities made them far more receptive to the change in the long run than their opponents.

The parliament which Nicolson entered in 1702 was still seething with the personal and party animosities stirred up by the Tories' impeachment in 1701 of four prominent Whig ex-ministers, Somers, Orford, Halifax, and Portland, for their alleged share in the Partition Treaties of 1698-1700. The impeachments, in the event, had foundered on the rock of a bluntly unco-operative House of Lords. But 'this matter', as a friend of Governor Pitt, the East India nabob, wrote in December 1701, 'hath made a feud that I fear will not die.'[29] Having been baulked in 1701 of one major prey, the former First Lord of the Treasury Lord Halifax, in the winter of 1702-3 the Tories attempted to run him to earth again, following a different scent. He was attacked by the party-dominated parliamentary Commission of Public Accounts for supposed malpractices committed as Auditor of the Exchequer, a post he had occupied since 1700. The charges were spurious, and although the House of Commons was persuaded to vote Halifax guilty of 'a breach of trust' in January 1703, the Lords, who had no illusions about the impartiality of the Commission, absolved him completely by a vote on 5 February, after a hearing which had begun on 2 February. This led to a bruising encounter between the two Houses whose echoes were still being loudly heard when the session ended.[30]

[27] For Nicolson's own view see Diary, 28 Nov.
[28] See Nicolson's account of his conversation with 'these two great men', both Union Commissioners, on 29 Jan.
[29] BL Add. MS 22851, f. 131.
[30] See Holmes, *British Politics*, p. 139. Rather more serious charges brought on 11 Nov. against Lord Ranelagh, a favourite of the late King's who had held the lucrative office of Paymaster-General of the Forces from 1691 to 1702, had resulted in his expulsion from the

Aside from the muck-raking of the Public Accounts commissioners, the likeliest source of opportunity for parliamentary enquiries into 'mismanagement' was now the Spanish Succession War, and the inevitable disappointment of too-sanguine expectations which it brought. But although members of both Houses were often activated by party malice in such matters, or indeed by party loyalty—Tories standing by Tory admirals, for instance, and Whigs by Whig generals, right or wrong—they were also influenced to some extent by their strategic predilections. For most Tories there was a natural prejudice in favour of a 'blue water' war, with the more adventurous prepared to argue the case for a supplementary strategy of 'combined operations' in southern Europe; while to the majority of Whigs a vigorous continental military commitment made much more sense. These predilections were brought out into the open quite early in the war by the Dutch request in the winter of 1702-3 for an 'augmentation' of Marlborough's army in Flanders. Although parliament did agree in January 1703 to an increase of 10,000 troops, the debate in the House of Lords on 9 January gave leading Whigs such as Townshend, Carlisle, Wharton, and Halifax the opportunity to accuse High Tory members of the Cabinet of having dragged their feet over bringing the request to parliament.[31]

A case which involved most of the currents and cross-currents set in motion by the war was the Lords' inquiry into the fiasco of the Cadiz expedition of July–September 1702,[32] the discreditable features of which had been subsequently masked, to some extent, by a successful action against the Spanish bullion fleet in Vigo Bay.[33] Set on foot by the Junto on 26 November, the inquiry absorbed a good deal of their lordships' time (mainly in committee), especially

Commons on 1 Feb. See below, 27 Nov., and *Parl. Hist.* vi, 97–127. Cf. Burnet, *History*, vi, 61–2 for a vindication of Ranelagh.

[31] A point worthy of notice about Nicolson's account of this debate is that it does not highlight the peculiarly Tory antipathy to the Dutch which became such a marked feature of politics in the second half of the reign, although distrust of the Dutch was already widespread among Tories up and down the country. On this occasion both parties joined in an address to the Queen, linking support for an 'augmentation' with the opinion that such reinforcements would be ineffectual 'unless all correspondence with France and Spain, by letters and otherwise, be totally prohibited by the States-General and all other your Majesty's Allies' (Diary, 13 Jan. 1703).

[32] The object of the expedition, which carried 14,000 troops, had been to seize a fortified naval base which would enable a permanent English naval presence to be maintained *via* the Straits, in the Mediterranean. It was also hoped that it would encourage Portugal to change sides and adhere to the Grand Alliance against France and Spain. There is a good account of the expedition, its hesitant leadership and the appalling indiscipline of the troops at Santa Maria, in Trevelyan, *Queen Anne*, i, 260-6, with a map of the environs of Cadiz which illustrates some of the points in Nicolson's diary.

[33] For Vigo, see below, 21 Nov. n. 85.

124

after Christmas, and plainly caught Nicolson's interest.[34] Fully
to understand the feelings which the affair aroused it is important
to remember that both the military and the naval commanders
involved, Ormond and Rooke, were Tory heroes, and that both
had been lavishly complimented by Speaker Harley in the House of
Commons for their 'most glorious expeditions'.[35] Tory peers, therefore, had no desire to see either of them censured, whatever the
merits of the case, at a time when Marlborough, the arch-exponent
of a Continental strategy, was basking in royal and parliamentary
favour following his first successful campaign in Flanders as Captain-
General.[36] Accordingly they strenuously resisted the original report
of the Duke of Bolton's committee, aimed against Rooke,[37] being
greatly helped by the fact that Ormond himself had been prevailed
upon to stifle his earlier resentment against his colleague.[38] Nicolson's
sympathies in this case appear to have been with 'the Admiral'
against 'his prosecutors',[39] although the verdict of most historians
has been uncomplimentary to the conduct of Sir George Rooke at
Cadiz.

When Nicolson left London by the York coach on 22 February,
bound again for his diocese, the rumblings of Cadiz were dying
away. But bad-tempered exchanges between the two Houses were
still souring the Westminster scene, and Nicolson left his proxy with
Archbishop Sharp of York, knowing that it would undoubtedly
be used if necessary to swell the Tory vote. In fact Queen Anne and
her closest advisers had already decided to bring this troublesome
session to an end. Only five days after Nicolson's departure parliament was prorogued. It was not to meet again for business until
the following November.

Nov. 14. *Saturday*. Six hillocks about half mile out of Stephenage.
Before five at London. After visits at Grey's Inn and Salisbury Court
conducted by my Brother[40] to my Lodgeings at Mr. Broughton's.[41]

[34] See below, pp. 186–7 (where Nicolson gets a first-hand account of the sack of Port
St Mary by Ormond's drunken troops); 23 Jan. (his account of the first full meeting of the
committee of inquiry).

[35] *Parl. Hist.* vi, 94–5.

[36] Marlborough received the formal thanks of the House of Lords on 30 Nov.

[37] Diary, 11 Feb.

[38] 'though the inquiry was set on by his [Ormond's] means . . . yet he came not to the
house, when it was brought to a conclusion.' (Burnet, *History*, v, 60).

[39] Below, 15 Feb. 1703.

[40] For Joseph Nicolson, see above, Chapter 1, p. 8.

[41] Probably John Broughton, an apothecary, who is recorded as living in the City of
London (poll books for 1710 and 1714). He was Upper Warden of the Apothecaries'
Company in 1714–15.

Nov. 15. *Sunday*. I waited, at the Queen's Chapple,[42] on the Archbishop of York [Sharp];[43] who (after Sermon by Sir W[illiam] Dawes[44] on *James* 4, 4. an excellent Discourse) introduced me to Kiss Her Majesty's hand: And carryed me to dine with Him. Dr A.[45] with his Grace the Day before; commending Dr Wake's Book.[46] The Insolent demand of the Lower House of Convocation to the Bishop of Bangor [Evans]—By what Authority he appeared in this Convocation; whether by the Queen's or the Archbishop's?[47]

After Dinner, with Mr Richardson,[48] to Lambeth.[49] Divisions amongst the Presbyters.[50]—In the Evening with Sir Christopher Musgrave;[51] who forewarned me of the Eyes that were, and would be, upon my behaviour and Voteing in the House of Lords. Whatever the expectations of men may be——*Det Deus ut mea sit semper mens Conscia recti*!

Nov. 16. *Munday*. I dined at Lambeth, with the Bishops of Salisbury [Burnet], Kilmore [Wettenhal] and Killalow.[52] My Lord Archbishop [Tenison] very Kind. Observed to me the preamble of the Bill against Occasional Communion;[53] that it asserted our Church's allowing of Toleration.[54] Likewise, that the Bill for Repair of

[42] At St James's Palace.   [43] See Appendix A.

[44] Master of St Catherine's Hall, Cambridge, see Appendix A.

[45] Possibly Dr Charles Alston (1681-1714), Archdeacon of Essex since 1689, and Treasurer of St Paul's in 1707.

[46] William Wake, Dean of Exeter (see Appendix A), was to publish his exhaustive answer to Atterbury's position in the Convocation Controversy, *The State of the Church and Clergy of England*, early in 1703. It was a work of monumental scholarship.

[47] Since 1534 Convocation met only by the authority of a royal writ addressed to the Archbishop of Canterbury. The Primate in turn issued his own mandate which was executed by the Bishop of London as Dean of the province of Canterbury. At the 1702 Convocation only the bishop appeared from the diocese of Bangor. The Lower House, therefore, censured the bishop for his supposed defect in the execution of the summons (Lambeth Palace, MS Conv. 1/2/8, f. 40a: copy of letter from the Lower House to Archbishop Tenison). For Tenison, see Appendix A.

[48] John Richardson (1675-1735), Prebendary of York, 1701-11, Archdeacon of Cleveland and Precentor of York, 1711-35.

[49] Lambeth Palace, residence of the Archbishop of Canterbury.

[50] Members of the lower clergy represented in Convocation.

[51] MP for Westmorland, see Appendix A.

[52] Edward Wetenhall, Bishop of Kilmore, 1699-1713; and Thomas Lindsay, Bishop of Killaloe, 1696-1713, and later Bishop of Raphoe, 1713-14, and Archbishop of Armagh, 1714-24.

[53] The great importance of the 'Occasional Conformity' issue is explained above in Session 1 introduction. The preamble to this first bill avers that 'nothing is more contrary to the profession of the Christian religion, and particularly to the doctrine of the Church of England, than persecution for conscience only'. The bill is printed in full in W. Pittis, *Proceedings of both Houses of Parliament . . . upon the Bill to Prevent Occasional Conformity* (1710), pp. 3-7, and reproduced in *Parl. Hist.* vi, 62-7.

[54] The word 'toleration' was nowhere used in the title, preamble, or text of the Act of 1689 which had become popularly known as the 'Toleration Act'. High Churchmen later

Churches[55] subjects the Ministers to their proportion in Repair of the
Body as well as Chancel. Bishop Burnet in good heart; not valueing
the Grins of the Lower House of Convocation.[56]

After setling points in Dr Gibsen's[57] Chamber, Dr Kennet[58] and
I with Mr Lloyd;[59] in danger of being taken into Custody by the
Commons (tho' a member of Convocation) for appearing against Sir
John Packington.[60] Our Northern Members to be applyed to. If not
kind, not to hope for Assistance from any Dependant on a Bishop
hereafter.

Nov. 17. *Tuesday*. I expected to have been admitted into the House
of Lords: But they had unlukily adjourned from Munday to Wednesday.—I dined with the Bishop of Worcester [Lloyd], who shewed
me several Libels against himself thrown about by Sir J. Packington;[61]

made much of this, preferring such words as 'indulgence' or 'exemption' to characterise
the concessions made to dissenters under this Act. See Holmes, *Sacheverell*, pp. 35-6.

[55] An 'Act for the more easy and effectual recovery of rates made for the repairs of
churches and chapels [of ease]' had been introduced from the Commons on 12 May 1702.
After its first reading on the following day there were no further proceedings. A similar bill
was to be reintroduced in Feb. 1703, but this too was rejected by the Lords on 9 Feb. 1703.
For the details of these bills, see HMC *Lords MSS* v, 38-9, 190-1.

[56] Burnet's *An Exposition of the Thirty-Nine Articles of the Church of England*, dedicated (somewhat provocatively in High Church eyes) to William III, had been attacked in
Convocation in 1701 as 'of dangerous consequences to the church'. See Burnet, *History*,
iv, 526; Lathbury, *Convocation*, pp. 376-7.

[57] Edmund Gibson, Chaplain to Archbishop Tenison, see Appendix A.

[58] White Kennett, Rector of St Botolph, Aldgate, see Appendix A.

[59] William Lloyd, son of the Bishop of Worcester, see Appendix A.

[60] Sir John Pakington (1671-1727) of West Wood, 4th Bt, MP for Worcestershire,
1690-5, 1698-1727 (Sedgwick, ii, 321). On 18 Nov. Pakington accused the Bishop of
Worcester and his son of interfering in the county election of Aug. 1702, by sending
threatening letters to the clergy and freeholders of Worcestershire. 'The good bishop', wrote
a local baronet at the time, 'charges his Clergy in his Visitation everywhere, upon theyr
canonicall obedience, not to give theyr votes for Sir J. Pak.' (BL Add. MS 29579, f. 401).
Pakington further accused the bishop that he 'refused institucion and induction unless the
party voted as ordered' (Berkshire RO Trumbull MS 50: T. Bateman to Trumbull, 8 Nov.
1702). Pakington's case against Lloyd was published by order of the Commons as *The
Evidence Given at the Bar of the House of Commons upon the Complaint of Sir John
Pakington, against William Lord Bishop of Worcester and Mr Lloyd, his Son Together with
the Proceedings of the House of Commons thereupon* (1702). Bishop Lloyd had performed
similarly in the Jan. 1701 general election. 'We do hear of some persons [wrote Charles
Stephens to Pakington, on 13 Feb. 1701] that have received letters from the Bishop of
Worcester; but it was to none he sent but such as he has some sort of obligation upon; so
that it will be difficult, if possible to gain any of his letters' (Worcester RO Pakington MS
705: 349/4657/iii/p. 7). The Commons resolved the Lloyds guilty of a breach of privilege,
and ordered the Attorney General to prosecute the son, while upon their address the
Queen removed Bishop Lloyd from the post of Lord Almoner. See A. T. Hart, *William
Lloyd* (1952), pp. 157-66; and below, 20 Nov. for the peeved reaction of the House of
Lords.

[61] Most notably, *The Character of a Low-Church-Man* by Henry Sacheverell.

who (nevertheless) is now persecuting him and his son, Mr Lloyd, for opposeing his Election in the County of W[orcester].

In the Evening with the Dean of Exeter [Wake]; who gave me his Elaborate Answer to Atterbury, and gave us (Dr Trimnel, Dr Stanhop[e], Mr Worth[62] and myself) an Account of the prepareing of Alterations in the Liturgy by Archbishop Sancroft's Committee before the Revolution.[63] Dr W[ake] himself was a member of that Body, and its Secretary, and the Book, corrected as far as they went, is now in the hands of the present Archbishop of Canterbury.

Nov. 18. *Wednesday*. I took the Oaths,[64] and my place,[65] in the House of Lords. An Appeal lodged; and adjourned. In the House of Commons Sir J. Packington's friends Voted the Bishop of Worcester Unchrist[i]an, Malitious, &c. and ordered an Address to Her Majesty to remove him from being Almoner.[66] His Son (Mr Lloyd) to be prosecuted by the Attourney Generall[67] when his priviledge of Convocation is out. Archdeacon Hutton[68] dined with me; resolveing to be good.

Nov. 19. *Thursday*. In the morning I waited on Sir James Stewart of Bute[69] and Dr Lancaster.[70]

[62] Francis Atterbury, Archdeacon of Totnes, leading High Church advocate in the Convocation Controversy, see Appendix A. Charles Trimnell, Archdeacon of Norfolk, and George Stanhope, Vicar of Lewisham (for both see Appendix A), and William Worth (1677-1742), classical scholar and divine, Fellow of All Souls, Oxford, 1702, and Archdeacon of Worcester, 1705-42.

[63] For Sancroft's plans for liturgical reforms in 1688-9 to comprehend moderate dissenters within the Church of England see Sykes, *Wake*, i, 48, and Wake's own account in *Parl. Hist.* vi, 862, and in his 'autobiography' in R. Beddard, 'Observations of a London Clergyman on the Revolution of 1688-9: Being an excerpt from the Autobiography of Dr. William Wake', *The Guildhall Miscellany*, ii, no. 9 (1967), 414.

[64] Of supremacy, allegiance, and abjuration. The new abjuration oath, devised by the Whigs in William III's last parliament, was tendered at the beginning of a parliamentary session for the first time in the autumn of 1702.

[65] The bishops sat on the right-hand side of the House viewed from the throne (see fig. 2). According to the Act of 1539, which established the post-Reformation seating arrangements in the Lords, the bishops sat in order of consecration to the episcopacy. In practice, however, the bishops sat promiscuously on their benches, and even occasionally strayed on to the benches of the lay lords. See C. Jones, 'Seating problems in the early eighteenth-century House of Lords: the evidence of the manuscript minutes', *BIHR* li (1978), 132-45.

[66] *CJ* xiv, 37. Lloyd's censure by the Commons did not deter him from electioneering in the future. 'The bishop is now here and doeing all the mischeff he can' (Worcester RO Pakington MS b706:349 BA657/i/p. 97: Sir Edward Goodere to Lady Pakington, 5 May 1705).

[67] Sir Edward Northey. He held the post from 1701 to 1707, but did not enter the House of Commons until 1710, when he was elected for Tiverton. See Appendix A.

[68] John Hutton (*c*.1649-1712), Archdeacon of Stow since 1684.

[69] MP for the county of Bute, 1685-93, 1702-3, a Commissioner for the Union, 1702-3, he was created Earl of Bute in 1703, and later opposed the Union in 1707. He died in 1710. *GEC Peerage*.

[70] William Lancaster, Fellow and later Provost of Queen's College, Oxford, see Appendix A.

In the House of Lords an Appeal brought by Nich[olas] Trott Esqr. late Governour of the Isle of Providence against some Dutch Merchants in Amsterdam who were Shiprecked and ill treated in 1695.[71] The Cause ever since depending in Chancery. Decreed for the Merchants; and the Decree affirmed this day: Notwithstanding Mr Dobbins's[72] parting suggestion that the Appellants Case might be the same with that of every Vice-Admiral or Lord of a Mannor near the Coasts.—A motion made by the Earl of Burlington (seconded by Lords Mohun, Wharton, &c.)[73] on behalf of the Bishop of Worcester. An Address Ordered, upon the Debate, to be presented to Her Majesty (by the Duke of Somerset and Earl of Burlington) to continue the Bishop in the place of Almoner, *till some Crime shall be legally proved against him*. This rightly observed, by Lord Nottingham to be limitting the Queen.[74] However it passed.

Nov. 20. *Friday*. The first day of my reading prayers in the House of Lords. Kindly cautioned, by the Archbishop of York, about the pronunciation of Jesus. The Queen's Answer to the Address,[75] Intimateing that (as yet) no Complaint was made against the Bishop of W[orcester], but *that it was her own undoubted Prerogative to retain or displace those that attended Her person*. Accordingly; soon after, She was pleased to signify to the Commons (upon their Address) that She *was sorry to have such a Charge against the Bishop but would discharge him of his Attendance as Almoner, and place another in that Office*.
The Lower House of Convocation appointed three Committees. 1. To Address the House of Commons, thanking them for their kind care of their priviledges in the Case of Mr Lloyd. 2. To form a Reply to the Bishop of Bangor's Answer to their Questions;[76] which Mr Moor (Lord Abingdon's Chaplain)[77] observed to be *unmannerly*. 3. To petition the Upper House to reverse, or cancel, the Obloquy on Dr Hooper (late Prolocutor)[78] by the Bishop

---

[71] For details of the cause, see HMC *Lords MSS* v, 55-6.

[72] Counsel for Trott.

[73] Brief biographical notes of most lay members of the House of Lords who figure in the diary are to be found in Appendix A.

[74] i.e. the Queen's prerogative of appointing and dismissing her servants and ministers of the Crown.

[75] For the address in reply to the Queen's speech, see *LJ* xvii, 169.

[76] Repl. 'Queenes'.

[77] William Moore, one of the representatives in the Convocation of the clergy of the Oxford Diocese, and possibly a son of the Earl of Drogheda. By 1708, Atterbury feared he was becoming inactive in Convocation (Westminster Abbey Muniments 62330: Atterbury to Needham, 2 Oct. 1708).

[78] George Hooper, Dean of Canterbury, see Appendix A. The Prolocutor, elected by the Lower House of Convocation, acted as intermediary between the two houses and

of Hereford's[79] chargeing him with prevarication: two years agoe.

I dined at Dr Lancaster's, with Archdeacons Skelton[80] and Hutton; all of a feather.—In the Evening visitted the Bishop of Hereford [Humphries]; who explained to me *pawb yn y arver* (the Motto under Sir Tho[mas] Herbert's[81] Arms in Mr Chancellor Watkinson's[82] house) i.e. *Every man in his way*.—Returning to my Lodgeing, I had a good account from my Landlord (Mr Broughton) of the Methods observed in the Hospital of Blew-coats,[83] in haveing all their lands and Houses Surveyed and Mapped; in a Book of Vellum, exactly Indexed.

— NB. when I left the House in the morning, I thought they had been goeing to Adjourn: but, hearing that Her Majesty had so far complyed with the Address from the Commons as immediately to turn out the Bishop of W[orcester] the Lords ordered the printing of their Address with the Queen's Answer, together with their farther Resolution (*Nem. Contrad.*) *That no Lord of this House ought to suffer any Sort of Punishment by any proceeding of the House of Commons, otherwise than according to the known and antient Rules and Methods of Parliament.*

Nov. 21. *Saturday*. An Appeal by the Earl of Orford; and carryed so far as to reverse so much of the Lord Keeper's [Wright's] Decree as respected two several Summs of 700 and 1300 *l.*, the former being paid after the Bill was filed.[84]—The Queen's Instructions (relateing to the Affair of Vigo)[85] ordered to be brought in on Tuesday as before.

comunicated *gravamina*, representations and messages to the Upper House. In practice he could exercise considerable influence on the proceedings of the Lower House.

[79] In 1700 the Bishop of Hereford was Gilbert Ironside (d. 1701), in Nov. 1702 it was Humphrey Humphries, for whom see Appendix A.

[80] John Skelton (d. 1704), Archdeacon of Bedford since 1689.

[81] Sir Thomas Herbert (1606–82), traveller and author, lived in High Petergate, York, after 1665.

[82] Henry Watkinson (c.1628–1712), of Leeds, Archdiocesan Chancellor of York, 1673–1712. Nicolson stayed at his house in York on his journey south. *N & Q* 2nd ser. xi, 238; *CW* ii (1902), 185.

[83] Christ's Hospital, the charitable foundation for the upbringing and education of the orphans of London freemen. By the 1720s it was said to be maintaining almost a thousand pupils at a cost of nearly £5,000 a year. See Defoe, *Tour*, i, 368–9; W. Trollop, *A History of the Royal Foundation of Christ's Hospital* (1834); E. H. Pearce, *Annals of Christ's Hospital* (1901).

[84] For details see HMC *Lords MSS* v, 52.

[85] In Oct. 1702 the English fleet under the command of Sir George Rooke, with the soldiery under the Duke of Ormond, after the disastrous failure to take Cadiz, attacked and destroyed the combined Franco-Spanish fleet in Vigo Bay. For the campaign see Trevelyan, *Queen Anne*, i, 259–72; and H. Kamen, 'The Destruction of the Spanish Silver Fleet at Vigo in 1702', *BIHR* xxxix (1966), 165–73.

The Commons had an Address from the lower House of Convocation, thanking them for the care they had taken of their priviledges in Mr Lloyd's Case. Whereupon, Resolved (on all occasions) to assert the just Rights & Priviledges of the lower Clergy.[86] *Sic Scabent mutuo Muli.*

Nov. 22. *Sunday.* At the Queen's Chapple, with the Archbishop of York, Bishops of Durham [Crew], Exeter [Trelawney], Hereford and Peterburgh [Cumberland]: Bishop of H[ereford] and I dined with the Bishop of Sarum [Salisbury]; who shewed me the Original Magna Charta of King John. On part of the Seal R— Joh— and Do. i.e. *Dom. Hibernia.* It wanted, in the beginning, the Article for the Church: And in the Conclusion, has a Provisional Commission to 25 Barons who (as Guardians or Guarantees of this Charter) are Empowered to distress the King or any of his Successors, by raiseing Forces, siezing his Castles, &c. upon every Infringement of it. Mr King (Author of the *Critical History of the Apostles Creed*, and a Member of Parliament)[87] gave us an Account of the proofs against Bishop Lloyd and his son. The hardest thing on the former was his affirming that Sir J. Packington had all the Vices of the Males of his Family without the Vertues of the Females; and on the Latter, that Sir John and his party[88] (in a former Parliament)[89] were in the Interests of France. The Bishop of Sarum assured us that (of his own knowledge) 14 of the Commoners of Scotland had so many half Crowns paid them, by Duke Hamilton the King's Commissioner,[90] every morning dureing a whole Session of Parliament as a sufficient pension and Hire for their Votes. Records in the Tower confused.[91]

Nov. 23. *Munday.* A long Report read in the House of Lords from the Commissioners of Trade.[92] Which done, the Lord Hallifax[93]

[86] *CJ* xiv, 40. For the solidarity between the Lower House of Convocation and the Tories in the House of Commons in the early part of the parliament of 1702-5, see Holmes, *British Politics*, p. 98.

[87] Peter King, MP for Bere Alston, see Appendix A. His *History of the Apostles Creed* (1702) attempted to trace critically, for the first time, the evolution of the creed, an extraordinary achievement for a practising barrister and future Lord Chancellor.

[88] The Tory party.   [89] The parliament of 1701.

[90] William Douglas, Duke of Hamilton (d. 1694), was Lord High Commissioner, i.e. the King's representative in Scotland, from 1689 to 1690.

[91] The Tower of London was one of several repositories for state records and contained mainly those of Chancery. For Nicolson's interest in the preservation of such records see above, Chapter 1, pp. 40-4.

[92] The Council of Trade and Plantations was formed in 1696. See J. C. Sainty, *Officials of the Boards of Trade, 1660-1870* (1974), pp. 3-6, 28, for their work. For the report see HMC *Lords MSS* v, 66-100.

[93] He had been *ex officio* a Commissioner of Trade as First Lord of the Treasury, 1697-9.

made a good Speech, Observeing how high the Improvement of the woolen Manufacture had been carryed (to at least a Million per Annum) in the late Reign,[94] beyond what it ever was in the so much applauded time of King Ch[arles] 2. That the Inspector Generall's books[95] (whereof he seemed to ascribe the Invention to himself) would put the Trade of this Nation into an infallible Adjustment. That, our Plantations would effectually ruine us if they get the Manufactures amongst them, as now endeavouring. That the Owling-Trade was effectually rooted in Kent and Sussex,[96] and flourished (scandalously) on the Borders of Scotland and the other Northern parts of this Kingdome.[97]—A Committee appointed, on all these Heads, to sit to morrow-morning in the Prince's Chamber;[98] and so adjourned.

Mr Lawson,[99] with me in the Evening, saies Sir Thomas Littleton[100] moved, in the Debate, about the Lower House of Convocation, that none but *just Rights* might be asserted; which Mr Finch[101] observed to be like *Right Rights*, but yet Sir Thomas carried his point. Joseph Musgrave[102] right in the Convocation-Dispute.

Nov. 24. *Tuesday*. The Earl of Nottingham brought in the Queen's Instructions to the Duke of Ormond and Admiral Rook;[103] which were ordered to be Considered on Thursday. Lord Hallifax sharp on Lord Nottingham's Delay for 17 dayes, what would not require the Labour of 12 Hours.

Orderd that Prayers be said exactly at Eleven.—An Appeal

[94] For detailed figures for the export trade in woollen cloth see R. Davis, 'English Foreign Trade, 1660-1700', *EcHR* 2nd ser., vii (1954-5), 150-66, where the national average for 1699-1701 is given as £3,045,000.

[95] The official trade figures compiled annually since 1696 by the Inspector General of Imports and Exports, William Culliford.

[96] Wool and sheep smuggling. See Defoe, *Tour*, i, 112, for such smuggling in southeast England.

[97] Smuggling has been described as 'the national vice of the Scots'. The favourite commodities smuggled into Scotland were wine, tobacco, sugar, prohibited English and Dutch cloth, and especially raw English wool which was re-exported. From 1701 to 1704 a Scottish Act restrained the export of wool from Scotland and thus discouraged imports from England. Cattle was the main commodity smuggled into England. See T. C. Smout, *Scottish Trade on the Eve of the Union, 1660-1707* (1963), pp. 38-41, 203-4, 214-16.

[98] A list of the committee is in *LJ* xvii, 171. The Prince's Chamber, the usual meeting place for committees of Lords, was adjacent to the House. See fig. 1.

[99] Gilfred Lawson, MP for Cumberland, see Appendix A.

[100] MP for Castle Rising, Norfolk, 1702-5, later Chichester, 1705-8, and Portsmouth, 1708-10.

[101] Hon. Heneage Finch, MP for Oxford University. Younger brother of Lord Nottingham, he was created Lord Guernsey in 1703. See Appendix A.

[102] Son of Sir Christopher Musgrave, and himself an MP in 1713. See Appendix A.

[103] Sir George Rooke (d. 1709), who, besides commanding the fleet at Vigo, was MP for Portsmouth, 1698-1708. For the instructions, etc., see HMC *Lords MSS* v, 104-24.

brought by J. Sharp Esqr. but the Decrees against him (both by Lord Chancellor Somers, and the present Lord Keeper [Wright]) affirmed.[104]

I dined with the Archbishop of York who very confident that the Convocation Broils will have a Speedy and happy Conclusion. *Det Deus!*

Nov. 25. *Wednesday*. In observance of yesterday's Order, Prayers begun at Eleven: present (besides the Lord Keeper) Lords Longvile, Herbert and G[u]ilford, and I their Chaplain. Lord L[ongueville] moved that we should immediately adjourn, in resentment of an Order not obeyed by those that made it: Which had been done, had not my Lord Bradford come in and interposed. After reading some petitions, and a private Bill, adjourned about half hour after twelve.

In Convocation, the Bishops gave their final Memorial to the Lower House (Refuseing them intermediate Sessions, as a *House*),[105] the Bishops of London [Compton], Rochester [Sprat] and Exeter, dissenting.[106]—The Commons (moved by Sir C. M[usgrave]) ordered the printing of the Bishop of Worcestor's Letters.[107]

Mr Worth gave me an account of my Oxford-Remonstrance[108] being drawn up by Mr Read of Christ Church[109] and Limburg's being discarded by the Bishop of Worcester as a Socinian.[110] Bishop of Hereford's visit.

[104] For details see ibid., p. 53.

[105] The Lower House of Convocation had claimed the right to sit as a house during the intervals in the sitting of the Convocation. The Upper House only agreed to the Lower House appointing committees to prepare matters for deliberation. For this controversy see above, Session 1 introduction, and in greater detail, Burnet, *History*, v. 67–8; Lathbury, *Convocation*, pp. 378–9.

[106] Compton, Sprat, and Trelawney had together been the focus of Tory-High Church opposition to the ecclesiastical establishment in the previous reign. See G. V. Bennett, 'King William III and the Episcopate', in *Essays in Modern English Church History*, ed. G. V. Bennett and J. D. Walsh (1966), pp. 124–6.

[107] These appeared in print, together with the proceedings of the Commons in the case, on 21 Jan. 1703 (BL Lansdowne MS 1024, f. 148: Kennett's Journal).

[108] Possibly a reference to the paper, published in London, which was drawn up by several Oxford dons objecting to the university conferring a doctorate on Nicolson. See Bodl. MS Ballard 4, f. 16: N. to Charlett, 9 July 1702, and for a list of the objections BL Add. MS 27440, ff. 21–6.

[109] Anthony Read (*c*.1661–1729), a fiery High Church don and preacher, and Canon of Exeter since 1696.

[110] Literally, one who subscribed to the subordinate view of Christ's status expressed by the sixteenth-century Italian, Faustus Socinus. 'Socinianism', the most popular anti-Trinitarian heresy in the late seventeenth century, had achieved something of a vogue among a section of the Anglican clergy, as well as among the laity, since the 1680s, much to the alarm of the orthodox. See H. J. McLachlan, *Socinianism in Seventeenth-Century England* (Oxford, 1951).

Nov. 26. *Thursday*. A deal of Instructions to the Duke of Ormond and Admiral Rook read in the House of Lords. In those for Cadiz, the Admiral was to preside in all Councils at Sea. In the Duke's Declaration, &c. all violence on Religion and Churches forbidden. Orders sent to Vigo; which, tho' they came too late, were exactly executed.——A full House. 20 Bishops; all the great Ministers; &c.[111] Adjourned without any Debate, the Duke of Ormond being absent.

The Bishop of Worcester pleasant upon the House of Commons haveing (yesterday) ordered the printing of Evidence against him. His story of Bishop Morely's[112] not pitying any that had the Tooth-Ach after 60 (why had they teeth?) applyed to a Scotchman's loseing 3000 *l.* in his way to Rotterdam.

Brother Joseph and's family with me (after Sir H[enry] Fletcher and Mr Dalton)[113] in the Evening. My Niece's present of her flowers.

Nov. 27. *Friday*. Before the sitting of the House, with Lord Longvile in the Prince's Chamber. The Customs, from Virginia and Mary-Land, in these two last years amounted to near 700,000 *l.*[114] a Trade into which Scotland will hardly be admitted. This good Lord's Family got nothing but Attaindure's by being related to the Crown;[115] the like Fate to be expected by Duke of H[amilton][116] if he claims the antient Kingdome.

[111] The presence list at the beginning of each day's sittings in the *Lords Journals* indicates that there were eighty-one lords (including nineteen bishops) present on 26 Nov. (*LJ* xvii, 173). To Nicolson's inexperienced eye this might seem a full House, but the chamber was capable of holding many more, e.g. 121 lords voted in person in giving their verdict on Sacheverell's impeachment in 1710, while 119 and 122 voted respectively in the divisions on the safety of the Protestant Succession on 5 and 13 Apr. 1714. For a discussion on the capacity of the House, see C. Jones, 'Seating problems', pp. 134–6.

[112] George Morely, Bishop of Winchester, 1662–84.

[113] Sir Henry Fletcher (*c.*1661–1712), 3rd Bt of Hutton, Cumberland. Nicolson was a close friend of his father, the MP for Cumberland, 1661–1700. Possibly John Dalton, of Queen's College, Oxford, who became Vicar of Deane, Cumberland in 1705.

[114] The imports from the plantations of North America consisted largely of tobacco. The average imports for 1699–1701 were valued at £249,000, but a far larger quantity, £421,000 worth, was re-exported to Europe in this period. The fall in the cost of tobacco had led to a prodigious increase in demand both in England and Europe during the second half of the seventeenth century. See Davis, 'English Foreign Trade', pp. 151–2.

[115] Henry, Lord Grey of Ruthin and Viscount Longuville, was directly descended, through two females, from the 7th Earl of Kent (d. 1623). There had been no attainders in the family of the Grey Earls of Kent, so Nicolson must be referring to the cadet branch of the family, the Grey Marquesses of Dorset and Dukes of Suffolk, the last of whom had married Henry VIII's niece and suffered attainder for his involvement in the attempted seizure of the Crown for his daughter, Lady Jane Grey.

[116] The Duke of Hamilton, who was descended from James II of Scotland, had pretensions to the Scottish Crown. The Act of Settlement vested the Crown of England, but not that of Scotland, in the House of Hanover, in default of heirs of Anne's body.

A private Bill read, and Lord Ranelagh's Accounts[117] to be laid before the House on Munday; to which time adjourned. NB. This Lord Scandalously expensive (to the Tune of 50 or 60,000 *l.* per annum in Gardening, Indian Ware, &c.) whilst Paymaster in the late Reign.

After Dinner with Joshua Barnes[118] at the Bishop of Norwich's [Moore's]. My Lord took occasion (on Mr B[arnes]'s Complaint) to teach us two infallible Remedies for bleeding at the Nose; 1. Inky Cotton, the older the better. 2. The Patient's standing up to the Knees in hot Water. Mr B[arnes] saies he lost 600 *l.* by his *Edward 3.*[119]

NB. The Bishop of Winchester [Mews] (He and I being the onely Bishops in the House, those of the Province of Canterbury being all, except himself, at Convocation) observed that, if either of us should leave the Room, the rest could not make a House; there being a Necessity of haveing Lords Spiritual as well as Temporal. This was contradicted by Lord Longvile and others;[120] and (indeed) two dayes agoe I was the onely Bishop in the House, for some hours, upon the same Convocation-Score.[121]

Nov. 28. *Saturday.* In the morning I waited on Sir James Steward; who agreed to my proposal about the Toleration of Episcopacy in Scotland,[122] instead of Establishing it forthwith. Thence to Lord Tarbat's;[123] where Duke of Queensberry[124] and Earl of Tullbardin [Tullibardine].[125]

Dined at Lambeth, with the Marquess of Anandale, Earl of Tiviot [Teviot],[126] Bishops of Hereford and Bangor. Occ[asional] Comm[union] bandyed.

[117] Richard Jones (1641-1712), 1st Earl of Ranelagh, MP for West Looe, 1701-3. See above, n. 30.

[118] Regius Professor of Greek at Cambridge University, 1695-1712.

[119] *The History of that Most Victorious Monarch Edward III*, published in Cambridge in 1688.

[120] Longueville is correct on this procedural point.

[121] However concerned he was at the proceedings of the Convocation of Canterbury, Nicolson as Bishop of Carlisle could not participate in them. Neither could the Bishop of Durham, whom the *Journals* also list as having attended the House of Lords on 27 Nov. (*LJ* xvii, 174), nor the Archbishop of York, whom Nicolson records he 'sate near' (HMC *Laing MSS* ii, 5).

[122] See above, sessional intro., pp. 122-3, and P. W. J. Riley, 'The Formation of the Scottish Ministry of 1703', *SHR* xliv (1965), 112-34.

[123] George Mackenzie, Viscount of Tarbat, later Earl of Cromarty (see Appendix A), recently (21 Nov.) appointed Scottish Secretary. See Riley, pp. 117-18.

[124] High Commissioner and leader of the Court party in Scotland. See Appendix A, for brief biographies of all Scottish peers who sat as representative peers in the Lords after 1707.

[125] John Murray, later Duke of Atholl. See Appendix A, and Riley, pp. 123-4.

[126] Thomas Livingston (*c.*1651-1711), a soldier who had served William III in Scotland against the Jacobites, and had been created Viscount of Teviot in 1696 (he was never an earl). Born in Holland, he was naturalized by act of parliament on 9 Dec. 1704.

Nov. 29. *Sunday*. After Dr Linford's[127] good Sermon at Westminster Dr Gibson and I dined with Brother Joseph. Hearing Dr Younger's[128] (grave) sermon at St Paul's, and haveing taken a glass of his Florence, I came home by Greys Inn; where onely Mr Lawson (somewhat indisposed) to be met with. NB. At Westminster the Litany read by two singing men as far as the Lords Prayer; which ended, they return to their seats, and the priest goes on in his stall. At St Paul's no versicle (of *O Lord save the Queen* &c.) before the prayer for her Majesty after Sermon.

Nov. 30. *Monday*. A 2d Letter to me from Mr Rymer published.[129] In the House of Lords, the Duke of Ormond[130] gave in his Journal; which, being long, was ordered to ly on the Table and be considered on Friday. Thanks to the Earl of Marlborough, moved by the Duke of Somerset and given by the Lord Keeper in the Name of the Lords Spiritual and Temporal. Lord M[arlborough] modestly imputed the whole Success[131] to Her Majesty's good Conduct and the Valour of her Troops, Himself being onely a Witness, &c.

I dined with the Earl of Nottingham; who is for the Union, opposed by Lord Weymouth.[132] With the Dean[133] and Sir W[illiam] Dawes, &c in the Evening. NB. Prophesied that the Earl of M[arlborough] should be a Duke and then beheaded. His 1st Rise from the Duchess of Cl[eveland].[134]

Dec. 1. *Tuesday*. The House of Lords adjourned before the Commons could bring up their Bill against Occasional Communion.[135] Mr Bell

---

[127] Thomas Lynford (*c*.1651–1724), Rector of St. Edmund-the-King, Lombard St., since 1685. He became Archdeacon of Barnstaple in 1709.

[128] John Younger, Canon of St Paul's since 1693. See Appendix A.

[129] Thomas Rymer (1641–1713), noted antiquary, and author of the *Foedera*, published two letters to the Bishop of Carlisle in 1702 'occasioned by some passages in his late book of the Scotch Library'. A third was to follow in 1706. The second letter contained an historical deduction of the alliances between France and Scotland. Sir Robert Sibbald, a Scottish antiquary and friend of Nicolson, published a refutation of Rymer.

[130] See above, n. 85.

[131] For Marlborough's campaign in which he had reconquered the lower Rhine and Maas valleys, see Trevelyan, *Queen Anne*, i, 235–45.

[132] Nottingham strongly supported the Union as the best safeguard of the Protestant Succession and proposed it in 1702 in opposition to the Whigs' abjuration oath. Weymouth typified the views of many English Tories who, fearing union with a Presbyterian kingdom, were lukewarm if not hostile.

[133] William Grahme, Dean of Carlisle, see Appendix A.

[134] Mistress of both Charles II and Marlborough, she is said to have influenced the King in Marlborough's favour. She was also rumoured to have given him £10,000 with which he purchased an annuity of £500 a year from the Marquess of Halifax. See BL Lansdowne MS 825, f. 121.

[135] The Commons gave it its third reading on 28 Nov. Bromley (see n. 138 below) was then ordered to carry it up to the Lords (*CJ* xiv, 14, 35, 51).

(of Newcastle)[136] dined with me; and the Evening spent with him a little idly.

Dr Hickes, in the morning, gave me a long History of (his School-fellow) Mr Rymer; whose father's Head is still to be seen at Doncaster, falling from his Body upon the Northern plott soon after the Restoration of Ch[arles] II.[137]

Dec. 2. Wednesday. The Bill against Occasional Communion brought up by Mr Bromley,[138] attended with 40 or 50 Members. Lord Wharton first moved against it, as *haveing nothing good in but its preface.* He was answered, somewhat pleasantly, by Lord North. The Third that spoke was Lord Haversham, who owned himself a Dissenter; but caressed the Bishops most highly. He concluded with a motion that it might be read a second time to morrow: which agreed to, and all the Lords to be Summoned.

Dec. 3. Thursday. After the Second Reading of the Bill against Occasional Communion, and its being voted to be Committed, the Lord Somers moved that it might be an Instruction to the Committee that *this Bill extend to no other persons than the Test-Act.*[139] After many long and warm Debates, the Question was at last put; and the House Divided upon't. *Contents,* 46. and *Not Contents,* 46. Amongst the former was the Archbishop of Canterbury and 10 of his Suffragans;[140] amongst the latter the Archbishop of York and 9 other Bishops, viz. London, Durham, Winchester, Exeter, Rochester, Norwich, Litchfeild [Hough], Lincoln [Gardiner] and Carlile. There being five proxies produced,[141] four of 'em fell to the *Contents*; and then they were 50 against 47. I had prepared the following Speech, on the Occasion: but there was no Room for it.

"My Lords. I am abundantly Sensible 'tis much too early for me to meddle in the Debates of this House: But the wise man tells me

[136] Probably Robert Bell, an officer in the Newcastle customs. See *CW* ii (1902), 195.

[137] Ralph Rymer (father of Thomas) was hanged at York (Jan. 1664) after his part in the abortive rising of 1663. Thomas Rymer and Hickes had been schoolfellows at Thomas Smelt's school at Danby-Wiske.

[138] William Bromley of Baginton, MP for Oxford University. See Appendix A.

[139] The Act of 1673 which required all office-holders under the Crown to swear the oaths of allegiance and supremacy, to take the sacrament according to the Church of England, and to sign a declaration against transubstantiation. The point of Somers's amendment was, of course, to remove 'Corporation men' from the scope of the bill.

[140] The Bishops of Worcester, Salisbury, Hereford, Ely, Peterborough, Gloucester, Bath and Wells, Bristol, Chichester, and Bangor (*LJ* xvii, 178).

[141] Peers absent from parliament could leave their proxies with a fellow-peer (see above, Chapter 1, pp. 32–6). Records of the proxies entered for use by peers are in the 'proxy books' in the HLRO. Those for the 1702–3 session of parliament have, however, been lost.

there is a time to Speak; and I know not that, in my whole Life, I shall ever be under a more pressing Obligation to trouble you with any Sentiments of mine than I am at this present.

My Lords, The blessed Sacrament of our Lord's Supper is usually called a Communion; and ought to be a certain Symbol of our being firmly united in the Mystical Body of our Redeemer: And therfore surely there cannot be a more dreadful profanation of that Sacred Ordinance than the breaking of this Bread for Secular Ends and purposes. The fixing Ones Eye upon Worldly Advantages in places of Honour and profit (which I take to be the Case of an Occasional Communicant) must hinder him from discerning the Lord's Body; and I am well assured such a man Eats and Drinks his own Damnation. For this weighty Reason, Out of a tender Compassion for the Souls of our Dissenters (as well as for the Honour of God and the Established Religion) I am now For the Committing of this Bill; as I shall be, in due time, for the passing of it into a Law."

NB. Prince George[142] came into the House to countenance the Bill; and Divided with the *Not Contents*. Lord Hallifax's Memorial from the Founders of the Charity without Bishop-gate; where 400 poor provided for. Lord Somers, never at a Conventicle.[143]

Dec. 4. *Friday*. After Prayers, and a few Private Bills, the House resolved into a Committee on the Bill against Occasional Communion. The Instruction of yesterday was read; and, in pursuance of it, the same persons were put into the preamble of this Bill which are reckoned up in the Test-Act,[144] and the rest struck out.[145] Then

[142] George, Prince of Denmark, husband of Queen Anne, sat in the Lords by virtue of his English title of Duke of Cumberland. As he was Lord High Admiral and a Lutheran it was necessary for him to conform occasionally to the Church of England. In voting for the Occasional Conformity Bill on 4 Dec. he deferred to the wishes of his wife, remarking to Lord Wharton, a strong opponent of the bill, 'My heart is vid you' (Burnet, *History*, v, 55, 109). According to Lord Shaftesbury, the prince was forced to go to the House to vote for the bill despite being ill with asthma (PRO 30/24/22/7: Shaftesbury to Sir John Cropley, 24 July 1710).

[143] A dissenting meeting-house.

[144] These were 'Peers or Commons, who have, or shall have, any office of offices, civil or military, or receive any pay, salary, fee, or wages, by reason of any patent, or grant from Her Majesty, or from any of Her Majesty's predecessors . . . or shall be admitted into any service or employment in Her Majesty's household or family.' Quoted from the Occasional Conformity Bill, see Pittis, *Proceedings*, p. 4. See 25 Car. II c. 2 (*Statutes of the Realm*, v, 782) for the original 1672 Act.

[145] These were the 'Mayor, alderman, recorder, baliff, town-clerk, common-councilman, or other person bearing any office of magistracy, or places of trust or other imployment relating to, and concerning the government of the respective cities, corporations, buroughs, cinque ports', etc. See Pittis, *Proceedings*, pp. 4-5.

an Amendment was proposed, That *Every one bearing office might receive the Sacrament four times a year; and come to Church, at least, once a Month*. This (by the Duke of Leedes, Archbishop of York, &c.) was observed a farther prostitution of the Sacrament. Upon the Question—*Contents*, 47. *Not Contents*, 48. So the Clause was rejected by one Vote; no Proxies being allowed in a Committee. In the latter Class were the Archbishop of York with the Bishops of London, Durham, Rochester, Exeter, S. Asaph[146] and Carlile: The Archbishop of Canterbury (and 11 of his Suffragans) on the other side. Prince George (a little reflected on by Lord Hallifax for his Occasional Communion) voted with us.

Dec. 5. *Saturday*. After a short visit to the Archbishop of York I called on our Dean; and (with him and the Archdeacon of Durham)[147] went to dine with the Bishop of Durham, who obliged me to salute his fair Lady.[148] Mr Alston, his Nephew, a very ingenious young Gentleman. Returning to the Dean's chamber, with the Archdeacon and Dr Dent,[149] disputed sharply the Case of Archbishop of Canterbury and his Suffragans;[150] most vilely misrepresented.

The House of Lords did not sit this day; being adjourned, last night, till Monday.—Upon Recollecting the choicest passages in the Speeches Yesterday, Lord Raby handsomely Apologized for his change of sides; the Bill offering at a *persecution*, and the Clause at an *Inquisition*: Lord North's Case of a Box on the Ear just before a Test-Sacrament, which either loses the place (if not forgiven) or Honour: Duke of Leedes glad the motion for a stricter Reformation came from the young men. Duke of South[amp]ton cajouled by Lord P[rivy] S[eal] [Normanby].[151]

Dec. 6. *Sunday*. I received the Sacrament, from the Bishop of Rochester, in the Church of Westminster;[152] after a grave Advent-Sermon by Dr Gee.[153] In the Afternoon, the Dean of St. Paul's Son (Mr Sherlock)[154] gave us an ingenious sermon on *Romans* 1, 22.

[146] Edward Jones (1641-1703), Bishop of St Asaph, 1692-1703.
[147] Robert Boothe (c.1662-1730), Archdeacon of Durham since 1691, became Dean of Bristol in 1708.
[148] Dorothy, Lady Crew (1673-1715), had become the bishop's second wife in 1700.
[149] Thomas Dent (d. 1722), Canon of Westminster since 1694.
[150] Probably in connection with the current dispute in Convocation, see above, sessional intro., pp. 121-2.
[151] Created Duke of Buckinghamshire and Normanby on 23 Mar. 1703, see Appendix A.
[152] St Margaret's.
[153] Edward Gee, Rector of St Bennet's, Paul's Wharf, see Appendix A.
[154] William Sherlock (c.1641-1707), Master of the Temple, 1685-1705, and Dean of St Paul's since 1691, and Thomas Sherlock (1678-1761), Rector of Therfield, Herts.

shewing the Folly of Irreligion and the wisdome of Rel[igion]. Sermon done, the Bishop of Hereford came to me; and acquainted me with his thoughts of bringing in a Clause (into the Bill against Occasional Communion) to prevent the Academyes of Dissenters.[155] Approved.

London before the Romans. Trenobant, is the Town in the Vally. Bre-gant (whence Brigantes) the Mountain-Borderers; as Cant (now Kent) Borderers on Gaul. He [the Bishop of Hereford] has the whole Remainder of the Impression of large Welsh Bibles:[156] those in 8° worse: the *Whole Duty of Man, Practise of Piety*, Dr William's's[157] Catechisms, &c. all in Welsh.

Dec. 7. *Munday*. In the Committee of the whole House of Lords on the Occasional Bill, moved (and agreed) that a Clause requireing the prayer for the Queen and Princess Sophia[158] in all private Assemblies be added, &c. The grand Debate—*Whether the penalties (of 100 l. forfeiture and 5 l. per diem so long as the Office continued) be left Out. Yeas,* 54. *Noes,* 46. Of the latter were the Archbishop of York, Bishops of London, Rochester, Exeter, Bangor and Carlile. The Archbishop of Canterbury and 7 other Bishops on the other side. This agreed, on all hands, to be (in effect) a throwing out of the Bill; since the Commons will not allow an Amendment in the Money part. After this, Every thing altered as Lord Sommers pleased to propose; without opposition.[159] I went off, before the End of the Debates, with the Archbishop of York to Supper; after 7 o'clock. The Bishop of Sarum assureing me that he'd move, and prove, that the Church of England was a persecuteing Church.

1701-34, who succeeded his father as Master of the Temple, and later became Dean of Chichester in 1715, and successively Bishop of Bangor (1728), Salisbury (1734), and London (1748).

[155] Dissenters had contrived since the 1660s (though without explicit legal authority) to educate their children in their own schools and to establish and maintain a growing number of academies for higher education, including the training of their ministers. The design of the Schism Bill of 1714 was to make this practice illegal.

[156] For Humphrey's interest in Welsh literature, particularly in the production of a new edition of the Welsh Common Prayer Book, see E. G. Wright, 'Humphrey Humphreys, Bishop of Bangor and Hereford', *Journal of the Historical Society of the Church in Wales*, ii (1950), 72-86; and G. M. Griffiths, 'Eight Letters from Edmund Gibson to Bishop Humphreys, 1707-9', *National Library of Wales Journal*, x (1957-8), 364-74.

[157] Probably Thomas Williams (1658-1726), cleric and translator.

[158] Granddaughter of James I, the Electress Dowager of Hanover was heir to the English throne by the Act of Settlement of 1701 should Queen Anne die childless.

[159] For details of the amendments added see Pittis, *Proceedings*, pp. 3-9; *CJ* xiv, 76-7. For a brief account of the progress of this bill through the Lords until Jan. 1703, see HMC *Lords MSS* v, 157-9.

Dec. 8. [*Tuesday*.] The House of Lords did not sit; the Committee of the whole House riseing late the last night. I visitted Cousin Shelton, dined with Brother Joseph, and came home to write Letters. Dr Gibson presented me with his Answer to Atterbury's *Parlam[entary] Rights* &c.[160]

Dec. 9. *Wednesday*. After a few private Bills, that against Occasional Conformity was read the 3d time and (with its Amendments) sent back to the Commons. Immediately a Debate began (much heated the Earl of Sunderland's affirming that the Commons were just now considering how to tack this to a Money-Bill) which brought on a Division of the House, 51 against 47. and ended in the following Order: That, *the Annexing any Clause or Clauses to a Bill of Aid or Supply, the matter of which is foreign to and different from the matter of the Said Bill of Aid or Supply, is Unparliamentary and tends to the Destruction of the Constitution of this Government.*[161] All Lords that please had leave given to subscribe this Order;[162] which is to be added to the Roll of Standing Orders.[163]

In the Debate, Lord Sommers, more passionate than usual, for *discharging a good Conscience and leaveing it to posterity to Judge of the Cause.* The Lord Treasurer [Godolphin], Duke of Leeds, Earls of Nottingham, Rochester and Marlborough, argued that (tho' the thing was just in it self) it was now *unseasonable.*—The Duke of L[eeds] called on by the Earl of Mountague to explain himself; but the House thought there was no Occasion.[164] However, some little

---

[160] In *The Parliamentary Original and Rights of the Lower House of Convocation cleared*, published in Oct. 1702, Atterbury tried to draw a parallel between the rights of parliament and Convocation, arguing that the latter had a right to sit independently of the former. Gibson's reply was *The Pretended Independence of the Lower House upon the Upper, A Groundless Notion*. For a summary of these two pamphlets, see Sykes, *Gibson*, pp. 39–40.

[161] See *LJ* xvii, 185 for this historic motion. The point of annexing, or 'tacking', a controversial bill or some of its clauses to a financial bill—the ideal candidate being the Land Tax Bill, with its utterly indispensable yield of around two million pounds in wartime—was that the Lords were, for practicable purposes, if not in theory (see Diary, 22 Dec. 1702), inhibited by long-standing convention from amending money bills. They could only accept or reject them, and the right of rejection was scarcely ever exercised. Consequently they would be unable to get rid of any offending 'foreign' clauses without imperilling essential supply.

For the implications of another 'tack', to Prince George's settlement bill, see below, 11 Jan. 1703. Lord Rivers, like most Whigs, was 'abundantly satisfyed', that the Commons were 'designing hereafter to alledge it as a precedent of that kind'. The final Lords' debate on that bill, on 19 Jan. is described in considerable detail by Nicolson.

[162] Sixty-three lords did sign, see *LJ* xvii, 185.

[163] As no. 97, see HMC *Lords MSS* x, 22.

[164] Ill-feeling between Leeds, the former Earl of Danby, and Montagu went back to 1679 when the then Ralph Montagu, as ex-ambassador in Paris, provided the evidence of secret negotiations with the French which led to Danby's impeachment.

Repartees 'twixt the Duke and Lord Hallifax, in defence of his Chief.[165] NB. Amongst the 47 were the Bishops of York, London, Durham, Rochester, Exeter, St Asaph and Carlile.

Dec. 10. *Thursday*. Upon complaint made to the House, by the Earl of Montague, that a Quarrel had happened betwixt the Lords Osburn[166] and Hallifax on occasion of Yesterday's Debate, and that Lord H[alifax] was confined by the Queen, they were both sent for. The latter came presently in; and it was long debated—Whether he might not to be committed to Custody of (or attended by) the Black-Rod,[167] for prevention of Evil, till the Lord O[sborne] could be likewise siezed. Whilst this was argueing, the Lord O[sborne] came in, and protested he knew of no Quarrel (but in Relation to a Suit at Law) that was between them. He confessed he had written a Letter last night, on this last mentioned Subject, to the Lord H[alifax] but never intended it, as it appeared to be understood, for a Challenge. However, The Commands of the House were given that they should both declare (upon their word and Honour) that no future Quarrel should be between 'em on occasion of any thing that was past: Which was obeyed.

Before the Committee, in the Morning, Lord Longvil gave me a pleasant Account of the Earl of Peterborough's turning himself into all Shapes (of Porter, Chairman, &c.) to firret out Intrigues: A man unsteady, and so embroyling that (at any rate) to be sent off.

Dec. 11. *Friday*. In the morning at the Parliament Office; which carries the Rolls no higher than the 12th of Hen[ry] 7. Till that time, as Prynne saise, it was the Treasury; robbed by the Monks of Westminster.[168] The Journals in Paper keep better than in Vellum. The warrant for beheading King Ch[arles] 1 (under the hands and Seals

[165] i.e. the Earl of Montagu, Halifax's cousin and mentor of his early years. According to Lord Coventry, 'The Duke of Leeds told Halifax publickly in the House that his family was raised by rebellion but his own suffered by it' (HMC *12th Report, Appendix ix* [Beaufort MSS], p. 96: Coventry to [his wife], 10 Dec. 1702).

[166] Lord Osborne was the eldest son of the Duke of Leeds, see Appendix A. For another account of this quarrel, see Fitzwilliam Museum, Cambridge, Spencer Perceval Bequest, Packet B: N. to Thoresby, 10 Dec. 1702.

[167] Sir David Mitchell was also an admiral and combined his duties as Black Rod, 1698–1710, with an active career as a member of the Board of Admiralty. M. Bond and D. Beamish, *The Gentleman Usher of the Black Rod* (1976), p. 6.

[168] The Jewel Tower, Westminster, which acted as the Parliament Office, where the records of parliament were stored, from 1621 to 1864, was built in 1365–6 as a store for the King's private and personal treasure. When the Court moved to Whitehall in the early sixteenth century, this use ended. William Prynne (1600–69), the puritan pamphleteer, was appointed Keeper of Records in the Tower at the Restoration. See M. F. Bond, 'The Formation of the Archives of Parliament, 1497–1691', *Journal of the Society of Archivists*, i, no. 6 (1957), 151–8.

of 56 of his Judges) taken from the Quaker [?Quarter][169]-Widow of Col. Hacker; to whom (with two others) it is directed, and who is supposed to have been the Executioner. It will be printed in some of the Lord Chancellor Hide's future Volumes.[170]

In the House of Lords, a Tryal betwixt the Lady Anderson (Appellant) and Mr Harcourt,[171] of the Crown Office.[172] When half the Counsel were heard, and many of the Lords gone, an Adjournment till Munday carryed upon the Question, 29 against 25.

Dec. 12. *Saturday.* In the morning with Mr Rymer; who wants nothing, but an allowance out of the Treasury, for the publishing the Treaties of England. He kindly lent me several of his Transcripts relateing to the old Scottish Charters, &c. In the Evening, with Dr Gibson, at Dr Hickes's. No French Charters, in their own Language, could be found (by Mabillon)[173] higher than the 12th Century: But the Dr in his Sept. Grammars, will publish one of W[illiam] the Conq[ueror] in the Normannie Saxon.[174] Lord Hollis' Observation that, unless the Commons allow the Lords to Vote in Elections, they are unreasonable in pretending to Tax them: since, for this reason, they do not now dispute the Right of the Clergy to vote.[175]

Dec. 13. *Sunday.* After preaching at the Savoy,[176] I dined at Cousin R. Nicolson's[177] with Mr Skelton, Dr Pratt[178] and brother Joseph. In the Evening visitted by Sir Philip Sydenham,[179] who invited me to preach before the Commons at St Margaret's, and Dr Dent.

---

[169] Word blotted.

[170] Edward Hyde, 1st Earl of Clarendon, had started his *History of the Great Rebellion* in 1640 and finished it in exile after 1671. It was designed to be published as it stood, and is a kind of manifesto addressed to posterity to vindicate the role of the constitutional royalists. It was published from 1702 to 1704 in three volumes by Clarendon's son, the Earl of Rochester, and intended as a Tory manifesto, as Rochester's introduction makes clear.

[171] For this cause see below, 14 Dec.

[172] The office which transacted the common law business of Chancery.

[173] Jean Mabillon (1632–1707), noted French scholar and historian, sometimes credited with the foundation of the science of diplomatics. His *De re diplomatica* appeared in 1681.

[174] George Hickes, the non-juror Saxonist, was at work on the *Linguarum veterum septentrionalium Thesaurus*, which included among other things a series of Saxon grammars and many printed documents. His work led to a brief skirmish with Mabillon. See D. C. Douglas, *English Scholars, 1660–1730* (1951), pp. 87–95.

[175] The clergy had finally surrendered the right to tax themselves in 1664.

[176] The palace built between the Strand and the river by Peter of Savoy in 1246. It became a royal possession, and in 1509 Henry VII endowed it as a hospital and a chapel was erected. The hospital was dissolved in 1703, though the chapel remained.

[177] Possibly Robert, brother of James Nicolson of Penrith, an attorney.

[178] Samuel Pratt (d. 1723), Vicar of Tottenham High Cross, 1693–1707, and former Master of the Savoy. He became Dean of Rochester in 1706.

[179] Sir Philip Sydenham (c.1676–1739) 3rd Bt., MP for Somerset 1701–5.

Dec. 14. *Munday*. The Second part of the Lady Anderson's Appeal against Mr Harcourt.[180] Sir Thomas Powis[181] urged in her favour the Case of Mr Stystede;[182] who, a few years agoe, used to seduce young masters into Oaths before a M[aste]r in Chancery that they had (bonafide) borrowed the whole Summs on his Sham-Securities. This, he said, was by Surprize; and, had he not been detected, he might have proceeded to a higher piece of Villany: *viz.* the prevailing with them to give Answers, on Oath, to Bills in Chancery. Notwithstanding this great man's [Powys's] Eloquence, and the pains taken by some young Lords for the fair Lady, the Decree was affirmed by a great Majority. Mr Dobbins's Complement to Sir Simon Harcourt;[183] that he would dy sooner than do any thing that might make him blush. This Lord Keeper advanced for his goeing thro with Serjeant Pratt's[184] part of pleading, when he swooned, at Sir John Fenwick's Tryal.[185]

Dec. 15. *Tuesday*. After a Couple of private Bills, a Letter read from the Secretary of the Admiralty[186] to the Clerk of Parliament;[187] acquainteing him that the Journals of the Flag-Officers, ordered to be laid before the House yesterday, were makeing ready and some of 'em would be prepared against Wednesday.—The Earl of Torrington observed that this was [an] odd way of obeying their Lordships Orders; to talk of *prepareing* matters, when the *Original Journals* were required. Whereupon, Ordered that the Secretary attend the House with the *Originals* themselves on Thursday-morning; to which time Adjourned.

In Convocation Sharp Repartees 'twixt the Bishops of Salisbury and Exeter; about the Opinions of the two Chief Justices[188] and Attorney General [Northey], concerning the paper lately subscribed

---

[180] For the case of Mary Sherard, widow of Sir Richard Anderson, Bt., and her husband Brownlow Sherard, against decrees in Chancery concerning Sir Richard's will, see *LJ* xvii, 190.

[181] Lady Anderson's counsel and MP for Ludlow, see Appendix A.

[182] Edward Stystead, described in 1695 as the 'notorious cheat of the town'. HMC *Lords MSS* ii, 120.

[183] Solicitor General and MP for Abingdon, see Appendix A.

[184] John Pratt (1657–1725), Serjeant-at-Law, 1700, MP for Midhurst, 1711–14, knighted and appointed a judge in King's Bench 1714.

[185] Tried for treason after a plot had been discovered to assassinate William III, he was executed by act of attainder in 1696. Pratt was a counsel for the bill of attainder and Powys a counsel for Fenwick.

[186] Josiah Burchett, Secretary to the Lords Commissioners of the Admiralty, 1695–1742.

[187] Matthew Johnson (1637–1723), Clerk of the Parliaments, 1691–1716. J. C. Sainty, *The Parliament Office in the 17th and 18th centuries* (1977), p. 17.

[188] Sir John Holt, Chief Justice of the Queen's Bench, 1689–1710, and Sir Thomas Trevor, Chief Justice of the Common Pleas, 1701–14.

by the Lower House asserting the Divine Apostolical Right of Episcopacy.[189] [Whether a Premunire?].[190]

In the House of Commons the Duke of Marlborough desired that the Queen's kindness[191] to him might be waved; rather then be displeaseing to any one single Member.

In the Evening, with the Archbishop of Canterbury and Dr Gibson at the Bishop of Hereford's. The Bishop of Hereford's Story of the late Marquess of Hallifax's[192] moveing against a Coal-fire in the House—*Nolumus Loggos Angliae mutare*. It[em]—his own desireing to see the Bishop of E[xeter]'s[193] Nails, when he sits next him in Convocation. The Archbishop in good hopes of the Union.

Dec. 16. *Wednesday*. By Lord Treasurer's and Sir H[enry] Fletcher's to Grey's-Inn. Sir C. M[usgrave] (in our way to Mr H[arle]y's[194] and Lord Rochester's) acquainted me with Mr Finch's Remark on the Queen's expression, in Her Message, that the Duke of Marlborough had *established an entire Confidence and good Correspondence betwixt Her Majesty and the States Generall, viz.* the Queen must therfore have been misrepresented, as her friends certainly were, by the late Ministry as friends to France. Visits over to Sister Rothery[195] and Dr (Togry) Smith,[196] who differs with Capt. Hatton[197] about the Atterburian Faction,[198] I dined with Lord Thanet; who, with Coll. Grahme,[199] had been Solliciteing Lord Treasurer for Mr Brathwait

[189] On 11 Dec. 1702 the Lower House of Convocation had, with malicious intent addressed the bishops declaring the order of bishops as superior to presbyters because of their divine apostolical institution. Some moderate and Low Church members of the Lower House protested against making such a declaration without royal license. The Upper House made their answer on 20 Jan. 1703. For this dispute see Lathbury, *Convocation*, pp. 379-83.

[190] Nicolson's brackets.

[191] Marlborough had been created a duke on 14 December and had been granted £5,000 a year for life from the Post Office revenue for his victories in Flanders in the summer. The Tory House of Commons had voted that he had 'retrieved the ancient honour and glory of the English nation'.

[192] William Saville, 2nd Marquis of Halifax, died in 1700.

[193] E[ly]'s?

[194] MS blotted. Robert Harley was MP for New Radnor and Speaker of the Commons, see Appendix A.

[195] Nicolson's younger sister Frances, who had married an E. Rothery. She apparently lived in Dorset and looked after the daughters of Henry Thynne, only son of Viscount Weymouth.

[196] Thomas Smith (1638-1710), non-juring divine and scholar. He settled in the house of Sir John Cotton and had looked after his library for several years. According to Nicolson, he was almost blind by this time, see Bodl. MS Ashmolean 186, ff. 530-1: N. to Lhwyd, 29 Dec. 1702. He had gained the name of 'Rabbi' or 'Tograi' Smith at Oxford after a visit to the East.

[197] ? Jonathan Hutton, Capt.-Lt. in Col. William Seymour's regiment of marines since 1698. Dalton, v, 135, 137.

[198] i.e. followers of Francis Atterbury in Convocation.

[199] James Grahme, MP for Abbleby, Westmorland, see Appendix A.

of Warcop[200] to succeed Major Christian.[201] Mr Grandorge[202] and I made a Short Visit to the Bishop of Litchfield; immoderate in his Concern for the Honour of King William.[203]

Dec. 17. *Thursday*. Mr Birchet, Secretary of the Admiralty, brought in the Original Journals of the Flag-Officers; with an Account of the Stores in the Navy when they came ashore. A month's provision good, in the shortest Article, of Beef and Pork. This Debate adjourned till Munday. A Message from the House of Commons, desireing a Conference on the Bill against Occasional Conformity. Managers appointed; mostly the same with those who had opposed it.[204] On the behalf of the Commons, the Conference opened by Mr Bromley; and reported by the Lord Stewart [Steward], Duke of Devonshire. Repeated, afterwards, by the Lord Keeper [Wright]. An Adjournment moved, *Noes*, 52 *Yeas*, 47. Among the latter, the Archbishop of York, Bishops of London, Durham, Winchester, Rochester, Exeter, Hereford, Chichester [Williams], St Asaph, Bristol [Hall] and Carlile.

The Reasons of the House of Commons read.[205] Some (of small moment) agreed to. The main Article, now considered, the penalty of 100 *l*. and 5 *l. per diem*.[206] Lord Hallifax observed that the Commons had disguised their Stile; concealing the Reasons (*which they might alledge and from which they will never depart*) upon the late Order of this House never to allow of tacking. The alteration (from 100 *l*. to 20) insisted on. Adjourned till to morrow at 10[207] the Duke of Leedes wishing that the Lords (*if possible, and for the sake of Justice*, a Cause being to be heard) might, to preserve the onely Remains of their Grandeur rise early.

With Jos[eph] Mus[grave] and Tullies[208] in the Evening.

[200] ? Richard Brathwayte, appointed Customer at Newcastle-upon-Tyne by Godolphin in Nov. 1703. *CTB 1703*, p. 457.

[201] Major William Christian, Joint-Customer at Carlisle Port. By 1704 he was a Solicitor of Taxes in several northern counties. Ibid., p. 264; *CTB 1704–5*, p. 140.

[202] John Grandorge, Chaplain to the Earl of Thanet, see Appendix A.

[203] Bishop Hough had formerly been Master of Magdalen College, Oxford, and had been deposed by James II, and later reinstated.

[204] See *LJ* xvii, 192, for a list of the managers. No bishops were included on this occasion, though in the final conference, on 16 Jan., the Bishop of Salisbury was to play a prominent part.

[205] The reasons of the Commons given on 16 Jan. 1703, which must be similar to those of 17 Dec. 1702, are printed in Pittis, *Proceedings*, pp. 10–14; see also *LJ* xvii, 305–14, and *CJ* xiv, 180–3.

[206] For the original penalties proposed see above, n. 8. The Lords amended the proposed fine of £100 to a forfeit of £20 to be divided into three: one for the Queen, one for the poor, and one for the informer. The Commons rejected this amendment, but the Lords adhered, as did the Commons to their disagreement. See Pittis, *Proceedings*, p. 6.

[207] MS blotted. HLRO MS Minutes of the Lords, reads as follows: 'Ordered that the house be begun tomorrow 10 Clocke. Adj[ourned] till tomor[row at] 11 Clocke.'

[208] William, Isaac, and Philip Tullie were the brothers of Thomas Tullie, Chancellor

Dec. 18. *Friday*. After the Committee of the Bishop of Chichester's Bill for rebuilding his Houses in Chancery-Lane,[209] An Appeal (in the House) by Mr Price a young Gentleman of Herefordshire against his Brother in Law Mr Button.[210] He had Suffered a Decree to go against him, by Default, in Chancery; and his Counsel seemed to hope that the Lords would allow him to have the Merits of his Cause heard originally at their Bar. Agreed — that nothing but their own Order, to the contrary, stood in their way; But, it appearing that the Appellant's Case did not deserve so extraordinary a Regard as the dispensing with a solemn Rule, the Decree was affirmed.

The Bill against Occasional Conformity brought on; and the remaining Amendments, disagreed to by the Commons, insisted on. A Committee appointed to draw up Reasons for this insisting; and an Instruction given 'em that they Search precedents for Bills with Penalties begun Originally in this House; and others, sent from below, amended and altered in that part.[211] NB. The Lord Treasurer [Godolphin] sent for the Duke of Leedes, into the Prince's Chamber, before the Debate began: And they were both in the House afterwards, without offering an Objection or *Not content* to any one of the Questions. All passed *Nemine Contradicente*.

This ended, the Duke of Marlborough was introduced in his Robes, 'twixt the Dukes of Somerset and Ormond. The procession— The Black Rod, Garter King,[212] Lord Marshall [Carlisle],[213] Lord high Chamberlayn [Lindsey] the 3 Dukes, in their [*sic*].[214] The new Duke kneeling to the Lord Keeper gave him his patent; which was read by Mr Relf,[215] a little slovenly. The preamble set forth his great Exploits in the Low Countries; his freeing the Queen from the Scandals there charged upon Her, his beating the Duke of Burgundy, &c. *Ne tota*

(1683) and Dean (1716) of Carlisle. All three lived in London, William and Philip in Hatton Garden, and Isaac in Highgate, but the latter had his business in Covent Garden. See *CW* ii (1902), 166; iii (1903), 37. Philip Tullie had lived in Hatton Garden from at least 1693 (Corporation of London RO Assessments Box 42, MS 3: 4s. in the £ tax, St Andrew's Holborn assessment, Mar. 1693/4).

[209] For the Bishop of Chichester's Estate Act see HMC *Lords MSS* v, 150-1.

[210] For the case see *LJ* xvii, 194; HMC *Lords MSS* v, 57-8.

[211] There had been protests in the Commons that the Lords were acting unconstitutionally in amending fines, on the grounds that this was 'a meddling with money' (Burnet, *History*, v, 52).

[212] Sir Thomas St George, Garter King of Arms, 1686-1703.

[213] The Earl of Carlisle was Deputy Earl Marshal, 1701-6. The Duke of Norfolk, hereditary Earl Marshal, was legally incapacitated from performing his office as a Roman Catholic and (until 1704) a minor.

[214] These two words smudged. Possibly Nicolson meant to write: 'the 3 Dukes in their robes. The new Duke . . .'.

[215] John Relf (1643-1711), Reading Clerk in the Lords, ?1664-1711, previously a Clerk in the House, 1660-4. From Newbriggin, Cumberland, he had estates in the county, and is probably the 'cousin' Relf referred to by Nicolson. See Sainty, *Parliament Office*, p. 20.

Europa, quanta quarta, Gallia fieret. The patent read, the Duke was conducted to his Seat at the lower End of the Duke's Bench; where (as the old Lord Herbert[216] observed) *Consedere Duces — Vulgistante Corona*.

In the Evening, in Essex-street, with Dr Kennet, Dr Waugh,[217] Dr Gibson and Mr Grandorge.

Dec. 19. *Saturday*. After reading prayers, and hearing Lord Wharton's Petition[218] against Mr R. Squire,[219] I left the House; and went to dine at Lambeth. The Bishops of Worcester and Hereford, Sir John Wynne,[220] Sir Ralph Ashton,[221] Mr Stewart, the new Warden of All-Souls,[222] &c.——After Dinner, with R. Snow;[223] who gave me a Comical Account of the Contract 'twixt him and his man Roger, never to marry without mutual Consent. Roger first craved leave, on Condition to attend his Master from Munday-morning till Saturday-night: which has been punctually observed for some years. At my brother's in   [224] with my Sister, Niece and Daugher till 9.

[216] For Edward, 1st Lord Herbert of Chirbury (1583-1648), see *DNB*.

[217] John Waugh, Fellow of Queen's College, Oxford, see Appendix A.

[218] There was a suit in Chancery, Lord Wharton plaintiff, and Robert Squire, Charles Bathurst, etc., defendants, over the ownership of some lead mines, the crux of which was the boundaries of the manor of Helaugh in Swaledale, north Yorkshire. It became a *cause célèbre*, in part no doubt because of the value of the revenues involved (the later case of Wharton *versus* Marriot in 1708, also involving lead mines in Swaledale, was said to be worth £5,000 *p.a.* to the winner). In Nov. 1702 at a trial in Queen's Bench out of Chancery, Squire and Bathurst won by producing in evidence the record (survey) of the honour of Richmond and lordship of Middleham filed in the Court of Exchequer. On 19 Dec. 1702, therefore, Wharton was petitioning the Lords by way of appeal (though this was not an Exchequer case) and he obtained an order from the Lords for getting the record of the honour of Richmond taken off the file in the Exchequer. Later, as a consequence, at a second trial in Queen's Bench in Nov. 1703, Squire and Bathurst were unable to produce the record and lost their case. Squire maintained that Wharton's purpose in all this was to suppress a vital piece of evidence. On 28 Jan. 1704 the Commons voted that the proceedings of the Lords over the record 'is without precedent and unwarrantable, and tends to the subjecting the rights and properties of all the commoners of England to an illegal and arbitrary power'. For the case see HMC *Lords MSS* v, 170-3; *CJ* xiv, 288, 298, 306, 310; T. B. Howell, *State Trials*, xiv, 890-5; and below, 21-22, 25 Jan. 1703. See also Luttrell, vi, 300-1 for the immense value of the mineral rights in the Wharton–Marriot case; and *Memoirs of the Life of the most Noble Thomas, Late Marquess of Wharton* (2nd edn., 1715), p. 48.

[219] Robert Squire (d. 1707), MP for Scarborough, 1705-7.

[220] MP for Caernarvon, 1698-1705, and Caernarvonshire, 1705-13.

[221] Sir Ralph Assheton (1651-1716), 2nd Bt., MP for Liverpool, 1677-9, and Lancashire, 1694-98.

[222] Bernard Gardiner (d. 1726), had succeeded as Warden in Dec. 1702. He was Vice-Chancellor, 1711-15.

[223] Ralph Snow (*c*.1613-1707), Treasurer and Register to Archbishop Tenison, he seems to have been fond of drinking and horseplay (Bodl. MS Ballard, 6, f. 89: Gibson to Charlett, 11 Jan. 1704). He had been a tenant of the Bishop of Carlisle since before 1685, having leased the rectory of Newburn (Carlisle Dean and Chapter Library: Nicolson's MSS Collection, iv, 390). See also *Survey of London*, xxxiii, 106, 114.

[224] Two words indecipherable. Possibly Salisbury Court.

148

Dec. 20. *Sunday*. Dr Gibson and I attended the Bishop of Hereford; who preached a very good and pious Sermon (at Dr Kennet's Church)[225] against men's *loveing Darkness better than Light*. Dined with Mr Cradock; and returned to Westminster. Dr. G[ibson]'s story of the late Dean of Exeter's[226] Reply to the Earl of Dorset, on the Contest betwixt the Lord Chamberlain[227] and Church of Westminster[228] for the Scaffolds[229] at King W[illiam]'s Coronation. When the Earl alledged that the Chamberlain had 'em at King James's. *Yea*, quoth the Dean, *and we Crowned him accordingly*.

Dec. 21. *Munday*. Immediately after Prayers moved (by the Archbishop of Canterbury) that the Bishop of Carlile be desired to preach, before the Houses on the 30th of January:[230] which was done accordingly, by Order signed by the Clerk of Parliament. The Money-Bill[231] (of 206 sheets of parchment haveing the Names of 32000 Commissioners) read the first time, and ordered a Second Reading. An Appeal of S[amuel] Shepherd Esqr. against other Creditors of Kent a Goldsmith; with whom he had joyned in Chancery.[232] Four Decrees (two of Lord Sommers, and two more of the present Lord Keeper [Wright]) affirmed against the Appellant, *Nemine Contradicente*. Adjourned till to morrow-morning at 10.

Lord Archbishop of Canterbury observed to me the empty Objection against our Trade goeing into Scotland;[233] as if it were still to be a seperate Kingdome: A thoughtless way of Argueing which some of our English could not Overcome.

Dec. 22. *Tuesday*. The Money-Bill read a second time, and Committed to a Committee of the whole House; wherein 'twas read again

---

[225] St Botolph, Aldgate.

[226] Richard Annesley, Lord Altham, Dean of Exeter, 1681–1701.

[227] In 1689 it was the Earl of Dorset.

[228] The Dean and Chapter of Westminster Abbey.

[229] i.e. scaffolding.   [230] Anniversary of the execution of Charles I.

[231] The Land Tax Bill which each year declared that £2 million were to be raised. It contained a schedule of the counties and principal towns of England with the amount each had to pay to make up the £2 million. The local authorities obtained the money by charging four shillings in the pound nominally on the annual value of the land, but actually on certain old assessments which were often not half the true value. See *CJ* xiv, 90, for the 1702 Bill; and Trevelyan, *Queen Anne*, i, 293–4; Holmes, *British Politics*, pp. 160–2; W. R. Ward, *The English Land Tax in the 18th Century* (1953), pp. 17–29.

[232] See HMC *Lords MSS* v, 66. Probably Samuel Shepheard, senr., MP 1698–April 1701 and 1705–8 for Newport (I.o.W.) and London respectively, of whom it was said in 1710 he was 'an excellent merchant for shipping, and foreign trade by far the first in England, but no banker' (HMC *Portland MSS* iv, 559).

[233] For the economic background to the Union, see T. C. Smout, *Scottish Trade on the Eve of the Union, 1660–1707* (Edinburgh, 1963), pp. 257–75; and idem, 'The Anglo-Scottish Union of 1707, I. The economic background', *EcHR*, 2nd ser. xvi (1963–4), 455–67.

(paragraph by paragraph) and piece-meal assented to. The Chairman (Lord Longvil) putting the Question and I onely answering; for no other Lord in the House regarded what was doeing, this being onely (*pro forma*) to preserve a seeming Right to dissent from, or amend, any part of a Money-Bill as well as others.

A Bill brought from the Commons, and read the first time, *To prevent Escapes from the prisons of King's Bench and Marshalsea.*[234] The Lord Sommers moved that it might be well considered, and made effectual; as what was much wanted. Lord Steward (Duke of Devonshire) moved that all the Lords present in the House, when the Committee was appointed for the drawing up Reasons for insisting on the Amendments to the Bill against Occasional Conformity, might be added to that Committee; which was agreed to, and so Adjourned.

Dr Gibson and I dined at the *Sun* in Essex-Street.

Dec. 23. *Wednesday*. In the morning, at a Committee in the Parliament-Office; with the Lords Sunderland, Manchester, Anglesey, Herbert and Sommers. The Rols searched for precedents of Bills begun, with penalties, in the House of Lords. These, whilst I stayed with them, Examined.[235]

19.	H[enry]	7.	Against Cross-bows. Pen[alty]	40s.
—			Concerning Scavage.	20l.
—			Against Riots	20l.
—			Vagabonds	1s.
—			By-Laws of Corporations.	40l.
1.	Hen[ry]	8.	Concerning Coroners.	40s.
—			Reformation of Apparel.	20l.
3.	Hen[ry]	8.	Against Mummers	20s.
—			About Physitians	5l.
—			payment of Soldiers	All Goods.
—			For Subsidies: A proviso (in the Act, begun with the Commons) the Colleges shall pay no Fifteenths.	
—			About Cross-Bows: Extends the penalties of a former Act (19 Hen[ry] 7.) to new persons.	

In the House, the Money-Bill read a third time and passed: Another, about the Regulation of the Kings-Bench and Fleet-Prisons read a 2d time, and Committed to a Committee of the whole House, on Munday-sennight. After other (Private) Bills, the Queen came to the

---

[234] 1 Ann. St.1 c. 6., see *Statutes of the Realm*, viii, 164–6.
[235] For these acts see *Statutes of the Realm*, ii, 650, 653, 656–7; iii, 4, 14, 27, 32, 44, 632–3.

House; and, haveing given the Royal Assent in the usual form to the
Land Tax and some Private Acts, went off without Speaking. 'Twas
expected she should have moved for 10,000 more Land-men:[236] but
that matter otherwise concerted with the Speaker [Harley], who
presented the Bill with a short and eloquent speech; telling Her
Majesty that *Her Loyal Commons could not let this year End without makeing Provision for the next, and praying for a Continuance
of Her Victories.*—The House of Commons resolved on a Resumption of the Grants of the late Reign.[237] NB. A great many Lords,
Spiritual and Temporal, without their Robes: And indeed, the
House being so crowded with Ladies and other Strangers, 'twas
indifferent in what Habit we appeared.[238]

In the Evening, a Visit paid to Cousin Gregson; and received from
Mr Dean, who knowes nothing who will be Primate of Ireland, &c.[239]

Dec. 24. *Thursday.* With 4 other Bishops, Lords Brook and Pawlet,
on a Committee for three Private Bills; all made ready for Reporting.
—In the Evening, paid a Visit to Sir Philip Sydenham; who gave me
an Account of his Own Apoplectick Indisposition three nights agoe:
And of the Bishop of Bath and Wells's [Kidder's] offer at Carlile,
in Case Bishop Kenn would have taken the Oath to Her Majesty.[240]

Dec. 25. *Friday.* At Sermon (preached by a learned Divine, the
Bishop of Chichester, on 1 Timothy) and sacrament where were also
the Bishops of Rochester, Exeter and Hereford, Dean of Christ

[236] i.e. requested parliament to increase the army estimates by making provision for an
additional 10,000 soldiers, for the following year's campaign in Flanders. The Flanders
establishment in 1702 had been almost 40,000, although fewer than 19,000 of them were
British nationals. A further 3,500 subject troops and 6,500 mercenaries were subsequently
added in 1703. See I. F. Burton, *The Captain-General* (1968), p. 21.

[237] See *CJ* xiv, 95. The question of William III's land grants to his favourites, both in
England and Ireland, had long been a sore point with most Tories and some country Whigs.
It was to remain so until 1712, at least.

[238] Parliamentary robes were normally worn only on ceremonial or official occasions,
such as the Queen giving the royal assent, or state trials. It was such an infrequent occurrence
that Lord Suffolk took particular note of the fact that the peers sat all day in their robes
at Sacheverell's trial (Badminton House, Beaufort MSS 509.101.3: Suffolk to his sister,
2 Mar. 1710). Robes were obviously a costly item and when Wake succeeded Tenison at
Canterbury, he found that his predecessor's robes had been bought from Mrs. Tillotson,
the widow of the previous archbishop (Christ Church Wake MS 6, ff. 86–7: Gibson to
Wake, 14 Jan. 1716). It was not uncommon for bishops to lend their robes to impoverished
colleagues (e.g. NLW Plas yn Cefn MSS 2744–5: Tyler to Humphries, 16 & 23 Sept.
1706).

[239] Michael Boyle, Archbishop of Armagh and Primate of Ireland, 1679–1702, had
died on 10 Dec. 1702. He was to be succeeded by Narcissus March, Archbishop of Dublin,
in Jan. 1703.

[240] There had been rumours early in 1702 to the effect that Thomas Ken, who had been
deprived of his see of Bath and Wells in 1690 as a non-juror, would return and conform.
See *The Life of Richard Kidder, D.D., Bishop of Bath and Wells*, ed. A. E. Robinson
(Somerset Record Society, xxxviii 1922), p. 159.

Church [Aldrich] &c. Dined at Dr Lancaster's with Dr Waugh. In the Evening with the Bishop of Hereford; who shewed me a Letter from E. Lhwyd,[241] with the following Note in the Margin of a MS. Juvencus[242] in the public Library at Cambridge.[234]

> niguorcosam nemheunaur henoid / mitelu nit gurmaur / mi am [*franc*] dam ancalaur. / nicanăniguardam nicusam heoid / cet iben med nouel / mi amfranc dam anpatel. / namercit mi nep leguenid henoid / is discirr micoueidid / dou nam riceus unguetid.[244]

My Lord of Hereford observed several Welch words here (as *henoid* = old; *Gurmaur*, a Great Man; *isdis Gur*, a judge or, Man of the Law; &c.) but concluded, from the Character, that it must be a Dialect of the Irish.[245] Mr L[hwyd] saies he cannot unravel it: But Mr Baxter[246] (his friend) believes it to be a certain prophesy that Her present Majesty shall yet bear a Prince of Wales. *Utinam*!—NB. Yesterday morning, with my brother Joseph, visiting Dr Knipe;[247] of whom observed (by, the Bishop of Rochester, his brother in Law) that the French King and he, two great Tyrants, were born in the same year. His wife Mr Talbot's Sister.—Great Trees, Roots and all, removed by a rolling Lever of three men, in St. James's Park.

Dec. 26. *Saturday*. Invited to dine at Lambeth: where (as usual) were the Archbishop of York, Bishops of London, Worcester, Rochester,

[241] Edward Lhwyd or Lhuyd (1660-1709), celtic scholar, antiquary, and naturalist, and Keeper of the Ashmolean Museum, Oxford, 1691-1709. He published vol. 1 of *Archaeologia Britannica* in 1707.

[242] Gaius Vettius Aqualinus Juvencus (fl. 332), Christian Latin poet.

[243] The manuscript (now ULC MS Ff.4.42) was bequeathed to the university in 1648, and consists of a number of Latin paraphrases of the Gospels of Juvencus, with some Old Welsh glosses and twelve englynion. Three of these englynion are the marginalia noted here. They were written in the early ninth century, and first appeared in print in Lhwyd's *Archaeologia Britannica*, p. 221. They were thought by Lhwyd to be 'Old British', i.e. the language of the Picts. See *The Beginnings of Welsh Poetry: Studies by Sir Ifor Williams*, ed. R. Bromwich (Cardiff, 1972), pp. 89-121.

[244] The text in the original diary is partly illegible and a recent transcription is reproduced here. In translation (Bromwich, *Welsh Poetry*, p. 90) it reads: I shall not talk even for one hour tonight, / my retinue is not very large, / I and my Frank, round our cauldron. / I shall not sing, I shall not laugh, I shall not jest tonight / though we drank clear mead, / I and my Frank, round our bowl. / Let no one ask me for merriment tonight, / mean is my company, / two lords can talk: one speaks.

[245] Nicolson reported to Lhwyd that the bishop 'cannot tell what to make of the whole', but guessed it was a prophesy (Bodl. MS Ashmolean 1816, ff. 530-1: N. to Lhwyd, 29 Dec. 1702).

[246] William Baxter (1650-1723), nephew of Richard Baxter, the Presbyterian divine, was a master at the Mercers' School, London, and published an edition of Horace in 1711, and the *Dictionary of British Antiquities*.

[247] Thomas Knipe (1638-1711), headmaster of Westminster in 1695, and author of grammars. He was married twice; first to the sister of Bishop Sprat of Rochester (who died in 1685), and secondly to a widow, Alice Talbot (d. 1723).

Exeter, Salisbury, Hereford, Norwich, Peterborough, Lincoln, Chichester, Oxford [Talbot], Bangor and Carlile.[248]

—Given (of Course) to the Archbishop's Sewer 2s. 6d., Porter, 2s. 6d. Waterman, 2s. 6d. Item, a Porter at the Cloisters, 2s. Lord of Sarum's Account of the Earl of Rochester's applying to him to bring him into the late Queen Mary's favour, insisting upon the Gospel Argument because he had been alwaies the Bishop's Enemy. The Intrigues of the Earl of Clarendon and Bishop of Ely discovered to the Bishop of Sarum by a servant of his ordered to watch them.[249] Bishop of Bangor's story of the true Welsh gutturals; fetched so deep, that one wondered they did not some times *choose rather to speak out at the other End of their Bodies.*—Bishop of Hereford's Appeal to H. Wharton's Lives of the Priors of Durham (in Rob[ert?] Stewart)[250] whether the Royal family of Scotland be not descended from Wales. In the Evening, Sir James Steward (of Bute) with me complaining of the slow progress of the Union; and the Queen's caressing, too Trimmingly, the Fanaticks[251] of both Kingdomes. NB. Bishop of Sarum's Account of Dr Barwick's[252] being shown all the persons he called for (except O. Cromwell) in a Glass by a Servant maid, who called for an Apple, brought to her through the Air. The Archbishop of York witnesses the same.

Dec. 27. *Sunday*. I preached in the morning at St. Margaret's on Matthew 11. 4. Dined with Brother Joseph and Mr Lowther.[253] At Paul's; the Evening-Sermon by Mr Bramston;[254] the Dean of Windsor's former [i.e. former sermon] at St. Clement's: wrapt in Rags of Obscurity.—Visits to the Dean and Dr Covel.[255]

---

[248] The Archbishop of Canterbury traditionally held a Boxing Day dinner for all the bishops in London.

[249] Henry, 2nd Earl of Clarendon, and Francis Turner, Bishop of Ely, both non-jurors and close friends, were engaged in 1690 in a design to bring about a counter-revolution in favour of James II. Col. Grahme was another member of the design. See *The Correspondence of Henry Hyde, Earl of Clarendon*, ed. S. W. Singer, 2 vols. (1828), ii, 319; Burnet, *History*, iv, 122-7.

[250] Robert II, King of Scotland (1371-90).

[251] In English usage this means Presbyterians (or Dissenters in general). Here it seems more likely to embrace the Episcopalian 'Cavaliers' in Scotland and the High Tories in England.

[252] Peter Barwick (*c*.1621-1705), was physician to Charles II, and brother of John Barwick (d. 1664), whose life he wrote.

[253] James Lowther, MP for Carlisle until the 1702 election, see Appendix A.

[254] William Bramston (d. 1735), Rector of Woodham Walter, Essex, 1686-1720, later of St Christopher's, London, 1708-35.

[255] Gregory Haskard (d. 1708), Dean of Windsor and Wolverhampton since 1684, and Rector of St Clement Danes since 1678. John Covel (1638-1722), President of Corpus Christi, Cambridge, since 1688, and Chancellor of York since 1687.

Dec. 28. *Munday*. After Morning-Visits from Mr Kinglove and Mr Elstob[256] (who brought my Diploma from Oxford)[257] I dined with Mr Philip Tully; calling on Mr C. Musgrave[258] by the way. Mr Bridges[259] and Mr Craggs,[260] the Duke of Marlborough's Secretary, with him: Mr J. Musgrave and Mr Lawson at dinner. In the Evening with the Bishop of Hereford and Dr Gibson. My Lord presented me with a Welch Almanac: And took notice of five Bangors, whereof one in ye Isle of Bell. Q[uery] Whether Christianity first in Ireland or Britain? The Saints from Ireland to Wales.

Dec. 29. *Tuesday*. Dr Cove[l], with me in the Morning, recounting his Northern Travels: particularly pleased with Gingling-Cove and Reeking-Cove, near Ingleton, which (he saies) outdoe Oakey-Hole in Somersetshire and all the wonders of the Peak. His Opinion of Sir R[ichard] Sandford's[261] whifling with him, in the promises of a Plate and 20 Guinneas for the Chapple.

After two or three Committees for Private Bills, read in the House, Adjourned till Thursday-Sennight; in Resentment of the Commons adjourning themselves beyond our Day.[262]

Dec. 30. *Wednesday*. In the morning, visitted by Capt. Vesey;[263] who had been in the Expedition at Cadiz and Vigo, in Lieut. Generall Churchill's Regiment.[264] He saies that, at Port-St Mary, the soldiers were civil the first night But, finding the Town wholly abandoned and the Houses richly furnished, they began their plunder the next day; and that, for a week following, there was nothing but Drunkenness and Confusion amongst them. He had not yet heard of (his

---

[256] William Elstob (1673–1715), a noted Saxonist whom Nicolson had appointed his chaplain in 1702; he was Rector of St Swithen and St Mary Bothaw, 1702–15.

[257] For the difficulty Nicolson had in gaining his Oxford doctorate see above, sessional intro., p. 117. To end rumours that he was dissatisfied with the university, Nicolson had asked Elstob 'to call upon the Registrar of the University for my Diploma, and to pay his Fee'. The bishop was of the opinion that he owed his degree to Dean Aldrich of Christ Church, President John Rogers of Magdalen, and Arthur Charlett. See Bodl. MS Ballard 4, ff. 14, 16: N. to Charlett, 9 July and 24 Sept. 1702.

[258] Christopher Musgrave, MP for Carlisle, see Appendix A.

[259] Hon. James Brydges (1673–1744), MP for Hereford, 1698–1714, succeeded his father as 9th Lord Chandos in 1714; Earl of Carnarvon (1714) and Duke of Chandos (1719).

[260] James Craggs senior (1657–1721), MP for Grampound, 1702–13.

[261] Until the election of 1702, MP for Westmorland, see Appendix A.

[262] On 23 Dec. 1702 the Lords had adjourned for Christmas until 29 Dec., while the Commons on the same day adjourned until 4 Jan. 1703. Consequently on 29 Dec. the Lords adjourned themselves until 7 Jan. *CJ* xiv, 95; *LJ* xvii, 201–2.

[263] Theodore Vesey (d. 1736), was a lieutenant in 1695, and a captain by 1702. He was a colonel of a foot regiment in Spain in 1710. Dalton, v, 256.

[264] Prince George of Denmark's regiment of foot. Charles Churchill (1656–1714), brother of the Duke of Marlborough, Lieutenant-General in 1702 and MP for Weymouth, 1701–10.

Uncle) the Archbishop of Tuam's[265] being like to succeed to the Primacy of Ireland;[266] but requested my being present, on Saturday, at the Committee for a Bill of the Archibishop's 2d Son.[267] Which was promised.—My Sister Rothery and her Son[268] with me. J. Relf civil to her.

After attendance on the Committee for Private Bills, I dined with Mr Is[aac] Tullie; the same Company as on the 28th. Brother Joseph and's Family invited to dine with me on Newyears-day.

Dec. 31. *Thursday.* After morning-visit from Mr Addison[269] (who put into my hand a formal Order for his Son Wyvel's being made Gentleman Pensioner, ready for the Duke of St Alban's[270] Subscribeing) I went to St James's and dined, about three, with our Dean and Mr Whitfeild[271] at the Chaplain's Table.

Comeing thence, I jumped with the Bishop of Sarum, returning (in some Heat and Concern) from the Queen; before whom he had been laying the Mischief that would ensue from the Commons tacking a Clause to the Bill of Settlement on the Prince, provideing that He should be capable of Preferments after the Demise of Her Majesty, notwithstanding the late Act of Succession.[272] He owned to me that the Queen seemed set upon haveing that Bill pass; saying that She

[265] John Vesey (d. 1716), Bishop of Limerick, 1673-9, Archbishop of Tuam, 1679-1716.
[266] See above, n. 239. [267] See below, 2 Jan. 1703.
[268] Joseph Rothery (c.1690-1731), matriculated from Queen's College, Oxford, in 1706, he gained his BA in 1710 and his MA in 1714. He was appointed Vicar of Bromfield, Cumberland, in 1715, and appears to have acted as Nicolson's domestic chaplain, 1714-17. He was Archdeacon of Derry, 1719-31. *CW* iii (1903), 2; v (1905), 2, 24.
[269] Thomas Addison (b. 1641), of Torpenhow, Cumberland; Commissioner for Sick and Wounded, 1689-c.1694; executor of Sir Joseph Williamson's will; Cumberland Tax Commissioner (*Cumberland Families*, p. 1; Nicolson, *Miscellany*, p. 90; J. Ehrman, *Navy in the War of William III* (Cambridge, 1953), p. 176; Hopkinson, p. 318; *CTB 1702*, p. 980).
[270] Charles Beauclerk (1670-1726), illegitimate son of Charles II, was a Court Whig with a pension of £1,000 p.a., and held the office of Captain of the Band of Gentlemen Pensioners, 1693-1712, 1714-26. He had been created Duke of St Albans in 1684.
[271] William Whitfield (d. 1717), Canon of St Paul's since 1695, and of Canterbury, 1709.
[272] The bill provided a settlement of £100,000 a year on Prince George, should he survive the Queen. The Act of Settlement had stated that after the Hanoverian succession no foreigner, even though naturalised, should be capable of holding employment. It had no retrospective force on those, such as Prince George, already naturalised, but to clear away any possible doubts a clause was added to the Prince's settlement bill which would allow him to take office. There were two objections to this clause: first, that it was a 'tack' on a money bill, and the Lords voted (Feb. 1692) to oppose any such clause, and had only recently condemned tacking as gravely unconstitutional (9 Dec. 1702); and, secondly, the clause implied that the Act of Settlement did exclude previously naturalised citizens from their rights on the Hanoverian succession, though this was not intended by the Act. Burnet opposed the bill in the Lords, believing 'the clause was put in the bill, by some in the house of commons, only because they believed it would be opposed by those against whom they intended to irritate the queen' (Burnet, *History*, v, 54-6). Queen Anne pressed strongly for the bill, despite the 'tack', yet later she was to oppose the 'tack' on the Occasional Conformity Bill.

had rather an Affront were given to Her self than to the Prince. Yet The Bishop was so free as to move for a two dayes Prorogation, that the Contents of this might be put into two Bills.

With Dr Gibson and Mr Elstob in Essex-Street. The former assured me that Dr Chetwood[273] had brought his flattering Author of King William's Life[274] to Dr Hody;[275] desireing him to introduce him to the Archbishop of Canterbury.

[Jan.] 1. *Friday*. I attended the Archbishop of York in the morning, in order to wait on the Queen with the rest of the Bishops. Our Rendesvous was at the Bishop of Sarum's Lodgeings; whither all (that could) came, except the Bishops of London and Durham. An exceedingly throng Court. Her Majesty at[276] Her Levet [levée], had the Trumpets and Kettle Drums; at her passing to prayers addressed to by the Archbishop of Canterbury in the name of the other Bishops; on her Return, entertained with a Song composed by (Her Poet Laureat) N[ahum] Tate.[277] After this, the Prince immediately received the Compliments of the Bishops in his Bed-chamber; and, after them, the Masters of Christ-Church Hospital, who attended Him (as Lord High Admiral) with their blew-coat Boys; each of 'em presenting Him with a Curious Map of his own drawing. No New-years-Gifts to the Queen's servants all being forbid to ask or receive. —NB. The Archbishop of York agreed with me that the Prince's Bill was a private one, and so could have no Tacking Clause; And that the Queen could do nothing, in Answer to the Petition of the lower House of Convocation.[278]

Brother Joseph and Sisters (with their Children) dined with me; my own Daughter being disappointed, and kept at home, by her fright from the Fire at Serjeants Inn[279] in Fleetstreet. In the Evening, at my Brothers, Dr Waugh gave me a surprizeing account of a late

[273] Knightley Chetwood (1650–1720), Archdeacon of York since 1688, and later Dean of Gloucester (1707).

[274] *The Life of William III, late King of England and Prince of Orange*, published anonymously in Nov. 1702. See *Term Catalogue*, ed. E. Arber (1906), iii, 320.

[275] Humphrey Hody (d. 1707), Regius Professor of Greek, Oxford 1698–1705, Rector of St Michael Royal and St Martin Vintry, London (1695), and later Archdeacon of Oxford (1704).

[276] Repl. 'had'.　　　　　　　　　　　　　　　[277] Appointed Poet Laureate in 1693.

[278] On 23 Dec. the Lower House had presented a petition to the Queen stating that since 1700 several questions concerning the rights of the Lower House had arisen, but that the bishops had refused to join with them in an application to Her Majesty. They therefore prayed that the Queen would take the controversy into her consideration. The Queen in answer had promised to give 'an answer as soon as possible' (BL Lansdowne MS 1024, f. 147). See Lathbury, *Convocation*, p. 382.

[279] Headquarters of the serjeants-at-law situated on the south side of Fleet Street at the north-east corner of the Inner Temple. There was also a second Serjeants' Inn in Chancery Lane. See R. Megaray, *Inns Ancient and Modern* (1972), p. 24.

Letter of Archdeacon Pearson's[280] to Dr Lancaster; in which was asserted the Reasonableness of modalling our Episcopacy like that of Scotland, and of the Lower House of Convocation's[281] craveing protection in their Rights from the House of Commons: Adding that this, with some other particulars of like kind, was alwaies his Opinion.

[Jan.] 2. *Saturday*. Called out to a Committee, on behalf of the Archbishop of Tuam's Second Son;[282] ill treated by the Irish Commission for forfeited Estates.[283] Mr Vesey (his Cousin, sometime an Officer at Carlile)[284] returned with me to Dinner; and gave a large History of their late Expedition to Spain. Their Provisions very bad and Scanty; their Plunder at Vigo not great as the French Losses. Mr Harwood[285] saies, had they not gotten Goats and Sheep, from the Rocks near Vigo, they could not have brought their Crew into England.

[Jan.] 3. *Sunday*. After a good sermon (on Christ's fulfilling the Law) by Mr Moss,[286] at Grey's Inn, I dined at Mr Wenyeve's[287] with Sir Christopher M[usgrave] and his family.—Set home by Mr Christopher Musgrave in his Chariot.

The Bishop of Hereford tells me that Dr Davis (the Author of the greater Welsh Dictionary)[288] had his whole Education in Wales; haveing never seen an University till he took his Dr's Degree, performing all his Exercise[s][289] Regularly: And that Jones,[290] the publisher of that

[280] William Pearson, Archdeacon of Nottingham, was a 'cousin' of Nicolson, see Appendix A.

[281] The specific reference here is probably to Pearson supporting Atterbury's argument in his pamphlet *The Parliamentary Original and Rights of the Lower House*. Shortly after its publication the Commons had, on 21 Nov. 1702, voted to assert the just rights and privileges of the Lower House of Convocation.

[282] Agmondisham Vesey. For his case see HMC *Lords MSS* v, 170.

[283] See J. G. Simms, *The Williamite Confiscation in Ireland, 1690–1703* (1957), pp. 80, 144–5, 191.

[284] i.e. of the garrison of Carlisle Castle.

[285] Probably Richard Harwood, Ensign in Prince George's regiment of foot (the same as Theodore Vesey) since 1697. In 1705 he became a Lieutenant in the Grenadiers. Dalton, v, 54–5.

[286] Robert Moss (d. 1729), Preacher at Gray's Inn from 1698; later Lecturer at St Lawrence Jewry, London, 1708, and Dean of Ely 1713–29.

[287] John Wyneve of Brettenham, Suffolk, married in June 1703 Elizabeth, fourth child of Sir Chrisopher Musgrave (Nicolson and Burn, i, 598; Berkshire RO Trumbull MS 53: J. Bridges to Sir W. Trumbull, 15 June 1703).

[288] John Davis (c.1567–1644), eminent Welsh grammarian and lexicographer. He published his *Dictionarium Duplex*, in 1632.

[289] The conventional exercises required of a candidate for the DD degree. See, e.g., Holmes, *Sacheverell*, p. 16, n; G. R. M. Ward, *Oxford University Statutes* (1845); and W. M. Marshall, *George Hooper* (Sherborne, 1976), pp. 19-20.

[290] Davis's dictionary had been published in 1632 by Robert Jones, the King's printer in Scotland. In 1688 Thomas Jones, a bookseller in London and printer in Shrewsbury,

in 8°., was onely an Illiterate Taylor. The Name of Twelf-tide in Welsh is now *Ystwill*. i.e. The hounding out Darkness. *Cyrrig*, a little Stone; *Main* (from Magnus) a great one: And yet, they say *Main Mawr*.

[Jan.] 4. *Munday*. Visitted, in the morning, by Dr Thomas Smith; who's peevishly afraid of his being rejected by the Curators of Cotton's Library.[291] The Chronicle of Lanercost, he saies, deserves to be printed.[292] I shewed him a Letter, respectful to himself, from Sir R. Sibbald; whom (from his Treatise of Thule) he reckons a poor Contemptible man.[293] Dined at Mr W[illiam] Tullie's with Joseph Musgrave, G[ilfred] Lawson, &c. and setled the State till after 8 at night.

[Jan.] 5. [*Tuesday*]. I breakfasted with Mr Chamberlaine;[294] who had before him the Journal of the Society *De Propaganda fide*, and (in discourse) observed that the Letter G, in English words, was pronounced soft (as J consonant) in those we borrow from the Southern Nations, and harsh (as Gh.) in those from the North.

Calling on Mr Gregson and our Dean, I took Coach at St James's for Kensington. Till Dr Lamplugh[295] came home his Sons carryed me to the Gravel-pits and new discovered Spaw. The Water is exceeding clear, and drinks soft and well; but tasts of no Mineral. It's purging Faculty has been supposed to be communicated, in the Summer, by Art. The prospect from it very fine. In the Evening (after comeing home in a Stage-Coach to Sir Stephen Fox's[296] with Mrs Johnson)

1676–1718, who had first practised the trade of a tailor in London, published an enlarged edition of Davis's dictionary. W. Rowlands, *Cambrian Bibliography* (Llanidloes, 1869), pp. 112, 241–2; H. R. Plomer, *Dictionary of Booksellers and Printers . . . 1668 to 1725* (1922), p. 175.

[291] In 1702–3 Humphrey Wanley, Robert Harley's librarian, pressed unsuccessfully to be made Keeper of the Cotton Library in place of Thomas Smith who was nearly blind. He had tried to enlist Nicolson's help (BL Add. MS 3780, ff. 263, 267: N. to Wanley, 24 Sept. 1702 and 7 June 1703; Bodl. MS Ashmolean 1816, f. 530: N. to Lhwyd, 29 Dec. 1702). For a brief history and description of the Cotton Library, see above, Chapter 2, pp. 79–81.

[292] The Chronicle of Lanercost Priory contains a general history of England and Scotland 1272–1346. The original, now BL Cotton MS Claudius D.VII, was first published in 1839. See *The Chronicle of Lanercost, 1272–1346*, ed. H. Maxwell (Glasgow, 1913); and A. G. Little, 'The authorship of the Lanercost Chronicle', *EHR* xxxi (1916), 269–79; xxxii (1917), 48–9.

[293] Sir Robert Sibbald (1641–1722), Scottish physician and antiquary, had published his *Essay concerning the Thule of the Anchents* in Edinburgh in 1692.

[294] John Chamberlayne, Secretary to the Society for the Propagation of the Gospel, see Appendix A.

[295] Thomas Lamplugh (*c*.1661–1703), Rector of St Andrew-under-Shaft, London, 1701–3, was the son of Archbishop Lamplugh of York.

[296] Sir Stephen Fox (1627–1716), MP for Salisbury, 1661–79, 1685–7, 1714–15, Westminster, 1679, 1691–8, and Cricklade, 1699–1702. C. Clay, *Public Finance and Private Wealth: the Career of Sir Stephen Fox, 1627–1716* (Oxford, 1978).

visitted by Dr Woodward; who saies he has a Treatise (ready for the press) discovering the best and cheapest Wayes of Assaying and refineing all sorts of Metals; from certain Experiments of his own.[297] The Sale of the Earl of Clarendon's Library, notifyed in this day's public prints, occasioned by the Earl of R[ochester]'s not sending in the money charged upon it, as promised, a week agoe.

[Jan.] 6. [*Wednesday*.] Dr Gibson and I dined with the Archbishop of York who told us (*Sub Rosa*) that He had discoursed the Queen Her Self upon the Subject of the late Petition of the Lower House ·of Convocation and that She was satisfyed that She could not Act in that Matter; that my Lord of Canterbury was in the Right; &c. Good news to my friend, and me.

In the afternoon, at my Cousin Bosworth's[298] in Colemanstreet. Mr Barton (a French Merchant) acquainted us that four of his Countreymen, and profession, were newly siezed for helping the French King to Remittances of Money into Italy.

[Jan.] 7. *Thursday*. After some Private Bills, a Message from the House of Commons (by Mr Conyers)[299] with a Bill for Enabling Her Majesty to settle 100,000 *l.* on the Prince, in Case of His surviveing Her; together with Her Palaces of Kensington and Winchester.[300] This being read, a second Message (by the same) with a Bill for Continuance of the Duties upon Coal and Culm. The Earl of Nottingham brought a Message from the Queen (the same as, last week, to the Commons) about the Additional Forces requested by the States General:[301] And, after reading of Memorials and

[297] John Woodward (1665–1728), Professor of Physic at Gresham College, 1692–1728. A famous geologist (FRS, 1693) he founded the Woodwardian Professorship at Cambridge. He had startled the world with his speculations about the geology of fossils in his *Essay Towards a Natural History of the Earth* (1695). The work referred to here remained in manuscript (BL Add. MSS 25095–6). For his career see J. M. Levine, *Dr. Woodward's Shield: History, Science, and Satire in Augustan England* (Berkeley, 1977).

[298] Probably Richard Bosworth, who was the brother-in-law of John Relf, Reading Clerk in the House of Lords. He had married Catherine Relf, see PRO Prob. 11, 520, f. 88: John Relf's will, 1711.

[299] There were two MPs of this name in the Commons. This was John Conyers (1650–1725), MP for East Grinstead, 1695–1708, 1710–25, and West Looe, 1708–10, Chairman of the Committee of Supply and Ways and Means (since 1700), and a right-hand man of Lord Treasurer Godolphin in expediting public business. Sedgwick, i, 572.

[300] The Royal Palace of Winchester, designed by Sir Christopher Wren for Charles II, was left half-finished at that king's death. It was never occupied. There is a good eighteenth-century description in John Macky, *A Journey Through England* (1722), ii, 21–3. Macky also mentions (p. 24) Queen Anne's design 'to have finished it, as a Jointure-House to her Consort Prince George of Denmark, but an expensive war, and that Prince's death before her prevented it'.

[301] The States General of the United Provinces had applied to the Queen to augment

Letters on that Subject, Ordered to take it into Consideration on Saturday.—The Duke of Leeds handed in a Petition of R. Squire, &c. in Answer to a former Petition of the Lord Wharton: who, haveing first rub[b]ed upon the Duke for not acquainting him with his haveing (according to the mannerly Custome among the Lords of the House) such a Petition against Him, desired that a Copy might be given Him, with time to put in his Answer. Which was granted.

The said Lord Wharton moved that a Day might be appointed for the 2d Reading of the Prince's Bill; and that all the Lords (and the Judges) might be Summoned to attend.[302] He observed to them that *it was possible* there might be something in that Bill which might highly merit their Consideration: As being either 1. Touching upon the Priviledges and Peerage of that House. 2. Affecting the late Act of Succession;[303] which he hoped, they would ever inviolably preserve. 3. Interfereing with a very late Order of their House (against Tacking) which, being subscribed by most of their Lordships, would not be easily departed from. In the Evening the Bishop of H[ereford] and I read over Dr Gibson's short *Commentary on the Schedule &c.*[304] for the use of Gentlemen, not at leisure to meddle with the Controversy[305] at length; and approved it, if not too long.

[Jan.] 8. *Friday.* After some Private Bills, the Duke of Devonshire reported the Reasons for insisting on the Amendments made to the Bill against Occasional Communion.[306] The most remarkable, 1. Presedents (in a Quire of paper) of Bills begun by the Lords with Penalties; or, if begun by the Commons, altered by the Lords: from Henry 7. as high as the Parliament Office reaches, down to the last of King W[illiam] 3. These (on a Motion by the Earl of Sunderland) ordered to be put into the Journal. 2. This Bill confined to the Test-

the English forces in the Netherlands to combat the expected French attack in the following spring. See the Queen's message read to the Lords on 9 Jan. 1703.

[302] The judges were expected to attend when called upon to do so to help the House with its judicial proceedings. Negligence in attending led in 1694 to the Lord Keeper ordering that two of the judges at least should be present every day during term time (*LJ* xv, 364).

[303] The Act of Settlement of 1701.

[304] Gibson published his sixty-four page pamphlet *A Short State of Some Present Questions in Convocation: Particularly, of the Right to Continue or Prorogue. By way of commentary upon the schedule of Continuation,* towards the end of Feb. 1703, see *Atterbury Epist. Corr.* iv, 381.

[305] i.e. Convocation Controversy.

[306] The Lords had amended the Commons' bill and sent it back to them on 9 Dec. The Commons agreed to some of the Lords' amendments and disagreed with others, and on 12 Dec. appointed a select committee for drawing up reasons to be offered to the Lords at a conference. These were delivered on 17 Dec. at a conference requested by the Commons. The Lords, on 8 Jan. 1703, sent the Commons a message desiring a conference on the 9 Jan. at 12 o'clock.

Act;[307] because the extent of this understood, and found useful by Experience; the Corporation-Act not so.[308] 3. Setting up or encourageing the Trade of Informers (by giveing them the whole Pecuniary Mulct) would be a Blemish on the best Reign.[309] 4. Incapacity[310] too high a punishment for goeing to a Conventicle; since the Bill assures us that Toleration shall still be preserved. 5. 'Twill disgust the foreign Protestant Churches, to find our English Subjects so Severely treated for comeing at their Assemblies here. To be given in at a Conference to morrow at 12 o'clock.

The Bishop of Peterborough offering an Amendment to a Private Bill, whilst it was reading the 3d time, stoped by the Earl of Rochester; who said 'twas Irregular, and should have been offered sooner. After the Lord Keeper [Wright] had read the Title, before the Question put for passing, allowed that the Amendment (if Literal onely, and such as might be altered by the Clerk at the Table) might now be made: And, it appearing that 'twas onely the correcting a Mistake in transcribing a Sign, the Bear and Key for the Bear and ragged staff, it was accordingly amended by the Clerk of Parliament and passed.

[Jan.] 9. *Saturday*. After the first Reading of the Act for continuceing the Duties on Coal and Culm, with other Private Bills, the business of the Day called for: And the Queen's Message was read, as follows;

"Anne R. Her Majesty haveing received several Letters from the States General of the United Provinces, as also several Memorials from their Ambassadors, setting forth the great Apprehensions

[307] The Act of 1673 (25 Car. II, c. 2) which enforced an Anglican sacramental 'test' on the holders of offices in the gift of the Crown.

[308] The original bill from the Commons sought to prevent occasional conformity not only by office-holders in the national government and armed forces but also by the municipal officers covered by the Corporation Act of 1661 (13 Car. II, St.ii, c. 1). The Lords in their fifth amendment to the bill left out the references to local officials (see Pittis, *Proceedings*, pp. 4–5), in effect emasculating the bill by neutralising its electoral influence. The Whig peers argued that the scope of the Corporation Act—whether it was meant to apply to petty officials as well as to mayors, aldermen, and councillors—had always been in dispute; and in their reasons the Lords defended their action by stating that they 'would not by this bill deprive men of their birth-rights' (ibid., p. 15). This clause was restored to the bill on 16 Jan.

[309] In the original bill the whole of the fine went to the informer. The Lords amended this in their eighth amendment to a third of a reduced fine.

[310] The original Commons' bill stated that the offender should not only be fined and deprived of his office, but 'shall be adjudged incapable to bear any office or employment whatsoever'. The Lords' ninth amendment said that 'loss of office [was] a sufficient punishment, without any incapacity, [which] was too great a penalty, and that it is hard to imagine any offence that is not capital, can deserve it . . .' (Pittis, *Proceedings*, p. 15).

they lye under from the Extraordinary preparations of France to attack them early in the Spring, and the Necessity, as they conceived, of makeing an Augmentation of the Forces of England and Holland, as the onely means to prevent the immediate Ruine which threatned their countrey, was pleased thereupon to propose some Expedients to the States General, which She hoped might have been of Advantage to the Common Interest; and relieved them, in some measure, from their just Apprehensions, without haveing Recourse to Her Parliament: But those Expedients Proposed, by Her Majesty to the States General, not haveing produced the Effect she hoped for, and the States haveing again renewed their Applications to Her Majesty, with more earnestness than before, to assist them, in this time of their Danger, with an Augmentation of Her Forces, as the only Means to Disappoint the Effect of these great and early preparations which the French are makeing against them; Her Majesty has commanded the several Letters and Representations, which have passed betwixt Her and the States General upon this Subject, to be herewith transmitted to you, that you may the better Judge of the Danger which threatens them. Her Majesty conceives this Matter to be of such great Consequence, as indispensably obliges Her to acquaint you with the Present State of it, that She may have your Advice upon it; not doubting but it will be such as will most tend to the Honour and Advantage of Her Majesty and Her Allies. St. James's Jan. 4. 1702/3."

The first that spoke to this was the Earl of Torrington; who moved that the Queen might be Addressed with an Assurance of the Readiness of this House to comply (as the Commons had done) with the Proposal of the Dutch; provided they would immediately Prohibit all Commerce and Correspondence with France and Spain. The Lord Townesend agreed to this motion; but added, that he thought the Lords ought likewise to acquaint Her Majesty that she had been imposed on by those of Her Counsel[311] who had told Her (for Delay's sake) that this matter could not be moved in Parliament without a Prorogation; And that it was another Delusion to propose (as appeared from the Memorials) to the States their bringing about an impossible Accommodation betwixt the two Northern Crowns,[312] and calling the Duke of Bavaria to Reason. This was seconded by

[311] The Cabinet Council in which the High Tories were strongly entrenched.

[312] Sweden and Poland. After the defeat of Denmark in 1700 the following six years in the Great Northern War were taken up with Charles XII of Sweden trying to defeat Augustus II of Poland.

the Earl of Carlile, who offered a form of words, to this purpose, which were such as none seemed to regard.

The Lord Hallifax, pitying the Ministry and all that were engaged in it, declareing that *he did not Envy men in their Posts*, proved (from examples of the last Reign, which Lord Nottingham observed were commonly extraordinary) that the Commons had frequently, without a Prorogation, voted new Supplies after their first Resolution of raiseing a certain Number — not exceeding so many men, or so much money.—Lord Wharton said this was so notorious that it was impossible the Earl of Nottingham, who sat so many years in the House of Commons, could be ignorant of it; and therefore (said He, slylie) who ever gave this false Account to Her Majesty, this Noble Lord could have no hand in it.

A Debate ariseing about the words *further Delay* in the intended Address (intimateing that the Ministers had already occasioned *one Delay*) the Lord Rochester moved that the word *further* might stand; Acknowledgeing that there had been a Delay, but (he hoped) no Criminal one. He was one of those, he said, who gave Her Majesty his Advice in this matter: And he thought the whole Council was unanimous in it. The Duke of Somerset beged leave to say that Himself dissented. If so (saies the Earl of Rochester) the Dissent was so modest, that I believe no body took notice of it. The Earl of Nottingham said, He was sensible the most of this was aimed at him; but, tho' he owned himself one of the Queen's Advisers, he was not yet conscious that he had offended in the least. If he was to fall under the Censure of their Lordships, he had two Comforts: 1. That he had acted in a Crowd; and therfore might hope that all his Companions would be Fellow-Sufferers with him. 2. That he should have the Testimony of his own Conscience that he suffered innocently and undeservedly. This was said with so much Courage, and so good a Grace, that the Opposers were struck mute. An Address was ordered, in pursuance of the first Motion, and the House adjourned; without comeing in with the proposed Reflections.

The Lord Hallifax observed that the Memorial, objecting the Difficulties of bringing any new matter into Parliament, was signed in Holland, Nov. 24. the Very Day that the Commons agreed on their first Numbers of men. Bishop of Norwich honestly advised me never to give a forward Voice for or against an Adjournment. The Temporal Lords saies he, do not love to see a Bishop offer to interpose in that matter; and I, in my own practice, have ever forborn it.

[Jan.] 10. *Sunday*. I preached, for Dr Birch,[313] at St Bride's on *Is[aiah]* 60, 2 and 3.——Dined (with Sir C. M[usgrave], Col. Graham, Mr Musgrave, Sir Thomas Hales, Mr Rider, Mr Ryley, &c.) at Lord Thanet's. Brought home, by Mr Hawley's, Sir H. Fl[etcher]'s and Mr Southwel's, by Mr C. M[usgrave].[314]

[Jan.] 11. *Munday*. Before prayers, I entered two Proxies (to my self) from the Archbishop of York and the Bishop of Bath and Wells. They were in the following Form: "Pateat Universis per presentes quod Nos Joahnnes Providentia Divina Archiepus Eboracensis Angliae Primus et Metropolitanus Revdum admodum in Christro Patrem ac Dnum Dnum Guilielmum eadem Providentia Carleol Epum nostrum verum et legitmum Constituimus Procuratorem ad Comparndum et Interessendum pro Nobis et Nomine Nostro in Presenti Parliamento Serenissimae Principis ac Dnae Nostrae Annae Dei Gratia Angliae, Scotiae, Franciae et Hiberniae Reginae, Fidei Defensoris, &c. tento, apud Westmonasterium. Necnon Negotijs in dicto Parliamento Exponend et tractand une cum Praelatis, Magnatibus et Proceribus, hujus Regni Angliae consentiend. Ratum et Gratum habituri totum et quicquid dictus Procurator Noster fecerit seu consenserit, quatenus ad Nos attinet in Praemissis. In cujus rei Testimonium Sigillum nostrum Episcopale Presentibus apponi fecimus. Datum apud Westmonasterium undecimo de Mensis Janris Anno Domini. Millesimo Septingentesimo Secundo in Nostrae Consecrationis 12°."

After one or two Private Bills, the Earl of Carlile reported the Address to the Queen according to the Instructions of Saturday: and [it was] Ordered that the Whole House present it, and that the Lords with the White Staves desire to know Her Majesty's Pleasure when she will be attended with it.——The Prince's Bill read a 2d time and committed to a Committee of the whole House; into which the House resolved it self immediately, the Lord Viscount Longvil [Longueville] takeing the Chair. The whole Bill read over again, Entire. Then, by paragraphs. The Title and Preamble (as usual) postponed, the first 2d. 3d. 4th. 5th. and 6th. paragraphs agreed to; without any Amendments. The 7th (impowering the Prince, or putting him into a Capacity of sitting in the House of Lords,

---

[313] Peter Birch (?1652-1710), Vicar of St Bride's, Fleet Street, since 1694.

[314] Sir Thomas Hales (1666-1748), 2nd Bt, MP for Kent, 1701-5, and Canterbury, 1715-41, 1746-7. Sedgwick, ii, 96-7. Possibly Thomas Ryder (d. 1728), MP for Maidstone, 1690-5, 1696-8, who with his Kent connections could be well known to both Thanet, his host, and Hales. Possibly James Hawley (b. 1676) of Brentford, son-in-law of Sir Chrisopher Musgrave, having married Dorothy, Musgrave's 2nd daughter. Possibly Edward Southwell (1671-1730), MP for Rye, 1702-8, Tregony, 1713, and Preston, 1713-15.

being a Member of the Privy-Counsel, &c. notwithstanding any Incapacities from the Succession-Act) objected against by the Earl of Carlile; who said the agreeing to this was directly contrary to their Order (against Tacking) of the 9th of December. Seconded by the Earl of Scarborough; who observed also that the passing of this would be a giveing up the Right of other Lords, that were Foreigners born.

The Lord North's opinion was that this Clause could not be called a Tack, as not being Foreign to the Title; which was, to support the Prince's Honour: Nor could it interfere with the Order of the House which respected onely Public Aids and Supplies. Lord Carlile replyed in a Repetition of what he had offered before. Earl of Rochester moved that (before the Debate went farther) the Clause of the Act of Succession might be read. Which done, Lord North (a little too forwardly, as was thought by his friends) asserted that, by this, the Prince would be excluded the House, if no Provision were made to the Contrary. *Then* (quoth the Earl of Feversham) *be gar I am kick out too; and therfore I will stick to the Prince, and the Prince shall stick to me.* Moved, that a Bill be brought in to indempnify all that were Lords when the Act of Succession passed.

Lord Haversham (with great warmth, as usual) desired that the Clause under Debate might be thrown out, by Amendment; because now was the time to affirm our Rights when no clamour was raised about public Dangers and Necessities, and when the Subscription of the late Order (against Tacks) was fresh in every man's memory. He said he'd as soon part with an Article of his Creed as with any Clause in the Act of Succession: And yet (what seemed a little Inconsistent) he was for secureing the Strangers[315] of that House, to whom the Nation was so much indebted.—Lord Raby professed himself a Subscriber, and yet for admitting the Clause; because he did not think this a Money-Bill.—Lord President (Earl of Pembroke) thought it was no Tack, because a Necessary part of the Bill; since the Prince could not, without this, have the Benefit of the other Clauses. The other Lords, in his Opinion, were already safe as to their Peerage: But, in this particular, he desired the Judges (who were present, haveing been ordered to attend for this very purpose) might be requested to give their Opinions.—The Lord Sommers said the Judges would certainly be very cautious how they gave their Opinions in this matter; since their predecessors had alwaies been wary in what concerned the Priviledges of this House: And it was most certain, he said, that the Commons ought to make less free with them; or, if they did venture further, what was offered from them should be

[315] i.e. the foreign-born peers.

rejected with the same Indignation, wherewith they would be sure to throw back any thing that should be sent from hence relateing to their Priviledges and Rights.

After some Heats on this Debate by the Duke of Marlborough, Lord Cholmley, Lord Privy-Seal [Normanby] &c. The Earl of Torrington moved that an Expedient might be considered on, how to grant the Prince all that this Bill pretended to give him in another manner; such as might not occasion any Disputes betwixt the two Houses: And, withal, such as might be more for the Honour of his Highness; since this, if it passed at all, would be carried in this House by a very slender Majority.—Upon which, the Lord Steward (Duke of Devonshire) proposed a separate Declaratory Bill; explaining the Act of Succession, and declareing that neither the Prince (nor any other Foreigner born, who sat in the House at the passing of that Act) was included in any incapicitateing Clause thereof. And that, for this End, the House might immediately be resumed. Earl Ryvers [Rivers] seconded this motion pretty warmly; professing that he was abundantly satisfyed that the Commons intended this 7th Clause as a Tack, designing hereafter to alledge it as a Precedent of that kind. Earl of Rochester wished that the Expedient might be offered in the Committee; where Lords would have a greater freedome in their Debates.

Lord Wharton, out of pure honour to the Prince, and that every thing intended for him might be put into a Method of passing *Nemine Contradicente*, pressed earnestly for Resumeing. Whereupon, the Question was put — *Whether the House be now resumed*? *Contents*, 54. *Not Contents*, 46. In the latter Number were the Bishops of London, Durham, Rochester, Exeter, St. Asaph and Carlile.[316]

The House being resumed, a strong Debate arose (which continued till after 7 o'clock) whether the Bill to be brought in should be Declaratory or Enacting;[317] which occasioned a new Question *Whether this Debate should be adjourned till Wednesday*? *Contents*, 61. *Not Contents*, 61. Among the former of these were the forementioned Bishops, with the Proxies of the Archbishop of York and the Bishops of Winchester, Landaff [Beaw] and Bath and Wells.[318] The latter carried it, according to the Rules or Orders of the House; which preferr the Negatives, in all Equal Divisions.

---

[316] The point of all this jockeying was that the Whig peers, while determined to put paid to any suspicion of a tack, were anxious not to appear inimical to the Queen's interests and prepared to advertise their loyalty in a formal session of the House and in the *Journals*.

[317] A declaratory act is one which declares or explains what the existing law is, while an enacting statute is one in which new provisions are brought in.

[318] The figures were *Contents* 47 (plus 14 proxies), *Not Contents* 54 (plus 7 proxies). Proxies could not be used in the previous division because the House was then in a Committee of the Whole House. Voting figures from HLRO MS Minutes, 11 Jan. 1703.

The next Debate (or Branch of the same) was about asking the Opinion of the Judges; which was, at last, agreed to. Before the Proposition was formed for them, the Lord Chief Justice Trevor[319] (by the Lord Keeper [Wright]) desired to be heard on the behalf of himself and his brethren: Which was agreed to. He said, the Judges were loath to give their Opinions in a Question wholly relateing to the Priviledges of Peers, upon any *request* whatever; and hoped their Lordships would excuse them from doeing it: But, if the Lords would lay their *Commands* upon them, they were ready to give them. This latter Method the Lords seemed not inclinable to take; and they would not insist upon the haveing their *Request* answered: So that, after a little more brandishing of Arguments, a Bill (*Enacting* and *declareing*) was Ordered to be brought in by the Judges; and the Prince's Bill to ly on the Table.

Mrs Stedman brought me a foolish Testimonial for her Husband;[320] and I foolishly subscribed it. 'Twas a particular Direction to the Officers (or Commissioners) of Excise.

[Jan.] 12. *Tuesday*. In the morning, I visitted the Archbishop of York; very much disordered with such pains as alwaies precede his severe Fits of the Stone and Gravel. He told me the Queen had hinted to the Archbishop of Canterbury how grateful to Her his promoteing the Prince's Bill would be; but had no clear Answer from him. He likewise acquainted me that he had heard of Dr Gibson's new Book, which was now goeing to the Press; And that he was verily perswaded it would effectually silence that Controversy.

In the House, most of the Day was spent in hearing Counsel on an Appeal of the Earl of Huntingdon's, from a Decree in favour of (his Stepmother) the present Countess Dowager.[321] After the Counsel were withdrawn, the Lords fell upon great Debates, and were much divided in their Judgements; till the Earl of Scaresdale (who had been privy to all the Secrets of the Cause) gave the House a much better Light than all the Counsel could do: Whereupon, the Decree was Unanimously Reversed in favour of the Earl.—The Lords were acquainted that Her Majesty had appointed to morrow (at 4 in the Afternoon) to be attended with their Address.[322]—The Bill for secureing the Foreign Lords read the first time, and ordered to be

---

[319] Sir Thomas Trevor (1658-1730), Chief Justice of the Common Pleas, 1701-14, had previously been MP for Plympton Erle, 1692-8, and Lewes, 1701. Created Lord Trevor of Bromham in 1712.

[320] Cispian Stedman, appointed tidesman in the port of London in Oct. 1702. *CTB 1702*, p. 366.

[321] For the case see HMC *Lords MSS* v, 155-6; *LJ* xvii, 236.

[322] See below, 13 Jan. 1703.

read a 2d time to morrow; to which time the Members of this House are to be summoned, and the Judges ordered to attend.

In the Evening, Dr Waugh, Dr Gibson and I paid a visit to Dr Lancaster, who was laid up in the Gowt. Dr Alston's pleasant account of his Landlord in Northamptonshire, who had marryed a Widow. *I heard she was rich; and so I fell in Love with Her*.

[Jan.] 13. *Wednesday*. A deal of Private Bills read in hast. After which, two Money-Bills (the one for continueing the Duties on Coal and Culm, and the other for purchaseing Annuities in the Exchequer)[323] read a second time, committed to a Committee of the whole House, and (immediately) reported without Amendment.

The Bill for Security of the foreign Lords read a 2d time, Committed, Reported (without any Amendments) and ordered to be engrossed.

A Message from the House of Commons; by Mr Annesly,[324] desireing a Free Conference on the Subject of the last Conference about the Bill against Occasional Conformity;[325] and, after the Report, the Messenger called in and acquainted that the Lords agree to a free Conference, at one o'clock on Saturday next, in the Painted Chamber.[326] A Bill for makeing the River Derwent in Derbyshire Navigable read a first time.[327] The Title, by a blunder of the Engrosser for the House of Commons, had called it Derwent Esqr. which (by the Earl of Torrington) was observed to be an Amendment not consented to by either House but this passed off in a smile. The Duke of Devonshire and other great Lords were concerned against it;[328] and the Archbishop of Canterbury, Bishop of Lichfeild,

[323] For Godolphin's method of raising loans to finance the war by the sale of long annuities which were administered by the Exchequer, see P. G. M. Dickson, *The Financial Revolution in England* (1967), pp. 59-62.

[324] Arthur Annesley, MP for Cambridge University, see Appendix A.

[325] The Lords' reasons for adhering to their amendments to the bill (see above, 8 Jan.) were given to the Commons in a conference on 9 Jan., and were reported to the House by Bromley. On 11 Jan. the Commons insisted upon their disagreement with the Lords and called for another conference. See Pittis, *Proceedings*, p. 9. The conference took place on 16 Jan.

[326] See fig. 1.

[327] A bill for making the River Derwent navigable from its junction with the River Trent up to Derby in order to cheapen the rates for carrying lead and other merchandise, and incidentally to preserve the highways of Derbyshire. See HMC *Lords MSS* v, 181-2, 186-7; below, 1 Feb. There had been an outburst of parliamentary activity on river navigation following the Peace of Ryswick, but the Derwent measure was one of the bills which failed to pass (*CJ* xi, 366). Strong opposition from Bawtry and Nottingham prevented any Derwent Bill passing until 1719, see T. S. Willan, *River Navigation in England, 1660-1750* (1936), pp. 29-30, 40-5.

[328] Devonshire, whose seat was at Chatsworth House, was the leading aristocratic land-owner in Derbyshire. A clause was inserted into the bill that no works for making the river

&c. for it. Upon the Debate, the Question was put (in Order to let it sleep forever) *Whether it be read a Second time on this day fortnight? Contents*, 30. *Not Contents*, 38. Amongst the latter were all the Bishops the first time that I had seen them unanimous. Lord Nottingham brought in Copies of some Letters from Admiral Rook, in pursuance of an Order of the House to that purpose. Earl of Torrington observed that the Order was for the Originals; and the Lord N[ottingham] assured the House (in Reply) that they were true Copies, and that himself had compared 'em. This satisfyed every body but the good Lord Haversham; who said he knew no Minister too great to observe the Commands of this House, and therfore he hoped their Lordships would insist upon haveing their Order more punctually obeyed. The Lord N[ottingham] replyed, that these Letters were from Secretary Hedges's[329] Office, and not his own; that he had faithfully obeyed the Commands of the House in laying before Her Majesty their literal Order; that the Queen had thought it enough to make this Return, and that (tho' he should ever acknowledge himself obliged to obey the Commands of the House, yet) he also thought himself obliged to obey His Royal Mistress; and if the House thought fit to command him to let Her know that they were not satisfyed with this Return, he would do it *Non pas*. The papers ordered to be given to the Committee appointed to inspect the Journals of the Admiral and Flag-Officers.

After Dinner, I went (tho' a little too late) to attend the presenting Her Majesty with the following Address:

"We your Majesty's most dutiful and Loyal Subjects, the Lords Spiritual and Temporal in Parliament Assembled, do return your Majesty our most humble thanks for Communicateing the several Letters and Memorials of the States General to this House, and haveing taken Notice how much time has been already Spent in this Negotiation, with what repeated and pressing Instances the States General have represented the Apprehensions they are under from the extraordinary and forward preparations of the French, do take leave humbly to advise your Majesty, That, without any further Loss of Time, You will be pleased to agree to the Proposeals made to your Majesty by the said States General, for such an Augmentation of Forces as may disappoint the great and early Preparations of France, and effectually support and defend the Common Cause. And we do further humbly acquaint your Majesty

navigable should be carried out on the estates of the Duke of Devonshire and the Earl of Chesterfield without their consent.

[329] Sir Charles Hedges, Secretary of State for the Northern Department, see Appendix A.

that it is the Opinion of this House, That your Majesty's furnishing your Quota of the Augmentation of Troops in the Low Countries will be ineffectual, unless all Correspondence with France and Spain, by Letters or otherwise, be totally prohibited by the States General and all other your Majesty's Allies."

From St. James's I went to pay a visit to Dr Smith in Dean Street; but, not finding him within, returned to my Lodgeings.

[Jan.] 14. *Thursday*. After a few Private Bills, the two public ones (of continueing the Duties on Coal and Culm and for purchaseing Annuities upon Funds in the Exchequer) read a 3d time and passed.

The Judges being come, 'twas moved that their opinions be asked, Whether those Foreigners who are now Lords of Parliament, and were so at the passing the Act of Succession, would be under all the Incapacities of that Act when in force? Lord Hallifax opposed the putting of this Query, as needless; since the House seemed unanimously resolved (however that matter might be stated) to pass the Explanatory Bill, now before them, in their favour. The Duke of Marlborough and Earl of Rochester observed that the Judges were summoned for this purpose; and therefore the Doubt ought to be proposed.—'Twas agreed accordingly. And Lord Chief Justice Holt[330] acquainted their Lordships that He and his Brethren had consulted on the matter under Debate; and were much divided in their Opinions. His own, he said, was that none of the present Members of this House would be under any of the Incapacities of the Act; because neither the Intention nor the Reason of the Law could be supposed to reach them. The Design of the Legislature appeared to be the provideing a *Security to our Religion and Government from and after the Death of His Late Majesty and the present Queen without Issue*. 'Twas then only that the House of Hannover could come in; and, as might be feared, bring with it a great Number of persons that were strangers to our Ecclesiastical and Civil Constitution. The Act apprehends no Danger till then, and therfore does not speak of *Depriveing*, but only forecloseing the new *Admission*, of Foreigners. He put the Case, Suppose this Act had provided that (after this Limitation of the Crown should take place) no Foreigner should marry an Heiress of 100 *l. per annum* in England, this would not certainly occasion a Divorce of any Foreigner from his Wife, who had so marryed before the Law was enacted. The preamble, in short, shewed the Intention of the Lawgivers; and this taught the Judges how to expound the Words.

[330] Sir John Holt (1642–1710), Lord Chief Justice of the Queen's Bench, 1689–1710.

2. Lord Chief Justice Trevor declared himself to be of a Contrary Opinion. The Judges, he said, were to expound all Statute-Laws according to the literal and Grammatical sense of its Words; or otherwise they would be for construeing in such a manner as was the same thing with the makeing of a Law. The words in this Act are General and Negative: As, None who is a Foreigner, Denison or Naturalized, &c. And there's onely one Exception, *for those that are born of English Parents.* No Limitation of time, Therfore all Peers, even such as are made so before this Act takes place, shall not (when it does take place) be Privy-Counsellors, nor sit in either House, because his Capacity is taken away (He *shall not be capable,* saies the Act) nor shall he *enjoy* Offices of Profit or Honour; and therfore (surely) not *keep* them.

3. Lord Chief Baron Ward[331] agreed with Lord Trevor. 4. Mr Justice Powel[332] joyned with Lord Chief Justice Holt: affirming that no Inheritance could be taken away by indefinite Expressions, such as were those of this Act; and that the word *Be* was capable of signifying futurely, as 'twas plain the word has did in this Law. 5. Mr Justice Powis[333] went into Lord Chief Justice Trevor and the Chief Baron; adding that the Law being political, and aiming at the preservation of the Government, was so to be expounded as might best answer that End. 6. Mr Justice Gould[334] supported the Opinions of Chief Justice Holt and Jutice Powel; declareing that this Act left the Reigns of King William and Queen Ann as it found them, haveing only a *Prospect* and no *Retrospect.*

7. Mr Justice Tracey[335] joyned with Trevor and Ward. 8. Mr Baron Bury[336] with Holt and Powel. 9. Mr Baron Price[337] did the like (in a nervous Speech) proveing that the Lords in Being were not reckoned amongst the Mischiefs against which this Act was to guard; for that (then) they would have been immediately deprived. 10. Mr Baron Smith[338] accorded with Trevor and Ward; putting their Arguments

---

[331] Sir Edward Ward (d. 1714), Chief Baron of the Exchequer, 1695–1714.

[332] John Powell (d. 1713), Justice of the Common Pleas, 1695–1702, and of the Queen's Bench, 1702–10.

[333] Littleton Powys (d. 1732), Justice of the Queen's Bench, 1702–26, and brother of Sir Thomas Powys, the eminent Tory barrister and MP for Ludlow.

[334] Sir Henry Gould (*c.*1644–1710), Justice of the Queen's Bench, 1699–1710.

[335] Robert Tracy (d. 1735), Baron of the Court of Exchequer, 1700–2, Justice of the Common Pleas, 1702–26.

[336] Sir Thomas Bury (1655–1722), Baron of the Court of Exchequer, 1701–6, Chief Baron of the Exchequer, 1716–22.

[337] Sir Robert Price (1653–1733), Baron of the Exchequer, 1702–26, of the Common Pleas, 1726–33, formerly MP for Weobley (Herefordshire), neighbour and friend of Robert Harley. See HMC *Portland MSS* iii–iv, *passim.*

[338] John Smith (d. 1726), Baron of the Exchequer, 1702–26, later Chief Baron of the Scottish Exchequer Court.

into somewhat of a new Dress. 11. Mr Justice Nevil[339] was indisposed: But Lord Chief Justice Holt acquainted the House that he was present at their Consultation, and had allowed him to tell their Lordships that his Sentiments were the same with his own. 12. Mr Justice Blencoe[340] was not in Town. The Bill was read a third time; and passed *Nemine Contradicente*.—In the Intervals of Business, I applied for Subscriptions to Dr Hickes's Book; and got 30 *l*. promised by the Earls of Kingston, Bridgewater, Sunderland (ready) and Warrington, Lord Longvil and Bishop of Hereford.

In the Evening I supped at Brother Joseph's with Cousin James Nicolson and his wife.[341]

[Jan.] 15. *Friday*. Mr Kinglove, in the morning, acquainted me with the Earl of Dalkeith's onely Son (by the Earl of Rochester's daughter) being just then dying;[342] the Lord H[enry] Scot a modest creature, when sober;[343] &c.—Before the sitting of the House engaged by Mr Atwood,[344] Author of the *Jani Anglorum facies nova*;[345] who offered me the perusal of a perfect Collection of his (now in the hand of my Lord Sommers) of Saxon matters, relating to the Constitution of their Government. He saies, He has demonstrated (from Doomesday-Book, &c.) that the Burroughs, before the Conquest, sent their Representatives to Parliament; which he also thinks plain from some of the Charters in Ingulfus. This Gentleman is a sharking, little, Fellow; sent lately to New-York for a Judge or (as he called Himself) a Chief Justice: But, takeing too much upon him, he was recalled lately, upon a Complaint from (the Governour) my Lord

[339] Sir Edward Nevil (d. 1705), Justice of the Common Pleas, 1691-1705.

[340] Sir John Blencowe (d. 1726), Baron of the Exchequer, 1696-7, Justice of the Common Pleas, 1697-1722.

[341] There were two 'cousin' James Nicolsons who are mentioned in the diary. (1) James Nicolson, of Castlegate, Carlisle (d. 1708), who was mayor 1689 and 1699. In 1690 he married his second wife, Sarah Bendish, who died in 1723. Of his children by his first wife, Jeremy is often mentioned in the diary. (2) James Nicolson, of Penrith, an attorney. His wife was Bridget Fetherstonhaugh of Kirkoswald, and of their children, the eldest son, Fetherston, is often mentioned in the diary. See *CW* i (1901), 48-51.

[342] James Scott (1674-1705), Earl of Dalkeith, was the eldest surviving son of Charles II's illegitimate son, the Duke of Monmouth and Buccleuch. He held his title by courtesy of his mother, the Duchess of Buccleuch in her own right. In 1694 he had married Henrietta Hyde, second daughter of the Earl of Rochester, who died in 1730. The 'only son' of the marriage referred to here was apparently Francis (b. 1695), though he survived the illness and in fact succeeded his grandmother in the dukedom in 1732.

[343] Henry Scott (1676-1730), third son of the Duke of Monmouth, created Earl of Delorain in 1706, he was a Scottish representative peer, 1715-30.

[344] William Atwood (d. 1705?), Whig barrister, and sometime Chief Justice in New York, who had been discharged in 1702 by the Governor, Lord Cornbury, for gross corruption. He was attacked by Nicolson in his book, *Border Laws*, published in 1705.

[345] Or *Several monuments of antiquity touching the Great Councils of the Kingdom*, published 1680.

Cornbury;[346] and is now under the Consideration of the Privy-Council.

After the reading of some Private Bills, an Appeal heard (for about three Hours) from one Powel and his wife, about some Houses in Dublin.[347] The Counsel being withdrawn, the Duke of Leedes took notice how scandalously Remiss the Lords had been in hearing that Cause; telling them that it put him in mind of an Observation of the late Duke of Buckingham,[348] who moveing for haveing a Cause of his own heard, the House came to a Division upon the Question. The present Lords carried it against the Duke; But, Proxyes being called for, His Grace had the better. Whereupon, he told them that he was more obliged to those Lords who were out of the House and had heard nothing of the Merits of his Petition, than to those that did hear it; and therfore (makeing his Leg) begged leave to go and make his Acknowledgements to them. This had such an Effect upon the Conscious, that they withdrew into a Corner; and left 13 of us, who were more attentive, to determine the matter. We were divided: and 7 of us gave our Voices for Affirming the Decree, against the Duke, and five more of the Contrary Opinion.

In the Evening Mr [Gilfred] Lawson came to my Lodgeings, and gave me an Account of the throwing out our Bill in favour of the foreign Lords;[349] the Commons resolveing to lay this *under their Table*, since We had laid the Prince's *upon Ours*. They also came to a Resolution of keeping the Malt Tax in their hands; tho' passed yesterday, and then ordered to be sent up to the Lords. The Speaker [Harley], Mr How[350] and others, for sending it up; opposed by Sir Edward Seymour,[351] Sir C. Musgrave, Coll. Granvil,[352] &c. Where will these things end? And, when (at this rate) will this Session be brought to a Conclusion?

NB. Yesterday the Lords ordered the printing of their Address, together with Her Majesty's most Gracious Answer; which was as follows:

[346] Edward Hyde (1661-1723), son of Henry, 2nd Earl of Clarendon, whom he succeeded in 1709. He was Governor of New York and New Jersey, 1701-8.

[347] For the cause see HMC *Lords MSS* v, 160-1.

[348] George Villiers (1628-87), 2nd Duke of Buckingham, member of 'the Cabal'.

[349] Peers of foreign extraction, such as Schomberg and Portland, tended, by and large, to vote with the Whigs in the House of Lords. There is a strong hint of the Tories' resentment at this, as well as of a more general xenophobia, in the manœuvres of both Houses over the Prince's Settlement Bill. See also the renewed Lords' debate of 19 Jan. on this bill, especially Nottingham's speech.

[350] John Grubham Howe (1657-1722), popularly known as 'Jack How', MP for Gloucestershire, 1698-1701, 1702-5, and previously for Cirencester 1689-98.

[351] MP for Exeter, 1698-1708. Being in the Cabinet as Comptroller of the Household, his obstruction of the Malt Tax, was a particularly offensive example of partisan politics.

[352] Hon. John Granville (1665-1707), MP for Cornwall 1701-3. Created Lord Granville in 1703.

"My Lords, No time shall be lost in relation to the Augmentation of Troops, and the Prohibition of the Commerce by Letters, recommended in this Address."

[Jan.] 16. *Saturday*. In the morning, I had a Letter from the Bishop of Bath and Wells; desireing that his proxy, in my hand, might be superseded:[353] And that the Clerks of the House might be acquainted that this was his pleasure, I applyed to the Clerks accordingly; and had for Answer, That the Proxy could not be taken off the File, nor vacated otherwise than by his own Appearance in the House.[354] This I reported by Letter to him, sick at Kensington; And immediately he posted to us, tho' (that very morning) he had assured Mr Richardson, that he could not for a world come to Town.

The House did not sit till betwixt Twelve and One. A little before Two, a message came from the House of Commons to acquaint their Lordships that their Managers had attempted to get to the Bar in the Painted Chamber; but could not for the Crowd: And therefore they prayed their Lordships to give Directions to clear the way.[355] My Lord great Chamberlain [Lindsey] [was] desired to do this:[356] But he returning told their Lordships that the thing was Impracticable, unless the Commons would call off their own Members. A message was sent, by two Masters in Chancery,[357] to this Purpose: Which being obeyed, the Conference began about a Quarter before Three, and lasted till half an hour after Seven. The Speakers of the Commons were Mr Bromley (who opened the Conference),[358]

---

[353] See above, 11 Jan. 1703 for when Nicolson entered this proxy. Richard Kidder, Bishop of Bath and Wells, was opposed to the Occasional Conformity Bill, and Nicolson, no doubt, had made his support for it clear. At the vote later in the day Nicolson voted for the bill and Kidder against it (see H. L. Snyder, 'The Defeat of the Occasional Conformity Bill and the Tack', *BIHR* xli (1968), 189). The Earl of Nottingham, Kidder's patron, had expected him to support the bill (see Snyder, p. 187 n; H. Horwitz, *Revolution Politicks* (1968), p. 262).

[354] Proxies could be vacated by letter as well as by appearance in the House (see M. F. Bond, *Guide to the Records of Parliament* (1971), p. 175), but during the reign of Anne this is only recorded as happening seven times (see HLRO Proxy Books, vii–viii, *passim*). Other methods of vacating proxies were death of either the holder or giver, or by the giver changing his proxy and thus superseding his previous one (both rare methods).

[355] The low and narrow corridors of 'the Parliament-House' were often a source of embarrassment to members of the Commons trying to get from St Stephen's Chapel to other parts of the Palace of Westminster. See, for example, Holmes, *Sacheverell* p. 123.

[356] He was responsible for running the Palace of Westminster.

[357] In a full session of the House, four Masters in Chancery sat on the woolsacks with the judges.

[358] On the Occasional Conformity Bill. The 'free conference in the painted chamber . . .', wrote Burnet later, 'was the most crowded upon that occasion that had ever been known; so much weight was laid on this matter on both sides' (Burnet, *History*, v, 53). The reasons put forward by the two Houses for their respective positions on the bill during this conference are printed in Pittis, *Proceedings*, pp. 10–34.

Mr St John,[359] Mr Finch, Mr Sollicitor General (Sir Simon Harcourt) and Sir Thomas Powis. The Lords were Lord Steward [Devonshire], Earl of Peterborough, Bishop of Sarum, Lord Sommers and Lord Hallifax.

Upon resumeing the House, Lord Steward made the Report.[360] Lord Haversham acquainted their Lordships that, whilst the Conference was depending, he had cast his eye into the Book of Proxies and had observed there was one entered since Prayers this morning which (he hoped) they would not suffer to be made use of in the Questions of this night. 'Twas Duke Schomberg's, given to the Prince. Whilst this was debated, the Duke himself (being privately sent for) came in person; but what Lord H[aversham] moved, being an Order of the House before, was now Ordered to be added to the Roll of Standing Orders.[361]

The Next great Debate was, whether the Question to be put on Each Amendment should be *Insist* or *Adhered*. 'Twas said that if the former was used, the Debates might be continued in some future Conferences on the same matter; whereas the latter would make the present Determinations final, as to this House. It was, at last, resolved that (since, in all probabillity, the Lords would severally abide by such Resolutions as they should now come to) the Question put upon the Reading of each Amendment respectively, should be — *Is it your Lordships pleasure to Adhere to this Amendment?* And, *as many of your Lordships as are for adhereing say Content*; &c.

Upon the Amendment to the Clause relateing to the Corporation-Act the Votes were Equal; *Contents*, 64. *Not Contents*, 64.[362] Amongst the latter were the Archbishop of York, Bishops of London, Durham, Winchester, Landaff, Rochester, Exeter, St Asaph, Oxford and Carlile. *Praesumitur pro Negante*.[363] The next was the Amendment to the Penalty.[364] Upon this the Bishop of Oxford divided with the Contents; telling us that he could not agree to the Tempting an Informer with so much money as the Commons had baited him with. This made the Voices 65 against 63;[365] and, being

[359] Henry St John, MP for Wooton Bassett, see Appendix A.
[360] See *LJ* xvii, 305-14. For the Commons' report, see *CJ* xiv, 180-3.
[361] Entered as no. 98. See HMC *Lords MSS* x, 22.
[362] There were five divisions in the House on 16 Jan. on amendments to the bill. According to the Manuscript Minutes of the House, this division was the third that day. For a discussion of these five divisions, the voting pattern of the peers, and a comparison between the official version of the votes and those of Nicolson and Burnet (in *History*, v, 53-4), see Snyder, pp. 173-4, 187-90.
[363] The negatives carry the vote in a tie, consequently the clause penalising municipal officers was restored to the bill.
[364] See above, 17 Dec. 1702.
[365] According to the Manuscript Minutes of the House, this vote took place before the one Nicolson records above.

the Cardinal Question which determined the Fate of the whole Bill, the rest of the Points were given up without comeing to any Division.[366]

The Cause being thus lost, about Eleven at night, we came sneaking home to our Lodgeings.

[Jan.] 17. *Sunday*. I preached for Dr Lucas[367] at St Stephens in Colemanstreet, on *Romans* 12, 9. an old Sermon on part of the Epistle for the Day: But, so it happened, there were several particulars in it touching the Hypocrisy of Occasional Communion, which made it doubly Seasonable. As I came from the pulpit, Mrs   [368] put some Papers into my hand, which (she pretends) were intended for the use of the Queen *in scriptis*; but, being ill treated by the Yeomen of the Guard and disappointed, she now publishes them, in hopes that some or other will hand them to Her Majesty.

The Resurrection, on the South Door of the Church-yard, finely carved in wood.[369]

[Jan.] 18. *Monday*. Mr Davison[370] and Mr Hawley with me in the Morning. Dr Gee, in the Lobby, gave me an Account of the Rise of Lord Haversham's father[371] in the East-India-Company; one of his Daughters marryed to Mr Gregory, a Clergyman, and two more to two broken Brewers.

The Bill of the Malt-Tax brought up by Mr Conyers; attended chiefly by Whigs, to shew (forsooth) their zeal for the Support of the War.

Earl of Peterborough's Cause being put off till Wednesday, the Duke of Marlborough moved that the Prince's Bill might be considered to morrow: which was agreed to. The Duke of Bolton desired that a Message might be sent to the Commons for Leave to Sir G[eorge] Rook and Sir Thomas Hobson[372] to attend the

[366] There were three other votes that day, see Snyder, pp. 173–4, 187–90.

[367] Richard Lucas (*c*.1649–1715), the blind Rector of St Stephens, Coleman St., since 1678.

[368] Blank in MS.

[369] A Wren church, St Stephens, Coleman St., was bombed in 1940 and the ruins demolished.

[370] Possibly Thomas Davison (1682–1748), son of Mary (d. 1728), daughter and heir of Sir Richard Musgrave, 3rd Bt., of Hartley. *Armorial*, p. 97.

[371] Maurice A. Thompson (d. 1671), of Haversham, Bucks. A trader to Virginia, the West Indies, and Guinea in the 1640s, he was Governor of the East India Company 1657–9. *Calendar of Court Minutes of the East India Company, 1655–9* (Oxford, 1916), pp. 197, 267. He was the guiding spirit behind the 1651 Navigation Act. For an outline of his career see J. E. Farnell, 'The Navigation Act of 1651, the First Dutch War, and the London Merchant Community', *EcHR* 2nd ser. xvi (1963), 443–6.

[372] Sir Thomas Hopson (d. 1717), second in command under Rooke on the Cadiz expedition, he had led the van at Vigo Bay. Knighted in Nov. 1702, he had retired from the navy as Vice-Admiral of the Red.

Committee appointed to inspect the Journals of the Duke of Ormond, &c.

Coll. Grahme, Mr Dean and I dined at the Bishop of Durham's; where I innocently enquired, who was the Duke of South[ampton]'s Father in Law. My Lady Crew answered—thereby hangs a Story: Query. Whether Sir William Portman or H[enry] Guy?[373] A visit, in the Evening, to Dr Younger.

[Jan.] 19. [*Tuesday.*] Lord Keeper reported the Commons would send an Answer by Messenger of their own: which came not this day. The Malt-Bill read a 2d time, Committed and ordered a 3d reading. The Prince's Bill being called for, and the House resolveing it[self] (according to the Order of the Day) into a Committee to consider it.—The Duke of Marlbrough opened the Cause with an earnest Request that, since their Lordships had been unanimous in passing a Bill (rejected by the Commons) in favour of all the Foreign Lords, they would be as much one in shewing their Respects to the Prince.

Lord Carlile first Opposed the Clause; prefaceing his Speech (as all the rest of the Malecontents did) with high professions of Honour for the Prince: But insisted upon it that 'twas a Tack, and would be such a Declarative Explanation of the Act of Succession as would effectually conclude all the now foreign Lords under the Incapacities of that Statute. To the same purpose spoke the Lord Steward [Devonshire], Sommers, Townesend, Wharton, Haversham, Scarborough and Hallifax.

The Bishop of Sarum was under great perplexity, the highest Obligations of Duty and Gratitude to the Prince, to the education of whose hopeful Son (the late Duke of Gloucester)[374] he had Dedicated the whole Remainder of his Life; believeing that hereby he should have done a most acceptable Service to this Church and Kingdome: But Justice, he observed, was to take place of Gratitude, and he thought it would be an apparent Injustice to the other Foreign Lords, if this Bill should now pass in favour of His Highness. Who, said he, is the Son and Brother of a King;[375] and therfore the

---

[373] Sir William Portman (1644–90), Bt., MP for Taunton, 1661–79, 1685–7, 1689–90, and Somerset, 1680–1. Henry Guy (1631–1710) MP for Hedon, 1670–81, 1685–7, 1689–95, 1702–5. The father-in-law of the Duke of Southampton (who was a bastard son of Charles II) was, in fact, Sir William Pulteney, of Misterton, whose daughter the duke had married in 1694, having previously (1671) been married to the only daughter of Sir Henry Wood, Bt., Clerk of the Green Cloth (d. 1671).

[374] Burnet had been the unwilling tutor of Queen Anne's only surviving son from 1698 until the duke's death in 1700, see Burnet, *History*, iv, 385–6.

[375] Prince George was the second son of Christian V of Denmark (1670–99) and brother of Frederick IV (1699–1730).

sitting in this House or the being a Member of the Privy-Counsell (in any future Reign, if he and we should be so unhappy as to live to 't) could not be reckoned any Honour or Dignity to him.'

The Earl of Nottingham agreed with the Bishop in his *Doctrine*; but would not allow of his *Application*. He admitted that Gratitude was a very pressing Duty; and could not see how (in this Case) it was in Competition with Justice. If their Lordships had lately thought it a doeing Justice to all the Foreign Lords, in passing that Bill which they had sent to the Commons, he hoped they would now do the like Justice to the Prince; who, saies he, is not to be blamed for the miscarriage of your other Bill below, nor ought he to suffer for it. He craved leave to differ from the Reverend Prelate, in believeing that the Sitting in the House and the Enjoyment of [an] English peerage would be an Honour to the Prince; whose Dignity (in being the Son &c. of a King) he would not lessen: But he would take the Liberty to Say that His highest Title here was Duke of Cumberland, which would be much Eclypsed if he could not bring into this House. He thought it was the Interest of the other Six Lords[376] to give their Concurrence to this Bill; the passing whereof might pave the way for the like Respects to themselves hereafter.

The Earl of Feversham took this opportunity of returning his thanks to their Lordships for the care which they had taken of Himself and the other Foreigners; declareing that he should be sorry that His Royal Highness should suffer on their Accounts and therfore he was for passing the Clause. The Lords on the other side of the Question, with whom he had joyned before, raised a great Laughter; somewhat inconsistent (as I thought) with the Gravity of so wise and great an Assembly.—The Duke of Leeds closed the Debate with an Account of what he judged the true Definition of a Tack; which, he said, was ever understood to be such an unreasonable Demand upon either the Prerogatives of the Crown, or the Priviledges of this House, as the Commons could no otherwise compass than by crowding it into a Money-Bill for a Necessary Aid or Supply: And, since nothing of that kind was here, no more than what related to the Rights and Pretensions of a Private Person, he could not see why such an Objection should be offered against the passing of this Clause.

Hereupon the Question was put (by the Lord Viscount Longvil, who was Chairman) *Whether this clause shall stand part of the Bill? Contents,* 48. *Not Contents,* 48. So — The Committee (after a long struggle, who were the Negatives in this Case) laid it aside.

[376] Foreign-born peers, *viz.* the Duke of Schomberg, and the Earls of Albermarle, Feversham, Grantham, Portland, and Rochford.

The Bishop of London came in dureing the Debate, and after the first Division: But (upon the next Head, which was a Clause of Provision for the Security of Former Grants to several persons out of the Post-Office, Excise, &c.)[377] the Advantage was on the other side, *Contents*, 49. *Not Contents*, 43;[378] five of the latter, seeing their Cause lost, haveing left the House. Amongst the former were the Bishops of London, Durham, Rochester, Exeter, St Asaph and Carlile. Proxies were not called for. The House being resumed,[379] the Question was put — *Whether this House agrees with the Committee's in rejecting the Clause now read?* It passed in the Negative.[380] Whereupon, the Bill was read a Third time; and passed without any Amendments.[381]

[Jan.] 20. *Wednesday*. After a Third Reading and passing of a Couple of Bills, for the makeing the River Cam Navigable[382] and repairing the Pier at Yarmouth,[383] the Earl of Peterborow's Appeal: the Hearing whereof lasted 5 hours. The Appellant's Case was signed by Bowyer and Sloan,[384] but pleaded by Sir Simon Harcourt and Mr Cowper.[385] This gave occasion to Serjeant Hooper[386] (one of the Counsel on the Respondent's side) to observe that the Earl's Cause had quite another face at the Bar from what it had in the Paper: Which Remark wrought wonders in the Countenance of Mr Sloan, who was one of the By-standers, the rest laughing aloud or smileing abundantly. The Hinge of the Cause was upon two Deeds (of the

[377] The Dukes of Southampton, Grafton, and Northumberland (HLRO MS Minutes of the House of Lords, 19 Jan. 1703). These three were all the illegitimate sons of Charles II by Barbara Villiers, Duchess of Cleveland. She had secured various grants of land and pensions for herself and her sons, including £5,000 out of the Post Office (*GEC Peerage*).

[378] The vote was on 'whether the House shall be now resumed', and the voting was *Contents*, 43, *Not Contents*, 49. HLRO MS Minutes of the Lords, 19 Jan. 1703.

[379] Nicolson appears to be wrong here, as the vote above was against resuming the House.

[380] The question 'whether this clause shall stand part of the bill was resolved in the affirmative' without a vote. Ibid. Nicolson's errors of detail over the various votes may be due to his method of composition of the diary, see above, Chapter 3, pp. 109–13.

[381] The frustrated Whigs had to content themselves with registering protests in the *Journals*. See below, 20 Jan.

[382] Cam *alias* Grant River Navigation Act (1 Ann. 2, c. 11). See HMC *Lords MSS* v, 187–8; *LJ* xvii, 248.

[383] Yarmouth was the main port for providing ships for the Newcastle coal trade in 1702–4, and was the second port in Britain (excluding London) by number of ships (after Bristol) and fourth by tonnage (after Bristol, Ipswich, and Newcastle) J. H. Andrews, 'English Merchant Shipping in 1701', *Mariner's Mirror*, xli (1955) 232–5.

[384] According to HMC *Lords MSS* v, 176, the case was signed by James Sloane and John Chesshyre.

[385] William Cowper, MP for Beeralston, and later Lord Chancellor, 1705–10, see Appendix A.

[386] Nicholas Hooper (c.1654–1731), MP for Barnstaple 1695–1715; Serjeant-at-Law, 1700, Queen's Serjeant, 1702.

14th and 16th of Car[olus] 1.) by the former whereof the Lady Mary Mordaunt, sometime Dutchess of Norfolk and now one of the Respondents, claimed the Lands in Question; as the Earl of Peterborough did by the latter.[387] It was pleaded, by the Appeleant, that this of the 16th was upon *Purchase* and a *Valuable* Consideration; whereas the other was purely Voluntary, and therfore (tho' prior in Time) was much the less valid and preferable. Two Acts of Parliament had passed in favour and Establishment of that of the 14th. But to this it was said that the Common Exception in the End of all Private Bills (saveing to every one their just Rights) removed that Objection. When 'twas asked, *Why the Appellant had not laid his claim before the Parliament?* It was answered, He was a Minor and beyond the Seas. [This, by the way, might be true as to the passing of the first Act; but could not be so, at the second.][388]

The Counsel being withdrawn and the House resumed, the Lord Keeper [Wright] (at the Request of the Lords) gave his Opinion that both the Deeds *Voluntary*, and of Equal Regard in themselves, preferable onely according to their Respective Dates; that the Earl's Title (if he had any) was Maintainable at Common-Law; that, for these Reasons, he had dismissed the Cause out of Chancery. Hereupon, the House Ordered that one Counsel (on either side) should be heard on Friday next upon this single point — *Whether the Cause might be most conveniently tryed by Ejectment or a feigned Issue?*

NB. Whilst this Appeal was hearing, came a Message (by Mr Charles Boyle)[389] from the House of Commons; to acquaint their Lordships that, according to their Request, that House had given Leave to Sir George Rook and Sir Thomas Hobson to attend their Lordships Committee; they haveing desired the same their Selves: And that they would attend accordingly on Munday next.

After the Appeal was over, a Protestation was offered against the passing of the Prince's Bill; and was entered in the Journal, and subscribed, in the following words:

"We dissent from this Clause (that of Capacitateing His Highness to sit in the House of Lords &c.) because, 1. We conceive this

[387] Lady Mary Mordaunt (c.1659–1705), daughter and heir of Henry, 2nd Earl of Peterborough, had married in 1677 Henry Howard, 7th Duke of Norfolk (1655–1701), and had been separated (1685) and finally divorced (1700) from him by act of parliament for her misconduct with Sir John Germaine, whom she had married in 1701. In 1697 she succeeded her father in the barony of Mordaunt and in the family property of Drayton Manor, which her cousin, the 3rd Earl of Peterborough, unsuccessfully tried to obtain (see HMC *Lords MSS* iv, 67; v, 173–8; viii, 348–50, for the cause): Peterborough succeeded her in the barony, but she settled the disputed estate on her second husband.

[388] Nicolson's brackets.

[389] Hon. Charles Boyle (1674–1731), MP for Huntingdon, 1701–5, who succeeded his brother as 4th Earl of Orrery [I] on 30 Aug. 1703.

is a Bill of Aid and Supply, and that this Clause is altogether foreign to, and different from, the Matter of the said Bill; and that the passing of such a Clause is therfore Unparliamentary, and tends to the Destruction of the Constitution of this Government. 2. Because we conceive that a Parliamentary Expedient might have been found, whereby His Royal Highness might, by an Unanimous Consent, have had all the advantages designed him by this Bill, without the Lords being obliged to depart from what we conceive to be their undoubted Right. 3. Because we conceive that this Clause was not necessary to enable His Royal Highness to enjoy the Benefit of the said Grant. 4. Because this Clause, which pretends to Capacitate His Royal Highness to Enjoy His Peerage, notwithstanding the Act for the further Limitation of the Crown and better Security of the Rights and Liberties of the Subject,[390] and which makes no provision for other peers under the same Circumstances, we conceive may tend very much to their Prejudice."

Torrington Manchester
Say and Seale Kingston
John Lichfeild and Cov[entry].[391]

"We dissent from the Clauses relateing to the Grants, 1. Because the said Grants were not laid before the House (tho' desired) by which we are ignorant upon what Considerations the same were granted. 2. Because we conceive that the saveing Clauses are so far from haveing any Relation to His Royal Highness, that, if they signify any thing (without any Respect to him) they prefer their Payment before His."

Somerset Wharton
Carlisle E[arl] M[arshal]   Mohun
Stamford Lovelace
Devonshire Essex
Say and Seale   Bergavenny
Thomas Cantuar   Towneshend
W[illiam] Worcester   Pawlet
John Chichester   Berkley of Stratton

[390] Formal title of the Act of Settlement.
[391] This protest was also signed by Lords Ossulston, Portland, and Somers. It was entered in the Journals on the 19 Jan. 1703, see *LJ* xvi, 247. None the less, Nicolson is probably correct in stating that the protests were signed on 20 Jan. On 7 Feb. 1689, after the crucial vote on the abdication of James II on the previous day, 'In the morning several of the Lords met before the sitting of the House, to enter their dissent; which could not be done yesterday, the Journal-Book not being made up; but must (by the usage of parliament) be entered before the rising of the House the next sitting, as part of the proceedings of the preceding day.' A. Simpson, 'Notes of a Noble Lord, 22 January to 12 February 1688/9', *EHR* lii (1937), 95.

Huntingdon   Rockingham
Richard Petriburg.   John Lichf[ield] and Cov[entry]
Sunderland   Gilbert Sarum
Bolton
Rivers[392]

In the Evening, at Dr Lancaster's with Dr Alston and Archdeacon Drew.[393] Dr A[lston]'s Grandmother (who dyed at 82) lived to see 700 of her own Progeny. The Doctor's way of Digging ground for planting of Fruit-Trees; throwing in the Upper-Turf to the bottome of a Shaft's Depth, and fattening the Surface by sowing of Turneps for a year or two. Portugal-Snuff an Excellent Remedy for a Green wound.

[Jan.] 21. *Thursday*. Over the Door on the Inside of the House of Office[394] of the Commons-H[ouse] this Mottoe.

A F—rt's as good as Land,
Ile take my Oath.
We hold them both in Tail,
and let them both.

Discourseing, at a Private Committee, of the Reasons of the Protesting Lords, &c. Lord Chandois [Chandos] observed they were like that of the Spark upon the Road, *Your Horse has dashed me; therfore you are the Son of a Wh[ore]*. After the quick Dispatch of some Private Bills, Three several Messages (without Intermission) from the House of Commons, with more Bills.

Lord Wharton put in his Answer to the Petition of Mr Squire against a former Complaint of his Lordship's about a Record in the Exchequer which He would have this House to order to be taken off their File as forged and a Counterfeit. Ordered to be Argued at the Bar to morrow, with a Counsel on each side. Lord Radnor moved that as many other Lords as pleased might be allowed to subscribe the Protestation entered yesterday: which was assented to. He also acquainted the House that tho' he had formerly opposed the passing of a Bill for Regulateing the King's Bench-Prison (haveing a Mortgage upon its Revenues) yet He was so well satisfyed with the Honest Design, and great Necessity, of that before Their Lordships, that he would readily consent to it's being enacted: Whereupon,

[392] The following peers also signed this protest: the Earls of Rochester and Orford, Lord Herbert of Chirbury, and the Bishop of Bangor. Like its predecessor, this protest was also entered on 19 Jan., see *LJ* xvi, 247.

[393] Edward Drew (*c*.1644–1714), Archdeacon of Cornwall, since 1672 and Chancellor of Exeter since 1675.

[394] i.e. the closet or bog, see fig. 1.

Saturday appointed for a Committee of the whole House to sit upon it.

Duke of Richmond offered a Petition for the bringing in of an Appeal; which being Read, the Lord Rochester wished it might be withdrawn since 'twas not intended that (as the Duke himself owned) any Process upon the Decree in Chancery should be stopped, as it certainly would in case the Parliament should be prorogued before the Cause was heard. Lord Wharton said the House was already in possession of the Appeal, by Reading the Petition, which could not now be withdrawn: But yet, at the Request of the Promoter, 'twas allowed that it might be withdrawn; as it was, &c. An Order entered that no more Appeals be received this Session. An Appeal from the Company of Haberdashers,[395] patrons of a Charity at Newlands in Gloucestershire; which, it appeared, they had most vilely mismanaged. The Decree against them [was] affirmed; and 10 *l.* Costs awarded for this Hearing.

In the Evening, I visitted (my good neighbour) the Bishop of Hereford, ill in a Cold; who gave me his Welsh Translation of Dr Ashton's[396] Treatise against Swearing.

[Jan.] 22. *Friday*. After some Public and Private Bills, The Counsel of the Earl of Peterborough and Lady M[ary] Mordaunt (Sir Simon Harcourt and Sir Thomas Powis) were called in, and heard upon the Question stated on Wednesday last. The former observed that the House haveing reduced the whole Controversy to the two Deeds, (of 14. and 16. Car[olus] 1.) whether of these was to take place[397] would be most easily and readily determined by *a feigned Issue*; because, upon Tryal by Ejectment, a thousand other Incident matters might come under Consideration, and this point never be touched. Sir Thomas Powis (on the Contrary) alledged that the tyeing down a Defendant, in this manner, and restraining him from such other Defence as the Law allowed, was such a breaking in upon the Common-Law of England (and the property of the Subject) as, he hoped, would never be countenanced by their Lordships. The Opinions of the Judges present (Lord Chief Justice Holt, and three more) being asked, they unanimously agreed with Sir Thomas Powis: Whereupon, the Decree was absolutely affirmed against the Earl.

After this, The Preliminary Query on my Lord Wharton's Appeal against an Inter-locutory Order (as his friends called it) of the Barons

[395] HMC *Lords MSS* v, 152-3.

[396] Charles Ashton (1665-1752), classical scholar and theologian, he was Master of Jesus College, 1701-52, Vice-Chancellor of Cambridge University, 1702-3, and a Prebendary of Ely, 1701-52.

[397] i.e. precedence.

of the Exchequer for the fileing up of a Record in that Court (i.e. Whether such a matter as this could be brought before the Lords by way of Appeal?) was likewise argued by one Counsel on each side, according to the Order of Thursday last. Mr Cowper, on behalf of Mr Squire and Mr Thompson,[398] against whom the Lord Wharton had first petitioned, and they afterwards against His Petition, alledged that His Clients could no way be obliged to answer here; haveing had no dealings (in the Court of Exchequer) with this noble Lord: That, if any could be brought before their Lordships on the Subject-Matter of this Complaint, it was the Barons of the Exchequer who were to be made Respondents: That, even these had done nothing but what they were obliged, in Conscience and by their Oaths, to do; and what was the dayly practice of their Court: That, upon the Whole, this was purely an Original Cause; and ought not (as he humbly conceived) to be admitted to a Hearing by their Lordships at the first Instance.

Mr Sollicitor (Sir Simon Harcourt) was Counsel on the other side; and said little more than that here was a practice suggested, of forgeing a Record, which was well worth their Lordships' Enquiry after: And that the Noble Lord was Remedyless, unless they Relieved him. Mr Cowper Replyed that (in all appearance) the Record was Genuine, and therfore was not (indeed, could not) be parted with at any Suit of this Lord, who happened to be aggreived by it; since the Queen and all the Subjects of England had a Property in it, as well as the Barons of the Exchequer. As to the Objection of the Lord Wharton's being without Remedy, So (saies he) it may happen in many other Cases, as, in that of a Jury-man's withdrawing himself, of a Judge's giveing wrong Instructions, &c. wherein it never yet was pretended that there lay an Appeal to the Lords.

Upon the withdrawing of the Counsel these particulars were debated over again: And, at last, the Question being put, it was carryed (upon a Division)[399] in favour of the Lord Wharton. This occasioned the following Protestation:

22 Jan. 1703

"After hearing Counsel upon the Petition of the Right Honourable Thomas Lord Wharton, as also the Petition of Robert Squire Esqr. and John Thompson; the Question was put Whether the Petition of Robert Squire and John Thompson shall be dismissed,

---

[398] John Thompson, Attorney in the Queen's Remembrancer's Office in the Exchequer. HMC *Lords MSS* v, 170.

[399] No division recorded in MS Minutes of the House. The question, 'whether Squires and Thompsons petition be dismissed and they ordered to answer', was resolved in the affirmative.

and they ordered to Answer? It was Resolved in the Affirmative. Dissentient. 1. Because we conceive that by this we assume a Jurisdiction in an Original Cause; for these Reasons:

1. Because there has been no Suit between the Parties in the Court of Exchequer and consequently this Petition cannot be called an Appeal from that Court.
2. Although there was a Suit in the Court of Chancery, yet one of the Persons required to answer, was not a Party in that Suit and therfore, as to him at least, it must be an Original Cause.
3. Though all had been Parties in the Chancery, yet it never was heard that an Appeal lay from one Court that had no Suit depending in it, because there was a Suit depending in another Court.

2. Because no Court can take any Cognizance of a Cause, in which that Court cannot make an Order: But, in this Case, the House of Lords cannot make an Order, because very many are concerned in this Record who are not before this House. Therfore this House cannot take any Cognizance of it."

Leedes   N[athaniel] Duresme
Nottingham   Tho[mas] Roffen
Rochester   Jonat[han] Exon
Towneshend[400]   W[illiam] Carliol[401]
Weymouth Pawlet
            Dartmouth

[Jan.] 23. *Saturday.* A numerous Committee (Duke [of] Bolton, Chairman) met upon the Journals of the last Summer's Expedition, before whom Sir George Rook and Sir Thomas Hobson, by leave of the House of Commons, were ready to appear. About an Hour being spent in finding out and modelling the Questions, which both Houses thought had been in Readiness a week agoe, Sir George was called in; and, being acquainted with the Reason why the Committee desired his appearance, he requested that he might hear all their Questions read over; That, if they were of a simple and unmixt kind, he might either answer to them immediately; Or, if they were of a Complicated Nature and such as would require the Consulting his papers, he might be allowed a Copy of 'em, and he would return his Answers in writeing. This was agreed to; and, the Clerk haveing read them

---

[400] Lord Townshend was the only Whig to declare in writing against Wharton.
[401] This is the first of six protests Nicolson signed during the sixteen years he sat in the House. Three of the others were signed on 11 Jan. 1711 and the remaining two on 3 Feb. 1711, see Rogers, *Protests*, i, 167, 199–205.

accordingly, he told their Lordships that he had not observed (as far as he understood 'em) any Difficulty in any of these Question: So that he now desired that he might answer immediately.

I was obliged to read Prayers in the House, and twice or thrice called out on other occasions, so that I could not attend the whole Examination; but the Substance of what I heard was this:[402] *Question* 1. Why did you not call a Council [of] Warr, and Resolve in what manner Cadiz was to [be] attacked, before you came before the place? *Answer*. Our Instructions were otherwise; nor had we any Certainty of the Condition of the Town till we came there. Yea but (Objected the Earl of Torrington) you might have consulted; and come to Conditional Resolutions. *Reply*. If your Lordships' Reasons had been with us, no doubt they would have prevailed. *Question* 2. What Report did your Engineer and other Scouts, who were sent to S[an] Pedro, make upon their Return [?] *Answer*. That there was good Landing on the back of Isle. *Question* 3. Why did you not land in the Isle of Cadiz? *Answer*. Because the Council of War resolved that we should land in the Isle of Bulls.[403] Lord Torrington objected that it was as easy to land in Cadiz. *Reply*. Noe. The other a much better Shore; not to mention other Reasons. *Question* 4. Were all the Queen's Instructions communicated to the Council of War? *Answer*. Yes: and, at every Council, lay alwaies upon the Table. *Question* 5. Were the Council Unanimous for landing at the Isle of Bulls? *Answer*. Yes. Every one either openly assented, or was Silent. NB. It was observed that the Duke of Ormond's[404] hand was not subscribed to this· Resolution. In Reply to which, Sir George told their Lordships that His Grace often agreed, when he did not subscribe; as, when the matters before the Council were such as related chiefly to Sea-Affairs. The Duke, who was present, acknowledged it. *Question* 6. Why was not the Town of Cadiz bombarded? *Answer*. It could not be done from the Fleet till Fort de S[anta] Catharina[405] was taken; it being impossible for the Ships to ly betwixt these two, without being insulted from one or the other. To this the Earl of Torrington objected that these were five miles distant from each other; but, granting (said he, what was allowed by Sir George) that distance is only betwixt three and four, surely a ship may pass safely

---

[402] Cf. Rook's own record of this committee of inquiry in *The Journal of Sir George Rook*, ed. O. Browning, Naval Record Society, ix (1897), 241–8. This edition, however, should be used with care, see a review of the volume in *EHR* xiii (1898), 171–4.

[403] There is a useful map of the operations before Cadiz, Aug.–Sept. 1702, in Trevelyan, *Queen Anne*, i, 264.

[404] Commander of the troops on the expedition.

[405] This fort commanded the south-eastern tip of the Bay of Bulls and lay to the northeast of Cadiz.

enough 'twixt these without suffering from either. Sir George said, the Question was not now whether a Single Ship, under sail and upon Motion might pass that road, but whether a Bombardment could be made from thence; that requireing the bringing in of the whole Fleet, which must ly still and have a deal of Sea-Room. *Question* 7. Why were not some greater Ships sent in, since the small ones were found Insufficient? NB. This Question was not understood at first, on either hand: But, at last, the Lords observed that in one of the Journals (of an inferiour Flag-officer) it appeared that a Resolution was taken, after we were in possession of St. Catherine's Fort, to attempt the Bombardment of Cadiz; and that to this purpose some Light Ships were sent in: But, these proveing insufficient for the purpose, the Design fell. And, why then (say the two old Admirals, Torrington and Orford)[406] did you not send in larger? *Answer*. Because the biggest of these small ones were too large. There was onely 4 fathome of Water; in which a Ship of 60 Guns could hardly ride, without being put under such service. *Question* 8. Whether, when some of the Sea-men went on Shore with the Land-forces, any orders were given against plundring? *Answer*. Noe: For I never imagined that such a Thought could be in any of their Heads, since they knew the Contents of the Duke of Ormond's Declaration &c. But, as soon as I heard of their plundering, I gave immediate Orders Not to receive any more Plunder on board; and to sieze what was already there, for the Queen's Service and Use. Some friends have blamed me for neglecting an Opportunity, which (they say) my predecessors would not have slipt, of bringing Advantage to my self. *Question* 9. Was not a greater Liberty afterwards given of bringing Goods on Board? *Answer*. Nothing was allowed to be shipped, except Provisions and Stores; and we saw very little of either of these.

As Sir George was goeing away the Duke of Bolton called him back; and told him that the Committee had some more Questions to put, which they hoped he would be ready to answer on Munday. He said he knew not how far his Leave from the House of Commons might reach; but assured His Grace that he would petition for new Liberty to attend again, being very desireous to give their Lordships all the Satisfaction he could.

In the House the Bill for Regulateing the Prisons of Queen's Bench and Fleet, amended by the Lord Chief Justice Holt and Baron Price.

Carried to Dinner by Lord Weymouth; attended by five Members of the House of Commons. After Dinner, came in Duke Hamilton;

[406] The former Admirals Herbert and Russell, they had commanded the English fleet at Beachy Head (1690) and La Hogue (1692), respectively.

who observed that, if his Ancestors should put their Noses above ground, they'd not know the faces of half of the present Commissioners for the Union, nor acknowledge that their Names were heard of in Scotland.

At Mr Dean's Chamber, in my way home, Earnestly sollicited by Dr Stanhope to appear against the Bill for makeing Navigable the River of Derwent; tho' 'tis brought in by his own Nephew and Mr Harper[407] (whom I had just before met with at Lord Weymouth's) Burgesses for the Town of Derby.

[Jan.] 24. *Sunday*. I preached at St Martin's on *Psalms* 5,3. and administered the sacrament to the Lord Treasurer [Godolphin], Duke of Marlborough, Lord Pawlet, &c. Dined with Dr Hutton, of Ano[408] and Dr Alston, at Dr Lancaster's. Dr H[utton] gave a very entertaining Account of his studies in matters of Records and Registers, in the Tower of London, at York, Lincoln, &c. Mr Dean at my Lodgeings, contriveing how to compass the Deanry of Wells.[409]

[Jan.] 25. *Munday*. Sir George Rook again before the Committee. He took notice that, at his last Appearance, he was told that the Questions read to him were all he would be required to answer to; and yet he afterwards found that a great more were put: He therfore desired that he might now have all they had to ask him in writeing, and he would (as speedily as they pleased) give his Answers also *in Scriptis*. Agreed; and to bring in his Answers on Wednesday.

In the House Lord Wharton moved that Thompson's Name might be struck out of their Order of the 22d (as a mistake of the Clerk) and only R. Squire obliged to answer. Objected against by the Bishop of Carlile since both had been made Respondents in His Lordship's first petition and late Answer: But agreed, that it be made an Order of this day, as on a new Motion.

In the Evening, at the *Globe*[410] with Dr Waugh, Mr Crackenthorp,[411] Mr Johnson and Brother Joseph.

[407] Thomas Stanhope (c.1679–1730), of Elvaston, MP for Derby, 1702–5, a second cousin of General James Stanhope, and John Harpur (c.1665–1713), MP for Derby, 1701–5, 1710–13.

[408] Mathew Hutton (1639–1711), antiquary, and Rector of Aynho, 1677–1711, and of Croughton, Northants, 1689–1711.

[409] Dean Grahme of Carlisle was interested in moving to Wells, where Dean Ralph Bathurst was thought to be dying, see below, 31 Jan. Bathurst recovered, but died as a result of a fall in his garden on 11 June 1704. See *Atterbury Epist. Corr.* iii, 199, 202, 206.

[410] Possibly the tavern in the Strand opposite Salisbury Street, see B. Lillywhite, *London Signs* (1972), p. 217.

[411] Richard Crackenthorpe, patron and lord of the manor of Newbiggin, Cumberland, and High Sheriff of Cumberland in 1702, Nicolson, *Miscellany*, p. 64; *CW* ii (1902), 184 n.

[Jan.] 26. *Tuesday*. Bill for the more Effectual Punishing of the Wilful Receivers of Stolen goods, and Burners of Ships, &c. mended by B[aron] Price. An Amendment given me by some Merchants, for the Regulateing of Private Policyes of Assurance; the occasion of destroying many of their ships, assured (in several Offices) for more than they are worth.[412] The Judges and Attourney Generall allowed that it was fit to bring in a Particular Bill for that purpose; but feared it would too much load that now before us.

Mr Dean came, in the Evening, to enquire after the Encouragement given by my Lord Archbishop of York; And, notwithstanding his Respects for Dr Todd,[413] declared himself of Opinion that Dr Smith[414] would be a better Successor for him.[415]

[Jan.] 27. *Wednesday*. Answers given in writeing, by Sir George Rook, to all the Questions proposed by the Committee of Lords. Lord Hallifax, laughing at the Vote passed yesterday against him in the House of Commons,[416] assured us that he had done all (in Remittances to the Queen's Remembrancer)[417] which they pretended to want of him. Lord Wharton kindly agreed with the Archbishop of York and my self, that R. Squire's Agents should have time (till Tuesday next) to put in their Answer. An Appeal upon one of Dr Oates's[418] Awards, condemned in Chancery, heard (for above two Hours) onely on the Appellant's side, with a deal of notable Evidence from the Dr's Wife and Maid-servant of his refuseing a Bribe of 200 *l*. &c. The Respondent to be heard to morrow.[419]

After Dinner, and a short visit from (Mrs Blencow's daughter) Mrs Vincent, Mr Elstob and I went to see Mr Stonestreet;[420] who entertained very obligeingly with Remarks on Mezobarba,[421] &c. The Enlargements that Author has made upon Occo[422] (though

---

[412] Act for Punishing of Accessories to Felonies, etc., see *LJ* xvii, 258. Nicolson's amendment is not part of the Act (1 Ann. St. 2 c. 9), see *Statutes of the Realm*, viii, 168-9.

[413] Hugh Todd, Vicar of Penrith, see Appendix A.

[414] Probably a reference to John Smith, a native of Westmorland and Treasurer of Durham, see Appendix A.

[415] Nicolson favoured a local candidate for the soon-to-be-vacated deanery of Carlisle, and as he had had disagreements in the past with the two main local contenders, Todd and Chancellor Tullie (see James, chapter 7, *passim*), he pressed Archbishop Sharp to recommend Edmund Wickins, Rector of Kirby Thore, to the Queen. Lloyd-Baker MSS, Box 3, Bundle 3: N. to Sharp, 22 Mar. 1703.

[416] See above, sessional intro., p. 123.

[417] Officer who collected debts due to the sovereign.

[418] Titus Oates (1649-1705), fabricator of the Popish Plot of 1678.

[419] For the case see HMC *Lords MSS* v, 168-9.

[420] William Stonestreet (d. 1716), Rector of St Stephen's, Wallbrook, London, 1689-1716, later President of Sion College, 1710, and Prebendary of Chichester, 1712.

[421] Francesco Mezzabarba (1645-97), Italian antiquarian.

[422] Adolphus Occo (1524-1604), German numismatist, whose *Imperatorum Romanorum*

the best Collection on the Subject) have many many Mistakes, through the misinformations he had from others: But where his Additions are from his own Musaeum (marked with M.N.) they may be certainly relyed on. Monsieur Masson (a French Gentleman, at Oxford) is correcting this work; and, in due time, will considerably improve it. The Roman Coinage in greatest perfection about the time of Adrian. One of three Languages now spoken in Livonia seems to be that of the old Estij; whom Tacitus observes to come near the Britains of his time in Dialect. A Vocabulary of the Lithuanian Tongue sent to Mr Lhwyd to try whether that have any Affinity with the Welsh.

[Jan.] 28. *Thursday*. Seven Bills from the House of Commons; whereof two (1. for preventing Theft and the Burning of Ships. 2. Enabling the Bishop of Chichester to let Leases in Chancery Lane; both sent from the Lords, the latter Originally, the other with Amendments) were brought together by Mr Conyers. Lord Wharton agreed to his yesterday's private proposeal.

The second part of the Appeal about Dr Oates's Award; wherein it fully appeared that the Dr is (still) a very great Villain. The Decree, which destroyed and set aside the Award, was Affirmed; and 20 *l*. Costs ordered to be paid by the Appellant.

[Jan.] 29. *Friday*. In the Morning, I was visitted by the Lord Viscount Stairs [Stair],[423] and his Brother (Sir David Dalrymple)[424] Lord President of the Session.[425] My Lord S[tair] gave me a kind Letter from his brother Sir James;[426] upon the subject of my *Scottish Historical Library*.[427] These two great men are both in the Commission for the Union; and gave me an Account of their haveing finished their Debates, and come to agreement on all the Heads whereon

Numismata a Pompeio Magno ad Heraclium, originally published in 1579, Mezzabarba enlarged and published in 1683.

[423] John Dalrymple (1648-1707), 2nd Viscount (1695) and 1st Earl (1703) of Stair. As Lord Justice Clerk and a Lord of the Session, he was a strong supporter of William of Orange in 1688-9, later becoming King's Advocate [S], 1689-92, and Joint Secretary of State [S], 1690-5. He held further offices, 1703-7, and was a commissioner for the Union in 1702 and 1706. *GEC Peerage*.

[424] Nicolson appears to have confused Sir David with Sir Hew Dalrymple.

[425] Sir Hew Dalrymple (1652-1737), third son of James, 1st Viscount of Stair, he was a Scottish MP, Dean of the Faculty of Advocates, 1695, and was nominated by William III as Lord President of the Court of Sessions. Like his elder brother he was a commissioner for the Union in 1702 and 1706.

[426] Sir James Dalrymple (1650-1719), second son of the 1st Viscount of Stair, he was an antiquary as well as a lawyer, and published an edition of Camden's *Scotland*. Like Sir Hew, he was created a baronet of Nova Scotia in 1698.

[427] Published by Nicolson in 1702.

they had power to Treat. The Article of Religion, and Laws of Tenure, were excepted out of their Powers. They much commended the Constant Attendance, and fair Behaviour, of our two Archbishops;[428] and seemed for a happy Conclusion of the Matter. The States of Holland, they observed, were much startled at it, now that it was so far Advanced. They[429] apprehended themselves in some danger of loseing their Herring Fishing; And flattered them selves with the Hopes of insuperable Difficulties in bringing any such Treaty as this to a good Issue, dureing our present Circumstances. Their youngest Brother,[430] as they came up, stole from them at Durham; and got a View of the Scotch Charters in the Treasury there: With which he was mightily pleased.

In the House, the Duke of Devonshire Reported Precedents upon Adhering to Amendments; most of which had been declared to the Commons, without giveing Reasons. A long Debate arose about the Return that should be made on that Clause in the Bill against Occasional Conformity, whereon the Lords had resolved not to Adhere to their Amendments.[431] At last, the Question (warmly opposed by Lord Herbert, and others, as very Irregular) was put — *Whether Their Lordships would agree to let that Clause* (about the Corporation Act) *stand part of the Bill, as it came from the Commons?* It was carryed in the Affirmative by 34 against 20. There were no more than 7 Bishops in the House;[432] and onely the Bishop of Sarum dissented. After this, the Bill was ordered to be remitted to the Commons (at a Conference) on Munday next.[433]

At Dr Lancaster's, in the Evening, I met with Mr Moor (Chaplain and Steward to the late Earl of Abingdon) a great Champion in the Lower House of Convocation. Dr Stanhop's decl[aration] that he'd take preferment from Satan.

[Jan.] 30. *Saturday*. Prayers at the House, before 8 Bishops and Earl of Carnarvon, ajourned to Munday. In Procession to the Abbey at

---

[428] There were twenty-nine meetings of the Union commissioners in 1702/3 (at five of which no English commissioners turned up to form a quorum), and the Archbishops of Canterbury and York attended twenty and sixteen meetings respectively. *Acts Parl. Scot.* xi, Appendix, pp. 145-61.   [429] i.e. the Dutch.

[430] Sir David Dalrymple, fifth son of the 1st Viscount of Stair. See Appendix A.

[431] The clause determining whether municipal officers be subject to the penalties of the bill had been reinserted into the bill on 16 Jan. 1703.

[432] The House was very thinly attended this day. Hence the unexpected ease with which the Tory peers were able to secure this late, but unavailing, concession on the vital 'corporation clause'.

[433] At this conference on 1 Feb., the Lords acquainted the Commons that they adhered to all their amendments except the one concerning municipal officers. Four days later the Commons resolved to adhere to their disagreements with the Lords in the amendments made by them. Thus the bill was lost. *CJ* xiv, 183.

Westminster where I preached (by Order) before the Lords.[434] Sermon done, at Bishop of Hereford's (with the Bishop of Bangor, Brother Joseph and Dr Gibson) till Evening prayer. Bishop of Bangor disturbed with the Report of the Bed, at Lambeth. Dr G[ibson] supped with me, and went to the Archbishop of York; who kindly accepted his Abstracts of the Convocation-Controversy. My Lord Archbishop acquainted us with the Bishop of Worcester's Observation of the three Orders of Apostles, Prophets and (Evangelists, or) Teachers, answerable to Bishops, Priests and Deacons, throughout the whole New Testament. Presbyters a general Name for Prophets and Teachers; never to Apostles or Bishops.

In the Evening at Gray's-Inn, with Sir C. Musgrave and Coll. [James] Grahme. Dr Woodriff's[435] sermon presented to me. Mr Bridges, son to my Lord Chandos, brought me home in his Chariot.

[Jan.] 31. *Sunday*. At the Church of Westminster in the morning, Dr Dent preached an honest sermon against presumption, on *Let him that thinketh that he stands* &c. I dined with Brother Joseph who informed me that he had (this week) received a Return from Mr Ward of Lincolnshire;[436] but seemed still to complain of Brother John's[437] putting upon him too hard.

At St. Paul's, in the afternoon, Dr Trimnel[438] preached piously (like himself) upon Reliance on God's Power and Faithfulness. In the Evening with Mr Dean, newly returned from Fulham.[439] The Bishop of London's adviseing me to think of a new Dean for Carlisle was what his Lordship had not communicated to him. Agreed, that

[434] This was the anniversary of the execution of Charles I, and a solemn fast was observed according to the Statute of 1661. The small number of peers who attended is interesting. During the sixteen years that Nicolson was a member of the Lords the average attendance was between nine and ten. The largest number, twenty-two, attended in 1711, in the aftermath of the Sacheverell affair, and the smallest, five, in 1709. Emotive as this occasion was for many Tories, it rarely tempted them to endure the ritual tedium of an official sermon. This was the only formal parliamentary sermon Nicolson preached before the Lords.

[435] Benjamin Woodroffe (1638–1711), Principal of Gloucester Hall (Worcester College), Oxford, since 1692.

[436] Richard Ward (*c*.1654–1711), Rector and lessee (from Bishop Nicolson) of Mareham-on-the-Hill, Lincs., near the manor of Horncastle, which had been appropriated to the see of Carlisle around 1318 and remained so until the late nineteenth century. Nicolson visited him at Mareham in his journey south in Oct. 1705. *CW* iii (1903), 28.

[437] John Nicolson (d. 1717), the bishop's youngest brother, was a public notary at Carlisle, and had been Chapter Clerk since 1699. He also looked after the bishop's financial affairs. *CW* i (1901), 49–50.

[438] Charles Trimnell, Archdeacon of Norfolk, and later Bishop of Norwich, see Appendix A.

[439] Fulham Palace, the official residence of Henry Compton, Bishop of London.

the Dean of Wells [Bathurst] was dyeing; and that this Deanry was worth his Acceptance.[440]

Feb. 1. *Munday*. Immediately after Prayers, Lord Berkley of Stratton moved for Thanks to the Bishop of Carlisle for his Sermon on Saturday; and that he might be desired to print the same: Which was ordered accordingly.

Several Bills being read, the Cause of the River of Derwent (in Derbyshire) was argued by Counsel at the Bar;[441] Mr Dodd and Mr Pooley against the passing of the Bill, and Mr Phipps[442] and Mr Parker (Recorder of Derby)[443] for it.[444] The former pleaded the Damage it would bring to the Towns of Nottingham, Bawtree [Bawtry], &c. and some particular persons: And the latter argued for the General Benefit of Navigation, averring with all that Bawtree (particularly) could not lose by this Improvement of the Trade at Derby;[445] because the Carriage from the Low Peak would still go that way. The greatest Damage appeared to be at Nottingham; where, by the stopping of Derwent above, their passage on the Trent would be uncertain. Upon a Division, the Bill was thrown out by 27 against 19.[446]

The Archbishop of York gave me a Hint that the Archdeacon of D[urham?][447] would probably be our Dean.

[Feb.] 2. *Tuesday*. Several Witnesses, Officers in the Fleet, sworn, in order to give their Testimony in the Enquiries about the last Summer's Expedition. Some Lords were of Opinion that this was Administring the Oath *Ex Officio*, in a Matter wherein they might

[440] William Grahme had apparently refused the bishopric of Carlisle in 1702 because of the financial sacrifice it would have involved (*CW* ii (1902), 161; lxvi (1966), 301 n. 15). Besides the deanery, Grahme held the first prebendal stall at Durham, reputed to be worth around £800, which he would have had to relinquish on becoming a bishop. The deanery of Wells, with its attached livings, must have been worth more than that of Carlisle (Grahme could keep his prebendary at Durham on moving to Wells) for him to consider it 'worth his Acceptance'.

[441] For the bill, see above, 13 Jan.

[442] Constantine Phipps (1656-1723), eminent barrister of Jacobite sympathies. His performance as defence counsel at the Sacheverell trial, in support of Sir Simon Harcourt, earned him in 1710 a knighthood and the Lord Chancellorship of Ireland.

[443] Thomas Parker, later MP for Derby, see Appendix A.

[444] Repl. 'against'.

[445] By the navigation of the River Idle which flows from Bawtrey to the Trent. According to Defoe (*Tour* ii, 181), the town 'becomes the centre of all the exportation of this part of the country, especially for heavy goods', mainly lead from Derbyshire and wrought iron and edge tools from Sheffield and Hallamshire.

[446] For a discussion of the opposition to the bill see Willan, *River Navigation in England*, pp. 40-5, 47. It was supported by London and Newark merchants who wanted cheaper transport for food, see ibid., p. 137.

[447] Robert Boothe.

be obliged to accuse themselves: But, precedents appearing in the Journals, that Objection was over-ruled.

The Bill for appointing Commissioners to take and Examine the Public Accounts,[448] the Earl of Sunderland moved (in the Committee) that a clause might be added that the Commissioners should not enjoy any Office under the Crown, dureing their Continuance in this Commission: Which (being in the former Acts of that kind)[449] was agreed to by the House.

Lord Hallifax gave a long Account of his Management in the place of Auditor of the Exchequer;[450] acknowledgeing that his Practice had not been agreable to one Clause in the Act of Parliament (which he Read, in his place) relateing to the Return of the Impressed Rolls to the Queen's Rembrancer: But averred that this was not agreable to other parts of the Act, nor Consistent with the present condition of Affairs in the Exchequer. He observed that Accounts there were far more Voluminous than they used to be in former Times; That antiently 30 or 40,000 l, was a great Summ, to be told over (as it must be) at every half year's End; and that, at this present, there's above 900,000 l. there in ready Money; &c. Upon the whole, it was Ordered that a Committee (of all the Lords now in the House) should meet to morrow morning; that the Commissioners of Accounts should be ordered then to attend; and that this Affair (of the Lord Hallifax) should be the first thing examined.

The Earl of Nottingham wished it might be considered, whether (since the Commons had already ordered a Prosecution, against that Lord, by the Attourney Generall [Northey]) this procedure might not be Interpreted a Giveing Judgement before hand in a Cause, which might come before them hereafter, by way of Appeal.—The Lord Sommers Replyed, This Consideration might as well deterr Their Lordships from looking into any part of the Report made by the Commissioners; and that he did not see why the Lords were obliged to take any sort of Notice of what was done in the other House.

---

[448] The bill (later the Accounts Commissioners Act [1 Anne 2, c. 23]) was brought in from the Commons on 21 Jan. and given a first reading on 23 Jan. 1703 (*LJ* xvii, 250, 254).

[449] In William III's reign. The Commons' Commission of Public Accounts had been revived in 1691, by the Act of 2 Will. & Mar., Stat. 2, c. 11, and kept on foot by later Acts until it lapsed in 1697. Sunderland's clause formed section 7 of the 1703 Act. The Commons agreed to the amendment and it received the royal assent on 27 Feb. 1703. See HMC *Lords MSS* v, 190; *LJ* xvii, 320.

[450] He had been appointed Auditor for life in 1700, having resigned his offices of Chancellor of the Exchequer and First Lord of the Treasury in 1699. For the Commons' attack on Halifax, whose real offence in Tory eyes was that he was one of the hated 'Lords of the Whig Junto', see above, 27 Jan. A copy of Halifax's defence can be found in Hertfordshire RO Panshanger MS D/EP F95, ff. 30–45.

[Feb.] 3. *Wednesday*. Committee on the Expedition; and several of the Flag-Officers examined on Oath. Some of 'em Scrupled the giveing Evidence, in Matters wherein they might be presumed to accuse them selves; but were told (by some Noble and Learned Lords) that they were onely Examined for *Information*, not for *Accusation*. Very Nice!

Another Committee on the Remarks of the Commissioners of Accounts the first relateing to the Auditor of the Exchequer. Several Officers were called in, to give the History of the Usage there in transmitting of Impressed Rolls to the Queen's Remembrancer. After an Examination of more than two Hours, and the House reassumed, the Duke of Somerset reported that some Progress was made; but that, the Commissioners of Accounts not appearing, the matter could not be finished. The Committee, therfore moved that a Message might be sent to the House of Commons, to give those Gentlemen (who are all members of their House) to attend on Friday. Which was ordered.

Dureing the sitting of the Committee, the Lord Keeper [Wright] called me into his Chamber[451] to look over the Original Warrant for the Execution of King Charles the First (which I had taken Notice of in my Sermon)[452] and the other Proceedings in that Matter; which were brought to us, from the Parliament-Office, by Mr Walker.[453] The Warrant is as follows:

"At the High Court of Justice for the Trying and Judgeing of Charles Steuart King of England. Jan. 29. 1648.
Whereas Charles Steuart King of England is and standeth con-victed, attaynted and Condemned, of High Treason and other high Crymes, And Sentence upon Saturday last was pronounced against him by this Court, to be put to Death by the Severing of his Head from his Body, Of which Sentence, Execution yet remaineth to be done, These are therefore to Will and Require You to see the said Sentence Executed in the open Street before Whitehal upon the Morrow, being the Thirtieth Day of this instant moneth of January, betwist the Hours of ten in the Morning and five in the Afternoon of the same Day, with full effect. And for so doing this shall be your Warrant. And these are to require all Officers and Soldiers, and other the good People of this Nation of England, to be assisting to you in this Service. Given under our

---

[451] See fig. 1 for Lord Chancellor's chamber used by the Lord Keeper.
[452] Of 30 Jan. 1703.
[453] John Walker (c.1652–1715), Clerk Assistant to the House of Lords, 1682–1715. Sainty, *Parliament Office*, p. 24.

Hands and Seals. To Colonel Francis Hacker, Colonel Huncks and Lieutenant Colonel Phayre, and to Every of them."
Jo. Bradshawe
Tho. Grey
O. Cromwell.
Edw. Whalley. &c.

Their Seals of Arms follow their Several Subscriptions. This Instrument is repeated in the large Parchment-Roll of the Proceedings of that Court, Deposited in Chancery (and thence transmitted to the Parliament Office) by an Ordinance of the House of Commons. One Name, in the Original, is scratched out; but it appears, by the Roll, to be that of—Chaloner.[454] Lord Keeper [Wright] moved to get all this Printed.

[Feb.] 4. *Thursday*. Duke of Bolton, Earls of Torrington, Orford and Stamford, early at the Committee against Sir George Rook.—The Earl of Torrington's chief Grudge at him, because of his not acquainting him that he was to be Vice-Admiral; tho' he dined with him the Day he obtained his Commission.—This Earl saved the English Fleet at Bantry-Bay; designed for a Sacrifice.[455]

Two Bills brought up by Mr Coniers together: One for finishing of Paul's,[456] and the other for Repair of Churches.[457] *Diruit haec; aedificat illa*. The former (onely) being Read, the Business of the Day was called for. i.e. The Goeing into a Committee of the Whole House on the Bill, sent from the Commons,[458] for enlargeing the Time for takeing the Oath of Abjuration.[459] Lord Wharton, before

---

[454] Thomas Chaloner's (1595-1661) name remained on the warrant, so the scratched out name must be that of his brother James (1603-60), and the name of Gregory Clement was written over. The warrant remained, after the execution, in Col. Hacker's possession. In 1660, at the Restoration, Hacker, a prisoner in the Tower, was ordered by the House of Lords to surrender the warrant to them. It has since remained in their custody, at first in the Jewel Tower and since 1851 in the House of Lords' Library.

[455] Torrington had attacked the French fleet attempting to land reinforcements in Ireland on 14 Mar. 1689, but had been beaten off.

[456] The bill received the royal assent on 27 Feb. 1703. Work on the cathedral, started in 1675, was entering its final stage. The last stone was laid in Oct. 1708. Annual expenditure was to rise rapidly from £14,000 in 1702-3 to £37,000 in 1706-7. See J. Lang, *Rebuilding St Paul's after the Great Fire of London* (1956), pp. 221-44.

[457] Bill for 'the more easy recovery of monies for repairing churches' was read a first time on 9 Feb. 1703, and rejected on the motion for a second reading, see *LJ* xvii, 268, 274; HMC *Lords MSS* v, 190-1.

[458] On 28 Jan. 1703. *LJ* xvii, 261.

[459] See HMC *Lords MSS* v, 199-200. Cf. Burnet, *History*, v, 57: 'the Commons sent up a bill in favour of those who had not taken the oath, abjuring the Prince of Wales ['the Old Pretender'] by the day that was named [in the Abjuration Act of 1702]; granting them a year longer to consider of it.' For the Bishop of Salisbury's account of how the Whig peers

the Lord Keeper [Wright] left the Wool-Sack, moved for Leave to offer a Clause to prevent the ill Treatment of the Princess Sophia and the House of Hannover;[460] Lord Carlile, that the Oath might be extended to Ireland; and the Bishop of London, that Clergymen already Instituted into Vacant Benefices might not be deprived.

As soon as Lord Herbert had taken the Chair, and the first Enacting Clause of the Bill was read, the Lords Nottingham and Sommers (with Assistance of the Judges) added, in pursuance of the Bishop of London's motion, a Proviso—*Unless such Benefices, Offices, &c. were already Supplyed.*—Lord Wharton's Clause appeared to be a Charge of Treason upon such as should attempt the putting by the family of Hannover. Upon Debate on this, the Judges saying that the Law had never yet carryed Treason further than the next Heir, agreed that it should be so worded as to secure the next *Visible* Heir, according to the late Act of Limitation of the Crown.[461]—After some more Alterations,[462] Adjourned the Debate till tomorrow.

The Bishop of Lincoln gave me an Account of Dr Charlet's[463] foolish Entertainment of the French Officers at Oxford on the 30th of January. And, presently after, News was brought him (into the House) that his wife, sometime distempered, had thrown her self out of the Window of her Chamber in Dean's Yard, and was killed.[464]

[Feb.] 5. *Friday*. After the Reading of some public and private Bills, an Appeal of the Lord Roseberry (Primrose) against his Father-in-Law's second wife.[465] The Cause was adjudged in his Favour; contrary to my Sentiments.

The Duke of Somerset reported from the Committee appointed to look into the Book of public Accounts that the Commissioners had not yet appeared, notwithstanding the Message sent by their Lordships to the House of Commons: That they had Examined the Officers of the Exchequer touching the matter of the first Article:

ensured that this 'bill, that was begun in favour of the Jacobites, turned so terribly upon them', see ibid., pp. 57–8.

[460] Wharton's clause would have made it high treason to attempt to overthrow the succession to the Crown, as defined by law in 1701, or to challenge the claim of the legal Protestant heirs, Princess Sophia and, after her, George Lewis, Elector of Hanover. On the advice of the judges the treason was 'carryed [no] further than the next Heir'.

[461] Act of Settlement of 1701.

[462] For details see HMC *Lords MSS* v, 199–201.

[463] Arthur Charlett (1655–1722), Master of University College, Oxford since 1692.

[464] Anne Hall (*c*.1656–1703), wife of James Gardiner, Bishop of Lincoln, was said to have suffered from 'melancholy', see *The Diary of John Evelyn*, ed. E. S. de Beer (1955), v, 528; Luttrell, v, 266.

[465] For details of the case see HMC *Lords MSS* v, 153–5.

That they had come to a Resolution, declareing the Lord Hallifax a person Diligent and faithful in his Office of Auditor; To which they desired the Concurrence of the House.——The Attourney-Generall [Northey], by the Lord Keeper [Wright], desired that he might be heard before any Conclusion was come to upon this Debate; and was beginning to Speak. At which the Lord Wharton fired. Lord Nottingham hoped they would hear him; because it might be too late afterwards. Perhaps he might have something to acquaint them with from the Queen; and the Anticipateing of Judgement, in this Case, would hinder this Court's medling in it, hereafter, if it should be brought from below by Writ of Error; &c.——The Earl of Peterborough haveing jested a little, by way of Reply, the Question was carryed (without Division) in favour of the Lord Hallifax and all the Proceedings of the Committee ordered to be Printed.

Lord Mohun moved that an Address might be presented to Her Majesty that a List might be laid before this House of all such Persons as had had Licenses to come from France since March last. Lord Nottingham (tho' believeing that this was Levelled at himself) went readily in to it: So 'twas ordered to be made by the Lords with white Staves.

Lord Carlile Reported the Amendment to the Bill for Enlargeing the Time for takeing the Oath of Abjuration, extending the force of that Law to Ireland;[466] which was read, and agreed to. 'Twas a long one; drawn up by Mr Justice Powel. Adjour[n]ment till Munday.

[Feb.] 6. *Satuday*. The Queen's Birth-Day. I went to St James's with the Bishop of Hereford; and we called, by the way, at the Bishop of Norwich's. As we went thence to Court, the Bishops of Norwich and Chichester taught us to take Stains out of Books by Water and Vinegar, strengthening the Leaves afterwards by Allumwater; and to take off Ink by Aq[ua]-fortis mixed with water, useing Allum water as before.

After our Compliments, I returned home with the Archbishop of York with whom I dined. Dr Bently[467] would [not] allow his Grace to say that Graevias[468] (lately dead of a Apoplexy, from which Good Lord deliver me!) was a Toper; though he allowed that, upon Occasion, he could bear a great deal of Wine. The Dr was pretty full

[466] Carlisle's was the second Whig amendment which gave the bill teeth to bite its Tory sponsors.

[467] Richard Bentley (1662–1742), Master of Trinity College, Cambridge, 1700–42, Archdeacon of Ely since 1701, and later Regius Professor of Divinity, 1717–42.

[468] Johann Georg Graevius (1632–1703), celebrated German classical scholar, for many years professor at Utrecht, where he died on 11 Jan. 1703.

of himself after Dinner. He blamed Dr James[469] for offering to persuade me to take my Doctor's Degree by way of Creation; in which I must have kneeled before the Professor and from him received an Authority (forsooth) of expounding the New Testament which, as he truely observed, was inconsistent with the Episcopal Dignity. He ridiculed the Expensive humour of purchaseing old Editions of Books at Extravagant Rates; a Vanity to which the present Earl of Sunderland[470] and Bishop of Norwich much subject. The former bought a piece of Cicero's Works out of Dr Francis Bernard's Au[c]tion,[471] printed about 1480 at the Rate of 3 *l*. 2 *s*. 6 *d*. which Dr Bentley himself had presented to that physitian, and which cost him no more than the odd half Crown.

Lord Stairs a 2d time at my Lodgeings.

[Feb.] 7. *Sunday*. I preached for Dr Lamplugh at St Andrew's Undershaft; and dined with a good honest Church-warden, directly over against the parsonage. In my return, endeavoured to wait on my Lord Stairs and Sir James Steward.

[Feb.] 8. *Munday*. E. Settle,[472] the Poet, attended me Early, to know what I thought of the Poem (on the House of Hannover) which he had lately sent me, i.e. what present I intended to make the Author in Return? He went off with a Guinnea, too well paid: Tho' he assured me that he was prepareing a Copy for the Princess Sophia, the binding and Illuminateing of which would stand him in 35 *l*.

After the Reading of several Bills, and the passing of that for the Rebuilding of St Paul's, the Bishop of London brought in a Petition from the Lord Mayor[473] and Court of Aldermen desireing to be heard (by their Counsel) when the Lord Wharton's Appeal against Mr Squire came on: Which Lord Wharton assented to, *provided they be not made Parties in the Cause*; the very thing (as I understand 'em) that they Petition for. For, their Paper sets forth that the City of London haveing Mannors at Midlam, &c. bordering on the

---

[469] Henry James (d. 1717), Regius Professor of Divinity at Cambridge University, 1699–1717, and President of Queens' College since 1675.

[470] Sunderland was notorious for offering exorbitant prices for early printed books, see Humfrey Wanley's comment at the time of Sunderland's death in *The Diary of Humfrey Wanley*, ed. C. E. & R. C. Wright (1966), i, 125, 139.

[471] Bernard, a Fellow of the Royal College of Physicians and Physician in Ordinary to James II, was a well-known book collector and his library was auctioned at his death in 1698. W. Munck, *The Roll of the Royal College of Physicians* (1878), i, 449–50.

[472] Elkanah Settle (1648–1724), a former rival of Dryden's, was appointed City poet in 1691.

[473] Sir William Dashwood, Lord Mayor of London, 1702-3.

Honour of Richmond, they apprehend they have a Right in the Record, which this Lord prayes may be destroyed.[474]

A long Appeal of Mr Hayes of Winchelsea;[475] wherein he was overthrown by a single Remark of Mr Cowper's (not so much as hinted at in either of the Cases) that he had given his Agent no Letter of Attourney to act by in his Absence.—The Cause a while Interrupted by two Messages from the House of Commons; with the Bills for qualifying Members in future Elections,[476] and Regulateing those of the Burrough of Hindon.[477]

Duke of Devonshire reported the Queen's Answer about Her Licences to persons comeing from France. That She had ordered a List to be laid before their Lordships; who would find that they were but few. Lord Nottingham said he would bring in the List accordingly to morrow, betwixt Twelve and One, when he hoped there would be a full House.—Sir R[obert] Clayton[478] excuseing the City's opposeing so good a man as the Lord Wharton assureing the Bishop of Glocester [Fowler], that nothing short of the Obligation of an Oath would have prevailed with the Aldermen to do it.[479]

In Essex-street with Dr Hickes, Dr Waugh, Dr Gibson and Mr Grandorge. Dr H[ickes] referred me to Mr Battely Keeper of the Augmentation Office,[480] to see a Counterfeit Saxon Charter.— Mr Cowper's perswadeing his Mrs to think her self his *other wife*.[481]

[474] For details of the petition see HMC *Lords MSS* v, 173.

[475] See ibid., p. 128.

[476] The House of Commons (Qualification of Members) Bill laid down that MPs had to be native born, and had to hold land to the value of £500 (if a knight of the shire) or £300 (if a burgess). The Lords rejected it at the 2nd reading on 22 Feb. 1703. See ibid., pp. 200–1; *LJ* xvii, 300. This was the forerunner of the Qualification Act, which eventually became law in 1711, and was a Tory measure, with some country Whig support, aimed at reducing the political influence of 'monied men' and of non-landed army and navy officers and government officials.

[477] For this bill, originally intended to disfranchise the corrupt Wiltshire borough of Hindon but subsequently watered down, see W. A. Speck, *Tory and Whig: The Struggle in the Constituences, 1701-1715* (1970), p. 15.

[478] Sir Robert Clayton (1629-1707), had been an MP since 1679, and sat for Bletchingley, 1702-5, and London, 1702, 1705-7.

[479] For the close relations between the Junto, of which Wharton was a leading light, and the City Whigs, see Holmes, *British Politics*, p. 172.

[480] The repository of the records of the Court of Augmentations (where Charles Battely was Joint Clerk), established by Henry VIII for determining suits in respect of monastic lands and abolished by Mary I, it was situated in a building on the west side of Westminster Hall, facing St Margaret's Street. According to J. Strype (*Survey of the Cities of London and Westminster* (1720), book vi, pp. 53-4) is contained 'deeds, instruments and original writings belonging to the abbies, priories etc. . . . with the values of the lands and rents of those foundations: whence much light may be given into Churchlands, vicarages and such like'.

[481] Perhaps an early reference to Cowper's supposed crime of bigamy. He was to be charged by Atterbury with such a crime in eary 1707, as part of a general condemnation of the 'abominable impurities' of the Whig Junto and its allies. See J. P. Kenyon, *Revolution Principles: the politics of party, 1689-1720* (Cambridge, 1977), pp. 116, 228 n. 45.

[Feb.] 9. *Shrove-Tuesday*. Bill from the Commons, for Repair of Churches, being Read the first Time, the Archbishop of Canterbury observed that it was a very faulty one in every branch of it; and incapable of being Amended. It makes every Utensil of the Church (Nay, even the Elements for the Sacrament) depend on the humours of a Majority of the Parishioners; exempts Churchwardens from the Inspection of their Ordinaries, &c. Whereupon, it was (*Nemine Contradicente*) Rejected. The Archbishop promiseing, with God's Leave, to bring in a better at the next Session.

The Earl of Nottingham brought in his List, of five persons; and gave a particular Account of each of 'em. Lord Mohun excused his Motion; adding, that he was yet of Opinion that the Ministers ought to prosecute those who came without License. Lord Nottingham agreed; but was also of Opinion that every Lord, who knew of any such, was obliged to inform those Ministers.——Lord Abingdon said some had busily reported that the Court of Requests and Painted Chamber were full of them.——Ordered, that Her Majesty have an Address of Thanks for being so Spareing of her Licences; and that She be desired to issue out Her Royal Proclamation for the prosecuteing of Offenders, without a Licence.——Lord Longvil moved that a List might be also brought in of the Licences granted by King William; which the Lord Nottingham promised to do.[482]

An Appeal of some Stock-Jobbers, who had farmed the Conduit-water of the City of London,[483] heard; and Confounded by 5 Bishops and 3 Temporal Lords: all that were left.

In the Evening at Grey's Inn. Sir C. Musgrave no Lord.[484]

[Feb.] 10. *Ash Wednesday*. The Archbishop of York preached (a very moveing Sermon) on — *How we shall escape* &c. before the Queen. Dr Gibson came with me home, and (after Dinner) we went together to Hatton Garden and Charterhouse. In my Return, I visitted Archdeacon Skelton; who seemed pretty quiet in the Convocation-Controversy. Mrs Broughton bespoke a Scotch Galloway.[485]

---

[482] See below, 15 Feb.

[483] In 1694 the Corporation of the City had agreed that a pipe should be laid from the Banqueting House to the conduits in Cheapside and Stocks Markets to convey not less than nineteen tons of water per hour. The supply was leased to a group who found that the pipe only supplied six tons per hour. They had petitioned against the lease for a faulty supply, but the court had decreed them liable to the terms of the lease. HMC *Lords MSS* v, 151–2.

[484] Possibly a reference to earlier rumours of his promotion to a peerage. Four new peers were created at the end of the session in Mar. 1703, viz. John Granville (Granville), Heneage Finch (Guernsey), Francis Seymour Conway (Conway of Ragley), and John Hervey (Hervey).

[485] Horse of small strong breed.

[Feb.] 11. *Thursday*. A Grand Committee, on the Examination of the Report prepared for the House upon the Duke of O[rmond]'s and Sir George Rook's Journals. In the Draught offered by the Duke of Bolton (Chairman) some Observations were made which seemed to bear hard upon Sir George; and such indeed as could not be fairly drawn from any Matters of Fact, made out by Evidence. These were prefaced with the words—*It appears to this Committee*; and—*it does not Appear to this Committee*. From the word *Appear*, the Earl of Nottingham and others took Notice that the Committee gave their own *Opinion*; which the Order of the House did not impower them to do: Their Instructions being only to Inspect the said Journals, and haveing Considered them, to make their Report. Now; this Consideration was not to be farther extended than the picking out such select particulars in matters of Fact as to them seemed most worthy of a Debate in the House: But did not allow their drawing Inferences and Conclusions, previous to such a Debate. This was, at last, agreed to; and the whole Form of the Report ordered to be changed.

The House was resumed too late (after two o'clock) to go upon the Lord Wharton's Appeal; though most of the Judges (particularly all the Barons of the Exchequer who were chiefly concerned) were present, and acquainted the House that to morrow (being the last day of the Term) they could not be so. Notwithstanding which, the Appeal was adjourned till to morrow; ordered to take place of all other Matters.

Haveing in the morning presented my Sermon to the Queen and Prince, I carryed one this Evening to the Archbishop of York: And had there an Account, from Mr Aislaby,[486] of the long Remonstrance of the Commons (this Day) against the Ministry of the late Reign.[487]

[Feb.] 12. *Friday*. I sent over 6 Copies of my Sermon to Lambeth; and Ordered the rest to be carryed to the House, where I found that the Bishop of Bangor had not answered the Request of the House in printing his on November 5 and so others formerly.

In the House, Lord Wharton's Appeal argued stoutly by Sir Thomas Powis and Sir S. Harcourt; though reported that the Commons (as was said) had forbidden 'em to appear in that Cause. Sir Thomas said there Never was a Record so strangely taken off the File as this is said to have been; so that no man knowes when, or by

---

[486] John Aislabie (1670–1742), MP for Northallerton, 1702–5, and Ripon, 1695–1702, 1705–21. See K. Darwin, 'John Aislabie (1670–1742)', *Yorkshire Archaeological Journal*, xxxvii (1948–51), 262–324.
[487] See *CJ* xiv, 188–91.

whom, 'twas done: Nor is it such a Return to the Commission as it ought to be; haveing no Depositions, Verdict or Map, annexed to it. The Eight Skins have been all one Roll. If others (as objected) concerned, why were they not called before the Barons?

Mr Sollicitor (Sir S. Harcourt) observed that in 1700 Mr Squire, in his Answer in Chancery, calls this a *Copy*; and so it appears he then thought it. Afterwards practised with Thompson, a Sollicitor in the Exchequer, to get it privately filed. Next, the Case was dubious before the Barons; who made two Contrary Orders. The Lords have a precedent for giveing sentence, in 11 Henry 6 where a like Case (a false Survey of Hartlepool &c.) was carryed by the Bishop of Durham. That was Cancelled; which is more than's now asked: Nothing being Requested (NB.) but that it may be set aside till the Quarrel about the Lead-Mines is over. The Queen not concerned. If she had, though the Sollicitor [Harcourt] had overlooked it, the Attorney Generall [Northey] would have applyed to the House. Barons may Err; and the Lords proper Judges of Errours. Fileing of imperfect Records dangerous.

On the other side Mr Cowper exposed the Attempt. Lord Wharton, he observed, was not grieved by the Barons; who had fully heard his Objections below.[488] The precedent of Henry 6 (he said) was not to the purpose; since that was onely a contest of Right betwixt the King and Bishop of Durham, properly cognizable by the Lords. The Lord Wharton thought below that the sentence of the Barons in this case would be Final; and therfore made his outmost effort. The Rolls of the Exchequer are transcribed in a Book; where this Record is copyed *Verbatim*. The Holes on the Top of the Parchment are easily accounted for by those that know in what manner the Clerks use to take Transcripts of such Records; pinning them before them, &c. the Objection, about its being imperfect, of no Consideration: since every piece and fragment of a genuine Record ought to be preserved and kept upon the File.

Mr Phipps (on the same side) said Mr Squire could not reasonably be made a Defendant in a Case wherein the Barons of the Exchequer had acted *ex officio*. The Queen has a Fee-farm-Rent out of some of the Lands in Question: And She (at this Rate) must lose her Right in case Mr Squire makes a faint Defence. The cited Instrument of 11 Henry 6 is an Act of Parliament: and no Sentence of the Lords. My Lord Wharton has been already heard; the Judgement of the Barons was deliberate; the writeing of this Survey is in a hand that answers to its Date; it's entered in the Auditor's Book, and was copyed (by Mr Thompson) in 1674, when, 'tis certain, it was upon

---

[488] In the Court of Exchequer in Westminster Hall.

the File. [Hereupon, a Debate arose, whether that Copy might be produced in evidence: And, the Counsell withdrawing, the House divided on the Question. *Yeas*, 17. *Noes*, 31. NB. The Duke of Bolton was amongst the former.][489] It was perused afterwards, on the Files, by Mr Hawkins; and carryed a Cause of Marquess of Winchester.[490] 'Tis also known and offered to be proved, how Mr Grainger[491] got it off.

The Counsel being all withdrawn (those on behalf of the City not being allowed to argue) what had been said was at large repeated in the Debates of the House. At last, on the previous Question for *Reverse*, the House Divided; and the Voices were equal, 19 and 19. *Praesumitur pro Negante*.[492] So, the Lords sent it to be Tryed in the Courts below. The Earl of Nottingham was indefatigable in opposeing my Lord Wharton and the Bishop of Sarum and Lord Hallifax gave also their Voices against him, to his manifest surprize.[493] The House adjourned, about a Quarter before Twelve at night, to Munday.

[Feb.] 13. *Saturday*. After a visit to my sister Rothery, I called in at Charing-Cross; to view two Kaamaes[494] (as they called 'em) lately brought from the West Indies. The Description Which the printed papers gave of 'em, was—That they were as Tame as a Lamb, haveing a Trunk like an Elephant, Teeth like a man and Eyes like a Rinocerus; wonderful Ears, with a furr round 'em like Sable; a neck and main, like a Horse; a skin as thick as that of a Buffler,[495] and a Voice like a Bird. And the Figure they gave of it was this that is here subjoyned [*opposite*]. I found neither the proboscis nor the Penis, to answer this Representation: For the Snout was more like that of a Badger or Mole, and the Male was Retromingent. 'Tis the *Glama Peruvianus*, described by Mr Ray. *Synops. Animal. Quadrup*. p. 145.[496]

[Feb.] 14. *Sunday*. Waiting for Dr Gibson in the Cloysters, I observed the Earl of R[ochester] and the Dean of Christ Church [Aldrich]

---

[489] Nicolson's brackets.

[490] Possibly a reference to Charles Paulet, eldest son and heir of the 2nd Duke of Bolton (see Appendix A), though it is not clear which Marquess of Winchester is meant here.

[491] John Granger (Grainger), First Clerk to Viscount Fitzharding, a Teller in the Exchequer. *CTB 1702*, p. 62.

[492] For further details of this day's proceedings on this cause see HMC *Lords MSS* v, 170–2.

[493] Halifax was a fellow lord of the Junto and the Bishop of Salisbury a staunch Whig.

[494] Llamas. The picture, however, suggests they may have been tapirs.

[495] Buffalo.

[496] *Synopsis Methodica Animalium Quadrupedum et Serpentini Generis* (1693), by John Ray (1627–1705).

goeing in pretty Early to the Cabinet-Council in the Dean of
W[estminste]r's[497] lodgeings. New Resolutions to be taken in the
Convocation-Matters.[498]—Thence to preach for Dr Kennet, at St
Botulph's Aldgate: into which the Bishop of London had, that
week, given a vexatious Institution *in Curam Animarum*, tho'
the thing is onely a Curacy or Donative in the Disposeal of the
parishioners.[499]

In the Evening I called on our Dean at St James's; and found him
surrounded with a Troop of old Officers of the Army, &c. *Hinc
illae Lachrymae*!

[Feb.] 15. *Munday*. The Committee on Sir George Rook's Journal
was very full; And, the Report being prepared by the Duke of
Bolton, Chairman,[500] several Amendments were made which favoured
the Admiral and dashed his prosecutors. Ordered that the Report
be made to morrow, and considered on Wednesday.—The Earl

[497] Thomas Sprat, Bishop of Rochester, see Appendix A. For most of the late seventeenth
and the eighteenth centuries the Bishop of Rochester was also Dean of Westminster.

[498] For the 'new resolutions', once more aimed provocatively against the bishops by
the Lower House, see Sykes, *Wake*, i, 121.

[499] For Kennett's insecure title to St Botolph and the many attacks upon him made by
the vestry, who refused to recognise him as minister until 1707, see Bennett, *White Kennett*,
pp. 178-80. Kennett wrote to Charles Hinde on 6 Feb. 1703 that 'they are trying hard again
to turn me out from Aldgate'. BL Lansdowne MS 1014, f. 30.

[500] The full report is printed in *LJ* xvii, 280-92.

of Nottingham brought in a list of Licenses[501] granted to Papists &c. for comeing out of France, by King William: And the Number amounted to 547.

Upon hearing an Appeal of Warburton,[502] the Decree affirmed.

[Feb.] 16. *Tuesday.* After the Report about Sir George Rook (read, and referred to the Consideration of to morrow) a message from the Commons desireing a Conference; the Messengers acquainted that the House will return an Answer by Messengers of their own. The Bill for qualifying Members of Parliament[503] adjourned (in order to be finally rejected) to Munday.

[Feb.] 17. *Wednesday.* An Address to Her Majesty, thanking Her for Licenseing so few from France.

The House of Commons [were] acquainted that the Lords agree to a Conference immediately. The Managers bring in a warm Report from Col. Granvil, remonstrateing against the Lords medling in Accounts and protesting against their Resolutions in my Lord Hallifax's Case; *Which,* say they, *could have no other End than either to Intimidate the Judges or prepossess a Jury.*

[Feb.] 18. *Thursday.* I preached at St James's, and dined with (Dr Wake) the Dean of Exeter; who, amongst his other agreable Entertainment, gave me a pleasant story of the Scotch Commander who was *bashful in the face of his Enemy.*

I was not this day in the House; and so escaped the being concerned in the sharp votes against the Commons. 1. Asserting the Right of the Lords to Examine public Accounts. 2. Justifying their proceeding in Lord Hallifax's Case. 3. Declareing the ill Language of the Commons subversive of the Government.

In the Evening with Dr Waugh, Dr Gibson, Mr Richardson and Mr Hutchinson.[504]

[Feb.] 19. *Friday.* I was forced to leave the House (in the middle of a great Tryal betwixt the Towns of Nottingham and Warwick &c.)[505]

---

[501] Printed in HMC *Lords MSS* v, 203–8. The total granted, according to this source, was 447.

[502] Alice and Esther Warburton, see HMC *Lords MSS* v, 156–7.

[503] See above, n. 476.

[504] Possibly Michael Hutchinson (*c*.1677–1740), a native of Westmorland, and Fellow of Queen's College, Oxford, since 1701. Later he became Minister of the chapel of Hammersmith in 1712 and Rector of Newnham, Hants, in 1719.

[505] For details, see HMC *Lords MSS* v, 161–2.

by reason of a great swimming in my head: And, that night, fell into violent purgeing and vomitting.

[Feb.] 20. [*Saturday*.] My Distemper continued violent,[506] and kept me within till the Evening; when I got to Dr L[ancaster]'s.

[Feb.] 21. [*Sunday*.] I preached at St James's before the Queen; dined at the Archbishop of York's; with whom I left my Proxy.[507] Takeing leave (in the Evening) at Grey's Inn, &c. I lodged at my brother Joseph's.

[Feb.] 22. [*Monday*.] I took the Coach for York, in the Company of Mr Hutchinson of Newcastle[508] and Mr Wilson of Richmond . . .[509]

---

[506] Nicolson was not able to report that his health was restored until the end of the following month. See BL Harleian MS 3780, f. 265: N. to Wanley, 25 Mar. 1703.

[507] See above, chapter 1, pp. 32–6, for Nicolson's use of his proxy.

[508] Jonathan Hutchinson (d. 1711), Whig MP for Berwick-on-Tweed, 1702–11, was a Newcastle brewer and distiller.

[509] Nicolson travelled in the York coach as far as Ferrybridge in Yorkshire where, on 26 Feb., he changed to horseback, having been met at Doncaster by his man, Robin, with horses. On Sunday, 28 Feb., he preached at Aldborough and inspected the Roman remains. The bishop reached home (Salkeld) on 2 Mar. 1703. See *CW* ii (1902), 193.

Session 2

24 October 1704–15 January 1705

The eighteen months from February 1703 to October 1704 were Nicolson's longest period of absence from London during the whole of Anne's reign. As in 1709–10, when his stay in the north was almost as protracted, the reason was an episcopal visitation, that of 1704 being the first and most thorough he undertook in the Carlisle diocese.[1] Unfortunately his satisfaction at the completion of this mission was soon sullied. In the summer that followed he suffered a grave local embarrassment, when Francis Atterbury, his adversary of the Convocation Controversy and the obstructor of his Oxford doctorate, was nominated by the Queen to the deanery of Carlisle. Atterbury had most powerful backers—Lord Treasurer Godolphin, Secretary Harley, and Archbishop Sharp—in securing this, his first major preferment; so the bishop's ill-advised and fruitless attempts to black the new dean's institution merely added to the humiliation of his inescapable eventual surrender.[2] His rebuff, together with the death of his old neighbour and patron Sir Christopher Musgrave, in 1704, significantly advanced the cooling process already under way in relations between Nicolson and the High Church Tories, whom he blamed more than Godolphin for his plight.[3]

By the time that Nicolson was ready to set out for London on 12 October, in good time for the parliamentary session,[4] much had happened to frustrate the High Tory cause since his last appearance in town. Only in the field of Church preferments had they prospered; for in addition to Atterbury's step up the ladder, Hooper had received two bishoprics in quick succession (St Asaph and Bath and Wells) in 1703—though as a reward for moderation rather than extremism —and Beveridge had then been promoted to St Asaph, on Sharp's

---

[1] Nicolson, *Miscellany*.

[2] See, *inter alia*, HMC *Bath MSS* i, 57, 63; HMC *Portland MSS* iv, 98, 127–8, 131–2, 138–9; *Atterbury Epist. Corr.* iii, 215–50: Atterbury's letters to Bishop Trelawney, 6 July– 21 Sept., *passim*. 'When Dr. Atterbury kissed her Majesty's hand for the deanery of Carlisle', Harley had written on 8 July, 'she was pleased to tell him she was glad of the opportunity to show him the respect she had for him, and that what she had given him was but a beginning of her favour'; and Godolphin had just said much the same to Sharp (Lloyd-Baker MS Box 4, L121: 4 July).

[3] Below, p. 225.

[4] He spent twelve days *en route*, doing much sightseeing, including a visit to Chatsworth. See Diary, vol. 4 (unpaginated): 19 Oct. 1704, for Nicolson's description of Chatsworth. Cf. White Kennett's description in 1707 (BL Lansdowne MS 1013, ff. 290–1).

advice, in 1704.[5] Over the Queen's administration, however, the right-wing Tories were very far from achieving that dominance which Anne's accession had encouraged them to hope for. Indeed, by the spring of 1704 they were in retreat. The three most prominent of their leaders had gone out of office; Rochester and Nottingham having resigned in pique,[6] while Seymour had just been dismissed together with the Lord Chamberlain, Jersey. Although the Earl of Kent, a pallid Whig, had replaced Jersey, the main beneficiaries of these and lesser changes had not been the Whigs but the moderate Tory supporters of Robert Harley. Harley himself, already Speaker, had become Secretary of State for the Northern Department in May 1704.

Meanwhile in parliament during the session of 1703-4 the High Tories had seen their 'darling bill', that against Occasional Conformity, founder for the second time. But the most remarkable feature of the session which Nicolson had missed had been a further, and really serious, deterioration in relations between the two Houses. Queen Anne's ministry as first constructed had proved quite incapable of maintaining harmony between a House of Commons whose Tory majority was, putting it mildly, unreceptive to Court management and a House of Lords in which the Whigs continued strong and grew in confidence month by month. The Lords' rejection of the second Occasional Conformity Bill (a defeat in which the Whig and moderate bishops played a vital part)[7] had been but one instance of this deterioration. There had been disharmony, too, after the revelation of the so-called 'Scotch plot'[8] when the Commons had soft-pedalled their inquiry whereas the Whigs in the Lords had raised a storm and tried to implicate Lord Nottingham. Worse friction still had been produced by the Aylesbury election case, which stored up bitter resentments for the following session.[9] It remained to be

[5] Beveridge to Sharp, 17 July 1704, printed in Thomas Sharp, *The Life of John Sharp* (1825), ii, 43. Sharp also promoted the advance of another Tory churchman, the veteran George Bull, to St David's in Mar. 1705 (ibid., i, 322-3).

[6] The former in Feb. 1703, the latter in Apr. 1704.

[7] See, e.g., Holmes, *British Politics*, pp. 102, 308; *Sacheverell*, p. 40 (on the bishops); H. L. Snyder, 'The defeat of the Occasional Conformity Bill and the Tack', *BIHR* xli (1968), 175-6.

[8] An attempt in 1703 by Franco-Jacobite agents to raise the Highlands. There is an excellent account of its political repercussions in H. Horwitz, *Revolution Politicks: The Career of Daniel Finch, second Earl of Nottingham* (Cambridge, 1968), pp. 191-6.

[9] Behind the constitutional issues in the case of *Ashby versus White*, in which the Commons' claim to complete jurisdiction over all aspects of election disputes clashed with the subject's right to take his case as an elector to the courts and to the House of Lords, lay the party interests of two prominent politicians. Lord Wharton, Ashby's backer, was the Junto's chief electioneering magnate and head of the Whig interest in Buckinghamshire, and Sir John Pakington, Tory MP for Worcestershire, was lord of the manor of Aylesbury.

seen whether the remodelled administration of April–May 1704 could improve this deplorable situation.

One thing at least was in its favour. While Nicolson was busy feuding with Atterbury in the summer of 1704 the Spanish Succession War, hitherto not conspicuously successful for the Grand Alliance, had taken a dramatic turn. The Duke of Marlborough's astonishing victory at Blenheim (13 August) seemed a complete vindication of the land strategy which he and Godolphin had been pursuing, backed by the Whigs and Harleyites but heavily criticised by the High Tories. Many of the latter had reacted petulantly to Blenheim by seizing on the indecisive naval battle off Malaga (24 August), which had followed the capture of Gibraltar, and building up Rooke, the English commander, as a hero comparable to the great duke.

Yet if Blenheim had lifted one weight on pressure from the ministry a political event which had taken place at home in the same month threatened to expose it to fresh parliamentary difficulties in the autumn. On 5 August Godolphin, the Lord Treasurer, had to advise the Queen to give the royal assent to the Scottish Act of Security. This Act, born of the anti-English sentiment which had redoubled in volume since the collapse of the Union negotiations of 1702-3, had originally passed the parliament of Scotland in its session of 1703.[10] It empowered the Scottish parliament to choose its own successor to the throne after the death of Anne; and it indicated firmly that this nominee could not be a member of the House of Hanover unless Scotland received unqualified satisfaction of all her grievances and solid guarantees of her future freedom 'from the English or any foreign influence'. For twelve months after Queensberry, the Queen's Commissioner, had refused the Act the traditional 'touch of the sceptre' Scotland had seethed with unrest and defiance; and when the Act passed again in July 1704 Godolphin (who could not have anticipated that the miracle of Blenheim was at hand to transform the dangerous military situation on the Continent which the Scots had exploited) felt he had no option but to give way.

Of course Godolphin was not expecting to have to stomach the Security Act as a permanency; he was still looking to a full union of the two Kingdoms as the only foolproof way of preserving the Scottish succession against the Jacobites. But meanwhile, his humiliation exposed him in the Westminster parliament both to the rancour of the Tories, who were now openly bent on his downfall, and to the power politics of the Whigs, who had decided that it was time to

[10] W. Ferguson, 'The making of the Treaty of Union of 1707', *SHR* xliii (1964), 96–8; P. W. J. Riley, 'The Scottish parliament of 1703', ibid., xlvii (1968).

wrest from the Court some reward for their support in the House of Lords and saw the chance to exploit the government's embarrassment to this end.[11] Nicolson heard later, through a Scottish grapevine, that the Junto, provoked by the promotion of the Harleyites the previous spring, had secretly helped to urge on the Security Act, on the second occasion, through its 'Revolution Whig' friends in Scotland.[12]

Nicolson, in his border diocese, had more reason than most to be anxious about the situation. Yet although he resumed his seat in the House of Lords on 24 October 1704, only one day after the opening of the final session of this parliament, he had to wait until 23 November for the House to begin its momentous deliberation on Anglo-Scottish relations. Lord Haversham, a Tory convert who was preparing to open the attack on the ministry, had prepared his ammunition for 13 November; but the Junto Whigs, who needed time to work out their own strategy, secured a postponement.[13] Godolphin, for his part, put what faith he had, for the time being, in the presence of the Queen, whom he had persuaded to attend the Lords as a spectator for the first time in her reign;[14] the limit of his ambition was to keep in play until Marlborough's return in mid-December, which would bring the government the relief of the general's reflected glory.

Nicolson kept a most valuable record of the Lords' proceedings on Scotland (with some comments on those of the Commons) from the opening encounter on 23 November and the crucial debate of the 29 November until 19 December. Sadly for us he came to the end of volume 5 of his diary at precisely the point in January 1705 when the bills embodying the new policy towards Scotland, initiated in both Houses, were coming 'on the anvil'.[15] It would have been instructive to have Nicolson's account of their final stages (11 January to 2 February), not least because they were briefly placed in jeopardy by yet another constitutional quarrel.[16]

[11] Nottingham Univ. Lib., Portland MS PwA. 942: Halifax to Portland, Aug. 1704.

[12] Diary, 10 Dec. 1704. Dr Riley has found other evidence to corroborate these suspicions: P. W. J. Riley, 'The Union of 1707 as an episode in English politics', *EHR* lxxxiv (1969), 506–7.

[13] Below, 10 and 23 Nov.

[14] For the psychological effect of the Queen's presence on some peers, especially congenital 'Court' peers, see Holmes, *British Politics*, pp. 390–1. For the proposal to construct a gallery in the Lords' chamber, arising partly out of her decision, see Diary, 7, 8 Nov. etc., and Chapter 2, pp. 84–6 above.

[15] There is no hint of a reason for this hiatus at the beginning of volume 6 of the original manuscript, whose first entry is for 25 Mar. See *CW* iii (1903) 1, whose first entry is for 26 Mar. 1705.

[16] For these stages see *Parl. Hist.* vi, 373–4; Burnet, *History*, v, 183–4. This particular dispute centred on the House of Lords' right to initiate a bill which contained money clauses, even if these were only financial penalties. In this connection see below, 6 Nov.

211

Nevertheless it is still possible to trace through Nicolson's pages most of the essential preliminary steps of November and December 1704 which paved the way for the new, and this time conclusive, Union negotiations of 1706. We can observe the success of Godolphin and his colleagues in wriggling off the hook prepared for them by the High Tories; the vital decision of the Junto Whig peers under the guidance of Somers, Halifax, Wharton, and Sunderland to forsake a destructive attack on the ministry for constructive policies designed to settle the Scottish problem and safeguard the succession; and finally the emergence of their 'carrot and stick' prescription for such policies—the offer of fresh negotiations for an 'incorporating Union', combined with an Aliens Bill,[17] severe sanctions on the Scottish wool and linen trade, and military preparations in the north.[18] What these pages inevitably conceal from us is the hard bargaining between Godolphin and the Junto which had made this outcome possible: first, the negotiations during November, with Lord Monthermer[19] acting as intermediary; then the decisive twist given to the knife on 29 November when the Lord Treasurer, as Lord Dartmouth recalled years later, 'did not know which side would fall hardest upon him' and his only defence, at first, was to 'talk nonsense very fast'.[20] It was Wharton, we are told, who clinched the final deal on the floor of the House while the debate still smouldered, delivering 'Lord Treasurer's head in a bag' to his friends,[21] and it was probably Somers, in the end, who 'diverted the whole debate' into the new channels,[22] and turned the tide for the government— and for Scotland.

Godolphin could have been forgiven for feeling by the end of November that he had passed through the fire. For it was only on 28 November, the day before his ordeal in the Lords, that he and Harley, after weeks of careful management, survived the long-expected 'Tack' in the Commons by 251 votes to 154. 'The Commons, I find, are most firmly resolved on the bill of occasional conformity',

[17] See Ferguson, p. 101.

[18] See below, 6 Dec., 11 Dec., beating off the Tory attack in the Commons, 12 Dec., and the commitment of the Lower House to policies more or less consonant with those of the Lords, 16 Dec., 18–19 Dec.

[19] Later (1709) 2nd Duke of Montagu, and in 1705 Marlborough's son-in-law.

[20] Burnet, *History*, v, 182 and Dartmouth's note.

[21] It was afterwards understood that a key point in the bargain driven was Godolphin's agreement to the appointment of a leading Whig MP and lawyer, Sir William Cowper, as Lord Keeper of the Great Seal as soon as possible, as 'part of his penance [in Dartmouth's words] for having passed the Scotch Act of Security'. Note to ibid., p. 225.

[22] Rather than Halifax, as Dartmouth later recollected. Nicolson's version would seem to suggest so, and still more do the accounts of the debate sent to George Baillie by the Duke of Roxburghe and James Johnston, 30 Nov. and 2 Dec., *Jerviswood Correspondence*, pp. 12–15.

Atterbury had written to the absent Bishop Trelawney at the start of the session, 'and (it is said) if they have strength enough, will certainly tack it'.[23] From the time he arrived in town Nicolson, too, was kept well abreast, by his friends and acquaintances in the Lower House, of the hopes, fears, and manœuvres surrounding the third attempt of the High Tories to quash Occasional Conformity by statute. The Commons held the key to the situation; for although the bill was toned down, compared with that of 1703,[24] it was plain to everyone that it would not get past the Lords on its own account. Among the bill's advocators the principal dispute was between those who proposed bringing traditional pressures on the government, by holding up supply bills until the Court persuaded the Lords to give way,[25] and those extremists such as Robert Byerley, who told Nicolson on 27 October that he was 'strongly for consolidating the Bill against Occasional Conformity with the first money-Bill', the vital Land Tax Bill.

The ultimate crushing defeat of the Tackers, though a triumph for Harley, was less than that for Godolphin.[26] His main aim had been to prevent the bill being reintroduced in the first place, since once brought in it must pass the Commons, whatever the fate of the Tack, and therefore come up to the Lords again to embarrass himself and Marlborough.[27] As it happened, when the bill did reach the Lords on 15 December, the vote was so decisive that Godolphin's old dilemma attracted less attention than he had feared. The same could be said of our diarist, who still felt bound to vote for the bill although he had clearly disapproved of the 'great swaggerings' of its Commons' supporters and had no sympathy with the Tackers.[28] It is interesting, however, that Nicolson, in common with many others at the time,[29] did not anticipate the fact that the bill would not be seen in parliament for seven years.

It was almost inevitable that the Lower House of Convocation would use the Occasional Conformity issue as a weapon in its continuing battle with the bishops. But the very few references in Nicolson's diary this session to the proceedings of Convocation

[23] 28 Oct. 1704, *Atterbury Epist. Corr.* iii, 252.

[24] Itself less severe than its predecessor.

[25] See Godolphin's account of the Tory meeting at the Fountain Tavern on 6 Nov., in HMC *Bath MSS* i, 64.

[26] 'Nothing can be done, I find, without so much labour and pain as makes one very often of opinion that the play is scarce worth the Candles' (BL Loan 29/64/12: Godolphin to Harley, 'Monday at 2 [27 Nov. 1704]').

[27] HMC *Bath MSS* i, 64-5.

[28] Neither had his friend, Archbishop Sharp (*The Life of John Sharp*, i, 305-6).

[29] Sharp again, for example. See his diary account of a conversation with the Queen, quoted ibid.

reflect the fact that this campaign was losing something of its momentum:[30] a great disappointment to those 'young Oxford divines' whose 'common practice' it had become to 'pray (before sermon) for the House of Commons and the Convocation', and of course to the Lower House's doughtiest champion, Dean Atterbury, with whom Nicolson continued to joust in London during this winter.[31]

Because of the unfortunate break in the diary after 15 January we have no account from Nicolson's pen of the great culminating struggle between the Lords and Commons over the revived case of the men of Aylesbury, which was to bring the session—and the parliament—to a tempestuous end on 14 March.[32] The likelihood is that the bishop stayed in town until ten days or so before the prorogation: the assistant clerk of the House of Lords recorded his attendance as late as 3 March.[33] He would certainly have been present at the time of the first 'free conference' between the Houses on 28 February; but not at the time of the second on 13 March, which was also the day of the great Lords' address to the Queen on the Aylesbury case, an epic constitutional document on which Somers and his Whig friends left their indelible stamp. The Junto had been quietly angling for Nicolson throughout the session. Wharton went out of his way to oblige him in diocesan affairs, Halifax to show him his splendid library, Somers to listen to his sermons. His respect for Somers and also for Halifax, with whom he was closely engaged in the work of the Lords' Committee on the Public Records,[34] was already profound. Had he been present at the framing of the address of 13 February, with its eloquent vindication of the rights of the Upper House, Nicolson would doubtless have admired their handiwork.

[24 Oct. 1704] . . . we arrived [in London] about 5 in the Evening, and (haveing supped with my Brother in Salisbury-Court) were conducted to our Lodgeings at Mrs Beal's in the Old Palace-Yard at Westminster.

[Oct.] 25. *Wednesday.* I went, too forwardly, to the House; where I had the Congratulations of the Bishops, Lord Nottingham, Lord Keeper [Wright], &c. Address[35] reported by my Lord Wharton and Approved: Whilst Lord Chamberlain [Kent] went to know the

---

[30] Cf. Sykes, *Wake* i, 119–21; Bennett, *Tory Crisis*, pp. 77–9.

[31] Nicolson delayed going to Court for three weeks after his arrival in London because he was unsure how Queen Anne would receive him, below, 14 Nov.

[32] *Parl. Hist.* vi, 377–436; Burnet, *History*, v, 191–8.

[33] *LJ* xvii, 696.   [34] See above, Chapter 1, pp. 40–4.

[35] The Lords' address in reply to the Queen's speech of 24 Oct., see *LJ* xvii, 567, 569.

Queen's pleasure, when She would be attended, Lord Hallifax moved that an Order might be made against the Reading of any Private Bill, not first printed and delivered at the Doors of the House. Which was seconded, and agreed to *Nemine Contradicente*.

I dined with Sir C. Musgrave's three Sons[36] (together with my Fellow Lodger Mr Brewer[37] of Kent) in Swallow Street. Bishop of Norwich [Moore] removed.[38]

[Oct.] 26. *Thursday*. I dined with Dr Gibson, after Viewing the pottery at Carlile-House;[39] and afterwards waited on my Lord of Canterbury [Tenison] who assured me of Mr Toland's[40] being out of Countenance at Hannover. His first Reception was by carrying the Archbishop of York's [Sharp's] Coronation Sermon to the Princess Sophia; and he was cashiered by Mr Fermin[41] and others for his Knavery.—The Dean of Carlisle's [Atterbury's] father[42] a Favourite of the Earl of Nottingham. *Hinc illae Lachrymae. Non pas*. Kissing old R. Snow, and dispatching my Letters, I spent the Remainder of the Evening with Brother Joseph dismissing Robin, and's horses, for the North, &c.

[Oct.] 27. *Friday*. In the Morning, Mrs Jane Lawson,[43] and her young son, in Complaint against Sir Wilfrid.[44] She referred her Character

[36] Christopher and his half-brothers, Joseph and Thomas. For the first two, see Appendix A. Thomas (1679-1756) was a barrister-at-law of Lincoln's Inn. P. Musgrave, *Notes on the Ancient Family of Musgrave* (Leeds, 1911), p. 160.

[37] Possibly John Brewer (c.1654-1724), MP for New Romney, 1689-1710, Treasurer of the Prize Office and Receiver-General of Prizes, 1702-7.

[38] A rumour without foundation.

[39] Formerly the Bishop of Rochester's house in Lambeth, it had been given to the bishops of Carlisle in 1539 in compensation for the bishop's previous house in the Strand which had been acquired by John Russell, later Earl of Bedford. The house was sold in 1647, and occupied by Sir Edward Dering. It reverted to the see in 1660, but remained unused by the bishops. In about 1690 part of it was used as a pottery which closed around 1730. The house was demolished in 1827. See *Survey of London*, xviii, 120; xxiii, 75; *The Diaries and Papers of Sir Edward Dering, 2nd Bt., 1644-1684*, ed. M. F. Bond (1976), p. 4.

[40] John Toland (1670-1722), prominent deist, pamphleteer and controversialist, author of the notorious *Christianity not Mysterious* (1696). See J. G. Simms, 'John Toland (1670-1722), Donegal Heretic', *Irish Historical Studies*, xvi (1968-9), 304-20. Lord Macclesfield took him to Hanover in 1701 to present the Act of Settlement, which Toland had attacked in a pamphlet, to the Electress Sophia.

[41] Thomas Firmin (1632-97), London philanthropist. Hearne called him a 'ranck Socinian [who] was a great man with Dr Tillotson', but Burnet thought him 'really an Arian'. In 1687 he had published Stephen Nye's *A Brief History of the Unitarians, called Socinians*, and after the Revolution he financed the publication or distribution of numerous anti-Trinitarian books and tracts. Hearne, *Collections*, i, 102; Burnet, *History*, iv, 389.

[42] Lewis Atterbury (1621-93), Rector of Milton Keynes.

[43] Sister of Sir Wilfred Lawson.

[44] Sir Wilfred Lawson (c.1665-1704), 2nd Bt. of Isell, Cumberland. Sheriff of Cumberland, 1689-90; MP for Cockermouth 1690-5. *GEC Barts*.

to Dr Gibson; who presently came and approved it. He and I dined with Mr Provost Lancaster and Dr Alston; and, after Dinner, had the Conversation of Coll. Byerley,[45] who is strongly for Consolidateing[46] the Bill against Occasional Conformity with the first money-Bill.[47] He saies he has had the perusal of several Volumes of the Lord Strafford's Letter,[48] which shew the Villany of Court-Intrigues in the dayes of Charles 1.

[Oct.] 28. *Saturday*. This day spent privately, in writeing Letters, &c. saveing that, at night, I had a little of the Conversation of my Neighbour Mr Brewer; who protests against the humour of Consolidateing.

[Oct.] 29. *Sunday*. In the morning, at Westminster-Abbey, I heard an excellent Sermon, on the Case of the Thief on the Cross, by Dr Lynford; whence was inferred the certainty of the Soul's Immortality, the folly of Despair, the Unreasonableness of delaying Repentance, &c.

After I had dined at my Brother's, I went to St Paul's; where, in the Vestry, Dr Chetwood and his great Services (and slender Rewards) were my first entertainment. Dr Godolphin[49] kindly enquired after the Dean of Wells [Grahme] and Coll. Graham's Family. Dr Stanley[50] preached on *Psalm* 95, 8. *To day if*, &c. and very obligeingly Entertained me (after the Service) with Dr Younger, Dr Gee, Dr Pooley,[51] &c. where the Case of the Archbishop of Dublin's [King's] claiming Inthronization in Christ-Church (as well as St Patrick's) was discoursed, and His Grace censured.[52]

[Oct.] 30. *Munday*. In the morning, Mr Thomas Dowson (Mr C. Musgrave's Clerk)[53] gave me a Visit; And, in acknowledgement of my

[45] Robert Byerley, MP for Knaresborough, see Appendix A.

[46] Colloquially, the 'tacking' to a revenue bill, in committee, of a controversial 'foreign' bill or clause, leaving the Lords with little alternative but to accept or reject the whole. After their humiliation over the tack of the Irish Grants Resumption bill to the Land Tax Bill in 1700, the Lords had resolved (1702) that tacking was 'unparliamentary and tends to the destruction of the constitution . . .'.

[47] For the defeat of the attempted 'tack' of the third Occasional Conformity Bill to the Land Tax Bill see below, 28 Nov.

[48] Published 1739. Byerley must have seen the original MSS belonging to Lord Rockingham.

[49] Henry Godolphin (1648–1733), brother of Lord Treasurer Godolphin, Prebendary of St Paul's since 1683, and later Dean, 1707–26.

[50] William Stanley (1647–1731), Archdeacon of London since 1692, and later Dean of St Asaph in 1706.

[51] Giles Pooley, Rector of Wrington, Somerset, 1692–1709, and Vicar of St Leonard, Shoreditch, 1708–20.

[52] For the prolonged feud, 1703–24, between the reforming Primate and the Dean and Chapter of Christ Church, with their extensive Irish properties see *DNB*.

[53] Musgrave's under-clerk in the Ordnance Office.

Recommendation, made me a present of a handsome Table-Book. I dined (after attempting to wait on Mr Secretary Hedges) at Lambeth; whence (the Mist being pretty thick) we had a slender prospect of the Lord Mayor's[54] Cavalcade, by water, to Westminster and the Barges and Streamers that attended him. The Noise of the Guns and Musick (Trumpets, &c.) was more audible, than the shew was Visible. My Lord Archbishop entertained me kindly, with Remarks on the heedless Wills of Sir W. Petty and Dr Barthurst.[55] Dr Kennet and Dr Gibson earnest with me to prepare a Counter-Narrative to Dr Atterbury's.[56]

In the Evening, Mr Provost Lancaster, Dr Alston and I, at Coll. Byerley's; where not a word of Consolidateing.[57] NB. A Drum on Bastions or Counterscarps discovers the Mines of the Besiegers. Dr Alston had eleven Ripe pears, upon a Ciend[58] of this year's growth not two Inches long; which he presented (as an Extraordinary Rarity, with its fruit hanging upon it) to the Bishop of London [Compton].

[Oct.] 31. *Tuesday*. The House of Lords read some few petitions of Appellants; and adjourned to Thursday. The Commons voted a Supply; and adjourned till to morrow. The Lower House of Convocation, on the Debate about their Congratulatory Address to Her Majesty on the late Success of our Fleet and Army,[59] insisted on the Nameing of Sir George Rook as well as the Duke of Marlborough which was not agreed to by the Upper, and so the matter rested, without comeing to any present Conclusion.[60]

I dined at Mr C. Musgrave's; with Mr (Comptroler) Mansel, Mr G. Grandvil[61] (very angry at Lord Nottingham for his severities

---

[54] Sir John Parsons.

[55] Sir William Petty (1623–87), Surveyor-General of Ireland, see E. Strauss, *Sir William Petty* (1954); and Ralph Bathurst, Dean of Wells, who died on 11 June 1704.

[56] With regard to the recent Carlisle institution dispute. See above, sessional intro., p. 208. After seeking legal advice Gibson told Nicolson to publish a 'plain statement in order to avoid misrepresentation at Court to the detriment of the party'. *Nicolson Epist. Corr.* i, 106. Nicolson's *A True State of the Controversy between the Present Bishop and Dean of Carlisle in a Letter from a Northern Divine* appeared early in Dec. See Diary, 20 Nov., 4 Dec. 1704. Atterbury inevitably responded with *A Letter from the South, by way of an answer to a late letter from a Northern Divine.* Cf. Bennett, *Tory Crisis*, pp. 78, 317.

[57] The prospective 'tackers' were as yet unsure of their welcome even among High Tory MPs. See HMC *Bath MSS* i, 64; HMC *Portland MSS* iv, 363: Godolphin to Harley [8 Nov. 1704, misdated by ed. 1706]; and cf. *Marlborough–Godolphin Corr.* i, 398, no. 407.

[58] *Sic.* for 'cient', obsolete form of scion, a shoot or twig.

[59] At Malaga and Blenheim.

[60] The disappointment of the High Church activists at this setback is expressed in Atterbury's letter to Bishop Trelawney, 7 Nov., *Atterbury Epist. Corr.* iii, 253.

[61] Sir Thomas Mansel, MP for Glamorgan, and Comptroller of the Household since the Harleyite promotions in Apr. See Appendix A. George Granville (1667–1735), MP for

towards, this Gentlemen's brother, the Governor of Barbadoes) and Mr Knatchbul.[62]

Nov. 1. *Wednesday.* The Commons met; and, haveing received and approved the Vote of their Committee for a Supply,[63] presently adjourned.

I dined (with the two Mr Musgraves and Mr G. Lawson) at the *Blew-posts* in the Hay-Market: where Mr C. Musgrave declared his Inclinations to let the Bill of Occasional Conformity sleep. *Esto!*

[Nov.] 2. *Thursday.* After a visit from Mr Huddleston[64] and Mr Symson,[65] I went to the House; where a Couple of Appeals read, and adjourned. The Bishop of Lichfield [Hough], earnest for calling for the Advisers of passing the Scotch Act of Security.[66] Mr Cook, of Derbyshire, for bringing in his old Bill.[67] House of Commons on the Act for the Poor, brought in by Sir H. Mackworth.[68]

In the evening (after Dr Woodward's humble dinner with me) visits paid to Mr James Lowther at the Temple, Mrs Waugh[69] and the Chancellor's Brothers:[70] who declare (as their Cousin George does) for Sir G. Rook.

Fowey, 1702-10, another Harleyite. Later MP for Cornwall, 1710-12, and created Lord Lansdowne on 1 Jan. 1712.

[62] Sir Bevil Granville (d. 1706), Governor of Barbados, 1703-6. Edward Knatchbull (d. 1730), MP for Rochester, 1702-5, and later for Kent, 1713-15, 1722-7.

[63] Of £4,670,486, of which the land tax was expected to raise about £2 million.

[64] Andrew Huddleston (1637-1706) of Huttonjohn, Cumb., was the first Protestant in the family. He married a Lawson of Isell, and was 'much respected in the county, and a zealous promoter of the Revolution'; but was gaoled in 1698 for malpractices as receiver of the land tax. *CSPD 1698*, p. 54; Nicolson and Burn, ii, 369; W. Jackson, *Papers and Pedigrees mainly relating to Cumberland and Westmorland* (1892), ii, 331, 333, 339.

[65] Matthew Simpson or Symson (*c.*1675-?1742), later Rector of Moreby, near Horncastle, Lincs., in 1704 and ordained a canon of Lincoln by Bishop Nicolson in 1718. *Speculum Dioeceseos Linc.*, pp. 8, 89. 　　　　　[66] See above, sessional intro., p. 210.

[67] See Diary, 3 Nov. 1704. The estate bill of Thomas Coke was for the confirmation of an agreement between him and Thomas Smith, later Bishop of Carlisle, for the rectory of Melborne, Derbyshire, being vested in Coke and his heirs, upon the augmentation of the rents to the see of Carlisle and of the stipend to the Vicar of Melborne. The bill was read the first time on 9 Dec. 1704, and after several amendments, received the royal assent on 14 Mar. 1705. See HMC *Lords MSS* vi, 227-8. A similar bill had been introduced on 4 Feb. 1702, but had got no further than a first reading, probably due to the death of Bishop Smith on 12 Apr. 1702. See *CW* i (1901), 41.

[68] Sir Humphrey Mackworth (1657-1727), MP for Cardiganshire, 1701-5, a leading pioneer of poor relief in the eighteenth century. For Mackworth, and his important, but abortive, bill of 1704 (printed in HMC *Lords MSS* vi, 273-87), see Charles Wilson, 'The other face of Mercantilism', *TRHS* 5th ser. ix (1954), 81-101. The Lords subsequently promoted their own relief bill but it too lapsed after its second reading on 17 Feb. 1705. See M. Ransome, 'The parliamentary career of Sir Humphrey Mackworth, 1701-1713', *University of Birmingham Historical Journal*, i (1947-8), 232-47.

[69] Wife of John Waugh, for whom see Appendix A.

[70] Philip and William Tullie.

[Nov.] 3. *Friday*. In the morning, Mr Cook brought me a Draught of a Bill for setling the Rectory of Melburn into a Freehold by Act of Parliament; which is to be considered. The House of Lords ordered the Accounts of the Navy-Charge (for the 4 last years) to be laid before them.

In the afternoon, amongst the old Books in Moor-fields, I purchased Cressy's *Ch[urch] History*[71] for 7s 6d Cawel's *Interpreter*[72] for 1s. &c.

[Nov.] 4. *Saturday*. In the morning, Dr Lancaster; enquireing what I wrote to Dr Crost[hwait].[73] At the House, nothing but a Breach of Privilege; in Arresting the Duke of Devonshire's Master of the Horse. I thanked my Lord Somers; who believes the Queen never was rightly informed of my Dispute with Dr Atterbury. After Dinner, I visitted the Bishop of Norwich; who cautioned me against too great Freedome in the Company of Sir A. Fountain[74] (a bigotted Creature of the Dean of Christ Church [Aldrich]) who, that minute, left his Treatise of Coins for me at my Lodgeings. Dr Lynford saies Chedder-Cliffs (near Wells) are a finer sight than Ookey-Hole.—The Bishop of Sarum [Burnet] gave me his printed Charge to his Clergy;[75] very good.

[Nov.] 5. *Sunday*. The House met before Ten, in Order to the Procession on the Solemnity of the Day:[76] But my Lord of Canterbury, Bishop of Peterburgh [Cumberland] and my self, were the onely members that appeared. I read Prayers; which being over, and the

[71] *The Church History of Brittany [i.e. Britain] from the Beginning of Christianity to the Norman Conquest* (Rouen, 1668), by Hugh Paulin Cressy, Dean of Leighlin in Ireland, known as Serenus Cressy.

[72] *The Interpreter: or Booke containing the Signification of Words*, by John Cowell (d. 1611), first published in Cambridge, 1607. A recent edition of this law dictionary had been extended by White Kennett and published in London, 1701.

[73] Thomas Crosthwait (d. 1710), Principal of St Edmunds Hall, Oxford, 1684-5, Canon of Exeter 1678. According to Hearne (*Collections* i, 306; ii, 339), he was a non-juror who lived on a small inherited estate in the North. He was described by Charlett as a man whose opinions were regarded as of no 'value, weight, or Authority, among the sober men here [Oxford], but rather the Jest, and Diversion of the Town' (Lloyd-Baker MS Box 4, 0 46: Charlett to Sharp, 13 Nov. 1704). For the occasion of this attack see below, n. 93.

[74] Sir Andrew Fountain (1676-1753), connoisseur and collector. Educated at Christ Church, Oxford, under Dean Aldrich, he possessed an extensive coin collection as well as china, pictures, and antiques. He wrote 'Numismata Anglo Saxonica' and 'Anglo-Dorica breviter illustrata' for Hickes's *Thesaurus* of 1705. He was secretary to the Earl of Pembroke.

[75] *A Charge given at the Triennial Visitation . . . in October 1704*, published in London, 1704. In it Burnet reflected on the Lower House of Convocation as an enemy of the bishops, the Church, and the country. The Lower House in turn accused Burnet of breaking the secrecy of Convocation and of derogating the synod. Lathbury, *Convocation*, p. 395.

[76] The anniversary of the Gunpowder Plot and the landing in England of William of Orange.

House adjourned till to morrow, we three attended my Lord Keeper
[Wright] to the Abbey-Church: Where a Learned Sermon was
preached by the Bishop of St Asaph (Dr Beverege)[77] on *Esther* 9,
26 and 27. setting forth the Nature and Occasion of the Jewish
Festivals, and applying the whole to the former part of the Business
of the Day (the Remembrance of the Powder Plot) without one
syllable of the second, the Landing of His late Majesty and the
Deliverance he brought.

[Nov.] 6. *Munday*. A petition of Brewster (the Atturney) and
Devereux the plaintiff, taken into Custody for arresting the Duke of
Devonshire's servant ordered to ly on the Table till the Bayliff's were
likewise taken.[78]

The Judges (by Lord Chief Justice Holt) acquainted the House
that they had considered the Command given 'em (the last Session)
for bringing in a Bill for more effectual Relief of the Poor;[79] and that
they were unanimously of Opinion that no such Bill could be prepared but what must (in the first place) provide for the raiseing of
Money, and also inflict a pecuniary penalty for Non-Observance of
the Law: Both which particulars they humbly submitted to the
Consideration of their Lordships. On Debate, it was agreed that this
House had an unquestionable power of enforceing any Law by
a pecuniary Penalty. But it was doubted how far they could begin
a Bill for the raiseing of Money, tho' not directly in Aid of the
Crown.[80] On a motion (by the Duke of Buckingham) it was resolved
that the Order should rest on the Books, without renewing the
Day of Return. Which was a suspending the matter; in hopes of haveing something sent up (to the same effect) from the Commons.

Mr Dean Atterbury gave me a Visit; and seemed to move for an
Address in favour of Sir George Rook; which (I told him) was long
since done from Carlile.——In the Evening with Dr Lancaster, Dr
Adams[81] and Dr Alston.

[Nov.] 7. *Tuesday*. In the morning, Mrs Dunhall (late Mrs Jane
Lawson) in a great Anguish on hearing of Sir Wilfred's dangerous
Illness. R[obert] Nicolson desires my Intercession for a Land-Waiter's

[77] A recent High Church Tory elevation to the bench (July 1704). See Burnet, *History*,
v, 189. In view of Nicolson's comment on the neglect of 1688 in his sermon, it is probably
significant that Beveridge, a venerable scholar, had turned down a bishopric in 1690 out of
sympathy with the non-jurors.
[78] For details of the cause see HMC *Lords MSS* vi, 5–6.
[79] See above, n. 68.
[80] By custom money bills had to be initiated by the Commons.
[81] ? Fitzherbert Adams (*c*.1652–1719), Rector of Lincoln College, Oxford, and Prebendary of Durham since 1685. Hearne, *Collections*, i, 118.

place for Fetherston;[82] and Sir John Worden[83] to be courted by Colonel Byerley.

In the House, Archbishop of Canterbury moved for thanks to the Bishop of St Asaph; and he [was] desired to print his Sermon. A printed Copy of an Act (according to the late Order) for setling the Right of several parcels of Land and Fishing &c. with a Rent-Charge, on the Bishop of Derry[84] and his successors: which was Read the first time. Lord Treasurer [Godolphin] moved that Care might be taken to prevent those Confusions in the House which had been common of late when the Queen appeared in the Throne; which was seconded by Earl of Rochester, Earl of Sunderland and Lord Sommers: And a Committee Ordered to consider of Galleries for Foreign Ministers and other Strangers, on those Solem Occasions, and that the Officers of the Works attend the said Committee to morrow.

After an Attempt to wait on Sir R. Blackmore,[85] the Evening spent with my Brother, Sister and Niece.

[Nov.] 8. *Wednesday*. In the morning, I spent over Mr Wotton's[86] papers and Letter (to my Lord of Canterbury) by Dr Gibson; who obliged me, if 'twas fair, to preach at Lambeth on Sunday next.

After an Appeal, and the Bishop of Derry's Bill read a second time, the House resolved into a Committee (Lord Rochester Chairman) to consider of Galleries, &c. Lord Bradford moved for onely putting the old excludeing Orders[87] in Execution: and was seconded by Lord Pawlet; who said, he was not for turning the House into a *Sight*. This being Opposed by Lord Treasurer, Lord Steward [Devonshire] and Lord Sommers, the Surveyor (Sir Christopher Wren)[88] and master mason were called in; and they acquainted their

---

[82] Son of cousin Joseph and Bridget Nicolson (*née* Featherstonhaugh) of Penrith. Robert Nicholson was Fetherston's uncle. Fetherston was to be appointed a waiter (customs official) at Mostyn in Flint and Chester Port in May 1706. *CTB 1706*, xx, 610, 642; *CW* i (1901), 51.

[83] Sir John Werdon or Wordon (1640–1716), diplomat and MP for Reigate, 1673–8, 1685–7; Baronet 1672; Commissioner of the Customs 1685–92, 1702–14. *GEC Barts*.

[84] Charles Hickman, Bishop of Derry, 1703–14. For the dispute over fishing rights in the Derry diocese, see HMC *Lords MSS*, vi, 6; T. W. Moody and J. G. Simms, *The Bishopric of Derry and the Irish Society of London, 1602–1705* (Dublin, 1968), i, 6, 9.

[85] Sir Richard Blackmore (d. 1729), physician, writer, and poet. Physician in Ordinary to William III, knighted 1697, Physician to Queen Anne.

[86] William Wotton (1666–1727), Chaplain to Lord Nottingham, Rector of Middleton Keynes, Buckinghamshire, and a noted linguist.

[87] Standing orders 18 and 30 of the House forbade strangers to enter the chamber, conferences, or committees of the Lords while they were sitting unless commanded to attend. On 5 Apr. 1707, these orders were reinforced by standing order 109 which resulted from a committee of privileges looking into recent irregularities. The order forbade any but lords and their heirs and the assistants of the House to attend sittings. HMC *Lords MSS* x, 3, 5, 25.

[88] The great architect had been Surveyor-General of the King's Works since 1669.

Lordships that a Gallery for about a Hundred (and no more) might be erected, without altering the Roof or incommodeing the Commons at the Bar. On this, Lord Paulet observed that this would be against the known Rules of all Public Shews; where the Spectators are alwaies more in Number than those that make the Spectacle. The matter ended in Orders to Sir Christopher, &c. to bring in Schemes (this day sennight) of several Projects for Galleries;[89] and Lord Steward (who seemed to hint that he knew Sir Christopher's weakness in what he had employed him in) directed that the Absent Officers should be consulted with on this Occasion: Which Sir Christopher said was an Instruction more than needed; for that he alwaies did it.

In the Evening I paid a visit to the Dean of Exeter [Wake]; who gave me the History of Dr Atterbury's comeing in Residentiary with his Concurrence:[90] Of the wicked prosecution of Mr Blackburn by some of Sir E[dward] S[eymour]'s friends:[91] Of the Archbishop of York's good Advice to the Queen upon the Appeal of the Lower House of Convocation to Her Majesty:[92] Of Lord Guernsy's learned Judgement of the Continuance of the Marquis of Hallifax's Lease (after all the Lives were expired) because of the Continuance of the Habitancy, &c. The Cause at Queen's College given up by Mr Thompson.[93]

[89] For Wren's plans, see *Wren Society*, xi (1934), 120, and plates 37–8.

[90] Bishop Trelawney of Exeter, chief episcopal defender of Atterbury in the Convocation Controversy, had appointed him Archdeacon of Totnes in 1701 and in 1704 desired to add to this a residentary canonry, the election to which lay with the Chapter. Wake, his great opponent in the Controversy, was Dean of Exeter, but agreed to Atterbury's election. See Sykes, *Wake*, i, 166–8.

[91] Lancelot Blackburne had been forced to resign his subdeanery in 1702 because of rumours circulating of his having committed adultery with the wife of a prominent citizen of Exeter, a city in which the Tory leader Sir Edward Seymour had great influence. In Oct. 1703 the Dean and Chapter issued a report of their investigation of the charges which completely vindicated Blackburn, who resumed his subdeanery in July 1704. See N. Sykes, ' "The Buccaneer Bishop": Lancelot Blackburn, 1658–1743', *Church Quarterly Review*, cxxx (1940), 82–3. Details of the affair can be found in the Blackburne–Wake correspondence in Christ Church, Oxford: Wake MS 17, *passim*.

[92] The two Houses having failed to agree on a joint address of congratulation on the successes of the Queen's arms because the bishops refused to agree to the insertion of Rooke's name, the High Churchmen in the Lower House hoped to break the deadlock by persuading the Queen to receive separate addresses. For this incident, and Archbishop Sharp's statesmanlike efforts, in Nov.–Dec. 1704, to ease the tension in Convocation, see Luttrell, v, 484; Burnet, *History*, v, 179; *The Life of Archbishop Sharp* i, 349–50; *Atterbury Epist. Corr.* iii, 253–4: Atterbury to Trelawney, 7 Nov. 1704.

[93] On 15 Oct. 1704, Dr William Lancaster had been elected Provost of Queen's College, Oxford, but the election was disputed as being against the statutes of the college. The question was whether the right of voting extended to past as well as present fellows. Francis Thompson had challenged Lancaster's election in his *A True State of the Case concerning the Election of a Provost of Queen's College, Oxford, 1704*, in which he had been helped by Dr Crosthwaite (see above, n. 73), who had 'been passed by'. Archbishop Sharp, as

[Nov.] 9. *Thursday*. After a present from Mr Buchanan,[94] of his Treatise on the Holidayes, I attended the House; where nothing done but the humbling of the man concerned in the Arrest of the Duke of Devonshire's servant who were (on their Knees) Reprimanded and Dismissed, paying their Fees.

[Nov.] 10. *Friday*. Lord Treasurer [Godolphin] Reported what had been done in Observance of an Order of the House (in the last Session) about secureing the Records in Caesar's Tower; the Directions given for New Drawers, pasting the Records (with Colquintida-past, to prevent Mothes) in Books, &c. The papers laid before their Lordships; and a Committee appointed to meet to morrow (at 10 in the morning) to make a farther Enquiry and Report.

Lord Haversham desired that all the Lords might be summoned against Munday; he haveing several matters then to move, wherein the Honour and Security of the Nation and Religion were much concerned. Lord Sunderland proposed that the House might rather be called over; and that the Lord Keeper issue out his Letters to all absent Lords against Thursday sennight. Which was ordered accordingly.

The said Lord Sunderland moved also that an humble Address might be made to Her Majesty (by the Lords with white Staves)[95] that She'd please to have a Regard to the Protestant Refugees in the Gallies, upon the Exchange of the Bishop of Quibec and other Ecclesiasticks taken this Summer by the Dreadnaught and now prisoners in England.[96] Upon which, the Lord Treasurer observed (on the History of that matter) that the French King would look on the Refugees as his own Subjects, and would (therfore) hardly give them in Exchange: But, however, he approved the motion (manifestly concerted) as what might shew an acceptable Concern in this House

Visitor of the college, was appealed to and refused to confirm Lancaster until some 'difficultys or scruples' were removed. After investigation by Dr Thomas Bouchier (see below, 14 Nov.) Lancaster's election was confirmed. Thompson had written to Nicolson on 7 Nov. 1704, evidently worried that Lancaster's vote would ruin his 'interest for Charleton' (see below, 17 Nov.), and declared he now thought 'the Election to be valid . . . [for] if possible I would avoid every thing that might occasion heats, and partys for the future'. Lloyd-Baker MS Box, 4, O 57: Fr[ancis] Thompson to [N.], 7 Nov. 1704. See also ibid., O 45, T 84: Lancaster to Sharp, 26 Oct. 1704, and Sharp to Lancaster, 20 Oct. 1704.

[94] Possibly Charles Buchanan, see below, Diary, 1 Jan. 1706.

[95] The officers of the Queen's household whose badge of office was a white staff, e.g. the Lord Chamberlain, the Lord Treasurer, and the Lord Steward.

[96] Jean-Baptiste de La Croix de Chevrières de Saint-Vallier (1653–1727), Bishop of Quebec since 1688, had been captured off the Azores in 1704 while returning to Canada after four years in France. He remained a prisoner for five years until Louis XIV agreed to free Baron de Mean, Dean of Liege, whereupon Saint-Vallier returned to Paris. *Dictionary of Canadian Biography* (Toronto, 1969) ii, 328–45.

for the Protestant Interest. So — 'Twas Ordered: And then, adjourned till to morrow.

[Nov.] 11. *Saturday*. Mr Chancellor Tanner[97] with me in the Morning (jumping with Dr Gibson and Mr M. Symson) assures me that there's no comeing at the Cotton-Library; nor has there been any Access in five months past.—Mr Hudleston (bringing in an Appeal against his Tenants)[98] saies Sir W. Lawson's death will confound his family; my Lady[99] doteing on a London-Life.—Lord Sommers gave me the History of King William's good Design in uniteing the Libraryes about Town; whereof that of Gresham-College has the best Collection of eldest Editions, as that of the late Bishop of Worcester (Dr Stillingfleet) had of moderns: And this, after the Books had been first brought together at Somerset-House; was to be placed on a Riseing-part of St James's Park, near the Duke of Buckingham's House; the MSS. &c. of the King's Library being also designed to be put there.

The Committee for ordering the Records in the Tower being met, Lord Hallifax (as last session) was chosen Chairman. The Lord Treasurer's papers read, and Mr Petyt[100] ordered to attend, adjourned to Wednesday at 10 in the morning: In the mean time the Bishops of Chichester [Williams] and Carlile to see what done at the Tower.

In the House, onely two Private Bills brought from the Commons, three or four Appeals entered, and Adjourned to Munday.

Sir A. Fountain saies he never had any notice of Mr Sutherland's[101] Draughts of Saxon Coins; that Dr Hickes is goeing to Oxford, and will disperse some of his Books before Christmas.—Mr Madox[102] will shew me the Treasures of the Augmentation-Office.—Sir R. Blackmore repaid my visit; and Sir S. Harcourt satisfyed of no Writ of Errour against Mr How.[103]

[97] Thomas Tanner (1674-1735), antiquary, and Chancellor of Norwich since 1700; later Archdeacon of Norfolk in 1721 and Bishop of St Asaph, 1732-5.

[98] For details of the case see HMC *Lords MSS* vi, 52. The appeal was dismissed on 24 Jan. 1705. *LJ* xviii, 630.

[99] Elizabeth Preston (d. 1734), niece of 1st Viscount Lonsdale, had married Sir Wilfred Lawson in or before 1697. *GEC Barts.*

[100] William Petyt (1637-1707), Keeper of the Records in the Tower, 1689-1707, Treasurer of the Inner Temple, 1701-2. For biographical details see J. Conway Davies, *Catalogue of the Manuscripts of the Library of the Honourable Society of the Inner Temple* (1972), i, 11-27.

[101] James Sutherland, Scottish botanist, who was 'intendent of the physick garden' in Edinburgh, and who owned a large collection of coins. W. T. Lancaster, *Letters Addressed to Ralph Thoresby* (Leeds, 1912), p. 95 n.; Bodl. MS Rawlinson D 377, f. 46.

[102] Thomas Madox (1666-1727), legal antiquary, Joint Clerk in the Augmentations Office. He published *Formulare Anglicarum* (1702), and *The History and Antiquities of the Exchequer* (1711).

[103] John Howe, MP for Gloucestershire, 1702-5, had been accused by one, John Prinn,

In the Evening (after an hour and half's waiting) I met with the
Archbishop of York at his arrival in Petty-France. The Papers from
Queen's College were laid before his Grace; who has no Scruples
about the Confirmation that will be of any Continuance.[104] He's
against the printing my Case.[105] In the Evening,[106] I waited long for
the Archbishop of York's comeing to Town. He came to Petty-
France about five; and, being tolerably well satisfyed in the matter
of Queen's College, presses my makeing my Court at St James's
even (I think) to Mr Secretary Harley.

[Nov.] 12. *Sunday*. I preached for Dr Gibson at Lambeth; and dined
with Lord of Canterbury who believes (as I do) that Lord Treasurer
[Godolphin] did not approve of Dr Atterbury's being sent Northward.[107] The Dean's charge of my [having] taken measures from Lambeth, very false; as will appear from the Date of all my Letters.—
My Lord gave me a long History of the latter End of King Charles
the 2d's time; Lord Arlington a pretended Protestant to the last, and
a monthly Communicant; Nell Gwyn could hardly read; Duchess of
Portsmouth had no hand in bringing in the King's Cordial, which will
be heard off hereafter; Sir Edmund King[108] (as well as Dr Short)[109]
sensible of his Condition; Sir J. Lowther (of Whitehaven)[110] discovered
to the Chaplains that no Sacrament to be given; the Wafer stuck, till
Earl of Feversham brought water; the Letters of the strong Box not
in the King's own hand; Dr Short and Sir Charles Walgrave,[111] at that
time of Opinion that Queen Mary could have no child; &c.

[Nov.] 13. *Munday*. In the morning, with the Bishop of Chichester,
at the Tower; where we viewed (first) the Office of Records,[112] and

during the election of being a Jacobite. Howe had been awarded damages against Prinn,
who had then brought a writ of errour, which the Lords dismissed on 29 Jan. 1705. HMC
Lords MSS vi, 55–6.

[104] See above, n. 93.

[105] Against Atterbury, see above, n. 56.

[106] The repetition of the account of Nicolson's visit to Sharp probably results from his
method of compiling the diary. See Chapter 3, above, pp. 109–13.

[107] See above, Sessional intro., n. 2, and *CW* ii (1902), 197, 206.

[108] Edmund King (1629–1709), physician to Charles II, knighted 1686.

[109] Thomas Short (1635–85), became a Roman Catholic. Burnet (*History*, ii, 473–7)
records that Short thought he had been poisoned for speaking so freely of Charles II's death.

[110] Sir John Lowther (1642–1705), 2nd Bt. of Whitehaven, MP for Cumberland,
1665–81, 1685–7, 1689–1700; Commissioner of the Admiralty, 1689–96; he retired from
politics in 1700. Father of James Lowther, for whom, see Appendix A.

[111] Sir William Waldegrave (?1636–1701), physician to James II's Queen, Mary of
Modena, was present at the birth of the Prince of Wales in 1688. He accompanied the Queen
and Prince on their flight to France, and died at St Germain.

[112] Compare Nicolson's impressions with the report of Sir Christopher Wren to Godolphin,
in HMC *Lords MSS* vi, 39–40.

the Method wherein the new appointed Clerks (now at Work) are sorting the long neglected, and confused, Records into Baskets; which are Labeled with the Several Titles of the Matters (as well as time) of those that are thought worthy, on any Account whatever, to be preserved. This Course was first taken by Mr Prynne; whose indefatigable Industry has not conquered a Tenth part of the Work. In this Office are deposited such Rolls as chiefly related to the Court of Wards. A Close Roll of King John's is the oldest they have. The rest ly still (mostly) in Confused Heaps, within Caesar's (or St John's) Chaple in the Great Tower; from whence the Clerks fetch such Loads as they have occasion for. At the Entrance into this Tower we were shewn the place, at the foot of the Stairs, where (in 1669) were found the Bodies of King Edward 5. and his brother Richard Duke of York. When we got into the Chapple, 'twas a great Trouble to me to see so many Waggon-Loads of Records as are here in the most Dirty and perishing Condition imagineable; many peeping out of Heaps of Dust and Rubbish, a yard or two in Depth. *Spero meliora.* The present Keeper (Mr Petyt) takes no farther Care than to Receive his 500 *l.* Salary;[113] out of which he ought to have allowed (as his Patent obliges him) that 250 *l.* which the Queen has now gratiously given (as an Overplus) to the four Assistant Clerks.[114]

In our Return my Lord of Chichester promised me a printed Copy of his *Notitia Ecclesiae Cantuariensis*; as Mr Dale[115] likewise did of Mr Ainstis's[116] Corrections of Camden,[117] and a sight of his MS. State of the Question Whether the Earl of Carlile has any Title to precedency in Right of his now executeing the Office of Earl

[113] This salary had been first granted to Sir Algernon May as Keeper of the Record by Charles II out of the first fruit and tenths, but as May was absent in Ireland, James II appointed Robert Brady to be Keeper on a salary of £300 out of the privy purse. May still enjoyed his £500. Petyt replaced Brady in 1689, he was granted half May's salary and on May's death he received the full £500. Dean and Chapter Library, Carlisle, Nicolson MS i, inserted between p. 168 and p. 169: Memorial touching the Office of Keeper of Her Majesty's Records in the Tower of London.

[114] George Holmes (mentioned frequently in the diary, see below, n. 130), whose salary as Deputy Keeper was £100, and Thomas Jenkinson, Robert Dale, and William Prichard, who divided the remaining £150 between them. Davies, *Catalogue of the Manuscripts of the Inner Temple*, i, 17; A. Wagner, *Heralds of England* (1967), p. 321.

[115] Robert Dale (1666-1722), herald and antiquarian. He was Blanch Lyon, 1694; Deputy Register of the College of Heralds and Clerk in the Tower Record Office, 1704; Suffolk Herald Extraordinary, 1707; and Richmond Herald, 1721. Wagner, *Heralds of England*, p. 321.

[116] John Anstis (1669-1744), antiquarian, herald and MP for St Germains, 1702-5, St Mawes, 1711-13, and Launceston, 1713-22.

[117] *Curia Militaris; or a Treatis of the Court of Chivalry; ... containing some animadversions on two posthumous discoveries concerning the etymology, antiquity, and office of the Earl Marshal of England, ascribed to Mr Camden, and published in the last edition of the Britannia* (1702).

Marshal?[118] Negative. — In the House, Nothing but Appeals and Writs of Error.

[Nov.] 14. *Tuesday*. In the morning, waiting on the Archbishop of York (with Mr Yates[119] and Mr Hutchinson) about the Affair of Queen's College, his grace (first) acquainted me, in private, that the Queen expected to see me; and would give me a kind Reception. After the Business of the House (Nothing but Appeals and Writs of Error, the last given in by Lord Chief Baron[120] at the Bar) I returned to Dinner with my Lord of York; who (now) despises Dr Bourchier's[121] Opinion, and proposes — That the Queen may ratify the Exposition of the Statutes of Queen's College in favour of all the Fellows, removed and actualy as equally capable of being chosen Provosts. This approved by Dr Lancaster; but not by Dr Gibson, who wisely foresees the hazard of bringing in the Authority of the Crown. It may be appealed to by any prevailing faction hereafter. Dr Gibson carryed home with him the State of the Controversy 'twixt me and the Dean.[122]

This day, the Commons voted the Conformity-Bill to be brought in again. *Yeas*, 152. *Noes*, 126.[123]

[Nov.] 15. *Wednesday*. I missed the Committee about the Records, being forced (by Dr Lancaster) to the Archbishop of York; who is never like to give him Confirmation. The Proposeal of the Queen's Exposition will not doe; since the Founder seems to have provided against any such Authority, by obligeing the Visiter[124] to make his Confirmation *Summarie, et absque processu Iudiciario*.

I waited on the Archbishop to the Queen who received me very gratiously and with a Smile.

[118] In 1703 Anstis had published *Letters to a Peer, concerning the Honour of Earl Marshal, shewing that no Earl Marshal can be made during the Minority of an Heredity Earl Marshal*. In 1704 the Duke of Norfolk came of age but, as a Catholic, was unable to perform the functions of Earl Marshal. Anstis, therefore, published a second edition of *Letters to a Peer* in 1706 which dealt with this incapacity.

[119] Thomas Yates, Rector of Charlton-on-Otmoor, Oxfordshire in 1704.

[120] The principal judge of the Court of Exchequer, Sir Edward Ward (1638–1714).

[121] Thomas Bouchier (d. 1723), Regius Professor of Civil Law at Oxford, 1672–1712, Principal of St Alban's Hall, 1679–1723, and Commissary of the diocese of Canterbury.

[122] Presumably Nicolson's draft, offered for Gibson's comments. See above, n. 56; below, 20 Nov.

[123] Reflecting a significant decline of Tory enthusiasm for the bill, when compared with the big majorities the first two bills had secured in this Commons. 'All the strength of argument ran against it ten to one', wrote Mrs Burnet, and Godolphin believed more responsible conduct by some Tory placemen would have prevented the bill going any further. Blenheim MS E-30: Mrs Burnet to Duchess of Marlborough, n.d. [?16 Nov.]; HMC *Bath MSS* i, 64–5; H. L. Snyder, 'The defeat of the Occasional Conformity Bill and the Tack', *BIHR* xli (1968), 179.   [124] Archbishop Sharp.

At the House the Bishop of Derry's Bill finished by the Committee; and a Gallery ordered for Foreign Ministers, &c. in the mean time the old Order against Intruders to be put in strict Execution.

In the afternoon, with my Brother, Sister, Niece and Cousin Isabel[125] Nicolson, at the Monument and Billingsgate.

[Nov.] 16. *Thursday*. In the morning, I was carryed (by Mr Madox) into the Offices of both the Remembrancers,[126] where some few Memoranda as old as Henry 3's time.——Thence (with Mr Charles Battely) into the Augmentation-Office; where no such stores (now left) as I expected.

At the House the Case of Mr Strowde (an Appellant out of the Exchequer) was heard at the Bar:[127] Where his Counsel (Mr Cowper and Sir John Hawles)[128] not being able to prove their Allegations, the Petition was rejected, the Decree affirmed, and the Appellant condemned in 30 *l.* Costs.

After dineing with Mr Lister,[129] pretty late, Dr Gibson brought back my State of the Dean's Case; with News that the Archbishop of York was (at 1st) resolved to confirm Dr Lancaster's Election.

[Nov.] 17. *Friday*. Early in the Morning I called on the Bishop of Chichester; with whom I was at the Tower before Nine. About an hour after came the Earls of Westmerland and Stamford; and the Lords Pawlet, Grey, Sommers and Hallifax. We viewed the Method the Clerks were in (towards the putting the Records in good Order) and returned to the House before One. Before the Temporal Lords came, I examined the Calendars for Matters Relateing to the Contest betwixt the City of Carlile and my Tenants of Dalston; and found these following—*Confirm. Civibus Karliol. Cart. Hen. 3. de Immunit. Thelon. per totum Regnum et quod habeant Estoveria ad Ignem et Edificia Construenda. Pat. 21. ed. 1. Confim et Amplif. Libertatu et Privileg. Epi. Karl. Cart. 25. Hen. 6. N. 18. Inquisitio de Return, Breviu et de omnibus fere alijs Libertat. Privileg. et Consuetud. Civitatis Karliol. Esch. 25. Ed. 3. Num 42.* The Second

---

[125] Possibly the daughter of 'cousin' William Nicholson of Fishergate, Carlisle, and four times Mayor of the city. Born in 1684, she married a Joseph Jackson (d. 1732) in 1710. *CW* i (1901), 50.

[126] The King's Remembrancer and the Lord Treasurer's Remembrancer, two officers of the Court of Exchequer.

[127] See HMC *Lords MSS* vi. 1.

[128] MP for Wilton, 1702–5, and Stockbridge, 1705–10.

[129] Possibly Thomas Lister, one of the five Commissioners of Accounts (Commissioners for Army Debts) in 1704, and possibly a cousin of Christopher Musgrave. *CTB 1704–5*, p. 288; HMC *Portland MSS* iv, 126. He was from Grimsby and sat in the Commons for Lincoln, 1705–15.

of these Recites a Charter dated July 16. in the 15th of Henry 3. (which is also in the Original Records of that year) wherein the Immunities of the Bishop as well as the Prior and Convent (and particularly, an Exemption of them and their Tenants from all Tols, &c.) are specially provided for. The other two, plainly enough, prove the City's Rights to have been procured by the favour and Intercession of the Bishops.—Mr Petyt very obligeing to me: But not capable of serveing any body. Mr Madox, Mr Holme[130] and Mr Dole, the Supporters of this Treasure.

In our Return, my Lord of Chichester gave me his Queries in his Diocese; as also his Map of the Diocese of Canterbury.—In the House, Nothing more than a base Adjournment.

After Dinner, I carryed News (and found it there) to Dr Lancaster's of the Vacancy of Burgh under Stanemore. Mr Yates will take it with the Archdeaconry. See first, how Charlton is disposed of.[131]

[Nov.] 18. *Saturday*. After two private Naturalizeing Bills (for the Viscount Tiviot [Teviot] and Lady Cresset) were passed in a Committee, of the Earls of Stamford and Rochester and Bishop of Carlile, they were read a Third time in the House and passed.

I dined at Lambcth, with the Bishops of Worcester [Lloyd], Sarum and Litchfeild; which last is for bringing in a Bill to reduce his 30 Prebendaries to 8 Residentiaries. *Placet*.—At Mr Snow's, convinced that a Patent to two Registers in my Diocese would be void.

In the Evening, with Dr Lancaster at Archbishop of York where Mr Provost's Election was confirmed. NB. Mr Provost subscribed the Articles, and took the Oaths of Allegiance and Canonical Obedience; being confirmed by the Title of *Nunc aut Nuper Socius*.

[Nov.] 19. *Sunday*. A good honest sermon, by a Chaplain of the Lord Brook, in the morning at Westminster; and the Second part of this day Three-weeks's (*To day if ye will hear*, &c.) by Dr Stanley at St Paul's in the Afternoon. I dined with my Brother; who gives no good Account of his Patient Isabel.

---

[130] George Holmes (1661–1749), became a protégé of fellow-Yorkshireman Petyt and his clerk in the Tower in 1690, and lived with Petyt in Chelsea. Appointed Chief Clerk in Scpt. 1706, on Petyt's death (1707) he became Deputy Keeper under Richard Topham, MP for New Windsor, but was the real head of the office as the keepership now became a sinecure. He helped produce a new edition of *Foedera*, and in 1731 was finally appointed Keeper of the Records. Davies, *Catalogue of the Manuscripts of the Inner Temple*, i, 18–19; Musgrave, *Obituary*, iii, 237.

[131] Joseph Fisher (*c*.1655–1704), Vicar of Burgh-on-Stainmore since 1695 and Nicolson's successor as Archdeacon of Carlisle in 1702, had recently died. Thomas Yates decided to take Charlton in Oxfordshire and George Fleming took the archdeaconry in Mar. 1705.

[Nov.] 20. *Munday*. A kind promise, in the morning, from Mr Holme of the Tower; to have the Perusal of all Mr Petyt's Books and Papers, towards the furnishing out a Mantissa, in a Repertory of Records, to my Historical Library. In the Lobby, Dr Stanley gave me his Predecessor's (Dr Goodman's)[132] story of his being entertained by a Chancery-Clerk; who, that morning, had gotten an Annuity for's Life (of 20 *l*. per Annum) in a single Cause. Dr Gee seconded my Complaint to my Lord of Canterbury against their Dean (the Bishop of Rochester [Sprat]) for omitting the Exhortion at the Sacrament administring his petty-Canons before Bishops, &c.—I presented W. Churdon's Case to my Lord Treasurer [Godolphin].[133] Prayers Read, and one petition, the House adjourned.

In the Evening, Dr Kennett and Dr Gibson perused, and approved of, the State of the Controversy 'twixt me and the Dean; and I gave the Letter to Dr Kennett to be published at his Discretion.

[Nov.] 21. *Tuesday*. In the morning, I waited on my Lord Wharton;[134] whom I found crowded with members of the House of Commons. I first thanked His Lordship for his late generous kindness to the Church and Curate at Ravenstondale, and then requested his giveing Leave to have the Boyes at Shap taught in the Court-House, instead of the Church. He was pleased readily to assure me that he would, by that night's post, give Orders to John Smith accordingly.[135] Chief business in the House, Lord Halifax's Motion: That the Lord Treasurer be directed to lay before the Lords the Several Summs given by Parliament in the years 1702. 3. and 4. and how the same have been expended.

Dr Woodward dined with me, and shewed me a (reputed) Brittish Coin in Copper; which he presented to me, but borrowed again to shew it to one particular Gentleman. Very angry he is at the Archbishop of York for renounceing (in his Yorkshire way) all Belief,

---

[132] John Goodman (d. 1690), Archdeacon of Middlesex, 1686–90.

[133] William Churdon had been a customs official at Cardurnock and Port Carlisle, and had been murdered by James Carlisle, a Scotsman, whom he had caught smuggling brandy across the Solway Firth. His widow was finally granted a pension. *CTB 1704–5*, xix, 422–3, 517.

[134] Wharton's house was in Dover Street. The Junto's great 'manager' was preparing for battle on the case of *Ashby* versus *White* (see above, sessional intro., p. 209) and also on the Occasional Conformity Bill, both of which were on the Commons' agenda for this week.

[135] On his visitation in 1703 Nicolson had written that the schoolmaster had 'no certain Salary more than 6 *ll*. which is a Voluntary gift (rather than an Endowment) of the Lord Wharton's, allotted for the teaching of a particular Number of the Children of his poorest Tenants that Noble Lord will undoubtedly be easily prevail'd with to allow the teaching of these poor Scholars and others in the Town-Hall, lately built (for a Mercate-House) by his Father; but now of no other use than for ye keeping of the Mannour-Courts, which would be little or no Interruption to ye School'. *Miscellany*, pp. 75–6.

present and future, of the Hasty-Pudding-Doctrine in his Theory of the Earth.[136] In the Park I met with poor Togry Smith, in as much Chagrin and Hypp as ever; in wrath with all the Occasional Bishops; with the Speaker [Harley], for excludeing him out of the Cotton-Libray; with Thomas Crosthwait, for opposeing Dr Lancaster; &c.

A visit in the Evening from (Dr Wake) the Dean of Exeter; who has collected most of the public Instruments, relateing to Church Affairs, from the Conquest to the Reformation: And is of Opinion that this part of our Ecclesiastical History is more capable of being ascertained than that which followes, from Henry the 8th's Reign. Lord Hallifax, he saies, is beginning a vast Design in Collecting the publick Records, &c.

[Nov.] 22. *Wednesday*. In the morning with Dr Woodward at Gresham-College;[137] who shewed me Johann Jacob Scheuchzer's Natural History, in Latine, of Switzerland;[138] wherein are a great many fine Cut's in Colours, and the Text of the Book (whimsically enough) in Vermilion-Letters, instead of an Italic Character, where the Author's παθος comes in, In his Dedication to the Royal Society he talks great things of Dr Aglionby[139] and Dr Woodward; the former being envoy to the Helvetic Body, and the other his friend and Correspondent. But — The Society is slow in getting his Book printed here: Which seems to have been his principal Design. He has Translated Dr Woodward's Theory into Latine; of which, by the way, the Dr now forgot (as I did) the promise he made me, by Letter, of his haveing kept one Copy for me. I have the greater Reason to suspect the Non Performance of this Promise, because of the Brittish Coin (given me yesterday, and onely borrowed to gratify a Particular Gentleman) is now said to be left with my Lord President, the Earl of Pembroke; to whom (as the Archbishop of York acquainted me

---

[136] This was Nicolson's term for Woodward's theory that the Flood had disolved the earth in Noah's time, after which it took its present shape. Nicolson was much impressed by Woodward's theories but never quite persuaded; Woodward nominated Nicolson as a fellow of the Royal Society in 1705.

[137] Situated on the east side of Old Broad Street, it was founded in 1598, according to the terms of Sir Thomas Gresham's will, in his own house. An endowed foundation which offered instruction and research into law, rhetoric, divinity, music, physic, geometry, and astronomy, it survived on its original site until 1768 when the Crown erected the Excise Office. It was the meeting place of the Royal Society from 1660 to 1710 when the Society purchased its own building. See F. R. Johnson, 'Gresham College, Precursor of the Royal Society', *Journal of the History of Ideas*, i (1940), 413–38; J. Ward, *Lives of the Professors of Gresham College* (1740).

[138] Published 1700.

[139] William Aglionby, diplomat and Under-Secretary of State to Nottingham, May–Aug. 1702, who was Envoy Extraordinary to Switzerland, 1702–5. D. B. Horn, *British Diplomatic Representatives, 1689–1789*, Camden 3rd Series, xlvi (1932), 119, 128, 146, 155; J. C. Sainty, *Officials of the Secretaries of State, 1660–1782* (1973), p. 63.

last week) the Dr, when he made the like Present to His Grace, carryed the Remainder of his Treasure. — However it be, the Dr has invited me to spend a morning in Viewing the Method wherein he has disposed his Natural Curiosities; and I will (God giveing the Continuance of my health) accept the Invitation. I want chiefly to be Instructed in his way of Tribeing his Fossils.[140] He shewed me a Northern Monument (sent him by Dr Key of Newcastle)[141] the Inscription whereof had formerly been communicated to me by Mr Thoresby;[142] on which the *Ala 1ᵐᵃ Asturum*[143] was what the Dr chiefly wanted my assistance in. Amongst those Fossils, which I had heretofore sent him,[144] he seemed to value the Mica Nigra (as he calls it) found in the Rivulet 'twixt Salkeld and Edenhall, being a sort of Talc; and the Fossil Coral from Pott-gill near Hartley.

In my return, I steped into a Bookseller's shop on Grace-Church-street; where I encountered a Dissenting Preacher, enquireing for some sermons of old Mr Burgess;[145] whose Testimony, said he, will be ever valuable. I agreed: And returned, by water, to my Lodgeings.

A Letter, from Brother John, about Sir W. Lawson's Legacies, carryed me to Mrs Dunhil[146] at Lambeth; who was surprised at the dying kindness of her brother.

[140] Dr Woodward had the most important collection of fossils in his time and was a pioneer in fossil taxonomy. See his *Fossils of all Kinds Digested into a Method* (London, 1728). The manuscript catalogues of his collection were published as *An Attempt Towards a Natural History of Fossils* (1729), and the collection itself survives intact in the Sedgwick Museum, Cambridge University.

[141] Jabez Cay (1666–1703), well-known physician of Newcastle, and frequent correspondent of Thoresby, see W. T. Lancaster, *Letters addressed to Ralph Thoresby*, Thoresby Society, xxi (1912), p. 42.

[142] Ralph Thoresby (1658–1725), antiquarian and topographer of Leeds, Yorkshire. He was a regular correspondent of Nicolson. For their letters see Lancaster, *Letters Addressed to Ralph Thoresby; Letters of Emminent Men Addressed to Ralph Thoresby* (2 vols., 1832); *Nicolson Epist. Corr.*; Yorkshire Archaeological Society, Leeds: Thoresby MS 1 (Letterbook, unfoliated); MS 18 (Thoresby's index of letters received, includes brief abstracts). See also H. W. Jones, 'A Checklist of the Correspondence of Ralph Thoresby', *Thoresby Society Pubs.* xlvi (1959–63), 36–53.

[143] This inscription, reading the '1st cavalry regiment of the Asturians', may bear some relationship to several inscriptions found at Chesters on Hadrian's Wall, bearing the words 'ala II Asturian'. This second cavalry regiment of Asturians was a third-century garrison at Chesters. See R. G. Collingwood and R. P. Wright, *The Roman Inscriptions of Britain* (Oxford, 1965), i, 471–3.

[144] A list of Nicolson's donations to Thoresby is to be found in Yorkshire Archaeological Society, Leeds: Thoresby MS 27 (unfoliated).

[145] ?Anthony Burgess (d. 1664), Rector of Sutton Coldfield, Warwickshire from 1635, to 1662 when he was ejected. Author of sermons. Not to be confused with Daniel Burgess, the celebrated pastor of the Presbyterian meeting house at New Court, Lincoln's Inn Fields, sacked by the Sacheverell mob in 1710.

[146] Formerly Jane Lawson, see above, 27 Oct.

[Nov.] 23. *Thursday.* Mr Huddleston, of Hutton-John, peevish on the Account I gave him of Sir W. Lawson's kindness to his sister.

A Committee passed the Bishop of Derry's Bill, with Amendments; which, being Reported by the Earl of Rochester were agreed to by the House, and the Bill sent down to the Commons. The Call of the House,[147] beginning at the Puny Baron and ending with Prince George, was the first thing by Order of the day. That being over, the Lord Haversham (as he had promised) began his truely eloquent Speech;[148] Wherein, haveing first magnifyed the Goodness of God (beyond all Example in History) in Crowning the Counsels and Conduct of the Duke of Marlborough, and extoled the Unpresidented Secresy wherewith that Expedition was carryed on, he acquainted the House that (he thought) Sir George Rook had done his part also as an Admiral: And that we had likewise great Reason to bless God for the Success that he had in the late Sea-Fight; which, tho' perhaps it could not be called a Victory, was such a Deliverance and so wonderful an Escape, as sufficiently evidenced both the Courage and the Conduct of the Admiral. In the Sequal of his Discourse He shewed that all the Measures taken in the Admiralty were constantly (almost) discovered to the French; who had also that Countenance given them, by Secret Traffickers, that even their Fleet was Victualed from England or Ireland. The next thing he recommended to their Lordships Consideration was the mighty Exportation of Bullien and coined Silver; which had already very sensibly sunk our Current Species, and must of Necessity (if speedy care be not taken to prevent it) utterly beggar the whole Nation. The Third Particular insisted on was the passing of the Scottish Act of Security. This, he said, was the less Surprizeing; because, in the very beginning of the Parliament at Edinburgh, there was a Distinction made betwixt the Revealed and the Secret Will of a Prince, which reconciled the Lord Commissioner's touching with the Scepter[149] a Bill of Exclusion, instead of getting such an Act of Succession as the Queen desired in her Letter. He professed his Abhorrence of the Keeping up of a standing Army, in this Kingdome in the time of Peace;[150] and yet

---

[147] A device for increasing the attendance of the House by reading the roll of members on a day of which due notice was given. Members not answering to their names and not sending an adequate excuse by a colleague were regarded as defaulters. It was only used four times in the Lords in Anne's reign: 23 Nov. 1704, 12 Nov. 1705, 29 Jan. 1707 and 3 June 1714, see *LJ* xvii, 583; xviii, 15, 220; xix, 702.

[148] For another full account of this speech and of the State of the Nation debate of 23 Nov., see *Parl. Hist.* vi, 369–71.

[149] The form by which the Queen's representative in Scotland, the High Commissioner, gave the royal assent to Scottish Acts.

[150] For a valuable study of this deep-rooted English prejudice see Lois G. Schwoerer, *'No Standing Armies!': The Antiarmy Ideology in Seventeenth Century England* (1975).

he could not but think it necessary to desire their Lordships to consider of some ready Course for the secureing us against an armed Nation, who had now cut themselves off from us, and were (of themselves) a numerous, discontented and beggarly, people.

After a pause of about half an hour, Lord Rochester rose up; and, haveing warmly reflected on the little Concern that appeared in the House for any thing that was laid before them, seconded Lord Haversham in every particular. He proposed a Select Committee to examine into the State of the Fleet; and hoped the Lords would not be Nice in their Enquiries, even in those particulars wherein the Prince[151] himself might seem to be concerned.

After some few less considerable talk, Lord Nottingham (professing a retired Life, and his being a stranger to public matters) wished that the little Coin that was left might be, some way or other, secured. Lord Grey [of Warke], netled at the Scotch Act, foretels that Nation's over-running this as the Goths and Vandals did the Roman Empire. Lord Peterborough assures the Lords that when we live with out French Drink, the French must live without English Victual. He also smartly remarked the Different figures made by our Land and Sea-Commanders; an Admiral being forced to foot in, from Whitehall to Wapping, whilst a Field-Officer greater than a Lord.

Capt. Edwards[152] being sworn, gave in a Memorial; wherein he saies, that (being a Prisoner at Rochel, &c.) he saw a great many French and English Bottoms bring in Provisions &c. [A forward witness he seemed to be.][153]

Lord Rochester against a Committee of the whole House; because that was so like the House, that he feared 'twould do no business. A select one he desired now for the Coin: for, unless that be regarded, 'twill be with us as in the dayes of Noah. Lord Treasurer [Godolphin] in some warmth replyed, if these bones be thrown in to stop the giveing of money below, the Flood will surely come, &c.—Lord Hallifax observed the like Cry was in the late Reign; and yet money was then found to carry on the Warr. Wherefore he moved for an Adjournment. Seconded by Lord Scarborough and Duke of Buckingham. So the House did Adjourn; after they had first appointed a Select Committee to consider (on Munday next) the State of the

[151] Prince George, the Queen's husband and Lord High Admiral of England, 1702–8. The Admiralty was, in effect, administered, 1702–8, by 'the Prince's Council', on which the dominant figure was Admiral George Churchill, Marlborough's brother. It came in for frequent criticism, culminating in the winter of 1707–8.
[152] For the report of Benjamin Edwards, a merchant captain, see HMC *Lords MSS* vi, 111–15.
[153] Nicolson's brackets.

Navy,[154] and a Committee of the whole (on Wednesday) to debate the Scotch Affair.

The Commons Read the Occasional Bill for first time; and carried it (by a great Majority) for a Second Reading on Tuesday next.[155]

Thus both Houses are now entered on their Respective business in good Earnest; haveing been together, adjusting Preliminaries, a month and two dayes.

May the following Book give a happy Account of their future Proceedings; and a peaceful Conclusion of this Session and Parliament.[156]

[Nov.] 24. *Friday*. This day was heard an Appeal[157] of Mr Dymoke (an Attourney at Law) from a Decree in Chancery made in favour of Sir John Hobart an Infant;[158] of whose mother the said Dymoke had formerly bought the next Avoidance of the Rectory of Clifton in the County of Bucks: But, the Lady Hobart dying before the Liveing fell void, and haveing onely a Lives Estate in the Mannor to which the Advowson was Appendant, the Lord Keeper [Wright] Decreed the Return of the purchase-money (100 Guinneas) and the Infant, by his Guardians, to present. The Decree was affirmed; and the Appellant charged with 10 *l*. Costs.

I dined at Mr C. Musgrave's with Sir Thomas Franklin, Mr Hales[159] (brother to Sir Christopher Hales)[160] Mr Hawley and Mr Joseph Musgrave; where great Swaggerings about the Occasional Bill, especially after Coll. Byerley came in. Amongst the London-Cases, it seems, there's One (touching the Union of Protestants) written by Dr Tennison, now Lord Archbishop of Canterbury, wherein the Author compares an Occasional Communicant to a Wooden Leg; which is no sound or essential part of the Body, but is taken of and put on Occasionaly and to serve a Turn.[161] They seemed

[154] For the proceedings of this committee from Nov. 1704 to Mar. 1705, see HMC *Lords MSS* vi, 109–226.

[155] The vote was 192 to 138. *CJ* xiv, 433.

[156] Here ends vol. 4 of the original manuscript diaries. The next entry begins vol. 5.

[157] See HMC *Lords MSS* vi, 53–4.

[158] Sir John Hobart (1693–1753), succeeded as 5th Bt. in 1698, later MP for St Ives, 1715–27, Norfolk, 1727–8, Baron Hobart 1728, and Earl of Buckinghamshire 1746.

[159] Sir Thomas Franklin (*c*.1656–1728) of Dean, Middlesex, was a nephew of Sir Christopher Musgrave (d. 1704). His aunt, Elizabeth Franklin (d. 1701), had become Sir Christopher's second wife in 1671. She was Mr Christopher Musgrave's stepmother. Nicolson and Burn, i, 598. Possibly Edward Hales (d. 1720), who succeeded his brother in the baronetcy in 1717.

[160] MP for Coventry, 1698–1701, 1702–7, 1711–15.

[161] This pamphlet, first published in 1683, was *An Argument for Union taken from the True Interest of those Dissenters in England, who profess, and call themselves Protestants*. Though reprinted in 1685 and 1694, it was not reprinted again until 1718.

inclinable to get it Reprinted, for the help of his own memory, against the Bill comes up to the Lords: and yet, notwithstanding all this Noise, I have hopes that some of these merry Gentlemen will be against Tacking the Bill to that of the money.[162]—The Evening spent at my Brother's.

[Nov.] 25. *Saturday*. At my Riseing in the morning I received a kind present (from Mr Chamberlayne) of the *Edda Islandorum* published by Resenius,[163] the procureing whereof I had often attempted in vain; together with the Loan of Gormond Andreas's Islandic Dictionary,[164] whereon Mr Wotton has made many good Marginal Notes.

Nothing at the House, saveing Committees of Naturalization, &c. —Mr Joddrel[165] brought me the Copy of Mr Coke's Bill; which wants Amendments, especially a Clause for selling of the Distresses for Non-payment of Rent (as in the Bishop of Derry's) within five dayes.

Mr Wotton came (surprizeingly) upon me in the Evening; and seemed very thoughtful and pensive, full of something but said little or Nothing. After he was gone, considering how early this morning his friend (and mine) had sent me his book, &c. I began to fancy that possibly he might have his Eye upon the vacant Archdeaconry of Carlile, imagineing it to be a more valuable preferment than it is; and freer from a parochial Charge.[166]

[Nov.] 26. *Sunday*. I took a sleight purge, of purgeing Waters and Manna; and dined, after the working was over, in Salisbury [Court]; takeing leave of Cousin Isabel Nicolson, for a Return into the North (*re infecta*) the next Morning.—Mr Brewer zealous against Tacking.

[Nov.] 27. *Munday*. Sir H. Dutton-Colt's Appeal[167] against Young the Taylor; to whom Coll. Ed[ward] Colt (Sir Henry's younger brother)[168] dyed indebted about 600 *l.* an Arrear for cloathing his Regiment.

---

[162] Sir Christopher Hale like Byerley supported the 'Tack'.

[163] *Edda Islandorum . . . Islandiae, Daniae, et Latine* by Peder Hansen Resen, published 1665.

[164] *Lexicon Islandicum* by Gudmundus Andreae, published 1683.

[165] Paul Joddrell, Clerk of the House of Commons, 1683–1726. For a biographical sketch see O. C. Williams, *The Clerical Organisation of the House of Commons, 1661–1850* (Oxford, 1954), pp. 35–58.

[166] The archdeaconry, according to Nicolson, was worth £60 a year. See Diary, vol. 1b: 25 May 1702.

[167] MP for Westminster, 1701–2, 1705–8. For the case see HMC *Lords MSS* vi, 3–4.

[168] The youngest son of George Colt, one of Charles II's companions in exile, he was a captain in Col. Belasyse's regiment of foot and John Hale's regiment of foot in 1688, and became a colonel before 1694. Dalton, ii, 152; iv, 9, 213.

The Case (tho' very pressing on the poor Taylour) seemed to bear so hard on all Colonels, who are not now lyable to these Debts, that the Lords (after a long Debate) thought fit to Respite the Sentence till this day Sennight: when [if not agreed before][169] the partyes are to be heard again, as to some particulars, by one Counsel on each Side.

Before the House sat, I was a good while in the Augumentation-Office with Dr Hutton; who (amongst other matters) acquainted me that the Statutes of Queen's College were at length in the Tower 1. Pat. Ric. 2. p. 3. M. 24 to 18. After the House rose, I went to Dr Waugh's; where I was God-father to his daughter Bridget, Madame Hales (granddaughter in Law to Lord Chief Justice Hales) being one of the Godmothers. The Dr beginning (as supposed) with the small pox.

In my Return, the two Mrs Lowthers of Milbank came to me at my brother Joseph's; and brought me a Letter from Lady Lawson, for Advice in relation to her husband's Will.

[Nov.] 28. *Tuesday*. In the morning, first Mr R. Musgrave,[170] and (soon after) Coll. Graham, with assurances that neither of 'em would Vote for Tacking the Occasional. The former might possibly pay some Deference to my Opinion in this matter: But the latter (I was sensible) was entirely under the Direction and Influence of Mr Secretary Harley. After Dinner I waited on (my late Lord Lonsdale's sister) Madam Lowther at Milbank;[171] who shewed me a much longer Letter from her Daughter, my Lady Lawson, with a fuller Account of the Circumstances of his Death. He left about 6000 *l.* in Money; and 800 *l.* per Annum. Each of his five younger Children are to have 1000 *l.* with power to his Lady to advance any of 'em to 1500. His sister Jane's Annuity (of 42 *l.* per Annum) is augmented to 50 *l.* and the like for his sister Frances; giveing my Lady a farther power to turn the latter into 500 *l.* The Tithes of Blincrake and Redmain (all the Impropriations that he had) are setled upon the Vicar of Isell for ever. The 600 *l.* left to Her Majesty, in Recompence of all undue payments of his Land-Tax, 'tis hoped will be begged off; to my Lady's own use.

The Commons set this Evening till Eight o'clock, from one, warmly debateing—Whether the Occasional-Bill[172] should be

---

[169] Nicolson's brackets.

[170] Richard Musgrave, MP for Cumberland, see Appendix A.

[171] Mary Lowther, sister of 1st Viscount Lonsdale, widow of George Preston of Holker, Lancashire, and mother of Sir Wilfred Lawson's wife. Her second husband was John Lowther, a Commissioner of Revenue in Ireland. Nicolson and Burn, i, 435.

[172] This was the debate on the second reading of the bill.

committed to the same Committee with the Land-Tax? Which Question, being at last put, was carried in the Negative. *Yeas*, 134. *Noes*, 251.[173] This defeat sat very uneasy upon many of our High-flyers; who were ventureing the Parliament and Nations falling into any sort of Confusion, rather than not carry their point. When the Coaches began to move, I sent out my servant to enquire how matters went: And he presently returned with a lamentable story that *the Church has lost it*. This, he said, he had from several Clergymen; as well as others. With Submission, I am of a contrary Opinion.[174]

[Nov.] 29. *Wednesday*. In the morning, by appointment, I met Mr Wotton at Mr Chamberlayne's where we brushed up our Northern Learning for an hour or two, and I left my *Border-Laws*[175] to be farther considered.

In the House (as soon as the Queen was come [Incognito and without Her Robes][176] and handed to the Throne by the Duke of Somerset)[177] the Business of the Day was called for, and the Order read for the goeing into a Grand Committee on the State of the Nation, in Reference to the Scotch Act of Security. Earl of Stamford moved that the House might consider the matter sitting, because then the Debates would be more Regular and Solemn; which was understood as an intended Respect to Her Majesty: But the Order was observed, and (Lord Keeper [Wright] quitting the Wool-sack) the Earl of Sunderland was put into the Chair.

After a long Pause, as usual, Lord Rochester rose up and (as heretofore) prefaced his Discourse on the present Subject with a new Invective against the Careless, and even thoughtless, behaviour of most of the Lords on these Occasions. That done, he moved that (in the first place) the Printed Act of Security might be read.

This opposed by Lord Sommers and Lord Wharton; who took notice that this Act was not yet printed in Scotland; and therfore

---

[173] The government had canvassed and prepared with the greatest assiduity for this vital division, on which war supply and conceivably the whole success of the war was seen to hang; their efforts having culminated on 26 Nov. in 'a great meeting . . . at Mr. Secretary Hedges's'. See Snyder, pp. 181–4; P. M. Ansell, 'Harley's parliamentary management', *BIHR* xxxiv (1961), 92–7.

[174] Nicolson's attitude was very much in harmony with that of Sharp, who supported and canvassed for the government over the 'Tack' despite his sympathy with the bill itself. *Life of Archbishop Sharp*, i, 304–6.

[175] *Leges marchiarum or Border Laws*, published May 1705.

[176] Nicolson's brackets.

[177] This could well have been seen as a significant gesture by both government and opposition peers, since Somerset, the Master of the Horse, was one of only two active Whig members of the Cabinet Council at this stage. Kent, the new Lord Chamberlain, had not been called to the Cabinet.

was no more than a private paper: tho', they allowed, there was little or no Doubt to be made but that every member of this House was satisfyed that it was a true Copy of an Act which was passed in the neighbouring Kingdome, and would consider it as such.

Lord Ferrers observed that there were different Copies of this Act printed here; and produced one (in Quarto) wherein there was an Article about the Scots Tradeing to our Plantations; which was omitted in the more common paper, or (at least) much otherwise expressed: But this quickly appeared to be His Lordships Mistake; for his was a Copy of the Act offered to the Royal Assent in 1703 and not of that which had it on the 5th of August last.[178]

The Bishop of Sarum prefaced his Discourse[179] with owning his Birth in Scotland; but, haveing lived more years in this Kingdome and being now (by his post) one of ours, he hoped what he offered would not be thought partial to his Native Countrey. He enlarged on the unkind Treatment the Scots had met with, ever since the Union of the Crowns; and, at last, offered several Reasons for his hopeing that this Act might turn to the Advantage of the Protestant Succession in England. He seemed to undertake that (whenever the black day of the Queen's death should happen) the States of Scotland would set the Crown of that kingdome on the same head with ours. Lord Nottingham observed that this could not be; Since they were tyed up by this Act to do otherwise.

Lord Treasurer [Godolphin] gave the Necessary Reasons for adviseing Her Majesty to Assent to it; from the posture of our Affairs (at that time) both at home and abroad, and observed that the Highlanders (most disaffected to the Protestant Succession) were alwaies armed. Now the Low-landers, our friends, were put into the same Condition; which would be a Barrier, rather than a Terrour, to England.

After other less considerable Speeches, the Lord Nottingham reassumed the Argument and, reflecting on the late King's being hard on the Protestants in the lower Palatinate, in the Reswick-Treaty, was desired to explain himself by Lord Somers which being done, by a varying of his former way of expressing himself, the Objection was decently waved.[180]

[178] For the turbulent session of the Scottish Parliament of 1703 from which the future Act of Security emerged, see P. W. J. Riley, 'The Scottish Parliament of 1703', *SHR* xlvii (1968).

[179] There is an excellent account of Burnet's speech and of other contributions to this debate, notably Godolphin's and Somers's in *Jerviswood Correspondence*, pp. 14–15: James Johnstone to George Baillie, 2 Dec. 1704. See also *Parl. Hist.* vi, 371–2.

[180] While Somers was speaking, according to one account, the Junto follower 'Lord

Lord Haversham moved that the Question might be put—Whether the present posture of Scotland, in Consequence of this Act, was not dangerous to England? Lord Somers said this needed not; since the House seemed generally inclined to the Affirmative.[181] Hereupon, Upon Motion made to that purpose, the farther Debate was adjourned to this day Sennight.

This matter brought me a deal of Company (enquireing after the News of the Day) in the Evening. 1. Dr Gibson and Mr Tanner; who had supped with me. 2. Two Cousins Relf's[182] and their brother Bosworth. 3. Mr C. Musgrave and Mr Hales. 4. Mr Addison and his son Hutton, with Fed.[183] Nicolson. 5. Dr Younger.

[Nov.] 30. *Thursday*. Mr Dean Atterbury, in the morning, to know what I would do with his two fighting Petty-Canons.[184] He told me that they were already suspended *Ab Officio et Beneficio*; and that, if they were Excommunicated, that strict Censure of the Law would render 'em so scandalous that they could not hereafter be received into their Places. I wondered at the Doctrine; Since, if every *Ipso Facto* Excommunication were to deprive men finally of their Ecclesiastical Preferments, 'tis my Opinion that Mr Dean himself would (or should) have an ill time of it: Nor could I think it consistent with my Duty to leave so gross a Misdemeanour, in the very Body of the Cathedral-Church, to be punished onely by the Dean and Chapter.[185]—Mr Lee (of North-

Mohun consulted with several peers, whether they should move to send the earl of Nottingham to the Tower. But this being the first time the queen did the House the honour of coming to hear their debates, they thought fit to decline that motion out of respect for her majesty.' *Parl. Hist.* vi, 371; A. Boyer, *The History of Queen Anne* (1735), p. 165.

[181] '[Somers] went through all the errours committed in this reign, in Scotch affairs, and laid them home with great art and weight . . . and said it was of the highest consequence to provide for their own security against the danger they were in from such acts, and to prevent the like in time to come. He owned that this ought to be done in as calm a manner as possible; and therefore he proposed an adjournment, that they might have time to think on it; that is, to have time to treat with the Court about an understanding in English affairs; —and the tail will follow'. *Jerviswood Correspondence*, p. 15. Cf. Lord Dartmouth's note to Burnet, *History*, v, 182–3.

[182] John Relf, Clerk of the House of Lords and Joseph Relph, the Duke of Somerset's Steward at Cockermouth. He was virtual 'town manager' and all local government posts were in his hands. He sacrificed his health and fortune in Somerset's service until he abandoned that interest at the 1713 election. He was also a Land Tax Commissioner for Cumberland, 1692–9, 1705–10. Hopkinson, pp. 20, 132, 157, 318.

[183] *Sic*. ?Fetherston. See above, n. 82.

[184] John Calvert and Thomas Bewley, Minor Canons, were ordered to beg the pardon of the Dean and Chapter at a Chapter meeting on 23 Nov. 1704, for 'kicking, boxing and by word abusing' each other, and in the meantime they were suspended. After an apology, they were restored by the Vice-Dean and Chapter on 28 Apr. 1705. *CW* ii (1902), 216.

[185] Atterbury, on the other hand, regarded their restoration as an infringement of his rights and powers as Dean with regard to discipline. This was the beginning of the dispute

ampton)[186] and Sol[omon] Bray[187] met at my Lodgeings; And, upon the whole Debate, it appears that Mr Ireland has been very rash in gieving a new Lease of the School-Lands of Blencow to the Latter; who (even by his own Confession) is a Beggar, and, in the opinion of every-body else, a Knave.

This Hearing being over, I went to St Paul's; where the Society of Clergymen's Sons[188] were met, and an excellent sermon (on *James* 1, 27.) preached to them by Mr L. Butler,[189] heretofore of Edmund-Hall. Service ended, they went in procession to Draper's-Hall; where above 500 were treated at Dinner, very splendidly. The two Archbishops, five Bishops, &c. were present; and two Admirals (Dilks and Wishart)[190] made two of the twelve new Stewards for the ensueing year. In our Return home Mr Wotton and I called on his Bookseller Mr Godwin;[191] who is willing to undertake the printing of the *Border-Laws*.

Dec. 1. *Friday*. In the Lobby, Mr Holme and Mr Dale came to me and complained that there was like to be some backwardness in Mr Charles Bertie (Treasurer of the Ordnance)[192] in gieving way to all the Alterations designed about the White Tower. Upon this, I desired the Lord Hallifax to respite the makeing of his Report to the House, till this matter could be adjusted: And my Lord was pleased to assure me that no Report should be made till I allowed it.

In the House, an Appeal from the Exchequer concerning a Double Grant (from the Queen's Officers) of some Lands in Cornwal;[193] in which Cause the Barons (below) had been twice divided in their Judgements, and were (at last) forced to call in the Chancellor of the

between Nicolson and Atterbury and Todd which was to culminate in the controversy over the statutes of Carlisle Cathedral in 1708, for which see below, Session 5.

[186] He lived at Brixworth, near Northampton, and was visited by Nicolson on 7 Apr. 1708. He may be Henry Lee, Town Clerk of Northampton, 1662–88, 1690–1705. *VCH Northamptonshire*, iii, 15; *Records of the Borough of Northampton*, ed. J. C. Cox (1898), ii, 70, 570.

[187] A freeman of the borough of Northampton since 1676. Ibid., p. 43.

[188] The Corporation of the Sons of the Clergy founded in 1655 to give assistance to the widows and dependants of the clergy.

[189] Dr Lilly Butler (*c*.1651–1717), Rector of Farnham, Essex, 1701–6.

[190] Sir Thomas Dilkes (?1667–1707), Rear-Admiral of the White, and an Irish MP 1703–7, and Sir James Wishart (d. 1723), Rear-Admiral of the Blue, MP for Portsmouth, 1711–15, and a Lord of the Admiralty 1710, both of whom had been knighted on 24 Oct. 1704.

[191] Timothy Goodwin, a printer at the Queen's Head, against St Dunstan's Church in Fleet Street, 1683–1720. He printed Nicolson's book. H. R. Plomer, *Dictionary of Printers and Booksellers, 1668–1725* (1922), pp. 129–30.

[192] Hon. Charles Bertie (*c*.1640–1711), MP for Stamford, 1678–9, 1685–7, 1689–1711, Treasurer of the Ordnance, 1681–99, 1702–5.

[193] For the case see HMC *Lords MSS* vi, 2–3.

Exchequer who seemed to me to have favoured the Officers, against the antient Right and Customes of the Queen's Tenants in that Dutchy. But — Onely the Counsel for the Appellants was heard, their Harangues and Proofs lasting till after three o'clock, and the Remainder adjourned till to morrow.

My Rooms smokeing, I was forced to spend the Evening abroad; and Cousin R. Nicolson and I attaqued brother Joseph (in vain) on behalf of poor George Spooner.[194] He thinks he has already done his part for his indigent Relations. *Be not weary*, &c.

[Dec.] 2. *Saturday*. In the morning, Mr Charles Howard,[195] with Coll. Grahme, desireing that I'd appear at the Court of Delegates[196] (of which Notice should be given) in the Case of the marriage of E. Fenwick (of Bywell) with the Lady Grosvenor.[197]—The Coll. promises to soften the Earl of Thanet in the Case of Kirkbythore.[198]

Haveing read prayers in the House, and attended a little on some prefatory matters, I went to dinner with my Lord of Canterbury at Lambeth; where Lord Fairfax,[199] the Dean of Chichester,[200] and a great many more of the Laity and Clergy of Note. After we had dined, His Grace took me and Dr Gibson aside; and told us that the Archbishop of York had (this very day) told him that he had endeavoured to dissuade both me and my Dean from publishing our Case in print, and hoped he had prevailed. *Non pas*. His Grace likewise acquainted us that my Lord of York had, some dayes agoe, moved that He would allow Dr Atterbury to wait on him at Lambeth: Which was peremptorily refused. He shewed us a new Remonstrance which the lower House of Convocation had yesterday brought

---

[194] Probably a relation of Nathaniel Spooner (d. 1703), late Rector of Kirkland, who had been married to Nicolson's sister, Elizabeth.

[195] ?Second son of Philip Howard, the seventh son of the 1st Earl of Berkshire, related by marriage to Col. Grahme. He was lost at sea in 1705.

[196] The court of appeal in ecclesiastical cases.

[197] This famous case concerned Mary Davies, a considerable heiress in her own right, and widow of Sir Thomas Grosvenor (d. 1700) of Eaton in Cheshire, and her supposed marriage to Edward Fenwick, a Catholic and brother of Mary's friend Dorothy Turnour, with whom she had travelled to Rome and Paris on the death of Sir Thomas. Nicolson was one of the four bishops, along with Compton, Sprat, and Hooper, who were on the court which tried the case. The Delegates decided that Lady Grosvenor was not 'compos mentis at the time of the pretended marriage . . . only four civilians [civil lawyers] of the six dissented, the four Bishops and five Judges were unanimous'. Newsletter, 20 Feb. 1705, quoted in C. T. Gatty, *Mary Davies and the Manour of Ebury* (1921), ii, 181. For the details of the case see PRO Del. 2/32.

[198] Nicolson was endeavouring to undo a contract entered into by his predecessor Bishop Smith, with Thanet, the patron of the rectory of Kirkby Thore, which caused the rector to make over £50 of his income to the curates of Sowerby and Milburn. See *Misellany*, p. 29.

[199] MP for Yorkshire, 1689–1702, 1707.

[200] William Hayley (c.1658–1715), Dean of Chichester since 1699.

up to the President and Bishops:[201] Wherein they complain that Their Lordships have not yet answered their hopes in redressing their Grievances; nor satisfyed them of the condition of their Respective Diosceses in relation to what was humbly laid before them the last year: That no care was taken for condemning Pernicious Errors, Blasphemous, Heretical and Schismatical, Doctrines: That the House of Commons had endevoured to secure our Establishment by a wise and Religious Provision against Occasional Conformity, which had not yet received that Countenance from His Grace nor their Lordships that they could have wished: And, in Conclusion, they humbly recommend this last particular[202] to their present more serious Consideration.

[Dec.] 3. *Sunday*. I preached and administered the Sacrament, at the Savoy, for Dr Pratt; dined with Cousin R. Nicolson; and returned to my Lodgeings before Three.

In the Evening came George Thomas's son[203] to me for Letters to Queen's College. The young fellow, I found, had been in Town above a month; on no other Errand, but to see the place and to Enjoy the Conversation of his friends. An Extraordinary Frolick in a poor Child, and the son of a poor father.

[Dec.] 4. *Munday*. My brother's boy brought me some Copies of the Northern Letter, concerning my Controversy with the Dean;[204] and, immediately after, I found it on the Stals in Westminster-Hall. My Sentiments freely given (it may be, too freely) to Mr Elstob and Mr Buchanan touching our Partiality in asserting the Principles, Doctrine and Government, of our Church; which we ought to do equally against all her Enimies.—In the House, Nothing but private matters. I spent the Evening quietly at home.

[Dec.] 5. *Tuesday*. No Business in the House; which (after I had read prayers, as almost ever since the beginning of the session) was adjourned, after a small pause in Expectance of the Lords comeing from the Committee on Sea-Affairs: But they sat on.

[201] See Lathbury, *Convocation*, pp. 394–5. This was the first of two deliberately provocative addresses from the Lower to the Upper House in this session. For the second, on 11 Dec., see Sykes, *Wake*, i, 119–20.

[202] i.e. legislation against occasional conformity. The Lower House clearly, and rightly, expected an episcopal majority against the current bill when it reached the House of Lords.

[203] John Thomas (b. 1685), BA Queen's College, 1706, Vicar of Brampton, Cumberland, 1721.

[204] *A True State of the Controversy between the Present Bishop and Dean of Carlisle, touching the Royal Supremacy. In a Letter from a Northern Divine to a Member of the University of Oxford* (London, 1704). See above, n. 56.

After Dinner, Mr Lowther gave me a visit; and the History of his Father's good Deeds, and better Designs, for the Town of White-haven. He will, by no means, agree to Mr Lamplugh's Project at Parton.[205]

In the Evening, a Visit to Mr C. Musgrave whose pulse very low, but spirits pretty high.——Mr Holme, of the Tower, brought me a Note of some matters in the Records relateing to Horncastle: As, *Karliol Epus. de Ecclesia de Hornc. approprianet ut ibidem refugia habeat Adversus Depopulationes Scotorum. Rot. Rom. 12. E.2. m.9. Literae Rs. ad Papam. De Ecclesia de H. Lincoln. Dioc. cum Capellis Spectant. appropriand.* Pat. 8. E.2. m.17. p.1.

This day the Committee of the House of Commons reported the Bill against Occasional Conformity; And, the Question being put for Engrossing, the House divided. *Yeas*, 148. *Noes*, 129.

[Dec.] 6. *Wednesday*. I waited early on Lord Thanet; who, in the work of the day,[206] is for *Searching the Sore to the bottome*. I gave His Lordship the first Account of the late Speeches at Appleby; and taken he was with his Deputy Hall's Prowess.[207]

In the House, after a little private business and the Queen's being come, the Order of the day was Read, for putting the House into a Committee again to proceed in Consideration of the State of the Nation in Reference to Scotland.[208] Whereupon, the House adjourned dureing pleasure; and Lord Sunderland took the Chair.

The first that spoke was Lord Sommers; who observed that the Scots unreasonably complained of their Condition's being harder

[205] Sir John Lowther was closely involved in the rise of Whitehaven as a prosperous port at the end of the seventeenth century. See J. V. Beckett, *Coal and Tobacco. The Lowthers and the Economic Development of West Cumberland, 1660–1760* (Cambridge, 1981). Thomas Lamplugh, MP for Cockermouth (see Appendix A) planned to enlarge Parton, 'a small creek within a mile of Whitehaven' to threaten this prosperity, but he lacked the resources to meet such a risky venture. Despite the Parton Pier and Harbour Act of 1706 (*CJ* xv, 177, 199) Lamplugh was bought out by the Lowthers. See HMC *Lords MSS* vi, 398–402. Whitehaven's development was ensured by the Whitehaven Harbour Acts of 1709 and 1712 (*CJ* xvi, 121; and xvii, 123).

[206] The question of Scotland.

[207] Thanet was the hereditary Sheriff of Westmorland, and his Deputy Sheriff since 1696, John Hall, was the effective returning officer at the county elections. Hopkinson, p. 23. The by-election caused by the death of Sir Christopher Musgrave, MP for Westmorland had taken place at Appleby on 30 Nov. William Fleming had been elected, but Robert Lowther (MP for Westmorland after the general election in 1705) had taken advantage of the presence of a large number of freeholders to announce his candidature for the imminent general election. He warned them against those who were in favour of repealing the penal laws, bringing in a foreign power and subjecting England to popery and slavery. The speech was described as a 'very long schoolboy oration' for which 'Mr Lowther had not one shout for his long speech'. Levens Hall MS: Thomas Carleton to James Grahme, 2 Dec. 1704, quoted in Hopkinson, p. 63.

[208] Cf. the account of this debate in James Johnston's letter to George Baillie, London, 7 Dec. 1704: *Jerviswood Correspondence*, pp. 16–17.

since the Union of the Crowns than formerly: Whereas (not to mention the Advantages they had by the Act declareing the Rights of
the *Post-Nati*)[209] it was visible that they had now much greater
Liberties in bringing in their Sheep, black Cattle and Linnen-cloth,
than all their Antient Traffick[210] was worth. He proposed, that,
for the bringing them to an Understanding of their true Interest,
some Laws might pass here for the cutting off of all their Trade with
England; which Lawes, he said, might be limitted as to the
Commencement and Duration, so as not to be of any force if the
End was speedily attained, nor to continue longer than the Humour
lasted of their setting up for a different Prince.[211]

Lord Nottingham moved that (for Order's sake) the Question might
first be put—Whether these Acts were not of dangerous Consequence to the peace of England and the Hanover-Succession? Lord
Hallifax with great Gayety of Oratory and Elocution, said the Act
of Security was not the Distemper it self but a Symptom: That the
Darien miscarriage was that which galled all the Kingdome of Scotland, ever since uneasy:[212] And he insinuated that the same person
[meaning, Secretary Johnston][213] was the Adviser of passing both
the Darien Act[214] and this.

Lord Haversham said the Act, he was sure, is a Wound; and ought
not to be healed up before it was probed. He invcighed against the

[209] James I had failed to secure an Anglo-Scottish union in 1604–6, but by a collusive
action (Calvin's Case, 1606–7), the judges decided that all those born in Scotland after
James's accession (*post-nati*) were natural born subjects of the King of England.

[210] Traditionally the bulk of Scotland's trade had been with the Continent, especially
with France, Holland, Sweden, and the Baltic seaboard; but war with France and a sharp fall-
off of demand for Scottish coal, salt, cloth, and fish had caused a marked decline to set in
during the later years of the seventeenth century, and dependence on an expanding English
market had become proportionately greater. Hence the singular efficacy, as a hard bargaining weapon, of Somers's proposal for an 'Aliens Act' (see below, n. 211). See T. C. Smout,
Scottish Trade on the Eve of the Union, 1660–1707 (Edinburgh, 1963).

[211] '10 (Somers) proposed a law to make the Scotch aliens, and to forbid the coming in
of their catle—this law to commence after some time, and to determine whenever the
Succession should be setled.' *Jerviswood Correspondence*, p. 16. See also Halifax's speech,
below, on 11 Dec.

[212] The 1695 Act for establishing a company of Scotland trading to Africa and the
Indies. The hostility of the English government, on account of William III's desire not to
drive Spain into the arms of France, ensured the collapse of the Scottish trading colony
established in Spanish territory at Darien on the Central American isthmus. The best
account of the affair is G. P. Insh, *The Company of Scotland* (1932); for a short account see
Smout, *Scottish Trade on the Eve of the Union*, pp. 250–3.

[213] Nicolson's brackets. James Johnston (1655–1727), son of Archibald Johnston of
Warriston, cousin of Bishop Burnet. From 1692 to his dismissal by William III in 1696
he was first Joint-Secretary, then sole Secretary for Scotland. In 1704–5 he was Lord
Registrar and mainly resident in London, being associated politically with the *Squadrone
Volante*.

[214] Halifax apologised privately next day for having wronged Johnston in this case.
Jerviswood Correspondence, p. 17.

new mode of our princes haveing, in the weightyest matters, a very few Councellours; or perhaps but One.

Lord Ferrers was full of Resentment. The beggarly nation could not subsist without us; and yet they are for Insulting us. He was for humbling them immediately. The very prohibition of bringing in their Cattle, would effectually ruine them.

Lord Rochester moved for Addressing the Throne; as had been done (on occasion of the Darien-Act) both in 1695 and 99 as appeared by the Journal.[215]

Lord Nottingham moved again for the Question.

Lord Peterborough was for playing Act against Act; and all would be safe. Many Frights, he said, had siezed him lately; but all were over, as he hoped this would be. He was frighted, when the French General joyned Bavaria;[216] when the French Fleet bore down upon the English,[217] and (especially) at the late Noise of a Tack. All these blown over. But, Scotland was long since observed to be our little Sister; and she will Squawl till something's given her.

Lord Treasurer [Godolphin] for Lord Sommers's proposal; which would make the Scots wiser another time.

In Fine, Lord Wharton read a Paper; which was agreed to as the Unanimous Resolution of the House,[218] and is as followes: *Resolved; That, upon Consideration of the several Acts of Parliament lately passed in Scotland, and the dangerous Consequences that may follow from thence, as to the Trade and as to the Present and future Peace of this Kingdome, the most proper way to prevent those ill effects will be by some new Laws to be made for that purpose.*

Just as the Clerk was reading this Resolution, and the farther Order of the House to go again into a Committee (on Munday next) upon the same Subject, the Commons sent up the Bill for the Land-Tax; which was immediately Read a first time.

[Dec.] 7. *Thursday.* The Money-Bill read a 2d time and Committed. I dwelt within Doors all day.

[Dec.] 8. *Friday.* Mr Holmes brought me some Records from the Tower, relateing to Scotland and the See of Carlile; and promised

---

[215] 13 Dec. 1695 and 10 Feb. 1699: *LJ* xv, 611; xvi, 511.

[216] Tallard joined the Elector of Bavaria with 35,000 French troops in Aug. 1704.

[217] At the Battle of Malaga, Aug. 1704.

[218] There was some bipartisan dissent from Poulet and Devonshire, 'but the Lords were weary on foot to be gone, and so the motion was agreed to' (*Jerviswood Correspondence*, p. 17). It was the first fruits of the recent deal between Godolphin and the Junto.

a Volume of Mr Petyt's Collections,[219] on the former Title, in the beginning of next week.

In the House, Complaint made by the Attourney-General [Northey] that the late Bishop of St David's[220] being lately sentenced in the Exchequer had taken out a Writ of Errour returnable in the House of Lords; but had smothered and delayed its Execution so as that this Session was like to be over before he brought the Cause to a Hearing. The House to be summoned against to morrow, and the Judges Ordered to attend, for the takeing some proper Course in the matter. Money-Bill gone thro' in a Committee, and ordered a Third Reading to morrow.

[Dec.] 9. *Saturday*. Haveing given the Breviat of Mr Coke's Bill to Mr Hook, I went to Col. Grahme's; where I met with Mr White (a Gentleman in a Grey Suit, long Wig and a Sword) who proved to be Mr Lesley:[221] Who, upon Discovery, merrily observed that the Colonel was not afraid to confess what loose Company he kept. The Colonel and I (according to Parole) went to dine with the Bishop of London at Fulham; where we found an Essex-Gentleman and three or four Clergymen: Of the latter, a Son of the late Bishop Jones of St David's.[222] Before Dinner, My Lord Carryed us round his Gardens: where there's the greatest variety of Greens and other plants in any private hand (at least) in England. The more tender Exoticks are kept over a Stove; amongst which I observed a great many *Seda*, which I thought had been generally a more hardy kind. Of the healthyer Foreigners he has a whole Wilderness, without doors, and several large Groves within. One Orange-Tree, with pretty good store of fruit, he shewed us; which he raised from Seed (above thirty years agoe) when he was Master of St. Crosse's Hospital, near Winchester.[223] Among thousands of Cypress and Cedar (of diverse kinds) I cursorily took notice of the Cork-Tree, Green and

[219] The 386 volumes in the Petyt Collection of manuscripts are now in the Inner Temple Library. For a description, see Conway Davies, *Catalogue of the Manuscripts of the Inner Temple*, pp. 27–41.

[220] Thomas Watson, Bishop of St Davids, 1687–99, suspended 1694 and deprived 1699. Owing to a protracted legal battle, the see was vacant until the appointment of George Bull in Apr. 1705. For the case, see HMC *Lords MSS* vi, 228–9.

[221] Charles Leslie (1650–1722), the brilliant non-juring pamphleteer and editor of *The Rehearsal* (1704–9). Largely responsible for the revival of passive obedience and non-resistance doctrine in the first decade of the eighteenth century; fled to St Germains to escape arrest in 1711. Cf. Burnet, *History*, v, 436–7 on Leslie's remarkable influence, especially on the High Church clergy. See also J. P. Kenyon, *Revolution Principles* (Cambridge, 1977), *passim*, esp. pp. 63–4, 109–11.

[222] Nicolson here mistakes Edward Jones's diocese. He was Bishop of St Asaph, 1692–1703.

[223] Appointed Nov. 1667.

as hardy-looked as a Sea-Buckthorne, but cut in the Bol from the very root upwards as far as the Curiosity of the Spectators and their Arms could reach; Evergreen-Oaks, from the West-Indies, stout enough after they once take to growing; Variegated Ivy; the Irish Tree Strawberry, three or four yard's high, now in flower and Leaved like the Mock-willow; *Sedum Arborescens*, of Portugal; &c.

NB. Lord Register Johnson (as the Colonel his kinsman and Friend assures me) is the Author of the *Reflections on the Lord Haversam's Speech*;[224] and complains that he has not (in the last Session of the late Parliament of Scotland) cleared above 150 *l.* tho' his Equipage at his Entrance upon his new post, cost him 1000 *l.*

[Dec.] 10. *Sunday*. Haveing heard Dr Manningham[225] (at the Queen's Chapple) a good Sermon, on *Psalm* 119, 104. *Thro' thy commandments I get understanding; and therefore I hate all false wayes*; I went to dinner at Salisbury-Court. Joseph Rothery, as tall as I am. In the Evening, by Grey's-Inn (on foot) to Swallow-street where Col. Grahme and his son[226] met me by Appointment. The Colonel backward in joyning charges with Mr J. Musgrave. His Cousin Johnson (he averrs) is not in the Presbyterian Interest.[227] Qu[ery] if not in the Popish? The Letters written into Scotland (Mentioned in the *Reflections*) which influenced the Revolution-Party to come into the Measures of the Act of Security, suggested to have come from Lord Somers,[228] &c. 30000 *l.* was promised; which would have carryed the Succession-Bill: But that failed, because (as was said) the Duke of Savoy and other Allies called so fast for Money that none could be sent Northward. The New Scheme of Alterations at Court is said (by the Colonel) to run thus: Lord Pembroke to be Admiral: Lord Sommers President of the Council; Lord Sunderland Secretary of State, &c. Time will shew.[229]

[224] *Reflections on a late Speech by the Lord Haversham, In so far as it related to the Affairs of Scotland* (London, 1704). For the speech see above, 23 Nov.

[225] Thomas Manningham, later Bishop of Chichester. See Appendix A.

[226] Probably Henry Grahme, MP for Westmorland, see Appendix A. He had voted against the Tack on 28 Nov. 1704. The colonel's other son, William (d. 1718), was a naval officer, becoming a captain in 1713.

[227] In point of fact Johnston was a strong Presbyterian.

[228] For Junto intrigues with the Queensberry party and the 'Revolution Whigs' in Scotland in 1704, see P. W. J. Riley, 'The Union of 1707 as an Episode in English Politics', *EHR* lxxxiv (1969), 506-7.

[229] There follows the beginning of an entry for 11 Dec. 1704, which covers one page of the original manuscript and reads: '11. *Munday*. In the House (after a first Reading of Mr Coke's and some other private Bills) the Order of the Day was called for, the Queen being comed to the House as heretofore on all Debates on the State of the Nation in Reference to Scotland. Lord Sommers began the Debate; shewing, by an Historical Detail of the matter of fact, that the Complaints of the Scots had alwaies been groundless; That their Kingdome was now in a wealthier State than at the Union of the Crowns: &c. And

[Dec.] 11. *Munday*. After the Reading of Mr Coke's and some other Private Bills, the Queen came to the House; and, the Order of the day being read, Lord Wharton opened the Debate by observeing that our Circumstances (in Relation to Scotland) were truely Deplorable; and that our Misfortune was, in a great measure, to be attributed to the putting the late Treaty of Union into wrong hands, the hands of those who were ever Enemies to the Cause. This he shewed from the Minutes of the last Session of the Scotch Parliament and (in conclusion) moved that Her Majesty might be enabled to issue out a new Commission, with more effectual Powers; and he seemed to hope that this would fall into better and more successful hands.

Lord Nottingham apprehending himself reflected on in several Particulars of this Speech, appealed to all the Commissioners (of both Nations) whether he had not been zealous in promoteing that good work. He affirmed that the Scotch Commissioners themselves were more backward than the English; and foretold that the Nobility of that Nation would never agree to any Union, till the Parliament of England should first agree on the Numbers and Rank of such as they would admit into the Parliament of Great Britain. He therefore moved that our next Commissioners might be empowered to act singly; that is, to draw up such Overtures as they thought fit to offer to the States of Scotland.

My Lord Wharton opposed this project as too condescending (or too prescribeing) on our parts: But declared that he meant no Reflection on that Noble Lord, haveing no body in's Eye but those that were either dead or half-dead.

Lord Rochester affirmed that he knew not one Englishman that retarded the late Treaty; and could not imagine that any of the Commissioners (as far as he could readily recollect) were either Dead or Half-dead. Then quoth Lord Wharton *I meant No-body*. ['Twas the General Opinion that his dead man was Sir C. Musgrave and his half dead (tho' indeed he never was a Commissioner) was Sir E[dward] S[eymour].][230]

Lord Treasurer [Godolphin] seconded Lord Wharton's proposeal; but without those Additional powers offered at by Lord Nottingham. This agreed.

Lord Hallifax approveing this first Resolution, proposes that (since the Scots had thrown off Friendship) we might now think

therefore moved that, since the Advantages of the Lawes of *Postnati* were so lightly esteemed, they might be put into their Primitive Condition.'

The entry is a mistaken reconstruction of the beginning of the day's debate. For the reasons why Nicolson probably made this error see above, Chapter 3, pp. 109–11.

[230] Nicolson's brackets.

of treating them as Enemies; or, at least, as Aliens; and that, to this purpose, all English Privileges (at a certain distant day) might be taken away from the people of that Nation.

Lord Nottingham desired that, for our own sakes, we would not wholly exclude 'em out of our Plantations; nor (immediately) out of our Armies and Fleets. Lord Hallifax assented: But Lord Grey [of Warke] observed that the Scots were already excluded from the bearing Offices in our English Plantations by Statute 8. William 3.[231] which Law himself had put in Execution.[232]

However 'twas agreed likewise that (after the aforesaid distant day) no Scotch man should be capable of bearing any office (Civil or Military) within the Kingdomes of England and Ireland, or in any of our English Plantations; excepting such as are already setled here, before the passing of such Act.

The third Proposeal was made (by the Lord Ferrers) for Prohibition of the Importation of their Cattle and Sheep, into either of the Kingdomes of England or Ireland, to commence at the said Day: And this was also agreed to.

The Lord Torrington offered a fourth Proviso (quickly admitted) that our Admirals might have Instructions to sieze, and treat as Enemies, all Scotch Bottoms tradeing to France.[233]

Lord Moon [Mohun] proposes the Inhibiteing of Scotch Wool being brought into England or Ireland. Upon which Lord Hallifax observed that the most peevish Act was their late one for the Exportation of Wool;[234] which did England a Mischief without any Benefit to themselves. This likewise agreed.

Lord Nottingham took notice that all these Clauses were threatning and such as would provoke; and therfore desired that something might be offered that was Softer and more inviteing. He particularly proposed that it might be considered whether the Fishing on that Coast, managed joyntly by the English and Scots, might not be of Use to both Kingdomes, in breeding up Seamen, &c.

This was not Seconded; it being late and the Queen supposed to be sufficiently wearyed out. Wherefore — The House was reassumed;

[231] Probably a reference to the Act for Preventing Frauds and Regulating Abuses in the Plantation Trade (7 and 8 William III, c.22).

[232] Lord Grey of Warke had been Governor of Barbados, 1698–1701.

[233] Among the 'four Acts' of the Scottish Parliament of 1703–4 which caused such resentment in England was the 'Wine Act', which in effect gave legal authority to the renewal of Scotland's traditional trade with France, even though the countries were at war with each other.

[234] The Scottish Parliament had banned the export of wool in 1701, but it was again made legal by the 'Wool Act' of 1704. *Acts Parl. Scot.* x, 227; xi, 190. The English grievance was that much of the wool destined for export came from the backs of English sheep, a major item in the endless illicit traffic across the Border.

And, Lord Sunderland haveing made his Report, their Lordship's
adjourned the Debate to Friday next; and the House till to morrow.[235]

[Dec.] 12. *Tuesday.* In the morning Mr Joseph Musgrave (who
brought me the *True Tom Double*)[236] Mr Lister and Dr Covel; likewise Mr Madox, who kindly had transcribed several Records for me.

In the House the Duke of Albemarl's Executors answered an
Appeal by Sir Cloudesley Shovel, Mr Francis Nicolson,[237] &c. concerning their Accounts in the Wreck-Adventure by Grant from the
late King. The Decree of the Lord Keeper [Wright] (who had
favoured the Executors) was Reversed.

In the Evening, Mr Tanner and I, paid a visit to Dr Hickes; who
gives a mighty Character of Mr Parker (Recorder of Derby) and Mr
Fortescue,[238] as two of the most learned Lawyers of the Age. Mr
Tanner took notice of many fine Characters in the *Athenae
Oxoniensis*[239] (particularly that of Cardinal Woolsey) which were
penned by Mr Harrington.[240]

At my Return, I found the Result of the long Debates in the
House of Commons touching the Scotch Acts. The first Question
put was—*It appears to the Committee that the Acts lately passed
in Scotland are highly prejudicial to the Interest and Trade of this
Nation, tending to defeat the Protestant Succession setled in the
Illustrious House of Hannover, and of dangerous Consequence to
the Peace and Union of both Kingdomes.* Upon this the House
divided; *Yeas,* 152. *Noes,* 209. So — Rejected.[241] The Next was —
That the House be moved that a Bill be brought in for the effectual

---

[235] James Johnstone's summary of the day's proceedings, with the comment that 'all this
was proposed by 6 (the Whigs), and 7 (the Tories) acquiesed', is in *Jerviswood Correspondence*, p. 22.

[236] *The True Tom Double: or an Account of Dr Davenant's late conduct and writings
particularly with relation to the XIth section of his Essays on Peace at Home, and War
abroad* (1704). This pamphlet attacked Charles Davenant (1656-1714), economist and
pamphleteer, who in his *Essays* had urged all parties to unite to fight the war. He was
accused of abandoning his Tory position which he had established in 1701 with his *The
True Picture of a Modern Whig*, in which the character of Tom Double represents the Tory
view point.

[237] Sir Cloudesley Shovel (1650-1707), Admiral of the Fleet, and Francis Nicholson
(1660-1728), Governor of Virginia, 1698-1705. For the case see HMC *Lords MSS* vi,
59-60.

[238] ?John Fortescue (1670-1746), changed his name to Fortescue-Aland in 1704, MP
for Midhurst, 1715-16, Solicitor-General 1715-17, Justice of the King's Bench, 1718-27
and of the Common Pleas 1729-46, created Baron Fortescue 1746.

[239] By Anthony Wood, published 1691-2 in two volumes.

[240] James Harrington (1664-93) wrote the preface to the first volume of *Athenae
Oxoniensis* and the introduction to the second volume.

[241] 'The Whigs and the No-Tackers joined against it; for if it had carried, there would
have been an address to the Queen to know who of the English Ministry had advised the
Act [of Security].' *Jerviswood Correspondence*, p. 23: Johnstone to Ballie, 12 Dec.

secureing the Kingdome of England from the Apparent Danger that may arise from several Acts lately passed in the Parliament of Scotland. This was happily agreed to; and falls very well in with the Resolutions taken yesterday in the House of Lords.[242]

[Dec.] 13. *Wednesday*. In the House Mr Coke's Bill read a second time, and committed; but (as I told Mr Hooks, his Sollicitor) his Contract and mine is not yet so far adjusted as that its like to be brought to a third Reading. An Appeal (very vexatious) Against Decrees of Foreclosure, and almost 30 years silence: the Appellant condemned in 20 *l*. costs.[243]—I dined with Mr Grandorge, Dr Gibson and Mr Johnson.

[Dec.] 14. *Thursday*. In the morning, the two Archbishops and other Commissioners opened and read the Queen's Commission for setling the First-fruits and Tenths,[244] &c. The Secretary and Treasurer[245] being sworn, my Lord of Canterbury produced a Device (invented by Mr Wotton) for a Common Seal for the Corporation; which set aside what I had to offer (from Mr Dale) to the same purpose: And indeed my Draughts were rejected with some little warmth, both my Lord of Canterbury and the Master of the Rolls[246] observeing that the Gentlemen of the Herald's office were alwaies too medling and apt to prescribe on these Occasions. After this was a while Debated, the Question was adjourned (with the rest of the Business) to this day month, Jan. 11th when we are to meet again here (in the Prince's Chamber) or, if the Queen will allow it, at Whitehall. The two Archbishops to know Her Majesty's pleasure.

In the House (after the hearing of an Impudent Appeal, wherein the Appellant was condemned in 30 *l*. costs)[247] Lord Mohun moved for thanks to the Duke of Marlborough, newly arrived, at his first comeing to the House. This being agreed to, Duke of Sommerset moved farther that my Lord Keeper might be desired to be more

[242] See *CJ* xiv, 455, 457; *LJ* xvii, 596.

[243] See HMC *Lords MSS* vi, 57–8.

[244] The commission is printed in A. Savidge, *The Foundation and Early Years of Queen Anne's Bounty* (1955), pp. 120–34. See this and G. F. A. Best, *Temporal Pillars* (Cambridge, 1964), for a description of the Bounty (for the supplementation of poor livings in the Church), authorised by Act of Parliament in Apr. 1704. Unfortunately, because of his absence in Cumberland, Nicolson was able to leave us no record of these early stages. The General Court and Committee of the Bounty (Nicolson was an active member of both) met in 'the New Buildings adjoyning the Banqueting House in Whitehall' (Church Commissioners, QAB Minute Book, i, 5).

[245] John Chamberlayne, see Appendix A, and Edward Tenison, cousin of Archbishop Tenison, and Treasurer of the Bounty, 1704–8.

[246] Sir John Trevor, 1693–1717.

[247] *Harley* v. *Searle*, see HMC *Lords MSS* vi, 4–5.

full, than usual, in expressing the sentiments of their Lordships.

A Petition from Sir R. Clayton, the Patron, for divideing a large parish in Hampshire (by the concurrent Assent of the Diocesan and present Incumbent) into two.[248]

The late Bishop of St. David's (by the Lord Chief Baron) sent in his Writ of Error; and has, of course, Eight dayes for the Assignment of his Errors.

The Commons passed the Bill against Occasional Conformity: but divided upon the Question: *Yeas*, 178. *Noes*, 131. So 'twas carryed by 47 voices.

In the Evening, I went (with my Sister) to pay a visit to Mrs Waugh: and the Dr (from Dr Hans)[249] gave me the first News of my Lord C[arlisle]'s parting houshold's with his Lady.[250]

[Dec.] 15. *Friday*. Upon the Queen's comeing to the House (the Scotch Affair haveing been appointed for the Business of the Day) the Occasional Bill was brought up by Mr Bromley; attended with about 150 of the Commons. 'Twas unanimously ordered a first Reading; and, after a Debate of four Hours,[251] the Question was put for a second Reading. *Contents*, 33. *Not Contents*, 51. Proxies for the former, 17. for the latter, 20. So 'twas rejected by a Majority (in the whole) of 21.[252] The Bishops for the Second Reading were those of York, London, Durham, Winchester, Landaff, Rochester, Exeter, Chester, Carlile, Bath and Wells, and St Asaph.

The Earl of Warrington began the Debate with his Reasons (weak enough) for his being now against the Bill; tho', the last Session, he had been for it.

Lord Haversham moved for a Second Reading; declareing his Resolutions to be (as they had ever been) to vote for the throwing it out at last.

The Arguers for the Bill were Nottingham, Rochester, Anglesey, Abingdon, North, Pawlet, Guarnsey, Winchesea [Winchilsea], the

[248] Horne parish in Surrey, see HMC *Lords MSS* vi, 229–30. The diocesan was the Bishop of Winchester and the incumbent Owen Griffith (*c*.1673–1731), Rector of Bletchingley, Surrey, 1704–31.

[249] Sir Edward Hannes (d. 1710), Professor of Chemistry at Oxford in 1690, doctor to the late Duke of Gloucester, and first Physician to Queen Anne in 1702; he was knighted in 1705.

[250] There were rumours as early as 1698 that the earl and countess would part. Levens Hall MS E/W3: Weymouth to Grahme, 30 June 1698.

[251] According to Burnet, 'if it had not been for the queen's being present, there would have been no long debate on that head, for it was scarce possible to say much that had not been formerly said'. *History*, v, 187.

[252] Nicolson's figures for the *Contents* appear to be wrong, according to the clerk of the House's MS minutes: 37 voted in person with 17 proxies, thus giving the *Not Contents* a majority of 17.

Archbishop of York, Bishops of London and Bath and Wells. Against it—Wharton, Mohun, Scarbrough, Sommers, Hallifax and the Bishop of Sarum.

The Lord Treasurer [Godolphin] declared his opinion to be (the same it was last year) that the Bill was unseasonable: But, being brought up, he thought it might be made a good one; and therfore he voted for its being read a second time.

Lord Winchelsea seeming to threaten the House with being hereafter forced by the Commons to pass this Bill, was first called on (to explain) by Lord Wharton; and was afterwards said, by Lord Peterborough to *Bully* the House: whereupon, he replyed warmly to the Latter—*That he was neither for Bullying, nor would he be Bullyed*. On this, somewhat of a Challenge was whispered; which was wisely prevented by the Earl of Abingdon's over-hearing it, And (on His motion) the Houses Injoyning Peace.

Lord Guarnsey hard on the Bishop of Sarum; haveing (accidentally) his *Glasgow-Dialogue*[253] in his pocket, out of which he read two or three Pages very severe upon the Dissenters.

The Archbishop of York averred they were Schismaticks; and, Schism being a Sin, he protested that *as long as he lived he would be for this Bill.*[254]

Lord Hallifax took notice of the Queen's proposeing Queen Elizabeth for her Pattern; and takeing Her Mottoe. *Queen Elizabeth* (he observed, from the Journals) *alwaies discountenanced any bearing hard upon the Puritans*.

Lord Angelesey replyed, that he hoped that care would be taken that our Religion might be transmitted to posterity *semper eadem*. This concluded the Debate; and the Votes (*ultima ratio*) ended the Contest as above.

[Dec.] 16. *Saturday*. In the morning I carryed my *Border-Laws* to Mr Goodwine; who remitted 'em presently to Mr Roberts his printer at Stationer's-Hall:[255] And he sets on forthwith.—Thence to the Custome-H[ouse] where Mr Britton[256] told me that 25 *l.* was ordered for W. Churdon's widow.

[253] *A Vindication of . . . the Church and State of Scotland. In four Conferences Wherein the answer to the Dialogues betwixt the Conformist and the Nonconformist is examined*, published in 1673 while Burnet was Professor of Theology at Glasgow University.

[254] For the exchange between the Archbishop and Lord Peterborough, after the former had uncomfortably said that 'he was for so much of the bill as concerned the Church', see *Parl. Hist.* vi, 363.

[255] James Robert (*c.*1669–1754), Master of the Stationers' Company 1729–31. Plomer, *Dictionary of Booksellers and Printers . . . 1668 to 1725*, p. 255.

[256] ? Richard Breton, Comptroller of the Cloth and Petty Customs, and a Commissioner of the Customs.

In the House (the Queen present) the Grand Committee came to a Resolution to Address Her Majesty on the following Heads.[257] 1. To give speedy and effectual Order for the putting the Town of Newcastle into a condition of Defence; and for secureing the Port of Tinmouth, and for the repairing and strengthening the Fortifications of Berwick, Carlile and Hull. 2. To direct the Laws effectually to be put in Execution (in Respect to the Arms and Horses) against all Papists and reputed Papists, and all persons refuseing or neglecting to take the Oathes to Her Majesty and that she would be pleased to direct an Account of what is done therein to be laid before Her Majesty in Council. 3. To cause the Militia of the four Northern Counties to be disciplined; and care to be taken that they be provided with Arms and Ammunition, to be in a readiness upon Occasion. 4. To order a competent Number of Regular Troops to be kept upon the Northern Borders.——These being reported, and agreed to by the House, the Bill for Union[258] (and another for preventing the Importation of Scotch Wool)[259] was read the first time.

In the Evening I had a visit from young Sir C. Musgrave whom I accompanyed back to his Uncle's. This day the Commons came also to the following Resolution: *Resolved, That it be one head of the Bill for the effectual secureing the Kingdome of England from the apparent Danger that may arise from several Acts lately passed in the Parliament of Scotland, to enable Her Majesty to name and appoint Commissioners for England to treat with Commissioners for Scotland for an Union between the two Kingdomes.*[260]

[Dec.] 17. *Sunday.* At the Queen's Chapple, Dr Wickart (Dean of Winchester)[261] preached an excellent sermon on——*He that hath ears to hear let him hear:* setting forth the several wayes of God's speaking to Man; as, in the works of Nature, the various turns and Dispensations of Providence in our own Lives, and in the Death of our friends.

I dined with the Bishop of Durham [Crew]: where Lord Hinchingbrook,[262] Mr Carteret,[263] Mr Conyers, Mr Dawson, Mr Hutton, Dr Bowes[264] and Mr Pickering.[265]

Mr Dean of Wells [Grahme] visited in the morning; and, at night,

[257] See *LJ* xvii, 602.   [258] See HMC *Lords MSS* vi, 230-3.
[259] Ibid., pp. 233-8.   [260] *CJ* xiv, 462.
[261] John Wickart (d. 1722), Dean of Winchester since 1692.
[262] Edward, Viscount Hinchingbrook (1692-1722), eldest son of the 3rd Earl of Sandwich, later to be MP for Huntingdon, 1713-22. Sedgwick, ii, 267.
[263] Possibly Edward Carteret (1671-1739), MP for Bedford, 1702-5, and Bere Alston, 1717-21. Previously he had sat for Huntingdon, 1698-1700. Sedgwick, i, 533.
[264] John Bowes (*c*.1658-1721), Canon of Durham since 1696.
[265] Possibly Theophilus Pickering, Canon of Durham since 1692.

Mr Brewer came for the History of our Debates on the Conformity-Bill: Which, he saies, must pass the next year.

[Dec.] 18. *Munday*. The two Scotch Acts were read a second Time, and committed to a grand Committee. After which an odd Appeal of Mrs Doyly (now Fownes)[266] endeavouring to prove Her deceased Husband marryed to another wife; which, after hearing the Appellant's Counsel, was adjourned.

I dined at Lambeth, with Mr Lorn, Dr Cade,[267] Dr Kennet, &c. and, haveing paid an accustomed visit to old Mr Snow, Mr Wotton and I spent the Evening together at Dr Gibson's and my own Lodgeings.

[Dec.] 19. *Tuesday*. After a troublesome (and unfinished) Committee on Lord Howard's Bill for the Sale of Wheldrake, &c.[268] the former of the Scotch Bills (for appointing Commissioners and forbidding the Importation of their Cattle) was considered by the Committee, the Queen and prince both present, and (with some Amendments) reported and agreed to have a third Reading. NB. Lord Hallifax proposed the 1st of Jan. 1705[269] for the Commencement of the Prohibition of Cattle; which will (in Scotland) be reckoned to be the first day of this next month.[270]—In the Evening, at my Brother's.

[Dec.] 20. *Wednesday*. Finishing the Lord Howard's Bill in the Committee, I read prayers: And, soon after the House was sat, the Bill of Union &c. was read the third time and passed. The Earl of Rochester acquainted the Lords with his Apprehensions that this Law would rather provoke the high-spirited Nobility of Scotland, than compass the End proposed; but yet he assured their Lordships that, since it seemed so agreable to most Members of the House, he would not oppose its passing. Lord Haversham declared his Dissent; and Lord Thanet (with some few others) were Not Contents.[271]

An Appeal of Mr Laurence's being heard, and the Decree (hardly enough) affirmed,[272] I went to dinner with the Archbishop of York;

[266] See HMC *Lords MSS* vi, 51-2.

[267] ? Salisbury Cade (?1660-1720), educated Oxford, D. Med. 1691, practised at Greenwich, Physician to St Bartholomew's Hospital 1708.

[268] Lord Howard of Escrick was selling the Manor of Wheldrake for the payment of his debts. See HMC *Lords MSS* vi, 87; *LJ* xvii, 586-7, 589-90, 606, 608, 717.

[269] Old Style: i.e. 1 Jan. 1706.

[270] Since 1600 the Scottish calendar had used 1 Jan. as New Year's Day, while England still retained 25 Mar., Lady Day, as the new year, until 1752.

[271] Cf. *Jerviswood Correspondence*, p. 26, Johnstone to Baillie, 21 Dec., for the proceedings of 20 Dec.

[272] See HMC *Lords MSS* vi, 6-8.

where Mr Dean of Chichester [Hayley] in Consult, about erecting a Chapple or two more in the parish of St Giles.[273]

[Dec.] 21. *Thursday*. In the morning, Mr R. Musgrave giveing me an honest Account of his zeal in some of his sentiments different from those of the Lords in Relation to Scotland; pleading for some Lenitives, and against the Arming of our Militia, &c.

In the Lobby, Coll. Grahme hastening the Confederacy with Mr J. Musgrave. Mr Charles Bertie advises the Agreement with Mr Patteson, in the Contest at Melmerby.[274]

In the House, the Address to the Queen (on the State of Scotland) reported by Lord Sunderland;[275] and ordered to be presented to morrow by the whole House.—The Galleries seeming to darken the House, and (being unfinished) looking a little ugly, a Motion was made by Lord Guilford (seconded by Lord Townesend) that they be pulled down. The Question called for, the Lord Wharton moved that the Question (which ought to take place)[276] be, whether the House shall now adjourn? Upon this the House divided. *Contents*, 22. *Not Contents*, 13.

Mr Holmes and Mr Dale (putting me on calling for the Lord Treasurer's papers concerning the Order about the Records) dined with me at the *Talbot*; whither Mr Relf sent me those papers. NB. My Arms may be appropriated for 6 *l*. Agreed. Mr Holmes gave me a sample of Mr Prynne's Common-place.

[Dec.] 22. *Friday*. The Report for the Committee to inspect the Records, being (as to the Chamber of the Treasurer of the Ordnance) drawn up by Mr Holmes and Mr Dale, was by us three carryed to my Lord Hallifax Who agreed to it, and promises to draw up the whole in consort with me against the next meeting of the House.

Lord Bradford (after some Private Bills, and the first Reading of that for the Poor)[277] acquainted the Lords that the Lord Chamberlain [Kent] had desired him to acquaint their Lordships that the Queen had appointed two o'clock to be attended with their Address. The Duke of Buckingham said — This is so irregular that the Reporter

[273] The unmanageable size and population of the London suburban parishes was a source of constant concern to Church leaders. The alternative to the building of chapels of ease on local initiative was eventually found in the Fifty New Churches Bill of 1711.

[274] Possibly a reference to the free school which had been founded at Maughanby [?Melmerby] and was supported by lands sold illegally by Mr Pattenson's ancestors. Nicolson had advised, early in 1704, selling the estate and paying off the debts and settling the remainder for the support of the schoolmaster. *Miscellany*, p. 122. Thomas Pattenson (1673–1742) was the son-in-law of the Rector of Melmerby. *Armorial*, p. 226.

[275] See *LJ* xvii, 607.   [276] i.e. take precedence.
[277] See HMC *Lords MSS* vi, 245-7.

257

would (as a man jealous of the Orders of the House) have severely remarked on any other that should have brought such a Message. However, for a Compromise, he desired that the Journal might be thus worded: *This House was informed by one of the Lords with the white Staves that Her Majesty* &c. Accordingly, the House attended; and, being returned, the Lord Keeper reported the Queen's Answer which (with the Address) was ordered to be printed.[278]

The Bishop of St David's, haveing not assigned Errors his Writ was voted to Discontinue; and the Attourney-General [Northey] directed to take out Judgement. Mr Attourney saies, he may bring another Writt: but 'twill be so expensive, to run thro' all the Offices again, that he rather believes that he'l submit and that the Queen will shortly fill the vacant See.[279]

Dr Gibson and I (goeing to dine together) had the *Essay for Catholic Communion*,[280] a vile popish book, recommended to our joynt Examination by my Lord of Canterbury but, upon my undertakeing to preach for the Dr next Sunday, the perusal was referred to him alone. NB. Mr Speaker Harley for dropping the Boutefeau's in Convocation.[281] Dean of Christ Church [Aldrich] for any Bishoprick even St Asaph;[282] and Mr Dean of Carlile [Atterbury] reckons himself (by his advice to his Brother Lewis,[283] to send his son to Westminster)[284] secure of succeeding. My Lord of Canterbury wants Assistants among the Bishops of his Province, since the Bishop of Hereford keeps at home. Bishop of Norwich to be removed, either to London or Ely.[285]

This Evening, the Commons (in a Committee of the whole House) resolved on Heads of a Bill—for arming the Six Northern Counties;

---

[278] For the Queen's answer see *LJ* xvii, 608.

[279] The see was filled in Apr. 1705 by George Bull. Watson petitioned the Lords not to discontinue the writ on 22 Jan. 1705, but his petition was rejected, see HMC *Lords MSS* vi, 228–9.

[280] Joshua Bassett's *Essay towards a proposal for a Catholic Communion* (1704).

[281] Those causing discontent and strife. For Harley's attitude towards the Convocation disputes in 1704–5 and his pacifying influence over a reluctant Atterbury, see Bennett, *Tory Crisis*, pp. 78–9.

[282] Traditionally one of the poorer bishoprics in England and Wales, valued at £187 for first fruits and tenths as opposed to the deanery of Christ Church valued at £1,000. However, its real income had been raised by the shrewd stewardship of William Lloyd (bishop, 1680–92). See A. T. Hart, *William Lloyd* (1952), p. 40. Wake's contemporary estimate of its value at £800 placed it eighth from the bottom in the ranking of sees (along with Carlisle and Peterborough), but the richest of the Welsh bishoprics. See Christ Church, Wake MS 18, f. 393.

[283] Lewis Atterbury (1656–1731), Rector of Sywell, Northants., 1685–1707, and of Shepperton, Middlesex, in 1707.

[284] Both Francis and Lewis Atterbury had attended Westminster School under the great Dr Busby. Lewis's son was Bedingfield Atterbury (c.1694–1718).

[285] He was translated to Ely in July 1707.

prohibiting Scotch Linnen; &c. But 'tis believed (the Committee being thin) all these will come to nothing.

[Dec.] 23. *Saturday*. I dined with Mr C. Musgrave where were also Coll. Grahme, Mr R. Musgrave, Mr Joseph Musgrave, Mr Wenyeve and Mr Lawson. The Coll. and Mr J. Musgrave could not adjust the matter of their joynt Expence at the approaching Election for Westmorland; and therfore Mr Musgrave resolved not to stand, *Esto*.

At my return, I found a Proof of the first Sheet of the *Border-Laws*; which, I hope, will be published before the End of this Session of Parliament.

[Dec.] 24. *Sunday*. I preached for Dr Gibson at Lambeth, on *Matthew* 11, 4. and, after we had dined at his house, we went cross the water together, to Dr Lancaster's. Dr Gibson preached at St Martin's; where he and Mr Snapes[286] are in expectance of being (this week) chosen Joynt-Lecturers in a full Vestry. The Duke of Somerset and Lord Sommers are two of that body.

[Dec.] 25. *Munday*. I preached, yesterday's sermon, for the Bishop of Rochester; with whom I dined, together with the Bishops of Chester and Bath and Wells, Dr Hutton, Mr Duke and Mr Friend.[287] The Bishop of Bath and Wells earnest against the Archbishop of Canterbury's power of depriveing; and an Advocate for the Omission of the longer Exhortation before the Sacrament which the present Dean of Westminster [Bishop Sprat] saies has been the practice of his Church ever since the Restoration. So, I suppose, has the method of mixing the Clergy and Laity within the Rails, and administring to the Bishops after the prebendaries.

Dr Lancaster and T. Pearson[288] with me at night; in expectance of meeting Dean Grahme.

[Dec.] 26. *Tuesday*. The (abdicated) Bishop of St David's with me in the morning, consulting (or pumping) me about what passed against him in the House on Friday last. He saies, he's resolved to bring in another Writt of Errour forthwith; And I the rather believe

---

[286] Andrew Snape (1675–1742), later to be Rector of St Mary-at-Hill, London, 1706–37, Headmaster of Eton, 1712–30, Provost of King's College, 1719–42, and Vice-Chancellor of Cambridge University, 1721–4.

[287] Richard Duke (1658–1711), Prebendary of Gloucester since 1688; Chaplain to Queen Anne and the Bishop of Winchester. Probably Robert Friend (1657–1751), Rector of Turvey, Bedfordshire, 1700–5, later Canon of Exeter in 1706 and Headmaster of Westminster, 1711.

[288] Thomas Pearson, Rector of Nether Denton, Cumberland, see Appendix A.

it because he has since sent me his printed Case in a pretty thick 4 to.[289] At Lambeth, dined with my Lord of Canterbury, the Archbishop of York, with the Bishops of London, Durham, Rochester, Worcester, Sarum, Peterborough, Chichester, Chester, Carlile and Bath and Wells. Archbishop of Canterbury much in the Gowt; for which my Lord of York prescribes 50 drops of Spirit of Sal Armoniae and *Sal. Volat. Oleosu*, mixed in Equal Quantities; and the Bishop of Sarum (as infallible) an Infusion of Cloves in fair Water.

In the Evening with Dr Gibson; who (on Discourse on our late Proceedings in the House of Lords) took Notice of an Observation of the late Provost of Queen's College[290] That a man *might* do two Things, very *fruitless*: i.e. *Protest* and *Run his Head against a Wall*.

[Dec.] 27. *Wednesday*. In the Morning, Mr Madox carryed me into the Pipe-Office; where the eldest Roll is of the 5th of King Stephen, and has some Northern Accounts under the Title of *Carleolium*. Afterwards from Henry the 2d's time there are a great many excellent Records; wherein the Danegelt &c. is particularly accounted for. There are also *Corredies* to the Kings of Scotland, Archbishops and other great men, in their comeing to (and returning from) the English Court.

Hence we went to visit the Bishop of St Asaph (Dr Beveridge) (very much Indisposed) and to address him on behalf of Mr Ellis of Jesus College: But we came too late. This Bishop is mighty uneasy at the Bishop of St David's Case's being likely to be brought into the House of Lords; which (whatever their Determination may be) must, he thinks, have very dangerous Consequences.

After a short Visit from Mr Stonestreet, I went to dine with Dr Gibson; where were also Dr Kennet and Dr Waugh. Her Majesty's Proclamation (in the *Gazette of* Xtmas-day)[291] much regretted; Mr Vanburgh and Mr Congreve (two of the chief Debauchers of the Stage) being appointed Directors.[292]

---

[289] *The Extraordinary Case of the Bishop of St David's, further cleared and made plain, from the several views that have been made of it: wherein the articles against him are considered, and his lordship vindicated from them* (1703).

[290] Timothy Halton, Provost, 1677–1704, had died on 21 July.

[291] For 'establishing a new Company of Comedians under stricter Government and Regulations than have been formerly, in pursuance of her Royal Intentions for the better reforming the Abuses and Immorality of the Stage. Given at St James, 14 December 1704'. BL Lansdowne MS 1024, f. 161 v.; *The London Gazette*, No. 4082.

[292] John Vanburgh (1664–1726) had been recently described in a letter of protest addressed to Archbishop Tenison by the Society for the Reformation of Manners of 10 Dec. 1704 as 'a man who had debauched the stage beyond the looseness of all former times'. He had built the Queen's Theatre in the Haymarket (opened on 9 Apr. 1705) and became

After we had dined, Mr Worseley[293] (haveing travelled nine years) came to us; and gave an agreable Account of his Entertainment abroad, the Glories of Italy and the Greek-Islands, the just Principles of the Arabs, Princess Sophia's free Discourses, &c. He also assured us (of his own Knowledge, being particularly conversant in Lord Weymouth's Family) that Bishop Kenn had resigned to the present Bishop of Bath and Wells, and now alwaies wrote his name Tho. Kenn.[294] NB. 'Tis a common Practise in the young Oxford-Divines to pray (before sermon) for the House of Commons and the Convocation.[295]

[Dec.] 28. *Thursday*. Addressed in the morning by Mr Lawson, to countenance him in the next Election,[296] I went to dine with W. Tullie; where we had the agreable Conversation of Sir W. Bowes,[297] a hearty well-wisher to the Confederate Union of the two Kingdomes in Succession and Trade. W. Tullie observed (on the canvas of Notegeld) that the Accusers of some of Sir William's neighbours averred that the Delinquents were either Deer-stealers or Nout-stealers.[298] He also remembered the Answer given to a Reflection (by a Londoner) on a Northern County, asserting that *there were a great many Knaves in that Countrey: Yea*, quoth the Countreyman, *I believe we have more Knaves than you have honest men.*

At the *Griffin*, Sir William is of opinion (rightly enough) that had the Whigs been Courtiers the Tack had been carryed, because the Court could not then have influenced so many High-Churchmen, who now voted as they were directed.

the lessee and manager. He was joined in the management by William Congreve (1670–1729), who had been attacked in 1697 by Jeremy Collier in his *View of the Immorality and Profaneness of the English Stage*.

[293] Henry Worsley (c.1675-1740), diplomat; later MP for Newton (I. o. W.), 1705-15. He had travelled throughout Europe and the Near East and contributed to Dr Woodward's collections.

[294] After his deprivation in 1691, Ken lived chiefly at Lord Weymouth's house at Longleat. He was unwilling to see the schism of the non-jurors perpetuated; and though he regarded his successor at Bath and Wells, Richard Kidder, as a 'hireling' who 'ravaged the flock', upon Kidder's death in 1703 he urged his friend Hooper to accept the diocese, offering to cede his rights to him. Ken first dropped his formal episcopal signature in a letter of 20 Dec. 1703 to Hooper. W. M. Marshall, *George Hooper*, p. 99. The letters of Ken urging Hooper's acceptance of Bath and Wells are in the Walton MSS available on microfilm (M1 214) at the Warwickshire RO.

[295] 'The lower House of Convocation will upon all occasions find the House of Commons stands their friends . . .' Bodl. MS Ballard 38, f. 190: Thos. Rowney, MP for Oxford City, to Arthur Charlett, Master of University College, 26 Nov. 1702.

[296] For Cumberland.

[297] Sir William Bowes (1657-1707), MP for Co. Durham, 1680-1, 1695-8, 1702-7.

[298] i.e. neat or cattle stealers. 'Nout' is Old Norse for 'neat'.

[Dec.] 29. *Friday*. The morning being frosty, I walked from Westminster to the Tower; where I hoped (in vain) to have found the
Under-Clerks at Work: But, meeting Mr Holmes in my return, I
appointed a second Visit on Tuesday next. Hitting upon Mr Dowson,
at the Office of Ordnance, I was carryed first to the Armory to see
the Standards taken from the French and Bavarians at the late
glorious Battail of Blenheim; amongst which the most remarkable
was that of the Riseing Sun. Hence we went to the Jewel-House;
and viewed the Regalia, in the following Order: 1. The Imperial
Crown, wherewith (as is said) all the Kings of England have been
Crowned ever since the dayes of Edward the Confessor's time; which
nevertheless has Cross-Bars on the Top, and Flower-de-Lis's on the
Rim. 2. The Orb, or Globe, held in the Queen's left hand at her
Coronation; on the Top of which is an Amethyst (of a light purple
colour) near an Inch and a half in height. 3. The Royal Sceptre, with
the Cross; under which is another Amethyst of great value. 4. The
Scepter of Peace, with a Dove on the Top. 5. St Edward's staff, all
of beaten Gold, carryed before the Queen at her Coronation. 6. A
rich Salt-Sellar of State, in the figure of the Caesar's Tower, used on
the Queen's Table at the Coronation; whereon are four Turrets,
with Covers, which hold the Salt. Traytor's-Gate is well represented
in this: And the whole is beautifyed with curious work and rich
stones. 7. Curtana, or the (pointless) Sword of Mercy, carryed
betwixt the two Swords of (Spiritual and Temporal) Justice, at the
Coronation. 8. A Silver-Font, double Gilt, wherein Her present
Majesty and many of Her Royal predecessors were Christened; with
a large Basin, of the same work, wherein the Font is placed on those
Occasions. 9. A large Silver-Fountain, presented to King Charles the
Second by the Town of Plimouth. 10. The Queen's Diademe or
Circlet, wherein Her Majesty proceeded to Her Coronation; very
rich. 11. The Coronation-Crown, made for the late Queen Mary,
very thick set with Diamonds onely. 12. The Rich Crown of State
which Her Majesty wears on Her Throne in Parliament; in which
there's a large Emerald (green) of 7 Inches round; the finest Pearl in
the world, pawned by King Charles II to the Dutch for 40000 *l.* and
a Rubie (given by the Jewes of London to the late King James,
when he was Duke of York) of an inestimable value, somewhat like
a large French Bean. 13. A Globe and Scepter, made for the late
Queen Mary. 14. An Ivory-Scepter, with a Dove on the Top, for the
late King James's Queen. 15. The Golden Spurs and the Armilla's
(which are curiously enameled, and will fit any Arm) worn at the
Coronation. 16. The Ampulla, or Golden Eagle, out of which the
Holy Oyl is poured into the Golden Spoon; both which are Pieces

of great Antiquity. 17. A Crown of State made for the late King
James's Queen. All these are now Viewed by Candles set with a Grate:
Strangers being not allowed to take any nearer View, since Coll.
Blood made so free as to carry off the Crown of State.[299]

Hence we endeavoured (by help of the Master Smith) to get a
Sight of the Mint-House, but none were there at Work in the Holy-
daies.[300]

This failing, I went to see the Lions; which (at present) are Six
in Number.[301] Viz. 1. One presented, to Her present Majesty by
Lord Granvil. 2. Another presented to the late King by the Earl of
Orford, then Admiral Russel. 3. A Third, to the said King, by Sir
Thomas Littleton. 4. and 5. Two young Ones sent to Her Majesty by
the King of South Barbary. 6. A large One brought over (by Capt.
Ludman) for the late Duke of Glocester; who did not live to see it.

Here are also—1. King Charles the Second's old Leopard, lean and
Lazy. 2. A young (fierce) Leopard, lately purchased by the Mistress
of the House. 3. Two Cats of the Mountains; in nothing (that I could
observe) different from our Northern Wild-Cats. 4. Two large (Eared)
Owls from Sweden; as dull and Lumpish as all the foregoing are
fiery and fierce. 5. Three Eagles, of different Colours; none of which
seemed to be very large.

I dined (at two o'clock) with Mr Christopher Musgrave; where,
besides his sister Mary[302] and their Nephew and Niece from Chelsea,
we had Mr Harrison of Cotgrave with Mr Jennings of Rippon, and
honest Mr Lister. Mr Harrison told us of several Exorbitant Grants
in Ircland, and particularly, that the Countess of Orkney had as
much Land as worth 25000 l. per Annum tho' she made not above
4000 l. of it.[303]

[Dec.] 30. *Saturday*. In the morning, Mr Grandorge, for a Prebend
of Canterbury in lieu of his Fellowship in Magdalen's; Mr Buchanan,
advocate for the Bishop of St David's, who (he saies) has not disputed

---

[299] Thomas Blood (?1618-80), attempted to steal the Crown Jewels on 9 May 1671.
He was pardoned by Charles II.

[300] The Master of the Mint since 1699 had been Isaac Newton. See *The Correspondence
of Isaac Newton*, iv, 1694-1709, ed. J. F. Scott (Cambridge, 1967).

[301] On 29 Dec. 1711 a Mr E. Wright noted in his diary that 'The Four Lions [in the
Tower] are Dead—the Old one died First, they died of Bleeding at the Nose, now we have
none in the Tower, which has not happen this many Years.' Yorkshire Archaeological
Society MS 28: diary of E. Wright, 1709-13.

[302] Mary Musgrave, stepsister of Christopher, being Sir Christopher Musgrave's third
daughter by his second marriage. She died unmarried. Nicolson and Burn, i, 598.

[303] Lady Orkney was Elizabeth Villiers (d. 1733), sister of 1st Earl of Jersey and mistress
of William III, and had been married to George Hamilton, Earl of Orkney, since 1695.
On the 'extraordinary grants' see J. G. Simms, *The Williamite Confiscatons in Ireland*
(1956), pp. 92-5, 106-9.

the Archbishop of Canterbury's Jurisdiction in the Courts below; Young Mr Patteson. Sollicitor for A. Huddleston's Tenants.

I dined (with Mr C. Musgrave the Dean of Wells [Grahme] and Mr Nevinson)[304] at Coll. Grahme's; and spent the evening with the Dean.

[Dec.] 31. *Sunday*. After a dull Sermon at Westminster (by an obscure Substitute of Dr Dent's, whom no body knew) I went to dinner with my brother: where I met with the good News, in the last night's Postscript to the *Post-Boy*, of the Raiseing the Siege of Gibraltar, Admiral Lake's confounding Ponti,[305] &c. May this be confirmed!

Jan. 1. *Munday*. Sir W. Bowes, Philip Tullie, W. Tullie, &c. and I went to dine with Alderman Isaac [Tullie][306] at High-Gate; where, from his Garden, there's one of the most Noble Prospects that I have seen.[307] In our return (in Shandois-Street) Mr Harrison gave us a remarkable story of Sir Thomas Maleverey's Son being anatomized at the Bath, contrary to his Brother's Promise, and appearing to him afterwards in that gastly Shape.

[Jan.] 2. *Tuesday*. In the morning early I called on Mr George Holmes and Mr Thomas Madox, and went with them to the Tower; where I was shewn (by Mr Holmes) the following Records: 1. *Concessio W. Regis Scot. Maritagij Filij sui Alex. Johanni Regi Angl. ut Ligeo Dno Suo*. An Original. 2. A Provisional Nomination of Robert Bishop of Carlile (Successor to John) by Pope Boniface. A Fragment. 3. A Boundary, taken by Inquisition in 1245 'twixt England and Scotland. *inter Carram et Hawudend* viz. *a fluvio Twuede sicut Rivulus de Bowden ascendit versus Ausrum usque ad tres Carras, et ab illis tribus Carris sic linealiter directe versus Austrum usque ad Hoperichelaw, et sic de Hoprichelaw linealiter directe versus Austrum*

---

[304] Probably Thomas Nevinson, who had married Nicolson's youngest sister, Grace, in 1690. Educated at Queen's College, Oxford, he had been Vicar of Torpenhow, Cumberland, since 1697. James, p. 24.

[305] On 29 Oct. 1704 (O.S.) Sir John Leake, who had been refitting at Lisbon, destroyed a French squadron under the command of Admiral Pointis poised to attack Gibraltar. Trevelyan, *Queen Anne*, ii, 45–6.

[306] Brother of Chancellor Tullie. The prefix 'alderman' may have been a family joke. He was not an alderman nor even a common councillor of London (Corporation of London RO, Common Councillors Alphabetical List to 1880). Neither was he an alderman or councilman of Carlisle (Carlisle RO, Common Council Order Book, 1689–1710).

[307] According to Defoe, from the ground floor windows of Sir William Ashurst's house at Highgate, 'they see the very ships passing up and down the river for 12 or 15 miles below'. *Tour*, ii, 3.

ad Witelaw. In cuijus &c. Taken by Knights and Gentlemen, of both Kingdomes, therein named. 4. *Perambulatio facta inter Regnu Angliae et Regnum Scotiae; sc. inter Terram unde Contentio fuit inter Canonicos de Karram in Regno Angliae ac Bernardum de Haudene in Regno Scotiae.* Inquis. Ac. 6 Ed. 1 Num. 56. 5. An Instrument dated Anno 1291 whereby W[illiam] and R[obert] Bishops of St Andrews and Glasgow (in the name of Edward King of England — *et Dom. Superiris Regni Scotiae*) issue Demands from the Treasury under the Great Seal of Scotland. An Original part of the Seal appendant, in white Wax, haveing the Lion of Scotland on one Side and St Andrew's Cross on the other. 6. *Inquisitio facta ad fontem de Welleton die Jovis prox post Epiphaniam Ac. R. Ed. 20⁰ coram Vice-Com. Cumbr. si esset ad dampnu novum seu dampnu et nocumẹntum aliorum, si concedemus Venerab. patri Rad⁰. Karl. Ep⁰. quod ipse duci faceret quandam parte Cursus aquae fortis de Welleton qui est in Foresta nra de Engylwode ab eodem fonte usque ad Molendinum suum juxta Manerium de Rosa, et si esset ad dampnum et.* Inquis 20. Ed. 1. Num. 103. 7. Inquisitio 23 Ed. 1. N. 87 for the Enlargeing of Dalston-park. 8. Treaty at Berwick on the 3d of Oct. A⁰. 1354 'twixt John Archbishop of York, Thomas Bishop of Durham, Thomas de Musgrave, etc. with Commissioners of Scotland, for the Establishment of the Border-Laws. 'Tis in French. Rot. Scot. A⁰ 31 Ed 3. Membr. 2 *in dorso.* 9 Another French Charter sets forth (as is noted on the Margine, in the same hand with the Record itself) — *quod Rex Angliae nichil aliud exigere possit in Regno Scotiae, Herede apparente in eodem Regno, quam Homagium et ea quae ad Homagium pertinent.* 10. *Rex Eschaetori in Com. Cumbr. et Westmerl. Salutem. Cum Dno summus pontifex de persona dilecti Capellani nri Nicolai Cloos nuper Archid. Colecestr. in Ecclia Cathed. London Ecclie Karliol per Translationem Marmaduci Lumley ultimi Epi ibidem ad Eccliam Cathedr. Lincoln Vacanti providerit, et ipsum Nicolaum in Epum dicte Ecclie Karliol prefecerit et pastorem, sieut per literas Bullatas ipsius Dni summi pontificis nobis inde directas Nobis constat, Nos, pro eo quod idem Nicolaus omnibus et singulis verbis Nobis et Corone nre prejudicialibus in dictis literis Bullatis contentis coram Nobis palam et expresse renuntiavit, et Gratie nre humiliter se submisit, Volentes cum eo in hac parte agere gratiose, cepimus fidelitatem ipsius Nicolai, et Temperalia Episcopatus dicte Ecclie Karliol. prout moris est restituimus eidem. Et ideo tibi precipimus quod eidem Nicolao Temporalia predicta, cum pertinentiis in Balliva tua, liberes, habend. in forma predicta. Salvo jure Cujuslibet. T. R. apud Westm.* 14 Mar. Pat. A⁰ 28. Hen 6. par. 1 membr. 6.

I came to the House at Twelve: But, no business (excepting a few private Bills) being before their Lordships, they adjourned to the 10th by which time 'tis hoped the Commons (who sit two dayes sooner) will provide work. The late Bishop of St David's had put a Petition into the hands of the Bishop of Bath and Wells and Lord Guilford: But neither of 'em seemed to be forward in offering it. So—it droped.

I went to dine with my Lord Thanet: but found his Lordship and my Lady in trouble for my Lady Catherine, much indisposed.[308] My Lord indifferent as to Elections in Westmerland; but earnest on his Chancery-Dispute with Sir C. Musgrave not without some little Reflection on the late old Gentleman.[309] In the same generous Temper, as heretofore, towards the Episcopal Clergy in Scotland; but saies that Carlton[310] cannot answer Bills till after Candlemas. Mr Grandorge and I haveing called at Dr. Hickes's, went to Mr Lawson; who will have the Occasional Bill to pass the next Session. No Letter from Oxford to Mr Bromley,[311] as reported, to pass it now *Viis et Modis*.

[Jan.] 3. *Wednesday*. Visitants in the morning: 1. Cousin Forster, confident of his abilities in writeing and every thing else. 2. Os[   ] Bird,[312] more modestly desireous of being examined for a Lieutenant. 3. Mr Dowson, promiseing the Mottoes of all the Standards which are this day to be brought thro' the City in Triumph. 4. Mr Provost Lancaster and Cousin Pearson (from the Archbishop of York) with the *Lemmata* of the Oxford-Encaenia[313] on Newyears-Day. 5. Mr Twyman (Tutor to my Lord Hinchingbrook) brought me the Medal of *sine clade victor*.

At 12 I went into the Park, to meet the Triumph; which passed that way about two. The Hourse-Guards, with Trumpets and Kettle-Drums, marched first; in the Middle whereof were 32 Standards born by so many Cornets with green feathers. The Troopers that led 'em had red Feathers, and the followers white. After a Company or two of Fusileers, came the 128 Colours; some of which were torn to the very Staff. These were followed by the rest of the Foot-Guards: the

[308] Eldest daughter and co-heir to Lord Thanet. His three sons had died by 1691.

[309] The recently deceased 4th Bt.

[310] Thomas Carleton (*c*.1660–1731), Town Clerk of Appleby since 1686, and Mayor in 1685, 1696, 1709, and 1710. He was Thanet's steward and political agent in Appleby. He gradually opted out of active politics by 1708. Hopkinson, pp. 23, 160–1, 322; *Armorial*, p. 66.

[311] Bromley, one of the leading promoters of the bill since 1702, was MP for Oxford University.

[312] Possibly a member of the Bird family of Brougham, the head of which, James Bird (*c*.1637–1714), was attorney to Lord Thanet.

[313] Annual Commemoration of founders and benefactors at Oxford University held in June.

whole Cavalcade being near an hour in passing by. All these were carried from the Tower in the like Procession, being brought thro' the Stables at St James's for the Convenience of Her Majesty's viewing 'em out of my Lady Fitzharding's[314] Lodgeings, and were deposited in Westminster-Hall. The Mob personated the Shew before it came up, with Handkerchiefs and Clouts; and made pretty odd Attaques on their Bretheren that look on.

I retired to dinner with Mr C. Musgrave; whose other Guests were Coll. Byerley, Coll. Grahme, Mr Dean of Wells [Grahme] and his Brother Thomas. No Joseph in any farther Treaty with the Colonel. Colonel Byerley for the Dependency of Scotland; and (justly) angry at the Unsteddiness of some of his friends.

At my Return, a dismal story (from Dr Todd) of the arming of the Scots in the Western parts; to the Number of 108,000. Impossible!

[Jan.] 4. *Thursday*. Early to Lambeth; where I waited on my Lord of Canterbury in bed, much afflicted with the Gowt. Hence Dr Gibson and I to the Archbishop of York; who gracious and humble. Thence to Dr Lancaster's; where Mr Proctor Smith[315] and Thomas Pearson (both Scandalously powdered) goeing, with Mr Provost, to attend the Vice-Chanccllor[316] and the Heads of Houses to the Queen: To whom they were, this day, to present their Newyear's-Exercise in Honour of the Duke of Marlbrough and Sir George Rook. Mr Secretary Harley being desired (by Blunder and mistaken Finery in Politicks) to introduce them; tho' himself had never had any University-Education.[317] Thence to Dr Waugh's, by the way of Salisbury-Court: whence (dureing my Sister's getting ready) I went to the *White Horse-Inn*[318] to see the Casheware a very odd sort of Bird; of a variegated (black and red) Colour; in full length, from the Tip of the Bill to his Toes-end, about 16 hands; Head and Neck like a Turkey; the Body hairy, not feathered; No Wings, nor Tongue; but two Sharp Spears, like the Arrows of the Porcupine, wherewith he

[314] Barbara Villiers (c.1656-1708), wife of John, 4th Viscount Fitzhardinge, MP for New Windsor, 1695-1710, and a cousin of Godolphin.

[315] Joseph Smith (1670-1765), brother of John Smith, Fellow of Queen's College, Oxford, since 1698, and Proctor of the University in 1704 (along with Thomas Smith of St John's College).

[316] William Delaune, President of St John's College, 1697-1728, Vice-Chancellor of Oxford University, 1702-5.

[317] Harley was educated at a nonconformist school at Burford and at Foubert's Academy in London. White Kennett reported that the general feeling was that either 'the Bishop of London or some Oxford [educated] Bishop or at least some former Member [of the University] had been more Proper' to introduce the university's senior academic dignitaries to the Queen. BL Lansdowne MS 1013, f. 77: Kennett to Blackwell, 6 Jan. 1705.

[318] In Fleet Street.

defends himself; No back Claw. It[em] A little Pigmey Monkey, said to be 60 years of age, which mustered and threw a stone of a great weight, &c. An Antelope, somewhat bigger than a Roe-Buck; but his Horns not branched. Two Laplers, from the East Indies, with Beaks two Inches broad and nine in length, as thin as a Six-pence. Two Flamingers, from the same place, with beaks of the like length; but sharp and bending Inwards. They were fed with Sprats.

At the next Door (the *blew Boar*) I saw wondrous feats performed by one John Valerius, a German, born without Arms; who wrote with his Feet and Mouth very readily. Samples of these are in the Cover of this book.[319] He also (with his feet) makes pens; comb's his head; trims himself; fences, and darts his Rapier into a Door with that force that I had much adoe to pull it out; Charges and discharges a Musket; Shuffles, and playes at, Cards; threds a Needle; &c. and shewed Agillity of body beyond what I had ever seen from a professed Tumbler on the Stage. The strength he has in his Thighs, Legs and Toes, is Prodigious. He walks, and jumps on his great Toes; and hops on one. His seating himself on a little Square stool, of a foot Square, and thrusting that half over the Edge of the Table, without falling, was as Admirable as his placeing of a glass of wine on his brow and riseing with it, his standing on the stool and fetching the said Glass from under it and returning it again, &c.

Hence to dinner (by appointment) at Dr Waugh's; where onely Dr Gibson, Mr Worth and I (with my brother, Sister and Niece) were the prime Guests. Afterwards, Dr Kennet and Mr D'Oyley: upon the latter's giveing us a pleasant Account of his personateing a Country Farmer (some years agoe) in Dr Halley's[320] Company, Dr Kennet mentioned a picture in Lord Leinster's (Farmer's)[321] Family, reporting the Courtship of one of His Lordship's Ancestors, in the like Disguise, throwing his Hat into a fair Lady's Lap.

[Jan.] 5. *Friday*. Invited to dine with Dr Woodward, at Gresham-College, and comeing before his Return from his patients, I took a Turn in the Library and publick Museum.[322] In the former (amongst

---

[319] Not found.

[320] Edmund Halley (1656-1742), the celebrated astronomer, at this time Savilian Professor of Geometry at Oxford.

[321] William Fermor (1648-1711), 1st Baron Leominster (or Lempster), Tory MP for Northampton, 1670-9, had been created a baron in 1692 reputedly through the influence of his father-in-law, the Duke of Leeds. He was something of a collector having bought the Arundel Marbles from the dowager Duchess of Norfolk. *GEC Peerage*.

[322] Dr Woodward's quarters and collection were at Gresham College where he was Professor of Physic. The Royal Society also met on the premises and stored their collections there. Nicolson takes the opportunity to visit both.

the MSS.) Mr Hunt[323] shewed me an antient Gr[eek] Copy of the four Evangelists, the *Imagines Regum, Consulum &c. ab Urbe Condita ad Jul. Caesarem*, finely drawn (with a pencil) in four large Volumes, and the first Archive replenished with many pieces of choice English History. The printed Catalogue[324] is said to be very faulty and imperfect. In the Museum there's a very large Collection of Natural Curiosities; whereof Dr Grew[325] has published a Catalogue.[326] Great Variety of Loadstones: some of which (unpolished, and in huge Lumps) from Devonshire. The small Indian Birds, and the Sceletons of the Ostrich and other larger Ones, are very Curious. So are the four Tables of Sinews, Viens and Arteries, given by Mr Evelyn;[327] and the Chair out of the twisted Roots of the Mangrove, presented by the Lord Sommers. The Dr called me to his (as he thinks it) richer Museum, before I had half satisfied my self with haveing so full a View of this as I desired. At his Lodgeings I had likewise the agreable Conversation of Mr Harris[328] (Author of the *Lexichon Technicum*) and Mr Charlwood. Amongst the Dr's immense Collection of Fossils, I noted: 1. A large black Nautilus, from the Isle of Man; sent by Dr Wilson, the present Bishop,[329] a great favourer of these Studies. 2. A sort of a large petr[ified] *Equisetum*, Cane or Rush, from Sir Roger Bradshaw's Pits in Lancashirc.[330] 3. Undulated Flints; which the Dr will not have to borrow their diverting Furrows (as Mr H[arris] and I presumed) from the dropping or Impress of waters, but from some other unobserved Cause. 4. A sort of Star-stone (of which great plenty on Stanemoor)

[323] Henry Hunt (d. 1713), Keeper of the Repository and Librarian since 1696. Ward, *Lives of the Professors of Gresham College*, p. 233.

[324] *Bibliotheca Norfolciana* (1681) by William Perry, Librarian (1679), of the Royal Society, and Professor of Music (1681), Gresham College. The library had been given to the Society in 1666 by Henry Howard, later Duke of Norfolk. It had been purchased by his grandfather, Thomas, Earl of Arundel, and a large part of it had originally belonged to the King of Hungary. Ibid., pp. 232-3.

[325] Nehemiah Grew (1641-1712), educated Cambridge and Leyden, MD *c*.1671. Secretary of the Royal Society and distinguished botanist.

[326] *Musaeum Regalis Societatis; or a Catalogue and description of the rarities belonging to the Royal Society and preserved at Gresham College* (1681, reissued 1694).

[327] John Evelyn (1620-1706), the diarist.

[328] John Harris (?1666-1719) was a friend and protégé of Dr Woodward, Fellow of the Royal Society, and author of the *Lexicon Technicum, or an Universal English Dictionary of Arts and Sciences* (1704), an important early scientific encyclopedia.

[329] Thomas Wilson (1663-1755), Bishop of Sodor and Man since 1698, was a noted antiquarian.

[330] Sir Roger Bradshaigh (*c*.1675-1747), 3rd Bt., MP for Wigan, 1695-1747. He was the owner, near Wigan, of 'one of the finest works of coal called carrell [cannel] in England, which is so much admired for its heat and brightness'. BL Add. MS 24120, ff. 138-41, quoted in Sedgwick, i, 481-2. See also Defoe, *Tour*, ii, 266; *The Journeys of Celia Fiennes*, ed. C. Morris (1949), p. 185; M. Cox, 'Sir Roger Bradshaigh and the electoral management of Wigan', *Bulletin of John Rylands Library*, xxxvii (1954-5), 120-64.

with its Asteriae impressed in the Exact Order of the Quincunx; which he values as a most extraordinary humour in Nature. 5. A fine sort of *Linum Arbestinum*, from the Isle of Anglesey; which has not so long, nor so vigorous, stamina as that which I formerly procured for him out of Scotland. 6. Great variety of Brainstones, from the West-Indies. 7. A large Star-fish, of 12 Radii, found on the English shore. 8. Tree-Oysters, Fossil, from France. 9. Stalactites, formed like a mass of rusty Iron-Wire, from the Canary-Isles. 10. Agostino Scilla's Noble present to the Dr of the largest and most beautiful Echini fossiles of the flat kind; *Vermiculi Marini*, supposed by him to be Snakes, and haveing such heads made for 'em; the Buchardites fine and large, with the natural shell agreable; the petrifyed Morse-Tooth or Ivory, which (saies Seignor Scilla, very probably) is as useful in physick as its prototype; &c. 11. Worn sea-shells in the Body of Stones; which the Dr supposes to have been the Exuviae of their proper Animals, and long tossed on the Shores, before the All-dissolveing Deluge. 12. A large fossile Muscle, in *Ludo Helmontii*; which last Term hee bestowes on all such stones as have any regular Apartments by such Sutures or Veins of Heterogeneous Matter as strike quite through their whole Mass. 13. Pori Corallini (very like Dr Plot's Entrochi)[331] in fine polished marble; the same with that at Chattesworth.[332] 14. A Drawer of most curious English Agats, finely polished; with Saphirs, Cornelians, &c. of our own Growth. 15. Amongst the Micae and Talks (which will both endure the Fire) he shewed us some of the former glittering ware that was brought from the Coasts of Africa in Queen Elizabeth's Reign, by one of Purchas's Pilgrims,[333] for true Gold of Guinea. 16. Osteocella is a Name which the Dr gives onely to such petrifactions as are made (by Cold Springs in Limestone Quarries) about the leaves and branches of Trees and lesser plants. 17. All the Pyritae (and Marchasites, which he makes to differ onely from the former as they are more regularly formed) are apt to loose their binding Salts, when expressed to the Open and Moist Air, and to fall into dust. 18. Not any of the many Samples he has of the Tinn-Ores, from Cornwall and Devonshire, are (as he averrs) to be found in the Northern parts of England. 19. The Coarse Coralline Mixtures, in the Rocks of Pot-gill near Hartley and other parts of Westmerland, he reckons very pretious. 20. Amongst his Vegetables from our peat-Mosses,

[331] Robert Plot had included fossils in his *Natural History of Oxfordshire* (Oxford, 1677, 2nd edition 1705).

[332] Nicolson had visited Chatsworth on his journey south to London in Oct. 1704, see above, Sessional intro., n. 4.

[333] Samuel Purchas (a contemporary of Richard Hakluyt) collected descriptions of voyages under the title *Hakluytus Posthumus or Purchas his Pilgrimes* (1625).

he shews a Whitish Moss (in the uppermost Turff of several of 'em) which he saies is composed of the Juli of the Hasel-Tree; which he takes for an infallible Argument that the Deluge happened in May. In this frolicksome Debate, and just as we came to the first Drawer of his *Cornua Ammonis*,[334] it grew a little Dark; and so we withdrew to Dinner.

After our being generously feasted, we retired again into the Dr's Library; where he shewed us several of his finished pieces: As, 1. A Catalogue of the Rarities in his Museum with discourses on the Chief of 'em, in a good method.[335] 2. His History of America; wherein he endeavours to point at the certain time when those people went out of Europe, from that Share of our most early Inventions and Knowledge which they have in Common with us: And here he takes occasion to run down the Egyptians, as mistaken Masters of antient Learning.[336] 3. History of Metals in two Parts;[337] whereof the former shews the Natural position of 'em in the Earth, their prognosticks and the several wayes of digging for 'em, and the latter directs how to roast and melt 'em. This last is Transcribed and wholly ready for the Press: But the Author seems to think his former Labours so slenderly rewarded by the Publick that he will needs (in Chagrine) withhold this Benefaction. Mr H[arris] and I were both very plain with him; assureing him that a more effectual Course could not be taken for the injureing his own Reputation, the disobligeing his friends and the gratifying of his Enemies. And—with this friendly Advice we left him.

[Jan.] 6. *Saturday*. In the way to my brother's in Salisbury-Court (where I had promised to end Christmas) I called on Mr Coke; and gave him a Copy of the Articles, before my consent to his Bill. In Fleetstreet, I was over-taken by the Duke of Marlborough (and his splendid Attendance of 70 Officers, in about 40 Coaches) goeing to dine with the Lord Mayor and Aldermen.[338] The Huzzars were not very great, not the Throng such as I expected. After Dinner, I returned early home to write Letters, &c.

---

[334] A fossil shell long thought to have had magical properties.

[335] Published in 1729 as *An Attempt Towards a Natural History of Fossiles*.

[336] The 'History of America' has disappeared; a discourse on the Egyptians was printed in *Archaeologia*, iv (1777), 212–311, a work 'seemingly prepared for the press'.

[337] This appears to be the work which remained in manuscript and is to be found in BL Add. MSS 25095–6.

[338] Cf. Luttrell, v, 506: 'This day his grace, in one of her majesties coaches, with the duke of Somerset and lord treasurer, accompanied by about 60 of the nobility and general officers of the army, were mett at Temple Bar by the citty marshal, and conducted to Goldsmiths Hall, where the lord mayor and alderman, was subscribed 800 *l*. for charge of a dinner, gave them a noble treat, the queens musich playing all the while, and everything performed in great splendour.'

[Jan.] 7. *Sunday*. At St Martin's, I received the Sacrament for the Test;[339] and heard a good sermon from Mr (Proctour) Smith of Queen's College. After Dinner, with Mr Provost, Dr Gibson preached; and came home with me. Sir Philip Sydenham brought me the News of the great Advantages of the Imperialists in Hungary, and the Savoyards against the French at Verrue;[340] and Mr Dowson presented me with the Descriptions and Mottoes on the Standards and Colours lately carryed in Procession: Which Mottoes are—1. *Arduus ad Solem*, under a Sun in full Splendor and a Snake salient from the Ground. 2. *Concussus Surgo*, under a Granado-shell &c. 3. *Adhuc Spes durat Avoru*, under a decayed Tree with a young sprout. 4. *Nec pluribus Impar*, under a Sun in Splendour; and on the Sinister, *Poso duri Pasche Sinalzi*. 5. *Audentior*, An Eagle surrounded with Thunder. 6. *Nec pluribus Impar* (which is on several others, in the Sinister, but here in the Dexter) under a Sun of Orange and Gold: And in the Sinister, *Jovis obruit hostes*, under an Infant lying on the Ground. 7. *Victoria pinget*, on a White Silk. 8. *Ingenito Solem adoratur amore*, under an Eagle riseing towards the Sun. 9. *Alter post fulmina Terror*, a Granadoe-shell breaking in the Fire. 10. *In Regnum et pugnas*, Under an Eagle on her Nest. NB. All these on the Standards; some of which have their Mottoes torn off. None of the Colours had any Mottoes: But these are　　　　[341]

[Jan.] 8. *Munday*. Visitants in the morning: 1. Mr Proctour Smith and Cousin T. Pearson; who (engageing with Dr Gibson) agreed that not four of the members of the University had read Dr Atterbury's Book, when his Degree was given for it.[342] 2. R. Nicolson; a witness

---

[339] By the 1672 Test Act all holders of civil and military offices had to be communicants of the Anglican Church, and had to repudiate transubstantiation.

[340] After Blenheim Prince Eugene was able to transfer forces from Bavaria to Hungary, where since 1703 the Emperor had been faced with a rampant rebellion of the Magyars under Rákóczi. During the winter of 1704–5 the tide was turned against the rebels. Verue was a Piedmontese fortress—one of a string which the hard-pressed troops of Britain's new ally, Victor Amadeus of Savoy, was trying to defend against French armies under Vendome and La Feuillade. Luttrell (v, 506) noted on 9 Jan. the news of 'the garison of Verue sallying out upon the French, and nailing up most of their cannon'. But hopes that 'Vendome will be forced to raise the siege' proved unfounded, and not until 1706, with Eugene's intervention did the war in Italy go decisively against the French.

[341] Blank in MS.

[342] Atterbury had been awarded his DD in May 1701 for his book the *Rights, Powers and Privileges of an English Convocation stated and vindicated* published in Mar. 1700. It had not happened without some sharp practice for 'the warmist Sticklers for it were apprehensive it would meet with some Opposition, and therefor the Business was carried on with a great deal of Privacy and Cunning. That it may not be looked on as an unanimous Act of the whole Body of the University, I think myself obliged to acquaint you, that, the Day when it was to be proposed being industriously kept secret, the Convocation-House was filled almost only with Xt-Church-men and those of the sam-party.' Corpus Christi College, Cambridge, MS 585, f. 220: Wallis to Postlethwayt, 11 May 1701.

to all the former Discourse. 3. Mrs Addison and Brother Nicolson; pressing for Fetherson. 4. The Bishop of London; mistakeing the Day of Session. 5. Capt. Studholm;[343] hard on the memory of Sir C. Musgrave. After my private Dinner, I steped into the Court of Request; where Col. Stanwix[344] exp[ostulated] with me for giveing him the Character of a Presbyterian. I hope he will never deserve it. M[ajor] Orfeur[345] saies the Dispute 'twixt Lord C[arlisle] and's Lady is an old Sore of 7 years standing.[346] Mr L[awson] mentions a Resolve newly passed by the Commons[347] — To perpetuate the Victory of Blenheim. Dr Charlett brisk and young.

In the Evening Dr Woodward, reflecting on the freedome taken by his friend Harris, whom he represents now as a forward Scribler not to be imitated. He affirms that Every body is (without farther Illustration) convinced of the Truth of his Hypothesis in his Theory; and that (particularly) Mr Moreton[348] of Northamptonshire had found out, by the Dr's book compared with its self in different Paragraphs, what was the Natural Agent which dissolved the whole *Compages* of the Earth at the Deluge.

[Jan.] 9. *Tuesday*. In the morning, Mr G. Holmes; advised to carry his papers (about the Union) to Lord Sommers. A Committee (of Lord Sarum, Peterborough, Chester, Carlile and Lord Escrick)[349] for Sir R. Clayton's Bill of disuniteing the parishes of Blechingley and Horne in the County of Hampshire.

Mr Key and I dined in Exeter-street: and, returning, I had the Company of Mr Symson (who assured me of the good Progress of the *Border-Laws*) Dr Younger and Mr Dean of Wells [Grahme]. The last forced me upon presenting him and the Dr with *Northern*

[343] Eliakim Studholme, lieutenant in the Earl of Macclesfield's regiment of horse in 1702, and a captain in Lord Windsor's in 1705. He was commissioned captain-lieutenant in Dublin in Mar. 1706. Dalton, v, 232, 248, 276. He was later an unsuccessful parliamentary candidate for Carlisle in 1708. Hopkinson, p. 149.

[344] Thomas Stanwix, MP for Carlisle, see Appendix A.

[345] John Orfeur (d. 1741), of High Close, Plumbland, Cumb., a major (1703) in Viscount Shannon's regiment of marines; lieutenant-colonel 1706; col. 1712. Dalton, v, 135-6. He stood against Gen. Stanhope at Cockermouth in 1710, being the gentry (anti-Duke of Somerset) candidate of Sir William Pennington and Sir Richard Musgrave, and engaged in a costly petition against his defeat. Hopkinson, pp. 50, 131, 281; Ferguson, *Cumberland and Westmorland MP's*, pp. 86-7; B. Williams, *Stanhope* (Oxford, 1932), p. 127 n.; W. Jackson, *Papers and Pedigrees mainly relating to Cumberland and Westmorland* (1892) i, table after p. 190.

[346] See above, n. 250.   [347] *CJ* xiv, 472 (8 Jan.).

[348] John Morton (?1671-1726), botanist and historian, Rector of Oxendon, Northamptonshire 1707-26. Published *The Natural History of Northamptonshire* (1712) in which he defended Woodward's geological theories. The problem here was just what agent had dissolved the earth at the time of the Flood; in fact Woodward suggested later that it was a temporary suspension of gravity that was the cause and not a solvent at all.

[349] The Bishop of Chester and Lord Howard of Escrick were not on the original committee, see *LJ* xvii, 588, 604.

Letter; and assures me that he'l shortly give me a Reason [such as he uses to give!] [350] for his calling for it.

[Jan.] 10. *Wednesday*. Sir J. Doiley's cause heard out: [351] wherein two Clergymen (Needham [352] and Cornelius) appeared very vile, and unworthy of their Character. Mr Dobbins makeing a long Harangue after all the Lords were satisfyed of the Justice of his Cause, was animadverted on by the Duke of Buckingham, who, observeing him afterwards to spin out his Discourse as before, said of him—*That he was a perfect Top, that ran the longer for being lashed*. In Conclusion, the Decree was unanimously affirmed.

Dr Waugh, who has zealously attended and was much pleased with the Issue, supped with me at my Lodgeings; and assured me that the *Northern Letter* (Stateing our Dean's Case) was generally applauded.

In a Letter sent open to me from Mr Lhwyd (for Dr Molyneux [353] in Dublin, near Ormond-Gate) I find that Mr Morton of Northampton-shire practices Physick; and is ready to publish his Natural History by way of Subscription; that the Professors in Gresham-College are in a Confederacy against the Royal Society; that Dr Hook's [354] post-humous Pieces are Printing in Folio; and That Mr Dale is publishing a Supplement to his *Materia Medica*. [355]

[Jan.] 11. *Thursday*. Haveing attended the Commission of First-fruits, &c. in the morning, and read prayers in the House, I went to dinner at Dr Kennet's with Dr Gibson; where we met Dr Waugh, Mr Lloyd and Mr Worth. Mr Lloyd very warm; and Mrs Kennet [356] very witty. Dr Atterbury's Letters to a certain Citizen and Lady, full of Slips of his Pen. In return the 2 Westmorland-Drs [357] and I at Mr Langhorn's; [358] innocently and freely. Mr Coke moves for con-

---

[350] Nicolson's brackets.

[351] Case of a double marriage of Sir John D'Oyly's son Chomley to (1) Margaret, daughter of Andrew Needham, and (2) Elizabeth Cabell. See HMC *Lords MSS* vi, 51-2. Sir John had been MP for Woodstock, 1689-90.

[352] Andrew Needham (*c*.1642-1711), Rector of Beverston-with-Kingscote, Gloucester-shire, 1685-1711.

[353] Thomas Molyneux (1661-1735), eminent physician.

[354] Robert Hooke (1635-1703), philosopher and Professor of Geometry at Gresham College.

[355] Samual Dale (?1659-1739), published *Pharmacologia, seu manuductis ad materiam medicam* in 1693. The supplement appeared in 1710.

[356] Dorcas Fuller was White Kennett's third wife. They were married in 1703. According to Hearne she 'wears the breeches, as his haughty, insolent temper deserves'. *Collections*, ii, 9.   [357] Waugh and Gibson.

[358] Probably some relation of Dr Gibson as his mother was Jane, daughter of John and Eleanor Langhorn of Hilton-end in the parish of Askham. Sykes, *Gibson*, p. 6.

tinueing his Committee to Munday next; against which time (he saies) his Leases will be here.

Dr Gibson assures me that I and the Dean of Durham[359] are struck out of the List of Lent-Preaches; and the Dean of Carlile's [Atterbury's] put in the place of the Latter. W[ha]t Mr Secretary Harley pleases!

[Jan.] 12. *Friday.* In the House the Bishop of St David's petition (brought in by Lord Guilford) ordered to ly on the Table till Wednesday; and all the Lords be summoned against that time. It assigns onely the General Error—*Quod judiciu redditum est pro Dna Regina ubi reddi debuisset pro dicto Tho. Watson &c.* A deal of Discourse I had (on this Subject) with Lord Guarnsey; who will have this Deprivation to be a hardship on all us ecclesiasticks. The Judges below, he allowes, have considered the Jurisdiction; and unanimously believe that Sentence has been given according to the Common-Law of England. That the Primitive Church proceeded against a Bishop by a Synod of Bishops I allow; But our opposers aim at such a Synodical Determination (mixed of Bishops and Presbyters) as the antient Church never knew. The Archbishop of Canterbury had the Assistance of 4 Bishops which is as many as ever the Archbishop of York can have &c.[360] A Cause called for 'twixt Dibble, &c. wherein, the Appellant not appearing by his Counsel, the writ (of Errour) abated; and the Appellant was sentenced in 40 *l.* Costs.[361] A Money-Bill, &c.

In the Evening, after Enquiry after the two Musgraves, I waited on Mr Dean of Wells [Grahme]; who (before his brother the Coll.) gave me a full account of the Practices upon him by the Dean of Carlile's [Atterbury's] friends. He saies—On Wednesday last (the 10th) he, by Appointment, waited on Mr Secretary Harley, at his House; where he found Mr Sollicitor Harcourt, Dr Eddisbury[362] and Mr Dean of Carlile. The proposeal made him was, That he should sign a Resignation of the Deanry of Carlile bearing Date the 8th July; in order to countenance Dr Atterbury's Letters Patents, dated the 15th of that Month: Whereas he knew that he had formerly signed a Resignation (on the 5th of August) before a public Notary. He had soe much presence of mind as to desire time to consider, and advise with his Friends; assureing them that he'd give his Answer the next Morning. Haveing advised with his Brother (the Coll.) and

---

[359] Hon. John Montague (?1655–1728), Dean of Durham since 1699.

[360] The four bishops of the Northern province (besides York) are Carlisle, Chester, Durham, and Sodor and Man.

[361] See *LJ* xvii, 614.

[362] John Edisbury (*c.*1646–1713), Master in Chancery, 1684–1709. He was MP for Oxford University, 1679, and Chancellor to diocese of Exeter, 1692–?1709.

Dr Bramston, he wrote a Letter to the Dean of Carlile (a Copy of which was shewn to me, both by the Coll. and himself) signifying that he could not comply. This Letter was sent to Mr Dean of Carlile yesterday (the 11th) early in the morning; and, as I believe, occasioned that private Application to the Archbishop of York which I observed to be made by my good Dean, at our Meeting, on Occasion of the Queen's Donation of the Tenths and First-fruits, at Whitehall that morning. NB. This whole matter was first moved to Mr Dean of Wells by Mr Stratford, the Speaker's Chaplain,[363] sent on purpose by his Patron to the Dean, on this Message and Errand, upon Tuesday the 9th of this month.

The Bishop of Bath and Wells this day (in discourse with me, in the House) observed, from the *Northern Letter*, that the Dean of Carlile's Letters Patents were wrong; and that (for his security) he thinks he ought to have a second Presentation and Institution.[364]

Lord Nottingham and Lord Thanet expostulated with me (in the House) the Fancy of Mr Joseph Musgrave's declineing his standing for Westmerland: To which I could onely answer *He's the best Judge of the weight of his pocket; and, when he put's the Debate on that head, I have nothing to reply.*

[Jan.] 13. *Saturday.* In the morning early, I went over to Lambeth; to consult with Dr Gibson (my friend) on the subject of last night's Conversation with the Dean of Wells [Grahme]. The Dr afterwards brought me my Lord of Canterbury's caution to the Dean, to get his Case (stated in writeing) to be put into the Queen's hand; to avoid Misrepresentations. After a long Case in the House (about Cole-Mines in Somersetshire)[365] Dr Gibson and I called on Dr Lancaster; and all three went to dine with Major Orfeur, who treated us Neatly. There we met with Mr Payne (the Agent of my Lord Shannon's Regiment) and my Cousin R. Nicolson. My brother was also invited. Mr Payne is a very ingenious and well-bred Gentleman; and enter-

---

[363] William Stratford (*c*.1672-1729), Archdeacon of Richmond since 1703.

[364] According to Atterbury it was the 'Lord Keeper [who] started a doubt about the Legality of a Clause in it [Atterbury's patent dated 15 July], which expresses the Deanery of Carlisle to be Vacant *per Translatiorem* of Dr Grahme to the Deanery of Wells; whereas his Lordship says that a Translation to a Second Deanery doth not make the first voyd, without a Resignation'. Grahme had formally resigned on 31 July and Atterbury had received the resignation on 8 Aug. 1704. The possible invalidity of Atterbury's patent caused him early in 1705 to obtain a legal settlement of the matter. He reported in May 1705 that 'I have by Warrant from the Queen adjusted my Patent to the true time of it's passing the Great Seal the Second time, viz: the 15th of Aug. so that now the Resignation is precedent to the Grant, and the Grant to the Institution [on 29 Sept.] and there can be no possible Dispute on that head.' Lloyd-Baker MS Box 3, N2; Box 4, V7, V15: Atterbury to Sharp, 27 July, 8 Aug. 1704, 25 May 1705.

[365] *Horner* v. *Hilliard*, see HMC *Lords MSS* vi, 54-5; *LJ* xvii, 615-16.

tained us very agreably. One severe Remark made by Lady Dor-chester[366] on the Duke of Marlborough's Victories this last Summer, in Conjunction with Prince Eugene of Savoy. *So*, saies she, *Dr Radcliff*[367] *and I can cure a Feaver*. She would also, under a Family-piece of that great General, have this Mottoe: *O Generation*, &c.[368]

NB. In the way to the House, I went (with Mr Holmes and Mr Dale) to my Lord Hallifax; who kindly carryed me into his Library, a Gallery nobly furnished with curious Books placed under Statues as in Cotton's. His Lordship has Transcripts of all the Rolls of Parliament, Journals of the Lords and Commons, &c. and has inter-leaved Thuanus's Catalogue[369] for shewing the Rarities and Defects of his own Collection.

[Jan.] 14. *Sunday*. I preached in the morning at St Martin's (Lord Sommers present) on *Psalm* 145, 15. Thence to Dinner, after a Conversation with Mr A. Addison[370] full of his own Deserts and Interest; at Mr C. Musgrave's; where Sir C. Musgrave,[371] Mr Joseph and Mr Thomas Musgrave, Mr Davison and Mr Eustace. Sir C. Hales and Mr Lister afterwards.

In return, I spent the Evening with the Dean of Wells [Grahme]; who gave me Minutes of his whole Interview at Mr Speaker's on Wednesday last, to be drawn up into Form for the Queen's View upon Occasion. He also shewed me two Letters (from Dr Atter-bury and Mr Warr)[372] dated the 27th of July, solliciteing his Resigna-tion; and a third from Mr Secretary Hedges, of the 3d of August, pressing him to hasten it.

[Jan.] 15. *Munday*. Haveing drawn up a Paper for Mr Dean of Wells, and sent it to him, I waited on the Archbishop of York; who doubts whether the Queen will give a Satisfactory Answer to Lady Lawson.

The Case of Supremacy argued with Mr Richardson. The Negative of the House of Lords or Commons does not prove their being

---

[366] Catherine Sedley (1657–1717), mistress of James II, created Countess of Dorchester in 1686.

[367] John Radcliffe (1650–1714), physician and benefactor of Oxford University.

[368] 'O Generation of vipers, who hath warned you to flee from the wrath to come?' *Matt.* 3: 7.

[369] *Catalogus bibliothecae Thuanae*, published in 1679. Jacques-Auguste de Thou (Thuanus) was a French historian and statesman (1553–1617).

[370] Anthony Addison (*c*.1658–1719), Rector of St Helen's, Abingdon, since 1698, Chaplain to the Duke of Marlborough, and brother of Thomas.

[371] The 5th Bt., see Appendix A.

[372] Probably Richard Warre, Under-Secretary of State at various times between 1676 and 1713. See J. C. Sainty, *Officials of the Secretaries of State* (1973), p. 114.

Sharers in the Legislature; makeing them onely Necessary Instruments, or *Causae sine quibus Non*, not Efficient Causes.

· In the House, a Writ of Error brought by Mr Prinn against Mr How; who had recovered 400 *l.* below, by a Verdict, on an Action on the Case for Scandalous words.[373] Counsel for the Plaintiff (in Error) were Mr James Montague[374] and Mr Lechmore;[375] and for the Defendant Sir Thomas Powis and Sir Simon Harcourt. Mr Montague took notice that in the Declaration mention was made of the Parliament held in the 12th of King William 3. and, since there were two Parliaments in that year,[376] it could not be known which of the two was referred to: which was an Error. He also said that, in the Verdict of the Jury, referring to the words—*in Narratione primo et sexto mentionat*! there was an unintelligible Ambiguity; since it could not be understood whether the first and sixth words, sentences, &c. were meant. Haveing distinguished the Case into two Parts—1. Are any words found? 2. Are those words Actionable? He desired the first point might be stated. This was opposed by Sir Thomas Powis; who desired that, as usual, the whole Cause might be opened. The Counsel with drawn, this point was a while debated: But, on a motion from the Earl of Rochester, agreed to.

Counsel called in, Mr Lechmore was ordered to proceed on the first point onely. Accordingly, he said that the word Narration was as ambiguous, as *primo et sexto*: For it might signify either the whole Declaration or any Paragraph of it. But his main Objection was—In the common Books of Entries [and he had already Rostal and Coke][377] no Verdicts appear on Actions of slander, where the words are not particularly recited.

Sir Thomas Powis and Sir Simon Harcourt said the *primo et sexto* were Adjectives, and had *Colloquio* (understood) for their substantive; and that Mr Lechmore's objection was not offered below.

To which he Replyed, *Nor could it be: For there the whole Record was not, as here, before the Judges; but onely the Postea.*

In Conclusion, the Judges were directed to give the House an Account how the Precedents of Verdicts in these Case[s] appear in their Books.

[373] John Prinn had called John Howe, MP for Gloucestershire, a Jacobite and had used abusive language. Howe had been awarded £440 damages. See HMC *Lords MSS* vi, 55-7; *LJ* xvii, 577.

[374] Later Attorney-General, and elected MP for Carlisle in 1705. See Appendix A.

[375] Nicholas Lechmere, later MP for Appleby, see Appendix A.

[376] The first sat from 6 Feb. to 24 June 1701, and the second from 30 Dec. 1701 to 23 May 1702.

[377] John Rastell (d. 1536), printer and lawyer, and Sir Edward Coke (1552-1634), judge and law writer. Nicolson's brackets.

In the Evening, Mr Botel;[378] has all our English plants. The Insects in Moorfields; With a Dissenter, who draws Patterns for the Silk-weavers. A. Addison (Mr Thomas's brother) with me at my Brothers full of Emptyness.[379]

---

[378] Adam Buddle (d. 1715), distinguished botanist, Rector of North Fambridge, Essex, since he had conformed in 1703, after being a non-juror, and a Reader at Gray's Inn, 1702-15.

[379] End of vol. 5 of the original manuscript. See above, sessional intro., n. 15.

26 October 1705–5 March 1706

After the middle of March 1705 Nicolson spent seven months in his diocese. Politically the summer was dominated by the second general election of the Queen's reign, which turned out to be one of the most fiercely contested of any of the seventeen elections held from 1679 to 1722, in the first age of party. The 1705 election was a statutory necessity, Anne's first parliament having come this spring to the end of its legal term. It was welcomed by all, for all had something to hope for from it. Many High Tories firmly believed that notwithstanding the recent attitude of parliament to the Occasional Conformity Bill, the electorate—whenever it was free to make its wishes felt—would respond with gut emotion to their cry of 'the Church in danger'. The Godolphin–Marlborough–Harley triumvirate which controlled the ministry hoped to strengthen its parliamentary base by eliminating as many of the notorious 'Tackers' from the new parliament as possible and supporting in the constituencies the cause of both amenable Whigs and moderate Tories known to be well disposed to the Court.[1] The Junto looked to the campaign with high expectations, as the best opportunity the Whigs had had since 1695 to turn back the Tory tide decisively and thereby fortify their own and their party's claims to office. In the event all had some ground for relief or satisfaction, though only the Junto could indulge in unqualified self-congratulation. The Tories lost nearly sixty seats but salvaged ninety of the 134 Tackers and clung on to a slender majority over their rivals. The Court's offensive against the Tackers enjoyed most success in the 'popular' constituencies[2] and it, though not without uneasiness, took comfort in the hope that many of the Tory, as well as the Whig, placemen who had kept their seats would continue to support its *via media* in the next parliament. The Junto not merely wiped out the losses of 1702 but clawed back all the ground it had lost since the dissolution of 1698, and what is more had realistic hopes of having a united party at its back after their heroic deeds in opposition since 1701.[3]

[1] For the Court strategy in this election and a lucid brief account of the whole campaign see W. A. Speck, *Tory and Whig* (1970), pp. 98–109.

[2] 'Few men attempt such rash measures', St John cynically commented, 'but such as are almost certain of being elected again, either by the prevalency of their party or the absolute dependancy of their corporation.' BL Blenheim MS A1–20: to Marlborough, 25 May 1705.   [3] Speck, *Tory and Whig*, pp. 108, 123.

To this crucial Whig achievement Nicolson made his contribution. For the first time at a general election he threw his local influence unequivocally into the scales against the High Church Tories. The Whigs did well in the north-west in 1705. Of the two Tory Knights for the Shire of Cumberland in the last parliament, the more moderate, Richard Musgrave, survived; but Gilfred Lawson of Drayton, who had voted for the Tack, was forced to yield his seat (though, in the end, without a contest) to a Junto-supported army officer, George Fletcher. More significant, in terms of Nicolson's change of allegiance, was the defeat at Carlisle by 145 votes of the other Musgrave who had sat in the last session of the 1702-5 parliament, Christopher. In the city election, in which there was a record turnout of freemen, the bishop mobilized his personal and episcopal interest not only behind the old Whig member, Colonel Stanwix, but behind the prominent Junto lawyer, Sir James Montagu, who as the Earl of Carlisle's nominee had had a fleeting connection with the borough in the last short parliament of the reign. Sir James was the younger brother of the man who, of all the Whig leaders, Nicolson probably admired most, Lord Halifax, and the bishop greeted his victory with evident satisfaction.[4]

During the summer and into the early autumn the Whig lords renewed their efforts to get more of their party into office and in particular into the Cabinet. The only significant concession the ministry had made to the Whigs before the election had been the replacement of the High Tory Duke of Buckingham (the former Marquess of Normandy) as Lord Privy Seal by John Holles, Duke of Newcastle; and the appointment of Newcastle, a landowner and borough magnate of prodigious wealth but with no pretensions as a working politician or a statesman, had been urged by Harley on the grounds that he was more likely to follow a Court than a Junto line in office. Now, however, the Junto concentrated their fire on one of the most obnoxious High Tory survivors in the Cabinet, Sir Nathan Wright, who as Lord Keeper since 1700 had been responsible for some notorious purges of Whig magistrates from the county commissions of the peace. His prospective replacement, the brilliant barrister and Queen's Counsel Sir William Cowper, was a man of the Junto's own kidney; and although both Anne and Harley were deeply unhappy with the change, Godolphin and Marlborough recognised it as the price that had to be paid for the Whig support they were bound to ensure in the next parliament,

---

[4] Diary, 18 May 1705. The polls for Carlisle at the contested elections of 1700, 1702, 1705, 1710, 1721 (B-E), and 1722 are given in Robert Hopkinson, 'Elections in Cumberland and Westmorland 1695-1723' (University of Newcastle Ph.D. thesis, 1973).

281

and the Queen finally conceded it in October, on the eve of the opening session.[5]

With every prospect that parliamentary forces, in the Commons at least, would be finely balanced, parliament's meeting was awaited with unusual expectancy and Nicolson determined to be in London early. He rode south from Rose on 15 October not entirely happy in his mind, for although Dean Atterbury had managed to alienate most of the Cathedral Chapter during his recent summer residence (and never in fact visited Carlisle again) he had left behind him a redoutable ally in opposing Nicolson's episcopal authority in the person of Dr Hugh Todd, possibly the most energetic and influential of the prebendaries.[6] For the moment, however, it was his London friends and above all London politics which claimed his attention. During the early autumn it had become clear that there would be a crucial trial of strength in the Commons on the first day of the session over the election of a Speaker, with the Tories pitting their strength, and their candidate William Bromley, against the joint nominee of the ministry and the Junto, Jack Smith. Unprecedented efforts were made by the unofficial Whips of both sides in the weeks before the opening to ensure the maximum attendance of members. As a leading Westmorland landowner told James Grahme, MP for Appleby, Whigs and Tories alike were convinced that the issue would be 'so near that one vote may save or lose it'.[7] The bishop himself caught the whiff of excitement as he butted his way through heavy rain storms down the Great North Road. At Doncaster he met up with 'a great throng of Commoners (Sir R. Eden, Sir W. Bowes, Sir W. Robinson, Mr Aislaby and Mr Carr)'; and choosing to pass the night before the vote at Peterborough, he tossed and turned in his bed for hours, unable to sleep for the constant 'posting up of Commoners', clattering into the inn yard and out again, urgently bound for Westminster.[8] The outcome was an attendance of 459, including tellers and candidates, the largest John Evelyn could ever recall on the first day of a parliament in all his eighty-five years,[9] and a victory for Smith and the Whigs by a margin of forty-three votes.[10]

[5] Harley would have preferred Chief Justice Trevor, while Anne, with an uneasy eye on the Lord Keeper's Church patronage, held out stubbornly for 'a moderate Tory'. BL Loan 29/237, ff. 97–8; Add. MS 28070, f. 12; HMC *Bath MSS* i, 67; Longleat MSS Portland Papers vii, f. 23: Godolphin to Harley, 1 Oct. 1705.

[6] Bennett, *Tory Crisis*, p. 90. The skirmishes were to continue both at Carlisle and in London during the winter, with Nicolson entertaining at one point vain hopes of the Dean's speedy removal. See below, 15, 17, and 20 Nov.; 7 and 27 Dec.; 4 and 26 Jan.; and 11 and 16 Feb.   [7] Levens Hall MS: Lord Thanet to Grahme, 25 Sept. 1705.

[8] Diary, 18 Oct., 25 Oct. 1705.

[9] *The Diary of John Evelyn*, ed. E. S. de Beer (1959) v, 614.

[10] For an excellent account of the struggle and a division list, see W. A. Speck, 'The Choice of a Speaker in 1705', *BIHR* xxxvii (1964).

Nicolson reached London on the following day, in good time to hear the Queen's 'excellent and healing' speech from the throne on Saturday 27 October, and he remained in town for four months and ten days, by which time there was only a fortnight left of the session before the prorogation. His diary is therefore a very valuable source of information on a parliamentary winter in which, even for Anne's reign, the House of Lords played an exceptionally prominent part. The outstanding issues of this first session of the 1705 parliament were the great 'Church in Danger' debates of December 1705; the repeal of the Aliens Act and the preparing of the ground for the opening of negotiations for a Union between England and Scotland; the renewed agitation over the Protestant Succession originating with the attempt of the High Tories, in the course of a 'State of the Nation' debate on 15 November, to persuade the Lords to invite the statutory heir, Electress Sophia of Hanover, to come to England; and the sequel of this abortive move, the introduction and eventual passing early in 1706 of one of the two great pieces of legislation of this parliament, the Regency Act; and, finally, the remarkable tussle in both Houses, but especially in the House of Commons—cutting for once across party lines—over the attempt to insert in that Act the 'whimsical clause' drastically reducing the number of government office holders who would be allowed in future to hold seats in the Commons. On all these issues Nicolson's diary has much of value to tell us; his account of the protracted procedures on the securing of the succession in the Regency Bill (26 November 1705–19 February 1706) is the fullest we have; and his version of the Lords' debate on 'the Church in Danger' (6 Dec.) is one of the best three extant.[11]

The loss of the speakership, the defeat shortly afterwards of their candidate for the chair of the most vital committee in the Commons, that of Supply and of Ways and Means, and the beginning during November of what was to be a series of defeats in disputed election cases at the hands of the combination of Whigs and placemen,[12] all combined early to persuade the High Tory leaders, Rochester and Nottingham—perhaps unwisely[13]—that if they were to keep the ministry under pressure their main offensive would have to be launched

[11] The other two are Archdeacon White Kennett's account (BL Lansdowne MS 1024, ff. 168-9) printed by C. Jones in 'Debates in the House of Lords on "the Church in Danger", 1705, and on Dr Sacheverell's Impeachment, 1710', *HJ* xix (1976), 764-9; and in *Parl. Hist.* vi, 479-507 (based largely on the contemporary account of Abel Boyer).

[12] The most significant was that for St Alban's, heard on 24 Nov., when the attempt of the Tacker John Gape to unseat Admiral Killigrew, a Whig recommended by Sarah, Duchess of Marlborough, failed on petition. *CJ* xv, 37-9.

[13] Marlborough must have thought so. The size of the Tory vote against John Smith on 25 Oct. had come as an unpleasant surprise to him. See *Marlborough-Godolphin Corr.* i, 509.

in the Upper House. And so it was (as Burnet wrote) that 'the main debates that were in this session began in the House of Lords; the Queen being present at them all'.[14] For roughly three weeks from 12 November 'the Church party' attempted to seize and hold the initiative, with Lords Rochester and Nottingham strongly supported from the floor by Haversham (an ex-Whig convert), Anglesey, Guernsey, and Buckingham,[15] and backed by other High Tory stalwarts such as Weymouth, Granville, Jersey, and even the veteran Duke of Leeds. From the second week of December, however, they were reduced to stubborn and often desperate defence as the Whigs and the Court took charge of the session, whose equanimity thereafter was more disturbed by the repercussions from sallies of Whig independents in the Commons than by efforts of the Tories.

In so far as the latter had a coherent strategy, as opposed to a general determination to embarrass the ministry at every opportunity, that strategy had two main aspects. These were, first, to follow through their election campaign by trying to expose in parliament the threats to which the Church of England was supposedly vulnerable under a government which relied on the Whig party for support; and secondly, to try to refurbish their own somewhat tarnished image on the succession issue while at the same time attempting to exploit the one possible chink in their opponents' succession armour, namely, the Queen's personal tepidity towards the House of Hanover and her acute sensitivity towards any suggestion of a personal Hanoverian presence in England during her lifetime.[16] As a moderate Tory still in office[17] wrote later, 'we all knew the Queen was little satisfied with the hands she was fallen into'; and behind the muddled thinking of the Highflyers evidently lay the hope of feeding her discontent and restoring, to some extent, their own lost favour. But in both respects their tactics rebounded on their own heads and antagonised the Queen far more than they placated her.

More foresight and less purblind factiousness would have served them better, and not least in the case of the Church, the issue which finally destroyed their brief offensive in the first week of December. For although they had been spoiling for a fight on this question long before the session started, and the way had been prepared for it by the publication of the notorious pamphlet *The Memorial of the Church of England*, which arraigned not only the Whigs but (much to

[14] Burnet, *History*, v, 230-1. For Nicolson's references to the Queen's presence at debates see Diary for 15, 19, 20, 21, 23, 27 Nov. and 6 Dec. See also *Diary of Earl Cowper*, pp. 16, 22.

[15] For these see Diary *passim*. For Guernsey, see Burnet, *History*, v, 247.

[16] See ibid., pp. 232-3, 233 (Dartmouth's note).

[17] Lord Dartmouth, Commissioner of Trade. See his note to ibid., p. 242.

his dismay and anger) Lord Treasurer Godolphin as enemies of the Anglican establishment,[18] the speech from the throne at the opening of parliament (27 October) had made it fairly clear that the Queen would take personally any intimation that the Established Church was in danger from her ministers.[19] Moreover, they might have taken warning from the fact that the Whigs were eager for an opportunity to justify themselves, after their defeat of the Occasional Conformity Bills, and that Godolphin too was ready for a showdown. 'Whether the Parliament approve of all the noise that is fomented in the Kingdom of the Church's danger', he told Harley, 'is, in my humble opinion, the first thing that ought one way or other to be cleared upon their meeting.'[20] In the circumstances the Tories would have been wiser to leave the campaigning to their friends in Convocation, where Dean Aldrich raised 'the dangerous growth of heresies and schisms' as early as 7 November. At most they should have been content to show their concern obliquely, when the opportunity arose in the debates on the Regency Bill at the end of November, by trying to get a new legislative security for the Act of Uniformity and other ramparts of Anglican monopoly after the Queen's death.[21] During one of these debates, however, as Nicolson observed, Lord Rochester declared 'with such a peculiar zeal and emphasis that tho' he would not *say* the Church of England was in Danger dureing her Majesty's Life, he could not help *thinking* that it would be so upon Her Demise',[22] that when Halifax dangled the bait of a full-dress debate on 'the Church in Danger' before the House on 30 November, he must have known that Rochester would gobble it up. He duly did so, and it is clear from Nicolson's Diary that some of Rochester's fellow Tory peers were uneasily aware that he had led them into a trap even before the disastrous debate on 6 December.[23]

The silence Nicolson records at the start of the debate, before Rochester's speech, is itself significant, as is the fact that Rochester himself was untypically cautious (a fact noted with some glee by

[18] Published anonymously, this pamphlet, it later transpired, had been written by Dr James Drake. See below, 6 Dec., n. 241. For Godolphin's shocked attitude see *Life of Sharp*, i, 366; for the rather more detached anger of Marlborough, who also suffered at Drake's hand, see *Marlborough–Godolphin Corr.* i, 474: Marlborough to Godolphin, 13/24 Aug. 1705.

[19] *LJ* xviii, 7–8.

[20] HMC *Bath MSS* i, 76: 19 Sept. 1705.

[21] See below, Diary, 29–30 Nov.

[22] Ibid., 29 Nov.

[23] Dartmouth later recalled how the occasion 'was brought on by Lord Rochester's passion, without consulting any body, and as ill timed as it could well be'. Note to Burnet, *History*, v, 242.

Halifax, who followed him) and while 'he professed himself of opinion, *That the Church is in danger*' studiously omitted to end with a motion to that effect.[24] Even more significant was the fact (not mentioned by Nicolson) that 'when that noble lord had done, the House sate still a quarter of an hour, expecting some body would second him' before Halifax's intervention.[25] It is hardly surprising that throughout the rest of the long debate Nicolson could afterwards recall only four brief speeches from lay Tory peers,[26] and two of these—including Nottingham's—were made directly in support of the only motion to emerge from the Tory side, a narrow and relatively innocuous one from the Archbishop of York 'for a Committee to consider the wayes for the effectual suppressing of Pamphlets'; and for consulting the judges on how to bring dissenting academies more effectively under Church control.[27] The Tory bishops were particularly embarrassed by the proceedings. Archbishop Tenison had primed the members of the bench most carefully and the moderates and Low Churchmen had agreed at Lambeth on 3 December 'that every bishop say something, of the state of his own diocese' during the debate; something which Burnet, Hough, Patrick, and Moore did partly at the expense of drawing attention to the insubordination of the High Church parish clergy and the Cambridge dons and students as the principal source of 'danger'.[28] Less than three weeks earlier six Tory bishops had divided against their party in an important vote in the House[29] and now only three High Churchmen, including Sharp, offered qualified support to Rochester and all were careful to dissociate themselves from any political implications in expressing their fears for the Church. Compton of London, for instance, 'prefaced his discourse with professing his entire confidence in the Queen and in the present ministry'.[30]

Soft-pedalling was of no avail, however. The Lord Treasurer intervened late in the debate to insist that the archbishop's motion 'about seminaries' ought to give way to the main question before the committee; and the lords in the end divided on a question previously rehearsed between Godolphin and the Junto, that

[24] See below, Diary, 6 Dec.; cf. Jones, 'Debates in the House of Lords', p. 766; *Parl. Hist*. vi, 492–3.
[25] *Parl. Hist*. vi, 481.
[26] Nottingham, Anglesey, North and Grey, and Leeds. According to Kennett there was one other, the Marquess of Carmarthen (Leeds's son) who 'stood up and talks of fighting for the Church &c'. Jones, 'Debates in the House of Lords', p. 768.
[27] Cf. Jones, 'Debates in the House of Lords', p. 766; *Parl. Hist*. vi, 492–3.
[28] Cf. Jones, 'Debates in the House of Lords', pp. 767–8; *Parl. Hist*. vi, 492, 495–7.
[29] See below, Diary, 20 Nov.
[30] Ibid., 6 Dec.; Jones, 'Debates in the House of Lords', p. 765. See also ibid., p. 766, for Sharp and *Parl. Hist*. vi, 497–8 for Hooper of Bath and Wells.

It is the opinion of this Committee that the Church of England, as by law established, which was rescued from the extremest danger by King William III of glorious memory, is now by God's blessing, under the happy reign of Her Majesty, in a most safe and flourishing condition; and [that] whosoever goes about to suggest and insinuate, that the Church is in danger under Her Majesty's administration is an enemy to the Queen, the Church and the Kingdom.[31]

The second part of the question, especially, revealed the confidence and uncompromising spirit of the Whigs, and when the resolution was carried by the crushing margin of sixty-one votes to thirty[32] many Tories must have shared Nottingham's view, expressed at the end of the debate and marvellously caught in all its frustration and dejection by Nicolson's pen, that now 'some of us have nothing to doe but to *goe home and say our prayers*'.[33]

Prayer was all the more necessary since by this time it was already clear that High Tory succession strategy, too, had run on to the rocks. It had been launched in the Lords on 13 November, when Lord Haversham had moved for a day on which the House in committee could consider the state of the nation. Nicolson learned from Bishop Moore of Norwich that Rochester had been plotting a Hanover motion ever since the summer; but Moore believed that the design was to try to procure an invitation for Sophia's grandson, the Electoral Prince, to come and reside in England as a resident guarantor of the Protestant Succession who would serve as a rallying-point whenever Anne died.[34] None the less, when Haversham unmasked his 'great guns' on 15 November Godolphin had apparently had less than forty eight hours' notice of what was really intended, namely a motion to invite over the Electress herself.[35] Haversham's motion, promptly supported by Rochester, Nottingham, and other High Tory spokesmen, was as squalid as it was mischievous. It 'had no other purpose than to damage the standing of Marlborough, Godolphin and the Whig chiefs, either with the Queen, if they

---

[31] *Parl. Hist.* vi, 507. Cf. the slightly different wording below, 6 Dec. and in Kennett (Jones, 'Debates in the House of Lords', p. 769).

[32] The tellers were Earl Rivers for the majority and the Earl of Denbigh for the minority. See HLRO MS Minutes, 6 Dec.

[33] On 8 Dec. the Commons considered the Lords' resolution. The ministry and the Whigs moved that the House should endorse it. The Tories tried first to get it referred to a Committee, but were defeated by 220 votes to 159. After a long debate, lasting until 8.00 or 9.00 at night, they then attempted to amend the resolution by omitting the final clause, but were again beaten by 212 votes to 162. The result was a joint address of both Houses to the Queen on 18 Dec. *CJ* xv, 58, 65, 68; BL Add. MS 17677AAA, ff. 578–9: L'Hermitage to the States General, 11 Dec. 1705. See also below, 8 Dec. and notes.

[34] See below, 13 Nov.

[35] BL Loan 29/237, f. 115: Godolphin to Newcastle, 13 Nov.

supported the invitation to the Electress, or with Hanover and the rank-and-file Whigs, if they opposed it'.[36] Late in the four-hour debate[37] the Lord Treasurer rolled out his counter-motion, the first stage of a plan carefully concerted with the Whig lords on the previous day.[38] There is no doubt that every Whig in the chamber would have been seriously embarrassed by having to vote *directly* against Haversham's motion,[39] so Godolphin first proposed on 15 November what Nicolson called 'an accommodation, by altering the motion to that of appointing a day for [considering] the better security of the Protestant Succession . . .', having laid particular stress on the need to make provision by law for the dangerous interlude that would ensue between the Queen's death and the arrival in England of the Hanoverian heir.[40] The Tories, finding that their motion that the previous question be put was shouted down, did not dare to press a division on their own question when the Court-Whig motion had been approved. The day thus ended in tarnished reputations if not disaster for them. Nicolson was particularly shocked by Rochester's hypocrisy, but it was Nottingham whom the Queen, having heard the Tory speeches in the debate with stern disapproval, never forgave. He was never given office by her again.[41]

Following their shrewd delaying tactics on 15 November the Whigs revealed the second, and crucial, part of their antidote to the Hanover motion on 19 November. Then, in a further Grand Committee on the state of the nation, Wharton, at his most ironically incisive, moved for a new bill to secure the succession[42]—the bill that was to find its way on to the statute-book early in the New Year as the Regency Act. Nicolson attended at Westminster religiously during the bill's passage through the Upper House (19 November–3 December),[43] and he chronicled quite fully the attempts of the Tory peers to

[36] Holmes, *British Politics*, p. 114 and n. for references there cited. Sophia's reactions had already been sounded and had been found to be favourable to an invitation. See Sophia's letter to the Archbishop of Canterbury, 3 Nov. (new style) 1705, printed in *Parl. Hist.* vi, 520–1. [37] Ibid., p. 463.

[38] Godolphin to Newcastle, 13 Nov., *loc. cit.*

[39] For the attitude of the bulk of Whig MPs in the Commons at this time, see BL Loan 29/191, f. 349: [Godolphin to Harley], 'Sat. night at 11' [Nov. 1705], printed but misdated in HMC *Portland MSS* iv, 154. See also Add. MS 4291, f. 38; Blenheim MS A 1–26: James Brydges to Marlborough, 4 Dec. 1705.

[40] Although Nicolson refers to this as 'Lord T[reasurer]'s motion', cf. Burnet, *History*, v, 232, where the Bishop of Salisbury writes of the proposal 'to make an effectual provision against the disorders that might happen in such an interval': 'This was proposed first by myself, and it was *seconded* by the Lord Godolphin [our italics], and all the Whigs went into it . . .'

[41] Ibid., p. 233 Dartmouth's note, for the reasons.

[42] Cf. ibid., pp. 234–5 for another, and excellent, account of Wharton's speech.

[43] 19, 20 and 21 Nov. were spent debating resolutions that were then worked into the bill by the Judges.

obstruct it indirectly, especially by bringing forward 'clogging' clauses[44] in committee.[45] These tactics, and other moves such as a spiteful vote forced on 20 November with the object of excluding the Lord Treasurer from the list of *ex officio* Regents who were to take charge of the interim government after the Queen's death, proved counter-productive. That six Tory bishops, including Compton and Hooper, should vote against the Rochester and Nottingham party on this proposal is a measure of how desperate the Tory opposition to the bill became. 'I never knew anything in the management of the Tories [Burnet wrote], by which they suffered more in their reputation than by this [opposition].'[46] Things became even worse when, after a third reading in which Nottingham made a last attempt to secure the Test Acts during a Regency,[47] the bill was sent down to the Commons. There it was subjected to all conceivable harassment.[48] As early as 19 December things became so heated that for indiscretions uttered during a debate which lasted until nearly midnight, Charles Caesar, MP for Hertford, was sent to the Tower to cool off. The Junto concerted the management of the bill in the Lower House closely with their lieutenants, and other leading Whigs such as Sir Richard Onslow.[49] Nicolson stumbled on two of their management meetings early in the New Year[50] and noted how Somers's barrister brother-in-law ditched a case he was handling in the House of Lords on 15 January in order to flee to the Commons where the debates were 'high and hot'.

However, the Tories alone could not have endangered the Regency Bill but for the well-meant endeavours of a strong group of Country Whigs who saw it as a golden opportunity to limit the influence of the Crown over the House of Commons, over which there had been mounting anxiety since the days of Charles II. Well over a hundred 'placemen'—ministers and officials of the government and royal household—held seats in the new parliament; and in addition there were many army and navy officers in the Queen's pay and some government contractors and pensioners. With the executive much expanded since 1689 independent members of both parties concerned for parliamentary independence viewed the future with

[44] *Diary of Earl Cowper*, p. 22.
[45] See in particular the proceedings on 30 Nov.
[46] *History*, v, 238.
[47] Below, 3 Dec. 1705.
[48] The most authentic contemporary account of the long Commons' proceedings, lasting altogether from the middle of Dec. to the middle of Feb. 1706, is in 'An Anonymous Parliamentary Diary, 1705-6', ed. W. A. Speck, *Camden Miscellany*, xxiii (1969), 49–81, though it unfortunately ends on 21 Jan.
[49] Burnet, *History*, v, 235 n: Speaker Onslow's note.
[50] Below, 5 and 7 Jan.

foreboding. Before the passing of the Act of Settlement in favour of the House of Hanover in 1701 a clause had been inserted to the effect that all placemen were to be excluded from the Commons on the Queen's death. It had been clear almost from the start that so radical a measure would never be enforceable; but the Country Whigs[51] now argued that the 'regulating and altering' of this clause by the substitution of a substantial for a universal exclusion of placemen in a new succession bill, a bill which neither the Court nor the Whig leaders in the Lords, nor indeed the Queen, could afford to lose, would be a truly effective way of realizing the most cherished of Country objectives.[52]

Thus was hatched the so-called 'Whimsical clause', introduced at the committee stage of the Regency Bill in the Commons on 21 January 1706,[53] which between then and 19 February engaged the attention of both Houses, and seemed likely at one stage to promote another rift between them and even to jeopardise the succession legislation itself.[54] It was among the amendments to the Regency Bill which were incorporated before the bill was sent back to the Lords on 26 January. The Bishop of Hereford's hopes of an easy compromise between Junto and Country Whigs[55] were soon shown to be vain. 'Much pains were taken . . . to heal this [breach]', Burnet observed, and Wharton's 'smooth' proposal on 29 January, supported by Sunderland, for deferring consideration of the Whimsical clause for a while[56] was a sure indication that cajoling and tough bargaining was already going on behind the scenes. Nevertheless, when the big debate did take place in the Upper House on 31 January, it transpired that the Junto, arguing successfully for the repeal of the self-denying clause of the Act of Settlement but not its amendment, were prepared to call the Commons' bluff, while offering them only minor sops.[57] For almost a fortnight after the Commons rejected the Lords' amendment by 205 to 183 on 4 February stalemate—or worse—threatened; but, eventually, tireless negotiations produced a 'bargain' sealed at Halifax's house between

[51] Their leaders at this time were Sir Richard Onslow, Robert Eyres, Sir Peter King, and James Stanhope.
[52] BL Loan 29/64/3: Godolphin to [Harley], 'Friday at 12' [15 Feb. 1706]; Burnet, *History*, v, 240.
[53] See below, 21 Jan., n. 420 for its provisions.
[54] For a full account of this epic struggle, the most important clash between Court and Country in a reign dominated by Whig and Tory divisions, see G. Holmes, 'The Attack on "the Influence of the Crown", 1702–16', *BIHR* xxxix (1966); Holmes, *British Politics*, pp. 132–4.
[55] Below, 27 Jan.
[56] Below, 29 Jan.; Burnet, *History*, v, 240.
[57] The bishops' bench overwhelmingly supported them. Below, 31 Jan.

the Junto and a splinter group of the 'Whimsical Whigs',[58] and on 19 February a delighted Nicolson was able to record a 'happy accommodation' which gave 'a certain prospect of a speedy and joyful conclusion of this session'.[59]

Certainly by the session's end there had been little joy on any front for the Tory opposition. The finance bills so crucial to the continued vigorous prosecution of a war whose scale and unprecedented geographical range was becoming increasingly unpalatable to dyed-in-the-wool right-wingers, they dared not oppose; and they went through both Houses with great dispatch. Very early in the session a factious attempt by Tory peers to censure the Duke of Marlborough, indirectly, for the alleged 'disappointments' of the 1705 campaign on the Moselle had ended in humiliating failure.[60] In any case frustrations in Germany were at once forgotten when news reached Westminster immediately after the debate of the first successes of the allied cause in the new Peninsular campaign, notably the fall of Barcelona (3/14 October 1705) to the forces of the Earl of Peterborough and the Habsburg candidate for the Spanish throne Archduke Charles.[61] Peterborough's erratic conduct and 'rashness', which had already caused annoyance in naval circles,[62] might look ominous to the discerning eye—as might the strained relations between him and the Carlist camp. But for a while all went well on the surface, and by February virtually the whole of Valencia was in allied hands.

Much nearer home there was one other major development this winter to encourage the triumvirs, the Whigs and all sincere well-wishers to the Protestant succession. By the end of the session prospects of a successful solution to the vexed problem of Anglo-Scottish relations appeared much brighter than had been the case when the new parliament met in October. At that stage the Earls of Nottingham and Rochester and their allies in the Commons were hopeful of an outcome which would placate Westminster on the question of the succession while doing nothing positive to promote a full union between an Anglican England and a Presbyterian Scotland. This was what was in Nottingham's mind when he called for a Lords' inquiry into the state of Scotland *and* the succession on

[58] Kent Archives Office, Chevening MS U1590 C9/31: Sir John Cropley to James Stanhope, 19 Feb. [1706].

[59] For the details of the crucial 'accommodation' on the self-denying provision, see Burnet, *History*, v, 240–1; Luttrell, vi, 17–18; Holmes, 'Attack on "the Influence of the Crown" ', pp. 58–9.

[60] Below, 22 Nov. See also Burnet, *History*, v, 245–6; *Parl. Hist.* vi, 476.

[61] In general, see Trevelyan, *Queen Anne*, ii, 66–75.

[62] Below, 13 Dec.

12 November (three days before the 'Hanover motion') and evoked a
nervous response from Godolphin. However, as their other hopes
crumbled in the early weeks of the session, they decided that over the
Union they would have to cut their losses and use the issue to try and
recover their credibility. The decisive steps were taken in the House
of Lords between 23 and 29 November. After the Queen had laid
before parliament the recent decisions of the Edinburgh estates,[63] including the address calling for repeal of the penal clauses of the
Aliens Act of 1705 before negotiations for a Union should be started

> the Tories . . . to make themselves popular, after they had failed in
> many attempts, resolved to promote this; apprehending that the
> Whigs who had first moved for that act, would be for maintaining
> their own work; but they seemed to be much surprised when, after
> they had prefaced their motions in this matter with such declara-
> tions of their intentions for the public good, that showed they
> expected opposition and a debate, the Whigs not only agreed to
> this, but carried the motion further, to the other act relating to their
> manufacture and trade. This passed very unanimously in both
> Houses; and by this means way was made for opening a treaty as
> soon as the session should come to an end.[64]

In a revealing conversation in January with the Bishop of Carlisle, Lord
Somers indicated that at this stage his own instincts were to move towards a full Union only by careful stages, with parliamentary and commercial union preceding any religious, legal, and administrative
settlement; a course which Nicolson (whose attitude towards the
Scottish problem was understanding and devoid of political cynicism)
interestingly agreed with.[65] But once they had secured their control
over the English negotiating commission appointed on 10 April—after
parliament had gone into recess—the Junto were able to contemplate
a more speedy and thoroughgoing process with far more equanimity
than were the High Tories, who now had to face being left with the
baby of the succession without being able to throw out the bathwater
of Court influence over Scotland's representatives at Westminster and
of the feared Presbyterian threat to the Church of England.

To make matters worse for them Convocation by March 1706

[63] Sept. 1705. See P. W. J. Riley, *The Union of England and Scotland* (Manchester,
1979), pp. 148–51.

[64] Burnet, *History*, v, 246–7. Cf. below, 23 and 29 Nov. For the latest account of the
complex manœuvres which provided the background to these parliamentary steps, and a
view of Junto motives more cynical than that of Burnet and Nicolson, see Riley, pp. 151–2,
161–8.

[65] Below, 19 Jan. Somers was the last man to be prey to the 'half-baked' ideas Dr Riley
attributes to him in this contest and his scheme was not the fruit of 'desperation'. Cf. Riley,
p. 165.

was even less capable than parliament of protecting the interests of the Church, as the High Churchmen conceived them. Convocation had opened promisingly enough that winter, with the election of Rochester's nominee, Dean Binckes, as Prolocutor instead of Atterbury, whom Harley had coaxed before the session into a more moderate stance, and with both Binckes and Aldrich making conciliatory noises towards the bishops.[66] But this time the bishops, smarting under ferocious attacks upon them by their diocesan clergy during and after the general election, were sternly resolved to bring their recalcitrant presbyters to heel. Nicolson was, of course, involved in their tactics only indirectly;[67] but from Trimnell and Sharp he was kept fully informed of the final showdown on 1 March and its aftermath which effectively ensured the subordination and then the silencing of Convocation for the next four years. The Queen by this time needed little encouragement from Tenison and Godolphin to assert her royal supremacy against the High Churchmen of the Lower House, and when parliament rose even moderates such as Harley and Sharp, let alone extremists such as Rochester and Aldrich, must have been dismayed by the realisation that the Junto had carried their bargain with the Lord Treasurer not only into the field of parliamentary tactics and civil appointments, but also into the crucial sphere of church patronage.[68]

[Oct.] 26. *Friday*. By Ware, Chaston, Waltham-Cross, Edmundton, Tattenham, Newington, &c. to London; and thence conducted by my brother to Mr Hallet's in Manchester Court, where I presently found my self so happy as to have Sir W. Fleming for my Neighbour: who presently welcomed me, and appears very brisk in his new Honour.[69]

[Oct.] 27. *Saturday*. In the morning I paid my first Duty (after that to God) to my Metropolitan the Archbishop of York [Sharp] and went thence to Mr C. Musgrave's in Swallow-street, but found him not within. In my Return, I called on the Bishop of Lincoln,[70]

[66] See below, 7 Nov. and n. 108.
[67] e.g. on 29 Jan., being consulted by Tenison about 'a printed state of the present disputes betwixt the Upper and Lower Houses of Convocation'.
[68] See G. V. Bennett, *Tory Crisis*, pp. 83–5.
[69] William Fleming of Rydal, Westmorland, MP for Westmorland until the 1705 election (see Appendix A), had been created a baronet on 4 Oct. 1705.
[70] William Wake, nominated 16 July and consecrated 21 Oct. 1705.

who yet wants the Restitution of his Temporalities[71] (tho' Homage is done) and his parliamentary Writt.[72]

At the House, I read prayers; and (haveing Congratulated the new Lord Keeper Cooper [Cowper])[73] took the Oaths together with the Lords Newport,[74] Guilford and Howard of Escrick. About two, the Queen came; and, haveing approved the Choice of the Commons,[75] made an excellent and healing Speech to both Houses from the Throne.[76] Which done, her Majesty withdrew; and the Session began with Reading a Bill for the better Maintenance of the Poor, the same (*pro formâ*) wherewith several former Parliaments have been opened. After this, Lord Sommers moved that Committees (as usual) might be appointed for Privileges, Inspection of the Journals, &c. and particularly, that the antient Custome of nameing *Tryers of Petitions*[77] might be revived. All which was assented to. Then the Queen's Speech was reported and read by the Lord Keeper, and afterwards (Paragraph by Paragraph) by the Clerk of the Committees; and a Committee appointed to draw up an Address of thanks, to be presented to Her Majesty by this House. Adjourned.

After I had dined at home, I was visitted by Dr Gibson (in pain for his good wife,[78] newly delivered of a dead child) Mr Wotton, &c.

[Oct.] 28. *Sunday*. Haveing heard a good Sermon from Mr Dean of Carlile [Atterbury] at the Queen's Chapple (in Defence of Moses and the Prophets) I dined at Brother Joseph's; whence, at night, by Cousin R. Nicolson's home again.

[Oct.] 29. *Munday*. The Committee for the Address (and the House likewise, presently after I had read prayers) adjourned to Wednesday;

[71] Wake himself estimated their value, despite the vastness of his see, at no more than £900 a year. They had reverted to the Crown since Bishop Gardiner's death on 1 Mar. 1705. See Sykes, *Wake*, i, 158, where the total income of the bishopric at Wake's succession is put between £1,000 and £1,100.

[72] Wake received his writ of summons to parliament on 1 Nov. and took his seat on 5 Nov. 1705. See ibid. i, 159.

[73] The Whig barrister and MP, William Cowper, had succeeded Sir Nathan Wright on 11 Oct. 1705, after stiff resistance by Harley and the Queen to the combined pressure of Marlborough, Godolphin, and the Junto. See Appendix A; Holmes, *British Politics*, p. 204.

[74] Nicolson means Francis Newport, Earl of Bradford, who before 1694 had been Viscount Newport. *LJ* xviii, 6.

[75] Of John Smith, as Speaker. See above, p. 282.

[76] *LJ* xviii, 7.

[77] From the reign of Edward I the King, or Lord Chancellor on his behalf, had nominated triers to see whether the remedies sought in petitions to parliament were reasonable and fit to be propounded.

[78] Margaret Jones, daughter of the Rev. John Jones, Rector of Selattyn, Salop. She was sister of the wife of John Bettesworth, Dean of the Arches. Sykes, *Gibson*, pp. 62–3. In *DNB* she is erroneously said to be Dr Bettesworth's sister. She married Gibson in July 1704.

this being the day of the Lord Mayor's Shew, and obligeing the Lord Keeper [Cowper] to make a quick Return to Westminster-Hall.

I dined at Lambeth; together with the Archbishop of Dublin [King], Sir Gustavus Hume,[79] Mr Archdeacon Kennett, Dr Fuller of Hatfield,[80] &c. The Impudent Forgery of the History of Formosa[81] occasioned the mentioning of the Counterfeit Petronius, Caesar's Commentaries, and others: And the Archbishop of Dublin confidently averred that Ludlow's Memoirs are of that Kind.[82] *No*; saies my Lord of Canterbury [Tenison]. *Ludlow indeed left his Works, in Slingsby Bethel's hand, much larger than they are; but nothing was cut of[f], save his long Citations out of Scripture and some canting Digressions.*[83]

Mr Archeadon K[ennett] and I haveing made a short visit to Dr Gibson, I came home; and (soon after) met Coll. Grahme at the Dean of Well's [Grahme's]: Where Mr Dent[84] in pain for the East-land Fleet.[85]

[Oct.] 30. *Tuesday*. In the morning, Visitted by Mrs Donning,[86] Mr Grandorge, Mr Buchanan, Mr Thomas Pearson, Mr Smith and Mr Hutchinson. I waited on Lord Thanet; with whom was his Neigh-

---

[79] Sir Gustavus Hume (*c*.1670–1731) 3rd Bt. of Castle Hume, co. Fermanagh. MP [I] Fermanagh, 1713–14, 1715–31.

[80] Thomas Fuller, Rector of Bishop Hatfield, Hertfordshire, 1685–d. 1712.

[81] At the end of 1704, one George Psalmanagau published an *Historical and Geographical Description of Formosa* with a long introduction in which he claimed to be a Formosan. Long afterwards he published an autobiography, admitting the fraud which is here suspected.

[82] Edward Ludlow (?1617–92), regicide and republican. His memoirs were first published in three volumes in 1689 and 1699, nominally at Vevey in Switzerland, but in fact in England.

[83] But see Edmund Ludlow, *A Voyce from the Watch Tower*, ed. A. B. Worden, Camden Soc. 4th ser. xxi (1978), pp. 17–35 for conclusive evidence that the editor of the Memoirs was John Toland, and that he subjected the original manuscript to massive cuts and highly significant editorial distortions. Cf. the hitherto accepted view of C. H. Firth, in the introduction to his edition of *The Memoirs of Edmund Ludlow*, 2 vols. (Oxford, 1894), i, pp. vii–xiv.

[84] George Dent, Whig Chamberlain and Senior Common Councilman of Appleby, 1700–1, 1708, 1714. Hopkinson, p. 183.

[85] The ships of the Eastland Company's merchants trading with ports in the Baltic, sailing in convoy since the outbreak of the Great Northern War in 1701. At the end of Oct. 1705 reports reached London from both Hull and Dunkirk of the depredations of Saint Paul, the French privateer captain. One referred to his 'taking 3 of our men of war and 12 merchant ships, with several stores [from the Baltic]'. Luttrell, v, 605–6. For this trade see R. W. K. Hinton, *The Eastland Trade and the Common Weal in the Seventeenth Century* (Cambridge, 1959).

[86] Jane Donning (also called by Nicolson 'Dunhall' and 'Dunhil') was a sister of Sir Wilfred Lawson. Nicolson explained to Atterbury, who was later pestered by her, that she had 'suffered a long imprisonment on account of her untoward behaviour to (her late brother) . . . and, since his death, she has been as troublesome to (a very worthy lady) his widow. A fancy has gotten into her head, that my Brother [-in-law] Nevinson and I have

bour, Mr Toke,[87] for excludeing all the Commissioners of the Land-Tax.[88] After a Cool Turn with Mr C. Musgrave in the Park, I returned to dinner at my own Lodgeings; and, in the Evening, visitted Dr Lancaster and Salisbury-Court.

[Oct.] 31. *Wednesday.* After prayers, the Address Reported.[89] Sir W. Fleming (not in hast for Wedlock)[90] dined and spent the Evening with Capt. Studholme, a mighty Collector of Bibles &c.

Nov. 1. *Thursday.* After a walk to Knights-bridge, I returned to read Prayers in the House; where the Duke of Newcastle[91] reported the Queen's haveing appointed Two o' clock for the Attendance of the Lords with their Address. Accordingly, after an Adjournment to Munday next, their Lordships (whereof 7 Bishops, in their Habits) went to St James's; where the Lord Keeper, as usual, read and presented the Address, and received Her Majesty's gracious Answer.

After Dinner, Robin dismissed; in Order to his Return homewards, in the morning, with the Horses.

NB. I had this day a great deal of Discourse (in the House) with Lord Sommers, about our Records. He assured me that, before he was Lord Chancellour, there were no Treaties Registered in Chancery after that for Dunkirk; which the French King, or some others concerned in that matter at home, had taken care to have very particularly inrolled: That, on the Treaty of Reswick [Ryswick], no precedents could be found in the Paper Office wherein our Kings had the Title of France allowed: That Sir Joseph Williamson was treated with, a little before his death, to transmit his Books and Papers into that Office; which he promised, but did not perform.[92]

combined with this good lady to cheat her of a Legacy left to her by her said brother; and to defraud a neighbouring School of a like bequest.' *Nicolson Epist. Corr.* ii, 408: N. to Atterbury, 18 Feb. 1710. She continued to pester Nicolson until 1709, and then tried to use Atterbury to deliver a petition to the Queen against Nicolson. Ibid., p. 407; *CW* iii (1903), 52.

[87] i.e. Thanet's Sussex neighbour John Toke (1671–1746), MP for Grinstead, 1702–8.

[88] Possibly from sitting in the House of Commons. By 1705 the Commissioners (unpaid) nominally included most of the principal and middling gentry in every county; but only a very small proportion were active. There was a considerable campaign for fresh 'place' legislation in the years 1705 and 1706, though in the session of 1705–6 it did not openly revive until after Christmas. See G. S. Holmes, 'The Attack on "the Influence of the Crown", 1702–16', *BIHR* xxxix (1966), 52–4.

[89] *LJ* xviii, 11.   [90] He did not marry until 1723.

[91] 'Appointed Lord Privy Seal, *vice* Buckingham, as a concession to the Whigs before the general election of 1705.

[92] Williamson, Secretary of State, 1674–9, had died in 1701. He was a Cumbrian and former patron of Nicolson's. James, pp. 8, 16–20 *passim.*

[Nov.] 2. *Friday*. At a meeting of the Commissioners for Queen Ann's Bounty in the morning: present Lord Archbishop of Canterbury, Lord Keeper, Bishops of London [Compton], Worcester [Lloyd], Sarum [Burnet], Litchfeild [Hough], Chichester [Williams], Bangor [Evans], and Carlile, Lord Paget, Lord Chief Baron [Ward], &c. The Lord Treasurer [Godolphin] haveing (on Petition of the Commissioners) ordered 500 *l*. for the payment of the Officers,[93] &c. an Order was made for 100 *l*. of that Summ to be immediately paid to (their Secretary) Mr Chamberlain; who was also to bring in an Account of his Disbursements in order to a farther Allowance. Accounts of Liveings under the value of 80 *l*. to be presently given in by the Bishops.[94]

After Dinner, I visitted Dr Gibson's; whither came also Dr Hody and Dr Sydel,[95] the former returning with me (cross the water) to Temple-stairs: whence to my brother Joseph's, where the Evening spent at Ease.

[Nov.] 3. *Saturday*. In the morning Sir W. Fleming sent me a Copy of his Baronet's Patent; which stiles him *Virum familias Patrimonio Censu et moru probitate spectatum, qui Nobis Auxilium et Subsidium satis Amplum Generoso et liberali animo dedit et prestitit ad manutenend et Supportand triginta viros in Cohortibus Nostris Pedestribus in dicto Regno nro. Hibernicae per tres annos integros* &c. And the Honour is granted—*Habend sibi et Haered Masculis de Corpore suoe legitime procreat. et pro defectu talis exitus Haeredibus masculis de Corpore Danielis Fleming Mil. defunct.*[96] *(nuper patris dicti Gulielmi Fleming) procreat. et Haered Mascul. de Corporibus taliu. Haeredu Masculoru. in perpotuum.*[97] Haveing visitted sister Rothery (and occasionally seen Mr Thynn's[98] Medals) I dined with Mr C. Musgrave, Mr Hales, the other Guest[s] Mr Burton and Coll. Grahme.

[93] The original establishment of the Bounty office consisted of a secretary (John Chamberlayne, for whom see Appendix A), a treasurer (Edward Tenison), and their respective clerks. See G. F. A. Best, *Temporal Pillars* (Cambridge, 1965), pp. 112–17.

[94] Ultimately they discovered 5,082 such livings, charged for taxation. For the work of the commissioners see Best, *op. cit.*, ch. 5, especially pp. 78–84; A. Savidge, *The Foundation and Early Years of Queen Anne's Bounty* (London, 1955).

[95] Elias Sydall (d. 1733), chaplain to Archbishop Tenison, later Bishop of St David's (1730) and Gloucester.

[96] Sir Daniel Fleming, (1633–1701) of Rydal, MP for Cockermouth 1685–7.

[97] In accordance with this special remainder, Fleming was succeeded by his brother George Fleming, then Bishop of Carlisle, 1735–47.

[98] Hon. Henry Thynne (1675–1708), son of 1st Viscount Weymouth, was MP for Weymouth and Melcombe Regis, 1701, 1702–8 and Tamworth, 1701–2. Nicolson's sister looked after Thynne's two daughters.

[Nov.] 4. *Sunday*. At the Queen's Chappel: Dr Stanhop, Dean of Canterbury, preached on (a part of the Gospel for the Day) forgiveing of Private Trespasses; proportioning 1000 Talents to 100 pence at the difference of 600,000 to one. Her Majesty received the Sacrement after the two Archbishops and five Bishops had it given 'em in both kinds, from the Dean of Chappel [Bishop Compton]: And the Organ and Voices assisted (before consecration) at *Holy, Holy*, &c. and (after the Administration) at the Gloria in excelsis.

To Dinner at the Archbishop of York's where also Dr Bently and Mr Laughton;[99] the latter a hearty Defender of Mr Hoadley's Sermon at the late Election of the Lord Mayor.[100] Dr B[entley] much for an Incorporated Union[101] of both Scotland and Ireland with England; foretelling that, without this, we should (in 50 years time) see an Independent King at Edinburgh, and another in Dublin. *Absit*!

[Nov.] 5. *Munday*. Procession, after prayers and Adjournment, to Westminster Abbey; where the Bishop of Lincoln preached a hearty Sermon against the *Teachers* (of the Roman Church) *in Sheeps-Clothing*, and their Dissimulation and Treachery.[102] In the Evening, a visit paid to Lady Lonsdale; who purposes to return to Lowther in the Spring.

[Nov.] 6. *Tuesday*. I walked, in the morning, round the Park with the Archbishop of York who in better Cheer than a week agoe; and waited on His Grace to the House: where prayers were read (the first time) by the Bishop of Lincoln. After which, the Queen's Answer to the Address reported by the Lord Keeper;[103] and (on the motion of the Earl of Rochester) the Call of the House ordered on Munday next. Young Lord Lonsdale brought in by Lord Wharton,[104] Lord Weymouth haveing not been acquainted with his Design of

---

[99] Probably Richard Laughton (?1668–1723), a Cambridge Fellow and a friend of Dr Bentley. An ardent supporter of the Newtonian system, he became Vicar of Quy-cum-Stow, Cambridgeshire in 1709.

[100] For Benjamin Hoadly, see Appendix A. His sermon of 29 Sept. 1705, on the text, 'Let every Soul be subject to the higher powers', was a violently controversial attack on the doctrine of unlimited passive obedience (see Bennett, *Tory Crisis*, p. 106), for which he was condemned by the Lower House of Convocation and criticised by Bromley in the Commons and Compton in the Lords. For Hoadly's defence, and his early career in general see E. R. Bingham, 'The Political Apprenticeship of Benjamin Hoadley', *Church History*, xvi (1947), 157–8.

[101] i.e. a fuller 'incorporating' union, with a common parliament, as opposed to a federal union.

[102] A sermon appropriate for the day.   [103] *LJ* xviii, 13.

[104] A carefully premeditated piece of Junto sponsorship, as the subsequent reference to Weymouth underlines. Weymouth was Lonsdale's uncle.

comeing thither, though he and's mother Suped with his Lordship the night before.

After I had dined, came to me Dr Gibson and Mr Wotton; the latter haveing gotten a Prebend in the Church of Salisbury and the Tuition of the Lord Finch[105] (eldest son to the Earl of Nottingham) not so well taken care of at Christ-Church. His Lordship also declares, That he'l send no more of his sons to Oxford.[106]

[Nov.] 7. *Wednesday*. I walked in the morning to Kennington. This day the lower House of Convocation presented (Dr Binks, Dean of Litchfeild)[107] for their Prolocutor, by Dr Aldrich his predecessor;[108] who complained hard of the long Sleep of Convocations, and their being under disturbances ever since the time (about 5 years agoe) that they awaked. He avowed the Rights of the Lower House; but seemed willing that those Disputes might be posponed for the present, that greater matters (the dangerous Growth of Heresies and Schisms) might be considered. The Prolocutor's speech followed; wherein the great services and sufferings of some Bishops in view (in King James's Reign) were magnifyed, and a hearty Obedience to the whole Order promised. The Archbishop of Canterbury concluded with a Fatherly Admonition to beware of Suggestions of Danger, to serve undutiful Purposes.[109]

In the House of Peers, I brought young Lord Lonsdale to my Lord of Canterbury. Dr Gibson and Mr Grandorge dined with me at our old Landlord's; where Measures adjusted in favour of the Latter. The Evening at my Brother's in Salisbury-Court; whence Mr Wotton accompanyed me to Charing-Cross.

[Nov.] 8. *Thursday*. Dr Hickes, in the morning, brought a memorial from Mr Grascome about the Tithes of Newburn.[110] The Lease shall

[105] Daniel Finch, fourth but first surviving son of 2nd Earl of Nottingham, who succeeded his father in 1730; MP for Rutland, 1710-30. He matriculated at Christ Church, Oxford, in 1704, but did not take a degree, and Nicolson, on his journey home in Mar. 1706, found him with his new tutor at Middleton Keynes Rectory.

[106] It is interesting that Nottingham preferred a sound scholarly education to the High Church Tory indoctrination in which Christ Church notoriously excelled.

[107] William Binkes, see Appendix A.

[108] Aldrich, as the leader of Lord Rochester's faction among the Tory clergy, had manœuvred Binkes into the chair to check-mate Atterbury. He had a majority of fourteen votes over Dr Stanhope. Luttrell, v, 604; Bennett, *Tory Crisis*, p. 83.

[109] Tenison and the Whig bishops were soon to dig a pit for the high-flying clergy, using the latter's 'Church in danger' agitation of the past year as bait. Bennett, *Tory Crisis*, pp. 83-5.

[110] The tithes of Newburn in Northumberland had been granted by Henry I to the priory of Carlisle in 1123, and ten years later the church formed part of the endowment of the newly formed bishopric of Carlisle. In the late seventeenth century the vicarage was valued at £30. The impropriation in 1736 was worth £300. M. H. Dodds, *A History of Northumberland*, xiii (Newcastle, 1930), 119-20.

not be renewed without his Consent. The House adjourned, and Dinner over, I went to view Brother Joseph's Dispensations for *Dioscordium* and Venice Treacle. The chief of the many Ingredients, Beaver's Codds, Cakes of Saffron, English Vipers or Adders, two Skinks or fine Lizzards, Agorick, &c. Thence to Dr Waugh's Barrel of Oysters. Straitned in my writeing of Letters by Mr Buttle; ful of Dr Plukenet and his own Collection of Grasses and Mosses.[111]

[Nov.] 9. *Friday*. I went, with Mr Dean of Wells [Grahme], to Kensington: where, after Prayers were ended and the Queen had touched four Children for the Evil,[112] I kissed Her Majesty's hand. She was, pleased to enquire what weather and Roads I met with in comeing to Town, &c. Afterwards, I waited on the Prince; who healthy and pleasant, beyond what I expected.[113] When we came, we found his Highness on Horse back; and the Queen in Her Chaise. Haveing spent two Hours in walking about the fine Garden, Wilderness and Green-House, I dined with Mr Dean and (one of the Dressers) Mrs Cowper:[114] And, returning by Coll. Graham's, got to my own Lodgeings about Nine. NB. The Queen's Dressing-Room hung with Neddle-work, in Satin, of the late Queen's ordering (and joynt assistance) by Dutch women: And the great Gallery stored with excellent Pictures. The whole much Superiour to the Palace at St James's.[115]

[Nov.] 10. *Saturday*. Mr Le Neve[116] kindly called on me in the morning; and carryed me to the Tally-Office in the Exchequer: Where he shewed me several Bundles of antient Fines and Recoveries in the Counties of Cumberland and Westmerland (sent in hither from the King's Bench &c.) which may [be] of great use in the History of my Diocese. The House of Lords not sitting, I went to dine at Lambeth; where I found the Archbishop of Dublin (thought by every body to be strangely paradoxical and a little crazed) the Bishop of

---

[111] For the botanical interests of Adam Buddle (d. 1715) and Leonard Plukenet (d. 1706), see *DNB* on both men.

[112] Scrofula. Anne was the last English sovereign to 'touch' for 'the King's Evil'.

[113] Prince George of Denmark was subject to chronic asthma. It killed him in 1708.

[114] One of the Queen's bedchamber women, later awarded a pension of £200 'being a poor Old Sickly Creature that is quite starving'. ULC Cholmondeley (Houghton) Papers 53, item 37.

[115] St James's, the Queen's normal winter residence, was notoriously inconvenient and inadequate.

[116] Peter Le Neve (1661–1729), Norroy King-at-Arms, FRS, 1711, President of the Antiquarian Society, 1717-24. At this time he was Deputy Chamberlain of the Exchequer (resigned 1706).

Chichester, Sir H. Ashhurst,[117] Sir Isaac Newton, Dr Bentley, Dr Mandevil,[118] &c.

After Dinner, Dr Gibson and I withdrew to his House from Dr Sydel's Chamber: And thence, being furnished with a Cloak, I had a rough Passage to Manchester-Court. I called on Sir W. Fleming; who had been visitted, for an hour and half before, by the great Earl of Portland. Mr Thomlinson from Rose.

[Nov.] 11. *Sunday*. At the Queen's Chapple, Dr Blackhall[119] made an Excellent sermon on the nature of Presumptuous Sins; very casuistical and Scholastic.[120] My Lord of York invited me again to Dinner: but I declined, and fed at h[ome]. After a fruitless search for Lady Lawson in Smith-street, I went to Dr Lancaster's: where I had the conversation of the Bishop of Killalow [Killaloe] (Dr Lindsey) the Arch-Deacons of Essex and Colchester,[121] and Dr Hutton, all High Church. The Bishop saies the 1200 *l.* per Annum on the Irish Civil-List, given by King William, is continued by the Queen; notwithstanding the late Vote of their Commons for its being withdrawn.[122]

Dr Hutton acquaints me that Mr Secretary Harley has purchased Sir Symonds Dewes's Library,[123] and has a great many Original Saxon Charters, as there are also in the Custody of Dean and Chapter of St Paul's, not hitherto examined: And Dr L[ancaster] assures me that he has seen the Original Instruments of Collation &c. of Dr

[117] Sir Henry Ashurst (1645-1711), 1st Bt. of Waterstock, Oxfordshire. A merchant, he had been MP for Truro, 1681-95, and Wilton, Wiltshire, 1698-1702.

[118] Probably John Mandeville (*c.*1655-1725), Chancellor of Lincoln, 1695-1713, Archdeacon of Lincoln, 1709-25, and Dean of Peterborough, 1722-5.

[119] Offspring Blackall, Rector of St Mary, Aldermary, London, later Bishop of Exeter, see Appendix A.

[120] A less 'scholastic' but more notorious sermon on the same theme was later preached by another High Churchman, Henry Sacheverell (*The Nature, Guilt and Danger of Presumptuous Sins*, Oxford, 1708).

[121] Charles Alston and Jonas Wanley, Archdeacon of Colchester, 1704-22.

[122] This refers to the *regium donum*, an allowance paid yearly to the Presbyterian ministers in the north of Ireland. Granted first by Charles II, suspended by James II, it had been restored by William III, who doubled the annual sum to £1,200. It was a constant source of irritation to High Church Tories in Ireland during Anne's reign, and payment was eventually suspended in 1714. The Irish Commons voted the allowance 'an unnecessary branch of the establishment' in Oct. 1703. *CJ Ireland*, ii, 346-7; *CSPD 1703-4*, pp. 163-4; J. C. Beckett, *Protestant Dissent in Ireland, 1681-1780* (1948), pp. 106-10.

[123] Sir Simonds D'Ewes (1602-50), famous antiquary. Harley acquired the collection (which included well over 600 MSS) on 4 Oct. 1705 for £450 from the antiquary's grandson, Sir Simonds D'Ewes (*c.*1670-1722), 3rd Bt. The purchase was negotiated by Humphrey Wanley, who had inspected the library for Harley at D'Ewes's seat at Stowlangtoft in Suffolk in Oct. 1703. See C. E. Wright, 'Humfrey Wanley, Saxonist and Library-Keeper', *Proceedings of the British Academy*, xlvi (1960), 99-129; *Diary of Humfrey Wanley*, ed. C. E. and R. C. Wright, 2 vols. (1966), i, p. xv; and for Harley's book collecting C. E. Wright, *Fontes Harleiani* (1972).

Langbain to the Vicarage of Crosthwait, by Archbishop Usher, Commendatory Bishop of Carlile.[124]

[Nov.] 12. *Munday*. In the morning; visitted by Thomas Hall, turned Brandy-Merchant;[125] Cousin Joseph Briscoe, as poor as ever; Mr Grascome (with Mr Bell) for paying off the Mortgage on the Lease of Newburn, or selling the whole; Mr Dean of Carlile [Atterbury], kindly disposed towards Mr Whittingdale.[126]

After the Call of the House was over, and the Standing Orders were read, Lord Nottingham moved for an Address to Her Majesty humbly desireing Her to lay before the House the present State of the Kingdome of Scotland in Relation to the Succession and Union.[127] A long Debate followed hereupon: Which [was] accommodated at last by Lord Treasurer's [Godolphin's] moveing that the question might be stated—*For Her Majesty's laying before 'em what had passed in the Parliament of Scotland (since the last Session of the late Parliament in England) in Relation &c.* This unanimously agreed to; and a Committee appointed to meet in the Prince's Chamber, at Ten to morrow, in Order to draw up an Address Accordingly.

The Evening spent at Brother Joseph's in [Salisbury Court].[128]

[Nov.] 13. *Tuesday*. An Early Visit from Cous. Bridget Nicolson; who in eager hast for her son Fetherston's promotion. My Godson Charles,[129] she saies, is now in the straits; and bids fair for being Mate to a Barbadoe's Merchant-man.

At the Committee for the Address, Lord Nottingham Chairman; besides whom were onely present, the Duke of Beaufort, the Earls of Winchelsea, Anglesey, Rochester, Lord Viscount Weymouth, Bishop of Carlisle and Lord Grandvil [Granville].[130] On the Report,

---

[124] Gerard Langbaine, of Westmorland, had been Provost of Queen's College, Oxford, 1645–58. James Ussher, had been Bishop of Carlisle, 1642–56, which he held *in commendam* while Archbishop of Armagh, 1625–56.

[125] The embargo on French trade during the Augsburg and Spanish Succession Wars had a stimulating effect, 'to a prodigious degree' on English domestic production of brandy and spirits. D. Defoe, *The Complete English Tradesman* (London, 1745), ii, 218–20.

[126] Christopher Whittingdale (d. 1719), had been appointed to the lectureship at St Mary's, Carlisle, in Nov. 1703. His presentation by Nicolson to the living of Castle Sowerby caused a dispute between Atterbury, the Cathedral Chapter and the Bishop, which eventually led to the controversy over the validity of the Cathedral statutes. Ultimately Whittingdale was presented by the bishop to Sowerby, and in 1708 he was elected a minor canon of Carlisle. *CW* iii (1903), 15.

[127] A prelude to the 'Hanoverian motion' on the succession question, now being concerted by the High Tory opposition in the Lords.   [128] Illegible.

[129] Son of Bridget and James Nicolson of Penrith, born 1683. *CW* i (1901), 51.

[130] It is significant that, apart from Nicolson, the only lords to turn up were warm Tories.

an Amendment made [instead of *lay before this House*, which too disrespectful, *Order to be laid*, &c.][131] which easily admitted; tho' the other more agreable to the Order of the House yesterday. Lord Haversham moved that the Lords might be summoned, for that he had something more to offer. Lord Bradford objected, that something should be specially proposed. *Noe*, said the Earl of Rochester, *but the motion ought to be seconded*: Which was done by that Lord himself. To gratify Lord Bradford (however) in his own way, Lord Haversham pitched on the State of the Nation, as a copious Subject: Whereupon the House ordered to be summoned for Thursday, but adjourned (for takeing in Appeals) for to morrow.

At Lord of York's, I met with Sir Andrew Fountain; who collected Lord Pembroke's Roman Weights. [His Dipondium, he saies, weighs 3 *l.* and cost 15 pistols, tho' Copper.][132] *Item*. Mr Dean of Carlile, half in a passion about the Vice Dean [Tullie] and Chapter's presenting to Sowerby.[133] *Item*. The Bishop of Norwich [Moore]; who expects that the Addressing Lords[134] will move for sending for the young Prince of Hanover:[135] projected by the Earl of Rochester who busyed this Summer in makeing proposals of that kind. *Credat Judaeus!*

[Nov.] 14. *Wednesday*. The Lord Chamberlain [Kent] reported the Queen's Answer to the Address: That, Her Majesty had ordered the Secretary of Scotland [Mar] to lay before this House the Papers desired; and hoped they would be so, in a few dayes.[136] The Convocation made an Address on the Assurances, given by Her Majesty, to continue Her Countenance to the established Church.[137] Mr Dean of Wells and I dined with Coll. Grahme (still fond of his eldest son) and, after Attempts to visit the Dean of Salisbury [Younger], &c. spent the evening, with Brother Joseph at the *Greyhound*.

[Nov.] 15. *Thursday*. In the morning at Whitehall, at the Committee for Queen Ann's Bounty; where Dr Edward Brown[138] bound for Mr Tennison the Treasurer, and 100 *l.* ordered to Mr Chamberlaine.

---

[131] Nicolson's brackets.
[132] Nicolson's brackets.
[133] See above, n. 126.
[134] Those who had moved for the address on the succession and the union on 12 Nov.
[135] The 'Electoral Prince', the future George II.
[136] The address for proceedings relative to a union between Scotland and England since the last session of parliament is printed in *LJ* xviii, 17. The Queen's answer in ibid., p. 18.
[137] For the dispute between the two houses of Convocation over the addresses to the Queen see Lathbury, *Convocation*, pp. 397–8.
[138] Edward Brown (1644–1708), Physician in Ordinary to Charles II, President Royal College of Physicians 1704–8.

The Bishop of Sarum's account of the dull head of Generall Monk; who would have his Son Kit instructed no farther than to make Speeches in Parliament.[139]

In the House, the Duke of Montague introduced by the Dukes of Ormond and Bolton; the Earl of Manchester supplying the place of Earl Marshal. The Queen being come *Incognito*, the Lord Haversham made a long Speech;[140] which ended in a Motion for bringing hither the Presumptive Protestant Heir. He was backed by the Earls of Anglesey, Rochester and Nottingham, the Duke of Bucks, &c. and opposed by Duke of Devonshire, Lords Sommers, Halifax, &c. Lord Treasurer proposed an Accomodation, by altering the Motion to that of appointing a Day for [considering] the better security of the Protestant Succession in the House of Hannover. After a Tedious Debate, the 1st Question was stated; and the Previous Question (*whether that Question should now be put?*) passed in the Negative by so great a majority, that the first Movers did not think fitt to insist upon a Division. Then the Second was put, and carryed; and Munday next appointed for a Grand Committee to consider of Lord Treasurer's motion.

Dr Gibson undertakes the drawing up of a protestation for our Chapter, against Dean Atterbury's Constituteing a Vice-gerent.[141] Sir W. Fleming's visit from 10 til 12 at night. His great respect for Lady Thanet.

[Nov.] 16. *Friday*. Early in the morning pestered with Mrs Donning; whom I was forced to turn off in a passion. In the House, a few Lords Entered their Dissent against the throwing out of the former yesterday's Question,[142] two petitions of Appeals read, and the House adjourned to Monday. Coll. Grahme, the Dean of Wells and I, dined with Mr C. Musgrave, with whom I stayed on till Dr Lancaster

[139] Christopher Monck (succ. as 2nd Duke of Albermarle, 1670) made his first and only recorded speech in the Commons on 16 Nov. 1667 at the tender age of 13! A. Grey, *Debates of the House of Commons* (1769), i, 41; E. F. Ward, *Christopher Monck, Duke of Albermarle* (1915), p. 9.

[140] Subsequently printed. A version appears in *Parl. Hist.* vi, 457–61, and Burnet (*History* v, 231) notes how he made use of the Scottish situation to advance his case for inviting the Electoral Prince to England. The Court and Whigs had skilfully prepared their 'defences against my Lord Haversham's great guns' on the previous day. See above, sessional intro., pp. 287–8.

[141] Atterbury argued that the Chapter of Carlisle could take no action without the consent of the Dean, even in his absence, and that the logical corollary was that the Dean had the right to give his proxy to one of the members, in this case Hugh Todd. Vice-Dean Tullie and Nicolson's party in the Chapter objected, maintaining that in the absence of the Dean, the Vice-Dean and a majority of the Chapter could carry on business. See James, pp. 162–7 for the dispute.

[142] See *LJ* xviii, 19.

and Dr Alston came (with Mr Lake) for Evening-work; which continued, very pleasantly by Dr A[lston] till near 12 at night. NB. The present Lord Keeper's being led thro' Chancery-Lane by a Farmer in Kent.

[Nov.] 17. *Saturday.* In the morning, I walked to Kensington with my modest Kinsman Thomas Pearson; who is well pleased with his Curacy at Oxenden-Chapple. Haveing treated him at Dinner, I fell upon my dispatches: And Dr Gibson came in luckily with an Account that the Form of Protestation and Appeal was ready. I presently sent for it to Doctors' Commons;[143] and, haveing transcribed it, sent the Original to our Vicedean [Tullie].

[Nov.] 18. *Sunday.* After I had dined with my brother Joseph I went to St Andrew's-Holburn;[144] where I preached an Evening-Sermon, to the Stewards for poor girls Catechized, on *Psalms* 145, 15. *Meat in due Season.* The Church very full.

[Nov.] 19. *Munday.* In the way to the House, I waited on Lady Lawson; who fully instructed me in the Case betwixt Her and her Sister Donning:[145] That the reason of the writeings being still in Mrs Beak's hand is, because they contain a Demise of 120 *l.* per Annum for the Security of her 42 *l.* and her Trustees would never yet so far concern themselves as to seal the necessary Re-Demise.

After I had read prayers, the Queen being come and the Order of the day read, Lord Stamford took the Chair; and Lord Wharton opened the Debate with a pretty long Speech:[146] in which He took notice of Her Majesty's working *Miracles* by Her Speech, in bringing all men to be zealous for the Hannover-Succession; or Mr Dodwel's late book[147] about the *illegally deprived* Bishops, affirming that (by the same Rule) the man might affirm the Queen's Title to be *illegal.* He proposed several Heads for the intended Bill;[148] as, the appointing

[143] The hall of the College of Doctors of Civil Law in London, south of St Paul's Cathedral, housing the Court of Arches, Prerogative Court of Canterbury, Court of Faculties or Disputations, the Consistory Court of London, and the High Court of Admiralty. The site also included the chambers of the leading civil lawyers and many of their private residences.
[144] The great Wren church at the east end of Holborn, to which Dr Sacheverell was preferred in 1713.   [145] See above, n. 86.
[146] It began with a masterpiece of political irony on the Tory 'conversion'—'in a manner which charmed the whole house' (Burnet, *History*, v, 234). Cf. the good account in ibid., pp. 234–5; HMC *Lords MSS* vi, 322.
[147] Henry Dodwell (1641–1711), non-juror, had published in 1705 *A Case in View considered . . . to show that in case the then invalidly deprived fathers should all leave their sees vacant, either by death or resignation, we should not then be obliged to keep up our separation from the bishops who are in the guilt of that unhappy schism.*
[148] This was to become known as the Regency Bill. It 'provided for a caretaker govern-

of Lords Justices on the Queen's Demise, Amendment of the Deficiencies of the present Laws about the Succession, Naturalization of the Princes intitled to the Crown, &c. Lord Treasurer moved for the sending for the Judges: which was done by the Committee, without (as was moved) resumeing the House. Duke of Bucks seconded Lord Wharton's motion;[149] adding, that provision be made for the immediate declareing of the Succesor by Proclamation. Lord Sommers mentioned the particular Justices; as Archbishop of Canterbury, Lords Keeper, Treasurer, &c. Lord Haversham moved that, the Great Offices might be in Commission.[150] Lord Treasurer that the 1st Question might be stated (for Order's sake) about the Lords Justices. Lord Nottingham, That the Laws might first be rectifyed; and none of the chief Ministers be Justices.

In Conclusion — Resolved, *That on Demise of the Queen (whom God long preserve) the Privy-Counsel immediately direct the proclaiming of the next Protestant Heir on pain of High-Treason: And that, in Case of the Absence of such Successor, Lords Justices be appointed for the Administration of the Government (in the name of such Successor) till he or she arrives or gives Directions to the Contrary.* This being unanimously agreed to, and reported, was (in like manner) assented to by the House: And the Judges undertook to bring in, to morrow, their Observations on the Defects of the present Laws touching the Succession.

In the Evening — I waited on Lady Lonsdale, with my thoughts of the person sent to me for French-Master at Lowther; who (wanting Greek) is not qualifyed to answer my late Lord's Directions,[151] in teaching Alternately with Mr Lodge: And my Lady scrupulously adheres to Her deceased Lord's Rules. Sir J. Wentworth[152] wishes, as I do, that the Masters might have separate Tasks.

[Nov.] 20. *Tuesday*. In the morning, I waited on the Archbishop of York with the papers relateing to the controversy 'twixt our Dean

ment (the Lords Justices) and for an automatic summons of Parliament to bridge the critical time-gap between the Queen's death and the arrival of the Hanoverian heir, [and] was the brain-child of the Junto'. Holmes, *British Politics*, p. 84.

[149] An unexpected move by a High Tory only recently dismissed from Cabinet office.
[150] See Burnet, *History*, v, 236-7 for the disputes, now and later, over the composition of the Lords Justices.
[151] See J. V. Beckett, 'Lowther College, 1697–1740: "For none but gentlemen's sons" ', *CW* lxxix (1979), 103–7. Described by Nicolson as the best-endowed school in his diocese but 'not like to be of any long continuance'. *Miscellany*, pp. 36, 73. The school had been orignally designed as a factory and was to revert to one in 1739. See J. V. Beckett, 'Eighteenth-Century Origin of the Factory System', *Business Hist.* xix (1977), 57.
[152] Sir John Wentworth (1673–1720), 1st Bt. of Elmshall, Yorkshire, son-in-law of 1st Viscount Lonsdale.

and Chapter; which Satisfyed His Grace that the matter had been mis-represented to him. He intimated that Mr Dean insisted on the 33. Hen. 8. cap. 27, whence he would (incongrously) inferr that the Common-Law presumes the Dean's Consent necessary in all Grants.[153]

The Queen being come to the House, the Lord Sommers (in the Grand Committee)[154] proposed the Lord Archbishop of Canterbury for the first Lord Justice; who, after a short Debate, was agreed to. After a long struggle, Six more were named and added; viz. the Lords Keeper, Treasurer, President, Admiral, Privy-Seal and Chief Justice of the Queen's Bench: To whom the Successor impowered to add an unlimitted Number of other[s] (unknown) to Act by vertue of a Commission (Variable at pleasure) Tripartite; One to be lodged with the Resident Minister of the Court of Hannover, a Second with the Archbishop of Canterbury, and a Third with the Lord Keeper.[155] The House divided onely on two Questions. 1. Shall the Lord Mayor be one? *Contents*, 21. *Not Contents*, 50. 2. Shall the Lord Treasurer? *Contents*, 53. *Not Contents*, 18. On the latter, all the Bishops were with the Contents:[156] And, on the former, onely the Bishops of London and Bath and Wells for the Lord Mayor.

Sir W. Fleming with me in the Evening.

[Nov.] 21. *Wednesday*. The Queen present again (after I had read prayers, at the Desire of the Bishop of Lincoln, as yesterday and formerly) the Grand Committee proceeded on the subject of the Hannover Succession. Lord Chief Justice Holt reported the Defects of the present Laws in Being, in Relation to the Succession of the Crown: Which being severally considered, and proper Amendments proposed, the Judges were directed to frame a Bill on the Resolutions of the House; and to bring in another for the Naturalization of the whole House of Hannover, for the better enabling Her Majesty to confer Honours on any of that Family upon their comeing into her Kingdome.

In the Evening (after Enquireing for Mr Wanley[157] and Mr Gran-

[153] The 'Act for Leases of Hospitales, Colleges and other Corporations' laid down that in the rules of some colleges the dissent of one member shall prevent any grants. See *Statutes of the Realm*, iii, 867.

[154] On the intended Regency Bill.

[155] The Lord Keeper/Chancellor's copy of the Electress Sophia's secret list of nominees was later sealed up in what became known as 'the black box'. There was to be intensive speculation about its contents in the months preceding Anne's death, and some Jacobite members wanted the House of Commons to authorise its opening. J. Macpherson, *Original Papers*, 2 vols. (1775), ii, 618.

[156] See above, sessional intro., p. 289 for the voting of six Tory bishops against Rochester and Nottingham.

[157] Humfrey Wanley (1672–1726), Anglo-Saxon scholar, palaeographer, and librarian. He was appointed assistant librarian at the Bodleian in 1695, and from 1702 to 1708 was

dorge) I visitted Dr Hickes; who satisfyed, by Mr Roger North,[158] that *Soc* and *Sac* signify *Court-Leet* and *Court-Baron*. Thence to Mr Joseph Musgrave at Grey's Inn, who is much offended at his Tutour Todd's Impertinent politicks.

[Nov.] 22. *Thursday*. In the morning, Mr Wanley came to return my last night's visit; and expressed himself discouraged, as well as diverted, from his Design on the Saxon Scriptures. He saies, there are not above five or six Saxon Charters in all Sir Symonds Dewes's Collection; but some thousands of pretty antient Grants since the Conquest. Whilst he was with me, came in Dr Covel; who entertained us with a very agreable Discourse on Eastern Manuscripts and Amulets. In the former of these, he observed, there was commonly the Age noted, according to the Grecian Epoche from the Creation: which (this year 1705) is 7213, so that they reckon the world to have been 5508 years old on the birth of our Saviour. The Doctor also shewed us his great Skill in antient and modern musick.

In the House, Lord Nottingham began the Debate in the Committee, for Considering the State of the Nation, and concluded with a motion[159]—*That the Queen might be Addressed to lay before the House what had occasioned our Disappointments the last Campaign, on the Moselle, at OverIsche* [Overyssche], &c. After 4 hours Dispute (chiefly 'twixt His Lordship and the Lord Treasurer [Godolphin]), the Question was put by the Lord Herbert, Chairman, and carried in the Negative. *Contents*, 20. *Not Contents*, 53. Then Lord Wharton moved to Address Her Majesty *to preserve Her Alliances with the present Confederates, especially the States General; and to excite them, and all the rest, vigorously to prosecute the War against France*. This, being unanimously resolved and agreed to, was the onely matter Reported to the House: But Lord Rochester (in Order, as Supposed, to bring it and a protestation against its being carried in the Negative upon the Journal-Books) moved again Lord Nottingham's Question *in terminis*. This Lord Wharton would needs (with more Assurance than Authority) affirm to be un-parliamentary; and therfore before it could be seconded, moved for an Adjournment; which, being a little tumultuously seconded by Lord Halifax, prevailed.[160]

secretary of the SPCK. In 1705 he became Harley's librarian. An FRS and a founder member of the Society of Antiquaries, he supplied Nicolson with materials for his account of Harley's Library for the second edition of *The English Historical Library*. See *The Diary of Humphrey Wanley*, ii, 464–5.

[158] Roger North (1653–1734), lawyer and historian.
[159] Cf. *Parl. Hist.* vi, 475, where the motion is attributed to Haversham.
[160] See ibid., pp. 475–6 for the failure of this 'attempt . . . against the duke of Marlborough'.

[Nov.] 23. *Friday*. After prayers read (by me) in the House, the Queen being come, the Order of the Day was read. Lord Haversham opened the Debate;[161] and, in conclusion, moved for Repealing the Clause declareing the Scots Aliens. This was seconded by Lord Nottingham. Lord Sommers moved for the Repeal of the whole Act (that part onely excepted which related to the Empowring the Queen to name Commissioners for the Union)[162] and was seconded by Lord Rochester. The whole House readily assented; haveing first, in the Preamble of their Vote, resolved—*That the Queen had done Her Utmost for the settlement of the Protestant-Succession in Scotland and the Union of the Kingdomes.* The Bishop of Sarum (as a Scotchman) thanked the House for their Generous Vote; and, privately invited all to an 100 *l*. Treat on, this day Sennight, St Andrew's day.

In the Evening, Mr Grandorge with me at the Dean of Wells's Lodgeings; whence Mr H[enry] Grahme called home by his amorous Lady.[163]

[Nov.] 24. *Saturday*. The morning proved cold, and stormy with Snow; and this discouraged Lord Lonsdale from his design of dineing at Lambeth. Whereupon, I went in Quest of Dr Woodward at Gresham-College: But, not meeting with him, I returned to my Lodgeings, and spent the Day in privacy and writeing of Letters. In the Evening, Mr Chamberlain brought me News of an Express arrived from Barcelona; where our General had much adoe to save the French Garrison from being Massacred by the Inhabitants.[164]

[Nov.] 25. *Sunday*. At the Queen's Chapple, Mr Verney[165] preached on the Duty (*Job*. 2, 15) of submitting to all the Dispensations; well applyed to Courtiers and Great men. In the Evening, visitted by Mr Dean of Wells, Mr Vaughan and Mr C. Musgrave.

[161] 'The queen having laid between the two Houses the Addresses of the Scots Parliament against any progress in the Treaty of Union, till the Act which declared them aliens should be repealed.' Ibid., p. 476. For the Tory tactics in this debate, and the Whig counterploy, see ibid., pp. 476-7.

[162] 'The Whigs not only agreed to this, but carried the matter further to the other act [repl. 'clauses'?] relating to their manufacture and trade.' Ibid.

[163] Henry Grahme (for whom see Appendix A) had married, on 23 May 1705, Mary Tudor, the illegitimate daughter of Charles II and widow of the 2nd Earl of Derwentwater, who had been his mistress during her husband's lifetime. His father, Col. James Grahme, strongly disapproved of the match, and Henry St John called it 'so irretrievable a folly'. *CW* lxviii (1968), 123-4: St John to J. Grahme, 23 June 1705.

[164] See Trevelyan, *Queen Anne*, ii, 75.

[165] Probably George Verney (1661-1728), who succeeded in 1711 as 4th Lord Willoughby de Broke and was appointed Dean of Windsor in 1714. At this time he was Rector of Southam, War., and Canon of Windsor.

[Nov.] 26. *Munday*. In the morning, I went to the Tower; where the Alterations (both about the Office of Records, and in the White Tower) in a good forwardness. I found Dr Hutton (of Ayno) hard at work; haveing taken Abstracts of all Ecclesiastical matters in the Charter and Patents Rolls as low as the middle of Richard the Second's Reign. He was so kind as to communicate to me several of his notes relateing to the Diocese of Carlile; and to shew me his Corrections on Goodwin's book *De presulibus*;[166] which he finds to be a loose performance. The Charter-Rolls in the Tower, haveing marginal Directions, are quickly run over: But the patent and Close Rolls are more troublesome. Mr Holmes very kind in proffering his services to me.

At Dinner (together with Mr Comptroller Mansel and Mr Bond) at Mr C. Musgrave's; whence to Salisbury-Court. Dr Woodward will have me a Fellow of the Royal Society.

[Nov.] 27. *Tuesday*. Morning, Mr Rook[167] with a Letter from Mr How[168] of Carlile; desireing the Removeal of the present School-master, or a new one Licensed.[169] Cousin Joseph Briscoe; starveing for want of a place in Chelsea.

The Queen made a Speech from the Throne[170] on Occasion of Letters[171] received from the King of Spain and Earl of Peterborough upon their Success in Catalonia; and ended with Application to the Commons for an Enlargement of their Supply, and to both Houses for a speedy Dispatch. Being disrobed, She returned to the House *Incognito*; and heard an Unanimous Vote passed for a Congratula-tory Address and Request to print the Letter. Then three Acts were given in by the Judges and Read: 1. For the better Security of the Protestant Succession.[172] 2. Naturalization of the House of Hannover. 3. Repeal of the Scotch Interdict of Traffick, &c. Adjourned.

NB. Two Judges, being sent with the Address to Her Majesty (of the 22d) to the Commons, desireing their concurrence; they

---

[166] *De Praesulibus Angliae Commentarius* (1616), Bishop Francis Goodwin's own trans-lation of his work *A Catalogue of the Bishops of England since the first planting of Christian Religion in this Island* (1601).

[167] W. Rook was an attorney and Town Clerk of Carlisle. *CW* iv (1904), 15.

[168] Probably the Alderman, John How, who was five times Mayor of Carlisle. He was sometime organist of Carlisle Cathedral. *CW* i (1901), 20–1. He may also be the John How who was Lord Lonsdale's agent in the Burgh Barony and who was Westmorland Land Tax Commissioner, 1692–1702, and Cumberland Land Tax Commissioner, 1710–14. Hopkinson, pp. 158–9, 320–1.

[169] For the trouble caused by the various masters at Carlisle Cathedral School, including John Stephenson (Master, 1704–10), see James, p. 152; *ĆW* iii (1903), 33, 46.

[170] See *LJ* xviii, 29–30.

[171] Translations printed in ibid., pp. 30–2.

[172] i.e. the Regency Bill.

withdrew as usual; and, a Debate ariseing about their present Agreement, they waited (till after the Lords were risen) above an Hour, and were then dismissed with — *We will send an Answer by Messengers of our own.* Query. Ought they not to have left the Address, as they do Bills, and to have returned immediately? No; saies Lord Stamford.

[Nov.] 28. *Wednesday.* Three Bills read a Second time; and Committed for to morrow. Lord Hartington[173] brought up the Message from the Commons; who agreed to the Address without any Alterations: Soon after which a Message was sent to them to acquaint 'em that Her Majesty had appointed half an hour after two (to morrow) to be attended by both Houses, with their Address, at St James's; and that the Lords resolved to be there at that hour. The House was moved for leave to bring in an Appeal, notwithstanding the 14 Dayes were lapsed: which motion (from Lord Hallifax) opposed by Lord Nottingham, alledgeing that the Appeal was vexatious, &c. and therefore not to be countenanced by breach of a Standing Order.[174] 'Twas proposed that one Counsel might be heard on each side, waveing the Merits, on the Circumst[ant]ials; so far as to inform their Lordships what Room there was for their Admittance of it to a Hearing: But Lord Treasurer observed that this method was new, and might be of inconvenient Consequence; and therfore moved that this motion might be considered on Saturday, against which Time some Noble Lords would be able to give greater Light. Which was unanimously assented to.

[Nov.] 29. *Thursday.* A motion being made for the Order of the Day's being Read, Lord Nottingham moved that it might be an Instruction to the Grand Committee (now goeing to take into their Consideration the Bill for the better Security of the Protestant Succession) to make provision against certain Laws (reckoned up) being Repealed, after the Demise of the Queen, by the Lords Justices; which occasioned a long Debate. In the End, Lord Rochester (with a warmth more than common) moved that, at least, the Act of Uniformity might be Intrenched; declareing that (unless this was done) tho' he would not *say* that the Church of England was in Danger dureing Her Majesty's Life, he could not help *thinking* that

[173] Whig MP for Yorkshire, succeeded in 1707 as 2nd Duke of Devonshire, see Appendix A.

[174] Standing order no. 69 of 1678 stated that appeals had to be presented to the House 'within fourteen dayes, to be accounted from, and after the first day of every Session, or Meeting of Parliament, after a Recesse'. HMC *Lords MSS* x, 15–16. For the appeal see ibid. vi, 328. An appeal was also allowed if made within fourteen days of the judgment from a court sitting concurrently with parliament.

it would be so upon Her Demise.[175] This was spoken with such a peculiar Zeal and Emphasis, that it had a Notable Effect upon the House; who presently ordered the Judges to attend to morrow, with their Advice how to provide against any such hazard.

Bill for Repeal of the Clauses against Traffick with Scotland was read a Third Time; passed and sent down to the Commons. Betwixt two and three in the Afternoon, both Houses of Parliament waited on the Queen at St James's; a Rarity not seen since 1692. The Lord Keeper [Cowper] read the Address; the Speaker of the House of Commons[176] standing on his left hand.

In Charles-street Westminster I treated (with Mr Hornsby's Vennison) Dr Waugh, Mr Smith and Cousin Thomas Pearson, with my brother Joseph, and afterwards sent off twelve Letters by the Post.

[Nov.] 30. *Friday*. St Andrew's day. Mr Elstob calling on me in the morning, I took him with me to Sir Andrew Fountain's Lodgeings; where we were most agreably entertained with a sight of a most valuable Collections of Medals and Coins, Greek, Roman, Saxon, &c. The chief remarkables: 1. Ten Nummi Restituti of Galienus. 2. Thirty-two of the said Emperour; with Reverses of different Birds or Beasts, or in different postures. 3. Nineteen Legions, and Twenty-six Divinities, of the same. [All or most of these he had from one person in Bishop-Gate-street: the same, I suppose, whom my Lord Pembroke mentioned to me the last winter].[177] 4. Three Salonina's, with three several Veneres (Venus Victrix, Faelix and Genetrix) on the Reverse. 5. The XXXᵃ Ulpia Legio of Galienus; a Duplicate of which (very Rare) he gave to Lord Pembroke. 6. Another of Galienus with *Vict. aet. s. p.* on the Reverse: in one of the Samples whereof (for he has three of 'em; all somewhat differing) the *p* is put 'twixt e and t: which occasioned Monsieur Vaillant's[178] reading it Nept. as if the Medal had been struck in Memory of Some Sea-Victory. 7. Pescenius Niger. 8. Julia Mameias Aug. 9. Caracalla; with a Julia Augusta on the R[everse]. 10. Caracalla and Severus. [Capita Juguta][179] 11. Theodobertus Franconum R. in Gold. small. 12. Patin's[180] Καισαρ Σεβαστος (in brass) and three more cost him

---

[175] Cf. Burnet's rather different recollection of Rochester's speech: 'in his positive way said, if this was not agreed to, he should still think the church was in danger, not withstanding what they have heard from the throne, in the beginning of the session.' *History*, v, 237–8.

[176] John Smith, Speaker since Oct. 1705. See Appendix A.

[177] Nicolson's brackets.

[178] Jean Vaillant (1632–1706), French author of many numismatic works.

[179] Nicolson's brackets.

[180] Charles Patin (1633–93), French antiquary and numismatist.

about 80 *ll*. He also bought up the whole Collection of the said
Patin at Padua. 13. A Roman Head in Gold, set in a Ring, the Con-
vex side being out; under which the Concave, of the same face,
makes an Impression finer than the Prototype. 14. A Coin of Attila,
King of the Hunns, in Gold. 15. Two Hundred and Thirty-Six Saxon
Coins in Silver with Ten or Twelve of the Northymbrians in brass.
[He gives 2s. 6d. for each piece of Saxon; which brings him in the
Monopoly][181] 16. A Series of the Roman Coins de aere minimo
(called also Sextula); which convinced me that Dr Smith's Medal of
Caravsius and Allectus are of this Class, and not (as he would have
'em) de aere medio. 17. Thomas Simon's[182] Tryal-piece of Charles
the Second's Crown; with his petition round the Rim. 18. Henry
the 7th's Shilling; the full weight of three of his Groats. [The Archbishop of York has a Couple of these.][183] 19. Half-Crown, Shilling
and Six-pence, of the Common-wealth of England, finely milled, by
Simon, who sets round the Edge of the Half-Crown *In the third year
of Freedom by Gods blessing restored.* [The remembrance of this
threw him out of King Charles the Second's favour.][184] 20. A XX^S
X^S and Crown-pieces of Charles I coined at Oxford 1642. 21. A
Three-Shillings piece of the Carlile-Coin (in the Siege 1645) very
fair. 22. King Philip's Coin after the death of Queen Mary, with
Phil. R. Ang. Fr. Neap. Pr, and, on the Reverse, *Fidei Defensor* in
a Laurel. One Shilling, value. 23. Half-Crown of the same (with the
Arms of England) after the Queen's Death. 24. Queen Elizabeth's
Scutu Fidei in Gold; as finely milled as Her Shillings and Sixpences.
25. A true Nero; with a Counterfeit Adlocutio carved on the Reverse.
Sir Andrew shewed us also a lovely Wolf (with Romulus and Remus)
which he had, cast in Brass, from Mr Wrenn; Monsieur Molinet's
Cabinet de la Biliotheque de Saint Genevieve,[185] richly stocked with
Antiquities, particularly a Draught of the Dipondiu, which Sir
Andrew himself lately transferred (with many more choice Rarities)
from his own Cabinet to Lord Pembroke's; &c. He gave us a pleasant
Account of the Italian plowmen imposeing on Travellers, by pretend-
ing to find Medals just as come up to 'em; and of Dr Battely's[186]

---

[181] Nicolson's brackets.

[182] Thomas Simon (?1623–65), English medallist and seal engraver.

[183] Nicolson's brackets. Sharp had helped Nicolson over certain numismatic problems
in his *English Historical Library*, see London UL MS 66, f. 100: MS of Sharp's 'Of the
Silver Coins of England'.

[184] Nicolson's brackets.

[185] Claude du Molinet (1620–87), French antiquary and writer, and librarian of the
Abbey of Ste Geneviève at Châlons-sur-Marne. He established a cabinet of curiosities
described in *Le Cabinet de la Bibliotheque de Ste-Geneviève* (1692).

[186] John Batteley (1646–1708), Kentish antiquary, Archdeacon of Canterbury since
1687 and collector of Roman antiquities.

Labienus (with Cingulum on the Reverse) being onely a Copy of a Counterfeit.

In the House (the Queen being come, and the Order of the day read) the Judges were directed to give their Opinions—*Whether the same Law that made Lords Justices might not limit and restrain them in the exercise of their power?* They were Divided, as usually, in their Determinations, For, 1. Chief Justice Holt, Chief Baron Ward and Mr Justice Blencow, doubted whether any such Restrictions could be made; because these officers were the same (in Effect) with the antient *Custodes Regni*; who were Invested, *pro tempore*, with Regal Authority: Which, acting in Conjunction with a Parliament, could not be restrained. And, Chief Baron Ward gravely compared this Authority with a Tenancy in Fee-simple; which could not be made unalienable for that would be to destroy its Nature. 2. The other Eight Judges (Chief Justice Trevor, Justices Powel, Powis, Gould, and Tracy, Barons Bury, Price and Smith) were of Opinion, and thought, beyond Dispute, that these intended Justices (as they were onely *Occasional Creatures* of this present Parliament), so they might have powers in such a proportion, and with such Limitations, as should be thought most proper: That the *Custodes Regni* of Old, in the Absence of our Kings, were frequently restrained from Calling of Parliaments and could never Act beyond their Instructions. Mr Justice Powis observed, in Return to the Chief Baron's Argument, that (though Lands in Fee-simple could not be wholly unalienable, yet) a man might tye up his Heir Specially, That he should not convey it to John a Stiles.[187]

Hereupon, the Lord Rochester repeated his motion, *That it should be an Instruction to the Committee to receive a Clause of restraining the Lords Justices from Repealing or altering the Act of Uniformity*, This, after a short Debate, was Unanimously assented to: But, the Lord Nottingham offering at the like Security for a great many other Laws,[188] the Question was put — *Whether any more Instructions?* and carryed in the Negative by 53 against 27.

The House [being] adjourned,[189] and Lord Stamford in the Chair, the Lord Nottingham moved for his Laws being secured; and (first) the Test-Acts were proposed as fit to be guarded against any Change under the Justices: Which was put to the Question, and (this being carryed in the Negative upon Division) the rest were severally proposed and rejected, without insisting on a Scrutiny. The House being

[187] Fictitious name for a party to a legal action.
[188] Including the Habeas Corpus Act, the Triennial Act, and the Trial of Treasons Act (see Luttrell, v, 618; Burnet, *History*, v, 238) and the Test Acts of 1673 and 1678.
[189] Into a Committee of the Whole.

resumed, Lord Stamford Reported — That the Committee had made a Good Progress: And, an Order being made for their goeing again into a Committee to morrow, the House was Adjourned near seven at night. NB. The Queen had the patience to sit out all these long Debates; bringing St Andrew's Cross, and the other Badges of the Order of the Thistle, with her.

Upon some words that dropped in the Course of these Debates, Lord Hallifax took notice that a great deal of pains had been taken to mis-represent several Persons of Honour and Quality as disaffected to the present Establishment of the Church of England; and moved that a Day might be appointed to consider of that Matter. This Motion was forthwith seconded by Lord Rochester; who desired that the Order might stand on the Book for appointing Thursday next to take Her Majesty's Gracious Speech into Consideration, and that the Lords would understand that part of it which related to Reports spread of the Church's being in danger.[190]—After Lord Nottingham had run over all his Acts which (as he thought) wanted the Guaranty of this Bill, and the House was about to adjourn, the Duke of Richmond beged their Insurance of King William's Act for the Preservation of the Game;[191] which was thought too light a motion for the place, and his coupling it with those concerning the Sacramental Test seemed to be the most extraordinary Circumstance in it.

Memorandum. This day, being the chief Anniversary Day of Meeting of the Royal Society, I had the Honour to be named one of their Members;[192] being proposed (without any Allowance or Consent of my own) by, my friend, Dr Woodwoard. Je vous remercy.

Dec. 1. *Saturday*. In the morning, Mr Maul[193] with a Letter from the Bishop of Cloine;[194] who is pestered with his Chancellor's[195] insolent giveing of Institution, without his Privity or Commission, as Vicar-General. The matter is now before the Queen's Bench at Westminster; being removed hither by Writt of Errour. Lord Chief Justice Holt

[190] For the debate on 'the Church in danger' see below, 6 Dec.

[191] Richmond, a Whig grandee, was doubtless indulging in a little mild fun at the expense of the archetypal High Tory squire, of whom Addison wrote: 'he affirmed roundly, that there had not been one good law passed since King William's accession to the Throne, except the act for preserving the Game' (*The Freeholder*, No. 22, 5 Mar. 1716).

[192] Seven other Fellows were elected that day along with Nicolson, including Archbishop William King of Dublin, see *Records of the Royal Society of London*, 4th edn. (1940), p. 390.

[193] Henry Maule (c.1687-1758), Prebendary of Lackeen, Cloyne, 1702-20, later Dean and Bishop of Cloyne.

[194] Charles Crow, Bishop 1702-26.

[195] Edward Sayers or Sayres, Chancellor of Cloyne, 1693-d. 1730.

seems (as yet) to incline to the Chancellor which is a point of Law that agrees with his forementioned Opinion about the power of the *Custodes Regni*.

In the House, the Hannover-Bill was gone through, Reported and Ordered to be Ingrossed. The Weather and Business again stopped my goeing to Lambeth with Lord Lonsdale.

[Dec.] 2. *Sunday*. I preached at St Martin's (present Lord Sommers and Rockingham) and dined, with Mr Arundel and his Lady,[196] at the Vicarage. Visitted in the Evening by Sir Philip Sydenham; who gives a dismal Account of the Lewdness of. Mr Blackburn (alias Martin) Dean of Exon, and of the Bishop's loseing himself in the Opinion of his Clergy.[197]

[Dec.] 3. *Munday*. After I had dispatched Cousin Joseph Briscoe and his brother Frank with a Letter to Coll. Fletcher,[198] I was called on by W. Rook; who sollicites for J. How's succeeding Mr Eglesfield, for whom (it seems) Mr Gilpin[199] stands bound. I directed him to enquire how Bishop Smith's School-money was setled at Carlile; and he (on talking about the Suit 'twixt the City and the men of Dalston)[200] assured me that he moved onely for a new Tryal against those of Linstock and Crossby, who had no liveing Testimony for 'em.

In the House, the Duke of Argyl[201] (Argwytheel, Argathelia i.e. Over against Ireland saies the Bishop of Hereford [Humphries]) was

---

[196] Probably Francis Arundell of Stoke, Northamptonshire, MP for Northampton since Nov. 1704, and his wife Isabella Wentworth, sister of Lord Raby, a former maid-of-honour to Queen Anne, whom he m. in July 1703. Luttrell, v, 321.

[197] For the strained relations between Bishop Trelawney and his High Church clergy in the Exeter diocese during 1705, see HMC *Portland MSS* iv, 176-7, 213-14: Lord Poulet and Daniel Defoe to Robert Harley, 2 May, 30 July 1705; N. Sykes, 'The Cathedral Chapter of Exeter and the General Election of 1705', *EHR* xlv (1930), 260-72.

[198] George Fletcher, MP for Cumberland, see Appendix A.

[199] William Gilpin (1657-1724), barrister, Deputy Vice-Admiral of Cumberland, principal adviser in law and business to Sir John and James Lowther of Whitehaven. (His abundant correspondence with the Lowthers is in Cumbria RO, Carlisle, Lonsdale MSS.) He succeeded John Aglionby as Recorder of Carlisle in 1718. It was Gilpin who drew up the Act 'for preserving and enlargeing the harbour of Whitehaven', 1708. In 1695 Gilpin had stood surety for Eaglesfield and in July 1706 petitioned for the discharge of all proceedings on his bond (*CTB 1705-6*, p. 697; below, n. 430).

[200] About 1698 a suit in Chancery was started between the Corporation of Carlisle and the bishop and his tenants of Dalton, Crosby, and Linstock concerning their paying tolls to the corporation. The issue was settled (after more than £1,000 had been spent by the bishop's tenants) on 7 July 1707. See Nicolson and Burn, ii, 312.

[201] John Campbell, 2nd Duke of Argyll, had on 26 Nov. 1705 been created Earl of Greenwich in the peerage of England. This was the price the ministry had to pay for ensuring his support of the Union. See W. Ferguson, 'The Making of the Treaty of Union', *SHR* xliii (1964).

introduced by the Earls of Kingston and Rivers, the Duke of North-umberland supplying the place of Lord High Chamberlain; and his patent was read for Earl of Greenwich and Baron of Chatham. Soon after he was Seated, the Queen came to the House; and His Grace bore the Sword before Her to the Throne, appointed thereto by the Duke of Northumberland as Chamberlain.

Her Majesty haveing given the Royal Assent to the Bill for enabl-ing the House of Hannover to be Naturalized,[202] went away; and the House (according to Order) had the Bill for Security of Her Majesty's person and the Protestant Succession read a Third Time. Before the Question was putt for its passing, the Earl of Nottingham offered a Rider for Security of the two Test-Acts. Upon this Debate, a Question was putt; and carryed (upon Division, 52 against 22) in the Negative. Several Others had the like Fate; but without divideing. Lord Nottingham then moved for an enlargement of the power of the Lords Justices, that they might supersede Commissions in the Army: which (said Lord Sommers) may, if need were, be provided for by an Amendment at the Table; but there's no Occasions the Bill in express terms investing them with *Regal power*. The Bill, at last was passed, the Duke of Bucks claiming a Right to protest, for himself and his friends.[203]

The House adjourned, the Bishops of Sarum, Hereford, and I, went to dinner with my Lord of Canterbury where (after a Natural Dis-course of the Bishop of Sarum's on the immaculate Conception and the unknown Author of Thomas de Kempis)[204] resolved that every Bishop say something, of the State of his own Diocese, on Thursday.[205]

[Dec.] 4. *Tuesday*. An Appeal heard at Barr; and, upon Lord Keeper's [Cowper's] Report and laying an Accent on the word *excite*, the whole house turned Round and reversed one of the late Lord Keeper's Decrees.[206] Whilst the Lords were in a Committee on

[202] 'There being an act in King James the 1st time, which says, no bill shall be brought into either House for naturalizing any person before a certificate be produced of their receiving the sacrament according to the church of England; which in this case is impossible to be done . . . without this dispencing act.' Luttrell, v, 619.

[203] Buckingham and fifteen other Tories protested at the rejection of the four riders, and then he and nine others protested at the passing of the bill. Rogers, *Protests of the Lords*, i, 174–7. Apart from Rochester and Nottingham, Nicolson's friend, Lord Thanet, and two Tory bishops, Compton and Hooper, signed the first protest.

[204] Thomas Hemerken (c.1380–1471), born at Kempin, near Cologne, is, according to the usual and most probable tradition, the author of the *Imitation of Christ*. E. F. Jacob, 'The *Imitatio Christi*', *Bulletin of John Rylands Library*, xxii (1938), 493–509.

[205] i.e. during the impending 'Church in danger' debate in the Lords. Tenison clearly expected his party on the bench to stand up and be counted on this critical occasion.

[206] See HMC *Lords MSS* vi, 301–2.

the Naturalization Bill (of the House of Hannover) I was called off to Dinner by Lord Pembroke,[207] who shewed me Apianus's Collection of Inscriptions (the first Ground-work of Gruterus's larger work)[208] which his Lordship had been 25 years in compassing. Sir Philip Sydenham, who dined with us, recommended Dr Fleetwood's *Epitome of Gruter.*[209] Lady Pembroke mistaken for one of her Daughters; my Lady Sawyer (her mother) being at the Table. Quietly home at Seven, to write Letters.

[Dec.] 5. *Wednesday.* Haveing procured a Skin of Stamped parchment, I was goeing to Ingross my Commission for Mr Whittingdale's Collation to Sowerby;[210] when Mr Rook came to me, offering to ease me of that trouble. Agreed. I went with him to Mr Chamberlain's; to enquire after Dr Aglionby's Circumstances: But found him not at home. The House not sitting to day, I went (after Dinner) to Gresham-College: Where I happily found the Royal Society met, and haveing a lucky Opportunity of being admitted a Fellow by (the President) Sir Isaac Newton. A Letter was read, by Dr Sloan the Secretary, from a Chirurgeon at Harwich, giveing an Account of an extraordinary involution of the Gutts; which occasioned such an Invincible Stoppage, that the patient had not a Stool in Seven months before his Death. A Livonian Bible in 4 to (printed at Riga in 1687) was presented, from a member resideing in those parts. Dr Cockburn[211] gave in a Discourse of his own, touching the weight of Humane Blood; and the proportioning of Medicines according to the different gravity of that in several Bodies. This was ordered to be published in the next monthly Transactions. These matters being over, the President and Fellows removed into the Adjoyning Gallery; where Mr Hawkesby,[212] who had formerly entertained them with

[207] He was undoubtedly the greatest collector of classical antiquities of his generation. There are catalogues of his collections in BL Stowe MS 1018; and by James Kennedy, Richard Cowdray, and anon., *The Marble Statues of the Right Honourable Earl of Pembroke at Wilton* (n.d.). The coins were engraved by N. F. Haym but not published. A modern description of the antiquities at Wilton is A. Michaelis, *Ancient Marbles in Great Britain* (Cambridge, 1882), pp. 43 ff.

[208] Jan Gruter (1560–1627), was the Dutch author of *Thesaurus Inscriptiorum* (c.1601) and *Inscriptiores Antiquae totius orbis Romani* (1602–3), the standard work on Roman inscription.

[209] In 1691 Fleetwood had published *Inscriptionum Antiquarum Sylloge* but it was not a mere epitome of Gruter.

[210] See above, n. 126.

[211] William Cockburn (1669–1739), was appointed Physician to the Navy in 1694. Having invented a specific for dysentry he made a fortune by his London practice, and was Swift's doctor.

[212] Francis Hawksbee (d. 1713?) experimenter with electricity, who had been made an FRS the same day as Nicolson, 3 Nov. 1705. He published *Physico-Mechanical Experiments on various subjects, containing an account of several surprising phenomena touching*

raining of Fire (in his Air-pump) and some other Curious Experiments on Mercury, now shewed 'em as odd phaenomena in strikeing fire *in vacuo*. Before any Air was drawn out the Sparks were Numerous and flameing; when half the Air was gone they were of a deep fiery (red) colour; and when all was drawn out none fell from the Flint, its surface onely appearing bright and enlightened. I had forgotten Mr Pettiver's[213] Petrifactions, in the Liver of an Oxe; which were presented in the other Room. They had the Appearance of such Sheaths of stone as are upon the Grass at (and near) the petrifying Well at Knaresborough.

Before I waited on the Society, I met with (at Dr Woodward's Lodgeings) Mr Hutchinson, the Duke of Somerset's master of the Mines;[214] who saies he has run Black-Lead (by it self, refuseing the Assistance of all Fluxes) into a hard mettal, *sui generis*, like Steel. This, he saies, is now a dear Commodity, worth 20 *s.* per pound in London. He also discovered fine Fernslatt at the far End of Bransty-Brow (with in Sea-mark) near Whitehaven; which, he saies, Dr Smart can also shew me. He got a deal of Letters from old Mrs Heckstetter at Keswick;[215] and the Duke himself has the Book, of their Accounts and clearings, which was formerly in Mr Aglionby's[216] possession.

Dr Woodward shewd us Samples of several Fossils sent to him from the East Indies; most of which (as the Cubical golden Pyrites, *Mica Aurea*, Spars of several Kinds, &c.) were of the same kinds and faccs with those that are found in England, and the onely Rarity was a sort of red *Arsenick*, solid and ponderous. Mr H. Worsley gave us the History of the Cheat of the Monks or Grecian priests at Jerusalem, and their bringing of Fire from heaven for the sanctifying of the Torches wherewith the holy Shirts are marked. Mr Mandrel's Travels[217] thither have nothing in 'em extraordinary; but many borrowed Accounts which are false.

light and electricity, producible on the attrition of Bodies (1709), e.g. electric light produced by shaking mercury in a glass.

[213] James Petiver (1663-1718), botanist and entomologist.

[214] John Hutchinson (1674-1737), Steward to the Duke of Somerset, was also employed by Dr Woodward in 1706 to collect fossils; later author of the *Moses Principia* (1724), and the founder of a theological party of 'Hutchinsonians'. Somerset had mines in both his Cumberland and Northumberland estates. It appears that, unlike other magnates (e.g. the 1st Duke of Devonshire), he preferred to work them directly rather than lease them out.

[215] The Hecksetter family was descended from Daniel Hecksetter (d. 1581), a Dutchman, who had settled in Keswick in 1564 as work master of the Company of Royal Mines in Cumberland, which was concerned with the mining and smelting of copper. J. F. Crosthwait, 'The colony of German miners at Keswick', *CW* original ser. vi (1883), 344-54.

[216] Either John Aglionby (1642-1718), Recorder of Carlisle, or Richard Aglionby, younger brother of the Recorder, who was Registrar of the diocese.

[217] Henry Maundrell, *A Journey from Aleppo to Jerusalem* (Oxford, 1703).

[Dec.] 6. *Thursday*. The Queen[218] being come to the House of Lords, the Order of the Day was read; and so was Her Majesty's Speech.[219] After a short silence, the Debates began; and were carried on in the following Order: 1. Lord Rochester applying himself to (the Earl of Stamford) the Lord in the Chair observed that a Speech from the Throne was not (neither ought) to be reckoned the Soveraign's own Composure: and Ministers were not *Infallible*. They might mistake, even where they were very faithful; as did (in Charles the 1st's time) the Duke of Bucks and Archbishop Laud. This he offered to prevent those Insinuations which might be made, as if all that was offered against the Speech were levelled at the Queen. He professed himself of Opinion, *That the Church is in danger*; nor did he think it the less so, for the pains that were taken to stop mens mouthes on that head. He remembered when 'twas made high Treason to call King Charles the Second a Papist; and yet the Event shewed (at that Prince's death) how little falshood there was in such an Assertion. There was, he said, Danger from Scotland; from the next Heir's not being here; and from the miscarriage of the Bill against Occasional Communion. The Queen's Example he allowed to be a great Barrier; but that (we see) cannot secure us against the prevailing Growth of Atheism, Socinianism, &c. He concluded with protestations against Ambition, &c. desireing nothing but (what a Noble Lord had for his Mottoe) *Otium cum Dignitate*. 2. Lord Hallifax[220] thought himself obliged to Reply: And, haveing made the Demand for this day's Debates, hoped no Lord would tax him with *Stifling* of matters, or *stopping mouthes*. As to the Scots, the most of our Danger seems to arise from their Act establishing[221] Presbytery;[222] which had the Royal Assent when Lord Rochester was in the Ministry.[223] He said, the Occasional Bill was not insisted on as an Argument to prove the

[218] For another manuscript account of the important debate of this day, see C. Jones, 'Debates in the House of Lords on "the Church in Danger", 1705, and on Dr Sacheverell's Impeachment, 1710', *HJ* xix (1976), 764–9.

[219] The speech from the throne at the opening of parliament had complained forthrightly that 'there have not been wanting some so very malicious as even in print to suggest the Church of England, as by law established, to be in danger at this time'. After re-affirming her own continued devotion to the Church's interests, Anne had continued with the warning 'that they who go about to insinuate things of this nature must be mine and the Kingdom's enemies, and can only mean to cover designs which they dare not publicly own . . .' *LJ* xviii, 8.

[220] Before Halifax stood up to speak, 'the house sat still a quarter of an hour expecting some body would second him [Rochester]'. BL Add. MS 28252, f. 82.

[221] Repl. 'establishment'.

[222] The Act for securing the true Protestant religion and Presbyterian government, passed in Scotland in 1703, ratified that of 1690 which had re-established Presbyterianism as the established religion.

[223] The Act actually received the royal assent in Sept. 1703, whereas Rochester had resigned in Feb. of that year. *Acts Parl. Scot.*, xi, 104.

Church's being in danger; nor did he know what Occasional Communicants there were in Office, any where.[224] To speak plain, said he, there's alwaies a Cry for the Church, when a certain Faction is disregarded.[225] 3. Bishop of London prefaced his Discourse with professing his entire confidence in the Queen and in the present great Ministry at Court; particularly Lord Treasurer.[Godolphin] and Lord Marlborough But complained that the Minds of the Inferiour Subjects were debauched by Atheistical and lewd Pamphlets. He lamented his own fruitless Struggle with Hickeringill,[226] &c. He then took notice (in an odd manner) of Reports that had passed in Relation to Briberies in Election of Members of the other House; *Memorial of the State* of England;[227] Calves-Head-Club;[228] the Scots; &c. 4. Bishop of Sarum began his Discourse with a long story of the French Holy League; which ended with Stabbing of the Duke of Guise. He produced Tilly's Sermon[229] of the 3d Edition; and cited also one of Mr Mathor, of the same College.[230] He likewise quoted the Exeter-paper; which saies the *Church was never so much in Danger* (as now) *since 41*.[231] He did not forget Mr Dodwel's Sugges-

---

[224] So far as *state* office was concerned there was much to justify Halifax's cynicism. See Holmes, *Sacheverell*, p. 39.

[225] Halifax was later congratulated on 'turning their own Canon upon those Persons whose real Grief it has been that the Dangers of the Church, & the Dangers of the Protestant Succession are only Imaginery and Chemerical'. BL Egerton MS 929, f. 90: John Chamberlayn to Halifax, 27 Feb. 1705[/6].

[226] Edmund Hickeringill (d. 1708), Vicar of All Saints Church, Colchester. In early life he had been a baptist, quaker, and free-thinker. Compton had been in legal conflict with him since 1681, and in Nov. 1705 had brought Hickeringill to the Court of Arches over the indecency of a published work, *Survey of the Earth*. See E. Carpenter, *The Protestant Bishop* (1956), pp. 233–5; cf. Luttrell, v, 607 (1 Nov. 1705) where the offending pamphlet is titled *The Vileness of the Earth*.

[227] A pamphlet by the well-known deist, John Toland, preaching toleration and praising the ministry for its moderation in religious matters, which was written in answer to the *Memorial of the Church of England* (see below n. 241).

[228] A fabled Whig society, which was supposed to have celebrated the anniversary of Charles I's execution by drinking toasts to the regicides from 'a calf's skull, filled with wine or other liquor'. Edward Ward, 'The Secret History of the Calves-Head Club', in *Harleian Miscellany*, vi (1810), 600. The club was probably an invention of Ward, a Grub Street hack, see J. P. Kenyon, *Revolution Principles* (Cambridge, 1977), pp. 76–7.

[229] William Tilly was an Oxford hothead of the Sacheverell stamp. In *The Nature and Necessity of Religious Resolution, in defence and support of a good cause in times of danger and trial*, preached at the assizes and before the University of Oxford on 9 July 1705, he 'brought in the same thing of occasional conformity, and his sermon was very much approv'd of' by the High Church dons. After its publication on 10 Aug. 'the Whigg Members of Parliament [are] much displeas'd . . . and . . . they will order it to be burnt'. Hearne, *Collections*, i, 10, 27, 70, 92; *Parl. Hist.* vi, 492.

[230] John Mather (*c*.1677–1748) had preached a sermon on *John* 5: 14 before the University of Oxford on 29 May 1705, the anniversary of Charles II's restoration. It was in print by 22 Nov. 1705. The college was Corpus Christi, where Tilly and Mather were fellows. Hearne, *Collections*, i, 311; *Parl. Hist*, vi, 492.

[231] This may be a reference to a sermon of John Agate (*c*.1677–1720), Rector of

tion, That the present Bishops were compounding for their Temporalities; upon giveing up their Order. Instances of the Church's now flourishing Condition he gave from the Frequent Communions; the many Emissaries sent to the Plantations; the Care taken for Catechiseing; and the Queen's Bounty to the poor Clergy: Concludeing, That whoever could shew where our Danger lay, should *Speak now or for ever hold his peace.* 5. The Archbishop of York[232] declared that he apprehended no Danger from the Queen, the two Houses, nor the Ministry; but thought there was some from the Dissenters of all kinds: Who, he said, were very *Uppish* since the miscarriage of the Occasional Bill. He moved, for a Committee to consider of Wayes for the effectual Suppressing of Pamphlets;[233] for Instructions to the Judges to Enquire into the Laws for subjecting the Seminaries of Dissenters[234] to Ecclesiastical Discipline; and for Regulation of the Act of Toleration. 6. The Bishop of Bath and Wells made his Acknowledgements to the present Ministers for their Favours to himself;[235] and their Encouragement of the Bill against Occasional Communion. Falling on our Dangers, he took notice that the Scots call us Anti-Christian; and they'l be joyned by their Brethren in England. He enlarged on the Skill of the *Western Shepherds* in discerning the Face of the Sky; and that they now saw a Cloud gathering in the North. High-Church he made Papists, and Low-Church Fanaticks and Commprehension-men;[236] setting the true Church of England-man in the middle. At last, after a Rambling (but elaborate and sett) Discourse upon Nothing, he concluded with a proposeal——That the Church might be secured by a Revival of the Occasional Bill. 7. Bishop of Sarum Remarked sharply on some

Stamley, Somerset, 1701–20, who published several contentious High Church sermons in Exeter from at least 1707 to 1713. See Kenyon, *Revolution Politics*, pp. 72, 223 n. 27.

[232] For another account of this speech see T. Sharp, *Life of John Sharp*, i, 363–4.

[233] The outpouring of anti-clerical, heterodox or 'atheistic' pamphlet literature had been an acute source of concern to the clergy since the expiry of the Licensing Act in 1695. The Blasphemy Act of 1697 had proved totally ineffectual and the Church Courts were powerless.

[234] It is not clear whether Sharp had in mind here schools, as well as dissenting academies, i.e. places of higher education. Possibly only the latter, since it was there that new dissenting ministers were trained. But see Wharton's speech (no. 10) below, which in another version of the debate (*Parl. Hist.* vi, 492–3) is said to have immediately followed Sharp's.

[235] He had good cause to be grateful, especially to Harley. Atterbury never forgave him for (as he believed) selling out the High Church cause in Convocation in return for two rapid steps up the preferment ladder. See W. M. Marshall, *George Hooper* (Sherborne, 1976), pp. 87–103; Bennett, *Tory Crisis*, pp. 68–71.

[236] Hooper complained that the Church had been damaged by bringing these terms, embodying 'an invidious distinction, tending to set us at enmity' into currency. For a version of this passage notably different from, and more plausible than, Nicolson's, see *Parl. Hist.* vi, 497–8.

passages in this Speech; and ended with inveighing against the Uncharitable Notion of a Low-Church-man, and the dangerous Heats in the Universities.[237] 8. Lord Nottingham,[238] haveing briefly remarked on the Scotch Act for the Establishment of Presbytery and the Mischief of Occasional Communicants voteing in Corporations, Seconded the Archbishop of York's motion about Seminaries. 9. Bishop of Litchfeild thought the Debate hitherto ran upon a wrong Topick; makeing the Chief point of Consideration to be the Modish Censures of the present Ministers and Bishops as addicted to Presbytery; And prayed a Redress of this. 10. Lord Wharton began with Reflections on what was said by my Lord of York who in his Discowrse on Seminaries took no notice of those that Educated their Children with Jacobites; that Blasphemy in pamphlets [meaning, as supposed, a Sermon of the present Prolocutor's][239] had been rewarded with a Deanry;[240] and that the Archbishop's moveing for monthly Communicateing of Men in Office had broken the Neck of the Occasional Bill. He knew no Dissenters in either House of Parliament. All the Danger mentioned in the *Memorial of the Church of England*[241] was that[242] the D. of B. and E. of R.[243] were not in the Ministry; and perhaps those Letters[244] might point at Men that were in the King James's High Commission for the better Establishment of the Church of England. 11. Archbishop of York sensible that his first Reflection was darted at his Grace's haveing had a Son with Mr Ellis of Thistleworth, declared that (when he found that person obstinately refused to comply with the Government) he removed his Child; who had now been, for a good while, instructed elsewhere. 12. Bishop of Norwich, haveing avowed the Quiet of his own Diocese,

[237] The White Kennett version of this debate has a speech here by the Bishop of Ely who expanded on the dangers in the universities, especially 'in the last election at Cambridge where young Masters and Soph[ister]s abused Persons of quality in the rudest manner'. Jones, 'Debates in the House of Lords', p. 767; cf. *Parl. Hist.* vi, 496 ('moved that the judges also might be consulted what power the Queen had in visiting the Universities'). For the election at Cambridge in May 1705 when the Court candidates were defeated by supporters of the 'Tack' see Speck, *Tory and Whig*, pp. 100–1, 107.

[238] His notes for this speech are in the Leicestershire RO Finch MSS, Political Papers 126.

[239] That preached by Binkes before the Lower House of Convocation, 30 Jan. 1701, in which he not only drew a parallel between the execution of Charles I and the crucifixion of Christ, but asserted that the former was the greater crime as Christ had not claimed any temporal powers. The Lords had voted it a 'just scandal and offence to all Christian people'. *Parl. Hist.* vi, 22–4. Nicolson's brackets.

[240] Lichfield.

[241] By the High Church pamphleteer James Drake (1667–1707). The book, having given great offence to Godolphin and Marlborough, had been presented as a libel by the grand jury of the City of London in Aug. 1705, and burnt by the common hangman.

[242] Repl. 'from'.

[243] Duke of Buckingham and Earl of Rochester. In Kennett's version Wharton also included the Earl of Nottingham. Jones, 'Debates in the House of Lords', p. 767.

[244] The version in *Parl. Hist.* vi, 495 does fuller justice to Wharton's wit.

acquainted the Committee that the Protestants beyond sea were generally bringing in the use of our English Liturgy; and that Offers were now made for the consecrateing of some Bishops for them here.[245] 13. Earl of Anglesey desired the Archbishop of York's Question about Seminaries, haveing been the first seconded, might now be put. 14. Lord Treasurer said the Main Question, for which this ought to give place, was *Whether the Church was in Danger*? [Hereupon[246] a long Debate arose about the Orders of the House; about *principal* and *Incidental* Questions; no previous Question in a Committee; the Duty of the Lord in the Chair, to note Questions as soon as seconded, &c. At last the whole Committee agreed that the Archbishop's motion should stand as the first Resolution, to this propose — *That the Judges be directed to search how the Laws stood in Relation to Seminaries of Papists and other Dissenters, and make their Report.* Before the main Question was put, several other Lords spoke to it; as] 15. Lord North expressed his Dissatisfaction in the latter part of the Question declareing Censurers to be *Enemies* &c. saying that if any Single Lord gave him such a Character he knew how to resent it; but was at a loss how to deal with the whole House. 16. Lord Sommers at large set forth the Liberties taken in Reproaching men as Fanaticks and Whigs; concludeing that the short of the Dispute was——Whether it was necessary, for the preservation of the Church, that three or four particular Lords should be in the Ministry? If so, he thought there ought to be a Bill brought in, not onely for the restoreing of them, but for the continueing them there for ever, and makeing them Immortal. 17. Duke of Leedes directed his Artful Speech towards the Queen; reminding Her of the great Concern she was under for the carrying of the Occasional Bill, and Her expressing Her own Sense of the Danger the Church was in if that should miscarry. He observed that this Bill was not yet passed; and therfore could not see how She could think the Church out of Danger, &c.[247] 18. Lord Nottingham concludeing, said——If the latter part of this Question stands, some of us have nothing to do but to *Goe home and say our prayers*. Then the Question was Read and put to this Purpose: *'Tis the Opinion of this Committee that the Church of England*

---

[245] Probably a reference to plans for creating bishoprics in the American Colonies. The SPG and Bishop Compton strongly supported such a plan. In Nov. 1705 missionaries in New Jersey had petitioned for a bishop. Though the SPG produced a draft bill in 1712 for 'the establishment of bishops in America', nothing came of it. See Carpenter, *The Protestant Bishop*, pp. 278–80.

[246] This passage is in square brackets in Nicolson's MS.

[247] Kennett's account records a speech here by the Marquess of Carmarthen, Leeds's son, who 'stood up and talks of fighting for the Church'. The following day he attempted to fight a duel with Halifax in Hyde Park. Jones, 'Debates in the House of Lords', p. 768; Luttrell, v, 622.

Established by Law, as rescued by His late Majesty King William of ever Glorious Memory and preserved by Her present Majesty, is now in a most Glorious and flourishing Condition; and that whoever insinuates or Suggests that the Church is in Danger, under Her present Majesty and Her Administration, is an Enemy to Her Majesty, the Church and the Kingdome. Upon a Division, the *Contents* were 61. *Not-Contents*, 30. The House being Resumed, both these Resolutions were agreed to: And the latter ordered to be sent to the Commons for their Concurrence.

[Dec.] 7. *Friday*. Visitted in the morning by Mr Dean of Carlile [Atterbury], Dr Kennett, Dr Gibson, Mr Smith, Mr Thomas Pearson and Mr Hutchinson. Item. Mr R. Musgrave brought to me Mr Charles Porter, a Convert from Popery. Mr Dean and I adjourned to my Lord of York's; where we debated the Controversy in Chapter[248] before His Grace. The Dean produced several precedents (out of the Chapter-Books) of such Proxies as he had granted to Dr Todd; but, in conclusion, offered to draw the Case fairly and referr it to any Counsel. Haveing dined with his Grace, and finding Dr K[ennett] and Dr G[ibson] who had stayed for me till now, otherwise engaged, I took Water at Whitehall and went (through the Bridge, at high water) to the Lime-Kilns in Southwark, over against the Tower; where I purchased some formed stones of the women who (at 1*d*. for 16 little baskets) chop the chalk and bear it up stairs to the Kilns. I presently returned the same way; not without Jealousy of haveing catched a cold.

[Dec.] 8. *Saturday*. An Appeal (betwixt Cole and Rawlinson)[249] heard, as far as the opening of the Cause (by Mr Sollicitor Harcourt and Serjeant Brodrick)[250] for the Appellant: Which done, Lord Wharton moved for an Adjournment. The Cause alledged (though now onely two o'clock) was the ease of the House, fatigued with tedious Days-works. But the true Reason seemed (to me) to be the sending three members of the House of Commons to their posts,[251] on this extraordinary day, being all of 'em persons confided in by His

---

[248] See above, sessional introduction, p. 282.

[249] See HMC *Lords MSS* vi, 303–4.

[250] St John Brodrick, Serjeant-at-Law, 1705.

[251] The Lower House this day staged a major debate on 'the Church in danger'. Two of the 'three members' were Whig lawyers, Sir Thomas Parker and Wharton's right-hand man, Nicholas Lechmere, briefed to support Broderick in the case of Cole versus Rawlinson. The third was Solicitor-General Harcourt, leading counsel in the same case. HMC *Lords MSS* vi, 304.

Lordship. The Success was answerable to his Lordship's hopes: For the Commons, after haveing debated till after Eight at night,[252] agreed to the Vote of the Lords on Thursday last. *Yeas*, 212. *Noes*, 162.[253] This Evening, the Tide (driven in by a strong Easterly wind,[254] and meeting with Floods of fresh water from above) overflowed all the lower streets of Westminster, the Hall and Palace-yards, to such a heighth as could not be remembered.

[Dec.] 9. *Sunday*. I went to Sermon at the Banquetting-House in Whitehall; where Mr Marshall[255] (Lecturer at St Ann's) preached very seasonably on *John* 3. 19. against mens loveing the Darkness of sin rather than the Light of the Gospel. Haveing dined at my Brother's (as once before) with Dr Beaufort's[256] Tory wife, I went to Christen Cousin James Nicolson's son Joseph; my brother Joseph and Mr Kensey Chirurgeon[257] being Godfathers. When I got home I found my man James very drunk; abused by my brother's Beau-Apprentice.

[Dec.] 10. *Munday*. In the Writ of Error (Cole against Rawlinson) counsel for the Defendant was heard;[258] and the Judgements below unanimously affirmed. As soon as I had dined, I went to Lambeth; with an Intent to visit Mrs Gibson, who will not be churched before Wednesday. Dr Gibson carryed me to Mr Snow's Chamber; whither Dr Waugh and Dr Sydal came to us. We were all too few to cure the old Gentleman's Hyp[ochondria]. Archbishop Sheldon[259] knew the Secret of King Charles the Second's Religion; expressing it to Dr Spencer[260] in this melancholy sentence—*We must fly; but, whither shall we fly?* This raised the Dr's Curiosity, to make farther Enquiry; but had no other Information at that time, save onely (that saying of

[252] Luttrell (v, 622) noted: 'debated from 2 till 9 at night the resolution of the Lords in relation to the Church of England.'

[253] *CJ* xv, 58. See Coxe, *Marlborough*, i, 373: Harley to Marlborough, 11/22 Dec. 1705, for a more precise definition of the question voted upon.

[254] 'Extraordinary tempestious and rainy weather the weeke before.' *The Diary of John Evelyn*, ed. E. S. de Beer (1959), v, 617, 9 Dec. 1705. Parts of Westminster were notoriously subject to flooding before the embankment was built in the nineteenth century. Easterly winds and heavy rain were the usual cause. Cf. *The Diary of Samuel Pepys*, ed. R. Latham and W. Matthews, 11 vols (1970–83), i, 92–3, 19–20 Mar. 1660.

[255] ?Thomas Marshall, one of the six chaplains appointed to preach at Whitehall in 1707.

[256] ?John Beaufort (*c*.1666–1750), educated Cambridge, BA 1687, MD 1728, admitted a candidate of the College of Physicians in 1729. He was said to have been at one time a non-juror (W. Munk, *Roll of the Royal College of Physicians* (1878), ii, 110), which would account for the long delay in his acquiring his formal medical degree at Cambridge.

[257] ?William Kensey, listed as a barber surgeon in the City of London in 1710. *London Poll 1710*, p. 12.

[258] Sir Thomas Parker and Nicholas Lechmere. HMC *Lords MSS* vi, 304.

[259] Archbishop of Canterbury, 1663–77.

[260] ?John Spencer, Dean of Ely, 1677–d. 1693.

Pliny) *periculosissimus morbus, qui a Capite diffunditur.*[261] Sir
Edmund King[262] being Knighted for alleviateing that King's first
Fitt of his Apoplexy, Fleetwood Shepherd[263] wrote under his
picture: *This Dr's skill may surely be relyed on, Who cured the King
of the Disease he dyed on.* When I came home, pretty late, I was
seized with a Fitt of Gravel; which gave me an uneasy and sleepless
night.

[Dec.] 11. *Tuesday.* Finding no Ease within Doors, I went to
the House: Where the onely matter of Consequence was a Message
brought from the Commons (by the Lord Woodstock)[264] desireing a Conference, which was had immediately in the Painted
Chamber; where the Lords were acquainted that the Commons
had agreed to their Resolution of Thursday last. In the Evening
Brother Joseph brought me some Syrrup of Marsh-Mall[ow] and
liquid Laudunum.

[Dec.] 12. *Wednesday.* A few private Bills being read, and a Message
or two brought from the Commons on the same head, I left the
House; and went to dine with Mr Christopher Musgrave and his
Brother Mr Joseph. A Copy of the Lieutenant Governour's Answer
in Council[265] was shewn me; wherein Sir C. Musgrave's Family is
maliciously, and Mr Gilpin scandalously, reflected on. Sir W. Fleming
after dinner; uneasy and fierce against Coll. Grahme. Haveing missed
of my brother and sister in Salisbury-Court, I went to Mr Elstob's;
where Mr Sommer's[266] MS. on the Saxon coins. Nothing of the
.[267] Dr Elstob informed about the Danger from Scotland.

[Dec.] 13. *Thursday.* Early visitted by Coll. Studholme; who heartily
in the Whig-Church Interest, as he calls it. As soon as he had invited

[261] 'The most dangerous disease which spreads from the head.'

[262] Edmund King (*c.*1629-1709), Charles II's doctor.

[263] Fleetwood Sheppard (1634-98), Steward to Nell Gwyn and her son, the Earl of
Burford (later Duke of St Albans), Gentleman Usher of the Black Rod and knighted in 1694.

[264] Henry Bentinck, Viscount Woodstock, MP for Southampton, succeeded as 2nd Earl
of Portland (1709), see Appendix A.

[265] The Lieut.-Gov. of Carlisle was Col. Thomas Stanwix (see Appendix A). In July
1705 William Gilpin reported to the Council 'abuses offered to him by Mr Stanwix and
also concerning the obstructions to officers of the Salt Duty at Carlisle'. *CTB 1705-6*,
p. 142. On 11 Dec. 1705, William Lowndes, Secretary to the Treasury, reported to the
Customs Commissioners on Stanwix's answer to the complaints made against him, and the
Commissioners reported to the Treasury Board on the complaint on 2 Jan. 1706. Ibid.,
pp. 182, 188, 496. The *CTB* notes that Stanwix's answer is missing.

[266] William Somner (1598-1669), Anglo-Saxon scholar.

[267] Word illegible.

me to the eating of his Cygnet, came in Major Orfeur; newly returned from Barcelona. He gives a sorry Account of the Rashness, &c. of the Earl of Peterborough under whose Conduct no Englishman (at Land or Sea) will be any more desireous to engage.[268] Sir Cloudesley Shovel[269] sick of him. The Garrison were all prisoners, to the Burghers, when our men entered the Town. The King of Portugal, he saies, is a very weak Prince; alwaies toying with his Pages and Blacks. Our Queen Dowager[270] managed the Government well and zealously for a while: But grew discouraged by the Tricking of the Ministers.

In the House—I read prayers—and had a petition putt into my hand (which I presently returned) wherein Dr Woodrofe (an Appellant) craves the deferring his Cause,[271] this day to be heard; on pretence that Lord Rivers, one of the Respondents, had brought over his Counsel. The Dr (on calling in the Counsel, as usual) appeared personally at the Barr; and handed in his own petition. He and the rest being withdrawn, the House agreed (by consent of the Lord R[ivers])— to put off the Hearing to this day sennight.

Dr Gibson dineing with me, Mr Loste [L'Oste] (a Frenchman) came from Lady Lonsdale[272] to be examined for the School at Lowther.[273]—An Invitation to Mrs Gregson's Funeral to morrow.

[Dec.] 14. *Friday*. In the morning Mr Dean of Carlile [Atterbury] repeated his Invitation for Tuesday next; and saies the Universities are offended at the Bishop of Ely's moveing for their being visitted by the Queen. *Esto!* The work unfinished in the House, I went to dine with Cousin Studholme; where was also Mr R. Tolson, my old School-fellow,[274] who full of Philosophy on the Deluge, Pre-Adamites, &c. Thence to my Brother's; and adjourned to Dr Beaufort's Lodgeings, in   [275] till after Eleven.

[268] See H. T. Dickinson, 'The Earl of Peterborough and the capture of Barcelona, 1705', *History Today*, xiv, No. 10, Oct. 1964. Peterborough employed Dr John Freind to justify his conduct in the campaign of 1705-6 in *An Account of the Earl of Peterborow's Conduct in Spain* (1707).

[269] Appointed joint Commander-in-Chief with Peterborough in 1705.

[270] Catherine of Braganza (1638-1705), Charles II's Queen, had returned to Portugal in 1692. She had been appointed Regent for her brother Peter II.

[271] See HMC *Lords MSS* vi, 315-16, 351-2.

[272] Katherine Thynne (1653-1713), sister of Viscount Weymouth, had married 1st Viscount Lonsdale in 1674.

[273] Charles L'Oste was tutor to the Lowther family and a master at Lowther College, 1706-12, and was later admitted to Anglican orders and became the Rector of Louth, Lincolnshire, in 1711. *CW* iii (1903), 36; *Speculum Dioeceseos Linc.* pp. 28, 71, 84; J. V. Beckett, 'Lowther College', *CW* lxxix (1979), 103-4.

[274] Nicolson had been educated at the school at Dovenby. *Miscellany*, p. 84.

[275] Two illegible words.

[Dec.] 15. *Saturday*. Haveing dispatched Mr Buchanan, R. Eglesfield and Cousin Grainger, I went to the Parliament Office to consult (in Vain) the Papers relateing to the Scotch Plott;[276] wherein 'twas said a Memorial of Secretary Melfort[277] chalked out the Politie of Representing the *Church of England to be in Danger*, as a proper Expedient for advanceing the Interests of the Court at St German's.

In the House Lord Hallifax (as concerted) proposed the Revival of the Committee for Inspecting the Records, with an Account of what was done the last Winter (and is still doeing) at the Tower; And his Lordship, at my Request, moved that the same Committee might be impowered to enquire likewise into the present State of the Cotton-Library. Lord Sommers moved for another Committee to Inspect the Laws, and to Report which were to be Abrogated or Amended; and also to look into the Modern Practice in Courts of Law and Equity.[278] His Lordship instanced in Several Laws (relateing to Wills and Testaments, Frauds and Perjuries, Recoveries of Debts on Bond, &c.) which he thought capable of Amendment: And, in the practice in the Court of Chancery, he took special notice of the Villany of Attourneys in carrying down Blank Commissions (for their own filling up with Names in the Countrey) and shreds of any Antiquated Parchment Deeds instead of their Useless Close Copies of Bills. I had the Honour to be very early named, both by my Lord President [Pembroke] and several other Noble Members of the House, for one in each of these Committees.

I waited on my Lord of Canterbury to dinner at Lambeth; where were also the Bishop of Hereford, Dean of Lincoln [Willis], Mr Jervaise [Jervoise][279] and Mr H. Worsley (of the House of Commons), Dr Covel, &c. Mr Worsley and Dr Covel agreed that Moses coasted the Red Sea; haveing gone into it, and out again, on the Asian side: And the former saies he was three dayes in goeing up to Mount Sinai (in *Arabia petraea*) where he lodged, and had thence the most delightful prospect in the world. Bishop of Hereford and Dean of Lincoln came home with me.

---

[276] For a lucid brief account of the 'Scotch Plot' of 1703, and its parliamentary repercussions in the session of 1703-4, see H. Horwitz, *Revolution Politicks* (Cambridge, 1968), pp. 191-6.

[277] The outlawed John Drummond (*c*.1650-1715), as Earl of Melfort, was Scottish Secretary of State under James II; cr. Duke of Melfort by James in 1692.

[278] For Somers's project of law reform and its legislative outcome, see W. L. Sachse, *Lord Somers: a Political Portrait* (Manchester, 1975), pp. 239-42; W. S. Holdsworth, *History of English Law* (2nd edn. 1938), xi, 519-25, for a discussion of the final Act of 4 Anne c.16.

[279] Thomas Jervoise (1667-1743), Whig MP for Hampshire, 1698-1702, 1705-8, 1709-10, also for Stockbridge, 1691-5, Plympton Erle, 1702-3, and Hindon, 1704-5.

[Dec.] 16. *Sunday*. I preached for Dr Waugh at St Peter's Cornhill; and, after Dinner, returned (by my brother's) to my Lodgeings quietly in the Evening.

[Dec.] 17. *Munday*. Morning-Visitants, Mr Dean of Carlile [Atterbury]; fixing me for dineing with him to morrow; and Mr Michael Hutchinson,[280] in prospect of being Chaplain to the Bishop of London. After attendance on the Committee for Naturalization, and half of an Appeal in the House, I accompanyed Lord Lonsdale to the Archbishop of Canterbury's barge; and to dine with His Grace. Here I met with (the first time I had seen him) Coll. Francis Nicolson, Governor of Virginia; who saies the late Description of that Countrey was written by (his back-friend) Mr Blair,[281] too much favoured by the Bishop of London; that the Judas-Tree or Red-Buds, are a common Shrub; they have no Cabbage-Tree; the Bears make good bacon; &c. He has been much on the Coasts of Africa, and in Spain; and saies that at Toledo the water is drawn from the Tagus to the top of the high Rock on which that City stands, and that Sir Samuel Morland[282] had thence his Device of drawing it up (in like manner) from the Thames to the Castle of Windsor. Here dined also Dr Verney, Dr Gee, Dr Mandevil, Dr Lloyd, Mr Patrick,[283] Mr Clavering,[284] &c.

Haveing landed my Lord Lonsdale at Whitehall, I went to enquire for the Chancellor's brothers; and spent the Evening with them and their Club, of Northern friends, at the *Globe*. The Alderman as vain, in his aery promises of Golden Mountains out of their Coalery [i.e. colliery] in the County of Durham, as ever.

[Dec.] 18. *Tuesday*. Haveing given the best advice I could to Mr G. Holmes, on his Mr Petyt's Indisposition, I went to the Quarterly Meeting of the Commissioners for Queen Ann's bounty; where it appeared that the clear yearly Revenue of the First-Fruits and Tenths

---

[280] Michael Hutchinson (d. 1740), Fellow of Queen's College, Oxford, 1701.

[281] James Blair (1665–1743), Founder and first President of William and Mary College, Virginia, and joint author of *The Present State of Virginia and the College* (written for the Board of Trade in 1697, published in 1727). He went to Virginia in 1685 at the request of Bishop Compton, and his disputes with Col. Nicolson resulted in the latter's recall in 1705. *Dictionary of American Biography*.

[282] Sir Samuel Morland (1625–95), Bt., diplomat, inventor, and mathematician.

[283] ?Simon Patrick (b. 1680), son of the Bishop of Ely, educated at Queen's College, Oxford, and ordained priest on 23 Dec. 1705.

[284] Robert Clavering (1671–1747), of Tilmouth, co. Durham, Fellow of University College, Oxford. Later Professor of Hebrew at Oxford, and Bishop of Llandaff and Peterborough.

was about 17,000 *l.* the annual Incumbrances upon 'em, 10,950 *l.* and the Arrears of these, 17,000 *l.* The two Archbishops and 8 Bishops, Lord Coningsby,[285] Lord Chief Justice Trevor, Lord Chief Baron [Ward] and three more Judges (with as many Deans) were present. *Agreed,* That Tenths are a *Real,* and First-Fruits onely a *Personal,* Debt upon the Incumbents: And Ordered that the Sub-Collectors give in a List (to their respective Bishops) of the former of these, noted which are *Sperate* and which *Desperate.* A Committee was also appointed (for the 7th of January next) to treat with those that claim Arrears; and another General Meeting on the 21st of the same month.

From hence I went (together with Dr Deering[286] and Mr Richardson) home to Chelsea, with Mr Dean of Carlile; who treated us very decently at Dinner. He lives in a pretty Box, with good Gardens;[287] and shewed us a Neat and Well furnished study, wherein the Drawers under his Books &c. were mighty convenient. Dr D[eering]'s story of the man sent for the Key of the Cellar; who (when the Company thought him returned) wanted the Bridle.

This day, the Lords and Commons waited on Her Majesty with their Joynt Address;[288] wherein they lay before Her their Resolution touching the Safety of the Church, *beseeching Her to take effectual Measures for the makeing the said Resolution publick, and for punishing the Authors and Spreaders of these Seditious and Scandalous Reports* [of the Church's being now in Danger][289] *to the end that all others may, for the future, be deterred from endeavouring to distract the Kingdome with such Unreasonable Distrusts and Jealousies.*

[Dec.] 19. *Wednesday.* At a Committee for inspecting the Navy, it appearing that the chief Information was to come from Members of the House of Commons, the Lord in the Chair (Lord Torrington) directed to give Notice to those Gentlemen; that they might consider whether they were at Liberty to attend without Leave. In the House, the Scotch Bill[290] brought up from the Commons, with an Amendment in the Prefatory part in these words: *And whereas, since the makeing the said Act, an Act hath been made and passed*

---

[285] Whig MP for Leominster, see Appendix A.

[286] Heneage Dering, Archdeacon of the East Riding of Yorkshire, see Appendix A.

[287] In 1704 Atterbury moved into a house on the east side of what is now Danvers Street. The house had a frontage of 30 feet and a garden 113 feet long. H. C. Beeching, *Francis Atterbury* (1909), p. 51. See also Bennett, *Tory Crisis,* p. 119.

[288] *LJ* xviii, 54.

[289] Nicolson's brackets.

[290] i.e. the bill repealing (in effect) the Aliens Act. *LJ* xviii, 57.

in the Parliament of Scotland enabling Her Majesty to appoint Commissioners to treat with Commissioners for the Kingdome of England, of and concerning an Union of the said Kingdomes of England and Scotland; Now, to the End that the good and friendly Disposition of this Kingdome towards the Kingdome of Scotland may appear, Be it enacted, &c. This was immediately thrice Read, and agreed to.

The Lord Keeper [Cowper] reported the Queen's Answer to the Address of both Houses, as followes: *My Lords and Gentlemen, I shall readily comply with your Address, and am very well pleased to find both Houses of Parliament so forward to joyn with me in putting a stop to these Malicious Reports.* The Commons being Reading the Bill for the Land-Tax a third Time, the Lords waited for its comeing up till after four; when (haveing before adjourned during pleasure) the House was re-assumed and adjourned. It afterwards appeared that the Commons were in no Disposition to rise for they sate till Twelve at night: When (on Debates about the Hannover Bill)[291] Mr Caesar, Burgess for Hartford,[292] was sent to the Tower for words reflecting on a great Minister of State.[293]

The evening spent at Salisbury Court.

[Dec.] 20. *Thursday.* Morning visits from Mr Richardson, rouzed by his Brother Wickins;[294] and Mr Maule well pleased with my brother John's Copies of Patents to Vicars Generall, &c.

In the House, the Bill for the Land-Tax brought up; and read a First and Second time: Dr Woodroff's Appeal heard, and himself allowed (though he had now two Counsellors at the Bar) to plead for himself; but (notwithstanding his oratory) the Decree was affirmed, with a proviso (in favour of Lord Rivers) that this Judgement should not injure any procedure upon Subsequent Orders in Chancery.

I went to dine with Mr C. Musgrave not well; who had the matter of my granting a Patent to R[ichard] A[glionby] most villanously represented, as my being secretly in Interests against him. Here I met with young Sir Christopher, a perfect Smoaker.

---

[291] i.e. the Regency Bill, sent down from the Lords.

[292] Charles Caesar (1673–1741), MP for Hertford, 1701–8, 1710–15. Sedgwick, i, 513.

[293] During a debate characterised, according to Harley, by 'the foulest Billingsgate language I ever heard', Caesar, 'in a long and tedious speech of railing', had spoken of 'a noble lord [Godolphin], without whose advice the Queen does nothing, who in the late reign was known to keep constant correspondence with the court of St Germans'. Coxe, *Marlborough*, i, 353; Harley to Marlborough, 22 Dec./1 Jan. 1705/6; Luttrell, v, 625.

[294] Richardson's brother-in-law, Edmund Wickens (*c.*1660–?1722), Prebendary of York, 1695–1722, and Rector of Kirbythore, Westmorland, 1699–1722.

[Dec.] 21. *Friday.* Visitted by Sir W. Lawson, Mr Madox and Mr Holme, Mr Porter and Major Orfeur. The last kept me till the Lords sent for me to read Prayers; which was done (an hour sooner than, of late, usual) before twelve: But the Money-Bill wanted to go through the Committee, and to have a Third Reading. This done, the Queen came to the House, gave the Royal Assent to that and some other Acts; and made an excellent Speech.[295] After Her Majesty was gone, on a Motion from Lord Hallifax, the Committee for Inspecting the Records, &c. was revived, and impowered to sit dureing the Recess; and then the House adjourned to Tuesday the 8th of January.

Memorandum. Lord Dartmouth's Receipt of a present from a West-Indian King,[296] to Her Majesty, in Return for a Bible sent to Him by King Charles the 2d. 'Tis a Tobacco Pipe; which, He saies, came from the Gods; and wherein *he prayes that Her Majesty may smoak in the Great Hunting-Room of the God's above.* Item. Sir Charles Hara's[297] little son taught (by Sir W. Clargis)[298] to watch for the Bishop of Sarum's vaulting over the Pulpit. At the Request of Lord Thanet, I gave my Lord Keeper an Account of young Raesbeck.[299]

In the Evening (after a short visit to Mr Bell)[300] with Mr Madox at Mr Holme's Chamber; where a deal of agreable Entertainment about Mr Atwood's Scandale, Dr Hutton's ringing of the Bells, Mr Rymer a merry Whigg, Mr Tyrrel's[301] respect for Sir A. Fountaine, Mr Petit's Original Letters on the Contests 'twixt Archbishops Laud and Williams &c.

---

[295] *LJ* xviii, 59.

[296] i.e. North American Indian.

[297] Lieut.-Gen. Sir Charles O'Hara (?1640-1724) cr. Baron Tyrawley [I], 1707.

[298] Sir Walter Clarges (1654-1706), Bt. Tory MP for Westminster, 1702-5. Son and heir of Sir Thomas Clarges (d. 1695), one of the leading House of Commonsmen of the post-Restoration and early post-Revolution period.

[299] Possibly John Raisbeck, son of the Tory coroner of Appleby, 1703-15, John Raisbeck senior. Previously his endeavours to become a clergyman had been frustrated by Bishop Smith of Carlisle and Archdeacon Nicolson. Hopkinson, p. 183. In 1705 he became the incumbent of Kelsey St Mary, Lincolnshire. *Speculum Dioeceseos Linc.* pp. 71-2.

[300] Possibly David Bell (d. 1730), Vicar of Askham, Westmorland., 1690-5, Rector of Kirklinton, Cumberland, 1694-1706, Vicar of Aspatria, 1706-29 and Rector of Great Orton, 1709-30. Alternatively the reference is to David Bell's brother, Thomas, who had been deprived of Askham in 1690 for refusing to take the oath of allegiance to William and Mary. The Bells were connected with Nicolson through David's marriage to Susanna, daughter of John Brisco of Crofton. *CW* iii (1903), 17, and iv (1904), 61.

[301] James Tyrrel (1642-1718), Whig historian and political theorist, educated at Queen's College, Oxford was the author of a three volume *History of England* (1696-1704). D. C. Douglas, *English Scholars* (1951), pp. 134-5. See also J. W. Gough, 'James Tyrrell, Whig Historian and Friend of John Locke', *HJ* xix (1976), 581-610; Kenyon, *Revolution Principles*, pp. 36-7, 47-50.

[Dec.] 22. *Saturday*. After I had [eased] the scruples of Archdeacon Bowchier (about the loss of his Induction-Fee on the consolidateing of two Liveings) to his own and Dr Waugh's satisfaction, and given Mr Grandorge a Certificate to Lord Keeper on behalf of Mr Raesbeck, I went to the Committee (for Records) in the Prince's Chamber: where Lord Hallifax, in the Chair, directed to apply to Lord Keeper [Cowper] and Chief Justice Holt for Information concerning the State of the Cottonian Library; and Mr Relf ordered to give the like Notice to Mr Cotton[302] and Mr Hanbury:[303] Mr Tucker,[304] to give an Account of the present State of the Paper-Office; and the Master of the Rolls [Trevor] (at his Convenience) of the Records in his keeping. Adjourned to Friday. Now present, Lords Rochester, Townesend, Paulet, Dartmouth, Sommers, Hallifax and Bishop of Carlile. Hence I went (on Invitation) to dine with Mr Is[rael] Fielding; where was Sir C. Musgrave his Uncle confined with a great cold.

[Dec.] 23. *Sunday*. I preached for Dr Gibson at Lambeth; and, after Dinner, visitted my Lord of Canterbury in the Gowt. His Grace shewed me Sir George Wheeler's[305] Devotions newly published; in the front of the Preface whereof is the *Gloria in Excelsis* on a Roman Altar, and in the Body of the Book twelve Halleluiah's makeing a Cross with IHS in the Center. My Lord gave also a particular of the Story of Robert Ferguson's[306] being supposed to be a Papist; his goeing to Spain, and officiateing there as a Priest, after the Defeat of the Duke of Monmouth; who (within an hour before he was beheaded) represented him, as a bloody Rascal, to my Lord himself; his haveing a Son a Novitiate in the Jesuit's College at Naples, attested by Dr Gee; Orders given to let him escape, on the Rye-Plott; &c. From my Lord's Chamber Dr Gibson and I adjourned [to] old Mr Snow's; where cheerfully entertained with Lord Ranelagh's Remark on Lord Newport's[307] being two yards and a half about;

---

[302] Either Philip or Robert Cotton, two of the trustees of the Cotton Library who had been called into the Committee on Records on 22 Dec. 1705. See HLRO Minutes of Committees 1704-10, vii, 108.

[303] William Hanbury (1665-1737), brother-in-law of Sir John Cotton, 4th Bt. (d. 1731), he was one of the trustees of the Cotton Library and lived at Cotton House in order to take care of the Library. See Wright, *Fontes Harleiani*, p. 178.

[304] John Tucker, Chief Clerk and then Under Secretary in the Secretary of State's office, 1694-1706, Keeper of State Papers, 1702-14. J. C. Sainty, *Officials of the Secretaries of State* (1973), p. 111.

[305] Sir George Wheler (1650-1723), Vicar of Basingstoke, Hampshire, 1683-1702, and Rector of Winston, co. Durham, 1706, and Houghton-le-Spring, 1709.

[306] One of the chief contrivers of the Rye House Plot, he acted as Monmouth's secretary. d. 1714.

[307] ?Richard, Viscount Newport, succeeded as 2nd Earl of Bradford in 1708, see Appendix A.

And Poet Waller's[308] observation on Lord Paston's[309] (fat) motion for adding 500,000 *l*. to the Two Millions desired by the King (Charles 2.) *that the Gentleman looked as if he had the money about him*; Dr Manningham's Notion of true Mirth, a man's being Dissolved in Pun.

—Visitted at night by Lord Lonsdale and Sir John Wentworth; who brought me the ill news of the death of (my Sister Rothery's Charge) Mr Thynne's onely Son. Sir John is now reading Mr Beaumont's *Book of Apparitions*;[310] a Subject wherein he's not over Credulous: But tells a Remarkable story of his Uncle Wentworth's voice being heard calling his Steward (*Ned, Ned, Ned*) some hours after he was dead at above 30 miles distance. R. Threlkeld[311] willing (in Gratitude) to hold Lowther *in Commendam* with Aiketon.

[Dec.] 24. *Munday*. Visitted in the morning by Mr Chamberlayne, and his Fellow-Stewards of the Charity Schools in Westminster,[312] to secure my preaching on the 13th of next month; also by my brother Joseph with an Invitation to dine with him. I moved not down stairs all day.

[Dec.] 25. *Christmas-Day*. At Sermon and Sacrament in Whitehall; where an indifferent preacher, Mr Swinfenn of the City.[313] Communicants Bishop of Lichfield, Lords Holderness, Bulkley,[314] Digby,[315] &c. and Ladies (even Lady Oxford) in abundance. At Dinner with brother Joseph whither Coll. J. Orfeur brought by Cousin R. Nicolson. Lord Peterborough still in disesteem with the Soldier.

[308] Edmund Waller (1606–87).

[309] William Paston (d. 1732), 2nd Earl of Yarmouth, styled Lord Paston, 1679–83.

[310] John Beaumont (d. 1731), geologist, theologian, and spiritualist, published *An Historical Physiological, and Theological Treatise of Spirits, Apparitions, Witchcrafts, and other Magical Practices* (1705). Bishop Fowler of Gloucester gave Thoresby a copy in 1712 remarking that 'this curious threatise has done much good in this sceptical age'. Thoresby, *Diary*, ii, 103, 124.

[311] Richard Threlkeld (d. 1707), Rector of Aikton, Cumberland, since 1694. Nicolson called him 'the lazy parson', and early in 1706 he tried to involve the bishop in mitigating a sentence which was to be passed by Chancellor Covel of York. *CW* iii (1903), 46, 55; lxvi (1966), 304; *Nicolson Epist. Corr.*, p. 295; *Miscellany*, pp. 22, 160.

[312] On the rapid progress of the Charity School movement in the early eighteenth century, especially in London and Westminster, and the importance of sermons in raising subscriptions, see M. G. Jones, *The Charity School Movement in the Eighteenth Century* (Cambridge, 1938), *passim*. John Chamberlayne was Secretary to the main sponsoring body, the SPCK.

[313] John Swinfen, one of the six chaplains appointed to preach at St James's, 1704.

[314] Richard, 4th Viscount Bulkeley [I] (1682–1724), had succeeded in 1704; MP for Anglesey, 1704–5, 1722–4; member of the October Club, he became an open Jacobite. Sedgwick, i, 505.

[315] William, 5th Baron Digby [I] (d. 1752), MP for Warwick, 1689–98.

[Dec.] 26. *Wednesday*. The two Archbishops and 13 Bishops dined together at Lambeth; the Bishop of Lincoln being the onely Bishop in Town (inexcusably) absent.[316] My Lord of Canterbury acquainted us, That he had newly received a Letter from Lord Galway[317] in Portugal; notifying to His Grace that he had disbanded one Ranklyn (Chaplain to His Regiment) for very dissolute Practices. The like Notice His Grace will give to the Bishops of Ireland. His Grace shewed us also a Volume of the Valuations of Ecclesiastical Benefices (Real, and as they stand Taxable in the King's Books) in the several Dioceses in England; which seem to have been collected in the beginning of Archbishop Sheldon's Time: For that of the Diocese of Carlile I easily observed to be the same which was drawn up by Chancellor Lowther,[318] five or six years after the Restoration of Charles the Second, and is very faulty. Here are several Volumes (about 14) of Parliament-Surveys, which will be of a more certain Use. The Bishop of Sarum (occasionally) observed that the Northern Bishops, of Sweden and Denmark, as well as the Super-Intendants of Germany, had onely their Call from their Respective Princes; haveing no higher Ordination than that of Presbyters.

Returning to my Lodgeings, I met (by Appointment) Mr Madox and Mr Holmes; to whom I gave an Account of the Proceedings of the Committee of Lords for Inspecting the Records, &c. Mr Holmes brought me a paper of Mr Le Neve's, wherein was the State of those in the Custody of the Chamberlains of the Treasury; which ran in such a stile, as seem's not to promise any Finenesses in his *History of Norfolk*. The Inquisitions of the Court of Wards are said to be in a private hand, some where within the Liberties of Westminster; and either Mr Lownds[319] or Mr Grimes[320] (or both) know where they are. An old painted Legend of St Guthlac,[321] with Marginal Explanations, is in the possession of Mr Le Neve; who will part with it, or any thing else, on a valuable Consideration. A great Number of antient Final Concords are in the Tally-Court: But the present Forms of Recoveries are no elder than Edward the Fourth's time. Both my friends agree that the Officers at the Rolls Chapple are much alarmed with this Committee.

---

[316] Wake was involved in church business the whole day. Lambeth Palace MS 1770, f. 9.

[317] Henry de Massue (1648-1720), Marquise de Ruvigny [France], Earl of Galway [I] (1697), was the commander in Portugal and, later, Spain, 1704-10.

[318] Robert Lowther, Chancellor of Carlisle (1666).

[319] William Lowndes (1652-1724), Secretary to the Treasury, 1695-1724; known as 'Ways and Means Lowndes'; was MP for Seaford, 1695-1715, and St Mawes, 1715-22. Sedgwick, ii, 225-6.

[320] William Grymes, one of the six Clerks of the Rolls Chapel in Chancery, appointed to inspect and report on records, Apr. 1704. *CTB 1704-5*, pp. 22, 228.

[321] Anglo-Saxon monk who died at Crowland in 714. Nicolson had visited the abbey there on his journey south this session. Diary, 24 Oct. 1705.

[Dec.] 27. *Thursday*. In the morning (as agreed) I called on Mr Madox and Mr Holmes and went with them to the Tower: where I found Caesar's Chapple furnished with shelves and Boxes as ordered. Here will be room for all that concerns Chancery Matters; and Wakefield Tower may be reserved for Rolls of a more valuable Kind. Here are now Parliament-Rolls, beginning at the Reign of Henry the Second, and ending with that of Edward the Fourth; with Petitions in Parliament and Chancery, Inquisitions *ad quod Dampnum*, Privyseals, Patent and Close Rolls, of the same Extent. The *Inquisitiones post mortem* (or Escheat-Rolls) fall lower, takeing in the Reign of Richard the Third; and of these there are good Abstracts. Here's also the *Taxatio Beneficiorum*, of the 20th of Edward 1., not to mention the Associations in the late Reign,[322] &c. Amongst the oldest Charters, I took notice of those that related to the Monasteries of Holmcoltram in Cumberland and St Trinity's in London. I was particularly (this day) Inquisitive after the Records that touched upon the Tryal of Bishop Merks, one of my predecessors,[323] but found that the best Account of that matter was to be had from the Plea Rolls at Westminster (in the hands of Mr Le Neve) and a particular Treaties on the Subject, the Property of Mr Petit. However, something I saw to this purpose; as Thomas Merks's his pardon, Pat. 2. Hen. 4. p.1. m.13. wherein his whole Indictment is recited; and *Idem Tho. Merks, Theologiae Doctor, nuper Epus Karl. translatus ad Ecclesiam de Samaston per Papam, in qua Clerus seu pipulus non habetur*. Pat. 2. Hen. 4. p.2. m.11. Other Records, relateing to the Diocese of Carlile and now found (accidentally) on the foresaid search, were — Rot. Claus. 2. Hen. 4. p.1. m.11. for the Bishop of Carlile's Fishery in Eden: and Pat. 2. Hen. 4. p.1. m.13. wherein are the Restitution of the Temporalities of William Strickland, Bishop of Carlile,[324] the immediate successour of Thomas Merks; who is also a Witness (W. Karliol) to another Roll, Claus. 2. Hen. 4. p.2. m.20. Whilst I was busyed with these, my kind friend (Mr Madox) wrote out two particulars to my purpose; Viz. Claus. 1. Hen. 4. p.2. m.6. *De recipiendo nuper Epum. Karliol. in Abbatiam Westmon*. And a Warrant to the Constable of the Tower (Cl. 1. Hen. 4. p.2. m.7.) *De Thoma. nuper Epo. Karliol. liberando*. After this, I believe, there's nothing in the Patent-Rolls; for we searched to the End of the Second Roll of this King's fifth year.

This done, a little before One o'clock, I took Coach; and went to

---

[322] To defend the person of William III at the time of the Fenwick assassination plot in 1696.
[323] Thomas Merks, Bishop of Carlisle, 1397–9.
[324] Bishop, 1399–1419.

Dinner with Mr Philip Tullie in Hatton-Garden: where were his two brothers, and their wives, Sir William Bowes, Mr Allanson,[325] Mr Clavel, &c.

[Dec.] 28. *Friday.* In the morning, at the Committee for Records; present, Lord Hallifax (in the Chair) Lord Rochester, Lord Sommers and my self. Lord Hallifax brought in his Catalogues of Cotton-Library, the Paper-Office, &c. but Mr Tucker (the Keeper of the latter) being called in, gave in a paper which better represented the State of what was in his Custody;[326] and his Clerk produced another (ordered to be copyed) of Mr Raymund's,[327] wherein the many Chasms and Defects (in his time) were reckoned up. Upon the whole story, it appeared that the Office had been alwaies neglected by its Keepers; and by none more than (my old Patron) Sir Joseph Williamson: Whose late Bequest (in his Will) of some Trunks full of Papers to this place proves onely a restoreing of 'em to the Cells from whence they had been borrowed. Mr Tucker told us that here are no Original Treaties though their proper Lodgeings: And that the Treaty of Breda (sought for on Occasion of the late Treaty of Ryswick) is not onely missing, but that even the Treaty of Ryswick it self is wanting. Hereupon The Lords Committees resolved to move the House that the Queen might be petitioned on this occasion; and Lord Rochester seemed to hope that that of Breda might be recovered from the Executors of the late Secretary Coventry,[328] in whose time it was concluded. Mr Tucker was directed to get the Office into a proper Condition to be viewed: And 'twas promised that this should be done with all possible expedition. — Lord Keeper and Lord Chief Justice Holt came to us, at the Request of Lord Hallifax; in order to the acquainting the Committee with the Present Condition of the Cottonian Library: And two Mr Cottons attended on the same Score. Mr Le Neve was also at the Door, with a larger View of the Records under the care of the Deputy-Chamberlains of the Exchequer than that which Mr Holmes had given me: But, before these Gentlemen were admitted, I was called away (by Dr Gibson) to dine with the Archbishop of York.

We found there Coll. Grahme and (his brother) the Dean of Wells,

---

[325] Possibly Robert Allanson, schoolmaster at Warwick, Cumberland. *Miscellany*, p. 51.

[326] For his report see HMC *Lords MSS* vi, 41–3. Nicolson's copy is in Carlisle Dean and Chapter Library Nicolson MS iii, 341–3.

[327] Thomas Raymond, Keeper of State Papers up to 1661. Nicolson's copy of this is also in ibid., p. 344.

[328] Henry Coventry (1619–86), Secretary of State, 1672–80. As special envoy he negotiated the Peace preliminaries of Breda with the Dutch in 1667.

Dr Lindford, Mr Potter,[329] &c. My Lord of York (in discourse with Dr Gibson, Mr Potter and my self, after the rest of the Company were gone) assured us that Lord Chief Justice Holt was previously acquainted with what his Grace had said (in the House of Lords) touching the Seminaries of Dissenters; and approved it. His Grace likewise highly approved Dr G[ibson]'s observation on the Canons of 1603 that we wanted a Commentary on 'em, to shew that they were agreable to antient Usages in the English Church, which would be of more weight with our Judges in Westminster-Hall than all the Authority which they now derived from their Sanction in Convocation; and passionately moved the Doctor himself to undertake the Work,[330] promiseing him all the Assistance that could be had from his Register-Books at York, &c. His Grace also heartily commended Mr Wall's *Treatise of Baptism*;[331] which, he saies, has fairly put (and effectually answered) all the Objections of the Quakers, Anabaptists and other Heretical Opposers, and occasionally[332] solved a great many other Doubts. The Doctor as zealously praised a late Edition of the old English Translation of the Psalm, with Critical Notes; which he guesses to be written by Dr Battely, Archdeacon of Canterbury.

Returning, I enquired of the Doctor whether he knew any thing of a late Letter (dated Nov. 3. 1705) from the Princess Sophia to the Archbishop of Canterbury quoted by the Lord H[aversham] in his Vindication (this day published) of his Speech in Parliament:[333] wherein he saies there are these words, *I am ready and willing to comply with whatever can be desired of me by my friends, in Case that the Parliament think that it is for the good of the Kingdome to invite me into England.* He told me, That he did believe there was a Correspondence betwixt the Princess and His Grace; but he knew nothing particularly of this Letter.[334]

[329] John Potter, Domestic Chaplain to Archbishop Tenison, see Appendix A.

[330] Thus was planted the seed of Gibson's magisterial work, published in 1713, *Codex Juris Ecclesiae Anglicanae.*

[331] *The History of Infant Baptism* (1705), by William Wall (1647–1728), Vicar of Shoreham, Kent, 1674–1727, a staunch supporter of infant baptism and a High Churchman zealous in Atterbury's cause.

[332] i.e. 'incidentally'.

[333] *The Lord Haversham's Vindication of his Speech in Parliament, November 15, 1705.* For the speech, see above, 15 Nov. The *Vindication* is reprinted in *Parl. Hist.* vi, 461–8.

[334] The letter is to be found in Lambeth Palace MS 930, f. 214. The rest of the Sophia-Tenison correspondence (from Aug. 1701 until Aug. 1707) is in ibid., ff. 181, 185–6, 189, 212–18, 224. The letter of 3 Nov. 1705, which does contain the passage given by Nicolson (though the original is in French), was printed in 1706 and created a furore. Tenison's reply (ibid., f. 189) expressed the view that the invitation 'carrys with it a great deal of danger . . . Nor has it yet to Me appeared that her Majesty has, in this Juncture, been consulted about it: And each stop taken by the most well meaning of your Servants without knowing her mind, is sett in a wrong way . . . [this invitation is] promoted by Some as a means to embroyl both Courts'.

I spent the Evening (at St Martin's) in conversation with Dr Lancaster and Mr Arundel.

[Dec.] 29. *Saturday*. Mr M. Hutchinson with me in the morning; and, after a walk through the Park, we drank a glass of Mead together: And then I went (as promised) to dine with Mr W. Tullie. Here, as at Mr Philip's, we had the Company of Sir William Bowes and the rest of Mr Chancellor's Relations; as also that of Mr Bray (Burgess for Tewksbury)[335] Brother in Law to Mr Isaac Tullie, an ingenious and honest young Gentleman. Comeing before the rest, I had the Advantage of being Instructed by the Lady of the House in the price of China-Dishes, &c. as, a stand of half a dozen of the finest Tea-dishes and Sawcers (at 18*d*. each) 18*s*., Japaned Iron-Kettle, with Lamp and Stand, 30*s*. The four Seasons of the year finely carved in Alabaster (easily cleansed with a brush and Lather of good Soap) 40*s*.

At my Return to my Lodgeings I found that I had been Enquired for by Sir Philip Sydenham, Mr C. Musgrave, Dr Waugh, Dr Woodward, &c. There was also left for me (by Mr G. Holmes) the whole process on the Tryal of Bishop Merks; and (by an unknown Bookseller) Mr Flaherty's MS. *Ogygia Vindicated*,[336] against Sir George Mackenzy's 2d Book of the *Defence of the Royal Line of Scotland*.[337] To this (after a Couple of Dedications, to the late King James and the Nobility and Gentry of Scotland) is prefixed King James's Genealogy gradually drawn from Adam in 125 Generations. Then follow the Twenty Chapters of the Work it self; which are—
1. *General Exceptions and Evasions answered*: wherein the Irish Historians (particularly the two Friers, Wardaeus and Colganus)[338] are avowed to be more credible than any of the modern Scotland.
2. *The Foundation on which the Irish Antiquities rely*: Which he acknowledges to be mainly Tradition, though (he saies) he has seen a manuscript of St Columb's own hand writeing, and does not think it improbable that there might be some Irish Books 1000 years before. 3. *Of the Scotish Nation in Britain, their Original*; and this, from their antient Language and Letters, appears to be Gaidelian or Irish. 4. *Sir George Mackenzy's Objections against Irish Authors answered*; where the old Genealogical poetry of that Island is

---

[335] Edmund Bray (1686–1725), Whig MP for Tewkesbury, 1701–8. Sedgwick, i, 483–4.

[336] Roderick O'Flaherty (1629–1718), Irish historiographer. For Nicolson's view of the historical and chronological part of this manuscript see his *Irish Historical Library* (1736), p. 23; and Bodl. MS Ballard 62, pp. 173–4: N. to Lhwyd 3 Jan. 1705/6.

[337] Published 1686. For this controversy see Nicolson's *English Historical Library* (1736), pp. 93–4; and Douglas, *English Scholars*, pp. 197–8.

[338] Luke Wadding (1588–1657) and John Colgan (d. 1657), Irish writers and historiographers.

strenuously defended. 5. *An Accompt of the Modern Scotish Writers*; exposeing the Follies of Fordon, Major, Boethius, Dempster and Camerarius. 6. *A further Discovery of the modern Scotish History*; shewing in what particulars Buchanan is ashamed to follow his Leaders. 7. *The Real Royal Line of the British Scots, and their lawful Right of Succession*; derived from Lourn, son of Eire, succeeded by his brother Fergus. 8. *Sir George's Contrivance on the onely Authentick Record he could produce*; maiming the honest Genealogy of King Alexander the Third, admitted by both Nations. 9. *Of St Columb's Abbey of Hy, St Adamnan Abbot of Hy, and other Authors; able alone to overturn Sir George and His Historians their Stories*. Amongst these is reckoned the *Codex Lecanus*; an Irish MS, in Velon, in the Library of the College at Dublin.[339] 10. *Malcom the Third's Poem Vindicated*; as the oldest Scroll, now extant of the Scotish Kings in Britain. 11. *Beda's Reuda and Dalreudini explained;*[340] wherein 'tis shewn that *Dal* (as well as *Clann, Kinel, Mac,* &c) is a patronymic particle in the Irish Tongue. 12. *That Scotland in Great Britain, nor any part thereof, was ever called Ireland*; which is a fancy, occasioned by a misunderstanding of a certain passage in Bede. 13. *That neither Jerna nor Juverna, was ever any part of Scotland*; the former of these Conceits being borrowed from Camerarius and the latter Sir George Mackenzy's own. 14. *That Scotland in the North of Great Britain is not an Island*; as Sir G. M[ackenzy] has surprizeingly endeavoured to prove out of *Tacitus*. 15. *Of Palladius Archdeacon of the See of Rome, and Bishop, his Mission to the Scots*; in whose Dayes no Scots were ever heard of, besides the Inhabitants of Ireland. 16. *Of the Fabulous early Conversion of the Scotish Nation in Britain, and their Grecian Easter*; wheras the Romans themselves kept Easter at the same time with the first British Christian till the new Paschal Tables were finished by Dionysius Exiguus in the year 532. 17. *What signifies the word Romani?* Some times the old Ethnic Inhabitants and Subjects of the Roman Empire, as in Tertullian: And sometimes Writers in the Latin Tongue, as in Ogygia. 18. *Of Marianus Scotus, and his Countrey*; proved out of Harpsfield, to be an Irishman. 19. *Ubbo Emmius vindicated.* 20. *Achaius, King of the Scots in*

---

[339] This manuscript, a compendium of Irish antiquities written in the early fifteenth century, and generally known as the Book of Lecan, arrived in Trinity College, Dublin, with Archbishop Ussher's library in 1661. In 1690, however, it was carried off to France, and in the late eighteenth century it turned up in the Irish College in Paris and was presented to the Royal Irish Academy in 1787, where it still is as MS 535. (We should like to thank Mr W. O'Sullivan, Keeper of MSS, Trinity College, for this information.)

[340] The Venerable Bede's explanation is incorrect, see *Bede's Ecclesiastical History of the English People* ed. B. Colgrave and R. A. B. Mynors (Oxford, 1969), p. 18 n.

Britain, his League with Charles the Great Fabulous: For the British Scots were too remote, and too inconsiderable, a people for Charles the Great to confer with.

[Dec.] 30. *Sunday*. At the Queen's Chapple, preached Mr S. Clark[341] (Chaplain to the Bishop of Norwich) on 1. *John* 4. 21. an excellent Sermon, by heart, on the grand Christian Duty of Love and Charity; from the Nature of God's Love to Mankind, and the Tyes of the Gospel.——The Bishop of Norwich knowes nothing of Princess Sophia's Letter to the Archbishop of Canterbury but thinks the Report Groundless.

In the evening (haveing dined at home) I went, with Mr Chamberlayne, to meet the Archbishop of Dublin at the Gray-coat-Hospital in Tothill-fields, Westminster;[342] his Grace and I[343] haveing promised to preach their two next Anniversary Sermons on this day fort'night. We were present, with great Numbers of the Neighbourhood, at their usual Sunday-night's exercise: Which began with two Collects (*Prevent us O Lord*, &c. and *O God who has caused all holy Scriptures*, &c.) and a Chapter read by one of the Boyes. This was followed by a psalm sung. Then the Master examined twelve of the Girls throughout the Church-Catechism; and six of the Boyes in an Introductory Explanation of the English Liturgy. This done, there was another psalm sung and an Anthem; and then (concludeing with an Evening Ditty in verse, and two or three Collects) the Children sat down to their Suppers of baked pudding. The Trustees presented my Lord of D[ublin] and me with a written Account of the present State of this Charity-School; which followes:

The said School was first set up about Christmas 1698 for the Christian Education of 40 poor Boyes of the parish of St Margaret Westminster, and instructing them in the Liturgy and Discipline of the Church of England, as by Law established; and for teaching them to write and cast Accompt, and (when fit) binding them Apprentices. The said school haveing, by God's blessing, met with Encouragement, the Trustees agreed with the Vestry of the said parish (about Xtmas 1701) to take several of the poor parish-

---

[341] Samuel Clark (1675–1729), Rector of Drayton, Norfolk, 1699–1706, of St Benet's, Paul's Wharf, 1707–9, and of St James's, Westminster, 1709–29.

[342] A charitable foundation of 1698, in 1706 maintaining seventy poor boys and forty poor girls of the parish of St Margaret's, Westminster.

[343] King's involvement is of interest. In the recent Lords' debate on 'the Church in danger' Burnet had forthrightly criticised the High Church party for their tepid interest in the work of the SPCK and concomitant Anglican voluntary activity in the field of social and educational reform. See *Parl. Hist.* vi, 491.

Orphans under their Care; and, besides the Instructions above mentioned, to keep them in Meat, Drink, Washing, Lodgeing, &c. provided they allowed the Trustees the usual Parish pay of 6s. per Calendar month for each Child, and a large House in Tothil-fields for that purpose. To which the Vestry agreed. Accordingly, the said Hospital being fitted up and Furnished, the Trustees have from time to time taken in several parish-boys and Girls as herein set forth, and provided for their education and maintenance: And there are now under their Care 110 poor Children. The Charge of this undertakeing has, for these four years past, amounted to up-wards of 800 l. per Annum. To defray which there is at present no other Foundation than the usual parish-pay as aforesaid, and the voluntary subscriptions and Benevolences of charitable persons. That the said school or Hospital being designed for a Nursery of sober and honest servants and Apprentices, it is humbly hoped, 'twill meet with all suitable encouragement, help and Assistance, from pious and charitable persons. The Revd Dr Onley[344] hath allowed two sermons to be preached Annually, viz. in the morning and afternoon of the Second Sunday in January; at which times there have been Collections at the Church-Doors for the said poor children, which have amounted to up-wards of 70 l. yearly, for these four years past. The Account of the Numbers of Children, taken into the said School and Hospital from Xtmas 1698 to Xtmas 1705 stands thus:

	Boyes	Girls
Admitted from Xtmas 1698 to Xmas 1701	62	00
From Xtmas 1701 to Xmas 1705	80	81
In all—		223
Thus disposed of—		
Deceased within the time above mentioned	7	3
Dismissed, as being no Objects of the Charity	5	11

[344] Nicholas Only (d. 1724), Minister of St Margaret's, Westminster.

Taken away by their parents, not willing that they should work	13	00
Taken away by Parents, grown able to provide for 'em	9	00
Run away—	3	00
Bound Apprentices—	44	18
Now in the Hospital—	61	49
Of these last—	142	81
On the parish Account about	90	
Maintained by Voluntary Contributions	20	

[Dec.] 31. *Munday*. I went in the morning to Gresham-College; where Dr Woodward (for several Hours) entertained me very agreably with a great variety of his own Composures in MS. several of which are completely ready for the Press. As, 1. His History of English Fossils; which are no fewer (in his own Collection) than 1760. 2. The Like History of the Foreign Fossils. Each of these Treatises is divided into two parts; whereof the former considers the proper Earths, Stone, Mettals, &c. and the other the Extraneous fossils (as parts of Vegetables and Animals) which are often found mixt with those. 3. Presages of the weather from Foggs and Vapours. 4. Observations relateing to the Natural History of Metals and Minerals. 5. Of the Practice, antient and modern, in Assaying of Metals. 6. Of the Learning of the old Egyptians. 7. Of the Origine of all Nations, from Noah and his Sons: Wherein he shews that all the Blacks (of Africa and America) sprang from the same stock with our selves; how long the General Correspondence of all Nations, after the Flood, continued; &c.[345] We also particularly viewed the Texture and other phaenomena of some of his choicest; As, the *Ludus Helmontii*, whose Cubes and Quincunces are severed by a double Treasure of waxen marcasite, interspersed with fine Spar; the *Lapis Syringoides* (from Theophrastus's Syrinx, or, old pastoral pipe) with its Tubuli separated by the like Walls of partition with the former; the pectuncalus (fossil) perforated, in its prime state, by the Purpura; Diamonds,

[345] For items 1, 2, 4, 5, and 6 see above, Diary, 5 Jan. 1705. Items 3 and 7 have been lost.

Cinnaber, Yellow Antimony, Scandaracha or yellow Arsenic, &c. not found in England. We have several Mucho-stones, found in our own Gravel-pits.

I returned to dine at my own Lodgeings; and walked to Dean Graham's afterwards: But, not finding him at home, ended the year at my private Study, &c.[346]

[Jan.] 1. *Tuesday*. Clients, at my Levees of several sorts; as first, Mr Ch[arles] Buchanan[347] and Susan Orfeur,[348] private petitioners; Dr Deering, with the Compliments of the Day; Mr James Lowther, with certificates against the intended port at Parton; Mr James Tyrrel, in an uneasy wrath at Mr Atwood; and Mr G. Holmes, as impatient to know when the Lords Committees will visit the Tower.

These over, I went to St James's to pay my own Duty (with the rest of the Bishops) to the Queen. When Her Majesty was gone to prayers, the Archbishop of Canterbury and the rest of the Bench (the Archbishop of York and Bishop of Durham [Crew] onely excepted) went to the Prince's Bed chamber; and there waited (His Highness being at his own Devotions)[349] till the Chapple-prayers were done, before they had an opportunity of makeing their Honours. This was certainly all wrong: Since this part of the Cere-mony should have given place to the Divine Service of the Day. NB. The Dean of Lincoln (Dr Willis, a true Courtier) was the onely person of his Character,[350] that I saw in either of the Drawing-Rooms.

Hence to Dinner, with Mr C. Musgrave in Swallow-Street; where were also Mr Wenyeve and's Lady. Unanimously voted, That G. Langstaff[351] ought to be at an Expence in his own Vindication; though nothing be got by 't but an Honourable Exit.

The Evening spent at Brother Joseph's; from whence I wrote a short Letter to my wife, and sent my News-papers under Covers.

[Jan.] 2. *Wednesday*. In the morning visitted by Mr Patrickson[352] (strangely broken) and Mr Leicester, late Surveyor of Excise; the

---

[346] End of vol. 6 of the original manuscript Diary. Vol. 7 begins with the following entry.

[347] ?Charles Buchanan (fl. 1661–?1718), son of James, Vicar of Appleby, 1661–80, Rector of Ditchingham, Norfolk, 1709–18.

[348] Either Susannah Orfeur (d. 1728), wife of Francis, fourth son of William Orfeur (d. 1681), Sheriff of Cumberland, or her daughter Susan (1682–1728). See the pedigree of the Orfeur family in W. Jackson, *Papers and Pedigrees* (1892), i, between p. 190 and p. 191.

[349] Prince George of Denmark was a Lutheran and had his own private chapel.

[350] i.e. the only Dean or High Church dignitary below bishop's rank.

[351] George Langstaff, acted as Deputy Chapter Clerk and Deputy Receiver and Treasurer to the Carlisle Chapter. He was married to Margaret, daughter of John Brisco of Crofton, a 'cousin' of the bishop. *CW* ii (1902), 173; iv (1904), 1.

[352] ?Richard Patrickson, Customs Searcher of Carlisle. *CTB 1702*, p. 348.

former solliciteing my Countenanceing of the latter, in his Aim at a Foot-Company, and thanking me for my (late) underserved Favour to his son-in-law R. A[glionby]. Item. Roger Briscoe, sent (by Cousin Gilpin) to Mr James Lowther; in Expectance of, he knowes not what, preferment.[353] Item. Charles Porter, another Seeker; but in a more discourageing prospect.

Parting with these, I took Coach and went to Dr Hickes; whom I found hard at's pen in his study, and was afterwards told (by Mr Grandorge) that he's upon answering Mr Dodwel's new project for healing the Schism. Our Discourse was chiefly on the genuine Caedmon, and Mr Wanley's Specimen of it out of the Bishop of Norwich's Manuscript,[354] which (being much Danish) ought not to be believed (I think) to have been penned in Northumberland before the Danes came over; Of the old Swedish Laws, whereof Sir Thomas Parker and Dr Sloan have procured Copies; Of the Hetruscan Inscriptions, in the Arundel Library, and the Doctor's late (much abused) Letter thereon, in the Transactions;[355] the Earl of Warrington's wanting his Book,[356] though one of the first that paid his 5 Guinneas; &c.

From hence to dine with Lord Thanet; whom I found kind and cheerful. His Lordship seems resolved to continue his Charity in Scotland; but will not be prevailed on to promise any Abatements to poor Mr Wickins, whose singular Respects to Sir R[ichard] S[andford] (at the last Election)[357] are not forgotten. Sir C. Musgrave pretended a Grant, of the Common now in Controversy, from Lady Pembroke; but his grandson (and his Guardian) insist onely on a prescription.

Mr Grandorge haveing accompanyed as far as Holburn-Bridge (with a doleful Account of his Noe-Hopes from Lambeth, the Duel 'twixt Lord Th[anet] and Duke of N[ewcastle],[358] &c.) I went to Coleman-street; where Cousin Bosworths entertained me very

[353] After ten months imprisonment in France, he hoped for employment in the Salt Office. See *CW* iii (1903), 10. A Roger Briscoe is listed as a messenger to attend the Lord Chancellor or Lord Keeper between *c*.1703 and 1709. Bedford RO Lucas (Wrest Park) MS L29/110, f. 11.

[354] Wanley's specimen of the Anglo-Saxon poet (Cædmon's hymn) was taken from Bishop Moore's manuscript of Bede's *Ecclesiastical History*. It is now believed to be of continental origin.

[355] Printed in the Royal Society's *Philosophical Transactions*, No. 302 (1705).

[356] Hickes's *Thesaurus*, five guineas being the subscription for the large paper copy.

[357] Sandford (see Appendix A) had been an unsuccessful candidate in June 1705 for Westmorland, where Thanet had extensive electoral interest.

[358] In the 1690s the two men had been involved in a prolonged wrangle over the disposal of the Cavendish estates, which had led to a duel in 1692 (Luttrell, ii, 451). Both married daughters of the last Cavendish Duke of Newcastle. See, e.g., HMC *Portland MSS* ii, 172: Lord Spencer to Newcastle, 7 Mar. 1695; BL Loan 29/236, f. 585: Newcastle to Spencer (draft), 11 Mar. 1695. See also O. R. F. Davies, 'The wealth and influence of John Holles, Duke of Newcastle, 1694–1711', *Renaissance and Modern Studies*, ix (1965), 29.

kindly; and sent for Mr Ogilby (their Curate and Lecturer) who pleasant on the Affairs of the antient Kingdome, blind Dr Lucas's Horsemanship and playing at Tables, &c.

[Jan.] 3. *Thursday*. In the morning, I made a fruitless Journey (with Mr Dale, full of Heraldry and Records, and Cousin Roger Briscoe) to Mr Lowther's Chamber in the Temple; whence I returned quietly to my lodgeings, with my Swoln Neck, and had onely the Company of Mr Thomas Brougham and his brother John[359] in the Evening.

[Jan.] 4. *Friday*. Confined with the Anniversary Bile in my neck; but much relieved with the Conversation of (my worthy and kind friend) Dr Gibson, who agrees with the Reporters that the Dean of Peterburgh[360] stands fair for the next small Bishoprick. I gave him a Copy of Dean Atterbury's Dispensation;[361] and, upon our Talk of a Royal Visitation's breaking in upon the Ordinary, he informed me that the Case of Exeter-College was at large in Sir Bartholomew Shower's Reports from the House of Lords.[362] He also gave me an obligeing History of their good Set of Register-Books (all in Vellum) from the dayes of Archbishop Peckham; with very few Chasms, We had new occasion joyntly to bemoan the want of a *Formulare Ecclesiasticum*; which betrays our present Bishops into very lame Acts.

In the Evening, Mr Dowson (one of Mr C. Musgrave's Under Clerks in the Ordnance) shewed me the State of the Train of Artillery, now fitting out for the Attendance of 12,000 men designed for Catalonia,[363] with the pay of all the Officers and others there in employed for the year Ensueing; Which, in the whole, amounted to 34,030 *l.* 10*s.* 08*d.*

---

[359] The sons of Henry Brougham of Scales Hall, Cumberland. Thomas (1663–1716) was Receiver of the Aids and other taxes in Cumberland and Westmorland from 1698, and Sheriff of Cumberland, 1715–16, while John (1677–1741) was Secretary to the Excise Commissioners from 1702, and a Commissioner himself, 1715–24. C. R. Hudleston, 'The Brougham Family', *CW* lxi (1961), 139–47.

[360] Samuel Freeman (*c*.1644–1707), Dean of Peterborough since 1691. One of the leading Low Churchmen of the day and likely candidate for a bishopric under a Whig government.

[361] One of Atterbury's first acts as Dean of Carlisle was to obtain, through Secretary Harley, a dispensation from his statutable residence so he could continue to live in London.

[362] For the Exeter College case, beginning in 1690 with the visitation of the college by Bishop Trelawney and not finally resolved until 1696 by the House of Lords, see Bennett, *Tory Crisis*, pp. 33–4. Shower, who acted as counsel for the deposed Rector of Exeter, Arthur Bury, published *Cases in Parliament resolved and adjudged upon Petitions and Writs of Error* (1698).

[363] In response to a message from the Queen on 27 Nov. the Commons' Committee of Supply had next day voted £250,000 for an expedition to Catalonia to support the cause of Charles III, the Hapsburg claimant to the Spanish throne.

[Jan.] 5. *Saturday*. With Mr Dale, in the morning, to Lord Hallifax's: where we found His Lordship[364] engaged with the Speaker and other Members of the House of Commons. I was directed to wait in his Library; and there I found Mr Laughton,[365] who acquainted me that Ramazini's book[366] was translated into English by one Saint-Clare a Scotchman, and might easily be had for 1s. or 1s. 6d. My Lord Treasurer [Godolphin] comeing in to us, I concluded there would be no Room for our little business; which was onely to advise about an Ornament over the Door of the Office of Records in the Tower: So that I desired one of my Lord's Servants to acquaint His Lordship that I'd attend another time, and presently went (with Mr L[aughton]) to Lambeth. Here dined with us the Bishop of Bangor, Sir Francis Masham,[367] Dr Brown, Mr P. King,[368] Dr Burnet,[369] Dr Kennet, Dr Lloyd, Dr Mandevil, &c. My Lord of Canterbury told me that the Frenchman his Grace intended for Lowther understood no Mathematicks; and therefore we must now resolve on Monsieur Loste. Dr Lloyd came to my Lodgeings, in his way; and carryed off two Copies of Dean Atterbury's Dispensation. NB. John Laughton's punn (pretended to be borrowed from Archbishop Usher) of *Quidam Homo* Latine for a certain man. Mr Postlethwait (Master of Paul's School)[370] tells me that Mr Johnson's Commentaries on Lilly's Grammar are foolish;[371] and their Author a great Jacobite.

[Jan.] 6. *Sunday*. Epiphany. I preached and administered the Sacrament, at St Brides, for Dr Birch; who sent his Chariot, the morning being very wet, to carry me thither. I dined (with Dr Waugh, Mr

[364] Clearly a Whig management meeting. The Commons were to reassemble after the Christmas recess on Monday, 7 Jan. The fact that Godolphin called on Halifax the same morning is likely to have been connected with this.

[365] John Laughton (1650-1712), Cambridge University Librarian, 1686-1712, whose own private library was renowned.

[366] *The Abyssinian Philosophy confuted* (1697), by Bernardino Ramazzini (1633-1714), Italian physician.

[367] Sir Francis Masham (1646-1723), 3rd Bt., Whig MP for Essex, 1690-8, 1701-10, and father of Samuel Masham, husband of the Queen's favourite Abigail Masham.

[368] Peter King, MP for Bere Alston, see Appendix A. As well as being a brilliant barrister and an outstanding parliamentary speaker, King was very much at home in clerical company.

[369] Thomas Burnet (?1635-1715), philosophical and scientific author. Master of Charterhouse since 1685. His *The Sacred Theory of the Earth* (1684), which questioned the biblical account of the Creation, on geological grounds above all, was one of the most revolutionary books of the day and caused much alarm to orthodox clergy. See John Redwood, *Reason, Ridicule and Religion* (1976), pp. 118-23.

[370] John Postlethwayt (d. 1713), Cumbrian-born High Master of St Paul's since 1697, formerly Master of Archbishop Tenison's School, St Martin-in-the-Fields.

[371] *A Treatise of the Genders of Latin Names: by way of explanation of Lilly's Grammar rules, commonly called Propria quae maribus* (1703), by Richard Johnson, Master of the Free School, Nottingham. William Lilly (d. 1522) had himself been High Master of St Paul's School, 1512-22. His *Grammatices Rudimenta* was first printed in 1527.

Standard and Mr Johnson) at my brother's; where our main Entertainment, after and at a good Dinner, was the State of the Case (to be heard before the Lords on Tuesday next) 'twixt this parish and the Dean and Chapter of Westminster.[372]

[Jan.] 7. *Munday*. In the morning, once more, with Mr Dale to wait on Lord Hallifax; whom we found, as before, surrounded with Members of the House of Commons, and (amongst the rest) both our Carlile Representatives:[373] But His Lordship kindly admitted us, and cheerfully encouraged all our proposals.

After Dr Gee's Exchange of the Cases of St Bride's, I went with Mr Dale to the Tower; where I dined and had the agreable Conversation of Mr Madox and Mr Holmes. The Books that are drawn, or bound, up in Mr Petyt's time are challenged as his property: And so Sir H. St John's (Garter)[374] deals with the Office of the Heralds. The old Calendar of the Inquisitions is dark; and the Abstracts so very short as to give little light to the Contents of any of 'em.

[Jan.] 8. *Tuesday*. After the Reading of some private Bills, a great Cause was brought on at the Bar of the House of Lords wherein the parishioners of St Bride's London appealed from a late Decree in the Exchequer in favour of the Dean and Chapter of Westminster, Impropriators of the Rectory: Who ([by] vertue of an Act of Parliament and Decree of the 37th of Hen. 8.) demand 2s. 9d. *per lib.* of the Improved Rents of Every House in that Parish; which would amount to an Immense Sum. On a full Hearing of Counsel, the House ordered the Report to be made (by the Lord Keeper [Cowper]) on this day fortnight: In prospect that the parties concerned will (before that time) compromise the matter; by the help of Lord Sommers and Lord Hallifax, with the Archbishop of Canterbury for Umpire.

In the Evening, at the *Greyhound* in Fleetstreet, with Mr Grascome and Mr Bell[375] (as also Brother Joseph) vainly treating about the Lease of Newburn;[376] which kept me (together with the coldness of the night) from writeing any Letters by this post, the first I missed since my comeing to Town.

---

[372] See W. II. Godfrey, *The Church of Saint Bride, Fleet St.*, Survey of London Monograph No. 15 (1944), pp. 5–6; HMC *Lords MSS* vi, 307–8; Lambeth Palace MS 640, ff. 693–749.

[373] Thomas Stanwix and Sir James Montagu (Halifax's brother).

[374] Sir Henry St George (1625–1715), Garter King of Arms, 1703–15.

[375] Probably Matthew Bell (1677–1748), of Mersington, Berwickshire, and of Newcastle-upon-Tyne, merchant. M. H. Dodd, *A History of Northumberland*, xiii (1930), 207–8.

[376] See above, p. 299.

[Jan.] 9. *Wednesday*. In the morning, Francis Partis; who now laments nothing but the Deteinure of his Brother Matt's person.[377]

In the Prince's Chamber sat the Committee of Lords (Lord Sommers in the Chair) for Inspecting the Deficiencies of the Laws and Abuses in process; and the Judges (the Lord Keeper being also present) brought in a paper, which, with some Amendments, is designed to be reported to the House; in order to the Bringing in a Bill, for the Remedying of such Defects and Abuses, pursuant to the said Report.[378] NB. The Lord Chief Justice Holt and the Chief Baron [Ward] differed in their Opinion about the Validity of the Evidence of an Inroled Deed; the former allowing it to be onely Good against those that had *acknowledged* it, and the latter admitting it against all the *Grantors*. — In the House a long Appeal against a purchase (on a Decree of Fore-Closure) made by the Bishop of Ely [Patrick]:[379] for whom Judgement was given, the Lord Guarnsey [Guernsey] offering several Reasons for his dissent; which were not seconded.

[Jan.] 10. *Thursday*. After a Turn in the Park with Mr Richardson (my Lord of York's Chaplain, acquainted with the expected vacancy of Rothbury) I went to attend Committees of Naturalization, &c. Amongst the rest, Mr S. Harcourt's was called; but, several Lords remembring Objections (three years agoe) about a supposed Forgery of a Deed, and some of the persons concerned not appearing, the Committee was droped.

Dr Gibson dined with me at the *Dog*:[380] where Assurances given me of my Lord of Canterbury's haveing consulted the Lord S[omers?] on the Dean of Carlile's Dispensation, &c. Princess Sophia's Attendants discover Her Letters to the Archbishop.

[Jan.] 11. *Friday*. Lord Thanet, Dr Gibson and Brother Joseph called on me in the morning; before I went to the Prince's Chamber: Where

[377] Francis and Matthias Partis, tobacco merchants of Newcastle-upon-Tyne, were in debt to the tune of over £6,700 on customs and salt duties and on tobacco bonds because of the great losses they had suffered by the war. Both had been imprisoned in Carlisle gaol, but Francis was discharged in Nov. 1705 and Matthias was either discharged or else escaped, for in May 1706 he had 'secured himself in Scotland and thereby prevented the execution of any process upon his person'. He was discharged from complying with his composition for the salt duty, but part of his estate was leased to William Gilpin for his debt. *CTB 1700–1*, p. 398; *1702*, pp. 158, 192, 292; *1705–6*, pp. 153, 170, 658, 670.

[378] For the proceedings of this committee see HMC *Lords MSS* vi, 355–7.

[379] For the case see ibid., pp. 308–9.

[380] Almost certainly the *Dog* tavern in Palace Yard, Westminster. See B. Lillywhite, *London Signs* (1972), no. 5853. Described in 1690 as 'in pallis yard . . . the doge' (BL Harleian MS 4716, f. 18), it had often been used by Samuel Pepys between 1660 and 1668, see, e.g., *Diary of Samuel Pepys*, ed. Latham and Matthews, i, 82, 8 Mar. 1660.

the Committee for Inspecting the Laws Examined the particulars given in by the Judges. In several of these, the Lord Keeper [Cowper] eloquently observed the Lord Chief Justice Holt's offering at the bringing some of the *Sweets of the Chancery* to his own Judicature: But both His Lordship and the Lord in the Chair (Lord Sommers) thought it most adviseable to keep the Courts of Law to *Law*, and the Chancery to matters of *Equity*, for the better avoiding of all clashing in Jurisdiction. To which all the other Lords assented.

In dined at my Brother's in Salisbury-Court, it being my Niece's Birth-Day, and stayed out the Evening there.

[Jan.] 12. *Saturday*. Visitants in the morning; Mr James Lowther, who bought the printed Case of the port at Whitehaven, and assures me that Lord Wharton and Lord Hallifax are his friends;[381] Mr Grascome and Mr Harding, for the Renewal of the Lease of Newburn set at 100 *l*; Cousin Roger Briscoe and's wife, turned away by my being engaged in other Company; Mr Man, who has lost (his Sheet-Anchor) his late Chaplainship in a Man of War; Mr Charles Porter, to be certifyed for as a Convert; and Mr Ch[arles] Buchanan, in his heretofore conditions.

Two Bills, for Naturalization of about 100 Foreigners, gone through at the Committee; present the Lord Stamford (in the Chair) the Earl of Westmerland and Bishops of Sarum, Peterborough [Cumberland] and Carlile. The Lords sat not: but the Commons kept together late on the Succession Bill, which ('tis hoped) will be finished on Tuesday next. An Evening Visit from Dr Woodward; who is not pleased with the Archbishop of Canterbury and downright angry at my Lord of York. He extols Lord Colrain's skill in English Coins;[382] and promises me a kind Reception from His Lordship.

[Jan.] 13. *Sunday*. In the afternoon, I preached at St Margaret's Westminster (as the Archbishop of Dublin did in the Forenoon) at the Anniversary Collections for the poor Children of the Gray-Coat Hospital. The Congregation was Exceeding full, both Morning and Evening: And, whereas the Sums collected on this Occasion had usually (for three years past) amounted to about 70 *l*. which was thought very Considerable, the Collectors this day brought in 97 *l*. 3*s*. 1*d*. which shews that the Charity in this place (notwithstanding the present general Scarceity of money) still increases. *Laus Deo*!

[381] For the proceedings of the House on the Parton Pier and Harbour Act, regarded by Lowther and the Whitehaven merchants as a threat to the rapidly growing prosperity of their port, see HMC *Lords MSS* vi, 398–402.

[382] Henry Hore (1636–1708), 2nd Baron Coleraine [I], well-known antiquary who lived at Tottenham.

[Jan.] 14. *Munday*. After the dispatches of Cousin Bridget Nicolson, Mr Buchanan and Mr Porters, in the morning, I went to visit the Archbishop of York; whom I found much dispirited with his Stone-Cholick and Spleen.

At the House, after a long Committee on Marine Affairs (where Sir Cloudesley Shovel, Admiral Churchill, Sir George Bings [Byng] and Sir John Jennings[383] were present) and some private Bills read, the Appeal of Mr H[enry] Clavering, against his Nephew Sir James,[384] was heard, by his Counsel Sir Joseph Jekill and Serjeant Cheshire;[385] and the Respondent's Counsel (Sir Thomas Powis and Sir S. Harcourt) deferred till to morrow: With this previous Order, That no private Bills should be read on a Day appointed for Hearing of any Cause; till after the Cause was so heard.

In the Evening (first) at Mr C. Musgrave's; where, with his two younger brothers,[386] all fair and good humoured. Thence to Mr Thynne's; where the Evening spent with Sister Rothery and Mr Martin. NB. Before the sitting of the House, I acquainted the Earl of Carbury[387] that I had read Mr Beaumont's Book (dedicated to His Lordship) concerning Spirits; and desired to know something of the Author's Character. His Lordship told that all the Knowledge he had of him was that he was a Fellow of the Royal Society, and had sometimes applyed (as such) to him, when he was president of that Body:[388] Whence I found 'twas (as I supposed) Mr B[eaumont] of Somersetshire. This brought us into a Discourse about the several Systemes of Dr Burnet, Dr Woodward, &c. and his Lordship ingeniously enough observed that, since Des Cartes led the way, Every New Philosopher thought himself wise enough to make a World.[389]

[383] George Churchill (1654–1710), Admiral and younger brother of the Duke of Marlborough. At this time effective head of the Prince's Admiralty Council—the rough equivalent (while Prince George was Lord High Admiral) of the Board of Admiralty. Sir George Byng (1664–1733), Vice-Admiral and MP for Plymouth, 1705–21, who had commanded the fleet at Malaga and the capture of Gibraltar, 1704. Sedgwick, i, 511. Sir John Jennings (1664–1743), Rear-Admiral. Luttrell (vi, 5) records that Sir Stafford Fairborne was another admiral called before this committee, the purpose of which was 'to find out a better way of manning our fleet'. Lord Torrington was in the chair.

[384] Sir James Clavering (1668–1707), 2nd Bt. of Axwell, Co. Durham. For the case see HMC *Lords MSS* vi, 309–10.

[385] Sir Joseph Jekyll (*c*.1662–1738), Welsh judge and MP for Eye, Suffolk, 1697–1713, and Lymington, 1713–22, was the brother-in-law of Lord Somers, King's Serjeant, 1700, Master of the Rolls, 1717–38. Sedgwick, ii, 174–6. John Chesshyre (1662–1738), Serjeant-at-Law, 1705, Queen's Serjeant, 1711, King's Serjeant, 1714.

[386] Thomas and George.

[387] John Vaughan, 3rd Earl of Carbery [I], Baron Vaughan [E].

[388] Carbery was President of the Royal Society, 1686–9.

[389] In general see Redwood, *Reason, Ridicule and Religion*, ch. 5 ('The Origin of the Earth') *passim*. For John Woodward's theories, developed in *An Essay towards a natural history of the Earth* (1695), ibid., pp. 124–8. For Burnet, see above, n. 369.

Memorandum. The Bishop of Lincoln this day told me that his own wife (Mrs Wake, with her Sister and brother in Law) was carryed by Mr W. Chafinch[390] into a dark Chapple of King Charles the II soon after that Prince's death, into which there was a privy-door out of his Closet; and in which they saw a popish Altar, and all Sorts of priest's Vestments, and were assured that here (for many years) he had assisted at Mass so privately, that Mr Ch[iffinch] himself knew nothing of the matter till after he was dead. But—He and's son knew of the Hoord of Gold which was in his Closet: which the Bishop sais amounted to near 100,000 Guinneas.

[Jan.] 15. *Tuesday*. In the morning Dr Nicolson (an Ingenious Physitian and my Neighbour)[391] was brought to me by Mr M. Hutchinson. — After they (and others) were gone, I went to attend the Committee for Regulation of proceedings at Law; and found that the Lord Keeper [Cowper] and Chief Justice Holt still differ in Proposeals, the latter catching at a Share in Equity, and the former loath to part with any. It was unanimously agreed that the Common-Law is wrong in the Case of Collateral Warranty; and that it ought to be changed. A proposeal was made, by the Chief Justice, that Juries might have Refreshment in long Trials; which Lord Rochester observed would hazard the prolonging of a Cause from 24 hours to 6 or 7 dayes.

In the House (Notwithstanding the freshness of yesterday's Order) the hearing the Residue of the Council on Clavering's Cause was put off till to morrow: Which was done at the Instance of Sir Joseph Jekyll, who (being a Member of the other House) was afraid, on this busy day,[392] to be censured for attending an Appeal at the Bar of this. In the House of Commons, the Debates went high and hott (on the Succession-Bill)[393] and were farther adjourned till Saturday next.

[Jan.] 16. *Wednesday*. First Visitant Mr Raesbeck, haveing gotte Institution into his Lincolnshire-Liveing, and goeing to take possession.

[390] William Chiffinch (1602?-88), Closet-Keeper to Charles. See also D. Allen, 'The political function of Charles II's Chiffinch', *Huntington Library Quarterly*, xxxix (1976), 277-90.

[391] ?John Nicholson (c1661-?1710), licenciate Royal College of Physicians in 1687, and candidate in 1692. Lived in the parish of St Margaret's Westminster.

[392] In the Commons.

[393] The chief debate on 15 Jan., in the Committee of the Whole House, was concerned with whether the meeting of parliament on the Queen's death should be immediate (as the Whigs wished) or delayed. 'After several hours pro and con, they divided and carried it for immediately, 195 against 160.' Luttrell, vi, 6. See also 'Anon. Parliamentary Diary, 1705-6', ed. W. A. Speck, *Camden Miscellany*, xxiii (1969), 66-71. For the progress of the Regency Bill in the Commons and the struggle over the 'Whimsical clause', see above, sessional intro., p. 290.

The name of the place is Kelsey, not far from Great Grimsby; and 'tis valued at about 50 *l.* A Charge given him (before Mr Harrison) to look to his Steps.

At the Committee for Records, the Master of the Rolls brought in the State of his several Offices in an humble Strain; kindly certifying their Lordship's that he apprehended even the Examiner's Trust (though nothing therein but papers) to be within their Commission. None of the Lords seemed to make any Question about the Extent of their powers: But, His Mastership being Ordered to withdraw and called in again, he was acquainted that the Lords would take time to consider of his Report, and that (if there was occasion) he should have farther Notice of their pleasure. Friday next being appointed to Inspect the Exchequer Records, the Committee adjourned to that day: And I presently (as I had promised) gave Mr Le Neve, one of the Vice-Chamberlayns and Norroy King at Arms Notice of the time.

In the House the Residue of Council was heard (at length) on the Appeal of Mr H. Clavering; and, after mighty Expectations, the Lords unanimously Affirmed the Decree; thinking it unreasonable to destroy a voluntary Deed without powers of Revocation (and uncanceled) to make good a Secondary Settlement, though never so well intended.

In the Evening, on the way to Salisbury-Court, I met with Mr James Lowther; who acquainted me that he had (this Evening) a Letter from Mr Gilpin, that his Father (Sir John) was Expireing when the Post came away:[394] And that therfore he expects to post for Cumberland about Saturday next, and leave the Cause of the New Haven at Parton to the mercy of the Parliament. Calling at Cousin R. Nicolson's, and promiseing him to preach at the Savoy on Sunday next, I went on to my brother's; and thence walked home again, by the Moon-shinc: Haveing had his Account of the Remainder of my Lincolnshire-Fines (25 *l.*) being paid in,[395] &c.

[Jan.] 17. *Thursday.* Called on in the morning by Mr G. Holmes, I sent (to Cousin Relf) for Mr Le Neve's elegant Return to the Committee of Lords concerning the Condition of the Records in the Treasury-Offices; which proved pretty long, and were presently given to James Hoodless to be copyed. Memorandum. To acquaint the Lords to morrow with the Inquisitions (*post-mortem*) in the Fishmonger's keeping; and the Books, belonging to the Old Court of Requests, over the Prince's Chamber.

---

[394] Luttrell (vi, 7) recorded in his entry for 19 Jan. the death of Sir John Lowther of Whitehaven.
[395] Entry fines payable by tenants on the bishop's Lincolnshire estates.

At the Committee for Regulating proceedings at Law, &c. Lord Keeper took notice of Sir Edward Cook's Defence of Collateral Warranty; that 'twas backed with a Reason somewhat like that which was given for the Romans wanting a Law against parricide.

In the House, Lord Hallifax Reported (from the Committee for Records) the Deficiencies in the Paper-Office, by the neglect of late Secretaries of State, in not transmitting thither the public papers:[396] Which (after Lord Nottingham had cleared himself, by observeing that he had parted with some which he ought to have kept for his own Security) ended in ordering an Address to Her Majesty to take some Effectual Course for the retrieveing of such of these as could be had again, if embezeled, or otherwise detained. Lord Sommers reported Resolutions from the Committee on Law; whereon the Judges were ordered to bring in a Bill.

After I had dined, I went to visit my Lord of York; whom I found newly returned from walking in the park. Here I met with Mr Grabe;[397] who laughs at the Conceit of the LXX's being Inspired, since there are so many mistakes in their Translations manifestly their own: But allows there was a great providence in haveing the Old Testament (to which the Apostles alwaies Appeal) thus turned in the Common Language of Greek, just before our Saviour's comeing.

In the Evening (late) I was first visitted by Coll. Francis Nicolson, Governour of Virginia; which Countrey (he sais) [is] in entire peace and security, none of the Neighbouring Indians being in any Condition to disturb its quite: And, whilst he was with me, Sir William Fleming came to take his last Farewell. He proposes to the Coll[onel] an approved way of makeing the Marines a Fund for Seamen, by Registring and Disbanding 'em every two years; and is justly offended at a late contract made with Mr Hutchinson (of Newcastle) and others, by the Commissioners of the Excise, for the fetching off the Collections in Cumberland (in Specie) from Penrith.

[Jan.] 18. *Friday.* Whilst Dr Scott[398] was with me in the morning (accounting the Sums he had in prospect for the Relief of his dis-

---

[396] Leading politicians such as Halifax missed few opportunities of scoring party points, however apolitical or academic the exercise. In fact, the neglect had been general since the Restoration, and extended to the Whig ministers of the 1690s.

[397] John Ernest Grabe (1666–1711), German scholar and divine who had settled in England, becoming chaplain of Christ Church, Oxford in 1700. He was employed in printing the Alexandrine manuscript of the Septuagint then in the Royal Library at St James's. In 1705 he published an account of the *Codex Alexandrinus*, and in 1707 the *Septuaginta Interpretum Tomus I* (vol. 4 followed in 1709, and vols. 2 and 3, edited by others from Grabe's translation, in 1719–20).

[398] Possibly Robert Scott (1641–after 1707), son of Sir William of Clerbington, Minister of Cannongate, Edinburgh, before 28 Nov. 1676, Prebendary of Hamilton, and Dean of

tressed Brethren in Scotland,[399] from Deans and Chapters, Arch-deaconryes, &c. in England) came poor distracted Mr Glaisters; with a Revelation (as he called it) of the French landed at Southampton &c.

At the Committee for Records, Mr Tucker brought in a full Catalogue (in a pretty thick Folio-Book) of all matters under his care in the Paper-Office; together with a Schedule of what seemed to be withdrawn, and in private hands. This latter is to be annexed to the Address designed for Her Majesty. Lords Rochester, Sunderland, Anglesey, Stamford, Townesend, Pawlet, Sommers, Hallifax and Bishop of Carlile, adjourned to the Chapter-House in the Cloister at Westminster; the Roof and windowes whereof they found in a very ruinous Condition. Sir Christopher Wrenn, Surveyour of the Queen's Works, was with us; and was directed to look after the Speedy Repairs of the Fabrick. Here are the Leagues and Foreign Treaties, which Mr Rymer is publishing; as also Term Reports (out of the King's Bench and Common-pleas) as high as Edward 2. The Golden Seal and Illuminations of the old Treaty with Alphonsus King of Castile (of which there's a Cutt in Mr R[ymer]'s first Volume) is very curious; but the Workmanship of the Seal is much outdone by the Golden Box over the Seal of Francis King of France; which hangs at a beautiful Treaty betwixt that King and our Henry the 8th. Amongst other Rarities, Mr Le Neve shewed me the pretended Homage of Malcolm; which has occasioned the spoiling of so much paper by Mr Atwood and my self.[400] 'Tis a very rotten and thin piece of parchment; and there lyes, in the same Box with it, a fair Seal of Scotland, with a double Treasure of Flowers de Lis, which is said to have been droped from it. To me it look fresher than the parchment; and is fastened to a hempen string, which (I think) would sooner have failed than that. However, Mr Le Neve will have it to be its proper Seal; and makes this the most certain Demonstration (in his way) of the Instruments being a Counterfeit, since the Scotch Arms were not thus Charged till long after Malcolm Canmore's time.

On my Return to the House, I met with Sir Andrew Fountaine;

Glasgow, c.1686–?90. *Fasti Ecclesiae Scoticanae,* ed. H. Scott (Edinburgh, 1915–61), iii, 259. Dr Scott was described by Nicolson as 'late Dean of Glasgow' (*CW* iii, 51: 12 July 1706).

[399] Episcopalian ministers, subjected to serious harassment, especially since 1704, by the Kirk and Presbyterian-dominated Scottish ministries.

[400] In 1704 Atwood had published *The Superiority and Direct Dominion of the Imperial Crown of England over the Crown and Kingdom of Scotland.* Nicolson dismissed the claim that the homage paid by Scottish kings to the English kings was for anything more than the English counties which the Scots held in fee, see *English Historical Library* (1736), p. 193.

who assures me that my brass Hadrian is undoubtedly genuine, and a very valuable medal. My Lord of Canterbury saies he'l shew me a good deal of Roman Medals, in Brass, in his own possession. His Grace (soon after) gave me a large Account of the Discourses he had lately had about our Dean's Dispensation: Which, he thinks, will necessitate his Speedy Removeal, and seems intended (by himself) to this purpose; and, in case he leaves us, His Grace repeats the Assurance of his utmost Endeavours for Mr Chancellor T[ullie]. The Business of the Day, with the Lords, was onely the Reading of a few private Bills and petitions: But the Commons had a Message from Her Majesty, concerning the Discovery made of the Author of the *Memorial of the Church of England*, which occasioned Debates of greater Weight.[401]

In the Evening, I made visits to Dr Lancaster and Mr Smith; and (returning to my Lodgeings, about Eight, with Mr M. Hutchinson) I had a kind visit from the Archbishop of Dublin; who saies Dr Whitby[402] has left the Discipline of the Church very Loose in his Discourses on ye 10th of the *Hebrews* and on *Titus* 3, 10. He likes not Mr Wall's compareing of the Emperour Constantine to Henry 8. nor his makeing Baptism a Covenant; whereas he thinks (with Dr Scott) that 'tis onely a Command, and joyned with Faith (by our being Taught) to keep us from attributeing too much merit to that Grace, which (saies he) is of no more Efficacy than the washing in a little cold water, if so commanded by God. His Grace highly commends Vossius's[403] *Votum Pro Pace*: and thinks most of the Controversies in the Christian Church (even ours with the papists about Transubstantiation) are more in *Name*, and words, than *Thing*.

[Jan.] 19. *Saturday*. Cousin B. Nicolson impatient for her son's promotion;[404] and Roger Briscoe despiseing the Offer (made him by Mr Musgrave and Mr Lowther) of being Clerk to a Train of Artillery.

I dined at Lambeth; together with the Bishop of Chichester, Lords Sommers and Hallifax, Dr Verney, Mr James Tyrrel, Dr Mandevil, Coll. Nicolson, Archdeacon Griffith,[405] &c. Lord S[omers] discoursed

---

[401] *CJ* xv, 98; Luttrell, vi, 7–8. The depositions of Edwards the printer implicated three members of the House. For the real author see above, n. 241.

[402] Daniel Whitby (1638–1726), anti-Catholic polemist and Rector of St Edmunds, Salisbury since 1669.

[403] Isaac Vossius (1618–89), Dutch philosopher and divine who settled in England in 1670.

[404] Nicolson was at this time in negotiations with Christopher Musgrave and Mr Bretton, a Commissioner of the Customs, for a place for Fetherston Nicolson. See Tullie House Library, Carlisle: Nicolson's Account Book for 1706, abstract of letters 15, 21, and 22 Jan. 1706.

[405] Roger Griffith (d. 1708), Archdeacon of Brecknock since 1704.

me singly, with great kindness and Freedome, on the subject of the Union; and we both agreed that, if Scotland were now admitted to a Community of Trade with England, paying their proportion of the public Taxes and haveing a like proportionable Number of their Lords and Commons at the passing of Money-Bills, 'twould be sufficient for the present: For that a farther Union (in Religion Laws and Civil Government) must be the Work of time.[406] The same Noble Lord gave me an Account of his pressing (when he was President) Dr Wallis[407] and Dr Hook to write a full History of the Royal Society; and concluded with some (easy and wel-bred) Reflections on the unaccountable Covetousness of the Latter, not dareing to sleep in the same Room with his Hoord of Guinneas till the Neighbourhood were risen, &c. His Grace of Canterbury (at parting) promised me to desire His Lordship's opinion on our Dean's Royal Dispensation.

In the Evening, Mrs Lamplugh[408] desireing me to attend her Cause on Tuesday: And, soon after, Mr Tucker and Coll. Francis Nicolson; who stayed with me till Bed-time. The former bemoaned the uncertain Post of a Dependant on a Secretary of State, who commonly brings into the Office a whole Sett of his own Creatures:[409] And the latter made free with the present King of Portugal, his whoreing with Pocky Negroes, &c. The Fortifications at Breda and Bergen op zoom the best in Europe; the latter by Cohorn, who a much better Engineer than Vaubun.[410]

[Jan.] 20. *Sunday*. I preached at the Savoy; and dined (with Mr Hobby,[411] Coll. Orfeur, &c.) at Cousin R. Nicolson's. My brother Joseph could not stay dinner; being hastily called to attend the Lady Ramsden,[412] siezed with the small pox. After Dinner, haveing

[406] An important insight into the private thinking of the Whig leader on the subject of Anglo-Scottish relations. See above, sessional intro., n. 65.

[407] John Wallis (1616–1703), FRS, Savilian Professor of Geometry at Oxford (1649–1703). Lord Somers was President of the Royal Society in 1698.

[408] Mary Lamplugh, widow of Dr Thomas Lamplugh, won her case which was heard on 24 Jan. 1706, see HMC *Lords MSS* vi, 312–13.

[409] Tucker's accusation certainly appears to be true at the level of Under-Secretary, very few of whom continued in office upon the change of the Secretary of State. Tucker himself had been employed by Trenchard, Trumbull, and Hedges, but not by Shrewsbury and Vernon. At a lower level it may also have been true, certainly Charles Delafaye was brought in as Chief Clerk in Dec. 1706 by Sunderland. See Sainty, *Officials of the Secretary of State*, pp. 24, 28, 111.

[410] Merro van Coehorn (?1632–1704), Dutch engineer and general, and Sebastien le Prestre, Seigneur de Vauban (1633–1707), French military engineer and a Marshal of France.

[411] Probably Thomas Hoby (1642–*c*.1706), Whig MP for Great Marlow, 1681, and Salisbury, 1689–98, who was a JP, 1702–6, and Deputy-Lieutenant, 1699–1706, for Hampshire.

[412] Elizabeth Lowther (d. 1764), daughter of 1st Viscount Lonsdale, married Sir William Ramsden (1672–1736) of Byron, Yorkshire, in 1695.

had Mr H[obby]'s history of the misbehaviour of B. Brougham[413] towards the Duke of Bolton, and Mr Gale[414] towards the Earl of Manchester, in the late Elections for Hampshire[415] and the University of Cambridge,[416] I returned home; and had the Evening in quiet.

[Jan.] 21. *Munday*. After Mr M[usgrave] and I had been with the Commissioners of the Customs, solliciteing (in vain) for F. Nicolson, I attended the Commission at Whitehall for Queen Ann's Bounty: Where the Lady Wal[de]grave had a proposeal (like to be closed with) for the paying her 2000 *l*. per Annum till her Arrear is run off.[417] The Bishops still pressed to make returns of the value of Liveings in their Dioceses under 80 *l*.

With my Lord of Canterbury (in his Barge) to the House; where a full appearance of Lords (expecting the Dutchess of Shrewsbury[418] to be sworn, in order to her Naturalization), but nothing done more than the Reading a few Private Bills. The Sheriff's Bill, from the Commons, expected to be read a first time; but not mentioned. Philip Tullie applyed to Lord Treasurer [Godolphin] upon't; and I fancy it will be droped for this Session.[419] The Commons on the Hannover-Act.[420] I introduced Mr Grandorge (who afterwards dined

[413] Bernard Brougham (1670-1750), brother of Thomas and John, and Vicar of Holy Rood, Southampton, 1702-50. C. R. Hudleston, 'The Brougham Family', *CW* lxi (1961), 146.

[414] ?Charles Gale (*c*.1678-1738), Chaplain of Trinity College, Cambridge, 1703-6, and brother of Roger Gale, MP for Northallerton, 1705-13.

[415] Bolton was the leading Whig landowner in Hampshire, and was Lord Lieutenant of the county, where the Whigs captured both seats in 1705. One of the successful candidates was Bolton's nominee, Richard Chaundler.

[416] For the great struggle between the candidates at the Cambridge University election in May 1705 see W. A. Speck, *Tory and Whig* (1970), pp. 100-1, 107. Manchester was the Whig High Steward of the University, 1699-1722.

[417] The arrears were a pension granted from the revenue of the first fruits and tenths (now allocated to the Bounty). Lady Waldegrave, an illegitimate daughter of James II and Arabella Churchill, was paid off in 1712 with £8,644. See A. Savidge, *The Foundation and Early Years of Queen Anne's Bounty* (1955), pp. 33, 52, 83.

[418] Adelaide Paleotti (d. 1726), daughter of the Italian Andrea, Marquis Paleotti, had married the Duke of Shrewsbury in Sept. 1705. A lady of exotic mien (hence the 'full appearance' of peers), she was naturalised by Act of Parliament on 18 Feb. 1706. Their marriage had 'been the wonder, and discourse of everybody'. Berks. RO Trumbull MS 50: T. Bateman to Trumbull 11 Oct. 1705.

[419] This bill, designed to facilitate the passing of sheriffs' accounts and in other ways to ease the burden of their office, is printed in HMC *Lords MSS* vi, 268-73. Its first reading was postponed until 17 Feb. and it was killed on 27 Feb. *LJ* xvii, 662, 666, 678.

[420] This was the day on which the 'Whimsical clause' was accepted in committee. It would have had the effect of disqualifying all but thirty office-holders (approximately) in the present House of Commons if the Queen died while it was still in being, and of putting an absolute ceiling of between forty and fifty on the number of placemen who could at any time hold seats after the Hanoverian Succession. G. Holmes, 'The Attack on "the Influence of the Crown", 1702-16', *BIHR* xxxix (1966), 55; Luttrell, vi, 8-9,

with me) to the Archbishop of Canterbury who objected his giveing Intelligence to my Lord of York of a Dissenter's baptiseing in his Grace's Diocese, &c. but, upon what I had to offer in his just Vindication, assured us that 'twas answered.

In the Evening I fetched Dr Hickes to the Bishop of Hereford's; where we had the Conversation of Archdeacon Griffith, a thorough Welshman and Hollander. On discourse about the Saxon *yul* or *eol* being borrowed from the Welsh *gwŷl*, he gave me in writeing the various use (and Declination) of that word: *viz*. *Gwŷl*, a Holyday; *yr wŷl* (κατ᾽ ἐξοχην) Christmas; *yngŵyl Nadôlig*, in the Christmas time. Other Discourses we had on Scrieckius's[421] fond stretch of bringing all the old Names of Men and places from the Low Dutch; the Welsh Derivations of *Trinovant* (the Town on the River), *Dobuni*. *Bondvica*, &c.

[Jan.] 22. *Tuesday*. After a Condoleance with B. Nicolson and her brother Robin, on our ill success at the Custome-House yesterday, I went (with my brother) to visit Cousin Relf; who has a dangerous dry Cough. — I dined with Lord Thanet; and had, from His Lordship, the first Account of the Town talk touching the Earl of C[arlisle?]'s being a Papist;[422] which occasioned my recollecting of his Son's being committed to the Conduct of his Kinsman on the Road.

Mr Grandorge and I visitted Archdeacon Bowchier in my way home: where I had a Second Visit (the first unreturned) from Lord Lonsdale and Sir John Wentworth. Their Business was to acquaint me with Monsieur Loste's design of carrying a Companion with him to Lowther: And we all agreed, that the thing might be allowable on Supposition that nothing more was intended than the haveing a friend in a strange Countrey till a new Acquaintance was made. To know the bottome on't, he's to be sent to me; and I am to make my Report.

[Jan.] 23. *Wednesday*. At the House, a frivolous Cause; preceded by a warm Debate on a Petition (preferred by Lord President [Pembroke], at the Request of Lord Nottingham) on behalf of Annuitat's [annuities] on the late Marquess of Hallifax's Estate; which is 7000 *l*. in Arrear.[423] The secured Estate, it seems, will not defray this Charge

listing the exempted officers; 'Anon. Parliamentary Diary', ed. W. A. Speck, *Camden Miscellany*, xxiii, 78-81.

[421] Adriaen van Scrieck, early seventeenth-century Flemish etymologist.

[422] Cf. *CW* xlvi (1946), 207 for Dr Todd's assurance that 'Ld C. had a popish priest, Mr Lawson, for his Companion' (4 Oct. 1703).

[423] The petition largely concerned the manor of Fotheringhay, Northamptonshire, of William Savile, 2nd Marquess of Halifax. See HMC *Lords MSS* vi, 380-1.

without Sale; and, the Lady Stanhop[424] haveing the Reversion after the
three Lives and 500 years (which is not worth Six pence) refuses her
Consent. NB. To day the Italian Dutchess of Shrewsbury took the
Oaths in the House; haveing a Chair set for Her Grace (whereof she
made no use) at the End of the Clerk's Table, before the Bishops Bench.

After Dinner, not finding any at home in Salisbury-Court, I went
to Mr Bell; with whom (haveing had his Relation of poor Mr
Buchanan's Adventures with his wife, &c.) I spent the Evening.

[Jan.] 24. *Thursday*. After the Committee for Regulateing of Law-
proceedings (wherein Lord Keeper [Cowper], still loath to resign up
the Chancery to the Queen's Bench) a long Appeal against Mrs
Lamplugh; who, in the End, had her Decree unanimously affirmed.
Haveing treated Dr Waugh, after his long attendance on the said
Cause, I retired to my writeing of Letters; haveing onely two sleight
Interruptions by Mr Lamplugh[425] (sollicitous for Ebenezer Gale)[426]
and my neighbour R. Thomlinson.

[Jan.] 25. *Friday*. St Paul's day. It snowed hard, all day long.[427] — I
was the onely Bishop in the House, for some time after its sitting: And
then the Bishop of Sarum came in with the news of Sir Francis Russel's
dropping down dead.[428] A few Private Acts being read, I drew home
to Dinner; which done, and some Transcripts made out of Prynne's
2d Tome,[429] I went and concluded the Evening in Salisbury Court.

[Jan.] 26. *Saturday*. My chief Morning Guest, Mr Wotton; who cannot carry on his Design on a plurality. Robert Eglesfield saies his
Father is indebted above 3000 *l*. to the Crown.[430] *Euges Bone!*

---

[424] Elizabeth Savile (d. 1708), sister of 2nd Marquess of Halifax, had married in 1692
Philip, Lord Stanhope (1673-1726), who succeeded as 3rd Earl of Chesterfield in 1714.

[425] Probably Thomas Lamplugh of Lamplugh, Cumberland, MP for Cockermouth (see
Appendix A).

[426] Ebenezer Gale was the leader of opposition in Whitehaven to the Lowther family.
See *Memoirs of Dr Richard Gilpin, CW* extra series, ii (1879), pp. 26–8. Nicolson had
written to him on 22 Jan., 'Mr C. M[usgrave] and I useless at the Customs'. Tullie House
Library, Carlisle: Nicolson's Account Book for 1706.

[427] Even Narcissus Luttrell, normally indifferent to the climate, was moved to record
'a very great snow the whole day' (Luttrell, vi, 10). Rain and a rapid thaw followed
immediately. *Diary of John Evelyn*, ed. E. S. de Beer, v, 622, 27 Jan.

[428] Sir Francis Russell (*c*.1638–1706), 2nd Bt. of Wylley, Worcestershire, MP for Tewkes-
bùry, 1673-90.

[429] Possibly a reference to *An Exact Chronological Vindication and Historical Demonstration of our British, Roman, Saxon, Danish, Norman, English Kings Supreme Ecclesiastical
Jurisdiction* . . ., published in three volumes by Prynne in 1665-8. The copy referred to
here belonged to Wake (see below, 28 Jan.), and is to be found in Christ Church Library,
shelfmark W.b.3.1-3, bound as 'Prynne's Records'.

[430] Robert Eaglesfield was to become an ensign in Col. Thomas Stanwix's regiment of

At a Committee for Confirming Pareyra's[431] Contract for cloathing the Forces in Spain, the Envoy of Portugal[432] had a Chair; comeing to attest the Bargains as concluded by his Master. NB. He did not appear personnally at the Committee of the Commons; but onely sent in a paper. — Next came on the Committee for Law-Proceedings; whereat Lord Keeper proposed the explaining of the Act of Frauds and Perjuries,[433] &c.

In the House, the Commons brought up the Hannover-Bill with Amendments. Appointed to be considered (and all the Lords summoned) on Tuesday next. The Malt-Bill, read a first time; and several Private Acts. Lord Sunderland took notice of the suspitious Contents of one of these; and the Lord Keeper (a little Irregularly) of another. — Lord Archbishop of Canterbury saies he has consulted Lord Sommers on our Dean's Dispensation; and I shall have his Instructions how to proceed upon the Appeal of the Chapter. Lord Keeper also kindly promised that the Tenants of Dalston should not be defrauded of their Benefit of this Term; though (upon Suggestion of several Affidavits comeing up, that would set aside their late Verdict) a short Delay could not be refused the Citizens.

After Dinner, I waited on my Lady Lonsdale; where I met with Mr Loste, a little Maudlin (as I suspected) and weeping on the Remembrance of his Happiness at Geneva. Returning, I had a terrible Fall by a slip down the Stairs from the High-Terass in St James's Street; in which my left hand was a little strained, but (as yet) I feel no other ill consequences.

[Jan.] 27. *Sunday*. The Frost broke, and no Hackney-Coach to be had, I walked through the Dirt and Rain to St James's; where I preached (as promised) for the Bishop of Lincoln. In the Vestry, the Bishop of Hereford, goeing to dine at Lady Sunderland's;[434]

foot in Aug. 1707, and was still serving in the army in 1740. Dalton, vi, 193, 337–8. A Richard Eaglesfield was a Collector of Customs at Carlisle Port, and was dismissed in Jan. 1706, and in Apr. 'died deficient in his accounts'. *CTB 1705–6*, pp. 560, 634.

[431] Possibly Francis Pereira, a Jewish merchant, and by 1725 the largest holder of Bank of England stock. See P. M. G. Dickson, *The Financial Revolution in England* (1967), pp. 263, 278–9, 318, 498, J. A. Giuseppi, 'Sephardi Jews and the early years of the Bank of England', *Transactions of the Jewish Hist. Soc. of England*, xix (1955–7), 59–61. Isaac Pereira of the great Dutch firm of Machado and Pereira, who had supervised the commissariat of William III's expedition to England and his Irish campaigns in 1690, and who was still concerned in army contracts as late as 1710 (*CTB 1710*, p. 46), seems to have specialised in the provision of bread and forage.

[432] Dom Luis da Cunha, Portuguese envoy (1697–1710).

[433] 29 Cha. II c.3. See *Statutes of the Realm*, v, 839–42.

[434] The dowager Countess and mother of the 3rd Earl. A lady said to be 'distinguished for her subtile wit and admirable address', A. Collins, *The Peerage of England* (1735 edn.), ii, 242. She died in 1715.

and he hopes the two Houses will easily adjust the Differences about the Hannover-Bill.

Mr Wotton dined with us; and, before we sat down, sealed and delivered a Presentation to my Lord of L[incoln] for his Kinsman Mr Saul:[435] Whereupon His Lordship made him a voluntary promise of Cornelius Fuller's Liveing. Mrs Wake saies her Countrey (though born in Town) is Norfolk; of which King Charles the Second observed that 'twas a County fit onely to be cutt into Roads for the service of the better parts of England. After Dinner, my Lord carryed us into his choice Library;[436] plentifully furnished with the best Editions of Fathers, Councils, Historians Ecclesiastical, &c. He has a complete Collection of all our English Historians and Law-Books; amongst which the Year-Books in Ten fair Volumes, which (he saies) may be had for 5 *l*. He shewed us Tullie's works (in four Volumes, Folio) printed at Venice 1537[437] which he values at 15 *l*. The Salamanca-Edition of the Canon-Law,[438] Dedicated to the Image of the B[lessed] V[irgin], and an Italian History of all the Miracles[439] wrought by the said Virgin, in Honour of her Image, in several parts of Christendome; the French Memorials in the Council of Trent,[440] with a ratling Renuntiation of Pope Pius the IV by the French King's Minister in that Council, &c. — In a Press in his Dineing-Room, he has near Twenty Volumes (in Folio) of Transcripts of Records of Parliament, Register-Books of several Dioceses, Journals of Convocations down to the present Time, &c. Amongst the first, he shewed me the Award made by Richard 2 in favour of the Archbishop of Canterbury's Metropolitical Right of visitting the two Universityes; which is also confirmed by King and Parliament in the 13th of Henry 4 and there Inrolled· And hereupon, in the year 1636, Judgement was given (at the Council Board) in favour of Archbishop Laud; the Sentence the Chancellours (who are commonly of the highest Rank of Nobility)[441]

---

[435] Edward Sale (*c*.1677–?1754), formerly Fellow of Magdalen College, Oxford 1698–1704, he became Rector of Harlaxton, Lincolnshire, in 1706.

[436] Surprisingly, this appears to have been Nicolson's first sight of Wake's library, which now forms the basis of Christ Church Library, Oxford.

[437] *M. Tullii Ciceronis opera*, ed. by Petrus Victorius, now Christ Church Library, W.o.2.4–7.

[438] Probably Fray Juan de Pineda, *Los treynta libros de la Monarchia Ecclesiastica*, 5 vols. (Salamanca, 1588), now Christ Church Library, W.N.3.1–5.

[439] Don Felice Astolfi, *Historia Universale delle Imagini Miracolose delle Gran Madre de Dio riverite in tutti le parti del Mondo* (Venice, 1624), now Christ Church Library, W.N.53.

[440] Probably *Instructions et Lettres des Roi Tres-Chrestiens, et de leurs Ambassadeurs, et autres actes concernant le Concile de Trente*, 4th edn. (Paris, 1654), now Christ Church Library, E5, 4.

[441] The Chancellors of Oxford and Cambridge Universities in 1706 were the Dukes of Ormond and Somerset.

to appear at such Visitations by their Proxyes. Here are also Spelman's two Volumes of Councils, with Marginal Notes (in the Bishop's own hand) out of Somner's MSS.[442] &c., and his own Observations on Godwin's History of our Prelates,[443] through the whole Province of Cantcrbury, Emendations on his History of Convocations.[444] He had the use of Dr Hutton's Notes;[445] and found that their being very concise had led Dr Atterbury (who never consulted the Records themselves) into a Multitude of Errours.[446] He has all the several Tracts that passed on that Contraversy;[447] and has prefixed a List,[448] wherein Dr Atterbury's and those of his friends are in Red, and they of his own Side in black. Dr Hody's (as not surely to be ranked on either side)[449] stands on the Margine; with a black Title, struck under with Red.

The Bishop of Landaff is dead;[450] and yesterday (in my Lord's hearing) the Earl of Sunderland assured the Archbishop of Canterbury that His Grace might name whom he pleased for a Successor.[451] The Bishoprick he saies is worth 400 *l.* yearly Rent; and brings in a Fine of 1300 *l.* once in every seven years.[452]

[Jan.] 28. *Munday.* Haveing returned the Bishop of Lincoln's two Volumes of Prynne's Collections, I went to attend (for him) at the

[442] *Concilia Decreta Leges Conctitutiones in re Ecclesiarum orbis Britannici* (2 vols., 1639–64) by Sir Henry Spelman. Wake's copy at Christ Church Library MS ccclvii a and b.
[443] *De Praesulibus Angliae Commentarius* (1616) by Francis Godwin, with Wake's marginal notes in Christ Church Library MS cclxv.
[444] Wake's *The State of the Church and Clergy of England*, published 1703. His own copy with notes in Christ Church Library MS ccc.
[445] The notes of Matthew Hutton (1639–1711), the antiquary.
[446] Especially in *The Rights, Powers and Privileges of an English Convocation* (1700, 2nd edn. 1701).
[447] 1696–1703.
[448] Wake's list is still to be found bound at the beginning of his collection of 'Convocation Controversy' pamphlets. Christ Church Library, WT4, 17. The editors would like to thank H. J. R. Wing, Assistant Librarian at Christ Church, for his assistance in the identification of Wake's books.
[449] Humphrey Hody's *A History of the English Councils and Convocations, and of the Clergy's Sitting in Parliaments* was published around Feb. 1701 (*Atterbury Epist. Corr.* iii, 18–20). While a supporter of the Upper House, Hody, in Nicolson's words, 'pretends not to give any decisive judgement in any one point of the controversy . . . Nor did either side ever complain of his partiality', *English, Scotch and Irish Historical Libraries* (1776), ii, 164. Hody also contributed, anonymously, *Some Thoughts on a Convocation* (1699), and it is this pamphlet which Wake places in the margin of his list.
[450] William Beaw actually died on 10 Feb. 1706.
[451] John Tyler succeeded to the bishopric on 30 June 1706. For the circumstances of Beaw's replacement by this 'austerely Whiggish divine', an appointment bearing out Sunderland's confidence, see G. V. Bennett, 'Robert Harley, the Godolphin ministry and the bishoprics crisis of 1707', *EHR* lxxxii (1967), 730–2.
[452] Beaw valued the see of Llandaff at £230 a year 'in old Rents . . . and not one farthing more' (Beaw to Tenison, 21 Aug. 1699: Lambeth Palace MS 930, f. 49), while Wake valued it at £300 (Wake MS 18, ff. 393–4) and Brown Willis at £680 in 1719 (Wake MS 9, unfoliated).

House; which sat late, by reason of a Chancery-Cause 'twixt the Duke of Hamilton and Lord Mohun.[453] Waiting for the end of this, I had the agreeable Company of Mr Wotton and Mr Wanley in the Lobby; where the former better half perswaded to enter on the Translation of Junius's *Caedmon*,[454] as the latter to resume his thoughts of publishing all the Fragments of the Old Testament in Saxon. The Psalms, he saies, are to be entirely done anew; J. Spelman's Edition[455] haveing jumbled several Versions, in different Dialects. The like is to be said of the Gospels. The Remains, that are to be picked out of the several Homilies, not to be forgotten. Mr Wanley tells us that Mr Secretary Harley has gotten (in Sir Symonds Dewes's Library)[456] above 8000 Original Charters and Grants; wherein there's an entertaining Variety of Seals appendant, which shew the multiplicity of Fancies (amongst the Nobility and Great Men) before they bore Coats of Armour on their Seals.

In the House, onely Private Bills read; tho' an Order of yesterday had appointed the goeing into a Grand Committee on a Bill for bringing hither some French wine from Copenhagen:[457] But Lord Wharton thought fit to move for Adjournment till to morrow; which, upon the Question, was carried by 27 against 16. Of the latter were the Bishop of Chichester and I, the onely Members present on our Bench.

Buying Mr Willymot's Book[458] in the Dean's yard, I gave a short visit to Mr Postlethwait; who has a good walk, on the Leads over the School,[459] and 300 Scholars. He agrees with Mr Johnson that *Quae Genus* (and a good share of *Propria quae Maribus*) should not be read to Boyes. The Evening (after a fruitless Attempt to pay a visit at the Herald's Office) pleasantly spent at my Brother's.

[Jan.] 29. *Tuesday*. In the morning, a Visit to My Lord of York who very much over-run with the spleen. He's for Dr Wynne's being

---

[453] Mohun was left the personal estate, worth £20,000, of the Earl of Macclesfield in 1701, but the real property was subject to an excessively protracted, complicated, and fluctuating lawsuit both with the Crown and the Duke of Hamilton. See *GEC Peerage*. The lawsuit was the direct cause of the fatal duel between Hamilton and Mohun in 1712. For the duel see H. T. Dickinson, 'The Mohun–Hamilton Duel: Personal Feud or Whit Plot?', *Durham University Journal*, lvii (1965), 159–65.

[454] *Caedmonis monachi paraphrasis poetica Genesios* (Amsterdam, 1655), by Francis Junius (1589–1677).

[455] Sir John Spelman (1594–1643), eldest son of Sir Henry, published from the manuscripts in his father's library *Psalterium Davidis Latino-Saxonicum Vetus* (1640).

[456] See above, n. 123.

[457] French Wines Importation Act, see HMC *Lords MSS* vi, 390–1. There was a general prohibition on French wine imports during the Spanish Succession War which the 'claret lobby' (largely Tory) from time to time attempted to erode.

[458] William Willymot (d. 1737), grammarian, published in 1705 *The Peculiar Use and Signification of Certain Words in the Latin Tongue*.

[459] St Paul's School.

Bishop of Landaff.[460] Before I came hither, I followed Mr Christopher Musgrave to St James's where I gave him his Cousin R. Musgraves's Letter on behalf of Mr Langstaff.[461]

In the House, Debates on the Amendments of the Commons to the Hannover-Bill. The first (about the Great Officers happening to be in Commission) agreed to with a small Variation, shewing the Distinction 'twixt a Lord Treasurer of England and a Treasurer of the Exchequer. The second, proposeing the excludeing of other Officers from the House of Commons, was smoothly opposed by Lord Wharton; who observed there were yet many Defects in the first Succession-Act,[462] which wanted the Consideration of both Houses, most happily (at time) inclined to Unity and a good Correspondence, and therfore moved the Debate on this Clause might be Adjourned. This motion was seconded by Lord Sunderland; who hinted at the hast wherein the Lords were forced to pass the formentioned Bill, without Amendments. Accordingly, the Debate was adjourned (*Nemine Contradicente*) till Thursday; and the House, for meeting to go in Procession to Church, till to morrow.

In the Evening a kind visit from Dr Trimnel and Dr Gibson; the former observeing the Misrepresentation made by the Oxford-Antiquary[463] of the Assertion of the Archbishop of Canterbury's power of visitting the Universities. Memorandum. Whilst the Debates on the former Amendment of the Commons was depending, I was employed (by the Archbishop of Canterbury) in reading over a Printed State of the present Disputes betwixt the Upper and Lower Houses of Convocation in the Province of Canterbury[464] which seemed too particular in recounting what was said by (this and the other) single Members. This Censure I gave of it to His Grace; but, at the same time, declared my self well satisfyed with the Discourse in the main. 'Twill be dispersed, after Friday next; when, upon the Meeting of both Houses after their Christmass-Adjournment, my Lord thinks of makeing another Adjournment by a Schedule sent to 'em by his Commissary.[465]

---

[460] John Wynne, Tory divine. See Appendix A. This was one instance in which Sharp's influence with the Queen in matters of high preferment could not prevail.

[461] George Langstaff, besides his other duties (see above, n. 351), appears to have been an officer of the salt duty in Carlisle. Lord Carlisle was to complain later in the year of the officers, including Langstaff, and wished him displaced. *CTB 1705–6*, p. 748.

[462] Act of Settlement, 1701. For the tactics of the Whig peers in the 1701 parliament in declining at that time to wrangle over the anti-prerogative clauses of this Act, see H. Horwitz, *Parliament, Policy and Politics in the Reign of William III* (Manchester, 1977), p. 284; *The Divided Society*, ed. G. Holmes and W. A. Speck (1967), p. 23. For a full discussion of the 'Limitations', D. Rubini, *Court and Country, 1688–1702* (1967), ch. 8 and Appendix C.　　　　　　[463] Possibly Anthony Wood (1632–95).

[464] *Proceedings in the Present Convocation: relating to the Dangers of the Church, and the Protestation against the Irregularities of Some of the Lower-Clergy* (1706).

[465] The two Houses of Convocation had been in dispute over the Primate's right of

[Jan.] 30. *Wednesday*. I read Prayers at the House; and (after Adjournment to Eleven to morrow) the Lord Keeper [Cowper] was attended by the Duke of Northumberland and Earls of Westmerland and Bath, together with the Bishops of Exeter [Trelawney], Sarum, Peterborough, Bangor and Carlile, to Westminster Abbey; where the Bishop of St Asaph [Beveridge] preached an honest and pious sermon[466] on St Paul's Confession of his being present and consenting to the Death of St Stephen. — Before we went from the House, Sir Richard Holford (Master in Chancery) told me that old Coll. Lewis, yet alive, had assured him that he was at Rome when King Charles 1 was beheaded; and, some months before the execrable day of his Martyrdome, was there informed (and convinced) that the Conclave had resolved on his Death. He likewise assured me, by as good Testimony, that (upon the signification of this) O. Cromwel went to the Spanish Ambassadour in England; and endeavoured to perswade him that (without this bloody method) the Catholic Cause might be better served: But the Reply was onely — *He must die. He must die*. A Third story he gave me, as well attested, of several Popish Priests attending the King's Scaffold in the habit of Troopers; the better to enable them to certify that the Romish Sentence was executed.

I dined (at three) with Mr C. Musgrave together with Sir Christopher, Mr Joseph, Mr Thomas, and (their Cousin) Mr Lister; who highly commends the Sermon preached (this day) to the Commons by Dr Kennett.[467] Dr Moss,[468] Mr Musgrave saies, did not (as was expected) preach before the Queen, being confined by the Gowt; but sent his Deputy, one Mr Brown,[469] a stout Asserter of the old Doctrine of Passive Obedience. We shall see all their Sermons: As also Mr Dean

adjournment and prorogation ever since 1701. Tenison had insisted from the start 'that Convocation had always been prorogued by a schedule signed by the archbishop with the consent of his brethren and sent by the hands of the Registrar to the Prolocutor, who then intimated it to the lower clergy'; but until the marked swing of the Court towards the Whigs in 1705 he had not felt secure enough to take this line unequivocally. N. Sykes, *From Sheldon to Secker* (Cambridge, 1959), pp. 48–9.

[466] This being the anniversary of Charles I's execution. The state of Tory morale is perhaps reflected in the pitiful attendance of peers on this supposedly most emotive of High Church occasions.

[467] Even Thomas Hearne conceded that this sermon was 'suitable to the occasion . . . and was much different from that he preached formerly upon the same occasion'. *Collections*, i, 175. For the earlier sermon of 31 Jan. 1704, which had provoked much Tory animus, see Bennett, *White Kennett*, pp. 90–4.

[468] Robert Moss (*c*.1666–1729), Fellow of Corpus Christi, Cambridge, 1686–1714, Chaplain in Ordinary to the Queen, Dean of Ely, 1713–29.

[469] Francis Browne (*c*.1670–1724), one of the six chaplains at St James's and Whitehall; Vicar of Shalford, Essex, 1694; Canon of Windsor, 1713.

of Carlile's [Atterbury's] before the Lord Mayor and Aldermen at St Paul's.[470]

[Jan.] 31. *Thursday*. In the morning, I called on Sir A. Fountain; who shewed me his English Coins and Medals in proper Classes of Turkey-Leather, at 3*s*. a piece. Amongst these, he has a fair Sett of Gold-pieces: And, in the Middle of these, a massy Medal (of about 40 Guinneas in Weight) given him by Princess Sophia; with her Head, on one side, and an Inscription gieveing Her Titles and notifying the time of her being Nominated Successor to the English Crown, and (on the other) the Head of our Maud the Empress, from whom the House of Hannover derived their Descent. He shewed me a Shilling of Charles the first (for so the Inscription calls it) with a fair pourtraicture of his Father King James. He likewise produced, in Mediobarbus's Edition of Occo, two of Hadrian's Coins nearly resembling mine with the Britannia. He supposes all those of Carausius and Allectus to have been struck here; and most of 'em at London.

Endeavouring to wait on the Archbishop of Dublin in my Return, I went to the House: where, after the Committee for regulateing Law-Proceedings had made an Amendment to the Bill (in favour of the poor Clergy sueing, by English Bill, in the Exchequer) the Business of the Day came on,[471] in a full Appearance of Lords and Commons. The Debate was opened by Lord Wharton, who pressed the transmitting that Monarchy to the next Successor, without any Clogg.[472] He was seconded by Lord Sommers; who, with great Eloquence, enlarged on the same subject; and concluded with a motion — To repeal the Self-denying Clause in the old Succession-Act,[473] instead of qualifying and explaining it in the manner as it now stands in the Amendment of the House of Commons. This, after a great many weighty Arguments *Pro* and *Con*, was carryed upon the Question; by 68 against 25.[474] In the latter Number were the Bishops of Durham and Bath and Wells, the Archbishop of York and the Bishop of London being withdrawn; and the Archbishop of Canterbury, with ten of the Bishops, went with the Majority. Afterwards, the Clause requireing the Privy-Counsellers (in the former

[470] Atterbury's sermon does not, however, appear to have been printed (Bennett, *Tory Crisis*, p. 317). Kennett did publish (by order) *A Sermon preached before the Honourable House of Commons at St Margaret's Westminster ... Jan 30, 1705–6* (1706).

[471] The Regency Bill, as amended by the Commons.

[472] i.e. any further limitation of the royal prerogative.

[473] The 'place' clause in the 1701 Act of Settlement provided for an unqualified exclusion of office-holders and pensioners from the Commons, in practice (though not explicitly) to take effect on the accession of the first Hanoverian. See Rubini, *Court and Country*, pp. 175–7, 283.

[474] See also Luttrell, vi, 11–12.

Act) to subscribe to all Acts of Counsil[475] was likewise Repealed;
and a Proviso added against the Commissioners in the Prize-Office,
and others in new erected Places.[476] NB. In the Management of
these Debates, several Noble Lords made sharp Reflections personal:
As, Lord Cholmley observed that the Lord Haversham acted as
honestly and honourably when in Office, as out of it: The like
(with a new Turn) was remarked on the Duke of Bucks by Lord
Wharton: And, Lord Nottingham objecting against the power given
to the Lords Justices, as far too great for Subjects, Lord Sunderland
said this Arrainging, of what had already obtained the *Fiat* of the
House, was not Parliamentary; and that, he well remembered, the
House of Commons had sent one Jennings to the Tower for the like
Crime. Betwixt Six and Seven, all Alterations over, the House
Adjourned.[477]

Feb. 1. *Friday*. After I applyed (at the Admiralty) to Sir Cloudesley
Shovel for the Prince's Letter for Jack Nicols,[478] and gotten a favourable Answer, I attended several Committees: Which being over, the
House sat and a great many Private Bills were read, and Amendments
to the Law-Bill reported by Lord Sommers. Lord Wharton applyed
to me (a second time) about the Parton-Bill; and I promised that
Mr Dale should attend His Lordship to morrow.

Dr Gibson dined with me; and the Evening was spent with Dr
Hutton, Mr Hare,[479] Mr Holms and Mr Dale, in learning the Abuses at
the Herald's Office: Wherein most of the Lords of the Committee,
for Inspecting Public Records, are principally concerned.

[Feb.] 2. *Saturday*. At my Lord Wharton's *Levèe*, with Mr R.
Lowther and Mr Dale, on the matter of the Port at Parton: On
which we had a fair Audience, and good Encouragement to expect
His Lordship's countenanceing of Mr James Lowther, notwithstanding that Mr Lamplugh had been (this very morning) before
us. We found with my Lord the Duke of Argyle, Lord Mordaunt,[480]

---

[475] For the wording of this clause (4), see Rubini, *Court and Country*, p. 283.

[476] For this very limited disqualification, in place of the sweeping exclusions of the
'Whimsical clause', see Holmes, 'The Attack on "the Influence of the Crown" ', p. 56.

[477] Nicolson wrote to his wife that evening, 'Long day's Session. Weary'd out'. Tullie
House Library, Carlisle: Nicolson's Account Book for 1706.

[478] Nicolson had been in regular correspondence with his brother John in Carlisle since
mid Jan. about Jack Nicols, and was to spend considerable sums on the case in Feb. (see
Appendix D). The Prince's letter alone was to cost the bishop £3 4s. 6d.

[479] John Hare (c.1668-1720) had been Richmond Herald since 1704.

[480] John, Lord Mordaunt (c.1681-1710), MP for Chippenham, 1701-8, eldest son of the
Earl of Peterborough.

and pickled Mr Minshall;[481] the last an Advocate for Mr Fletcher.[482]

I dined at Lambeth, with Sir J. Cook,[483] the Dean of Lincoln, Mr Chamberlayn, Mr Clavering, &c. and, after Dinner, had a long Account (from my Lord of Canterbury) of Algernoon Sidney's[484] Natural Inclination to write speculatively of Government.—In the Evening, after the Dispatch of my Post-Letters, I got Mr Provost's[485] Recommendation of Joseph Rothery to the Tuition of Mr Hill;[486] and (at my Brother's) gave the boy 40 s. to bear his Charges to and from Oxford, this next week.

[Feb.] 3. *Sunday.* I preached, and consecrated the Sacrament, at St Botulph's Aldgate; and had the Company of Mr Gardiner (Subdean of Lincoln)[487] at Dinner, Dr Kennett haveing forgotten my promise, and invited him to preach. Dinner being late, I posted down to Sir W. Fleming at the *Bell* in Warwick-Lane; and went with him to Christ-Hospital,[488] where about 700 boyes are kept at School and 100 Girles: the former being taught Grammar, Writeing, Arithmetick, &c. and the latter Reading, Writeing and Plain Work. The Girls lodge all in one Ward (where they also eat) and the Boyes in several; each Ward being under the Inspection of an Elderly Matron, who is called its Nurse, and carves out their Commons at Table. The Writeing-School (very large, with five Benches on each side) was built at the sole Expence of Sir John Moor,[489] late Lord Mayor; who is said to have laid out, in his Life-time, 40,000 *l.* in Charitable Uses. The Mathematical School[490] is also spatious; and adorned with Globes, Ships, &c. Here the Queen's Navigation-Lads are instructed; and each of these wears a Silver-Badge on his left side, with the pourtraictures of Arithmetic, Geometry and Astronomy. 'Tis among Mr Evelyn's Medals. In the Common-Hall are two pieces of Fine

---

[481] ?Richard Minshall of the Inner Temple, Reader at St Clement's Inn in 1705. *Calendar of Inner Temple Records*, ed. F. A. Inderwick and R. A. Roberts (1896–1936), iii, 219, 396.

[482] Thomas Fletcher was a supporter of the Parton Harbour Bill. HMC *Lords MSS* vi, 399, 401.

[483] Sir John Cooke (1666–1710), Vicar-General and principal officer to the Archbishop of Canterbury.

[484] Whig politician and political theorist, executed for his part in the Rye House Plot, 1683.

[485] William Lancaster, Provost of Queen's College, Oxford, see Appendix A.

[486] Probably John Hill, Fellow of Queen's College, who helped to get Lancaster elected Provost in 1704. Hearne, *Collections*, ii, 32.

[487] James Gardiner, son of Bishop Gardiner of Lincoln, Subdean and Prebendary of Lincoln, 1704–d. 1732.

[488] Founded by Edward VI in 1553 as a home for orphans and poor children, it soon became a school. It was largely rebuilt, by Wren after the Great Fire, in Newgate Street.

[489] Sir John Moor (1620–1702), President of Christ's Hospital and Lord Mayor in 1681. The writing school was endowed and built in 1694 to Wren's design at a cost of £10,000.

[490] Founded in 1674 to qualify forty boys for service at sea.

Paint: the one (Signior Verrio's[491] Work) at the upper End, representing King Charles the Second, the Governours, Boyes and Girls, &c.
in their proper Habits; and the latter King Edward the Sixth
(surrounded with his Nobles) handing out their first Charter to the
Lord Mayor and Aldermen. Mr Brerewood, the Treasurer[492] entertained us with an Anthem sung by the Boyes from the Organ-Loft,
as soon as Supper was ended: And then we saw the Boyes and Girls
go off (in procession, two and two, with their Nurses and Baskets)
to their respective Apartments.

[Feb.] 4. *Munday*. From the Committee of the Commissioners of
Queen Anne's Bounty at Whitehal (where the Lady Wal[de]grave
waited for in vain by my Lords of Canterbury and Bangor and my
self) to those at the House of Lords; after the Archbishop of Canterbury had entertained us (very agreably) with a thorough Comparison
of the Libels of the present time with those of former Reigns. In
the House the main matter a Difference 'twixt the Bishops of Sarum
and Lichfeild, touching the Latter's Bill[493] for the Augmenting of
the Numbers of his Canons, &c; upon which, Thursday appointed for
its Second Reading; and the Lords to be summoned. The Evening
spent (in Disputes 'twixt High and Low Church) with Mr Thomas
Bell[494] and Mr Hutchinson.

[Feb.] 5. *Tuesday*. Shrove-Tuesday. Kept for the Queen's Birth-day;
the Solemnity whereof I could not attend. Morning Visitants, Mr
Clavering, Mr R. Thomlinson, Mr Dale, Robert Eaglesfeild and Roger
Briscoe. Letters written (whilst the rest of the Lords were paying
their Compliments at St James's, the Queen's Birth-day being now
observed instead of to morrow) I went to Moorfields, and picked up
a few old English Historians: Which done, I brought my brother
(with his wife and Daughter) to meet Sister Rothery at my Lodgeings; where we supped together, and spent the Evening cheerfully.

[Feb.] 6. *Ash-Wednesday*. The Court in Mourning for Q[ueen]
Dowager.[495] The Bishop of London preached at St James's on the
Working out Salvation with Fear and Trembling; a very Meagre Lent-

---

[491] Antonio Verrio (?1639–1707), Italian painter who worked in England from around
1671.
[492] Francis Brerewood, Treasurer of Christ's Hospital, 1700–7.
[493] Cf. below, 6 Feb., where it is described as the *Dean* of Lichfield's Bill.
[494] Formerly Vicar of Askham, 1681–90, deprived as a non-juror, he was succeeded by
his brother David. *CW* iii (1903), 17.
[495] Catherine of Braganza, who died on 31 Dec. 1705.

Sermon. The Queen was at Chappel; but born thither, being lame in the Gowt. After Dinner, I was visitted by (Mr Prolocutor) the Dean of Litchfeild [Bincks]; who is in pain for his Bill, now depending in the House of Lords. Another Visit, of the like kind, I had from Mr Lamplugh; who's as earnest for the Success of his Port at Parton. – In the Evening, at Dr Nicolson's with Mr Hutchinson and Mr Davis; treated with Yorkshire-Ale and Devonshire-Cheese.

[Feb.] 7. *Thursday*. In the Morning, Dr Scott, in warm Quest of the like Contributions from the Bishops as he got the last year: Mr Madox, not satisfyed with Mr Petyt's no progress.

At the House, the Bishop of Litchfeild prevailed on to delay the Reading his Bill:[496] The Commons, at a Conference,[497] gave Reasons why they could not agree to some Amendments made by the Lords to their Amendments on the Succession-Bill; which being Read, their Lordships unanimously agreed to Insist on their Amendments and appointed a Committee to draw up Reasons for their so doeing: The Bishop of Sarum moved for the throwing out a Private Bill in favour of Mr Asgil, the Translatour;[498] but, several Noble Lords observeing that his Family ought not to suffer for such a Fault, 'twas ordered a Second Reading.

The Evening (by Appointment) at Dean Graham's; where, with the Collonel and Mr Vaughan, Sir Thomas Dyke;[499] Who very sharp on Archbishop Tennison's Dispute with Pulton;[500] with a long History of the Attempts of his School-fellow Mr Meredith on Dr Busby,[501] &c.

[496] The bill was designed to augment the number of canons and to improve the prebends. It had progressed through the Commons between 10 Dec. 1705 and 26 Jan. 1706. Nicolson was on the committee which amended the bill and it passed the House on 22 Feb., the Commons agreeing to the amendments on 26 Feb. 1706. *CJ* xv, 59, 115, 167, 175; *LJ* xviii, 98, 119.

[497] In the Painted Chamber. Opposition in the Commons had predictably focused on the 'place' clause, and on 4 Feb. the House 'carried it by 22 against concurring with their lordships, 205 against 183; and ordered a committee to draw up reasons to be offered at a conference on the same'. Luttrell, vi, 13.

[498] The bill was for John Asgill's relief in relation to his purchase of forfeited Irish estates and subsequent bankruptcy (see J. G. Simms, *The Williamite Confiscations in Ireland*, p. 155). The bill received the royal assent on 16 Feb. 1706. *LJ* xviii, 107.

[499] Sir Thomas Dyke (*c*.1650-1706), 1st Bt., MP for Sussex, 1685-7, and East Grinstead, 1689-98.

[500] Andrew Pulton (1654-1710), a Jesuit, had been in controversy with Tenison in 1687, while Tenison was still Vicar of St Martin-in-the-Fields, over the 'corporal presence'. Pulton was imprisoned in 1688 and on his release joined James II at St Germain.

[501] Edward Meredith (1648-?89), Roman Catholic controversialist who took part in the Tenison–Pulton controversy. Richard Busby (1606-95), celebrated Headmaster of Westminster School, academically the most successful school of the late seventeenth century. See the vivid cameo in Bennett, *Tory Crisis*, pp. 24-5.

[Feb.] 8. *Friday*. J. Nicols brought to me, in the morning, by Mr Thomlinson: And an Account of the Bishop of Cloyne's [Crow's] advantages over his Vicar General before the Queen's Bench; the whole Court agreeing that no Vicar Generall can legally execute any power of giveing Institution, *ratione Officii*, without an Express Grant (to that purpose) in his Patent. At the Committee for Records, the Surveyor (Sir Christopher Wren) brought in an Estimate of the Charge of repairing the Chapter-House at Westminster; which amounted to above 1400 *l.* and is to be laid (by Petition) before the Queen.

In the House, a throng Appearance; but no business besides Private Bills. Lord Keeper [Cowper] acquainted me with the Order he had given for a New Tryal of the Issues betwixt the City of Carlile and Tenants of Dalston; pursuant to a standing Rule of the Court of Chancery, provideing that where two Issues have been tryed whereon Different Titles are to be Decreed, and the Verdicts are Equal, a New Tryal (on petition or motion of either party) is not to be refused. Coll. Francis Nicolson and Dr Kennett dined with me; the former notably versed in the Alliances of our Nobility, severely treated by Blaire and Beverley in Virginia,[502] who have miserably (in many things) imposed on the Bishop of London. The Evening at my Brother's in Salisbury-Court.

[Feb.] 9. *Saturday*. In the morning, forced to Address Mr Breton once more for F. Nicolson, through the endless Importunity of his mother; and obliged to send a Copy of the Dean's Dispensation to Archdeacon Trimnel. After setling of the Lease of Newburn (in project) with Mr Grascome and Mr Bell, I got Mr Crosfeild[503] to go with me to the Office of the Admiralty, to enquire after Capt. Hancock:[504] To whose House (at Poplar) young Mr Buchanan conducted J. Nicols, but they did not meet with him.

In the House, the Complaint (in Errour) of Williams against Offley[505] was heard; and the Complainant's Counsel insisting on the Reading of Affidavits brought below to support Motions for a new Tryal, the Lords refused to allow 'em to be Read here, as haveing Nothing of Fact (but Judgement onely) before 'em. — Archbishop of Canterbury acquainted me with the Queen's Appointment of a Fast, on Wednesday in Passion-week; desireing my Assistance (with others) in prepareing the Form. His Grace likewise took notice of the

---

[502] Robert Beverley (*c.*1673–1722), Clerk of the General Court, the Council and the General Assembly of Virginia, 1696–1705. *Dictionary of American Biography.*

[503] Robert Crosfield, Clerk at the Admiralty Office, 1700–15.

[504] Robert Hancock (d. 1707), Captain in the Royal Navy 1691.

[505] See HMC *Lords MSS* vi, 330.

true Reasons for the Thanks of the Lower House of Convocation to Mr Wall for his late Book on Baptism;[506] *viz*. The Author's lashing all the Bishops, in a Quotation out of St Austin [Augustine]; and his disrespectful Treatment of Archbishop Tillotson and Bishop Burnet (the Expositor) in particular.

In the Evening, I visitted Dr Lancaster; who's angry, very angry, at Dr Kennett's preaching down the *Libellous Pamphlets* that (in Charles the 1's dayes) *artfully distinguished betwixt the King and his Ministers, &c.*[507]

[Feb.] 10. *Sunday*. I preach[ed] at Covent-Garden; and, haveing been generously treated at Dinner by Mr Dean of Peterborough [Freeman], walked (in the Evening) to and from Kensington, without stop or calling, and returned sufficiently weary to my Lodgeings.

[Feb.] 11. *Monday*. Morning-visits from Mr Man, in prospect of another Ship; Mr L. Simpson, in great wrath against Dr Todd;[508] &c. With the Archbishop of Canterbury, the Bishops of Peterborough, Chichester and Bangor, and Dean of Lincoln, at a Committee in Whitehall; where several Proposeals agreed on for payment of Arrears on Pensions out of the Tenths; and the Arrears of the Bishop of Winchester [Mews] (3060 *l*.) and of the late Bishop of St Asaph[509] (upwards of 2000 *l*.)[510] considered.

In his Grace's Barge to the House: where the Reasons for the Lords Insisting on their Amendments[511] reported, and given to the Commons at a Conference: The chief of which were, 1. The Exclusion of Officers from being Members of the House of Commons will be Injurious to the Soveraign; who is hereby debarred of the Choice of such to serve Him or Her, as may be thought best qualifyed, if already Members of Parliament. 2. The like hardship will be upon the Electors, in Counties or Corporations; who must forgoe the Choice of suitable Representatives, if Officers under the Crown. 3. When any Inconvenience appears, from the sitting of such Members of Parliament, the Triennial Act gives the Electors an Opportunity if choose-

---

[506] See above, n. 331.   [507] See above, 30 Jan. and n. 467.

[508] Lancelot Simpson (1643-1711), of Allerthwaite, near Penrith, was Clerk of the Peace for Cumberland, 1690-1711. He resigned at the end of a court case, and was succeeded by his son Hugh. He was also a local agent for Lord Carlisle. E. Stephens, *The Clerks of the Counties, 1360-1960* (1961), p. 72; Hopkinson, p. 165. On 5 Feb. Nicolson had written to Hugh Simpson 'with a Copy of Dr Todd's Charge. Guilty, or not', and on 16 Feb. he was to write to Todd, 'My method with him and H. S[impson] fair. The Archbishop will do what's fit.' Tullie House Library, Carlisle: Nicolson's Account Book for 1706.

[509] Edward Jones (d. 1703).

[510] Cf. the case of Lady Waldegrave, above, n. 417.

[511] To the Regency Bill.

ing others.[512] 4. The chief Clamour, on this Head, has been since the Revolution; and yet, in this time, more Acts have passed for the Security of the Subject's Liberties than (in the like Number of years) in any forgoeing Reign. 5. By the Amendments of the Commons, many Elections must be had immediately on the Queen's Demise; a very improper time for such Numerous Congresses[513] as are usual on those Occasions: And, if (for Instance) Portsmouth, as is probable, should be obliged to make a new choice, the Garrison is to march out, and all who pretend to the Right of Electors are to come in; which may endanger the Surrender of that Important place to any Pretender to the Throne. 6. The Exceptions which the Commons have made, of the chief Court-Officers,[514] looks like appropriateing those Offices to themselves; whereas the Lords have hitherto had their share in 'em. — The Bishop of Litchfeild's Bill was posponed its Second Reading; in hopes of haveing all its Particulars better setled, by Consent. Most of the Lord (Spiritual and Temporal) were invited to dine with the new Judge, Mr Justice Dormer;[515] whose Serjeant's Motto, given by the Bishop of Sarum, is *Imperium Oceano, Famam Astris*: For which his Lordship saies, he lately read over Virgil. At the House, I received (by the Penny-post) a Letter, subscribed by one who writes his name Thomas Smith, and dated from Leaden-Hall-Street; wherein the Writer banters me with strange Matters hatching in the North, to my dishonour, &c. *Magna est Veritas, et praevalebit*!

In the Evening (after a Walk into Hyde-Park with Cousin Thomas Pearson and Mr Holm) at the Dean of Sarum's [Younger's] with the Dean of Wells [Grahme] and Mr Vaughan: Where the Story of the Queen's laying aside her Staff, in goeing to Council on Her predecessor's death, a *Certain Cure for the Gowt, but hard to come by*; and Mr Subdean Battle's[516] Account of his being directed to putt his Letters from hence to Rome into the Pacquet of Mr Pen, a Brother of the Society of the Jesuits.

[512] Six general elections had already been held since the passing of the Triennial Act in 1694, on which see *The Divided Society*, ed. Holmes and Speck, pp. 10-11.

[513] i.e. gatherings of people.

[514] The officials excepted from the general disqualification included the Treasurer, Comptroller and Vice-Chamberlain of the Household; two principal Secretaries of State; the Chancellor of the Exchequer and up to five Treasury Commissioners; and the Chancellor of the Duchy of Lancaster. For the full list see Holmes, 'The Attack on "the Influence of the Crown" ', p. 55 n. 4.

[515] Sir Robert Dormer (1649-1726), MP for Buckinghamshire, 1701-2, 1705-6, and Northallerton, 1702-5; Chancellor of Durham. His appointment as a Judge of the Court of Common Pleas, in lieu of the late Sir Edward Nevill, was a fresh mark of favour for the Whigs. See Luttrell, vi, 15.

[516] Ralph Battell (1649-1713), Sub-Dean of the Chapel Royal, and Sub-Almoner to the Queen, 1689-1713.

[Feb.] 12. *Tuesday*. In the House, on Reading a Private Bill[517] sent from the Commons, which appeared to be fraudulent for the Sale of an Estate left to Infants by their Father, and the Purchase-money ordered into the Mother's hand. The Lord Keeper [Cowper] laid such an Emphasis on the peccant parts of the Breviat, that the Lords took notice of the Roguery; and threw it out with Indignation. Hereupon Lord Sommers made an excellent Speech against the perfunctory and careless passing of such Bills;[518] and the Lord K[eeper] observed that the Breviats of many of 'em were so un[in]telligible often times (by way of blind) as never failed of discovering to him the Villany that was in them. Lord Hallifax took this occasion to inveigh against the Archbishop of Dublin's Bill;[519] which, he said, was one of the many Instances of the Loss that came to the Crown by the false Titles in Conveyances of the forfeited Estates in Ireland: And that too many Revocations of this kind had already passed in Parliament.

Dr Gibson dined with me: And Mr Maul, in the Evening, took Leave for Ireland, with my Letter to the Bishop of Cloyne.

[Feb.] 13. *Wednesday*. In the morning, I waited on the Archbishop of Dublin; who thankfully took my advice of goeing immediately to inform my Lord Hallifax and found his Account in it. The said Lord soon after kindly acquainted me, in the Prince's Chamber, that some [of the] Lord[s'] committees for examineing the Records, would be to morrow (at Ten) in the Paper-Office; and desired my makeing one of the Number.

After the last Money-Bill[520] was brought up from the Commons, I went (with Mr Chamberlayne) to dine with the Royal Society at *Pontac's*;[521] where Sir John Cope,[522] Sir Thomas Crisp,[523] Mr Herbert,[524] Dr Woodward, Dr Cockburn (and four more) were our

---

[517] See HMC *Lords MSS* vi, 396.

[518] For the efforts of Somers and Cowper this session to control the abuses of private legislation, see in general Burnet, *History*, v, 249–50.

[519] Bill for making effectual a grant of their late majesties, King William and Queen Mary, of the town and lands of Seatown, and for restoring the same to the see of Dublin. It received the royal assent on 19 Mar. 1706. *LJ* xviii, 162. See J. G. Sims, *The Williamite Confiscations in Ireland*, pp. 154–5.

[520] The Annuity Bill.

[521] Pontack's in Lombard Street was a famous dining place and tavern, named after a M. Pontack (or Pontacq), a vintner of Lombard St. It was established in the 1670s and lasted until the 1780s. See B. Lillywhite, *London Coffee Houses* (1963), pp. 450–4.

[522] Either Sir John Cope (d. 1721), 5th Bt., of Hanwell, Oxfordshire, MP for Oxfordshire, 1679–90, and Banbury, 1699–1700; a Director of the Bank of England, 1695–8, 1700–2; or Sir John Cope (1673–1749), Kt., of Branshill, Hampshire, eldest son of the above, MP for Plympton, 1705–8, Tavistock, 1708–27; elected to the Board of the Bank in 1706. Sedgwick, i, 575–6.

[523] Sir Thomas Crisp (1703), Kt., of Dornford, Oxfordshire, FRS 1666.

[524] ?John Herbert, FRS 1677.

fellow Guests. Thence we adjourned to Gresham-College; where Mr Burnet,[525] and three more, were (by Ballot) chosen Fellows, Mr Edward Howard (of Berkshire) offered a Nonsensical Paper for the Improvement of Navigation; which was, more Civilly than it deserved, rejected: And Mr Hawkby shewed us an Experiment of Light formed by a swift Motion of Quicksilver *in vacuo*, very entertaining; especially, as explained by Sir Isaac Newton. In the Repository, the Wind-Gun; which kills at 100 yards distance: And the Contracted MS. by the fire of London. Buchanan's[526] picture (from Sir Thomas Povey)[527] with others of the Presidents, from Sir W. Murray, in the Council-Room.

In the Evening, at my Brother's where Mrs Pinfold and Mrs Brewer guests.

[Feb.] 14. *Thursday*. In the Morning, I went to the Paper-Office; where I found the Lords Rochester, Grey, Sommers and Hallifax. This place is in better Order than I ever saw it; and Mr Tucker promises me a Copy of a Paper (which I found in his new Catalogue) that gives a better View of its Contents, than what he first gave in to the Lords Committees. Sir J[oseph] Williamson, in a Letter of his to my Lord Arlington, shews that Mr Secretary Maurice[528] sent nothing in hither, dureing the 10 or 12 years of his being in the Ministry; and that the Original Treaty of Breda was in his Custody.

At my Return, Mr Buchanan gave me a visit, and a pleasant Account of Generall Dalyel's[529] marching in his Polish Habit through the Streets of London, followed by a Mob of Boyes to a Tavern; where, at entrance, he courteously thanked the young Gentlemen, and acquainted them that he should go abroad again about four in the afternoon.—Lease of Newburn sealed to Mr Husband.—In the House, onely Private Bills.

This day was published Mr Dodwel's scandalous Book entitled— *An Epistolary Discourse, proveing from the Scripture and the first fathers that the Soul is a Principle naturally Mortal; but immortal actually by the Pleasure of God, to Punishment or to Reward, by its Union with the Divine Baptismal Spirit: Wherein is proved that none have the power of giveing this Divine Immortalizeing Spirit, since the Apostles, but onely the Bishops*. This was sold publickly at the Doors of both Houses of Parliament and many of our

[525] William Burnet, FRS 1706.
[526] George Buchanan (1506-82), Scottish historian, presented by Thomas Povey in 1696. *The Records of the Royal Society of London* (4th edn., 1940), p. 155.
[527] Thomas Povey (neither knighted nor created Bt., contrary to Nicolson), FRS 1663.
[528] Sir William Morrice (1602-76), Secretary of State (North), 1660-8.
[529] Thomas Dalyell or Dalzell (?1599-1685), General and C.-in-C. Scotland, 1666-85.

Temporal Lords (particularly my good Lord President [Pembroke])
expressed to me their hearty abhorrence of the Doctrine.

[Feb.] 15. *Friday*. Forced out by Mr Tyrrel (together with Mr Dale
and Mr Holmes) to attend Mr Le Neve at the Chapter-House of
Westminster where we saw several of King David the First's forms of
Hommage, &c. As, 1. The Homage he made on the 2d of June, in
the first year of his Reign; wherein mention is made of the *Custumae*
and the *Tres status* of that Kingdome; which Mr T[yrrel] will not
allow to be of so old standing in that Countrey. 2. Another dated
Nov. 1. in the 5th year of that King's Reign: *Apud Halyrodehowse,
in pleno parliamento Triū Statuū*. There's a Duplicate of this; both
under Seal. The one seems to have undeniable Marks of Forgery
upon it; haveing neither the same seal, not being written in the same
hand, with the other. 3. A Third in French, upon the Ransome of
this King. 'Tis without a Seal; but allowed to be Genuine. 4. A Fourth
in Latine, fairly sealed as the two first, and bearing date the 20th of
March in the 26th year of his Reign. 5. A Trewse in old English,
dated April 12 1352. 6. Another, of the like kind, in French. 1359.
Neither of these are sealed; but both conceived to be Genuine. Mr
Le Neve again obliged me with a Sight of the Treaty 'twixt Francis
the first of France and our Henry 8. which is in Latine, and the most
beautiful MS. that I ever saw. The Golden Seal is curious work; and
so are the Embellishments on the first Page of the Treaty, where is
Francis's picture to the Life with his Salamander in Flames under
the Mottoe of *Nutriseo et Extinguo*. The Book of the Statutes of the
Order of St Michael, sent by the said King to Henry 8 is also very
fine: And so is the Indentured Book, of the like kind, betwixt
Henry 7 and the Abbot of Westminster, &c. upon the Erection of
that King's fair Chapple. The Protestation of our Nobility against the
Pope's Determination of the Cause of Henry 8th's Divorce is also
a Curiosity of good Note; the Seals being appendant.

In the House, several private Bills rejected; and some Resolutions
taken, in a Grand Committee, for the more safe and honourable passing
of such Bills for the future.[530]—Whilst my Dinner was getting Ready,
I went to see a Couple of Yellow (spotted) Leopards, an Hyaena very
fierce with bristles, a Civet-cat, a little Squirrel-mouthed Egyptian
Panther, &c at a Neighbouring-House; where was also a great Variety
of all sorts of Singing Birds, as Bull-finches, Canaries, Nightingales,
&c. and Parakeets (male and female), Turtles, &c.

In the Evening at Dr Gibson's, whence I brought home with me Mr
Smith and Mr Hutchinson, and had their Company till Bed-time.

[530] See also above, 12 Feb. and n. 518.

[Feb.] 16. *Saturday*. At the House, the Queen gave the Royal Assent to the Annuity-Bill and Malt-Tax, with several Private Bills: Which done, Her Majesty made a Gracious Speech;[531] extolling the Dispatch that was already made, and pressing the bringing of this Session to a speedy Conclusion. Report was made of the Rules and Orders to be hereafter observed in passing of Private Bills in the House;[532] and (on Motion of the Earl of Rochester) one added, That these should be alwaies given in Charge to every Committee on Private Bills.

The Archbishop of Canterbury acquainted me with his Letter of Complaint from Dr Todd; and told me that, he found, another was written to my own Metropolitan: Which my Lord of York owned to me, but declined the giveing me any satisfactory Light into't. — The Bishop of Hereford, in discourse, observed that *Brie-Gant* (in Welsh) signifies the High Borders; and *Pen-y-gant*, the Hill on the Borders.

[Feb.] 17. *Sunday*. The Bishop of Norwich preached at the Queen's Chapple on *Job*, 21, 15: an argumentative Discourse on the Nature of Divine Providence, and the Necessity of Prayer. I dined, with Coll. Byerley, at Mr C. Musgrave's where the Collonel gave us a pleasant Relation of some late remarkable Speeches of Sir Thomas Meers:[533] One of which compared the present Comptroller[534] with (his predecessor) Sir E. Seymour; of the latter observeing that he used to sit in the same Corner, yet now—*The Staff*[535] *is there, but the Man is not.*[536]

[Feb.] 18. *Munday*. In the morning, with Mr Grisdale[537] and Mr Yates, waiting on the Archbishop of York; to set the Reports of their extortion of Parish-Fees in a fair Light. I expected His Grace would have taken Notice to me of Dr Todd's late Letter to him, with new Complaints; but—*ne Gru.*

In the House, Coll. Rice's Bill for Debentures of 11,000 *l*. in consideration of his bringing over a French Regiment of Horse after the

---

[531] *LJ* xviii, 107.

[532] For the standing orders relating to private bills see *LJ* xviii, 105–6; HMC *Lords MSS* x, 23–4.

[533] The veteran Country Whig, Sir Thomas Meers (1634–1715), MP for Lincoln, 1659, 1660–81, 1685–7, 1701, 1702–10 was 'the father of the House'. See D. T. Whitcombe, *Charles II and the Cavalier House of Commons* (Manchester, 1966), p. 205.

[534] Sir Thomas Mansel, Comptroller of the Household since 1704. See Appendix A.

[535] i.e. the Comptroller's white staff.

[536] Sir Edward Seymour, though still MP for Exeter, was in poor health and made few appearances in the House between 1706 and his death in 1708.

[537] Possibly Robert Grisedale of Westmorland, educated at Queen's College, who was Clerk of St Martin-in-the-Fields.

Reduction of Limerick, passed (with some appearance of Difficulty) in a grand Committee. Sir Thomas Pendergest,[538] one of his Captains, his chief Witness. This occasioned some hard Reflections on the Archbishop of Dublin's depending Bill; which was observed to be of the like kind: But the Earl of Rochester warded off that blow for the present, with — *Sufficient unto the Day is the Evil thereof.*

[Feb.] 19. *Tuesday*. In the morning, I sent (as desired) my man to Lord Hallifax; who sent me Mr Rymer's Second Volume of Treaties, and promised to procure me the former also from Lord Treasurer [Godolphin].

In the House, the Amendments of the Commons to the Security-Bill[539] (given in at a Conference) were immediately agreed to by the Lords:[540] Which happy Accommodation gives a certain prospect of a Speedy and Joyful Conclusion of this Session.[541] Catterick Birkbeck's Appeal[542] came on against his Brother in Law Speerman; and his Creditor Wilkinson was also allowed to appear by his Counsel: Which occasioned the deferring of part of that Cause to another Day.——By Lord Wharton's Directions, I brought in the Petitions of the Gentlemen and Freeholders of Cumberland (together with that of the Citizens of Carlile) against the Bill for Enlargement of the Harbour at Parton: And, upon my motion, the Lords ordered the Petitioners to be heard by their Counsel at the Barr of the House on Thursday next.[543]

In the Evening, Mr Bell came to me; bemoaning the Misbehaviour of Mr Dodwel in his late Book of the Natural Mortallity of the Soul. Afterwards, I went (by appointment) to Johnston's Court in Fleet-street; where Mr Madox shewed me Nine large Volumes (in Folio) of his own Collections out of Records and MSS. Dr Hutton pleasant in the History of his Amours with his D.C.B. but a little more dumpish in relateing the cool Answer given by the Queen to the

[538] Sir Thomas Prendergast (d. 1709), 1st Bt., MP [I] for Monagham 1703-9, Brigadier-General, was killed at Malplaquet.

[539] For these amendments, carried by twelve votes in a House of over 400, see Luttrell, vi, 17-18; Holmes, 'Attack on "the Influence of the Crown" ', pp. 58-9. On the vital 'place' provision they represented a compromise between the 'Whimsical clause', on the one hand, and the Lords' amendments on the other.

[540] *LJ* xviii, 111-12. The way for the compromise had been paved by intense behind-the-scenes negotiations between the Junto lords, with Townshend and Cowper in support, and the leading Country Whigs. For these manœuvres, and the crucial secession of Sir Richard Onslow and Robert Eyres from the opposition to the Court—which probably saved the bill, see Holmes, 'Attack on "the Influence of the Crown" ', pp. 53-8.

[541] On this day Nicolson wrote to Receiver Aglionby in Carlisle that the 'Session at an End'. Tullie House Library, Carlisle: Nicolson's Account Book for 1706.

[542] See HMC *Lords MSS* vi, 360-2.

[543] For the petition see ibid., pp. 398-9.

Archbishop of York's on his Application for the Professor's Chair at Oxford.[544] Dr Smalridge will not be the man: But (probably) Mr Potter.[545]

[Feb.] 20. *Wednesday*. Early at the Committee for the Bishop of Litchfeild's Bill for the better Regulation of his Cathedral-Church. The Bishop of Sarum, with the Earls of Sunderland and Stamford, severe upon Dean Bincks; and, upon their Insisting on the Queen's giveing Her formal Consent for the Uniteing of a Liveing (of her Majesty's Patronage) to the Deanry, the Committee was adjourned. —Mr Palmes's Appeal against[546] the men of York was half heard; and Adjourned till to morrow.

The Bishop of Exeter's lending me a MS. copy of Bede's life of St. Cuthbert occasioned my promiseing Lord Herbert an Account of St Herberht[547] his reputed Kinsman. Called from my brother's in the Evening by Mr Grascome and Mr Bell, I went to adjust Accounts with them: Which done, I found they both agreed in crying up Mr Johnston's Grammar and crying down Mr Dodwel's Divinity.

[Feb.] 21. *Thursday*. By Instructions from the Archbishop of Canterbury I went Very early to attend a Committee on the Bill for setling the Rectory of St Bride's: which was read afterwards a 3d time, and passed with a few Literal Amendments. Afterwards, came on the long and large Remnant of Mr Palmes's Appeal; and it appeared (from several of his own and his wife's Letters) that he had taken up Clipt money, on the turn of the Coin in 1696,[548] to the value of above 5000 *l.* under such Promises and Conditions as were not yet performed. The Counsel being withdrawn, there was a long Silence; a Majority being loath to give sentence against a man of Mr Palmes's

---

[544] The Regius Professorship of Divinity at Oxford was held by William Jane, who did not die until 1707. His ill-health, or anticipated retirement, may account for these early manœuvres over his prospective successor.

[545] John Potter, the future Archbishop of Canterbury, currently Fellow of Lincoln College and Domestic Chaplain to Archbishop Tenison (see Appendix A), was Marlborough's candidate for this important ecclesiastical patronage prize, and was favoured by the Whigs; George Smalridge, Fellow of Christ Church and at present Deputy Professor (see Appendix A), was the candidate of Sharp and Harley. When William Jane died in 1707 the contest became entangled with the broader 'Bishoprics crisis' of that year, and the post was not finally filled (by Potter) until Jan. 1708. See G. V. Bennett, 'Robert Harley, the Godolphin Ministry and the bishoprics crisis of 1707', *EHR* lxxxii (1967); HMC *Portland MSS* iv, 388, 473–4: Smalridge to Harley, 12 Feb. 1707, 8 Jan. 1708; Coxe, *Marlborough*, ii. 101, 161: Marlborough to Duchess of Marlborough, 12/23 June 1707, 8/19 Sept. 1707.

[546] See HMC *Lords MSS* vi, 305–6. For Palmes see below, n. 549.

[547] ?St Herbert (d. 687), friend of St Cuthbert, who had visited Carlisle.

[548] For the Recoinage see J. K. Horsefield, *British Monetary Experiments, 1650–1710* (1960), pp. 37–90; Ming-Hsun Li, *The Great Recoinage of 1696 to 1699* (1963).

kidney.[549] At last, some Lords began to whisper *Affirm, Affirm*, &c. which occasioned a motion from the Duke of Devon that the Loss might be divided 'twixt the Appellant and Respondents. This being Impracticable, the Decree was affirmed *Nemine Contradicente*.

This being over, Lord Rochester moved for dispensing with the Standing Order of allowing 14 dayes after the Commitment of a Private Bill; and was seconded by Lord Sommers and Lord Nottingham. On the other side were Lord Wharton, Lord Hallifax, Lord Treasurer [Godolphin] and Duke of Marlborough, which last made two or three earnest Replies to the Earl of Nottingham. After a warm Debate, Lord Treasurer proposed that part of the Orders for the future Management of Private Bills, might presently take place. *Viz.* That all that were now before the House might now be referred to the Judges, for their Opinion of such as were fit to be passed: But, the Judges being immediately to enter on their Circuits, this was thought Impracticable. Whereupon, the Question was put—*Insist or not Insist on the Standing Order?* and carried for *Insisting.*—I had Dr Gibson's company at Dinner. He knowes nothing of Mr Potter's being designed for Professor at Oxford.

[Feb.] 22. *Friday*. The Committee on the Bishop of Lichfeild's Bill sate early; and the Lord President [Pembroke] brought Her Majesty's consent to the annexing the Rectory of Tattenhal to the Deanry of Lichtfield. Upon which, the Bill was gone through; and (with some Amendments) reported to the House, and passed. At a Conference, the Commons gave Reasons for their disagreeing to an Amendment made to Mr Cary's Bill for bringing in some French wines from Copenhagen, shiped in France before the late Prohibition; by which Amendment general Leave was given for the Importing of such Wines, either from Ireland or Holland, for four months. These Reasons (chiefly insisting on our present Engagements with Portugal)[550] were such as had their present Effect and the Lords immediately returned the Bill, with a Message, *That they did not insist on their Amendment*. After the Reading of a few Private Bills, The Counsel were called in on the Bill for Parton-Harbour; Mr Dodd[551] and Mr Phipps appearing against the Bill, and Mr Serjeant Chesshire for it. The Chief Witness produced by the former was

---

[549] William Palmes (b. *c.*1638), MP for Malton 1668–85, 1689–1713, a Yorkshire landowner of great wealth with strong Whig (especially Junto) connections.

[550] Portuguese wines received most-favoured-nation treatment under the terms of the Methuen Treaty of 1703.

[551] Samuel Dodd, 'an ancient practiser' of the Court of Exchequer, who specialised in commercial law and had negotiated the merger of the Old and New East Indian Companies. John, Lord Campbell, *Lives of the Lord Chancellors* (8 vols., 1845–69), iv, 350.

Mr G[ilfred] Lawson, who gave an account of the falsyfying of hands at the Cockermouth-Sessions, &c. and, on the other side, Mr Justice Addison declamed against the monopolizeing Oppressions of the Late Sir John Lowther, whose Interests in and about Whitehaven were those onely that were Superiour to his own. There was some Debate (the Counsel being withdrawn) whether this Gentleman's Evidence should be heard, since it appeared that he had petitioned below for the bringing in the Bill, and was one of the Trustees nominated in it: And the Lord Keeper [Cowper] (haveing his Opinion asked) declared that he thought not to be admitted in any Tryal either at Law or in Equity; but that the Lords, in their Legislative Capacity, were (he thought) at greater Liberties. [This was certainly wrong; For the man was here upon his Oath, and a party, and 'twas giveing way (if not a sort of Invitation) to those Stretches which he made in his Testimoney.][552] Admitted he was; and a modest story he told of himself, &c. Counsel and Witnesses withdrawn, Lord Wharton pressed the Contents of the Petitions against the Bill; and was seconded by the B[ishop] of C[arlile] who observed there were the Subscriptions of 15 (out of 17) of the Justices of Peace and Deputy Lieutenants resideing in the County, and almost all the Citizens of Carlile that could write their Names. Hereupon, Lord Mohun and others moved that the Bill might be immediately thrown out: And the House seemed generally inclined to doe soe. But Lord Rochester desireing that the Commissioners of the Customs might first be heard (and Lord Wharton being willing to let the Bill fall as easily as we could, since the Duke of S[omerset] seemed to espouse it)[553] Munday next was appointed for the said Commissioners to appear.

Mr Lawson, Dr Gibson, Mr Dale and Mr Hare, dined with me: And the Evening was spent with my Brother, Sister and Niece, in Salisbury-Court.

[Feb.] 23. *Saturday*. Visited in the morning by Mr Buchanan and Capt. Garret; both Beggars. In the House, amongst other Private Bills, Mr Goulston's[554] appeared to be sent in with such a Breviate as concealed the purport of a Deed of Trust whereon the whole Equity of the Bill depended: Which being observed by Lord Keeper, the House ordered the Sollicitor to be immediately called in,

[552] Nicolson's brackets.

[553] The duke and Lord Wharton were uneasy political allies in Cumberland—they were at open loggerheads over the Cockermouth election in 1713—and Somerset had apparently been converted to the support of the bill by Thomas Lamplugh, one of the present members for Cockermouth.

[554] See HMC *Lords MSS* vi, 429-30.

reprimanded at the Barr, and commanded to prepare a more full Breviate. He alledged for himself that this Br[eviate] was drawn by the Clerk of the House of Commons; and was here the same as below. — The Archbishop of Dublin's Bill being considered (according to Order) in a grand Committee, Lord Hallifax moved that the Endowment might either be transferred towards the Augmentation of some English Bishoprick or the Price refunded out of the Revenue of Ireland; and was seconded by Lord Sunderland. On the Archbishop's behalf appeared Lords Rochester, Nottingham, North, &c. Lord Sommers moved for Amendment of the Title, in Honour of King William the Donour; which was unanimously assented to. Upon a motion, for throwing out the Refunding Clause, the House divided; and the Archbishop carried the Question by 30 against 28. In the former Number were all the Bishops except Sarum. The House being Resumed, and the Amendments reported and agreed to, one Motion was made for the Bill's being read a 3d time on Munday; and another for its being read immediately. The Question being put on the former of these, it was carried by 25 against 22, the Lords Rochester, Weymouth and Townsend, with the Bishops of Hereford and Carlile being of the former Number, though with the Archbishop in the former Question. NB. They feared the provokeing the Opponents Lords; who (on sending back the Bill to the Commons) might hinder an Agreement to the Amendments, and so lose the Bill in the other House. — C. Birbeck's Appeal (in the name of Mr Wilkinson) came on again: But it being late before this new Appellant's Counsel was heard, and the Judges not appearing as ordered, the Remainder was again Adjourned.

In the Evening, a Visit to Mr Buttle of Grey's Inn; who shewed me 14 vollumes of dryed English Plants; the fairest I had seen. His Mosses are remarkably Curious and Numerous. Most of our Northern Trees, he saies, are in Suffolk; and many of 'em (as the *Fraxinus Silvestris, Alnus,* &c.) in the woods about Hampstede. Mr Dandridge, a Drawer of Patterns for the Silk-Weavers in Moor-fields, has the most complete Collection of Insects; which he breeds in Boxes, preserves dryed in double Glasses, &c. Mr James Pettiver has lately lost 800 *l.* by the breaking of one Airay, a Northern Quaker and wholesale Silk-man.

[Feb.] 24. *Sunday.* At Whitehall morning-Service: where Lords High Chamberlain [Lindsey], Carnarvon, Bath, Holdernes, Guilford, &c. and the Bishop of Peterborough. At Dinner, young Mr Buchanan; assisting the setting forwards of J. Nicols.[555] Evening at D. Relf's in

[555] Nicolson had written to Capt. Robert Hancock at Portsmouth 'Recommending

Colman street,[556] with all the Family; celebrateing this day for (Sunday next) Midlent.

[Feb.] 25. *Munday*. Mr King's[557] Bill paid, and Mr Henley[558] brought and carryed off by Brother Joseph, I went to the House: where the Archbishop of Dublin's Bill passed without any farther Amendments. The Commissioners of Customs (by Mr Godolphin)[559] were heard on the Parton-Bill; and gave in some necessary Amendments (as they thought) to secure the Harbour to Coal onely. These were received and, notwithstanding my Motion on Lord Wharton's request for Thursday or Friday, a Committee of the whole House appointed for its Consideration (after a 2d Reading) to morrow. Messenger dispatched hereupon to Winchenden:[560] And, after Dinner with Mr Dale in Exeter-street, the evening spent (in bemoaning the evil Success of the Day) with Brother and Sister in S[alisbury]-Court.

[Feb.] 26. *Tuesday*. To Mr Secretary Hedges' Office in the m[orning] to sollicite for Capt. Benson,[561] prisoner at St Malo's. The last Money-Bills brought up, and an Appeal heard at the Bar, the Lord[s] (in a thin House) read the Parton Bill a second time, and the Grand Committee (Duke of Somerset Chairman) went through it; rejecting all Clauses offered by me, and even those brought in by Mr Godolphin. Read a third time, and (on the Question) carryed by 11 against 10.[562] NB. Lord Weymouth failed us; or else we had thrown it out.[563]

J. Nicols to his Care and good Advice'. Tullie House Library, Carlisle: Nicolson's Account Book for 1706.

[556] Possibly Dorothy Relf, sister to John and Joseph Relf. PRO Prob. 11, 520, f. 88: John Relf's will, 1711.

[557] Probably Charles King, bookseller at the Judge's Head in Westminster Hall. H. R. Plomer, *Dictionary of Printers and Booksellers, 1668 to 1725* (1922), p. 179.

[558] Anthony Henley (c.1666–1711), Whig MP for Andover, 1698–1700, Weymouth and Melcombe Regis, 1702–11.

[559] Charles Godolphin (1651–1720), Commissioner of Customs, 1691–1715, Assay Master of the Stannaries, 1681–1720, and MP for Helston, 1681–1701, and brother of the Lord Treasurer.

[560] One of Lord Wharton's two Buckinghamshire mansions. Wharton had written to Nicolson to try to prevent the passage of the bill until he could attend the House (Carlisle RO Lonsdale MSS Miscellaneous Letters, 1692–1715, bundle 27: Thomas Littleton to [James Lowther], 2 Mar. 1705/6). Wharton was back in the House on 28 Feb.—too late! (*LJ* xviii, 129). Nicolson's message to Wharton on 25 Feb. was 'to appoint other proxies in Parliament'. Tullie House Library, Carlisle: Nicolson's Account Book for 1706.

[561] George Benson, Captain of Dragoons in 1704, was later to be related to Nicolson when a Benson cousin of his married the bishop's eldest daughter, Mary. By Dec. 1706 he had been exchanged for a French prisoner and was in London. Dalton, v, 111, 167; Nicolson's Account Book for 1706.

[562] The only vote recorded by the Clerk on 26 Feb. was on whether the House shall be adjourned during pleasure and the figures were *Contents* 13 (including one proxy), *Not Contents* 10, see HMC *Lords MSS* vi, 400. But Nicolson is unlikely to have erred, on a

[See p. 386 for n. 562 cont. and n. 563]

[Feb.] 27. *Wednesday*. Adjusted an Account With Mr C. Musgrave in the morning; and paid him 85 *l*. I just called at the House; and afterwards, takeing a Walk, met with Major Generall Wood[564] at the Corner of Hide-Park, but did not address him. Afternoon, at the Lime-Kilns at Pickle-Herring in Southwark; some of which have been continually burning for 20 years past. The Chalk is brought from Green-Hith near Gravesend; and in it the Labourers find *Echinitee* and *Glossopetrae*, which they call *Flint-Eggs* and *Crows-Bill*. By Dr Waugh's to the *Globe* in Holburn; where Sir W. Bowes and Philip Tullie full of purchases.

[Feb.] 28. *Thursday*. Prepareing (with Mr Grisdale's Assistance) in the morning Trunks, Shoes, &c. for carrying home. In the House, the Bishop of Chester's [Stratford's] Cry against Popery;[565] and Mr Birkbeck's Appeal quashed. In the Evening, Sleddale with the Horses; and T. Bell and J. Pearson my guests.

Mar. 1. *Friday*. In the morning with Dr Gibson, who carryed me to my Lord of Canterbury, in the Gowt: To whom Dr Trimnel brought an Account of the Day's proceedings in Convocation, in great Contempt of the Queen's Letter.[566] Haveing in the Evening attempted to

matter which so closely involved him personally, in stating that there was a division on the question 'that the Bill do pass' and that the opponents of the new harbour lost it by one vote. The reference to Lord Weymouth, which immediately follows seems conclusive.

[563] According to Thomas Littleton, who had been 'soliciting the Lords [to oppose the bill] but all to little or no purpose', the bill 'past even in the Lords house without so much as one amendment for fear it should have miscarryed for want of time. Never did so unreasonable a bill make so swift a passage thro both houses or had so great an Interest made to Support it, the Duke of Somerset espoused it, heartily.' Carlisle RO Lonsdale MSS Miscellaneous Letters, 1692-1715, bundle 27: Littleton to [James Lowther], 2 Mar. 1705/6.

[564] Cornelius Wood (d. 1712), said to be the son of a Staffordshire clergyman, had risen from the ranks to distinguish himself as a cavalry leader in Ireland and Flanders, becoming a Major-General in 1704. Dalton, v, pt. ii, p. 3.

[565] An event worthy of some remark, for Bishop Stratford rarely troubled the House. Here he was speaking in support of a petition of the gentry and clergy of South Lancashire at their monthly meeting, 12 Feb. 1706, in Wigan for suppressing profaneness and immorality. The judges were ordered to bring in a bill on the following day to prevent the further growth of popery (*LJ* xviii, 129-30, 133); but it failed to pass into law, to the intense disappointment of Burnet, who complained darkly of 'very weighty intercessions' by leading Papists 'with the considerable men' of the House of Commons. *History*, v, 250-1.

[566] On 25 Feb. the Queen had written to Archbishop Tenison, on the advice of the government, expressing her concern over the increasing differences between the two houses of Convocation, and making plain her resolve 'to maintain our supremacy, and the due subordination of Presbyters to Bishops, as fundamental parts thereof'. She instructed the Primate to have the letter read to both Houses on 1 Mar. and then to order them to prorogue. See *The Letters . . . of Queen Anne*, ed. B. Curtis Brown (1935), p. 182; Lathbury, *Convocation*, p. 398; Bennett, *Tory Crisis*, pp. 84-5, for the scene of confusion which followed.

visit Dr Burnet at the Charter-House, I stayed till Bed-time at my Brother's.

[Mar.] 2. *Saturday*. The morning bestowed on my Lord Treasurer's Sadler in Suffolk-street, who is to get me new Furniture. At the House, the Complaint against the Proprietors of Carolina, their High-Commission, Arbitrary Laws, &c.[567] The Lord Granvill,[568] being alone to answer, had Wednesday given for the being heard by Counsel.

In the Evening, I had the Company of Mr De la fay;[569] who brought me a Copy of a paper, relateing to the present State of the Paper-Office, from Mr Tucker.

[Mar.] 3. *Sunday*. I dined at Salisbury-Court, with my Sister Rothery and her Son; and spent the Evening, with Sir Thomas Franklyn, at Mr C. Musgrave's.

[Mar.] 4. *Munday*. I was visitted in the morning by Mrs Wenman, Sister Rothery and Mr Martin, &c. &c. I went to take Leave of Lord Lonsdale and the Archbishop of York; who was just returning from the Queen at Kensington, in great wrath with the lower House of Convocation. Haveing waited on His Grace to the House, I went immediately, with Dr Kennett, to Lambeth. We dined with Dr Gibson; but presently adjourned to the Palace: where haveing had a kind Blessing from my Lord Archbishop of Canterbury (in Bed) I gave a short visit to Mr Salkeld[570] at the Temple. Thence to Lord Thanet's, &c. on the *Congée*; and lastly took a second Farewell at Salisbury Court.

[Mar.] 5. *Tuesday*. About Nine in the morning, I took horse; and, being accompanyed as far as High-Gate by my brother and Cousin R. Nicolson, I lodged at Dunstable; the night after the Judges.[571]

---

[567] The inhabitants of Carolina accused the Lords Proprietors in a petition of infringing the charter of 1663 which granted religious toleration. See HMC *Lords MSS* vi, 406–13.

[568] One of the Proprietors.

[569] Charles Delafaye (1677–1762), Clerk in the Secretary of State's office, *c*.1700–6, Chief Clerk, 1706–13, Under Secretary, 1717–34. For his career see J. C. Sainty, 'A Huguenot Civil Servant: the career of Charles Delafaye, 1677–1762'. *Proceedings of the Huguenot Society of London*, xxii no. 5 (1975), 398–413.

[570] ?William Salkeld (*c*.1672–1715), of Embledon, Northumberland, was called to the bar in 1698 and appointed Serjeant-at-Law in 1715. *Register of Admissions to . . . the Middle Temple* (1949), i, 230; Musgrave, *Obituary*.

[571] Nicolson proceeded northward by way of Leicester, Nottingham, Rotherham, and Leeds, reaching Rose on 15 Mar. 1706 (*CW* iii (1903), 45). The journey was used by Nicolson not only to see the country homes of three fellow members of the Lords (Lord Byron's Newstead Abbey, the Duke of Newcastle's Bolsover Castle, and the Duke of Leeds' Kiveton) but to visit three of his scholarly friends: William Wotton, Rector of Middleton Keynes, John Morton of Oxenden, Northamptonshire, who had a fine fossil collection, and Ralph Thoresby of Leeds, who presented Nicolson with some coins from his fine collection after a morning spent browsing in his library. See Diary, 6, 7, 9, 10–11 Mar. 1706.

Session 4

20 November 1706–24 March 1707

The year 1706 saw the allied cause in the Spanish Succession War prospering as never before, and to a degree that was never equalled thereafter. It is true that in Spain itself the hopes raised in June by the capture of Madrid by an Anglo-Portuguese army under Galway and Das Minas were dashed in the months that followed: national and personal jealousies prevented any effective co-operation between this army and the allied forces in Valencia, where Peterborough and the Archduke Charles were at loggerheads, and disease completed their mutual frustration.[1] But Spain could still, it seemed, be won—if only on the fields of Flanders and Italy. Marlborough's resounding triumph at Ramillies in May 1706 made the French position in the Spanish Netherlands untenable, and a series of brilliant sieges between then and October left Louis XIV's troops with no more than a toe-hold in the territory. Moreover, King Louis, by denuding his Italian army to reinforce his stricken forces in the north, left northern Italy exposed to the onslaught of Prince Eugene, whose defeat of Orleans at Turin in September destroyed the whole French position in this theatre.

The news of these exhilarating victories helped to enliven Nicolson's nine-month residence in his diocese between 15 March and 7 November 1706, which was one of the quietest he was to experience. So too did distant noises of alarms at Court, where the Queen's relations with her *ci-devant* favourite, the Duchess of Marlborough, suffered strains this summer and autumn from which they were never fully to recover. These were closely connected with the main political battle fought 'behind the curtain' during the parliamentary recess. Towards the end of the summer the Junto made it plain to the duumvirs that continued Whig support for the ministry next session was contingent on the admission of Lord Sunderland, Sarah's son-in-law, to the Cabinet as Secretary of State for the South. This was a move which had been in their minds, and Godolphin's, for at least a year;[2] but from July to early December 1706 the Queen, her resolution stiffened by the private advice of Harley, the Northern Secretary, stubbornly

[1] The disappointments of 1706 in the Peninsula, and not least the controversial Peterborough's role in them, were to be the subject of important Lords' debates in the session of 1707–8, and of a full-dress 'inquiry' by the House in Jan. 1711.

[2] See *Marlborough–Godolphin Corr.* i, 478 n.

held out against a change which seemed to her the thin end of the wedge of Whig monopoly of her government (as indeed it was). In the end she did not give way to the arguments and bullying of Godolphin and the Marlboroughs until the very day on which parliament met for business, 3 December.[3]

From the high drama abroad and the crucial tussle at Court, Carlisle diocese stood tranquilly remote. Between the spring and autumn of 1706 only the grumbling dispute between Nicolson and Hugh Todd ruffled the placid surface of routine ecclesiastical business and pleasant social intercourse of which the bishop's life was chiefly compounded. There were already some signs, however, that this quarrel was the precursor of a much more serious storm ahead. Todd strenuously sought the support of Archbishop Sharp of York and aroused Nicolson's understandable resentment by presenting his sister, Elizabeth Carlile (formerly Spooner), before the consistory court on a charge of adultery. Before Nicolson set out for London in November he persuaded the three remaining prebendaries to 'exclude Dr Todd from offices, of all kinds, for the year ensuieing'.[4] During the winter he was due to begin his preparations for his second visitation of the diocese, in 1707;[5] and, ominously, Dean Atterbury left no one in doubt that he, for his part, would resist any attempt to include the cathedral in the visitation, on the grounds that, as a royal foundation of Henry VIII's reign, the Queen alone could act as Visitor (and likewise appoint to canonries and prebends).[6]

On 26 October Nicolson received 'Notice of the Session of Parliament on the 21 of the next month; and pressing instances to be at Lambeth some dayes before'. After rapid preparations he set out for London on 7 November. As he travelled south via Appleby, Settle, Wakefield, and Doncaster, and on to Nottingham by 15 November, the weather turned from poor to abominable; and on the 16 November he took nine hours to navigate seventeen miles of flooded road into Leicester. When he reached London on 20 November it was 'raining still'.[7]

[3] The best-documented account in print of the Sunderland affair is in Coxe, *Marlborough*, ii, 1-24. See also Trevelyan, *Queen Anne*, ii, 167-71; *Marlborough–Godolphin Corr.* ii, 603 n., 638-86 *passim*, 700, 728 and n. 6.

[4] For Nicolson's period of residence at Carlisle in 1706 see *CW* iii (1903), 45-56. York Minister Lib. Hailstone Collection QQ 2.7, pp. 25-31, 'Representation of the Grievances of the Diocese of Carlisle', expresses Todd's view of the dispute at this time, sent to Sharp on 16 Oct. 1706 (copy).

[5] He had his visitation articles printed while in London (below, 17 Mar.).

[6] See below, 22 Dec. and 12 Mar. For the questions at issue, to which Sharp was already alerted (below, 17 Dec.), see Bennett, *Tory Crisis*, pp. 89-91; James, pp. 163-6.

[7] *CW* iii, 55-6: Diary, 7-20 Nov. The final stages of the journey took the bishop through Northampton and Dunstable.

The parliamentary session of 1706–7 was dominated in its later stages by the debates on the articles of Union between England and Scotland, culminating in the eventual ratification of the treaty by the Act of Union (6 Anne c.11). But the session also proved to be of no small significance for Church as well as State, since, as an essential by-product of the Union, it saw the passage of an 'Act for securing the Church of England as by Law established'. In the House of Lords (where Nicolson never missed a sitting until two weeks before he left for the north in March 1707) these two issues highlighted the impregnability of the ministry, so long as its partnership with 'the Whig lords' and with the Low Church divines worked—as it did this session—with well-oiled smoothness. The High Tories tried hard to keep alive the flames of opposition: but the fire was continually doused by one heavy adverse vote after another (e.g. below, 14 January, 3 February, 3, 4 March). The Queen's attendance at some of the Union debates, to signify her firm support for the Treaty (e.g. below, 3 and 15 February) made their task the more hopeless.

The twenty-five articles of the Treaty had been signed the previous July, after negotiations between the two sets of commissioners (Whig-dominated on the English side) lasting since mid-April 1706. The basic *quid pro quo* was the concession by the Scottish representatives of a common parliament for the new United Kingdom of 'Great Britain' (and an end, therefore, to Scotland's legislative independence) in return for the guarantee, crucial to their country's wilting economy, 'that all subjects of the United Kingdom shall have full freedom and intercourse of trade and navigation within the United Kingdom and Plantations [the English colonies] thereunto belonging'.[8] The Scots had made no more than a token attempt, as a sop to hostile opinion at home, to secure a loose federal union embodying two separate parliaments, but they knew that this was bound to be rejected by the Junto lords (all five of whom were commissioners) as being an inadequate guarantee of Scotland's acceptance of the Hanoverian succession. The other salient points settled—all, in varying degrees, favourably to the Scots —concerned the distribution of the tax burden,[9] the allocation of Scottish representation at Westminster (forty-five members and sixteen elected peers),[10] the preservation of the Scottish legal system[11] and, *pro tem*, of the Edinburgh Privy Council, and the payment to Scotland of an 'Equivalent' of more than £398,000 as compensation for the Scots taxpayer's inheritance of the English national debt.[12]

[8] Article 4.
[9] Articles 7 to 13.
[10] Article 22.
[11] Articles 18 and 19.
[12] Article 15. There is a full and fair—if Whiggish—account of the negotiations in Trevelyan, *Queen Anne*, ii, 265–9; cf. the contemporary narrative in Burnet, *History*, v, 280–3.

'There was no provision made in this treaty, with relation to religion', wrote the Bishop of Salisbury: 'for in the acts of parliament, in both kingdoms, that empowered the queen to name commissioners, there was an express limitation that they should not treat of those matters.'[13] However, during the stormy three-month passage of the articles of Union through the Edinburgh Estates (12 October 1706-16 January 1707)[14] the Scottish parliament insisted on carrying in November an 'Act for Securing the Protestant Religion and Presbyterian Church Government'. This Act, which identified 'the true Protestant religion' with 'the form and purity of worship presently in use within this church, and its Presbyterian church government and discipline, that is to say, the government of the Church by kirk-sessions, presbyteries, provincial synods and general assemblies', and guaranteed that it should 'remain and continue unalterable' in Scotland, was unquestionably necessary to appease the ministers of the Kirk: indeed, the Treaty would never have been ratified in Scotland without it.[15] But it naturally caused deep concern in England, both in Tory and moderate Whig circles; and above all it placed the bishops in a real quandary since they could not now put their seal of approval on the Union in the House of Lords without laying themselves open to the charge of appearing to condone the Presbyterians' claim to embody 'the true Protestant religion and purity of worship'.[16]

Consequently as early as 4 January 1707 (twelve days before the final ratification of the Union in Edinburgh) Archbishop Tenison told Nicolson that he would 'insist on an Act of Security for Episcopacy [in England] previous to the Union'. The urgency of such a measure was underlined on 14 January when Lord Nottingham, backed by Rochester, Haversham, and Buckingham, unsuccessfully moved the House of Lords to 'provide betimes against the dangers with which the Church, by law established, was threatened, in case the Union was accomplished'.[17] Between 23 and 27 January there was a series of meetings between the Primate and his episcopal

---

[13] Ibid., p. 283.

[14] For the political background to the Union see P. W. J. Riley, 'The union of 1707 as an episode in English politics', *EHR* lxxxiv (1969), 498-527; P. W. J. Riley, 'The structure of Scottish politics and the Union of 1707', in *The Union of 1707*, ed. T. I. Rae (Glasgow, 1974), 1-29; W. Ferguson, 'The making of the Treaty of Union of 1707', *SHR* xliii (1964), 89-110; P. W. J. Riley, *The Union of England and Scotland* (Manchester, 1978).

[15] From the time the Act was passed, on 12 Nov. 1706, it came to be regarded as an integral part of the Treaty. See *Acts. Parl. Scot.* xi, 320-2; ibid., pp. 402-3, for the text of the Act.

[16] See the later speeches of Lord Haversham and Bishop Talbot of Oxford in the Lords, *Parl. Hist.* vi, 564, 571-4.

[17] H. Horwitz, *Revolution Politicks* (Cambridge, 1968), p. 208; *Parl. Hist.* vi, 554-6; Luttrell, vi, 126-7.

friends, either at Lambeth or at the house of the Bishop of Norwich, to hammer out the first and second draft of a bill for the security of the Church of England. Among those chiefly involved in the consultations, apart from Bishop Moore, were Wake, Dean Willis of Lincoln, and Edmund Gibson, and not least Nicolson himself, who records one of the meetings in his diary and was given the charge of correcting the second draft (below, 27 January). The archbishop was also careful to take the Junto into his confidence, and the advice of Somers, in particular, was sought at every stage, for as Tenison explained to him on 27 January, 'we cannot pretend to accuracie in the Form of Law'.[18]

On 28 January the Queen at last laid the Union before parliament, and at once Tenison moved for leave to bring in the Security Bill, an invitation which seemingly 'stun'd many of the other side'.[19] Work on the bill was completed the following day at a meeting at the Earl of Sunderland's house at which 'one short amendment [was] agreed to, and measures concerted for the passing of it'.[20] Wharton, who attended along with Godolphin and Marlborough and two of his Junto colleagues (Somers being indisposed), was not formally noted for his Anglican devotion. But, as he realised, 'the bigoted part of our Church would have been a flame if the same care [as provided for the Kirk] had not been taken of them'; and like the shrewd politician he was, he could see that if the Security Bill passed before the Union came under close consideration it would frustrate the hopes of those on both sides of the border who believed that the Kirk Act could wreck support for the Treaty in England.[21]

Events very rapidly justified the prescience of the Junto and their Low Church allies. At its second reading in the Lords the bill gave rise to a major debate (below, 3 February), when the Tories, led by Sharp and Nottingham, moved for the explicit inclusion of the Test Act in the bill and Somers, who 'did his G[racc of Canterbury] and all the Bench a great deal of justice', opposed the motion as superfluous in view of the bill's comprehensive wording.[22] After the rejection of

[18] Surrey RO Somers MSS D12 and 13: Tenison to Somers, 23 and 27 Jan. 1707; Lambeth Palace MS 1770, ff. 34-5: Wake's diary, 24, 27 Jan. A draft of the bill, with alterations, is in Lambeth Palace MS 640, pp. 445-9. 'By it', wrote Burnet, 'all acts passed in favour of our church were declared to be in full force for ever; and this was made a fundamental and essential part of the union.' (*History*, v, 292.)

[19] NLW Plas yn Cefn MS 2772: Bishop Evans of Bangor to [Humphries of Hereford], 28 Jan. [1707].

[20] Lambeth Palace MS 1770, f. 35: Wake's diary, 29 Jan.

[21] HMC *14th Report, Appx. iii* (Marchmont MSS), p. 158: Wharton to Earl of Marchmont, 31 Jan. 1707.

[22] The Queen had tried in vain to persuade Archbishop Sharp to support the bill (T. Sharp, *Life of John Sharp* (1825), i, 390-2). For the debate of 3 Feb. see also Lambeth Palace MS 1770, f. 35; NLW Plas yn Cefn MSS 2779 and 2788: Evans to [Humphries], [4]

Sharp's amendment by sixty votes to thirty-three[23]—all the Tory bishops present, except Trelawney,[24] voting with the opposition—the bill passed its committee stage unamended, and after an uneventful third reading on 4 February it was sent down to the Commons. There the Tories under Bromley attempted a similar ploy to that of Sharp and Nottingham. Their 'whole design [according to Walpole] was to reflect upon the Archbishop and Bishops who drew up the Bill; but we would permit of no alterations'.[25] By 13 February it was ready for the royal assent. Tenison was able to reflect with satisfaction on one of the rare political triumphs of his archiepiscopate, and the Junto were equally content that their Scottish allies would find the bill 'conceived in such cautious and moderate terms as not to give any just occasion of offence in Scotland'.[26]

The ratification of the Union itself was now not long delayed. The Commons had begun debating the articles on 1 February and by 11 February they had completed their work. There was some Tory opposition. But Sir John Pakington's attempt to make mischief by referring to Convocation the apparent *impasse* between two Churches which both claimed divine institution was brusquely dealt with by the Junto's General Mordaunt;[27] and later, as Walpole reported, 'B[romley] spoke against the first article [that an incorporating union should take effect on 1 May 1707] . . . but could make nothing of it, so that we pushed through all the articles in the committee . . .'.[28] By 11 February the Lower House was ready to order Sir Richard Onslow to draw up a bill of ratification—the bill which,

& 11 Feb. [1707]; TCD King Corr. 1244: F. Annesley to Archbishop King, [15?] Feb. 1706[/7]; *Addison Letters*, p. 69.

[23] But cf. the larger majority given in *Parl. Hist.*, vi, 559.

[24] The reasons why, as Bishop Evans reported, 'the knight from Exeter turned on our side', were assumed to be closely tied up with his hopes of translation to the wealthy see of Winchester (NLW Plas yn Cefn MS 2788: Evans to [Humphries], 11 Feb. [1707]. We are grateful to Mr G. Milwyn Griffiths of the Dept. of MSS at the NLW for translating this passage from the original Welsh.)

[25] TCD King Corr. 1241: Annesley to King, 11 Feb. 1706[/7]; Luttrell, vi, 137; Kent Archives Office Chevening MS U1590 C707/5: Robert to Horace Walpole, 12 Feb. 1707. The Tory amendment was defeated by 208 to 167.

[26] For Tenison, see TCD King Corr. 1242 and 1244: Annesley to King, 11 and [15?] Feb., and below, 10 Feb.; HMC *14th Report, Appx. iii* (Marchmont MSS), p. 159: Somers to Marchmont, 11 Feb. A copy of the Act (6 Anne c. 8) can be found in *Statutes of the Realm*, vii, 562, and in *The Treaty of Union of Scotland and England*, ed. G. S. Pryde (1950), pp. 111–12.

[27] Pakington 'might, if he thought fit, consult the Convocation for his own particular instruction', Mordaunt replied; 'but . . . it would be derogatory from the rights of the Commons of England to advise on this occasion with an inferior assembly, who had no share in the legislature'. *Parl. Hist.* vi, 561.

[28] Kent Archives Office Chevening MS U1590 C 707/5: Robert to Horace Walpole, 12 Feb. 1706/7.

in Burnet's words, was to be 'prepared by Harcourt [Solicitor-General] with so particular a contrivance, that it cut off all debates'.[29]

While the bill was being drafted, the House of Lords opened its discussion of the Union articles in Grand Committee on 15 February. Joseph Addison was able to report that:

> the Queen present, and the Bishop of Salisbury in the Chair.
>
> They made the same progresse as the house of Commons had done before them at their first sitting on the Articles, having past the first four and entered on the fifth. The methods, objections and Exceptions of the Party opposite to it were much the same as had been made use of by their friends in the Lower House.
>
> They proposed the postponing of the first article till all the rest were agreed to[30] which was overruled. They then declared themselves against any Union but a Federal Union,[31] and after having canvassed the Proposition for some time the Question was put Content or not Content for a Federal Union,[32] and the Bishop of Salisbury having given the Majority for the Not Contents by a general Survey of the Votes, Lord Stawell demanded a division, which Lord Nottingham and others of his own side would afterwards have waved for fear of showing the Thinnesse of their Party, but Lord Wharton said since it had been demanded he joyned in the motion and accordingly the House came to a Division where the Contents amounted but to Twenty and the Not Contents to Seventy one.
>
> It was observed that the Bishops of York, Durham, and Rochester left their Friends in this division and appeared for the Union. The Finch family appeared the warmest against it (vizt) Lords Nottingham, Guernsey, and Winchelsea.
>
> Nothing was objected to the 2nd Article, but for the Third they would have postponed it till the 22nd had passed, which fixes the Number of the Lords and Commoners to sit in Parliament.
>
> There were several objections made against the Fourth and in particular it was urged that the Scots being allowed their present Liberty of Importing what they pleased into Scotland and afterwards having all the Privileges of English Merchants they might bring in before the First of May such Quantities of East India Goods from Holland as might ruine our owne Company's in England.

---

[29] Burnet, *History*, v, 295-6.
[30] Moved by Lord Anglesey, supported by Bishop Hooper (*Parl. Hist.* vi, 562).
[31] Haversham headed this forlorn hope (ibid., vi, 563).
[32] The vote was, in fact, on the postponement of the 1st Article (ibid., vi, 565; and see below, 15 Feb.).

This was allowed to be an Inconvenience. The Lord Wharton said that he beleived the Scots had never thought of it and perhaps would be beholden to the Noble Lord, who was Lord Guernsey, that put them in mind of it.[33]

Further articles were considered and accepted on 19, 21, and 24 February. There were divisions on the 9th Article (settling Scotland's Land Tax quota), forced by Lord North and Grey, and, according to Nicolson on 18 February, though it was the 15th Article (the Equivalent) which caused most debate on 21 February.[34] On the last day of the Grand Committee's discussions Bishop Hooper of Bath and Wells was the only bishop on the bench to 'argue strenously' against the Union.[35]

The Commons' bill for ratification was brought up and given its first reading on 1 March. Two days later, at the committee stage of the bill, a 'great debate' took place on the confirmation as part of the Union of the Scottish Kirk Act, and on the vote four other Tory bishops joined Hooper in opposition.[36] Having by fifty-five to nineteen failed to take the Scottish Act out of the Union, the Tory opponents on the third reading of the Ratification Bill on 4 March tried to add a rider explaining that 'nothing in this Ratification contained shall be construed to extend to an approbation, or acknowledgement of the truth of the Presbyterian way of worship, or allowing the Religion of the Church of Scotland, to be what it is stiled the True Protestant Religion'. This rider was rejected; and again Bishop Hooper found himself alone on the episcopal bench in voting for it.[37]

Frustrated on all points, the only move left to the Tory opposition was to sign a formal Lords' protest against the Union.[38] On 6 March the Queen gave her royal assent to the Act of Union,[39] which came

---

[33] Kent Archives Office, Chevening MS U1590 C474/10: encl. in Joseph Addison to Horatio Walpole, 18 Feb. 1706/7.　　　　　　　　　　　　　[34] *Parl. Hist.* vi, 565-7.

[35] TCD King Corr. 1244: Annesley to King, [15?] Feb. 1706[/7]; *Parl. Hist.* vi, 568 (24 Feb.). For Hooper's opposition, and the Queen's approval of the integrity of his stand (though she herself was 'of a contrary position'), see Warwick RO Microfilm MI 214 (Walton MSS): MS memoirs of Hooper (by his daughter, Mrs. Prowse), p. 28.

[36] Below, 3 Mar.; HMC *Lords MSS* vii, 20. Archbishop Sharp had been expected to come out in opposition. His son, John Sharp, MP for Ripon, had strongly opposed the Union in the Commons on 28 Feb., Bodl. MS Ballard 7, f. 7: Smalridge to Charlett, 1 Mar [1707]. For the basis of his opposition to the Scottish Act see T. Sharp, *Life of John Sharp*, i, 392-3.

[37] His supporters on the temporal bench included Beaufort, Buckingham, North and Grey, Anglesey, Northampton, Abingdon, Winchilsea, Nottingham, Scarsdale, Thanet, Stawell, Guernsey, Weymouth, Guildford, and Leigh (Bodl. MS Ballard 31, f. 61: William Bishop to Charlett, 17 Mar. 1707). See *LJ* xviii, 68; HMC *Lords MSS* vii, 20.

[38] *LJ* xviii, 268; Rogers, *Protests of the Lords*, i, 183-4.

[39] The Act (6 Anne c. 11) can be found in *Statutes of the Realm*, viii, 566-77.

into force on 1 May 1707. On that day 'without dissolving or pro-
roguing the Eng[lish] parliament died an early Death, with a Declaration only read by Commissioners in the H[ouse] of Lords, that the
two Houses should rise up in to a Part of the British Parliament',
Symbolically on that day White Kennett 'married a Scots Merchant
to an Engl[ish] young Lady by a Ring with this Motto *The Happy
Union.*'[40]

A session which began with the appointment of Sunderland and
ended with the Act of Union appeared to many, certainly to the
dejected High Tories, to portend unqualified triumph for the Whigs
in the near future. In fact, however, the political way ahead was less
clear than it seemed when Nicolson began his journey back to
Cumberland on 24 March. Sunderland's secretarial colleague, Harley,
was now resolutely opposed to any further concessions to the Junto,
and he was still influential with the Queen. Moreover, the Whigs'
next priority, to reward some of their leading clerical supporters with
high preferments, touched the very area of the Queen's prerogative
which she guarded most jealously; and it was one where she still
relied heavily on the advice of Archbishop Sharp. During the winter
Somers and his friends had grudgingly accepted Godolphin's commitment to the trimming Tory, Trelawney of Exeter, allowing him to
fill the shoes of the late Bishop Mews (d. 9 November 1706) at
Winchester (see above, n. 24). But this appointment was still un-
gazetted in March 1707, and towards the end of the 1706–7 session
the deaths in quick succession of Bishop Stratford of Chester and
William Jane, Professor of Divinity at Oxford, promised succour for
the Whig divines.

Nicolson left London convinced, as most Whigs were, that Dean
Freeman of Peterborough would get the prize of Chester and Marlborough's nominee, John Potter, the Regius chair (see below,
15 March). It also seemed that other slots then vacated, the see of
Exeter and the deanery of Peterborough, would be filled by two
more Low Church stalwarts, Charles Trimnell and White Kennett.
But the events of the summer were to lay bare the frailty of these
assumptions, and before the start of the next session were to throw
the world of Court and parliamentary politics into renewed confusion.[41]

---

[40] BL Lansdowne MS 1013, f. 101: Kennett to Blackwell, 1 May 1707; ibid., 825,
f. 78: [Kennett to   ?], 1 May 1707 (fragment).

[41] For the above, see the indispensable article by G. V. Bennett, 'Robert Harley, the
Godolphin Ministry and the Bishoprics Crisis of 1707', *EHR* lxxxii (1967), 735–7 and
passim.

[Nov.] 20. *Wednesday*. Rainy still: But the way good, the 30 miles from Dunstable to London passed merrily and quick. Mett at High-Gate by Brother Joseph with whom I supped; and (about 10 at night) returned to my old Landlord in Manchester-Court.[42] *Deo Laus*!

[Nov.] 21. *Thursday*. In the morning, Visits to Dr. Gibson (in a cold) and Lord Archbishop of Canterbury [Tenison] in the Gowt. His Grace consulted with me and Dr Potter about a Form of Thanksgiveing;[43] and desired my seeing Him again on Saturday. Parliament and Convocation Prorogued to December 3. I dined with Mr C. Musgrave's, where his Brother Joseph and two young Sisters.[44]

[Nov.] 22. *Friday*. Visitted in the morning by Mr Thomas Bell, still pressing for his brother David; and by Mr W. Johnson[45] and my brother Joseph, the former bringing me to Mr Taylor[46] at the Treasury and the latter goeing with me in fruitless Quest of Mr Dean of Wells [Grahme] and Mr Lee of Clifford's Inn.[47] Evening, with Dr Hickes and at my Brother's.

[Nov.] 23. *Saturday*. With Mr Johnson to Dr Gibson's about Mr Holme's[48] Dispensation: and thence to the Palace at Lambeth, where met by the Bishops of Sarum [Burnet] and Norwich [Moore], at ten, and (with His Grace) the Form of Th[anksgiving] finished.

At Dinner, Mrs Chancellors Lloyd and Mandevil, Archdeacon Hoddy, Mr Moor Son of the Earl of Drogheda, &c. After a short visit to Mr Snow, I went to Kensington; kissed Her Majesty['s] hand, and returned with Dr Verney and Dean Grahme.

[Nov.] 24. *Sunday*. In the morning at Lord Treasurer's [Godolphin's] Levy [levee]; where His Lordship kindly discoursed G. Langstaff's Case, and desired my farther Information. At the Queen's Chapple, Dr Verney preached, Bishops of Exon [Trelawney], Norwich, Bangor [Evans] and my self. I dined at Mr C. Musgrave's with Sir Thomas

---

[42] Mr Hallet, see above 26 Oct. 1705.

[43] A thanksgiving service was being planned in recognition of a year of triumph for the allies in Flanders and Italy. It was to be held at St Paul's on 31 Dec. (see Luttrell, vi, 122).

[44] Mary and Anne Musgrave. Nicolson and Burn, i, 598.

[45] Probably William Johnson, Solicitor in the Salt Office. Chamberlayne, *Present State 1707*, p. 506.

[46] John Taylor, Under Clerk 1690-5, Chief Clerk 1695-1714, and junior Secretary of the Treasury 1714-15. J. C. Sainty, *Treasury Officials* (1972), p. 154.

[47] The third of the Inner Temple's Inns of Chancery, dating from *c*.1345, it stood (to the east of) behind Serjeant's Inn in Chancery Lane.

[48] Richard Holme (*c*.1656-1738), Rector of Lowther, Westmorland, 1694-1738, Vicar of Aikton, Cumberland, 1707-38.

Franklin, Mr Bridges, Mr Lister and Mr Joseph Musgrave. In the Evening visitted by Mr James Lowther.

[Nov.] 25. *Munday*. Visitted in the morning by Cousin Grainger, Mr Henly, Mr Holmes, Coll. J. Orfeur and Mr Chamberlayne. Dr Waugh dined with me; and after Dinner, we paid visits to Mr Rymer, Sir A. Fountain (not within) Mr Holmes and Mr Maddox conclude-ing at my Brother's.

[Nov.] 26. *Tuesday*. Morning Visitants Mr Grisedale, Mr Yates and Mr Johnson; the latter appointing Thursday for our goeing to the Salt-Office.[49] At Cousin R. Nicolson's, I gave Sir T[homas] H[oby]'s[50] MS. to his great Grandson Mr Hoby. Sermon at St Paul's for the sons of the Clergy[51] preached by Dr Altham on *Galatians* 6, 10. — *the Houshold of Faith*. At the Dinner, the Bishops of Bangor, Carlile, St. David's [Bull] and Meath (Dr Morton),[52] Sir Thomas Meers, Sir Richard Levett,[53] &c. &c. A Deal of Meat, Musick and Mob.

[Nov.] 27. *Wednesday*. Morning Visit from Mrs Donning, as malicious as ever. Respects paid to Mr Delafaye and Earl of Sunderland. After Dinner, I carryed Archdeacon Pearson's Letters and Mr Wotton's to Dr Gibson; and visitted Cousin J. Relf and's Spouse. In the Even-ing brought Mr Buchanan; whose Son gives a sorry Account of my Admiral Nicols.

[Nov.] 28. *Thursday*. After waiting on the Commissioners of the Salt-Office with my thanks for G. Langstaff, I went to the Tower; viewed the fine (and costly) Repairs at both Repositaries of Records, and haveing dined with Mr Dale (full of Employments under the New Lord Marischal[54] [Bindon]) and Mr Holmes, returned to the writeing of Letters at my Lodgeings.

[Nov.] 29. *Friday*. Cousin R. Nicolson, in the morning, with a Narrative of the shirking poverty of our Cousin Mat[ilda?] R[owse].

[49] In York Buildings.
[50] Sir Thomas Hoby (1530-66), diplomat and translator.
[51] The Corporation of the Sons of the Clergy, an Anglican voluntary society involving (like the SPCK and the SPG) laymen as well as clerics, organised an annual anniversary sermon at St Paul's, among a number of other major fund-raising functions, to raise money for the widows and orphans of poor clergymen.
[52] William Moreton (d. 1715), Bishop of Kildare, 1682-1705, and of Meath, 1705-15.
[53] Sir Richard Levet (d. 1711), Alderman of London, 1690 and Lord Mayor, 1699-1700; a former director of the Bank of England, 1698-1700, and a current member of the com-mittee of the East India Company, 1701-9. A. B. Beaven, *The Aldermen of the City of London* (1908), ii, 118.
[54] Nicolson uses the Scottish spelling.

Mr. Morland (Cousin Lesley's Nephew) from St Giles's. Evening, at my Brother's with (Mr Sill's brother) Mr Smith.

[Nov.] 30. *Saturday*. Private all day. In the Evening, I called at my Lord of York's [Sharp's]; and immediately, His Grace arrived cheerful and Healthy. He told me, That he had received a long Letter from Dr Todd;[55] which he would not answer.

Dec. 1. *Sunday*. I preached at Lambeth; and dined with Dr Gibson. In the Evening, an hour and half with Lord of Canterbury in bed; who heartily discoursed of the Times of Charles 1 and promised me a Narrative of Mr Cook, on the King's confinement in the Isle of Wight,[56] The rest — with Mr Snow and my Landlord Hallet, successively.

[Dec.] 2. *Munday*. Morning, Visitted by Mr George Holmes, Mr James Tyrrel (who attempted the bringing me to the Cotton-Library) and Mr Dean Story;[57] who called just as I was goeing out with Mr C. Musgrave, to dine with him. Our company, his two Sisters; together with Mrs Lister[58] and her Daughter. In the Evening, Mr Delafaye; in hopes of being advanced by Lord Sunderland who will be Secretary to morrow.[59]

[Dec.] 3. *Tuesday*. Morning, visitted by Mr Lowther of Meaburn,[60] indifferent for all Religions; Mr Smith of St Martin's;[61] Mr Latus[62] and Mr Huddleston of Millum.[63]

[55] See above, sessional intro., p. 389.

[56] *Certain passages which hapned at Newport, in the Isle of Wight, November 29th, 1648, Relating to King Charles I* (1690). For a brief description of Edward Cooke's career see C. H. Firth and G. Davies, *The Regimental History of Cromwell's Army* (1940), ii, 578-9.

[57] George Story (d. 1721), Dean of Limerick, 1704-21, a Cumberland man and brother of the Quaker, Thomas Story; he had previously been Dean of Connor, 1694-1704.

[58] Wife of Christopher Lister, a cousin of the Musgraves.

[59] For Sunderland's appointment see above, sessional intro., p. 388. He promoted Charles Delafaye to Chief Clerk in his office.

[60] MP for Westmorland since 1705. See Appendix A *sub* Lowther, Robert.

[61] Possibly Joseph Smith who lived in London and had been appointed by Lancaster as Rector of St Martin's to the Russell Court Chapel in 1704. He was also chaplain to the 1st Earl of Jersey.

[62] Ferdinand Latus (1670-1738), Cumberland Land Tax Commissioner, 1698-1714. By 1723 he was Collector of Customs at Whitehaven, Hopkinson, p. 318; J. Chamberlayne, *Magnae Britaniae Notitia* (1723 edn), p. 520. He was also Steward to Lord Carlisle. *Cumberland Families*, p. 198.

[63] Possibly Wilfred Hudleston (1673-1729), a scion of the family of Hudleston of Millom Castle, who had been a sailor but had, by 1707, been for some years a merchant of Whitehaven, 'trading constantly every year to Virginia'. E. Hughes, *North-Country Life in the Eighteenth Century, II. Cumberland and Westmorland, 1700-1830* (1965), pp. 2-3.

The Queen's speech in the House,[64] much crowded; and Compliments from Lord Sunderland (this day Secretary) Lord Townesend Lord Somers, &c. Mr Archdeacon Rogers[65] with me at Dinner, in the old Ordinary.[66]

[Dec.] 4. *Wednesday*. Morning with Philip Tullie at Lambeth; fruitlessly seeking for a Deputation from (Sir J. Cook) the new Clerk of the Pipe. Lord Archbishop of Canterbury disturbed at the Bishop of E[xeter]'s being likely to have Winton [Winchester].[67] In the House Address reported; and the Queen appoints to morrow (at half hour after one) to be attended with [it]. The Evening spent, with Dr Adams, at Dr Lancaster's.

[Dec.] 5. *Thursday*. Morning, Dr Harris with his proposeals for 2d Edition of *Dictionarium Technicum*.[68] From the House to St James's with the Address, after Thanks to the Duke of Marlborough. Thence to dine with the Archbishop of York, where met (by chance) with the Dean of Carlile [Atterbury]; who warm on the Loose Books and Pamphlets.[69] In the evening, after Letters, visitted (till Eleven) by P. and W. Tullie.

[Dec.] 6. *Friday*. In the House, Queen's Answer Reported; and that ordered to be printed with the Address.[70] Mr Dale dined with me (after Lord Keeper's [Cowper's] order for Cotton's Library entered) at the Ordinary. Convocation this day unanimous in their Address; the Deans of Christ Church [Aldrich] and Carlile agreeing to the Church's *flourishing* Condition.[71] In the Evening, with Mrs Beaufort, at Brother Joseph's till after Ten. Letters abundance.

The head of the family at Millom at this period was Mrs Bridget Hudleston, whose estate was managed by Humphrey Senhouse. Ibid., *passim*.

[64] See *LJ* xviii, 174–5.

[65] John Rogers (*c*.1647–1715), Archdeacon of Leicester, 1703–15, and Rector of Seagrave, Leicestershire, 1682–1715.

[66] A tavern where meals were provided at a fixed price. Possibly meaning the *Dog*.

[67] Bishop Mews of Winchester had died on 9 Nov. 1706. He was to be succeeded by Trelawney of Exeter in Apr. 1707, who had been promised Winchester by Godolphin to keep the support of this influential boroughmonger of the south-west, and Trelawney secretly kissed hands for the appointment. For the political manœuvering behind his appointment and for Trelawney's earlier opposition to Tenison and his party, see G. V. Bennett, 'William III and the Episcopate', in *Essays in Modern English Church History*, ed. G. V. Bennett and J. D. Walsh (1966) pp. 124–30; G. V. Bennett, 'Robert Harley, the Godolphin ministry and the bishoprics Crisis of 1707', *EHR* lxxxii (1967), 726–46.

[68] *Lexicon Technicum: or an Universal English Dictionary of Arts and Sciences*, first published 1704; second edition appeared 1708–10.

[69] See Lathbury, pp. 401–2, for proceedings in the Convocation of 1705–6 on certain writings.

[70] *LJ* xviii, 178.   [71] See Lathbury, p. 402.

[Dec.] 7. *Saturday*. Short and Civil visit from Mr Dean Atterbury, goeing to wait on the Queen with Address of Convocation. Soon after, on the same Errand, Dr Gibson; who returned to dinner (with me and Mr Buttle) at our Ordinary.

[Dec.] 8. *Sunday*. Service ended at Whitehal, I dined (with Mr Johnson and Mr Brathwait) at my Brother's whither Sister Rothery and her Daughter came in the Afternoon. Setting them down at Sohoe, I returned to my Lodgeings at Seven: two hours and a half before my Man.

[Dec.] 9. *Munday*. In the morning, failing of getting into Cotton-Library, I visitted the Dean of Wells [Grahme]; yet in the Dark about Convocation-Matters. Returning, I met with Mr Tyrrel, Mr Hanbury, and Mr Leneve [Le Neve], all to meet at the Library to morrow; and found that Dr Hickes and Mr Grandorge had called at my Lodgeing. Mr Joseph Musgrave carryed me to the House; where a single Appeal. Mr Grandorge at Dinner; and Dr Woodward in the Evening.

[Dec.] 10. *Tuesday*. Morning, To Cotton-Library; where Mr Hanbury's Clerk (Mr Elphinston)[72] ordered to attend me with Books. Mr James Tyrrel finds he has misquoted the *Chron[icon de] Lanerc[ost]*.[73] The House, after first Reading of Lady North's Bill,[74] adjourned to Friday. Post-night. At home.

[Dec.] 11. *Wednesday*. At meeting of the Commissioners for the Queen's Bounty at Whitehall; where I gave in my Return of poor Liveings. Report from Dr Mew[75] of his Uncle's Circumstances; and proposeal from the Archbishop of Canterbury that the Queen would secure Arrears from Bishops hereafter removed [translated].[76] Afternoon, with Dr Waugh, attempting also to see Dr Kennett.

[72] John Elphinston, secretary to William Hanbury. By 1712 he was being paid to look after the Cotton Library. *CTB 1714*, xxviii, pt. 2, pp. 4, 6, 16, 86, 390.

[73] It was used by Tyrrell in writing his *The General History of England*, vol. iii (1704).

[74] For Lady North and Grey's Naturalisation Act see HMC *Lords MSS* vii, 2. Lady North was a Dutch national.

[75] Peter Mews (?1672–1726), nephew and heir of Bishop Mews of Winchester (d. 1706), Chancellor of Winchester diocese, 1698–1726, and Tory MP for Christchurch, Hampshire, 1710–26, he was knighted in 1712. Sedgwick, ii, 255.

[76] In 1706 the Governors of the Bounty found that great arrears of first fruits and tenths were due from certain bishops or their executors. The case of Mews was the first to be considered. He owed £3,065, some of it from Bath and Wells, which he had left in 1684. See A. Savidge, *The Foundation and the Early Years of Queen Anne's Bounty* (1955), pp. 43–4.

[Dec.] 12. *Thursday*. Morning in Cotton-Library with Mr Hanbury; who shewed me the [MSS][77] Charters, &c, and Lent me (home) the Chronicle of Lanercost. I dined with Lord Thanet; offended at the Address of Convocation.

[Dec.] 13. *Friday*. Morning-Visitants, Major Benson, Ensign Eaglesfield and Brother Joseph.

In the House, a Motion (by Duke of Bolton) for a Summons against to morrow; for his imparting of some matters of Consequence. After Dinner, Dr Gibson and Mr Grandorge; the latter accompanyed me (with the Dean of Wells [Grahme]) to the Dean of Sarum's [Younger's]; where the Evening spent *ad Clerum*. No Letters from Cumberland.

[Dec.] 14. *Saturday*. Morning, Mr Madox; adviseing about Subscriptions for his Book.[78]

In the House, Duke of Bolton moved for an Address to the Queen for setling (by Act of Parliament) the Duke of Marlborough's Honours on his Posterity.[79] Agreed, *Nemine Contradicente*. Evening, after a Ramble from the Bridge-End, at my Brother's, whence a single Letter to my wife.

[Dec.] 15. *Sunday*. I preached (a Charity-Sermon) at St Ann's; dined, at Mr C. Musgrave's, with Sir Robert Davers, Sir John Bland,[80] Coll. Graham, Mr Harvey[81] and Mr Knatchbole [Knatchbull]. In the Evening, visitted by Cousin Mat[ilda?] Rowse and her Nephew Stillingfleet. NB. She laments that her mother did not offer, once upon a time 500 *l.* as designed.

[Dec.] 16. *Munday*. In the House, the Address (in Honour of the Duke of Marlborough) sent to the Queen by the Duke of Bolton. An order from Her Majesty, by Lord Chamberlain [Kent], to attend Her to St Paul's on the last Instant.[82] Lord Great Chamberlain [Lindsey] to give the necessary Directions.

By Dr Lancaster's to Brother Joseph's, where supper and Mr Thwates,[83] bright and well.

[77] Word blotted.
[78] Possibly his *History and Antiquities of the Exchequer of the Kings of England* (1711).
[79] An Act received the royal assent on 21 Dec. which enabled Marlborough's title and estates to pass through the female line. See HMC *Lords MSS* vii, 8–9 for the Act.
[80] Sir John Bland (1663–1716), 4th Bt., MP for Pontefract, 1690–5, 1698–1713, previously for Appleby, 1681, a Commissioner of the Revenue [I], 1704–6.
[81] Probably William Harvey, MP for Appleby 1705–8 (see Appendix A).
[82] For the service of thanksgiving. See below, 31 Dec.
[83] Edward Thwaites (1667–1711), Anglo-Saxon scholar of Queen's College, Oxford, Regius Professor of Greek, 1708, and Whyte's Professor of Moral Philosophy, 1708.

[Dec.] 17. *Tuesday*. Morning, visitted by Mr Richardson, Chaplain to Lord [Archbishop] of York who (NB.) has been employed to search for the Visitations of our Prior and Convent at Carlile. Item, Mr James Tyrrel, full of his Scotch Records. Item, Mr Morland; for being a Tutor to some English Nobleman. In the House, Queen's Answer to yesterday's Address; and the Duke of Marlborough's proposeal about Woodstock and Blenheim.[84]

[Dec.] 18. *Wednesday*. Morning at the Committee for the Queen's Bounty; where the Dean of Carlile [Atterbury] fruitlessly opposed the Archbishop of Canterbury's motion (in writeing) for Addressing Her Majesty not to promote[85] till Tenths and First-Fruits cleared: Affirming that Every body might see at whom (meaning the Bishop of E[xeter]) this was levelled.

In the House, the Duke of Marlborough's Bill read a first time. Mr Hutchinson with me at the old Ordinary.

[Dec.] 19. *Thursday*. In the House, early, Money-Bill. Item, That for the Duke of Marlborough's Honours &c. Lord Treasurer [Godolphin], applyed to for G. L[angstaff?], ended kindly with — *Let it cool, and it will dye.*

Dr Gibson dined (with 2 Sharps[86] and Mr Hutton) with Lord of York, who obliged me to preach the Inauguration-Sermon, before the Queen, on March 8. *Dante Deo.*

[Dec.] 20. *Friday*. Morning, Governors of the Charity-School at St Ann's, with thanks for my Sermon, &c. Their Collection that day 98 *l.*[87] In the House, Two Money Bills[88] read a second time. Evening at my brother's. Item, NB. In the morning sealed Mr Ward's Lease.

[Dec.] 21. *Saturday*. Morning, Monsieur Lenier[89] answering Lady L[onsdale?]'s queries.

In the House, Lord Wharton acquainted me with His (intended) Visit at my Lodgeings last night. About two came the Queen; and

---

[84] Marlborough wished the estate to descend with the title after the death of his wife, upon whom it was settled in jointure. *LJ* xviii, 181-3.

[85] i.e. to bishoprics.

[86] Probably the archbishop's two sons, John Sharp, MP for Ripon (see Appendix A) and Thomas Sharp (1693-1758), currently attending St Paul's School, for whose later career see *DNB*.

[87] For the charity sermons see above, 24 Dec. 1705, note, and 13 Jan. 1706. At White Kennett's three schools at Aldgate the average sum raised was £36, which his biographer describes as a 'surprisingly high average'. See Bennett, *White Kennett*, pp. 189-90.

[88] The annual Land and Malt Duties Bills. *LJ* xviii, 185.

[89] One of the tutors at Lowther School. *CW* iv (1904), 1.

passed the Money-Bills, &c. This Dispatch (Mr Speaker [Smith] Observed) was like the Victory at Ramellies, Over before the Forces known to be in the Field. Her Majesty's Speech[90] obligeing to all; particularly to the Duke of Marlborough.

I dined with Dr Gibson at our old Ordinary. Archbishop of Canterbury will oppose the Bishop of E[xeter].[91]

[Dec.] 22. *Sunday*. At the Queen's Chapple; where onely the Archbishop of York and Bishop of Norwich. A good Sermon (on the *Messiah*) ill preached by Dr Resbury.[92] I dined at home. In the Evening (after Dr Gibson's Account of our Dean's Dispensation's being again in View) I visitted Mr Grisdale and Mr Yates; the former (honestly) against Dr A[tterbury]'s new Doctrines.[93]

[Dec.] 23. *Munday*. Morning, visitted by Dr Nicolson, Mr Holmes, and Brother Joseph. Committee at Whitehall, Archbishop of York, Bishops of Salisbury, Chichester [Williams]. St Asaph [Beveridge] and Carlile, Lord Chief Justice Holt and Deans of Lincoln [Willis] and Carlile. Adjourned to Friday-Sennight; after agreeing on Remission of Tenths to such as paid no First-Fruits. Day private. Evening, Mr Morland with me some hours; expecting more news from Scotland than the Post had for us.

[Dec.] 24. *Tuesday*. Morning, visitted by Fr[ank] Briscoe, begging for Cousin Grainger; and Mr Dean Story; full of Irish Improvements. I did not dress all day.

[Dec.] 25. *Christmas-Day*. The Bishop of Peterborough [Cumberland] and I communicated[94] with the Earl of Manchester, Lord Woodstock,[95] and &c., after a good Sermon (on our Saviour's takeing on him the *Seed of Abraham*) by Mr James,[96] Chaplain to the Earl of Northampton and Student of Christ Church. Late at Dinner (with Sir W. Bowes, Mr Philip Frowd,[97] Mr Wrightson,[98] &c.) at Mr W. Tullie's.

---

[90] *LJ* xviii, 187.   [91] See above, n. 67.

[92] Nathaniel Resbury (1643–1711), Rector of St Paul's, Shadwell, Middlesex since 1689, and Chaplain to William III and to Anne, 1691–1711.

[93] The initial letter is uncertain, but probably 'A'. If so, this is probably an ironical reference to Atterbury's stance over the local statutes of Carlisle Cathedral, see above, sessional intro., p. 389.

[94] Nicolson's parish church was St Margaret's, Westminster.

[95] See Appendix A. It is interesting that a Bentinck should now be an Anglican communicant.

[96] Ptolemy James (*c*.1672–1729), Rector of Whatcott, Warwickshire, since 1702 (near Compton Winyates, Lord Northampton's seat), Canon of St Paul's, 1713–29.

[97] ?Philip Frowde (*c*.1681–1738), poet.

[98] William Wrightson (*c*.1676–1760), of Cusworth, Yorkshire, later MP for Newcastle-upon-Tyne, 1710–22. Sedgwick, ii, 559.

[Dec.] 26. *Thursday*. Morning, visitted by Mr Hutchinson, Mr Dowson, Brother Joseph, Mr J. Tyrrel and Mr Watkinson. I dined at Lambeth; where both the Archbishop and Eleven Bishops, 13 in all. Onely Bishop of Exon wanting.[99]

[Dec.] 27. *Friday*. Evening, with Mr M. Hutchinson, Sister and Niece Rothery, at my Brother's (in Salisbury Court) till Eleven; after hard Labour at Sermons.

[Dec.] 28. *Saturday*. Morning, vissited by two Broughams and Mr Johnson. Item, by Sir Robert Harrison, whom I carryed (in Quest of Mr Smith) to Earl's Court. I dined (with Sir W. Bowes, &c.) at P. Tullie's; and bestowed the Evening on Mr Bell and Mr Buddle.

[Dec.] 29. *Sunday*. I preached, in the morning, and administered the Sacrament. Dined with Mr Vice-Chancellor Lancaster, as did Mr Sandys[100] and Mr John Smith. Directly home.

[Dec.] 30. *Munday*. Morning, preached (to the Societies for Reformation [of Manners])[101] at Bow-Church; and thence, a little after One, came directly to the House. The new Lords[102] had their patents read, and were admitted; that of the Lord Keeper [Cowper] being laid by himself (on his Knee) upon the Throne, and thence taken up again and delivered to the Clerk. After a late Dinner, Visits to R. Nicolson's and Mr C. Musgrave's. At the latter place I found Sir H. Fletcher and Coll. Graham whose elder son dyeing.[103]

[Dec.] 31. *Tuesday*. Accommodated with Robes by the Bishop of Lincoln, and a Seat in my Lord of York's Coach, I attended the

[99] Of those bishops then in town.

[100] Possibly Thomas Sandes, Canon of York, 1690–1718.

[101] On these societies, the most controversial of the post-Revolution Anglican voluntary associations, see T. C. Curtis and W. A. Speck, 'The Societies for the Reformation of Manners', *Literature and History*, No. 3 (Mar. 1976). Although there were sixteen such societies in London and Westminster as early as 1694, they very soon became a nationwide phenomenon. High Churchmen in general disliked them; and even moderates such as Sharp mistrusted their influence (A. T. Hart, *The Life and Time of John Sharp, Archbishop of York* (1949), pp. 179–85). Nicolson had earlier opposed the establishment of a society in Carlisle because it was supported by a number of prominent Dissenters (see James, pp. 52–5). But by 1706 he appears to have been converted to the favourable attitude common to most of his new Low Church friends.

[102] The Marquesses of Lindsey, Dorchester (formerly Earl of Kingston), and Kent, the Earls of Bindon, Wharton, Poulett, Godolphin, and Cholmondeley, and Lords Cowper and Pelham. *LJ* xviii, 188–91.

[103] Henry Grahme, MP for Westmorland. He died on 7 Jan. and was buried on 11 Jan. 1707.

Queen in Her glorious Procession to St Paul's;[104] the Weather Good, and the Shew unspeakeably fine. From the House of Lords to the Church 3 hours and a quarter. Decorum of both Houses, &c. very extraordinary. After the Bishop of Sarum's Elegant Harange,[105] I dined with the Dean of St Asaph [Stanley], and was brought home by (his Uncle) the Bishop.

Jan. 1. *Wednesday*. Morning. After Mr Buchanan, &c. Mr Watson[106] (Brother to Lord Rockingham) Mr Jervase [Jervoise], Mr Wind-ham,[107] &c. desireing me to print my last Munday's Sermon.[108] With Archbishop of York and Bishop of Exon to St James's; whence, Duty paid to the Queen and Prince, back again to Dinner (with the Dean of Salisbury [Younger] and Mr Ellis) with His Grace. Evening at S[alisbury] C[ourt].

[Jan.] 2. *Thursday*. Morning, Visitted by Mr Grandorge, with his Case; and designing to visit Lord Wharton. That failing, Lord Halifax effectually waited on; my man bringing away 3 voll. of Mr Rymer's. Mr Stonestreet, at Dinner with me, explained the *Entrochi*,[109] &c. Dr Gibson, with a sneaking Letter to himself from Dr Todd. Evening, at Milbank; where young Mrs Lowther mightily for Monsieur Lenier.

[Jan.] 3. *Friday*. Morning, With the Bishop of Norwich offering Visits to Lords Somers and Wharton; paid to Dr Trimnel,[110] with whom Lord Sunderland. Evening, Visit to Mrs Brougham: And, the Remainder, with Mr Bell and Mr Buchanan.

[Jan.] 4. *Saturday*. I dined at Lambeth with the New Earl Marshal [Bindon], Sir J. Cook, Dean of Canterbury [Stanhope], Dr Harris, &c. NB. After the Company gone Lord Archbishop of Canterbury

[104] For the thanksgiving service for Ramillies. The coaches of the Lords spiritual and temporal immediately preceded the Queen in the procession. The Commons, in their coaches, went first.

[105] Before Burnet's sermon there 'was a fine anthem sung'. Luttrell, vi, 123. Nicolson wrote to his wife 'I am very weary with the Glories of the Day', Tullie House Library, Carlisle: Nicolson's Account Book for 1706.

[106] ? Hon. Thomas Watson Wentworth (1665–1723), MP for Higham Ferrers, 1703–13, 1722–3, third son of 2nd Lord Rockingham.

[107] Possibly Ashe Wyndham of Flebrigge, Norfolk, who sat in the next parliament as Knight of the Shire for Norfolk.

[108] It was printed as *A Sermon Preached December 30, 1706 before the Societies for the Reformation of Manners*.

[109] The name sometimes given to the wheel-like plates of which certain crinoid fossils are composed.

[110] Charles Trimnell (for whom see Appendix A) had been tutor to Lord Sunderland.

assured me and Dr Gibson that he'd insist on an Act of Security for Episcopacy, previous to the Union.[111]

[Jan.] 5. *Sunday*. Morning, Very Rainy, I kept within; transcribeing my Reformation-Sermon for Mr Jervase [Jervoise]. At Dinner with my Brother, Sister and Niece; and directly back to my Lodgeings. Private and Quiet.

[Jan.] 6. *Munday*. Morning, Visitted by Sir H. Fletcher; and visitting (his Neighbour) the Bishop of Bangor; to whom I gave a copy of my Sermon for Mr Jervase. Dined at Lord Thanet's, with Sir John Mordaunt[112] and his Family.

[Jan.] 7. *Tuesday*. Morning, visitted by M. Hutchinson. After the H[ouse] had ordered the Bishop of Landaff [Tyler] to preach on the 30th,[113] &c. I dined with Dr Gibson, together with Dr Sydel and Dr Potter. Evening, Letters dispatched, at Sir H. Fletcher's; where Coll. Grahme, Mr Vice-Chancellor Lancaster, Dean of Salisbury [Younger], Mr Fisher and I, most Sumptuously entertained in Silver and Gold at Supper, &c.

[Jan.] 8. *Wednesday*. Morning, at Gresham-College; and thence, with Dr Woodward, visit to Mr James Lowther. Evening, Mr Muth-land's company till near Bed-time. Lords sat not.

[Jan.] 9. *Thursday*. Morning, Visitted by Mr Holme of Childrey; and by Mr George Holme and Mr Dale, with News of renewal of Committee for Records. Qu[ery]. Dined at Mr C. Musgrave's with Sir Christopher, Mr Joseph and Mr Lister. Lords sat not.

[Jan.] 10. *Friday*. Morning, Visitted by Mr Bell, and Mr Dean of Carlile [Atterbury]; with whom I went to the Committee at White-hall, where nothing done to any purpose.

At the House a petition for a Private Bill rejected on Report of the Judges:[114] And on Second Reading of the Bill against Burning in the Cheek,[115] Bishop of Sarum moved for the removeal of the *Farce*

[111] See above, sessional intro., p. 391.

[112] Sir John Mordaunt (*c*.1650–1721), 5th Bt., MP for Warwickshire, 1698–1715.

[113] The choice of so uncompromising a Whig prelate to preach on Charles I's day of martyrdom was yet another unpleasant pill for the Tories to swallow.

[114] A petition against Opie's Estate Bill had led the House to seek the judges' opinion. They reported (HMC *Lords MSS* vii, 4–5) that it would be difficult to put the bill into effect.

[115] The Housebreakers Act of 1707 amended that of 10 Will. c.12, 'for the better apprehension, prosecuting and punishing' of burglars and housebreakers. The clause in this

of Benefit of the Clergy,[116] Seconded by the Bishop of Oxon [Talbot].
Evening private.

[Jan.] 11. *Saturday*. Morning, After visits from Susan Orfeur,
Brother Joseph and R. Nicolson, I went to Lord Wharton's and (at
my Lady Lonsdale's Instance) to Lord Weymouth's; and thence to
the House: Where, at Lord Nottingham's motion, the Lords ordered
to be summoned for Tuesday next.

I dined (my Niece's Birth-day) at my Brother's, and bestowed the
Evening at H[enry] Graham's Funeral; together with the Duke of
Norfolk, Earl of Clarendon, Marquess of Huntley,[117] Lord H[oward]
of Effingham, Mr St John, Mr Granvil, Mr Prior,[118] Sirs H. and G.
Fletcher, Mr C. Musgrave, Mr Vice-Chamberlain [Coke][119] &c.

[Jan.] 12. *Sunday*. I preached at the Savoy; and dined (with Coll.
Orfeur, Mr Cavel, Mr Ramsey, and Sister Rothery) at R. Nicolson's.
Evening, sent a Query to Archbishop of Canterbury, Whether not fit
for moveing to morrow (in His Name) for a bill of Security to the
Church? Dr Gibson came over upon it; sent by His Grace, &c.

[Jan.] 13. *Munday*. Morning, Visitted by Mr R. Musgrave (for bringing in Irish Wool at W[hite]haven) and's Brother James. Nothing, of
moment, in the House. Afternoon, Mr James Tyrrel; satisfyed that
the Union will pass.[120] Evening, at Lambeth, with Lord of Canterbury,
very cheerful and kind; and, afterwards, with Dr G[ibson] and Dr
Sydel, at R. Snow's chamber: Whose story's of Queen Elizabeth's
Mayor of Queenborough and King Charles 2d's of Feversham, good.

bill authorising punishment by burning in the cheek was removed because it had proved not
to be a deterrent; rather the contrary, since the burning prevented those convicted from
living subsequently by lawful gain or employment. HMC *Lords MSS* vii, 8.

[116] This was the privilege of exemption from trial by a secular court, allowed to or
claimed by clergymen arraigned for a felony, which had developed into the privilege of
exemption from the sentence which, in the case of certain offences, might be pleaded on
first conviction by everyone who could read. On 22 Jan. 1707 a clause was added to the
bill which made it no longer necessary for a person claiming benefit of clergy to prove his
capacity to read. See *Statutes of the Realm*, viii, 563 (6 Anne, c.9).

[117] Alexander Gordon (*c*.1678–1728) styled Marquess of Huntley, 1684–1716, later
2nd Duke of Gordon, 1716, was a Roman Catholic and a Jacobite who was imprisoned
in 1715.

[118] Matthew Prior (1664–1721), poet, placeman, and diplomat, closely associated with
Harley and St John. Part of his correspondence is printed in HMC *Bath MSS* iii.

[119] Thomas Coke (1674–1727), MP for Derbyshire, 1698–1700, 1701–10, and Grampound, 1710–15, Vice Chamberlain of the Household, 5 Dec. 1706–27, Teller of Exchequer,
1704–6.

[120] After a protracted struggle since the previous November (see above, sessional intro.,
p. 391) the Treaty of Union was finally ratified by the Scottish parliament on 16 Jan. The
news took a week to reach London (see below, 22 Jan.; Luttrell, vi, 130).

[Jan.] 14. *Tuesday*. Morning, Visitted by Mr Thomas Bell, Mr Grandorge, Mr Grisdale, Dr Deering, Mr Hutchinson, Mr Gibson, Mr Richardson and Mr Elstob.

In the House, Lord Nottingham's Motion for the Articles of the Union was quashed by Lord Treasurer [Godolphin] without a Question.[121] Dr Gibson and Mr Elstob treated at the old Ordinary; the Latter fully satisfyed with Archbishop of Canterbury's cause in Convocation.

[Jan.] 15. *Wednesday*. Morning, Visitted by Mr Joseph Smith, Mr Hutchinson and (in hopes of the Schoolmaster's place at St Alban's)[122] Mr Rumney.[123] The House adjourned the Cause 'twixt Lewis and Fielding, to Tuesday next.[124] Evening, with Mr Hutchinson and Mr Buttle.

[Jan.] 16. *Thursday*. I went by water, with Mr Hutchinson, to Chelsea; and paid an Hour's Visit to the Dean [Atterbury]. At my Lord of York's (with the Bishop of Chester [Stratford], Dr Smallridge, Dr Gatforth,[125] &c.) at Dinner; and afternoon at Lord Howard of Effingham's, concludeing finally with Monsieur Leniere. In the Evening, unseasonably and too long, visitted by Coll. Francis Nicolson, Mr Bell and Mr Buchanan; after I had (whilst unfortunately at Lord Howard's) been called for by Lord Somers.

[Jan.] 17. *Friday*. Morning, visitted by Dr Waugh, Dr Harris and Mr Grandorge: At the House, Randolf's Appeal about Taxes.[126] The Decree, on Lord Somers's disagreeing with Lord Rochester, affirmed. Evening, with Mal. Rothery,[127] at Salisbury-Court.

[Jan.] 18. *Saturday*. The Lords not sitting, I went (with Mr. Hutchinson) to see the New Hospital at Greenwich;[128] which will be a most

---

[121] See *Parl. Hist.* vi, 554–6, and Luttrell, vi, 127, for speeches, and for the support given to Godolphin by Somers, Halifax, and Wharton.

[122] St Alban's Grammar School, founded in the mid-sixteenth century, was endowed by the corporation of the borough. The mastership carried in the 1670s the relatively high salary of £52 *p.a.* W. A. L. Vincent, *The Grammar Schools . . . 1660–1714* (1969), pp. 36, 170.

[123] ?Robert Rumney (1686–1743) of Kirkoswald, Cumberland, gained his BA from Queen's College, Oxford, 1707, and was Vicar of St Peter's, St Albans, 1715–43.

[124] For the case see HMC *Lords MSS* vii, 10.

[125] Lionel Gatford (d. 1715), Rector of St Dionis Backchurch since 1680; later Archdeacon of St Albans, 1713, and Precentor and Treasurer of St Paul's, 1714.

[126] See HMC *Lords MSS* vii, 1.

[127] Probably Nicolson's niece, Mary Rothery.

[128] Greenwich Palace had been turned into a hospital for superannuated and disabled seamen in 1694.

Magnificent Structure, far (as yet) from being finished. We also visitted Mr Flamsted's Observatory;[129] whence a glorious View of London, The Thames, &c. His *Motus Annuus* (made by Tompion[130] 1676, the same year Sir Jonas More[131] got the Observatory reered) is much neglected and out of Order; and his *Motus Perpetuus* wholly ceased. His Quadrant-House mean; and the Well long since filled up.[132]

[Jan.] 19. *Sunday*. At Whitehal, a very good Sermon concerning ou[r] Saviour's Miracles, on (part of the Gospel for the Day) *John* 2, 11. by Mr Marshal, Lecturer at St Ann's. In the Evening, a kind (dry) visit from Mr James Lowther; who stoutly (and reasonably) resolved to have the Patronage of Whitehaven, if a parish.[133]

[Jan.] 20. *Munday*. Morning, A visit from Mr Grahme, Junior, of Newbiggin.

At the House, the New Erected Mill at Tiverton (by Appeal from the Exchequer)[134] occasioned the remitting the Consideration to all the Judges, against Tuesday Sennight, whether these Tithes were Predial, Personal or Mixt. The Barons had given Sentence for the Parson; allowing 'em to come under the first Tribe. After a late Dinner, Mr Richardson and I a while at Dr Nicolson's: And the rest, with Mr Newt, Parson of Tiverton.[135]

[Jan.] 21. *Tuesday*. Morning, Visitted by Mr Madox and Dean Story; the latter for ventureing 500 *l*. on a manufacture at Carlile. In the House cause heared on the Appeal against Is[rael] Fielding. Decree affirmed. Evening, Treating Mr Buttle and Letters.

[Jan.] 22. *Wednesday*. Morning, Mr James Musgrave and Brother Joseph both treated (at Story's)[136] with a pint of Mumm.[137]

[129] Built in 1675 by Wren, it was occupied by John Flamsteed (1646–1719), the first Astronomer Royal in 1676.

[130] Thomas Tompion (1639–1713), clockmaker. The *Motus Annuus* was inscribed 'Sir Jonas Moore caused this movement to be made with great care Anno Domini 1676 by Thomas Tompion'.

[131] Sir Jonas Moore (1617–79), mathematician and Surveyor-General of the Ordnance 1663.

[132] Over 100 feet deep and equipped with a tube, it was constructed in 1676 to measure the parallax of the star *Gamma Draconis*. Only one, unsuccessful, observation is recorded, in 1679. The well was rediscovered in 1965.

[133] For the Lowthers' involvement in the appointment of a minister in 1694 see R. Hopkinson, 'The appointment of the first minister of St Nicholas' Church, Whitehaven', *CW* lxxii (1972), 283–302.   [134] See HMC *Lords MSS* vii, 6–7.

[135] John Newt (?1655–1716), Rector of Tiverton, 1680–1715.

[136] Storey's Gate Coffee House, Westminster. B. Lillywhite, *Coffee Houses* (1963), pp. 553–4.

[137] A beer imported from Brunswick in the seventeenth and eighteenth centuries. Nicolson

After a short Attendance on the Commissioners of the Queen's Bounty, at the House: Where News of the Union finished;[138] Duke of Marlborough's Bill passed; and that for takeing away the *burning on the cheek* gone thro' (bunglingly enough by the Judges) in a Grand Committee. Item, A long Report (by the Earl of Rochester) rejecting a Petition against Ob[adiah] Sedgewick.[139]

Evening, at my Brother's. NB. Lord Wharton's Letters from Dr Fl[eming?][140] and Mrs Gregory.

[Jan.] 23. *Thursday*. Called to Lambeth by Mr James Musgrave[141] who fancies he ought to succeed Dr H[ody?].[142] Reg[ister] *Warham*[143] returned to Dr G[ibson].

In the House, Jermyn's Divorce adjourned on the Woman's Petition.[144] Bill for takeing away Burning in the Cheek (with an amendment at the Table, strikeing out *and moderate*) read a 3d time and passed. Evening, Mr Murthland with me; on the finished Union.

[Jan.] 24. *Friday*. Morning, Two Musgraves impetuously upon me again; and on Dr Gibson: Who (after the Reversal of one of Lord Keeper Wright's Decrees,[145] directing a wrong Issue) dined with me. Evening, at Salisbury-Court.

[Jan.] 25. *Saturday*. Morning, After seeing Mr Tilson[146] and writeing to Lord Treasurer [Godolphin], I made my Appearance at the House; and then went to Dinner (as desired) at Lambeth: Where Bishops of Worcester [Lloyd], Sarum, Oxford and Bangor. Lord Archbishop of Canterbury shewed us his Design for a Bill of Security

may have acquired a taste for it on his trip to Germany in 1678. While at Brunswick on 5 Sept. he tried both types available: that for home consumption, and the better brew for export. It was made 'out of Barley and hops, with a small mixture of wheat'. Queen's College, Oxford, MS 68 (unfoliated): Diary of Nicolson's journey to Holland and Germany.

[138] See above, n. 120; *Acts Parl. Scot.* xi, 406–14.

[139] For the case and report see *LJ* xiv, 601, 657, 672; xviii, 200–2.

[140] Henry Fleming (c.1661–1728), fourth son of Sir Daniel Fleming of Rydal, Westmorland, and brother of Captain Michael and Archdeacon George Fleming. He became a close friend of Nicolson's at Queen's College, Oxford (see James, pp. 6–7, 17–18). He was Rector of Grasmere, Westmorland, in 1685 and of Asby, 1694–1728.

[141] James Musgrave, third son of Sir Richard Musgrave of Hayton, MA Queen's College, 1705, Vicar of Kirby Moorside, Yorkshire, 1707, Rector of Little Gransden, Huntingdonshire, 1714.

[142] Dr Humphrey Hody (1659–1707), Regius Professor of Greek at Oxford since 1698, whose death was reported by Luttrell (vi, 130) on 23 Jan.

[143] The register of Archbishop William Warham, still in Lambeth Palace Library.

[144] See HMC *Lords MSS* vii, 40–1.

[145] See *LJ* xviii, 204.

[146] Christopher Tilson, Chief Clerk of the Revenue, 1695–1714. He had been a Clerk in the Treasury since 1684. Sainty, *Treasury Officials*, p. 154.

for the Church. Very Good. Lord of Sarum and I warm on the time of passing that in Scotland. He in the wrong.[147] Dined also with us, Drs Claget,[148] Mandevil, Turner,[149] Torriano[150] (goeing to Venice), Gibson and Snapes.

[Jan.] 26. *Sunday*. Morning, Mr Dowson, from the Tower, went with me to St James's: where I met with Mr James Musgrave, disappointed, and (with him) offered a Visit to Dean Grahme, and paid one to Mr R[ichard] M[usgrave]. At the Queen's Chapel Dr Brady[151] preached a polite Sermon on the *Unum Necessarium*. With the Bishop of Exon (brisk) about the Park, home to Dinner. Evening, Visitted by Lord Thanet; who put Mrs Grandorge's Letter into my hand for Lord of Canterbury. Afterwards, at Salisbury Court, takeing leave of M. Rothery.

[Jan.] 27. *Munday*. Morning, At Sir A. Fountain's Request, I endeavoured to sollicite my Lord Archbishop of York in favour of Mr Thwaites, for the Greek Professor's place: But His Grace was gone to Kensington. At the Bishop of Lincoln's and Bishop of Chester's in the way to the House; where, after Justice done to Mr Ward of Leicestershire,[152] in my Lord of Canterbury's Closet[153] correcting the designed Bill for Security for the Church. Carryed by His Grace again to Dinner at Lambeth, with Dean of Lincoln [Willis], Archdeacons of Huntingdon [Kennett] and Norwich [Trimnell], &c. Evening, the Deans of Wells [Grahme] and Salisbury [Younger] at my Lodgeings.

[Jan.] 28. *Tuesday*. Morning, Early to Dr Kennett's; where an Eyewitness of his Immoderate Pains in Schemas of Bishops and other Dignitaries of England,[154] Critical Notes on Liturgy and Canons, Memoirs of Centuries,[155] &c. He carryed me and my Ref[ormation of Manners'] Sermon to Mr Churchil's,[156] and I, him and's wife to

---

[147] For Burnet's views, see *History*, v, 289–90.

[148] Nicholas Clagett (1654–1727), Archdeacon of Sudbury, 1693–1726.

[149] Probably Thomas Turner (1646–1714), President of Corpus Christi College, Oxford, 1687–1714, Precentor of St Paul's, 1690–1714.

[150] Alexander Torriano (*c*.1668–1717), Professor of Astronomy, Gresham College, 1691. He was Domestic Chaplain to Lord Manchester who was sent as envoy extraordinary to Venice in 1707.

[151] Nicholas Brady (1659–1726), Chaplain to Queen Anne, Rector of Clapham, Surrey, 1706–26.

[152] For the case see HMC *Lords MSS* vii, 4.   [153] See fig. 1.

[154] Now BL Lansdowne MS 935. In 1708 Kennett placed his collection at the disposal of John Le Neve, who published his *Fasti Ecclesiae Anglicanae* in 1716.

[155] For an assessment of Kennett as a historian see Bennett, *White Kennett*, pp. 158–77.

[156] Awnsham Churchill, printer, bookseller, and MP for Dorchester, see Appendix A.

the House of Lords: Where the Queen passed the Duke of Marlborough's Act, &c. and then laid the UNION before the Parliament
in a moveing Speech.[157] Archbishop of Canterbury to bring[158] in
a Bill for the Security of the Doctrine, Liturgy, Rites, &c. of the
Church of England.[159]

I dined with Mr Musgrave where Sir Christopher and Mr Joseph.

[Jan.] 29. *Wednesday*. Morning, After Visits from Mr Donning and
Dr Gibson, I went to the Committee at Whitehall; where Bishops
of Norwich, Chichester and Oxford, Mr Attorny Generall [Northey],
Sir J. Cook, and the Deans of Lincoln and Carlile [Atterbury]. Orders.

At the House, the Call:[160] Which over, Dean Story's Cause half
heard:[161] The Residue refered to Friday, with a Proviso, That the
Respondent's Counsel (who opened) should be allowed to Reply.
NB. Evening private.

[Jan.] 30. *Thursday*. Morning, visitted by Mr Grisdale for a Remove
by the Favour of Archbishop of Canterbury. From the House to
Westminster Abbey; where Sermon (a very good One) by Bishop
of Landaff on *Ecclesiastes* 8, 14. Present Lord Keeper [Cowper],
Earl of Rochester and Ten Bishops. Archbishop of Canterbury's
Reply in the Evening to Lord Thanet's Message.

[Jan.] 31. *Friday*. Morning, Visitants, Cousin R. Nicolson and
Philip Tullie; the latter Mr Joseph Musgrave's Sollicitor. A Visit
attempted to the Earl of Carlile; and Mr Tilson called on, not worth
the while: Mr Hewston being appointed Mr. Patrickson's Successor.[162]
At the House Lord of Canterbury's Bill for the Church, read; and
ordered a second Reading (Lords summoned) on Munday. Dean
Story's Cause, for him. Evening at Salisbury Court.

Feb. 1. *Saturday*. Morning Brother Joseph and Mr James Musgrave.
After a Walk, Mr Ward (of Leicestershire) had his Decree Unanimously

---

[157] *LJ* xviii, 207.

[158] i.e. he moved for, and was granted, leave to bring in.

[159] For the bill see HMC *Lords MSS* vii, 22–3; and above, sessional intro., p. 392, for the
finishing touches put to it the following day at a meeting at Lord Sunderland's house.

[160] The Lord Keeper's letter·was sent to eighteen peers, as a result of the call, requiring
them to attend 'upon extraordinary business'. The occasion was considered so important
that the absent peers were required, if they could not attend because of sickness or some
other reason, to 'send up two persons to attest the Same upon Oath'. *LJ* xviii, 220–1. At
the call seventy-nine peers were recorded in the *Journal* as present. See below, n. 176.

[161] See HMC *Lords MSS* vii, 2–3.

[162] Maurice Houston was appointed Searcher at Carlisle Port on 27 Jan. 1707 in the
place of Richard Patrickson, lately deceased. *CTB 1706–7*, p. 159.

affirmed. The Commons first debated the Union-Articles in Generall.[163] Evening, Cousin Thomas Pearson from the Election at Queen's.

[Feb.] 2. *Sunday*. After Sermon at the Abbey, I went to dine with my brother; intending to preach for Dr Waugh: But he haveing provided an excellent Discourse on the *Purification*, I desired to hear that; reserveing my Services for a Common Day. After Prayers, the Dr and I paid a Visit to Mr Bernard; whose Library and frank Entertainment very fine.[164]

Afterwards, hearing poor Mrs. Beaumont's Complaints at my brother's till almost Nine.

[Feb.] 3. *Munday*. In the House, the Archbishop of Canterbury's Bill (the Queen and Prince present) had a Second Reading: And, before Committing, was Teezed by—1. Lord Scarborough; who gave the History of Motions towards Union on the Affairs of Glengow [Glencoe], Darien and Act of Security: Concludeing, that all the Acts concerning Religion (in both Kingdomes) be enquired for. 2. Lord Ferrers, Violent against the Admission of Cameronians[165] and Covenanters into our Parliaments. 3. Lord Nottingham, Angry at the Archbishop for not consulting the Convocation.[166] Proposes Test-Act, Apostolical [Succession],[167] &c. 4. Lord Rochester, For Care of the Universities[168] and True Prot[estants]. 5. Archbishop of York for adding onely the Test-Act.

For the Bill, without Amendments. 1. Lord Somers, provision already made for all demanded: The present Archbishop of Canterbury a Glory to our Church: Who was chief Minister when Presbytery set up in Scotland.[169] 2. Lord Wharton, As much Care ought to be had of our Pure Religion as the Scots have taken of theirs — odd.

[163] 'This day the Commons . . . went into a committee upon the Union, Mr [Spencer] Compton chairman; and read the articles, and voted to consider them paragraph by paragraph, every Tuesday, Thursday, and Saturday.' Luttrell, vi, 134.

[164] Charles Bernard (1650–1710), a strong High-Churchman, was the surgeon who had saved Benjamin Hoadly's crippled leg. He was Serjeant-Surgeon to the Queen, 1702, and Master of the Barber Surgeon's Company, 1703. His library was sold at his death, and Swift bought some of his books at the auction, see *Journal to Stella*, i, 219, 227, 240, 242, 244.

[165] Scottish reformed presbyterian followers of Richard Cameron.

[166] The Convocation was about to be prorogued (12 Feb.) for three weeks to prevent its reported intention of addressing the Commons against the Union. See Lathbury, p. 402.

[167] Nottingham's proposal was that these should be explicitly guaranteed by the bill.

[168] The draft of the bill included a clause, omitted from the act, to ensure that all persons connected with the universities should conform to the Church of England. Lambeth Palace MS 640, p. 446.

[169] Reference to either Nottingham, who was Secretary of State, or to the Duke of Leeds, who as Lord Carmarthen was Lord President of the Council, in 1690, when the Act passed in Scotland restoring Presbyterianism as the state religion.

Fundamental part and Condition not different. 3. Lord Sunderland, the like. 4. Lord Hallifax, Glad to hear that *True Prot[estants]* in good Esteem. 5. Archbishop of Canterbury, Agreed with Lord Nottingham that our Church Government *Apostolical*; but no need of saying it here.

Question[170]—*Whether Test-Act be part? Contents, 33. Not Contents*, 60. The Bill, gone thro' without any Amendments, Reported by Bishop of Salisbury; and ordered to be Ingrossed. NB. Amongst the Contents, Archbishop of York, Bishops of London [Compton], Rochester [Sprat], Chester,[171] Durham [Crew], and S. Asaph. Evening, Mr Murthland.

[Feb.] 4. *Tuesday*. Morning, Visitted by Cous. Br[idget] Nicolson, in great heart, and Mr Buchanan; with whom at the *Queen's Mead-House*.[172] At Westminster Archbishop of Canterbury's Bill (after an Amendment of 13 for 14 C. 2.)[173] passed. At Dinner, with Mr C. Musgrave, Mr Crowther and's Lady.

[Feb.] 5. *Wedenesday*. Morning, Visitted by J. Grainger, Dr Torriano (Goeing to Venice, and presenting me with his Sermon), Dr Gibson and Brother Joseph. At the Committee at Whitehall. In the House Writt of Error, brought by Lady Strode, heard; and Judgement Reversed.[174] Evening, Cousin Thomas Pearson and W. Senhouse.[175]

[Feb.] 6. *Thursday*. Morning, After Visits to Mr R. Lowther and Lord Herbert, I went to pay my Duty (with the Archbishop of Canterbury and 12 other Bishops) to the Queen and Prince. Afternoon, Visitted by Mr Vice-Chancellor Lancaster (newly arrived from Oxford) hinting at Designs in Convocation against the Archbishop's Bill. Caution given to Dr Gibson.

[Feb.] 7. *Friday*. Morning, With Mr Hutchinson, thro' the Park, to the Mead-House. Lords debated on the Union; but ended in calling for the Answers of the Absents[176] on Tuesday next. Leave for a Divorce to Mr Jermyn.

[170] ' a clause . . . offer'd by the archbishop of York, and seconded by the earl of Nottingham.' Luttrell, vi, 134.

[171] Nine days later Bishop Stratford of Chester died. Extraordinarily, Nicolson does not mention the fact.

[172] In Hyde Park Road, B. Lillywhite, *London Signs* (1972), p. 437.

[173] The bill mistakenly referred to the Act of Uniformity as 13 Char. II, c.4, whereas it was 14 Char. II, c.4. See HMC *Lords MSS* vii, 22, note.

[174] See HMC *Lords MSS* vii, 7.

[175] William Senhouse had been a lieutenant in Ireland in 1706. He became a captain in 1708. Dalton, iii, 319; iv, 133; vi, 254.

[176] The Lord Keeper was ordered to give the House the answers of the absent lords on

After Dinner, Dean of Peterborough [Freeman] Archdeacon Trimnel, Dr Gibson and Dr Bearcroft:[177] the three first of the Committee, to consider what to do on the Archbishop of Canterbury's Bill;[178] which will probably pass both Houses before they come to any Resolution. Evening, with Sister Rothery, at Brother Joseph's.

[Feb.] 8. *Saturday*. Morning, After a Walk in the Park (and a Glass of Mum) with Mr Smith and Mr Musgrave, at the House; where News of all being Calm in Convocation upon apprehensions of the Bill being to pass the Commons on Munday. The Judges not ready, in the Case of Tiverton-Mills, till Thursday next. Misrepresentations of the Lords in Coffee-Houses refered to a Committee.[179] Evening, With Dr Lancaster.

[Feb.] 9. *Sunday*. Morning, I preached for, and dined with, Dr Kennet; who is sure that the Bishop of E[xeter] will not be removed to Winton. Evening, at Mr Hoadley's;[180] preaching for the Bishop of Lincoln, a Charity-Sermon. Both Churches crowded.

[Feb.] 10. *Munday*. Morning, With W. Senhouse at Mr Walsh's;[181] for's Letter to Sir M[atthew] Dudley.[182] Granted. In the Committee, Dr Kennet and others examined about the false News. In the House,

the following Tuesday, 11 Feb., when only four letters (from Rutland, Warrington, Coventry, and Gower) were read. *LJ* xviii, 229, 233. Only Coventry appears to have followed the original request of the House to provide two witnesses of inability to attend (see above, n. 160). And even in this case 'my Lord Manchester (at my Lord Bindon's request)', had to acquaint, 'the house that your Lordship had sent 2 servants to testifie that your Honour was under a course of Phisick and that 'twas your Doctors opinion you could not with safety attend the house'. Badminton House Beaufort MSS Drawer 30: Bern[hard] Rice to [Coventry], 11 Feb. 1706.

[177] William Barcroft (*c.*1656–1712), Treasurer of Chichester, 1691–1712, Prebendary, 1705–12, Proctor for the clergy of Chichester in the 1707 Convocation.

[178] For proceedings in this committee see BL Lansdowne MS 1013, f. 95: Kennett to Samuel Blackwell, 13 Feb. 1707.

[179] Papers, distributed in coffee houses and purporting to be the proceedings of the House of Lords, had stated 'that in the Bill for the Security of the Church, a clause was carryed in the House by a great majority for a repeal of the Test-Act as to Protestant Dissents' (Bodl. MS Ballard 6, f. 105: Gibson to Charlett, 8 Feb. 1707). The committee ordered the arrest of four people including William Rowlands (below 11 Feb.) for writing these libels, and in late Mar. a person was arrested for their distribution, only to be later discharged. See *LJ* xviii, 230, 233–4, 244, 305, 309; HMC *Lords MSS* vii, 50–2.

[180] The church of St Peter-le-Poor.

[181] Probably William Walsh of Abberley, Worcestershire, MP for Richmond, Dec. 1705–8, formerly MP for Worcestershire, 1698–1701, 1702–5, a close associate of Lord Somers; vigorously backed in Worcestershire elections by Bishop Lloyd.

[182] Sir Matthew Dudley (d. 1721), 2nd Bt., MP for Northampton, 1702–5, and Huntingdonshire, 1713–15, was a Commissioner of the Customs, 1706–11, 1714.

Waveing of Privilege[183] adjusted 'twixt the Earls of Derby and Anglesey.

At Lambeth, dineing with the Archbishop of Canterbury, who mightily pleased with the Commons passing his Bill (in their Committee) this day, without Amendments; notwithstanding the contrary Endeavours of Dissenters of all Denominations.[184] At Mr Snow's chamber, &c.

[Feb.] 11. *Tuesday*. Morning, Visitants, Cousin R. Nicolson, W. Rook, W. Senhouse and Monsieur Leniere.

At the Committee, Rowland (a News-monger) detected, and, by the House, taken into Custody of the black Rod. I dined (with Dr Sydale and Dr Potter) at Dr Gibson's; and returned to my Letters. NB. The Archbishop of Canterbury's Bill sent up, without Amendments, from the Commons; who approved all the Articles of Union, and order Sir R[ichard] Onslow,[185] &c. to bring in a Bill of Ratification.

[Feb.] 12. *Wednesday*. Morning, Lt. Leethut[186] and Joseph Smith. At the House, a Trivial Welsh Appeal. Dr Potter, at Dinner. Evening, with Archdeacon Fleming and Brother John; from Oxford.

[Feb.] 13. *Thursday*. Morning, Visits by Mr G. Holmes and Mr Black. After bringing Archdeacon Fleming and brother John to the Archbishop of York's, and to see the Queen in Her Robes, I went with [them] (by water) to Brother Joseph's: Where we dined, and I walked home. Archbishop of Canterbury's Bill had the Royal Assent.

[Feb.] 14. *Friday*. Morning, Forced from me by Mrs Donning, unsufferably pressing, Mr Buchanan, Mr Stedman and W. Senhouse. At the House, Another Welsh Decree affirmed: And the Printed Act for the Security of the Church (together with the Bishop of Landaff's Sermon, on Jan. 30) dispersed.

[Feb.] 15. *Saturday*. With Archdeacon Fleming to the House; where (the Queen Present) the Union considered, and Five Articles read

---

[183] On 10 Feb. Derby voluntarily waived his privileges as a peer in all suits relating to the case of the Dowager Countess v. the Earl of Derby. Anglesey had married the daughter and heiress of the 9th Earl of Derby. For this and the sequel, see *LJ* xviii, 228-31, 270, 275; HMC *Lords MSS* vii, 29, 62-3.

[184] A move to insert a clause on the Test Act was defeated by 211 votes to 163 (Luttrell, vi, 137).

[185] Sir Richard Onslow (1654-1717), 3rd Bt., MP for Surrey, 1689-1710, 1713-15, also Guildford, 1679-81, 1685-7, and St Mawes, 1710-13, Speaker of the Commons, 1708-10, Chancellor of the Exchequer, 1714-15, cr. Lord Onslow 1716.

[186] Richard Leathut, 2nd lieutenant in a marine regt. 1704, 1st lieutenant 1707. Dalton, v, 140, 142.

and approved.[187] Bishop of Sarum in the Chair; and the Gallery full of Commoners. Lords Rochester, Nottingham, Haversham,[188] Scarborough, Garnsey [Guernsey], Anglesey, &c. for Amendments. Answered by Wharton, Somers, Hallifax, Treasurer, Marlborough, &c. One Question put — Whether the First Article[189] postponed? *Contents*, 21. *Not Contents*, 71. Amongst the former, Bishops of London and Bath and Wells [Hooper].

[Feb.] 16. *Sunday*. Archdeacon Fleming and Brother John (after our hearing a good Sermon, by Mr Fr[ancis] Brown, at Whitehall against immoderate Love of the Things of this world) dined with me. In the Evening, we visitted Mr Vice-Chancellor Lancaster; full of his new Building at Queen's.[190]

[Feb.] 17. *Munday*. At the House, The eight Judges of the Queen's Bench and Common Pleas gave their Opinions on the Case of the New Erected Mill at Tiverton;[191] and Seven of 'em thought the Tith[e] of Mills to be Personal, Mr Justice Powel alone affirming 'em to be Predial; because ariseing from an Inheritance, which payes in the Parish where fixed and not where the Miller dwells, &c. The Lords hereupon Reversed the Unanimous Decree of the Barons of the Exchequer who had given the parson the 10th Toll-Dish, and ordered the Tenth of the Clear product, Repairs and other Incidental Charges deducted. In the Evening, Archdeacon Fleming my brother John and Thomas Bell with me.

[Feb.] 18. *Tuesday*. Morning, happily comforted by Brother Joseph in my Splenetic Fears. Visitted by Dr Hickes, Mr R[ichard] and James Musgrave. Mr Elstob, &c. With the Commissioners at Whitehall; and Lord Keeper [Cowper] (on the Cause 'twixt Carlile and Dalston) in the House. Archdeacon Fleming and W. Rook dined with me at the *Talbot*;[192] and the former walked with me afterwards to Kensington. O. Dykes.[193]

[187] For the debate see above, sessional intro., p. 394.

[188] His speech is printed in *Parl. Hist*. vi, 562-5. See ibid., pp. 561-2 for other speeches.

[189] 'That the two kingdoms of England and Scotland shall, upon the first day of May, ... 1707, and for ever after, be united into one kingdom, by the Name of Great Britain. . . .' *LJ* xviii, 208.

[190] William Lancaster was responsible for building the front quad at Queen's College, the west range, 1709-11, and the hall and chapel, 1714. See J. Sherwood and N. Pevsner, *Oxfordshire*, The Buildings of England (1974), p. 187.

[191] See HMC *Lords MSS* vii, 6-7.

[192] There were two taverns of this name, one in the Strand and the other at the Gravel Pits in Kensington. Lillywhite, *London Signs*, pp. 546-7.

[193] Oswald Dykes (c.1670-1728) of Warthole, Cumberland, and Queen's College, was keeping a boarding school at Kensington by 1708.

[Feb.] 19. *Wednesday*. Morning, Visits from Brother Joseph, Mr Tyrrel, Archdeacons Worth and Fleming, Sister Rothery.

At the House (the Queen Present) the 13th Article [of Union][194] agreed to; after a Division, on the 9th,[195] *Contents* 70. *Not Contents*, 23. All the Bishops in the former. Chief Opposers, Lords Nottingham, Ferrers and North.[196] Evening, Archdeacon Fleming and I at Dean Grahme's; where Sir John Talbot (with his Story on the Trick put on Archbishop Sandys by Stay Stapleton),[197] Coll. Grahme and his son the Captain.[198]

[Feb.] 20. *Thursday*. Morning, Dr Scott and Mr Chamberlayne, At the House, the Appellant Dey (a rascally Attourney) charged with 50 *l*. costs.[199] In the Evening, at the *Globe*,[200] with two Tullies, Archdeacon Fleming, Brother John and W. Rook.

[Feb.] 21. *Friday*. Morning, After a Walk to Hide-park (where Dr Lancaster met, goeing to Oxford) with Archdeacon Fleming, visitted by Coll. Grahme, &c.

At the House, the 18th Article[201] agreed to, after a Division on the Question; *Contents*, 58. *Not Contents*, 21. Lord Scarbrough apprehensive of the Decay of Trade at Leeds and Hallifax.[202] Lord Nottingham concerned for the Habeas-Corpus-Act; which (say both

[194] 'That, during the continuance of the Duty payable in England on Malt, which determines the 24 Day of June, 1707, Scotland shall not be charged with that Duty.' *LJ* xviii, 209.

[195] 'That when £1,997,763 raised in England by Land Tax, Scotland shall be charged with £48,000 as Scottish quota to Tax and so proportionaly for any greater or lesser sum charged.' *LJ* xviii, 209.

[196] There is a brief summary of the speeches of North and Nottingham, also of Lord Halifax's replies to both, in *Parl. Hist.* vi, 565–7.

[197] Sir John Talbot (*c*.1630–1714) of Lacock, Wiltshire, was a distant cousin to the Duke of Shrewsbury and first cousin to Bishop Talbot of Oxford. D. H. Somerville, *The King of Hearts* (1962), p. 18. Sir Robert Stapleton, in order to get advantageous leases from Archbishop Sandes of York (1577–88), surreptitiously introduced a woman into the archbishop's bedroom. Her husband rushed in followed by Stapleton who offered to prevent a scandal. Sandes fell for the trick, but later reported the outrage to the Council and was cleared.

[198] William Grahme (1680–1717), second son of James Grahme, and a captain in the navy.

[199] See HMC *Lords MSS* vii, 11.

[200] Possibly the tavern in Holborn (see above, p. 386), though there was one by this name in the Strand, and a coffee house on Fleet St. Lillywhite, *Coffee Houses*, p. 234.

[201] 'That the laws concerning regulation of trade, customs . . . to be the same after the Union, as in England and that all laws in Scotland remain in force except those contrary to the treaty, but alterable by the Parliament of Great Britain but that no alteration be made in laws concerning private rights, except for the good of Scottish subjects.' *LJ* xviii, 210.

[202] In the event, the prosperity of the Yorkshire woollen and worsted cloth industries, based on these two towns, which had been stimulated by the wars with France, was unimpaired by the freeing of trade with Scotland. See Defoe, *Tour*, ii, 197–208.

Chief Justices) is in no Hazard. Archdeacon, Brother John, &c. at Salisbury Court in the Evening.

[Feb.] 22. *Saturday*. Archdeacon Fleming and I dined at Lambeth; where also Bishop of Sarum, Dr Bentley, Dr Lloyd, Dr Linford, Dean of Limerick, &c. My Lord of Canterbury had from me the Valuation of the Bishoprick of Chester, as sent from Mr Commissary Waite;[203] which (with the Rectory of Wigan, set at 300 *l.*) makes 1160 *l.* clear.[204] After a pipe with Mr Snow, home to write Letters.

[Feb.] 23. *Sunday*. I kept private all the day; at my Sermon. Archdeacon and Brother John at Salisbury Court.

[Feb.] 24. *Munday*. After a walk round the Park, with Mr Hutchinson and Thomas Pearson, I dined at the *Talbot* with Archdeacon Fleming and Brother John.

At the House, the last 7 Articles (the Queen present) agreed to: the Debates chiefly managed by Lord Nottingham and Lord Somers. Incidental, Bishop of Bath and Wells singly against the Union;[205] Lord Haversham, alwaies a Churchman; Lord Thanet for Rights, which Lord Wharton calls Tyranny and Oppression; &c. Past Seven to my Lodgeings; where (with the Archdeacon and Brother John) News of the Appleby-Election.[206] On the 22d Article[207] the House divided. *Contents*, 71. *Not Contents*, 22. The two Archbishops and all the Bishops (except Bath and Wells) amongst the former.

[Feb.] 25. *Shrove-Tuesday*. Morning, After a walk in the Park with Mr Archdeacon Fleming and Mr James Musgrave, with the Commissioners at Whitehall; present both the Archbishops, &c. A

---

[203] Thomas Waite (b. *c.*1662), a cousin of Bishop Cartwright of Chester (1686–9), had been appointed Commissary of the Archdeaconry of Richmond. F. Gastrell, *Notitia Cestriensis*, ed. F. R. Raines, Chetham Soc. (1845), i, 29–30; *Diary of Dr Thomas Cartwright*, ed. J. Hunter, Camden Soc. (1843), pp. 21, 27, 70.

[204] From 1662 to 1707 the Rectory of Wigan was held by the Bishops of Chester from the Bridgeman trustees. In 1661 Sir Orlando Bridgeman had bought the advowson with the object of creating a rural living for the bishop. In 1707 Lord Nottingham's brother, Edward Finch, was appointed to Wigan (see below, n. 240), partly because of the 'bishoprics crisis' which left the see of Chester unfilled for a year (see Luttrell, vi, 190–1). Bishop Gastrell also valued Wigan at £300 p.a. in 1717. *VCH Lancashire*, iv, 60–3. Wake's valuation of Chester was scarce £1,000 (£1200 with Wigan). Christ Church, Wake MS 18, ff. 393–4.

[205] For Hooper's stand see above, sessional intro., p. 395. For his speech on 24 Feb., *Parl. Hist.* vi, 568; ibid., pp. 567–9 for the debate as a whole.

[206] The Westmorland by-election, to fill the seat left vacant by the death of Henry Grahme, took place in Appleby on 20 Feb. 1707, when Michael Fleming was elected.

[207] This provided for sixteen representative peers and forty-five members of the Commons to represent Scotland in the British parliament.

Draught offered;[208] and Adjourned to March 18. Thence to the House; where Counsel and Civilians[209] heard at Length on the Divorce of Mr Jermyn. Upon the Question, the Bill (for his marrying again) thrown out. Home, to Letters.

[Feb.] 26. *Ash-Wednesday*. Morning, With the Archdeacon and brother John to Whitehall; where we heard Mr Higgins's Tory Sermon (on *Revelations* 3, 2 & 3) in honour of the Church and Government of Ireland and vilely bespattering both in England.[210] Brother dined with me. Evening, Visitted by Mr Buddle and Coll. Fletcher.

[Feb.] 27. *Thursday*. Morning, Visits from W. Senhouse and Coll. Orfeur. I dined, at the *Talbot*, with Archdeacon Fleming and brother John. In the House, the Report of the Articles agreed to; with Threats of Protests. Lord of Canterbury saies, Dr Chetwood will be Dean of Gloucester. His Grace enquired earnestly after Mr Higgins's Sermon.[211]

[Feb.] 28. *Friday*. Morning, Visitants, Mr Watson (Lord Rockingham's Brother) and Mr Jervaise, Mr Joseph Musgrave, Mr Madox, Dr Gibson, &c. After Archdeacon Fleming had dined with me, in my Lodgeings, at the House: where Lord Kingsland's (stultifying) Appeal half heard;[212] and adjourned till to morrow. Evening, with the Archdeacon, visits at Bernard's Inn,[213] S[alisbury] C[ourt].

---

[208] The Commissioners of Queen Anne's Bounty had asked the Attorney General to prepare a draft bill for discharging the first fruits and tenths of all livings with cures of souls not exceeding £40 a year in the improved value. The bill was approved by the Commissioners and they asked Lord Coningsby to introduce it into the Commons, which he did on 7 Mar. 1707. It was amended in the Commons and passed on 21 Mar., and agreed to by the Lords on 28 Mar. In its final form the Act (6 Anne c.54) discharged all livings up to £50. Church Commissioners QAB Minute Book, i, 40–1; *CJ* xv, 327, 337, 353, 366; *LJ* xviii, 302.

[209] i.e. civil lawyers.

[210] Francis Higgins (1669–1728), fiery High Church preacher, known as the 'Irish Sacheverell', was a Prebendary of Christ Church Cathedral, Dublin, in 1705, and later Archdeacon of Cashel, 1725–8. See Holmes, *Sacheverell*, pp. 45, 96–7. In this sermon he asserted, not for the first time, the Church to be in danger from favour shown to the champions of heterodoxy, Puritans and Presbyterians. On 28 Feb. 1707 he was arrested and in Apr. the grand jury of Middlesex found against him for sedition, but in May the Attorney-General entered a '*nolle prosequi*'.

[211] Tenison seems to have tried to persuade Higgins to alter his tone, shortly before his arrest in 1707. He was, however, obdurate and published his sermon with a postscript, giving a very partial report of his interview with the Primate. See HMC *2nd Report*, Appendix, p. 244.

[212] See HMC *Lords MSS* vii, 7–8.

[213] Gray's Inn's only remaining Inn of Chancery, situated on Fetter Lane, was founded *c.*1454. R. Megarry, *Inns Ancient and Modern* (1972), pp. 41–4.

Mar. 1. *Saturday*. Morning, Visits from Mr Hutchinson and L. Simpson. Archdeacon Fleming and Brother John dined with the Dean [Atterbury] at Chelsea. At the House, the Remainder of Lord Kingsland's Appeal heard, and Decree affirmed. Lord Treasurer [Godolphin] spoke in favour of the Appellant; who marryed Lady M[arlborough]'s Niece.[214] The Bill for Ratification brought up, and Read a first time; and ordered a Second Reading on Munday. Evening, Mr Paul[215] and Leniere.

[Mar.] 2. *Sunday*. All day, at home, writeing out my Sermon. Evening (after a Visit from the Dean of Peterborough [Freeman], Bishop intended of Chester,[216] and Dr Gibson) with Brother John at Sohoe-Square.

[Mar.] 3. *Munday*. Morning, Broke in upon, after Copying part of my Sermon, by Os[wald] Dykes and (his Scholar) James Nicolson; who with Dr Gibson, Archdeacon Fleming, Brother John, Mr James Musgrave and Cousin R. Nicolson, dined with me at the *Talbot*.

At the House, Act of *Ratification* read a second time, and Committed. Great Debate on Confirmation of the Scotch Act for their Kirk; and of all *Clauses and Matters therein contained*. On the Question, *Contents*, 55. *Not Contents*, 19. Amongst the latter, Archbishop of York, Bishops of London, Durham, Bath and Wells, and St Asaph.

[Mar.] 4. *Tuesday*. Morning, Attempting, with W. Senhouse, to wait on Lord Wharton. Dinner, at the *Talbot*, with Archdeacon Fleming and's Brother Capt[ain].[217] At the House, the Union-Bill read a third time, and (after the Rider for Explaining the Assent to the Kirk-Act rejected by 55 against 19) passed. After a walk round the Park with the Archdeacon, Letters, franked, 17.

[Mar.] 5. *Wednesday*. After a long Remainder of an Appeal in the House, I and Brother John went to dine with Mr C. Musgrave and his

---

[214] In 1688 Lord Kingsland had married Mary Hamilton (d. 1736), whose mother was Francis Jennings (the Duchess of Marlborough's sister), subsequently Countess of Tyrconnell.

[215] ?George Paul, Fellow of Jesus College, Cambridge, 1704–14.

[216] Dean Freeman was to be disappointed. See Bennett, 'Bishoprics crisis of 1707', pp. 736, 746.

[217] Michael Fleming, MP for Westmorland, 20 Feb. 1707–8 (see Appendix A). At this time a captain in the 16th Foot, he spent most of his time abroad with Marlborough, becoming a major in 1709. He had been put up at the by-election (see above, n. 206) by his brother Sir William, and had been unopposed. At the 1708 general election he was disqualified from standing by the Qualification Act because he lacked a landed estate.

brother Joseph, where much banter on High and Low Church. Evening-Visit from Dr Woodward; earnest for Dispensary and my Brother Joseph.

[Mar.] 6. *Thursday*. At the House, Part of Mr Annesley's Writ of Errour[218] (on being Ejected from a purchased Estate from the Trustees for Irish Forfeitures) heard; and Adjourned. The Queen gave Her Royal Assent to the UNION-Act; and made a Gracious Speech[219] on the Occasion. Guns fired from the Tower, &c. I went home with my Niece; and dined at Salisbury-Court. Brother John and Sister Rothery there. Home to write Letters.

[Mar.] 7. *Friday*. At the House, Dispute (about waveing Privilege) betwixt Earl of Derby and Earl of Anglesey; Adjourned till to-morrow. I left Mr Vachell's Appeal,[220] to dine with the Archdeacon, brother John and W. Rook, at the *Talbot*. Evening, at Coll. Orfeur's; with Archdeacon, my two brothers, Mr Martin and Sister Rothery.

[Mar.] 8. *Saturday*. Her Majesty's Inauguration, entering her 6th year. I preached before the Queen at St James's, on *Leviticus* 25, 20, and 21. The House sitting, few Lords were present. Onely the two Archbishops and Bishop of St Asaph in the Chapple and Bishop of Exeter in the Vestry, Lord Treasurer [Godolphin], Earl of Chol-mondely, &c. Archdeacon Fleming and I dined with my Lord of York; who very cheerful.

[Mar.] 9. *Sunday*. After Ordination-Sermon at St Paul's (by Mr Brown, against the Socinians)[221] at Dinner with Brother Joseph, with Archdeacon Fleming, brother John, Sister Rothery, Mr John-son, &c. Evening, at Christ's Hospital, treated by Mr Monford Schoolmaster.

[Mar.] 10. *Munday*. Called early to the House to attend the Duke of Beaufort's Committee.[222] Mr Annesley's Purchase in Ireland

---

[218] See HMC *Lords MSS* vii, 43. For the work of Francis Annesley with the Forfeiture Trustees in Ireland, which led to his expulsion from the Irish Commons, see J. G. Simms, *The Williamite Confiscation in Ireland, 1690–1703* (1956), pp. 98–157 *passim*.

[219] *LJ* xviii, 272–3.   [220] See HMC *Lords MSS* vii, 38.

[221] The growth of Socinianism, a unitarian heresy, had caused great alarm among orthodox Anglicans since the early 1690s. The views of the Socinians, more extreme than those of the Arians in calling into question the divinity of Christ, had their origins in the thought of Faustus Socinus, an Italian theologian of the late sixteenth century, who denied the divinity of Christ.

[222] A select committee on the Duke of Beaufort's Estate Bill, see HMC *Lords MSS* vii, 37–8.

condemned; and the Judgement of both the Queen's Benches Affirmed. After Dinner (at the *Horn*,[223] with Archdeacon Fleming, brother John, Cousin Thomas Pearson and Mr Ar[thur?] Atkinson)[224] the Archdeacon and my brother and I went to visit Dr Gibson.

[Mar.] 11. *Tuesday*. Morning, Visits from Mr James Musgrave, Mr Madox, Mr Grisedale, Cousin T. Pearson, Mr Ar[thur] Atkinson, &c. In the House, Servants Bill[225] thrown out on the 1st Reading; and *Game* narrowly escaped.[226] Both Houses attended the Queen with their Address.

[Mar.] 12. *Wednesday*. Morning, By Water (with the Archdeacon) to Salisbury-Court; whence to Aldersgate, giveing Earnest[227] for the Stage-Coach to Warrington. I dined (with the Archdeacon and brother John) at the *Talbot*; and this day, the first in the Session, did not go to the House.

Evening, Mr Dean of Carlile [Atterbury]; protesting against my Visitation,[228] as (this day) against the Queen's prorogueing of the Convocation.[229] Supper (with Archdeacon, my brothers and two Broughams) at Mr W. Johnson's. NB. At the *Archimedes*,[230] fine Microscropes; which shewed us the Circulation of the Blood in Newts.

[Mar.] 13. *Thursday*. The Archdeacon and I walked round the Park; thence crossed the water to Carlile-House, where Potters very entertaining;[231] thence (by the way of Salisbury-Court) to New Bedlam:

[223] Either the one in Fleet St. or in New Palace Yard. Lillywhite, *London Signs*, pp. 288-9.
[224] Arthur Atkinson (b. *c*.1684) of Queen's College, Oxford, MA, 1707, Fellow of Queen's, 1710, Rector of Sulhampstead Abbot and Barrister, Berkshire, 1722.
[225] Servants (Regulation of Wages) Bill, see HMC *Lords MSS* vii, 64-7.
[226] The Game Preservation Bill was brought from the Commons on 10 Mar. The vote, on 11 Mar. on whether the bill should be read a second time was *Contents*, twenty-eight (including six proxies), *Not Contents* sixteen (with eight proxies). The poulterers of London had their petition against the bill dismissed, and the bill received the royal assent on 24 Mar. HMC *Lords MSS* vii, 68.
[227] i.e. deposit.
[228] See above, sessional intro., p. 389, for Atterbury's campaign against the local Carlisle Statutes. In general see Bennett, *Tory Crisis*, pp. 89-91, 94, 96-7, where it is emphasised that this was a test case, with a great fund of patronage at stake for both High and Low Churchmen and their Tory and Whig allies.
[229] The Convocation had been prorogued on 12 Feb. for three weeks to prevent a clash over the Union. The Lower House had been allowed to meet again on 5 Mar. and a relatively restrained representation to the bishops, against prorogation during the sitting of parliament, followed on 19 Mar. Ibid., p. 87; Lathbury, pp. 402-3.
[230] Possibly the *Archimedes and Globe*, an optician near St Anne's Church, Soho, though there was also one in Ludgate St. Lillywhite, *London Signs*, p. 16.
[231] Carlisle House, Lambeth, owned by the see of Carlisle, was a pottery at this time.

And, haveing dined in Pater-Noster-Row, home by Brother Joseph's. Cousin Susan and brother John goeing to the Play-House.[232]

[Mar.] 14. *Friday*. Morning, visits by Mr Hutchinson, Mrs Donning, &c. In the House, the Game-Bill passed in the Committee: One Question put, *Contents* 41. *Not*, 23. Archdeacon and I dined together at the *Talbot*; and, after a walk into Hide-Park, Spent the Evening (with wine and Oysters) at Salisbury Court, takeing leave of Brother John and W. Rook.

[Mar.] 15. *Saturday*. Morning, Visitted by Mr Morton of Northamptonshire. At the House, Lace-Bill amended.[233] Dinner, with Dr Gibson (sure of Chester for the Dean of P[eterborough] and the Chair for Dr P[otter])[234] and Archdeacon Fleming. With the latter, for pleasure, up the Water to Paul's Wharff; and back again to our (14) Letters.

[Mar.] 16. *Sunday*. At Twelve, I went to Dinner at Salisbury Court; where, Indisposed, I slept near two Hours afternoon. My brother accompanyed me home, on foot, 'twixt five and six.

[Mar.] 17. *Munday*. After a long Ramble with Archdeacon Fleming to Black Fryers (with my Articles),[235] Broad Street, &c. we dined and went to the Lobby; and thence to Dr Gibson, who concerned to have my Sermon printed.[236] At night, a Multitude of Letters; of which the Sharpest (on Archbishop of Canterbury) from Mr Chancellor Tullie.

[Mar.] 18. *Tuesday*. Morning, Visits from Mr. James Lowther (designing to be Knight [of the shire] for Cumberland),[237] Mr Elstob and Mr Paul. Afternoon, Mr Murthland and Archdeacon Fleming

---

[232] Also called The Duke's Theatre, Whitefriars, south of Salisbury Court, it was opened in 1671.

[233] A bill to repeal all the laws prohibiting the importation of foreign lace made of thread. It gained the royal assent on 24 Mar. HMC *Lords MSS* vii, 67–8.

[234] i.e. the Regius Chair of Divinity at Oxford, now vacated by the death of Dr Jane. For the significance of Potter's candidacy and that of his rival, Smalridge, see above, 19 Feb. 1706.

[235] Nicolson's Visitation Articles for his second triennial visitation which was to take place later in 1707.

[236] *The Blessing of the Sixth Year, a Sermon preached before the Queen on the Anniversary of Her Accession*, given on 8 Mar.

[237] At present Storekeeper of the Ordnance Office, James Lowther was to resume his parliamentary career in 1708 and sit almost continuously until his death in 1755, including forty-two years as Knight of the Shire for Cumberland. See Appendix A.

successively. All the day at home; partly Indisposed, and (chiefly) writeing a Multitude of Letters.

[Mar.] 19. *Wednesday*. After seeking for Morning-Gowns with the Archdeacon and hearing the News of the Convocation-Address to the Bishops,[238] we dined at the *Talbot*, spent the Afternoon with Sister Rothery and Evening with Brother Joseph.

[Mar.] 20. *Thursday*. I kept within all day; packing up Goods, and writeing Letters. Visitted by Brother Joseph, Mr James Musgrave, Lord Carlile (with a gracious Invitation to Henderskelf)[239] Cousin M. Rowse, for presenting the Queen with a Manual of Devotions. NB. In the morning, Letter from Lord Chamberlain [Kent]; signifying the Queen's pleasure that my Sermon (on the 8th Instant) be printed.

[Mar.] 21. *Friday*. In the morning, my Sermon put into Dr Gibson's hand for the Press. After purchaseing of paper, and a Visit from Sister Rothery, the Archdeacon and I dined at the *Short Dog*; went by water to pay for my Visitation-Articles at Black-Fryers; bought Gowns in Ludgate-street; paid Visits at Aldgate, Dr Waugh's and Brother Joseph's, and returned weary home.

[Mar.] 22. *Saturday*. Morning, Visits from Cousin Bridget Nicolson, Mr Holmes, Mr Buchanan, Mr Hutchinson, Mr Grisedale, Mr Richardson, Cousin J. Relf, Mr Liniere. Item, Letters from Lord [Howard of] Effingham and Coll. Grahme answered; others unanswered.

    After Dinner with the Archdeacon, leave taken at Lambeth; where the Prolocutor (Dr Binks) in attendance on the Archbishop of Canterbury, bespeaking his Grace's favourable Construction of that part which he had in the late Remonstrance of the Lower House of Convocation.

[Mar.] 23. *Sunday*. After a Ramble with Archdeacon Fleming in the Park, to his brother Captain's Lodgeings, &c. I dined at Brother Joseph's with Mr Johnson and Sister Rothery. Haveing taken a short Nap there in the Afternoon, and stayed till nine at night, I took leave; and went to Lodge (unadvisedly) at the *George-Inn* without Aldersgate, where little or no sleep that night, and ...

[238] See above, n. 229.

[239] The site in North Yorkshire where the 3rd Earl of Carlisle was building Castle Howard. Begun in 1700, it replaced Henderskelfe Castle, rebuilt 1683 but destroyed by fire in 1693. The site had been Howard property since 1571. See N. Pevsner, *Yorkshire: the North Riding*, The Buildings of England (1966), pp. 106–9.

[Mar.] 24. *Munday*. Hence I began my uncomfortable Journey,[240] encouraged by my brother, with the Archdeacon, Mr Sinclare (from Leghorn) with his wife and daughter, and Mrs Holme of Manchester.

---

[240] Nicolson was suffering from an attack of the stone, and because of the inflammation caused he left the coach at Dunstable, intending to return to London. He changed his mind, hired horses and overtook the coach at Newport Pagnell. He continued his journey on horseback via Northampton, Coventry, Nantwich, Warrington, Preston, and Oxenholme, arriving at Rose on 3 Apr. 1707. At Preston Nicolson had met Lord Anglesey, returning from the Lancaster assizes, together with Dean Henry Finch of York and his brother Edward, 'newly presented and Instituted to the Rectory of Wigan'. *CW* iii (1903), 58; MS Diary, 24 Mar.– 3 Apr. 1707. The parliament continued to sit until 24 Apr.

Session 5

24 December 1707–5 April 1708

Nicolson's eight and a half months in his diocese from 3 April to 15 December 1707 were almost completely overshadowed by his quarrel with Hugh Todd, Prebendary of Carlisle, and Dean Francis Atterbury over the validity of the local cathedral statutes. This issue, which was to result in the Cathedrals Act of 1708, was also, for Nicolson, to dominate the parliamentary session of 1707–8.

Both Todd and Atterbury were old adversaries of Nicolson's and personal animosities were at the bottom of the dispute. The 'Book-quarrel', as Todd termed the clash between Atterbury and Nicolson during the Convocation Controversy, and both Todd's and Atterbury's criticisms of the Bishop's scholastic performance in his *English Historical Library*,[1] had soured relations before Atterbury was nominated to the deanery in 1704. Nicolson's attempt to obstruct the Dean's institution had turned dislike into a near feud. Atterbury had recruited Todd as his aide-de-camp in the field upon his appointment to Carlisle, and since then the Chapter had been seriously disturbed by quarrels between Atterbury and Todd on the one hand (Todd holding the Dean's proxy)[2] and Thomas Tullie, George Fleming, and John Atkinson, the three remaining prebendaries, on the other. The Bishop at first had tried to remain aloof, but inevitably had been drawn into the fray on the side of Tullie and his allies.

While at Carlisle in 1704, Atterbury's researches amongst the Chapter archives had convinced him that the Foundation Charter of Carlisle Cathedral, given by Henry VIII in 1541 and sealed with the great seal, was its sole legally valid constitution. The statutes of 1545, by which the collegiate body was usually governed, had no

[1] Bodl. MS St Edmund Hall 7/2, p. 266: Todd's History of the Bishopric of Carlisle, vol. 1. Todd's version of the quarrel and the subsequent parliamentary activity can be found in ibid., pp. 265–77b (his brief life of Atterbury); York Minster Library Hailstone Collection QQ 2.7 (copies of documents from 1706 to 1708 formerly belonging to Todd); his 'The Case of Dr Todd, Prebendary of Carlisle', excerpts from which are printed in J. E. Prescott, *The Statutes of the Cathedral of Carlisle* (2nd edn., 1903), p. 10, and in *CW* iv (1904), 12, 14, 15, 19, 20. Nicolson's 'Case of the Bishop of Carlisle as Local Visitor of his Chapter' is printed in *Nicolson Epist. Corr.* ii, 341–56 (excerpts printed in *CW* iv, 10–11). The quarrel can be followed in James, pp. 152–69; and the national political importance of the dispute is covered in Bennett, *Tory Crisis*, pp. 88–97.

[2] Atterbury had been excused by royal licence in 1705 from further attendance at Carlisle. See Lloyd Baker MS Box 4, V15: Atterbury to Sharp, 25 May 1705. Todd's papers in York Minster Library Hailstone Collection QQ 2.7, show how closely Todd worked with Atterbury.

legal status at all for they had not passed the great seal and were therefore null and void.[3] If Atterbury's interpretation was correct it not only gave Atterbury himself, as Dean, supreme power in the Carlisle Chapter but it had wide-ranging implications at a national level. Similar statutes, also not under the great seal, had been given to the twelve other cathedrals of the 'new foundation' (see below, 31 December, n. 40), and if Atterbury were right the appointments to all their canonries and prebends and the right to act as their visitor would belong to the Crown and not to the individual bishops. Thus an invaluable hoard of ecclesiastical patronage lay in the balance which a future Tory government might use to consolidate its support at a local level. Atterbury soon communicated his ideas to his friend and associate Robert Harley, Secretary of State.[4]

Since then there had been a number of skirmishes—for example, on the Dean's right to issue Todd with his proxy[5]—but it was Nicolson's second triennial visitation of the Chapter in 1707 which brought matters to a head. In a conciliatory letter to Atterbury in June, Nicolson assured the Dean that:

> I shall never Encourage the Abridgeing you of any of those powers (in their utmost extent) which the Foundation-Charter has loged in you; Nor will you, I know, seek to withdraw any of those which it leaves (as it found 'em) in the Bishops of this See.[6]

But Atterbury was unappeased: and with Todd's help he set about challenging the statutes' validity with the clear aim of making the Foundation Charter the legal basis for his control of the Chapter.

Despite a promise of future obedience from Todd in late July 1707, the doctor, under instructions from the 'Pilot of Chelsea', protested on 20 August against the Bishop issuing his monition for his visitation of the Chapter.[7] Atterbury then protested that Nicolson had no authority under the 'pretended local statutes'; only the Queen was the visitor and he was determined nothing should be done to damage the royal prerogative and supremacy. On 29 August the Dean drew up his legal case and a formal petition and sent them both to Harley to lay before the Queen.[8]

On 25 September Nicolson went ahead with his first visitation of

[3] See Prescott, *Statutes of the Cathedral Church of Carlisle*, pp. 1–6 for the legal background. [4] HMC *Portland MSS* iv, 138–9.
[5] See Lloyd Baker MSS Box 4, V15–16: Atterbury to Sharp, 25 May, and Todd to Sharp, 9 Sept. 1704; York Minster Library Hailstone Collection QQ 2.7, p. 5: Atterbury to N., 20 Jan. 1706 (copy).
[6] Bodl. MS Add. C217, f. 40: N. to Atterbury, 14 June 1707; *CW* iv (1904), 3.
[7] Ibid., pp. 5, 8.
[8] HMC *Portland MSS* iv, 437–8. The documents are in BL Loan 29/313/35 and 29/194/208–9.

the Chapter. Todd protested vigorously on behalf of himself and the Dean whose proxy he held. Nicolson suspended Todd for a month for his contumacy.[9] After taking legal advice and giving notice on 11 October, Nicolson made a second visitation of the Chapter on 21 October, 'where Dr Todd continued his Insolence, and was suspended' until 24 November. Both men seem to have lost their tempers and insults were bandied.[10] Todd now decided to act and he sent up affidavits to the Court of Common Pleas in London in order to gain a prohibition against Nicolson to relieve him of any penalties that might ensue. As a result on 22 November Nicolson was served with an order by the Court to show cause within the week 'why a prohibition should not be awarded to stay proceedings in my Visitation'. Ignoring this ruling Nicolson visited the Chapter a third time on 24 November and again Todd refused to submit. Three days later the Bishop, losing all patience, used his ultimate spiritual penalty of excommunication against his adversary, and on 4 December he received a second ruling of the Court of Common Pleas (dated 28 November) stopping all proceedings till the first day of the next term.[11]

This was how the dispute stood when Nicolson left for London on 15 December 1707. The first parliament of Great Britain had opened on 23 October and the fact that the Bishop had not sent off his proxy suggests that he had not expected to be delayed so long by his dispute with Todd. As he journeyed south on horseback Nicolson must have wondered how he was to extricate himself from this impasse. His route took him via Appleby, Richmond, Ferrybridge to Stamford, where he preached on Sunday, 21 December, and visited Lord Exeter's seat, Burghley House. The following day he dismissed his servants, who returned with the horses, and took the York coach for London via Huntingdon, a flooded St Neot's, Biggleswade, Stevenage, and Barnet, reaching London on Christmas Eve.[12]

Though Nicolson's legal case against Todd was weak, as he found out on his arrival in London, political events had so far shifted in the autumn of 1707 that the Bishop was to find himself more than compensated by the strong political backing of the Junto lords. In November Nicolson had suspected that an unseen hand was directing Atterbury and Todd.[13] This hand was Harley's, and between September

[9] Nicolson's detailed account of the first visitation can be found in *Nicolson Epist. Corr.* ii, 354–6; and in *CW* iv (1904), 10–11.

[10] For Todd's detailed account of the second visitation see ibid., p. 12.

[11] Ibid., pp. 13–15; *Nicolson Epist. Corr.* ii, 362–6. For Nicolson's view of the dispute see BL Add. MS 6116, ff. 6–7: N. to Wake, 29 Nov. 1707.

[12] Ware transcripts, xxiii, 64–7.

[13] BL Add. MS 6116, ff. 6–7: N. to Wake, 29 Nov. 1707.

and December 1707 his position within the ministry, long distasteful to the Junto, was called seriously into question.

The bishoprics question of the previous spring had developed into
a full-blown political crisis during the summer of 1707, after the
Queen had privately promised Exeter and Chester to the Tory divines
Blackall and Dawes. As the time for parliament's meeting approached
the crisis was still far from being resolved.[14] Anne was standing firm
by her promises and rejecting the claims of Trimnell and Freeman.
Lord Treasurer Godolphin was pressing hard for Whig promotions
to these sees and for the appointment of John Potter rather than
Harley's candidate, George Smalridge, to the Divinity Chair at
Oxford, in order to appease the Junto, who in their turn were
working hard for Harley's dismissal. They, of course, blamed him
(wrongly) for the Queen's choice of Blackall and Dawes. Harley for
his part was planning to lay the foundations of a 'moderate Scheme'
in which Whigs and Tories would participate to save the Queen from
the bondage of the Junto. Atterbury's plan for the new legal basis of
the new foundation bishoprics formed part of this scheme, since the
Tories for whom Harley was angling required some gesture of public
favour from the Queen. Consequently Harley on 7 September 1707
had presented Atterbury's petition to the Queen. Having finally
come out into the open over ecclesiastical affairs, Harley received
a stern rebuke from his cabinet colleagues. Badly rattled,[15] he saw
Atterbury on 10 September and indicated that he wanted to drop
the latter's plan. Even Atterbury was shaken by the ministry's
reaction, and in a change of tack proceeded to publish a collection
of his sermons whose preface, designed as a manifesto to the Tories,
indicated that the Queen was ready to change her policies towards
the Church.

By the time that Nicolson reached town in late December, Harley,
aided by the Queen's obstinacy and by the Junto's tactics in parliament, aimed at embarrassing the *duumvirs*, had regained some
lost ground and Godolphin and Marlborough were prepared to
consider bringing a new mixture of moderate Tories and Whigs
into the administration. At the beginning of January it was publicly
announced that the bishoprics of Exeter and Chester were to
go to Blackall and Dawes, with Trimnell getting the consola-
tion prize of Norwich, after Moore's translation from there to

[14] For the crisis see G. V. Bennett, 'Robert Harley, the Godolphin ministry, and the
bishoprics crisis of 1707', *EHR* lxxxii (1967), 726–46.

[15] Hertfordshire RO Panshanger MS D/EP F60, f. 25: Harley to Cowper, 12 Sept. 1707
(endorsed by Cowper: 'Secr. Harley's Lre . . . abt Ld Treasurer chiding him at Windsor for
prefering Dr Aterburys Petition'). This paragraph is largely based on Bennett, *Tory Crisis*,
pp. 91–3.

Ely,[16] and Potter the Oxford chair. By now Harley's 'scheme' hung in the balance: many of the Tories held out against it, while the Junto was determined to force Godolphin and Marlborough to drop Harley. It was probably with this in mind that the Whig lords approached the Bishop of Carlisle with an offer to bring forward a bill to secure his shaky legal case by giving legislative force to customary statutes (see below, 12 January). As they saw it, this would, at one blow, undermine Harley's scheme in parliament and also destroy Atterbury's plan for the Church.

At this critical juncture Harley's personal position had been seriously weakened by the discovery that one of his confidential clerks, William Greg, had been engaged in treasonable correspondence with France (below, 7 January, n. 48). At the end of January 1708 Godolphin, after some weeks of uneasy reconciliation with 'Mr Secretary', suddenly decided to break with Harley and end their long alliance, suspecting (probably correctly) that the Secretary was by now scheming his own dismissal from the Treasury.[17] Marlborough refused to abandon his friend in the face of pressure from the Queen and lures from Harley, and after a dramatic cabinet council on 8 February, Harley knew that all was lost. He resigned on 11 February, taking with him out of office Henry St. John, Sir Simon Harcourt, and Sir Thomas Mansell. Nicolson was doubtless as relieved at 'the Court changes' as the Archbishop of Canterbury. Boyle replaced Harley, Walpole replaced St. John as Secretary at War, and eventually Sir James Montagu replaced Harcourt as Attorney-General and Lord Cholmondely replaced Mansel as Comptroller of the Household.

Meanwhile Nicolson's case in the Court of Common Pleas, which incidentally was to cost him £70,[18] did not go well (see below, 26 January, 6 February), and Todd carried the court with him and procured a final writ of prohibition against the episcopal sentence. The Bishop came under strong pressure from influential MPs and peers to be lenient and to restore Todd without undue humiliation. But in parliament he was triumphant. Here the Whig bishops rallied round him, stirred up a little tardily by Archbishop Tenison, who on 2 February issued a circular letter to his suffragans calling on them to support Somers's project for a Cathedrals Bill.[19] Atterbury claimed to have the votes of all the Tory bishops (York, London, Bath and Wells, Rochester, and St Asaph—and presumably Chester, but see

---

[16] The death of Bishop Simon Patrick of Ely offered this way of breaking the bishoprics deadlock.

[17] See G. Holmes and W. A. Speck, 'The fall of Harley in 1708 reconsidered', *EHR* lxxx (1965), 673–98. [18] CW iv (1904), 46.

[19] Printed in *Nicolson Epist. Corr.* ii, 355, note. Copies can be found in HMC *Portland MSS* iv, 476; BL Lansdowne MS 1039, f. 65; Christ Church Wake MS 17, f. 185.

16 February), and that when the bill went down to the Commons its 'warm reception' there would probably sink it.[20] There was indeed a heated debate in the Lords on 19 February, in which there were signs of a revival of Tory unity; and in the Commons the bill did receive some rough handling from the Tories (below, 24, 28 February, 9 March), now led by Harley and St. John as well as by Bromley and Hanmer. But although the bill did not escape without amendments, these were accepted by the Lords on 19 March and the measure went on to the statute-book the following day.[21]

The Whig attack on the ministry had started in November, shortly after the parliament opened. The Godolphin–Marlborough coalition was unexpectedly vulnerable, for the great successes of the war in 1706 had given way to grievous disappointments in 1707. The main allied army in the Peninsula, 15,500 Anglo-Portuguese troops under Galway and Das Minas, had been crushed at Almanza in April. In August a vital part of Marlborough's grand strategy, the land and sea attack on France's underbelly at Toulon, had failed. The Captain-General himself, plagued by the Dutch, had been forced to endure his most inactive campaign of the entire war.[22] Having entered into a temporary alliance with the Tories against the government, the Junto had no lack of targets; but they had good reason to choose to open with a debate on the state of the nation, particularly in regard to the fleet and trade, while keeping their options open meanwhile on Spain. On 19 November the Committee of the Whole House considered the petition of many London merchants whose trade had suffered hardships through the lack of protection afforded by the Admiralty. A committee was appointed, under the Duke of Bolton, a Junto lieutenant, to consider the petition, and during the next three months Bolton's committee made an exhaustive inquiry into the convoy system and the state of the navy in general.[23] Statements were called for from the Admiralty and other departments of state. The committee first reported on 17 December, accusing the Admiralty of mismanagement. Prince George of Denmark as Lord High Admiral was nominally in charge of the Admiralty Council, but the dominant influence there was Admiral George Churchill, Marlborough's less than competent brother. The Whigs' strategy was to remove Churchill,

---

[20] *Atterbury Epist. Corr.* iii, 284–5: Atterbury to Trelawney, 6 Feb. 1708.

[21] For Nicolson's lobbying campaign on the bill's behalf see above, Chapter 1, pp. 45–9.

[22] For the war in 1707 see Trevelyan, *Queen Anne*, ii, 293–309.

[23] For the debates and the evidence used for and against the Admiralty see HMC *Lords MSS* vii, 99–334; *Parl. Hist.* vi, 597–600, 612–13, 618–62; *LJ* xviii, 366–92, 405–23, 466–72; Burnet, *History*, v, 342–7; *Addison Letters*, p. 83. See also Trevelyan, *Queen Anne*, ii, 321–4.

or to force Marlborough to make terms in order to save his brother; but a substantial minority of the party in both Houses, including Robert Walpole (himself a member of the Admiralty Council) regarded such naked power politics with disfavour.

One of the main accusations made by the merchants was against Commodore William Kerr, who commanded a squadron in Jamaica. It was alleged that Kerr demanded a *douceur* of £800 in return for providing a convoy and that a ship had been lost because a merchant had refused to pay. Kerr denied the charges (below, 8 January), but Bolton's committee found Kerr guilty (below, 28 January) and drew up an address to the Queen asking for steps to be taken to check corrupt practices.

The Admiralty's reply to the committee's first report, presented on 9 January 1707, consisted of a general vindication of their naval policy. The final report of Bolton's committee drawn up on 16 February strongly censured the Lord High Admiral's reply to their first report. This final report, presented after the fall of Harley when the Junto Whigs were somewhat mollified, was agreed to by the House and the two reports were presented to the Queen together with an address which excused her husband and laid the blame at the door of his advisers (below, 1 March).

The Junto Whigs' second line of attack in November and December 1706, this time the 'Squadrone' Scots being their allies, was against the Scottish Privy Council. Though it had been left intact at the Union, the negotiations of the treaty had contemplated its abolition. The 'Squadrone', the opposition party in Scotland, sought a rapid end to the Council to damage the new Secretary of State for Scotland, the Duke of Queensberry, whose main prop in Scotland it was. The ministry was in favour of retaining a body that was a useful tool of Court interest in Scotland.[24] In December there was a majority in the Commons for abolition and a committee was appointed to draw up a bill. The Court continued to fight the bill by adopting the tactic of trying to delay the date of proposed abolition. 1708 was an election year, and the opponents of the ministry proposed to end the Council on 1 May 1708 before the elections took place thus striking hard at the Court's influence in the campaign. The date 1 May was carried by a majority of sixty-one and an attempt to amend the date to April 1709 at the third reading in the Commons on 23 January 1708 was defeated.[25]

In the Lords the combination against the Court was the Junto,

[24] For a discussion of the Council's abolition see P. W. J. Riley, *The English Ministers and Scotland, 1707-27* (1964), pp. 92-5; and Trevelyan, *Queen Anne*, ii, 266, 336-7.
[25] *CJ* xv, 461, 512; *Addison Letters*, p. 88.

Lord Rochester and his friends, and the four Scottish 'Squadrone' peers: Montrose, Roxburghe, Sutherland, and Tweeddale. In committee on 5 February, while the outcome of Harley's attempted ministerial *coup* was still in doubt, the Court tried again to postpone the Council's abolition, this time until 1 October 1708, the Lord Treasurer speaking five times against the bill. The government amendment, however, was defeated by five votes (below, 5 February) and the bill, with the original date of 1 May, passed its third reading on 7 February.[26]

Meanwhile, in December 1707, the Junto Whigs widened their attack on the ministry still further to include criticism—cautious at first—of the conduct of the war in Spain. The Tories, under Rochester, opened the attack on 15 December in the Lords. Peterborough, recalled by the ministry from Spain for his erratic conduct, threw himself into the arms of the Tory opposition and persuaded them to press for a policy of giving higher priority to the war in Spain at the expense of the Netherlands. It was on this cue, though not with any sympathy for Peterborough or for the neglect of the Netherlands theatre, that Somers successfully moved on 19 December the ill-fated motion of 'No Peace without Spain'.[27] Four years later the Junto had still not recognised the fact that Charles III's Habsburg cause in Spain had been lost at Almanza.

In January the Earl of Peterborough's conduct was examined at such length (below, 13 January–16 February, *passim*), and the show turned into such a virtuoso performance by the Earl himself that 'people often attend it as they do a play—for entertainment', and eventually the House wearied of the matter: 'so, without coming to any conclusion, or to any vote, they let all that related to him fall'.[28] It was three years before another inquiry into Peterborough's actions were raised, and then from a different quarter and with very different motives.

The main attack on the ministry's conduct of the war in the Peninsula took place in the Commons. Tories and Country Whigs combined in the first Almanza debate on 29 January 1708 severely to censure the government for the apparently glaring discrepancies between the numbers of men voted by parliament and those actually in Spain

[26] HMC *Mar and Kellie MSS* p. 426; *Vernon Corr*. iii, 341–2; *Addison Letters*, pp. 89–90; PRO 30/24/21/145, 148: Cropley to Earl of Shaftesbury, 4 & [5] Feb. 1708 (this second letter is undated and is wrongly listed under 20 Feb.).
[27] For the debate on 19 Dec. see HMC *Egmont MSS* ii, 219–21; *Parl. Hist.* vi, 605–9; *Addison Letters*, pp. 83–6; *Vernon Corr*. iii, 300–2.
[28] Burnet, *History*, v, 348. See also *Addison Letters*, pp. 86–7; *Court and Society from Elizabeth to Anne*, ed. Duke of Manchester (1864), ii, 277: S. Edwin to Manchester, 6 Feb. 1708.

at the time of the battle.[29] Harley's lack of enthusiasm on the ministerial side in the second debate, 3 February, was a further indication of the now irreparable breach between him and Godolphin and Marlborough. By the time of the third Almanza debate in the Commons on 24 February, Harley had gone and the ministry, now moving once more towards the Whigs for support, was rescued by them from a decisive censure of its Spanish policy.

[Dec.] 24. *Wednesday.* Pretty early, on a wet morning, towards London; where (baiting at Barnet on an Anchovy, it being Fasting-Day) we arrived safe about Five in the Evening. Met at the *Black-Swan*[30] by Brother Joseph; and by him, after supper, conveyed to our Lodgeings at Mr Fitzgerald's[31] in the Old Palace-Yard at Westminster.

[Dec.] 25. *Christmas Day.* Haveing (with the Bishop of St Asaph [Beveridge], &c) received the Sacrament at St Margaret's Church, I dined at my brother's; where Sister Rothery, and my two Attourneys, Mr Johnson and Mr Heatley.[32] In the Evening, an Attempt made to visit Mr C. Musgrave.

[Dec.] 26. *Friday.* In the morning (with Dr Gibson) to Mr Serjt Cheshyre; who of opinion that Dr Todd's Forty dayes, towards a Writ *de Excom[municato] Capiendo*,[33] are goeing on. He was much surprised to hear of the Statute of 1. Elizabeth to the same purpose with that of Queen Mary.[34] From the Temple, we returned to dine

[29] See Trevelyan, *Queen Anne*, ii, 324–8.

[30] Possibly the one in Holborn.

[31] Possibly Gerald Fitzgerald (c.1666–1718), copying clerk to the House of Lords, who had entered the Parliament Office by 1706, J. C. Sainty, *The Parliament Office in the Seventeenth and Eighteenth Centuries* (1977), p. 16. He was Nicolson's landlord for the session of 1710–11 (see BL Harleian MS 3780, f. 281), and possibly also in 1717 and 1718.

[32] Acting for Nicolson in the case brought by Todd in the Court of Common Pleas. See above, sessional intro., p. 430.

[33] This old writ was used against serious offenders who had first been formally excommunicated. The person who remained forty days under the sentence of excommunication, and who had not submitted, could, at the request of his diocesan, be arrested and imprisoned. R. Phillimore, *The Ecclesiastical Law of the Church of England* (2nd edn., 1896) ii, 1089–90. Nicolson had excommunicated Todd twenty-seven days previously on 27 Nov. 1706.

[34] The Act of Mary I (1 Mary, sess. 3. cap. 9) declared null and void the statutes given by Henry VIII to the several cathedrals which he had founded because they were not indented according to the form of the foundation of the corporations. Power was, therefore, given to the Queen during her life to make statutes and ordinances under the great seal. The same power was given to Elizabeth I (1 Eliz. c.22) soon after her accession. See J. E. Prescott, *The Statutes of the Cathedral Church of Carlisle* (1902), pp. 4–6; and Phillimore, *Ecclesiastical Law*, i, 146–9, for a discussion of this point. See also Nicolson's comment that the

at Lambeth; where the two Archbishops and fourteen Bishops.[35] My Cause much encouraged.

[Dec.] 27. *Saturday*. Morning, with the Archbishop of York [Sharp] who denies his *wishing Success* to my Adversaries; and hopes that the Statute of 1^O Elizabeth will work peace. At Dinner again at Lambeth; where Lord Fairfax, Sir John Holland (a very learned and worthy Gentleman),[36] the Dean of Exeter [Blackburne], &c. Lord of Canterbury [Tenison] wishes for a new State of my Case and its Consequences, &c. but (withal) gave too broad Hints that Lord Treasurer [Godolphin] was consenting to its being carried into Westminster-Hall.[37]

[Dec.] 28. *Sunday*. I dined at Mr C. Musgrave's (himself ill in a cold) with Sir Christopher, Mr Joseph, Mr Thomas, Mr Watson and Mr Johnson, brought home in the (Rainy) evening by Sir Christopher.

[Dec.] 29. *Munday*. We dined at home; after a short visit to Dr Lancaster, goeing to Fulham. Afternoon, Mr B[enson][38] with me at Coll. Grahm's. He saies, our Dean [Atterbury] disowns the Cause of Dr T[odd].

[Dec.] 30. *Tuesday*. Morning, Visitted by Mr G. Holmes, Mr Dowson and (lastly) Mr James Lowther; who continues his Resolution, to stand for the County of Cumberland.[39] We dined at Brother Joseph's with Dr Waugh and his wife, Mr Standard and his, and Mr Johnson: all Innocent and good.

[Dec.] 31. *Wednesday*. Morning, I carryed over my Case to Dr Gibson; and returned the MS. of Queen Elizabeth's Commissioners.

Elizabethan Act 'is every whit as destructive to the Statutes of several of our Cathedral Churches (particularly that of Durham) as Queen Mary's is of ours at Carlisle: or, if you please, they equally threaten, and are equally insignificant' (*Nicolson Epist. Corr.* ii, 338).

[35] Durham, London, Rochester, Lichfield, Salisbury, Ely, Bangor, Peterborough, Bath and Wells, Chichester, Llandaff, St Asaph, Lincoln, and Carlisle. Lambeth Palace MS 1770, f. 54^V: Wake's Diary.

[36] Sir John Holland (d. *c*.1724), 2nd Bt. of Quidenham, Norfolk, MP for Norfolk, Dec. 1701-10; Comptroller of the Household, 1709-11.

[37] Godolphin, it would seem, was still disposed to give cautious encouragement to Harley's moderate Tory 'scheme'. See Bennett, 'Bishoprics Crisis', pp. 745-6.

[38] Thomas Benson (*c*.1679-1727), educated Queen's College, Oxford; Vicar of Stanwix, 1705-27, and of Dalston, 1714-27, Prebendary of Carlisle, 1716-27. He married Nicolson's eldest daughter, Mary, on 2 Mar. 1714. James, pp. 208-9; *CW* iv (1904), 70.

[39] Cumberland was represented in the current parliament of 1705-8 by Richard Musgrave (Tory) and Capt. George Fletcher (Whig).

Dr Gibson, dineing with me, carryed back Queries for the Churches of the New Foundations.[40] In the Evening, the Chancellor's [Tullie's] Letter (about Dr Todd's Insolent Demeanour in the Cathedral on Xmas-Eve, &c) sent to the Bishop of Lincoln [Wake]; who will give me his thoughts of it tomorrow.

Jan. 1. *Thursday*. Morning, Wishes of the New-Year to Archbishop of York; who continues his promise, not to intermeddle in my Dispute with the Dean.[41] Thence to the Bishop of Lincoln; who heartily approves our Chancellor's conduct against Dr Todd. Afternoon, visitted by Mr Joseph Smith, who seemingly offended at Dr Todd. Alwaies a *coxcomb*.[42]

[Jan.] 2. *Friday*. Morning, With Dr Gibson, getting his few corrections on my Case;[43] which my Lord of Canterbury advises to lay (in MS.) before Lord S[omers]. In the evening, I first visitted Dean Grahme; who, as his Brother the Colonel, who was with him, cold in the Affair with the Dr. Thence to Brother Joseph's: where more hearty, till Bed-time.

[Jan.] 3. *Saturday*. Morning, visits from Mr M. Hutchinson and Mr P. Le Neve (Norroy)[44] not allowed to visit.

[Jan.] 4. *Sunday*. Morning, I went to the Abbey-Church; where Mr Richardson preached, and I received the Sacrament. Mr B[enson] preached at St Margaret's. Evening, a Visit to Coleman-Street; and found Mrs Relf returned from Daventry.

[40] The thirteen cathedrals founded by Henry VIII at the Reformation fall into two groups. Eight were conventual cathedrals prior to the Reformation, having monks or regular canons. These were changed, when the monasteries were suppressed, into chapters of deans and canons, corporate bodies under a royal charter and governed by royal statutes. They were Canterbury, Carlisle, Durham, Ely, Norwich, Rochester, Winchester, and Worcester. Henry also founded five new bishoprics, each with a chapter of a dean and canons: namely, Bristol, Chester, Gloucester, Oxford, and Peterborough.

[41] Two weeks earlier, however, the Archbishop had been taken into the Queen's confidence concerning her intention of forging a new partnership in government with responsible Tories. T. Sharp, *Life of Sharp* (1825), i, 323.

[42] During the heated exchanges in the cathedral when Nicolson suspended Todd on 21 Oct. 1707 the Bishop had called Todd a 'coxcomb'. See *CW* iv (1904), 12.

[43] Published on 17 Feb. 1708. There is a copy in Nicolson's hand, of a text called 'The Case of the Statutes of the Cathedral Church of Carlisle' in Herts. RO Panshanger (Cowper) MS D/EP F168, ff. 88-9. This text was later published, and is probably the 'case' referred to here (there is a printed copy in the Bodleian Library). For a different text see 'Case of the Bishop of Carlisle' printed in *Nicolson Epist. Corr*. ii, 341-56.

[44] Le Neve was the third of the Kings-at-arms in the Heralds Office with a jurisdiction over the counties north of the Trent.

[Jan.] 5. *Munday*. Morning, After Reading my Case to the Bishop of
Ely [Moore][45] (who goeing to Lord Sunderland but will any time
carry me to Lord Somers) I went on with it to Archbishop of York;
who answers all, but the Amendments and Confirmation. Then to
Serjeant Cheshire; who against the printing of it: Because, 'twill
disgust the Court.[46] Dined and sup[p]ed (with Brother and Sister)
at Dr Waugh's.

[Jan.] 6. *Tuesday*. Mr B[enson] dined with me at Lord of York's;
where Lady Sharp, Mr Palmes, Mr Fairfax, &c. Mr Sharp too pert on
the Cause of Prohibition, failure of Bishopricks on the North of Trent,
&c. Archbishop himself fair and Courteous. Evening, an hour's visit
from Mr C. Musgrave; who laments Mr Wybergh's[47] fate.

[Jan.] 7. *Wednesday*. Morning, I waited on the Bishop of Sarum
[Burnet], who gave me the Character of Gregg (committed to
Newgate) and his Master, equally good;[48] thence to Sir Joseph
Jekyll, who approves my cause; and to Serjt Cheshire, who for seeing
the Proofs at large; [to] Dr Lancaster, with whom to dine tomorrow.

Both Houses sitting, I took the Oaths; and (in the House) had
special encouragements in my Cause against Dr Todd from Lord
Somers, Lord Sunderland, Lord Hallifax, &c. Afternoon, a visit from
Mr R. Lowther, for standing again in Westmerland;[49] and (takeing

---

[45] He had been translated from Norwich in June 1707 on the death of Simon Patrick,
see Appendix A.

[46] i.e. the government: a further indication of the way the political wind appeared to be
blowing before Godolphin's break with Harley.

[47] Jeffrey Wybergh (*c*.1671–?1727), of Cumberland, educated at Queen's College,
Oxford; Rector of Caldbeck, 1700–27; he had been Chaplain to Bishop Smith, and was
imprisoned because of debt and nearly lost his rectory through sequestration. James,
pp. 130–1; *CW* ii (1902), 169.

[48] William Greg (biographical information on whom is to be found in T. B. Howell,
A Complete Collection of State Trials (1816), xiv, 1380–7) was arrested on 1 Jan. He was
a talented but spendthrift Scot whom Harley had used as a government agent in Edinburgh
in 1705 and who was later employed on highly confidential work in the Secretary's Office
in the Cockpit—work which brought him into fatal contact with Chamillart, the French
Minister of War. In his *History* (v, 352) Bishop Burnet described him as 'a clerk, whom
Harley had . . . taken into a particular confidence, without enquiry into the former parts
of his life; for he was a vicious and neccessitous person, who had been secretary to the
Queen's envoy in Denmark, but was dismissed by him for those ill qualities. Harley . . .
came to trust him with the perusal and sealing up of the letters which the French prisoners
here in England sent over to France: and by that means he got into the method of sending
intelligence thither.' See A. McInnes, *Robert Harley: Puritan Politician* (1970), pp. 75–85
for an effective vindication of Harley's secretarial record against all charges save that of slack
security.

[49] Robert Lowther, of Maulds Meaburn, Whig MP for Westmorland, 1705–8. He did
stand, but was defeated by James Grahme, and subsequently succeeded his cousin, James
Lowther of Whitehaven, as Storekeeper of the Ordnance after the latter's election for
Cumberland. See Appendix A.

Sohoe in our way) Mr B[enson] and I passed the evening at the *Globe* with Mr Joseph Musgrave and Philip and Joseph Tullie, all grumbling; the last especially warm on the flourishing of the East Indian Companies and declineing of Silk-Weavers,[50] to the Ruin of 60,000 famm[ilies].

[Jan.] 8. *Thursday*. Morning, At Dr Gibson's; with Account of my Encouragements. Thence to the Banquetting-House; where the Secretary's Accounts passed. New Bishops, Regius Professor &c,[51] to the satisfaction of my Lord of Canterbury, who very kind in Recommendation of my cause to Sir J. Cook.

At the House, Capt. Kerr's Answer to his black Charge;[52] to be considered to morrow. I dined at Dr Lancaster's, with Dr Gibson, Mr Smith and Mr Benson; all seemingly pleased with the new professor. Before I went to the House, Mr L. Sympson's cause[53] brought to me by Mr Salkeld; who will help in drawing my Breviats.

[Jan.] 9. *Friday*. Morning, My Affidavits delivered to Mr Heatley; and Breviat sent to Serjt Cheshire. A Visit from the Bishop of Bangor [Evans]; who astonished on the Reading of my case, presently delivered (in the House) to Lord Sommers. On Lord Haversham's Motion,[54] the Writer of the *Post-Boy* (Mr Bowyer [Boyer]) sent for, to give his Authority for asserting (in his Paper of Jan. 1) that the Earl of Galway had *positive Orders* to fight at Almanza. To which he said, He was prompted to write this by Common-Fame[55] and his own Desires to support the Earl's Honour. Dismissed. Tuesday next appointed for the Consideration of our late misfortunes in Spain.

[50] English silk weavers—many of them of Huguenot or Walloon origins and concentrated in particular in Spitalfields and Canterbury—had been protected from French competition since 1689 but heavily exposed to competition from cheap East Indian fabrics. The 10% duty on imported Indian calicoes and silks of 1685 was doubled in 1690 and made permanent in 1711, but a great deal of smuggling went on. There had been riots by weavers in 1697 caused by their economic plight, but in fact the industry survived its periodic crises and expanded, with the help of protective acts of parliament in 1701 and 1721. See A. Plummer, *The London Weavers' Company, 1660–1970* (1972), pp. 292–4; Defoe, *Tour*, i, 118.

[51] On 6 Jan. the Queen closed the last chapter of the protracted 'bishoprics crisis' by announcing the appointments of the new Bishops of Exeter (Blackall), Chester (Dawes), and Norwich (Trimnell), the Regius Professor of Divinity, Oxford (Potter), and the Dean of Peterborough (Kennett). See Bennett, 'Bishoprics crisis', pp. 726–46.

[52] See above, sessional intro., p. 434. For the case and Kerr's answers see also HMC *Lords MSS* vii, 100, 102–10, 168–70.

[53] Lancelot Simpson was Clerk of the Peace in Cumberland, 1690–1711, but he was suspended in Feb. 1710 and eventually succeeded by his eldest son, Hugh. There was conflict between father and son over some bonds, and Hugh was excluded from the real or personal estate in Lancelot's will. See *CW* xxxv (1935), 121; lxix (1969), 226–9.

[54] This marked the resumption of the Lords' inquiries into the state of the war in Spain, begun before Christmas. See *Vernon Corr*. iii, 303–4; above, sessional intro., p. 435.

[55] '. . . he said he had it from about 40 officers.' Luttrell, vi, 254.

Afternoon, visitted by Dr Burnet of the Charter-House; who sollicites for Thomas Nicolson.[56] The Evening bestowed in Salisbury-Court; where Mrs Beaufort in the same Opinion of the Dr [Todd] as heretofore.

[Jan.] 10. *Saturday.* Morning, At the Bishop of Ely's, my friend (Dr Kennet) the new Dean of Peterborough. The Bishop carryed me, in his coach, to Lord Somers's, but his Lordship was gone out. After I had likewise endeavoured (in vain) to meet with Dr Trimnel and Mr Heatley, I went to dine with Mr W. Tullie; where also Philip and Isaac, Mr Allison, Mr M. Hutton, Mr Wrightson. Home at eight.

[Jan.] 11. *Sunday.* After hearing an empty Sermon on the Peace-Makers (by Mr Ramsey) at the Abbey, we went to dine at my brothers; where, it being my Niece's Birth-Day, were also Dr Waugh's Family and Mrs Beaufort.

[Jan.] 12. *Munday.* Morning, visitted by Mr Grisedale and Mr Yates; and (whilst I was at the Coffee-House with them) by Dr Deering and Mr Richardson.

In the House, Lord Somers assured me of his Readiness to bring in a Bill for Security of our Chapter-Statutes;[57] and impowering Her Majesty to appoint Commissioners (of Bishops) to inspect and correct those we have. The two Archbishops, Bishop of London [Compton] and Lord Chief Justice Holt, being to consult on a Bill against Libels, my design of goeing to Lambeth broken. Lord Cardigan, haveing renounced the Popish Religion[58] and received the Sacrament yesterday at St James's church, this day took the oaths and his Seat in the House of Lords.

Evening, Visits (at Grey's Inn) to Mr Browham[59] and Mr Johnson; the latter pestered with Letters from Jeoffrey Wybergh.

[Jan.] 13. *Tuesday.* Morning, Single Visit from Col. Grahame. In the House (till seven at night) papers read, in a Grand Committee, relateing to the Earl of Peterborough's conduct in Spain;[60] and his

[56] ?Thomas Nicolson (*c.*1672–1749) ordained deacon (Carlisle) 1697. He was probably the Vicar of Grindon, Durham, 1699–1706, and Rector of Great Stainton, Durham, 1706–49. J. Peile, *Biographical Register of Christ's College* (Cambridge, 1913), ii, 109.

[57] For Somers's commitment to the bill, see below, 15 Jan., 2, 19 Feb. See also W. L. Sachse, *Lord Somers: a political portrait* (Manchester, 1975), p. 253.

[58] He had been brought up a Roman Catholic by his grandfather, the 2nd Earl of Cardigan. He renounced catholicism on 11 Jan. 1708. *GEC Peerage.*

[59] ?John Brougham.

[60] For the papers read see HMC *Lords MSS* vii, 409–56, and for the whole investigation into the conduct of the war in Spain see ibid., pp. 357–517. There are accounts of the

Lordship's Declamatory Replyes.[61] The Heads on which his Lord-
ship is chiefly charged by the Ministry are these: 1. His diverting the
King of Spain from hastening to Madrid.[62] 2. Refuseing to joyn the
Earl of Galway; who had a Superior Commission. 3. Takeing up great
Sums, at Genoa, without Orders.[63] 4. Sending back the Queen's
Revocation of his Credentials, unopened. 5. Not attending Her
Majesty on his Return,[64] &c. Farther Debate adjourned to Thursday.

[Jan.] 14. *Wednesday*. Fast-day. At the House, onely seven Bishops
(Archbishop of Canterbury one) and two Northern Lords, the Duke
of Montros[e] and Marquess of Tweddale; which (as observed by
the Bishop of Bangor) a sign that our Church was in least danger
from that Quarter. Bishop of Litchfeild [Hough] preached (an
excellent Sermon) on *Psalms* 75, 15. *Wait on the Lord*. Afternoon,
rainy, at home: drawing up an Act for Cathedrals, &c.

[Jan.] 15. *Thursday*. Morning, To Lambeth; where Mr Snow dying,
and my Lord Archbishop in bed, with yesterday's cold. His Grace
wishes Lord Sommers and me to consider on a Bill against Saturday;
and then to dine with him. In the House, my Draught[65] given to Lord
Sommers who very kind. Grand Committee a second time on the
Conduct of the Earl of Peterborough; who asserted his own Innocence
with a deal of Bravery, in challenging his Accusors[66] here or elsewhere, &c.

Evening, Visits from Mr Vice-Chancellor Lancaster, Mr Dean of
Wells [Grahme], Mr Brewer, Mr Hutchinson and Mr Ar[thur]

proceedings on 13 and 15 Jan. in *Addison Letters*, pp. 86–7: Addison to Manchester,
16 Jan. 1708; and in *Vernon Corr*. iii, 303–8: Vernon to Shrewsbury, 13, 15 Jan. 1708.

[61] Peterborough spoke for nearly three hours all told, showing 'a more than ordinary
gaicty in his behaviour both in the House and out of it'. Luttrell, vi, 256; Addison to
Manchester, 16 Jan., *loc. cit.*

[62] In reply to this charge, Peterborough 'made it appear how he prest King Charles to
goe to Madrid, but he [Charles] took contrary council'. Luttrell, vi, 256.

[63] After the failure of the 1706 campaign in Spain Peterborough had left for Italy, at
his own suggestion and without the Queen's commission, to raise a large loan at high rates
of interest from Genoese bankers. He claimed in the House on 15 Jan. to have given
£30,000 of his own money to Charles. *Vernon Corr*. iii, 308.

[64] Peterborough's trump card was a letter from Secretary Sunderland, 'acquainting him
that her Majesty did not think fit to admit him to her presence till he had given her satisfaction in some points specified'. Ibid., p. 306.

[65] Of a Cathedrals Bill (see above, 14 Jan.).

[66] Since the settlement of the bishoprics crisis, and the arrest of Greg (opening up the
possibility of discrediting Harley), the Junto lords and their followers had been more cagey
in their attitude to the Spanish inquiry; on 13 Jan. 'Lord Sunderland desired notice might
be taken that he was not his [Peterborough's] accuser.' At the same time the main High
Tory spokesmen began to show themselves 'well-wishers to his Lordship's cause'. *Vernon
Corr*. iii, 306; *Addison Letters*, pp. 86–7.

Atkinson. NB. Mr Dean of Carlile [Atterbury] called (the first time) at my Lodgeings; just after I was gone out.

[Jan.] 16. *Friday*. Morning, James sent with Letters to Scrjcant Cheshyre and Mr Salkeld: with Brother John's Affidavit on Dr Todd's refuseal of a Copy of the Statutes, and a larger Breviate of my case.

In the House, the Earl of Peterborough's papers again under consideration; wherein his Letter to the Prince of Hesse contradictory to his protestations in the several Councils of War. The Booksellers, printers and Author,[67] of *Remarks on the Narrative* of his Lordship's Conduct in Spain, sent for in custody; the Book being scurrilous and scandalous.[68] In the evening, at Salisbury-Court; as usual on Friday-nights.

[Jan.] 17. *Saturday*. Morning, Feeing Mr Salkeld; who affirms the Bishops [are] Local Visitors of their Chapters, where others not appointed. In the House, Dr Kingston[69] (the impudent writer of the *Remarks against Dr Friend*)[70] continued in Custody till Munday; when the Bishop of Winchester [Trelawney] to attend the service of the House, to prove Kingston not ordained. Evening, a while with Dr Gibson; at the *Dog*.

[Jan.] 18. *Sunday*. Morning, At Christ-Church; where Mr Cook preached on *John* 8. 36. *Evangelical peace*. Dined at my Brother's, with Mr Cummin; who's Guardian to Mrs Belwood, well acquainted with R. Squire's Circumstances, &c. Afternoon, Dr Waugh's Repetition of his very good Fast-Sermon. In the Evening, Visits to Mr Smith and Mr Yates; concludeing with Mr Vice-Chancellor Lancaster, for Oxford tomorrow. NB. Mr Smith assured me that Dr Todd came this morning to Trinity-Chappel, with the Dean of Wells [Grahme]; who preached there for Mr Sandes, and had the moveing comparison to Two Dogs fighting, &c.

[Jan.] 19. *Munday*. Morning, Visits to Lord Hallifax; who presented me with Mr Rymer's Fifth Volume.[71] In the House, R. Kingston

[67] 'Brisco the printer, and Dr. Kingston the author.' Luttrell, vi, 257. For Kingston see below, n. 69.

[68] See HMC *Lords MSS* vi, 358; *Addison Letters*, pp. 86–7.

[69] Richard Kingston, Rector of Royden, Suffolk, author of *Remarks upon Dr Friend's Account of the Earl of Peterborow's Conduct in Spain* (1708).

[70] John Friend (?1677–1728), Professor of Chemistry, Oxford, 1704; physician to the army in Spain, 1705, and in Flanders, 1712. He wrote *An Account of the Earl of Peterborow's Conduct in Spain* (1707).

[71] Of the *Foedera*, published 1708.

avowed (by the Bishop of Winchester) to have counterfeited Orders, &c. was dimitted to prosecution by the Attourney Generall [Harcourt]. In the Evening, at Mr Thynne's, supping with my Sister Rothery's two little mistresses, Mr Martin, &c.

[Jan.] 20. *Tuesday*. Morning, At the Temple with Mr Salkeld; who saies Serjt Cheshyre is perfectly master of my Cause. With the Commissioners of Queen Anne's Bounty at Whitehall. After Dinner, at the House (dureing the Reading of Earl of Peterborough's Letters and papers) a long conference with Lord Pembroke; who saies, the Irish Coin of King John puts his Head in an old fashioned Harp.

[Jan.] 21. *Wednesday*. Morning, With Mr Rook, attending the pleasure of S[erjeant]s Jekyll and Cheshyre; who (at six in the evening) met at Lincoln's Inn, and joyntly agreed there was matter enough in the Acts of Court (on the Deposition of the Prebendaries) to set aside the Doctor's Suggestion. In the House, a Bill from the Admiralty (for a Register for Seamen)[72] iregularly begun to be read in a Grand Committee on the same Subject.[73] Evening, at the *Greyhound*[74] with Mr Johnson, Rook, Brother, &c.

[Jan.] 22. *Thursday*. Morning, visitted abundantly by Cousins Bridget and Robin Nicolson; and likewise by Coll. Studholme full of being a Representative.[75] Capt. Wedhill,[76] moveing me (in vain) to present his Memorial to the Duke of Marlborough.

At the House, Commodore Ker pressed hard in the Committee; and other matters adjourned in the House. Evening, Mr Morland with a second and third Letter from Cousin Lesley; and Mr James Lowther, repeating his purpose of standing for our County. NB. A Decoction of the Roots of Rest-Harrow, Licoras, Twitch-Grass, and the Marine Marsh-Mallows the most effectual Cure (saies C. Studholme) for the Gravel.

[Jan.] 23. *Friday*. Morning, Being ready to attend the Court of C[ommon] P[leas], Mr Rook and Mr Heatley brought me word that the Hearing (at Sir Thomas Powis's Request) was put off till Munday. After attending Capt. Ker's Committee, I dined (with Mr Benson and Mr Rook) at the *Dog*; and, with them and Sister Rothery, bestowed the evening with my Brother Joseph's Family.

[72] The Encouragement of Seamen Bill, see HMC *Lords MSS* vii, 518–39.
[73] The Bolton Committee. See above, sessional intro., p. 433.
[74] Probably the one in Fleet Street. B. Lillywhite, *London Signs* (1972), no. 8033.
[75] Probably for Carlisle, at present represented by Sir James Montagu and Thomas Stanwix. In the event Carlisle was uncontested in 1708.
[76] ?William Weddall, captain in Irish regiment of foot, 1704–15. Dalton, v, pt. ii, 54.

[Jan.] 24. *Saturday*. Morning, Haveing published Mr L. Simpson's Award (and franked a dozen Covers for his Grandchild Wybergh) I went to Lambeth; where after a long discourse with Lord of Canterbury, on the subject of our Dean's Collegiate church, I dined with the Steward; And, walking afterwards in the Park, met with the Archbishop of York; who assures me that he has not yet seen Dr Todd. His Chaplains cannot say so.

[Jan.] 25. *Sunday*. I preached for Dr Lancaster at St M[artin]'s, present Lords Bindon, Towneshend, Sommers, Rockingham and Berkley. Haveing dined with Mr Grisedale, Mr Smith, John King,[77] &c. I went to Mr C. Musgrave's; where Mr Comptroller Mansel, for the S[cottish] privy-counsel, and Coll. Grahme against it.[78] NB. Dr Todd has made no visit here; Mr Joseph refuseing to bring him.

[Jan.] 26. *Munday*. Dr Todd's suggestion argued at the Bar of the Common-pleas: where Mr Serjt. Cheshire plainly, and Sir Joseph Jekyl more smoothly, exposed the Obstinacy of the Doctor's behaviour in my late Visitation, and the Hypocritical Slyness of the Dean's. However, Upon Reading a long (and false) Affidavit made by the Doctor himself (wherein amongst other Untruths, he asserted that he *never intended to oppose my Ordinary Jurusdiction*) the Lord Chief Justice Trevor, Mr Justice Blenco[w]e and Justice Tracy, declared that the matter of the Suggestion, *quoad Statuta* and the powers of the Bishop as Local Visitor, ought to be argued ten dayes hence. Mr Justice Dormer frankley avowed, That this cause did not properly lay before that Court: But ought to be remitted to be heard in the ordinary method of Ecclesiastical procedure by way of Appeal.

After dineing (with Dr Waugh, Dr Gibson, Brother Joseph, Mr Rook, &c) Mr Benson went with me to repay a Visit to Dr Hickes; who pretty cheerful, and now publishing more of his Saxon Remains.

[Jan.] 27. *Tuesday*. Morning, with Dr Gibson at the Palace of Lambeth where the Archbishop still confined in the Gowt; and (after

[77] ?John King (1652–1732), writer, Rector of Chelsea, 1694–1732, and Prebendary of York, 1718–32.

[78] See above, sessional intro., p. 434. There had been a decisive division on the Privy Council clause of the bill 'for completing the Union' two days earlier in the House of Commons, carried against the government by 197 votes to 118. Luttrell, vi, 259–60; *Addison Letters*, p. 88: Addison to Manchester, 24 Jan. 1708. For the alignment of forces, see Holmes, *British Politics*, pp. 111, 234, 242, 341.

a Recital of the hardship of my case) unwilling to stir so much as his Tongue for me, till it will be too late. In the House, Lord Peterborough's Papers finished; and the Debates on them appointed for Saturday. In the evening, with Serjt. Cheshire; who (in vain) presses me to go upon the Defence of the Statutes.

[Jan.] 28. *Wednesday*. Morning, After a walk to (near) Kensington, I went to the Committee on the Examination of Commodore Ker; whose Charge was voted to be just, in contracting for 800 *l*. Convoy-Money. *Contents*, 28. *Not Contents*, 18.[79] Amongst the latter were no fewer than 14 of the Scotch Lords.[80]

In the evening, at Cousin R. Nicolson's; where Mr Clavel (of Dorsetshire) and voluble Mrs Dykes, who saies her Husband is impatient to see me and to have my Censure on his Book.[81]

[Jan.] 29. *Thursday*. In the House after a Committee on Trade, where the Merchants severe on the Admiralty, the Report against Capt. Ker made by the Duke of Bolton; and, on the Question, agreed to. *Contents*, 27. *Not Contents*, 15. Bill from the Commons, for takeing away the Scotch Privy-Counsel,[82] read a first time; and ordered a 2d Reading this day 7 night.

On Invitation, I dined with Lord Hallifax; where Lord Sunderland, Lord Sommers, Bishops of Ely and Litchfeild and Dr Bentley. Lord Hallifax's paints in his Dineing and Drawing Rooms exceeding fine; especially that of King Charles 1 on Horseback, taken amongst the Furniture of the Duke of Bavaria.[83] In his Library, Antique Statues (or Porphyry and marble) from Rome, of Marius, &c. very valuable; as also Brass-Figures of a Gladiator, Hermaphrodite, &c. exceeding curious.

NB. The Sollicitor Generall (Sir James Montague) brought us in a running Account, from the House, that the Commons (in their

[79] According to HMC *Lords MSS* vii, 105 the vote was twenty-eight to seventeen. Confirmed by James Vernon, *Vernon Corr.* iii, 334.
[80] '. . . and the other two absent [adds Vernon]; the other three were the Duke of Bucks, Lord Torrington and Lord Carmarthen.' Ibid.
[81] *Moral Reflections upon Select English Proverbs; familiarly accommodated to the Humour and Manners of the present Age*, published in Nov. 1707 by Oswald Dykes, a Kensington Schoolmaster.
[82] See above, sessional intro., p. 434. The bill had passed the Commons the previous day.
[83] This is a puzzling reference. The picture is probably the Van Dyke portrait of Charles I (now in the National Gallery) which was looted from the Bavarian collection by the Emperor Joseph I and given by him to the Duke of Marlborough by 8 Nov. 1706. It is not known exactly when it reached England and it could have been housed temporarily for the Duke by Halifax. (We should like to thank Sir Oliver Millar, Surveyor of the Queen's Pictures, for commenting on this passage.)

Debates on the Affairs of Spain)[84] were very warm on Secretary Harley, H[enry] St Johns and Arthur Moor.[85] *Esto*!

[Jan.] 30. *Friday*. Morning, The House of Lords, as usual proceeded to Westminster-Abbey; where an excellent sermon by the Bishop of Lincoln, on *Matthew* 26, 51 and 52, against drawing the sword in Defence of Religion. The Evening, at Salisbury-Court, where W. Rook &c.

[Jan.] 31. *Saturday*. Morning, Mr Richardson, a pure visit; Mr Johnson and Mr Haines, about Mr A[tterbury]'s Dispensation; Mr Rook, with a copy of Dr Todd's Affidavit. In the House, fruitless Reading of more papers brought in by Lord Peterborough. The rest (supposed by Lord Treasurer [Godolphin] not to be yet in being) referred to next Wednesday. Lord Sommers appoints Munday-morning, at nine, to attend the Archbishop of Canterbury with our Bill. A single pint, at the *Dog*, with Dr Gibson.

Feb. 1. *Sunday*. At home, with my great cold. Mr B[enson] preached at St Peter's Cornhil. Evening, visitted by Dr Gibson, Mr Walker and Brother Joseph.

[Feb.] 2. *Munday*. Morning, called on early by Lord Sommers, who went with me to Lambeth; where the Archbishop's circular Letter (on my behalf)[86] and the Bill for the House against tomorrow, read and approved. At Dinner, and the evening, with Brother and Sister, Mr Benson at Dr Waugh's; celebrateing his Birth-day.

[Feb.] 3. *Tuesday*. Morning, After a walk in the park, visitted by Coll. Grahme, Cousin James Nicolson (Apoth[ecary]) and W. Rook.

---

[84] *CJ* xv, 520; *Vernon Corr*. iii, 328–30; above, sessional intro., p. 435. For the inevitable dilemma of Harley and his friends in the first Almanza debate of 29 Jan. 1708, see G. Holmes and W. A. Speck, 'The Fall of Harley in 1708 reconsidered', *EHR* lxxx (1965), 678, 691 and n. 4.

[85] Arthur Moore (*c*.1666–1730), MP for Great Grimsby, 1695–1700, 1701–15, 1721–2, and Comptroller of Army Accounts, 1704–7, and a Lord of Trade, 1710–14. Sedgwick, ii, 270–1.

[86] See above, sessional intro., p. 432 and n. 19. The letter was sent to every bishop of Canterbury province, declaring 'the case of the Bishop of Carlisle . . . to be a common cause, and of great concern to the Church; which will never be quiet so long as that evil generation of men who make it their business to search into little flaws in ancient charters and statutes, and to unfix what laudable usage hath well fixed, meet with any success'. Tenison's hesitancy in taking this step (complained of by Nicolson in his diary, above, 27 Jan.) may be partly explained by the fact that Carlisle was in Sharp's province.

In the House after Lord Bindon's Tryal,[87] Lord Sommers brought in a Bill *for the avoiding of Doubts and Questions touching the Statutes of diverse Cathedral and Collegiate Churches;*[88] which, being introduced with a pathetic[89] speech was read a first time, and ordered a Second Reading on Friday next. In the Evening with Serjt Cheshire; who, as before, full of Scruples: But still peremptory that the Dr cannot rub off his Excommunication.

[Feb.] 4. *Wednesday*. Morning, Visits by Mr Martin and Mr Maddocks. In the House, Spanish Officers[90] produced by Earl of Peterborough to assert his good Conduct. Evening, after a Glass with Dr G[ibson] at the *Dog*, Mr B[enson] and I attempted Visits to Mr Dean of Wells [Grahme] (newly marryed) and to Mr R. Lowther, Mr Brewer, &c.

NB. This morning, I attended Sir Joseph Jekyl with my 2d Breviat; who kindly foretold that no use would now be made of it, and therefore he refused to take any Fee. He also promised to farther my Bill, the best he could, in the House of Commons; Lord Sommers,[91] as he added, haveing already desired him to do it.

[Feb.] 5. *Thursday*. Morning, Long visit from Mr C. Musgrave; who irreconcileable to Mr R. Lowther.

In the House, The Bill for takeing away the Scots privy-council, &c. Lord Chancellor [Cowper], Lord Treasurer and the Generality of the Court, for preserveing it to October but carryed on the Question (as it came from the Commons) to end May 1. *Contents*, 50. *Not Contents*, 45. NB. This difference was in the Committee. Had the House voted, the Advantage would have been yet greater on the side of the Majority; who had Ten proxies for the others Four.[92] Lords Sunderland, Sommers, Hallifax, &c. joyned in with Rochester, Nottingham, &c. So did all the Bishops; except Winchester and Oxford [Talbot].[93]

[Feb.] 6. *Friday*. Morning, Called surprizeingly from Lambeth, to attend the Common-Pleas; where Lord Chief Justice Trevor and Justice Blenco[w]e (but most immoderately Justice Tracy) for Prohibiteing me. Be it so! Hence, with the Bishop of Lincoln, in attendance on my Lord of York to Kensington; where (being Her Majesty's Birthday) the Queen, lame and Indisposed, and Prince,

---

[87] An appeal against a decree in Chancery. *LJ* xvii, 344, 444; HMC *Lords MSS* vii, 99.
[88] For this bill see HMC *Lords MSS* vii, 544–5.   [89] Moving.
[90] Brigadier Hans Hamilton and Colonel Bisset, who gave evidence on oath.
[91] His brother-in-law.   [92] Proxies could not be used in committees.
[93] Nicolson's account agrees in substance with those of James Vernon (*Vernon Corr.* iii. 341–2) and Joseph Addison (*Addison Letters*, p. 89). Vernon adds, 'It was observed the Bishop of Ely withdrew from the question.'

complimented by a Numerous Court. Evening, as usual, at my Brother's.

[Feb.] 7. *Saturday*. After a good morning's walk, to the House; where the Lord Sommers's Bill (for secureing the future Quiet of Cathedrals) read a 2d time; and, on the motion of Lord Rochester, committed for this day sennight. The Annuity Bill,[94] Succession Bill,[95] &c. from the Commons. Then, the Scotch Council again debated; and some of the Northern Lords very loath to part with their Regalities, contrary (as averred) to the 20th Article of Union:[96] But carryed on the Question against them. *Contents*, 51. *Not Contents*, 44. Whereupon the Bill was read a 3d time; and passed without any Amendments.[97]

Evening, I dined (at the *Dog*) with Dr Gibson, Mr Benson and Mr Rook.

[Feb.] 8. *Sunday*. I attended my Metropolitan to St Stephen's Chapple; where His Grace consecrated (Sir W. Dawes) the new Bishop of Chester, assisted by the Bishops of Winchester, Rochester [Sprat] and myself. We all dined (as did also the officers of Doctor's Commons, &c) with the Archbishop. The Sermon was preached by Mr Milner,[98] on 2 *Corinthians* 3, 6. − *The Ministry be not blamed*. The Discourse very good, and ordered to be printed. I waited long [for] my neighbour (the Bishop of Rochester's) company homewards; haveing sate out our first companions, as also the Bishops of London, and Ely, from Lambeth; where were consecrated the new Bishops of Exeter [Blackhall] and Norwich [Trimnell].

[Feb.] 9. *Munday*. Morning, Mr B[enson] and I walked to Kensington; and returning had a visit from Joseph Smith, Inquisitive after an imaginary Week-Lecture at Lambeth.

In the House, after a warm Report that the Queen was not to

---

[94] Act for raising a further Supply to Her Majesty, for the Service of the Year 1708, and other uses, by Sale of Annuities . . . *LJ* xviii, 449.

[95] An Act for the Security of Her Majesty's Person and Government, and of the Succession to the Crown of Great Britain in the Protestant line. See HMC *Lords MSS* vii, 572-3. It was a post-Union restatement of the provisions of the English Regency Act of 1706.

[96] Viz. 'That all Heretable Offices, Superiorites, Heretable Jurisdiction, Offices for life and Jurisdiction for life, be reserved to the Owners thereof, as Rights of Property, in the same Manner as they are now enjoyed by the Laws of Scotland, notwithstanding of this Treaty.' *LJ* xvii, 258. The present bill established the system of JPs in Scotland as well as abolishing the Edinburgh Council.

[97] See *Addison Letters*, pp. 90-1: Addison to Manchester, 7 Feb. 1708. There was a protest against it by the Court lords, see *LJ* xviii, 450-1; Rogers, *Protests of the Lords*, i, 184-5.

[98] William Milner (d. 1713), Vicar of Shephall, Hertfordshire, 1691-1713.

be prevailed on by the Duke of Marlborough and Lord Treasurer's united Requests to part with Secretary Harley,[99] Lord Wharton made a motion to enquire into the matter of Gregg's Condemnation: Whereupon the House (by Ballotting) chose the following seven Lords as a Select Committee to examine the man, &c. viz. Duke of Somerset, Duke of Bolton, Duke of Devonshire, Earl of Wharton, Lord Viscount Towneshend, Lord Sommers and Lord Hallifax.[100]

Evening, Dr Waugh and Dr Gibson supped with me; and the former walked along with me afterward to my Brother's.

[Feb.] 10. *Tuesday*. Morning, The Queen's Writ of Prohibition was served on me by Mr Taylor's Clerk;[101] who also delivered a Message to this purpose. *Dr Todd gives his Duty, and desires to know when he may wait on you for Absolution.* To which my Answer was. *As soon as we come into the Countrey; For, here I have no Jurisdiction.*[102] This allowed by Lord Sommers and Mr Serjt. Cheshyre. Lease renewed to Mr Henley; who shewed me a Map of Carlile-place,[103] with the Gardens, &c. Mrs Fetherson vainly solliciteing my Interest towards the getting a son of Hers into the Charter-House.[104]

Scene changed at Court: Mr Harley being laid aside, and other Removes expected.[105] — The House of Lords quietly proceeded on the Bills for the Choice of the 16 Peers of Scotland.[106] Evening,

[99] See Holmes and Speck, 'The Fall of Harley in 1708 reconsidered', pp. 694–7.

[100] This was a 'packed jury' of the Whig Junto and their friends obviously intended to 'frame' Harley and ruin him for good. In this it failed, but it was probably decisive in persuading the Queen to accept his resignation. Ibid., p. 697.

[101] Thomas Dayes. John Taylor was probably the Deputy Register in the Faculty Office. Chamberlayne, *Present State 1708*, p. 554.

[102] Thomas Dayes' report of the meeting is as follows: 'I went on Tuesday morning the 10th of February 1707/8 between 8 and 9 o'clock to the Bishop of Carlisle's Lodgings and acquainted his Lordship that the copy of the Rule which I gave his Lordship was a copy of the Rule of the Court of Common Pleas for a prohibition and this is the writt (which I gave him at the same time) directed to your Lordship to restore Dr Todd to his Office in the Church of Carlisle and to Absolve him from his Excomunication.

Respons I shall *or will* observe it

Then I presented Dr Todd's most humble duty to his Lordship and desired to know when he would be pleased to give him leave to wait on him to receive his Lordship's Absolution.

R[esponse] I shall talk with him when we come into the Country. No Judge can compell me to give Absolution here.'

York Minster Library Hailstone Collection QQ 2.7: Thomas Dayes to -?-, n.d.

[103] Near Carlisle House in Lambeth.

[104] The early seventeenth-century school founded by Thomas Sutton. There is no record of a Fethersone entering the school, see *Alumni Carthusiani*, ed. B. Marsh and F. A. Crisp (1913).

[105] See below, 11 Feb.

[106] The Representative Peers of Scotland Act (HMC *Lords MSS* vii, 558–9) which provided for the election and summoning of the sixteen representative Scottish peers to sit in the Lords as laid down in article 22 of the Act of Union (see *LJ* xvii, 259).

Dr Gee and Mr Freeman;[107] desireing the latter might preach, instead of me, on Sunday next at St Margaret's. Letters by the Post, northwards; and by Mr Benson, for Oxford.

[Feb.] 11. *Wednesday*. Morning, Mr Warner Goldsmith,[108] sent to Brother Joseph with Mr Hill's Bill for 30 *l*. At the House, sure news of the quitting of Secretary Harley, Mr Comptroller Mansel, &c.[109] More of the Earl of Peterborough's Spanish officers examined; and all stoutly for him.

After Dr Gibson had dined with me, Dean Atterbury (with Dr Deering) came to give me a Visit; stayed some hours, in a peaceful Temper, and carryed off some Queries for the Civilians in the Case of Dr Todd's excommunication.

[Feb.] 12. *Thursday*. Morning, with Lord of Canterbury, cheerful on the Removes at Court;[110] and hearty in my Cause. In the House Money-Bill and the Peers of Scotland. Our Dean with me again in the Lobby; but peremptory against Dr Todd's Kneeling at his Absolution. Never otherwise from me. After Dr Gibson had dined with me, in order to settle my paper for the Commons, I had a kind Visit from Mr Seton of Pitmeden;[111] an ingenious Gentleman.

[Feb.] 13. *Friday*. Morning, Visits from Cousin R. Nicolson, Mr Holme of Berkshire and Mr Buchanan.

In the House, Annuity-Bill, &c. had the Royal Assent by Commission;[112] most of the Lords sitting bare[113] which severely checked by the Earl of R[ocheste]r. Evening, at Salisbury-Court with Mr Rook.

ND. Lord Chancellor [Cowper] acquainted me that the Archbishop

[107] Charles Freeman (d. 1722), later Perpetual Curate of St Botolph's, Aldersgate, 1714–22.

[108] ?John Warner, elected Liveryman of the Goldsmith's Company in 1698, and elected to the court of the Company in 1714. W. T. Prideaux, *A List of Wardens . . . of the Worshipful Company of Goldsmiths Since 1688* (1936), pp. 8, 40.

[109] Harley and his friend Sir Thomas Mansel resigned on 11 Feb; Henry St. John, Secretary-at-War, and Attorney-General Harcourt followed their example on 12 Feb. Three other junior ministers believed to be involved in Harley's 'scheme' (James Brydges, Thomas Coke, and Henry Paget) were the subject of speculation, but chose to survive and were not dismissed.

[110] Addison wrote exultantly of the Whig reaction to 'this Revolution', that it 'has already had the good effect to unite all old friends that were falling off from one another, and in all probability will produce a good new Parliament'. *Addison Letters*, p. 92: to Manchester, 13 Feb. 1708.

[111] ?William Seton (1673–1744), 2nd Bt., MP for Scotland, 1707–8, Commissioner of the Equivalent, 1707, of the Union, 1706.

[112] For the procedure and the text of the commission see *LJ* xviii, 460–1.

[113] i.e. without hats.

of York had informed the Queen that the Judges of the C[ommon] P[leas] had already condemned the Statutes of the Church of Carlile; which had inclined Her Majesty to oppose the Bill now depending, since the 3d of this month: But His Lordship (on receiveing my case, &c.) promises to set Her Right.

[Feb.] 14. *Saturday*. Morning, I visitted, and secured, the Bishops of Norwich and Lincoln: But, when we came to the House, Lord Chancellor advised the Adjourning of our Committee to Thursday, which was approved by Lord Sommers and proposed by Lord Treasurer [Godolphin]. All the Judges ordered to be then present. This (surely) the best way to set the Queen at Rights, and to prevail for a ready Dispatch in the House of Commons. Dr Gibson and I dined (as also yesterday) at the *Dog*. Letters at night.

[Feb.] 15. *Sunday*. Morning, I preached at Lambeth (haveing sent the Bishop of Landaff [Tyler] to Crutched Fryers)[114] and dined at his House. After Dinner, with my Lord Archbishop who is my hearty well-wisher against the Insinuations of my own Metropolitan.[115] His Grace, on Discourse told me that Dr South,[116] on his Return from Poland, had acquainted him that King Charles 2 had then a project for the abolishing of all Free States; and that, particularly, the P[rince] of O[range] was then intended to be made King of the Netherlands. After prayers in the Chapple, and visits to Mr Snow and Mr Tennison, home to my Lodgeings.

[Feb.] 16. *Munday*. Morning, Dr Todd (attended with Mr Taylor's clerk) came to me, without bending either his knee or his Head, and *demanded and desired* (in the Queen's name, I suppose, and his own) Absolution. Answer. Not till I am farther commanded. Next to him Visitted by Francis Bugg[117] and Thomas Ducket. To relieve

[114] The area near Tower Hill where the convent of the Crutched Friars formerly existed. They were so called from their bearing or wearing a cross. They appeared in England in 1244 and were suppressed in 1656.

[115] i.e. Archbishop Sharp of York.

[116] Robert South (1634–1716), Prebendary of Westminster, 1663–1716, who had travelled to Poland in 1676 as Chaplain to Laurence Hyde. He had also been Chaplain to Charles II.

[117] Francis Bugg (1640–1724?), writer against quakerism who had formerly been a Quaker. He may have called to see Nicolson in connection with his petition to the Commons presented two days later called 'Some reasons humbly offered against the Quakers unreasonable request touching elections of members to serve in parliament, that their afirmation may be without the words *As in the Presence of Almighty God*'. The Quakers presented their own petition to have the words removed 'because it seems to much like an oath' and it was read and rejected on 27 Feb. 1707. BL Lansdowne MS 1024, f. 184^V: Kennett's Journal; *CJ* xv, 578.

me, the new Bishop of Chester brought me a pair of Consecration-Gloves; and read over and approved my Case.[118]

At the House, the Spanish Enquires half drop[p]ed;[119] and onely Bills read. After I had given my Case[120] to Mr Powel (at Black-Fryers)[121] to be printed, and had dined at home, I walked up to Covent Garden: And thence, the Alderman[122] being engaged, to Salisbury Court; where the remaining part of the Evening.

[Feb.] 17. *Tuesday*. Morning, At Dr Gibson's correcting my Case; and afterwards visited by two Brou[g]hams, Mr Joseph Smith and Mr W. Johnson.

At the House a severe Report from the Committee on the Admiralty by Duke of Bolton;[123] whereon an Address moved by Lord Wharton, supported by the Earls of Rochester and Orford and Lord Sommers.[124] A faint Opposition from Lord Treasurer but carryed without a Division.

Cases brought at three; and some distributed. After Dinner, I carryed one to my Lord of York; who (more frankly than kindly) told me that he'd opposed my Bill; because I had declined the Sentence of the Court of Common Pleas. An Excellent Reason for a Metropolitan!

[Feb.] 18. *Ashwednesday*. Morning, Borrowing the Bishop of Lincoln's coach I carryed my Cases to Lords Rochester, Sommers, Sunderland, Pembroke, Roxborow, Queensberry, Twe[e]ddalc, Montross, Wharton, Bishops of Norwich and Peterborough [Cumberland], Earls of Marr and Lowden [Loudoun]. In the Court of

---

[118] The vote of the Tory Bishop Dawes was a valuable one for Nicolson and the Whigs to capture, especially in view of the attitude of his mentor, Sharp.

[119] There were no further proceedings during this session, see HMC *Lords MSS* vii, 359. On the exhaustion of the House under the bombardment of papers and witnesses to which Peterborough had subjected it, see Burnet, *History*, v, 348.

[120] Possibly *The Case of the Statutes of the Cathedral Church of Carlisle, shewing them to be good and valid, notwithstanding they were not intended* which Kennett lists in his Journal under 4 Feb. 1707 [/8]. BL Lansdowne MS 1024, f. 184ᵛ.

[121] Edmund Powell, printer and bookseller in Blackfriars, 1708–11. H. R. Plomer, *Dictionary of Booksellers and Printers, 1668–1725* (1922), p. 243.

[122] Nicolson's title for Isaac Tullie.

[123] Printed in *LJ* xviii, 466–72. See also *Parl. Hist.* vi, 647–62.

[124] The High Tories and the Junto Whigs maintained their alliance of convenience in the attack on the Admiralty on 17 Feb., the latter—according to one Whig MP—from 'anger that the present great charges [the offices of Harley and his friends] have been fill'd with creatures of the Court ['Treasurer's Whigs', notably Boyle and Walpole], and not some of theirs'. In hammering out the address, however, they parted company over whether to lay the blame for naval miscarriages on the ministry or Cabinet as a whole, or (as the Junto wished) merely on the Admiralty Council. PRO 30/24/21: Sir John Cropley to Lord Shaftesbury, 20 Feb. 1708; Burnet, *History*, v, 346–7.

Requestes. Sir Joseph Jekyell informed me that the Queen would probably be at the Hearing of my Case tomorrow; and that the Judges would unanimously declare for me. *Faxit Deus*!

After Dr Gibson had eaten a little salt-fish with me, I took a Hackney-Coach; and carryed more of my Cases to the Lords Seafield, Argyle, Ilay, Chief Justice Holt, Chief Justice Trevor, Chief Baron Ward, and the Bishops of Sarum, Lichfield and Ely; the last very obligeing, but so pained in his cheek that I fear his confinement.

[Feb.] 19. *Thursday*. At the House, after the committee for drawing up an Address to the Queen (on the Severe Report upon the Affairs of the Admiralty) the Cathedral-Bill[125] was called for by the Order of the Day; Her Majesty and the Twelve Judges[126] being present on this Occasion. The Debates in the Grand Committee (Lord Stamford in the Chair) were begun, in a Heat, by the Archbishop of York who passionately insisted on the Bill's touching on the Queen's Prerogative, &c. His Grace was (in conclusion) cool enough on the Sharp Replyes that were made by Lords Somers,[127] Halifax, Towneshend, &c. And the Bill was agreed to, on the Question, by such an Irresistible Majority, that no Lord had the Hardyness to call for a Division.[128] *Deo Gratias*!

[Feb.] 20. *Friday*. Morning, I waited, with the History of my Success, on my Lord of Canterbury; who is willing that I should give copies of his Letter in the House of Commons, but not call it Circular.[129] In the House, an Appeal (very vexatious) heard, touching Sir J. Alston's Will;[130] and the Ingrossed Cathedral-Bill deferred till tomorrow.

After Dinner Mr Benson went with me to Mr Churchill's; to pay for Archdeacon Pearson's Sermons: And Mr Awnsham [Churchill][131]

---

[125] Cathedral and Collegiate Churches Bill. See HMC *Lords MSS* vii, 544–5.

[126] It was reported the judges had refused to give their opinion on the bill without seeing the statutes of Carlisle and the grant of Henry VIII. Bodl. MS Ballard 39, f. 33: James Harris to [Charlett], 24 [Feb.] 1708.

[127] 'My Ld Sommers, I hear, exerted himself more than ever he had done before on this occasion.' *Addison Letters*, p. 92: to Manchester, 20 Feb. 1708. There is some evidence that Nottingham and Guernsey opposed the bill. Bodl. MS Ballard 39, f. 33.

[128] For another account, see *Addison Letters*, p. 92. Addison heard 'that the Queen express'd herself entirely satisfied with the merits of the Bishop's cause', staying till the end of the debate 'after six o'clock in the evening'. Bishop Wake confirmed in his diary that the House 'sate till after 6 a Clock upon the bill about Cathedralls'. Lambeth Palace MS 1770, f. 57^v.

[129] See above, 2 Feb.

[130] See HMC *Lords MSS* vii, 346–7.

[131] He combined bookselling with the representation of Dorchester in the Commons. See Appendix A.

assured me of his best Assistance in the House of Commons. Evening, we supped (with Dr Waugh and his wife, and Sister Rothery) at Salisbury-Court; being cheerful on my Success.

[Feb.] 21. *Saturday*. Morning, Lords not sitting, I attended Sir R[ichard] Onslow and others of the House of Commons with my Case; and (after furnishing Mr James Lowther and Mr Dale with six apiece) went down to the Tower with Mr Benson, returning onely to write Letters. Joseph Smith, our companion, much netled at the Insects.

[Feb.] 22. *Sunday*. I preached for, and dined with, Dr Onley; whose Daughters on Dr Atterbury's side. Evening, Cases deposited with Lord Seafield and Bishop of Ely; and endeavoured to be left with C[olonel] Grahme and Mr R[ichard] Musgrave.

[Feb.] 23. *Munday*. Morning, with Mr C. Musgrave, warm on the Whigs Commissioners for the Queen's Bounty at Whitehall. Her Majesty at the House, passing Bills. After Dinner (at the *Dog*) with Dr Gibson and Mr B[enson] Cases deposited at the Temple with Mr Salkeld and Mr Denton[132] and one given to R[obert] Lowther.

[Feb.] 24. *Tuesday*. Morning, Attending Mr Speaker [Smith], Sir Joseph Jekyll, Bishop of Sarum, Sir D[avid] Dalrymple, Mr Seton, and the Bishop of Lincoln, with my Cases; which are greatly encouraged. The Scots most zealously, and unanimously, my friends.[133]

The Lords read the Cathedral-Bill a 3d time; and, on putting the Question, there were onely three Voices (of 68) that were Negative. Hereupon, the Bill was sent down to the House of Commons by two Judges (Mr Justice Dormer and Mr Baron Smith) instead of so many Masters in Chancery: And (on the motion of Mr Nevil,[134] seconded by Mr Jervoise) that House gave it immediately a First Reading, and ordered it a Second on Saturday next.[135] NB. Mr Harley saies, He

---

[132] Alexander Denton (1679-1740), laywer and client of Lord Wharton and MP for Buckingham, 1708-10, 1715-22. Sedgwick, i, 610-11.

[133] This was amply confirmed by the division in the Commons on 28 Feb. *Vernon Corr.* iii, 358.

[134] Probably Richard Neville (1655-1717), MP for Berkshire, 1695-1710, a prominent Country Whig who had parted company with the Junto on occasions this session (see *Addison Letters*, pp. 93-4: Addison to Manchester, 24 Feb.). It was reported that Sir William Whitlock (MP for Oxford University) forced a division upon the first reading. Bodl. MS Ballard 39, f. 33: Harris to [Charlett], 24 [Feb.] 1708. No division was recorded (*CJ* xv, 568-9). [135] See below, 28 Feb.

will demonstrate to the House that the passing of this Bill into a Law will put the Election of 28 members into the hands of the Bishops.[136] *Papae!*

Evening, Dr Gibson dined with me. Letters.

[Feb.] 25. *Wednesday.* Morning, I visitted Mr P[eter] King at his chambers in the Temple; and he assured me of his utmost care in carrying the Church-Bill thorough the House of Commons,[137] but objected the Harshness of Dr Tod's sufferings. Dr Gibson and I to see him again on Friday. Thence to Lambeth; where the Archbishop of Canterbury much concerned at the odd behaviour of his brother of York.

In the House, Duke of Bolton reported the Address touching the Admiralty;[138] which ordered to be presented by the whole House. After Dinner, Mr B[enson] and I went to hear Mr Clinch of Barnet;[139] who admirably well personates the French or Italian Mountebank, the Drunken man and the old woman, as his danceing son well mimicked the Taylor, Shoemaker and Baker. He playes fine on the Violin and, with that and his Voice, curiously imitates the Organ and Quire, a pack of Hounds, &c.

[Feb.] 26. *Thursday.* Morning, To Dr Gibson; who disturbed with wife's Indisposition. At the House, private Bills read; and two rejected. NB. This day, our Dean dispersed his pretended Reasons against the Church-Bill;[140] on which I immediately wrote short *Remarks,*[141] which were printed the same night. Mr Denton, of the Temple, went with me and Mr B[enson] to Dr Hickes, Bishop of Sarum, Mr Eyres,[142] &c.

---

[136] Robert Harley was the chief organiser of the fierce opposition to the Cathedrals Bill in the Lower House. Since his resignation, it was said that, 'Mr Harley has taken his old part, the management of the House, the torys his abject slaves'. PRO 30/24/21/148: Sir John Cropley to Lord Shaftesbury, 20 Feb. 1708.

[137] Like Neville, King had been a prominent Country (or 'Whimsical') Whig this session; but he recognised the Cathedrals Bill for what it was, a crucial 'party cause'. He was prominent on the Whig side in the debate of 28 Feb. *Addison Letters*, pp. 96–7.

[138] *LJ* xviii, 482.

[139] He was performing at the *Swan Tavern* in Fish Street. BL Burney Newspaper Collection, vol. 144b: *The Daily Courant*, no. 1878, 24 Feb. 1708.

[140] *Reasons humbly propos'd against the Passing a Bill, entituled, An Act for avoiding of Doubts and Questions touching the Statutes of divers Cathedrals and Collegiate Churches.*

[141] *Short Remarks on a Paper of Reasons against the Passing of the Bill for avoiding of Doubts and Questions touching the Statutes of divers Cathedral and Collegiate Churches*, dated by White Kennett as 27 Feb. 1707, BL Lansdowne MS 1024, f. 184^v.

[142] Robert Eyres (1666–1735), Kt., MP for Salisbury, 1698–1710, Solicitor General in 1708.

[Feb.] 27. *Friday*. Morning, After enquiries for Lord Wharton, Mr Montgomery,[143] &c. to the House; where notice of Dr Todd's Libellous Case.[144] At Dinner, with Mr C. Musgrave, called by the Bishops of Litchfeild and Bangor with a message from the Lord Sommers; who's earnest for my immediate Absolution of Dr Todd. I went forthwith to Doctors Commons: where neither Sir J. Cook nor Mr Tillot[145] could find any precedent for such a Case. At Mr King's, Lord Chief Justice Holt's, Sir Thomas Parker's and thence back to Sir J. Cook's, till much wearyed; but called on Lord Sommers at Northumberland House, where Duke of Devonshire and His Lordship very pressing for the Absolution.[146]

[Feb.] 28. *Saturday*. Morning, Sir James Montague attended with my Papers, Statutes, &c. and part of the Dean's Oath left for Mr King. Haveing provided an Absolution in Form for Dr Todd the Instrument was given at the House (by the Duke of Devonshire) to Sir Thomas Parker; who thereupon promised his Assistance to the Church-Bill.

Well! On it came, to a Second Reading, in the House of Commons; where, after a long Debate 'twas (on the Question) committed by 166 to 138.[147] Evening, I had the Congratulations of Dr Gibson, Dr Gee, Dr Sydale, &c. All agree, we must be more diligent against Thursday.[148]

[Feb.] 29. *Sunday*. The Prince's Birthday, Kept once in four years; but yet more remarkable for being the 5th Sunday in February, the like to which I shall hardly see again. In King Henry 7th's Chapple

[143] Probably Francis Montgomerie (b. aft. 1691–d. before 1729) of Giffen, MP for Scotland, 1707-8, Ayrshire, 1708-10; second son of Earl of Eglinton.

[144] This may be a reference to a pamphlet written by Atterbury putting forward Todd's case. It was reported to be printed on 27 Feb. (Bodl. MS Ballard 39, f. 33 and may be *The Case of Dr Todd, Prebendary of Carlisle, In relation to a Bill . . . now depending in Parliament*).

[145] Thomas Tillot, Deputy Actuary in the Court of Arches, and Clerk of the Convocation of Canterbury. Chamberlayne, *Present State 1707*, p. 555; ibid. *1708*, p. 552.

[146] With an eye, no doubt, to clearing the decks for the major Commons debate on the second reading expected on 28 Feb. Somers had changed his opinion on this point (cf. above, 10 Feb.). The concession certainly won votes: see the case of Sir Thomas Parker, below, 28 Feb.

[147] For the debate of 'several hours' (Luttrell, vi, 273) and the main spokesmen on either side, see *Vernon Corr.* iii, 357-8; *Addison Letters*, pp. 96-7: Addison to Manchester, 2 Mar. 1708. Addison observed that 'the managers on one side were Mr Harley, Sr. T. Hanmore [Hanmer], Mr Bromley, Mr Harcourt and St. John. On the other were Peter King, Sr. J. Jekyl, Sr. J. Montagu, Sr. T. Parker and Spencer Cowper'.

[148] Addison (*ubi supra*) explained that 'the season of the year drawing the lawyers off to their circuits [every one of the main Whig 'managers' on 28 Feb. was a lawyer], it is feared the superiority may not be kept up in the next debate'; while Vernon forecast, rightly, that the bill 'will still be endeavoured to be clogged' in committee (to Shrewsbury, 28 Feb., *loc. cit.*)

I ordained (5 priests and two Deacons) for the Bishop of Lincoln; who preached at Court.[149]

Dr Mandevil who dined with me, gave me the excuse made by our Dean for treating the said Bishop [of Lincoln] and others so barbarously,[150] *'Twas to inspirit a dull and dry Subject*. Evening, Sir James Montague came to me; and gave me a Account of the yesterday's Intemperate behaviour of Mr Harley, Mr Harcourt, and (especially) Mr Sharp, against the Cathedral-Bill.

Mar. 1. *Munday*. Morning, picking up the statutes of New Cathedrals at Lambeth, to be laid before the Commons. The Lords carried their Address, touching the Admiralty, to the Queen. News from Dunkirk.[151] Evening, Shareing the Members (for the Church-Bill) with Dr Gee, Dr Gibson, Dr Waugh, Mr Bradley and Mr Benson; at the *Dog*.[152]

[Mar.] 2. *Tuesday*. Morning, coached about to Sir Joseph Jekyll, Sir James Montague, Lord Sommers, Mr Martin, &c. solliciteing. My Lord of Canterbury sent in his 8 copies of Cathedral-Statutes by Mr Bradley; who, after they had been considered by Lord Sommers, Mr Sollicitor Montague and Mr Cowper,[153] delivered 'em to the Commons. Evening, after the Report against R. Harley,[154] at the *Crown* on Ludgate-Hill; correcting Bishop of Lincoln's Letter.[155]

[149] Wake records in his diary that he 'preached at St. James Chappell: The Queen not there, nor any One Bishop'. He had asked Nicolson on 26 Feb. to ordain for him. Lambeth Palace MS 1770, f. 58.

[150] i.e. in the Convocation Controversy.

[151] See Luttrell, vi, 273–4, 28 Feb., 2 Mar. Six thousand French infantry and thirty ships were preparing to sail with the Prince of Wales to Scotland. They left Dunkirk on 6 Mar. 1708, and Sir George Byng was already in position to intercept them. See Trevelyan, *Queen Anne*, ii, 341–2.

[152] Wake recorded that Nicolson visited him 'after dinner, and is full of preparing for his bill to be committed Thursday next in the House of Commons'. Lambeth Palace MS 1770, f. 58.

[153] Spencer Cowper (c.1670–1728), MP for Bere Alston, 1705–10, Truro, 1715–27, brother of the Lord Chancellor. Sedgwick, i, 590.

[154] This was the report of the Lords' select committee appointed to examine William Greg (see above, 7 Jan., n.). It was presented by the chairman, the Duke of Somerset, and took three hours to read (Luttrell, vi, 274); but it failed seriously to incriminate Harley. See *Addison Letters*, pp. 97–8: Addison to Manchester, 5 Mar. For the report *Parl. Hist.* vi, 670–724; *LJ* xviii, 516–42.

[155] Wake recorded on 3 Mar., 'In the morn[ing] the Bishop of Carlisle sent me some of his printed letters to disperse' (Lambeth Palace MS 1770, f. 58). This 'printed letter' may be the one listed by Kennett in his journal as *A Letter to a Member of the H[ouse] of Commons in Answer to the Reasons against the Church Bill* (BL Lansdowne MS 1024, f. 184[v]).

[Mar.] 3. *Wednesday*. Morning, Solliciteing Mr A[wnsham] Churchill, Lord Pawlet [Poulet], Mr Seton, Sir Thomas Burnet;[156] &c. all encouraging. Bishop of Lincoln's Letter dispersed.

House of Lords, Sir R. Strickland's Case[157] and Bill for Scotch Peers.[158] Dr Todd's petition to the Commons[159] (on the Riseing of the House) to be heard, tomorrow, by's Counsel. As false as his *Case*. The Dean and Chapter of Durham (saies Dr Smith) appear for the Bill. Evening, with my new *Case of the 12 Cathedrals*,[160] to Sir Joseph Jekyll and Sir James Montague.

[Mar.] 4. *Thursday*. Morning, Disperseing my printed *Remarks on the Statutes of 12 Cathedral-Churches*, to Mr Churchill, Mr Denton, &c.

A message from the Queen, to both Houses, acquainting them with the Embarking of the Pretended Prince of Wales with 15,000[161] French Forces at Dunkirk: Upon which they joyntly Addressed Her Majesty very Loyally.[162] This delayed the Committee on the Church-Bill to Tuesday next, after some Instructions proposed by Mr St John's and others, on behalf of Dr Todd's side of the Question, had been first over-ruled. Strength enough for the Bill!

Letters after a late Dinner at the *Dog* with Dr Bentley and Dr Potter, and the Vote of the Lords to concur with the Commons in their Address.

[Mar.] 5. *Friday*. Both Houses, at two, attended Her Majesty with their joynt Address; which was numerously attended: And 'twas observed that they came resolved to stand by Her.[163] At Supper, with Sister Rothery, in Salisbury-Court.

---

[156] Sir Thomas Burnett (d. 1714), 3rd Bt., MP for Scotland 1707–8; Commissioner for the Equivalent, 1707–8.

[157] No such case went before the Lords. Perhaps Nicolson confused the case with Sir Ralph Mibank's Estate Act, see *LJ* xviii, 493; HMC *Lords MSS* vii, 562–3.

[158] Representative Peers for Scotland Act, see HMC *Lords MSS* vii, 558–9. On 3 Mar. the bill was amended in the Committee of the Whole House, the Bishop of Salisbury in the chair.

[159] *CJ* xv, 586. The petition is printed in *Nicolson Epist. Corr.* ii, 377, and Nicolson's views on it are given in ibid., p. 378

[160] Probably the publication listed by Kennett as '*Remarks on the Statutes of the Cathedral Church of Henry VIII Foundation now laid before the Honourable House of Commons.* – to promote the Bill depending and to answer the Reasons urged against it.' BL Lansdowne MS 1024, f. 184ᵛ.

[161] But cf. below, 12 Mar.   [162] *CJ* xv, 590; *LJ* xviii, 496–7.

[163] The joint address of 5 Mar. included the undertaking that 'we, on our parts, are fully and unanimously resolved to stand by and assist your majesty with our lives and fortunes, in maintenance of your undoubted right and title to the crown of these realms . . .' (it also included a renewed commitment to 'No Peace without Spain', cf. above, sessional intro., p. 435). *LJ* xviii, 496–7.

[Mar.] 6. *Saturday*. Morning, Visit to Archbishop of Canterbury, in the Stone.[164] The Lords, after Report of the Queen's Answer[165] to the Address, an Appeal against Mr Gardiner of Derbyshire (for a *modus*) Reversed, on the Question, by 29 against 23 by the Court and the Northern Lords against 16 Bishops.[166] Bishop of St Asaph dyed last night.[167]

[Mar.] 7. *Sunday*. Morning, Dr Woodroff preached at St Margaret's on *Romans* 6, 1 and 2. *What shall we say*, &c. Less Action than 40 years agoe. Evening, I walked (with Mr B[enson]) to Kensington-Gravelpits, to see O. Dykes; and returned, on foot, by Knight's Bridge.

[Mar.] 8. *Munday*. Morning, Cases to Sir J. Swinton,[168] Sir J. Wentworth, &c. House of Lords heard the claim of Mr Cary, to the Barony of Hunsden,[169] argued, which adjourned to Thursday. Evening, with Mr Buddle; and his mosses.

[Mar.] 9. *Tuesday*. House of Commons in their Committee on the Church-Bill:[170] previous to which these two Motions were made and Questions thereon put, and both passed in the Negative.

   1. *That it be an Instruction to the Committee to receive a Clause for preserveing to the Crown, and the Queen and her Successors, the Right of Local Visitation of those Churches which were found by King Henry the 8th to which no Statutes have been granted since that time. Yeas*, 136. *Noes*, 179.[171]

   2. *That it be*, &c. *That they have power to receive a clause admitting*

---

[164] i.e. suffering from stone in the bladder.

[165] *LJ* xviii, 498.

[166] See HMC *Lords MSS* vii, 548.

[167] William Beveridge, a much-respected High Churchman who had refused a see after the Revolution, was already sixty-seven when he accepted St Asaph in 1704. He was succeeded by a Whig divine, William Fleetwood, later Bishop of Ely (see Appendix A), on 6 June 1708.

[168] Sir John Swinton (d. 1724), MP for Scotland, 1707–8; Commissioner for the Equivalent, 1707–8.

[169] For the case see HMC *Lords MSS* vii, 560–1. Carey won his case on 11 Mar. and he took his seat in the Lords on 22 Mar. 1708, *LJ* xviii, 547.

[170] Nicolson had written to William Seton, MP for Scotland, on 8 Mar.: 'As long as the Church Bill is depending in your House, so long (at least) you are to look for continued troubles from me.

'This second memorial renews my former request: that you will please to put our Northern Members in mind of the strength that will be formed against this Bill to-morrow. I would gladly hope, that a very great majority will always be ready to withstand such attempts, as nothing but a Dunkirk Squadron ought to countenance.' *Nicolson Epist. Corr.* ii, 378.

[171] Tellers for the yeas were St John and Sharp, and for the noes Lord William Powlet and Wortley. *CJ* xv, 598.

an Appeal from the Bishop's Local Visitation, as in Cases of Ordinary Jurisdiction. Yeas, 112. *Noes*, 162.[172]

Then Mr Wortley-Montague (for his Remarkable speech on Dean Atterbury's way of clearing himself of Oathes)[173] being called to the Chair, the Committee heard Dr Todd's Counsel; who, roveing from the Petition, were soon dismissed. Mr Speaker [Smith] resumeing the Chair, a few Amendments were made to the Bill (for Indemnity, &c.) by its Friends; who ordered 'em to be Reported on Thursday.

NB. The Supporters of the Bill were chiefly, Sir Joseph Jekyll, Sir James Montague, Sir John Holland, Sir R. Onslow, Mr Speaker Smith and Mr Lowndes. Its Opposers, Mr Harley, Mr St Johns, Sir Thomas Powis, Mr Bromley, and (spit-fire) J[ohn] Sharp. Rejoyseing, at Dinner, with Dr Kennet, Dr Gibson, Dr Waugh, and Mr B[enson]. Evening, Capt. Fleming, Dr Gee, &c.

[Mar.] 10. *Wednesday*. Morning, Thanks returned to Lord Somers, Hallifax, Sir R. Onslow &c. The Lords gave a First and Second Reading to a Bill for enforeceing (speedily) the Oath of Abjuration in Scotland;[174] and received the Report[175] concerning Mr Harley's Spyes. Evening, Returning thanks to Sir Joseph Jekyll, Mr Sollicitor Montague and Mr A. Churchill.

[Mar.] 11. *Thursday*. House of Lords heard farther Counsel for the Claimant of the Barony of Hunsden; and agreed his Title good. They prepared several Bills for the Queen; who came to them about Four and (haveing given the Royal Assent to Several, and Rejected that for Modelling the Militia in Scotland)[176] acquainted both Houses that the Pretender was on[177] the Suffolk-Coast, that Sir George Bing was near him, and 10 Squadrons on Board at Ostend ready to follow him. New Addresses Voted, for the farther Security of Her Majesty's person,[178] &c.

[172] The tellers in this vote were Aislabie and Caesar (yeas) and Pelham and Lowther (noes). Ibid.

[173] Edward Wortley Montagu (1678-1761), MP for Huntingdon, 1705-13, 1722-34, Westminster, 1715-22, Peterborough 1734-61, another leading Country Whig spokesman, had been a teller for the majority in the division on the second reading, 28 Feb. (*CJ* xv, 580). 'That part of yesterday's vote [on the Jacobite invasion attempt] that glances on the late Secretary [of State]', wrote Addison on 12 Mar., 'was put in at Mr. Wortly's motion, who likewise spoke incomparably well in the controversy about the Church statutes, for which reason they put him in the Chair.' *Addison Letters*, p. 101.

[174] Security of the Queen's Person Act, see HMC *Lords MSS* vii, 573. Clause 7 concerned the oath in Scotland.

[175] Of the Committee of Seven. See above, 9 Feb.

[176] So passes the last exercise of the royal prerogative of vetoing legislation. For the bill see HMC *Lords MSS* vii, 552-3.

[177] i.e. 'off'.   [178] *LJ* xviii, 506. See above, 5 Mar.

[Mar.] 12. *Friday*. Morning, At Lord Radnor's Committee.[179] Both Houses Reported their Respective Address, wherein *the Affronts put upon this Kingdome in sending a handful of 5000 men to Invade it*, was Resented with Indignation. The Evening, at Salisbury-Court with Mr B[enson] and Mr Johnson; eating a Barrel of Oysters from Mr Heywood of Colchester.

[Mar.] 13. *Saturday*. Morning, Visits at Lambeth. Both Houses (at two) waiting on the Queen, I went to dine (with Mr B[enson] and Mr Johnson) at the *Dog*. Evening, with Mr Seton. No news.

[Mar.] 14. *Sunday*. Morning, I preached at Lambeth, dined at Salisbury-Court, with Mr Benson; who, afternoon, preached at St Brides. Short Visits to Dr Gee, and from Mr Jenkins after Mine. Invasion, Amusement.

[Mar.] 15. *Munday*. The Lords voted an Address to Her Majesty (*nemine contradicente*) on the Debate of the House for the Execution of Gregg;[180] the Declareing Valière and Barrow [Barra] in the Interests of France,[181] and Betrayers of the Navy and Secrets of this Kingdome to its enemies, &c.

The Church-Bill delayed till Wednesday; upon a Treacherous Attempt of bringing in a Clause for Appeals from the Local Visitors by J. Sharp.[182] Evening, with Dr Waugh and Mr Benson, at the *Castle* in Pater-Noster Row.

[Mar.] 16. *Tuesday*. Morning, Assurances given me (from Duke of Bolton, Lords Sommers and Hallifax) that the Appeal-Clause should be over-ruled, if not withdrawn, tomorrow. After Dinner in Southampton-Street, Mrs Wenman's son (secretary to the Duke of

---

[179] This committee on the address to the Queen met at 10.00 a.m. at the Prince's Chamber. The address is printed in *LJ* xviii, 507–8, and that of the Commons in *CJ* xv, 608.

[180] Greg was executed on 28 Apr. 1708. The address to the Queen is printed in *LJ* xviii, 510–11.

[181] Alexander Clerk (*alias* Valière) and J. Barra were two smugglers employed for espionage by Harley. They had acted as double agents. See Burnet, *History*, v, 352–3, 356–7.

[182] Nicolson objected to this clause, which stated that 'any person aggrieved by the sentence of the Bishop [as local visitor] may have liberty to appeal, in such a manner as is allowed from the Bishop's Ordinary Jurisdiction', because it was 'intended for the utter overthrow of the Bill; and will be of no other use whatever: since the Bishops always visit by their *ordinary* power'. *Nicolson Epist. Corr.* ii, 378, note.

Newcastle)[183] brought us the Joyful news of Sir G. Bing's comeing up with the French Fleet.[184]

[Mar.] 17. *Wednesday*. Morning, After several Letters to the worthy members of North-Britain and Consults with Dr Gibson and Mr Sollicitor Montague, to the House; where News of the Fleets being Engaged, &c. Eight Bishops, at St James's with the Oxford-Address.[185] At four, congratulated (by C[apt]. Fleming and two Churchills) on the passing of the Church-Bill without the Rider.[186] Evening, with Dr Waugh and Brother Joseph, at A. Richmond's.[187]

[Mar.] 18. *Thursday*. Morning, Waiting on my Lord of Canterbury; who heartily thanked me for my Services to the Church, in carrying forward the Bill: *Which*, said, he *I would not have seen miscarryed for 500 l.*

In the House, the Address (against Harley) Reported;[188] and ordered to be presented by the whole House. A Writt of Errour against the City of London, on a Fine of 400 *l.* for Sherriff, argued; and the Judgement affirmed.[189] Letters.

[Mar.] 19. *Friday*. The Church-Bill brought up to the Lords; and the Amendments immediately read and agreed to. Clause for the covering the Cupola at St Paul's with Brittish Copper rejected, as were several Bills. Others prepared for the Royal Assent Tomorrow.

At Brother Joseph's with Dr Waugh and Thomas Pearson; the Latter from Dr Gibson; accosted by Dr Todd.

[Mar.] 20. *Saturday*. Her Majesty gave the Royal Assent to the Church-Bill[190] (with others) much to my comfort. At dinner with

---

[183] William Wenman (d. 1749) was one of the Duke's five righthand men (the others were Thomas Farr, Peter Walter, William Jessop, and Thomas Hewitt) in the business of running the largest private estates in Britain. O. R. F. Davies, 'The Dukes of Devonshire, Newcastle, and Rutland, 1688–1714' (Oxford, D Phil thesis 1972), pp. 149–55.

[184] Byng caught the French fleet in the Forth on 13 Mar. and forced it to flee. See Trevelyan, *Queen Anne*, ii, 344–5.

[185] 'An Address of the University of Oxford to the Queen against the pretended Prince, Attainted of High Treason, Educated in Romish Superstition, and Supported in this Attempt by a French Army', printed in *The London Gazette*, no. 4419, 15–18 Mar. 1707 [8].

[186] Sharp's clause, see above, 15 Mar.

[187] ?Andrew Richmond (b. 1667), youngest son of Christopher Richmond of Highland, by his second marriage to Magdalen, daughter of Andrew Hudleton of Hutton John, Cumberland. He had married and settled in London. W. Jackson, 'The Richmonds of Highland', *CW* original series ii (1874–5), table between p. 144 and p. 145; *CW* lxix (1969), 233.

[188] *LJ* xviii, 516.

[189] See HMC *Lords MSS* vii, 561.

[190] 6 Anne c. 75, printed in *Statutes of the Realm*, viii, 840. *LJ* xviii, 546.

Sir James Montague, in whose presence and Coll. Grahme's (as attested under their hands) Dr Todd declared, That *he would behave himself dutifully and respectively to the Bishop of Carlile, according as the Canons of the Church, the local Statutes of the Cathedral and the Laws of the Land do require; and with all Readyness do every thing that can be expected by a Bishop from a Dutiful Son.* And, in Return, the Bishop likewise declared, that *he would treat* Dr Todd *with all the paternal Affection that can be expected from a Bishop to one of the members of his Church; and that he will forget and forgive all that has been hitherto taken amiss.* Amen, Amen.

[Mar.] 21. *Sunday.* I preached for Dr Waugh, in the morning, at St Peter's, and, in the Afternoon, at St Bride's. In the way home, with Dr Lancaster; who very kind to my son and his Servitor,[191] Jackson. Dr Todd came in, whilst I was there, civilly.

[Mar.] 22. *Munday.* As the Lords were ending their Grand Committee on the Scotch Exchequer Bill,[192] I went to dine with Lord Thanet; where I met with Mr Tufton, the Heir presumptive,[193] and heard the (mistaken) news of the French landing in Wales. Dr Waugh, Mr J. Brougham, Mr Benson, my Brother and I, sup[p]ed late with Mr Johnson at Grey's-Inn.

[Mar.] 23. *Tuesday.* Mr B[enson] and I dined (by Appointment) with Coll. Grahme at Mr C. Musgrave's; where Mr Joseph owned his Design of offering his Service at Appleby,[194] without desireing any of my Assistance. He was exalted with Her Majesty's dark Answer to the Address of the Lords concerning Secretary Harley.[195] Letters.

[191] i.e. at Oxford. Joseph Nicolson, the Bishop's son, matriculated at Queen's College on 20 Mar. 1707 and gained his BA in 1709.

[192] Bill for establishing a Court of Exchequer in Scotland, see HMC *Lords MSS* vii, 573–90.

[193] Sackville Tufton (1688–1753), nephew and heir male of the 6th Earl of Thanet. He succeeded his uncle in 1729. Thanet's three sons had all died at birth. *GEC Peerage.*

[194] Joseph Musgrave's decision to stand at Appleby was something of a gesture of defiance, an attempt to assert his independence from the acting head of his family, his brother Christopher, who considered that Joseph 'ran too fast into the proposal of standing which was agreed on before I was consulted . . .'. Levens Hall MS D/M: Christopher Musgrave to James Grahme, 9 Sept. 1708. Joseph Musgrave, however, came bottom of the poll, with Nicolas Lechmere (backed by Lord Wharton) capturing a seat for the Whigs.

[195] The Queen answered, 'I am sorry that any who have been employed by those in My Service should have proved false to their Trust, and injurious to the Public. The Examples you lay before Me will, I do not doubt, be a sufficient Warning to keep all Matters of Importance as secret as may be; and to employ such only as there shall be good Grounds to believe will be faithfull.' *LJ* xviii, 548.

[Mar.] 24. *Wednesday*. Morning, I wrote over my Return of Liveings under 50 *l.* for the Barons of the Exchequer who refuse to take it without Oath. After a Tedious Attendance on Ordinary business in the House, and dineing the Bishop of Norwich on a Dish of Green-Fish,[196] visit attempted to S. Usher, but paid to C. Studholme. The year ended in a walk (by Moon-light) in St James's Park, till after Nine at night.

[Mar.] 25. *Thursday*. Morning, with the Archbishop of York, who received me very Kindly, desireing that our warmth in the House of Lords, &c. might be mutually forgotten. At Lieut. Generall Earl's[197] (with Mr C. Musgrave and Mr James Lowther) the groundless news of the Pretender's being taken: which too forwardly reported at Lambeth and in the House; where an Address[198] voted on the Arrears upon the Civil and Military Lists in the Reign of King William, &c.

At Dinner with me, Dr Gibson neither approves of my visit to my Lord of York nor of my Easyness to Dr Todd; but especially execrates all Reconciliation with the Dean [Atterbury].

NB. My Lord of Canterbury assures me that Dr Short, Sir Charles Scarborough[199] and Dr Windebank,[200] knew that the late King James's Queen could not bear a Live child; and that she miscarryed on Easter-Munday before the pretended birth of her Son on Trinity-Sunday following. Dr Harris'saies the same.

[Mar.] 26. *Friday*. Morning, Mr Benson and I walked to the Hospital at Chelsea, and returned by water. Dr Waugh at Dinner with me. After viewing the Repository at Gresham, Bedlam, &c. to my Brother's where met by Sister Rothery, whose Company home.

[Mar.] 27. *Saturday*. Morning, After my vain Attempt to wait on Lord Sommers, I was visitted by Mr Anderson[201] newly come from Scotland; as also by Mr Maddox, who brought me Mr Lhwyd's proposeal (for Celtic Lecture) and his own Specimen of the History of the Exchequer.[202]

---

[196] A fish allied to the cod, sometimes called Coal fish.

[197] Thomas Erle (?1650–1720), MP for Wareham, 1679–81, 1685–7, 1689–98, 1701–18, and Portsmouth, 1698–1701. He was Governor of Portsmouth, 1694–1712, 1714–18, C.-in-C. in Ireland 1702–5, Lieutenant-General of the Ordnance, 1705–12, 1714–18. He had just returned from Spain, having commanded the centre at the battle of Almanza in Apr. 1707. Sedgwick, ii, 12–13.   [198] *LJ* xviii, 552.

[199] Sir Charles Scarburgh (1616–94), physician to Charles II.

[200] John Windebanke (1618–1704), also physician to King Charles.

[201] James Anderson (1662–1728), genealogist and antiquary, who collected facsimiles of Scottish charters which he published under the title *Diplomata Scotiae* (1729).

[202] Published in 1711.

In the House, the Bill for prolonging the Time of our Returns of our Liveings under value,[203] &c. After I had dined late, Evening-Visitants were Mr Buddle the Mossman, and Mr C. Musgrave, not averse from comeing into Parliament.

[Mar.] 28. *Sunday*. Morning, I preached at the Savoy, and dined with Cousin R. Nicolson; whose Lodger, Dr Beeston,[204] good ingenious Company. Evening, Visitted by Mrs Roose, who wants the Queen's touch for Her Daughter;[205] and Mr Wenman, concerned to have his Brother[206] chosen from Eaton.

[Mar.] 29. *Munday*. Morning, Visitted first by Dr Todd; who freely dealt with as to his past and future behaviour. He was just gone, when Mr Dean Atterbury came in; and, washing his own hands, was for chargeing all former mistakes on the other 3 Prebendaries.[207]

At Lambeth Dr Gibson and I appointed a Visit to Mr Churchill to morrow in the Evening. From the House, on Messages from the Commons,[208] to dine at Mr C. Musgrave's; where Mr Crowther and I kindly treated. Both Sir Christopher and Mr Joseph abroad. Evening. Mr B[enson] and I treated by J. Relf at the *Dog*.

[Mar.] 30. *Tuesday*. Morning, Visitted by the Bishop of Bangor. Chief Business of the House the Cochineal Bill; now passed, tho' little different from one rejected this very Session.[209] Orders! Orders![210] After Dinner, Dr Gibson with me at the *Black Swan*; returning my Solemn Thanks to Mr A. Churchill. Evening-Visit from the Dean of Sarum [Younger]. Letters.

[Mar.] 31. *Wednesday*. Early at the House, on a Committee of Privileges upon a Complaint of the Lord Langdale, who committed,

[203] *LJ* xviii, 555.

[204] ?John Beeston (born c.1675), educated New College, Oxford, MA 1698, D Med 1708.

[205] Presumably a victim of scrofula.

[206] George Wenman (born c.1692), educated at Eton 1704–8, and at Merton College, Oxford, BA 1713, MA 1717; Rector of Kingsley, Staffordshire, 1717.

[207] Of Carlisle: Thomas Tullie, George Fleming, and John Atkinson.

[208] Concerning various bills which were brought up from the Commons. *LJ* xviii, 557–8.

[209] Bill for the importation of cochineal from any ports in Spain during the present war and six months after (HMC *Lords MSS* viii, 592). The bill was brought from the Commons on 25 Mar., there was a Committee of the Whole House on 29 Mar., and the bill received the royal assent on 1 Apr. 1708 (*LJ* xviii, 551, 553, 555, 566). The earlier bill brought from the Commons on 20 Feb. 1708, was rejected on 4 Mar. upon the petition of the Spanish merchants who wanted the Navigation Act enforced (HMC *Lords MSS* vii, 557, 562).

[210] The Lords dealt with a great volume of business this day, and twelve orders (an unusually high number) concerned with legislation and causes resulted (*LJ* xviii, 558–60).

as a suspected Papist, by the Deputy Lieutenants of the East-Rideing of Yorkshire.[211] The Lords (after a long Debate) voted this no Breach of Privilege; but, on the Contrary, directed the Duke of Newcastle[212] to let the Deputy Lieuts. know that their Lordships highly approved of what they had done. Bills read, &c.

After Dinner, with the Dean of Peterborough [Kennett]; who treated us with Hermitage-wine,[213] from his brother in Italy.[214] Thence (by my Brother's) to Coll. George Fletcher's Funeral at St Martin's;[215] where the Coffins piled up in the Chancel (at 8 *l.* to the Vicar, 18 *s.* to the Clerk, &c) in an extraordinary manner. The Coll. buryed as a Batchelour; born by Lord Berkley, Mr C. Musgrave, Mr James Lowther, &c. in white Scarves.

Apr. 1. *Thursday.* Morning, With Dr Waugh and Mr Benson at Dr Woodward's, who offended at the Church-Divines, less grateful to him (in their Sermons) than the Dissenters. In the House, Bills (public and private) hurryed on till after Four; when the Queen came, and (haveing given the Royal Assent) made a Gracious Speech,[216] wherein she thanked both Houses for their Respective Services, pressed the Execution of the Laws against Papists and Non-Jurors, &c. Which ended, Lord Chancellor [Cowper] Prorogued the Parliament to the 13th Instant.

[Apr.] 2. *Good Friday.* Morning, I preached and Administered the Sacrament, for Dr Lancaster; and, haveing dined on Red Herring[217] at home, spent the Evening with Sister Rothery. NB. The Shod-Egg.[218]

[Apr.] 3. *Saturday.* Morning, With Mr Madox, in bed, giveing him Account of Subscribeing Lords, and Subscribeing (for two of his Books, one in larger and the other in Common paper) for my self:

[211] Marmaduke (d. 1718), 3rd Baron Langdale of Holme since 1703, was a Roman Catholic who appears never to have qualified himself to take his seat in the Lords. On 17 Mar. 1708 he was arrested and imprisoned in Beverley, being suspected of an intention to join the attempted invasion of Scotland by the Pretender. He appealed in vain to the Lords to protect him from this breach of privilege, for in their view he was not a member of the House. *LJ* xviii, 560-1; HMC *Lords MSS* vii, 594; Luttrell, vi, 285-6.

[212] Lord-Lieutenant of the East Riding.

[213] A French wine produced near Valence, so called from a nearby ruin supposed to have been a hermit's cell.

[214] Basil Kennett (1674-1715), author and younger brother of White Kennett. From 1706 to 1713 he was Chaplain to the British factory at Leghorn.

[215] The member for Cumberland was one of four MPs to die in the last three weeks of the session. The others were Edward Strode, Charles Goring and Thomas Bulkeley. Luttrell, vi, 285.

[216] *LJ* xviii, 567-8.   [217] Smoked herring.   [218] Scrambled egg.

Thence to Mr Sollicitor[-General] Mountague, with my Thanks and to receive his commands for Carlile, where again he offers his Service,[219] and will accept my help and another Char-pye.[220]

Thence to Lambeth; where (at parting) my Lord of Canterbury assured me that in Secretary Harley's Disbursements of money for Secret Service there was frequent Repititions of Hire (3s 4d) to a Messenger sent to Dr Atterbury at Chelsea. After Dinner, with the Vice-Chancellor [Lancaster] (promiseing to preach for him again tomorrow) and thence to Salisbury-Court; whence up to the Cupola of St Paul's. Evening, Mr Brown[e] Willis; still zealous in beautifying Blecheley-Church.[221]

[Apr.] 4. *Easter-Day*. Morning, I preached and administered the Sacrement for Dr Lancaster; who very hearty in serveing E. Llwyd. At Dinner, with Sister Rothery, in Salisbury-Court. Evening, Visits to Mr C. Musgrave and Archbishop of York; who very frank in Assurances of a steady Friendship. At home, I found Mrs Wenman waiting for me; with her daughter and youngest son. Leave of our own Family, Mr Jenkins. &c.

[Apr.] 5. *Munday*. After Accounts adjusted, we took Coach (at nine) in Salisbury-Court, my brother being detained at home by Mr W. Johnson's Indisposition . . .[222]

---

[219] As prospective member of parliament.

[220] Potted char, the char being a small trout-like fish.

[221] Browne Willis (1682–1760), antiquary and MP for Buckingham, 1705–8, spent £800 between 1704 and 1707 on Bletchley Church in memory of his parents who were buried there in 1699 and 1700.

[222] Nicolson travelled north via St Albans, Dunstable, Woburn, Stony Stratford, and Northampton, where he visited Mr Lee's 'fine house at Brixworth'. He proceeded via Leicester, Nottingham, Doncaster, Wetherby, Boroughbridge, and Appleby, reaching Rose on 14 Apr. 1708.

Session 6

5 February 1709–29 April 1709

Nicolson's ten months in his diocese between April 1708 and January 1709 were fairly quiet ones. The month after he arrived back at Rose saw the general election, which produced the first and only clear majority for the Whigs in Anne's reign. There is little in Nicolson's printed diary about the preparations for the elections in the north-west. He makes no mention of his refusal to support the Tory, James Grahme, in Westmorland county,[1] but does record the possibility on 15 April of Recorder Richard Aglionby (with Christopher Musgrave's support) standing for Carlisle, provided Lord Carlisle, Sir James Montagu, and Joseph Reed (powerful Whig clerk of the fraternity of butchers)[2] consented. Nicolson refused to enter into the plan.[3] He no longer supported the Musgraves in local politics and Christopher Musgrave wrote of him in May 1708: 'he pretends to put me up at Carlisle, which I take to be only a bamboozle, and end in nothing.'[4] Musgrave was right, for Nicolson had previously committed himself to Sir James Montagu, the Solicitor-General, on 3 April 1708. Musgrave did not stand, and at the election on 20 May Montagu and Thomas Stanwix (both Whigs) were returned and Eliakim Studholme, an army officer who had been invited to stand as Stanwix was absent serving in Portugal, was defeated.[5] Montagu's promotion to the post of Attorney-General on 22 October 1708 was followed by his peaceful re-election at Carlisle in December.

The triumph of the Whigs at the polls in May led at last to the long-delayed breakthrough of the Junto in government, although only after more months of frustrating resistance from the Queen. On 25 November Lord Somers was appointed Lord President of the Council and on 4 December the Earl of Wharton became Lord Lieutenant of Ireland. The death of Prince George of Denmark, the Queen's husband, on 28 October (Nicolson received the news on 1 November) left the post of Lord High Admiral vacant. It was filled

---

[1] The Bishop explained his decision to Christopher Musgrave on the personal ground of Grahme's refusal to support him over the Cathedrals Bill in the Commons (Levens Hall MS D/M: Musgrave to Grahme, 15 and 27 May 1708).

[2] See below, 23 Jan. 1712.   [3] *CW* iv(1904), 30–1.

[4] Levens Hall MS D/M: Musgrave to Grahme, 15 May 1708. As late as Nov. 1707 Nicolson had regarded Musgrave as his favourite candidate for Carlisle. *CW* iv (1904), 13–14.

[5] From information supplied by Eveline Cruickshanks on behalf of the History of Parliament Trust.

not by a Whig but by Nicolson's friend Lord Pembroke who had previously held the lord presidency and the Irish viceroyalty simultaneously.

The new parliament began sitting on 16 November 1708, and on the following day, at dinner, Nicolson received the good wishes of his friends for his London journey.[6] However, he was not prepared to leave his diocese while the question of the local cathedral statutes was undecided: the Cathedrals Act had not, as he had expected, 'secured Peace to me (in my Cathedral Church) for the Remainder of my Days'. In an effort to clear the way for the future Nicolson had demanded an attested copy of the local statutes. The comparing of the various transcripts was left until the last minute, however, and this enabled the indomitable Dr Todd—who, in Nicolson's words, treated the Cathedrals Act 'with a great deal of contempt, and some coarse epithets'—to rock the boat again with a claim that one copy gave the Archbishop of York joint visitorial powers over the Chapter with the Bishop. Todd failed to substantiate his claim at a Chapter meeting on 23 November, and Nicolson hoped that this would end all his disputes with Dean Atterbury, though he could not 'help expecting a fresh Assault very speedily'.[7] Atterbury, when he met the Bishop in London, confined himself to asserting that the 'Local Statutes [were] not worth *one Farthing*', while Todd vented his spleen in a 'villanous Letter' to Sir James Montagu (below, 19 February, 7 March).

By early December, the statutes being largely settled, Nicolson had decided to postpone his journey south until after Christmas and he warned Wake that even then he might not be able to stay until the end of the session. 'I reckon', he added 'you will have such an entire Harmony in the House, that such an insignificant Creature as I am may well be overlooked.'[8]

The winter of 1708–9 proved exceptionally severe[9] and in mid-January Nicolson heard the startling news that Joseph Relf had taken thirty days to travel from London to Cockermouth. Nevertheless, on 26 January Nicolson set out from Rose on horseback. He proceeded in deep snow via Appleby, Bowes, and Richmond to

[6] *CW* iv (1904), 42.

[7] Todd's detailed objections are to be found in BL Add. MS 6116, ff. 9–10: N. to Wake, 9 Oct. 1708; see also Gloucestershire RO Lloyd Baker MS Box 4, V23: N. to Sharp, 18 Oct. 1708; BL Lansdowne MS 1038, f. 30: N. to Kennett, 9 Oct. 1708; and, for the denouement in late Nov. *CW* iv (1904), 43; BL Add. MS 6116, ff. 10–11: N. to Wake, 4 Dec. 1708. An attested copy, in Nicolson's hand, of the local statutes is to be found in Lloyd Baker MS Box 4, L9.

[8] BL Add. MS 6116, ff. 10–11: N. to Wake, 4 Dec. 1708.

[9] See below, 9 Feb. The Thames froze over in early Jan. 1709. See Trevelyan, *Queen Anne*, ii, 418–19.

Boroughbridge and Bolton Percy, where he stayed with Archdeacon Pearson. Unable to meet a London coach in Yorkshire, he continued south on horseback down the Great North Road to Ware, and having dutifully viewed the Great Bed, completed his journey by coach on 5 February.[10]

With the Whigs now close to the high tide of their fortunes, the 1708-9 session was, as the Bishop had anticipated, one of the easiest in Anne's reign, the Tories putting up no serious resistance in either House. Yet Anglo-Scottish friction over the Treason Bill meant that the session was not, after all, one of 'entire Harmony'. Nicolson, with his considerable Scottish acquaintance, found himself closely involved with this controversial Whig bill, as he was with two other pieces of public legislation which passed during this session, and with James Lowther's private bill for Whitehaven harbour.[11]

Early in 1709 the Whigs began their campaign to facilitate by law the naturalisation of foreign Protestants driven from their own countries by religious persecution. This long-cherished aim of their party[12] aroused high feelings, those in favour arguing that the influx of people would advance the wealth and strength of the nation, and that in particular trade would benefit, as it had from the Huguenot immigration of the 1680s. The Tory opponents of the legislation objected, partly on economic grounds but mainly on religious ones: the large number of aliens who would take advantage of the Act would flood the market with cheap labour causing a reduction in wages, and as non-Anglicans would prove a danger to the Church. It was with this last point that Nicolson was particularly concerned. Having been shepherded through the Commons by Edward Wortley Montagu,[13] the bill was first read in the Lords on 11 March and committed on 15 March. It obviously gave rise to considerable concern among some of the bishops and on 14 March an unusual debate between them over the bill took place in the lobby of the House. On 15 March, before the committee-stage, legal counsel for the City of London were heard in support of a petition against the bill on the grounds that by it they would lose the ancient duties which were levied on the goods of all alien merchants, and that part of this revenue was granted for the benefit of orphans. It was found upon examination that these duties had lately yielded no more than £20 a year, most of the foreign merchants being already naturalised, and the petition was rejected. In the Committee of the Whole House a group of bishops, led by Dawes of Chester (who, as Burnet said, 'spoke as zealously against' the bill 'as I spoke copiously for it') and

[10] *CW* iv (1904), 44; Ware transcripts, xxiv, 92-4. [11] See below 4 Mar., n.
[12] Burnet, *History*, v, 410. [13] *Parl. Hist.* vi, 780-3.

by Nicolson, who was similarly concerned by the bill's implications for the Church, tried to amend the bill by inserting *Parochial church* instead of *some Protestant Reformed Congregation*. This would have meant that foreigners seeking naturalisation could only qualify by taking the Anglican sacrament. The amendment was rejected by forty-five to fifteen (ten of the latter being bishops) but it is instructive to find Nicolson (along with three other moderate Whig bishops)[14] siding here with the High Church prelates against the bulk of the Whig bishops. He was following consistently his principle of voting with the High Church party on most issues where he believed the security of the Church to be *genuinely* at stake, and he took the defeat hard, dining with Edmund Gibson that evening, he tells us, 'in the chagrin' (below, 15 March). The bill finally passed without amendment, only the Tory Earl of Abingdon protesting, and it received the royal assent on 23 March 1709.[15]

Nicolson was also personally to intervene in the progress of another bill this session. The Stamp Bill, which originated in the Commons, was designed to prevent frauds in the imposition of the stamp duties on vellum, parchment and paper, and one of its provisions was that every person who should perform or assist in performing any service, form or ceremony of marriage without banns or licence should forfeit £100. The Quakers had petitioned the Commons against the clause, asking for the addition of the words *except the marriages of the people called quakers their usual certificates being stamped with a five shilling stamp*. The Commons agreed that the penalty on clandestine marriage should not extend to the Quakers, and the clause was also confirmed by the Lords despite the opposition of all the bishops in the House (below, 6 April). However, the Bishop of Carlisle, who had just been under attack for his attitude to Quaker marriages (below, 30 March), persuaded the House to adopt an amendment adding the words *or pretended marriages* after the word *marriages*. The bill passed its third reading on 8 April and was returned to the Commons. The Quakers, dissatisfied with Nicolson's amendment, petitioned the Commons and the consequent delay led to the bill being lost by the prorogation of parliament on 21 April 1709.[16]

Constitutionally, the session's most important piece of legislation

[14] Evans of Bangor, Tyler of Llandaff, and William Wake.

[15] HMC *Lords MSS* viii, 285–6; *LJ* xviii, 668; Bodl. MS Ashmolean 1816, f. 554: N. to Lhwyd, 15 Mar. 1709. For the background to the Act see H. T. Dickinson, 'The poor Palatines and the parties', *EHR* lxxxii (1967), 464–85; 'The Tory party's attitude to foreigners: a note on party principle in the age of Anne', *BIHR* xl (1967), 153–65.

[16] *LJ* xviii, 687, 692, 699, 701; *CJ* xvi, 193, 198, 201, 205, 209; BL Lansdowne MS 1024, f. 193.

was the inaptly titled 'Union of the Two Kingdoms Improvement (Treason) Act'. The bill was a direct result of the abortive invasion attempt by the Pretender in March 1708, which was the subject of inquiry by the House of Lords on 25 February and 1 March 1709. The failure, largely on technical grounds, to convict those arrested on suspicion during the invasion scare in Scotland, particularly the Jacobite gentlemen of Stirlingshire,[17] had aroused alarm in Whig government circles. It was decided, therefore, that for the safety of the United Kingdom it was advisable that the Scottish law and procedure in treason trials should be brought into line with those of England. The Queen's Speech had recommended legislation to this end, but the opposition of Scottish MPs meant that the bill initiated in the Commons was dropped in committee.[18] After the second debate in the Lords on the attempted invasion, the judges were ordered to prepare a bill to provide that 'there be the same law as now in England throughout the United Kingdom in respect of high treason'.[19] But it was already clear that all the Scottish representatives in the Lords, as in the Commons, would oppose the bill as an infringement of Article 18 of the Union.[20]

Introduced into the Lords on 11 March 1709, the bill was read a second time and committed to the Committee of the Whole House on 16 March with one of its chief opponents, Bishop Burnet (a Scot), in the chair. Seven further meetings of the Committee in which the bill was debated and amended took place from 18 to 26 March. At the second of these Lord Stamford replaced the 'blundering' Burnet as chairman for the rest of the Committee's meetings.[21] When the bill passed its third reading on 28 March Nicolson, along with all the other bishops, except Burnet, opposed a second attempt to amend the bill by Lord Guilford (giving the accused five days' notice of the witnesses which were to be produced at the trial). As a consequence, he stood in bad odour with the Scottish peers (below, 29 March). Nicolson had by this time, however, along with Lord Halifax, come to regret the existence of the bill (below, 2 April).[22] His continuing preoccupation with it carried him several times into the Commons' gallery to follow its progress through the Lower House, where it was piloted by Wharton's client, Nicholas Lechmere, now member for

---

[17] See Trevelyan, *Queen Anne*, ii, 392–3.

[18] *LJ* xviii, 6; Burnet, *History*, v, 403.

[19] *LJ* xviii, 651.

[20] For the legal grounds for the opposition see Burnet, *History*, v, 403–7.

[21] For debates on the bill see *Parl. Hist.* vi, 794–9; Burnet, *History*, v, 403–9; HMC *Lords MSS* viii, 286–8.

[22] Cf. Baillie of Jerviswood's comments, SRO Montrose MS GD220/5/203: Baillie to Montrose, 9 Apr. 1709.

the Westmorland borough of Appleby.[23] The Commons added two new conciliatory clauses,[24] and it passed its third reading on 9 April 1709, 'for tho the Scots had been against the Bill as sent down they were obliged to go in to it as amended or have lost their [Whig] friends'.[25]

The bill returned to the Lords and on 14 April the Commons' amendments were debated:

> My Lord Halifax spoke at large against the Amendments of the Commons, as unseasonable, after one Descent and under the apprehensions of another,[26] and, in conclusion, moved that the Amendments might not take place till after the death of the Pretender, and offered a Clause of two lines to that effect.[27] My Lord Se[a]field said, he did not think that the life of the Pretender was to be regarded longer than the present War should last, and therefore moved that the Amendment of the Commons should take place upon the Peace with France.[28] After many Speeches on both sides, it was carried for my Lord Halifax's Proposition; upon the Article of not forfeiting, by 4[7] to 27; and upon the second Article concerning the Indictment and names of Witnesses to be delivered 10 days before, by 42 to 34; some of the Lords who were against the first amendment of the Commons reck[on]ing the other a just and equitable relief to the Innocent, without any damage or danger to the Crown. This is Substance of what passed: the particulars will, noe doubt, be transmitted to your Lordship, by some of your own Brethren of your Bench; who in the first division, were unanimous, the Bishop of Roch[este]r [Sprat] not excepted; and also in the 2[nd] except only the Bishop of Sarum [Burnet]. I think, eleven were present.[29]

The Lords' amendment was consented to by the Commons after they had, in turn, altered the time when the clauses would come into effect to three years after the House of Hanover has succeeded to the

[23] *Lockhart Papers*, i, 300.

[24] (a) Giving a prisoner 10 days' notice of the witnesses to be called at his trial; (b) providing that no estate be forfeit upon a judgment of high treason. See Burnet, *History*, v, 407–8; *CJ* xvi, 193.

[25] SRO GD220/5/203: Baillie to Montrose, 9 Apr. 1709. Government and party pressure carried it against Scottish opposition, see *Wentworth Papers*, p. 83.

[26] For the fear of another invasion in 1709 see Luttrell, vi, 426–7.

[27] Halifax was seconded by Townshend (NLS Yester MS 7021, f. 171: Yester to Tweeddale, 14 Apr. 1709).

[28] There is some evidence that here Seafield contravened an agreement between the Scottish peers and Halifax. He is described as speaking 'Backward and forward' (ibid.).

[29] Christ Church Wake MS 17, f. 204: Gibson to Wake, 14 Apr. 1709. See also BL Add. MS 6116, f. 11: N. to Wake, 14 Apr. 1709; Burnet, *History*, v, 408; and below, 14 Apr.

throne.[30] This final Commons' amendment was accepted by the Lords on 19 April.[31] The bill received the royal assent on 21 April, the last day of this parliamentary session.

It is interesting to compare the acquiescent attitude to the harsh English treason laws of the bishops' bench in 1709 with that of their predecessors to the passage of the Trial of Treason Act in William III's reign. Politically, however, the significance of the 1709 Treason Act lay in the overriding of the unanimous Scottish opposition by the Whig-dominated Westminster parliament.[32] This created the precedent exploited by the Tories to bring in their Toleration and Patronage Acts in 1712. The method by which all these acts were brought in and passed placed a great strain on the Union.

[Feb.] 5. *Saturday* . . . From Ware, the Horses sent back; and my fellow-Traveller[33] and I went by Coach to London; whence, after Dinner in Salisbury-Court, to my last year's Lodgeings in the Old Palace Yard. Dr Gee my first Visitant.

[Feb.] 6. *Sunday*. Morning, First Visit to Archbishop of York [Sharp], who kind and pleasant on the Juncto and Flying Squadron;[34] Mr C. Musgrave not within, and Sir C[hristopher] in bed. Dined at my Brother's where M. Rothery and A. Spooner.[35] Evening with Lord Archbishop of Canterbury [Tenison] and Dr G[ibson] at Lambeth; where the History of Lord Wharton's brisk Reply on

[30] *CJ* xvi, 205; Burnet, *History*, v, 408. The date which the rest of the bill came into effect was 1 July 1709.

[31] Nicolson says there was 'faint opposition'; but Burnet writes of 'great opposition' and claims the amendment was carried in the Lords by a small majority (*History*, v, 408-9).

[32] Trevelyan, *Queen Anne*, ii, 273, 280.

[33] 'Mr Knight, Lord and patron of Warksop [Worksop (Notts.)]'. Diary, 2 Feb. 1709: Ware transcripts, xxiv, 93.

[34] The Squadrone, or *Squadrone Volante*, was a Scottish political party, formed in 1704. Its chief members among the peers were Roxburghe, Montrose, Rothes, Marchmont, Tweeddale, Haddington, and Sutherland, though only the first three sat among 'the sixteen' in the parliament of 1708-10. It was strong in the Commons after the Union, accounting for at least eleven members in 1707-8 and eight or nine between 1708 and 1710. Its parliamentary alliance with the Junto, originally a marriage of tactical convenience in the first session after the Union, but cemented by their co-operation in the 1708 general election, was put under strain from Jan. to Mar. by the Junto's determination to change the Scottish treason law. This had first been displayed in the Commons on 28 Jan. 1709, just over a week before Nicolson's arrival in London. *CJ* xvi, 74; Holmes, *British Politics*, pp. 242-4; P. W. J. Riley, *English Ministers and Scotland 1707-27* (1964), pp. 119-20.

[35] Probably a relation of the Revd. Nathaniel Spooner, the Bishop's late brother-in-law.

Lord Chancellor [Cowper][36] and condoleing on the death of my God son.[37]

[Feb.] 7. *Munday*. Morning, Visitants, Mrs Donnel (for Anabaptism) and her son Mr Robinson,[38] Mr Martin, Mr Hutchinson the miner, Mr Richardson, Lord Bishop of Chester, not marryed,[39] Dr Fall,[40] troubled at the usage of his Duke. Dined at Lambeth; with Bishop of Lichfield [Hough], Dean of Peterborough [Kennett], Dr Bentley, Dr Mandevil, &c. after haveing taken the Oaths in the House. Evening, with the Bishop of Lincoln [Wake].

[Feb.] 8. *Tuesday*. Morning, Visits paid to Lord President Sommers,[41] Lord Wharton, &c. with the two Archbishops, Bishop of Ely [Moore] and Norwich [Trimnell] &c. At Whitehal where my Arrears of Tenths cleared. Thence to the House;[42] where I read Prayers, and was friendly treated by Lord Chancellor. Dined at Mr Chamberlayne's; with Sir James Dalrymple, a street Presbyterian, Mr Mackenzy a Church-Clerk of the Session,[43] and (my friend) Mr James Anderson, to whom I communicated a Coin of David I. Letters.

[36] Although the Junto had firmly supported Cowper's appointment as Lord Keeper in 1705 and subsequent promotion, the latter remained, for the next four years at least, a somewhat unpredictable ally. He had, for example, gone his independent way on a number of occasions in the session of 1707–8, when he believed Wharton, Somers, and their friends to be putting power politics before principles. See, e.g., *Addison Letters*, p. 90 for his clash with Somers over the Scottish Privy Council Bill. In general, Holmes, *British Politics*, p. 242.

[37] This is the first reference in the diary to the death of his godson. He had at least five godsons: Charles Nicolson (see above, 13 Nov. 1705), H. Fisher (see Diary, 10 Dec. 1708: Ware transcripts, xxiv, 82), William Robinson (*CW* iii (1903), 8), W. Richardson and a son of a Mr Proctor of Bromfield, of whom the last two were alive in May and Aug. 1709, respectively (*CW* xxxv (1935), 107).

[38] Thomas Robinson (d. 1719), Rector of Ousby, Cumberland, 1672–1719, and naturalist, who published *The Anatomy of the Earth* (1694), *New Observations of the Natural History of this World of Matter and this World of Life* (1696), which defended the Mosaic system of Creation, in opposition to such controversial works as Thomas Burnet's *The Sacred Theory of the Earth*, and was dedicated to Nicolson, and *An Essay Towards a Natural History of Cumberland and Westmorland* (1709). He had invested in and had been concerned in the management of a colliery at Bolton in Cumberland belonging to the Duke of Somerset, but his literary and mining ventures were not prosperous and he fell into debt. After a period of refuge in London, 1708–9, and a spell as a naval chaplain, 1709–10, he returned in 1711 to Cumberland where he encouraged village football. J. Greenop, ' "The Anatomy of the Earth", by Thomas Robinson, Rector of Ousby in Cumberland, 1694 — with a Note on the Author', *CW* v (1905), 243–8; see also *CW* iii (1903), 6; iv (1904), 42, 44–5.   [39] Sir William Dawes's wife had died in 1705.

[40] James Fall (*c*.1647–1711), Precentor of York, 1691–1711, and Archdeacon of Cleveland, 1700–11.

[41] See above, sessional intro., p. 469 for Somers' appointment.

[42] Thoresby 'met with my long expected friend the Bishop of Carlisle, in the House of Lords, where we discoursed till the House being full, prayers and business began'. *Diary*, ii, 38.

[43] ?John Mackenzie, a Clerk of the Session. Chamberlayne, *Present State 1708*, p. 732.

[Feb.] 9. *Wednesday*. Morning, Visitted by Mr H. Watkinson and his Niece Pearson, Mr Al[len?] Chambers,[44] &c. and visitting Lord Hallifax, who wondrous sweet. In the House, a long cause on Partnership;[45] Decree affirmed. Dinner at home. Evening, A visit to Mr Thomas Benson (at the *White Horse Inn* in Fleetstreet) laid up [w]ith Gowt. Floods in the North. Snow here.[46]

[Feb.] 10. *Thursday*. Morning, To Mr Richard Thomlinson in Lombard-street, to pay for Swedish Books; and thence (by the Admiralty-office with Mr Robinson) to the House; where no great Business. Dined at Mr C. Musgrave's, with Sir Christopher, Mr George and Mr Crowther.

[Feb.] 11. *Friday*. Morning, Mr Thoresby early with his Album; like Noah's Ark.[47] With him, Sir James Dalrymple, Mr Mackenzy, Mr Anderson and Mr Semple, to the Cotton-Library; where Mr Wanley shewed us the Rarities of Origen's Genesis,[48] MSS Charters, 2 Marie's Letter to Bothwell &c. At the House, onely private Acts. Lord Sunderland obligeing.

P.m. Mr James Lowther; jealous of the Court and Bank.[49] Evening, at my Brother's; whence A. Spooner carryed home.

[Feb.] 12. *Saturday*. Morning, Visits paid to Coll. Grahme, Dr Fall and the Bishops of Bangor [Evans] and Norwich. Dined with Dr Fall, at the Archbishop of York's; and returning, I waited on the Bishop of Ely. Evening, Lord Lonsdale (with Mr Liniere) gave me a visit, to my shame, before I had waited on Him.

[Feb.] 13. *Sunday*. Morning, Mr Swinfin preached at Whitehall on the reasonableness of *dilatory Judgement* in God. Very well.

[44] Allen Chambre, Recorder of Kendal, 1695–9, and Westmorland Tax Commissioner, 1694–9, 1705–14.

[45] The case of *Morgan v. Digby*, partners in the manufacture of flint glass. See HMC *Lords MSS* viii, 8.

[46] This followed three days of extreme frost in London. Luttrell, vi, 405, 407, 409–10; Thoresby, *Diary*, ii, 40–1.

[47] Thoresby was with Nicolson from 8.00 to 10.00 a.m. and noted that 'the Bishop, Sir James, and Mr Anderson . . . writ in my album, as also Mr Mackenzy'. *Diary*, ii, 40. This 'travelling album' does not appear to have survived. See *Letters addressed to Ralph Thoresby*, ed. W. T. Lancaster (Leeds, 1912), p. 55 n. A similar album, covering 1696 to 1707, contains signatures and Latin tags of the visitors to Thoresby's museum. Nicolson wrote his name and 'Non Nobis, Sed Deo et Patriae' on 4 Nov. 1701. Yorks. Archaeological Society MS 17, p. 24.

[48] 'Homiliae Origenis super vetus testamentum', originally from the library of Thomas Barlow, Bishop of Lincoln, 1672. *Catalogue of MSS in the Cotton Library* (1802), p. 614. Cf. Thoresby, *Diary*, ii, 40.

[49] For Lowther's fiercely independent 'Country' Whiggery, see Holmes, *British Politics*, pp. 125–6, 127, 223.

P.m. Visits to Mr Vice Chancellor Lancaster, much pleased with my Son and Nephew; and to Sister Rothery, attended by Mr Furman[50] and two Nieces. Mr C. Musgrave and the Dean of Wells [Grahme], in my absence.

[Feb.] 14. *Munday*. Morning, After Mr Robinson (full of his Book[51] and Dirt) visitted by Mr Henley, Mrs Wenman, Mr Wilson, Dr Smith and (the Antiquary) his namesake,[52] Mr Francis Montgomery, well-wisher to the Marquess of Lothian.[53] From the House to dinner with M. Hutchinson. P.m. with him and T[reason] Bill.

[Feb.] 15. *Tuesday*. Morning, Mr Lindsey,[54] Mr J. Browham [Brougham?], Mr Forster. Dined Mr A. Chambre, from the House. P.m. Cousins J. Relf and his brother[-in-law] Boswell [Bosworth].

[Feb.] 16. *Wednesday*. Morning, Visitted by Mr Vice-Chancellor Lancaster and Dr Gibson. The former brought me the Oxford-verses; and the latter accompanyed me (on foot) to Sir J. Dalrymple's, Lord Lonsdale, Mr Attorny Generall [Montagu] and 6 cl[erks] office.[55] We dined together at the *Dog*. Dr Waugh, all the evening, for my Son's comeing. NB. Lord Wharton's two Simple men. Lacy's Message.

[Feb.] 17. *Thursday*. Morning, Eleven Temporal Lords (whereof nine North Brittains,[56] and Seven Green Ribbands)[57] accompanyed the Lord Chancellor and the Bishops[58] to the Abbey-Church; where

---

[50] Possibly a servant of Lord Lonsdale. He was also a naturalist. *CW* iv (1904), 9.

[51] See above, n. 38.

[52] John Smith, Treasurer of Durham and his kinsman Robert Smith (1682–1760), of Morton House, Durham, antiquary and student of northern languages. The latter was the author of 'Observations upon the Picts Wall' (1708–9), and judged by Nicolson to be 'an extraordinary person' (Thoresby, *Letters* ii, 144: N. to Thoresby, 12 Mar. 1709).

[53] Lothian had recently lost his place as a Scottish representative peer on petition. See HMC *Lords MSS* viii, 2–7; *LJ* xviii, 626. For the background to the election and disqualification of Lothian and three other peers see Riley, *English Ministers and Scotland*, pp. 103–15; C. Jones, 'Godolphin, the Whig Junto and the Scots: a new Lords' division list from 1709', *SHR* lviii (1979), 158–74.

[54] Possibly the Cumberland attorney, who had been to school with one of Nicolson's sons. *CW* iv (1904), 65.

[55] Part of the Court of Chancery.

[56] Scottish representative peers. The *Journal* lists only nine peers as attending the House before they adjourned to the Abbey, and of these only seven Scottish peers are listed. *LJ* xviii, 638.

[57] Holders of the order of the Thistle. Of the seven Scottish peers listed in the *Journal*, Hamilton, Annandale, Mar, Orkney, Loudoun, and Seafield held the order. The other peer listed was Glasgow.

[58] Peterborough, Exeter, Chester, Norwich, and Carlisle.

an excellent Thanks-giveing Sermon preached by the Bishop of Norwich on *Psalm* 20, 6. Evening, visitted by Dr Dowson, Mr Robinson &c. Letters.

[Feb.] 18. *Friday*. Morning, Visits to Mr Wilson, Mr Smith, Lord Seafield, Sir David Dalrymple and Lord Lonsdale. In the House, an extraordinary Appeal of the Lady A. Russel,[59] &c. about Sir W. Litton's humoursome Will: A cause numerously attended,[60] but onely half heard. Evening, at Salisbury-Court, with Sister Rothery and Mrs Beaufort.

[Feb.] 19. *Saturday*. Morning, Visitted by Mr Dean of Carlile [Atterbury]; who bewails the Church's Hazard, on a Second Invasion, decryes the Church Act,[61] and is still of opinion that our Local Statutes not worth *one Farthing*.
  The Lords gave Sentence in Mr Litton's great Cause, Affirming the Decree; because all Sir William's Lands were *out of Settlement* at his death, and the Depositions explaining his Intentions (contrary to the words of his Will) ought not to be admitted. Evening, Letters.

[Feb.] 20. *Sunday*. Private, and within doors all [day]. Evening, Visitted by Dr Gibson; in pain for the unsetled State of Lord Sommers.

[Feb.] 21. *Munday*. Morning, An Attourney with 6 Queries from Mrs Donning; to three of which I could onely answer, nor in those to her satisfaction. Visit to my Lord of York; abundantly satisfyed with what I left with him concerning my being *Expounder* of our Statutes. After the House had heard counsel, and respited judgement till Wednesday, I dined at Lambeth, and thence waited on Lord Chancellor, mighty courteous and Kind. From Mr Benson, home.

[Feb.] 22. *Tuesday*. Morning, Visitted by Dr Deering, Mr Sanderson the Antiquary,[62] Dr Gibson, Brother Joseph, Sir W. Fleming, &c. No House. After dinner, Letters. Supper at Mrs Wenman's; her Son George goeing for Oxford tomorrow.

[59] See HMC *Lords MSS* viii, 20; *LJ* xviii, 638–40.
[60] Ninety-nine peers attended. *LJ* xviii, 638.
[61] i.e. the Cathedrals Act of 1708. See above, sessional intro., p. 470.
[62] Robert Sanderson (1660–1741), historian, Clerk of the Rolls Chapel; contributor to Rymer's *Foedera* and published vols. 16 to 20 after Rymer's death, 1715–35; FSA, 1717.

[Feb.] 23. *Wednesday*. Morning, To Chelsea; Mr Dean [Atterbury] very mild. Visits, on Return, from Bishop of Norwich and Mr Maddox.

In the House, the Twelve Judges gave their Opinions of Sir N. Sherburn's Declaration;[63] whereof 8 (Lord Chief Justice Holt, Chief Baron Ward, Justice Powel, Justice Powis, Justice Blencoe, Justice Gould, Baron Bury and Baron Lovel)[64] made it bad; but 4 (Chief Justice Trevor, Justice Tracy, Baron Price and Justice Dormer) said 'twas good.[65] Lord Guarnsey with the former; Lord President Sommers with the Latter. Judgement in Q[ueen's] B[ench] affirmed. Lord President Sommers moved that a Bill for Regulation of Proceedings at Common Law might be brought in. Agreed.

Evening, private.

[Feb.] 24. *Thursday*. Morning, Visitted by James Tyrrel, who invites me and Mr Anderson to a Club of Antiquaries.[66] After the House had passed the Malt Bill,[67] &c. Dr Gibson, at dinner with me, stateing the Bampton-Cause.[68] P.m. In a Court of Delegates[69] in Serjeant's Inn in Chancery-Lane; where Cause half heard, and Adjourned to Friday Sennight.

[Feb.] 25. *Friday*. Morning, Mr Robinson, with his Book; Mr Forster renewing his Lease;[70] Brother Joseph, with Mr Rose's Debenturs; Mr Thornton and W. Senhouse Candidates.

In the House Lord H[aversha]m on the Scotch Invasion;[71] which

---

[63] See HMC *Lords MSS* viii, 22–3.

[64] Sir Salathiel Lovell (1619–1713), Serjeant-at-Law, 1688, and made 5th Baron of the Exchequer at the age of ninety in 1708, he was 'distinguished principally for his want of memory'.

[65] Cf. Wake's impression that 'Seven were of one Opinion; four of Another; and one of both sides'. Lambeth Palace MS 1770, f. 75ᵛ.

[66] For a history of the development of the Society of Antiquaries of London see J. Evans, *A History of the Society of Antiquaries* (Oxford, 1956).

[67] *LJ* xviii, 647.

[68] The Minister of Brampton, Thomas Wearing, presented the schoolmaster, Thomas Jackson, to the ecclesiastical court in 1707 as unsuitable for not being in holy orders which the original endowment deed of Brampton Grammar School required. The Court of Chancery eventually (1709–10) barred Jackson, but an amicable agreement was reached in 1717 through the intervention of Thomas Gibson, who gave £200 to the vicarage, and by the sacrifice of a portion of the School's endowment. The Vicar thereupon freed the schoolmaster from the necessity of preaching in the parish church. See M. E. Noble, *A History of the Parish of Brampton* (Kendal, 1901), pp. 100–4.

[69] The court of appeal in ecclesiastical and admiralty cases.

[70] Possibly the Mr Foster of Reading who had leased the Newcastle tithes in Mar. 1708. Ware transcript, xxv, 4. Cf., however, below, 4 Mar.

[71] Papers on the intended invasion of Scotland in 1708 had been laid before the House on 3 Feb. as a result of a debate on 12 Jan. 1709 on the state of the nation. They were taken into consideration on 25 Feb., when Haversham spoke at inordinate length in criticism of the ministry's defence preparations. See *Parl. Hist.* vi, 766–74; HMC *Lords MSS* viii, 33–264, for the printed papers.

ended in an *Union* of the Ministry.[72] Dined with Dr Gibson at the *Dog*. Evening, Dr Grandorge had the true History of my Case at Appleby. Visits to Bishop of Lincoln[73] and Vice-Chancellor Lancaster, with Dr Alston.

[Feb.] 26. *Saturday*. Morning, With Mr Receiver Rose, Mr Forster's Goldsmith, &c. After dinner and Letters, with Dr Waugh to my brother's, where my Son and Nephew Rothery from Oxford.

[Feb.] 27. *Sunday*. Dined at St Martin's, with Monsieur Wilkins,[74] Dr Hide,[75] Dr Smith and Mr Sands. Ret[urned] Visit to Dean of Wells [Grahme].

[Feb.] 28. *Munday*. Morning, Visitted by Mr Grisdale, Mr Elstob, my Son and Nephew, Mr Usher,[76] &c. After Lord President [Somers] and Lord Hallifax's favours in the House, at dinner with the two Oxon philosophers. P.m. Visit to Dr Gee; of the same year with Bishop of St Asaph [Fleetwood]. Evening, with Mr Anderson to the College of Antiquaries (Dr Hutton, Mr Maddox, &c.) at Mr Ibbet's.[77]

Mar. 1. *Tuesday*. Morning, Visits from Brother Nicolson and W. Senhouse dayly orator. Mr Forster's money paid me in Guinneas, I returned by Salisbury-Court; where the two boyes (past 10) in bed.

In the House, long Debates (all on a side) about the present Forces in Scotland, what money paid on the Equivalent,[78] Trials of Treason,

[72] The debate was adjourned until the following Tuesday, with a view, it would seem to producing a palliative motion from the Court side which would turn the flanks of the Tories. See below, 1 Mar.

[73] Wake had been prevented from attending the House by the Convocation and private business. Nicolson's visit informed him 'of what had been done at the House to day'. Lambeth Palace MS 1770, f. 75v.

[74] Possibly D. Wilkins, a Prussian student at Bodley, 1707–9, who was reported as 'mightily caressed in London by the Archbishop of Canterbury, the Bishops of London, Sarum and Ely, and Dr Grabe' in Jan. 1709. Hearne, *Collections*, ii, 34, 162, 198, 342. He was working on a book on the history of the Church in Alexandria, and left London for Vienna and Rome in May 1709.

[75] Possibly Robert Hyde (c.1662–1723), Fellow of Magdalen College, Oxford, 1681–1722, DCL 1707, or his brother Lawrence, also Fellow of Magdalen, and DD 1707.

[76] ?Charles Usher of Cumberland, BA (Oxon), 1697, barrister-at-law, Gray's Inn, 1709.

[77] Benjamin Ibbot (1680–1725), librarian (later chaplain) to Archbishop Tenison. An able scholar and preacher, his Boyle Lectures (1713–14) provided one of the Church's most effective replies to the notorious freethinker, Anthony Collins. M. C. Jacob, *The Newtonians and the English Revolution 1689–1720* (1976), pp. 171–2.

[78] For the details of the payments of the 'Equivalent' see HMC *Lords MSS* viii, 297–9. The 'Equivalent' was the sum of money which England agreed to pay Scotland at the Union in compensation for the collapse of the Darien enterprise and in reimbursement for Scottish customs duties and excise used to pay off pre-union English debts.

&c. At last, an Address to Her Majesty (moved by Lord Hallifax) that, on a Treaty of Peace, the Queen's Title and the Protestant Succession be secured and Guaranteed[79] by the Allies; and the French King obliged [to] send off the Pretender.[80] Concurrence of the Commons.[81]

[Mar.] 2. *Wednesday*. Morning, Mr Hutchinson for Oxford; against E. Llwyd.[82] In the House, Haydon's Committee[83] and Th[anks] to the Duke of Marlborough.[84] Dined with Mr C. Musgrave; to whom I paid 117 *l.* for the Release of my Bond, and Payment of my last Debt.[85] *Deo Gratias*! Guests at Dinner, Sir C. Musgrave, Coll. Dobbins[86] and Mr G. Musgrave. Visitors there, Coll. Grahme and his nephew Medcalf. Evening, with my Brother, Mr Benson, my Son and J. Rothery at the *Greyhound*. In my absence, enquired for by Sir James Mountague and Dr Wotton.

[Mar.] 3. *Thursday*. Morning, Visits from Mr Richardson, Cousin R. Nicolson, Mr Ogle,[87] without an Estate, Dr Wotton and Mr Twyman. Paid to Lord Wharton and Dr Fall. No sitting of the Lords. Mr James Tyrrel, begging for his friend Mr Cook; Author of *Arg[u-mentum] Anti Norm[annicum]*.[88] Dined, Mr Benson with me, at home, and Dr Gibson; against the Removeal of our Dean to Wells.

No Company admitted, being a Post night.

[Mar.] 4. *Friday*. Morning, With my Lord of York about Mr Capstack;[89] and Dr Deering, with Mrs Talbot's just complaint against

---

[79] Repl. 'Quaranted'.

[80] i.e. to expel the Pretender from French soil. The address is printed in *LJ* xviii, 651. It must be seen in the context of the critical peace negotiations in 1709, which were soon to open with the arrival of the French plenipotentiary, Rouillé, in Holland. For the diplomatic objectives of the ministry in engineering the address see M. A. Thomson, 'Louis XIV and the Grand Alliance, 1705–10', *BIHR* xxxiv (1961), 16–35.

[81] On 2 Mar. 1709 the Commons agreed to the Lords' address with amendments, and the Lords then agreed to the amendments. *CJ* xvi, 130–1; *LJ* xviii, 654.

[82] Lhwyd was a candidate at Oxford for the office of Superior Beadle of Divinity. He was successful despite Woodward's opposition. He died 30 June 1709.

[83] Bill for vesting Gideon Haydon's estate in trustees, see HMC *Lords MSS* viii, 18–19.

[84] For his campaign of 1708 in Flanders. *LJ* xviii, 652.

[85] Here Nicolson is breaking the last formal tie between himself and the Musgrave family.

[86] William Dobbins, Capt. and Lieut.-Col. in 1st Foot Guards, 1702–5, appointed Lieut.-Governor of Berwick, 1705. Dalton, v, 158, 163.

[87] Probably Samuel Ogle, Whig MP for Berwick-on-Tweed, 1689–1710.

[88] For the thesis of this book about the Norman Conquest see D. C. Douglas, *English Scholars* (1951), p. 122.

[89] Thomas Capstick (d. 1738), Vicar of Newburn, Northumberland, 1694–1738. He had succeeded Thomas Tullie at Newburn, the advowson of which belonged to the diocese of Carlisle. See *History of Northumberland*, ed. M. H. Dobbs (Newcastle, 1926), xii, 118–21, 130.

Mr Johnson. In the House Blen-Karn's Appeal;[90] and the Duke of Somerset's Kindness in the Whitehaven-Bill.[91] The Bishop of Bangor and I with the other Delegates (after I had dined at home with Mr Murthland) ending Forster's Cause at Serjeant's-Inn.[92] Evening, with Dr Waugh and Dr Woodward, &c. Dean Atterbury called in my absence.

[Mar.] 5. *Saturday*. Morning, Visitted by Cousin Br[idget] Nicolson and Mrs Senhouse, poor. At the House, the Whitehaven-Bill hardly allowed (by Duke of Somerset) to pass the Grand Committee. Dr Fuller[93] excused me at Lambeth. Dined. My brother with his two nephews treated with a Single Quarter of Lamb. Evening, 12 Letters.

[Mar.] 6. *Sunday*. Morning, Sermon (by Mr Evans on *Job* 1. 8) and Sacrament at the Abbey. Dined with Mr Commins, &c. at Salisbury-Court. Afternoon, I preached for Dr Waugh, had the Conversation of Dr Birch; and, in the evening, Mr C. Musgrave's (very Frank) for three hours. NB. Coll. Grahme's 8000 *l*. Subscriptions by Mr C. Musgrave to the Bank, Silesia,[94] &c.

[Mar.] 7. *Munday*. Morning, Visits to Mr Attourney General [Montagu] (at home) who shewed me Dr T[odd]'s villanous Letter;[95] and to the Bishop of Sarum [Burnet] and Lord Seafield ab[roa]d. Dined at Lambeth, with Duke of Bedford, Earl of Westmorland, Lord Charlemont,[96] Dean of Lincoln [Willis], Drs Wotton, Green,[97] &c.

[90] See HMC *Lords MSS* viii, 269–70.

[91] The Act for Preserving and Enlarging the Harbour of Whitehaven was James Lowther's response to the Parton Harbour Bill. Read the first time on 25 Feb., debated in committee on 5 Mar. and agreed without amendments, it finally passed the House on 12 Mar., receiving the royal assent on 23 Mar. *LJ* xviii, 648–9, 657, 664, 680. For a detailed study of the Lowthers' exploitation of Whitehaven see J. V. Beckett, *Coal and Tobacco. The Lowthers and the Economic Development of West Cumberland, 1660–1760* (1981); and J. E. Williams, 'Whitehaven in the eighteenth century', *EcHR* 2nd ser. viii (1956), 393–404.

[92] See above, 25 Feb.

[93] Thomas Fuller (*c*.1652–1712), DD (Camb.), 1689, Rector of Bishop Hatfield, Hertfordshire, 1685–1712.

[94] For the great Bank subscription of 1709 (£2,200,000), filled up in five hectic hours on 22 Feb., see Luttrell, vi, 410; *Parl. Hist.* vi, 786; P. G. M. Dickson, *Financial Revolution in England* (1967), pp. 260–70. The treatment of the Silesian Protestants, by which the Emperor had taken their churches from them and had infringed their liberties contrary to the treaties of Westphalia, was causing some concern in Britain. See Trevelyan, *Queen Anne*, ii, 290, 379.

[95] See above, sessional intro., p. 470.

[96] William Caulfield (d. 1726), 2nd Viscount Charlemont [I] in 1671, soldier who had served in Ireland and Spain and had reached the rank of Major-General in 1708.

[97] Thomas Green (1658–1738), Archdeacon of Canterbury, 1708–21, Master of Corpus Christi College, Cambridge, 1698–1716, later Bishop of Norwich, 1721–3, and of Ely, 1723–38. He was Bishop Trimnell's son-in-law.

Evening, Dr Wotton with me; promiseing to answer for himself and me to morrow at Mr Chamberlayne's, to send me a List of his Northern Books, approveing my *praemunientes*, &c.

[Mar.] 8. *Shr[ove] Tuesday*. Morning, Visits from young Buchanan, with Mrs Nicol's money and begging for his Father; Mr Thornton, afraid of being pressed; Cousin James Nicolson, ill used by his Father. Dined with my Brother's Family, Mr Provost of Oriel,[98] Mr Fitch[99] &c. at Dr Waugh's; where Letters written, and (thro Bonfires) home.

[Mar.] 9. *Ash Wednesday*. Morning, Mr Charles Buchanan, begging for himself, Mr Robinson, sea-sick; Ensign Senhouse, with his mother's petition. Visits paid to Mr Danvers, engaged to Lord Carlile, to Lord Seafield, accompanyed with the Duke of Queensberry, &c; Mr Montgomery, who hires a Chair at 25s per week; Sir James Dalrymple, gone out. Dined at home. P.m. Visit endeavoured to Dr Joseph Smith; who gone to Oxford, in Battle-Array against poor E. Lhwyd.[100]

[Mar.] 10. *Thursday*. Morning, To Dr Gibson; against any costs for Mr Wearing,[101] or applying (on any occasion) to the Archbishop of Canterbury. *Vale!* Visits from C. Buchanan, impudently begging the Loan of a Guinnea after I had but yesterday given him one; Mr Tyrrel, in fret for his friend Cook's doctrine of *Co-ordination*[102] not haveing my countenance; and Mr Thomas Wybergh,[103] about the F[irst] Fruits of Clifton. In the House, Decree of Lords of the Session[104] (in favour of Duke Hamilton) Reversed;[105] in Justice to Sir James Gray. Mr Dugal Stewart Advocate[106] made the best of the Duke's plea. Evening, Mr Walker; in praise of Earl of Portland and Lord Osulston.

[Mar.] 11. *Friday*. Morning, Visits to Dr Woodward, angry at Langius[107] and Brother Joseph, Lincolnshire Bill rejected. In the

---

[98] George Carter (c.1673–1727), Provost of Oriel College, Oxford, 1708–27.

[99] Possibly William Fytch, MP for Maldon, 1701–8, 1711–12. He was an old student of Queen's College, Oxford. [100] See above, 2 Mar., n. 82.

[101] ?T. Wearing, Vicar of Bampton, Westmorland, in 1704 when Nicolson made his first visitation. *Miscellany*, pp. 75, 189. [102] See above, n. 88.

[103] Thomas Wybergh (1685–1753) of Clifton, Town Clerk of Appleby. *Armorial*, p. 333.

[104] Scottish judges in charge of civil cases.

[105] See HMC *Lords MSS* viii, 12–3.

[106] Dougal Stewart (d. 1712), of Blairhall, MP for Buteshire and Perthshire, 1708–9, brother of 1st Earl of Bute, became a Lord of Judiciary in 1709.

[107] Carolus Nicolas Langius was a friend of Lhwyd, and his recent *Historia Lapidum Figuratorum Helvetiae* (Venice, 1708) was hostile to Woodward's theories.

House, Bill for General Naturalization[108] read and appointed a second Reading on Tuesday; when the Lords Summoned. Dined with me, the two Oxonians. After waiting on my Sister to the Surprizeingly moveing picture from Germany, the Evening merrily spent in Fetter lane.

[Mar.] 12. *Saturday*. Morning, Joseph Rothery, for's Dispatches to Oxford; Mr Lindsey, with an indifferent Account of Mr Robinson and's Son. In the House (*inter alia*) the Whitehaven Bill read a 3d time and passed; to the great ease of Mr James Lowther and my self. Dined, Mr Buddle; sent off, when time to write Letters.

[Mar.] 13. *Sunday*. Morning, Mr Robinson, with the present of his Natural History in two parts. I preached at St Martin's in the Forenoon, and Dr Snape in the Afternoon. Dined with Mr Grisdale. After prayers with Mr Browne Willis, and his young Lady.

[Mar.] 14. *Munday*. Morning, With Dr Gibson; who for[109] the Deanery of Rochester by Lord Sunderland, &c. Thence to Marquess of An[n]andale, to further the Bridges on the Borders;[110] and the Earl of Leven, for Cousin Lesley.
    In the House, a Scotch Appeal,[111] wherein Sentence Affirmed, and, in the Lobby, Debate on Naturalization.[112] Dined, Mr Murthland and my son; and with the latter, in the evening, to visit Cousin Boswell.

[Mar.] 15. *Tuesday*. Morning, Visitted by Mr Robinson and's son with Mr Pearson from the D[uke] of S[omerset?]; Mr Smith (with King James's Charter) and Mr Dean of Carlile [Atterbury] goeing to Lord Wharton.
    In the House, the Bill for General Naturalization Read a second Time, and (on a Division upon the Question, *Contents* 65, *Not Contents*, 20) Committed. City-Council heard against it for the Orphans; and their petition (as being better Gainers another way) Rejected. In the Committee, the word *Parochial* being offered by

---

[108] See above, sessional intro., pp. 471–2.
[109] i.e. recommended for. Surprisingly the deanery of Rochester was not vacant at this time. It was held by Samuel Pratt from 1706 to 1723.
[110] Annandale was a major landowner in south-west Scotland. The bridges under discussion were presumably to span the rivers Esk and Sark.
[111] See HMC *Lords MSS* viii, 14–15; Luttrell, vi, 418.
[112] Wake reveals that this informal debate, preceding the second reading debate due on the following day, was between the Archbishop of York and the bishops. Lambeth Palace MS 1770, f. 76^V.

the Bishop of Chester [Dawes] (and myself) as an Amendment,[113] Ten Bishops against Seven on the Question.[114] The Former, Archbishop of York, Bishops of Durham [Crew], Winchester [Trelawney], Rochester [Sprat], Bangor, Carlile, Lincoln, Landaff [Tyler], Exeter [Blackall] and Chester: And the latter, Archbishop of Canterbury, Bishops of Sarum, Litchfeild, Ely, Peterborough [Cumberland], Chichester [Williams], and Norwich. Of which Chichester by mistake.[115]

Dinner, at the *Dog*, with Dr Gibson; in the Chagrin. Letters.

[Mar.] 16. *Wednesday*. Morning, Mr Thomas Morland,[116] Candidate for Priest's Orders, for my Letter to Dr Sydal; Mr Alsop, about his purchase at Bugden; Lord Wharton's Gent[leman] for W. Senhouse; Mr Sully, with Dr Fenton's son.[117] Mr Smith carried me to Mr Leneve [Le Neve]; who shewed us Doomsday-Book, the Rolls of 20 Edward 1. *Testade Nevil*, &c. Vid. *Amanack*.[118]

In the House, a Grand Committee (Lord Bishop of Sarum in the Chair) on the Treason-Bill;[119] which referred to Friday. After Dinner, alone, a Visit to Mr Walker; full of his Fox-Hunting, but disgusted with yesterday's work. My Neck began to swell.

[Mar.] 17. *Thursday*. Morning, Mr Lindsey. At the House, the Bill for the Middlesex-Register[120] Committed for Saturday. Dined at Dr Gibson's; with Dr Waugh and our two Sons. Evening, takeing Leave (in Salisbury-Court) of my son; for Oxford, in the morning.

[Mar.] 18. *Friday*. Morning, Mr Fenton for a Letter to the Bishop of Lincoln; W. Senhouse, to wait on Lord Wharton as a servant; Dr Fuller, of Hatfield, marrying his daughter with 8000 *l*. wants 27 *l*. of Mrs Stockdale and her Family.

In the House the Treason-Bill in a Grand Committee, Bishop of

[113] The purpose of the amendment and the line of division among the bishops is discussed above, sessional intro., p. 472.

[114] T. Sharp, *Life of John Sharp* (1825), i, 369 gives the figures as six against ten, identifying three of the ten as Sharp, Dawes, and Nicolson. The bill finally passed without amendments. *LJ* xviii, 668.

[115] Bishop John Williams may well have been ailing at this time. He was to die on 24 Apr.

[116] ?Thomas Morland, from Lasenby, Cumberland. Educated at Oxford, BA 1707, he became Vicar of Bapchild, Kent, in 1709.

[117] James Fenton (*c*.1654–1714), educated at Queen's College, Oxford, and at Cambridge, was Vicar of Lancaster, 1685–1714. His son, James (*c*.1688–1767), at this time an Oxford undergraduate was to succeed his father as Vicar of Lancaster, 1714–67.

[118] Nicolson's Almanack for 1709 has not survived.

[119] See above, sessional intro., p. 473. For the Committee's proceedings, see HMC *Lords MSS* viii, 286.

[120] Act for the Public Registering of all Deeds, Conveyances and Wills, that shall be made . . . within the County of Middlesex. For the bill and the proceedings see HMC *Lords MSS* viii, 278–84. It received the royal assent on 21 Apr. 1709.

Sarum (blundering) in the Chair; the onely Question put, on the first paragraph. Whether the English statutes be particularly enumerated?[121] *Contents*, 23. *Not Contents*, 45.[122] Amongst the Former all the Northern Lords; but not one Bishop. Dined.

[Mar.] 19. *Saturday*. Morning, Mr Fenton, not to be admitted to Orders till he's 23 *complete*.

In the House, Two Orders of the Day. 1. Register-Bill for Middlesex. Counsel Heard for the Clerks of Inrollments; who like to succeed. 2. Scotch Treason-Bill; in which provision to be made for Dukes of Argile and Hamilton,[123] &c. NB. Lord President Sommers hard on the present Lords of Justiciary for slipping the Tryal of 16 Treasonable Rioters;[124] not finding so much as Room for a Tryal.[125] Query. Dined, Dr Gibson, justifying Dr Gee's conduct in Relation to Mr Chamberland and his Clerk Cousin Robert Ponsonby.[126]

[Mar.] 20. *Sunday*. Morning, My Brother brought Mr Kelway a Surgeon; who opened the swelling in my neck with a Caustic, and promises a Thorough Cure in a month. P.m. Dr Gibson, from St Martin's; Mr Robinson, for Portsmouth; W. Senhouse, to attend Lord Wharton by his own Directions to me.

[Mar.] 21. *Munday*. Morning, Cousin R. Ponsonby for purchaseing a Common Trooper in the Guard's Horse at 100 *l*. Mr Chancellor Tanner, who saies the Registers at Norwich are entire since 1299; Mr B. Culme, in the Gravel; Mr Sanderson, from finishing the last sheet of the 8th vol. of the Foedera; Mr Kelway (with my brother) opening my sore, with good encouragement.

In the House, the Treason-Bill, in several particulars amended;[127]

---

[121] 'whether, after the words (Crimes and Offences) shall be added the Statutes following, that is to say, the Statutes as in the Judges' Schedule.' HMC *Lords MSS* viii, 286–7. The amendment was proposed by the Scots peers, for reasons explained in Burnet, *History*, v, 403.

[122] HMC *Lords MSS* viii, 287, gives the figures as twenty-three against forty-seven.

[123] Section 3 of the Act 7 Anne c.21 (see *Statutes of the Realm*, ix, 93), concerning the rights of Justice Generals who existed before the Act to be ex officio on the Commission of Oyer and Terminer.

[124] A reference to the group of Stirlingshire and Perthshire gentlemen and their servants who had risen too early in 1708 before the Prince of Wales's invasion force arrived. They had been sent to London to be examined and then returned to Scotland for trial. The verdict of 'Not proven' resulted from a common reluctance in Scotland to testify. See Trevelyan, *Queen Anne*, ii, 392–3, 347, 349; HMC *Lords MSS* viii, 85.

[125] The Committee of the Whole sat on the Treason Bill until after 9.00 p.m. (SRO Ogilvy of Inverquarity MS GD 205/36: Grey Neville to Sir W. Bennet, 19 Mar. 1709).

[126] The Robert Ponsonby who was Ensign in Col. Richard Kane's regiment of foot in 1716. Dalton, *George I*, i, 144.

[127] See HMC *Lords MSS* viii, 287.

and the Grand Committee adjourned for tomorrow. Evening, Mr
Thomas Bell; advocate for W. Senhouse and wishing his brother
D[avid] to Orton.

[Mar.] 22. *Tuesday*. Morning, Mr Kelway, at my neck; Capt. Crow,[128]
for waiting on Lord Wharton; Dr Gee, with Bishop of St Asaph's
Answer to E. Lh[wyd].

In the House, Duke of Argyle's motion for admitting that part
of the Scots Law which gives the Party Accused a List of Witnesses
15 dayes before Tryal, on the Debate reduced to *Five* or *Two*, and
the Question, put for *Five*, was carryed (for the N[orthern] Lords
against the Court) by 37 against 31. In the Majority were the Bishops
of Sarum, Peterborough, Chichester, Carlile, Landaff and Exeter.
On the Court-side; Litchfield, Bangor and Norwich. The Cucumber
thus cooked, Lord Chancellor [Cowper], Lord Treasurer [Godolphin]
and Lord President [Somers] earnestly moved for the throwing out
the whole Clause, as makeing a Dangerous Change (at this Juncture)
in the Laws of England. Whereupon, a Second Question threw it out
accordingly by 44 against 27.[129] NB. I was this day Chairman in a
Grand Committee on the Bill for preventing of Mutiny and Desertion.[130]

Dined at Sir A[ndrew] Fountain's; where Mr H[enry?] Worsley
and Mr Chancellor Tanner. Sir Andrew has now 370 different sorts
of Saxon Coins.

[Mar.] 23. *Wednesday*. Morning, Mr Philip Nanson[131] with a Complaint about his Curate Rose; which I undertook to adjust with the
Bishop of Winchester.

Mr Kelway haveing dressed my Neck, at the House: where
(after a Committee about the Records) the Scotch Bill of Treason,
till near six at night, brought a Question. 42 against 23.[132] No
Bishop with the North Brittains, except the Bishops of Sarum (who
against all Forfeitures but *personal*)[133] and Peterborough. Evening,
private.

---

[128] ?Edward Crowe (d. ?1715), Capt. in Col. Edward Jones regiment of foot, 1708;
possibly sent to Spain with the regiment 1711–12. Dalton, vi, 254–5.

[129] See HMC *Lords MSS* viii, 287, for the day's proceedings. A clause giving the prisoner
ten days' notice of witnesses was restored by the Commons to the bill, see Burnet, *History*,
v, 405–7; below, 8 Apr.

[130] Passed without amendment. *LJ* xviii, 676. This is the first time Nicolson chaired a
Committee of the Whole House, see above, Chapter 1, p. 37.

[131] 'hanson' in transcript. Possibly Philip Nanson of Appleby, Rector of Dogmersfield,
Hampshire, since 1680, and formerly of Queen's College, Oxford.

[132] See HMC *Lords MSS* viii, 287–8.

[133] Burnet explains why in his *History*, v, 406.

[Mar.] 24. *Thursday*. Morning, My neck dressed, I went with Capt. Crow to wait on Lord Wharton; who met with at the House: where long case of the Duke or Richmond for the Earl of Kildare's Estate and Tenants.[134] Evening, Mr Murthland, takeing leave for Holland. The year ended with writeing ten long Letters.

[Mar.] 25. *Friday*. Morning, Visits to Lord Archbishop of York, tortured with the Gowt in's Knee; Mrs Lamplugh, desireous of a Fellowship for her eldest son;[135] Lord Townshend, not at home. Visitted by Mr Anderson, who designs to keep my Scots Coins; Mr Maddox, despiseing James Tyrrel. In the House, the Treason-Bill in a Grand Committee;[136] wherein, after long Debates, a proposeal made by Lord Seafield (and approved by Lord Chancellor) to consider upon the Scots Settlements[137] till to morrow. On the Question, *Contents* 36. *Not Contents* 32. Amongst the former (with Lords Chancellor and Treasurer, Bishops of Sarum, Peterborough, Chichester, Carlile, Landaff, Lincoln and Exeter. With the Latter (with Lord President, Lord Sunderland, &c.) Bishops of Winchester, Rochester, Litchfield, Bangor and Norwich; the last in great warmth, at his Lord's[138] Disappointment. The Evening at Salisbury-Court; my Sister's Birthday.

[Mar.] 26. *Saturday*. Morning. Letters and Messages dispatched, I went to the House; where Lord Seafield's proposal Rejected; but Lord Guilford's, for the prisoners haveing a List of Witnesses for five dayes, after a Bill found by the Grand Jury, came to a Question. 30 against 30.[139] *Pro Negante*: Eight Bishops equally divided. Dined, At Mr Walker's, with Mr Johnson (Clerk of Parliament) and his son,[140] very cheerful.

[Mar.] 27. *Sunday*. Morning, After Mr Kelway, brother Joseph against takeing more Nieces into his House. Dined At my Brother's with Mrs Beaufort and Mr Talbor: whence, haveing given my Lincolnshire-Bill to Dr Waugh, I presently returned to my Lodgeings.

[134] See HMC *Lords MSS* viii, 275-6, for the case.
[135] Thomas Lamplugh, son of Thomas, Rector of St Andrew Undershaft (d. 1703), of Queen's College, Oxford (BA 1708), later Canon of York (1712) and Rector of Bolton Percy, Yorkshire, 1716.   [136] See HMC *Lords MSS* viii, 288.
[137] The issue here was the validity of Scottish marriage settlements under the new treason law. Burnet, *History*, v, 406-7.
[138] i.e. his patron, Sunderland.
[139] HMC *Lords MSS* viii, 288, gives the vote as thirty-two against thirty-two.
[140] Matthew Johnson, Clerk of Parliament, 1691-1716, and his son, Matthew Johnson (c.1683-1725), Reading Clerk, 1711-15, and Clerk Assistant, 1715-24. J. C. Sainty, *The Parliament Office in the Seventeenth and Eighteenth Centuries* (1977), p. 17.

[Mar.] 28. *Munday*. Morning. Mr James Gordon; shewing me an Address to the Queen from 33 Episcopal Ministers in the Diocese of Aberdene,[141] persecuted notwithstanding the Act of 95 in their Favour.[142] In the House, Lord Guilford's Clause offered again as a Rider, on the Third Reading of the Treason-Bill; but Rejected (on the Question) by 40 against 25.[143] Bishop of Sarum, the Single man of the Bench, with the Latter. Lord Scarborough moved for the prohibiteing the Exportation of Corn;[144] 5000 Q[uarte]rs of Wheat being lately carryed from Portsmouth to France, in a Swedish Bottome. Evening With Mr Anderson, who shewed his Diplomata and Scots Coins; a Crown of King James 6 after he came to England; his Ounce of Gold (1575 and 76) no Medal; Luckius (of Strasburgh)[145] his Numismata, whence Mr Evelyn had his of Queen Mary, Queen Elizabeth and the Earl of Leicester.

[Mar.] 29. *Tuesday*. Morning, A second Visit attempted to Lord Townshend, I read prayers at the House; where (for some time) alone on the Bench, and frowned on by the Northern Lords, angry at yesterday's Vote.[146] Lord Carlile took the Oaths; and desired that He and I[147] might settle the Affairs of Cumberland.[148] Dined At

---

[141] James Gordon (d. 1732), Minister *de facto* of Foveran, 1692–6, preacher at an episcopal meeting house at Montrose, 1696–9, Minister at Hawnby, Yorkshire, until his death. His father, James Gordon senior (d. 1714), Minister of Banchory-Devenick, 1666–1714, had decided upon an address from the episcopal clergy in the diocese of Aberdeen who were qualified in law stating their grievances under Presbyterian domination, which should be presented to the Queen. The Duke of Queensberry, Scottish Secretary of State, proved unco-operative, and Gordon junior presented the address to the Queen on 25 May through the auspices of Bishop Compton. See *James Gordon's Diary, 1692–1710*, ed. G. D. Henderson and H. H. Porter, Spalding Club, 3rd ser. (Aberdeen, 1949), pp. 22–4, 177–9. Gordon had first met Nicolson on 15 Dec. 1702, and they corresponded thereafter. See ibid, pp. 116, 119.

[142] The Act of 1695 which protected the livings of episcopal clergy who took the oaths to the government and submitted to the Presbyterian polity. They were also admitted to the jurisdiction of the Church. *Acts Parl. Scot.* ix, 449–50. For trouble in the diocese of Aberdeen over the persecution of episcopalians in 1711 see HMC *Portland MSS* x, 393–402.

[143] This vote is not recorded in HMC *Lords MSS* viii, 288. See *LJ* xviii, 689 for the rider.

[144] The very bad harvest of 1708, followed by the savage frosts of the late winter, had led to a steep rise in the price of wheat in most home markets. The London price reached 57s 6d per quarter on 25 Mar. 1709, more than double the price on Lady Day 1708. The Commissioners of Customs informed the Lords on 6 Apr. that wheat prices at thirty-five different outports on 17 Mar. had varied from 32s to 64s. Alarm in official quarters was to increase further over the next six months as another miserable summer and harvest sent up the price of bread to its highest level since 1660; and parliament finally took legislative action against corn exports in Dec. 1709. M. Beloff, *Public Order and Popular Disturbances, 1660–1714* (Oxford, 1938), pp. 68, 70, 159; HMC *Lords MSS* viii, 306.

[145] Johann Jacob Luckh (d. 1653), German genealogist and numismatist.

[146] See the protests in *LJ* xviii, 689.   [147] 'I' omitted in transcript.

[148] Probably with particular reference to revising the commission of the peace of the county. See below, 12 Apr.; Bodl. MS Add. C.217, f. 41: N. to Carlisle, 19 Mar. 1709; *CW* xxxv (1935), 100 (10 June 1709).

Mr C. Musgrave's where Sir Christopher, Mr Fleetwood[149] and Mr Crowther. Political Oathes rightly understood in Flanders. Evening Visitted by Sir W. Fleming; getting his Brother Michael made a Major, and J. Fisher a Justice.[150]

[Mar.] 30. *Wednesday*. Morning Attempt to visit Lord Carlile; who afterwards told me that he had received my Letter. Charles Buchanan and young Patrickson, beggars. At the House, Orders signed for the Orange-Brief;[151] on which already remitted to the King of Prussia above 18000 *l*. George Whitehead[152] attacked the Bishop of Chester and me on behalf of the Quakers-Marriages.[153] To no purpose. Lord Thanet heard, by his Counsel, against his being obliged to find a New Under-Sheriff yearly;[154] Lord Hallifax (to make the work short) proposed the throwing out that clause, as a Tack.[155] Seconded by Lord Wharton. NB. Viponts Sherifs of Westmorland ever since 5 John.[156] After Dinner, at Dr Gibson's, where his two Voll. of Ecclesiastical Digests[157] very entertaining: And thence to Mrs Thynn's, where met by Mr Fürman and kindly treated till 10 by Mrs Martin.

[Mar.] 31. *Thursday*. Morning Visitted (takeing physick) by my brother and Mr Elstob; the latter with Cuts for his sister's Saxon

---

[149] ?Henry Fleetwood (?1667–1746), Tory MP for Preston, 1708–22. Sedgwick, ii, 39.

[150] ?John Fisher, Sheriff of Cumberland, 1711–12.

[151] This may possibly be a reference to the treaty of 28 Nov. 1704 between Britain and Prussia whereby Prussia provided a contingent of troops for service in Italy, while in return Britain paid Prussia a subsidy and promised to 'employ her credit on behalf of the king of Prussia with the Emperor and States General' over the Prussian claim to the succession of the principality of Orange. The treaty was initially for one year but was renewed three times and expired on 18 Apr. 1709. On 25 June 1709 £13,333 was paid to Prussia for arrears due under this treaty, while in Nov. £45,000 was paid 'in full arrears'. *The Consolidated Treaty Series*, ed. C. Parry (Dobbs Ferry, N.Y., 1969), xxv, 215–25; *CTB 1709* xxii, pt. 2, pp. 22, 228, 405. The 'Orange Brief' was of some interest to Nicolson for it is mentioned several times in his letters to his brother John in 1706. See Tullie House Library, Carlisle: Nicolson's Account Book for 1706.

[152] George Whitehead (1636?–1723), leading Quaker, from Orton, Cumberland.

[153] The question was raised by the provisions of the Stamp Bill currently before parliament. See above, sessional intro., p. 472.

[154] The Stamp Bill, or 'Attorneys' bill' contained a clause on under-sheriffs and specifically referred to Thanet's position as Hereditary Sheriff of Westmorland. *LJ* xviii, 687, 692.

[155] The House reaffirmed declarations of 9 Dec. 1702 and 28 Mar. 1707 against tacking and ordered that such lords as had not signed the previous declarations might sign as they saw fit. Nicolson did so. *LJ* xviii, 692; Luttrell, vi, 424.

[156] The Earls of Thanet became Hereditary Sheriffs of Westmorland in 1678 when the 3rd Earl succeeded to the barony of Clifford in the right of his maternal grandmother, Anne Clifford, *suo jure* Baroness Clifford. The shrievalty had been hereditary in the Clifford family since 1291, when they inherited it from the Viponts. It continued so until the death of the last Earl of Thanet in 1849. *GEC Peerage*, iii, 296–8.

[157] A reference to Gibson's as yet unpublished *Codex Juris Ecclesiastici Anglicani*, which appeared in two volumes in 1713.

Homily.[158] Dr Deering, Mr Lindsey, &c. sent off. In the House, an Appeal (from Hambden, a Villainous Clerk in Chancery) rejected.[159] Lord Wharton promises fair for W. Senhouse; but, in return, expects Crosthwait for Mr Gregory. The Commons (On the Second Reading, by a Majority of 8 as on the first) committed the Treason-Bill.[160] Dinner Mr Thomas Benson returning home; Dr Waugh, with an Account of the Exhibitions in Dr Kennet's disposeal. Evening Mr George Holmes, pressing for Records from the Rolls. Dr Smith, sending his Nephew to Cambridge.

Apr. 1. *Friday*. Morning On an April-Errand to Lord Hallifax just goeing to the Treasury. I read Prayers in the House, but, soon after, called on by Dr Gibson and Dr Grandorge, went to Dinner at the *Dog*: Leaveing the great Testamentary Cause of Hedges to the Lords, who (by a Division of 15 against 11) Reversed the Decree.[161] Evening Visits attempted (with Dr Grandorge) to Drs Smith, Waugh and Kennet; concluded, with Mr Johnson and A. Spooner, in Salisbury Court.

[Apr.] 2. *Saturday*. Morning Visit paid to the Archbishop of York; who's pretty cheerful. Visitted by W. Senhouse, for the Customs here; and Mr Richardson, directed to write to Mr Spark not to prosecute Mr Capstack. In the House, The Bill for Middlesex-Register finished in the Committee. NB. My Fall from the Corner of the Throne, just before my Reading of prayers. Lord Hallifax agrees with me that 'tis best to drop the Treason-Bill.[162] Dined Mr Fitzgerald, with some of Mr Jenkin's Oysters.

[Apr.] 3. *Sunday*. Rainy. All the day Private. Evening my brother; with the story of Archbishop of Canterbury's discourageing the weekly Lecture of Conformists at Maidstone.

[Apr.] 4. *Munday*. Morning With Mr Fürmane to Gresham-College; where Dr Woodward shewed us his last Rare Fossils: Amongst which

[158] Elizabeth Elstob (1683–1756), Anglo-Saxon scholar, published her *English Saxon Homily on the Nativity of St. Gregory* with a translation in 1709.

[159] See HMC *Lords MSS* viii, 284–5.

[160] The vote was 149 against 141, while the vote on the first reading on 29 Mar. was 116 against 108. *CJ* xvi, 178, 181.

[161] Hedges v. Hedges, see HMC *Lords MSS* viii, 277–8.

[162] Disagreement between Halifax and his Junto colleagues over this question foreshadowed a growing strain in relations between them during the course of the next twelve to eighteen months. See, e.g., BL Add. MS 34521, ff. 39–40: Halifax to Somers (transcripts of two letter), n.d. [1709]; *Marlborough–Godolphin Corr.* iii, 1560–1: Godolphin to Marlborough, 7 July 1710.

1. Hippocephaloides, from Portland. 2. Fossil-Shells (particularly Dr Lister's[163] Cochlea fluviatilis vivipara) from Limmington in Dorsetshire. 2. Native Lead from Mendip; and Native Copper from Cornwall. 3. Spina Raij petrifyed. 4. From my Diocese, Ludus Helmontij from Strickland-Head; the Sea-Fann, from Stainton; Mr Lhwyd's Lithonstrata and Coralline Marble from Lowther. He saies, Sulpher, Vitriol and Allum, are all the same Mineral Salts variously modifyed. Query. Hard on Mr Lhwyd, Dr Richardson[164] and Mr Rowlands. In the House, Bishop of St Asaph took the Oathes, introduced by me:[165] Lord Clanrickard's and Lord Lindsey's Bills read;[166] but both like to meet with warm Opposition. Lord Thanet very friendly. With Mr W. Tullie at the Treasury of Queen's-Bench;[167] where the highest Roll of 1. Henry 6. Downwards Entire. O. Cromwells in English. Every Term in Queen Elizabeth's with her picture illuminated. In the Evening Mr Thomas Bell being paid for his Books, I carryed Mr Holmes's Letter to Dr Gibson; and thence to my brother's till Bed-time.

[Apr.] 5. *Tuesday*. Morning Visits to Mr Lawson, and Mr Usher, and attempted to Lord Carlile and Mr J. Brougham. After Dinner (at the *Dog*) with Dr Gibson, and an Appeal overthrown in the House, I went to the Commons-Gallery; where I heard learned Debates on the Treason-Bill. On the side of the Dyeing Laws of Scotland appeared Sir David Dalrymple, Mr Baillie,[168] Mr Carnegie,[169] Mr Dugal Steward, Mr Cockburn[170] and Sir J. Hawles; And, on the behalf of Oyer and

---

[163] Martin Lister (?1638–1712), zoologist and antiquary, Physician to the Queen, 1703–12. His *Historia sive Synopsis Methodica Conchyliorum* (1685–92) was the standard work on sea shells.

[164] Richard Richardson (1663–1741), botanist, antiquary, physician, and close friend of Thoresby, who lived at North Bierley, Yorkshire, and Henry Rowlands (1665–1723), divine, antiquary, and geologist. Woodward was hard on them because they were all critical of his theories about fossil shells.

[165] Bishop William Fleetwood, a Low Church Whig, had succeeded to St Asaph, on the death of Beveridge, the previous May (cons. 6 June 1708). His first appearance in the Lords had been delayed by his primary visitation.

[166] Both estate bills. See HMC *Lords MSS* viii, 302–4.

[167] William Tully was Deputy Clerk of the Inner Treasury of the Queen's Bench and was a clerk for making up the records throughout England. Chamberlayne, *Present State 1708*, pp. 638–9.

[168] George Baillie (1664–1738) of Jerviswood, MP for Berwickshire, 1708–34, previously for Scotland, 1707–8, he was one of the ablest of the Squadrone Commoners, and son-in-law of the 1st Earl of Marchmont. He was a Lord of Trade, 1710–12, of the Admiralty, 1714–17, and of the Treasury, 1717–25. Sedgwick, i, 427–8.

[169] John Carnegie (c.1680–1750), MP for Forfarshire, 1708–16, Solicitor-General, 1714, later became a Jacobite. Sedgwick, i, 531.

[170] John Cockburn (c.1679–1758), MP for Haddingtonshire, 1708–41, previously for Scotland, 1707–8, a Lord of Trade, 1714–17, and of the Admiralty, 1717–32, 1742–4. Sedgwick, i, 562. See Holmes, *British Politics*, p. 338 n. for the broad spectrum of Scottish opposition. 'Every man of them [in the Commons]', noted Abigail Harley, 'was against the Bill.' HMC *Portland MSS* iv, 523.

Terminer, Sir Thomas Powis, Mr Sollicitor Eyres, Mr Cowper, Mr Smith, &c. Two Divisions were carried by the latter onely by Six Voices; but the main Question, at last, by 116 against 93.[171] Letters.

[Apr.] 6. *Wednesday*. Morning Visitted by Cousen R. Nicolson; who for my preaching at Savoy. Failing of Lord Hallifax, I went to Lambeth; where Archbishop very lame in the Gowt. His Grace shewed me a New Edition, with Enlargements and better Method, of Gruter's Inscriptions.[172] In the House, the Quaker's Clause voted to stand part of the Stamp-Bill. *Contents*, 31. *Not Contents*, 16. whereof 9 were Bishops, all that were in the House and of these the Bishop of Ely and my self spoke.[173] This done the Earl of Rochester moved for inserting *pretended*: Opposed by Lord Stamford: The two Noble Lords reconciled (and the whole House agreed) and a motion of mine, from the words of the St[atute] of 6 & 7 W[illiam] 3 c. 6.[174] for inserting after the word *Marriages, or pretended Marriages*. Evening With Lady Lonsdale; who will not spare my Lord, on any tedious Tour, long out of her sight. This day he and's brother had been at Greenwich.

[Apr.] 7. *Thursday*. Morning, After my second purgeing was (as I thought) over, and visits declined from Lord Carlile, Bishop of Lincoln, Coll. Studholme, &c. I went to the Committee of Records, and thence to the House. Private Bills. Afternoon, my purgeing renewed with Violence. Evening Letters.

[Apr.] 8. *Friday*. Morning Visitted by Lord Marquess of Anandale; who brought me the News of the Amendments made in the Committee of the Commons (carried by 27)[175] to the Treason-Bill; allowing 10 Dayes Notice of Witnesses, and confineing Forfeitures to the Persons.[176] Enquired for Mr Blencow and Capt. Phillips,[177]

[171] No vote is recorded for the beginning of the committee stage in *CJ* xvi, 188.

[172] *Inscriptiones Antiquae totius orbis Romani* by Jan Gruter had recently been republished at Amsterdam in 1707.

[173] See above, sessional intro., p. 472.

[174] Act for granting to his Majesty certain rates and duties upon Marriages, Births and Burials and upon Batchelors and Widowers for the terms of Five years for carrying on the War against France with Vigour. *Statutes of the Realm*, vi, 568–83. Nicolson is probably referring to clause 57.

[175] By 137 to 110, according to Luttrell, vi, 427.

[176] 'added a clause, that no person in England or Scotland upon conviction of treason forfeit his estate, but [it should] descend to his heirs.' (Ibid.). This was the amendment Burnet had unsuccessfully contended for in the Lords.

[177] A Capt. Phillips was connected with running the House of Lords. Gibson was let into the House to hear a debate 'by the favour of Capt. Philips', and Luttrell reported on 8 Sept. 1709 the death in Flanders of 'Captain Phillips, which last belonged to the house

after I was gone to wait on Sir William Cunningham; with whom I met with the Bishop of Sarum (his Cousin) who told us two free stories of Sir G. Mackenzy's being feed by a Traytor (Greydon-Hume)[178] to bring him off, if he'd bring some to swear that they *did not see* him at Bothwel-Bridge; and the other of Sir E. Coke's[179] giveing 600 *l.* (of his 1200) in presents of Plate to the Judges Wives. After I had dined, to the House; where Counsel for and against the Destillers of the Oyl of Turpentine, &c. Thence to the Gallery of the House of Commons; where yesterday's Clauses agreed on the Question. *Yeas*, 164. *Noes*, 112.[180] With the former, Mr Harley,[181] Mr Scobel,[182] &c. with the latter Mr Smith, Mr Walpool,[183] &c. Evening. With Sister Rothery, at Salisbury-Court.

[Apr.] 9. *Saturday*. Morning Rescued from Mrs Donning's Clamours, I Endeavoured a Visit to Lord Carlile: And afterwards, dismissed from Attendance on Lord William Pawlet's Bill, I had the Company of Mr Laurence Echard[184] (recommended to me by the Bishop of Lincoln) with his Introduction and List of Writers for the History of Charles 1 to the Restoration, as also a Letter from Charles 2 to Monsr. Testard concerning his Father's Ἐικων Βασιλικὴ[185]

of lords'. He left for Holland in late Apr. 1709. Christ Church Wake MS 17, f. 204: Gibson to Wake, 14 Apr. 1709; Luttrell, vi, 486; Berks RO Trumbull MS 50: T. Bateman to Trumbull, 1 May 1709. There was also a Capt. Phillips who was probably a member of the Carlisle garrison whom Nicolson met in Carlisle between 1705 and 1713. *CW* iii (1903), 51; iv (1904), 68; xxxv (1935), 135.

[178] George Hume (d. 1679) of Graden, Berwickshire, Covenanting son-in-law of Archibald Johnstone of Warriston, who fought at Bothwell Bridge in 1679. See R. C. Bosanquet, 'Cavaliers and Covenanters', *Archaeologia Aeliana*, 4th ser. ix (1932), 29–30.

[179] Sir Edward Coke (1552–1634). [180] *CJ* xvi, 193.

[181] For Harley's exertions in the Commons to soften the bill's severity, and their unexpected success, see HMC *Portland MSS* iv, 521: Abigail Harley to [her aunt] Abigail Harley, 19 Apr. 1709.

[182] Francis Scobel (1664–1716), MP for St Germans, 1708–10, Mitchell, 1690–5, Grampound, 1699–1708, Launceston, 1710–13, and St Mawes, 1713–15.

[183] Robert Walpole (1676–1745), MP for King's Lynn, 1702–12, 1713–42, Castle Rising, 1689–1700. Remarkably enough, it is his first appearance in the diary. The prominence of the Chancellor of the Exchequer and the Secretary-at-War, and later the Vice-Treasurer of Ireland, Lord Coningsby (below, 9 Apr.), among the minority suggests the ministry still favoured as hard-line a bill as possible. For the final vote in the Commons, on agreeing to the Lords' revised amendments, 18 Apr., 'they assembled all their forces, the lame and the blind and all, and yet it was carried but by six'. Abigail Harley, 19 Apr. *loc. cit.*; Luttrell, vi, 431, giving the vote for the ministry as 152 to 146.

[184] Laurence Echard (?1670–1730), historian and divine, Prebendary of Louth, 1697. He published the *History of England from the first entrance of Julius Caesar and the Romans to the end of the reign of James I* in 1707 and two further volumes in 1718 bringing the history down to William and Mary.

[185] Subtitled *The Portraicture of His Sacred Majestie in His Solitudes and Suffering*, it was supposed to have been written by Charles I and appeared at the time of his execution. It is usually attributed to Bishop John Gauden.

communicated by Mr Elstob. Dr Bray, promiseing an Increase of the parochial Libraryes in my Diocese.[186] *Credat Judaeus*! Mr James Gordon, solliciteing the Cause of the Aberdene-Clergy: for whom I drew up a paper for the Duke of Dover and Bishop of London [Compton]. As I had dined, I was called on by Dr Woodward; to acquaint me that Lord Lonsdale and I should be waited for on Munday. To the House of Commons; where the Treason-Bill read a 3d time; and (notwithstanding Lord Coningsby's Remark, that noe Traytour could now forfeit either Life or Estate) passed upon the Question. *Yeas*, 141. *Noes*, 73.[187] To Enquire for Dr Gibson; who not at home. Letters.

[Apr.] 10. *Sunday*. Morning. Hearing Dr Dent (woefully dull and squeeking) in the Abbey, with the Bishop of St Asaph, I dined in Salisbury-court; and, after Evening Service at St Paul's, and some Tey drunk with the Deans of St Asaph [Stanley] and Sarum [Younger], I took leave of Cousin A. Spooner goeing to Wiltshire. NB. The Bishop of St Asaph observed the three Noble Structures of England (The Chapples of Westminster, King's College and Windsor) to have been built in the time of Henry 7. Qu[ery].

[Apr.] 11. *Munday*. Morning. I waited on Lord Lonsdale and Mr Lowther to Gresham-College; where Dr Woodward presented my Lord with his *Essay*,[188] and gave us handsome Discourses on his Rarities. See my Almanack.[189] Bringing my Lord home, we called at the *Spectacles* in Paul's Church-yard; where short Telescopes for the Pocket (at 8*s*. with one Sight, and 16*s*. double) Microscopes with Views on the Circulation of the blood in Newts and Gudgeons, Mites in rotten Cheese, Pepper-water, &c. To the House; where the Marquess of Lindsey's Bill (after the Queen's Counsel heard against it) thrown out, on the Question, by 33 against 19.[190] After I had dined, about Five, I went to visit the Archbishop of York; whom I found cheerful with the Duke of Roxborough, M[ajor] G[eneral] Fairfax,[191] &c.

[186] Thomas Bray (1656–1730), Vicar of St Botolph's without Aldgate, and the originator of the SPG. For the work of Bray through the SPCK to erect 'parocial libraries in the meanly endowed cures' see W. K. Lowther Clarke, *A History of the SPCK* (1959), pp. 77–80. The Act for the Better Preservation of Parochial Libraries received the royal assent on 21 Apr. 1709. The libraries reached Carlisle a year later. *CW* xxxv (1935), 124 (27 Mar. 1710).

[187] *CJ* xvi, 195 gives the figures as 141 to 75.

[188] *An essay towards a Natural History of the Earth* (1695, 2nd edn. 1702).

[189] No almanac for 1709 has survived.

[190] HMC *Lords MSS* viii, 303 gives the figures as eighteen against thirty-three. See ibid., pp. 302–3 for the bill.

[191] Thomas Fairfax, second son of Sir William Fairfax, Kt. of Steeton, Yorkshire. He had commanded a regiment of foot in Ireland before the Revolution, served in Flanders in 1697, and died, 1710, as a Major-General and Governor of Limerick. Dalton, iii, 74; v, 276.

[Apr.] 12. *Tuesday*. Morning After visits from Mr Anderson (who will return my Coins) Mr Eachard (who submits to my Advice and correction of his Preface &c.) and Mr Maddox introduceing Mr Tolman, goeing to Travel in Italy,[192] I waited on Lord Carlile; and gave him a List of six to be added to the Commission of Peace.[193] His Lordship promises fair in that, and other matters for the Chancellor &c.[194] Thence to Mr Chamberland [Chamberlayne] (at Whitehall) who shewed me a List of his Islandic, Frisian, Lithuanish, Rhetian and Curlandish, Bibles, with others; To Sir W. Fleming, deep in the Settlement of Affairs in Court and Country; with the Committee of Records in the Queen's Bench and Court of Wards, the latter most Scandalously neglected and abused by Mr Grimes. In the House, Counsel heard for and [against] Lord Clanrickard's Bill; to be farther considered on Friday. Dined. Dr Gibson carryed me into the Gardens and Park at Lambeth, till Archbishop at leisure; who very Frank in shewing me his Letters from Dr Lloyd, &c. and discoursing on our Differences in Parliament.

[Apr.] 13. *Wednesday*. Morning. After Mr Henley's visit (with his Thimble-full of Formality) I waited on Lord Hallifax; who upon kind Intentions towards the Cotton-Library and my self. Mr Attourney in the Gowt. The Court of Wards shewn (open) to Mr Smith, but soon shut up by me and Capt. Philips, with a Hang-Lock. The Fire-Bill[195] being gone through in a Grand Committee, I went to dine (at the *Dog*) with Dr Gibson, and Dr Waugh; the latter (in pain about the Rights of his Parish-Clerk) relieved with my Company to Smithfield (where a Bill of 38 *l.* paid me from Mr Ward) and Mr Johnson's Chambers, which the Evening past merrily.

[Apr.] 14. *Thursday*. Morning. Visited by my Brother, Mr Patrickson, still in Beggary; Mr Dean Stanley, and Dr Gee, assureing me that the Bishop of Lincoln was gone;[196] Mr Maddox, in want of more Subscriptions; Mr R. Lowther, in doubts about the Amendments made

[192] John Tolman (1677–1726), amateur architect and artist, left England for Italy in Sept. 1709. On his many foreign travels he formed a remarkable collection of prints and drawings and became the first Director of the Society of Antiquaries in 1717. H. M. Colvin, *Biographical Dictionary of English Architects, 1660–1840* (1954), pp. 589–91.

[193] See above, 29 Mar.

[194] Both Chancellor Tullie and Archdeacon Fleming were added to the commission of the peace in 1709 upon the recommendation of Nicolson. See Bodl. MS Add. C217, f. 41: N. to Lord Carlisle, 19 Mar. 1709; James, pp. 148–9.

[195] Mischiefs by Fire Prevention Act. See HMC *Lords MSS* viii, 305.

[196] Wake left London on 14 Apr. for his annual visit to his diocese (he usually spent most of the summer at his palace in Buckden). He returned to London on 5 Oct. 1709. Lambeth Palace MS 1770, ff. 78, 85: Wake's diary. Nicolson visited him at Buckden on 30 Apr. 1709, see below, n. 229.

by the Commons.[197] These (in the House) agreed to, with a Proviso; not to take Place till after the Death of the Pretender. On the Question, 47 against 27. All the Bishops with the former; and all the Scots with the latter.[198] Evening. Letters a while retarded by Mr Walker and Mr Relf.

[Apr.] 15. *Friday*. Morning Calling on Mr Smith (in M[anchester?] Court) we Rowed to Dr Gibson's; and paying a dry visit to Mr Henley at Carlile-House in the view of his High-way, we went (by Mr H. Watkinson's) to the Tower: where both the Repositories of Records shewn to Mr S[mith]. At the House, Lord Clanrickard's Bill, passed with a sleight Amendment. Evening. By Dr Lancaster, newly returned from Oxford, to Salisbury Court.

[Apr.] 16. *Saturday*. Morning. Two places taken (for the 28th) in the York-Coach, I went to visit Mr Elstob and his Sister; to whom I paid in four Subscriptions to their Saxon Homily.[199] He shewed me also his Stock of MSS. Laws of those Time; King Ælfred's Translation of *Orosius*;[200] King Ch[arles] the Second's original Letter[201] to Monsieur Testard (the French Protestant-minister) in defence of his Father's Ἐικων Βασιλικη &c. In my absence, a visit designed me by Sir William Cunningham: And, after my return, Dr Gee (with Dr South's Declaration in favour of the Statutes of Westminster)[202] Coll. Gledhil[203] and Mr Whittingdale, both lately returned from Carlile. In the House, till after Three, attending on Private (and Money) Bills; in pure Duty. Evening Cousin M. Orfeur; with a Ring for her mother.

[197] To the Treasons Bill. The two clauses added by the Commons on 8 Apr., after further amendments, became sections 13 and 14 of the Act. See HMC *Lords MSS* viii, 288; *LJ* xviii, 708, 714.

[198] For this debate see above, sessional intro., p. 474.

[199] See below, n. 208.

[200] This is probably a reference to King Alfred's translation of the six books of the world history of Orosius which had been in the Cotton Library since 1621 (Cotton Tiberius B.i.). It was not unknown for scholars to borrow manuscripts from the library.

[201] See above, 9 Apr.

[202] After the passing of Nicolson's Cathedrals Act doubts arose as to whether it affected the Westminster Abbey statutes, whose legal validity had been questioned. The Attorney-General, Sir James Montagu, and Sir Edward Northey gave their opinion that the Act only applied to the foundations of Henry VIII and not to an Elizabethan foundation such as Westminster.

[203] Samuel Gledhill, appointed Lieutenant-Colonel in 1707, having served in Flanders with distinction. Later he was to be appointed Lieutenant-Governor of Carlisle. He stood unsuccessfully for Carlisle at the election of 1710 and submitted a celebrated petition against the return of Sir James Montagu and the involvement of Nicolson in the election (see below, Sessional intro., pp. 512–14). Dalton, vi, 158.

[Apr.] 17. *Palm-Sunday*. I preached at Lambeth, dined at Dr Gibson's with Dr Sydal, went thence to St Martin's; where I accompanyed Dr Lancaster (in prospect of Relief from the Gowt) whilst Dr Gibson preached, and returned by water (and Dr Gibson's Study) home to my Lodgeings.

[Apr.] 18. *Munday*. Morning. After Mr Richardson's Account of Lord of York's Indisposition and his Brother Wickins's uneasyness, I went to Chelsea; forgetting that the Dean could not probably be returned from London. In our Return I had time to call at a Colour-Mill, which grinds (at a time) for the use of the Potters 28 several Sorts of compositions of Litharge of Tin, Lead, &c. with Ochres and other Earths; from whence I brought Samples of their Green-Whites, Sleight-whites and White-whites. The rest are most sent to them. But these they mix on the Spot, as I understood the young man that shewed me the Grinders and Pounders, &c. all carryed on by the wind. Visitted, upon my Return, by Dr Grandorge, to whom I gave Mr Wickins's State of his Liveing; and Mr Chamberlayne, who promises a List of Swedish Books. With the Latter to Dr Bentley; who improves every place as his last, undertakes (on Lord Hallifax's proposeals) to purchase in all the new Books of Europe with 500 *l.* per Annum and approves the Register-Bill following that of Naturalization, as what will bring in buyers of Land. The House, after Hearing Counsel in Sir Ar[thur] Shaen's Case,[204] the Bart. condemned in 20 *l.* Costs. Dined with Mr C. Musgrave where his Brother George and Mr Morley;[205] Sir Christopher and Mr Joseph both gone Northwards. Evening Dr Gee; with the empty Replyes of their Dean and his Party to Dr South's Paper about their Statutes.

[Apr.] 19. *Tuesday*. Morning Visitted by Sister Rothery and Cousin R. Nicolson. Item. Mr James Gordon called in my short Absence in the Hall; and Dr Grandorge (who followed me to the House) discourageing my waiting on Lord Thanet, throng in order to's Journey to morrow. The Amendments of the Commons (for the Clauses commenceing three years after the Queen's death)[206] agreed to without Division on the Question: Notwithstanding some faint Opposition by the Duke of Buckingham and Earl of Marr. Dined. Mr Smith with me; after three o'clock. Letters. NB. Lord Hallifax's Report from the Committee of Records was read in the Prince's

[204] See HMC *Lords MSS* viii, 275-6.
[205] ?George Morely (*c.*1664-1711), MP for Hindon, 1701-2, 1705-8, 1710-11.
[206] For the Commons' debate of 18 Apr. on the Treason Bill, when 'The Torys and most of the countrey Whigs stood ferm to us [the Scots]. But the Court and juncto were very diligent.' See NLS Yester MS 7021, f. 172: Yester to Tweeddale, 19 Apr. 1709.

Room to Lord Orford, &c. and, some Amendments being made at my Request, it was afterwards Reported to the House.[207]

[Apr.] 20. *Wednesday*. Morning With Mr James Gordon (by water) to St Swithin's; whence Mr Elstob (after I had given him Subscriptions from my self and Mr Thoresby)[208] accompanyed me to Bur-street in Wapping to repay a Visit to Cousin A. Pearson; thence to Black-Fryers, where Addenda to the Statute-Book bespoke; thence by Dr Gibson's, home. After this, Morning-Visitants, Dr Gibson and Mr James Lowther. At the House, Lord Sunderland delivered in Her Majesty's Gracious Act of Indemnity;[209] which had a single Reading (all the Lords sitting Bare) and was then put to the Question. Every Lord stood up, as he gave his *Content*; and continued standing till all had voted.[210] All other Bills finished. Dined at home, about Four. Evening (with honest Dr Waugh) eating a Barrel of Oysters at Salisbury Court. He saies, Dr Smaldrige highly commends Timothy and Philatheus.

[Apr.] 21. *Thursday*. Morning Cousin B. Nicolson; begging for her eldest Daughter and Mrs Roose; Mr How, Ship-Lieut, for a Capt's Commission; and Dr Gee, in despair of Right from his Dean. In the House, Royal Assent given (by Commission) to 22 public and 31 private Acts.[211] After which Lord Chancellor [Cowper] Prorougued the Parliament to Thursday, May 19. Duke of Marlborough arrived about Three.[212] Evening, with Mr Smith, to Ormond-street; whence,

[207] It was reported to the House on the following day, 20 Apr., see *LJ* xviii, 715–17. For the work of the select Committee on Records in this session see HMC *Lords MSS* viii, 27–8.

[208] The subscriptions were to the book by 'our Saxon nymph', Elizabeth Elstob. Nicolson also 'procured a few from my brethren of the bishop's bench, and some of my country-men in town'. Thoresby, *Letters* ii, 160: N. to Thoresby, 26 Apr.

[209] *LJ* xviii, 717. For a more detailed description of its passing the Lords see BL Add. MS 6116, ff. 11–12: N. to Wake, 21 Apr. 1709.

[210] See ibid. for a more detailed description of this procedure. This very comprehensive Act of Grace, pardoning all treasons, except those at sea, committed before 19 Apr., was largely designed as a sweetener for the Scots who had been forced to stomach the Treasons Act. Burnet, *History*, v, 409–10. For the intriguing, but unsubstantiated, suggestion that the true motive for the haste with which the Act was introduced and rushed through at record speed was to protect Lord Treasurer Godolphin from incriminating evidence of correspondence with St Germains, contained in a 'miraculous manuscript' recently acquired by Lord Wharton from the Marquess of Annandale, see Charles Hamilton, *Transactions during the Reign of Queen Anne* (1790), pp. 111–12, 120–1. Wharton had left London on 6 Apr. *en route* for Ireland (Luttrell, vi, 427).

[211] See *LJ* xviii, 719–24.

[212] At St James's (BL Add. MS 6116, ff. 11–12: N. to Wake, 21 Apr. 1709). The Duke had left England at the end of Mar. to hold a watching brief over the French–Dutch negotiation at The Hague. He reported home, and returned again on 4 May. *Marlborough–Godolphin Corr*. iii, 1234–47.

in very dirty wayes and weather, we were forced to walk home at Eleven, no Coach to be had. Dr H[ickes] highly offended (as his neighbour Nelson,[213] reputed Author of the late Letter to Lady Berkley) with the Looseness of our Grandees; in pain, and good humour otherwise: but, for Antiquities and Controversies, *Dixi*. Accounts not yet made up with E. Thw[aites] who, he finds, ought not to have been trusted — *de magno tollere acervo*.

[Apr.] 22. *Good-Friday*. Morning I preached and Administered the Sacrament for Dr Lancaster; who complains of Dr P[otter?]'s misrepresenting him (in the Case of Mr Caswel)[214] at Lambeth, his neglect in Reading, his *ab omnibus sequendum*. &c. In the Evening, after I had dined at home, I waited on the Archbishop of York who came cheerfully from the Queen; talked with me (about Mr Whiston's Arianism,[215] &c.) very Frankly; and gave me Dr Nichols's *Defensio Eccl[esiae] Angl[icanae]*.[216] Thence to Mr Chamberlain's. His Lacquered Ware, from the Indies, very fine; a rich return for an old Watch.

[Apr.] 23. *Saturday*. Morning. Parting with my Surgeon, visitted by Capt. Philips, Mr Whittingdale and Mr Sewel, who brought Mr Serjeant Wybergh with his promise of 30 *l.* per Annum to his Brother Jeoffrey, but no 70 *l.* ready money; Mr Thomas Todd,[217] like to lose (as he saies) the value of 80 *l.* by his Agent in Town; Mr Madox and Mr Tolman, projecting Cuts of antient Seals; Mr W. Johnson, with news of another Vacancy like to happen on our Borders; my Brother, not able to make up his Michaelmas-Accounts till the Sum of Tenths adjusted. After Dinner; Mr Dowson, presenting me with Tobacco

---

[213] Possibly Robert Nelson (1656–1715), non-juror and religious writer.

[214] John Caswell (c.1655–1712), Vice-Principal of Hart Hall, Beadle of Divinity, had been elected in Feb. 1709 as Savilian Professor of Astronomy at Oxford. At the convocation on 11 Mar. to elect his successor as Beadle, Lancaster had been defeated in his efforts to have one of his supporters elected. Hearne, *Collections*, ii, 171–2, 174–5.

[215] William Whiston (1667–1752), succeeded Newton as Lucasian Professor of Mathematics at Cambridge in 1703, and along with Richard Bentley and Samuel Clarke did much to popularise Newtonian theories. After his successful Boyle Lectures in 1707 he succumbed increasingly to the influence of Clarke and other anti-Trinitarians. Bishop Lloyd made strenuous efforts in Apr.–May 1709 to deter him from publishing his theories, but without success (Gloucester RO Lloyd-Baker MS: Lloyd to Sharp, 4 May 1709), and in 1710 he was to be banished from the university for an essay in which he expounded Arian doctrines. There is much valuable information on Whiston in J. Redwood, *Reason, Ridicule and Religion* (1976), *passim*.

[216] Published in London in 1707 and 1708. William Nicholls (1664–1712), author and divine.

[217] ?Thomas Todd, of Hutton, Cumberland, brother of Hugh, educated at Queen's College, Oxford, and perhaps Vicar of Corbridge, Northumberland, 1709.

and a Box; Dr Gee, desireing my Company to Lord Sommers; and Sir W. Fleming, free with old Lady Essex[218] and all her Family.

[Apr.] 24. *Easter-Day*. Morning I preached in the Abbey at Westminster to the Bishops of Rochester, Peterborough and St Asaph; Drs South, Bentley, Gee, &c. Dined with the Bishop of Rochester; where also Dr Bentley, Dr Knipe, Mr Friend and his Brother,[219] as also Archdeacon Sprat[220] and Mr Wilcock's (of Magdalen College Oxon.)[221] who preached in the afternoon on 1. *Corinthians* 15, 20.

[Apr.] 25. *Easter Munday*. Morning Running visits to Lord Towneshend, Lord Lonsdale, Lord Anandale, Dr Lancaster and Dr Yates. By water to the Chalk-Kilns in Southwark; and from Billingsgate (by Dr Waugh's) to Moorfields, where a Purchase of old Historians. Dined. At my Brother's, takeing Leave of Sister Rothery and Mrs Martin. Enquired for by 3 Tullies, Dr Gee, Dr Gibson, &c.

[Apr.] 26. *Tuesday*. Morning Mr Henley's visit over, I went with Mr Fromaine to Gresham-College, where Dr Woodward stuffed us with Metals, but was spareing of his Formed stones [fossils]. After Dinner I went to Lambeth; and took leave of Archbishop of Canterbury (kindly Inquisitive after Lord Lonsdale) and Dr Gibson's family. Evening. A surprizeing Visit from Lord High Admiral, the Earl of Pembroke, who (attended by Sir A. Fountaine) entertained me with a particular Account of Monsieur Mont-facon's New Book *De Re Diplomatica Graecorum*;[222] and the Inscription on the Middle-stone in Cornwal, mistaken by Cambden, but better explained (before him) by Mr Cary.[223] Afterwards, Mr Smith; bidding Farewel, for his

[218] Elizabeth Capell (1636–1718), wife of Arthur, 1st Earl of Essex, who had committed suicide in the Tower after the Rye House Plot.

[219] John Friend and his brother Robert.

[220] Thomas Sprat (c.1679–1720), Prebendary and Archdeacon of Rochester, 1704–20, also Canon of Winchester, 1712, and Westminster, 1713. He was the son of Bishop Sprat of Rochester (d. 1713).

[221] Joseph Wilcocks (1673–1756), Fellow of Magdalen College, 1703–22, DD 1709, Chaplain to Earl of Galway, Ambassador in Portugal, 1709, later Bishop of Gloucester, 1721, and of Rochester, 1731.

[222] Possibly a reference to *Palaeographia graeca* published in 1708 by Bernard de Montfaucon (1665–1741), the French scholar and antiquary.

[223] Here Nicolson appears to be confused. The stone in question is called 'The Otherhalf Stone' and the interpretation of the inscription *Doniert: rogavit pro anima* in Hiberno-Saxon minuscules was correctly given by Camden in his 1607 edition of *Britannia*. Camden's cut of the stone is, however, much inferior to Carew's in his *Survey of Cornwall* published in 1602. Carew, however, refrains from interpreting it. See R. G. Collingwood's note, *CW* xxxv (1935), 94.

Journey to morrow. Item. A Letter from Mr Chamberlayn; with the Lord's prayer in Finnish, Lappish, Lettish, Estish and Danish, from Mr A. Grub of Stockholm.

[Apr.] 27. *Wednesday*. Morning Visits to Lord Sommers, Lord Carlile and Lord Hallifax who presented me with the 8th Vol. of Rymer's Collection. The Journal examined by Bishop of Ely, Lord Hallifax and my self, to St Paul's day inclusive.[224] After dinner, visitted by Dean Atterbury; and, after a View of Mr Harley's Choice Library, and kind Treatment by the Owner, the Evening spent with 3 Tullies, Dr Bowes, &c. at the *Globe*.

[Apr.] 28. *Thursday*. Morning. Leave taken of Mr Chamberlayne, Bishop of Ely, Sir A. Fountain, Lord Carlile and Mr Attourney General [Montagu]. Dined At Lord Pembroke's; with Sir A. Fountain, Dr Swift,[225] &c. By the Vice-Chancellor's [Lancaster's] and Cousin R. Nicolson's to my brother's; and thence to the *Black-Swan*,[226] where Dr Waugh, my Brother, Mr Wenman and Mr Haddock[227] Companions to near Twelve. No Attendance on the Bishop of Chichester's Funeral.[228]

[Apr.] 29. *Friday*. Morning. Rainy. Set forward with Mr Adams, Mr Holdesworth, Mrs Lister and her maid and Child; and got, in good time to Bigleworth. 35 Miles.[229]

---

[224] The Lords' Journal was also examined up to 25 Jan. 1709 (St Paul's Day) by Lords Delawar and Dartmouth. *LJ* xviii, 615.

[225] Jonathan Swift (1667–1745), writer and satirist, later Dean of St Patrick's, Dublin. For Swift's association with Pembroke, the former Lord-Lieutenant of Ireland, see his letter to the Earl of 13 June 1709, *Swift Corr.* i, 139–41. Swift had been in London since mid-Dec. 1707 and left for Ireland on 5 May 1709. See ibid., pp. 56–9, 140 n. 5, 145 n. 1.

[226] Probably the one in Holborn, near the Fetter Lane end, see B. Lillywhite, *London Signs* (1972), no. 3484.

[227] Possibly James Haddock, a citizen of Carlisle. See *CW* ii (1902), 173; iv (1904), 36.

[228] Bishop John Williams had died on 24 Apr. at Grey's Inn and was buried on 28 Apr. in St Mildred Poultry.

[229] Nicolson travelled north to Stamford, calling on Bishop Wake at Buckden, Huntingdonshire., on 30 Apr. He continued via Doncaster to Bolton Percy in Yorkshire where he stayed with Archdeacon Pearson. On 5 May he visited Thoresby at Leeds, crossing the Pennines on 6 May to Oxenholm near Kendal. On 10 May 'apprehensive of a Fit of Gravel' he travelled via Penrith to Rose, where he arrived 'about 8 in the Evening. Very weary. *Deo Triuni Gloria*.' *CW* xxxv (1935), 95–6.

Session 7

8 December 1710–5 April 1711

After leaving London in April 1709, Nicolson was to spend nineteen continuous months in his diocese. It was to be his longest break from Westminster politics since the winter of 1703–4. As a consequence of this extended period in the north, Nicolson was to miss the second —and, as events turned out, the final—session of the parliament of 1708–10. He has left no clear record of his reasons for absenting himself from the whole of this session of 1709–10, though he was apparently very unwell when it opened.[1] It is true that in the spring of 1710 he undertook his third triennial visitation of the diocese, but this began only after the parliamentary session had ended.

The year and a half away from Westminster were filled with the usual mixture of ecclesiastical, social, and political business, with an occasional antiquarian visit thrown in.[2] One of Nicolson's first important visitors in the summer of 1709 was Bishop Dawes of Chester who was passing through Carlisle during his primary visitation of the second largest diocese in England.[3] The late summer and autumn brought news of the Pyrrhic victory of Malplaquet, Marlborough's bloodiest and most controversial triumph, the sequel to the breakdown of the peace negotiations at The Hague earlier in the year, and the decisive turning-point in the alienation of the Tories, and of much of British public opinion, from the Spanish Succession War. Carlisle also heard the first rumblings of the trouble in Scotland over the use of the English liturgy in Episcopalian churches.

By the time parliament opened on 15 November 1709, Nicolson had decided not to attend, though he wrote to Wake to request that 'if anything of moment comes in view you will please to give some short hint of it; that I may either bring you my corporal appearance, or send my representative'. By mid-December he had supplied Wake with his proxy.[4]

With Tory country members reluctant to leave their estates and the morale of the whole Tory party at Westminster manifestly low, the Whigs in November had high expectations of a smoothly

[1] He had pleaded 'my great Indisposition in the beginning of this Session' and the great distance between Carlisle and Westminster (Bodl. MS Add. C.217, f. 44: N. to Portland, 1 Jan. 1710).
[2] Nicolson's diary for these months is printed in *CW* xxxv (1935), 96–139.
[3] Ibid. pp. 103–4; BL Add. MS 6116, ff. 12–13: N. to Wake, 18 July 1709.
[4] BL Add. MS 6116, ff. 16–17: N. to Wake, 19 Nov., 15 Dec. 1709.

triumphant session. Scarcely anyone anticipated the appearance this winter of an affair of such 'moment' as to change, more dramatically than any single event of Queen Anne's reign, the whole complexion of British politics. This was the impeachment and trial of Dr Henry Sacheverell for printing the sermon he had preached at St Paul's on 5 November 1709 against 'false brethren in Church and State'. First news of the case appears to have reached Rose on 21 December. By early February 1710, with the opening of the trial still some weeks away, Nicolson had put himself on a state of 'alert' and informed Wake and Gibson 'that my Horses were ready for Saddling on an Hours warning; and that on a lawfull Call, I should not be backward in venturing my carcass'. He still thought, however, that there would be 'no necessary Occasion for such a Jaunt', despite the fact that his proxy could not be used in any judicial vote. The Bishop was kept in touch by Wake with the progress of the trial, but the call never came and Nicolson felt at liberty to stay in the country for the rest of the session (parliament was prorogued on 5 April 1710).[5]

Nicolson's triennial visitation opened on 24 April at Carlisle and he proceeded around his diocese until 5 May. His work closed with his visitation of the Chapter: 'I went to the Deanry as three Years Agoe [he wrote to Wake]; and met with a much kinder Reception than at that time . . . when (after Prayers) we came to the Chapter-House all went on very calmly . . . without any manner of Protestation or Demur.' The lack of conflict this time was probably due to Dean Atterbury's last-minute decision to be absent. The deserted Todd, angling as ever for the next vacancy in the deanery, not only behaved himself, but as Treasurer for the year, provided dinner 'in a splendid Manner . . . the Plenty and Choice of Dishes was beyond what I ever saw in that Place'.[6]

The summer of 1710, following the trauma of the Sacheverell trial, saw a basic reconstruction of the Queen's government. In mid-June Sunderland, a linch-pin of the Junto and the Marlboroughs' son-in-law, was replaced as Secretary of State by a moderate Tory, Dartmouth. On 12 August Nicolson received the chilling news of Lord Treasurer Godolphin's fall from power. In September most of the leading Whigs still left in the Cabinet followed him out of office, with the resignation or dismissal of Boyle, Somers, Devonshire, Cowper, Wharton, and Orford, who had been appointed First Lord of the Admiralty only the previous November. These events were the

[5] CW xxxv (1935), 117, 123-4; BL Add. MS 6116, ff. 19, 20-1: N. to Wake, 2 Feb., 23 Mar. 1710. See Holmes, Sacheverell, for the background and aftermath of the trial.
[6] CW xxxv (1935), 126, 130; BL Add. MSS 6116, ff. 24, 26-7: N. to Wake, 25 May, 1 July, 31 Aug. 1710.

climax to Harley's 'great scheme' (unfolded in April when Shrewsbury replaced Kent as Lord Chamberlain) to overthrow the Godolphin
ministry and his Whig Junto supporters, without, he hoped, opening
the door for the extreme Tories to seize control of a new administration.

For Nicolson also the summer of 1710 was an eventful one politically, despite the fact that the effects on his diocese of the trial and
of Sacheverell's subsequent triumphal tour proved, fortunately for
him, to be minimal.[7] On 8 July he had advance warning from Lord
Carlisle that Harley and the Queen intended to call a new parliament. For at least a month thereafter he declined to believe that
there would be a dissolution, misled by the remoteness and false
perspective of his diocese, and convinced that the most favourable
time for the Tories, 'whilst the Spirit of the Dr was most vigorously
upon us', was past. Even if events were to prove him wrong, he predicted 'that the County of Cumberland would (as at present) send up
five Whigs for One Tory'. By late August, however, Nicolson found
himself involved in discussing Whig strategy for the forthcoming
elections. At a meeting on 28 August at Naworth, the Earl of
Carlisle's home, the mayor and aldermen of Carlisle 'unanimously
assured him that they'd continue their present Representatives (Mr
Attorney General [Montagu] and Brigadier Stanwix) if a Dissolution
happened'. Three days later at the quarter sessions, Lord Carlisle,
more sensitive than the Bishop to the national climate, decided to
bid for a renewed compromise between the parties in the shire.
'After dinner [Nicolson wrote of the Earl], proposes the Peace of the
County in Election of Knights. Agreed that the two present [James
Lowther and Gilfred Lawson] *neither directly nor indirectly assist
a Third.*'

In the event, at Carlisle a Tory, Colonel Samuel Gledhill, formerly
a client of Lord Carlisle, who allegedly owed him £200 for the
purchase of a commission and refused either to reimburse him or to
put him up at Carlisle in lieu, was to stand for election as a burgess
along with Montagu—the brother of the Bishop's friend, Lord
Halifax—and Stanwix. Official news of the dissolution of parliament reached Rose on 27 September and the election at Carlisle was
held on 16 October. Stanwix, a 'favourite son' of the city 'rabble',
came top of the poll with 395 votes, Montagu was second with 276,
and Gledhill trailed behind with 167. This result was clearly against
the national trend where the Tories won a crushing victory. Although
Nicolson refused an invitation to attend in person, he had cam-
paigned vigorously for Montagu against Gledhill, and the election

[7] Holmes, *Sacheverell*, p. 237.

at Carlisle was to have important repercussions in parliament, agitating Nicolson's political life both in the 1710–11 and the 1711–12 sessions of parliament (see, for 1710–11, below, 20 Feb., 3, 8, 10, 14–15 March).[8]

The case of James Greenshields was to bulk almost as large as that of Carlisle in Nicolson's London experience in 1710–11. The Bishop was well known as a channel for Scottish lobbying and as a source of information on Scottish affairs at Westminster, and it was as such that he was contacted by Greenshields in person in September 1710. Nicolson had heard as early as August 1709, through his many unofficial contacts in Scotland, of the storm clouds that were gathering round Edinburgh and were destined to drift south; and the man at the centre of the storm later wrote to him describing his case and condition.

Born and bred in Scotland, James Greenshields had been ordained an Episcopalian priest in 1694 by the Bishop of Ross, thereafter taking a parochial cure in Ireland, which he still held. While visiting friends in Edinburgh, the citadel of Scottish Presbyterianism, in February 1709, he was prevailed upon to set up a meeting house with the English liturgy. On 21 August the Act of the Commission of the General Assembly against innovations in worship was published, and on 7 September Greenshields was cited before the Presbytery and suspended. He continued to preach and read the liturgy, in defiance alike of the Kirk's censure and the ban of the city magistrates, and was therefore committed to the Tolbooth Prison on 15 September. Greenshields found Nicolson sympathetic to his cause and in favour of wider and more secure toleration for Scottish Episcopalians. The Bishop hoped 'that some Expedient were found out for the Setting our Liturgy on an equal Foot in Scotland with the Presbyterian Worship in England', though he feared that 'this project', which was likely to attract much more Tory than Whig support south of the border, 'will hardly be carried on without blows'. Greenshields took his case on appeal first, unsuccessfully, to the Lords of the Session, and then to the House of Lords in February 1710; but the noise it might normally have made was 'drowned with the Huzzaes on Dr S[acheverell]'s Triumph'. Although this dampened Nicolson's desire to see any Experiments tryed on the Scots for the present: ''Tis enough [he thought] at once to be Stark mad on one side of the Tweed', he remained well

---

[8] *CW* xxxv (1935), 130, 133–6; BL Add. MS 6116, ff. 25–6, 26–7: N. to Wake, 7 and 31 Aug. 1710; Levens Hall MS D/T: Todd to Grahme, 26 Sept. 1710; Kent Archives Office, Chevening MS U1590 C9/34: Gledhill to Stanhope, 17 Sept. 1714; HMC *Portland MSS* iv, 565, 578–9.

disposed, and Greenshields left Rose after a week's visit in September 1710 with a recommendation to Wake 'that both the Man himself and his Cause have a just title to our Compassion'.[9] William Nicolson was to fight hard in the 1710–11 session, against a good deal of opposition (not least from Harley and his ministerial allies), for the successful conclusion to the Lords' hearing of the case which was at length obtained.[10]

By the time that Nicolson received his parliamentary writ, on 7 October 1710, the Tories were in control of the Queen's government and had won a spectacular victory at the polls. Harley had been able to complete his Tory appointments to his cabinet, finding places for the moderates Dartmouth and Poulet, for two friends who had shared his defeat in February 1708, St John and Harcourt, and for three High Tories, Rochester, Buckingham, and Ormond. And although the transactions were kept a complete secret even from their colleagues until the following April, Harley and his co-manager Shrewsbury, had already made the first cautious moves in the long negotiations with France which were to culminate, first in the preliminaries of September 1711, and finally in the Utrecht Settlement of 1713. Nicolson had seen the writing on the wall for his party by late August 1710, and recognised its implications for himself: 'This I do believe [he wrote to Wake] that your Lordship, and my other Governors will scarce allow me to keep at home this next Winter; and therefore I am prepareing to obey your Summons.' He duly began his journey south on 28 November 1710, three days after parliament had opened. Travelling via Appleby, Boroughbridge, Ferrybridge, Doncaster, and Newark, much of the way through storms and floods, he proceeded to Stamford and Huntingdon, and thence 'to Buntingford, 22 miles; whereof 17 the worst in England'; and he reached London on 8 December.[11]

Although confined to his lodgings for some days after his arrival with what appears to have been a cyst on his neck, Nicolson was immediately briefed by Gibson on proceedings so far in parliament and Convocation (see below, 10 December). In the wake of the

---

[9] *CW* xxxv (1935), 107, 134–5; BL Add. MS 6116, ff. 15–22, 26: N. to Wake, 29 Aug., 13 Oct., 19 Nov., 15 Dec. 1709, 5 Jan., 2 and 25 Feb., 23 Mar., 3 Apr., 18 Sept., 1710. For the background to the Greenshields case see Trevelyan, *Queen Anne*, iii, 236–9; W. L. Mathieson, *Scotland and the Union: a history of Scotland from 1695 to 1747* (Glasgow, 1905), pp. 195–9. An excellent contemporary account, from a strong episcopal Tory standpoint but very revealing, especially on Harley's attitude, is in *The Lockhart Papers*, ed. A. Aufrere (1817), i, 339–41, 345–8.

[10] For a discussion of Nicolson's parliamentary activities during the Greenshields case see above, Chapter 1, pp. 49–50.

[11] BL Add. MS 6116, ff. 25–6: N. to Wake, 7 and 31 Aug. 1710; *CW* xxxv (1935), 136, 139.

Sacheverell affair and of the fall of Godolphin, new heights of Tory fervour and the battle-cry of 'the Church in danger' had produced not only a 'country Tory' majority in the Commons—the largest since the Revolution[12] and soon destined to be further swollen by the unseating of Whigs in disputed elections, such as that for Devizes (see below, 17 December); it had also given rise to a rampant High Church majority in the Lower House of Convocation. Atterbury, who was recognised on all sides as by far the strongest candidate for the prolocutorship of the Lower House, designed to use the synod to put into effect an ambitious programme of measures for the revival of the Church's influence, in which he counted on the co-operation of the Commons under their new Speaker, William Bromley, his friend and a true son of Christ Church. On 25 November, despite the concerted opposition of Tenison and the bishops, the Dean of Carlisle was triumphantly elected Prolocutor. The Queen, fearful of further internecine broils among the clergy, ignored Tenison completely and arranged through Harley, Rochester, George Hooper, and Archbishop Sharp that the agenda of Convocation should be limited to a discussion of heretical books, the practice of excommunication in Church courts, and the project of a union between the Anglican Church and the Lutheran church of Prussia.[13]

The royal licence and letters of business read in the Upper House on 24 January 1711 were, however, Atterburian in tone and content, and they shocked the Archbishop's party, who had already been warned not to resort to procedural devices to block the Queen's policies. Yet it was not long before the work of the Convocation, skilfully obstructed in its more controversial aspects by White Kennett and a dedicated minority of Low Churchmen, was overwhelmed by detailed committee work and disputes over the implications of the new form of royal licence (see below, 24 January, n. 171).[14] It dragged on through the months of February to April, and little was achieved beyond the scheme for a number of churches, chapels and meeting-houses in and near the cities of London and Westminster. On 26 January Convocation petitioned the Queen to favour the project, and she commended it to parliament, where the Commons had, in fact, already taken an independent initiative. Such were the origins of the Act for the Fifty New Churches of 1711. After the Easter recess (Nicolson having by this time departed

[12] For the English results see W. A. Speck, *Tory and Whig: The Struggle in the Constituencies 1701–1715* (1970). Roughly two-thirds of the forty-five Scottish members returned in 1710 were expected to support the new ministry.

[13] T. Sharp, *Life of Sharp* (1825), i, 351–3; BL Lansdowne MS 1013, ff. 142–3: Kennett to Blackwell, 13 Jan. 1711.

[14] Cf. BL Lansdowne MS 1024: Kennett's diary, 18 Jan.

for the north) the High Churchmen in Convocation were unwisely side-tracked into an investigation of the heretical works of William Whiston, and when the assembly was prorogued on 12 June it was clear that the High Church project had failed.[15]

Though a non-participant Nicolson closely observed the conflict among the clergy of Canterbury province, his interest doubtless accentuated by Atterbury's dominant part in it. There was news, however, early in the session of a possible end to Nicolson's formal relationship with his troublesome Dean (see below, 18 December). On 14 December Dean Aldrich of Christ Church, Oxford, died. The reversion of the deanery had been promised to Atterbury by Harley as early as 1704. But Sharp's decision to campaign on behalf of George Smalridge, unsuccessful candidate for the Regius Chair of Divinity in 1707-8,[16] and the Queen's procrastination caused a long delay, and it was September 1711 before Francis Atterbury landed his rich prize.

The seven-month parliamentary session of 1710-11, the longest of the reign so far, was given dramatic unity in the House of Commons by the struggle of the new Prime Minister, Robert Harley, to hold in check the extremist wing of the massive Tory majority in St Stephen's Chapel. By the time that Harley came face to face with this first parliament of his ministry three overriding aims had begun to take precedence over all other considerations in his mind, the third being, as he saw it, a necessary consequence of the other two. Most basic was his determination to end the war at the earliest feasible opportunity, but to do so (as the Queen's speech made clear) from a position of military strength. This policy was backed by almost the whole Cabinet, for as St John later put it, 'the worse condition we are in, the worse peace we are likely to obtain';[17] but not all his supporters accepted Harley's own conclusion that if the record supplies needed to support another year of war were to be voted, nothing—and certainly not controversial partisan legislation or protracted vendettas against the Whigs—must be allowed to obstruct them. The second and most immediate task which Harley set himself, very much his personal responsibility as Chancellor of the Exchequer and the guiding spirit at the Treasury Board, was the resolution of the serious credit crisis inherited from the Godolphin regime and the establishment of the new administration on a financial

---

[15] For a full discussion of the Convocation of 1711, see G. V. Bennett, 'The Convocation of 1710: an Anglican attempt at counter-revolution', in Studies in Church History, vii, ed. G. J. Cuming and D. Baker (Cambridge, 1971), pp. 311-19; Bennett, Tory Crisis, pp. 125-38.

[16] See below, 18 Dec.

[17] HMC Portland MSS v, 676: to Harley, 19 Apr. 1711.

foundation that would be thoroughly secure. Emergency measures taken the previous August had been purely palliative; the disease remained, with stocks depressed and the City nervous, if not hostile, and when Nicolson came to town he found Whig friends who claimed some knowledge of the market cheerfully pessimistic about the ministry's financial prospects (see below, 12 December).[18] Quite apart from Harley's own inbred aversion from extreme courses and the knowledge that the Queen was even more apprehensive than he was himself of a total surrender of her government to the High Tories, both his peace aims and his financial priorities dictated the adoption right through the session of 1710-11 of a domestic policy of 'moderation'. It was not so much a question of letting sleeping dogs lie—for the obvious reason that most of the Tory hounds were only too wide awake—but rather of turning a deaf ear, much of the time, to their barking and throwing them an occasional meagre bone on which to gnaw away their frustrations.

Frustrations on the Tory benches there certainly were; and more than that—suspicions, hardening with every week that went by in December 1710 and January 1711, that a first minister who seemed unwilling to purge scores of surviving Whigs, including many MPs, from their offices, and who was known to be still on good terms with some leading figures in the Whig party, notably Newcastle and Halifax, was no more to be trusted now by the true sons of 'the Church party' than he had been in the days of 'the Tack'. For a while the energies of the malcontents were spent in traditional 'country' channels, such as the promotion of a new Place Bill, aimed at severely curtailing the number of office holders entitled to sit in the Lower House. But measures of this kind, which had always claimed substantial support from backbench Whigs, as well as Tories,[19] and (as Nicolson found from his fellow-Cumbrian, James Lowther) still did so (see below, 23 December), could not appease the deep partisan hunger of the Tories; especially when their suspicions were sharpened by the defeat of the Place Bill, whose summary rejection in the House of Lords by an unholy alliance of ministerial peers and Junto followers was deeply resented (see below, 2 and 3 February).

The result was a new political phenomenon, to which Nicolson was introduced, somewhat misleadingly, on 6 February. From the

---

[18] Cf. Lord Halifax's prophecy to the Duke of Newcastle on 26 Oct. that the government's credit was 'past retrieve' (HMC *Portland MSS* ii, 223). The best treatment of the credit crisis is in B. W. Hill, 'The Change of Government and the "Loss of the City", 1710-1711', *Ec.HR* 2nd Ser. xxiv (1971).

[19] For the 'Place' campaigns of 1692-1714, and the involvement of the Country Whigs in Anne's reign, see Holmes, *British Politics*, pp. 130-6.

first week in February until the early summer, politics in the Commons were dominated by the efforts of Harley and his supporters to keep at bay, not the Whig opposition, which was for the most part powerless as an independent force, but the October Club. This club, originally with near seventy members rising to 150 by April, constituted 'the largest and the most powerful of all the parliamentary pressure-groups to develop within either party in the years before 1715'.[20] Its avowed aims, developed at its Wednesday meetings in the *Bell* Tavern, were 'to force partisan policies on the Harley administration and to institute an anti-Whig vendetta, and they were fully prepared to use fair means or foul to attain these ends, including the systematic obstruction of supply and ways and means.'[21]

It was one of the earliest surges of the October Club—a minor one, compared with what was to come—which caught up Bishop Nicolson in its frothing wake. On 2 December 1710 Colonel Gledhill had petitioned the Commons against the return of Sir James Montagu for Carlisle, alleging partiality on the part of the mayor, Thomas Brougham, and bribery by Montagu's agents. The petition was referred to the Committee of Elections, where, taking its place in the queue along with another three score, its hearing was put back until the following March. The impatient Gledhill, after two fruitless attempts to get preferential treatment, at last persuaded Charles Eversfield, Tory knight of the shire for Sussex and one of the most prominent of the new October men, to raise the matter in the Commons on 19 February 1711.

Eversfield's tactic was to complain to the House of a letter written by Montagu to the Bishop of Carlisle after the former's removal in September 1710 from the post of Attorney-General. Gledhill's party in Carlisle had been quick to allege that Montagu's dismissal was a sure sign that the Queen did not wish to see him re-elected to parliament. Montagu's response had been to tell Nicolson that 'though the Queen had thought fit to put another in his Place, yet he was so far from having incurred her Majesty's Displeasure, that, on the contrary, her Majesty had graciously been pleased, in consideration of former services, to bestow on him a Pension of 1000 *l.* per annum'.[22] Nicolson circulated copies of this letter without

---

[20] Holmes, *British Politics*, p. 342. See below, 6 Feb. The earliest reference to the club, by 'the name of the Loyal Club' is in early Jan. 1711. 'Near 70', met on 2 Jan., 'to be honest and oppose the measures of the Court party.' Suffolk RO, Ipswich, Gurdon MS M142 (1), vol. 2, p. 149: R. Berney to T. Gurdon, 3 Jan. 1710[/11]. We should like to thank David Hayton for this reference.

[21] Holmes, *British Politics*, p. 342.

[22] This is the Whig journalist Boyer's version of the contents of the letter, in *Political State*, i–ii (1711), 247.

Montagu's knowledge (or so Nicolson later averred, below, 14 March). Gledhill objected that since Montagu 'had a place of profit, meaning the pension, he could not be chosen Member', to which Montagu responded with a second letter to Nicolson, again made public by the Bishop, 'intimating, that he had no Place of Profit, but only a Pension for Life, which qualifyed him to be chosen'. Eversfield's charge was that in this second letter Montagu claimed that the Queen had given him the pension 'to enable him to carry his Election'.[23] Since Montagu was not in the House on 19 February, the attack was renewed the following day, to the great interest of a new Scottish member, Mungo Graham, soon to be the victim himself of a Tory election petition:

> Mr Eversfield accordingly made the complaint, and made no other use of it then to bring the house in to order the Committee to hear the merits of the election within a short day. . . . Sir Ja[mes]'s friends upon tableing the Complaint told that this being a reflection upon the Q[ueen] it was a matter of far greater consequence than any elections, and theirfor insisted to have the matter immediately enquired into . . .
>
> Upon this the house agreed that the Gentleman [Gledhill] should be called to the bar. Accordingly being brought he repeated the accusation, as Mr Eversfield had represented it, and being askt how he came to know of such a letter, he said that it was handed about at the election, that he had seen it then, and had taken notes of it. Being askt if he had these notes upon him he pulled out of his pocket book, and read them. These notes spoke of Sir Ja[mes] haveing got a pension of £1000 to enable him to serve her Majesty, but not on[c] word about securing elections. Being askt if he saw any such words in the letter, he said no, but that a gentleman who told him that he had read it informed him so. Upon which he was ordered to withdraw, and the question was moved that Mr Gleddel for haveing prevaricated in his evidence should be taken into custody.[24] This debate lasted long (about 4 or 5 hours). At last Mr Gleddell being called in again told, that he had no other way to prove his accusation but by witnesses, and so craved 3 weeks time to bring them up.[25] Then the debate run if he shall have that time

---

[23] *Political State*, i–ii (1711), 247.

[24] This was moved and seconded by Generals Webb and Erle. See NLS Wodrow Letters Quarto v, item 91;   ? to R. Wodrow, 22 Feb. 1711, which is another account of this debate.

[25] Gledhill on being called in again (according to Wodrow's correspondent in ibid.) said he had two witnesses at the door who 'could satisfy the house there was such a letter. Being called in one of them said he only heard a letter read upon Sunday after Service by the

allowed, and upon a division of 154 to 151 it carryed that he should. Its to be observed that in this division Whig and Court were joyned, and Clear [i.e. pure] October [Club] carried it against both.[26]

Mr Harley was in the house all the time, and spoke very warmly for Sir James.[27] The Whigs left the debate to the Court, so it went betwixt them and October. I forgot to tell you that before they came to the question Mr Walpole told them that the Bishop of Carlisle was at the door, and had the original letter, and desired to be allowed to come in, and he would give the House a full account of that matter. Accordingly a chair was brought in, but before the Bishop was called, the question was put, and thereby the Bishop had not the opportunity to tell his story.[28] Its said theirs not on[e] word of elections in the letter and that Mr Gladhill can make nothing of it. It seems he's a man of the army but of a bad character their, which General Earle and General Web told out in the house . . .[29]

It was 14 March before Nicolson appeared before the Commons, and the result was his condemnation by the House for concerning himself in the Carlisle election and thus infringing the liberties and privileges of the House. Gledhill failed to carry his charge against Montagu, though the House resolved that he had sufficient grounds for bringing it.[30] It may be doubted whether Nicolson fully shared one Whig MP's view of the outcome, as 'a deadly blow to the October-men' (see below, 19 March).

His censure had no long-term effect, none the less, on the irrepressible Nicolson. At the time of the 1713 election he wrote to James Lowther:

Curate of Carlisle, said to be Written by the Bishop of that place, which had some such words. The other witness could not be found.'

[26] See below, 20 Feb., n. 248. Sir Simon Harcourt, the Lord Keeper, thought that Gledhill had not 'well concerted' his case and that the October Tories would have been prepared to drop his flimsy accusations, but that the fury of Montagu's party made them contend for Gledhill to have time to substantiate his charges (Bodl. MS Ballard 10, f. 125: Harcourt to Charlett, 23 Feb. 1711).

[27] For a variety of reasons. He was anxious not to give gratuitous offence to the many Whigs still in minor offices, of whom he later wrote (HMC Portland MSS v, 464), 'it was impossible, as well as inadvisable to remove them, but by degrees'; he valued his continued friendship with Halifax; and he was concerned about the Queen's involvement in the case, especially since he had himself recommended Sir James's pension.

[28] Harley was also in favour of hearing Nicolson's testimony (NLS Wodrow Letters Quarto v, item 91).

[29] SRO GD220/5/808/22: Graham to Montrose, 22 Feb. 1711.

[30] HMC Portland MSS iv, 595, 632; v, 628; Political State, i-ii (1711), 246-9; M. Ransome, 'Church and dissent in the election of 1710', EHR lvi (1941), 83-4; information supplied by Dr Eveline Cruickshanks on behalf of the History of Parliament Trust.

One that has been so remarkably buffetted (by your Honourable House) for intermedling in Elections ought not to be fond of thursting [sic] into such crowds; and yet, so little Impression had that discipline on me, I would venture very far to serve so good a[nd] great a man as General Stanhop [at Cockermouth].[31]

Nicolson had had an opportunity to demonstrate his admiration for Stanhope two and a half years earlier in the House of Lords, at a time when the general, who had commanded the British forces in the Peninsula from 1708 to December 1710, had just fallen into French hands as a prisoner of war. For possibly the most strident issue to arise in the Lords during the session of 1710–11 was the re-opening of the grand inquest into the war in Spain, of which little had been heard in parliament since its initiation in the winter of 1707–8.

The House of Lords held a key place in Harley's political strategy in 1710–11, a place dictated partly by the balance of party forces there, but even more by the unruliness of the Commons. Even before the first election results had confirmed the expected temper of the new House of Commons, the Queen's first minister had been busy calculating the strength of his support among the peers. On 3 October he had drawn up three lists,[32] one of peers expected to oppose the administration (among them a squad of moderate or Low Church bishops),[33] a second of doubtfuls (mostly Court Whigs), and a third of reliable supporters. As a hypothetical exercise this was quite re-assuring, since it appeared to show that with the addition of sixteen representative peers of Scotland, where Harley expected, correctly, a clean sweep for the government's 'list' of candidates, there would be seventy-seven firm administration supporters at the beginning of the new parliament, slightly more than the totals for doubtfuls and firm opponents combined. Yet, in fact, the paper position was mis-leading, as the uneasiness of both Harley and his chief Cabinet ally, Shrewsbury, before the opening of the session[34] makes clear. There were too many old or ailing Tory peers for comfort—by December they had already begun to 'drop apace'[35]—and some of the rest

[31] Cumbria (Carlisle) RO Lonsdale MSS D/Lons/W/26: N. to [Lowther], -?- Sept. 1713.

[32] BL Loan 29/10/19.

[33] Canterbury, Winchester, Worcester, Salisbury, Hereford (query), Lichfield, Ely, Peterborough, Gloucester, Oxford, Bangor, Lincoln, Llandaff, Norwich, and St Asaph. There was one bishop among the doubtfuls (Chichester) and eight reliable supporters (York, Durham, London, Rochester, Bristol, Bath and Wells, St Davids, and Exeter). The missing bishops are Nicolson and Dawes of Chester. Nicolson may have been omitted because he was absent from the previous session.

[34] HMC Bath MSS i, 199: Shrewsbury to Harley, 20 Oct. 1710; Miscellaneous State Papers, ed. 2nd Earl of Hardwicke (1778), ii, 487: memo by Harley for the Queen, 30 Oct.

[35] HMC Portland MSS v, 127: Dr Robert Freind to Edward Harley, 9 Dec. [1710] (mis-dated 1711).

were habitual absentees. Almost from the start, therefore, Harley was convinced that the success of the session (and, if the Commons' Tories turned ugly, perhaps even the survival of his administration) depended on how many of some thirty Whig peers of doubtful allegiance[36] could be persuaded, either by the ties of offices still carefully preserved in their hands or by their sensitivity to Treasury pressure, to support a Tory-dominated, but moderate-faced, ministry rather than risk, by adherence to the Junto, delivering the Queen into the hands of High Church or even Jacobite extremists. In the end Harley succeeded in holding the votes of roughly a dozen—invaluable alike in smothering controversial legislation sent up from the Commons (e.g. the Place Bill and the bill to repeal the General Naturalization Act of 1709, see respectively below, 2–3 February and 5 February) and in preventing the well-organised forces of the Junto from capturing the initiative in the House of Lords; and in this success the issue of Spain played a very important part.

Right up to the Christmas recess both Junto and ministry trod extremely warily in the Lords, both sides being anxious to choose the ground carefully for the first big clash of this parliament, and Harley especially so, because he needed to find an issue which would attract some moderate backing from the Whig side. He was working explicitly on the assumption that since the Junto 'have most of their strength . . . and most of their able men' in the Lords, they would 'attempt to unite themselves at first by some vote'; so that it was imperative for the government party 'to secure those who are to be had before they are engaged too far the other way'.[37] That Spain should provide the issue he was looking for early in the New Year was certainly not the ministry's desire from the start. On the contrary, ever since Stanhope's victory at Saragossa in the summer there had been plenty of confident talk in Tory circles about 'pushing' the war in Spain as the surest way of bringing Louis XIV quickly to terms;[38] and both the pointed reference to the Peninsula in the Queen's Speech at the opening of parliament[39] and Harley's private correspondence, especially a remarkable confidence he exchanged with William Stratford,[40] indicates that he and many of his fellow

[36] Twenty-five of them listed thus by Harley on 3 Oct., plus a few other Court Whigs, e.g. Schomberg, Grafton, Kent, and Fitzwalter, whom he had at that time over-optimistically placed on his 'safe' list.

[37] Hardwicke, *State Papers*, ii, 487.

[38] *Private Correspondence of the Duchess of Marlborough* (1838), ii, 11; Berkshire RO Trumbull MS 54, f. 38: Ralph Bridges to Sir W. Trumbull, 8 Nov. 1710.

[39] *CJ* xvi, 403.

[40] 'The news from Spaine proves better than the first report. I look upon that country as conquerd once more, and if we don't take pains to manage it away, it wil bring a Peace.' (BL Loan 29/171: 16 Sept.; see also Loan 29/238, f. 373: Harley to Newcastle, 14 Sept.)

Cabinet ministers shared some of this euphoria. So the news which reached London on 24 December that Stanhope's army had been disastrously defeated, and many of its survivors forced to surrender at Brihuega[41] was a double shock to the ministers. On the one hand they were stunned by the wreckage of their war-peace strategy by 'this dreadful turn';[42] but on the other they were extremely apprehensive that the Whigs would exploit the defeat with a censure vote in the Lords that might gravely damage the government's reputation and destroy its still precarious credit.[43] Such a strong possibility must have been very much in the mind of Rochester, the Lord President of the Council, who Nicolson discovered had been 'forwarning' Court supporters in the Upper House immediately after Christmas 'of warm-Work on the Affairs of Spain' (see below, 27 December). And it clearly prompted the decision, taken over the next two or three days, that since the ministry's best chance lay in taking the initiative itself, as much attention as possible should be distracted from Brihuega and focused instead on the disaster at Almanza in 1707, which could plausibly be depicted as the true source of the allies' tribulations in the Peninsula. This course had the additional attraction of providing some vicarious excitement for the Tory hounds in the Commons who were baying for Whig blood, without unleashing them directly.[44]

Such was the context of the debates on Spain in the Lords in January and early February 1711, which Nicolson attended and in which he dutifully voted on the Whig side, as most of the bishops present did (see, e.g., below, 9 January).[45] The Court and Tory design was to lay the blame for the mismanagements which had culminated in Brihuega squarely on Marlborough and Godolphin, on those Whig ministers who were in the Cabinet as early as 1706–7, and on the Whig generals in the Peninsula, notably Galway (a Huguenot), Tyrawley and Stanhope. Lord Peterborough, whom the Godolphin ministry had recalled from his command in 1706, was to be portrayed as the neglected genius who, had he been kept in Spain, could have saved the Habsburg cause there. Galway, the Commander-in-Chief of the British forces at the time of the Almanza defeat, and Sunderland, who as Secretary of State for the South had conveyed the Cabinet's order for a vigorous offensive in Spain, bore the brunt

---

[41] For this battle see Trevelyan, *Queen Anne*, iii, 85–7.

[42] Trumbull MS 54, f. 46: Bridges to Trumbull, 29 Dec.

[43] See J. Swift, *The Examiner*, No. 24, 4 Jan. 1711.

[44] BL Add. MS 17677 EEE, f. 31: l'Hermitage to the States-General, 5/16 Jan. 1711.

[45] Nicolson also kept in close touch with Lambeth during the proceedings, e.g. see below, 3, 4, 5, 22 Jan. Argyll, with his customary rudeness, told the bishops they had no right to meddle at all in such a secular issue! (l'Hermitage, 12/23 Jan., f. 42).

of the onslaught in the House; but Stanhope, as a participant in the fateful council of war at Valencia in 1706 which took the military decision for an offensive strategy, was not spared. It is significant that the first government motion put to the House in the course of the inquiry and debates, that of 9 January, was as mild as could be devised, without any direct censure element. It represented a very tentative exploration of the temperature of the water. Its outcome —a majority of fourteen in their favour, including (just as Harley had hoped) a significant Court Whig element—almost certainly exceeded their expectations and came as a rude shock to the Whig Junto;[46] and but for this it is unlikely that the ministry would have risked the outright censure motions of 11 January (initiated by Poulet, First Lord of the Treasury) and 12 January. They were carried by even larger margins, with the Queen present on the second occasion to indicate her support for the censures. Nicolson, apart from mentioning the recording of his protests on 11 January, does not comment on the dubious morality of the way the 'enquiry' was conducted on the government side. But Burnet wrote: 'I never saw anything carried on in the house of lords so little to their honour as this was; some who voted with the rest, seemed ashamed of it'; and he reported the Lord Privy Seal (Buckingham) as having 'said in plain words, that they had the majority, and would make use of it, as he had observed done by others, when they had it on their side'.[47]

Subsequently the proceedings meandered on into February, generally in a less acrimonious style, though the defection of Lord Cholmondeley, the Whig Treasurer of the Household, from the Court side on 3 February was a sure signal to Harley, Shrewsbury, and Poulet that, as the attack had now been taken over by Nottingham and some Tory hotheads outside the Cabinet, the time had come to bring down the curtain on this particular play.[48] Their decision was strengthened by awareness that Nottingham, still a respected and influential figure among High Church Tories, but excluded (to his disgust) from the ministry by the Queen's animosity, was making trouble for them on other fronts (see below, 5 February).[49] Perhaps by deliberate policy this elaborate set-piece on Spain in the House of Lords had taken up a great deal of parliamentary time and absorbed energies which the Whigs had feared would be thrown into far more serious parliamentary attacks on the leaders of the fallen administration.

However, the October Club Tories in the Commons who in late

[46] *Wentworth Papers*, p. 173. [47] *History*, vi, 28, 29.
[48] The final address on Spain, presented on 10 Feb. and probably drafted by Nottingham, was too sweeping for the ministry's liking, and it received a cool reply from the Queen (*Parl. Hist.* vi, 997).
[49] See also Dartmouth's note to Burnet, *History*, vi, 41-2.

February decided to press for a bill reviving that old war-horse, the Commission of Public Accounts (below, 24 March, n. 332), had clearly not given up hope of finding material for impeachments. Indeed, as the month drew to a close, with the club becoming increasingly aggressive and financial business languishing, the ministry's difficulties mounted and some Tories began to talk openly of compelling Harley's resignation unless he surrendered to their demands for office and for the punishment of the Whigs.[50] In these circumstances what seemed at first a near-catastrophe, when Harley was stabbed at a council meeting on 8 March by a French spy under interrogation, turned out to be a marvellous stroke of fortune for the victim. During his long, and in the end tactically protracted, illness involving seven weeks' absence from the Commons, the government certainly had its tribulations: for example, a vital supply measure, a revived duty on leather, almost foundered on 26–7 March through a combination of backbench Tory faction and front-bench ineptitude.[51] But these were far outweighed by the emotional reaction in Harley's favour which gradually disarmed both his parliamentary opponents and his Cabinet rivals and made his return to politics, on 27 April 1711, a triumphant one, and his subsequent promotion to the Earldom of Oxford, and to the office of Lord High Treasurer a matter of general acclaim. Even Rochester, the veteran Lord President, had come out decisively in support of moderation— and Harley—before his sudden death in May.

Nicolson, however, had left for the north early in April, before the long denouement to the session which did not end until 12 June. By so doing he missed Harley's masterly *coup*, the bill establishing the South Sea Company to liquidate £9 million of the floating debt, which silenced all his critics; and a major defeat for the October Club with the rejection of a measure that would have been political dynamite had it succeeded—a bill to resume the land grants of William III. Shortly before he left London Nicolson dined at Bishop Trelawney's along with the cream of the Whig clerical élite (see below, 2 April), where they were 'nobly entertained, as friends to the old Establishment and Ministry'. Thanks to the divisions among the Tories, and the determined pursuit of moderate measures by Harley and the Queen, they had rather more to celebrate this session, and a good deal less to deplore, than they could reasonably have expected.

[50] BL Add. MS 22231, f. 105: Sir John Cope to Lord Raby, 2 Mar. 1711. See also Robethon to Bernstorff, 10/21 Mar., in O. Klopp, *Der Fall des Hauses Stuart* (Vienna, 1875–88), xiv, 673–5.

[51] Unfortunately Nicolson takes no notice of this incident, although it caused a stir at the time. See *Wentworth Papers*, pp. 189–90: Peter Wentworth to [Raby], 27 Mar. 1711; Burnet, *History*, vi, 31–2.

[Dec.] 8. *Friday*. To London, 28 miles, in good time. Mr Philip Tullie dispatched at the Inn, and supper over at my brother's. I came joyfully (swelling in my neck excepted) to Mr Fitzgerald's. *Deo Laus*!

[Dec.] 9. *Saturday*. Morning Visitted by Mr Dowson, Mr G. Holme, Cousin J. Relf (joyful Father of a Son) Dr Hutton and my brother.

[Dec.] 10. *Sunday*. Morning. My Brother brought Mr Keilway; who opened my Neck with a Caustic, and approved of the Digestion &c. much better than two years agoe.[52] P.m. Dr Gibson, Recounting the Transactions in Parliament and Convocation; and paroling for the Staunchness of the Bishop of Lincoln [Wake]. Evening, my Brother pleased with the Discharge from my Neck.

[Dec.] 11. *Munday*. Morning Mr Keilway, still more satisfyed. Dined. Mr Greenshields;[53] who commends the Earl of Eglinton and Lord Balmerinoch[54] as truely Episcopal; but doubts the Bishop of Edinburgh[55] has too much Influence over the rest;[56] that Mr Carstairs[57] and others are comeing to Remonstrate against our Liturgy; that Mr Dumbrake (a Non-Juror)[58] is here solliciteing a Connivence for his Brethren; that some Addresses for the Complyers are comed up, and more may be had; &c. P.m. Mr M. Hutchinson, in new Broyls: Mr Leiut. Leethwait, refitted. Evening. Bishop of Bangor [Evans], Archdeacon Rogers, Archdeacon Gibson and Mr Walker; the last till Bed-time.

[52] Nicolson's trouble with his neck had first occurred on 16 March 1709 and had reached a climax in July 1710 when the tumour 'so much affected my Head that for about fourteen Days, I was neither able to write or read'. BL Add. MS 6116, f. 24: N. to Wake, 7 Aug. 1710; *CW* xxxv (1935), 115, 131.

[53] See above, sessional intro., pp. 507–8.

[54] Both were Scottish representative peers, 1710–15. Richard Dongworth (see below, n. 100) had classified them as 'Court Tory' and 'Episc[opal] Tory' respectively in a letter to Wake of 11 Nov. 1710: Christ Church Wake MS 17, f. 269ᵛ.

[55] Alexander Rose (1647?–1720), Bishop of Moray, 1686–7, of Edinburgh, 1687–1720. Deprived on the abolition of the prelacy in 1689, he was the last of the pre-Revolution Scottish bishops to survive and was in sympathy with the English non-jurors. He had not licensed Greenshields.

[56] Of the sixteen representative peers listed by Dongworth, seven are classed as Episcopal Tories, eight as Court Tories, and one (Loudoun) as a Presbyterian Court Tory. Wake MS 17, f. 269ᵛ. Dongworth defines Episcopal Tory as one who is 'always Episcopal, and mostly Enemies to the Union and Hanover Succession', and Court Tory as 'Episcopal or Presbyterian upon Occasion, who depend on and are moved by the Court Ministers'.

[57] William Carstairs (1649–1715), Scottish statesman and divine; Moderator of the General Assembly, 1705–11; Principal of Edinburgh University since 1703; largely responsible for overcoming the opposition of the Presbyterian clergy to the Union.

[58] Patrick Dumbreck, ordained in 1696 by the Bishop of Moray, was Chaplain to the 8th Earl Marischal by Nov. 1711. HMC *Portland MSS* x, 393–402.

[Dec.] 12. *Tuesday*. Morning. With Mr K[eilway] (and after my Lord of York's [Sharp's] Visit by Mr Richardson) Mr James Lowther; still very sure that the New Ministry cannot support the Public Credit. P.m. Cousin Jer[emy] Nicolson,[59] wanting to be entertained by Mr Provost Lancaster.

[Dec.] 13. *Wednesday*. With Mr K[eilway]'s leave, I dressed; and waited first on my Lord of York, and then on Sir James Mountague. The latter desires my meeting Sir Thomas Frankland[60] to morrow. Evening. Dr Deering, with the story of his being robbed at Stevenage.

[Dec.] 14. *Thursday*. Morning. Interview at Sir J. M[ontagu]'s with Sir Thomas Frankland, and Visit to Lord Hallifax, kept me too late to take the Oaths in the House. P.m. Visit to Bishop of Lincoln; who hard at work in answering the Queen's Letter.[61] Evening. Mr R. Smith of Durham, studying Islandic. Called today at my Lôdgeings, Mr Chamberlayne, Dr Joseph Smith, Dr Waugh and Mr Grisedale. Item with me in the morning Mr Addison, Confirming the ill news from Whitehaven.

[Dec.] 15. *Friday*. Morning. Mr K[eilway] saies Sir C. Musgrave had 10000 *l.* for getting the same Civil List setled on the Queen which King William had.[62] Visitted by Mr Wilkinson; and paid to Dr Lancaster, who tells me the Dean of Christ Church [Aldrich][63] dyed this morning. P.m. Mrs Hudgebutt (quondam Crackanthorp) on a cold Scent after a Debt due to her from (her Brother)[64] Thomas Denton. Visit to Mrs Penington;[65] and the Evening (as by Friday-Custome)

[59] Son of cousin James of Castlegate, Carlisle, baptised Jan. 1681. *CW* i (1901), 48. Matriculated at Queen's College, Oxford, 1697, under the name 'Jeremiah' (called Jeremy by Nicolson), BA 1702, MA 1705. Vicar of Bromfield, Cumberland, 1718–33.

[60] Frankland was Joint Postmaster-General and the meeting apparently concerned the misconduct and/or replacement of the postmaster of Carlisle. See below, 16, 21 Dec.

[61] To the Archbishop of Canterbury, warning the Upper House of Convocation not to allow procedural disputes to frustrate the business of the synod. It was read to the Lower House on 13 Dec. 1710. See *The Letters of Queen Anne*, ed. B. C. Brown (1968), p. 311; Bennett, *White Kennett*, pp. 71–3, for Tenison's ignorance of the intended letter and Low Church suspicions that it had been dictated by Atterbury. It caused a difference of opinion between the two houses concerning the address of thanks to Her Majesty.

[62] No evidence has been uncovered to support this extraordinary statement, and it is intrinsically highly improbable.

[63] The deanery was one of the wealthiest in the Church. With the rectory of Wem (Shropshire), Aldrich was reputed to have enjoyed an income of £1,200 *p.a.* Luttrell, vi, 666.   [64] Repl. '(her h Br)'.

[65] Very probably one of the Pennington family of Muncaster, Cumberland, the head of which was Sir William Pennington (d. 1730). The reference may be to Margaret, daughter of 1st Viscount Lonsdale, who had married Joseph Pennington in 1706. Nicolson was related by marriage to the family through his wife's brother. *CW* i (1901), 2.

at My Brother, with Capt. James Nicolson, &c. This day called, in my Absence, Mr R. Lowther; devested, say some, of his Government of Barbadoes.[66]

[Dec.] 16. *Saturday*. Morning. Visitted by Cousin Jeremy Nicolson; in no favour with Dr Lancaster. Dined at Lambeth; where in private with the Archbishop [Tenison] for half an hour (with great Freedome) before prayers. At Dinner, Dr Beckwith [Bettesworth] Dean of the Arches,[67] Mr Crow,[68] Mr Chamberlayne, Drs Willis, Wotton, Waugh, Gibson, &c. &c. P.m. with Sir James Mountague, on joynt Resolution to leave the Postmaster at Carlile to the Justice of the Commissioners.[69] Evening at the *Castle*, in Fleetstreet, with Dr Waugh, Dr Wotton and Brother Joseph.

[Dec.] 17. *Sunday*. Morning. Mr K[eilway] comeing a little too late, I got not to Church. He saies the Election at the Devises[70] bore hard on Lord Sunderland who proved to have ordered 700 *l.* from the Treasury, for manageing against Sir Fr[ancis] Child.[71] Dined At my Brother's with Mrs Beaufort. P.m. To St Paul's; where only Dr Hare,[72] a stranger to me. Thence fruitlesly to enquire for Dr Kennett; and, in Return, visitted Cousin R. Nicolson.

[Dec.] 18. *Munday*. Morning Mr Dean of Peterborough [Kennett] visitted and accompanyed me to the House; where I took the Oathes,

[66] Robert Lowther of Maulds Meaburn was appointed Governor of Barbados on 16 Aug. 1710. *CTB 1710*, pp. 465-5. He held the post until 1714, and was reappointed 1715-20.

[67] John Bettesworth (c.1678-1751), eminent civil lawyer, BA (Cantab) 1700, LLD 1706; Dean of the Arches, 1710-51, Judge of the Prerogative Court in succession to Sir Robert Raines, 1714-51. For Bettesworth, see G. D. Squibb, *Doctor's Common* (Oxford, 1977), pp. 117, 187.

[68] ?Mitford Crow, 'late governor of Barbados', for whom see Luttrell, vi, 664: 12 Dec. 1710.

[69] See above, n. 60. The reference here is probably to the Commissioners of the Treasury.

[70] There had been an exceptionally expensive struggle for the control of this corrupt Wiltshire borough, with its corporation electorate, between the previous Whig members, Paul Methuen and Josiah Diston, and their Tory challengers, Sir Francis Child and Serjeant Thomas Webb. It ended in a double return and the unseating of Methuen and Diston on petition. Diston, a wealthy Blackwell Hall cloth factor, had been heavily backed both by Lord Sunderland and by the Whig electioneering *supremo*, Wharton. See *CJ* xvi, 407, 436.

[71] (1642-1713). Son of a Wiltshire clothier who became one of the wealthiest private bankers in London and by 1710, though originally a Whig, a dominant voice among 'the monied citizens on the Tories side' (*Addison Letters*, p. 229). Knighted, 1689, MP for Devizes, 1698-1702, 1705-8, 16 Dec. 1710-13, London, 1702-5.

[72] Francis Hare (1671-1740), educated Cambridge, DD 1708; Chaplain-General to Duke of Marlborough (see Holmes, *British Politics*, p. 50 and *passim*). Prebendary of St Paul's, 1707, Dean of St Paul's, 1726-40, Bishop of St Asaph, 1727-31, of Chichester, 1731-40.

&c. Archbishop of York's endeavours failing for Dr Smalridge,[73] His Grace acquainted me that Dr Atterbury was to be removed from the Deanery of Carlile to that of Christ Church. *Esto*! Dutchess Dowager of Beaufort's Appeal heard;[74] and the Decree unanimously Reversed. Evening Dr Gibson, startled at our Dean's Remove; and Mr Thomas Bell, recounting his good Services to his Brother David.

[Dec.] 19. *Tuesday*. Morning. Dismissing Mr K[eilway] my brother and R. Leeth[wai]t I went to visit Lord Sommers, Wharton and Godolphin; the last whereof remembers the Queen's promise to me concerning our Deanry,[75] but doubts of the Effect. Mr Lawson, calling on me in his way to the House, wishes for Mr Gibbon;[76] but, in the Evening, assures me Dr Smalridge will be the man.

[Dec.] 20. *Wednesday*. Morning. I called on Mr Greenshields; who saies he's censured by his friends for being too *Low*. Thence to Lord Wharton; who frank on the School at Kirby Stephen[77] and all other matters. At the House, Nothing done; the Land-Tax not being ready. P.m. With Dr Lancaster, who commends Lathes; but thinks him too young for a Schoolmaster. Calling at Dr Smith's, I walked on to Dr Waugh's; where the Evening well bestowed.

[Dec.] 21. *Thursday*. Morning Mr K[eilway] dismissing me, I visitted Mr G. Lawson; offended with the Musgraves, and for pleasureing me with a Dean: Sir James Mountague; who adheres to his not medling with our Postmaster. At the House called on again by Sir Thomas Frankland; who for James Haddock, sooner than Timothy How. So be it! P.m. Mr Goodman, no Assistant of Col. Gledhil's; and Mr Greenshields, with farther Instructions in his Case.

[Dec.] 22. *Friday*. Morning. In search of Dr Woodward and Mr James Lowther. At the House, Bill for better Performance of Quarantine[78]

[73] See above, sessional intro., p. 510.   [74] See HMC *Lords MSS* ix, 2–4.

[75] Godolphin had written to Sharp on Atterbury's appointment to the deanery of Carlisle that the Queen had done it 'as an earnest only of her intention to give him [Atterbury] a better preferment when an occasion shall happen of it, which will likewise give her an opportunity of pleasing the Bishop of Carlisle'. Gloucestershire RO Lloyd-Baker MS Box 4, L121: Godolphin to Sharp, 4 July 1704. See also *CW* ii (1902), 197. In 1708 the Queen had apparently promised that Chancellor Tullie would succeed Atterbury, see below, 3 Jan.

[76] Thomas Gibbon, Rector of Greystoke, Cumberland, see Appendix A.

[77] The free grammar school at Kirkby Stephen, Westmorland, had been established (1568) by Wharton's ancestor, Thomas, Lord Wharton. Nicolson had been involved in Dec. 1709 in replacing the schoolmaster, who had proved incompetent. See *Nicolson Epist. Corr.* ii, 402–4: N. to Wharton, 29 Dec. 1709.   [78] *LJ* xix, 179.

read thrice. P.m. Dr Gibson, saies Mr Finch[79] will be my Dean, and Dr Smalridge have his Prebend at York. Evening, at my Brother's, Visits designed me this day (in my absence in the City) by the Bishop of Bangor, Mr Henley and Cousin M. Chambers.[80]

[Dec.] 23. *Saturday*. Morning. Mr James Lowther, earnest for the passing of the Officer-Bill;[81] Mr Wilkinson not yet provided for; Mr John Brougham, with Order for instructing J. Hoodless. In the House, the Queen gave the Royal Assent to the Land-Tax and Quarantaine-Bill:[82] After which both Houses adjourned to January 2. P.m. Mr Dowson. Item. Bishop of Lincoln's Secretary; desireing me to Ordain for him to morrow.

[Dec.] 24. *Sunday*. Morning. I ordained seven Priests (Mr Yates of Plumland[83] one of 'em) and four Deacons for the Bishop of Lincoln in Henry 7th's Chappel, Assisted by the Dean of Peterborough (as Archdeacon of Huntingdon) and two of the Prebendaries of Lincoln. We four dined with the Indisposed Bishop and his good wife.[84] Evening Prayers and Sermon Ended in the Abbey, Dr Kennett came with me to my Lodgeings; where M. Hutchinson treated us with a long Deatail of his Riotous and expensive Cause.

[Dec.] 25. *Christmas-day*. Morning. I went to Church at the Abbey, where Dr Fowk (Canon of Exon)[85] preached an excellent Sermon:

[79] Edward Finch (1664–1738), younger brother of the Earl of Nottingham and of Henry, Dean of York; Rector of Wigan since Feb. 1707; Prebendary of York, 1704–38.

[80] Mal (?Mary) Chambers of Kendal, sister to Archer Chambers (d. 1711), Vicar of Askham, 1707–11. They were probably related to Nicolson's wife. See *CW* ii (1902), 184; iv (1904), 44; below, 5 Jan. and 9 Feb.

[81] House of Commons (Officers) Bill, which provided for the exclusion of all but about thirty-five specified placemen and army officers from the House, had been introduced into the Commons on 7 Dec., sponsored mainly by Country Whigs, led by Edward Wortley Montagu, but at once espoused with almost indecent enthusiasm by the bulk of independent Tories. (*CJ* xvi, 423; BL Loan 29/321: Dyer's Newsletter, 7 Dec.; Add. MS 17677 DDD, ff. 683–4). It been committed on 21 Dec. by 239–76 (Luttrell, vi, 668). It eventually passed the Lower House on 29 Jan. 1711, with all but three government members voting against it, the Tory MP, Sir Arthur Kaye, noting with obvious satisfaction, that 'Harley had the mortification to see wt. the country Gentlemen's Interest may do, if they don't suffer themselves to be trick'd out of that Union they ought to preserve inviolable' (Staffordshire RO Dartmouth MSS D1778 v. 200, Kaye's MS diary, p. 2). It was, however, rejected by the Lords on 1 Feb. HMC *Lords MSS* ix, 86. For James Lowther's earlier support of 'Country' policies, see *The Divided Society*, ed. G. Holmes and W. A. Speck (1967), pp. 134–5.

[82] *LJ* xix, 181. The Land Tax Bill, crucial to the government's credit-worthiness, had gone through rather less rapidly than had been hoped.

[83] Obadiah Yates (c.1687–1765), Rector of Bolton All Saints', Cumberland, 1710–52.

[84] Wake recorded that 'being afraid of my Teeth the Bishop of Carlisle did me the favour to Ordain for Me'. Lambeth Palace MS 1770, f. 102v.

[85] Peter Foulks (1676–1747), MA (Oxon) 1701, DD 1710; Canon of Exeter, 1704, later (1724–36) Chancellor and Precentor of Exeter, Canon and Sub-dean of Christ Church.

After which six Bishops (of Rochester [Sprat], Peterborough [Cumberland], Carlile, Bath and Wells [Hooper], Exeter [Blackall] and St Asaph [Fleetwood]) at the Communion. I dined at my Brother's; and went to Prayers in the afternoon at St Paul's. Cousins Robert, James, Jeremy and Ja[mes] Jun[io]r[86] Nicolsons (with Mr Greenshields) a short while with me, in Return, at Salisbury-Court. Evening, Bishop of Lincoln's Secretary, sealing Letters of Orders.

[Dec.] 26. *Tuesday*. Dined At Lambeth; where the two Archbishops and 17 Bishops (Nineteen in all) dined at one Table. The greatest Appearance that had been known.[87] Onely Lord Crew of Durham[88] and the Bishop of Lichfield [Hough] (on occasion of his wife's Indisposition) absenting. Lord Archbishop of York whispered me that Dr T[odd] will not be my Dean.[89] Τίς Ποτε; Bishops of Winton [Trelawney], Norwich [Trimnell] and I, private with Dr Gibson. Institution, to the Rectory of Bolton, given at Lambeth; Mr Hayes acting for, and takeing the Fees of my Secretary. Evening. A second Visit from Cousin J. Relf; who saies his brother Joseph[90] set out for the North this Morning. Called this day, in my absence, Mr Willis, Dr Lancaster and Dr Woodward.

[Dec.] 27. *Wednesday*. Morning Visits from Mr Keilway (the last) Mr Johnson, Dr Smith and Mr Greenshields. With the last to wait on the Earl of Eglinton; with whom the Earl of Seafield, Sir Robert Pollock[91] and Sir Thomas Montgomery: Thence to Lord Balmerinoch, latcly visited (this morning) by the Earl of Rochester forwarning him of warm-Work on the Affairs of Spain:[92] Thence to Earl of

---

[86] Son of James Nicolson of Castlegate, Carlisle, baptised May 1676, and brother of Jeremy. See above, n. 59; *CW* i (1901), 48. Their father had died in 1708, so the 'James' mentioned here must be James Nicolson, the Penrith attorney, and the 'Robert', his brother.

[87] A glance at Wake's diary confirms this: in 1707 sixteen bishops attended and in 1709 and 1712 only nine. Lambeth Palace MS 1770, ff. 54, 90, 128.

[88] He may have been ill. In Sept. 1710 there had been rumours of his death. See *Journal to Stella*, i, 23; Luttrell, vi, 630, 633; Bedfordshire RO Lucas MS L30/8/29/1: Godolphin to Duke of Kent (Bishop Crew's nephew by marriage), 24 Sept. 1710.

[89] In July 1711, with Atterbury still at Carlisle, Todd was professing confidence and claiming the support of Sharp, and in Aug. he rashly 'removed his Family to the Cathedral, in sure Hopes of succeeding here' (Levens Hall MS D/T: Todd to Grahme, 10 July 1711; BL Add. MS 6116, f. 28: N. to Wake, 6 Aug. 1711). He was to be disappointed in Sept. when the Queen finally made Atterbury Dean of Christ Church and Smalridge Dean of Carlisle. Nicolson's choice had been Thomas Tullie, see below, 3 Jan.

[90] Joseph Relf was Steward to the Duke of Somerset at Cockermouth. Having sacrificed his health and fortune in Somerset's service, he began in 1710 to differ politically from the Duke. See Hopkinson, pp. 20, 132, 157.

[91] Of Pollock, Renfrewshire, created bart. (Scotland), 1703; Whig MP for Renfrewshire, 1707-22.

[92] See above, sessional intro., p. 517; below, 2 Jan.

Leven, who immediately attended by the three last mentioned
Northern Lords and the Earl of North-Esk. Dined. Mr Gr[eenshields]
with me, with his printed Cases;[93] and a promise from the Earl of
Cromarty to see me shortly, and sustain 'em. Before I came in, Lord
Portland called at my Lodgeings; moved, as I guess, by Dr Todd.[94]
Evening. Visits attempted to Dr Lancaster and Mr Grisdale; and a
long one paid to Dr Joseph Smith, his wife and son.

[Dec.] 28. *Thursday*. Morning. Calling on the Bishop of Bangor,
I went with him (in his Coach) to visit Lord Cowper, in the Countrey;
Bishop of Litchfield, in Dread of a Rheumatism; Lord Portland,
not within. Dr Woodward giveing me Notice of his dineing abroad,
I dined privately at home. P.m. Mr Tickell of Queen's College[95] who
speaks well of my Son; and highly of Cousin Rothery. Evening Mr
Wilkinson, with two Sons (Charles and John) of his Uncle Sanderson.

[Dec.] 29. *Friday*. Morning After a fruitless Attempt to wait on
Lord Hallifax I went to a meeting of the Commissioners of Queen
Anne's Bounty at Whitehall; where the Archbishop of York, Bishops
of Ely [Moore], Bangor, Carlile, Exeter, St Asaph, Chichester
[Manningham], and St David's [Bisse]; Lord Chief Baron [Ward],
Mr Attourney General [Northey] &c. The chief thing debated and
ordered, the makeing out of New Books of Tenths for the several
Dioceses. Bishop of Winton's long Arrears (for Bristol and Exeter)
to be paid in twelve months. This matter over, I went to Gresham-
College where Dr Woodward's other Guests (at Dinner) were Coll.
King,[96] comed to Town last night (with the Duke of Marlborough)[97]
from Flanders; Mr Dummer, an Ingenious Citizen, Mr[98]   a
learned young German bread at Leipsick, &c. Evening at my Brother's
with Mr Fiddis and his Sister &c.

[93] Probably a reference to Greenshields' *A true state of the Case of the Rev. Mr Greenshields . . .* (London, 1710), though he was shortly to publish *The case of Mr Greenshields
fully stated and discussed in a letter from a commoner of North Britain to an English peer*
(London, 1711).

[94] The 2nd Earl of Portland had an estate in Cumberland, near Penrith.

[95] Thomas Tickell (c.1686–1740), of Bridekirk, Cumberland, MA (Oxon) 1709; Under
Secretary of State, 1717–24.

[96] Richard King, an artilleryman and engineer, had served in several campaigns under
Marlborough and was appointed colonel in Feb. 1710. Dalton, v, pt. ii, 10.

[97] The Duke had visited the Queen immediately, his first audience with her since the
ministerial revolution of June–Sept. According to Godolphin, 'My Lord Marlborough
had carry'd [it] Mildly, assuring the Queen that he would serve her as long as he could do
her any Service, and that it was not a time now to take notice of any mortification given
him . . .'. *The Diary of Sir David Hamilton 1709–1714*, ed. P. Roberts (Oxford, 1975),
p. 23. Cf. below, 31 Dec.

[98] Name blank in MS. Nicolson clearly could not remember it by the time he came to
write up his diary.

[Dec.] 30. *Saturday*. Morning Mr Wenman (Postmaster of Merton-College) petitioning for a promise of my seeing his mother next Wednesday in the Evening. P.m. Mr Le Neve, with a Loan of Abstracts of Records (in the Exchequer) relateing to the County of Cumberland;[99] and a long story of a Contest like to happen betwixt Lord Hallifax and him concerning the keeping the Keys of the Reacords in the Treasury. The *Auditor*, he saies, is the same Thing with (the antient) Treasurer's Clerk; who used to have a Third Key, as Each Chamberlain's Deputy had one. Evening Mr Greenshields and Mr Dungworth[100] (Chaplain to the Dutchess of Monmouth) with papers relateing to the true State of Religion in Scotland.

[Dec.] 31. *Sunday*. Morning. To St James's Church; where Dr Clark preached an Excellent Sermon on *Galatians* 4, 4 and 5—*When the fulness of Time was come*, &c. NB. Mr Speaker Bromley, with (his Clerk of the Closet) Dr Kymberley.[101] Hence to dine at my Brother's with Mr Cummins and Mrs Bathurst. Afternoon to St Paul's; where also a good sermon by Mr[102] Prebendary. Invited to Warwick-Court by Dr Brabant, my brother's friend; who as much bitten with Educateing a Son[103] in the University as my self. He assures me that the Duke of Marlborough was highly caressed, Friday and yesterday, both by Her Majesty and the whole Court. Be it ever So![104] Amen.[105]

Jan. 1. *Munday*. I waited (according to custome) on the Archbishop of York; who carryed me, in his coach, to St James's; where a great Court. The Duke of Marlborough newly returned from Flanders, much caressed; and, next to Her pert Grace of Shrewsbury, made the chief Figure there. In the Chapple 10 Bishops (whereof I the fourth) besides the Archbishop. Sword carryed by the Earl of Marr. Invited to Dine with the Bishop of Winton; but returned with my Metropolitan,

---

[99] Possibly the 'Abstracts out of Mr Le Neve's Records Dioc[ese of] Carl[isle]' in Nicolson's antiquarian notebook. Bodl. MS Gen. Top. c. 27/1.

[100] Richard Dongworth (or Dungworth), MA Edinburgh 1695; Curate of Kirkby *cum* Osgarby and Owerby-End, Lincolnshire, 1698; Wake's informant on Scottish politics (see above, n. 54). *Catalogue of the Graduates of . . . Edinburgh* (1858), p. 150; *Speculum Dioeceseos Linc.* i, 24, 73, 75, 94. He was alive in 1730 (St Andrews UL Gibson MS 5277).

[101] Cf. Luttrell, vi, 659, 28 Nov. 1710: 'Mr. Bromley, speaker of the house of Commons, has made Dr. Kimberly, a member of the convocation, and rector of St. Michael's in Coventry, his chaplain.'

[102] Name blank in MS.

[103] Dr Brabant's son Robert had entered University College, Oxford, in Oct. 1710. His son Henry matriculated at Trinity College, Oxford, in Feb. 1711.

[104] It is ironical that Nicolson should have written these words on the last day of the old year. On 31 Dec. 1711 Marlborough was disgraced and stripped of all his offices.

[105] End of the 'Mansergh volume'. The last entry is followed by three blank folios.

who is now for makeing Dr Higden my Dean.[106] Dined with us, the Dean of Bristol [Boothe] and Mr Whitfield. Item young Mr Paul, a pert Cambridge-Master. In the Evening, Mr Dungworth and Mr Greenshields repeating the State of the Church in Scotland.

[Jan.] 2. *Tuesday*. Morning, Visit paid to Mr James Lowther; and attempted to Mr R. Lowther, Dr Gibson, Lord Hallifax, Lord Sunderland and Lord Portland. In my absence, Lord Sommers called at my Lodgeing. In the House, A message brought (by the Duke of Dover) from the Queen[107] in writeing; whereby was Intimated the late misfortune in Spain, the Care taken to send Recruits,[108] &c. and concludeing — That Her Majesty hoped that what She had done in this matter would be approved by Her parliament. Duke of Beaufort moved for an Address of Thanks; for which a Committee appointed, to Report tomorrow. Not a word of the Duke of Marlborough.[109] Dr Smith dined with me; in his way, hard on the late Ministry. NB. In the House the Duke of Somerset brought me a grateful Answer from Her Majesty in favour of Mr Chancellor Tullie.

[Jan.] 3. *Wednesday*. Morning, After short visits from my Brother and Mr Keilway, I went to wait on the Queen; to whose presence I was Introduced (as was promised) by the Duke of Somerset. Haveing Kissed Her Majesty's hand, I craved leave to remind Her of the promise made to Mr Tullie, three years agoe, in her name. She was not yet (She said) Resolved how to dispose of the Vacant Deanry; nor could she particularly promise me any Thing for Mr T[ullie]; but she would assure me that, on Dr Atterbury's Removeal, some provision should be made for him.

To the House with Mr Tickel; where the Address Reported and Approved.[110] Upon Debate, on the Clause about Enquiries into

---

[106] William Higden (*c*.1663–1715), a favourite of Lord Nottingham's (see below, 23 Jan.). Later Rector of St Paul's, Shadwell, Middlesex, 1711–15 (cf. below, 19 Feb.), Prebendary of Canterbury, 1713–15. Sharp was still in favour of Higden succeeding Atterbury in the summer of 1711 (Levens Hall MS D/T: Todd to Grahme, 19 July 1711.).

[107] *LJ* xix, 182; *Parl. Hist*, vi, 935.

[108] Reinforcements for Spain had left Portsmouth, with an escorting fleet commanded by Sir John Jennings, on 29 Dec. 'Major general Harvey, and other officers here in the service of Spain, are ordered to be at their several posts by 17th February, on pain of being casheered.' Luttrell, 30 Dec. (vi, 672).

[109] An unconcerted attempt, prompted by the independent Whig, Lord Scarbrough, to persuade the Lords to vote Marlborough thanks for his services in the 1710 campaign had already flopped (28 Nov.). BL Add. MS 17677 DDD, f. 665; Boyer, *Queen Anne*, p. 482; *Wentworth Papers*, pp. 158–9. When she saw the Duke on 29 Dec., Anne is said to have told him bluntly 'not to suffer any vote of thanks to you to be moved in Parliament this year, because my ministers will certainly oppose it'. Coxe, *Marlborough*, iii, 172.

[110] *LJ* xix, 183.

Miscarriages,[111] ordered that the House go into a Grand Committee on Friday next.[112] Account carryed to Lambeth before I dined. P.m., Dr Gibson for news, and paying me his Bill. Evening, By Dr Lancaster's to Mrs Wenman's; and thence to Philip Tullie. Called (in my absence) Sir James Mountague, twice, and Col. Orfeur.

[Jan.] 4. *Thursday*. Morning, Mr Henley, in want of his high way to the River. Another fruitless Attempt to wait on Lord Sommers; Thence to Sir James Mountague, pleased with our Recorder's full Certificate on behalf of M. Pattinson and my Management for the Deanry: Thence to my Brother's to invite my Sister and Niece, the latter indisposed: Thence, in vain to Mr R. Lowther's. In the House, an Address to the Queen[113] to stop the Earl of Peterborough a few dayes, from goeing to Vienna; His Lordship being thought able to give a good Account of the management in Spain. This Reported to my Lord of Canterbury and Dr Gibson. Evening, Letters.

[Jan.] 5. *Friday*. Morning, Mrs Donning; will have me to swear in her Case, as her Agent directs: Mal. Chambers, solliciteing the Duchess of Monmouth. Mr Thomas Gibson (born at Horncastle) introduced by Cousin Relf, wants a pension; Jeremy Nicolson, Lecturer at Newington;[114] Mr Hutchinson, the Dukc of S[omerset]'s operatour; Mr Goodman, presageing the Duke of M[arlborough]'s suddain Removeal; Dr Lancaster, from the Duke of O[rmond]'s Levee. Dined, Dr Waugh and Dr Gibson. In the House, Earl of Peterborough repeateing Dr Friend's *History* of His Lordship's Wonders in Spain; in answer to the following Questions[115]—1. How was your Lordship furnished with mcn and money; and to whom did you apply in want? A[nswer]. Not a Third of cither. My Applications to Lord Treasurer [Godolphin] and Secretary Hedges. 2. What provisions in your Marches? [Answer]. All wrong (as in the Book). 3. What Advices

[111] The passage concerned, clearly emanating from ministerial peers, read: 'as this misfortune may have been occasioned by some *preceding* mismanagement [editors' italics], we take the liberty to assure Your Majesty, we will use our utmost endeavours to discover it, so as to prevent the like for the future.'
[112] The Duke of Beaufort, almost certainly set up by the Court party, originally asked the House to appoint a *select* committee rather than sit in Grand Committee, an indication of the government's uneasiness, even at this stage, about having the matter debated on the floor of the House. It was Beaufort who later moved (see below, 4 Jan.) that the Queen should be asked to delay the Earl of Peterborough's departure for Vienna, so that he could 'assist' the House in its deliberations—an obvious 'Court-juggle', as Boyer remarked (*Queen Anne*, p. 485).   [113] *LJ* xix, 184.
[114] Jeremy was presumably a candidate for the lectureship of £80 *p.a.* at Newington Butts to which that parish had elected Dr Sacheverell during his imprisonment a year earlier. Sacheverell had since resigned the post. Holmes, *Sacheverell*, p. 256.
[115] Cf. HMC *Lords MSS* ix, 19-21.

from Lord Galway? A[nswer] None. 4. Why did the King of Spain march into Arragon, instead of Valencia? A[nswer]. This falsely charged on me. I Appeal to our Letters. 5. What forces taken from him by the King? A[nswer]. Most of what he had. 6. What Orders had he from England when in Valencia? NB. This Question put by the Duke of Argile;[116] but not well understood. There could be none. After some puzzling Remarks by the Duke of Devonshire and Lord Godolphin, ordered that the Queen be desired to give leave to the Earl of Peterborough to speak fully;[117] and that Lord Galway and Lord Tyrawly attend to morrow. Report of this carryed to Lambeth; and the Evening at my Brother's with Mrs Waugh and her daughter and A. Spooner.

[Jan.] 6. *Saturday*. Morning, Visits from Cousin Br[idget] Nicolson, in great heart on her Son's Advancement; Mr. Fowler, begging (as two years agoe) for the Redemption of his Medals; Bishop of Bangor, a pure Visit; Lord Balmerinoch, explaining Sir James Stewart's Act against Intruders into vacant Stipends;[118] Mr James Lowther, offering to call again (with his chariot) to carry me to Sir James Mountague's: where we both dined together with Lord Castlecomer,[119] Sir R. Sandford, two Tullies &c. Brigadier Stanwix detained from us, by an Accidental meeting of Portugal-Officers. In the House the two Irish Lords (from the Bar) gave different, Accounts of Spain from that of yesterday.[120]

[Jan.] 7. *Sunday*. Morning, prayers and Sermon at Whitehall. Evening, Visitted by Mr Chancellor Lloyd, with (his Brother in Law) Mr Thompson and Archdeacon Goodwin;[121] who report the Bishop of Worcester [Lloyd] to be in better health than seven years agoe, and caution me against Dr Brabant.

[Jan.] 8. *Munday*. Morning, Cousin M. Chambers, farther consulting; Mr Joseph Haddock, afraid of his brothers being put upon; Col.

[116] This Whig general, bitterly jealous of Marlborough, had defected from his party in Mar. 1710, adhering since then to Harley's 'juntilla'.

[117] He had spoken on this day for about an hour. Luttrell, vi, 677.

[118] A Scottish act of 1685 called the 'Act concerning vacant stipends' required patrons of livings to employ the vacant stipends in pious uses, such as building, or otherwise they would lose their right of presentation to the living. This Act was reinforced by the 'Act concerning Patronages' of 1690. *Acts Parl. Scot.* viii, 474; ix, 196.

[119] Christopher Wandesford (1684–1719), 2nd Viscount Castlecomer [I], Whig MP for Morpeth, 1710–13, Ripon, 1715–19. Sedgwick, ii, 518–19.

[120] See HMC *Lords MSS* ix, 21–2 for the accounts of Lords Galway and Tyrawley. See *Wentworth Papers*, pp. 170–3 for the day's proceedings.

[121] Timothy Goodwin (?1670–1729) Archdeacon of Oxford, 1707–14, and Chaplain to the Duke of Shrewsbury.

Orfeur, in great hopes; Dr Smith, on a pure visit; and so Mr Dowson. With Mr Greenshields to Dr Gibson; who will tomorrow Introduce him to His Grace. Dined Mr Greenshields on our Return from the Drs.

In the House Lord Peterborough and Lord Galway gave their Narratives in writeing;[122] and both ordered to be read to morrow. Archbishop of York and Lord Eglinton encourage me to undertake Lord Ilay in the Law-part of Mr Greenshields's Case; which I readily agreed to. Duke of Argile offers 200 *l.* and Irish preferment for his dropping it. Noe. In the Evening, Dr Gibson and Mr Thomas Bell; argueing for and against Mr Lesley &c. Mr Dungworth, with a kind Message from the Duchess of Monmouth, and Lord Cromarty's hearty Remarks on the case of Greenshields.

[Jan.] 9. *Tuesday.* Morning, Visited by my Brother, with a present (of one of Sister Rothery's cheeses) from my Niece Susan; M. Chambers, very earnest for a Service; Mr Wilkinson, the like for an Office; Mr Grisdale, Mr Gibson, Mr Ellison[123] and Cousin Jeremy Nicolson (all Queen's-men) pure Respects; Mr Elstob, with a new present (of an Old Saxon Homily) from his Sister; Mr Paul, returning to Cambridge. In the House (the Queen present)[124] papers of the Earl of Peterborough and Earl of Galway read, Earl of Tyrawley[125] examined, &c. on the Affairs of Spain;[126] and (after a long Debate till Ten at night) Voted on the Question in the Committee, *That the Earl of Peterborough hath given a just, Faithful and Honourable Account of the Council of War held at Valentia before the Battle of Almanza. Contents,* 59, *Not Contents,* 45.[127] Among the former 4 Bishops, and, amongst the latter, 9. viz. Winton,[128] Sarum [Burnet], Ely, Peterborough, Bangor, Carlile, Lincoln, Landaff [Tyler] and S. Asaph.[129]

---

[122] HMC *Lords MSS* ix, 23–32. Lord Galway's narrative is printed in *Parl. Hist.* vi, 939–47.

[123] Possibly Robert Ellison (1665–1726) of Hebburn. See *The Correspondence of Sir James Clavering,* ed. H. T. Dickinson, Surtees Soc. vol. clxxvii (1967), pp. 29, 117.

[124] On the advice of her ministers, and undoubtedly with the votes of Court Whig office-holders and pensioners mainly in mind. [125] Mistake for Baron Tyrawley.

[126] See HMC *Lords MSS* ix, 32–8; *Parl. Hist.* vi, 938–61: the very full account of Abel Boyer, who heard and took extensive notes on the whole debate (later censured by the Lords), with somewhat dramatic effects—see below, 5 Mar. and n. 288).

[127] The vote took place on the question of whether 'the House shall be now resumed?'. It was resolved in the negative: *Contents* forty-five, *Not contents,* fifty-nine. For the key significance of this vote for what followed, especially on 11 and 12 Jan., see above, sessional intro., p. 518.

[128] Bishop Trelawney's continued adherence to the Whigs in this session is especially noteworthy.

[129] In addition Nicolson may well have forgotten to list Trimnell of Norwich and Hough of Lichfield on the Whig side. Both registered protests against the Tory vote of 11 Jan. *LJ* xix, 190–1.

[Jan] 10. *Wednesday*. Morning, After a good long walk in the Park, I visitted Lord Hallifax; and left with his Lordship Mr Greenshields's paper about the Regularity of his Appeal. Visitted by Lord Leven and Dr Lancaster. Dined Mr Wilkinson, whom I afterwards accompanyed to the *Miter* in Fanchurch-street, to visit his Cousins George Sanderson and Highm[o]r. By my brother's home to Westminster, at 10.

[Jan.] 11. *Thursday*. Morning, Visitted by Mr Wanley, who invites me to Mr Harley's Library; where my Benefaction (in giveing the old Cartulary of the Abbey of Dunmow) is to be amply acknowledged.[130] In good Time! Visitted by Dr Smith, who accompanyed me to the House: where, after a long (very long) Debate,[131] this Question carried by 64 against 43. *That the Earls of Galway and Tyrawley and General Stanhop's*[132] *voteing for an offensive War, in the Council at Valentia, was a Great Occasion of the Loss of the Battle of Almanza, the Miscarriage at Thoulon, &c.* Dureing the Speeches,[133] I stole off (at three) to my Brother's, it being my Niece's Birth-Day, and (after dineing there with Dr Waugh and his daughter Fiddis) returned, to make one of the Ten protesting Bishops.[134]

[Jan.] 12. *Friday*. Morning, Attended by Mr Dungworth and Mr Greenshields, each takeing an Abstract of the Answer of the Magistrates of Edinburgh. Dinner. Mr Greenshields, resolved to take a copy of the said Answer.

In the House strong Debates[135] (the Queen present from 7 till 10 at night) which ended in a Question,[136] carried by 68 against 48.[137] *That a Cabinet Council*[138] *held in February 1706 ought to be blamed*

---

[130] *The Registrum Cartarum Prioratus de Dunmowe in Com. Essex incaeptum A.D. 1274* (now BL Harleian MS 662) had been given to Harley in 1709. See BL Harleian MS 662, f. 1: N. to Wanley, 28 Apr. 1709.

[131] It lasted until between 8.00 p.m. and 9.00 p.m. For the proceedings see HMC *Lords MSS* ix, 38–43; *Parl. Hist.* vi, 961–9.

[132] James Stanhope (1673–1721), MP for Cockermouth, see Appendix A.

[133] The main speakers for the government were Peterborough, Argyll, Poulet, Buckingham, Rochester, Nottingham, Shrewsbury, Guernsey, Ferrers, and Lord North and Grey; for the Whigs, Somers, Devonshire, Cowper, Wharton, Halifax, Godolphin, and Marlborough.

[134] There were two protests on this day, and in both Nicolson was one of the eleven bishops protesting. See *LJ* xix, 190–1.

[135] See HMC *Lords MSS* ix, 44–6; *Parl. Hist.* vi, 969–81.

[136] Proposed by the Tory peer, Lord Scarsdale (not in the ministry).

[137] Burnet, who was present during all the debates of 9–12 Jan., wrote later that 'some were more easily drawn to concur in these votes, because, by the act of grace [Act of Indemnity, 1708], all those who had been concerned in the administration were covered from prosecution and punishment: so this was represented to some as a compliment that would be very acceptable to the queen, and by which no person could be hurt'. *History*, vi, 29–30.

[138] These words were in the original question proposed by Scarsdale, but in the final

for adviseing an Offensive war in Spain; this being a great Occasion of the Loss of the Battle of Almanza, the Disappointment at Thoulon, and our other misfortunes. After which, another was moved[139] (and carryed) in favour of the Earl of Peterborough who had the Thanks of the House given him by Lord Keeper [Harcourt] for his Conduct in Spain four or five years agoe;[140] and thereupon immediately (near Midnight) went on Board for Vienna.[141]

[Jan.] 13. *Saturday.* Morning, With Mr Wanley, who gave me a couple of Inscriptions; one of 'em Runic. Thence to Whitehall; where Mr Chamberlayne reported (from Mr Cardonel,[142] as pretended) that the Duke of Marlborough was displaced, and the Dukes of O[rmond] and A[rgyll], the Earl of Orkney, and L[ieutenant] G[eneral] Lumley[143] Commissioners in his Room. Thence (with the Dean of Lincoln [Willis]) to Lambeth; where dined with the Dean of the Arches [Bettesworth], Mr Farrer,[144] Mr Pocklinton,[145] Drs Lindford, Lloyd, Mandevil, Gibson, Mr Cook, &c. My Lord Archbishop shewed me a Summons to the Duke of Marlborough (with others) to a Cabinet Council tomorrow; which not consistent with Mr Chamberlayne's Report.[146] Visit to Mrs Gibson in my way home.

[Jan.] 14. *Sunday.* Morning, At the Chapple of Whitehall; where an Excellent Sermon preached by Dr Snapes on *Psalm* 51, 22. against

version delivered by him to the Grand Committee they were changed to 'the ministers'. For the prolonged wrangle about the significance and aptness of these terms, see *Parl. Hist.* vi, 971–5.

[139] By the Duke of Argyll. He was soon afterwards 'rewarded' for his support of Harley and the new ministry by being given the thankless task of commanding the remnants of the British Army in Spain.

[140] See *Parl. Hist.* vi, 981–3.

[141] On a diplomatic mission. Peterborough had served his purpose; for the rest of the Oxford ministry's life he was a political embarrassment, especially in view of the Queen's determination not to employ him at home. Holmes, *British Politics*, p. 202.

[142] Adam Cardonnel (d. 1719), Secretary to the Duke of Marlborough and MP for Southampton, Nov. 1701–Feb. 1712 (expelled the House).

[143] Henry Lumley (c.1660–1722), Tory brother to the 1st Earl of Scarbrough and uncle to Richard Lumley (titular Viscount Lumley), Whig MP for Arundel, 1710–15; represented Sussex, 1701, 1702–5 and Arundel, 1715–22; rose from rank of Captain (1685) to Lieutenant General in eighteen years; promoted General of Horse, 1711.

[144] ?Henry Farrent, Register and Actuary of the Court of Arches. Chamberlayne, *Present State 1710*, p. 645. This seems a more likely identification than William Farrer, the lawyer and long-serving MP for Bedford, for whom see Sedgwick, ii, 26–7.

[145] ?John Pocklington, Whig barrister, MP for Huntingdonshire, 1705–13; a Welsh judge since 1707 (removed 1711), and later (1714–32) a Baron of the Exchequer in Ireland. Client of the Earl of Manchester.

[146] Marlborough continued to attend Cabinet meetings periodically until he returned to Flanders for the next campaign on 20 Feb. Staffordshire RO D1778/v/188: Cabinet minutes of Lord Dartmouth, June 1710–June 1711.

compareing God's Nature with our own. *Thinking him such an One as our selves.* P.m. I visitted, for two hours, Mr Addison and's wife; fond of their witty Grandchild Hutton. Cousin Lesley, in quest of me.

[Jan.] 15. *Munday*. Morning, My Brother &c. In the House, Return of Absent Officers at the Battle of Almanza read and adjourned to Wednesday.[147] Dinner at home. Evening at my Brother's, private.

[Jan.] 16. *Tuesday*. Morning, Visitted by Mr Wilkinson and Alderman Tullie; and summoned (by Dr Lancaster, in my absence) to preach for him on Sunday next. Dined Alone. Evening, Dr Gee and Cousin Lesley; the latter seeking promotion, either from the Duke of Marlborough or Lord Chief Baron Smith.[148]

[Jan.] 17. *Wednesday*. Morning, Mr Greenshields complaining of the Court's bringing Delayes upon him; Mrs Gibson and Atkinson,[149] returning to Queen's; Mr G. Holmes, paid for Ryley's prepar[ation]; Brigadier Stanwix, very obligeing to my Friends and inviteing me to dine with him tomorrow; Cousin Lesley, carrying me to wait on the Earl of Hindforth;[150] and I also paid Visits (in the same street) to the Earl of Leven and Lord Balmerinoch; Philip Tullie, pleased with the Brigadier's offers to his nephew. After Dinner, the House (for want of more Letters &c) presently adjourned.[151] I went home with the Bishop of S. Asaph: Thence, with Dr Waugh, to visit Dr Lancaster and Mr Elstob: Whence, in my Return home, I came to Cousin James Nicolson's in Fetterlane.

[Jan.] 18. *Thursday*. Morning, My brother John's Account of the Tenths of my Diocese put into Mr Chamberlayne's hand at Whitehall; to be restored. In the House, Reading of Lord Galway's papers, &c.[152] I dined with Brigadier Stanwix; as did also Sir James Mountague

---

[147] HMC *Lords MSS* ix, 46–61.

[148] John Smith, Chief Baron of the Scottish (not the English) Exchequer Court, but also an English judge.

[149] Arthur Atkinson, of Morland, Westmorland; educated Queen's College, Oxford, BA 1703, MA 1707; later Rector of Sulhampstead Abbot and Bannister, Berkshire, 1722.

[150] James Carmichael (d. 1737), succ. as 2nd Earl of Hyndford [S] in 1710; Brigadier General of Dragoons, 1710. He was not a Scottish representative peer.

[151] See HMC *Lords MSS* ix, 63–6.

[152] Ibid., p. 66. Galway had been denied by the Tories the right, which he had petitioned for on 11 Jan., to put his full case *before* the votes were taken on the censure motions of 11 and 12 Jan.

and Sir R. Sandford. Called in my absence, Mr J. Churchill,[153] Dr
Gibson, &c. Evening, Cousin M. Orfeur, solliciteing for her friend to
be Steward to some Nobleman. NB. My first Visitant in the morning
was Master Stephenson,[154] not yet provided of a place; but Mr Dean
(he saies) promises to labour together with me, for his Advancement.

[Jan.] 19. *Friday*. Morning, Mr Paul, for writeing the Life of Sir
Philip Sidney and getting to the Secretary's Office; Bishop of Bangor,
drinking Coffee called in my Absence, Lord Balmerinoch and Dr
Gibson. Dined Cousin Lesley, for a place in their Exchequer by aid
of Baron Scroop.[155] Evening, Visits paid to Mrs Fetherstons and Mr
Isaac Tullie; and attempted to Dr Lancaster and Mr Greenshields.
Mr Walker's company from the Committee on the Gilford-
Election.[156]

[Jan.] 20. *Saturday*. Morning, New Gown and Cassock. Governors
of Queen Ann's Bounty at Whitehall; where the officers brought in
a sample of Books for the several Dioceses. Thence by water, very
cold, towards the Tower. Mr Holmes shewed me an Abstract of
Prynne's Reg[iste]r[157] on the Calling of members for Cities and
Burroughs corrected; promiseing me a Copy, and catalogue of
Spanheim's Book.[158] After we had dined together, we visitted Mr
Rymer; who will help me (if Lord Hallifax fails) to his 3 last volumes.
Dr Smith angry at his drinking a health to Prince Eugene; and Dr
Hickes unaccountable. Above 100 Rolls, of Treaties, Charters, &c.
from Edward 4 to Charles 1 inclusive, found under the Leads of
the Chapple at the Rolls by Mr Sanderson.

[153] John Churchill, bookseller at the Black Swan in Paternoster Row, 1690-1714, was
the brother of Awnsham Churchill, MP (see Appendix A), with whom he was in partnership.
H. R. Plommer, *Dictionary of Printers and Booksellers 1668-1725* (1922), p. 70.

[154] John Stephenson had been Master of the Carlisle Cathedral School, 1704-10.
Accused of incompetence after the 1710 visitation by the Dean and Chapter, he resigned on
a pension of £4 a year. See *CW* iii (1903), 33.

[155] John Scrope (c.1662-1752), Baron of the Court of Exchequer in Scotland, who in
1724 succeeded William Lowndes as Secretary to the Treasury. Sedgwick, ii, 413-14. He
was one of the most influential men in Scotland from 1708 to 1724, particularly in matters
of patronage. See P. W. J. Riley, *The English Ministers and Scotland* (1964), *passim*.

[156] Two Whigs Denzil Onslow and Brig. Robert Wroth had been returned for Guildford, but upon a petition of Morgan Randyll and the recommendation of the Committee
of Elections (19 Jan.) this was amended by the order of the Commons, on 3 Feb. 1711, by
substituting the name of Randyll for Wroth. *CJ* xvi, 476-7; Luttrell, vi, 680.

[157] The *Brevia Parliamentaria Rediviva* or *Brief Register of the several kinds of Parliamentary Writs* was published in 4 parts by William Prynne between 1659 and 1664.

[158] Ezechiel Spanheim's *Dissertationes de praestantia et usu numismatum antiquorum*
(London, 1706). He was the Prussian Ambassador in London, 1702-10.

[Jan.] 21. *Sunday*. Morning, I preached at St Martin's and (before Second Service) was carryed in Dr L[ancaster]'s coach to Salisbury-Court; where I dined, and (in the afternoon) preached at St Bride's and walked back to Westminster. Frost and Snow.

[Jan.] 22. *Munday*. Morning, Mr Greenshields, after his Report, walked with me almost to Kensington, and returned to Dinner. In the House the Grand Committee pursued the Affair of Spain;[159] and (after some calm Debates, wherein the Duke of Marlborough discovered his Superior Abilities to the Duke of A[rgyll][160] and his great Integrity) resolved that the Lord in the Chair[161] demand of Lord Galway — Whether the Forces of the King of Portugal, after their March out of that Kingdome, had the post of Honour in the Field, in preference to the Brittish?[162] The Committee adjourned to Wednesday. Evening, Finding that the prolocutor [Atterbury] and Dr Smalridge &c. were with my Lord of Canterbury I carryed the good news of our Proceedings to Dr Gibson; called afterwards on Isaac Tullie and Thomas Bell, and fixed (till nine) with Dr Lancaster and Mr Arundel at St Martin's.

[Jan.] 23. *Tuesday*. Morning, Visit to Mr Chamberlain; with whom I found Mr Whiston, who read us his Letter to Dr Sacheverel,[163] avowing his being refused by Sir Charles Holt[164] (patron of a Liveing where the Dr was Curate in 1696) because even among servants, he ridiculed the Reality of Hell-Torment.[165] Mr Whiston being gone, Dr Higden came in; with whose view Lord Nottingham jumps. The House onely met to adjourn. In my absence, called on by Cousin Lesley, Mr Le Neve, Mr Madox and Mr Israel Fielding; also Mr M. Hutchinson, with a Letter from his mother. In my way home, I called on Cousins Penington and Chambers; the former in pain for an absent Husband, and the other for a sick Brother. After I had dined alone, I went to the House; where, nothing appearing from the Select Committee, we were soon adjourned. Prayers done at the Abbey, I went home with Dr Gee; who severe on the Ingratitude of

---

[159] See HMC *Lords MSS* ix, 65–79, and *Wentworth Papers*, pp. 176–8.
[160] There is a certain relish in Nicolson's comment, understandable in the light of Argyll's anti-clericalism and his remarks about the bishops earlier in the Spanish debates (see above, sessional intro., n. 45).
[161] Earl of Abingdon.
[162] Galway was bound to yield this by the terms of treaty with Portugal ('otherwise', he claimed, 'they would never have stirred out of Portugal'), and was nominally subordinate to the Portuguese General, Minas. *Parl. Hist.* vi, 991–3; Burnet, *History*, vi, 30.
[163] See Holmes, *Sacheverell*, p. 301 (n. 20).
[164] Sir Charles Holt (*c*.1649–1722), 3rd Bt. of Aston, MP for Warwickshire, 1685–7.
[165] See Holmes, *Sacheverell*, pp. 9–10.

the Dean of Wells [Grahme] to me, in assisting Dr T[odd]. Mr King the Bookseller's company,[166] with professions of Moderation.

[Jan.] 24. *Wednesday*. Morning, Mr W. Rook, Schoolmaster in the Panther, for Orders; my brother, adviseing physick; Mr M. Hutchinson, for application to the Dean of the Arches [Bettesworth]; Mr Leneve, offended at Mr Anstis and Mr Dale; Mr James Lowther, on the old string; Mr Little-John (introduced by Mr Greenshields) for a favour in Baliol College from the Bishop of Rochester;[167] and Mr Wilkinson, for a Letter to Lord Sussex. Dined Alone. After Dinner, in a Grand Committee[168] (on the Question 64 against 44. Duke of Bucks with 9 Bishops amongst the latter) Lord Galway's giveing the post of Honour to the Portugal Forces voted *contrary to the Honour of the Imperial Crown of Great Brittain*.[169] This day the Convocation met (the Archbishop of Canterbury present) and a Licence was read from the Queen, impowering the Bishops (whereof the Archbishop the Bishop of London [Compton][170] and the Bishop of Bath and Wells of the Quorum) with the other Clergy of the province to expedite all such matters as within their cognisance. NB. The Bishop of Bath and Wells protested against the Innovation;[171] as never communicated to him, &c. Evening, Mr Bell brought to me Mr Cambel (an ingenious Scotch Gentleman)[172] who was bred at University College where (and at Lord Preston's[173] afterwards) unjustly treated by Dr T[odd] who falsley quoted Bishop Turner[174] for's Informer,

[166] Charles King, bookseller at the Judge's Head, Westminster Hall, 1707-25. Plommer, *Dictionary of Booksellers and Printers 1668-1725*, p. 179.

[167] Probably George Littlejohn, son of Charles of Edinburgh, who matriculated at Balliol College, Oxford, on 27 Oct. 1710, aged 15.

[168] HMC *Lords MSS* ix, 80; *LJ* xix, 202. See also *Wentworth Papers*, pp. 178-9.

[169] Cf. above, 22 Jan., n. 162. That the Duke of Buckingham, a High Tory member of the Cabinet, sided with the Whigs on this vote throws some light on its injustice.

[170] The choice of Bishop Compton at this juncture is curious. Only six days before he was said to be lying 'dangerously ill'. Luttrell, vi, 680.

[171] The innovation was that the Archbishop of Canterbury was not named as president but that he and the two bishops named were to be a quorum before whom all matters were to be brought. Canterbury and London were both ill and Bath and Wells refused to act so that a new licence was sent on 21 Feb. 1711 appointing Canterbury president and adding other bishops to the quorum. The original licence, suspected to be the work of Atterbury and Harley, revealed the ministry's intention to give official approval to the Lower House's doctrine that the Archbishop was president by royal grant and not by right of his metropolitical office. See Lathbury, *Convocation*, p. 409; Bennett, *White Kennett*, p. 75; Bennett, *Tory Crisis*, p. 131; BL Lansdowne MS 1024, f. 254ᵛ.

[172] Archibald Campbell (d. 1744), grandson of Archibald, Marquess of Argyll, was consecrated a bishop of the Scottish Episcopal Church at Dundee in Aug. 1711; Bishop of Aberdeen, 1721-4.

[173] Edward Grahme (c.1679-1710), 2nd Viscount Preston, had matriculated University College, Oxford, 1693. He was the nephew of Col. James Grahme and the Dean of Wells.

[174] Francis Turner (?1638-1700), Bishop of Ely, 1684-90; deprived as a non-juror.

and afterwards cheated the Family of the better part of Lord Preston's Library. After they left me, the Remainder of tHe evening at Salisbury-Court.

[Jan.] 25. *Thursday*. Morning, To Dr Gibson's, with Archdeacon Pearson's Letter; shewing that my friend had better Knowledge of the proceedings in Convocation than Archbishop of Canterbury. Thence to Whitehall; where onely the Bishop of Bristol [Robinson] and myself. The Deputy Auditors Instructed about the List of my Diocese. In the way to the House, Abel Roper[175] rightly reported the Changes at Court.[176] Lord Hallifax, called on, saies he will procure Rymer's three last Volumes. In the House, An Appeal heard (Green against Green) and the Decree unanimously affirmed.[177] Dined Alone. Evening, visitted by Dr Woodward much in starch; Mr Smith, my brother Antiquary, full of Willeramus, Tatian,[178] &c. Dr Dent, of Emptiness.

[Jan.] 26. *Friday*. Morning, Mr R. Wenman, returning to Oxon. Mr Redman's son, with a Letter from's Father, for Preferment.[179] Dined with me Dr Lancaster and Dr Waugh, both earnest friends to the Duke of Marlborough. After a walk in the park with Mr Sandes &c. I spent the Evening at St Martin's with Coll. Orfeur, for the General. NB. The Earl of Carlile met with in the House; where no Report from the Committee.

[Jan.] 27. *Saturday*. Morning, My Brother and R. Leethwait. In my way to Whitehall, I met Mr Moody;[180] who told me our Books of Tenths would be finished against this day Fortnight. Mr Madox returned with me to the House: where Sir P. King (in maintenance of a Writ of Errour about Imposts on Prisage-Wines) very learned

---

[175] Abel Roper (1665–1726), Tory journalist who started the *Post Boy* in 1695 and continued to be associated with the paper until *c.* 1712.

[176] The changes consequent on the Duchess of Marlborough's resignation of all her places on 18 Jan., notably the appointment of the Duchess of Somerset as Groom of the Stole and of Abigail Masham as Privy Purse.

[177] HMC *Lords MSS* ix, 11–12.

[178] Willeram, Abbot of Ebersburg, wrote a paraphrase of the Song of Songs (*c.*1060), which was published in 1598 as *In Canticum Canticorum paraphrasis gemia*. An East Franconian version from a manuscript in the Bodley of Tatian's Gospel Harmony (*c.*835) called *Tatiani Harmonia Evangeliae antiquissima versio Theotisca* was published at Greifswald in 1706.

[179] This may be A. Redman, who was offered the post of Clerk to the Justice of the Peace in Cumberland in mid February. See below, 19 Feb.

[180] Possibly James Moody, Deputy to the Auditors of the Imprest in the Court of Exchequer, who was involved in Queen Anne's Bounty. *CTB 1711* xxv, 213; Chamberlayne, *Present State 1710*, p. 575; Church Commissioners QAB Minute Book, i, 148.

on the Antiquity of Purveyances, Subsidies &c. One side heard, the Cause adjourned to Munday;[181] the Grand Committee, on the Affairs of Spain, being postponed to Wednesday. Dined Alone. Evening, Cousin Lesley, not for crossing the Seas.

[Jan.] 28. *Sunday*. I took a Dose of purgeing pills; which wrought long and violently. Visitted onely by my Brother in the Day-time; and, at night, by some Gentlemen of the Vestry of St Botulph's Bishopgate desireing a Charity-Sermon on the 3d Sunday in March. Yes, if I stay.[182]

[Jan.] 29. *Munday*. Morning Mr Cambel (cousin German to the Duke of A[rgyll]'s father) whom I durst not, for the cold,[183] as yet attend to Lambeth. He gave two sharp stories of the Bishop of Sarum his physico-Theological Letter to the Duke of Lauderdale on King Charles II's takeing a new wife;[184] and the old Marchioness of Montrose's maids spying the Gallows 'twixt his een. An old Scotch Coin given me; and others, with Ave Maria, shewn. Mr Ar[thur] Atkinson, returning to Queen's, speaks well of my son. Mr J. Orfeur called after I was gone to the House; where I read prayers, and returned to Dinner: And lost Mr Watkinson's call, whilst I waited for it. The Duke of Northumberland's cause about Prisage-wines ended; after the Twelve Judges had, at length given their opinion: Ten for the chargeing with them with Tunnage, and two (Lord Chief Baron [Ward] and Baron Bury) against it. Lord Guarnsey, on the Debate, joyned the two Barons; and had, on the Question, 26 against 40. Amongst his Followers, the Bishop of Bristol; whose endeavour to put an Antedated Resignation into the Archbishop's hand (of his prebend of Canterbury, in favour of the same Family) was thereupon told me by the Bishop of N[orwich] [Trimnell]. Evening, bestowed on the Chancellor's two Brothers in Holburn.

---

[181] *LJ* xix, 205–6.

[182] Although Nicolson remained in London, he did not preach the sermon. See below, 18 Mar.

[183] The weather at this time was exceptionally severe. Luttrell (vi, 687) reported the deaths of five men drowned this week when their boat was overturned in the Thames by floating ice.

[184] In answer to Lauderdale's request for Burnet's opinion on divorce in 1671, Burnet wrote a paper entitled 'Resolution of two important cases of conscience, viz: (1) Is a woman's barrenness a just ground for divorce? and (2) Is polygamy in any case lawful under the gospel?'. Burnet answered both questions in the affirmative, but later retracted the paper. See T. E. S. Clarke and H. C. Foxcroft, *A Life of Gilbert Burnet* (Cambridge, 1907), pp. 103–4.

[Jan.] 30. *Tuesday*. Morning, Mr Robinson Vicar of Berwick, Chaplain to the Garrison,[185] with Mr Greenshields. The House, after prayers and Adjournment, proceeded (9 Bishops and as many Temporal Lords) to the Abbey-Church;[186] where a Loyal, and honest Sermon, preached by the Bishop of Chester [Dawes]. After a walk round the Park, I returned to Evening-Prayer; and thence to my Dinner at four.

[Jan.] 31. *Wednesday*. Morning, With Mr M. Hutchinson to Dr G[ibson] who will apply to the Dean of the Arches [Bettesworth] for Dispatch. At the House, I was called to the Chair of the Grand Committee for passing the Malt-Bill; which had the Royal Assent by Commission.[187] The Committee for Affairs of Spain agreed (*Nemine Contradicente*) that 29,000 was the Establishment and onely 15,000 in that Kingdome when the Battle of Almanza fought.[188] Who in fault, see tomorrow. The Convocation had a Letter of Instructions from the Queen requireing their opinion on the Occasion of the Growth of Irreligion; their frameing of Forms of prayer with condemned Criminals, Consecration of Churches, &c. modelling of proceedings in Excommunication and Commutation.[189]

In the Evening, at the Remembrancer's office with Mr Madox; to whom subscriptions delivered in, &c. Thence to Brother's till Ten. NB. Lord Carlile (in the House) put into my hand a paper of vile matters, of Corruption, against Mr Goodman.

Feb. 1. *Thursday*. Morning, Cousin M. Orfeur, renewing her suit for Mounsey. Let me see him. After fruitless waiting for Mr R. Smith, I went to the House, and, haveing read prayers, returned to Dinner. P.m. The Affairs of Spain, considered more particularly: And, tho' mismanagements hinted at, nothing could be carried save this— *That two Regiments, twice Reckoned, had not been supplyed as*

---

[185] Probably Patrick Robertson, MA Edinburgh 1672, incorporated Oxford 1712; Vicar of Berwick, 1686–1726. See also BL Add. MS 6116, ff. 34–5: N. to Wake, 14 Nov. 1715.

[186] The attendance was remarkably low in view of the fervour shown in London on the same day twelve months previously. Cf. Holmes, *Sacheverell*, pp. 118–19.

[187] *LJ* xix, 207–8.

[188] The figures given were an establishment of 29,395 of which 13,759 were in Spain, leaving a deficiency of 15,636. See HMC *Lords MSS* ix, 85; *LJ* xix, 208–9; *Parl. Hist.* vi, 993–5.

[189] See Lathbury, *Convocation*, pp. 408–9 for the full list of heads of subjects for discussion by the Convocation. It is mistakenly dated by Lathbury as 29 Jan. 1710. One of the Queen's doctors noted of an interview with Anne on 12 Feb.: 'I mention'd how the Pious part of the people were pleas'd with taking the Convocation off from Hereditary Right, and Passive Obedience, to fix their thoughts against Immorality and Atheism, hoping this would strengthen the endeavours after Reformation. To which the Queen said, that would be very well.' *The Diary of Sir David Hamilton*, p. 30.

they ought to have been; yet it appeared that four were sent in lieu of them; that all the money given [by] parliament was honestly disbursed; and that Eleven Millions had been expended in Spain, to the value of less than 11d. The Question carryed by 52 against 49.[190]

[Feb.] 2. *Friday*. Morning, Mr M. Mounsey with certificates from Lords Carlile and Lisburn;[191] Mr Farish,[192] with a presentation to the Rectory of Plumland; to be held with Isale, if the Bishop of Chester's Letter prevails for his Degree at Cambridge. Mr Cambel, with me to Lambeth, to search for (what we found not) Archbishop Sharp's being ordained Decon and Priest, as well as Consecrated Bishop, in 1661. My Lord Archbishop very lame, but cheerful. At dinner with Dr Waugh, his Birth-day. At four, I came back to the House, but found it adjourned, haveing onely read and thrown out the Office Bill.[193] Evening, With Dr Waugh, by appointment, at my Brother's.

[Feb.] 3. *Saturday*. Morning, Mr Greenshields, to meet Mr Little-John returning to Edinburgh. Being at a Committee, Mr Lawson came for Advice about the place of Elections in our County; and expressed his own Resentment and that of other Gentlemen against the Lords for throwing out the Bill against Officers, blameing (especially) some for giveing it the Epithet of Whimsical and others for saying 'twas sent up by the *Dregs of a discontented party*.[194] This news to me. He also reported to me Mr Hungerford's observation, That the present Ministry differed from the last as a *Cat in a window from a Cat out of it*.[195] In the House, after long Debates, voted on the Question (62 against 46) That *the great Deficiencies in the Forces in Spain were to be charged on the Great neglect of the Ministry*. This to be drawn into an Address; and laid before the

---

[190] See HMC *Lords MSS* ix, 85.

[191] John Vaughan (*c.*1670-1721), MP for Cardiganshire, 1694-8, created Viscount Lisburne [I] in 1695 in consequence of his marriage in 1692 to the daughter of John Wilmot, Earl of Rochester.

[192] Peter Farish (Faresh), MA Trinity College, Dublin, 1712; Rector of Plumbland, Cumberland, 1711, and of Moresby, 1720.

[193] By a majority of seventeen (46-29). HMC *Lords MSS* ix, 86; Luttrell, vi, 686. See above, sessional intro., p. 511 for the Place Bill, and Tory reactions to its defeat.

[194] Probably Poulet's words. See HMC *Portland MSS* iv, 657.

[195] John Hungerford (*c.*1658-1729), standing counsel for the East India Company and a leading Tory Commoner (MP for Scarborough, 1692-5, 1702-5, 1707-29) was, like Lawson, a member of the October Club which (significantly, in the light of this resentment) first erupted in the House of Commons the following week. SRO GD 220/5/808/15: Mungo Graham to Duke of Montrose, 6 Feb. 1711. See also above, sessional intro., p. 512; below, 6 Feb.

Queen.[196] NB. Lord Treasurer of the Household (Earl of Cholmley) one of the 46 because—*He would be loath to see the present Ministry condemned on such evidence.*[197]

[Feb.] 4. *Sunday*. I preached at the Savoy; and (with the Dean of Rochester [Pratt] Mr Clavel, &c) dined at Cousin R. Nicolson's. Evening Cousin Lesley.

[Feb.] 5. *Munday*. Morning, Mr Wilkinson, Knows nothing of his succeeding Mr How:[198] Mrs Fr[   ] Hutton, with a begging Petition: Earl of Hindforth, for moderation in Mr Greenshields's Case: Mr James Lowther, protesting against the Schemes of Mr Lawson for the place of Election:[199] Mr Chamberlayne, with the Dutch Abstract of the Gothic Grammar. After Dinner, in the House; where the Bill for Reversing the Act of General Naturalization read for the first time.[200] Lord Hallifax moved the throwing it out, in a strain of eloquence becomeing himself. After a long Debate (wherein Lords Nottingham, Guarnsey, Ferrers, North, Anglesey, &c. earnest for it) the Question put for a second Reading, *Contents*, 42. *Not Contents*, 52.[201] Amongst the former 8 Bishops (with the Archbishop of York one) and with the latter 10, whereof I was one. The Commons as hard on the hitherto prevailing party. I carried the news to Archbishop of Canterbury who denies (what the Earl of Nottingham charged on him)[202] a Correspondence with the King of Prussia, and letting it cool; and assures me that the Palatines were invited by W. Penn.[203] Dr G[ibson]'s story of H. Cross's being an unaccountable man under Lord Chancellor Cowper; not so under Lord Keeper Wright. Evening, Visitted by Cousins Penington and Chambers. In my absence, Dr Gee and Mr Dowson.

[196] HMC *Lords MSS* ix, 86–7; *LJ* xix, 212–13; *Parl. Hist.* vi, 994.
[197] Cholmondeley, though not a member of the Cabinet, was one of the more important Whig peers preserved in office by Harley and the Queen, and had supported the ministry in the votes of 9–12 Jan.
[198] ?John Howe, Surveyor of the Window Duties in Cumberland. Appointed in Sept. 1710, he was replaced by Lord Thanet's candidate, Thomas Lamb, in Sept. 1711. *CTB 1710*, p. 445; *CTB 1711*, pp. 402–3, 459.
[199] The topography of Cumberland made the choice of a polling place in shire elections a contentious matter. Speck, *Tory and Whig*, p. 83.
[200] See HMC *Lords MSS* ix, 87–8; *LJ* xix, 215.
[201] This Act had been an emotive measure, unacceptable to the majority of the Tories, when it had passed in 1709. The repealing bill, promoted largely by Nottingham's friends outside the ministry, was too partisan a measure at this stage for Harley and most of the Cabinet. But their use of the Lords—and Whig votes—to kill it added more fuel to the discontent of the October men.
[202] i.e. in the debate.
[203] William Penn (1644–1718), Quaker and founder of Pennsylvania.

[Feb.] 6. *Tuesday*. Morning, In my way to Court, visits paid (and attempted) to Lord Carlile in the Gowt; Lord Sommers gone to St James's;[204] Lord Eglinton perswaded that (after tomorrow) Mr Greenshields's Bill may be seasonably moved. Mr Dungworth of the same mind for new Reasons of fresh Banishments. The Queen's Levee full of the most glittering Appearance of fine cloathes &c.[205] She born in a Chair (open) to the Chapple: When the Bishop of Exeter and I went home to dinner with the Bishop of Ch[ester?] at Kensington; where Sir J. Cotton and his son (a member of the House of Commons) explained[206] the October-Club,[207] as made of old Beer-Drinkers, as Sir Thomas Willoughby[208] &c; Tory-Discourse; The Freeholder of Cambridgeshire's Reply to Lord Cuts's[209] Agent in the County-Election—That *their Poor never were consulted in setting Parish Rates*. The Bishop of Exon brought me back.

[Feb.] 7. *Wednesday*. Morning, Visitted by my Brother with account of Lord Portland's Court-suit valued at 40000 *l*. Dr Lloyd, with a Case to be heard tomorrow; Mr Paul, one of M. Orfeur's clients. In the House, A Writt of Errour heard; and Judgement (by consent of Lord Guernsey, Lord Cowper and all the Judges) reversed.[210] The Representation on Saturday's Vote not ready till tomorrow. P.m., Mr Addison and Mr Hornsby, on a pure Visit. Dr Gee, in some pain for his 1200 *l*. in the Exchequer. He saies the Convocation, met today, could not proceed in Business for want of one of the Quorum; yet the lower House were under Deliberation whether they were obliged to take any notice of that Defect.[211] He mounts the value of

[204] Somers had remained on good personal terms with the Queen since his dismissal the previous September.

[205] See Luttrell, vi, 688 for a description. It was said to be the most dazzling show seen at Court since the Restoration.

[206] Sir John Cotton (d. 1713), 2nd Bt. of Madingley Hall, Cambridgeshire, had been MP for Cambridge, 1689-95, 1696-1702, 1705-8. For his son, John Hynde Cotton (*c*.1688-1752), who succeeded as 3rd Bt., and was MP for Cambridge, 1708-22, see Sedgwick, i, 584-5.

[207] See above, sessional intro., p. 512. The club had existed as a social club since the early weeks of the session. It was only at this juncture that it assumed such a marked political significance. In general, see H. T. Dickinson, 'The October Club', *Huntington Library Quarterly*, xxxiii (1969-70), 155-73. John Hynde Cotton, an able young Tory of Jacobite leanings, was a member (see ibid., p. 171).

[208] Thomas Willoughby (*c*.1670-1729), Tory MP for Newark, 1710-12; Baron Middleton (cr. 1712). He is not listed by Dickinson, 'The October Club', pp. 170-3, as a member.

[209] John Cutts (1661-1707), a soldier who had distinguished himself at the Boyne and had been created Baron Cutts [I] in 1690. A Major-General in 1696, he was third in command at Blenheim, and became C.-in-C. in Ireland in 1705. MP for Cambridgeshire, 1693-1702, and Newport, I.o.W., 1702-7.

[210] *LJ* xix, 216.

[211] The weather was so bad and there was so little expectation of business that even Kennett did not attend Convocation. The Archbishop's commissary (Bishop of Lichfield)

Lord P[ortland]'s Accoutrements to 80000 *l.* of which his Sword onely 600 *l.* John Abbat with the men of Cockermouth.[212]

[Feb.] 8. *Thursday.* Morning, Cousin R. Nicolson, with Rumney's Petition; Sir James Montague, with the History of yesterday's fruitless endeavour of C. Gledhil to get the Hearing of his senceless cause appointed for February 26 instead of March 8, to which I gave him a Counterpart from my Letters from Carlile-Election.[213] W. Rook fair in Lord C[arlisle]'s opinion.

At the House, the Representation Read and Approved. One Division on the word *Profusion*, 58 against 32.[214] At a second Dinner with Mr Walker; whose Guests also Mr Johnson and his two Sons. Mrs W[alker] commends Quince and Bacon (partee p[ ] pale) baked, as a most agreeable Dish. NB. In the morning I again attempted a visit to Lord Carlile who in bed. Mem[orandum]. Reply of Capt. Steel to Dr A[tterbury?]. The Tatler in Commission.[215]

[Feb.] 9. *Friday.* Morning, Mr M. Hutchinson, fraught with the praises of the Dean of the Arches [Bettesworth]; who has proved expeditious in doeing him Right: In the House, the Reason of the Lords protesters (against the Vote of the *Great Neglect* of the late Ministry) expunged;[216] by 52 against 33[217] as all Reasons for the future will probably be, so as onely to leave Room for a plain Dissent. In the Evening I carryed M. Chambers the news of her Brother's death;[218] thence to Salisbury-Court, till Bed-time.

---

prorogued Convocation until the following Friday, but the Lower House referred consideration of this to the Committee for Rights and Privileges. BL Lansdowne MS 1024, f. 266[r].

[212] Col. J. Orfeur, the unsuccessful candidate in the 1710 election, had petitioned against Gen. Stanhope. The Commons heard the petition on 6 Mar. 1711 (*CJ* xvi, 537), and declared a void election. Abbat was possibly one of the witnesses on whom the Duke of Somerset spent £641 to fight Orfeur's petition.

[213] See above, sessional intro., p. 512.

[214] The Representation to the Queen was that called for on 3 Feb., concerning the war in Spain. *LJ* xix, 218–19. The vote was fifty-eight against thirty-three.

[215] Richard Steele (1672–1729) had started *The Tatler* on 12 Apr. 1709. After 271 numbers it came to a sudden end on 2 Jan. 1711. On 4 Jan. a spurious No. 272 was published by John Baker and on 6 Jan. No. 273 appeared. On the same day John Morphew began another series with what purported to be Nos. 272 and 273 of the original *Tatler*. These continued until 19 May and No. 330, under the editorship of Harrison and the sponsorship of Swift. See *Journal to Stella*, i, 54, 162–3.

[216] The vote on the *Great Neglect* took place on 3 Feb. 1711. The original protest (including the subsequent expunged section) is printed in Rogers, *Protests of the Lords*, i, 204–5. For the expunged protest as it appears in the Journal see *LJ* xix, 213.

[217] 'The lord Somers and others of the late ministry made speeches, that the protestations might stand, but the Scotch lords, being all of a side, over ballanced the rest.' Luttrell, vi, 689.

[218] Archer Chambers, Vicar of Askham, 1707–11.

[Feb.] 10. *Saturday*. Morning Mr Farish, returned from Cambridge without a degree, for Institution next week. In the Committee at Whitehall; where the Officers not ready with our Books. Sir N. Lloyd's[219] story of the Engineer's nameing a half-demolished Fortification a *Twentyfication*; in answer to mine of S[ergeant] Maynard's[220] *Pugnabo fortiter*. Visitted by Lord Sunderland and Lord Hallifax. At Dinner with me Mr M. Hutchinson and Cousin Lesley. Evening private, at Letters &c.

[Feb.] 11. *Sunday*. I kept private all day (being Rainy) in provideing Charity-Sermon. Evening, I went with Mr Greenshields to seek for Dr Lancaster; and, not finding him, returned to the perusal of his papers.

[Feb.] 12. *Munday*. Morning, P. Tullie to be Commissioner for the Lottery.[221] Mr Greenshields, for a Letter to Dr L[ancaster]. Mr Wilkinson, prepareing for the Country: Mr Ar[thur] Redman, unprovided. A Visit paid to Lord Hallifax where Sir James M[ontagu] gave me the story of his being Decoyèd into the House by Mr Caesar. Coll.[222] saies Lord Galway did not licence the lame Account of his conduct. In the Lobby, the Bishop of Man [Wilson] has brought me more Runic from his Island.[223] Dr Moss, fair. Sir Alexander Rigby,[224] to assist him and's fellow-Commissioners in Scotland.[225] Bishop of Ely, observations on the Queen's new Quorum,[226] the Charge of his Justices and the Statutes of Trinity-College. In the House, Her Majesty's Answer to the *Representation* Reported, and ordered to be printed:[227] The expunged Reason repeated in the Journal (with new Entries of Dissent) referred to a Committee.[228] Dined Alone. Evening, Mr Greenshields and Cousin Lesley, cheerful Antagonists.

---

[219] Sir Nathaniel Lloyd (1669–1741), Admiralty Advocate, 1704–17, Master of Trinity Hall, Cambridge, 1710–35, Vice-Chancellor of Cambridge, 1710–11.

[220] Sir John Maynard (1602–90), judge and MP.

[221] A bill for raising a loan through the establishment of a state lottery was currently going through the Commons. When it was launched in Mar. it proved a striking success (below, 13 Mar.).

[222] Name blank in MS.

[223] For details see Nicolson's notebook, Bodl. MS Gen. Top. c. 27/1.

[224] A London merchant, formerly MP for Wigan, 1701–2, and protegé of the Earl of Macclesfield, he died in 1717. See M. Cox, 'Sir Roger Bradshaigh, 3rd Bt., and the Electoral Management of Wigan, 1695–1747', *Bulletin of the John Rylands Library*, xxxvii (1954–5), 126 n.

[225] Rigby had been appointed one of the Commissioners of Customs for Scotland in May 1707. Luttrell, vi, 173. For his career, see Riley, *English Ministers and Scotland*, pp. 131–4.

[226] See above, n. 171.

[227] *LJ* xix 222. See above, n. 214.

[228] *LJ* xix, 223.

[Feb.] 13. *Tuesday*. Morning Arthur Redman, sent (with my Letter) to Mr Chamberlayne: Dr King of Chelsea, with his Defence of Bishop Atherton:[229] Mr Elstob, with an Account of the continuance of his and his sister's Labours. A Visit to Dr Gibson, who has parted with a Tooth. Thence to the Archbishop who well pleased (tho' confined to his Bed) with the Discovery of Chalk stones in his sore Toe. I dined, at the Steward's Table, with the Dean of the Arches, Dr Sydale, &c.

In the House, An Appeal ('twixt Docksey and Docksey) heard; and the Decree affirmed.[230] *Reasons* &c. effectually expunged.[231] Evening, my Brother and Sister (and two Nieces) supped with me; and a coach, at Eleven, procured for them with great Difficulty.

[Feb.] 14. *Ash-Wednesday*. Morning, Hearing Dr Higden preach (a very good and plain Sermon) at Whitehall: His Text the Resolution of the Prodigal Son, *Luke* 15 and's Subject the danger of a late Repentance. Present, the Dukes of Bucks and Leedes, Lord Hide[232] and three Bishops. Evening, Cousin Lesley; who saies the Duke of Marlborough is goeing off, but has not spoke to Lord Hindford.

[Feb.] 15. *Thursday*. Morning, Mr Farish, for goeing back by the way of Oxford; Mr Chamberlayne, with the Queen's second Letter to the Convocation;[233] Mal. Chambers, apprized of the Custome at Abbey-Holme; Mr Greenshields, for bringing in his petition to day; Dr Scott, with the Account of a new Fast appointed by the presbytery of Edinburgh; Mal. Orfeur, impatient for her friend's success with Lord Carlile.

In the House, Lord North assured me of his moveing for Mr Greenshields on Saturday; and Lord Sunderland undertook to sollicite Lord Hindford for Cousin Lesley: who with me in the evening, to learn the Success.

[Feb.] 16. *Friday*. Morning, After Mr Farish's goeing off for Oxford; I went to preach a Charity-Sermon at St. Catharine's Hospital;[234] where prayers were read by (the plain-Englishman, and famous

---

[229] John King (1652–1732), Rector of Chelsea, 1694–1732, Prebendary of York, 1718–32. The *Case of John Atherton, Bishop of Waterford, fairly represented* had been published anonymously in 1710. Atherton (1598–1640), Bishop of Waterford and Lismore in 1636 had been executed for an 'unnatural crime'.

[230] HMC *Lords MSS* ix, 10.

[231] *LJ* xix, 224; above, 9 Feb.

[232] Henry, Lord Hyde, MP for Launceston, later 2nd Earl of Rochester, see Appendix A.

[233] For the letter see above, 31 Jan. The letter was published in the *Post Boy* on 15 Feb. 1711. BL Lansdowne MS 1024, f. 268^r.

[234] Founded in 1148 to the east of the Tower.

eldest Brother of the three) Mr Bisset.[235] He saies the extended Rents of their House would amount to 6000 *l.* per Annum. But they are so miserably under-Rented that 500 *l.* in the hands of the late (deprived) Bishop of Norwich[236] paid onely 13*s* 4*d*. The Society was abolished and Reinstated by Lord Sommers, when Lord Chancellor, who deprived the then Master succeeded by Dr Newton.[237] I returned about one to the Lobby; but, finding nothing more to do than the hearing of a Writ of Error, went not into the House. Here Mr Chancellor Lloyd gave me an Account of the prolocutor's [Atterbury's] makeing a couple of Deputies proprio jure &c.[238] Evening, Mr M. Hutchinson, inveighing against Mr Collins's Letter (as he called it) to Sir J. Banks.[239] Mr R. Smith, and Mr Willis, the latter much Hypped. The Remainder at My Brother's.

[Feb.] 17. *Saturday*. Morning, With Gr[eenshields] endeavouring to wait on Lord Cromarty; who in Bed. We were more fortunate in meeting with Mr Archibald Cambel; whose Collection of Scotch Books, Coins and other Rarities, noted in my old Almanack. After a walk, to Dinner at my Lodgeings. Evening, C. Lesley, takeing Leave.

[Feb.] 18. *Sunday*. After dineing (with Ch[arles] Buchanan) at my Brother's and hearing Dr Waugh preach, I went to preach at Bow-Church; where an Excessive Crowd. After a Dish of Coffee with the Bishop of Man, I returned home at almost Nine. The Bishop will have the small Pox an Indian Distemper.

[235] William Bissett (d. 1747), Low Church pamphleteer; Rector of Whiston, Northamptonshire, 1697-1747; author of *The Modern Fanatick* (1710), the most lengthy and uninhibited of all the Whig attacks on Dr Sacheverell.

[236] William Lloyd (d. 1710), Bishop of Norwich, 1685-90, was deprived of his see for being a non-juror.

[237] Henry Newton (*c.*1651-1715), civil lawyer. Advocate of Doctor's Commons, 1678; Chancellor of the diocese of London, 1685-1715; Admiralty Advocate, 1695-1714; judge of the High Court of Admiralty, 1714-15. According to *DNB* he was appointed Master of St Katharine's Hospital during his absence from England on a diplomatic mission to Italy 1706-9, but this is at odds with Bisset's evidence (Somer's tenure of the Lord Chancellorship ended in 1700).

[238] For this fresh altercation in Convocation, which led to a walk-out by Archdeacons Kennett and West, see Bennett, *White Kennett*, p. 76; BL Lansdowne MS 1024, f. 268[V].

[239] Sir Jacob Banks, MP for Minehead (High Tory), 1698-1714, a former Tacker, owed his Minehead seat to his marriage to the widow of Col. Francis Luttrell. In 1711 the following pamphlet was published: *Letter to Sir J[acob] B[anks], by birth a S[wede], but naturalized, and now a M[embe]r of the present P[arliamen]t; concerning the late Minehead doctrine, which was established by a certain free parliament of Sweden, to the utter enslaving of that Kingdom*. It was written by William Benson, High Sheriff of Wiltshire in 1710, who published *A Second Letter . . .* later in the year. See also below, 23 Feb.; Luttrell, vi, 696 for the protest of the Swedish Resident.

[Feb.] 19. *Munday*. Morning W. Tate,[240] with a great Cargo of Spermacete (100 *l.*) brought from Scotland; for which the Druggists (who sell it to the Apothecaries at 55*s.*) offer him 32*s.* per pound. He bought it at 15*s.* A. Redman,[241] offered to be made Clerk to a Justice of Peace: Dr Smith, with an Account of the Queen's giveing Lutterworth[242] (sought by Mr Dungworth) to Dr Higden: Mr Greenshields to the House; where his Appeal, on the unopposed motion of Lord North, appointed to be heard on March 1.[243] After half-hearing a Cause, Mr G[reenshields] back with me to Dinner. P.m., Sir James Mountague, with an Account (which was given me before by Mr Lowther and Mr Lawson)[244] of C[oll.] Gledhill's impudent Accusation of him and me in the House of Commons. This carried by me to Lord Carlile: From whom, with Mr R. Smith, to Rendezvous of the Antiquaries at the *Fountain*.[245]

[Feb.] 20. *Tuesday*. Morning, Sir J. M[ontagu] peruseing my Letter to Mr Lawson; which Lord Hallifax thinks better let alone: Mr Leneve, with the *Pedes Finiu.* of Westmerland: Cousin James Nicolson and his wife, with Mr Higgins Def[endan]t in a Writ of Error. After a Visit to Bishop of Lincoln (who communicated *Remarks* on Mr G[reenshields]'s case)[246] I went to the House; and, after the Remainder of an Irish Cause,[247] had tacit Leave to attend the House of Commons; where a Chair set for me at the lighting of Candles. But, Mr Gledhil's friends moveing for an Adjournment of the Debate for 3 weeks carried it (so as to save the Coll[onel] from Bondage) by 154 against 151.[248] Thus leave given for the Man's running away, I retired to Lord Hallifax's where I dined with Lord Castlecomer, &c.

[240] Related to Nicolson, see *CW* ii (1902), 173; 1 (1950), 128.

[241] See above, n. 179.

[242] A market town in Leicestershire where the parish living was in the Lord Chancellor's gift.

[243] *LJ* xix, 228; see HMC *Lords MSS* viii, 356–9 for the case.

[244] They were tellers for the minority of the vote on 20 Feb. It is interesting that Lawson chose to support Montagu and the Bishop over the Carlisle election despite his association with the October Club.

[245] The revived Society of Antiquaries, which had been meeting for three years with Le Neve as chairman, had moved in 1709 from the *Young Devil* tavern in the Strand to the *Fountain*, outside Temple Bar in Fleet Street. For a discussion of these meetings see J. Evans, *A History of the Society of Antiquaries* (1956), pp. 45–6.

[246] *Remarks on a pamphlet, entitled, A true state of the case of the Revd. Mr Greenshields* (1710) was an anti-Greenshields pamphlet.

[247] The case of the Bishop of Raphoe. See HMC *Lords MSS* ix, 80–1.

[248] See the letter of Mungo Graham quoted above, sessional intro., p. 514. In the minority the Harleyites and some other Tories voted with the Whigs against the October Club. In the debate, Gen. John Webb, bluntly accused Gledhill of fabricating his charges and suggested he should be taken into custody, and he was seconded by a Whig placeman, Gen. Thomas

[Feb.] 21. *Wednesday*. Morning, Dr Scott, fishing for what he caught not: Mr R. Smith, with whom I went to Dr Bentley's; but he could not (in Mr Elphinston's Absence) let us into the Library. NB. His observation on the cold N.E. winds, from the melting of the Snowes in Tartary and Muscovy; comeing on the opening of our Fruit-Blossoms. The like Influences, and for the same Reason, it has on the Bodies of our Men and Beasts.

In the House, much complimented on C[oll.] Gledhill's Blunders: A Writ of Errour heard (on the Case of the Warden of the Fleet) and Judgement affirmed.[249] Bishop of Bangor and Dean of Peterborough [Kennett] came home with me: The latter haveing Demureley reflected, in Convocation, on the Prolocutor.[250] Evening, Dr Gee, alarmed with the wording of yesterday's Votes, set right.

[Feb.] 22. *Thursday*. Morning, Mr Winder, with a Letter from Dr L[ancaster] recommending him to the Duke of Argyle: Mr Thomas Machel's[251] youngest Daughter, in poverty: Cousin Tate goeing to his sister. In the House, I spoke to the Duke of A[rgyll] and shewed him Dr L[ancaster]'s Letter. His Grace ordered the young man to wait on him in the morning. I left the Grand Committee (at Three) debateing and passing the Qualification Bill;[252] and went to dine at Sir J. M[ontagu]'s where Cousin Tate and Mr Wilkinson, the Lawyer, stuned at my nameing Dr A[tterbury] for Bishop of London.[253] In Return, brought by Sir James to Lord Carlile; who still in the Gowt. His Lordship fears not the haveing Coll. Gl[edhill] for a Lieut. Governour.

Erle, BL Add. MS 17677 EEE, f. 95, Staatsarchiv Hannover, Cal. Br. 24 (England) 99: Kreienberg's despatch, 23 Feb./6 Mar. 1710; *CJ* xvi, 508.

[249] See HMC *Lords MSS* ix, 15–17.

[250] See Bennett, *White Kennett*, pp. 76–7.

[251] Thomas Machell (1647–98), Cumberland antiquary, Rector of Kirkby Thore, left his manuscripts in the care of Nicolson for his wife, son, and four daughters. The Bishop organised and bound them. See HMC *2nd Report*, Appendix, pp. 124–5, for a description; J. Rogan and E. Birley, 'Thomas Machell, the Antiquary', *CW* lv (1955), 132–53; and for Machell's will, *CW* original series iv (1880), 4–5.

[252] Attempts to impose a property qualification on parliamentary candidates had failed (on two occasions in the Lords) in 1696, 1697, and 1703. The present bill, which stipulated that a knight of the shire must have £600 a year in real estate and a borough member £300 a year, was so dear to the hearts of the hard-pressed 'landed interest' that, although it originated from the Country Tory back benches in Dec. 1710, it was quickly appropriated by the ministry; and it passed the Commons without a division and with only minor amendments. After their defeat over Spain, from 9 Jan. to 3 Feb., the Whig peers did not dare oppose it this time, as they had in Feb. 1703. For the issue in general see Holmes, *British Politics*, pp. 178–82.

[253] A distinctly premature speculation, since Compton recovered from his present illness and survived until 1713.

[Feb.] 23. *Friday*. Morning, Mr Winder, for my Letter to the Duke of A[rgyll]: John Abbat, for a Testimonial: Mr Loste (goeing to Barton on Humber) for the like: Mr Dean of Peterborough, much offended with a Tricking Prolocutor. No Business in the House, Dr Waugh and I (after dineing together) went to visit Dr Gibson; with whom Dr Kennet and Dr Mandevil. The former gave us the History of Lord Mayor's promise to insert the Bishop of Bristol's Story of the Clergyman at Stockholm's laying 9 years in prison for averring that true Kingly Government was not to be had in *Samuel* but *Deuteronomy* into the next edition of the Letter to Sir J[acob] B[anks].[254] Hence (with Dr W[augh]) to And[rew?] Bell's; where Treated with madera, and Jul[ ] Johnson's Works. The Evening at my Brother's.

[Feb.] 24. *Saturday*. Morning, Mrs Hutton, fancying that she's to attend on Maundy-Thursday. Lord Balmerinoch, with Mr Greenshields and his Case:[255] Mr Lawson, with news of C[oll.] Gledhill's order from the speaker to bring up B[rothe]r Carlile, Mr Brathw[ai]t and Mr Green:[256] Mr Winder, Kindly received by the Duke of A[rgyll]. Cousin Tate and M. Chambers with me at Dinner.

[Feb.] 25. *Sunday*. Morning, At Whitehall, where a good Sermon on late Repentance preached (*memoriter*) by Dr Lamb, elder brother to Mr Charles Lamb,[257] Defender of Dr S[acheverell] against Mr Bisset. P.m. At the Abbey, Sermon (on the Secrets of the Lord, &c) by Dr Onely's pert Reader. Evening, With Archdeacon Rogers and Archdeacon Frank, at Dr Gee's; both full of the praises of their good Bishop.[258] Mr Greenshields, with his Proof of the printed Case.[259] *Apage*!

---

[254] See above, 16 Feb.

[255] Probably *The Present State of Mr Greenshield's case now before the right Honorable the House of Lords in a Letter from a Commoner of North Britain to his Friend in Edinburgh dat[ed] Lond[on] Feb. 3. 1710 [11]*. Noted by Kennett under 1 Mar. 1711: BL Lansdowne MS 1024, f. 276[V]. See also above when Greenshields sees a Mr Littlejohn returning to Edinburgh on 3 Feb. 1711.

[256] These were probably witnesses in the case against Montagu's election. Edward Carlile was Nicolson's brother-in-law. Braithwaite may have been George Braithwaite, a minor Canon of Carlisle and Curate of St Mary's, Carlisle, *CW* iii (1903), 2. A George Braithwaite, with Jeremy Reed, had hindered pro-Gledhill voters on election day, see Ferguson, *Cumberland and Westmorland MP's*, p. 89; *CJ* xvii, 106–7. For Green, see below, 6 Mar.

[257] Henry Lamb, or Lambe (*c*.1674–1729), LLD Cambridge, 1709; Vicar of Impington, Cambridgeshire, 1709 and Lecturer at St Mary Magdalene, Bermondsey; Charles Lamb [Lambe] (d. ?1733), Vicar of Impington, Cambridgeshire, 1704, Rector of Trottiscliffe, Kent, 1709; author of *A Vindication of the Reverend Dr Henry Sacheverell from the . . . Aspersions cast upon him in a late infamous Pamphlet, entitled The Modern Fanatick* (London, 1711, 2 edns.).

[258] Thomas Frank (*c*.1663–1731), Archdeacon of Bedford, 1704–31. The good bishop is Wake of Lincoln.   [259] See above, n. 93.

[Feb.] 26. *Munday*. Morning, A present of six pint-Bottles of Sack, from Mr Winder, by Dr Lancaster's Footman. Bishop of Bangor, who accompanyed me to the Bishop of Lincoln's (where we hoped to have concerted the matter of the Scotch Case with him and the Bishop of Norwich) and thence to the Bishop of S. Asaph; who much delighted with the *Medley* of this day, written by Mr Manwaring.[260]

In the House, Dispute with Lord Guarnsey about the Church of a Majority of the Bishops who not of his Faith, because not of his Opinion.[261] Duke of Hamilton, for bringing in Claret; because Port is (as the other will be) counterfeited.[262] Sir James M[ontagu] and Lord Castlecomer's Accounts of new Lies from C[oll.] Gledhill about a Regiment promised, &c. P.m., By water, paying a Visit to Mr H. Watkinson's Family; whence, on foot, to Coleman-street. Merry with Cousin Relf's sisters till after 8 at night.

[Feb.] 27. *Tuesday*. Morning, Mr Greenshields, with notice of the original of the Commission of Generall Assembly from Guthry[263] &c. Young A. Toppin Book-Keeper to a Gentlewoman-Salter in mourning for his Mistress. Mr Fowler, with a parcel of new Medals: Mr Thomas Fletcher, Cousin Joseph Relf and Dr Smart, on a Running Visit; there being then with me Lord Sommers, Lord Cowper and the Bishops of Bangor, Lincoln and Norwich, consulting on the Case of Greenshields; which is to be restrained to the Civil part, without touching on the Authority of the Kirk.[264]

In the House, the Recruit-Bill read a first and second Time, and committed for Tomorrow.[265] P.m., Enquiry made for Dr Lancaster; but not yet (at 5 o'clock) returned from Oxford, but expected this night.

[260] Arthur Mainwaring (MP for West Looe, 1710–12) edited, and largely wrote, the *Medley*, which he had started on 5 Oct. 1710. It ceased publication in July 1711.

[261] This dispute should possibly be seen in the light of the disillusionment of the Finch family with a Church hierarchy over which they (and above all, Guernsey's brother, Nottingham) had had considerable influence in the 1680s and early 1690s. See G. V. Bennett, 'King William III and the Episcopate', *Essays in Modern English Church History*, ed. G. V. Bennett and J. G. Walsh (1966), pp. 104–31.

[262] The 'Claret Bill', or bill for the importation of French wines, an October Club measure with government blessing, was at this time in its committee stage in the Commons. It passed the Lower House and was sent up to the Lords on 10 Mar. Luttrell, vi, 694, 700; *CJ* xvi, 514, 529.

[263] Probably a reference to a publication by James Guthrie (1612?–61), Scottish Presbyterian divine. On 1 Mar. 1711 Kennett recorded buying '*A Letter concerning the Affair of Mr Greenshields after reading the Appeal and the Magistrates Answer to it dat[ed] Feb. 27 1710–11 with the Act of the commission of the General Assembly against Innovations in the Worship of God*. Lond[on]. 8VO 1710–11.' BL Lansdowne MS 1024, f. 276^V.

[264] The Whig lords, while wishing to accommodate their Low Church allies on the bench over the Greenshields case, must have been equally anxious not to alienate support among the Scottish Presbyterians. [265] *LJ* xix, 238.

[Feb.] 28. *Wednesday*. Morning, C[ousin] Tate, desireing to be let into the House of Lords: Mr R. Smith, with whom I went to the Cotton Library and made collections out of the Chronicle of Gisburn.[266] In the House, Her Majesty passed the Qualification and Recruit Bils; with some private Acts.[267] P.m., At Dr Gibson's, giveing Account of this day's Business in Convocation; where the Queen's Answer to the two Queries 1. None of her Quorum to preside; Nor 2. to have a negative.[268] Thence to call on Mr E. Watkinson, not within. Evening, With Mr Maddox and Mr Holmes at the *Fountain*.

March 1. *Thursday*. Morning, Mr Greenshields in good heart, with Copies of Dr Strachan's and Mr Gedderer's Books.[269] Sir James

---

[266] This chronicle, more correctly the chronicle of Walter of Guisborough, survives in whole or in part in ten different copies, two of which were in the Cotton Library. Nicolson probably used the older and better of the two texts in MS Cotton Tiberius B iv, ff. 19–210^V. See *The Chronicle of Walter of Guisborough*, ed. H. Rothwell, Camden 3rd ser. lxxxix (1957), pp. xii–xiii.

[267] *LJ* xix, 239.

[268] This was a gratifying development for the Low Church party, thus far almost entirely on the defensive. Kennett writes in his Journal for 28 Feb. 1711: 'In Jesus Chamber, there had been a Stop or Demurr to Proceedings, upon a Report that had been made from a Committee of three Bishops, Ely, Lincoln, Norwich, appointed to consider how the late Licenses did agree with those that had been granted to Convocations by her Majesties Royal Predecessors who . . . had found reason to raise some Queries about the Sens of the two Licenses granted to the present Convocation. 1) Whether it was her Majesties Intention that Any of the Persons by Her nominated in the Archbishops Absence, should take place of the Archbishops Commissary, and Preside over the Upper House. [Tenison's illness had necessitated the substitution of the Bishop of Lichfield, Tenison's commissary, as President on 23 Jan. 1711.] 2) Whether if Any of the Said Bishops so Nominated by her Majesty in the absence of the Archbishop did not Preside, He had notwithstanding a Negative upon the Majority of the other Bishops . . . This Matter on the last Synodical Day had occasioned some debate and divisions among their Lordships: but before the present Session, upon a Meeting of Some Bishops at the House of the Bishop of Lincoln, the Matter was very well and wisely accomodated.' It was agreed, Kennett explains, to put the queries 'into a Dutifull Address or Message in writing to her Majesty which was accordingly done and agreed to by the House this Morning, and immediatly carried to her Majesty by the Lord Bishop of St Davids, who within a little time (the Matter having been before concerted) brought back a Gracious Answer in Writing That her Majesty by requiring some One of such a Number of Bishops to supply the Absence of the Lord Archbishop of Canterbury did not intend that such Bishop should *Preside* over the Convocation or should have any Negative over a Majority of the other Bishops. Upon which Royal Declaration their Lordships proceeded cheerfully upon the Business recommended by her Majesty'. BL Lansdowne MS 1024, ff. 275^r–275^V. Bishop Wake's copy of the minutes of the committee of the Upper House appointed to consider the licences (24 Jan.–17 Mar. 1711) is in Christ Church Wake MS 18, f. 292. It shows that Lords Cowper and Somers attended some of the committee meetings, the latter being particularly active.

[269] Probably a reference to *Some remarks upon a late pamphlet, entitled, An Answer to the Scots Presbyterian Eloquence wherein the innocence of the Episcopal Clergy is vindicated and the Constitution . . . of our Church of Scotland defended*, published in 1694 by William Strachan DD; and the *Right of Succession to the Kingdom of England* (1703), a translation from the Latin of Sir Thomas Craig's unpublished work, by James Gadderer (1655–1733), later Bishop of Aberdeen in the Scottish Episcopal Church.

Mountague, with W. Rook's Letter of Comfort: Mr P. Tullie, inviteing Sir J[ames] and me to dine with him on Saturday: Mr James Lowther, pleased with the passing the Qualification Bill.[270] In the House, Mr G[reenshields]'s Case heard;[271] and the Sentence of the Magistrates and Decree of Lords of Session, unanimously Reversed.[272] There was little or no Debate on the main Subject. But a Division happened on a Question for Adjournment, after half the Counsel were heard; which was carryed (for sitting on) by 68 against 32.[273] Some weak efforts were, after the Lawyers had done, made for Adjournment of the Sentence till tomorrow; but the Cry was so loud for *Reversing* (20 Bishops present and Concurring)[274] that the Curate prevailed against the Lord Provost and Magistrates of the good Town of Edinburgh, who were undeniably in the wrong. NB. The first point (i.e. Whether the Appeal lay Regularly before the Lords?) was quickly agreed, almost *Nemine Contradicente*; and then the Great Lords divided (as above) for goeing to Dinner. The Second part, being the Merits, held till near 7 at night; when my Land Lord and I dined together at home.

[Mar.] 2. *Friday*. Morning, Mr Brodrick,[275] with proposeals for a History of the war: Dr Lancaster, with slender encouragement to Mr Greenshields from Oxford. My brother Joseph with misrepresentations of our yesterday's work. Mr Goodman pretendedly offended

---

[270] For the support of Country Whig opinion for the principle of a landed qualification for MPs, see Robert Molesworth's Reflections on Politics [c.1711], printed in *The Divided Society*, ed. G. Holmes and W. A. Speck (1967), pp. 137–8.

[271] *LJ* xix, 240; HMC *Lords MSS* viii, 357. See also NLS Wodrow Letters Quarto v, items 100, 97: ? to R. Wodrow, 1, 10 Mar. 1710/11.

[272] The 'Duke of Buck[ingham] rejoyced with the Bishop of Sarum it being the first time that they ever agreed in opinion Since they had the honour of setting in that house'. Herefordshire RO Brydges MS A81/23a: William to Francis Brydges, 6 Mar. 1710[/11].

[273] Lord Ilay, who opposed Greenshields and who moved the adjournment, wrote of the debate: 'I knew very well that our english friends would never be our champions but when att the same time they were their own and promoted their own interest as well as ours, thus all their bishops left us and the rest declared it was none of their buissiness, and when I moved A delay which might possibly have been of some use to us, they all left my brother [Argyll] and me to debate against the whole house; They knew the loss of the cause would do them more good in their politick conjunction than An affirmation of the decree, judging very right how irreconci[l]able the Tories would make themselves to the presbiterians by making A stretch in that tender point, and that they might easily save their own reputation by saying they were overpowered.' Edinburgh University Library Laing MS II 577: Ilay to Carstairs, 30 Mar. 1711. The Duke of Hamilton was reported as voting against the appeal, 'but that was to keep up his Interest'. Herefordshire RO Brydges MS A81/23a: William to Francis Brydges, 6 Mar. 1710 [/11].

[274] According to William Brydges the 'Bishop of Oxon and Winchester were the onely two Bishops that voted against an appeal from the Lord Justiarys'. Ibid.

[275] Possibly Thomas Brodrick (1654–1730), Joint Comptroller of Army Accounts, 1708–11, later MP for Stockbridge, 1713–22. Sedgwick, i, 491–2. A Thomas Brodrick did publish *A Compleat History of the late War* in 1713.

with Mr Gledhill. After attendance on two private Committees, in the House, where Lord Delaware proposed to me the getting the Queen to provide a Subsistence in England for Mr Gr[eenshields]. This I communicated to the Archbishop of York who ready to assist. Lord Pembroke has no Memoirs of Sir Philip Sydney;[276] but recommends the cutt of him in Holland's Icones.[277] His Lordship has a Coin of David I and Queen Mary's Atchinsons.[278] An Appeal (from Creditors of the old Duke of B[uckingham] heard,[279] and the Decree unanimously affirmed. Mr Greens[hields] for goeing to Oxford.

P.m. Cousin Tate, with copy of Sir J. M[ontagu]'s Letter; so far as communicated by me. Give it to Sir James. Evening, With Mr Smith at Dr Hickes's. Hearty and Free.

[Mar.] 3. *Saturday*. Morning, Dr S[acheverell?]'s Uncle,[280] not admitted; nor Mrs Trelawny, another Beggar. At a Committee, Lord Wharton complained to me of his Trustees at Kirby-Stephen; and sent me with a petition to the Bishop of Lincoln, about re-building of a church in Bucks. A Commission shall be Issued. In the House Lord Guilford's bantering way of sounding me about the contest 'twixt Sir J. M[ontagu] and C[oll.] Gledhill; who, being a new Convert, has (he saies) a Title to be set at the Head of High-Church. The Lottery-Bill read a first time.[281] With Sir James Mountague, to dine at Mr P. Tullie's; where we had the company of Mr Farrer, Mr Alanson and Mr W. Tullie. NB. Coll. Byerly (as well as Sir R. Onslow) disqualifyed by the late Act.[282] Sir J. M[ontagu] brought me home.

[276] Possibly a reference to Fulke Greville's *The Life of the renowned Sir Philip Sydney* (1652).

[277] Henry Holland (1583–1650?), the compiler and publisher, brought out *Herωologia Anglica*, a collection of sixty-five portraits of eminent Englishmen in 1620. It contained an engraving of Sydney by Simon Pass.

[278] The atchinson was a copper coin coated with silver coined in the reign of James VI, equal in value to eight pennies Scots or two-thirds of an English penny.

[279] See *LJ* xix, 241–2; HMC *Lords MSS* ix, 89–90. The debts contracted by Buckingham were largely in connection with the building of Cliveden.

[280] Henry Sacheverell's father, Joshua, had two half brothers, Benjamin and Samuel, both of whom followed the dissenting tradition. This is probably a reference to Benjamin, a dissenter with a business in London, who published *Sacheverell against Sacheverell* in 1711. Holmes, *Sacheverell*, pp. 4–6.

[281] *LJ* xix, 243.

[282] The reference is obscure. It would seem to allude to the recently passed Qualifications Act (which did not come into force until the end of the current parliament). But even as a hypothesis of what might happen to the two members involved, it is credible neither in the case of Robert Byerley (see Appendix A), who had large estates in Yorkshire and Durham, nor in the case of Sir Richard Onslow (see ibid.), who was one of the wealthiest commoners in Surrey.

[Mar.] 4. *Sunday*. Morning, Sermon by Mr Kimberley on the Wages of Death &c. The Rt Revd Dean not at the Sacrament I dined at my brother's; and (the weather being wett) returned directly home, without performing my Conditional promise (to the Dean of St Asaph [Stanley]) in goeing to Evening Prayer at St Paul's. Mr Jermyn's Bill read, and considered.[283]

[Mar.] 5. *Munday*. Morning, D. Rumney with Reply to Mr How: Visits paid to the Duke of Somerset gone to Court; Lord Eglinton, for a Toleration in Scotland (of the very Frame of ours) and, as is also Lord Ilay, for Resumption of Patronages;[284] Lord Balmerino, gone out: But (met with in the House) declares himself against Toleration at present.[285] Duke of Rutland, his Father's patent (for Duke) being now first exhibited and Read; was Introduced in Form; and, after the Reading of his Writt, took the Oaths.[286] A. Bowyer ordered to attend; Baker taken into Custody of the Black-Rod;[287] and Lord Great Chamberlayne [Lindsey] ordered to pull down the Gallery.[288] P.m., Mr Cambel, Mr Thomas Bell, Mr Greenshields, Mr Gedderer and Mr Dennison; all true Episcopal Scots. They leaveing me, I attempted Visits to Dr Lancaster. Mr John Browham and Mr W. Johnson.

[Mar.] 6. *Tuesday*. Morning, Mr R. Smith, designing to view the Parliament-Office: Dr Lancaster, in Quest of Contributions towards his new Buildings:[289] Sir J. M[ontagu] and Mr Lowther, with

[283] The divorce bill of Stephen Jennyns committed by the Lords on 27 Feb. On 5 Mar. the committee was put off. See *LJ* xix, 246; HMC *Lords MSS* ix, 97.

[284] Both an Act for the Toleration of the Scottish Episcopal Church and a Scottish Patronages Act were to pass in the 1712 session of parliament. See Trevelyan, *Queen Anne*, iii, 236–9.

[285] According to William Brydges, 'Lord Balmerinno Spoke well [in the debate on Greenshields' appeal on 1 Mar.], toleration of Episcopacy in N[orth] Britain says he is what ought to be there being noe Law in Scotland against it. Shew any act that forbids reading the Common prayer in Private familys, and if toleration on Principle be good in one Case or places tis good in all.' Herefordshire RO Brydges MS A81/23a: William to Francis Brydges, 6 Mar. 1710[/11].

[286] See *LJ* xix, 245. John Manners, 9th Earl of Rutland had been created a duke in 1703, but he never sat in parliament again and died 10 Jan. 1711. His successor, the former Marquess of Granby, had been an active Whig MP, except in the parliament of 1702–5, since Jan. 1701 and was sitting for Leicestershire at the time of his father's death.

[287] Abel Boyer was the author of *The Political State of Great Britain* and John Baker was its printer. They had printed the proceedings and debates of the House of Lords on the War in Spain contrary to standing orders, see *LJ* xix, 245–6; HMC *Lords MSS* ix, 106–7.

[288] *LJ* xix, 246. For its building see above, Chapter 2, pp. 84–6. The work of demolition was begun in Sept. 1711. See *CTB 1711*, p. 94.

[289] The Queen's College, Oxford, was completely rebuilt between 1672 and 1765. Provost Lancaster was responsible for the Front Quad, and the west range was built in 1709–11. See J. Sherwood and N. Pevsner, *Oxfordshire* (1974), pp. 184–7.

their Informations from Carlile: W. Tate, proves the hand of I. Green. The last went with me to the House; where he and D. Relf &c. lett in to see the Queen passing the Lottery Bill, &c. Lord Hallifax moved for Reviveing the Committee for Records.[290] The Election of Cockermouth entered upon by the Commons;[291] and adjourned to Saturday-sennight. P.m. I walked into Hide-Park with Mr Sands, who saies the Attourney Generall and Sir Thomas Powis are both displeased with the College;[292] and afterwards round St James's with Mr Richardson, much pleased with my management of the Case of Greenshields. Evening, Dr Gee; in want of a Northern Horse.

[Mar.] 7. *Wednesday*. Morning, After two or three begging petitioners had been with me, I went to walk in the park; and so missed the intended Visit of (my Reg[istra]r) R. A[glionby]. To Lambeth, where Dr Gibson takeing Physick and his wife delivered of another Boy; the Archbishop under strict confinement to his Bed, hands and Face in the Gowt yet merry on Greenshields's — *Lumina caeca duo*. Onely private Bills in the House. Mr Smith (after dineing with me) carryed me to seek for Mr Wanley[293] and Count Guldenberg;[294] and thence to Mr Madox, with whom the Evening merrily spent on his *Instrumenta* and *Ingenia*, i.[e.] State-Tools and Engines. NB. The walks in the Middle Temple beautifyed by I ^{I} S (i.e. John Sommers Treasurer) AD 1691.

[Mar.] 8. *Thursday*. Morning, Joshua Price, Glass-painter, with his Proposeals for the East window at St Paul's.[295] Petitioners for a Charity-Sermon from old Fish street: Mr Gibson, the old School-master, in Quest of his pension. At the Queen's Chappel, Bishop of Bristol preached (on *Psalm* 21, 1) a very honest Theologico-Political Sermon; giveing a just preference to our well proportioned Constitution, before the *Arbitrary will* of a single person, or a *popular Anarchy* in other parts of Christendome. Her Majesty not seen by

[290] See above, Chapter 1, p. 43.

[291] *CJ* xvi, 537. See above, n. 212.

[292] Both Sir Edward Northey and Powys, a prosperous Tory barrister, were graduates of Queen's College, Oxford, as was Thomas Sandes. Sandes was also a close friend of William Lancaster, the Provost of Queen's. See *Diary of John Evelyn*, ed. E. de Beer (1955), v, 376.

[293] Smith and Nicolson were seeking an appointment to see Harley's library but Wanley was not at home. The attempted assassination of Harley on 8 Mar. meant that Nicolson did not meet Wanley this session. BL Harleian MS 3780, f. 271: N. to Wanley, 9 Mar. 1711.

[294] Count Karl Gyllenborg, Swedish minister to England, 1710–17. He was arrested in 1717 on a charge of conspiring with the Jacobites and was deported to Sweden.

[295] Joshua Price was to produce the stained glass for the east window of Queen's College Chapel, Oxford, in 1717, Sherwood and Pevsner, *Oxfordshire*, p. 87.

any Body, being (as given out) in a cold: But the true Cause of Her privacy appeared at night, when Count Guiscard assaulted Mr Harley in Council;[296] of which my Information as yet Imperfect. Mr Archdeacon Rogers dined with me; and saies some of the Convocation Reports (that particularly about Terriers) will be given in to-morrow.[297] P.m. Sir J. Mountague, with a Letter from W. R[ook] which tells him that Gledhill's witnesses Know not their errand to Town.

[Mar.] 9. *Friday*. Morning, Short visit from Mr Prolocutor [Atter-bury], who saies there's no danger of (his Friend) Mr Harley: Mr R. Smith, with whom I went first to the Parliament Office; and thence, to settle matters with M. Chambers. At the House Lord Dorchester's long Bill at a Committee;[298] Mr Jermyn's Bill passed a Grand Committee, Bishop of Sarum in the Chair and ill treated by the Duke of A[rgyll]. Both Houses joyn in an Address in honour of Mr Harley &c.[299] News carried to Dr Gibson, who fears the Archbishop's Recovery; and the Evening at Salisbury-Court.

[Mar.] 10. *Saturday*. Morning, Mr Loste, goeing to a sorry Liveing at Barton on Hull; if it were vacant, which (since 'twas begged for him of the Lord Keeper [Harcourt]) he finds it is not. The principal of Brazen-Nose's Bill[300] wofully wrong in Clerk-ship. After long waiting in the House (for a Answer from her Majestry about the Address which came not at last)[301] I went to dine at Mr W. Tullie's; where were his two Brother's and Sir James Mountague, who brought me home. He's in pain, on the Apprehension of haveing his Original Letter produced.[302] NB. A beer-glass of simple distilled water of sea and Garden Scurvy Grass (with the juice of Orange) sovcraign Medicine for the Gowt.

[296] Harley was stabbed by Guiscard, a French adventurer under examination by the ministry, at a meeting of the Committee of the Cabinet Council at the Cockpit. Harley's subsequent illness and acquisition of heroic status had vital personal and political consequences. S. Biddle, *Bolingbroke and Harley* (1975), pp. 200–7.

[297] On 9 Mar. Convocation discussed a report from the joint committee of both houses concerning the second head recommended by her Majesty, which was largely about excommunication. See BL Lansdowne MS 1024, ff. 279^r–81^v.

[298] An estate bill, see *LJ* xix, 250; HMC *Lords MSS* xix, 95.

[299] *LJ* xix, 251.

[300] See ibid., p. 252; HMC *Lords MSS* ix, 95–6. The principal was Robert Shippen (1710–45).

[301] The Queen had been deeply upset by the attack on Harley and appears to have also had influenza. Sir David Hamilton, her physician, reported in his diary: 'March. In this month the Queen's Feavour, took away the opportunity of converse.' *The Diary of Sir David Hamilton*, ed. P. Roberts (1975), p. 30.

[302] See below, 14 Mar.

[Mar.] 11. *Sunday*. Morning, I preached for Dr Gibson; dined with him; and heard him (on *Colossians* 3, 5) at St Martin's in the Afternoon. Thence to Mrs Grisedale's with Mr Hudson[303] and Mr Elletson. Dr G[ibson] came home with me; where encountered by Mr Dungworth, in quest of a Hospital for Mrs Fowke. Mr Greenshields with the *Review* of Thursday last, highly reflecting on the Lords for their Judgement in that Cause.[304]

[Mar.] 12. *Munday*. Morning, My Bill paid by Mr E. Watkinson; from whom I came to the Temple, to enquire for Mr James Lowther: By water (from Somerset-Street) to Lambeth, where a good Account of my Lord Archbishop. In the House Mr Calvert's Bill[305] wanted a Lord willing to take the chair, since the Bishop of Salisbury had fared so ill on Mr Jermyn's and therefore (*Re infecta*) the House was Resumed, the two Prisoners Released, &c. Cousins Tate and Chambers dined with me; and were caught by Sir J. M[ontagu] who (as Lord Hallifax in the House) in good Confidence of tommorrow's Success.

[Mar.] 13. *Tuesday*. Morning, J. Robinson dispatched to the Excise-office, I went to Mr Leneve at the Treasury; where 250,000 *l.* subscribed to the Lottery (in less than two dayes) more than its compliment. In the House, abundance of Talk (about Scotch coins) with my Lord of Pembroke; who has obliged me to send him a Scotch penny (and Atchinson) of Copper. Mr Gledhill's cause to be heard by the Commons tomorrow; on occasion of both Houses waiting on the Queen with their Address about the Assault on Mr Harley. NB. Onely the two Speakers called in. P.m., Mr R. Smith, for goeing to visit Mr Harley. Letters.

[Mar.] 14. *Wednesday*. Morning, Mr Ogle,[306] with a cheerful Account of peace, in the parish of Holm-Cultram, since the change of his Curate: Mr W. Tullie, notice of the meeting of Committee for Records: Mr Leneve, for the Court of Wards (Fabrick and all) to the College of Heralds: Mr Elstob, with Saxon Catalogue of Northern Bishops. In the Upper Treasury of Queen's Bench, with Lord Chief Justice Parker, who set upon getting things into Order. At the

---

[303] Possibly George Hudson (*c.*1679–1749), educated Queen's Collegé, Oxford, MA 1703, DD 1718, from Cumberland, he was Rector of Great Stanmore, Middlesex, 1715–49.

[304] The *Review* was the London newspaper edited by Daniel Defoe. It appeared three times a week.

[305] Another divorce bill, see *LJ* xix, 253; HMC *Lords MSS* ix, 98.

[306] John Ogle, educated Queen's College, Oxford; Vicar of Holme Cultram-with-Newton, Cumberland, since 1695.

House, two Committees attended; Report of the Queen's Answer yesterday[307] &c. Bishop of Chester ashamed of haveing Dr S[acheverall] to read the prayers on Thursday last.[308] P.m., Lord Castle-Comer came (from the House of Commons) to desire me to be in Readiness, if occasion offered, to attest what Copies I gave of Sir J. M[ontagu]'s Letter. Soon after, I was called on by Sir James himself; who pressed me to desire Admittance into the House of Commons. This was opposed by (my true friend in this whole matter) Mr Lawson; foretelling that 'twould be to my own prejudice, and could be of no Benefit to Sir James: Against whom there was no Evidence. However, at his Earnest Intreaty, I did go in twice; being (at first) not well apprized of the Forms of the House, which do not allow the Speaker to ask any questions of a Lord. At my second goeing in, I acknowledged the Transcripts of Sir J. M[ontagu]'s Letter to be my proper hand-writeing; that I had faithfully copyed them; that I had sent for the Original, which was not to be found; that these words [*To enable me to carry my Election*][309] were not in it; nor did Sir James give me any Directions to publish his words in the manner I had done. After I withdrew, a Debate began; which (about a Quarter before Eleven) ended thus: Resolved, *That it appears to this House that William Lord Bishop of Carlile hath dispersed several Copies of a Letter pretended to have been received from Sir James Mountague (a member of this House) in order to procure Sir James Mountague to be elected a Citizen of the City of Carlile, reflecting on the Honour of Her Majesty; And, by concerning himself in the said Election, hath highly infringed the Liberties and privileges of the Commons of Great Britain.*[310] This Heavy Censure was occasioned by the Depositions of R. Aglionby and E. Walker (my Profligate Reg[istra]ı and Quondam Bayliff) that they saw a Copy, in my writeing, wherein were the words *To Enable me*, &c. *Miserere Deus*! —*Lay not this sin to their charge*! Mr Briscoe and Mr Green had certifyed the contrary. But — 'Twould not do.

[Mar.] 15. *Thursday*. Morning, Compliments (some of congratulation, others of Condolence) paid me by the Bishop of Bangor, Lord Sunderland, Lord Somers, Lord· Hallifax, Lord Cowper, Sir

---

[307] *LJ* xix, 255.

[308] At St Botolph, Aldgate, to celebrate the opening of a charity school built over the church porch by Sir John Cass, MP for London. The occasion was used to stage a popular demonstration of the Tory–Anglican cause in the City. See Holmes, *Sacheverell*, p. 258.

[309] Nicolson's brackets.

[310] *CJ* xvi, 548. The vote was 156 to 136; tellers for the minority being Lawson and Lowther. See also the account of L'Hermitage in BL Add. MS 17677 EEE, f. 124, 16/27 Mar. For the Scottish vote, see below, 18 and 20 Mar.

J. M[ontagu], Mr Lowther, Mr Lawson, &c. P.m., Dr Gee and Mr R. Smith, the later for goeing Secretary to some Ambassador.

[Mar.] 16. *Friday*. Morning, I carried my thanks to Mr Lawson, who gave me Cousin Briscoe's Letter, &c. From him (by Sir J. M[ontagu]'s chambers in Lincoln's Inn) to Serjeant Wynne's;[311] where Mrs M. Sandford, attended by Mr Wilson, not to be had from her cousin. In the House, the Claret-Bill[312] (amended in a Grand Committee) Read a 3d time and passed. The Amendments presently agreed to by the Commons.[313] Bishop of Bristol very ready to assist in getting Mr R. Smith to attend on some Ambassador. P.m. The Bishop of Exeter and I walking in the Park, Lord Leven siezed me; and told me of prayers in the Jacobite Meeting-Houses at Edinburgh on Sunday-sennight *For a person goeing on a Dangerous Voyage*.[314] A Cargo of Pewter bespoke with Cousin R. Nicolson; with whom, and my Brother, the Evening spent at the *Castle*.

[Mar.] 17. *Saturday*. Morning, My first Visitant (presumptive) R. Aglionby; to whom I refused Admission. Mr Dungworth went with me to Whitehall; where Mr Chamberlain promised us his Assistance to Mrs Fowke. Books of Tenths not yet Ready. I carried my Story of my late Vile Usage by the Commons to Dr Gibson; who thinks a printed St[ate] of the Case necessary. Lord Hallifax sought for in vain: But Sir J. Mountague agrees with the Dr and will procure me their minutes. I thanked Coll. Grahame, Mr Harcourt,[315] Mr Lauhern,[316] &c. for their Kind Adherence to me. Lord Stamford, in a private Committee sharp on the Low-Church's[317] roasting a priest the last-winter; and High-Church's Carbanodoeing a Bishop in this Session. P.m., Dr Torriano, Hankering after the Deanry of

---

[311] Richard Wynn (1655–1719) MP for Boston, 1698–1700, 1705–19. Son of a London merchant; barrister of the Inner Temple, 1682; Welsh Judge in early years of Anne, dismissed Jan. 1706; Serjeant-at-law, 1705. Sedgwick, ii, 565.

[312] *LJ* xix, 258; HMC *Lords MSS* ix, 109–11.

[313] *CJ* xvi, 554.

[314] Reports had reached London from Paris on 12 Mar. 'that the court of St. Germains are getting ready for a journey, some say to Switzerland, others that the chevalier St. George is only to go thither in his way to Rome . . .'; and on 22 Mar. he was said to have spent some days at Calais (Luttrell, vi, 701, 705). But there was no serious expectation of a landing in Britain.

[315] Probably Simon Harcourt, junior (1684–1720), MP for Wallingford, 1710–13, Abingdon, 1713–15; but could be Simon Harcourt (d. 1724), MP for Aylesbury, 1702–5, 1710–15.

[316] John Laugharne (?1665–1715), MP for Haverfordwest, 1702–15. It is noteworthy that Grahme, Harcourt, and Laugharne were all friends or followers of Harley in 1711. The same was true of Foley (see below, n. 324), and probably of Dr. John Hutton (below, n. 325).

[317] This page (page 73 of volume xxvi) is repeated in the Ware transcript.

Carlile, had my Engagements freely imparted; and Mr R. Smith, sent to make his Acknowledgements to my Lord of Br[istol]. NB. This day the Royal Assent given to the Wine-Bill, Bank-notes, &c. by Commission;[318] the Lord Keeper [Harcourt], Lord President [Rochester], and Dukes of Bucks, Shrewsbury and Ormond, on the Bench.

[Mar.] 18. *Sunday*. I kept private all day. Evening, Visitted by Mr Greenshields; who sets out for Oxford on Wednesday. He saies, All his Countreymen (in the House of Commons) would have served me, if I'd given up Sir J. M[ontagu]. *Non tanti emam*. He's in hopes of a Good Liveing in the Diocese of Durham, on the Intercession of Lord Pr[esident] and the Duke of B[uckingham]. The Translation of the Liturgy into the Highland-Irish will go on.

[Mar.] 19. *Munday*. Morning, Dr Lindford, introduceing Dr Gaitsgarth; whom he modestly Recommended to me for a Dean: Lord Carlile (called on) confined again to his Bed; and Bishop of Sarum removed to Smithfield. Mr R. Smith (the onely person found in my Circuit) shew me five Voll. of Goltzius's *Numismata*[319] whereof 4 of the Brugis-Edit[ion] and the 5th (at Antwerp) with Nonnius's *Commentaries*, on the Greek Coins.[320] Item. O. Verelij[321] *Index Ling[uae] vet[eris] Scytho-Scandicae*, &c. Fol. Elpsal. 1691. Item. The Swedish Edition of Ulphila's[322] Gospels 4°. Dr Onely, desireing a Sermon for Easter day.

In the House, a Scotch Appeal[323] (about Tithes and Patronages) left to the Decision of their own Lords. I dined at Sir James Mountague's, with Mr Harcourt, Mr Wortley, Mr Foley,[324] Mr Lawson, Dr Hutton[325] and Mr Lauhern; all my good friends in the House of Commons. Sir James brought me to Lord Carlile's (where Lord

---

[318] *LJ* xix, 261.

[319] Hubrecht Goltzius (1526–83), Flemish antiquary. This may be a reference to *H. Goltzii opera omnis* [with commentaries, additions etc. by A. Schotius, L. Nonnius, and others] (5 vols., Antwerp, 1645).

[320] Louis Nonnius (1553–) also Flemish. His *Commentarius in H. Goltzi Graeciam Insulas, et Asiam Minorem* was republished in 1708.

[321] Oluf Verelius (1618–82), Swedish archaeologist.

[322] Ulphilas (322–83), Gothic bishop and writer.

[323] HMC *Lords MSS* ix, 17–18.

[324] Possibly Thomas Foley (?1670–1737) of Stoke Edith, MP for Hereford, 1701–22 (later 'Auditor Foley', see Sedgwick, ii, 41), who was close to Harley. But there were two other Foleys in the Commons: Thomas Foley (1673–1733) MP for Stafford, 1699–1712, cr. Lord Foley in 1712; and Edward Foley (1676–1747), MP for Droitwich, 1701–11, 1732–41 (ibid., pp. 40–1).

[325] John Hutton (d. 1713), MD, MP for Dumfries Boroughs, 1710–13; royal physician under William III and Anne.

Cornwallis, C[oll.] Graham &c.) and thence home. Agreed, That the Duke of Shrewsbury introduce me to the Queen.

[Mar.] 20. *Tuesday*. Morning Ar[thur] Redman for accepting any thing: Mr Capstack, with Mr Cuthbert's opinion about his Augmentation: Mr Greenshields, Mr Gedderer and Mr Grey,[326] with a Letter of Thanks to me from the Bishop of Edinburgh [Rose], for my Assistance in the House of Lords. At the House (after Sentence on the Appeal about Tacks and patronages) the Duke of Athol and Lord Balmerino came to me; and expressed themselves much grieved with the Behaviour of their countreymen, in my Case. P.m., Mr R. Smith and I walked twice round the Park. Evening, Dispatches for Oxford given to Mr Greenshield's.

[Mar.] 21. *Wednesday*. Morning, A Visit to Mr James Lowther, who furnished me with papers necessary for a right State of my case in the House of Commons: Thence (fruitlessly) to Sir J. M[ontagu]'s chambers in Lincoln's Inn: Lord Castlecomer assureing me that the Vote against me has given a Deadly Blow to the October-men.[327] P.m. Mr R. Smith and I went first over to Dr Gibson (who had called at my Lodgeings in the forenoon) and thence to Mr Wanley's; but met with neither. Evening at my Brother's.

[Mar.] 22. *Thursday*. Morning, Mr H. Simpson with his Father's Resign[ation].[328] Mrs W. and J. Churchill, comforting and Reporting; Jer[emiah] Tullie,[329] in no hast for Portugal: Mr R. Sanderson, for Keeping the Records of the Court of Wards. At a Committee of Records (Lord Hallifax in the Chair) Resolved to begin with those of the Queen's Bench, in the first place; and to go thorough with them. Lord Hallifax gave us the Story of the hazard of the best MSS. in Cotton Library, by Elphinston's Easiness. In the House, after I had read prayers, an Irish Writ of Errour[330] which was brought directly

---

[326] Probably James Gray (b. 1659), native of Aberdeen, Minister of Muirkirk of Kyle, 1684–90, who became the agent of the episcopal party in London for which he received from the government £100 a year. In 1705 he was intruded at Logiebridge, Perthshire (*Fasti Ecclesiae Scoticanae*, iii, 59). He may be the James Gray who had in 1714 been the family chaplain to Lord Balmerino for some years. SRO Montrose MSS GD220/5/1851: Balmerino to Montrose, 11 Nov. 1714.

[327] See above, sessional intro., p. 514.

[328] Hugh Simpson (d. c.1728), was Clerk of the Peace in Cumberland, 1711–28 (an appointment Nicolson opposed—below, 23 Mar.), in succession to his father Lancelot. He was also Mustermaster of the Cumberland militia and County Treasurer in 1702. E. Stephens, *Clerks of the Counties* (1961), p. 72.

[329] Jeremiah Tullie, Ensign in Thomas Stanwix's regiment of foot, 1710. The regiment had gone to Portugal in 1707 and was disbanded in 1712. Dalton, vi, 173.

[330] See *LJ* xix, 264; HMC *Lords MSS* ix, 96.

from their Court of Exchequer to their Lordships whereas it ought first to have comed to our Queen's Bench. However, Judgement affirmed. The Archbishop of York, in his Condolence, assured me of his's being for me: which he was not, in effect. P.m. A Visit to the Archbishop of Canterbury who hearty in a good way of doeing well.

[Mar.] 23. *Friday*. Morning. To the Rolls-Chappel; where met by (the Usher of the Rolls) Mr Trevor, a curious person, and Mr R. Sanderson; who shewed me the Lame Condition into which Mr Grimes has brought that place. No Calendars of Things or places; save two or three County-Books lately discovered accidentally by Mr Trevor. Mr S[anderson] and I went hence to the Tower; where Mr Holmes helped to somewhat relateing to my Fishery at Linstock, &c. At the Mint we saw 'em coin Union-Shillings (with the Roses) for the Maunday; and Mr Croker[331] shewed us all his Dyes for Coins and Medals. A set of those of Queen Ann in Copper, I bought of him; at 4*s*, 2*s* and 1*s* 6*d*. After we had dined together I came home; and was presently attacked by H. Simpson, for my consent to his succeeding his Father. I cannot give it. Evening, Mr Smith carryed me in Quest of Mr Madox, not found.

[Mar.] 24. *Saturday*. Morning, Cousin R. Nicolson, for directions for's pewter; calling for Brother John's four Guinneas, and Interest for's son amongst the Commissioners of Accounts;[332] and giveing me the History of Ch[arles] Lamb's foolish spite at the Archbishop of Canterbury and myself: Dr Scott, with printed Account of the Scotch Contributions: F. Bugg, with more work for the Quakers. The Bishop of Peterborough, Bishop of Landaff and I, went over the Journals of this Session (in a Committee) as far as the end of January;[333] to Mr Johnson's great satisfaction. Evening, Cousin M. Chambers; bemoaning my hard usage by R. A[glionby] and E. W[alker] and assureing me of her being in Readiness for a Journey.

---

[331] John Croker (1670–1741), was born in Dresden and trained as a jeweller and die sinker. He came to England in 1691, and was employed at the Mint *c*.1696 where he succeeded Henry Harris, 1704, as Chief Engraver. See *The Correspondence of Isaac Newton*, ed. J. F. Scott, iv (Cambridge, 1967), 351, 420.

[332] The Commission of Accounts was reconstituted this session, on the initiative of the October Club, intended as an agent of partisan attacks on the late ministry. The bill authorising it passed the Commons on 12 Mar. and the club packed the Commission with its own members at the ballot on 19 Mar. *CJ* xvi, 562; *Lockhart Papers*, i, 325; Berkshire RO Trumbull MS 51, f. 63: Ralph Bridges to Trumbull, 16 Apr. 1711.

[333] See *LJ* xix, 210.

[Mar.] 25. *Sunday*. Morning, Kept within. Being my Sister's Birthday, I dined at Salisbury Court whence my Brother returned with me to Westminster at three, to visit dying Dr Knipe.[334] Evening, With Sir Edward Lawrence (an honest young Courtier)[335] at Dr Dent's; and, with him and's son, to Mr Carteret's Funeral in the Abbey.

[Mar.] 26. *Munday*. Morning, Visit to the Archbishop of York; who resolves to make Archdeacon Pearson his Chancellor on the Resignation of his Archdeaconry:[336] With Mr Smith, from the Parliament Office, to Lambeth-Library: Thence to the House, where the Royal Assent (by Commission) to the Act against Mutiny and Desertion.[337] Dr Gibson, at Dinner with me, Reports the Queen's Answer to the Address of the two Houses of Convocation concerning the Building of Churches.[338] *My Lords, and Gentlemen of the Lower House*, &c. No Hoods or Caps, as Mr Prolocutor [Atterbury] had ordered. P.m. Mr Thomas Bell, not ordered to see R. A[glionby]. Visit to Lord Carlile, who has accepted L. S[impson]'s Resignation; and given it to Hugh. His Lordship is for Newmarket the next week. Evening With Cousin R. N[icolson] and Mr Clavell.

[Mar.] 27. *Tuesday*. Morning, To Mrs Sandford, with her Father's orders to come down with me: Thence to Lincoln's Inn, where Sir J. M[ontagu] much incensed at Lord Carlile's failing W. Rook: Thence to the *Black-Swan*, where four places taken in the York-coach: Dr Lancaster and Dr Smith, with me at my Lodgeings, had the particulars of my case read to them. In the House, onely private

---

[334] He died on 6 Aug. 1711.

[335] Sir Edward Lawrence (d. 1725), Kt. 1701, FRS 1708, Gentleman-Usher of the Queen's Privy Chamber.

[336] Henry Watkinson, the Chancellor of the diocese of York, did not die until 22 Apr. 1712. He was indeed succeeded by William Pearson on 29 Apr. 1712, though Pearson did not resign his archdeaconry. Borthwick Institute CC. Ab.5/13, pp. 16-21.

[337] *LJ* xix, 266-7.

[338] On 26 Mar. the address of both houses of Convocation was presented to the Queen. It was occasioned by reports that the Commons' committee on the building of new churches had come to a stop. The Lower House of Convocation had addressed the Commons on 28 Feb. without reference to the Upper House, the House of Lords, or the Queen, and Atterbury had been informed by Henry St John that the Court took that address ill (BL Lansdowne MS 1024, ff. 275-6, 291, 292). The Commons had originally appointed the committee to examine the petition of the minister and churchwardens of Greenwich, who wanted relief for the rebuilding their church, the roof of which had collapsed on 28 Nov. 1710 damaging the walls. The committee was instructed to consider what churches were wanting within the cities of London, Westminster, and the suburbs on 14 Feb. 1711. The resulting bill for fifty new churches was ordered on 14 May 1711, and finally passed on 28 May and was agreed to by the Lords on 31 May. *CJ* xvi, 495, 529, 580-3, 662, 671-2, 681, 685; *LJ* xix, 312-13, 315.

Acts. Bishop of S. David's Kind wish for Unanimity on our Bench.
P.m. Mr Capstack, putting in for a plurality at Pont-Eland.[339]

[Mar.] 28. *Wednesday*. Fast Day. Morning, Mr Dungworth, for a
certificate in favour of Mrs Fowke. From the House in Procession
to the Abbey; where a good Sermon (on *peace* and *Righteousness*)
by the Bishop of Bristol: present Lord President [Rochester], Lord
Steward [Buckingham] and seven more Temporal Lords with the
Bishops of Winchester [Trelawney], Peterborough, Bangor, Carlile
and Norwich. After Evening-Prayer and Dinner, Mr Smith and I
went to Mr Maddox at the Remembrancer's office; with whom we
continued (till Ten) at the *Horn*.[340]

[Mar.] 29. *Thursday*. Morning, I waited on Lord Hallifax; who Knows
not yet how to judge of the Interests at Court; the Queen still indisposed;[341] &c. He gave the 9th and 10th of Rymer's voll. Thence with
Dr Waugh to Lambeth; where the Archbishop still in Hazard: At the
House, Lord Chief Justice Parker told me of the want of a parenthesis
in the printed Act (2d) for Dissolution of Monasteries which is in the
Records, and (but for Sir W. Dugdale) had been Fatal to the Tenants
of Croxden: At the Committee for Records, Lord Hallifax and Lord
Chief Justice promised me to procure a warrant to sieze Mr Grimes's
papers, &c. Mr Jodrel gave us a plan of the Buildings about the Court
of Wards.[342] P.m., Visitted by Dr Grandorge and Sir James Mountague.

[Mar.] 30. *Friday*. (Good) Morning, From Whitehall, before Dinner,
to Chelsea; whence I returned very weary. P.m., to Dr Gibson's
where an Account of Lord F[alkland?]'s declaring (at Rome) for
King James 3.[343] and the Bishop of Gl[asgow]'s[344] Letter thereupon
to the Archbishop of York who bid him mind his *Revelations*. Item,

---

[339] The Vicar of Ponteland, Northumberland, had died in 1710 and was succeeded by
Richard Parker on 17 Mar. 1711. He, however, resigned the same year and his successor was
instituted on 12 Sept. 1711. *History of Northumberland*, ed. M. H. Dobbs, xii (Newcastle,
1926), 431-2.

[340] In New Palace Yard, B. Lillywhite, *London Signs* (1972), no. 8905.

[341] For the stress within the ministry during Harley's illness, see HMC *Portland MSS*
v, 655; Burnet, *History*, vi, 31n; G. Holmes, 'Harley, St. John and the death of the Tory
Party', in *Britain after the Glorious Revolution*, ed. G. Holmes (1967), pp. 221-3. Cf.
below, 31 Mar.

[342] The committee appointed to consider of the methods of keeping records was looking
into the possibility of using the old Court of Wards, which adjoined Westminster Hall, as
storage space for records. See Halifax's end of session report from the committee to the
House on 31 May 1711, *LJ* xix, 314.

[343] Probably Henry Cary, 6th Viscount Falkland, a faithful and devoted Jacobite he was
created Earl of Falkland in 1722 by the titular James III.

[344] John Paterson, Bishop of Glasgow, 1687-1708.

the Medal sent to the Bishop of Bangor, from an unknown hand. Qu[ery]. Thence to supper at my Brother's.

[Mar.] 31. *Saturday*. Morning, Foreign Grammars from Mr Chamberlayne: Visitted by the Bishop of Bangor, who much afraid of the Times; on account of the Behaviour of our Grandees about the Chaplain at Leghorn,[345] &c. Notice carryed to M. Chambers to be ready against next week. P.m., Bishop of Lincoln, takeing Leave on his goeing to Dorsetshire on Munday: Mr R. Smith (disappointed of his goeing to the Parliament-office) walked round the Park. NB. The Bishop of L[incoln]'s story of our B[rothe]r of S[arum]'s warning to Her Majesty on the change of her Ministry, the Growth of the Pretender's Interest; &c. Item. The prayers of our friends for Mr H[arley]'s safety.[346]

April 1. *Easter Day*. I preached for Dr Only, and dined with him and his son, Mrs Grove and her daughter, &c. Afternoon, at the Abbey; where Mr Cornweall (censured by Sir J. Jekyll in Shropshire)[347] preached on *Departing* from *Iniquity*. Evening, With Dr Smith and's nephew.

[Apr.] 2. *Munday*. Morning, After a few dispatches at home, I waited on Lord Carlile and Lord Wharton; who introduced me to His Grace the Duke of Shrewsbury and to him I gave two memorials Relateing to the Censure of the House of Commons and the Deanry of Carlile; both which His Grace Kindly undertook to lay before the Queen. NB. The fine marble Table Antique, out of a cemented Mass of old Fragments. With the Bishop of Norwich, Deans of Exeter [Blackburne] and Peterborough [Kennett], Archdeacon of Surrey [Gibson], &c. at Dinner with the Bishop of Winton at Chelsea: Where nobly entertained, as friends to the old Establishment and Ministry. A Letter from the Duke of M[arlborough] saies the Duke of A[rgyll] passed thro' Holland without notice either of the States, or General. Memorandum. The fine Furniture, and two Tables of

---

[345] Basil Kennett, the chaplain at Leghorn, 1706–13, had decided to return home in the autumn of 1710 as the new ministry was not prepared to protect him. For White Kennett's use of the case of his brother to embarrass the Harley ministry, see Bennett, *White Kennett*, pp. 118–20.

[346] Whig anxiety can be seen in the light of the situation at Court and in parliament, see above, n. 341.

[347] Frederick Cornwall (*c*.1677–1748), Vicar of Bromfield, Shropshire, had preached before Jekyll at Welshpool against Sacheverell's impeachment. Jekyll ordered his indictment, but the grand jury had thrown out the bill. The Queen then ordered the Bishops of St Asaph and Hereford to proceed against him in their consistory courts. Luttrell, vi, 565; Holmes, *Sacheverell*, pp. 237–8.

Egyptian porphyry. Gr[ ]. After setling the Bill for the new writt *de Contumaci capiendo*[348] with the Dean of Exon and Dr G[ibson] (neither of which agree with the Speaker for putting all into the Justices hands) I went by Cary-street, &c. to my Brother's for the evening.

[Apr.] 3. *Tuesday*. Morning, Called on by Mr Capstack, Capt. Leethwait, M. Chambers, &c. At the Committee for Inspecting the Journals, with the Bishop of Peterborough and Landaff. P.m. Visits from Mr Highmore, Mr Stanwix, Mr Greenshields; with the last of which I went to the Bishop of Sarum's (with his Thanks and Mr Holme's Letter) and returned by St Martin's.

[Apr.] 4. *Wednesday*. Morning, Visits from Cousin B. Nicolson, Mr D. Curwen and his sister Musgrave,[349] &c. Mr R. Smith (struck dead with the news of my goeing away) with me at Mr Chamberlayne's; where also Col. Taylor and Mr Newman) all Projectors. The Journal read (to this day) in a Committee; myself Chairman, present Lords Clarendon and Yarmouth, Bishop of Peterborough and Lord Delaware.[350] Dined At my Brother's with A. Spooner; where Lord Mayor,[351] &c. from the Spittle Sermon[352] by Dr West.[353] Thence Farewells to the Bishop of Salisbury, Sir J. M[ontagu], Bishop of Bangor, Archbishop of York, and (finally) Peter-street.

[Apr.] 5. *Thursday*. Morning, I set out for the north, in the Yorkcoach, with Mrs M. Sandford and Cousin M. Chambers; and had the agreeable Company of Capt. Wilson and his well-bred Lady, from Jamaica. To Stephenage at night.[354]

---

[348] A writ by which minor recalcitrants might be committed to prison until they promised obedience.

[349] Darcy Curwen (1643–1722), and his sister Mary (1649–1715), who had married Humphrey Musgrave. See W. Jackson, 'The Curwens of Workington Hall and Kindred Families', *CW* original ser. v (1881), 215, and table following p. 232.

[350] *LJ* xix, 269.

[351] Sir Gilbert Heathcote (1652–1733), Governor of the Bank of England, 1709–11; MP for London, 1701–10; Whig merchant prince and 'monied man'. Sedgwick, ii, 123.

[352] The sermon preached on Easter Monday and Tuesday from a special pulpit at St Mary Spital, outside Bishopsgate.

[353] Probably Richard West (*c*.1670–1716) Archdeacon of Berkshire, 1710–16.

[354] The coach party rose at six o'clock the following morning and travelled all day reaching Huntingdon at 7.00 pm. Nicolson proceeded north via Stamford, Newark, Doncaster, Ferrybridge, and Tadcaster, where he met Archdeacon Pearson, who accompanied him as far as Catterick on 12 Apr. Nicolson then travelled over Stainmoor to Appleby, reaching Rose on 14 Apr. 1711. *CW* iv (1904), 51–2; Ware transcripts, xxvi, 90–4.

1 January 1712–2 April 1712

Nicolson passed the months from the middle of April 1711 to early November in unremarkable diocesan business. The highlights appear to have been a great reception of the Bishop by the garrison, church dignitaries, and corporation of Carlisle on 23 April, intended as a demonstration in favour of the Bishop after his censure by the Commons on 14 March 1711, and the replacement of Dean Atterbury by George Smalridge in September, which caused Chancellor Tullie, Nicolson's own candidate, to be 'in some wrath against Court-Promises'. Notification of the new Dean's institution reached Rose on 7 November, the day before Nicolson left for Westminster.[1]

The summer had seen a further change in the complexion of Oxford's government. In June there was a cabinet reshuffle brought about by the death on 2 May of Lord Rochester (who was replaced as Lord President by Buckingham), and at the same time many Tories, including some October men, were appointed to junior offices. In July the Duke of Newcastle died, and on 31 August he was succeeded as Lord Privy Seal by Bishop Robinson of Bristol. Thus there were no genuine Whigs remaining in the cabinet, for Somerset (Master of the Horse) had ceased attending, in protest against ministerial changes, in September 1710. Too many Whigs still clung to the lower rungs of the administration (for instance, in the Household, the Ordnance, and the Board of Trade) for the peace of mind of the High Tories. But whether this was deliberate policy on the new Treasurer's part, or whether he was more inhibited by the Queen's determination to pursue 'moderation' than his Tory critics allowed for, was something even his closest confidants were unsure about.

In one respect, however, both the Queen and her first minister had cause for profound satisfaction. September 1711 saw the secret peace negotiations between Britain and France brought to a successful conclusion with the signing of preliminaries between them. By the autumn it was obvious that the coming parliamentary session was going to be critical. The Whigs had been angered, and their unity restored, by the news of a private deal with France, especially when they realised that this involved the abandonment of Spain to

[1] *CW* iv (1904), 52–4; BL Add. MS 6116, ff. 27–8, 30: N. to Wake, 9 June, 17 Sept. 1711.

the Bourbons. Their morale was also lifted by the knowledge that the Dutch and the Hanoverians, as well as the new Emperor, Charles VI (the former Archduke Charles), were strongly opposed to certain features of the *fait accompli* that was to be presented to them at a general peace conference in the New Year. They were also much encouraged, in view of the fact that parliament would have to consider the preliminaries at the beginning of the new session, by the news that Lord Nottingham was exhibiting strong discontent with the peace terms. (Indeed, the man who for so long had been the lay conscience of the High Church Tories, who had been the *eminence grise* behind much of the October Club agitation in the 1710–11 session, finally broke in November 1711 from a ministry which had once again, the previous summer, spurned his claims to office.) Thus the Whigs mustered in earnest and with growing confidence for the fray, pinning their hopes on regaining their control of the House of Lords; and on 7 November 1711, Nicolson recorded in his diary that his brother-in-law Edward Carlile, had unexpectedly 'brought summons for my journey tomorrow'.[2]

With the entry for 7 November, Nicolson ended a volume of his diary, closing with the following words: 'N.B. I set out for Westminster Nov. 8 1711, from which day to the end of that year (Dec. 31) the Journal is in my Almanack for 1711.'[3] This almanac has not been traced,[4] consequently we not only have no information as to Nicolson's journey south, but none of his reactions to the political events of December 1711. Parliament had met on 13 and 27 November only to be prorogued until 7 December. Nicolson's first recorded attendance was on this first day of business. From then until 22 December, when the House adjourned for Christmas, it met on twelve days and Nicolson attended on each.[5]

During these twelve days much happened that was to affect proceedings in the New Year, when Nicolson's surviving diary restarts. The Whigs opened their attack on the ministry on the first day of the session by narrowly defeating it in the Lords on a motion of 'No Peace without Spain' (the Utrecht conference was to open in January 1712).[6] With many of his friends in panic or despair, Oxford resolved

[2] *CW* iv (1904), 54. Hugh Todd confirms that Nicolson left in haste: 'The Bishop went for London last Thursday the 8th at the desire of his Friends. He went away in hast; knowing nothing of certainty of his Journey, till the day before.' (Levens Hall MS D/T: Todd to James Grahme, 10 Nov. 1711.)

[3] See *CW* iv (1904), 54.

[4] Its loss was noted as early as 1904 (ibid.).

[5] *LJ* xix, 335–48.

[6] Nicolson appears to have voted with the Whigs for the motion, BL Add. MS 22908, f. 88: ? to Colebatch, 11 Dec. 1711. For an analysis of Harley's defeats in the Lords on 7 and 8 Dec. see C. Jones, 'The Division that never was: new evidence on the aborted vote

this crisis at the very end of December through the novel expedient of creating twelve Tory peers *en bloc* (see below, 1 January) to gain control of the Upper House. He further appeased the Tory party by dismissing Marlborough, against whom the Commissioners of Public Accounts (see above, 24 March 1711) had just produced serious charges, from his post as Captain-General on 31 December. Marlborough had been open in his condemnation of the government's peace policies, as had Somerset who in January was also removed from his office at Court. Meanwhile, shortly before the Christmas recess the Whigs had paid their debt to Nottingham for supporting their peace offensive by agreeing (much to the dismay of many members of the party, though probably to the relief of most of the bishops) to the Earl's revived bill against Occasional Conformity.[7] Consequently a measure which had caused so much bitter political controversy, in Church as well as State matters, in the years 1702–4 (see above, sessions 1 and 2, *passim*) passed at length quietly into law.

This winter also saw the first major crisis in Anglo-Scottish relations since the Union of 1707. The cause was the Hamilton peerage case.[8] On 20 December the Lords rejected the Duke of Hamilton's right to sit in the Lords by virtue of his title of Duke of Brandon (created 11 September 1711) in the peerage of Great Britain. The sixteen Scottish representative peers, justifiably angered at this rebuff, temporarily coalesced into a united group and after the failure of a Committee of the Whole House, on 18, 21, 25 January and 4 February, to find a solution, organised a 'walk-out' from the Lords on 31 January and an intermittent boycott of the House's proceedings between 7 and 26 February 1712. This attempt to prise satisfactory terms out of the ministry or out of the Whigs was a failure, partly because the government's parliamentary position (thanks to Oxford's 'dozen') was now less dependent on the Scots, but also because of the introduction into parliament of the Toleration Bill for Scotland, to which most of the sixteen peers (being

in the Lords on 8 December 1711 on "No Peace without Spain" ', *Parliamentary History* ii (1983). For the corresponding proceedings in the Commons see G. S. Holmes, 'The Commons' Division on "No Peace without Spain", 7 December 1711', *BIHR* xxxiii (1960), 223–34.

[7] Burnet, *History*, vi, 85 and Dartmouth's note; John Oldmixon, *History of England* (1735), p. 481; BL Add. MS 17677 FFF, f. 3. See also SRO Montrose MSS GD220/5/256/20: George Baillie to Montrose, 13 Dec. 1711 for the view that the Nottingham-Junto pact merely forestalled a much stiffer bill from the ministerial side.

[8] For a full treatment see G. S. Holmes, 'The Hamilton affair of 1711–12: a crisis in Anglo-Scottish relations', *EHR* lxxvii (1962), 257–82. Nicolson voted with the Whig leadership in opposing Hamilton's right to sit. See Holmes, *British Politics*, p. 434.

Episcopalians) were closely committed. By mid-March the affair was over.

The Whig campaign against the 'Tory peace' was doomed to disappointment virtually from the time when the Court, reinforced by the new creations, won its trial of strength in the Lords on 2 January. French obduracy at the Utrecht conference table did, however, revive some hopes in the breasts of Whig supporters (Nicolson included) before Nicolson left London in early April (see below, 29 March).[9] The other political events which were chiefly to occupy Nicolson between January and early April 1712 were Colonel Gledhill's second petition against the Carlisle election of 1710, the second, and this time successful, attempt to repeal the 1709 General Naturalization Act, a new Place Bill, and the Toleration Bill for Scotland.

Colonel Samuel Gledhill, the defeated Tory candidate at the Carlisle 1710 election, whose petition to the Commons in December 1710 against the return of Sir James Montagu had eventually led to the Bishop's censure by the Commons, had re-presented his petition against Montagu on 10 December 1711. He claimed that several qualified persons had not been allowed to vote for him while unqualified voters had been allowed to vote for Montagu. The report of the Committee of Privileges and Elections was heard by the Commons on 23 February 1712.[10] One of Gledhill's witnesses charged the Bishop with threatening to turn out any choristers who would not vote for Montagu, to which it was replied that the Dean and Chapter not the Bishop appointed the choir. Montagu was decisively vindicated by the Committee of Elections and again voted duly elected by a majority of fifteen votes in the full House (see below, 1 February) through the management of Lord Oxford, who, as in 1711, was acting in deference to Lord Halifax, Montagu's brother.[11]

The Tory attempt to repeal the General Naturalization Act of 1709, which had resulted in the influx of poor Palatines, had foundered in February 1711 in the Lords. In the new session, as an olive branch to the Tory zealots during the peace crisis, Oxford's ministry undertook to support a new repeal bill. Though it was probably distasteful to the Treasurer he judged it a necessary sacrifice to ensure a smooth passage for government business in the Commons. So when the bill

---

[9] There were occasional Whig successes in the Lords, such as the passing of Halifax's motion on 15 Feb. (see below, 15 Feb. and n.); but these were purely temporary and there was no stopping the broad flow of the tide.

[10] Ferguson, *Cumberland and Westmorland MP's*, pp. 87–94; *CJ* xvii, 5, 98, 106–8.

[11] M. Ransome, 'Church and dissent in the election of 1710', *EHR* lvi (1941), 84; unpublished constituency article on Carlisle supplied by the History of Parliament Trust.

was introduced into the Commons on 22 December 1711, a junior minister, John Manley, was associated with Heneage Finch and the Octobrist, Henry Campion, in its preparation. By 22 January it had passed its third reading without a division, and at the end of January government forces turned out in force to help it over its much stiffer hurdle in the Lords. Nicolson is disappointingly cryptic about the Lords' proceedings, and we do not even know how he himself voted on an issue of some concern to the clergy because of its implications for the Anglican Sacramental Test. On 1 February the Commons accepted the Lords' decision to retain the clause that children of natural-born subjects born out of the Queen's allegiance were to be considered natural-born subjects, and on 9 February the bill received the royal assent.[12]

The Place Bill, which was thrown out by the Lords on 29 February 1712, was more or less a carbon copy of the previous abortive bills of 1710 and 1711 designed to lessen the influence of the Crown in parliament. In each parliamentary session between November 1709 and July 1714 a new Place Bill was introduced and lost; but the one introduced in February 1712 was the only one, save that of 1714, to come close to success.[13] It had passed in the Commons with the minimum of opposition, and the Junto Whigs, in the hope of seriously embarrassing Oxford's ministry, for the first time came out in support of such a bill in the Lords. Oxford, to draw the Whig attack, submitted an amendment which would make the Act effective from the end of the reign and not from the end of the existing parliament in 1713. Desertion to the government of the Junto's Scottish and independent Tory allies at a critical moment led to a carrying of the amendment by five votes on 29 February, and the bill was lost on its third reading, with the Junto no longer interested in pursuing it now that its teeth were drawn.

Because of Nicolson's close association with Scottish émigrés in London, and with James Greenshields in particular the Toleration Bill of 1712, or more correctly the Episcopal Communion (Scotland) Bill, became for him the most important piece of legislation in the 1712 session. The bill resulted directly from Greenshields's case in 1711 (see above, Session 7 intro., pp. 507–8). The need for a statutory Toleration to protect the Episcopalian services in Scotland had been seen as early as 1709. At that time the understanding

---

[12] See H. T. Dickinson, 'The Tory Party's attitude to foreigners: A note on party principles in the age of Anne', *BIHR* xl (1967), pp. 162–4; 'The Poor Palatines and the Parties', *EHR* lxxxii (1967), 483–5.

[13] For a discussion of this and other Place Bills, see G. S. Holmes, 'The attack on "The Influence of the Crown", 1702–16', *BIHR* xxix (1966), 47–68; Holmes, *British Politics*, pp. 134–5, for the special political context of the 1712 bill.

by which Episcopalians were tolerated in practice, though not in law, began to break down, a process accelerated when the implications of Greenshields's appeal to the Lords became clear to the Presbyterian establishment in Scotland.

The bill passed the House of Commons on 7 February 1712 and was first read in the Lords on 8 February. It was vigorously opposed by many Presbyterians as contrary to the Union, and William Carstairs petitioned both the Queen and the Lords (see below, 11 February). The bill as it arrived from the Commons contained the oath of allegiance and assurance, to which many Episcopalians (including the Bishop of Edinburgh) were opposed. Carstares, who feared all Episcopalians were Jacobites, persuaded Lord Ilay to move on 13 February to replace this oath with a modified oath of abjuration of the Pretender, in which the words 'as limited' were replaced with 'which is limited'. This alteration was done to meet Presbyterian objections 'that by swearing to the Queen and Succession *as Limited* by the Acts of parliament was swearing to every thing in the acts, namely that the Queen or her Successors should be of the Church of England'.[14] All clergy, Episcopalian and Presbyterian, were to be obliged to take the amended oath.

As a result of a further change in the bill, prompted by Ilay (Argyll's brother), the Episcopalian desire to be exempted from the censure of the Kirk was extended so 'that no Magistrate should putt in Execution any Ecclesiastical censure of the Kirk against any person either of the Episcopal or presbyterian Communion'.[15] This was seconded by Lord Cowper on the grounds that otherwise all Presbyterians who were censured by the Kirk would join the Episcopal church. This clause, strongly objected to by Nicolson as destructive of ecclesiastical discipline (see below, 13 February), was opposed by nine bishops (nearly two-thirds of those present) 'because they feared it might be an ill president, to deprive them sometime or other of the Magistrates assisting in Executing their Censures'.[16]

On 15 February the bill was ready to be returned to the Commons for their approval of the Lords' amendments, but Greenshields (who had been keeping Nicolson in close touch with Scottish opinion throughout the progress of the bill) reported that the Tory and pro-Episcopalian Commons would not accept the abjuration oath.[17] On 21 February, however, the Episcopalian Scottish MPs contented

[14] Bodl. MS Ballard 36, f. 122: Greenshields to Charlett, n.d. [endorsed, 1 Mar. 1711/12]. Our italics.
[15] BL Add. MS 22908, f. 89: Greenshields to Colebatch, 1 Mar. 1711/12.
[16] Ibid.
[17] See below, 15 Feb. For confirmation see SRO GD220/5/268/8: [George Baillie] to Montrose, 16 Feb. 1712.

themselves with restoring 'as' to the abjuration oath, thus restoring the very implication to which the Presbyterians had objected. Fortunately, they were sensible enough to add a proviso that if the Lords would not agree, the Commons would yield rather than lose the bill.

When the Lords considered the Commons' amendments on 26 February the peers who spoke for restoring their pro-Presbyterian amendment were opponents of the ministry, including Nottingham and Bishop Burnet, while those who spoke for accepting the Commons' pro-Episcopalian alteration were ministerial Tories together with six Scottish lords (among them Mar who seems to have changed his mind). Some of the Scottish peers

> affirmed that the Presb[yterian] clergy would all take it [the oath] with the As. Had there been any to gain say it possibly it might have gone otherwise, but it seems the rest of the Scots [particularly Ilay and Loudoun] were not then determined to return to the house as all of them did next day except D[uke] H[amilton] and M[arquess of] An[nandale].[18]

The pro-Episcopalians prevailed and the House passed the bill as it had come from the Commons by fifty to forty-six, the bishops dividing as follows: for the bill York, London, Durham, Rochester, Chester, St Davids and Exeter; against Salisbury, Lichfield, Peterborough, Oxford, Bangor, Carlisle, Lincoln, Norwich, and St Asaph. It seems extraordinary that Nicolson, 'State-Whig' and friend and mentor of Greenshields, should have in the end opposed the bill. He apparently was about to leave the chamber to vote for the bill when, wrote Greenshields, 'he was stopt when he was going out by the Bishops of Lincoln [Wake] and Bangor [Evans]'.[19] Nicolson gives no hint as to why pressure from his fellow Whigs should have prevailed with him to vote against his principles.

The Scottish Toleration Act received the royal assent on 3 March 1712. Its sequel was another anti-Presbyterian measure, the bill which restored the lay patronage of livings. Introduced into the Commons in mid-March, it finally passed the Lords on 28 April, after Nicolson had departed for the north, becoming law on 22 May 1712.[20] It is possible that he sympathised with the measure. With

[18] SRO GD220/5/268/9: 28 Feb. 1712; Bodl. MS Ballard 36, f. 122. Mar, Eglinton, Rosebery, Kinnoull, Home, and Kilsyth were the peers who did speak.

[19] Bodl. MS Ballard 36, f. 122. For the course of the bill through both Houses, see *CJ* xvii, 33, 73, 92, 99, 103–4; *LJ* xix, 373, 376–7, 379, 384–5, 392. For Nicolson's strong views in favour of toleration in Scotland see BL Add. MS 6116, f. 17: N. to Wake, 15 Dec. 1709.

[20] *CJ* xvii, 143, 202; *LJ* xix, 420, 432, 455. For the Patronage Bill see Trevelyan, *Queen Anne*, iii, 239–40.

one set of developments on the ecclesiastical front, at least, he was well content: the 1712 session in Convocation had seen nothing but frustration for the High Churchmen, thanks partly to the mystifying tactics of their leader, Atterbury (see, e.g., below, 20, 27 February).

After Nicolson had left Westminster on 2 April, parliament continued to sit until 8 July 1712; so that Nicolson was not present to witness the final failure of the Whig attack on the government's peace policy, notably their failure to censure the 'Restraining Orders' issued to the British army in Flanders (May), and the emphatic endorsement of Oxford's policies by both Houses (June), which was just as well for his peace of mind, for the June vote represented the nearest point to a collapse of Whig morale in the House of Lords during the whole of Anne's reign.

[Jan.] 1. *Tuesday*. Morning, Visitted by Cousin Br[idget] Nicolson, Mr Thomas Pattinson and Brother Joseph. With the two latter to St James's; where Her Majesty confined in the Gowt called in 9 Bishops in their Turn.[21] A Thin Court; the Duke of Marlborough, &c. being displaced last night; 13 new Lords provided for tomorrow;[22] &c. Dined with my Brother and till near 7 at night. Letters.

[Jan.] 2. *Wednesday*. Morning, From Islington Mr E. Johnson (salesman) fetched back to Smithfield, to pay my 15 *l*.
House, 12 new Lords introduced.[23] Queen's message for

[21] It is very probable that, as well as exchanging New Year pleasantries, the Queen canvassed the bishops' votes in preparation for the trial of strength in the House of Lords next day. Between 28 and 31 Dec. Oxford and his friends had been hard at work on the reconversion of the Court Whig apostate peers who had reverted to their party loyalties and leaders during the Peace votes of early Dec. (for the process of reconversion see BL Loan 29/10/16, memo., 29 Dec.; Swift, *Journal to Stella*, p. 28, 30 Dec.; *Wentworth Papers*, p. 224).

[22] Between 28 Dec. 1711 and 1 Jan. 1712 twelve new peers were created in order to re-establish a majority in the Lords for Oxford's administration's Peace policy. The Lord Treasurer had originally considered twenty names as possible candidates for promotion (BL Loan 29/10/16, paper dated 'Dec. 27: 1711'), including some wealthy members of the October Club, e.g. Thomas Strangeways, sen. (MP for Dorset) and George Pitt (Hampshire). Only twelve were eventually chosen; but a thirteenth whose promotion was intended, but who declined the offer, was an old friend of Oxford's, Sir Michael Warton, MP for Beverley (HMC *Dartmouth MSS* i, 308). These creations caused some dismay, on constitutional grounds, even among one or two of Oxford's own Cabinet colleagues, but the Queen herself, utterly committed to the Peace, was undismayed by this use of the prerogative (see Burnet, *History*, vi, 94; *Hamilton Diary*, pp. 35–7).

[23] *LJ* xix, 353–6. They were in order of creation 28 Dec., Lord Compton (heir of the Earl of Northampton), summoned in his father's barony; 29 Dec., Lord Bruce (heir of the Earl of Ailesbury), also summoned in his father's barony; 31 Dec., George Hay (styled Lord Dupplin as heir to Earl of Kinnoull [S]) cr. Baron Hay; 1 Jan., Thomas, Viscount

Adjournment to the 14th carried by 81 against 68.[24] Evening, with Dr G[ibson] at the *Dogg*.

[Jan.] 3. *Thursday*. Morning, Visitted by Mr Greenshields and Mr Jennys, for the Congress.[25] Visits intended and paid to Lord Carlile and Mr G. Lawson; who went with me to dine at W. Tullie's, where the other two Brothers and Sir James Mountague.

[Jan.] 4. *Friday*. Morning, Mr Henley,[26] to be attended on Munday; young Pool,[27] out of place. Visits to Mr and Sir C. Musgrave. Item. Mr Ar[chibald] Campbel; who shewed me Books and Medals, in my N[ote] B[ook].[28] Dinner, with me, Mr Robert Sanderson; whose gift a Brittish medal of Severus. Evening, With Sister Rothery at my Brother's, new present of Mountain-Wine &c.

[Jan.] 5. *Saturday*. Morning, Visitted by Mr Wilson, Mr Chambre and Mr Pattinson; the last for Oxford. With the Bishop of St Asaph [Fleetwood] to dine (with the Bishop of Winton [Trelawney]) at Chelsea; where also the Bishops of Sarum [Burnet], Lichfeild [Hough], Ely [Moore], Oxon [Talbot], Bangor [Evans] and Norwich [Trimnell]— Bishop of Glocester [Fowler] not dead.[29] Evening, (returned from my son at Oxford) Mr Nicols.

Windsor [I], cr. Baron Mountjoy; Henry Paget (heir of Lord Paget), cr. Baron Burton; Sir Thomas Mansel, Bt., cr. Baron Mansel; Sir Thomas Willoughby, Bt., cr. Baron Middleton; Sir Thomas Trevor, cr. Baron Trevor; George Granville, cr. Baron Lansdowne; Samuel Masham, cr. Baron Masham; Thomas Foley, cr. Baron Foley; and Allen Bathurst, cr. Baron Bathurst. See *GEC Peerage*, i, 61, note d, and ii, 28, note b. It did not escape notice that over half of Oxford's 'dozen' were relatives, followers, or friends of the Treasurer himself (Foley, Dupplin, Mansel, Paget, Trevor, Granville, Masham). In addition another friend, Warton, declined, and Oxford's nephew, Francis Popham, was considered for promotion.

[24] *LJ* xix, 356; *Parl. Hist.* vi, 1060-2. To make the path of the errant peers back to the Court camp as easy as possible, Oxford chose to present the House with a simple message from the Queen, desiring their adjournment until 14 Jan., with the promise that 'matters of great importance' would then be laid before both Houses jointly. Despite this (though Nicolson strangely omits to record the fact), eleven out of fifteen bishops voted against the adjournment—a remarkable display of Whig solidarity (Trumbull Add. MS 136/3: Ralph Bridges to Trumbull, 18 Jan. 1711/12), as did five Nottinghamite Tories. Even with the new creations, the ministry would have been in some trouble had not seven Court Whigs succumbed to Oxford's blandishments, either by voting with the government or abstaining.

[25] A Mr Jenny accompanied Bishop Robinson of Bristol, the Lord Privy Seal and one of the two chief British negotiators, to the peace conference at Utrecht (Bodl. MS Rawlinson C.392, f. 330).

[26] Possibly Anthony Henley, MP for Weymouth.

[27] Possibly W. Pool, Vicar of Isell, 1711–19, previously Curate at Caldbeck, 1708, who may have married a niece of the Bishop's. *CW* iv (1904), 39.

[28] See below, Appendix B.

[29] The infirm Edward Fowler, who had staggered up from his diocese to oppose the Tory peace in Dec. but had been taken ill in the House before the critical division (Holmes, *British Politics*, p. 410), did not die until 26 Aug. 1714.

[Jan.] 6. *Sunday*. I preached (and administered the Sacrament) at St Bride's; and dined (with Mrs Beaufort, Mr Evans and Mr Brian) at my Brother's. Evening, Dr Gee.

[Jan.] 7. *Munday*. Morning, visitted by Cousin Jer[emy] Nicolson and young Pool. After a view of the way from Carlile-House, I went to dine at Lambeth; where also Generall Nicolson, the Deans of Glocester [Chetwood] and Peterburgh [Kennett], Mr Brigstaff, Drs Lloyd, Gee, &c. The last with me afterwards at Dr Gibson.

[Jan] 8. *Tuesday*. Morning, After fruitless attendance on the Committee at Whitehall,[30] walking in the Park with Sir Joseph Jekyll and my warm Neighbour Nicols. I dined (with Dr Gibson) at Dr Gee's. Letters.

[Jan.] 9. *Wednesday*. Morning, with Mr A. Chambre and his son to the Bishop of Bangor's and thence (on a Visit) to the Bishop of Chester's [Dawes's] pleasant House. Mr Gibbon dined with me, in quest of a new Institution; and he and I spent the Evening, with Mr Madox and Mr Holmes, at the *Horn*.

[Jan.] 10. *Thursday*. Morning, Mr Henley, Cousin S. Goldsmith and Mrs Hume.[31] In Scotland Yard, two Quakers (P. Fearon and J. Bowstede) with Proposeals for makeing their *Yea* and *Nay* Oaths in Law.[32] Two Broughams dined with me; and accompanyed [me] to Lord Carlile's and Mr James Lowther's.

[Jan.] 11. *Friday*. Morning, with Mr Greenshields to thank the Dean of Carlile [Smalridge] for his Sermon. Dined with Dr Waugh, Mrs Hans and Mrs Fiddis, at Salisbury-Court; my Niece's Birth-Day.

[Jan.] 12. *Saturday*. Morning, At Mr Chamberlayn's. After a walk (with him) in the Park, to Whitehall; where a Committee. Bishops of Carlile, Chester, Norwich and St Asaph, with Baron Price, passed Mr Chamberlayn's Accounts and ordered no pay for *Quietus*. P.m. Lord Cromarty, Dr White and Mr Greenshields.

[30] Queen Anne's Bounty Committee. See under 12 and 28 Jan. 1712.
[31] Possibly the widow of the incumbent of Aspatria, who died in 1706, and sister to David and Thomas Bell. See Levens Hall MS C/G1: William to James Grahme, 26 June 1706.
[32] The Affirmation Controversy was growing towards the end of Anne's reign, with a Tory House of Commons, generally hostile to the Quakers, and with 1715, the date for the expiration of the Affirmation Act of 1696 (renewed in 1702), drawing close. See W. C. Braithwaite, *The Second Period of Quakerism* (Cambridge, 1961), pp. 190–5.

[Jan.] 13. *Sunday*. Morning, I preached a Charity-Sermon at (Mr Freeman's Church) St Botulf's Aldersgate;[33] being fetched, and brought home, in a Chariot, &c.

[Jan.] 14. *Munday*. Morning, Visits from Dr White, with his new Book, Mr M. Hutchinson, Jeremy Nicolson, Mr Madox, &c. Attempting to wait on Prince Eugene,[34] by accident came to (his Brother General's) the Duke of Marlborough's whence, with the Bishops of Oxon, Bangor and Norwich, to Whitehall; and thence to the House. Lord Keeper [Harcourt] brought a Message for Adjourning to Thursday;[35] which done immediately. Dined with me, Mr Campbell. P.m. I went, with Mr Pattinson, to Covent-Garden and Fetterlane; where the evening with my Niece, &c.

[Jan.] 15. *Tuesday*. Morning, Mr Wilson, for his Brother; Young Pool for himself; and Mr C. Musgrave for his Nephew. Dined with me, Mr Lawson and Mr Gibbon; with whom to Dr Smith's, Lord Carlile's, Greys-Inn, &c.

[Jan.] 16. *Wednesday*. Morning, Fast-Sermon heard at Whitehall from young Mr Marshall, a very ingenious man, on *Romans* 13, 13. *Let us walk honestly, as in the day*.

P.m. Sir Christopher Musgrave, with hearty offers of Friendship to Lord Carlile and myself. *Esto*!

[Jan.] 17. *Thursday*. Morning, Calling at Sir J. M[ontagu]'s with false news from Sir C. Musgrave I came too late to the Bishop of Litchfield for the seeing of Dr Sloan's Library.[36]

House. Queen's Message concerning Peace, Scotch Lords and Libels.[37] Bill for precedency of the Family of Hannover brought in (from Her Majesty) by Lord Treasurer [Oxford].[38] Hard words

[33] Kennett was a great protagonist of the Charity School movement. See Bennett, *White Kennett*, pp. 187–90.

[34] The great Imperial general, and friend of Marlborough, had arrived in England on 5 Jan. (Luttrell, vi, 712) on a diplomatic mission, aimed at repairing the badly damaged relations between Britain and the Court of Vienna. The Emperor was deeply aggrieved by the peace policy of the Oxford ministry. For Eugene's visit, see Trevelyan, *Queen Anne*, iii, 201–2; D. Mckay, *Prince Eugene of Savoy* (1977), pp. 136–8; also below, 6 Feb., 2 Mar.

[35] *LJ* xix, 357.

[36] Hans Sloane lived in Bloomsbury Square from 1689 to 1741. His collection, which had cost him £50,000, was left to the nation and forms the basis of the British Library. A catalogue of his manuscripts (*c*.1701), by Wanley, is in BL Sloane MS 3972B.

[37] *LJ* xix, 358. The message concerned the recently begun peace negotiations at Utrecht, the best method of settling the question of Scottish peerages (the after effects of the Hamilton case), and the printing and publishing of anti-governmental libels.

[38] A bill 'for settling the precedence of the most excellent Princess Sophia Electress and

'twixt the Duke of Bucks and Earl of Anglesey about the Tuition of a child.[39]

The Commons (about Eleven at night) sent Mr Walpool to the Tower.[40]

[Jan.] 18. *Friday*. Morning, Visitted by John Taylor,[41] Isaac's Uncle; and Mr James Lowther, still jealous of his Fellow-Knight.[42] House. The Address (on yesterday's Message) Reported and agreed to.[43] The Grievances of the Scottish Lords, hard to Redress,[44] adjourned to Munday. News of the hopeful Stand,[45] carryed to Lambeth.

Evening, at Salisbury-Court; with A. Spooner and M. Jackson.

Duchess Dowager of Hanover, of the Elector her son, and of the Electoral Prince the Duke of Cambridge'. The leave to bring in the bill, originally a Whig measure, sponsored by Devonshire, was granted on 22 Dec. 1711. That it was actually brought in on 17 Jan. by the Treasurer, and with the Queen's imprimatur, was the result of some crafty negotiations between Oxford (who needed to reingratiate himself with Hanover) and the Whig leaders. See the five letters from Halifax to Oxford, three of them dated 7, 10, and 11 Jan., in BL Loan 29/151. Oxford's reward was to see the bill pass through both Houses in two days (17–18 Jan.) and to have the satisfaction of sending his cousin, Thomas Harley, to carry it to Hanover. A. Boyer, *The History of Queen Anne* (1735), p. 542; Burnet, *History*, vi, 99; *LJ* xix, 351, 360–1, 374; *CJ* xvii, 32.

[39] The Duke of Buckingham and his wife—widow of the 3rd Earl of Anglesey (d. 1702) and thus sister-in-law to the 5th Earl, Arthur (succ. 1710) — were guardians to Arthur's niece the 4th Earl of Anglesey's daughter Catherine. The Duke's case was discussed by the Committee of Privileges on 19 Jan. See HMC *Lords MSS* ix, 184.

[40] Robert Walpole was accused, on the basis of a recent report of the Commissioners of Public Accounts, of corruption in his late post of Secretary-at-War (1708–10). He was found guilty, committed to the Tower, and expelled from the Commons, see J. H. Plumb, *Sir Robert Walpole* (1972 edn.), i. 178–82. The attack was supported by the ministry, Oxford seeing it both as a sop to the Tories and as a necessary step to facilitate government business in the Commons by removing the opposition's chief financial expert and one of its ablest debaters. However, thanks to poor parliamentary management, for which, it seems, St John was largely to blame, it almost ended in fiasco, with many Tories deserting and the government's majority falling disastrously (W. Pittis, *The History of the Proceedings of the Second Session of the Present Parliament* (1712), pp. 23–4; Berkshire RO Trumbull Add. MS 136/3: Ralph Bridges to Trumbull, 25 Jan. 1711/12; HMC *Portland MSS* v, 139).

[41] Possibly the John Taylor who was Chief Clerk to the Treasury, 1695–1714.

[42] i.e. the other knight of the shire for Cumberland, the Tory Gilfred Lawson.

[43] *LJ* xix, 360. The address thanked the Queen for the message that peace negotiations were in progress.

[44] HMC *Lords MSS* ix, 174. The Lords met in committee on four days, 18 Jan.–4 Feb., to try to thrash out the tangled problems of the Scottish peers, raised in acute form before Christmas by the Hamilton case (see above, sessional intro., p. 570). The ministry had been making a sincere effort to find a solution (SRO Dalhousie MSS GD45/14/352/12: [Lord Balmerino] to [Henry Maule], 15 Jan. [1712]) but none of its expedients, including Oxford's scheme of substituting some form of hereditary system for the present elected one of parliamentary representation, proved acceptable to the House.

[45] The Whigs had some hopes of turning alienated Scottish votes in the Lords against the peace, as had Lord Nottingham. See Northamptonshire RO Finch-Hatton MSS FH281, ff. 10–13: [Nottingham] to [his wife], [late Jan. 1712].

[Jan.] 19. *Saturday*. Morning, With the Bishop of Litchfeild to Dr Sloan's Museum; the richest in Europe.[46] Thence to Dinner at Lambeth; where Sir P. King, Mr Wortley-Mountague, Dr Harris, Mr Clavering, &c.

[Jan.] 20. *Sunday*. Morning, Sermon (by preacher unknown) on *Luke* 15, 10. *Joy over one Sinner* &c. Evening, Visitted by Mr Walker; his wife being engaged with Ladies.

[Jan.] 21. *Munday*. Morning, Visitted by Mr Henley, Mr Jennis, Jeremy Nicolson, Mr Hutchinson, Dr Lindford, Mr Madox, Mr Cuper, &c. (about the Marsh-way at Lambeth),[47] Dr Harris, Mr Chambers, &c. &c. for Charity-Sermons.

House. In a Committee on the Grievances of Scots;[48] fixed by Parliament, which not to be restored. Meeting of their Peerage Hazardous; not to dictate to this House.[49] Evening, with Lord Carlile, to whom Mr C. Musgrave's Letter shewn; and with Sister R[othery] who has had onely one Letter from her son, since I came to Town.

[Jan.] 22. *Tuesday*. Morning, Cousin Br[idget] Nicolson, Mr Lamplugh and my Brother with a Bill for my son. With the last to Sir J. Mountague; who beged Mr C. Musgrave's Letter to me. House. I read Prayers. Adjourned till Friday. Bishop of Chester and I cooked Dr Dent's Bill. P.m. Dr Gibson.

[Jan.] 23. *Wednesday*. Morning, Visitted by Mr Grisdale, Capt. Dalrymple,[50] J. Hume, Dr Smith, and (from Carlile) Mr Rook, Brother Carlile and Mr Jeremy Reed,[51] sollicited by Sir C. Musgrave. P.m. Mr James Lowther in good hopes of Sir J. M[ontagu]'s success.

[46] See below, Appendix B.

[47] Probably the son of Boydell Cuper, gardener to the Earls of Arundel. The father took many of the mutilated marbles, at the time of the demolition of Arundel House in the 1670s, and placed them in Cuper's Garden in Lambeth, a place of popular amusement until 1753. The site of the garden was originally part of Lambeth Marsh where Waterloo Bridge now stands. H. B. Wheatley, *London Past and Present* (1891), i, 483; *Survey of London*, xxiii, 25–6.　　　　[48] See above, n. 44.

[49] For the fears of the English peers see G. S. Holmes. 'The Hamilton affair of 1711–12', *EHR* lxxvii (1962), 267–8, 273.

[50] William Dalrymple, captain in the 3rd regiment of foot guards in 1710. A younger son of 1st Earl of Stair, he resigned his commission on the accession of George I. Dalton, vi, 59, 61.

[51] The chief witnesses for Sir James Montagu against Col. Gledhill in the revived Carlisle election case, and described by Montagu as 'Three substantial persons of the [Carlisle] corporation'. See Ferguson, *Cumberland and Westmorland MP's*, p. 93; *CJ* xvii, 106–8. Jeremy Reed was the son of Joseph Reed, the powerful Whig Clerk to the Fraternity of Butchers in Carlisle, who had great influence at elections. *CW* ii, 74; iii, 7; iv, 30–1; xxxv, 136; Hopkinson, p. 137.

[Jan.] 24. *Thursday*. Morning, Visitted by Mr Forster, lately in Durance; Dr Waugh, waiting for his wife and Mrs Hans; Mr Rook who accompanyed me to dinner at the *Griffin*; where three Browhams [Broughams], Brothers Joseph and Carlile, and Mr Reed. Evening, Brother C[arlile] and I wrote Letters at my Lodgeings; and the Commons roasted the Duke of Marlborough.[52]

[Jan.] 25. *Friday*. Morning, Bishop of Bangor, treated with a dish of Soup.

House. In the Committee, Resolved *that the sitting of the Scottish peers by Election Alterable at their Request*.[53] This not pleaseing to themselves. Evening, Dr Gee, Mr Bell and Cousin R. Nicolson. With the last to Salisbury-Court.

The Election of Carlile put off till Munday by Mr Freeman; fatigued by last night's work.[54]

[Jan.] 26. *Saturday*. Morning, Visitted by both our Knights (Mr Lowther and Mr Lawson) together; goeing amicably to support the Whitehaven Bill.[55] Dined at Lambeth; where the Bishop of Oxon, Dr Betsworth, Dr Lindford, Mr Gee, Mr Lushington, &c. By Dr Gibson's (where Mrs Betsworth) home to Brother Carlile.

[Jan.] 27. *Sunday*. Morning, Mr Marshall, senior, preached at Whitehall, on *Matthew* 13, 24, 25.—*Tares*.

[Jan.] 28. *Munday*. Morning, To wait on the Archbishop of York [Sharp]. From him to Whitehall; where Mr Ecton[56] complained of a Slanderous passage in the Printed Report of the Committee.

House. Act conc[erning] General-Naturalization[57] Adjourned

---

[52] Marlborough had been accused of peculation by taking money from the contractors for bread and bread wagons for the army in the Netherlands. Though standard practice, this was declared 'illegal and unwarrantable' by a crammed and feverish House of Commons, the vote being 265 to 155. *CJ* xvii, 37–8; Boyer, *Queen Anne*, p. 538. The Treasurer, plainly determined to avoid the fiasco of the previous week, took over the parliamentary management of the censure himself. See Holmes, *British Politics*, p. 310; also ibid., pp. 140, 142, 302. [53] *LJ* xix, 365; HMC *Lords MSS* ix, 174.

[54] i.e. the protracted Marlborough debate, which lasted from 3.00 p.m. to almost 11.30 p.m. Ralph Freman (*c*.1665–1742), MP for Hertfordshire, 1697–1727, was the Chairman of the Committee of Privileges and Elections, 1710–13. Sedgwick, ii, 54.

[55] This Whitehaven Bill enlarged the terms for the payment of certain duties granted by the Act of 1709 'for preserving and enlarging the Harbour of Whitehaven'. See *CJ* xvii, 39, 123.

[56] John Ecton (d. 1730), compiler, antiquary, and musician, he worked in the first fruits department of the office of Queen Anne's Bounty, becoming in 1718 Receiver of the Tenths of the Clergy. He has been described as 'among the best civil servants of his day'. G. F. A. Best, *Temporal Pillars*, p. 83.

[57] See above, sessional intro., pp. 511–12.

to Thursday. Committee of the Commons went thro' some of Col. Gledhil's witnesses.[58] Adjourned to Friday.

[Jan.] 29. *Tuesday*. Morning, Visits from Mr Henley and Mr Hutchinson. At Generall meeting of Queen Ann's Bounty where the Archbishop of York and four Bishops, Lord Chief Baron, &c.

House. Scottish Debate further adjourned till Munday; as their Toleration-Bill,[59] by the Commons, to Saturday. Evening, at Mr Walker's; with a Welsh Divine, full of second Sight and St George's Ducks.

[Jan.] 30. *Wednesday*. Morning, I walked round the Park with Mr Greenshields; who (after Evening-Prayers) dined with me. With the House to hear the Bishop of Norwich's admirable sermon on *Proverbs*, 17, 14. Evening, with Mr Madox, Mr Ecton and Mr Holmes at the *Horn*.

[Jan.] 31. *Thursday*. Morning, Visitted by Mr Forster in Quest of a Protection. With Mr Greenshields to wait on Balmerino, not within; Lord Eglington, pleased with exemption of Episcopal Clergy from Presbyterian Discipline; Lord Cromarty, for Toleration: Mr Loddington, with his father's Lease.[60]

House. Bishop of Norwich's Sermon censured, by Earl of Abingdon.[61] Generall Naturalization Repealed.[62] P.m. At Dr Lancaster's; where Dr Sacheverel, angry at Lord Clarendon's History.[63] Evening, with Dr Gibson at the *Dog*.

[58] See *CJ* xvii, 106–8 for a list of witnesses.

[59] See above, sessional intro., pp. 572–4, and HMC *Lords MSS* ix, 196–7.

[60] Either Thomas or Pickering Loddington, whose father, Thomas, was Rector of Hornchurch, Lincolnshire, 1679–1724. The rectory and manor of Hornchurch had been appropriated by the see of Carlisle in c.1318 and remained so until 1869, see *CW* iii (1903), 28.

[61] Of the sermon which Nicolson deemed 'admirable', Swift wrote that Bishop Trimnell 'preached yesterday before the house of lords, and today the question was put to thank him, and print his sermon; but passed against him; for it was a terrible whig sermon'. *Journal to Stella*, ii, 476. See J. P. Kenyon, *Revolution Principles* (Cambridge, 1977), pp. 74–5, 78–9, for Trimnell's sermon, and for the embarrassment which the emotive occasion of 30 Jan. caused to conscientious Whig preachers.

[62] The Repeal Bill was carried in the Lords by fifty-seven votes to thirty-nine. For the government's attitude, see above, sessional intro., p. 571. See also *Wentworth Papers*, p. 261; Swift, *Journal to Stella*, ii, 476–7. It was a bad defeat for the Whigs in view of a walk-out during the debate by the Scots peers.

[63] As Professor Kenyon has pointed out, although two of Lord Rochester's prefaces to the three volumes of Clarendon's *History of the Great Rebellion* (1702–4) were Tory party manifestos, the *History* itself possibly proved, in the long run, a more acceptable source of material for Whig than for Tory divines. *Revolution Principles*, pp. 80–2, and n. 55, p. 224.

Feb. 1. *Friday*. Morning, Mr Hutchinson, Mr Hill, Mr Hemmings, Mr Morton, &c. Dr Waugh, Mr Sanderson, Mr James Lowther; with an Account of his Trapping the Serjeant's Evidence about Mr Gilpin.[64] Visits attempted to Sir J. M[ontagu], Mr C. Musgrave and Sir C. Musgrave.

The House sat not. Dined with me, Brother Carlile and Mr Morton, designed for Dr Sloan's: But—He was called to Eaton [Eton] yesterday. P.m. With brother Carlile in quest of Dean Smalridge; and (with the Bishops of Bangor and Norwich) to Lambeth.

Evening, Committee of the House of Commons voted Sir J. Mountague duely elected. *Yeas* 74. *Noes* 45.

[Feb.] 2. *Saturday*. Morning, Mr Haines helped me to dispatch Mr Loddington's Lease. Visits from Sir A[lexander] Rigby, Mr Greenshields, Brother Carlile, &c. Dined at Dr Waugh's (his Birth-Day) with Mr Glanvil, Mr Hungerford, &c.[65]

House. Onely an Appeal heard for Sir E[dward] Seymour.[66]

[Feb.] 3. *Sunday*. I dined (with Brother Carlile, &c.) at Salisbury-Court and preached, in the afternoon, at St Bride's. Evening, with Sister Rothery, at Cousin R. Nicolson's.

[Feb.] 4. *Munday*. Morning, Visitted by Mr Jenney, for his Letter to Utrecht; and Mr Smith, who walked with me to Hyde-Park. Afterwards, by Dr Harris, to remind me of Sunday; and Brother Carlile, goeing to dine with Mr Dean [Smalridge].

House. The Malt-Bill read a 3d time:[67] The Scots Lords quitted their claim, and the Committee drop[p]ed.[68] P.m. The news carryed to my Lord of Canterbury [Tenison]; with whom the Deans of Durham [Montague] and Exon [Blackburne], Archdeacons West, Godwin, &c. Evening, Mr James Lowther, with an Account of their strange Votes on our Allies;[69] and still Jealous of Mr Lawson.

[64] William Stagg, a Serjeant-at-Mace for thirty years with the corporation of Carlisle, had stated to the Commons' committee on the Carlisle election that Mr Gilpin, who had voted at elections for the past seven or eight years, was not a freeman. Stagg claimed to have lost his job because of his pro-Gledhill role in the election. *CJ* xvii, 106.

[65] Two indecipherable words.

[66] Son of the famous Tory politician, and MP for Great Bedwyn, 1710–15. For his appeal see HMC *Lords MSS* ix, 170–1.

[67] Bill 'for charging and continuing the duties upon malt . . . to pay the deficiency of the value of plate coined, and to pay for the re-coining the old money in Scotland'. *LJ* xix, 371.

[68] HMC *Lords MSS* ix, 175, where no further proceedings are recorded.

[69] A Committee of the Whole House of Commons, by two hundred and thirty-five votes to ninety, had on 4 Feb. condemned the States General for not observing their agreed 'quotas', i.e. proportions of subsidies. Staffordshire RO D.1778. v. 200: MS diary of Sir

[Feb.] 5. *Tuesday*. Morning, Mr Campbell and I attended Mr Kemp, and his rich Collection of Antiquities;[70] where Col. Finch and Mr Wanley. Dined, at the *Dog*, with Mr Hill; with whom, by Mrs Lamplugh's to St Martin's: where Dr Lancaster (still in the Gowt) gave me a good Answer for Joseph Rothcry; and a bad one for Mr Thompson of Burgh.[71] Evening, Brother Carlile, Mr F. G[   ] and Mr Nicols.

[Feb.] 6. *Wednesday*. Morning, After a short visit from Mr Pattinson, I went (in the Bishop of Lincoln's coach, with him and the Bishop of St Asaph) to Court: which (the Queen's Birth-Day) was very throng. Returning I met Prince Eugene in the Pall-Mal; where his Highness's Chariot was stoped directly over against my Hackney. I had a full view of that Lively and martial-looked General.

Dined at Sir J. M[ontagu]'s with two Mr Broughams, W. Rook and E[dward] Carlile. My Lady[72] recommended to my Reading *Isaiah* 22, 15, &c. Evening, With my said Carlile-friends; and Mr Thomas Fletcher, at the *Griffin*.

[Feb.] 7. *Thursday*. Morning, Brother Joseph, Mr Greenshields (for the Rectory of Whickam) Mr Chambre, takeing leave; Mr Lawson and Mr Gibson, with the Attourney Generall's [Northey's] Letter; Lord Eglington, Bishops of Oxon and Bangor, Mr Lowther (with Letter from Whitehaven) and Dr Gibson, with Account of the Decree about the School at Bampton. House. Bill for Weight of Billet-wood.[73] Petition from Hammersmith unsigned. Dined with me Mr Hutchinson, Mr Hill and Mr Hemmings. Evening, An hour at Dr Gibson's.

[Feb.] 8. *Friday*. Morning, Visitted by Mr Henley, on the High way; Mr Greenshields, from Duke Hamilton; Mr W. Johnson, Commissioners Waite and Col. Grahme. House. Case of Privilege (once waved, reassumed in the same Session) argued, 'twixt Duke of Brandon and

Arthur Kaye, p. 8. Swift wrote the same night, 'all agree that it was my book *The Conduct of the Allies* which spirited them to these resolutions'. *Journal to Stella*, ii, 480. Cf. *CJ* xvii, 68–70, 5 Feb.

[70] See below, Appendix B. John Kemp (1665–1717), antiquary, FRS 1712, whose museum was described in *Monumenta Vetustatis Kempiana* (1720) by Robert Ainsworth. By Kemp's will his museum was offered for £2,000 to Lord Oxford. He refused it and in 1721 it was auctioned for £1,090.

[71] Francis Tompson, MA, BD (Oxon.), Rector of Borough-under-Stainmore, Westmorland, 1705.

[72] Tufton Wray, Lady Montagu (d. 1712), had married Sir James in 1694. Montagu's second wife was his cousin Elizabeth, daughter of the 3rd Earl of Manchester.

[73] *LJ* xix, 372.

Lord Mohun.[74] Dined at the *Dog*, with Mr Fletcher, Mr Brougham, Dr Waugh and Mr Gibbon. After Archdeacon Richardson had made us a short visit, Mr Gibbon and I spent the evening in Salisbury-Court. ·

[Feb.] 9. *Saturday*. Morning, F. Bugg, with Case of the Quakers; whose petition this day thrown out by the Commons.[75] Archdeacon Bowchier, full of the Bishop's Blunders: Bishop of Winton, Kind to Jeremy Nicolson. House, The Queen passed the Malt-Tax, Hannover-Bill, &c.[76] Prince Eugene present. Warm Rencounter with Sir C. Musgrave and his Uncle, in the Court of Requests. Dined with me Mr Hill; goeing (that very afternoon) towards Oxford; and Cousin F. Nicolson (with Roman Coins and Salamander-Knives) from North-Wales. Evening, Mr Mack met with in the Park, Mr Nicols and Brother Carlile, reporting News.

[Feb.] 10. *Sunday*. Morning, I preached a Charity Sermon at St Mildred's;[77] and dined at Dr Harris, with Mr Knight an ingenious (and honest) Director of the South-Sea-Trade.[78] Evening, Visitted by Dean Chetwood, Dr Dent and Mr Dungworth; setling the Toleration in Scotland.

[Feb.] 11. *Munday*. Morning, Cousin F. Nicolson with old Coins and Rarities from North-Wales, promised on Friday; Mr Morton, bespeaking for tomorrow; Brother Carlile, from takeing Leave of our Dean [Smalridge]; Mr G. Wenman, returning to Oxford; W. Rook, pressing the Delivery of Mr Recorder's[79] Paper to Lord Portland; Mr Lawson and Mr Gibbon, for new Institution into Greystock: which was given.

House. On the petition of Mr Carstairs,[80] &c. to be heard by

---

[74] On 20 May 1710 the Duke of Hamilton (and Brandon) obtained a decree in Chancery against Mohun over the Gerard estate. For subsequent proceedings, see HMC *Lords MSS* ix, 187–9.

[75] The petition of the Quakers in 'relation to the present solemn Affirmation' was rejected on 9 Feb. 1712 by 101 to 80. *CJ* xvii, 74. Bugg's pamphlet was probably *Some Remarks on the Quaker's Case, relating to their Solemn Affirmation; humbly presented to the consideration of the High Court of Parliament* (1712).

[76] *LJ* xix, 374.

[77] Probably St Mildred's, Bread Street, rebuilt by Wren in 1673. There was also St Mildred the Virgin, in the Poultry, rebuilt by Wren in 1676.

[78] Robert Knight (1675–1744), Cashier to the South Sea Company since its establishment (1711). His subsequent career hardly justified Nicolson's confidence in his honesty. See J. Carswell, *The South Sea Bubble* (1961), p. 281.

[79] John Aglionby, Recorder of Carlisle.

[80] Carstairs's two co-petitioners were Thomas Blackwell, Professor of Divinity at Aberdeen, and Robert Baillie, Minister at Inverness. HMC *Lords MSS* ix, 196; *LJ* xix, 376.

Counsel against the Scotch Toleration. Question, Whether on Friday or Wednesday? Agreed for the latter. Dined with me Brother Carlile. P.m. The Transactions of the day reported to the Bishop of Lincoln and Archbishop of Canterbury.

[Feb.] 12. *Tuesday*. Morning, Mr Greenshields, with Armour for tommorrow; Mr Madox, with a paper of Complaint of his own Losses; Mr Rook, news from Carlile; Mr Lawson and Mr Gibbon, completeing the Instruments for Greystock; Mr Lowther, new Appointment from the Bishop of Chester. P.m. Mr Morton (who dined with me) accompanyed me to Dr Sloan's; where a second view of the Museum.[81] Evening, With Mr Madox and Mr Morton at the *Horn*: from the former of whom I learned that Mr D. Parry was not E. Lhwyd's Executor, nor a man of Industry enough to finish his Labours.[82]

[Feb.] 13. *Wednesday*. Morning, Cousin R. Nicolson, bespeaking me for Sunday next; Sir A. Rigby, for the Bishop of Sarum's visitting his Lady; Mr Dean Smalridge, with offers of mediation on the behalf of Sir C. Musgrave; Sir James Mountague and W. Rook, with news of the Project to declare Gledhil chosen; Mr Lowther, calling me to meet the Bishop of Chester.

House. Toleration-Bill finished (with several Amendments) in a tedious Committee.[83] I spoke against the 9th Clause, as destructive of all Ecclesiastical Discipline;[84] *sed—Frustra*. Evening, First a while, at the *Griffin*; takeing Leave of our Carlile Witnesses;[85] And afterwards at Mr S. Brougham's;[86] whence I conveyed Mr T. Fletcher's two sisters to their Lodgeings in Marlbrough-street.

[Feb.] 14. *Thursday*. Morning, Visits received from Mr Forster and Mr Greenshields, I attended the Commissioners of the Queen's bounty; where Archbishop of York, Bishops of Ely, Bangor, &c. Mr Attourney Generall [Northey], Dean of Carlile [Smalridge], &c.

---

[81] See below, Appendix B.

[82] For David Parry (?1682–1714) of Cardigan, Celtic philologist, who succeeded Edward Lhwyd as Keeper of the Ashmolean Museum, Oxford, 1709, see *Dictionary of Welsh Biography* (1959), pp. 731–2; E. Rees and G. Walters, 'The Dispersion of the Manuscripts of Edward Lhuyd', *Welsh History Review*, vii (1974), 150–2.

[83] For the proceedings in the committee on the Scottish Toleration Bill see HMC *Lords MSS* ix, 197.

[84] See above, sessional intro., p. 573. The clause referred to here was the twelfth of the Act passed into law (see *Statutes of the Realm*, ix, 559).

[85] See above, 23 Jan.

[86] Samuel Brougham (1681–1744), brother of Thomas and John, C. R. Hudleston, 'The Brougham Family', *CW* lxi (1961), 143, 148.

Report from the Committee's way made easy, on Discourse with Sir C. Musgrave and's Uncle in the Court of Requests. House. An Appeal being hearing,[87] I left it; and went to Dinner with Mr Gibbon at his Brother's where Mr Lawson, Mr Aislabie, &c. expected; but the Barrier-Treaty kept them from us.[88] Visits attempted to Dr Woodward and Dr Laney;[89] and paid to Dr Waugh, who presented me with a fair Goa-stone.[90] Sir A. Rigby.

[Feb.] 15. *Friday*. Morning, Second Letter, for a Guinnea, from Mr Forster. Noe. Mr Greenshi[e]lds; with Assurance that the Commons will not accept the Clause for Abjureing in the Scotch Act.

House. Lord Ab[ingdon] moved for altering the Abjuration-Oath; but no more Amendments assented to. Lord Hallifax moved for an Address of Indignation against the French King;[91] which (after a faint Debate on the Court-Side) agreed to. Dined at Lord Pembroke's whose cabinet of Coins shewed (by Sir A. Fountaine) to the Kinsmen of the Czar and King of Prussia, the latter well versed in them. Evening, at my Brother's.

[Feb.] 16. *Saturday*. Morning, Haveing gotten a Copy of our yesterday's Address, at the Parliament-Office, I presently handed it to Dr Gibson, for the immediate use of my Lord of Canterbury. House. To attend the Queen presently with their Address. To Dinner, with Dr Waugh, at Lambeth: where Mr Dean of Arches [Bettesworth], Drs Bentley, Gee, &c. Evening, Mr Brougham and Mr Rook; the latter for the North, on Munday.

[87] See HMC *Lords MSS* ix, 167–8.

[88] The Commons, in a Committee of the Whole House, was considering the correspondence of Lord Townshend concerning the Whig-negotiated Barrier Treaty with the United Provinces (letters dated The Hague, 1 and 26 Nov. 1709). The Tories, with Secretary of State St John providing the lead from the Court, crushingly condemned the Barrier Treaty at the end of the debate by 279 votes to 117, probably the most impressive demonstration this session of the party's strength and solidarity. Staffordshire RO D.1778. v. 220: MS diary of Sir Arthur Kaye, p. 8.

[89] Edward Lany (*c*.1667–1728), Master of Pembroke College, Cambridge, 1707–28, Vice-Chancellor of Cambridge, 1707–8, Professor of Divinity at Gresham College, 1691–1728.

[90] A fever medicine, consisting of various drugs made up in the form of a hard ball, from which portions were scraped as required.

[91] See *LJ* xix, 379–80. This was the first important *coup* achieved by the Whig peers since before Christmas, following the arrival in London of news from Utrecht of the specific offers made by the French plenipotentiaries to the allies. These offers, reflecting the reviving ambitious confidence of the French, were a blow to Tory hopes of an early settlement; and after Lord Guernsey had intervened in the debate on the side of Halifax, the Court peers abandoned their embarrassed attempts to get the debate adjourned. 'The Ministry [Nottingham observed] were afraid of a train of Tory's following him.' Northampton RO Finch-Hatton MSS FH281, f. 14: [Nottingham] to [his wife], 20 Feb. 1712. Cf. Swift, *Journal to Stella*, ii, 489–90.

[Feb.] 17. *Sunday*. Morning, I preached at the Savoy; and dined (at Cousin R. Nicolson's) with the Dean of Rochester [Pratt] and Mr Sadler, Deputy-Clerk of the Pell, a great Lover (and Designer) of Medals. P.m. Mr Dean brought me home in his chariot.

[Feb.] 18. *Munday*. Morning, Vissitted by Mr Henley, Mr James Lowther and the Bishop of Bangor. House. Report by Lord Keeper [Harcourt] of the Contents of Muhl-meester's[92] Informations. Duke of M[arlborough]'s character of the man. P.m. With Mr Greenshields to visit Dr Lancaster and Dr Smith.

[Feb.] 19. *Tuesday*. Morning, Visitted by Mr Brome,[93] with another Treatise; Mr Ogle; Mr Audley, with a poem rejected; Mr Stanwix, with a Sessions-Brief; Mr Smith, with Presentation to his Liveing in Dioc. Linc.[94] Dined at Dr Gibson's; with Dr Betsworth (Dean of Arches) and his Lady. Evening, Visitted by the Bishop of Waterford;[95] who against the Dutch being Christians, and for the Convocation's ordaining: Mr Oughton,[96] for my Subscription; which readily given. Mr Madox's mournful Letter.

[Feb.] 20. *Wednesday*. Morning, Mr Ecton, for an Appointment to go to the Bishop of St Asaph. I went to the Archbishop of York with Mr Greenshields; who dined with me. P.m. Mr Dean of Peterborough [Kennett] and Archdeacon Frank; with Account of the Prolocutor's Speech (this day) against acting, by vertue of a Licence, after a prorogation of the Parliament.[97] Evening, Visit paid to Mrs Lamplugh (surrounded with the Archbishop of York's merry Daughters) in my way to Mrs Thynne's; where Kindly received (with my Brother and Niece) by the young Ladies, &c.

[Feb.] 21. *Thursday*. Morning, Mr Morland, for a Fellowship; Mr Madox, for marriage; Dr Waugh, a running Visit; Mr Greenshields, with his unfinished petition; Bishop of Bangor, confident of the

---

[92] A Monsieur Muell, who was Muster Master of the Marines Abroad, had been captured by the French while returning from Gibraltar in Sept. 1705. Luttrell, v, 592.

[93] Possibly William Brome (1664–1745) of Withington, Herefordshire, antiquary, and friend of George Hickes, to whose *Thesaurus* (1703–5) he contributed indexes.

[94] John Smith, ordained priest by Nicolson on 29 Feb. 1708, Chaplain to the Duke of Atholl, Rector of Raithby, Lincolnshire, 1707, Rector of Halton Holegate, 1711. *Speculum Dioeceseos Linc*. i, 65, 97.

[95] Thomas Mills (c. 1672–1740), Bishop of Waterford and Lismore, 1708–40.

[96] Possibly Thomas Oughton, Deputy Registrar of the Court of Delegates. Chamberlayne, *Present State 1710*, p. 645.

[97] On 20 Feb. 1712, the first day of assembly after the Christmas recess, Atterbury decided that all business must be recommenced afresh after a royal prorogation, a loss of many months' work. A minority of members protested vigorously against it. Bennett, *White Kennett*, pp. 82–3.

French King's being dead; Mr Lowther, with farther Sollicitations on his Bill.

House. The Whitehaven-Bill read a second Time, and committed to a Committee of the whole House.[98] On a Motion by Lord Godolphin, Question put for Adjourning to Munday: Carryed (in the Negative, by even Voices; 45 each) against Saturday. P.m. This Account carryed to Lord of Canterbury: who shewed me many Original Letters of the Reign of King Charles 1. Evening, Visitted by Dr Gee and Mr Nicols.

[Feb.] 22. *Friday*. Morning, Visit offered to me from Mr Forster; and admitted (onely) from Sir J. Mountague, who read over the Chairman's Report on our Election, and furnished me (from Lord Hallifax) with 3 last Vollumes of Rymer. Evening, First, with Mr Campbell; to whom promised two of my Welsh Knife-Hafts. Afterwards, at my Brother's with Sister Rothery.

[Feb.] 23. *Saturday*. Morning, Sir Alexander Rigby, thankful for the Bishop of Sarum's favour to his Lady; and desireous of future conference: To the Bishop of St Asaph, with Mr Ecton unpaid for his Book:[99] Mr Lowther, hauling me to the House, Where the Scotch Bill brought back, by Sir S[imeon] Steward [Stuart] with amendment of the Abjuration Oath.[100] Dined at home, with Mr Greenshields.

House of Commons agreed to the Resolution of their Committee— That Sir J. Mountague fairly elected. *Yeas*, 148. *Noes*, 133.[101]

[Feb.] 24. *Sunday* and St Matthias. Morning, Mr Marshall Senior [preached] at Whitehall, on (part of the Gospel) *Yoke easy* &c. Evening. Sir A. Rigby (and, his countreyman, Mr Nicols) with me till Bed-time.

[Feb.] 25. *Munday*. Morning, Mr Stone-street, bespeaking me for Sunday sennight; Mr Chamberlayne, bestowing on me *Heims Kringla*;[102] Mr Gibbon, for his papers; Mr Madox, with an Appointment from

[98] *LJ* xix, 382.

[99] *Liber Valorum et Decimarum, being an account of the valuations and yearly tenths of all such ecclesiastical benefices in England and Wales as now stand chargeable with the payment of first-fruits and tenths* . . . (1711).

[100] For the Commons' amendments of the oath see *CJ* xvii, 103–4 (21 Feb.). Sir Simeon Stuart (Stewart), MP for Lymington, Dec. 1708–10, Hampshire, 1710–13, was a frequent Tory speaker in this parliament and a prominent member of the October Club. He became one of the Chamberlains of the Exchequer later in 1712 and passed out of politics in 1713.

[101] See *CJ* xvii, 108.

[102] *Heimskringla* (published in Swedish and Latin in Stockholm in 1697) was by Snorri Sturlason (1178–1241), the Icelandic historian and poet. It comprises abbreviated king's sagas, and contains many references to English affairs in the tenth and eleventh centuries.

Mr Brittain; Mr Ecton, with wrong Representation of his Case; Sir James Mountague, with Lists of his friends and Enemies.[103] P.m. By Dr Gibson's, to the Temple; whence, with Mrs Madox and Ecton.

[Feb.] 26. *Tuesday*. Morning, After seeing the Rare Animals, &c. in Channon-Row (amongst which a Shank-bone of a man, cast on the Shore near Barcelona, of 3 feet and 10 inches in length and 37 lbs weight) I visitted Lord Hallifax, who earnest for removeing Records from the Rolls, to the Tower. *Esto*. Visitted by Dr Waugh, Brother Joseph, Mr Holm's son of Westward, &c.

House. Amendment of Commons (*As the same* for *Which*)[104] agreed to by 56 against 40.[105] P.m. After Mr Greenshields had dined with me, I waited on Lord of Canterbury where Generall Nicholson; and at Dr Gibson's set[t]led Bampton-School and Mr Thoresby's Book.[106]

[Feb.] 27. *Wednesday*. Morning, Mr Nelms,[107] returning (from the North) to Oxford; Sir A. Rigby, dayly Orator, Mr Brome, for his lean MS.[108] Dean of Peterborough [Kennett], from the idle Convocation, Mr Gibbon, who dined with me; and with whom (p.m.) I went to visit Mr Lawson, till Bed-time.

[Feb.] 28. *Thursday*. Morning, Cousin Bridget Nicolson and her son; Mr Holme's nephew; Mr Henley, on the old way.

House. Place-Bill read a First time (on the Question, 63 against 42) ordered a second tomorrow.[109] Evening, Letters.

[Feb.] 29. *Friday*. Morning, Cornet Nicolson, in Quest of his poor Knight's place; Mr Thomas Fletcher, for Oxford, &c; Mr Gibbon, goeing Northward.

House. The Place-Bill committed on the Question; *Contents*, 74. *Not Contents* (proxies included) 72.[110] Amendments of the Committee

[103] Apparently a lost division list of the House of Commons for 23 Feb. 1712.

[104] See above, sessional intro., p. 574.

[105] *LJ* xix, 385. See above, sessional intro., p. 574, for Nicolson's voting on this question.

[106] A reference to Ralph Thoresby's *Ducatus Leodiensis*, for which he had been collecting material since 1691 and which he had been writing since c.1705. It was published in 1715.

[107] Richard Nelms, MA (Oxon.) 1707, Rector of Skelton, Cumberland, 1711, and Vicar of Thedingworth, Leicestershire, 1714.

[108] See above, 19 Feb.

[109] See above, sessional intro., p. 572; HMC *Lords MSS* ix, 201–3; *LJ* xix, 388.

[110] According to HMC *Lords MSS* ix, 202, the voting figures were seventy-eight to seventy-two (*Contents* fifty-seven plus twenty-one proxies, and *Not Contents* fifty-eight plus fourteen proxies).

being reported to the House, the First (relateing to the Commencement on Her Majesty's Demise) agreed to, on the Question. *Contents*, 70. *Not Contents*, 65.[111] The Bill, on a 3d Reading, thrown out.[112] Evening, At my Brother's.

March 1. *Saturday.* Morning, Mr Forster, begging 2s 6d. With Mr Madox, to his wedding at the Chappel at Guild-Hall; where Mr Edwards, the Bride's brother,[113] &c. Returning from this office, I found Mr Ecton at my Lodgeings; with his paper for the Queen's Bounty. Dined at Lambeth, with the Bishops of Oxford, Bangor, and Norwich, the Dean of Lincoln [Willis], &c. The last and I went home with Dr Gibson; and took Boat a little unluckily.

[Mar.] 2. *Sunday.* Mr Nicols and I (haveing been at Prayers and Sacrament at Whitehall) went to Dinner at Ely-House; where Dr Canon,[114] &c. P.m. In my Lord's Library (of Seven Rooms, Walls and Floors)[115] where Prince Eugene, the Duke of Marlborough, Lord Townshend, &c, had been yesterday. Evening, With Dr Barton,[116] a Chaplain at Port o Porto formerly; and who refused the Bishoprick of Bristol.[117]

[Mar.] 3. *Munday.* Morning, Mr Thomas Morland, loaden with the Agues of Kent; Mrs Hutton, for more Charity; Brother Joseph, Pension for an Officer's Widow; Mr Ogle, for resigning on a year's Grace; Jeremy Nicolson, for Dr Grant's[118] curacy; Mr James Lowther,

---

[111] For the significance of this (Lord Oxford's) amendment, see above, sessional intro., p. 572. The voting figures given in HMC *Lords MSS* ix, 203 are *Contents*, sixty plus fifteen proxies (seventy-five), *Not Contents* fifty plus twenty proxies (seventy). For the Amendments see ibid., p. 202; *LJ* xix, 389.

[112] Without a division. For the proceedings of the day see L'Hermitage's dispatch in BL Add. MS 17677 FFF, ff. 91–2; cf. *Journal to Stella*, ii, 501; Burnet, *History*, vi, 114.

[113] Madox married Catherine, daughter of Vigarus Edwards. In 1756 Madox's widow left his collection of transcripts to the Cotton Library.

[114] Robert Cannon (1663–1722), Archdeacon of Norfolk, 1708–22, Sub-Almoner, 1716–22.

[115] John Moore's library was famous throughout Europe. At the time of his death in 1714 he had collected 29,000 books and 1,790 manuscripts. It was sold for 6,000 guineas to George I who gave it to the University of Cambridge. Cf. Thoresby, *Diary*, i, 334–5, 342; ii, 116.

[116] Samuel Barton (c.1649–1715), Vicar of Christ Church with the rectory of St Leonard, Foster Lane, London, since 1708.

[117] Bristol was, by common consent, the poorest of the English bishoprics, being worth at this time about £400. Christ Church, Wake MS 18, ff. 393–4. Barton, a Low Church Whig divine, had been offered it early in 1710 by the Godolphin ministry (Luttrell, vi, 555; HMC *Portland MSS* iv, 536); and after his refusal it remained vacant for several months until given by Harley to the moderate Tory, John Robinson.

[118] ?John Grant (d. 1736), Rector of St Dunstan-in-the-West, 1677–1736, Prebendary of Rochester, 1692–1736, Vicar of Kingsdown, Kent, 1710–36.

&c. Queen's Bounty at Whitehall; where onely a little Chatt with Dr Bray and Mr Ch[amberlayne?].

House. Four Bills passed by Commission.[119] P.m. Visit to Dr Lancaster; with whom Mr Clark (of the Admiralty)[120] and the Chancellor of Glocester.[121] Evening, Eating Oysters with Mr Nicols.

[Mar.] 4. *Tuesday*. Morning, Chars sent to Lord Hallifax and carryed to Sir J. M[ontagu] who pleased with his news from Carlile. Thence to Mr J. Brougham, to spur him northwards; to Lord Carlile, who also for the North; Sir C. Musgrave not yet to be seen. With Mr Morton to the Tower. Here medals bought of Mr Coker;[122] and (after an Attempt to see Mr Walpole)[123] dined with Mr Holmes and Mr Morton, the former repeating to me the story of Sir A. Fountaine's selling *Boccace* and *Virgil* to Prince Eugene for 35 guinneas. By my brother's home, to write Letters.

[Mar.] 5. *Ash-Wednesday*. Morning, A good Sermon (at Whitehall) by Dr Adams, on *Act[s]*, 17, 31, 32. *Now all to Repentance*. Evening, At Grey's Inn, with the two Broughams.

[Mar.] 6. *Thursday*. Morning, Visit to Mr Chamberlayne, jealous of Mr Ecton. At my Lodgeings, Mr Dean of Rippon [Dering], prepareing for the North; Mr Lamplugh, pleased with his Prebend;[124] Mr P. Tullie, guarding against the Bill for Sherifs-Accounts.[125] P.m., At Lambeth, returning J. Mabillon, I had a view of the present Case in Convocation. Evening, With Dr Gibson (receiving his Quarterage as Lecturer) in Long Acre.

[Mar.] 7. *Friday*. Morning, J. Cockson, with a new periwig: Archdeacon Bouchier, bidding Adieu: Dr Smith, moderate: Mr Morton, in quest of the Bishop of St David's [Bisse]: Mr Madox, for regulateing First-fruits: Mr Lowther, still angry at his Brother Knight; P. Tullie, on the Sherif's Bill.

[119] Including the Episcopal Communion (Scotland) Act, see *LJ* xix, 391–2.

[120] Dr George Clarke, Fellow of All Souls, 1680–1736 (DCL, 1708); Joint Secretary to the Admiralty, 1702–5, and a Commissioner, 1710–14. MP for Launceston since May 1711. Sedgwick, i, 554–5.

[121] Henry Penrice (1677–1752), Chancellor of Gloucester, 1711–52; Judge of the High Court of Admiralty and Kt., 1715.

[122] Probably John Croker, see above, 23 Mar. 1711.

[123] Walpole's imprisonment in the Tower had become something of a triumph as he was besieged by Whig visitors, and also visited by Marlborough and Godolphin. See Plumb, *Walpole*, i, 181–2.

[124] Thomas Lamplugh (d. 1747) had been installed as a Prebendary of York on 27 Feb. 1712.

[125] The Sheriff's Bill is printed along with the proceedings of the Lords on it, in HMC *Lords MSS* ix, 209–17.

House. Onely private Bills. P.m. With Mr Campbel; who shewed me Peschius's[126] Eng[r]aveing of James I and Charles I in large ovals, silver, valued at 20 and 24 Guinneas; Old Scotch Coin (Camb[ere]d in Mont[in]g) with *Ave Maria*; the incombustible Asbestos and yellow Talk; reported the manner of Blanching Wax, in broad and thin plates, watered in the Sun. Evening, At my brother's, with Col. Orfeur: when called for, at my Lodgeings, by Lord Carlile and Sir C. Musgrave.

[Mar.] 8. *Saturday*. Morning, The Bishop of Chester preached (the Queen's Accession) at Westminster and the Bishop of St David's at St James's where so throng a court (Prince Eugene present) as not usual. P.m. Mr L'Oste, Vicar of Lowth; Mr Glas,[127] a converted Scotch Clergyman, with his Case and Sermon. Evening, Letters.

[Mar.] 9. *Sunday*. After Service at Whitehall, I went (with Mr Walker) to dine with Mr C. Musgrave where Lord Downes,[128] Mr Lister, Col. Grahme, Mr J. M[usgrave] and Col. Dobbins. High Gentlemen all. The Cases of Lord Townshend and Mr Walpole compared with those of our present plenipotentiaries and excluded place-men re-elected.[129] Evening private.

[Mar.] 10. *Munday*. Morning, Mr Giles Redman, from the Isle of Ely. At a Committee in the Banquetting-House, with the Bishops of Chester and St Asaph. House. Private Bills; after Mr Johnson's Committee for the Journals.[130] Lord Keeper [Harcourt] successfully applycd to for Mr Oughton's Book. P.m., Visitted by Mrs Fetherston, Mrs Brougham, Cousin F. Nicolson and Dr Gee. Item. Thomas Bell.

[Mar.] 11. *Tuesday*. Morning, F. Nicolson, with whom (presently) to attend the Bishop of Bangor and Mr Shute;[131] the latter for

---

[126] One of the family of Pass (Van de Pas or Passe, Passaeus), famous engravers from the Netherlands, two generations of whom worked in England in the early seventeenth century.

[127] Adam Glas, whose *A sermon [on Hebrews, i, 5] preached upon Christmas day, 1711* was published in London in 1712. Having joined the Church of England after his desertion of his Presbyterian charge of Aberlady, he was reordained by Bishop Compton and became Rector of Lofthouse, Yorkshire, in 1712. *Fasti Ecclesiae Scoticanae*, ed. H. Scott (Edinburgh, 1915) i, 352.

[128] Henry Dawnay (1664–1741), 2nd Viscount Downe [I], MP for Pontefract, 1690–5, Yorkshire, 1698–1700, 1707–27. Sedgwick, i, 606–7.

[129] Townshend and Horatio Walpole (Robert's brother) had been involved in the Barrier Treaty negotiations of 1709, Townshend as Ambassador at The Hague, Walpole as Secretary to the Embassy and Under-Secretary of State. The 'present plenipotentiaries' of the Queen at Utrecht were the Earl of Strafford, formerly Lord Raby, and Bishop Robinson of Bristol, Lord Privy Seal.   [130] See above, Chapter 1, pp. 37–9.

[131] ?Nathaniel Shute (c.1648–1712), educated Queen's College, Oxford, Canon of Salisbury, 1704–12, he died before June 1712.

moderateing the Resentments of the Scots: Mr Turretine and Mr L'Oste, in my absence; as also, Mr Martin goeing into the Countrey: Col. Berry[132] and his mother, with a Letter from the Bishop of Cloyne [Crow], about an Irish Appeal: Jeremy Nicolson, on a cold Scent after a Liveing in Surrey. Dr Waugh brought Mr Smith of Queen's College[133] to be ordained by the Bishop of Winton; and, after my Letter written in's favour, dined with me at the *Dog*. P.m. The Dr and I made a Visit to the Provost; who cheerful, on Recovery from the Gowt. Evening, Letters.

[Mar.] 12. *Wednesday*. Morning, J. Clark, with his father's Letter to Mr Gibbon; which sent (as notifyed) to Mr Lawson: Mr Stonestreet, unwillingly excuseing my Service next Sunday: Mr Ecton, not pleased with the wording of his Summons: Mrs Hutton, with petitions to Lord K[eeper] [Harcourt] and Master of the Rolls [Trevor]: Mr Madox, with the like to the Lords Committees for Records. At dinner with me, Mr Morton; with some sheets of the last Chapter of his *Nat[ural] Hist[ory]*.[134] P.m. Visit paid (with my Niece) to Colemanstreet; whence home by Salisbury-Court.

[Mar.] 13. *Thursday*. Morning, Mr Greenshields, without a mask; Dr White, for Recommendatory Letter to Mr Harbin;[135] Dr Higden, with the Duke of Buck's Case. General meeting[136] at Whitehall; where Archbishop of York, Bishops of Peterborough [Cumberland], Chester, &c, Dean of Carlile [Smalridge], B. Lovel, &c. All things recommitted.

House. Long Cause twixt Duke of B[uckingham] and Lord Conway, on the Finishing the House at Ragley.[137] The Question put for Reverse — *Contents*, 27. *Not Contents*, 32. Evening, Kind visit from Dr Barton.

[Mar.] 14. *Friday*. Morning, Dr White, for a Letter to Mr Harbin; Mrs Donnel, on the old Grievances; Cousin R. Nicolson, from dunning

[132] Lieut.-Col. Richard Barry, commissioned in 1707 in Col. Alnutt's regiment of foot. Dalton, vi, 368.

[133] ?Thomas Smith of Appleby, Westmorland, matriculated Queen's College, Oxford, 1703, aged 17, BA 1708, MA 1711.

[134] *The Natural History of Northamptonshire, with some account of the Antiquities; to which is annexed a transcript of Domesday Book, as far as it relates to that County* (London, 1712).

[135] George Harbin (?1665–1744), non-juror; Chaplain to Bishop Turner of Ely and Chaplain and Librarian to Thomas Thynne, 1st Viscount Weymouth (d. 1714), and possibly to 2nd Viscount; author of *The Hereditary Right of the Crown of England Asserted* (for which Hilkiah Beford was wrongly imprisoned).

[136] Of the Bounty Commissioners.

[137] See HMC *Lords MSS* ix, 199–200; *LJ* xix, 397.

the Bishop of St David's. House. Mr Johnson's Committee ended, the Sheriffs-Bill read a second time; and committed for Munday. P.m. I waited on the Archbishop of Canterbury with Cousin Rothery's papers; and had leave to use his Grace's name to Dr King for Redress. Thence to visit Dr Gibson, in a sprained Ancle or the Gowt. Evening, With Sister Rothery (in great fear of the Mohocks)[138] at my brother's.

[Mar.] 15. *Saturday*. Morning, Visits attempted to Dr Waugh, Dr Woodward and Dr Kennet; the last gone to Greenwich. House Sat not. Onely Mr Egerton's Committee.[139] P.m. Walk, in the Park, with Mr Lamplugh. Letters.

[Mar.] 16. *Sunday*. Morning, At the Abbey-Church a good Sermon (on speedy Repentance) by Dr Linford. Dined With my Brother. P.m. A Sermon, by Mr Nicols in the Abbey, on the *Sin against the Holy Ghost*.

[Mar.] 17. *Munday*. Morning, Fr[ank] Briscoe, starveing and his son dyeing; Mr Stephenson, will be thankful for an Excise-walk;[140] J. Clark, marryed and in fear of Arrests. With the Bishops of Exeter [Blackall] and Chester, at Whitehall; where the Papers read, and Act ordered to be formed thereupon. Baron Bothmar[141] with Lord Hallifax. At the House, the Sherif's Bill committed; Counsel (for Lord Strafford and the pipe-officers) heard against it; and then the Committee adjourned to Thursday.[142] P.m. Visits to the Bishop of Ely (in an Ague) and Mr Lawson; attempted to Sir J. Mountague and Mr Thomas Browham.

---

[138] Aristocratic ruffians—Augustan muggers—who had recently begun to infest the streets at night. See *Journal to Stella*, ii, 509 (9 Mar. 1712); Hearne, *Collections*, iii, 326–7 (30 Mar. 1712), who thought they were 'all of the Whiggish Gang'. According to John Bridges, brother of the Bishop of London's Chaplain, the rumours of insults and disorders lately committed by 'a set of Men called Mohocks' in a great part proved entirely false on examination (Berkshire RO Trumbull MS 54, item 95: to Trumbull, 21 Mar. 1712).

[139] See HMC *Lords MSS* ix, 203–4, for the Egerton Estate Act.

[140] In the organisation of the Excise Office, two types of area were covered by the ordinary excise officers, or 'gaugers': the 'walk' was predominantly urban and the 'ride' predominantly rural. The 'walk' was generally the more sought after, on grounds of convenience and not having to maintain a horse.

[141] John Caspar, Baron von Bothmer, Envoy Extraordinary, 1710–11, 1711–12 to England from Brunswick-Luneburg (Hanover), and Minister Plenipotentiary, July–Aug. 1714. Stationed in The Hague, he kept a close watch upon affairs in England. He came to England in Dec. 1711 to deliver a Memorial from Hanover against the peace. See C. H. Firth and J. F. Chance, *Notes on the Diplomatic Relations of England and Germany* (Oxford, 1907), pp. 14–15.

[142] See HMC *Lords MSS* ix, 214–15.

[Mar.] 18. *Tuesday*. Morning, Visitted by Mr M. Hutchinson and Mr Hemmings, Mr Wilson, Mr Ogle, Cornet Nicolson, Jeremy Nicolson and Mr Smith, Mr Shute, Dr Potter, Mr Madox. Dined at the Chaplain's Table with Dr Younger, Dr Gee (the Inviter of Dr Potter, Mr Nicols and myself) and Monsieur Menard, the last preacher at Charenton.[143]

[Mar.] 19. *Wednesday*. Morning, Stateing Accounts with Dr Gibson, blamed for not goeing to Convocation; and reading Mr Henley's Plea to Lord of Canterbury who told me of the University of Cambridge's goeing to displace their Chancellor and old Snow being in Purgatory. P.m. Visits attempted to Mrs Lamplugh; Dr Deering and Mrs Wenman; paid to Mr Bateman and Salisbury-Court.

[Mar.] 20. *Thursday*. Morning, With Mr Nicols, viewing the Books for the Coaches of Chester and Wakefield; in the latter of which I took two places for April 2. House. Farther Progress in the Committee on the Sherif's Bill. Adjourned to Munday. P.m., and Evening, Sir W. Johnson[144] and Mr Lawson vainly expected.

[Mar.] 21. *Friday*. Morning, Mr Morton; who also came and dined with me. Evening, At my Brother's.

[Mar.] 22. *Saturday*. Morning, Mr Chamberlaine, Mr C. Musgrave, Mr Tirrick and Cousin Fetherston Nicolson; the last for a Remove to Biddiford. P.m. With Mr Nicols, bidding Adieu to the Bishop of Lincoln;[145] and thence a walk into Hide park.

[Mar.] 23. *Sunday*. Morning, Sermon at Whitehall, against Occasional Conformity; concluded with *Goe ye wicked* &c. P.m. At the Abbey, a good Sermon by Mr Freeman on *Watch and pray*, &c. From the Church, Dr Gibson came in with me; and stayed till six. After him, Earl of Cromarty (full of the French Silence, &c.) till nine.

[Mar.] 24. *Munday*. Morning, Visitted by Cousin R. Nicolson and (the now Clerk of the Patents) his son;[146] Messrs Greenshields, Dungworth and Hay, with projects for plenty of English and Irish

---

[143] ?Philip Menard, preaching Minister at the French Chapel at St James's.

[144] Sir William Johnstone (d. 1727), 2nd Bt., MP for Dumfries, 1708–10, 1713–15, Dumfriesshire, 1715–22. Sedgwick, ii, 181–2.

[145] Wake left London for Dorset on 24 Mar., returning on 10 May 1712. Lambeth Palace MS 1770, ff. 119–20.

[146] Possibly James Nicolson who was Chief Clerk of the Pells Office (see *The Laws of Honour* (1714), p. 42; Chamberlayne, *Present State 1716*, p. 115).

Common-prayer Books; Mrs Wenman; Bishops of Chester and Norwich, from the Committee at Whithall; Jeremy Nicolson, still in
hopes; Mr Morton, brought to the Bishop of St David's. House. The
Sherif's Bill impracticable, referred to a private Committee. P.m.,
Thomas Bell, with Mr Collier's proposeals.

[Mar.] 25. *Tuesday*. Morning, Mr Stephenson, for Excise, &c. House.
Act against Mutiny, and othefs, passed by Commission.[147] Dined and
Evening at Salisbury-Court; my Sister's Birth-Day.

[Mar.] 26. *Wednesday*. Morning, Jeremy Nicolson, hunting on a very
cold scent; Mr Morton, fetching away his old coins and bespeaking
Dinner; Mr Campbel, with Sir R. Home's Case;[148] Mr James Lowther,
provideing parochial Libraries;[149] Dr Higden, with Mr Pye's Case.[150]
Dined Mr Moreton; who (with me) once more disappointed by Dr
Sloan. P.m., Mr Thomas Bell and I paid a visit to Dr (or Bishop)
Hickes; and there met with Mr Harbine learned in our English
Histories. Thence to meet the Lord Privy Seal's [Bishop Robinson's]
Chaplain[151] (and his brother, the Advocate) at the *Five Bells*.

[Mar.] 27. *Thursday*. Morning, Sir William Johnson (brought by Mr
Lawson) on a fruitless errand to the House of Commons. House.
Scandalous Cause 'twixt Gorge Appellant and Pye Respondent.
Decree affirmed; with 40 *l.* costs. P.m. Visitted by Sir A. Rigby;
and paid to the Bishop of St Asaph.

[Mar.] 28. *Friday*. Morning, Visitted by Mr Dungworth, solliciteing
for Common Prayer-Books; and Visit paid (with the Bishop of
Bangor, Lords Carteret,[152] Haversham, &c) to Lord Hallifax in an
Ague, cheerful and Kind to Mr Madox. Dined Mr Morton, with whom
(fruitlessly) to Dr Sloan's thence (with Mr Madox) to the *Horn*.
Supped, with Dr Waugh's Family and Sister Rothery, at Salisbury-
Court.

[147] *LJ* xix, 406–7.
[148] See HMC *Lords MSS* ix, 179–82.
[149] This had been one of the principal objectives of the SPCK since 1699.
[150] See HMC *Lords MSS* ix, 204–5.
[151] Thomas Dibben or Dibden (*c*.1678–1741), Rector of Gt. Fontmell, Dorset, 1701–41,
was the Bishop of Bristol's Chaplain and accompanied him to Utrecht. He remained his
Chaplain on Robinson's translation to London. Berkshire RO Trumbull MS 55: R. Bridges
to Trumbull, 7 May 1714.
[152] John, 2nd Baron Carteret (see Appendix A), was a young Tory peer who on a
number of occasions this session (e.g. 2 Jan. 1712) had voted with the Whig opposition,
probably under the influence of Lord Nottingham or one of his friends, e.g. Weymouth.
He was to become a regular member of the Hanoverian Tory opposition group by 1714, and
was converted to acknowledged Whiggery under George I.

[Mar.] 29. *Saturday*. Morning, Col. Benson (from Spain) gave me an Account of the French Insolence at Utrecht, and C[ol.] Gledhil's sale of's commission to defray a Debt of 760 *l*. With Dr Waugh to the Archbishop of York thence to Chartreux, and to dinner in Fanchurch-strcet. At the Dr's takeing leave, till 8 at night.

[Mar.] 30. *Sunday*. Morning, Mr Marshall Junior pr[eached] at Whitehall on *Romans* 6, 8. P.m. Dr Gibson, lamenting the Archbishop's bloody water.

[Mar.] 31. *Munday*. Morning, Visits from Drs Smith, Higden, and Potter; Messers Dungworth, Greenshields, Henley, Broughton, &c. Cousin Bridget Nicolson.— paid to Sir James Mountague, Lords Carlile, Wharton and Duke of Somerset gone to Newmercate.[153] P.m. Leave taken at Lambeth; whence, to St James's Park, with Dr Potter. Letters.

April 1. *Tuesday*. Morning, Lodgeings discharged. Leave taken of Dean Smalridge, Bishop of Bangor, Lord Carlile, Mr Lawson, Mr Lowther and Mr Churchill. Dined With Sister Rothery at Salisbury-Court; whence (with Mr Nicols and my brother) to the *White Hart* in Aldersgate.

[Apr.] 2. *Wednesday*. Morning, At six I set out in the Coach for Leedes; in company of Mrs Benlowes (and her young son) from Dantzick, and Mrs Wheeler a Dry-salter. That night, at Bigglesworth, met with Mr Sill &c from Wakef[ield].[154]

---

[153] Newmarket races were a favourite resort of the Whig peers, especially during Mar. and Apr. (in the Easter recess or during a quiet period of a session) and in Oct. and thus often provided a venue for Junto conferences. See Holmes, *British Politics*, pp. 289–90 and (for 1712), 308–9.

[154] Nicolson continued north to Stamford on 3 Apr., reaching the town after eleven o'clock at night because the roads were so bad, and he had had a horse killed on the road. On the following day he travelled from 5.00 in the morning until "twixt one and two the next morning' reaching Barnaby Moor. On 5 Apr. he reached Leeds via Doncaster and Wakefield, where he was met by Thoresby. He spent Sunday, 6 Apr. preaching at Leeds. He then proceeded via Settle and Kendal reaching Rose on 10 Apr. *CW* iv (1904), 57.

14 March 1713–16 March 1713

Nicolson's summer, autumn, and winter of 1712–13, spent in his diocese, were dominated by the personal tragedy of the long illness of his wife, first recorded by the Bishop in May, and her death on 16 November 1712: 'the last day', he noted, 'of my 31st year in this Diocese; having been Instituted (into my prebend and vicarage of Torpenhow) Nov. 17. 1681. *Nigro Carbone*.' The loss of 'my chief Blessing' numbed Nicolson. The entry in his diary on the day of her funeral ends movingly with the word 'Help!'.[1]

The rest of the Bishop's months away from London were occupied with the usual local and diocesan business. He visited Lady Lonsdale in July (she was also to die that winter), and in September her son, Lord Lonsdale, recently returned from 'his Travels'. In late August Dean Smalridge made a visit to Carlisle; while in the same month Nicolson reaffirmed his commitment to the Protestant Succession by refusing to sign 'the new County-Address' which omitted any reference to it. In December 1712, upon the rumour of a possible removal of Smalridge to Christ Church, Oxford,[2] both Todd and Tullie solicited Nicolson for the Dean's place. Of the former's request, the Bishop recorded, 'I shall be passive', and of the latter, 'Esto!'[3]

As we have seen, Oxford's peace policy had been decisively endorsed by parliament in June 1712, and soon after the prorogation the Lord Treasurer had weeded out most Whig MPs remaining in civil offices. Nicolson was probably not surprised, therefore, particularly as peace with France was expected to be proclaimed in the New Year[4] to receive a pressing summons from Tenison to be at the opening of the parliament, expected in late January 1713.[5] Fortunately for his personal circumstances, the long drawn-out Utrecht negotiations were beset by further delays (the main Anglo-French treaty was not signed until March 1713) and parliament did not

---

[1] Nicolson was still under a great 'affliction; occasioned by the Loss of the best friend, and dearest companion' on the eve of his journey south in 1713 (BL Harleian MS 3780, f. 275: N. to Wanley, 23 Feb. 1713).

[2] Bishop Humphries had died on 20 Nov. and Gibson thought Dean Atterbury of Christ Church might be removed to Hereford (Bodl. MS Add. A269, p. 19: Gibson to N., 22 Nov. 1712).

[3] *CW* iv (1904), 57–62.

[4] Nicolson was kept particularly well informed during his absence by a series of letters from Gibson, see Bodl. MS Add. A269, pp. 9–22.

[5] Ibid., p. 19: Gibson to N., 30 Nov. 1712.

eventually meet until 9 April, thus the Bishop was 'reprieved till the roads are better and days longer'.[6]

He began preparations for his journey on 20 February 1713, and set out on 26 February, travelling via Skipton and Tadcaster, where he met Archdeacon Pearson, and on to Bolton Percy, where he preached on Sunday, 1 March. He spent from 3 to 6 March at Lincoln, dealing with his Horncastle tenants. On 7 March he left for Oxford with his son John, arriving on 11 March. While in Oxford he visited the Ashmolean Museum, which he described as 'short of Dr Sloan's', dined in Queen's College with the Provost, visited Dean Smalridge, and generally inspected the university and met friends. Nicolson left for London on 13 March arriving the following day.[7]

On his second day in town, while making a courtesy call on his friend, Lord Halifax, Nicolson accidentally stumbled on a piece of high-level political intrigue. During the winter the Whig leaders, acknowledging now that they could not prevent the conclusion of peace, had begun to sponsor a propaganda campaign aimed at arousing the widest possible suspicion of the ministry's future intentions towards the Protestant Succession once the peace was concluded: 'to open people's eyes, and to show them the snares that are laid for them', as Sunderland put it.[8] The campaign was spearheaded by George Ridpath's *Flying Post*, and both Whig bishops, from their pulpits, and Whig judges, on circuit, lent effective support.[9] The Lord Treasurer was worried by the rumblings of discontent in his Cabinet left over from a dramatic clash with St John the previous autumn,[10] and also by the frustration of the Tory country members, who had been kicking their heels in town for weeks, enduring numerous prorogations and the jibes of their opponents.[11] By mid-March Oxford was approaching the session nervously. It may be that these worries, plus a natural instinct for securing his lines of retreat, account for Oxford's strange contacts with individual Whigs on 15 and 16 March, one of which Nicolson inadvertently interrupted,[12]

[6] Ibid., p. 21: same to same, 23 Jan., 17 Feb. 1713.

[7] Ware transcripts, xxviii, 87–91; *CW* iv (1904), 62–3.

[8] Leicester RO Finch MS Box VI, bundle 24: to Nottingham, 12 Nov. 1712.

[9] HMC *Portland MSS* v, 266–7; *Wentworth Papers*, p. 310; BL Add. MS 17677 GGG, f. 107: L'Hermitage, 20/31 Mar.

[10] G. Holmes, 'Harley, St. John and the Death of the Tory Party', in *Britain after the Glorious Revolution, 1689–1714*, ed. G. Holmes (1969), p. 224.

[11] *Wentworth Papers*, p. 318; *Swift Corr.* i, 337–40: Swift to Archbishop King, 28 Mar. 1713; BL Add. MS 17677 GGG, f. 107.

[12] See below, 16 Mar.; *Diary of Earl Cowper*, pp. 54, 56 (15 Mar. 1712). For what may be a slightly over-coloured Tory version of the meeting between Halifax and Oxford which Nicolson records, see HMC *7th Report*, Pt. I (1879), p. 508: Ralph Palmer to Viscount Fermanagh, 24 Mar. 1713.

and for a secret meeting between the prime minister and all the five
Junto lords, together with Cowper, which seems to have followed
immediately afterwards.[13] On the other hand, it is not out of the
question that the initiative for these meetings came from the Whig
side, and that Oxford was being sounded on the possibility of a bill
being introduced in the new session to disqualify the Pretender
regardless of his religion.[14] That there was ever a serious prospect
of a 'coalition' (to use the Bishop's word) at this juncture can hardly
be entertained. But it is understandable that dismayed Tories should
lend an ear to industriously circulated Whig reports that 'the lord
treasurer intends after the peace to declare for the Whigs' and should
resent 'this sort of trimming'.[15]

Only two days of the 1713 session diary have survived, so that
we can only guess at what Nicolson thought about the politics of
this session. The major events—the Scottish revolt against the Malt
Tax and the Union, in which the ministry narrowly survived an
attack in the Lords from the Whigs and Scots (1–8 June), the defeat
of the government's French Commerce Bill in the Commons by
Whigs and rebel Tories, and the successful Whig 'Lorraine motion'
against the Pretender carried in the Lords, at the beginning of July—
all took place after Nicolson's departure from London. He attended
the first day of parliamentary business on 9 April, and between then
and his last recorded attendance on 19 May, he attended fourteen
of the twenty-two sittings. The session ended on 16 July 1713,[16] but
Nicolson probably left London shortly after 19 May for he was
back in the North by the end of that month, and at Rose by 8 June
at the latest.[17]

While in London Nicolson had had time before his 'very abrupt'
departure to indulge his antiquarian interests. He had visited Wanley
and given him advice about his project for printing a volume of
English history from materials in the Cotton Library. He also
borrowed Wanley's Cotton catalogue, which he then left with his
landlord, Mr Fitzgerald, to return, having spent several hours noting
materials for his next publication, the second edition of *English*

[13] *Wentworth Papers*, p. 324.
[14] Halifax seems to be preparing the way for a meeting in his letters to Oxford of 8 and
9 Mar. (HMC *Portland MSS* v, 270–1), and Hanover had for some time been urging such a
bill on the Whig lords (James Macpherson, *Original Papers* (1775), ii, 464 ff: Robethon to
Grote, 3 Jan.–14 Feb. 1713, *passim*). Cowper records that at their interview on 15 Mar.
Oxford, having 'written down heads on a paper', spent most of the time protesting his
continuing firmness to the Protestant Succession (*Diary of Earl Cowper*, pp. 54, 56).
[15] *Wentworth Papers*, p. 324; *Swift Corr.* i, 337–40: Swift to King, 28 Mar. 1713.
[16] *LJ* xix, 511–615.
[17] Cumbria (Carlisle) RO Carleton Papers: Carleton to Lutwych, 6 June 1713; BL
Harleian MS 3780, ff. 181–2: N. to Wanley, 8 June 1713.

Historical Library. Nicolson's publisher also called on the Bishop two or three days before his departure in an attempt to persuade him to have this second edition prepared by the next parliamentary session, when the presses would be ready for him. Nicolson promised to return next winter with the necessary emendations and additions.[18]

[Mar.] 14. *Saturday*. At six in the evening, we got to London; and I to Westminster,[19] from my brother's supper.

[Mar.] 15. *Sunday*. Dined with Sister Rothery at Brother's. Evening, Single visit to the Bishop of Lincoln [Wake] who assures that a Tripple League is engaged in by the Czar, King of Prussia and House of Hannover. *Stabiliat Deus*!

[Mar.] 16. *Munday*. Morning, Visits paid to Dr Gibson, Archbishop of York [Sharp], Lord Lonsdale, Sir and Mr C. Musgrave and to Lord Hallifax; with whom Earls of Sunderland and Orford. All three (of us) withdrew, on Lord Treasurer's [Oxford's] demanding Audience. Hence a Report of Coalition. P.m., Mr Greenshields.

From this 16th of March 1712/13 to the 6th of July 1713 (Inclusive) see the Journal in separate sticked Leaves.[20]

---

[18] BL Harleian MS 3780, ff. 278, 281-2.

[19] Nicolson stayed with his former landlord Mr Fitzgerald in Old Palace Yard. BL Harleian MS 3780, ff. 277, 281.

[20] A marginal note in the Ware transcript reads: 'This is not preserved. The Diary begins again at Rose Castle, July 7 1713.'

Session 10

31 March 1714–14 June 1714

Nicolson remained in his diocese from May 1713 to March 1714. In July Dean Smalridge was removed to Christ Church, Oxford, to replace Atterbury who had been grudgingly elevated to the bishopric of Rochester. In October Nicolson had learned that Thomas Gibbon, Rector of Greystoke, was to be the new Dean, and he saw him installed at Carlisle on 23 October.[1] On 24 November the Bishop made a visitation of the Dean and Chapter, and in the following month became embroiled in difficulties between Dean Gibbon and Chancellor Tullie and the indomitable Dr Todd.

September 1713 had seen the country go to a general election in the flush of enthusiasm for a Tory peace, and Whig hopes of gaining ground in the Commons faded as the results came in. Sir James Montagu did not stand again for Carlisle, and on 7 September Nicolson saw 'Sir C. Musgrave and Col. Stanwix elected', '*Nemine contradicente*'.

Death was to stalk this winter as it had the previous one. 16 November brought 'the Gloomy Aniversary of my dear wife's death. *Nox mihi penitus insomnis*', while on 26 December, Nicolson heard of 'the surprizeing news of Lord Lonsdale's death of the small pox'. Nicolson had seen much of the young 2nd Viscount since his return to the North, and he regarded 'this sudden snatching away of a young Nobleman (of so promiseing Goodness) [as] a heavy Affliction to the whole Country. Righteous art thou, O Lord!' A month after Lonsdale's funeral, Nicolson received the news of the death of his old friend and mentor Archbishop Sharp of York.

December 1713 also saw Nicolson's unsuccessful courting of Lady Hasell, sister-in-law to Dean Gibbon. The lady had seemed to encourage the Bishop before she rebuffed him, which left Nicolson in a state of 'Stunning Shock', but which greatly pleased his children. On 24 February 1714 Nicolson ordained seven candidates for the ministry, among them his son Joseph; and on 2 March, the day before the Bishop's journey south, Joseph conducted the

[1] Gibbon's promotion to the deanery was backed by Sir Christopher Musgrave as well as by Smalridge. See J. V. Beckett and J. A. Downie, 'Letters from Sir Christopher Musgrave to the Earl of Dartmouth, 1711–15: New Light on the Politics of Opposition in Cumberland and Westmorland', *CW* lxxviii (1978), 124–5. Tullie, Nicolson's candidate, had received strong backing from several peers including Halifax (BL Loan 29/151/7: Halifax to [Oxford], 22 Aug. 1713).

marriage of his eldest sister Mary to Thomas Benson, the Bishop's chaplain.[2]

During his absence from London, Nicolson had again been kept well informed of political events by Gibson.[3] What Gibson did not report was the growing rift between Oxford and Henry St John, Viscount Bolingbroke, in which the latter had been defeated in a struggle shortly before the election, for control of the ministry. Nor is there any mention of the growing estrangement that autumn between Oxford and the Queen over the former's request for the vacant Newcastle title for his son, nor of the serious illness of the Queen in December 1713, all of which were to prove decisive in the following year.[4]

The unstable political situation at home, and continued uncertainty abroad, where negotiations at Utrecht between Britain and Spain dragged on, where Hanover was becoming increasingly alienated, and Bolingbroke (at least) appeared to be envisaging new and controversial alliances for Britain, led Tenison to rally his episcopal troops early in preparation for what was expected to be a stormy parliamentary session. At the start of November Gibson reported that 'the Bishops in Town on our side are Ely, Lichfield, Peterburrow, St Asaph, Llandaff, Norwich. Bangor has proposed to be dispensed with this Winter, but the excuse is not admitted.' He broadly hinted that Tenison 'is very glad that he can undertake for your company when the Parliament meets'. Nicolson seems to have ignored this pressure and remained at home, no doubt hoping that Gibson's subsequent forecast that the meeting might be postponed 'till March, or February at soonest' would prove true.[5] By mid-January, however, Gibson was pressing Nicolson to be in London by 16 February for the 'bare possibility [of a parliament] at a juncture soe critical on many accounts is a full warrant to importune their friends to be ready'.[6] Whig hopes of the co-operation of a substantial number of 'Hanover Tories', in the Commons as well as in the Lords, lent a special urgency to such whipping, but although Nicolson apparently undertook to comply, in the event he postponed his departure, first until 22 February, and then —doubtless because of his daughter's wedding—until 3 March.[7] Parliament had, in fact, opened on 16 February, and two weeks later

[2] *CW* iv (1904), 63–70.

[3] Bodl. MS Add. A269, pp. 23–32.

[4] G. Holmes, 'Harley, St John and the Death of the Tory Party', in *Britain after the Glorious Revolution*, ed. G. Holmes (1969), pp. 225–6.

[5] Bodl. MS Add. A269, pp. 26–7: Gibson to N., 3 and 14 Nov. 1713. Lincoln was in London by late Dec. and Bangor was on the road (ibid., p. 28: same to same, 26 Dec. 1713).

[6] Ibid., p. 29: same to same, 14 Jan. 1714.

[7] Ibid., pp. 29–30: same to same, 6 Feb. 1714; Christ Church Wake MS 6, f. 168: Gibson to Wake, 7 Feb. 1714.

Gibson had written urgently of the pending address of the Commons 'to express the satisfaction of the House in the provision already made for the Hanover Succession as full and sufficient', hoping his friend would not 'loose one moment'.[8]

Nicolson's entry in his diary recording his daughter's wedding on 2 March 1714 was intended to be his last: 'Here [he concluded] . . . ends this Journal: None being intended to be continued hereafter, save in my Almanack.'[9] This decision to abandon the keeping of a regular diary means that the brief entries of 'visits received and given at Westminster' in his Almanac[10] give very little indication of the crises of the spring of 1714. There is no mention of the expulsion of Richard Steele from the Commons on 14 March for writings accusing the Oxford ministry of Jacobite sympathies, a natural extension of a campaign begun in the winter of 1712/13;[11] no mention of the critical debates in the Lords in March and April on the state of the nation in which the ministry was under attack from Whigs and Hanoverian Tories; and only the most oblique reference (see below, 8 April) to the narrow victory of the ministry when both Houses in April voted the Protestant Succession not in danger under the present administration.[12] The one major issue which is explicitly mentioned in the 1714 Almanac is the Schism Bill; but although it was a measure in which Nicolson obviously took a keen interest, it frustratingly receives only brief notices of its progress through the Lords.[13]

The prime object of this vicious bill was to strike at the roots of religious 'schism' by making it impossible for the dissenters to educate their children in their own schools or above all to train up a new generation of pastors in their own academies. But it had a dual political purpose also; to heal the breach among the Tories and to place Oxford, who was deeply committed to preserving the Toleration, in a serious dilemma. Although the moving spirit behind the bill

---

[8] Bodl. MS Add. A269, p. 32: Gibson to N., 2 Mar. 1714.

[9] *CW* iv (1904), 70; Ware transcripts, xxviii, 141.

[10] The 1714 Almanac is in vol. xxx of the Ware transcripts, and the brief 'diary' entries for the parliamentary session occupy pp. 6–14. There is no account of Nicolson's journey to London in March.

[11] There is, however, a list of MPs headed 'Mr Steele's Friends' in the Ware transcripts, xxxi, 48–54. It is the same as the list printed in *Parl. Hist.* vi, 1282–3, except that Nicolson's list is in alphabetical order and misses out four names: Edward Hopkins, Aubrey Porter, George Baillie, and John Campbell.

[12] There is some evidence that Nicolson opposed the calling of the Duke of Cambridge (the future George II) to parliament as a safeguard to the Protestant Succession (TCD MS 2532, p. 285: King to N., 8 May 1714). The Hanoverian envoy Schütz's demand for the writ on 12 Apr. had split the cabinet and angered the Queen. See Trevelyan, *Queen Anne*, iii, 277–9.

[13] See below, 4–11 June.

was Bolingbroke, the initiative probably came from, and the bill was probably drafted by, Atterbury. Formally introduced into the Commons on 21 May 1714 by Sir William Wyndham, friend of Bolingbroke, this ultra-Tory measure (described by Wharton as 'the most unreasonable, unchristian, and impolitick bill, that ever went through any English Parliament')[14] stated that all teachers, whether in schools or academies, were to be licensed by the diocesan bishop according to the intent of the Act of Uniformity. Further, they had to produce a certificate of having received the Anglican sacrament and to pledge to conform to the liturgy of the Church of England. Any licensed teacher who subsequently went to a Dissenting conventicle was liable to three months' imprisonment. The bill passed with a majority of 109 in the Commons on 1 June. Before its first reading in the Lords, Atterbury had agreed to an amendment proposed by Lord Anglesey that a new clause extending the scope of the bill to Ireland should be added.[15]

Bolingbroke himself introduced the bill into the Lords on 4 June in the face of opposition from the Junto lords and Lord Nottingham. In the Committee of the Whole House on 11 June, chaired by Archbishop Dawes of York, the clause extending the bill's operation to Ireland was added by a vote of seventy-five to seventy-four, Nicolson voting with the Whigs against the clause. Nicolson was probably under great pressure from his episcopal Whig colleagues (on 31 May Tenison, who opposed it, had summoned Nicolson to attend the House upon the bill). But while he supported them on 11 June, his general support, as one would expect from his previous stance on religious matters, lay with the bill. Nicolson saw Archbishop Tenison on the afternoon of 11 June, and was probably pressed to vote against his inclinations and the bill as a whole.[16] This may well have proved too much for him. His duty done to his colleagues on 11 June he hurriedly decided to leave London, and on 12 June visited Wake to leave his proxy. There is no indication in the Almanac of any other reason for this abrupt departure, as Nicolson was to proceed northwards at a leisurely pace, leaving London on 14 June, travelling via Lincoln, and not reaching Rose until 23 June. On 15 June the Schism Bill passed its third reading in the Lords by five

---

[14] BL Add. MS 57861, f. 173: Wharton to Coningsby, 15 June 1714.

[15] *CJ* xvii, 660; HMC *Portland MSS* vii, 186; Bennett, *Tory Crisis*, p. 178.

[16] It is strange that at this critical juncture Tenison, who appears not to have attended parliament during this session (BL Loan 29/8: Newsletter, 15 June 1714) probably owing to illness, did not provide a proxy. Neither did two other Whig bishops, Lloyd of Worcester and Fowler of Gloucester. There was no inconsistency in Nicolson's opposition to the bill's extension to Ireland while supporting the bill. The bill would divide the Protestant minority in Ireland and thus weaken the Protestant Succession.

votes, among which was Nicolson's proxy vote, cast by Wake in opposition to his own. This was contrary to the usual contemporary practice, though not unconstitutional,[17] and it can only have happened on explicit instructions from Nicolson, in full knowledge that the parties were so even that his vote might decide the bill's fate.[18]

Parliament was not prorogued until 9 July, and the fireworks did not end with the Schism Act. In July the Whigs opened an attack, with Oxford's connivance, on the illicit profits of Bolingbroke and his friends from the Spanish trade. Only the personal intervention of Queen Anne to prorogue parliament (she was concerned not just for Bolingbroke but for Lady Masham) stopped the inquiry. Gibson, as usual, kept Nicolson informed, but wrote (perhaps with a touch of resentment) 'your friends could have wished you at Westminster to give your testimony against the Spanish Treaty of Commerce concerted at Madrid'.[19] By some Whigs the Bishop's defection at so critical a juncture, with the ministry's fate and the fortunes of both parties in the balance, was not to be readily forgotten.

Visits received and given at Westminster.[20]

March 31. Morning, Dr Lancaster and I to the Bishop of London [Robinson], Archbishop of York [Dawes][21] and Lord Lonsdale,

[17] The only other known example, contemporary with Nicolson, of a proxy vote being cast on the opposite side of a division to the vote of the proxy-holder was on 20 May 1712 when 'Orkneys proxy [was] given by Loudoun against the [Land Grants] Bill tho he was for it himself'. Mellerstain Letters, v: [George Baillie] to [Roxburghe], 22 May 1712. In the sixteenth century, however, it was not uncommon for bishops to leave their proxies with fellow bishops who held opposing views. See V. F. Snow, 'Proctoral Representation in the House of Lords during the Reign of Edward VI', *Journal of British Studies*, vii, no. 2 (1969), 11.

[18] On 15 June 1714 the Lords voted on the third reading of the Schism Bill as follows: *Contents* fifty-six plus twenty-one proxies (seventy-seven), *Not Contents* forty-nine plus twenty-three proxies (seventy-two). The voting of the bishops on 15 June was probably identical to that on 11 June, with the exception of Nicolson's switch. The Earl of Notting-ham's estimate of the probable voting pattern for 15 June (Leicestershire RO Finch MS P.P. 161; see also Holmes, *British Politics*, pp. 423–4, 434–5) gives the bishops' votes as the same as the vote on 11 June given by Nicolson himself, with the exception of the Bishop of Winchester whom Nottingham classes as 'doubtful'. There is a list (Bodl. MS Fol. θ 666, fol. 68^V) which purports to give the voting pattern of the bishops for 15 June, though it incorrectly gives the overall voting figures as seventy-nine against seventy-one. This list corresponds with Nottingham's estimate for 15 June and with Nicolson's list for 11 June except in two respects. Winchester is given as voting with the *Contents* (Tories) as he had on 11 June. Nicolson also is shown as voting with the *Contents* (Tories).

[19] Bodl. MS Add. A269, p. 32: Gibson to N., 5 July 1714.

[20] At this point in the Ware transcripts there is a marginal note: 'Where spaces left, the entries of no interest.' Nicolson had taken the oaths for this session on 15 Mar. *LJ* xix, 636.

[21] John Robinson was confirmed as Bishop of London on 13 Mar. 1714 (and though

for Oxford. Dined Dr Gibson and Mr R. Smith. P.m. Dr Kennet, in the Park, with news of Ruptures.[22]

April 1. Morning, To the Bishop of Bangor [Evans], with Mr L. Lloyd, Great Great Grandson of Humphrey.[23] Com[mittee] at Whitehall. P.m. From Mr Campbel.

[Apr.] 4. Morning, With the Bishops of Hereford [Bisse] and Chester [Gastrell] to the latter's Consecration. Dined At the Archbishop of York. Evening, Visits to the Bishops of Rochester [Atterbury][24] and St Asaph [Fleetwood].

[Apr.] 8. Morning, Dr Gibson, Bishops of Bangor and Landaff [Tyler]. P.m. To Archbishop of Canterbury [Tenison] with the woful Journal, of all safe.[25]

[Apr.] 12. Morning, From Thomas Bell, Bishop of Bangor, Archbishop of York, Sir James Mountague, Dr Yates and wife. To Bishops of Bristol [Smalridge] and Lincoln [Wake], St Asaph's Bill,[26] the Queen with Address.[27] Dined Mr R. Smith; with whom (Evening) at Dr Hickes's.

no longer Lord Privy Seal, he was still called to the Cabinet), and Sir William Dawes, formerly Bishop of Chester, was promoted to Archbishop of York on 9 Mar. Dawes had emerged since 1713 as a prominent Hanoverian Tory.

[22] This may be a reference to Kennett's forthright views on the Hanoverian Succession which had made him unpopular at Court. He had published several pamphlets defending the Protestant Succession and on 30 Mar. 1714 he preached a Spital sermon entitled 'The Properties of Christian Charity' (published 19 Apr. 1714), which involved him in the associated lay baptism controversy. See Bennett, *White Kennett*, pp. 125-7.

[23] Humphrey Lloyd (1610–89), Bishop of Bangor, 1673–89.

[24] Francis Atterbury had held the bishopric since June 1713. Lord Dartmouth, at that time still Secretary of State, later recalled: 'I never knew the queen do anything with so much reluctancy, as the signing of his *congé d'élire*. She told me he would be as meddling and troublesome as the bishop of Salisbury, had more ambition, and was less tractable.' Note to Burnet, *History*, vi, 176.

[25] The allusion is to the proceedings of the last few days in the Lords, beginning on 5 Apr. with the great debate on the government's motion 'that the Protestant Succession was *not in danger* under her Majesty's government', in which the crucial vote gave the ministry a majority of fourteen, despite a notable defection of Hanoverian Tories, and ending on 8 Apr., with a Whig-framed address for the apprehension of the Pretender which was watered down in the House, and 'four stragling lords returned to us [the ministry]— Lord Anglsea, Arch Bishop of York, Lord Cartwright [Carteret] and Lord Ashburnham'. *Wentworth Papers*, p. 367: Peter Wentworth to Earl of Strafford, 8 Apr. 1714.

[26] A 'Bill for taking away mortuaries within the diocese of St Asaph, and giving a recompense therefor to the bishops of the said diocese' was extended to the other three Welsh dioceses in May 1714, becoming the 'Mortuaries in the Welsh Diocese Act'. See HMC *Lords MSS* x, 235-6.

[27] Address of the Lords, voted on 8 Apr., for a proclamation for apprehending the Pretender in case he should attempt to land, and asking the Queen to renew her insistence

[Apr.] 16. Morning, Mr Perkins and examiner, Mrs Williamson, Mr Brent, Jeremy Nicolson, Bishop of Bangor. Evening (after Ruined party) at my Brothers with E. Nevinson.

[Apr.] 20. Morning, Dr White, Dr Gibson. To Whitehall and the House. P.m. Mr Wanley, without pique.

[Apr.] 23. Morning, Bishop of Landaff, Archdeacon Gibson, D[ean] Gibbon,[28] Br[other] Nevinson. Dined Dr Joseph Smith. P.m. To Mr Grisdale, Sister Rothery and Brother Joseph. Coronation.

May 6. Morning, Mr Henley, Junior, Mr Hutton, Mr Lawson. Dined Brother Nevinson and his son John, with the Queen's Letter. Evening With the Dean, &c, at Mr Lawson's Ch[ambers] in Grey's Inn.

[May] 9. Morning, I preached in Basingstreet. Dined (at Mr Brent's) with Dean Kennet, Dr Rotherick, &c. P.m. I preached again at the Mineries. Evening, at Mrs Wester's and Mr Perry's.

[May] 12. Morning, Cousin R. Gilpin. I read prayers a second time, at the House. Dined at Sir C. Musgrave's with our Dean, Mr Lawson, Mr Fleetwood and Brother Nevinson. Evening, with Dr Lancaster and's Citron Water.

[May] 13. Morning, Dr Scott, Mr Madox, Dean Gibbon, Dr Todd, Mr Lamb, Dr Gibson, Sir C. Musgrave, Brother Nevinson. At the House the Divorce Bill[29] ordered to be Ingrossed. Adjourned to the 26th. Evening Dr G[ibson] again, with news from Han[ove]r.

[May] 18. Visit to Mr Walker at Hillington. ND. Hedge-Hogg-Holly, Bay 20 J.h. and 2 in Circumf[erence] Pomegranates. To me, Mr A. Lowther,[30] &c.

[May] 19. Morning, Jeremy Nicolson, Mr Chamberlayne, Fr[ank] Briscoe, Dr Todd, Dr Gibson, Dr Joseph Smith. To Monsieur Cranenburg,[31] Lord Lonsdale, &c. P.m. With son John to his Aunt, the

on his removal from Lorraine and to desire the Emperor and other princes to guarantee the Protestant Succession. The Queen gave her answer on 13 Apr. See *LJ* xix, 650, 654.

[28] See above, sessional intro., p. 603.

[29] The Loggin Divorce Bill. See HMC *Lords MSS* x, 313–14; *LJ* xix, 689.

[30] ?Anthony Lowther (b. after 1694–1741), third son of 1st Viscount Lonsdale; MP for Cockermouth, 1721–2, Westmorland, 1722–41. See Sedgwick, ii, 226.

[31] Christopher Frederick Kreyenberg or Kreienberg, the Hanoverian resident in England, 1710–14. He had the entry to prominent Whig circles and was a shrewd and closely informed observer of British politics, as his surviving dispatches, in the Staatsarchiv Hannover, reveal.

Tower and its Rarities, Exchange, &c. Evening, Two Sons and J. Rothery at my Lodgeings.

[May] 22. Morning, Dr Todd, my sons, &c. To Dean Kennet and the Bishop of Lincoln, with (his preacher) Mr Nicols.[32] Dined At Chelsea, with my boyes. P.m. To the Bishop of London, on his Letter for Confirmation.

[May] 23. Morning, Dr Kennet, goeing to the Ordination. I preached (and administered the Sacrament) at the Savoy. Dined At Cousin R. N[icolson]'s with Mr Saler, son Joseph, &c.

[May] 24. Morning, My sons, Mrs Hutton, Fr[ank] Briscoe, Mr Perkins, Cousin James Nicolson, Dean Kennet, Dr Lancaster. To Bishop of Lincoln's Institution, &c. of my son:[33] Mr Reading, with my copy: Dr Waugh. P.m. with our Dean to Dr Woodward, Lady Musgrave of H[ayton].[34] Thomas Bell. The *Vine*. NB. I waited on Mr Pelham[35] who promised G. Spooner E. Lamplough's place.[36]

[May] 25. Morning, Son Joseph for Lincoln immediately. Mr Madox. I confirmed at St James's. Dined (with the Bishops of Hereford, St David's [Ottley] and Bristol) at the Bishop of London's. Evening, Letters.

[May] 26. Morning, Son and Nephew, Dr Todd, with whom to Mr R. Smith. Archbishop of York, Lord Halifax. House, a Roguish Cause.[37] P.m. Mr R. Smith, Dean of Limrick [Story]: with whom to Dr Gibson's, Mr Child's,[38] my Brother's, Mr Lowther's and the *Bell*.

[32] Possibly Samuel Nichols, Rector of Gayton-le-Marsh, Lincolnshire, 1701-18. See Sykes, *Wake*, i, 151.

[33] Wake recorded in his diary for 20 May 1714: 'Bishop of Carlisle with his Son: the Gentleman to be Ordained, I sent them to the Dean of Peterborough who having examined them dined with Me.' Lambeth Palace MS 1770, f. 145. Joseph Nicolson, the bishop's son, was to be preferred to the living of Mareham, near Horncastle, in the diocese of Lincoln, but in the gift of the Bishops of Carlisle. Nicolson recorded in one of his almanacs that his son's preferment to Mareham had cost him £49 1s. 6d. Ware transcript, xxix, 3.

[34] Dorothy Jones (d. 1718), widow of Sir Richard Musgrave, 2nd Bt. of Hayton (d. 1710).

[35] Henry Pelham, of Stanmer, Sussex, MP for Lewis, 1695-1701, 1701-2; Clerk of the Pells in the Exchequer, 1698-1721.

[36] A 'Mr Lamplugh' is noted as one of the ten ordinary clerks in the Exchequer Pells Office in c.Dec. 1714. By 1716 a George Spooner is listed as a clerk in the Pells Office. *The Laws of Honour* (1714), p. 43; Chamberlayne, *Present State 1716*, p. 115.

[37] Possibly a reference to the case involving the Duchess of Hamilton and Lady Mohun, the aftermath of the bitter lawsuit between the two families and the appalling duel in 1712 in which both the ladies' husbands had been killed. Lord Mohun's estate had been taken by force by the Duchess. See HMC *Lords MSS* x, 314-15.

[38] ?Robert Child (d. 1721), City merchant, son of Sir Francis Child, the great Tory banker, MP for Helston, Dec. 1710-13, Devizes, 1713-15.

[May] 29. Morning, Sermon by Bishop of Ch[este]r. Dined with the Boyes, at the *Dog*. P.m. With the Bishop of Winton [Trelawney] at Lambeth; and with Dr Gibson at Clapham.

[May] 31. Morning, Bishop of Bangor, with a 3d pretender; Mrs Hutton, a Guinnea strong; Mr James Gordon, for a Return to Scotland. Dined (with Mr Nicols), at the Archbishop of York's at Kensington. NB. Letter from princess Sophia. Evening, At the *Bell*, with Mr Windham and F. G[   ]. Message from Archbishop of Canterbury by Dr Clarke, to attend the Schism-Bill.[39]

June 1. Morning, Mr Thoresby, Mr Grainger, Mr Wilson, Dr Joseph Smith. House, Scotch Cause.[40] Aff[irmed]. Dined Mr Nichols and the Boyes. P.m. comm[union] at St Paul's; Bank-Bill received at Mr Ashurst's; Visit to my sister from Kensington.

[June] 2. Morning, To the Boyes, Cousin Jane Scot, Bishop of Ely, *Three Cupps*, Mr Reading, Lord Carlile. House, Lord H[aversham]'s Cause.[41] P.m. Mr R. Smith. Coffee, &c. from Mrs Constable.

[June] 3. Morning, Joseph Briscoe, Dr Gibson, &c. To the Bishops of Lincoln and St Asaph. Dined At the *Greyhound* with my Brother, Sister, Son, Niece and nephews. Evening, Farewell to the Boyes, for Oxon.

[June] 4. Morning, Three Mr Bells, Mr Madox, Bishop of Bangor, Dean Gibbon. House, Schism-Bill, 1st Reading.[42] P.m. At Dr Gibson's with Dean Story. Evening, At my Brother's.

[June] 5. Morning, Mr Anderson, Mr R. Smith, Mr Greenshields. P.m. second coach-Hireing.

[June] 8. Morning, With Mr Smith to Lord Howard of Escrick, Dr Todd, Lord Halifax's Study. P.m. With the Stewards of the Clergy Comp[any] to Lambeth.

[39] For this controversial anti-dissenting bill, anathema to the lay Whigs, and Nicolson's attitude to it, see above, sessional intro., pp. 605–7. Proceedings in the Lords can be traced in HMC *Lords MSS* x, 334–47.

[40] See ibid., pp. 58–9.

[41] See ibid., p. 316.

[42] There was a long debate, the main speeches in which are summarised, from Boyer's contemporary account, in *Parl. Hist.* vi, 1351–4. The House did not divide against proceeding to a second reading; but it did reject, by seventy-two votes to sixty-six, a petition from the Presbyterians to be heard by counsel against the bill, some of Lord Oxford's friends voting with the Whigs, and the Treasurer abstaining.

[June] 9. Morning, Mrs Curwen on her Aunt M's petition; Dr Hutchinson,[43] for Dom[estic] Chaplain to the Bishop of London, Archdeacon Gibson goeing to Convocation. House, In a grand Committee; amending the Schism-Bill,[44] *prima vice*. Evening, Supper, at the *Dog*, with the Dean of Limrick [Story] and Mr R. Smith.

[June] 10. Morning, Cousin R. Nicolson, with his nephew's petitions; E. Selby, for Poultry-Custome. Dined At the Bishop of Lincoln's. House, Committee. Evening Dean of Limrick, &c.

[June] 11. Morning, Brother Joseph with Mr Line's 10 *l*.; Dean Gibbon; Mr Ch[arles] Howard; Lord Carlile. House, Schism-Bill by Instruction extended to Ireland.[45] P.m. With the Archbishop of Canterbury, Dr Gibson and the Dean of Arches [Bettesworth], now Judge of the Prerogative. Item. At my Brother's.

June 11, 1714.
Schism-Bill extended to Ireland, by Instructions, the Question being carried by 75 against 74. Amongst the former

Archbishop of York	*Not Contents*
London	Ely
Durham	Bangor
Winchester	Carlile
Bath and Wells.	Lincoln
Hereford	Landaff
St David's	St Asaph
Rochester	*Proxies —*
Bristol	Litchfield
Chester	Sarum
Proxies	Peterborough
Chichester	Oxon
Exeter	Norwich

[43] Probably Michael Hutchinson.

[44] There had been a short second reading debate on 7 June, during which it was agreed to insert a clause in favour of French Protestant churches and schools. The really vital struggle took place in committee on 9 June (Archbishop Dawes in the chair), when the bill was under scrutiny for seven hours, and on the next two days. The Whigs and their ally, Nottingham, set out to emasculate the bill clause by clause, and the Lord Treasurer, drawing on all his reserves of management skills and using his relatives and close personal followers (e.g. Foley and Poulet) as 'front men', lent them all the covert support he could.

[45] One of only two major amendments lost by the opposition. See above, sessional intro., p. 606; HMC *Lords MSS* x, 345–7; *Parl. Hist.* vi, 1355; *LJ* xix, 714. The figures were *Contents* seventy-five (including twenty-one proxies) to *Not Contents* seventy-four (twenty-two proxies).

Absent
Archbishop of Canterbury
Worcester
Glocester

[June] 13. Morning, Adieu to Westminster. Dined At my Brother's. Evening, With him and Mr Nicols to the *Three Cups*.

[June] 14. *Anno Consecrationis 13⁰*. Morning, Adieu to London in the Lincoln-Coach, with Capt Foulks and's wife (sister to Col. Bladen) Mrs Birch, &c. Evening, At Supper, &c. with Mr Thomson of Humbleton.[46]

---

[46] Nicolson travelled via Huntingdon, Stamford, and Grantham, arriving at Lincoln on 16 June, where he met his son John. Nicolson spent the following day in Lincoln, leaving on 18 June for a visit to Archdeacon Pearson at Bolton Percy, travelling via Gainsborough and Doncaster. On 21 June he set out for home via Boroughbridge, Richmond, and Penrith, arriving at Rose on 23 June. Ware transcript, xxx, 14–15.

25 March 1715–9 September 1715

Seven weeks after Nicolson had left London, Queen Anne died on 1 August 1714 and an era came to an end. The feared Jacobite reaction did not take place and King George I succeeded peacefully to his kingdom. His proclamation in Carlisle on 4 August elicited the comment 'Servet Deus' from Nicolson. The new King arrived in England on 18 September. But although Gibson urged his friend to hasten to London to greet him—for a translation to a more congenial see must surely be in the offing[1]—Nicolson decided to spend the winter at home, and on 20 October attended 'the Bonfires on the Coronation, Fireworks &c.'. However, he had reason to hope for rewards from the new regime, as a loyal friend to the Protestant Succession, as a good Whig in politics (despite his support for the Schism Act), and as one of the most active and long-serving bishops on the bench. Yet despite the triumph of the Whigs in government on the accession of George I, Nicolson was to be disappointed. Only the onerous and financially unrewarding post of Lord Almoner came his way, and this not until February 1716.[2]

The winter of 1714/15 was spent quietly attending to diocesan, political, and domestic chores. Nicolson reported in October 1714 that 'We continue here in the most profound quiet as to matters of election, every one taking it for granted there's no room for the disturbers of our peace to fix a foot amongst us'.[3] And so it proved. The general election of early 1715 went off quietly in both the county and in Carlisle. Both constituencies were uncontested and on 29 January Thomas Stanwix and William Strickland were returned for the city, while James Lowther and the 'Hanoverian Tory' Gilfred Lawson duly renewed their old tenancy of the two Cumberland seats on 8 February.[4] Nicolson had not been inactive in the elections, having deployed his interest successfully against Sir Christopher Musgrave, whom he persuaded not to stand, and supported Strickland, a Whig client of Lord Carlisle.[5]

[1] Bodl. MS Add. A269, pp. 33–4: Gibson to N., 10 Aug. 1714.
[2] See above, p. 58.
[3] HMC *Lonsdale MSS*, p. 248: N. to James Lowther, 9 Oct. 1714.
[4] *CW* v (1905), 3; Sedgwick, i, 221–2. The old parliament had been dissolved on 5 Jan. 1715.
[5] See the Nicolson/Musgrave letters printed in Ferguson, *Cumberland and Westmorland MP's*, pp. 101–4.

Nicolson had intended to be in London before the opening of the first Hanoverian parliament, which was expected early in April 1715. At the beginning of March, however, he heard from Gibson that the session would open on 17 March.[6] The Bishop left Rose on 11 March and travelled to York via Kendal (where he spent two days, one ordaining for the Bishop of Chester) and Castle Howard, the home of Lord Carlisle. Reaching York on 16 March, Nicolson spent one day there, leaving for Horncastle in Lincolnshire (where the manor was owned by the Bishops of Carlisle) on 18 March. He stayed three days at Horncastle, preaching for his son Joseph at Mareham. He left for London on 22 March, travelling via Bourne, Caxton, Royston, and Enfield, reaching the capital on 25 March, and taking the oaths in the Lords five days later.[7]

The first session under the new dynasty proved less stormy than many had expected, the Tories being chastened by their heavy losses at the recent general election from which they had emerged with barely 220 seats in the House of Commons, including Scottish members. The main generator of political excitement was the parliamentary attack by the Whigs on the fallen Tory ministers, Oxford and Bolingbroke, on the former Captain-General, Ormond, and on the chief Tory negotiator at Utrecht, Strafford. The first three were impeached by the Commons for treason, on 22 June and 2 July 1715, while Strafford was impeached on 3 July for high crimes and misdemeanours. Bolingbroke and Ormond escaped to France and were later proceeded against by act of attainder. The impeachment of Strafford was soon dropped. Only Oxford's impeachment proceeded, to the point of his being imprisoned in the Tower on 16 July 1715. After a two-year ordeal, he was at length acquitted by the Lords, on the failure of the Commons to put in an appearance against him, on 1 July 1717.[8]

Nowhere in the diary nor in any of his letters that have survived[9] does Nicolson display any opinions on Oxford's impeachment. Though a political opponent of the Lord Treasurer's while the latter had held the highest office, he had a genuine respect for Oxford as a collector and a person interested in antiquarianism, and during this session Nicolson twice visited his library. It seems very probable that

[6] Bodl. MS Add. A269, p. 38; Gibson to N., 1 Mar. 1715.

[7] Ware transcripts, xxi, 15–16. Parliament had met, as expected, on 17 Mar. (*LJ* xx, 21, 34).

[8] A detailed 'diary' of the impeachment proceedings from 9 July to 3 Sept. 1715 was kept by Bishop Wake: Christ Church Wake MS 19, ff. 1–6.

[9] Nicolson had written to Archbishop King in Dublin on 7 July 1715 about the impending impeachments but the letter has not survived among King's correspondence (TCD MS 2533, pp. 15–17: King to N., 16 July 1715).

Nicolson shared the attitude of Bishop Wake, that 'tho' I have all along had a very ill Opinion not only of the measures of the latter part of Her Majesty's reign, but of those who advised, and executed them . . . I could have been content to have let their faults die with their Interest . . .'.[10]

[Mar.] 25. Ten miles (post) to London; dined with my sister; Her Birth-Day.

[Mar.] 26. Private in my Lodgeings. Seen only by my Brother and Jeremy Nicolson.

[Mar.] 27. Still retired: But visitted by Mr Dowson, Mr Greenshields, and Dr Gibson.

[Mar.] 28. Morning, Visits to Archbishop of York [Dawes], Lord P[ortland]'s and Lord Hallifax in the House. Dined with Mr Greenshields. P.m. waiting (with Dr Potter, Dr Kennett and Dr Gibson) on my Lord of Canterbury [Tenison]. Visits from Mr J. Leneve,[11] Dean of Limrick [Story], Mr Chamberlayne, Mr Wilkins.

[Mar.] 29. I had the Honour to Kiss the King's hand, introduced by Lord Hallifax who Kindly reminded His Majesty of our Oxford Acquaintance 34 years agoe.[12] Lords, of both Nations, very obligeing. Visits from Mr Wilson,[13] Brigadier Stanwix, Dr Gee, Cousin R. N[icolson], Mr Chamb[erlayn]—To Lord Chancellor [Cowper] and Bishop of Lincoln [Wake].

[Mar.] 30. Morning Visits to Lords P[rivy] S[eal] [Wharton], Sunderland and Portland: From Drs Gibson, Waugh, Lancaster; Messrs Wilson, Strickland,[14] Browham, Manwaring, &c. Oaths taken at the House. Lord Bollingbroke gone.[15] Evening—To R. N[icolson], Isaac Tullie and Mr Browham.

[10] Christ Church Wake MS 19, f. 1ᵛ.
[11] John Le Neve (1679–1741), antiquary, Rector of Thornton-le-Moor, Lincolnshire, 1721–41, published *Fasti Ecclesiae Anglicanae* (1716), and *Monumenta Anglicana* (1717).
[12] George I, then hereditary prince (and heir to the dukedom) of Hanover, had briefly visited England in 1680–1, and he had been welcomed to Oxford by Nicolson in late 1680. At that time Nicolson had recently returned from a trip to Leipzig. See Bodl. MS Add. A269, pp. 33–4: Gibson to N., 10 Aug. 1714; James, p. 224; on the English visit in general, R. Hatton, *George I: Elector and King* (1978), pp. 39–40.
[13] Possibly Daniel Wilson, MP for Westmorland, see Appendix A.
[14] Possibly William Strickland, MP for Carlisle, see Appendix A.
[15] Bolingbroke had finally decided to flee the wrath of the Whig ministry after they

[Mar.] 31. Morning, Mrs Hutton, Mr Martin, Mr Green, Sir R. Sandford, Dean Story. Dr Simcock,[16] Dr Gee, Mr Maturin,[17] W. Tullie &c. Dined. Brother's Wedding-day. P.m. Dr Kennett and Dr Gibson.

April 1. Col. Graham, Mr Wilson, Mr Blencow, R. Eglesfield, C. Lister, Dean of Cloyne, Dr Gee, &c. Dined, Dean of Limrick and Dr Gibson. Evening, with Is[rael] Fielding at Dr Lancaster's as m[orning?] with Mr Greenshields at General Nicolson's.

[Apr.] 2. Morning, To Lords Lonsdale, Portland, &c. P.m. Archbishop of Canterbury cheerful. I stand fair.

[Apr.] 3. Morning, With the Bishop of Bangor [Evans]. P.m. at Dr Gee's, Dr Smith, Mr Wilkins and Mr Holms.

[Apr.] 4. Dr K[ennett], Dr Gibson, Dr Hutchinson, Col. Graham, &c. House, Committee on the standing Orders.[18] Evening, at the Tower.

[Apr.] 5. Morning, By Mr Wilkins, Dr Gibson, Mr Madox, &c. To Lord Hallifax Whitehall, Brigadier Stanwix, Mrs Blencow. Evening, Mr R. Smith.

[Apr.] 6. By Dr G[ibson] and Dean Story. To the Bishops of Norwich [Trimnell] and Sarum [Talbot], Mrs Todd, Coll. Grahame, Lord Wharton, Mrs Story, Lord Lonsdale, &c. House, Committee and Lord Hallifax's Apol[ogy]. P.m. Rainy.

[Apr.] 7. Dined with the Archbishop of York at Kensington. Sir W. Lawson from Oxford.

[Apr.] 8. Committee (for Orders of the House) dropt. Evening, at Salisbury-Court.

had asked him to surrender his own papers, notably his secretarial correspondence of the years 1710–14. He left for France on 27 Mar. 1715 just in time to avoid arrest, while Oxford, true to his native stoicism and to the Providentialism of his Puritan stock, stayed to face his persecutors, telling his friends, 'I know how to die, but cannot fly'. See H. T. Dickinson, *Bolingbroke* (1970), p. 135; HMC *Portland MSS* v, 665–6.

[16] Thomas Simcocks (d. 1718), Dean of Cloyne 1714–18.

[17] Possibly Peter Maturin (d. 1741), son of the Revd. Gabriel Maturin, a Huguenot preacher in Paris, who was later Dean of Killala 1724–41.

[18] Nicolson had been appointed to the committee to consider the standing orders of the House on 1 Apr. 1715. *LJ* xx, 35.

[Apr.] 9. Carryed by Bishop of B[angor?] to the Prince and princess.[19] Dined With the Chaplains.

[Apr.] 10. Morning, St James's. Archbishop of York preached on *Philippians* 2, 5 for Christian Resolution.

[Apr.] 11. To Baron Mountague,[20] Lord L[onsdale], Sister Rothery; at the House petition of Lord Digby. Dined with me Bishop of Norwich, Mr R. N[icolson].

[Apr.] 12. All day at home. Visitted by Mr G. Lawson, Mr Madox, Dr Smith, &c. Lord Wharton, Privy Seal dyed.[21]

[Apr.] 13. Dr Brydges[22] preached at St James's; where the young princesses not waited on, by the Bishop of Norwich's withdrawing.

[Apr.] 14. Dined with me Dr Gibson; with whom to the Bishops of Norwich, Lincoln [Wake] and Litchfield [Hough].

[Apr.] 15. Good Friday. I preached, &c. at St Bride's. P.m. at St Paul's. Dined with my Brother.

[Apr.] 16. Morning, At Lord Oxford's Library.[23] Dined with me Mr Greenshields with whom p.m. at the Glassworks, &c. at Foxhall [Vauxhall?].

[Apr.] 17. Easter-day. I preached at Lambeth. P.m. with the Archbishop of Canterbury's Becofigo's.[24]

[Apr.] 18. Morning, Whitehal. Dined with Mrs Townley, Mr Carpenter, &c. P.m. Kensington.

[19] Prince George of Wales (the future George II) and Princess Caroline.

[20] Sir James Montagu, appointed a Baron of the Court of Exchequer on 22 Nov. 1714.

[21] The Marquess of Wharton had been in indifferent health for some months; but his friends believed that his end was hastened by a bitter quarrel with his son Philip, who contracted a disastrous Fleet marriage in Feb. 1715. See J. Carswell, *The Old Cause* (1954), pp. 125–6.

[22] Possibly Henry Brydges (*c*.1676–1728), son of Lord Chandos, educated Oxford, DD 1711, Rector of Broadwell-with-Adlestrop, Gloucestershire, 1699–1717, and of Amersham, Buckinghamshire, 1721; Chaplain to Queen Anne; Archdeacon of Rochester, 1720.

[23] He took with him a catalogue of the Welsh and Cornish manuscripts which had belonged to the late Edward Lhywd. See *Diary of Humphrey Wanley*, ed. C. E. and R. C. Wright (1966), i, 9. Nicolson was apparently contemplating buying Lhywd's collection. See ibid., p. 10; E. Rees and G. Walter, 'The dispersion of the manuscripts of Edward Lhwyd', *Welsh History Review*, vii (1974), 151–4.

[24] Beccafico is a small migrant bird which was esteemed as a delicacy.

[Apr.] 19. Dined at North-holt, with Dr Lancaster, Mr Grisdale and Mr Sands, &c. &c.

[Apr.] 20. Morning, Visited by Dr Brown, D.D. Han[over?] Chaplain.[25] Dined At St Martin's.

[Apr.] 21. Morning, Visits by General Nicolson, Bishop of Clogher,[26] Archbishop of York, &c. Dined Home.

[Apr.] 22. Great Eclipse. Dined with Mr Blencow, &c. at the Tower. Evening, Brother's.

[Apr.] 23. Private all day, Visited by the two D.D. Gibsons,[27] Bishop of Bangor; &c.

[Apr.] 24. Morning, I preached at St Margaret's, dined at Mr Chamberlayne's. French.[28]

[Apr.] 25. Visits from Mr Brougham, Mr Blencow, Mr Grey, Col. Orfeur, &c. To Lord Carlile, Lord Lonsdale, Archbishop of Canterbury, Bishop of London [Robinson], &c. &c.

[Apr.] 26. Morning, With Mr Usher. Visits, Ditto. House, Mrs Forester's petition,[29] opposed by Archbishop of York, Bishop of Bristol [Smalridge], Lord Alesford, &c. Dined with me Bishop of Bangor.

. [Apr.] 27. Morning, Visits to Earl of Carlile, Earl of Orford, Mr Gumley, &c. Dined with me Dr Smith and Mr Greenshields. P.m., Mr Grey.

[25] ?Francis Browne.
[26] St. George Ashe (d. 1718), Bishop of Clogher, 1697–1717, and of Derry, 1717–18. He was a protégé of Archbishop King of Dublin.
[27] Edmund Gibson and possibly his half-brother John Gibson (c.1678–1730) educated Queen's College, Oxford, and Provost of that college, 1716–30; Canon of Lincoln, 1719. He was not, however, awarded his DD until 21 Mar. 1717. John was the son of Edmund Gibson, senior, by his second wife, see Sykes, *Gibson*, pedigree following p. 432. Thomas Gibson (d. 1722), uncle of the above, had an MD and was Physician-General to the Army in 1719.
[28] Presumably a reference to the cuisine.
[29] For a bill to end her marriage with Sir George Downing, which had not been consummated. They were married in 1700 aged thirteen and fifteen respectively. See *LJ* xx, 41–2. It was reported that all the bishops except London, Lichfield, and Rochester, and all the 'High Church men of both parties' as well as Lords Townshend and Carleton 'are violently against the divorce'. SRO Stairs MS GD135/145: [Cathcart?] to Stair, 28 Apr. 1715.

[Apr.] 28. Private. With J. Relf's works.[30] Evening, Mr Green, Mr Symson, &c.

[Apr.] 29. House, petitions; dined with me Mr Greenshields. Evening, My Brother's.

[Apr.] 30. Morning, Bishop of St Asaph [Wynne]; with whom to the Committee.[31] Query, if Bishops Peers?[32] P.m., With Lord Carlile and Bishop of Lincoln.

May 1. Mr E. Finch,[33] before the King on *Hebrews* 10, 35 and 36, for *Humble Confidence in God*. Dined at home.

[May] 2. Morning, Whitehall and Lord Digby's Committee.[34] Evening, with 3 Bells and Mr Forster.

[May] 3. Morning, Committee, Bishops Peers. House, No Bill for Mrs Forester.[35] P.m., Dean Kennet on my side. Evenings, Greys Inn.

[May] 4. Morning, Lord Lonsdale and Mr Blencow. P.m., Clergy-Court at St Paul's.

[May] 5. Dr Dixon,[36] Mr Lowther, &c. Dined (with the Bishop of Winton [Trelawney]) at Chelsea.

[May] 6. House, Fruitless, till tomorrow. P.m., Lambeth, Cornhill, Brothers.

[May] 7. Alderman Tullie, Dr Dixon, &c. House, Tax-Bill.[37]

---

[30] Probably the 'calendars' or original guides to the MS Journals consisting principally of books of tabulated entries under names and general subjects. They are known as 'Relf's Journals'. See HLRO *Memorandum No. 13* (1957), p. 8.

[31] The Committee on the Standing Orders had been dropped on 8 Apr. and revived on 11 Apr. (see *LJ* xx, 39).

[32] According to Standing Order 34 of the House 'Bishops are only Lords of Parlyament, but not Peeres, for they are not of trial by nobility'. HMC *Lords MSS* x, 5-6.

[33] Edward Finch, one of the Chaplains in Ordinary to the King.

[34] Nicolson was not appointed to the original committee on Lord Digby's petition concerning his son's insanity. *LJ* xx, 39; HMC *Lords MSS* xii, 152-5.

[35] *LJ* xx, 45. It was reported that the bill 'was thrown out by 2 voices, the Court Generally were against her for giving no handle to the High Church mobb'. SRO GD135/145: [Cathcart?] to Stair, 5 May 1715.

[36] ?George Dixon (c.1671-1728), educated Oxford, DD 1710; Rector of Brampton St Botolph, Northamptonshire, 1694-1728.

[37] Land Tax Bill. *LJ* xx, 47.

[May] 8. The Archbishop of York and I preached at Hackney. Dined with Mr Dawling,[38] Mr Cook, &c. conveyed to and from by Mr Ch[amberlay]n.

[May] 9. Lord Carlile, &c. To the Bishop of Chester [Gastrell], Whitehall, Mrs Lowther. P.m. *Eight Bells*.

[May] 10. House, Tax-Bill read a 3d time and passed; Lord Digby's committee enlarged.[39]

[May] 11. The King passing the 1st Money-bill.[40] Prince of Wales, Robed. Dined with the Bishop of London. Evening, with B[aron] Montague, Earl of Orford and Bishop of Clogher [Ashe].

[May] 12. Morning, Mr Lamplugh, Mr Grisdale, &c. Lord Oxford's Library. Committeee of Standing Orders.

[May] 13. Morning, Dr G[ibson] and I adviseing the Bishop of Lincoln. Committee on Lord Digby's petition. P.m. At Cupid's Garden.[41] Evening, Brothers.

[May] 14. Morning, With Mr Wilson to seek Sir W. St Quinton;[42] who Kindly came to the Prince's Chamber. To Lord Lonsdale and Sir R. S[andford]. Dined, Mr R. Smith.

[May] 15. Morning, I preached at Great Queen-street for the Bishop of Bangor. Dined, at my Brother's.

[May] 16. Morning, Mr Chancellor Tanner, &c. &c. House, Lord Digby's Bill.[43] P.m., Lambeth.

[May] 17. Morning, Dr Dixon, Mr Wanley, Mr Chamb[erlayn], Mr Wilkins, Mr Sharp, &c. P.m., Lord Hallifax enquired for (sick)[44] and Bishop of Lincoln Visited.

[May] 18. Morning, Mrs Harrington, Bishop of London, &c. Dined, Dr Hickes's. Evening, Dr Smith's.

[38] ?John Dauling (d. 1727), Rector of Ringwould, Kent, 1679–1727.
[39] *LJ* xx, 49.   [40] Ibid., p. 50.
[41] Cuper's Garden, Lambeth.
[42] Sir William St Quinton (c.1662–1723), 3rd Bt., Whig MP for Hull, 1695–1723; a Lord of the Treasury, 1714–17. Sedgwick, ii, 405.
[43] *LJ* xx, 52; HMC *Lords MSS* xii, 153.
[44] He had suddenly been taken ill on 15 May and died on 19 May of inflammation on the lungs. With Wharton already dead (see above, n. 21) and Somers mentally and physically decayed, the great Whig Junto was to all intents and purposes dissolved.

[May] 19. Morning, Bishop of Landaff [Tyler], Mr Lawson, Mr Wanley, &c. House, Lord Digby's Bill committed.[45]

[May] 20. Morning, Bishop of Bangor, F. Bugg, Mr Anderson: with whom to Mr Sharp and Dr K[ennett]. House, Committee. Evening, Duchess of Monmouth's.[46]

[May] 21. A Preventing Purge. Lord Lonsdale, Mr Lowther, Dean Kennet.

[May] 22. Morning, Dr Bradford[47] preached at the Abbey. Dined, my Brother's. P.m., Mr Watkinson's.

[May] 23. Morning, To Mr Ecton, Mr Madox, Mrs Wenman, Mr Burnet, Lord Carlile. House, Bill for Quartering of Forces.[48] Dined, Mr R. Smith. P.m., Bishop of Rochester [Atterbury], &c.

[May] 24. Morning, Dean Kennet, Mr Thompson, Mr Wanley, &c. &c. Dined, Bishop of Bangor and Dr Gibson. P.m., General Tatton,[49] &c.

[May] 25. Morning, Lord Carlile and Monsieur Bonet.[50] House, Lord D[igby]'s Bill. P.m., With the Dean of Arches [Bettesworth], Chancellor Tanner and at Dr G[ibson]'s.

[May] 26. Morning, Mr J. Brougham, Mr Wanley &c. P.m., Bishops of Glocester [Willis] and Bangor.

[May] 27. Morning, with Mr Wilkins to the Bishops of Oxford [Potter], Peterborough [Cumberland] and Llandaff. House, Bishop of Bath and Wells's [Hooper's] Case.[51] Evening, my Brother's.

[May] 28. King's Birth Day. Dined with the Clerk of the Closet.[52] Evening, Mr B. Willis.

[45] *LJ* xx, 53.

[46] Correctly speaking she should be called the Duchess of Buccleuch (d. 1732), widow of the Duke of Monmouth.

[47] Samuel Bradford (1652–1731), Prebendary of Westminster, 1708–23, who had turned down a poor bishopric in 1710, was to succeed Nicolson at Carlisle in 1718, and (ironically) Atterbury at Rochester in 1723.

[48] The Mutiny Bill. *LJ* xx, 54.

[49] William Tatton (d. 1737), had served in Ireland and Flanders under William III; Major-General in 1710, he held the governorship of Tilbury Fort at his death. Dalton, v, pt. 1, p. 64.

[50] Louis Frederick Bonet (Bonnet) de St Germain, the Prussian Resident in England, 1696–1720.

[51] A private cause. *LJ* xx, 58; HMC *Lords MSS* xii, 143–5.

[52] Charles Trimnell, Bishop of Norwich, was Clerk of the Closet, 1714–23.

[May] 29. Bishop of St Asaph preached on *Psalm* 147, 1. Dined with Mr R. Smith. Evening, Bishop of Lincoln.

[May] 30. From the Bishop of Landaff and Dean of Peterborough [Kennett] To Mr Wanley. House, Quartering Bill. 81 against 35.[53] Evening, with Bishop of St Asaph.

[May] 31. House, Lord Digby's Bill in long Committee.[54] P.m., Mr R. Smith, set on a Ramble.

June 1. Morning, Lord Oxford's Library. Parliament office, &c. House, Noise of Impeachments.[55]

[June] 2. Morning, Bishop of Bangor, Dean of Peterborough, Dr Gibson, &c. House, Scotch Cause.[56] P.m., Dr Cannon. To Sister Rothery, Mr. C. Musgrave.

[June] 3. Morning, Mrs Fetherston. To Lord Chancellor's; fruitless. House, The King's Assent to Malt and Recruits.[57] Dined, Mr Smith and Mr Wickins. Evening, Brothers and Sisters, &c, at Mr Richmond's. My Birth Day *Aet* 61. *Miserere Deus*!

[June] 4. Morning, To Dr Lancaster. P.m., Private.

[June] 5. Morning, Sp[ring?] Garden. Ch[urch?]. Dined, Brother's P.m., St Bride's. Nicolsons.

[June] 6. Morning, Mr Wanley, Duglas.[58] H. Farrington, Grascome, &c. With H. F[arrington][59] to the Bishops of London and Durham [Crew], the Tower, &c. P.m. To Dr T[odd], Mr Moreton, R. N[icolson].

[June] 7. With my sisters to Dr Waugh's at Ham. Mr Hodges &c. Late home.

[53] Dissenters to the vote are listed in *LJ* xx, 60.
[54] Ibid., p. 62; HMC *Lords MSS* xii, 154.
[55] 'While the Secret Committee were forming their Report [submitted to the Commons on 10 June], the House was every day amused with the great discoveries they had made; and that they might render themselves very terrible, Mr [Thomas] Harley and Mr Prior were by the Chairman moved to be taken into custody by the Serjeant at Arms . . .' (HMC *Portland MSS* v, 664).   [56] *LJ* xx, 65.
[57] Recruits refers to the Mutiny Act. Ibid., p. 68.
[58] Possibly Oley Douglas, MP for Morpeth, 1713–15.
[59] Possibly Hugh Farrington (*c*.1687–1739), Rector of Elsdon, Northumberland, 1715–39. See *CW* xxxv (1935), 108.

[June] 8. Morning, Mr Farrington, Clark, &c. with Dr K[ennett] to dine at the Bishop of Lincoln's. Evening, Mr B. Willis.

[June] 9. Morning, Mr Lewis, Capt. Phillips, &c. House, Foreign Lords C[lauses].[60] Report from sec[ret] Committee. Mob.[61]

[June] 10. Morning, Mrs Hodgson, M. Pearson, Mr Lawson, &c. P.m. Dowgate. Brother's.

[June] 11. Morning, Mr Chamberlayne. Lord Hallifax. House, Nothing. P.m., Dr Gibson's.

[June] 12. Morning, I preached a Charity Sermon at Trinity-Chapple. Dined, Dr Lancaster's.

[June] 13. Morning, Archdeacon Bowchier, Mr Lewis. Two Farringtons, &c. P.m., Mr Wanley and's Daughter, Mr Wilkins. Private.

[June] 14. Morning, Lord Viscount Strangford,[62] Bishops of Bangor and Landaff. Dean of Peterborough, &c. &c. House, Cause.

[June] 15. Morning, With Archbishop of York and Mrs L[   ] at Kensington. House, Nothing. Dined, Two Farringtons. Evening, Major General Tatton's.

[June] 16. Morning, With the Bishop of Landaff, to Lord Somers,[63] Secretary Stanhop and Lord Lonsdale. House. Woolaston and Preston. Half.[64]

[60] The House had taken into consideration the clauses relating to the incapacities on foreigners in the Act of Settlement of 1701, and in the Act for Securing the Queen and Government, and the Succession in the Protestant Line of 1707. By these clauses foreigners were barred from the Privy Council and parliament and were forbidden to hold civil or military offices or to receive grants of land from the Crown. The House decided to bring in a bill to declare that the clause in the Act of Settlement 'does not extend to Persons naturalized before Her Majesty's accession to the Crown'. *LJ* xx, 67, 69–70.

[61] The report was presented to the Commons by Walpole and on the evening of 10 June the House resolved to impeach Oxford and Bolingbroke. For popular Jacobite demonstrations in June 1715 see N. Rogers, 'Popular Protest in Early Hanoverian London', *Past and Present*, 79 (1978), p. 73. The mob violence on 9–10 June was associated with the celebration of the Pretender's birthday as well as with the unpopular activities of the Commons Committee, and resulted in the gutting of Wright's meeting-house in Blackfriars.

[62] Endymion Smythe (d. 1724), 3rd Viscount Strangford, bred a Roman Catholic. He conformed to the established Church in 1714 and took his seat in the Irish Lords in Nov. 1715.

[63] See above, n. 44. Somers did not die until Apr. 1716. That he was not totally incapacitated in the summer of 1715 is shown by the fact that between 31 Aug. and 23 Sept., after the outbreak of the Jacobite rebellion, he managed to attend five successive meetings of the Privy Council. W. L. Sachse, *Lord Somers* (Manchester, 1975), pp. 314, 319.

[64] See *LJ* xx, 76, and n. 65 below.

[June] 17. Morning, Col. Benson, Mr Winder, Mr Hornsby, &c. House, Furnes-Cause ended.[65] Evening, Dr G[ibson]'s; my Brother's.

[June] 18. Dined, Mr R. Smith and Mr Fiddis. Evening, Lord Portland; private.

[June] 19. Morning, I preached at St Peter's Corn[hill]. Dined, at my Brother's. P.m. Preached at St Bride's.

[June] 20. Morning, Mr Wanley, Mr Jefferson,[66] &c. House, Long Irish cause.[67] Evening, with Dr Gibson visitting Archbishop of Canterbury hearty; Col. Benson and cousin R. N[icolson].

[June] 21. Morning, Dr Smith, Dr Gibson, &c. House, Foreign-Lords.[68] Evening, Dr Todd.

[June] 22. Morning, Private, at Leland. House. Report of Orders.[69] Evening, With Dr Gibson at the Bishop of Bangor's.

[June] 23. Morning, Mr Lamplugh, Mr Wilson, Mr Ogle &c. Dined, With Mr Jefferson instead of Mr Winder. Evening, Mr Lowther.

[June] 24. Morning, Mr Wilkins, &c. House, Appeal. Evening, with Sister Rothery at my Brother's.

[June] 25. Morning, Mr Algood, Mr Ogle, &c. House. Irish Cause.[70] Evening, Letters.

[June] 26. Charity Sermon at Lambeth. Dined, with Dr G[ibson]. Evening, with Archbishop [of] Canterbury.

[June] 27. Morning, Capt Maurice, Dr Gibson, Dr Hutch[inson], Archdeacon Bowchier, Capt. Phillips, &c. &c. &c. Dined, At the *Dog*; after Archbishop of York and Mr Montgomery. Evening, Mark Lane.

---

[65] The Wollaston v. Preston case concerned the validity of a lease of 1695 to the site of the monastery of Furness. *LJ* xx, 77; HMC *Lords MSS* xii, 150–2.

[66] Possibly Thomas Jefferson, Rector of Holme Cultram, 1715, and of Lamplugh, Cumberland, 1731.

[67] See *LJ* xx, 78–9; HMC *Lords MSS* xii, 141–3.

[68] The House resolved in the negative a proposal to ask the judges whether the clause in the Act of Settlement extended to persons naturalised since that act and Queen Anne's accession. Twenty-two Tories protested. See *LJ* xx, 81.

[69] The report of the Committee on Standing Orders is printed in ibid. pp. 82–4.

[70] Ibid. p. 88; HMC *Lords MSS* xii, 187–8.

[June] 28. Morning, pretty Private. House. Cause, &c. Dined, At Mr R. Smith's with Dr Sm[ith].

[June] 29. Morning, To Mr Madox, Dr Woodward and Bishop of Ely [Fleetwood]. Mr Lawson, Col. B[enson], &c. House. Sc[otch] Cause.[71] Evening, to Lord C[arlisle?] and Chelsea for Brother Carlile.

[June] 30. Dined, With Archdeacon Gibson, &c. at his Uncle's. House sat not.

July 1. Morning, Capt Morris, Mr Thore[s]by, &c. Dined with me Col. B[enson], Mr Thompson and Mr Rook. House. Nothing. Evening, my Brother.

[July] 2. Morning, To Chelsea, General Erle, Mr Lawson. P.m. Dr Smith, &c.

[July] 3. Sacrament with the Bishops of Landaff and Chester. P.m. Dr Scot, No better for Dr Rate.

[July] 4. Morning, To Mr Burnet, Lords Portland, and L[ord] H[igh] Comm[issioner],[72] Brother Benson.[73] P.m. T. Pattinso[n], Chancellor Reynolds[74] and Mr Nicols.

[July] 5. Morning, Mr Thoresby, Dobbinson,[75] Att[orney?] Farringtons, Philips, &c. P.m. To Holburn, with Leland, Brother Benson, &c.

[July] 6. Morning, Mr Thoresby, Grisdale, &c. &c. Dined, Dr Gibson and Brother Benson. P.m. With the Bishop of Litchfield to Hackney. Brother's.

[July] 7. To Baron Mountague, B[rother?] B[enson?], Excise office,[76] Lord Portland. House. Nothing. P.m. Mr R. Smith, Dr Gibson, &c.

[71] *LJ* xx, 91; HMC *Lords MSS* xii, 163–4.
[72] Possibly a reference to Lord Carlisle who was a Lord High Commissioner for the Treasury, 23 May–11 Oct. 1715.
[73] Probably Mr Benson of Kendal, the father of Nicolson's son-in-law, Thomas Benson.
[74] Richard Reynolds (1674–1744), Chancellor of Peterborough, 1704–18, Dean, 1718–21, and later Bishop of Bangor, 1721–23, and Lincoln, 1723–44.
[75] A Mr Dobbison was a Carlisle attorney. See *CW* xlvi (1946), 215.
[76] Very possibly the Bishop was on a local patronage mission (see below, 1 Sept.). The Excise was by far the largest government department, with over 3,500 employees in 1715. Its headquarters was in the Old Jewry, 'in a very large house, formerly the dwelling of Sir John Fredrick, and afterwards of Sir Joseph Hern, very considerable merchants' (Defoe, *Tour*, i, 340).

[July] 8. Morning, With Mr Wilkins at Lord O[xford]'s Lib[rary].
House. Scotch Cause.[77] Evening, Mrs Elstob.

[July] 9. To Lord Hertford, Lord Portland, Mr Chamberlayn. House.
Impeachment.[78]

July 9. 1715. Impeachment and Articles from the Commons
(brought up by Lord Coningsby) of High Treason, &c. against the
Earl of Oxford: Three Questions
1 Adjourn the Reading till Munday
— Contents, 52. Not Contents, 86.
2 Call the Judges? —
Contents, 52.
Not Contents, 84.
3 Commit to the Black Rod?
Contents, 81.
Not Contents, 52.[79]
For Lord Oxford—
Lord Tr[evor] and Harc[our]t. Not Treason, Course of Negot[ia-
tion]. Lord Nott[ingham], Lord Ch[ancellor] [Cowper], Duke of
Argyle. Judges in good time. Grand Inquest. No Trusting. Bishops
of Rochester, Bristol and Chester New precedent. Old. No Treason
in Intention, save murder of the King.
    Lord O[xford]'s own Speech. Bishop of Rochester's new Prece-
dent.[80]

[July] 10. I preached at Aldgate. Dined at Mr Brent's, with Dr Waugh
and Mr Nicols. Home, weary.

[July] 11. Morning, Mr Burrough, Jeremy Nicolson, Mr Wilson, &c.
&c. Dined At the Earl of Portland's. P.m. Mr Grisdale, Mrs Howard.

[July] 12. Morning, Dr Brown (Valedic[tion]), Brother B[enson], Mr
Thoresby, &c. House. Lord O[xford] to the Tower.[81] P.m. With the
Bishop of Litchfield to Archbishop of Canterbury and Dr Gibson's.
Item. R. S[mith?].

    [77] LJ xx, 96; HMC Lords MSS xii, 162.
    [78] Of the Earl of Oxford. See LJ xx, 99–112 for the articles of impeachment. See HMC
Lords MSS xii, 195–201 for proceedings 9 July 1715–1 July 1717.
    [79] For the dissenters from these three votes, see LJ xx, 111–12.
    [80] For a full account of this day's proceedings, see Christ Church Wake MS 19,
ff. 2^r–3^v: Wake's 'diary' of the impeachment.
    [81] Harley did not enter the Tower until 16 July. LJ xx, 115. He was to remain there
until 1 July 1717. For an account of the debate on this day, see Christ Church Wake MS
19, ff. 4^r–4^v.

[July] 13. Morning, With Brother B[enson] to Chelsea. House. Scotch Cause.[82] P.m. To Bishop of Lincoln's and Brother's. King on the River.

[July] 14. Morning, D[ean] Simcocks, T. Bell, Mr Synge, &c. House sate not. P.m. With Mr R. Sm[ith] to Barn-Elms.

[July] 15. Morning, Mr Ibbet, Wilkins, Capt. Duguier, Lord Strangford, &c. &c. Dined at Col. B[enson]'s. Evening, my Brother's. NB. House. Paterson's Bill,[83] &c.

[July] 16. Mr A. Smith and Mr Manley for Ordination. Evening, Constitution Hill.

[July] 17. I preached and ordained at St Vedast's. Dined My Brother's. Evening, Dr Dungworth and Greenshields.

[July] 18. Morning, Mr Forster, Dr Gaitsgarth, &c. To Dr Cannon. House. Cause and Riot-Bill.[84] Dined, At Mr Chamberlayne's, with the Bishop of Litchfield, Mr Bonet.

[July] 19. Morning, At Whitehall. House. Pr[ivate] Bills. Dined. At Kensington, with Mr Green.

[July] 20. Morning, To Mr Benson, Smith, Brothers. House. King's speech.[85] Evening, With Archbishop [of] Canterbury. With me Baron Mountague and the Chancellor of Peterborough [Reynolds] and Mr Nicols.

[July] 21. To Woolwich (Mr Nash's) &c., with the Bishop of Bangor, Mr Ellis and Mr Hayley. Dined. Capt. Harlow's[86] at the King's Yard in Deptford.

---

[82] LJ xx, 116; HMC Lords MSS xii, 164–5.   [83] See LJ xx, 116–17.

[84] It passed the Lords without amendments on 20 July. See ibid. pp. 119, 121. Under the bill, which was introduced against a background of serious popular disorder in London, and here and there in the provinces, extending back to the time of the general election, a riotous assembly of twelve or more persons became guilty of a capital offence if they failed to disperse within one hour of being publicly ordered to do so by magistrates. Nicholas Rogers ('Popular Protest', pp. 74–5) sees it as 'a response to a tense political situation in which the credibility of the government was at stake'. But, naturally, both the Riot Act and the suspension of Habeas Corpus on 23 July must be seen against the background of a Jacobite invasion which was now considered a near-certainty and of the Whig conviction that 'the common people are so poisoned with Jacobitism and so much set against the present government', The Diary of Dudley Ryder, 1715–16, ed. W. Matthews (1939), pp. 61–2: 25 July 1715.   [85] See LJ xx, 122–3.

[86] ?Thomas Harlow (d. 1741), Captain in Royal Navy in 1690. Commissioned Sea Officers of Royal Navy, 1660–1815 (National Maritime Museum, 1954), ii, 407.

July 21, 1715
On board the new vamped *Queen*
(now *Royal George*) at Woolwich[87]

	f.	i.
Length on the Gun Dock [Deck?]	170.	3.
Extreem Breadth	49.	0.
Depth in Hold	20.	2.
Draught of Water	22.	0.
Height from the Kiel to		
the Gun-wail	44.	8.
Length Aloft	188.	0.

[July] 22. To Greenwich, with my Brother, sister and Niece.

[July] 23. Morning, D[ean] Simcocks, Mr Thoresby, &c. House. Habeas-Corpus Act rep[eale]d by King.[88] Dined At Chelsea, with the Bishop of Winchester.

[July] 24. Dean of Glocester [Chetwood] preached at Whitehall on *John* 21, 21 and 22, against Curious Enq[uiries]. Dined, Brother Benson.

[July] 25. Mr Philips, Capt. Morris, &c. House. Scotch Cause.[89] Dined, Bishop of Bangor. Evening Lincoln's and Grey's Inn, my Brother's.

[July] 26. Morning, Bishop of Landaff, Mr Rook, &c. House. Half of Touchet's App[eal]. P.m. Mr R. Smith and Brother Benson.

[July] 27. Morning, Mr Thoresby, with his book.[90] House. P[ar]t 2d.[91] Evening, Visits to Mrs Gibson.

---

[87] Dudley Ryder paid a visit six days later and left a good account in his diary (ed. W. Matthews, pp. 63–4). It was 'the largest [ship] that was ever built in England and . . . indeed of a prodigious bulk'. It had been on the stocks for two and a half years and was originally to have been named *The Royal Anne*.

[88] A bill was brought in from the Commons to suspend the Habeas Corpus Act. It was read three times immediately and given the royal assent on the same day. See *LJ* xx, 127–8. See above, n. 84.

[89] See *LJ* xx, 129; HMC *Lords MSS* xii, 145–6: Touchet v. Dowager Countess of Castlehaven.

[90] *Ducatus Leodiensis* published in May or June 1715. Nicolson had subscribed £1 11*s*. 0*d*. for a copy of each of the large and small size of the book. Yorkshire Archaeological Society MS 28 (unfoliated).

[91] Perhaps a reference to the conclusion of the Touchet Appeal case. See *LJ* xx, 130.

[July] 28. Morning, Mr C. Musgrave Hyp, Bishop of Bangor, Mr Chamberlayne, &c. House. Scotch Cause.[92]

[July] 29. Morning, With W. Rook to Bishop of Bristol and Baron Mountague. House. Bills. Dined, Brother Benson. Evening, My Brother's.

[July] 30. Morning, Captains Studholm and Morris, Mr Dowson, &c. House. Bills. Evening, Letters.

[July] 31. After Sermons at the Abbey and St James's, Dined with Mr C. Musgrave.

August 1. King's Accesion. Church and Court. P.m. With Archbishop of Canterbury and Mr R. Smith.

[Aug.] 2. Morning, Brother Benson, &c. House. R[oyal] Assent to Mutiny-Bill.[93] Dined, Dr Todd.

[Aug.] 3. Morning, To Lords Lonsdale and Portland. House. Earl of O[xford]'s Indisp[osition].[94] Duke of Ancaster introduced.[95] Dined, Brother's. Wet.

[Aug.] 4. House. Security-Bill.[96] Dined At Lord Portland's with Lord [Howard of] Effingham, &c.

[Aug.] 5. Morning, To Lord Carlile, Dr Todd, Col Grahme. House. Bill, Ditto. Evening, Mr Madox, and Mr Smith, &c.

[Aug.] 6. Morning, Mr Dowson, &c. House. Six Articles against Lord B[olingbroke][97] and the Black Rod[98] ordered to take him, &c.

[Aug.] 7. I preached at Lambeth. Dined at the Palace. Evening, Mrs Gibson.

[Aug.] 8. With my Brother, sister and Niece, to the Camp.[99] House. Duke of O[rmond] Impeached.[100] Evening, with Mr R. S[mith] at Battersey, &c.

---

[92] See ibid., p. 132.
[93] See ibid., p. 144.
[94] See ibid., pp. 144–5.
[95] Formerly the Marquess of Lindsey.
[96] See *LJ* xx, 146.
[97] Printed in ibid., pp. 149–53.
[98] Sir William Oldes.
[99] At Kensington. See *Diary of Dudley Ryder*, pp. 71–3.
[100] Printed in *LJ* xx, 155–7.

[Aug.] 9. Morning, Mr James Lowther &c. House. Lord B[oling-broke] *non inventus.*[101] Security Bill.[102] On the Question *Contents*, 45. *N[ot] C[ontent]*, 16.

[Aug.] 10. Morning, Mr Chamberlayne's. House. Sec[urity] Bill finished.[103] Dined with me, Bishop of Bangor. Evening, Lord Chancellor's [Cowper's], &c.

[Aug.] 11. Morning, Mr Grisdale, &c. House. Money-Bill[104] P.m. C[ousin] Jeremy Nicolson's.

[Aug.] 12. Morning, Mr Lowther, &c. To the Archbishop of Canterbury with Dr Gibson. House. Cause. Evening, To my Brother's and (with D[r] W[augh]) the *Bl[ack] Swan.*

[Aug.] 13. With Dr Waugh, Sir Thomas Manwaring, Mr Wilkins to Oxford.

[Aug.] 14. Morning Sermon at Christ Church by Mr White.[105] Dined with the provost [Lancaster], Dr Pearson, Mr Smith, &c. Magdalen College.

[Aug.] 15. Founders Day. Dined in the Hall[106] with the Bishop of St Asaph, &c. &c. Evening, Common-Room.

[Aug.] 16. Morning, Blenheim.[107] Dined, Jesus College. P.m. P[ublic] Library,[108] &c.

[Aug.] 17. Dr Waugh and I returned (late) from Oxford.

[Aug.] 18. Morning, Col. Grahme, Mr Wilson, Dr Todd, &c. House. Attainders.[109] P.m. with the Archbishop of Canterbury.

[101] See *LJ* xx, 158.

[102] For its amendment see ibid., pp. 158–60.

[103] Ibid., p. 161.

[104] Act for enlarging the fund of the governor and company of the Bank of England, relating to Exchequer bills. Ibid., pp. 160–2.

[105] John White, Student of Christ Church, 1700, Proctor, 1716. For his sermon, see Hearne, *Collections*, v, 96.

[106] This was the first dinner in the new Hall built by Provost Lancaster. Ibid.

[107] Blenheim Palace, at Woodstock, the seat of the Marlboroughs, was only eight miles from Oxford.

[108] i.e. the Bodleian.

[109] Against Bolingbroke and Ormond. See *LJ* xx, 171–2; Christ Church Wake MS 19, ff. 5^r–5^v.

[Aug.] 19. Treasury with Brother Benson. House. Cause. P.m. Mr James Lowther and Dr Gibson. Evening, Brother's.

[Aug.] 20. Morning, Brother Joseph. To the House. Royal Assent. Dined, Brother Benson and Dr G[ibson]. Evening, Bishop of Lincoln, against Lodington.[110]

[Aug.] 21. From Sermon in Spring-Garden, to dine (with Sister R[othery]) at my Brother's.

[Aug.] 22. Morning, In quest again of Sir W[illiam] St Q[uintin]. House, Scotch cause,[111] Lords Carlile, Ilay, &c.

[Aug.] 23. Morning, Dr Todd, &c. To Mr Green. House. Bills. P.m. Dr Barton's Fun[era]l.

[Aug.] 24. Morning, Mr Whetham, &c. To Duke of Montrose, Earl of Carlile, &c. House. Fr[ench] K[ing]'s death.[112] Evening, Col. Benson.

[Aug.] 25. Morning, King's Review in H[yde] Park. House. Cause. Dined with me, Bishop of Bangor.

[Aug.] 26. Morning, To Sir D. Heckstetter,[113] Mr Watkinson, &c. House. Mr Ramsey's Cause.[114] Evening, Dr Gibson's and my Brother's.

[Aug.] 27. Morning, Dr Gibson, &c. Dined, Dr Waugh from Mrs Bonelli. Evening, Letters, Letters.

[Aug.] 28. Morning, I preached at Russel-Court. Dined at my Brother's with Mr Johnson. Evening, R. N[icolson].

[Aug.] 29. Morning, Exeter-Change.[115] House. Scotch Cause. Evening, York-Coach.

[110] Pickering Lodington (c.1688–1742), son of the Vicar of Horncastle. He had been appointed Vicar of Thornton, Lincolnshire, on 22 Jan. 1715, but lived with his father. *Speculum Dioeceseos Linc*. i, 129.

[111] *LJ* xx, 178.

[112] The death of Louis XIV had been reported in London as early as 20 Aug. (*Diary of Dudley Ryder*, p. 81), though he did not die until 1 Sept. 1715. The assumption of control over French policy after Louis's death by the Regent Orleans made no practical difference to the failure of the Jacobite rebellion. It was already denied any hope of serious French aid. See Hatton, *George I*, pp. 174–5.

[113] Sir David Heckstetter (Hetchetter) (c.1659–1721), Hamburgh merchant of Southgate, Middlesex, knighted in 1714 as director of the Merchant Adventurers' Company. Musgrave, *Obituary*, iii, 187.

[114] See *LJ* xx, 182; HMC *Lords MSS* xii, 186–7.

[115] In the Strand from c.1676 to 1829 when it was demolished.

[Aug.] 30. Morning, Dr Melvil, &c. House. R[oyal] Assent.[116] Evening, Dr Gibson, to the Bishop of Lincoln.

[Aug.] 31. To the Tower, Ratcliff, &c. Evening, from Dr Gibson, to Col. Benson, Mr Walbank and Brother Benson. Item, Dr Lancaster.

September 1. Morning, with Brother Benson at the Excise-office. Dr I[ ]d. House. Impeachment of the Earl of Strafford.[117] Letters late.

[Sept.] 2. Morning, Bishop of Landaff, &c. House. Scotch Cause.[118] P.m. Lambeth and my Brother's.

[Sept.] 3. Lord O[xford]'s long Answer.[119] Dined, Dean Kennett and Dr Waugh. Bishop of L[incoln].

[Sept.] 4. With sister N[icolson] to the King's Charity Sermon by Dr Chandler[120] on *Confidence from Conscience*. Dined, A. Tullie, &c.

[Sept.] 5. House. Committee of Earl of O[xford]'s Answer and the Irish Palatines.[121] P.m. Bishop of Glocester [Willis], Mr Farrington, Mr Ascue, &c.

[Sept.] 6. With D[ean] Simcocks to Lord Galway's. To Mrs Lowther, &c. Dined with Sir R. S[andford], our Citizens,[122] Mr Jenkins and Mr Cholmley[123] at Lord Carlile's. Evening, Dr Gibson's.

[Sept.] 7. Morning, To Duke of Grafton, Lady Hertford, &c. House. Drawback-Bill rejected.[124] Evening, with the Bishops of Sarum and Bangor.

---

[116] For the acts see *LJ* xx, 189.

[117] Articles printed in ibid., pp. 192-7.

[118] See ibid., pp. 197-8.

[119] Printed in ibid., pp. 200-22. It took more than two and a half hours to read, see Christ Church Wake MS 19, f. 6ʳ.

[120] Edward Chandler (?1668-1750), educated Cambridge, DD 1701; Chaplain to Bishop Lloyd of Worcester, Prebendary of Lichfield, 1697, of Salisbury, 1703, and of Worcester, 1706; Bishop of Lichfield, 1717, and of Durham, 1730-50.

[121] See *LJ* xx, 222-3. This was a Committee of the Whole House, which was chaired by Nicolson.

[122] Thomas Stanwix and William Strickland, MPs for Carlisle, see Appendix A.

[123] Possibly Tobias Jenkins (1660-1730), Whig MP for York, 1695-1700, 1701-5, 1715-22; and Hugh Cholmley (1684-1755), Whig MP for Hedon, 1708-21. Sedgwick, i, 550; ii, 176.

[124] The 'Act for relief of merchants, importers of tobacco and wines, concerned in bonds

[Sept.] 8. Morning, Dr Gee, Mr Lowther, &c. Leave of Dr Lancaster, Archbishop of Canterbury. Dr Gibson. Supper at Brother's, *Black Swan*.

[Sept.] 9. 10. 11. 12. 13. In the stage-coach (with Brother Benson, Captains Du-Mar and Talbot) to York.[125]

given for part of the duties on the same' was not rejected, but ordered to be committed in three weeks. The prorogation of parliament on 21 Sept., however, meant that the bill was lost. *LJ* xx, 225, 237; HMC *Lords MSS* xii, 225–7. The 'drawback' was the amount of excise or import duty paid back on goods exported.

[125] Nicolson spent 14 and 15 Sept. in York visiting, among others, the Archbishop and Lord Bingley. On 16 Sept. he set out for Rose, via Kendal (where he preached on 18 Sept.), arriving home on 19 Sept. 1715. Ware transcripts, xxxi, 36; *CW* v (1905), 4.

Session 12

19 February 1717–22 July 1717

The winter of 1715/16 was to prove an eventful one.[1] The Jacobite rebellion in Scotland spilled over into north-west England as a detachment of rebels pushed south. On 27 October 1715 Nicolson heard that the 'Rebels joyn'd' and two days later received the 'Good News' that they were prevented by the flooded River Eden from giving him a visit.[2] In the true tradition of a marcher lord, the sixty-year-old Bishop decided to take the field, and on 2 November, along with Viscount Lonsdale, led the *posse comitatus* on to Penrith Fell. Upon the appearance of the Highlanders the *posse* ignominiously fled, abandoning Lonsdale who departed for Appleby leaving Nicolson and a few servants. Nicolson was driven to the safety of Rose by his coachman. Here on 14 November he received news of the defeat of the rebel column at Preston, and the decisive defeat of the Scots at Sheriffmuir was reported to him five days later.[3] Early in the New Year Gibson informed Nicolson that his courageous efforts were appreciated in London,[4] and Wake (soon to be Archbishop of Canterbury in succession to Tenison, who died 14 December 1715) hinted that he was to be rewarded with the post of Lord Almoner.[5] Meanwhile life soon returned to a normal pattern in the diocese.[6]

Originally the Bishop had been expected in London for parliamentary duty by Christmas. He scarcely needed Gibson to remind him that the next session would 'call for all imaginable dispatch both of persons and things', while the Tories were 'summoning their whole strength to Fight Impeachments and other affairs, inch by inch with the Government'; indeed, he confessed to Wake that he 'never yet had stronger Inclinations to be at Westminster Than I have at this

[1] Many of the letters Nicolson wrote to Wake from late 1715 to late 1716, concerning the rebel invasion and the subsequent trials (originals in the Wake MSS in Christ Church; and copies in BL Add. MS 6116), are printed in *Original Letters Illustrative of English History*, ed. H. Ellis (1824), 1st ser. iii, 357–96. Most of those written between 8 and 27 Dec. 1716 have also been printed in Scottish History Society, xv, *Miscellany 1* (Edinburgh, 1893), pp. 523–36, where they are mistakenly described as letters from Nicolson to Archbishop Dawes of York.

[2] *CW* v (1905), 5; *Original Letters*, iii, 360: N. to Wake, 14 Nov. 1715.

[3] *CW* v (1905), 6; James, pp. 218–19.

[4] Bodl. MS Add. A269, p. 53: Gibson to N., 10 Jan. 1716. See also ibid., pp. 44–5: same to same, 5 Nov. 1715.

[5] BL Add. MS 6116, f. 35: N. to Wake, 9 Jan. 1715/16; Bodl. MS Add. A269, p. 60: Gibson to N., 28 Feb. 1716. The appointment was duly made after Nicolson's arrival in London in 1716. [6] *CW* v (1905), 6.

present'. In the event, the news of the Pretender's landing delayed Nicolson's departure and he did not arrive in London until 25 February—parliament having met on 9 January.[7] His first appearance in the House was on 2 March 1716.

Nicolson's diary for 1716 (assuming he kept one) has disappeared. He remained at Westminster until the end of the session on 26 June, attending sixty-three out of a possible seventy meetings of the Lords.[8] His attitude to such weighty transactions as the execution of Derwentwater and Kenmure,[9] or the passing of the Septennial Act (April) which brought to an end the era of triennial parliaments, is unknown. However, the following letter (the sole survivor for this session) illustrates Nicolson's continuing parliamentary interests.

BL Add. MS 6116, f. 36 (Christ Church Wake MS 7, ff. 125–6). Nicolson to Wake, Westminster, 18 June 1716.[10]

My very good Lord,

It will be no unpardonable Interruption in me to acquaint your Grace with some acknowledgements, which (as having the Honour of your Proxy) I thought myself obliged to make (in Your Name) to my Lord Chancellor [Cowper] for a kind Piece of Justice which his Lordship did your Grace in the last Saturdays Debate. The Question under Dispute was,—Whether the Bill for appointing thirteen Commissioners of Enquiry into forefeited Estates &c, should be committed.[11] Lord Trevor made an elegant Speech, of about an Hour's Length, against the Commitment; And his Motion was seconded by the Duke of Bucks, who concluded, that, as a late Bill concerning Ecclesiastical Matters had been so effectually exposed by a most Reverend Prelate,[12] that there upon it was unanimously rejected, so he hoped that this, having been as thoroughly laid open by as proper a Judge of the Nature of its Contents,[13] would immediately (and

[7] Bodl. MS Add. A269, pp. 40, 47, 53, 59: Gibson to N., 10 Oct. 1715, 29 Nov. 1715, 10 Jan. 1716, 25 Feb. 1716; BL Add. MS 6116, f. 35: N. to Wake, 9 Jan. 1716.

[8] *LJ* xx, 242–397. Nicolson also attended seven meetings of the Governors of Queen Anne's Bounty between 13 Mar. and 1 June 1716. See 'Minutes of the Governours Proceedings from 17 Dec. 1715 to 7 July 1718': Christ Church Wake MS 15 (unfoliated).

[9] Nicolson was regarded by some Scottish Jacobites as a possible source of aid for their imprisoned relatives. See Blair Atholl Castle, Atholl MS 45a. xii. 114: Atholl to Lord James Murray, 6 Mar. 1716.

[10] Wake had left London for the visitation of his diocese on 12 June 1716, entrusting his proxy to Nicolson. (Lambeth Palace MS 1770, f. 176: Wake's diary, 12 June 1716).

[11] On 16 June 1716, see *LJ* xx, 382.

[12] Wake had opposed a government measure for the reform of closed vestries, introduced into the Commons, and brought up to the Lords on 25 May 1716. The bill virtually disestablished the clergy from participation in local government. Wake spoke successfully for its rejection on its second reading on 5 June 1716. See Sykes, *Wake*, ii, 112–14; *LJ* xx, 365, 372.

[13] Trevor was a former Chief Justice of the Common Pleas.

636

without any further Consideration) meet with the same fate. Lord Chancellor stepping from the Woolsack, confessed that what was said against the Vestry-Bill convinced him that there was not one sound part in its whole Composition; and therefore he was stil of Opinion that it was justly denyed the respect of a Commitment: But he beged Leave to say, that (tho' he had all due Regard to the Noble Lord's Learning and knowledge of the Law) he had not now met with the like Conviction that was forced upon him the other Day. Some of the Noble Lord's Arguments he confessed had so much Weight, that he could not see how they were to be Answered; Others he thought were not so weighty, and some of them, he begged Leave to say, did not appear to him to carry any Weight at all. He would not now give his Reason for such a sentiments: 'Twould be time enough to do that in the Committee, if the Matter was carryed that Length, and if the Bill was now Rejected, their Lordships would ease themselves of the Trouble which he took to be a little unreasonable at present. Hereupon the Question was put, and carried by a Majority as near two to one as has appeared this Session. *Contents 57. Not Contents 29.*

Your Grace will, after this Plain narrative forgive the Warmth of my Zeal, which presently hurryed me to Lincolns-Inn Feilds, where I had the comfort doubled by finding his Lordship at leisure, and not displeased with my Errand.

This Day, my Lord, has bestowed ('til six in the Evening) on the Register-Bill,[14] upon which a Grand Committee employed their Oratory for about four Hours, and both sides seemed to agree that there was Room for new Amendments on the Report to the House, which is to be on Wednesday. Tomorrow we are to engage again on the Bill for appointing the thirteen Commissioners; And that's likely to afford us as lasting Speculations.

What Success it has, my Brother of Lincoln [Gibson] (who dined or supped with me this Evening) has undertaken to account for to Your Grace.[15]

I can only Add my Prayers for the Continuance of Your Grace's Health; a Blessing highly valuable to us all, and to none more than to

My good Lord,
Your Graces
most Dutiful and obliged Servant
W: Carliol.

[14] Bill to oblige papists to register their names and real estates. *LJ* xx, 384.

[15] The bill after being amended by the Commons received the royal assent on 26 June (HMC *Lords MSS* xii, 290–2).

Nicolson returned north *via* York some time between the end of the session on 26 June and 16 August 1716 when he wrote to Wake from Rose. The unsettled times following the final eradication of the rebellion in Scotland led to a belief that parliament might sit again in late September 1716.[16] In fact the next session was not to open until 20 February 1717, the day after Nicolson's arrival in London.

Nicolson's winter was largely occupied with the trials at Carlisle of the captured Scottish rebels. The Bishop believed that Carlisle had been chosen as the venue because of the 'unsullied reputation of our singular integrity'.[17] Justice Tracy, at the opening of the trials in December 1716, confirmed this. Besides the practical consideration that Carlisle was the nearest place to the 'friends of those that were to be arraign'd; so that no just complaint could be made of their witnesses being at a great distance, etc. There was also, he said, a special regard had to the loyalty of this county; where, if anywhere, honest juries might be hoped for on this occasion.'[18]

Nicolson was not directly involved in the trials and had no direct personal contact with the prisoners, yet his concern with their welfare and his show of sympathy towards some of them[19] led English newspapers falsely to accuse him of consorting with the rebels. Paradoxically, some Scots thought him hard-hearted. On Christmas Eve, just after the trials had finished a tribe of lawyers dined with the Bishop before they left for the south.[20]

During the late autumn Thomas Gibbon, the aged Dean of Carlisle, had died and Nicolson lobbied as before to have his Chancellor, Thomas Tullie, promoted. This time he was successful and Tullie was appointed just in time for the Bishop's triennial visitation of the Chapter.[21] So when Nicolson departed for London in 1717 he left

[16] BL Add. MS 6116, ff. 36–7: N. to Wake, 16 Aug. 1716; Bodl. MS Add. A269, p. 61: Gibson to N., 4 Sept., 16 Oct. 1716.

[17] *Original Letters*, iii, 365: N. to Wake, 6 Sept. 1716.

[18] Scottish History Society, *Miscellany 1*, p. 523: N. to [Wake], 8 Dec. 1716.

[19] See James, pp. 219–20. William Murray, a prisoner, wrote to his father: 'My brother John was out the other day to the Bishop who received him very kindly and told that he had ane line from Sir James Dalrymple in my favours and he woud doe all the service possible to me. My brother was sent out by us all to begg that the Bishop woud send one to say prayers to us which he very readdily granted and said it would doe us much good and affoord him ane handle to write to Court in our favours. The Sheriff is the Bishops brother [John] and I have ground to beleive will doe us all the service possibly he can and he has it in his power to doe a great deall.' NLS MS Acc. 6026 (Murray of Ochtertyre MS), 26, 268/5: W. Murray to Sir Patrick Murray of Ochtertyre, Carlisle, 24 Sept. 1716. See also ibid., 268/6–8, 12: same to same, 9 and 29 Oct., 3 Dec. 1716, 15 Feb. 1717, for Nicolson's indirect contact with the prisoners.

[20] Scottish History Society, *Miscellany 1*, pp. 535–6: N. to [Wake], 24 Dec. 1716 (postscript dated 27 Dec., see BL Add. MS 6116, f. 52).

[21] BL Add. MS 6116, ff. 41–5: N. to Wake, 22 Oct., 25 Oct., 5 Nov., 24 Nov. 1716.

a peaceful diocese in the hands of 'the first Person in that Post [of Dean] with whom (for above a Dozen Years Past) I could converse with Freedom, as one having the same dutiful Regard for the present Constitution with myself'.[22]

Having scarcely recovered from a very severe fit of 'the gravel',[23] the Bishop left Rose on 7 February and travelled via Kendal, where a recurrence of the gravel, caused him to pass 'bloody water'. He stayed at 'Brother Benson's' in Oxenholme from 8 to 11 February. From Oxenholme, in snowy weather, the 'gravel still sticking', Nicolson continued his journey, passing through Settle, Bradford ('Gravel as before'), and Rotherham where he arrived on 13 February 'wet again to the skin'. From there on the traveller made steady progress, via Nottingham, Leicester, Northampton, and Dunstable, arriving at London on 19 February, where he stayed in his old lodgings in Old Palace Yard at Mr Fitzgerald's.[24]

The two things which were largely to preoccupy Nicolson in the 1717 session were interrelated. First, there was the attempted attack of the ministry on the Church and the universities. On the eve of the great schism between the Stanhope–Sunderland and the Walpole–Townshend factions[25] the administration planned both to repeal the Occasional Conformity Act of 1711, that old Whig bugbear, and to 'regulate' the universities of Oxford and Cambridge (regarded with some justification by the government as hotbeds of Tory/High-Church/Jacobite activity). Secondly, came Nicolson's brush with Bishop Hoadly of Bangor over his sermon of March 1717, which sparked off the Bangorian Controversy.

In 1716 Townshend had already been considering a scheme for controlling the universities in consultation with Archbishop Wake, Dean Prideaux of Norwich, Lord Chancellor Cowper, and Chief Justice Parker.[26] Wake's attitude towards reform and state control was ambivalent. In a letter to the Warden of All Souls he grudgingly supported the government's position in principle.[27] Elsewhere, however, he expressed opposition to any such measures against the

[22] BL Add. MS 6116, f. 43: N. to Wake, 8 Nov. 1716. Dean Smalridge's fleeting conversion to 'Hanoverian Toryism' had taken place after his translation to Christ Church in 1713.
[23] Ibid., ff. 53–4: N. to Wake, n.d. [?Jan. 1717], 31 Jan. 1717.
[24] Ware transcripts, xxxii, 4–7.
[25] Townshend was dismissed from the Lieutenancy of Ireland on 9 Apr. Walpole resigned from the Exchequer and the Treasury on 10 Apr., and was replaced as First Lord by Stanhope. For an account of the epic quarrel and its denouement, see J. H. Plumb, *Sir Robert Walpole: The Making of a Statesman* (1956), pp. 232–42; C. Jones, 'The Impeachment of the Earl of Oxford and the Whig Schism of 1717: four new lists', *BIHR* lv (1982), 66–87.
[26] See B. Williams, *Stanhope* (Oxford, 1932), p. 401.
[27] Wake to Gardiner, 21 Mar. 1717, quoted in Sykes, *Wake*, ii, 133.

universities in 1717, and apparent opposition to their revival in 1719.[28] He told Nicolson that he had advised that the proposed reform be left out of the King's speech to parliament on 20 February 1717 (see below, 3 March); yet in December 1718, when the bill was revived, Wake was to be present at a meeting of the Lords of the Council at the Cockpit, at which, on his own evidence, it was 'unanimously agreed that the King has a right to visit the Universities'.[29]

While Nicolson was still negotiating the midland roads, Wake had received a deputation on 16 February 1717 from the Bishops of Winchester, Lichfield, Salisbury, Norwich, Ely, Gloucester, Lincoln, and Exeter, and on 18 February, on the morning of the Council meeting, attended by the Archbishop, which probably gave final approval to the King's speech delivered on 20 February, he was again visited by Winchester and Exeter.[30] It seems very likely that the bishops had urged Wake to make a stand against university 'reform'; certainly Trelawney of Winchester was strongly opposed to it.[31] A bill was nevertheless drawn up. It deprived, for an unspecified term of years,[32] the universities and their colleges of their rights of appointment and patronage. These rights were to be vested in royal commissioners, and even the chancellors of the universities were to become removable at royal pleasure and replaceable by Crown nominees.[33] However, the proposed measures 'raised such a Ferment' that in the end they were 'posponed to another Session'.[34] Many lay peers, as well as the bishops, were strongly opposed to them. Even so strong a Whig as the Duke of Devonshire 'declared that he would as soon consent to a Bill for divesting Him of Chatsworth, as for depriving the Universitys of their Privileges'.[35]

Though the King was still pressing for the Universities Bill as late as May 1717, it is clear that by mid-March Sunderland and Stanhope had resolved to break off the attack on the universities and to concentrate upon the repeal of the Occasional Conformity and Schism Acts.[36] During the 1717 session Nicolson personally was to be far

[28] See Hertfordshire RO Panshanger MS D/EP F62, ff. 37, 103: Wake to Cowper, 14 Mar. 1717, 20 Oct. 1719.

[29] Lambeth Palace MS 1770, f. 211^V: Wake's diary, 10 Dec. 1718.

[30] Ibid., f. 186^V.

[31] See letters quoted in Williams, *Stanhope*, p. 402.

[32] The ministry probably had in mind a period of seven years.

[33] See Williams, *Stanhope*, p. 401. The text of the bill is printed in ibid., pp. 456–8. A copy with Cowper's amendments is in Hertfordshire RO Panshanger MS D/EP. F138, ff. 10–14.   [34] BL Lansdowne MS 1013, f. 220: Kennett to Blackwell, 30 Mar. 1717.

[35] Bodl. MS Ballard 7, f. 51: Smalridge to Charlett, 25 Mar. 1717.

[36] Hertfordshire RO Panshanger MS D/EP E56, f. 112: Sunderland to Cowper, 13 May 1717; Christ Church Wake MS 20, f. 347: Cowper to Wake, 14 Mar. 1717. Though revived again in the 1718–19 session, the Universities Bill finally perished in 1719 after the defeat of the Peerage Bill.

more involved in lobbying against the proposed repeal of the Occasional Conformity Act than with the move against Oxford and Cambridge.

Early in March 1717 Stanhope, Sunderland, Cowper, and Bernstorff (one of George I's leading Hanoverian ministers)[37] met and agreed upon the principle of repeal. Townshend and Walpole significantly did not attend the meeting, which was followed by the sounding-out of Archbishop Wake as to the views of the Church.[38] On 18 March Nicolson had an audience with the King at which he informed him that most of the bishops were against repeal, and amid growing evidence that the Cabinet was deeply divided over this issue,[39] Nicolson was one of the seven bishops invited, five days later to dine and confer with Cowper (see below, 23 March). At this vital meeting Cowper confessed that the bill of repeal would probably not be brought in 'if the greater part of the Honest [i.e. Whig] Bishops were against it'; and having been left in no doubt that this was the case, Cowper turned the thoughts of the prelates towards finding an 'equivalent' to repeal, some expedient which would both ease the condition of the Dissenters and please the King. The possibility of 'waiving' the sacramental test or radically amending the Corporation Act was raised.[40]

The repeal of the Occasional Conformity Act in due course (May) followed the Universities Bill into hibernation for the 1717 session, to be awakened the following year. The opposition of the bishops was partially responsible for scotching it. The deepening of the Whig schism which followed the dismissal of Townshend from the Lord Lieutenancy of Ireland (cryptically noted by Nicolson—who had dined with the minister only eight days before on 9 April), and the resignation of Walpole, must also have prompted caution. But a major cause of the postponement was the heated atmosphere of religious controversy, engendered by Bishop Hoadly's sermon preached before the King on 31 March 1717, an atmosphere inimical to religious reform of the type the government was proposing.

Ben Hoadly was the most uncompromising Revolution Whig in Anglican orders and a Low Churchman of extreme latitudinarian views. Even by 1710 his writings and sermons had inspired enough

[37] Andreas Gottlieb von Bernstorff or Bernsdorff (1649–1726). See J. M. Beattie, *The English Court in the Reign of George I* (Cambridge, 1967), chapter 7 for his role at Court.

[38] Christ Church Wake MS 20, f. 347: Cowper to Wake, 14 Mar. 1717.

[39] Devonshire, the Lord President, complained to Nicolson that Stanhope and Sunderland, 'know no more of the inclinations of the common people of Great Britain, than those of China and Japan'. See below, 22 Mar. 1717.

[40] See Cowper's notes on this meeting printed below as Appendix C (from the Hertfordshire RO Panshanger MS D/EP F131, f. 11).

controversy to last most clerics a lifetime. But in the autumn of 1716 he opened a fresh campaign with his tract *A Preservative against the Principles and Practices of the Nonjurors*. Erastian in tone, it was a counterblast to Hickes's deliberately provocative *Constitution of the Christian Church, and the Nature and Consequence of Schism*, which advocated excommunicating all but non-juring churchmen. Nicolson had acquired a copy of Hoadly's tract shortly before Christmas 1716 and what he read he did not like.[41] But he was still less amused when Hoadly developed the principles expounded in this tract in a sermon before the King on 31 March 1717, using the text, 'My kingdom is not of this world' (*John* 18: 36), to argue that the Gospels afforded no warrant for any visible Church authority. The subject was thought to have been suggested by the King himself. At all events, both the sermon, published at once as *The Nature of the Kingdom, or Church, of Christ*, and the *Preservative* led to the storm of protest and pamphleteering known as the Bangorian Controversy, which by the end of the year had showered almost a thousand tracts on the heads of a hapless public and a deeply disturbed clergy.[42]

The Lower House of Convocation soon became embroiled and on 3 May 1717 appointed a committee to consider the sermon, which reported on 10 May. According to Bishop Atterbury the Upper House of Convocation was prepared to condemn the *Preservative* while leaving the sermon alone 'considering before whom it was preached, and by whose Authority published'.[43] But a conflict between the two houses seemed inevitable when the Lower House's seering condemnation of Hoadly was sent up to the bishops for their assent, and it was in order to forestall it that the ministry took the step—a fateful one for the Church—of ordering Wake to prorogue Convocation until the following November, at the same time withdrawing the repeal legislation. Apart from a short meeting in 1741 Convocation was not to sit again until 1852.[44]

Nicolson's part in the controversy, apart from trying to persuade Wake to counteract the influence of Hoadly at Court (see below, 17 April), was more self-damaging than central. With a typical excess of enthusiasm Nicolson launched into what turned out to be an undignified and ill-considered public attack on Hoadly which generated much heat and little light, which severely strained his friendship with Kennett, and which possibly cost Nicolson his translation in 1717 to

[41] Scottish History Society, *Miscellany 1*, p. 534: N. to [Wake], 22 Dec. 1716.

[42] Bennett, *Tory Crisis*, p. 215.

[43] NLW Ottley Papers 1716: Atterbury to Ottley, 7 May 1717.

[44] Lambeth Palace MS 1770, f. 190: Wake's diary, 8 May 1717; NLW Ottley Papers 13: Wake to Ottley, 9 May 1717; A. Boyer, *Political State of Great Britain*, xii (1717), 515-33.

his much-desired richer see.[45] To be fair to Nicolson he was pitched into the controversy by Dr Andrew Snape, Headmaster of Eton College (below, 22 and 29 June). Snape accused Hoadly in his *A Letter to the Lord Bishop of Bangor* of changing the text of his sermon between delivery before the King and printing, resulting in a shift of emphasis so that it now looked as though Hoadly were attacking only the Roman Church rather than the Anglican. In answer to a challenge from Hoadly to name his source for this accusation, Snape announced that it was Nicolson, who publicly acknowledged himself as such in Snape's advertisement in the *Post Boy* on 29 June 1717. Challenged by Hoadly to prove his charge, Nicolson replied in an advertisement on 1 July that an unnamed person, whom Nicolson hoped would come forward, had caused the Bishop of Bangor to alter his sermon. Hoadly denied the charge on 2 July. Meanwhile Nicolson had written privately to Kennett on 30 June accusing him of causing Hoadly to make the changes and demanding a public admission.[46] Kennett's denial appeared in print on 6 July, and two days later Nicolson published his pamphlet *A Collection of Papers Scatter'd Lately About the Town*, in which he publicly named Kennett, and provided 'proof' in the form of the testimonial of a witness to the conversation between Kennett and Hoadly (see below, 6 July). Despite the public denial by Nicolson's witness that he had testified to Kennett's guilt Nicolson persisted in his story, and was preparing 'Additional Remarks' when Wake made it clear to him on 16 July that there had been enough of this open conflict between two divines who were already on the bench and another who was a leading aspirant to it. Nicolson ventured no more into print, and Kennett's last shot was fired after the Bishop had left London for the north (see below, 24 July).

The 1717 session also saw the reopening of Lord Oxford's trial in June on the charges which had sent him to the Tower two years previously. The Whig schism, which had seen Townshend and Walpole leave the government with their followers in April, altered the prospects for Oxford. He and his supporters in the Lords—skilfully led by Harcourt—exploited the division in the Whig party and the section led by Townshend and Devonshire supported the Tories in order to embarrass the ministry. With the Whigs in the Commons deeply divided on the issue (Walpole was giving tacit support to

[45] There are hints in the diary that Sunderland may have had a translation in mind, see below, 11 Mar. 1717.

[46] The irony is that in 1704 Kennett had been accused of softening down, by textural alterations, his *Compassionate Enquiry into the Causes of the Civil War*. See J. P. Kenyon, *Revolution Principles* (Cambridge, 1977), pp. 71, 223 n. 23.

Oxford), the managers failed to appear at the trial and the accused was formally acquitted on all charges against him on 1 July.[47]

On a personal as well as a professional level, the 1717 session proved a bad one. Nicolson's proposal of marriage to Baroness Gemmingen, German governess to the Prince of Wales's children, was rejected,[48] though they were to remain close friends until her death in 1723 (e.g. below, 14 June, 11 July).

NOTE ON THE TEXT OF SESSION 12

Two different texts for the diary of 1717 exist in the Ware transcripts. As the originals have disappeared and there is no indication in the transcripts of how the two texts were related, it has been decided to print both (even though there is some repetition). Text A (Ware transcripts, xxxiii, 3–19) is in the form of a continuous diary, with short entries, running from 20 February to 22 July. Text B (Ware transcripts, xxxii, 14–25) is a much fuller diary which amplifies text A but which is not continuous. It runs from 19 February to 24 July, with many gaps which are probably the result of the policy adopted by the Wares in transcribing from the originals (see above, Chapter 3, p. 106). The amalgamated text in this edition is identified in the margin by the letters [A] and [B].

[B] [Feb.] 19. Thence [from Dunstable] (30 miles) to London. Supper (with Dr Waugh, my son John, &c.) at my Brother's: and thence to my old Lodgings. *D[eus] G[ratia].*

[A] [Feb.] 20. King's Speech.[49] Evening, at Cousin R. N[icolson]'s.

[Feb.] 21. King, prince and princess, attended. Dined, Mr Hill and son John.[50]

[Feb.] 22. On the D[uke] of B[olton?], &c. and the princess. Address.[51] Dined with the Bishop of L[incoln][52] at the Bishop of Norwich's [Trimnell's].

----

[47] For a full discussion of Oxford's impeachment and the ministerial crisis, see Jones, 'The impeachment of the Earl of Oxford'.

[48] For Nicolson's courtship see Diary entries, 28 Mar.–9 June *passim*.

[49] The opening day of the session. *LJ* xx, 412–13.

[50] John Hill senior had been John Gibson's opponent in the recent elections for the provostship of Queen's College in Feb. 1717, and had accompanied the Provost-Elect to London for Gibson's confirmation by the college's visitor, Archbishop Dawes of York. See Hearne, *Collections*, vi, 22–3.

[51] For the address on the King's speech see *LJ* xx, 417.

[52] Edmund Gibson since Feb. 1716.

The Bishop of Lincoln heard pleas of *Jus patronatus*, at St Martin's [B]
Library; where Mr Attorney General [Northey] and Mr Cowper for
those that had a Decree for Equity of Redemption: Sir Fr[ancis]
Page,[53] for Serjeant Selby[54] the mortgagee: And Mr Kettleby,[55] for
a fraudulent Grant (suit in Chancery depending) by the mortgager.
The first seemed best supported.

[Feb] 23. Dined (with the Bishop of Lincoln, provost and 8 Fellows) [A]
at the Archbishop of York's [Dawes's].
The Archbishop of York treated the Provost[56] and Fellows of [B]
Queen's College in a very generous (and nicely neat) manner. [NB.
6000 *l.* fortune to his daughter.][57] His Grace had, that morning
confirmed the Election of Mr Gibson.

[Feb.] 24. Morning, King's Chapel, Mr Egerton.[58] Dined with me, Mr [A]
Hill, Hudson and Tickill.

[Feb.] 25. Dined, Mr Provost, &c. P.m. at Serjeant's Inn to Salisbury
Court.
At the Request of the Bishops of Gloucester [Willis] and Lincoln [B]
(both Indisposed) I attended a Cause in the Court of Delegates,
being in the Commission:[59] But, Informations of 4 hours Reading
being hear[d] at the last Session, to avoid a tedious Repetition,
Adjournment was made to Thursday; when (if the said Bishops could
not appear) Application to be made to Lord Chancellor [Cowper]
for a Commission of Adjuncts.

[53] Francis Page (*c.*1661–1741), called to the bar (Inner Temple), 1690, called to the
bench, 1713; MP for Huntingdon, 1708–13; Serjeant and knighted, 1715, Baron of the
Exchequer, 1718, a Justice of the Common Pleas, 1726, of the King's Bench, 1727. *Masters
of the Bench of . . . the Inner Temple* (1883), p. 63.
[54] James Selby (d. 1724), admitted Inner Temple, 1676, called to the bar, 1683, Serjeant-
at-Law, 1700. Ibid., p. 58.
[55] Abel Ketelbey (?1676–1744), called to bar (Middle Temple), 1699, Agent and Attorney
for S. Carolina, 1712–16; Recorder of Ludlow, 1714–43; MP for Ludlow, 1722–7; Bencher
(1724) and Treasurer (1735) of Middle Temple. A Tory, he defended the Jacobites
imprisoned at Carlisle after the 1715 rebellion, and Christopher Layer during the Atterbury Plot in 1723. Sedgwick, ii, 189.
[56] John Gibson, half-brother of the Bishop of Lincoln, was provost of Queen's College,
Oxford. William Lancaster, the previous Provost, had died on 4 Feb. 1717.
[57] Nicolson's brackets. In view of the size of the fortune it should be remembered that
Dawes, as well as being Archbishop, was a baronet and a landowner in his own right.
[58] Henry Egerton (*c.*1689–1746), was the son of John, Earl of Bridgwater, BCL (Oxon)
1712, DCL July 1717; Rector of Dunnington, Yorkshire, 1713, Canon of Christ Church,
1716, Bishop of Hereford, 1724–46.
[59] The Court of Delegates was the highest ecclesiastical court for the hearing of civil
cases. 'A court which consists of Commissioners delegated or appointed by the King's Commission to sit upon an appeal to him in the Court of Chancery . . . The Judges are appointed
by the Lord Chancellor, under the Great Seal of England, *pro illa vice.*' G. Miège, *The New
State of England*, 3rd edn. (London, 1699), pt. iii, p. 68.

[A] [Feb.] 26. Dined, At Dr Dent's, with the Archbishop of Dublin [King], Bishops of Derry [Ashe] and St Asaph [Wynne], Col. Bladen, Mr Mollineux,[60] &c.

[Feb.] 27. House. Swedish Bill read twice, and (without Committing) ordered a Third Reading tomorrow.[61]

[Feb.] 28. Royal Assent.[62] Dined with Mr Green, &c. at Dean Kennett's.

March 1. Princess's Birth Day. Dined at St James's. Evening, Brother's.

[Mar.] 2. Private. Morning, Mr Lawson, for Mr Bolton to Greystock. P.m. Sir Thomas Samwell,[63] &c.

[Mar.] 3. Rains Kept me within. Dined, Bishop of Lincoln [Gibson] and I at the Archbishop of Canterbury's [Wake's].

[B]   Archbishop of Canterbury saies Visitation of the Universities was once part of the King's last Speech, but left out by Advice of himself, Lord Chancellor, Lord Orford, &c. against Lord Sunderland, Secretary Stanhope, &c. In the Northern Exp[edition] Generals Earl and Lumley[64] slighted (Lord G[odolphin]'s *old women*) and two enemies sent.[65]

[60] Possibly Samuel Molyneux (1689–1728), of Dublin and St Martin-in-the-Fields; MP for Bossiney, 1715–22; Secretary to the Prince of Wales, 1715–27, nephew of Dr Thomas Molyneux. Sedgwick, ii, 263–4.

[61] A bill to enable the King to prohibit or restrain commerce with Sweden. *LJ* xx, 421. Hanover had been openly involved in the Great Northern War since Oct. 1715 and this measure was part of the anti-Swedish policy of George I designed to force the Swedes into submission by prohibiting all trade until 31 Mar. 1718. Parliament's support was ensured by the revelation in Jan. 1717 of Swedish intrigues with the Jacobites ('Gyllenborg Plot'), but the effectiveness of the ban was nullified by the unwillingness of the Dutch to co-operate in it. See R. Hatton, *George I* (1978), pp. 188, 199, 218–19. For a full account of this plot, see J. J. Murray, *George I, the Baltic and the Whig Split* (1969), ch. 11.

[62] *LJ* xx, 422.

[63] Sir Thomas Samwell (1687–1757), 2nd Bt., Whig MP for Coventry, 1715–22, son-in-law of Thomas Fuller of Hatfield. Sedgwick, ii, 406.

[64] Gen. Thomas Erle, Lieut.-Gen. of the Ordnance and MP for Warham, and Gen. Henry Lumley, brother to the Earl of Scarbrough and MP for Arundel. Both were to be involved in June 1717 in the parliamentary attack on Gen. Lord Cadogan by the Walpole Whigs, and Lumley's participation in this attack and his sale of his regiment and virtual retirement later in the year can be partly explained by professional resentment at favours shown by the government to Cadogan. Sedgwick, i, 12–13, 229.

[65] A British naval expedition sailed to the Baltic in Mar. 1717 under Sir George Byng, but there seems to have been no question of troops accompanying it. Wake may, therefore, have been making a retrospective reference to the Scottish campaign against the Jacobites in the winter of 1715/16, when Cadogan was brought over from Holland with Dutch troops to join the forces under Argyll. Alternatively the reference could be to the Preston campaign of 1715 in which the King's troops were commanded by Generals Wills and Carpenter.

[Mar.] 4. Morning Mr Lawson, presenting Mr Bolton to Greystock. [A]
Dined with me, the Dean of Peterborough [Kennett]. Evening,
Cousins Fishers, &c.

Mr Stephenson — with his order of Ch[apter], August 17. 1710, [B]
for 10 *l.* yearly till (*by Judgment and Approbation of the Bishop and
Dean) he be well and sufficiently provided for.*

[Mar.] 5. House. Francis Partis's Cause.[66] Evening, With Mr Harris[67] [A]
at Whitehall.

[Mar.] 6. Morning, To Archbishop of Dublin, Bishop of Norwich,
&c. Sermon at St James's by Subdean.[68] Evening, To Bishop of
London [Robinson], Lord Chancellor [Cowper], &c.

Visitting the Bishop of London, he told me that Varelius[69] had [B]
set up a Runic Monument for himself on the Top of a Hillock in
the open Field. NB. His own Inscription at Cleasby[70] is

ᚤᚨᛈᛘᛉ . ᛂᚺᚱᛁ . ᚦᛁᚱᛏ . i.e.

I.e. *Homo Humi Incrementu. prov.*
'Tis, on a second perusal of the original, written thus by his Lordship   ᛏᛂᛈᚱ:ᛏᚱ . ᛁᛘᚱᛏᚱ . ᛏᛘᛁᛏ .

[Mar.] 7. House. Half a Cause.[71] Dined, Dr Dent's. P.m. His Grand- [A]
daughter's Christening.

[Mar.] 8. House. Other half of Ash's Cause. Dined at the Bishop of
Lincoln's. Evening, my Brother's.

[Mar.] 9. Morning, To Dukc of Argylc. Dincd with mc Mr Harris.
Evening, Letters many.

In two Letters (from Mr Borneman and Mr Bircherode, two [B]

---

[66] See *LJ* xx, 423; HMC *Lords MSS* xii, 312–13.

[67] He was Clerk of the Closet to the Prince of Wales (Hertfordshire RO Panshanger MS
D/EP F62, f. 22).   [68] Possibly John Doben, Subdean of the Chapel Royal.

[69] Oluf Verelius (1618–82), Swedish archaeologist.

[70] Bishop Robinson had had a stone inscription erected at Cleasby in North Yorkshire
to commemorate a benefaction made by him in 1716. The same inscription had been set
up by him in Oriel College, Oxford. The runes (innacurately cut) are taken from verse 14 of
the Norwegian Runic Poem, which Robinson would have had access to in either Worm's
Danica Literatura or Junius's *Gothicum Glossarium*. The inscription read 'Ma͡r er moldar
auki', which means 'Man is the augmentation of dust'. The same inscription is to be found
in Hearne's manuscript diary for 12 Dec. 1719 (Bodl. MS Hearne's Diaries, lxxxiv, 76). See
J. A. W. Bennett, 'The history of Old English and Old Norse studies in England in the
time of Francis Junius till the end of the 18th century', Oxford, D.Phil., 1938, p. 418;
B. Dickins, *Runic and Heroic Poems* (Cambridge, 1915), pp. 26, 32.

[71] See *Ashe* v. *Ashe. LJ* xx, 424–5; HMC *Lords MSS* xii, 313–16.

Danish Gentlemen) communicated by Mr Chamberlayne, mention is made of the following writers (on Antiquities of their Country) and some of their books unknown to me; As —

Petri Claudij vera *Descriptio Norvegiae et vicinaru Insularu* 4⁰.[72]

Petri Risenij *Atlas Daniae*; ubi omnes celebriores Daniae et Norvegiae Urbes aeri incisae dantur.

Snorronis Sturlaesonij *Chronicon Norvegiae*. Fol. et 4to. Vertente P. Claudio et Edente Ol. Wormio.[73]

Eric. Ol. Tormij *Effigies Regum Danorum cum Chronologia* &c.

Tormodi Torfaci *Series Regu. Danorum.*[74] Hic Tamen caute legendus, quippe cum omisit quosdam Reges. 4to.

Tho. Bartholini, sen. *Dissertatio de Ordine Danebrogico* Fol.[75]

Tho. Bartholini, jun. scripsit [praeter Antiquitates Dan. de causa mortis, &c][76] libru de Antiqitatibus Daniae Ecclesiasticis, luce publica dignissimu, qui adhuc in manibus est filii eius Tho. Bartholini, Tho. fil. Tho. Nep. professoris philosophiae Haun, qui in Cogitationibus suis de nomine Regni Daniae, 4to, passim illud opus edere pollicitus est.

Jo. Bircherodij *Dissertationes de Antiquitatibus Danicis ante natum Christum.*[77]

Otton. Sperlingij *Commentarius de Danicae Linguae et Nominis antiqua Gloria* &c. 4to. Hafn. 1694.[78]

Tho. Bircherodij *Specimen rei monetariae de nummis ante Familiam Oldenburgicam*. 4to.[79]

Willichij Westhovij *Urbes et Oppida Selandiae*. 4to. Haun. 1707.

Tho. Bartolini *Numismata Danorum vicinarumq Gentium, a Joh. Mulenio collecta*. 4to. Haun. 1670.[80]

[72] Peder Claussen's book *Snorre Chronicae Sturlesons in Linguam Danicam Versio, et Descriptio Insularum Septentrionalium* had been published in 1633.

[73] Snorri Sturluson (1178-1241) was an Icelandic historian and author of the *Edda, Heimskringla* and *Chronicum Regum Norwegorium*. The edition of the *Chronicum* referred to here was published in Copenhagen in 1633. Oluf Worm (1588-1654), was the Danish author of *Lexicon Runicum* (1650) and *Monumenta Danica*.

[74] Thormond Torvesen (1636-1719), Icelandic historian, published his *Series dynastarum et regum Daniae . . .* in 1702.

[75] Thomas Bartholin, eminent Danish antiquary and legal historian, published *De Equestris ordinis Danebrogici, a Christiano V insturati origine* in 1689.

[76] Nicolson's brackets.

[77] Johannes Bircherod, professor of history and geography at Copenhagen, published eight *Disputatio . . . circa disqvisitiones antiqvitatum patriae Daniae gentilis* between 1701 and 1718.

[78] Otto Sperling (1634-1715), Danish jurist and historian, who published *De danicae linguae et nominis antiqua gloria et praerogativa inter septentrionales commentariolus* at Copenhagen in 1694.

[79] Thomas Broder Bircherod's *Specimen antiqvae rei monetariae, Danorum . . .* was published in 1701.

[80] *J. Mulenii Numismata Danorum et vivinarum gentium edita a T. Bartholino* (Hafniae, 1670), 8⁰.

Jani Laur. Wolfij *Norvegia Illustrata*. 4to. Hafn. 1657.[81]

Jonae Rami *Nori Regnum. sc. Norvegia Antiqua et Ethnica*. 4to. Christianiae, 1689.[82]

Descriptio Fodinaru Norvegiae. 4to. Hafn. 1649.

Biblia Islandica. Fol. Holae Island. 1584 et 1644.

Snebiorni Torphaei Islandi, *Annales Omniu praesidium Islandiae*, 4to. 1656.

Thoranini Erici Islandi *Historia de Haldano Nigro Rege Oplandoru in Norvegia*. 4to. Hafn. 1658.[83]

Claud. Christopheri *Chronican Groenlandiae*. 4to. Hafn. 1622.[84]

Dan. Fabritij *Tractatus de Islandia et Groenlandia*. 4. Rostock.1625.

J. Birchevodij *Arctos Alexandriae sc. de prisco Septentrionalium in urbe illa mercatu*. Hafn. 1685.

MSStu Lubecense Anonymi Authoris de profectione Danoru in Gerram Sanctam a Theodorico Monacho dicatum Augustino Archiepiscope Nidrosiensi, Editum a Bernh. Casp. Kirchmanno, Amstel. 1684.[85]

NB. The same day Mr H[arris] assured me that the Doctrine of the *Preservative* (on the Text — *whose sins &c.*) was advanced *verbatim* in a Sermon preached by the Bishop of Norwich 20 years agoe.[86]

[Mar.] 10. I went by water (thro' Bridge) to St Olave's; and preached [A] Charity-Sermon. Dined with Archdeacon Boulter.[87] P.m. Dr Bennet.[88]

---

[81] Jens Wolf, *Norrigia illustrata* . . . (Copenhagen, 1641), 4⁰.

[82] Jonas Ramus, *Nori Regnum: hoc est Norvegia antiqua et ethnica* . . . (Christianiae, 1689), 4⁰.

[83] Thoraninus Kricius, *Historia de Haldano cognomento Nigro, Rege Oplandorum in Norvego, translata elingua veteri, toti feri Septentriori olim Communi in Latinam a Thoranino Erico Islando* (1658), 4⁰.

[84] Claus Christophersen Lyschander (1557-1623), Danish scholar, who first published his 'Chronicle of Greenland', in Danish verse, in Copenhagen in 1608.

[85] *Commentarii historici duo hacterus inediti: alter de regibus vetustis Norvegicus, (a Theodoricus monacho Nidrosiensi conscriptus) alter de profectione Danorum in Terram Sanctam circa annum MCLXXXV, susceptam, eodem tempore ab incerto autore conscriptus: cura olim et opera J. Kirchmanni* . . . *nunç primum editi ab hujus nepote Bernh. Casp. Kirchmanno*, published in Amsterdam in 1684.

[86] The preacher in question was probably Charles Trimnell, then Bishop of Norwich, and not John Moore, who was Trimnell's predecessor from 1691 to 1707. The reference to 'the Doctrine of *Preservative*' reflects the recent controversy over Bishop Hoadly's *A Preservative against the Principles and Practices of the Nonjurors* (1716). See above, sessional intro., p. 642.

[87] Dr Hugh Boulter (1672-1742); Archdeacon of Surrey; MA (Oxon) 1693, Fellow Magdalen College, 1689-1709; Rector St Olave's, Southwark, 1708-22, Archdeacon since 1716. Later Bishop of Bristol and Archbishop of Armagh.

[88] Thomas Bennet (1673-1728); MA (Cantab.) 1696, DD 1715; Fellow St. John's College, 1694-1705; Rector St James's, Colchester, 1700-13; Rector of St Giles's, Cripplegate, 1716; controversialist and oriental scholar.

[Mar.] 11. Rainy. Dined with Archbishop of Canterbury very Kind; And so, saies he, is Lord S[underland].

[B]   My good Lord of Canterbury (after I had dined with him) acquainted me with the Applications made this morning, by our Great men severally and diversly, touching methods for *Reformation of the Universities* by creating a Trust in the King or His Commissioners for . . . years; and for *easing the Dissenter*.[89] It[em], Lord S[underland]'s new scheme in my favour. *Metuo Danaos*.

[A] [Mar.] 12. Morning, Duke of Devonshire (in the House) exceeding Kind to me. P.m. Dr Waugh.

[Mar.] 13. Morning, Dr Green's Sermon at Court. Dined Home, with Dr D[ent]. Evening, Bishop of Lincoln.

[Mar.] 14. Mrs Jackson and Mrs Licence, &c. Dined with me Cousin F[isher].

[Mar.] 15. House. Nothing but Adjournment till Tuesday. Evening, my Brother's.

[Mar.] 16. Morning, Bishop of Lincoln, Archbishop of Dublin, Sir R. S[andford], &c. &c. Evening, Dr Cannon, with Kind message from Lord T[ownshend].

[B]   Archbishop of Dublin tells me that the late Governors in Ireland have run the K[ingdom] 2,000,000 *l*. in debt: So that none cares to enter upon't.[90] Church Leases there have half the Improved value reserved Rents.[91] NB. Two parts of cost in Building.

[A] [Mar.] 17. From St Margaret's to dine with the Bishop of Lincoln. Evening, with Archbishop of Canterbury.

---

[89] See above, sessional intro., pp. 639–41.

[90] The figure of 2 million may be a mistranscription. The gross debt of the Irish administration in mid-1717 was £248,483; the net figure (balances in collectors' hands, arrears of revenue, etc., having been subtracted) was £98,283 (*CJ Ireland*, iii, appdx, pp. civ, cviii). The late governors were the Duke of Grafton and the Earl of Galway. Archbishop King had not co-operated fully with the administration.

[91] Bishops in Ireland had the option, invariably exercised, of taking a fine, i.e. a lump sum, at the setting of a lease which could not exceed 21 years, and reducing the annual rent in proportion. Legislation (10 & 11 Car. I, c. 3), designed to protect their successors, prevented bishops from reducing their rents by more than half, so that no matter what fines tenants paid, leases which did not oblige them to pay at least half the full annual value of the land were not valid.

[Mar.] 18. Morning, To Duke of Devonshire, King, &c. Evening, Mrs License's.

I waited (with Mr Secretary Methwin [Methuen])[92] on the King; [B]
and acquainted His Majesty that 18 or 19 of the Bishops (in 25 the Bishop of Worcester [Lloyd] absent, with out Proxy) would be against Repealing the Act against Occasional Communion.[93] K[ing]. For what Reasons? A[nswer]. Probably because so lately, and unanimously, agreed to. K[ing]. Have not the Dissenters deserved well since? A[nswer]. The honest and deserving will have no Benefit by the Repeal.

[Mar.] 19. House. Adjourned till Friday. Dined, Dr Smith. Evening, [A]
princess Anne,[94] &c.

[Mar.] 20. Dined, Bishop of St Asaph and I with the Archbishop of Canterbury. Whence we went to Duke of Devonshire.

The Bishop of St Asaph and I sent for to dine with the Archbishop [B]
of Canterbury who acquainted us that the Earl of Sunderland, Mr Secretary Stanhop and Baron Bernsdorff, had newly declared the King's earnest desire to have the Dissenters eased, &c. Proposed to be done on a *political foot*, by a Sacramental Test in their own Congregations. This also will justly raise Jealousies and Disquicts; and cannot be assented to by Bishops.

[Mar.] 21. Dined at Bishop of Peterborough's [Cumberland]. P.m. [A]
Dean K[ennett]'s, Duke of Devonshire and I counter.

[Mar.] 22. Morning, To Lord President [Devonshire], Lord T[ownsh-end], &c. House. Mutiny-Bill.[95] Letters to Fleet-street.

I waited on the (Duke of Devonshire) Lord President; who gave [B]
me a most obligeing and open hearted Account of His Grace's haveing dealt freely with the King and foreign ministers in relation to the pernitious Advices given (in favour of the Dissenters) by two of

---

[92] Paul Methuen (*c.*1672–1757), diplomat and statesman; MP for Devizes, 1708–10, Brackley, 1713–14, 1715–47; employed on six diplomatic missions and embassies between 1694 and 1715, to Portugal, Turin, and Spain; a Lord of the Admiralty, 1709–10, of the Treasury, 1714–17, Secretary of State for the South, June 1716 to 21 Apr. 1717, when he resigned (*CTB 1717*, p. 287) to follow Walpole and Townshend into opposition. Sedgwick, ii, 254.

[93] See above, sessional intro., p. 641. As it turned out when the vote was taken two sessions later fifteen bishops opposed the repeal on 19 Dec. 1718. See N. Sykes, *Church and State in England in the Eighteenth Century* (Cambridge, 1934), p. 35. Both Archbishop Wake and Bishop Trelawney estimated that at this time twenty bishops opposed repeal (Hertfordshire RO Panshanger MS D/EP F62, f. 37: Wake to Cowper, 14 Mar. 1717; Christ Church Wake MS 15, unfoliated: Trelawney to Wake, 29 Mar. 1717).

[94] The eldest daughter of the Prince of Wales, born 1709. She died in 1759. .

[95] *LJ* xx, 428.

our own Grandees,[96] who Know no more of the Inclinations of the Common people of Great Britain, than of those of China or Japan.

[A] [Mar.] 23. Dined with six Bishop more, at the Lord Chancellor's [Cowper]. 4 against Occasional Conformity.

[B] Seven Bishops (Sarum [Talbot], Carlisle, Glocester, St Asaph, Lincoln, Bangor [Hoadly] and Exon [Blackburne]) treated at dinner by Lord Chancellor Cowper; who modestly told us, *That 'twas his misfortune to be pinned to the Wool-sack, so that he had not Access (as other Lords had) to the Bench of Bishops: And therefore he beged that we would now inform him, what was variously reported, how our sentiments stood about the Repeal of the Act against Occasional Conformity.* His Lordship was hereupon assured that 18 in 25 (As the King had been told) would be against the Repeal; which he easily credited, when he found Four of us (Carlisle, St Asaph, Lincoln, and Exon) were so.[97] He recommended to our perusal the Corporation-Act of 1661 as what might suggest a more allowable scheme.[98]

[A] [Mar.] 24. Morning, From Dr K[ennett]'s to hear the Bishop of Lincoln at Court. P.m. with Archbishop of Canterbury.

[Mar.] 25. Sister[-in-law] N[icolson]'s Birth-day. Royal Assent to the Mutiny Bill.[99]

[Mar.] 26. Private all day. P.m. Bishop of Lincoln for the Corporation-Act,[100] Dr Canon against it.

[Mar.] 27. Dined with me, at opening my pot of chars, Mrs Paton, Mr Maleverer,[101] J. Fisher, &c.

[96] Sunderland and Stanhope.
[97] Gibson of Lincoln and Blackburne of Exeter were to support repeal in Dec. 1718. Sykes, *Church and State*, p. 35.
[98] Cowper's notes of this meeting are printed below, Appendix C.
[99] *LJ* xx, 430–1. Six peers protested at the third reading.
[100] Gibson was to change his mind over this. By Nov. 1717 he was agreeing with several other bishops who wished to relieve the Dissenters that 'the more desirable method would be to abolish the Sacramental test so far as it concerned Corporations'. Nicolson believed it was Gibson's desire 'to prevent the undue returns of members disaffected to the present government' which converted him to a policy which would effectively readmit Dissenters in large numbers into municipal corporations. See Sykes, *Gibson*, pp. 72–3.
[101] Bellingham Mauleverer (1689–1752), of Arncliff, Yorkshire. A Cambridge graduate (MA 1715), he became Chaplain to Bishop Nicolson in Derry, secured preferment in Ireland and married Nicolson's daughter, Elizabeth, on 3 May 1722. J. B. Leslie, *Derry Clergy and Parishes* (Enniskillen, 1937), p. 259.

[Mar.] 28. Dined at Dr Dent's. Evening, Mr Harris and I with Lady Governess.[102]

At five in the evening, I went (with Mr Harris) to St James's [B] to kiss the hand of Princess Carolina;[103] and, missing of her, was most courteously entertained by the two Elder sisters.[104] The Lady Governess (as accustomed) read a *Spectator* in English; and Translated (*Ex Tempore*) a French Comedy read to her by my friend. With this excellent Lady we stayed two hours; till the Princesses went to Supper 'twixt 8 and 9.

[Mar.] 29. Dined with me, Mr W. Lawson.[105] House. Papers brought [A] in.[106] Evening, Brothers.

[Mar.] 30. Dined at Lord Townshend's, with Bishops of St Asaph, Lincoln, Mr Naylor,[107] Dean of Worcester [Hare], Dr Cannon.

[Mar.] 31. From Whitehall to dine with the Bishop of Lincoln at the Archbishop of Canterbury's [on the Oxon-Bill].[108] P.m. with the o[l]d Bishop [Cumberland] to Dean Kennett's.

April 1. Morning, To the Temple: House. Lord M[ontague]'s[109] Ap[peal]. P.m. with the Lady Governess, &c.

[Apr.] 2. Mostly within. Dined with me Dr Dent. Evening, Birthday-Visit balked.[110]

[102] Auguste Sophie, Baroness Gemmingen (1676–1723), Governess to the Prince of Wales's children. Daughter of Reinhard von Gemmingen, President of the Privy Council in Baden. Nicolson appears to have fallen in love with her and to have contemplated marriage (see below, 29 Apr. 1717), but nothing came of it. 'Adieu Pallas', the disappointed suitor wrote on 9 June. See James, pp. 235–6; *CW* v (1905), 9.

[103] Caroline (1713–57), daughter of the Prince of Wales.

[104] Anne (1709–59) and Amelia (1711–86).

[105] Wilfred Lawson (*c*.1678–1732), son of Henry, the fifth son of Sir Wilfred Lawson, 1st Bart. He became the Vicar of Warkworth, Northumberland, a living in Nicolson's gift, in Apr. 1717. See J. C. Hodgson, *A History of Northumberland*, v (1899), 186–7.

[106] Concerning the riot in Oxford in Nov. 1716 on the Prince of Wales's birthday. See *LJ* xx, 432; HMC *Lords MSS* xii, 359–64; Hearne, *Collections*, v, 333. For the initiation of the Lords' investigation into the riot see Bodl. MS Ballard 7, ff. 53–4: Bishop Smalridge to Charlett [25 Mar. 1717].

[107] Perhaps George Naylor, MP for Seaford.

[108] Nicolson's brackets. For the contentious topic of university reform, before and during this session, and the attitude of Wake and other bishops, as well as of Sunderland and Stanhope, towards it, see above, sessional intro., pp. 639–41.

[109] Henry Browne (before 1641–1717), 5th Viscount Montague. He became Secretary of State to James II in exile in 1691, succeeding to the title in 1708. He died 25 June 1717. For his appeal see *LJ* xx, 434, 439; HMC *Lords MSS* xii, 282–5.

[110] This was Baroness Gemmingen's forty-first birthday.

[Apr.] 3. House. Resolutions, after long Debate, on the Riot at Oxford.[111]

[Apr.] 4. Dined with me Bishop of Lincoln. Evening, presentation to Warkworth[112] and Commission for Instit[ution] to Greystock.

[Apr.] 5. Dined with me Mr L. Farrington.[113] House. Archbishop of York's complaint.[114] Evening, Brother's.

[Apr.] 6. House. Printers censured. P.m. with Mr Harris to Kiss the hand of the younger Princess Carolina &c.

[Apr.] 7. Bishop of Norwich preached, at Court, on 1 *Timothy* 4, 8. excellently.

[Apr.] 8. Dined, the Bishop of St Asaph and I with the Archbishop of Canterbury. P.m. At Mr H[arris]'s Lodgings.

[Apr.] 9. Dined, the Bishop of Lincoln and I with Dr Gee. P.m. Lord T[ownshend] displaced.[115]

[Apr.] 10. House. Royal Assent to Land Tax, &c.[116] Noise of new Removes.[117]

[Apr.] 11. All the day within Doors, at Maundy-Lists and Sermon.[118]

[111] See *LJ* xx, 436–7; *Parl. Hist.* vii, 430–4. Resolutions were passed by sixty-five to thirty-three censuring the university and the city of Oxford, and led to a protest by the university. According to Bishop Smalridge, 'Great Wrath is expressed against the Protestat[ion], but there has been no Motion for Obliterating it' (Bodl. MS Ballard 7, f. 56: to Charlett, 6 Apr. 1717).   [112] Of Revd. W. Lawson.

[113] Perhaps Laurence Farington of Kendal, Fellow of Queen's College, Oxford, 1712; Vicar of Monks Sherburne, Hampshire, 1722.

[114] Archbishop Dawes had complained about a piece in the *St James's Evening Post* which accused a 'Northern Prelate' of ordaining two men turned out of the Excise for disaffection to the government. The author and publisher were questioned before the House on 6 Apr. (the printer being too ill to attend). The author was put under arrest but the publisher, a woman, was discharged on the motion of the Archbishop. See Bodl. MS Ballard 7, ff. 55–6: Smalridge to Charlett, 6 Apr. 1717, for the details of the examination; see also *LJ* xx, 438–40.

[115] As Lord Lieutenant of Ireland (appointed 13 Feb. 1717). See Plumb, *Walpole*, i, 240–1.   [116] *LJ* xx, 443.

[117] Townshend's fall was followed immediately by an open split in the government party and especially by the resignation of Walpole from the post of head of the Treasury and of Paul Methuen from the Southern Secretaryship.

[118] On Maundy Thursday (18 Apr., q.v.), Nicolson, as Lord Almoner, was to wash the feet of as many poor men as the years of the King's life (in this case fifty-seven) and distribute the 'Maundy money' to them. He also had to preach in the Chapel Royal. Nicolson resigned the post upon his translation to Derry.

[Apr.] 12. Dined with me Mr Harris. Evening, At my Brother's where she-Capt. Pinfold.

[Apr.] 13. Morning, Labouring, with Dr Cannon, &c. at our Maundy-Lists. P.m. Letters.

[Apr.] 14. I preached at Queen's Square. Dined at Mr Green's with Dr Reynolds. P.m. At the King's Chapel and Bishop of Lincoln's.

[Apr.] 15. Morning, Finishing our Lists. P.m. I began to write my sermon fair for the King's Chapel.

[Apr.] 16. Both Houses adjourned (by the King's Directions) to May 6.[119]

[Apr.] 17. P.m. The Bishops of Lichfield [Hough], Lincoln and Exeter, with me; by Instructions of the Archbishop of Canterbury.
    The Bishops of Lichfield, Lincoln and Exeter (at the Request [B] of the Lord Archbishop of Canterbury) met at my Lodgings: where we unanimously agreed to lay before His Grace, as our humble opinion and Advice
1. That it is highly necessary (at this Juncture) that he more frequently attend the King in person, to prevent Misrepres[ent]ations.
2. That he privately call the Bishop of Bangor to him; and require him to explain the offensive propositions in his Sermon.[120]
3. That His Majesty be humbly addressed to beware of what commands he gives for the printing Sermons.
4. That no Business (if it may be avoided) he entered upon in Convocation, till the present Jumble is over.[121]

[Apr.] 18. Maundy Thursday. A wearisome day with me.   [A]

[Apr.] 19. Bishop of Glocester preached at the King's Chapel. Evening, at Salisbury Court.

[119] *LJ* xx, 445.
[120] The notorious sermon preached before the King on 31 Mar. 1717, *The Nature of the Kingdom, or Church, of Christ*, was designed as a preparation for the ministry's programme of repeal legislation. See, in general, above, sessional intro., p. 642. Hoadly concluded that private sincerity was the important thing in theological matters and that therefore there could be no compulsion in affairs of conscience.
[121] See above, sessional intro., p. 642.

[Apr.] 20. Private all day. Mr H[arris]'s Report from the Lady Governess.

[Apr.] 21. I preached at Court. King, prince and princess, communicated. Dined with Archbishop of Canterbury. Evening, Mr Lawsons.

[Apr.] 22. Morning, with Lord of Canterbury to Duke of Devonshire, &c. Dined with me Dr Smith. Evening, Harpagon.

[Apr.] 23. Private; seen only by Bishop of Lincoln and Dr Gee.

[Apr.] 24. Morning, Princess, on Hoadley. Dined with the Chaplains. Evening, Gemminghen.

[Apr.] 25. Morning, With Mr Secretary Addison,[122] &c. Dined, Bishop of Lincoln and I at Dr Waugh's. Evening, The Provost's Contract.[123]

[Apr.] 26. Morning, At Court, too early for the princess's prayers. Dined, At Home.

[Apr.] 27. Dined with the Bishops of Lincoln and Exon at the Bishop of Winton's [Trelawney's] in Chelsea.

[Apr.] 28. I preached at Great Queen Street. Dined at my Brother's with Dr Waugh, Mr Maleverer, &c.

[Apr.] 29. Morning, At Court, with secretary Addison. Evening, L[ady] Gemm[ingen] for Joyntures only.

[Apr.] 30. Visits to Archbishop of York, Duke of Devonshire, &c. Dined with me, Mr Hudson. Evening, Letters.

May 1. Dined At the Bishop of Lincoln's. Evening with Lady Governess and Lord Carlile, not Pr[incess].

[B]   Mr Beauvoire (Chaplain to the Earl of Stair)[124] gave a long History

---

[122] Joseph Addison (1672–1719), the man of letters, who as MP for Malmesbury (1710–19) held the Secretaryship of State of the Southern Department, Apr. 1717–Mar. 1718. Sedgwick, i, 407–8. He was appointed on 16 Apr. *vice* Paul Methuen, in the ministerial reshuffle following the fall of Townshend and the resignation of Walpole.

[123] See above, 23 Feb.

[124] John Dalrymple (1673–1747), 2nd Earl of Stair (1707), Scottish representative peer, 1707–8, 1715–34, 1744–7, and Ambassador Extraordinary to the Court of Versailles, 1715–20.

of the Many great Accomplishments, Courage, Skill in Languages, Civil Law, &c. of his Lord; and likewise of the great propensity in France (and Swisserland) to the use of our English Liturgy.

[May] 2. At the Temple, with Mr Lowther. Dined, Bedford-Row. [A] Evening, Letters.

[May] 3. Morning, To Bishop of Norwich and Dean of Peterborough [Kennett]. P.m. Dr Canons. Evening, Mr Sadler and B[rother]'s.

Mr Campbel (Lord Provost of Edinburgh,[125] visitting me with [B] Col. Cambel)[126] saies — The Army in the North is grievously oppressive to Newcastle: the Corporation paying 40 *l.* per week for extraordinary supplies, besides the sufferings of Inn-Keepers and other Householders: And that Alderman Ridley[127] is treated by the Officers there as if he were a professed Jacobite or Rebel. NB. This same Provost is a rigid presbyterian.

The same day Mr Chamberlayne sent me Andr. Ol. Rhyzelius's *Treatise de Sepultura Sueogothorum Ethnica et Christiana*, 8° Upsal. 1709, mostly borrowed from Wormius, Verelius, Rudbeck, and Bartholin. Some use is also made of the *Edda* and *HeimsKringla*. He sent me likewise a Copy of a Letter to himself (dated at Stockholm, Idib. Jun. 1716) from the said Rhyzelius, who stiles himself *Ad aulam Reg. Satell Regg. Ecclesiastes*; with a MS Copy of his *Diatribe de Skaldis Sueo Gothicis.* Herein he labours to prove the writeing of poems to be more antient than prose; and that the first Laws and Rules of Morality, as well as Civil Government, were in mccter. He observes that (contrary to Ol. Wormius's claim of Right for his Danes) the true Tribeing of the Skaldi is in this order: *Skaldi qui claruerunt sub Regibus, 1. Suio Gothiae. 2. Norvegiae. 3. Daniae.* and that they are thus duely placed in the *Skaldathal*, or *Catalogue of the Skaldi*, which is annexed to the *Konga-Sagor* published at Visingburg, 1670. Their Carols (sung at the Tables and merry-meetings of princes and great men) were called *Bragarbott, Bardadon,*

[125] John Campbell (1665–1739), Lord Provost of Edinburgh, 1715–17, 1719–21, 1723–5; MP for Edinburgh, 1721–3. Sedgwick, i, 522–3.

[126] Possibly James Campbell, youngest son of 2nd Earl of Loudoun; fought as a captain at Blenheim; colonel of Scots Greys, 15 Feb. 1717. As lieutenant-general (1742) mortally wounded at Fontenoy, 1745. Dalton, *George I*, i, 221–2.

[127] Richard Ridley (d. 1739) coal-owner, shipowner, and merchant of Newcastle upon Tyne; later of Heaton, Northumberland (1719); Mayor of Newcastle, 1713 and 1732; Governor of the Hostmans' Company, 1716–25. See E. Hughes, *North Country Life in the Eighteenth Century: The North-East* (Manchester, 1952), pp. 11, 69–70, 209–14, 247 n. and *passim*; *The Correspondence of Sir James Clavering*, ed. H. T. Dickinson, Surtees Soc. clxxviii (Gateshead, 1967), pp. 130, 132, 226.

Bardaquaed, Bardasong, &c. He concludes with an Epigram in praise of the old Swedish poets, which ends thus—
> *Graecia, da veniam, mihi fassit vera fateri,*
> *Quae patriae nemo dissimulavit amans.*
> *Plurima, tot populi quae te didicere Magistra*
> *Haec prius Arctoi se docuere viri.*

[A] [May] 4. Private all day. P.m. Mr James L[owther] with account of Election at Cockermouth.[128]

[May] 5. Dean of Chichester [Sherlock] preached at Court on *Be ye perfect*. Evening, Fen[   ] Tillotson.

[May] 6. King's Gr[eat] Speech.[129] Dined with me, Mr H[arris] and Mr Gilbert.[130] Evening, Mrs Crow.

[May] 7. Morning, Visitted by Duke of Devonshire and Lord T[ownshend]. House. Address reported.[131] Evening, Harpago[n].

[May] 8. Morning, Queen Ann's Bounty. Address presented to the King. Dined and Evening with Bishop of Lincoln.

[May] 9. Morning, To D[uke] of A[rgyll], Sir R. S[andford][132] and dined with Mr H[arris] at the Tower. Not at the House.

[May] 10. Morning, Thanking Secretary A[ddison]. Long Cause. Evening, With my Fellow-Executors[133] and Mr Freeman.[134]

[May] 11. Private (at Letters) till the evening when cheerful at St James's.

[May] 12. Morning, I preached Charity-S[ermon] at St Magnus. Dined at Mr Fetherston's. Evening open; with princesses, &c.

[128] At the by-election on 29 Apr. 1717 Thomas Pengelly, Serjeant-at-Law, legal adviser and nominee of the Duke of Somerset (lord of the manor), was elected *vice* James Stanhope, appointed to the office of Secretary of State. Pengelly defeated Sir Robert Raymond, the government's candidate. Sedgwick, i, 222–3; ii, 334–5; HMC *7th Report*, pp. 681, 683.

[129] Announcing that the fleet under Byng had reached the Sound, that there was to be a reduction of land forces by 10,000 men, and an Act of Grace. *LJ* xx, 447.

[130] John Gilbert (1693–1761), later Chaplain in Ordinary to George I, Dean of Exeter, Bishop of Llandaff and Salisbury, and Archbishop of York (1757).

[131] Address of thanks: *LJ* xx, 449.

[132] Repl. 'Sir R. St'.

[133] Nicolson was an executor for John Nicolson, whose funeral took place on 15 May 1717. John Nicolson's will can be found in abstract in Ware transcripts, xxxii, 32. It is dated 28 Apr. 1717.

[134] A beneficiary in John Nicolson's will.

[May] 13. Dined with the Deans of York [Finch][135] and Durham [Montague], &c. at St James's. P.m. Pensions. Evening, with the Bishop of Lincoln at Dr Dunster's.[136]

[May] 14. House. Half an Irish Cause. Evening, Huzza Science!

[May] 15. Dined at my Brother's. P.m. Mr John Nicolson's Funeral.

[May] 16. Morning, With J. N[icolson]'s Trustees. Dined At home. Evening, Bishop of L[incoln] and Letters.

[May] 17. House. Lawrence's Appeal. Decree affirmed with 30 *l.* costs.[137] Evening, St James's.

[May] 18. Mostly private. Visitted by Bishop of Lincoln and Dr Canon, &c. Dined, Mr Harris.

[May] 19. Dr Oldcomb preached at Court. P.m. Prayers and Tillotson ibid.

[May] 20. Vol[ume] contributions. House. Sunderland,[138] P.m. consult of Bishops[139] at Archbishop of Canterbury's.

[May] 21. Vol[ume] Contributions. House. Carter's Case.[140] Evening, With executors at the *Leg.*[141]

[May] 22. Vol[ume] contributions. House. Lord Oxford's petition.[142] Evening, Pallas.[143]

---

[135] Henry Finch (*c.*1664–1728), Lord Nottingham's brother, Dean of York since 1702.
[136] Samuel Dunster (d. 1754), DD (Cantab. 1713); Vicar of Paddington, *c.*1716 and Prebendary of Salisbury, 1717.
[137] *LJ* xx, 458; HMC *Lords MSS* xii, 344–5.
[138] The River Wear and Port of Sunderland Bill. *LJ* xx, 463; HMC *Lords MSS* xii, 387–9. For the rapid growth of Sunderland in the early eighteenth century and the Wear navigation project of 1717, see E. Hughes, *North Country Life*, pp. 12–13.
[139] The bishops involved were Lichfield, Oxford, Lincoln, and Carlisle. Wake also records that Lord Manchester visited him that afternoon. Lambeth Palace MS 1770, f. 190ᵛ: Wake's diary, 20 May 1717.
[140] *LJ* xx, 464; HMC *Lords MSS* xii, 367–9.
[141] Possibly in Palace Yard. B. Lillywhite, *London Signs* (1972), nos. 9952–3.
[142] Oxford had been imprisoned in the Tower since 16 July 1715. For his imprisonment see Auditor Edward Harley's 'Memoirs' in HMC *Portland MSS* v, 665–9, and Oxford's letters in ibid., pp. 529–32. Oxford now petitioned the House to take his case into consideration, and it was referred to a committee to search for precedents. *LJ* xx, 466; HMC *Lords MSS* xii, 197. For a discussion of Oxford's impeachment, see C. Jones, 'The impeachment of the Earl of Oxford and the Whig Schism of 1717: four new lists', *BIHR* lv (1982), 66–87.
[143] Nicolson's pet name for Baroness Gemmingen.

[May] 23. Dined with me Mr Harris and J. Rothery. House. Cause compromised.[144]

[May] 24. Morning, A while at Court. House. Notice of tomorrow's Report.[145] Evening, Brother's.

[May] 25. House. On the Question for Impeachments falling on prorogation. *Contents*, 45. *Not Contents*, 87.[146]

[May] 26. Dr Boulter preached at the Chapel. Bishop of Asaph and I dinner with him, &c. Evening, Princess with M[adam] Gemm[ingen].

[May] 27. House. Tryal for June 13 (against 6th) carryed by 85 against 44.[147] Evening, with Bishop of Sarum at Dr Dunster's.

[May] 28. King George's Birth-day. Dined Mr H[arris] with me at dinner and Salisbury Court. Attendance on Mr Lutwich.[148]

[May] 29. Dr Dunster preached for me. Dined with him at the Bishop of Sarum's. Evening, Bishop of Exon. Dr Hern[149] and Mr Harris with me.

[May] 30. Morning, Committee for Rotherhith-Church.[150] The rest private.

[May] 31. Morning, Visits to Lord C[arlisle?] &c. After dinner Mr H[arris] and I to Battersey. Evening, Brother's.

[144] Probably a reference to the appeal of Charles O'Hara which was withdrawn because it had not been presented within the time limit laid down in standing orders. *LJ* xx, 468; HMC *Lords MSS* xii, 445–7.

[145] On the Earl of Oxford's case. *LJ* xx, 469; HMC *Lords MSS* xii, 197.

[146] The report on Lord Oxford's case was given by Lord Trevor and quoted precedents between 1660 and 1699. It is printed in *LJ* xx, 472–4. The vote was on the question 'That the impeachment of the Commons against the Earl of Oxford is determined by the intervening Prorogation'. This vote supported a resolution of 19 Mar. 1679 (prompted by Danby's case), which affirmed the continuation of impeachments after a prorogation or dissolution, rather than the subsequent contrary resolution of 22 May 1685. See Rogers, *Protests*, i, 67, 236–7, for the protest of the *Contents* on 25 May 1717. See also HMC *Lords MSS* xii, 198.

[147] *LJ* xx, 478; HMC *Lords MSS* xii, 198.

[148] Thomas Lutwyche (1674–1734), Tory MP for Appleby, 1710–22, and an able lawyer and member of the October Club. Sedgwick, ii, 231.

[149] Thomas Hearne (d. 1722), Fellow of Merton College, Oxford, 1716, who took part in the Bangorian Controversy.

[150] A bill to enable the parishioners of Rotherhithe to finish the parish church was brought in from the Commons on 18 May, reported without amendments, and read a third time on 31 May, and received the royal assent on 22 June 1717. *LJ* xx, 460, 480, 485, 508.

June 1. House. Nothing. Morning, Evidence against T. Fl[   ]. Evening, Mr H[arris]'s Report.

[June] 2. Dr Carter, at St James's. Evening, Lord Archbishop of Canterbury's nar[rative?] from the princess.

[June] 3. My Birth Day. *A[nn]o Aet[atis]* 63. *Miserere Deus!* At my Brother's.

[June] 4. Dined with Archbishop of Canterbury. Evening, Way paved from my Return to Pallas.

[June] 5. Private till evening When openly again with &c.

[June] 6. House. Watchings. Dined with me Mr Plen[i]po[tentiary] Harris. Evening, with Bishop of Lincoln to Grove-H[ouse].[151]

[June] 7. Dined with me Ditto. House, orders for the Trial.[152] Evening, as on the 5th. Morning, J. N[icolson]'s will proved by four Ex[ecutors].

[June] 8. Morning, With Mr Warner, for's Letter to Dr Hartop. House. Cuningham's Appeal dismissed.[153] Evening, Letters.

[June] 9. Adieu, Pallas.[154] I preached at Court. Dined with the Chaplains. Bishop of Asaph and I home from prayers.

[June] 10. By water to Twittenham; and Lame home at midnight.

[June] 11. Private. Dined with me, Mr H[arris] and Cousin Rothery. P.m. Dr Clavering.[155]

[June] 12. House. Trial of Earl of O[xford] putt off to the 24th.[156] Evening, At my Brother's. NB. Messenger from Lady Gemm[ingen].

[151] Probably at Kensington Gore, on the site now occupied by the Albert Hall. See *Survey of London*, xxxviii (1975), 12.

[152] Of Lord Oxford. *LJ* xx, 491–2; HMC *Lords MSS* xii, 199.

[153] *LJ* xx, 493; HMC *Lords MSS* xii, 328–9.

[154] See above, sessional intro., p. 644.

[155] Robert Clavering (1671–1747), DD (Oxon) 1716; Rector of Bocking, Essex, 1714–19, and Regius Professor of Hebrew at Oxford, 1715–47. Later Bishop of Llandaff and Peterborough.

[156] *LJ* xx, 496; HMC *Lords MSS* xii, 199.

[June] 13. Morning, Mr H[arris] with me paying 100 *l.* &c. and at dinner. P.m. Letters.

[June] 14. Morning, With Pallas &c. seeing the Tombs. *A[nn]o Consecrat[ionis]* 16to. Evening, At my Brother's.

[June] 15. Private. Mr H[arris] at dinner with me. Complimented on supposed mar[riage].

[June] 16. Cousin Jer[emy] Nicolson and I preached for (and dined with) Dr Hutchinson.

[June] 17. Lame and private. P.m. Mr H[arris] with message from Princess Anne, &c.

[June] 18. Ditto. Saveing Visits from Bishops in abundance.

[June] 19. House. Bill for enlargeing pop[ists] subscr[ibing].[157] Dined, Mr H[arris] with whom at St James's.

[June] 20. At 10 in the evening Lady Carolina Lowisa (daughter to the Earl of Holderness) christned by me: The prince Godfather, and the Rograffin[158] and Countess of Essex Godmothers.

[June] 21. Fit of the Gravel. Evening, with Mr Croonfield, &c. at my Brother's Square Gravel-stone voided.

[June] 22. Morning, More Gravel. Dr Snape's Query.[159] Mostly private.

[June] 23. Morning, I preached at St Martin's. Dined with Mr Grisdale. Evening, preached St James's.

[June] 24. Lord O[xford] at the Bar. House. Treason tryed first, 88 against 56.[160]

[157] A bill for explaining an act of the previous parliament called 'An act to oblige papists to register their names and real estates', and for enlarging the time for such registering. *LJ* xx, 503.

[158] Louise (1661–1733), only surviving daughter in 1717 of Charles Louis (1617–80), Elector Palatine, by his second and morganatic marriage. All the children of this marriage bore the title Raugraf or Raugrüfin. She was the King's first cousin and sister-in-law to the Duke of Schomberg.

[159] Dr Andrew Snape, Headmaster of Eton, was about to embroil Nicolson in the Bangorian Controversy. See above, sessional intro., p. 643 and below, 29 June.

[160] *LJ* xx, 511–12. This vote, which virtually ensured Oxford's acquittal a week later,

[June] 25. Prosecution (on message) delayed till Thursday.[161]

[June] 26. Bishop of Lincoln and I (after dinner with the Archbishop of Canterbury) to Mortlack.

[June] 27. Reasons from the Commons against our Vote of the 24th rejected. Insist.[162] Dined with me Bishop of Lincoln and J. Rothery. Good news from Merton College.[163]

[June] 28. Morning, Bishop of Bangor's Advertisement.[164] House. Answer to Commons.[165] Evening, Brother's.

[June] 29. Dr Snape's Adv[ertisment] and Bangor's Answer.[166] P.m. from the House to Letter.

[June] 30. Dr Burscough[167] preached at St James's. Dined at home.

July 1. Earl of Oxford acquitted. My Advertisement published.

[July] 2. Bishop of B[angor]'s long Answer.[168] Visitted by too many. Mostly private.

was on a motion of Lord Harcourt's that the House should hear no evidence on charges of high crimes and misdemeanours until the charge of high treason had first been tried. The majority included many Whig peers, either openly sympathetic to the late Prime Minister, or prepared to vote with the Tories to embarrass the ministry. Nicolson, along with Wake and Trelawney, abstained in the vote. For details see Jones, 'The Impeachment of the Earl of Oxford', pp. 72-5, 80-6.

[161] *LJ* xx, 514.
[162] The reasons of the Commons had been presented at a conference held between the two houses on the trial. The Lords insisted on their former resolution for the Commons not to proceed on the other articles till judgement was given on those for treason. *LJ* xx, 515-16, HMC *Lords MSS* xii, 200.
[163] Possibly a reference to the outcome of the fellows' election at Merton in Mar. 1716, when the Warden, 'ruled by 2 Tory fellows', had denied admission to their fellowships of the six fellows-elect. One of them, Thomas Hearne (see above, n. 149), had had the support of three Whig bishops and Lord Somers. The case had been taken to the Court of Arches in May 1716. There is correspondence on the case in Christ Church Wake MS 15.
[164] In the *Daily Courant* in answer to Snape's *Second Letter to the Lord Bishop of Bangor*. For the context, see above, sessional intro., pp. 641-3. For the advertisement see A. Boyer, *Political State of Great Britain*, xiii (1717), 681-3; and for Snape's *Second Letter* see ibid., pp. 674-81.
[165] The Lords' reasons for insisting are printed in *LJ* xx, 518; HMC *Lords MSS* xii, 200.
[166] See above, sessional intro. p. 643.
[167] William Burscough (*c.*1676-1755), Fellow of Wadham College, 1699-1719, and Rector of Stoke-next-Guildford, 1712; Later Bishop of Limerick, 1725-55.
[168] Denying Nicolson's charge. *Political State*, xiii (1717), 686-90. See also his answer in the *Daily Courant* of 3 July and Snape's retort in the *St James's Evening Post* of 4 July. *Political State*, xiv (1717), 2-5.

[July] 3. House. Scotch Bill,[169] &c. P.m. Dean Kennett's Letters to Archbishop of Canterbury and me.[170]

[July] 4. Morning, Bishop of Lincoln's letter from Dr K[ennett].[171] P.m. Hard at my press-work.

[July] 5. Early Dinner. House. Turn-pike.[172] P.m. postscript, &c. to my printed Letter.[173]

[July] 6. Morning, At my Brother's getting Mr Henchman's certif[i-cate].[174] Dined (with the Bishops of Land[aff][175] [Tyler], Glocester, St Asaph, Oxon and Exon) at the Archbishop of Canterbury's. House. Sheriff's Bill,[176] &c.

[July] 7. Dined at my Brother's with Sister Rothery, &c. Evening, Introduction of my Letter censured.

[July] 8. Letter published.[177] Dined with me Mr H[arris]. Private on Letter to Dr K[ennett]. Presents.

---

[169] Bill for continuing the Equivalent in Scotland. *LJ* xx, 528.

[170] After receiving (30 June) a letter from Nicolson accusing him of having altered Bangor's sermon and demanding a public admission (see above, sessional intro., p. 643), Kennett wrote to Wake from Peterborough on 1 July denying any responsibility (Wake MS 20, ff. 402–3; see also Bennett, *White Kennett*, p. 141). He wrote by the same post to Nicolson and this letter was published in the *Daily Courant* and the *St James Evening Post* on 6 July. *Political State*, xiv (1717), 5–7. It asked Nicolson to withdraw his declaration, solemnly declaring he had known nothing of the sermon until after it had been preached and had not seen Hoadly between its preaching and publication.

[171] Kennett was, no doubt, hoping for Gibson's support, but he was to be disappointed. Gibson later confessed to Wake that 'I have not heard one syllable from Peterb[oro]w since I came hither; being, as I suppose, suspected of partiality to my L[or]d Almoner, from the Caution and Reserve with which I answered the Dean's Letter upon my L[or]d Almoner's first Challenge'. Wake MS 20, f. 411: Gibson to Wake, 20 July 1717. In fact Gibson believed in some degree of collusion between Hoadly and Kennett. See Bodl. MS Add. A269, p. 68: Gibson to N., 11 July 1717. See also Bennett, *White Kennett*, pp. 143–4; and below, 23 July.

[172] There were two bills on this day concerned with improving certain highways. *LJ* xx, 532–3; HMC *Lords MSS* xii, 425–8.

[173] See *Political State*, xiv (1717), 13.

[174] Appended to Nicolson's *A Collection of Papers* published on 8 July. In it Leonard Henchman, a Common Councillor for the Aldgate Ward of the City of London in 1715, asserted that he had been told by Timothy Child, the keeper of Child's Coffee House (much frequented by the clergy) that Bangor had discussed his sermon with Kennett in his coffee house. See *Political State*, xiv (1717), 20–1, for the certificate. On 11 July Child published a complete disavowal that he had ever testified concerning Kennett's guilt. Ibid., pp. 34–5.

[175] Repl. 'Lond.'. Wake in his diary (Lambeth Palace MS 1770, f. 192[v]) records that Landaff and not the Bishop of London was at this meeting. 'Lond.' must either be Nicolson's mistake or an error by the Wares' transcribers.

[176] Bill concerning the office, fees, patents, and accounts of sheriffs. *LJ* xx, 534.

[177] *A Collection of Papers scatter'd lately about the Town, in the Daily Courant, St James's-Post, &c, with some Remarks upon them, in a Letter from the Bishop of Carlisle to the Bishop of Bangor.* See *Political State*, xiv (1717), 8–21.

[July] 9. Letter to K[ennett] published.[178] I dined, &c. at home. Evening, Letters.

[July] 10. Dined at Mr H[arris]'s with Col. Innis.[179] P.m. Brother's and Fetterlane.

[July] 11. Dr W[augh] and I at dinner with my Brother. Evening, (*ultimum vale*) with Pallas.

[July] 12. Morning, At Whitehall, with the Governours [of Queen Anne's Bounty] for Mr Ecton. Evening, At the *Leg* with Mr Midwinter, &c.

[July] 13. Dined, with me Mr Maleverer and J. Rothery. Evening, my son.

[July] 14. Dr Snape preached at St James's on *what fruit*, &c. Dined with me Mr Harris.

[July] 15. End of the Session.[180] Dined with me my son and two nephews. Private, At *Add[itional] Remarks*.

[July] 16. Archbishop of Canterbury against my printing.[181] Dined with me J. Fisher and Jack. P.m. Visits.

[July] 17. Dined with me my son, J. Rothery and Mr Maleverer. Evening, R. N[icolson] and I at my brother's with the Sollic[ito]r N[   ].

[July] 18. Morning, Visits to Lady Haliburton. Dined with me Mr Harris. Private.

[July] 19. After dinner with the Watkinsons, Visits to Mrs Bellingha[m], Brother, &c.

[178] *A Letter from the Bishop of Carlisle to Dr Kennett, Dean of Peterborough.* See *Political State*, xiv (1717), 25–8.

[179] Robert Innes had served in the expeditions to Cadiz and in the West Indies as a lieutenant. He became a colonel in 1711, and served in the Canadian expedition of that year. See Dalton, *George I*, i, 364–5.

[180] Nicolson had not attended the House since 10 July and he did not attend on the final day. *LJ* xx, 533, 543–7.

[181] Wake made his opposition clear to Nicolson's publishing the 'Additional Remarks' he had been preparing the previous day to carry on his unseemly controversy with Kennett. See above, sessional intro., p. 643.

[July] 20. Morning Farewells. Dined with me, Mr Harris, Maleverer, nephew R[othery] and son John. Evening, late at St James's Farewell.

[July] 21. Dined At my Brother's. P.m. at Cousin R. N[icolson]'s whence (in a chair) home, no coach to be had.

[B]   Mr Fitzgerald acquainted me from the Bishop of Winton that Archdeacon Hoadley[182] was present at the beginning of a Conference twixt his brother (the Bishop of Bangor) and Dr K[ennett] before the publishing of his Sermon, &c.

[A] [July] 22. Cousin Rothery and I set out for Lincoln; and by the way of York,[183] &c. happily finished our Journey on — August 5. — when we were met at Penrith by a great many friends; who came with us to Rose.

[B]   At Hatfield a Reflecting Scroll in the window on the Lord Bishop.

[July] 23. The Bishop of Lincoln desires the Bishop of Bangor to answer clearly, Whether the Dean of Peterborough [Kennett] was not with him 'twixt *preaching* and *publishing*; and the Dean (who this day dined with him)[184] to explain what it was that, as he saies, led me into a Mistake. Till both these are done, he thinks my plea good.[185] I am sure it is.

[July 24.] Dr K[ennett]'s Advertisement in the *Dayly Courant* of Wednesday, July 24. 1717.[186]
    The Bishop of Carlisle never in my Study alone,
    without some other Company, for several months past.[187]
His wife present (I think) alwaies, some part of the time; but as often ordered to withdraw particularly, after her motion about the Bishoprick of N[orwich], May, 29.[188]

---

[182] John Hoadly (1678–1746), brother of Benjamin, Bishop of Bangor; DD (Cantab.) 1717; Prebendary of Salisbury, 1706–13, and Archdeacon of Salisbury, 1710–27. Later Archbishop of Dublin, 1730–42, and of Armagh.

[183] Nicolson probably arrived at Lincoln on 26 July, travelling via Buckden where he met Gibson (see below, 23 July). He left Lincoln, after visiting his son Joseph, probably on 29 July, travelled via Doncaster, arriving at York on 30 July. Nicolson left York on 1 August. See 'Letters on the Road, or after July 18, 1717', Ware transcripts, xxxii, 34–6.

[184] For the interview between Gibson and Kennett and the latter's tactical retreat to avoid meeting Nicolson, and farcial near encounter in a local inn see Wake MS 20, ff. 414–15: Gibson to Wake, 25 July 1717; extracts printed in James, p. 234.

[185] See above, n. 171.

[186] Printed in full in *Political State*, xiv (1717), 38–44. It was dated Peterborough, 18 July 1717.

[187] Quoted from the advertisement, see ibid., p. 41.

[188] See Wake MS 20, f. 423: N. to Wake, n.d., but in reply to one of 9 Aug. 1717,

—I never advised the Bishop of Bangor in amending, &c. any one word in his Sermon. [189]

Would not an explanatory preface [have] amended many words and expressions in it, by setting them in a better Light? Qu[ery] Mr Collins. [190]

— In some perplexity and Confusion of Mind. True; upon the Discovery of the hitherto unheeded Difference twixt *Preaching* and *Publishing*. Hope and suppose, &c.

For Answer to the Bishop of Bangor's charge of my being in Confederacy to slander him, see Dr Burnet's Coll[   ].

printed in Bennett, *White Kennett*, pp. 142–3. In this letter Nicolson gives a clearer account of his supposed meeting with Kennett on 29 May. There is no mention of this meeting in his diary under that date. At this time there was an 'expected vacancy at Norwich', presumably because of the illness of Bishop Trimnell.

[189] Misquoted from Kennett's advertisement, see *Political State*, xiv (1717), 43.
[190] Possibly a reference to Anthony Collins (1676–1729), deist and pamphleteer.

Session 13

11 January 1718–17 March 1718

After arriving home in August 1717 Nicolson spent a quiet and uneventful autumn and early winter in his diocese. Parliament re-assembled on 21 November,[1] and within the week the Bishop was discussing the speech from the throne and 'consulting on the Test-Act' with Dean Tullie and the Chapter at Carlisle.[2]

The possibility of abolishing the sacramental test and expunging the Corporation Act from the statute-book in addition to repealing the Occasional Conformity and Schism Acts, was certainly in the air in the autumn of 1717, as indeed it had been in the previous March.[3] The King in his speech had promised, in view of the attacks on Protestantism abroad, to 'strengthen the Protestant interest' at home. The King was known to support Stanhope's measures for unequivocally relieving the Dissenters of their civil disabilities.[4] The alarming development for moderate bishops like Wake, Trelawney, and Nicolson was that there was a small minority of bishops, led by Gibson of Lincoln, who were prepared to support Stanhope's policy of genuine toleration.

On 22 November, the day after the opening of parliament, this 'radical' group of bishops, consisting of Gibson, Talbot of Salisbury, Trimnell of Norwich, Willis of Gloucester, Chandler of Lichfield, and Hough of Worcester, held a conference at which they agreed to support the abolition of 'the Sacramental test so far as it concerned Corporations'.[5] The case of this group was frankly Erastian and practical as expressed by Bishop Willis to Lord Chancellor Cowper:[6]

---

[1] The original diary for this session has not survived. The Ware transcripts, xxxii, 40–7, are tantalisingly brief. Towards the end of the session Nicolson appears to have recorded only the most important events, see *CW* v (1905), 15. In Christ Church Library, however, in a bound volume of *Votes of the House of Commons* for 1717 to 1720 (shelfmark E.2.4.11) originally belonging to Archbishop Wake, there are notes and letters by Nicolson addressed to Wake concerning proceedings in the Lords between 25 Jan. and 20 Mar. 1718. These considerably enhance the diary and the more important ones have been incorporated in this edition, and are indicated by the marginal reference [C.C.]. The editors are indebted to Mr H. J. R. Wing of Christ Church Library for drawing their attention to this material.

[2] *CW* v (1905), 15; *LJ* xx, 554.

[3] Hertfordshire RO Panshanger MS D/EP. F62, f. 36: Wake to Cowper, 14 Mar. 1716[/7].

[4] B. Williams, *Stanhope* (Oxford, 1932), p. 390.

[5] Christ Church Wake MS 20, f. 480: Gibson to Wake, 22 Nov. 1717. All these bishops, with the exception of Lichfield, voted for the repeal of the Occasional Conformity and Schism Acts on 19 Dec. 1718. Lichfield opposed repeal. See N. Sykes, *Church and State in England in the Eighteenth Century* (Cambridge, 1934), p. 35.

[6] Panshanger MS D/EP.F138, ff. 18–21; endorsed by Cowper, 'Given me by Dr Willis

the Dissenters deserved to be rewarded for their fidelity to and zeal for the government, which needed their support at the next election. None the less, while trying to satisfy the Dissenters, the measures proposed had to be capable of passing both Houses and must not make the bishops who supported them and the government look like enemies to the Church. Outright repeal, therefore, of the Occasional Conformity Act was rejected in favour of a limited measure. A new bill would breach the Test and Corporation Acts only so far as they related to the receiving of the sacrament; and it would require the great officers of state and lesser officers down to JPs to renounce transubstantiation and make a declaration that they lived in communion with the established Church of England; and the Occasional Conformity Act would remain in force with respect to such officers as were bound to make this declaration, but would cease to apply to all others, in other words 'corporation-men'.

Nicolson's position on such a scheme was clear:[7]

1. The Dissenters are sufficiently rewarded, for all the Good Offices they did King William, or can do His present Majesty, by the continuance of Toleration.

2. If the King's promise and Honour require any new favour, it were better that the late Act against Occasional Conformity should be Repealed; than that the Test-Act be suspended in Cities and Great Towns, which (upon such suspension) will immediately be filled with Quakers, Anabaptists and other Hereticks and Schismatics, from all parts of the neighbouring Counties.[8]

3. No Declarations in favour of the Established Church, either in the Body of the New Bill, or any other Separate Act, can prevent these confusions.

Nicolson wrote to Gibson opposing the substitution of a declaratory test for the sacramental test, and Gibson replied that 'the Dissenters opened most Liberally [against the stronger terms of the declaratory

Bishop of Gloucester in the Session 1717'. It probably refers to the session 1717–18 and may well be the result of the bishops' conference in Nov. 1717.

[7] Expressed in his letter to Thomas Tullie, Dean of Carlisle, 26 Nov. 1717, 'on the Project for further Indulgence to the Dissenters', Nicolson's own abstract of which is in Ware transcripts, xxxii, 37–8. These same views were communicated to Archbishop Wake, along with Nicolson's proxy with instructions to use it 'on the same side of the Question as your own' (Wake MS 20, f. 484: N. to Wake, 28 Nov. 1717). Cf. Nicolson's letter of 21 Nov. to Wake (ibid., ff. 477–8), in which he called for the King to make a declaration against future favourable measures towards Dissenters. It will be recalled that he had been a 'hard-liner' both on the Occasional Conformity and Schism issues, from 1702 to 1704, and again in 1714.

[8] A curiously hysterical and unrealistic prophecy.

test]; to such a degree indeed, that I am of [the] opinion, nothing at all will be done this Sessions; especially all hopes being vanished of making matters easy at Court'.[9]

Gibson's forecast was to prove wrong: the 'Bristol Bill', introduced into the Lords on 13 February 1718 concerning the hospitals and workhouses for the poor in Bristol, contained a clause which exempted officials of the Bristol workhouse from the terms of the Test and Corporation Act. This attempted breach of the Anglican monopoly of local government was supported on the second reading, on 5 March, by all the radical group of bishops who had met on 22 November 1717 (with the exception of Worcester, but including Hoadly of Bangor). Nicolson was vigorously to oppose this bill, and his actions in the committee on the bill on 14 March led him to believe that he had forfeited his lucrative translation to Derry.[10]

No further action was taken this session to help the relief of Dissenters. This was partially due, as Gibson had pointed out, to the critical breach at Court between the King and the Prince of Wales. Relations had been strained for some years,[11] and Leicester House, the Prince's residence, became the rallying ground for Tories and discontented Whigs, now including Townshend and Walpole. The final breach between the King and his son came over an incident at the christening of the Prince's second son in early November 1717. The King had insisted on the traditional right of the Lord Chamberlain (the Duke of Newcastle) to be a god-parent, and the Prince, who detested the Duke as one of his father's servants, quarrelled with Newcastle and, according to the Duke, threatened his life.[12] A visit to the Prince by the Dukes of Roxburghe, Kingston, and Kent failed to settle the quarrel and the King, after placing his son for a short while under virtual house arrest, expelled him from St James's Palace but insisted that his children should remain behind. In January the King laid down proposals for a settlement;[13] but this ultimatum was unacceptable to the Prince and the estrangement of father and son was to continue until April 1720.

Politically it was of the first importance. From 1717 it encouraged the disaffected Walpole–Townshend Whigs in both Houses to launch a campaign against the ministry in combination with the Tories and

[9] Bodl. MS Add. A269, pt. ii, pp. 75–6: Gibson to N., 24 Dec. 1717.

[10] The bill passed the Lords on 17 Mar. 1718. The only bishops to sign the protest were Trelawney, Smalridge, Atterbury, and Robinson (*LJ* xx, 655–6).

[11] For the quarrel see J. M. Beattie, *The English Court in the Reign of George I* (Cambridge, 1967), pp. 268–71.

[12] See *Addison Letters*, pp. 394–5 for a description of the quarrel.

[13] See below, 18 Jan. A similar set of proposals are to be found in Panshanger MS D/EP. F134, f. 18.

with the Prince's favourite, Argyll. The major point of attack in the 1717–18 session was the Mutiny Bill which received a rough handling in the Lords before it finally passed on 24 February 1718. The quarrel naturally affected Nicolson personally, as he was a frequent visitor to the Prince's daughters and a close friend of their governess, Baroness Gemmingen.[14] The political battle in the Lords over the Mutiny Bill, however, makes no definite appearance in the diary, though the cryptic comments in Nicolson's letter to Wake of 23 February may refer to this matter.

Apart from the Bristol Bill, the only two pieces of parliamentary business recorded in the Bishop's 1718 diary and the accompanying letters are the agitation over the scarcity of silver coins and the *Annesley* v. *Sherlock* case.

On 16 January 1718 Lord North and Grey introduced the question of the scarcity of silver coins into the House of Lords, to embarrass the government, commenting that the great shortage occasioned a general stop of trade and very much distressed the poor. It was a sensitive issue, not least to those who remembered the 'great re-coinage' crisis of 1695–6. But a Committee of the Whole, which began considering the question on 23 January and heard evidence from Stanhope,[15] came to a healing resolution which resulted in the introduction of two bills on 28 January: one to prevent the melting down of coins, the other to ensure that silver plate be made with the same fineness as the current silver coin.[16]

The *Annesley* v. *Sherlock* case[17] (along with the case of *Ward* v. *the Earl of Meath*[18]) was of some constitutional significance. It was a dispute over forfeited land, in which a decree of the Irish Exchequer Court was reversed by the Irish House of Lords (1716), whose own was effectively reversed in 1718, on appeal by Maurice Annesley to the English House of Lords. An inflammatory situation was only settled by the Declaratory Act of 1719.

All this was in the future as Nicolson 'set out for Westminster in pleasant weather' on 30 December 1717. Travelling the west-coast route, through Kendal, Lancaster, Preston, and Chester,[19] Nicolson reached Towcester on 9 January 1718. There he wrote to his brother Joseph to expect him early on 12 January, and to his old landlord, Mr Fitzgerald, to 'Get my chamber &c. in readiness'. The last part

---

[14] See e.g. below, 28 Jan., 4 Feb. For his private feelings on the quarrel see TCD King Correspondence 1850: N. to King, 13 Feb. 1718.

[15] See A Boyer, *Political State of Great Britain*, xiv (1717), 602–8; xv (1718), 60, 101–3.

[16] *LJ* xx, 585–7; HMC *Lords MSS* xii, 476–88.

[17] For the case see J. G. Sims, *The Williamite Confiscation in Ireland, 1690–1703* (1956), pp. 145–6; F. G. James, *Ireland in the Empire, 1688–1770* (Cambridge, Mass., 1973), pp. 101–7. [18] See below, 1 Feb.

[19] Nicolson wrote at Chester that the 'Remaining 150 m. frightful. The end worse.'

of his journey took Nicolson through Stony Stratford, Dunstable, and St Albans, and he arrived, a day early, at London on 11 January 1718.[20] Both Houses reassembled after their Christmas break on 13 January. Nicolson's first appearance in the 1717–18 session was on 16 January.[21]

[C.C.] in the margin indicates text from Christ Church Library (shelfmark E.2.4.11), and [D] indicates text from the Ware transcripts (xxxii, 40–7) (see above, n. 1).

[D]　Letters from Westminster on or after January 11, 1717–18.

Jan. 11. [To] Daughter Catherine.[22] I am at my old lodgeings in health.

Dr Benson. Ditto. Letters and Visitors many. Blessing and good night.

Brother John. His and the Dr's (two in Twenty) received but not yet read.

Brother Benson. A Cheerful Companion has brought me safe.

Mr Bridges of Castleford.[23] Answer I was here on the 26th of June, &c. &c.

Jan. 12. Archbishop of York [Dawes] and Bishop of B[ango]r [Hoadly] favourites. *Children* of the *State*.	Bishop of Lincoln [Gibson][24]
Lord T[ownshend]'s caresses. Chancellor [Cowper] tottering.[25] So Gemm[ingen], Devon[shire], Cad[ogan][26] and Ban Tutors.	Archbishop of Canterbury [Wake].
[Jan.] 13. K[ing] to be Governor of South-Sea [Company] advised against by Sir J. B[ateman].[27]	at Archbishop of York's.

[20] Ware transcripts, xxxii, 36–40. Nicolson computed the journey to have cost him £19 8s 6d.　　　　[21] *LJ* xx, 572–3.

[22] Nicolson's second daughter born 19 Feb. 1691. She was still alive and unmarried in 1777. Ware transcripts, xxxv, 1; *CW* i (1901), 49.

[23] William Bridges (c.1670–?1729), Rector of Castleford, Yorkshire, 1696–1729, in succession to his father, also William Bridges (d. 1696). Yorks Arch. Soc. MS 17, pt. 3, p. 22.

[24] The people mentioned in this column are probably Nicolson's source for the information under each date. Nicolson certainly visited Archbishop Wake on 12 and 18 Jan. and both attended the Lords on 23 Jan. 1717. See Lambeth Palace MS 1770, f. 200.

[25] He was to leave office on 15 Apr. 1718 because of the quarrel in the royal family.

[26] William, Lord Cadogan (?1671–1726), MP for New Woodstock, 1705–16, returned on Marlborough's interest, had been the Duke's right-hand man in the campaigns of the War of the Spanish Succession. He was cr. Baron (1716) and Earl Cadogan in May 1718. Sedgwick, i, 513.

[27] A new election of South Sea Company directors, always a sensitive barometer of

[Jan.] 18. The King's new proposals to the P[rince][28] 1. Nom[ination] of his servants 2. Right claimed to the children, with 40,000 *l.*[29] 3. No Companions disagreeable to His Majesty. 4. Satisfaction in form to Dukes of Newcastle and Roxburgh.[30] 5. Fair with all the Ministry. V[ide] *Bracton*, p. 105 Inst. P.3.[31] P[rince]'s servants directed to Vote with the Ministers in the Cases of the 250,000 *l.* and Lord Cadogan.[32]	Archbishop of Canterbury
[Jan.] 20. Dukes of Bolton, K[ent] and Kingston[33] against the Court-Heats. Not one step more in favour of Diss[ent]. Agreed.	Archbishop of York
[Jan.] 21. My obs[ervations] on the Bishop of L[incoln]'s Disc[ourse] — That the King kept warmed by his Ministers and the Prince warms his Servants	At Lord Chief Justice King's[34]
[Jan.] 23. Duke of Devonshire and Earl of Pembroke must move the Prince to submission: 10 (of 12) Judges haveing given up the children.[35]	Archbishop of Canterbury in the Lobby

political changes, was due in Feb. 1718. At this time George I replaced the Prince of Wales as Governor. The Prince of Wales had succeeded Lord Oxford as Governor in Feb. 1715. Sir James Bateman, who died in Nov. 1718, was Sub-Governor of the Company from July 1711 and MP for East Looe, 1715–18. See J. Carswell, *The South Sea Bubble* (1960), pp. 73–5, 274, 278; Sedgwick, i, 443.

[28] See above, sessional intro., p. 670.

[29] On the expulsion of the Prince of Wales from St James's, the King had kept his children (see R. Hatton, *George I* (1978), p. 208). He now demanded £40,000 for their maintenance and education.

[30] For their involvement in the royal quarrel, see above, p. 670.

[31] Probably a reference to a point of law raised by the legal proceedings of the Prince to recover custody of his children, Jan.–Feb. 1718. See R. Hatton, *George I*, p. 208 and n. 85, p. 353.

[32] Six months earlier, on 4 June 1717, Lord Cadogan had been the object of the first full dress attack staged by the new Whig opposition under Walpole. He had been unsuccessfully charged with fraud and embezzlement over the transport of Dutch troops. Perhaps there was some hint now of a revival of the charges.

[33] Lord Lieutenant of Ireland, Lord Steward, and Lord Privy Seal respectively.

[34] Sir Peter King, Lord Chief Justice of the Common Pleas since 1714.

[35] i.e. the Prince's children to the King. On 21 Jan. 1718 the King had asked the judges

[Jan.] 24. Warning (by Mr H[arris]) to Duke of A[rgyll].[36]

At the House Archbishop of Canterbury unsatisfyed with Reasons of 10 Judges.[37] Earl of Sunderland Kind in his professions to me.

Evening with Mr Knaplock, &c. at the *Leg:* where J. N[icolson]'s effects (already in view) reckoned at 8,000 *l.*[38]

[C.C.]　House of Lords. Jan. 25.

Lord Clarendon[39] Reported the following Resolution from the Committee; which was unanimously agreed to by the House.

> Resolved That the present Standard of the Silver-Coin of this Kingdome ought not to be altered in Weight, Fineness or Denomination.[40]

It was moved by the Duke of Argyle, and Seconded by the Earl of Strafford, that Guinneas should be lowered to 20*s.* and 6*d.* but the Question not insisted on.[41]

[D]　[Jan.] 27. My Sub-Almoner [Cannon] hints that one Argument against parting with the children will be drawn from E[dward] 4's Queen giving up (from the Sanctuary) her younger son; who dyed with his Brother in the Tower. God forbid!

to give an opinion as to whether he could revoke the Prince's right to his £100,000 in the civil list, whether the Prince had the right to name his own servants, whether the King had the right to educate his grandchildren and to give his 'approbation of their Marriages'. See J. M. Beattie, *The English Court in the Reign of George I* (Cambridge, 1967), p. 271; Panshanger MS D/EP. F147, f. 23: Sunderland to Cowper, 20 Jan. 1718. A copy of the 'minority' report of the two judges is to be found in Panshanger MS D/EP. F134, ff. 20–2 (in Lady Cowper's hand). They agreed with the majority that the marriages of the children must have the King's approbation, but they must also have the consent of the Prince. They did not concur with the other judges about the care and education of the children, which they thought rested with the Prince.

[36] Argyll was one of the Prince's favourite advisers, while Harris, as Clerk of the Prince's Closet, was close to the Princess.

[37] For Wake's difficult position over his continuing to attend the Princess of Wales despite the King's prohibition, and for his attempts at a reconciliation see Sykes, *Wake*, ii, 114–15.

[38] John Nicolson's funeral had taken place on 15 May 1717. An abstract of Nicolson's will can be found in Ware transcripts, xxxii, 32. It is dated 28 Apr. 1717. Bishop Nicolson was one of the executors of the will.

[39] Clarendon had by this time established himself as the regular Chairman of Committees in the Lords, for which he received a pension of £2,000 a year on the Irish establishment. See J. C. Sainty, *The Origin of the Office of Chairman of Committees* in *the House of Lords*, House of Lords Record Office Memorandum No. 52 (1974), p. 3.

[40] *LJ* xx, 585; HMC *Lords MSS* xii, 477–8; see above, sessional intro., p. 671.

[41] 'On the Lowering of Guinneas a general Fancy prevaled [reported Nicolson] that an Advance (on the other hand) would presently follow, upon all the greater pieces of our silver-money; a crown to 5*s.* 4*d.*, half a Crown to Eight Groats, &c. This might perhaps be one cause of our Scarcity' (TCD King Correspondence 1850: to King, 13 Feb. 1718).

[Jan.] 28. M[adame] Gem[mingen]'s grateful account of the K[ing]'s Goodness to her; and the D[uchess] of M[unster]'s,[42] &c.

[Nicolson to Wake, 28 Jan. 1718]   [C.C.]
Haveing first beged pardon for the slovenly paper[43] sent to Your Grace last night, I beg leave to take notice of the Debates concerning the Coins being continued to day; and, no doubt, they'l be attended with the like Throng Appearance as Yesterday. They seem to point at the bringing in a Bill,[44] for the more effectual quieting of the minds of the Jealous folks without doors; and the different methods proposed threaten dividing on Questions, tho' nothing of that kind has yet happened.

I hear nothing of comfort from another Court; but what's not worth the relating.

[Jan.] 29. Bishop of Lincoln zealous against the Archbishop's free [D] declaring his Thoughts of the *Reasons* to Bishop of B[ango]r.

[Nicolson to Wake, 29 Jan. 1718]   [C.C.]
The Cause appointed for this day is upon a Writ of Error (Burk against Morgan or Blake) from Ireland.[45] There's another Irish Cause, of the same sort, wherein one Tyrrel (a Clergyman) is Defendant in the Room of his predecessor Carr, and Shirt plaintiff. This should be heard on Tuesday next; and I am Earnestly pressed, both by the Archbishop of Dublin [King] and Bishop of Meath [Evans], to attend it: But 'tis not likely that 'twill come on so soon.[46]

For—Today all the Lords are summoned to hear the Report from the Committee appointed to consider the point of Jurisdiction.[47] Their Opinion is, That the Sheriff be forthwith obliged to give possession in persuance of the Judgment of your [*sic*] House; and that the party dispossessed be at liberty to proceed at Law, *de novo*, if so advised.

What the Judges have really done (after the many various Reports that have flown abroad) I neither know, nor care for Enquireing. It shocked me too much, and struck me to the heart, when I was told of some precedents that had been searched into.

---

[42] Ermengarde Melusina (1667–1743), Baroness von der Schulenberg, mistress of George I, created Duchess of Munster [I] for life in 1716, and Duchess of Kendal for life in 1719.

[43] A short note dated 27 Jan. (included in Christ Church Lib. E.2.4.11.) with the resolution 'that the Gold-Coins of this Kingdome ought not to be further reduced'. Cf. *LJ* xx, 586; HMC *Lords MSS* xii, 478–9.   [44] See above, sessional intro., p. 671.

[45] See *LJ* xx, 589; HMC *Lords MSS* xii, 374–5.

[46] The case was not heard until 19 Feb. *LJ* xx, 565, 575, 615; HMC *Lords MSS* xii, 459.

[47] On the *Annesley* v. *Sherlock* case. See above, sessional intro., p. 671.

I can cheerfully assure your Grace that the young prince[48] has had a very good night; and all Apprehensions of danger are over.
[Postscript] I have such a Cold and hoarsness upon me, that I dare not cross the River.

[D] [Jan.] 30. G[emmingen]'s Hardships by consultation. N.B. Dr K[ennett?] at the Chapel.

[C.C.] [Nicolson to Wake, 1 Feb. 1718]
The Debates on the second of the inclosed Resolutions[49] were surprizeingly long and warm. Lord North (seconded by Lord Harcourt, Duke of Buckingham and others) moved that, in Consideration of the Respondent Sherlock's Trifling the last Session and Appealing since to the Lords of Ireland, the little likelyhood there was of her putting in any Answer after so many Affronts offered to the House, the necessity there was of the speedy asserting the Jurisdiction and Honour thereof, &c. Munday-Sennight might be appointed for the final hearing of this Cause.

Against this, Lord Coningsby, Lord Parker, &c. argued that Lords were not to suppose that the Respondent would not appear; that it had ever been thought reasonable to allow a month for an Answer out of Ireland; that to break that Rule now would have an ill face of Resentment; &c. and therfore they moved for the 5th of March, instead of the 10th of February.

The Lord Chancellor [Cowper] (on the same side) gave the whole History of the last year's proceedings in this Cause; and shewed that the Appellant Annesley had no Title to the favour of this House; haveing first Appealed to the Lords in Ireland, and not from them till the Time approached for his payment of 1,500 *ll.* that too much hast, in a Case of this Nature, was unbecoming the Dignity of so High a Court; Especially since the Appellant was already ordered to be put into immediate possession of the Estate in Controversy.

His Lordship haveing done, the Question was put (as first moved and seconded) for the 10th of February; and carryed in the Negative. *Contents,* 22. *Not Contents,* 44. Amongst the former were the Archbishop of York and the Bishops of Rochester [Atterbury] and Bristol [Smalridge].

[48] George William (2 Nov. 1717–6 Feb. 1718), second son of the Prince of Wales. For a description of his condition see TCD King Correspondence 1850: N. to King, 13 Feb. 1718.
[49] 'That a Peremptory Day should be appointed for hearing the Cause upon the Appeal of the said Maurice Annesley *ex parte*, if the said Hester Sherlock should neglect or refuse to put in her Answer in the mean time' (Christ Church Lib. E.2.4.11.: note not in Nicolson's hand). Cf. *LJ* xx, 593; HMC *Lords MSS* xii, 379–80.

After this was over, there followed as warm a Dispute concerning the proper methods of inforceing that part of the former Resolution which related to *Possession*. Lord Harcourt was of Opinion that His Majesty should be Addressed to, for his giveing Orders to the Sheriff: Which, by others, was thought to be New and Unparliamentary. The Bill for Enabling His Majesty to accept the Compliment of the South-Sea Company [to be its governor] comeing up,[50] the Duke of Buckingham (haveing first expressed his Earnest desire to spend the Remainder of his dayes in Ireland, where Honour and Courage flourished) moved that the matter [of *Annesley* v. *Sherlock*] might -be debated in a Grand Committee on Munday next; which was accordingly Ordered, *Nemine Contradicente*.

I forgot to acquaint your Grace that the proceedings in the Case of the Earl of Meath and Bishop of Derry, in 1699 were refered to, and (on the motion of the Earl of Abingdon) read by the Clerk. It thereby appeared, That the said Earl had put in a plea against the Jurisdiction of the Lords here, on Feb. 26 and that two dayes after (Feb. 28) their Lordships had asserted their own Jurisdiction by Rejecting the Plea,[51] and hearing the Cause *Ex parte*; which the Noble Lord urged as a precedent for comeing now to the like Speedy End. But—both parties being then present, no weight was laid on that Argument.

February 4. G[emmingen] in New Joy on the King's repeated Good- [D]
ness to Her and the Children. *Esto!*[52]

Feb. 4. [Nicolson to Wake]   [C.C.]
The Irish Affair adjourned again to Thursday.

This day spent in the Debates on the Bill for sale of the Lord Ranelagh's [estates][53] which (by the Lord Chancellor [Cowper], Report of the Judges, &c.) was observed to be hard on the Creditors, to want the Consent of several parties concerned, &c. The Question

[50] See *LJ* xx, 594; *Political State*, xv (1718), 180–3.

[51] Nicolson is in some confusion here. There were two separate cases: *Ward* v. *the Earl of Meath*, and *the Society of Ulster* v. *the Bishop of Derry*. Both were concerned with the right of appeal to the Irish House of Lords. The first came before the English Lords in Feb. 1699 and judgement was reached on 29 Apr., while the dates of Meath's plea should be 26 and 28 Apr. 1699. *LJ* xvi, 383, 452, 455. In both cases the English Lords decided that the Irish Lords had no appellate rights. For details see T. W. Moody and J. G. Sims, *The Bishopric of Derry and the Irish Society of London, 1602–1705* (Dublin, 1968), i, 6–9; F. G. James, *Ireland in the Empire, 1688–1770* (Cambridge, Mass., 1973), pp. 99–101.

[52] Baroness Gemmingen was to be dismissed as Governess to the Prince's children by the King on 4 Apr. 1718. Wake MS 20, f. 519: N. to Wake, 5 Apr. 1718.

[53] In Chelsea and Cranborne, Berkshire. *LJ* xx, 597; HMC *Lords MSS* xii, 431–2.

(on Second Reading) was—Commit or Not Commit. *Contents*, 43. *Not Contents*, 46. Rejected by Proxies.

Both Archbishops,[54] with the Bishops of St Asaph [Wynne], Oxford [Potter], Carlile, &c. for Rejecting. *Not Contents*.

The Bishops of Rochester, Bristol, Lincoln, &c. with Lord Coningsby and the Court, *Contents*.

[D]   [Feb.] 8. Bishop of Sarum [Talbot] complained to that an Anabaptist was buryed in the Church-yard without consent or knowledge of the Incumbent, asks Advice. Bishop of Lincoln would know whether any prayers, &c. used at the Interment.—Bishop of Glocester [Willis]. What harm if there was, considering there's a Toleration? *O Tempora*! [House of Lords][55]

[C.C.]   [Nicolson to Wake, 23 Feb. 1718]
Returning just now to my Lodgings from St James's (where I dined with the Chaplains, and stayed Evening Prayers) I meet with your Grace's Commands. 'Tis said that several Riders will be offered to morrow; and probably the Clause mentioned in your Grace's Letter may be one of 'em. We fully expected it yesterday. The strength of those that offer it is visibly greater in a House, than a Committee. If it appears, I am allowed to say that it will assuredly be countenanced by the Bishop of Oxford as well as by Your Grace's most obedient servant W. Carliol.[56]

[D]   [Feb.] 25. Cousin F[etherston?]'s[57] account of Grants to—Earl of Berkshire 1,000 *l*., Earl of Westmorland, ditto, Lord Tenham [Teynham],[58] ditto. Lords Abergavenny and Tamworth,[59] each 600. Earl of Rochfort, 500.[60]

[54] Wake was absent from the House because of illness, but Nicolson held his proxy (see below, 22 Mar.) and obviously used it on this occasion.

[55] Nicolson's brackets.

[56] On Sunday 23 Feb. Wake records that 'In the Evening I sent to the Bishop of Carlisle about the business of to morrow'. On 24 Feb. there took place the crucial third reading of the Mutiny bill (which passed eighty-eight to sixty-six; including twenty-one proxies on each side). The Tories and the disaffected Whigs under Townshend and Argyll had strongly opposed the bill since its introduction into the Lords on 12 Feb. on the grounds that it established martial law. The debates had been long and acrimonious. See *Parl. Hist.* vii, 538–48. Wake's comment on 22 Mar. and the material included here from Christ Church Lib. E.2.4.11., confirms that he and Nicolson worked closely together in this period. See also Lambeth Palace MS 1770, ff. 200^V–202^r.

[57] Fetherston Nicholson was a Collector of Customs and Salt Duties at Beaumaris in 1718, and had petitioned to be moved to London. *CTB 1718*, p. 217.

[58] Henry Roper (*c*.1676–1723), 8th Baron Teynham, had only taken his seat in the Lords in 1716, having then conformed to the Church of England.

[59] Washington Shirley (1677–1729), styled Lord Tamworth until 1717, when he had succeeded his father, a Tory, as 2nd Earl Ferrers.

[60] For these grants of pensions see *CTB 1717*, p. 466. The figures for Abergavenny,

March 2. I went with the Bishop of St Asaph to wait on the Earl of Pembroke; who discoursed very learnedly on the Antiquity of the Runic Alphabet, Coins, &c. His Lordship bespoke a Transcript of the Monn[ument] in the Isle of Man, &c. My old *Cato*; and the βουδτροφ [ηόον] in *Buraeus*.[61]

[Mar.] 5. Bristol-Bill was read a second Time; and Counsel heard thereupon.[62] On both sides agreed; That there was no want of Conformists (as suggested) to force the Admission of Dissenters, by takeing off the Test from the Governors, &c. Yet, on the Question for Commitment, six Bishops (Sarum, Norwich [Trimnell], Glocester, Lincoln, Bangor, and Litchfield [Chandler]) were *Content*. Ten *Not Content*.[63]

[Mar.] 8. A day of strange Occurrences. Morning. Bells ringing for Queen Ann's accession, motion made for her Happy Memory being recorded in the St. Giles's Bill, Rejected.[64] Dr Cannon reports the confusion of Pillonière;[65] and Dr Dent that of Lord S[underland?]. Duke of Bolton encourages hopes for Derry; and Archbishop of Canterbury confirms 'em.[66] L[ady] Gem[mingen] (by Mr H[arris]) sends me a despairing Answer to my Congratulatory Letter, on prospects of Peace.

[Mar.] 10. Morning. Mr Harris brought me Princess Ann's picture drawn by her own hand, and sent to me from herself. In the Evening,

Tamworth, and Rochford should be £1,000, £500, and £600 respectively. All the pensions, except those for Lords Berkshire and Tamworth, were continued in 1718, see *CTB 1718*, pp. 240, 305, 544, 548, 549.

[61] Johan Bure or Buraeus (1568–1652), Swedish antiquary and poet who produced many works on runic monuments in Scandinavia.

[62] See above, sessional intro., p. 670.

[63] The figures were *Content*, fifty-four; *Not Content*, thirty-one. HMC *Lords MSS* xii, 517.

[64] The bill empowered the commissioners for building fifty new churches in London and Westminster to direct the parish church of St. Giles-in-the-Fields, Middlesex, to be rebuilt instead of one of the original fifty. The motion to add the words 'of pious Memory' after the words 'Queen Anne' in the preamble to the bill was rejected by fifty-four to thirty-three. It occasioned a protest by nineteen Tory peers and bishops. The bill itself was passed, and this vote led seventeen Tory peers and bishops to protest. See *LJ* xx, 643–4.

[65] Francis de la Pillonnière, formerly a Jesuit priest but since converted to the Church of England, had been received into Bishop Hoadly's household. The controversy between Snape and Hoadly begun in mid-1717 had by early 1718 come to centre upon the sincerity of la Pillonnière's conversion. Kennett, in his last contribution to the Bangorian Controversy, in late Feb. 1718 defended Hoadly against the accusation that he kept a Jesuit in his household. See Bennett, *White Kennett*, p. 144.

[66] As early as Jan. 1717 there had been rumours that Nicolson was in line for an Irish see. Bodl. MS Add. A269, pt. ii, p. 10: Gibson to N., 24 Jan. 1717. It was rumoured in early 1718 that Hoadly of Bangor was a candidate for Derry. HMC *Portland MSS* v, 557.

Mr H[arris] and I waited on Her Highness; playing at Piquet with the Governess, and (A⁰ at 9) syllogizeing in true Mood and Figure, and appositly quoteing the 2d Punic war.

[Mar.] 14. In the morning Archdeacon Trimnell[67] sent to Lambeth with Assurances of my being Bishop of London-Derry, and his brother Green[68] Bishop of Carlisle. The former part of this account was presently confirmed in the House by the Bishop of Norwich; and thereupon I was complimented by all. The same afternoon the House was in a Grand Committee on the Bristol-Bill; wherein was a Repeal of a Clause in a former Act, provideing that the Governors of their Corporation for provideing for the poor should take the Test. Upon one Question, the Committee divided:[69] And five of the Bishops (Sarum, Norwich, Glocester, Lincoln and Bangor) voted against the two Archbishops and the rest of their Brethren. For my continueing with the latter, I was kept from my Irish Translation; and (the next morning) another took away my said presumptive Bishoprick, As was generally Reported. Yet on the—

[Mar.] 17th. (St Patrick's day) the King was pleased to nominate me to the Bishoprick of London-Derry; as was signified to me (in the House of Lords) by the Duke of Bolton Lord Lieutenant of Ireland. And, the next day, His Grace introduceing me, I had thereupon the Honour to Kiss His Majesty's hand.[70]

[C.C.]   [Nicolson to Wake, 20 March 1718]
Your Grace's message was delivered to Lord Parker; who gives his Duty, and desires that his own Indisposition (in a cold) may excuse, for a while, his not paying it at Lambeth.

After this day's free Conference,[71] the Lords receded from their Amendment; whereby the Penalty of Transportation was to be incurred by Killers of Deer in Forests, as well as private Parks.

The Committee threw out three or four more Clauses in the Smugling Bill, and adjourned the Consideration of the rest till tomorrow; when ('tis supposed) the whole will be droped.[72]

---

[67] Probably Dr William Trimnell (d. 1729), brother of the Bishop of Norwich, who did not become Archdeacon of Norwich until 1721. He is referred to by Wake as 'Dr Trimnell' when they dined together on Mar. 13. See Lambeth Palace MS 1770, f. 202.

[68] Thomas Green, Archdeacon of Canterbury, 1708–21.

[69] The vote was Content, forty-four; Not Content, twenty-five. HMC Lords MSS xii, 518.

[70] Nicolson's gratitude at his promotion was soon to be dampened by the King's 'extraordinary instruction' that he must reside in Ireland (see above, Chapter 1, p. 60). For Nicolson's reaction see Wake MS 12, ff. 259, 265: N. to Wake, 9, 10 May 1718.

[71] On the bill to prevent 'robbery, burglary, and other felonies'. LJ xx, 660; HMC Lords MSS xii, 506–8.

[72] The Clandestine Running of Goods Bill. The parliament was prorogued on 21 Mar. and

[Mar.] 22. P.m. I went, with the Bishop of St Asaph, to Lambeth. [D]
The Archbishop told us that he had, the day before, a visit from the
Bishop of Rochester, who accused me of giveing His Grace's proxy
in Parliament contrary to his Instructions.[73] Upon which, His Grace
declared to the Bishop of St Asaph (what, he assured him, he had
likewise said to the Bishop of Rochester) that I had ever faithfully
discharged the Trust reposed in me; and that *He should lose his
right hand* on my Removal to Ireland.[74]

there were no further proceedings on the bill. *LJ* xx, 660–4; HMC *Lords MSS* xii,
540–55.

[73] Nicolson held Archbishop Wake's proxy from 31 Jan. to 11 Mar. 1718. HLRO Proxy
Book, vol. vii (unfoliated). The reason was that on 29 Jan. Wake had caught a cold, which
brought on severe toothache and a fever. He continued ill into February, not leaving
Lambeth until 28 Feb. when he visited the Princess of Wales. He returned to the Lords on
11 Mar. During his confinement and absence from parliament Wake was visited regularly by
Nicolson (eleven visits during Feb. and early Mar.). The purpose of the visits, other than
social, was to keep Wake informed of political developments and for Nicolson to receive
instructions on voting.

[74] The London entries end here, though Nicolson was to remain in London until he set
out for Ireland at the end of May, taking his final leave of Wake on 21 May (Lambeth Palace
MS 1770, f. 204^v). Parliament had been prorogued on 21 Mar. 1718 (*LJ* xx, 661–4), so it
is probable that the preparations for his translation kept Nicolson in the capital. The next
entry in the diary is for 23 May 1718: 'I set out in the Chester-Coach with Lady Margaret
Davis, Mrs Sclater, Col. Irwin, etc'. The entry for 30 May reads 'On board the *Robert Snow*,
Matthews master' (Ware transcripts, xxxii, 48). Nicolson arrived in Dublin on 3 June 1718,
where he stayed a fortnight and then travelled on to Derry. He remained in Derry until
8 Aug. when he left for home arriving at Rose on 17 Aug. See James, pp. 240–1.

Appendices

Appendix A
Biographical notes

ABINGDON, Montagu Venables-Bertie (*c.*1672–1743), 2nd Earl (1699) of; Constable and Lord-Lieut. of the Tower 1702-5; Lord-Lieut. of Oxon. 1702-5, 1712-15; Chief Justice in Eyre South of the Trent 1702-6, 1711-15.

ALDRICH, Henry (1647-1710), architect, composer, with Bishop Sprat entrusted with the publication of Clarendon's *History of the Rebellion*; Dean of Christ Church, Oxford, 1689-1710.

ANGLESEY, Arthur Annesley (d. 1737), 5th Earl (1710) of; younger brother of 4th Earl; MP for Cambridge Univ. 1702-10, New Roll [I] 1703-10; Joint Vice-Treasurer and Treasurer at War [I] 1710-16.

ANGLESEY, John Annesley (1676-1710), 4th Earl (1702) of; Vice-Treasurer, Receiver General, and Paymaster of the Forces [I] 1710.

ANNANDALE, William Johnston (1664-1721), 1st Marquess (1701) of; previously 2nd Earl (1672); President of the Council [S] 1693-9, 1702-6; Lord Treasurer [S] 1696-1705; Lord Privy Seal [S] 1702, 1715-21; a principal Secretary of State [S] 1705; opposed to Union, but a Scottish rep. peer 1708-13, 1715-21; Lord Keeper Great Seal [S] 1714-16.

ARGYLL, John Campbell (1680-1743), 2nd Duke (1703) of; sat in Lords as 1st Earl (1705) and Duke (1719) of Greenwich; elder brother of Earl of Ilay; High Commissioner of Parliament [S] 1705; served with Marlborough 1708-10; General 1711; Ambassador to 'Charles III' of Spain 1711; Governor of Minorca 1712-14, 1714-16; Lord-Lieut. of Surrey 1715-16.

ATHOLL, John Murray (1660-1724), 2nd Marquess (May 1703) and 1st Duke (June 1703) of; cr. Earl of Tullibardine (1696); Lord Privy Seal [S] 1703-5, 1713-14; opposed Union, but Scottish rep. peer 1710-15.

ATTERBURY, Francis (1662-1732); Archdeacon of Totnes 1701; Preb. of Exeter 1704; Dean of Carlisle 1704-11, of Christ Church, Oxford, 1711-13, and of Westminster 1713-23; Bishop of Rochester 1713-23; deprived June 1723 and exiled after trial for favouring the Pretender. G. V. Bennett, *The Tory Crisis in Church and State 1688-1730: the career of Francis Atterbury Bishop of Rochester* (1975).

BALMERINOCH or BALMERINO, John Elphinstone (1652-1736), 4th Baron (1704); eminent lawyer opposed to the Union; rep. peer 1710-15; Governor of the Mint [S] 1710; Commissioner of the office of Lord Chamberlain [S] 1711.

BEAUFORT, Henry Somerset (1684-1714), 2nd Duke (1700) of; a staunch Tory who absented himself from Court until the accession of the Tory ministry in 1710; Captain of the Gentlemen Pensioners 1712.

BEAW, William (*c.*1617-1706); Major of a reg. of horse for Charles I; served abroad, particularly with the Swedish army; Bishop of Llandaff 1679-1706. J. R. Guy, 'William Beaw: bishop and secret agent', *History Today*, xxvi (1976), 796-803; Lambeth Palace MS 930, f. 49: Beaw to Tenison, 21 Aug. 1699 (autobiographical letter).

BERKELEY of STRATTON, William (d. 1741), 4th Baron (1697); Master of the Rolls [I] 1696-1731; Chancellor of the Duchy of Lancaster 1710-14; First Lord of Trade and Plantations 1714-15.

685

BERKSHIRE, Henry Bowes Howard (1687-1757), 4th Earl (1706) of; took seat in Lords Jan. 1710; Deputy Earl Marshal 1718-25; 1709 m. Catherine daughter of Col. James Grahme of Levens.

BEVERIDGE, William (1637-1708), Preb. of St Paul's 1674-1708, of Chichester 1673-1708, of Canterbury 1684-1704; Archdeacon of Colchester 1681-1704; Bishop of St. Asaph 1704-8.

BINCKES, William (c.1653-1712), Preb. of Lincoln 1683, and Lichfield 1697; Vicar of Leamington, Warwickshire, 1683-1712; Dean of Lichfield 1703-12.

BINDON, Henry Howard (1670-1718), 1st Earl (1706) of; succeeded as 6th Earl of Suffolk (1709); MP for Arundel 1695-8, Essex 1705-6; Commissary General of the Musters 1697-1707; Deputy Earl Marshal 1706-18; Lord-Lieut. of Essex 1714-18; First Lord of Trade 1715-18.

BLACKALL, Offspring (1654-1716), Rector of St. Mary, Aldermary, London, 1694-1708; Bishop of Exeter 1708-16.

BLACKBURNE, Lancelot (1658-1743), Subdean of Exeter 1685-1702, 1704-5, Dean 1705-17, Bishop 1717-24; Lord Almoner 1723; Archbishop of York 1724-43. N. Sykes, ' "The Buccaneer Bishop": Lancelot Blackburn, 1658-1743', *Church Quarterly Review*, cxxx (1940).

BOLINGBROKE, Henry St John (1678-1751), 1st Viscount (1712); MP for Wotton Bassett 1701-8, Berkshire 1710-12; Secretary at War 1704-8; Secretary of State North 1710-13, and South 1713-14; Ambassador to Paris 1712; Lord-Lieut. of Essex 1712-14. H. T. Dickinson, *Bolingbroke* (1970); S. Biddle, *Bolingbroke and Harley* (1975).

BOLTON, Charles Paulet (1661-1722), 2nd Duke (1699) of; Warden of the New Forest 1699-1710, 1714-22; Commissioner for the Union 1706; Governor Isle of Wight 1707-10; Lord Chamberlain of the Household 1715-17; Lord-Lieut. of Ireland 1717-19.

BOYLE, Henry (d. 1725), 1st Baron Carleton (1714); MP for Tamworth 1689-90, Aldborough 1690, Cambridge Univ. 1692-1705, Westminster 1705-10; a Lord of the Treasury 1699-1701; Chancellor of the Exchequer 1701-8; Lord Treasurer [I] 1704-10; Commissioner for Union 1706; Secretary of State North 1708-10.

BRADFORD, Francis Newport (1620-1708), 1st Earl (1694) of; Treasurer of the Household 1672-87, 1689-1708; 1st Viscount Newport 1675; Cofferer of the Household 1691-1702.

BRADFORD, Richard Newport (1644-1723), 2nd Earl (1708) of; Lord-Lieut. of Shropshire 1704-12, 1714-23; known as Lord Newport 1694-1708.

BRIDGWATER, Scroop Egerton (1681-1745), 4th Earl (1701) and 1st Duke (1720) of; Gent. of the Bedchamber to Prince George 1703-5, and his Master of the Horse 1705-8; Lord Chamberlain to the Princess of Wales 1714-17; 1703 m. Elizabeth third daughter of the Duke of Marlborough.

BROMLEY, William (?1663-1732) of Baginton; MP for Warws. 1690-8, Oxford Univ. 1701-32; Speaker of Commons 1710-13; Secretary of State North 1713-14. Sedgwick, i, 493-4.

BRYDGES, James (1674-1744), 9th Baron Chandos (1714), 1st Earl of Carnarvon (1714) and 1st Duke of Chandos (1719); MP for Hereford 1698-1714; one of the Council of Lord High Admiral Prince George 1703-5; Paymaster General of the Forces Abroad 1705-13.

BUCKINGHAMSHIRE and NORMANBY, John Sheffield (1648-1721), 1st Duke (1703) of; previously Marquess of Normanby (1694) and 3rd Earl of

Mulgrave (1658); Lord Privy Seal 1702-5; Commissioner for Union 1706; Lord Steward 1710-11; Lord President of the Council 1711-14.

BURNET, Gilbert (1643-1715), a Scot; Prof. of Divinity Glasgow Univ. 1669; visited The Hague 1686, and accompanied William III's invasion 1688; Bishop of Salisbury 1689-1715. T. E. S. Clarke and H. C. Foxcroft, *A Life of Gilbert Burnet* (Cambridge, 1907).

BYERLEY, Robert (*c*.1661-1714); MP for Durham County 1685-7, Knaresborough 1689-90, 1695-1714; Colonel 1689; Commissioner for Public Accounts 1702-5; Commissioner for the Privy Seal 1711-13; Deputy Lieut. West Riding, York, and Ainsty 1700-14, North Riding 1701-14.

CARLISLE, Charles Howard (1669-1738), 3rd Earl (1692) of; MP for Morpeth, 1689-92; Governor of Carlisle 1693-1738; Deputy Earl Marshal 1701-6; First Lord of the Treasury 1701-2, 1715; Commissioner for Union 1706; Constable of the Tower 1715-22.

CARTERET, John (1690-1763), 2nd Baron (1695); took his seat 1711; Gentleman of the Bedchamber 1714-21; succ. mother as Earl Granville 1744.

CHAMBERLAYNE, John (1666-1723), Gentleman of the Privy Chamber to Anne and to George I; Secretary of the SPCK to 1702; FRS 1702; took over his father Edward's *Angliae Notitiae* 1703; published in Amsterdam the Lord's Prayer in 100 languages with a preface by Bishop Nicolson; Secretary of SPG 1701-12; Secretary of Queen Anne's Bounty 1704-23.

CHOLMONDELEY, Hugh (*c*.1662-1725), 2nd Viscount [I] (1681), 1st Baron (1689), 1st Earl (1706) of; Comptroller of the Household 1708; Treasurer of the Household 1708-13, 1714-25.

CHURCHILL, Awnsham (born bef. 1657-1723), of Henbury, Dorset, son of Dorchester bookseller, had become a stationer and bookseller in Paternoster Row, London by 1681, and took his brother John, into partnership in 1690; MP for Dorchester 1705-10; a Whig; Commissioner for taking subscriptions to the Land Bank; brother of Joshua, MP for Corfe Castle 1719-21, and William, MP for Ipswich 1707-14, 1715-17.

CLEVELAND, Charles Fitzroy (1662-1730), 2nd Duke (1709), and 1st Duke of Southampton (1675); illegitimate son of Charles II by Barbara Villiers, Duchess of Cleveland.

COMPTON, Henry (1632-1713), younger son of 2nd Earl of Northampton; Master of St Cross Hospital, Winchester, 1667; Bishop of Oxford 1674, of London 1675-1713; Dean of the Chapel Royal 1675-85, 1689-1713. E. Carpenter, *The Protestant Bishop* (1956).

CONINGSBY, Thomas (1656-1729), 1st Baron [I] (1692), 1st Baron [GB] (1716), 1st Earl (1719); MP for Leominster 1679-81, 1685-7, 1689-1710, 1715-16; Vice-Treasurer [I] 1692-1710.

COWPER, William (*c*.1665-1723), 1st Baron (1706) and 1st Earl (1718); MP for Hertford 1695-1700, Bere Alston 1701-5; Lord Keeper 1705-7; Commissioner for Union 1706; Lord Chancellor 1707-10, 1714-18.

CREW of STENE, Nathaniel (1633-1721), 3rd Baron (1697); Bishop of Oxford 1671-4, of Durham 1674-1721. C. E. Whiting, *Nathaniel, Lord Crewe, Bishop of Durham* (1940).

CROMARTY, George Mackenzie (1630-1714), 1st Earl (1703) of; previously Viscount of Tarbat (1685); one of the Principal Secretaries of State [S] 1702-5; Lord Justice General [S] 1705-10; supporter of Union.

CUMBERLAND, Richard (1631-1718), Bishop of Peterborough 1691-1718.

DALRYMPLE, Sir David (*c*.1665-1721), 1st Bt of Hailes, Haddington; 5th son of

James, 1st Viscount of Stair; MP for Culross [S] 1698–1707, Scotland 1707–8, Haddington Burghs 1708–21; Solicitor-General [S] 1701–9; Commissioner for Union 1706; Lord Advocate [S] 1709–11, 1714–20; Dean of Faculty of Advocates 1712–21. Sedgwick, i, 600–1.

DARTMOUTH, William Legge (1672–1750), 2nd Baron (1691) and 1st Earl (1711) of; a Lord of Trade and Plantations 1702–10; Secretary of State South 1710–13; Lord Privy Seal 1713–14.

DAWES, Sir William (1671–1724) 3rd Bt; Master of St. Catherine's Hall, Cambridge, 1697–1714; Preb. of Worcester 1698–1708; Bishop of Chester 1708–14; Archbishop of York 1714–24.

DERING, Heneage (1665–1750), Archdeacon of the East Riding of Yorkshire 1702; Preb. of York 1705–50; Dean of Ripon 1711–50.

DEVONSHIRE, William Cavendish (1641–1707) 1st Duke (1694) of; MP for Derby 1661–81; succ. 4th Earl 1684; Lord Steward 1689–1707.

DEVONSHIRE, William Cavendish (c.1673–1729), 2nd Duke (1707) of; styled Marquess of Hartington 1694–1707; MP for Derby 1695–1701, Castle Rising 1702, Yorks. 1702–7; Lord Steward 1707–10, 1714–16; Lord President of the Council 1716–17, 1725–29; Chief Justice in Eyre North of Trent 1707–10; Lord-Lieut. of Derb. 1707–10, 1714–29.

DORCHESTER, Marquess of, see KINGSTON UPON HULL, Duke of.

EVANS, John (d. 1724), minister at Fort St George, Madras, 1692; Bishop of Bangor 1702–16, of Meath 1716–24. M. Martyn, 'John Evans — East-Indian Chaplain', *History Today*, xxvi (1976), 670–7.

FERRERS, Robert Shirley (1650–1717), 1st (or 8th) Baron (1677) and 1st Earl (1711); Steward to Queen Catherine Braganza 1685–1705; PC 1699–1714.

FEVERSHAM, Louis de Duras (1641–1709), 2nd Earl (1677) of; nephew of Marshal Turenne, naturalised 1665; succ. father-in-law in peerage; Lord Chamberlain to Queen Catherine Braganza 1680–1705; Master of St Katharine's Hospital 1698–1709.

FLEETWOOD, William (1656–1723), Rector of St Augustine, London, 1689–1706; Canon of Windsor 1702; Bishop of St Asaph 1708–14, of Ely 1714–23.

FLEMING, Michael (1661–1718), 6th son of Sir Daniel Fleming of Rydal, Westmld., brother of Sir William; MP for Westmld. 20 Feb. 1707–1708; a soldier, Capt. 1697; Capt. 16th foot 1702, Major 1709.

FLEMING, Sir William (1656–1736), 1st Bt of Rydal, Westmld.; MP for Westmld. 1696–1700, 1704–5; 1st surv. son of Sir Daniel, and brother of Michael; Commissioner of Excise 1698–1702; cr. Bt 4 Oct. 1705.

FLETCHER, George (c.1666–1708), MP for Cockermouth 1698–1701, Cumb. 1701–2, 1705–8; 2nd son of Sir George Fletcher, 2nd Bt; Colonel 1704–8; served under Marlborough in most of the Flanders campaigns.

FOWLER, Edward (1632–1714), Vicar of St Giles, Cripplegate, 1682–1714; Bishop of Gloucester 1691–1714.

GARDINER, James (1637–1705), Bishop of Lincoln 1695–1705.

GEE, Edward (c.1661–1730), Rector of St Bennet's, Paul's Wharf, 1688–1706; Canon of Westminster 1701–30; Rector of Chevening, Kent, 1707–30; Dean of Peterborough 1722, and of Lincoln 1722.

GEORGE of DENMARK, Prince (1653–1708), youngest son of King Frederick III of Denmark; husband of Queen Anne; Lord High Admiral 1702–8; sat in Lords as Duke of Cumberland (1689).

GIBBON, Thomas (c.1669–1716); DD (Cantab.) 1714; Rector of Greystoke, Cumb., 1693–1716; Dean of Carlisle 1713–16.

GIBSON, Edmund (1669–1748), Chaplain to Archbishop Tenison and Lambeth Librarian 1702; Archdeacon of Surrey 1710; Bishop of Lincoln 1716–23, of London 1723–48. N. Sykes, *Edmund Gibson, Bishop of London* (Oxford, 1926).

GODOLPHIN, Sidney (1645–1712), 1st Baron (1684) and 1st Earl (1706) of; First Lord of the Treasury 1684–5, 1690–6; Lord Treasurer 1700–1, 1702–10.

GRAHME, Henry (born aft. 1676–1707), son of Col. James Grahme; MP for Westmld. 1701–7; Groom of the Bedchamber to Prince George 1702–6; he had been defended by Nicolson in 1700 against an accusation of disaffection to the government (HMC *Le Fleming*, pp. 334–5); in May 1705 m. Mary Tudor, Lady Derwentwater, illegitimate daughter of Charles II; died 7 Jan. 1707.

GRAHME, James (1650–1730), of Levens, Westmld.; MP for Carlisle 1685–7, Appleby 1702–8, Westmld. 1708–27; Lieutenant-Colonel 1678; Keeper of Privy Purse to James II 1679–88; Judge of Admiralty Court 1711–14; Mayor of Appleby 1717–18. Sedgwick, ii, 76–7; J. F. Bagot, *Col. James Grahme of Levens* (Kendal, 1886).

GRAHME, William (c.1656–1713), younger brother of Col. James Grahme; Preb. of Durham 1684; Dean of Carlisle 1686–1704, of Wells 1704–13.

GRANDORGE, John (1670–1730), Rector of Hortfield, Sussex, 1698, of Ashurst 1707; Chaplain to the Earl of Thanet; Preb. of Canterbury 1713–30.

GUERNSEY, Heneage Finch (c.1649–1719), 1st Baron (1703), and 1st Earl of Aylesford (1714); MP for Oxford Univ. 1679, 1689–98, 1701–3, Guilford 1685–7; brother of 2nd Earl of Nottingham, q.v.; Solicitor-General 1679–86; PC 1703–8, 1711–14; Chancellor of the Duchy of Lancaster 1714–16.

HALIFAX, Charles Montagu (1661–1715), 1st Baron (1700) and 1st Earl (1715) of; a Lord of the Treasury 1692–4; Chancellor of the Exchequer 1694–9; First Lord of the Treasury 1697–9, 1714–15; Auditor of the Exchequer 1699–1714; Commissioner for Union 1706; Envoy to Hanover 1706; one of the five Junto Lords.

HALL, John (1633–1710), Master of Pembroke College, Oxford, 1664–1710; Preb. of St. Paul's 1664–1707; Bishop of Bristol 1691–1710.

HAMILTON, James Douglas (1658–1712), 4th Duke (1698) of; succ. mother who had surrendered the dukedom; opposed Union; Scottish rep. peer 1708–12; Lord-Lieut. of Lancs. 1710–12; PC 1710; cr. Duke of Brandon [GB] 1711, but Lords prevented him sitting by virtue of his new title; appointed ambassador to Paris 1712, but killed in duel by Lord Mohun before he took up the post; Master General of Ordnance 1712.

HARCOURT, Sir Simon (?1661–1727), 1st Baron (1711) and 1st Viscount (1721); MP for Abingdon 1690–1705, 1708–9, 1710, Bossiney 1705–8, Cardigan Borough 1710; Solicitor-General 1702–7; Kt 1702; Commissioner for Union 1706; Attorney-General 1707–8, 1710; Lord Keeper 1710–13; Lord Chancellor 1713–14.

HARLEY, Robert, *see* OXFORD and MORTIMER, Earl of.

HARVEY, William (1663–1731), grandson of a rich Turkey merchant, with an income of £5,000–£6,000 a year; MP for Appleby 1705–8, also Old Sarum 1689–1705, 1708–10, Weymouth and Melcombe Regis 1711–13, 1714–15, and Essex 1715–16, 1722–7; member of the October Club. Sedgwick, ii, 116.

HAVERSHAM, John Thompson (c.1648-1710), 1st Baron (1696); MP for Gatton 1685-7, 1689-96; Lord of the Admiralty 1699-1701.

HEDGES, Sir Charles (d. 1714), Kt; MP for Calne 1702-5, West Looe 1705-13, East Looe 1713-14; Secretary of State North 1700-1, 1702-4, South 1704-6.

HICKES, George (1642-1715), non-juror and antiquarian; Dean of Worcester 1683-91.

HOADLY, Benjamin (1676-1761), Lecturer of St Mildred's Poultry, London, 1701-11; Rector of St Peter-le-Poor, Broad St., 1704-21, and of Streatham 1710-23; Chaplain to George I 1715; Bishop of Bangor 1715-21, Hereford 1721-3, Salisbury 1723-34, and Winchester 1734-61.

HOOPER, George (1640-1727), Rector of Lambeth 1675; Dean of Canterbury 1691-1704; Prolocutor of Lower House of Convocation 1701; Bishop of St Asaph 1703-4; and of Bath and Wells 1704-27. W. M. Marshall, *George Hooper 1640-1727, Bishop of Bath and Wells* (Sherborne, 1976).

HOUGH, John (1651-1743), President of Magdalen College, Oxford, 1687, 1688-1711 (ejected by James II); Bishop of Oxford 1690-9, of Lichfield and Coventry 1699-1717, and of Worcester 1717-43.

HUMPHRIES, Humphrey (1648-1712), Dean of Bangor 1680-9; Bishop of Bangor 1689-1701, and of Hereford 1701-12.

HYDE, Baron, *see* ROCHESTER, 2nd Earl of.

ILAY, Archibald Campbell (1682-1761), 1st Earl (1706) of; younger brother of 2nd Duke of Argyll whom he succ. as 3rd Duke in 1743; Scottish rep. peer 1707-13, 1715-61; Lord of the Treasury [S] 1705-6; Lord Justice General 1710-61; Lord Clerk Register 1714-16.

KENNETT, White (1660-1728), Rector of St Botolph, Aldgate, 1700, of St Mary Aldermary and St Thomas Apostle, Vintry, 1708; Preb. of Salisbury 1701, of Lincoln 1708; Archdeacon of Huntingdon 1701; Dean of Peterborough 1708; Bishop of Peterborough 1718-28. G. V. Bennett, *White Kennett 1660-1728, Bishop of Peterborough* (1957).

KENT, Henry Grey (1671-1740), 11th Earl (1702), 1st Marquess (1706), and 1st Duke (1710) of; Lord Chamberlain of the Household 1704-10; Lord of the Bedchamber 1714-16; Lord Steward 1716-19.

KIDDER, Richard (1633-1703), Dean of Peterborough 1689-91; Bishop of Bath and Wells 1691-1703; killed in bed at the Palace, Wells, by the falling of a chimneystack in the great storm of 26 Nov. 1703.

KING, Peter (1669-1734), later 1st Baron (1725); MP for Bere Alston 1701-15; Recorder of London 1708-15; Kt 1708; Chief Justice of the Common Pleas 1714-25; Lord Chancellor 1725-33.

KING, William (1650-1729), Dean of St Patrick's, Dublin, 1689; Bishop of Derry 1691-1703; Archbishop of Dublin 1703-29. *A Great Archbishop of Dublin, William King, 1650-1729*, ed. Sir C. S. King (1908).

KINGSTON UPON HULL, Evelyn Pierrepont (c.1665-1726), 5th Earl (1690), and 1st Duke (1715) of, and 1st Marquess of Dorchester (1706); Lord Privy Seal 1716-18, 1720-6.

LAMPLUGH, Thomas (1656-1737), of Lamplugh Hall, Cumb.; MP for Cockermouth 1702-8; Sheriff, Cumb.. 1702-3; a Dissenter who 'occasionally conformed', he supported the Wharton interest in Cockermouth, and defeated Somerset's candidate, James Stanhope, at a by-election in 1702; an owner of coal mines, he sought an act to levy a duty on coal to improve his harbour of Parton as a rival to Sir John Lowther's Whitehaven; his Parton Harbour Bill was supported by Somerset, Thomas Stanwix, Christopher Musgrave, and

Sir Richard Sandford, and it passed in 1706 despite Lowther opposition, but Lamplugh's lack of financial resources meant that Parton never seriously rivalled Whitehaven.

LANCASTER, William (1650-1717), Vicar of St Martin-in-the-Fields 1694; Provost of Queen's College, Oxford, 1704-17; Vice-Chancellor of Oxford Univ. 1705-9; Archdeacon of Middlesex 1705-17.

LAWSON, Gilfred (?1657-1749), MP for Cumb. 1701, 1702-5, 1708-34; 1st son of Wilfred Lawson, nephew of Sir Wilfred Lawson 3rd Bt; succ. as 6th Bt 1743; member of the October Club. Sedgwick, ii, 200.

LECHMERE, Nicholas (1677-1727), MP for Appleby 1708-10, Cockermouth 1710-17, and Tewkesbury 1717-21; son-in-law of the 3rd Earl of Carlisle; Queen's Counsel 1708; Attorney-General 1718-20; Chancellor of the Duchy of Lancaster 1717-27; cr. Baron Lechmere 1721. Sedgwick, ii, 202-4.

LEEDS, Thomas Osborne (1632-1712), 1st Duke (1694) of; previously Earl of Danby (1674) and Marquess of Carmarthen (1689); Lord Treasurer 1673-9; Lord Pres. of the Council 1689-99. A. Browning, *Thomas Osborne Earl of Danby and Duke of Leeds 1632-1712* (3 vols., Glasgow, 1944-51).

LINDSEY, Robert Bertie (1660-1723), 4th Earl (1701) and 1st Marquess (1706), and 1st Duke of Ancaster and Kesteven (1715); summoned to Lords in father's barony of Willoughby de Eresby 1690; Lord-Lieut. of Lincs. 1701-23; hereditary Lord Great Chamberlain 1701-23.

LLOYD, William (1627-1717), Archdeacon of Merioneth 1668-72; Vicar of St Martin-in-the-Fields 1676-80; Dean of Bangor 1672-80; Bishop of St Asaph 1680-92, of Lichfield and Coventry 1692-9, and of Worcester 1700-17. A. T. Hart, *William Lloyd, Bishop, Politician, Author and Prophet, 1627-1717* (1952).

LLOYD, William (c.1674-1719?), son of Bishop Lloyd; Rector of Sunning-well, Berks., 1699-1705; Vicar of Blockley, Worcs., 1700-5, of Harwell, Berks., 1703-13; Rector of Ripple, Worcs., 1705-19, and of Fladbury, Worcs., 1713-19; and Chancellor of Worcester 1705-18.

LONSDALE, Richard Lowther (1692-1713), 2nd Viscount (1700).

LOWTHER, James (1673-1755), of Whitehaven; 2nd son of Sir John Lowther 2nd Bt; succ. to family estates 1706, and as 4th Bt 1731; MP for Carlisle 1694-1702, Cumb. 1708-22, 1727-55, Appleby 1725-7; Clerk to the Deliveries in the Ordnance 1696-1701, Principal Storekeeper 1701-8; PC 1714. J. V. Beckett, *Coal and Tobacco: the Lowthers and the Economic Development of West Cumberland, 1660-1760* (Cambridge, 1981).

LOWTHER, Robert (1681-1745), of Maulds Meaburn, Westmld.; cousin of James Lowther of Whitehaven and of the Lowthers of Lowther (Lonsdale); MP for Westmld. 1705-8; Principal Storekeeper of the Ordnance 1708-10; Governor of Barbados 1710-14, 1715-19.

MANNINGHAM, Thomas (?1651-1722), Rector of St Andrew's, Holborn, 1691; Dean of Windsor 1709; Bishop of Chichester 1709-22.

MANSEL, Sir Thomas (c.1688-1723) 5th Bt; MP for Cardiff 1689-98; Glamorgan 1699-1712; Commissioner of Treasury 1710; Teller of the Exchequer 1712-14; cr. 1st Baron Mansel of Margam 1712.

MAR, John Erskine (1675-1732), 6th Earl (1689) of; Secretary of State [S] 1705-9; Keeper of Signet [S] 1706; Commissioner for Union 1706; Scottish rep. peer 1707-15; Secretary of State for Scotland 1713-14; Pretender's C.-in-C. in Scotland 1715; attainted and title forfeit 1716; chief adviser to Pretender 1716-24, and cr. by him Duke of Mar (1715).

MARLBOROUGH, John Churchill (1650–1722), 1st Duke (1702) of; Captain
General of the English forces at home and abroad, Generalissimo of the allied
forces, and Master General of the Ordnance 1702–11; Master General of the
Ordnance and Captain General of the forces 1714.

MEWS, Peter (1619–1706), Pres. of St John's College, Oxford, 1667–73; Dean
of Rochester 1670–3; Bishop of Bath and Wells 1673–84, and of Winchester 1684–1706.

MOHUN, Charles (1672–1712), 4th Baron (1677); Colonel of reg. of foot
1702–12, Brigadier General 1707, Major-General 1708, Lieutenant-General
1710; killed in duel with Duke of Hamilton in which he also killed his opponent.

MONTAGU, James (1666–1723), brother of Lord Halifax, q.v.; MP for Tregony
1695–8, Bere Alston 1698–1700, Carlisle 1705–13; Kt and QC 1705; Solicitor-
General 1707–8; Attorney-General 1708–10; Baron of the Exchequer 1714–22;
Joint Collector of Tonnage and Poundage, Port of London, 1714–23.

MONTAGU, Ralph (1638–1709), 3rd Baron (1684), 1st Earl (1689) and 1st
Duke (1705) of; Master of the Great Wardrobe 1671–85, 1689–1709.

MOORE, John (1646–1714), Rector of St Andrew's, Holborn, 1689–91; Bishop
of Norwich 1699–1707, of Ely 1707–14.

MUSGRAVE, Sir Christopher (c.1631–1704), 4th Bt of Edenhall, Cumb.; MP
for Carlisle 1661–81, 1685–7, 1689–90, Westmld. 1690–5, 1701, 1702–4,
Appleby 1695–8, Oxford Univ. 1698–1700, Totnes 1701–2; father of Christopher and Joseph, and grandfather of Sir Christopher 5th Bt, q.v.

MUSGRAVE, Christopher (c.1663–1718), 2nd son of Sir Christopher 4th Bt;
MP for Carlisle 1690–5, 1702–5; Clerk of the Deliveries in the Ordnance
1689–96; Secretary to the Ordnance 1696–1714; Clerk of Privy Council
1695–1710.

MUSGRAVE, Sir Christopher (1688–1736), 5th Bt, of Edenhall, Cumb., succ.
grandfather 1704; son of Philip Musgrave; MP for Carlisle 1713–15, Cumb.
1722–34; Clerk of the Privy Council 1710–16; Commissioner for executing
the Privy Seal 1715. Sedgwick, ii, 286–7.

MUSGRAVE, Joseph (c.1676–1757), 5th son of Sir Christopher Musgrave 4th
Bt, but 1st by his 2nd wife; half brother of Christopher Musgrave; MP for
Cockermouth 1713–15; Secretary to Chancellor of Exchequer 1711–14.

MUSGRAVE, Richard (c.1675–1711), of Hayton, Cumb.; succ. as 3rd Bt
1710; MP for Cumb. 1701, 1702–8.

NORMANBY, Marquess of, see BUCKINGHAMSHIRE, Duke of.

NORTH and GREY, William North (1678–1734), 6th Baron (1691); a soldier
(Lieut.-General 1710); who lost right hand at Blenheim; Governor of
Sheerness 1705, of Portsmouth 1711–14; PC 1711–14; later a Jacobite and
cr. Earl North by the Pretender 1722.

NORTHEY, Sir Edward (1652–1723), Attorney-General 1701–7, 1710–18;
Kt 1702; MP for Tiverton 1710–22. Sedgwick, ii, 300.

NOTTINGHAM, Daniel Finch (1647–1730), 2nd Earl (1682) of; succ. as 7th
Earl of Winchilsea (1729); elder brother of Lord Guernsey, q.v.; Secretary
of State South 1689–93, 1702–4; Lord President of the Council 1714–16.
H. Horwitz, *Revolution Politicks, the Career of Daniel Finch Second Earl of
Nottingham, 1647–1730* (Cambridge, 1968).

ONSLOW, Sir Richard (1654–1717) 3rd Bt of Clandon, Surrey; MP for Guildford 1679–81, 1685–7, Surrey 1689–1710, 1713–15, St Mawes 1710–13;
Speaker of the Commons 1708–10; Chancellor (1714–15) and Teller (1715–
17) of the Exchequer. Sedgwick, ii, 310–11.

ORFORD, Edward Russell (1652–1727), 1st Earl (1697) of; nephew of 1st Duke of Bedford; Treasurer of the Navy 1689–99; Admiral of the Blue 1689, of the Fleet 1693; 1st Commissioner of the Admiralty 1694–9, 1709–10, 1714–17; one of the five Junto Lords.

ORMOND, James Butler (1665–1745) 2nd Duke (1688), of, in both the Irish and English peerage; General of the Horse 1702; Lord-Lieut. of Ireland 1703–7, 1710–13; Captain General in succ. to Marlborough 1712; attainted for favouring the Pretender 1715, exiled to France.

OSBORNE of KIVETON, Peregrine (1659–1729), 2nd Baron (1690) of; summoned to the Lords in his father's barony, but known by his father's courtesy title as Marquess of Carmarthen; succ. as 2nd Duke of Leeds 1712; Rear-Admiral 1697, Vice-Admiral of the Red 1703.

OTTLEY, Adam (c.1655–1723), Preb. of Hereford 1686–1723; Archdeacon of Salop 1687–1713; Bishop of St David's 1713–23.

OXFORD and MORTIMER, Robert Harley (1661–1724), 1st Earl (1711) of; MP for Tregony 1689–90, New Radnor Boroughs 1690–1711; Speaker of the Commons 1701–5; Secretary of State North 1704–8; Chancellor of the Exchequer 1710–11; Lord Treasurer 1711–14. A. McInnes, *Robert Harley, Puritan Politician* (1970); E. Hamilton, *The Backstairs Dragon, a Life of Robert Harley, Earl of Oxford* (1969); S. Biddle, *Bolingbroke and Harley* (1975).

PARKER, Thomas (c.1667–1732), MP for Derby 1705–10; Kt 1705; Serjeant-at-law and Queen's Serjeant 1705; Lord Chief Justice Queen's Bench 1710–18; Lord Chancellor 1718–25; cr. Baron Parker 1716, Earl of Macclesfield 1721.

PEARSON, Thomas (c.1659–?1722), of Orton, Cumb.; brother of William; Principal of St Edmund Hall 1707–22; Rector of Nether Denton, Cumb., 1703, of Sulhampstead Abbots, Berks., 1708.

PEARSON, William (c.1663–1716), of Orton, Cumb.; brother of Thomas; Preb. of York 1689; Archdeacon of Nottingham and Preb. of Southwell 1690; Subdean of York 1695, and Bolton Percy 1697.

PEMBROKE, Thomas Herbert (c.1656–1733), 8th Earl (1683) of; First Lord of the Admiralty 1690–2, 1701–2; Lord President of the Council 1699–1702, 1702–8; Lord Privy Seal 1692–9; Lord High Admiral 1702, 1708–9; Lord-Lieut. of Ireland 1707–8.

PETERBOROUGH, Charles Mordaunt (1658–1735), 3rd Earl (1697) of, and 1st Earl of Monmouth (1689); General of Allied Forces in Spain and Joint Admiral and Chief Commander of the Fleet 1705; Ambassador to 'Charles III' of Spain 1706–7; General of the Marines 1710; Ambassador to Vienna and Turin 1710–11, and to the King of Sicily 1713–14; Governor of Minorca 1714.

PORTLAND, Hans Willem Bentinck (1649–1709), 1st Earl (1689) of; First Gentleman of the Bedchamber, Groom of the Stole, and Keeper of the Privy Purse 1689–1700; Ambassador to Paris 1698; impeached for part in Partition Treaties 1701.

PORTLAND, Henry Bentinck (1682–1726), 2nd Earl (1709), and 1st Duke (1716) of; known as Viscount Woodstock 1689–1709; MP for Southampton 1705–8, Hants. 1708–9; Lord of the Bedchamber 1717–26.

POTTER, John (?1674–1747), Domestic Chaplain to Archbishop Tenison 1704–7; Regius Professor of Divinity, Oxford, 1707–37; Bishop of Oxford 1715–37; Archbishop of Canterbury 1737–47.

POULETT, John (c.1668–1743), 4th Baron (1679) and 1st Earl (1706); PC 1702–14; Commissioner for Union 1706; First Lord of the Treasury 1710–11; Lord Steward 1711–14.

POWYS, Sir Thomas (c.1649–1719), brother of Sir Littleton Powys, Baron of King's Bench 1700–26; Solicitor-General 1686–7; Attorney-General 1687–8; Queen's Serjeant 1702–13; Judge of Queen's Bench 1713–14; King's Serjeant 1714–19.

QUEENSBERRY, James Douglas (1662–1711), 2nd Duke (1696) of; cr. 1st Duke of Dover [GB] (1708); Commissioner of the Treasury [S] 1692–1704, 1705–7; Lord Privy Seal [S] 1696–1702; Extraordinary Lord of Sessions 1696–1711; Lord High Commissioner to Parl. [S] 1700, 1702, 1703, 1706; Scottish rep. peer 1707–8; Joint Keeper of the Privy Seal [S] 1709; Secretary of State Scotland 1709–11.

RABY, Baron, see STRAFFORD, Earl of.

RICHMOND, Charles Lennox (1672–1723), 1st Duke (1675) of; also Duke of Lennox [S]; illegitimate son of Charles II and the Duchess of Portsmouth; Master of the Horse 1681–5; Grandmaster of Freemasons 1696–7; Lord of the Bedchamber 1714–23.

RIVERS, Richard Savage (c.1654–1712), 4th Earl (1694); C.-in-C. of forces sent to Portugal 1706; General and C.-in-C. in GB (in the absence of Ormond) 1712; Envoy to Hanover 1710, 1711; Constable of the Tower 1710; Master General of the Ordnance 1712.

ROBINSON, John (1650–1723); Chaplain to the English Embassy at the Swedish Court (c.1680) where he remained for more than twenty-five years; successively Resident and Envoy Extraordinary; interpreter for Marlborough with Charles XII of Sweden; Dean of Windsor and Wolverhampton 1709; Dean of the Chapel Royal 1710–14; Bishop of Bristol 1710–14, of London 1714–23; Lord Privy Seal 1711–13; 1st English Plenipotentiary at Utrecht 1712–13.

ROCHESTER, Henry Hyde (1672–1753), 2nd Earl (1711) of; known as Lord Hyde 1687–1711; MP for Launceston 1692–1711; Joint Vice-Treasurer and Paymaster [I] 1710–16; High Steward of Oxford Univ. 1711–53; Lord-Lieut. of Cornwall 1711–14.

ROCHESTER, Lawrence Hyde (1642–1711), 1st Earl (1682) of; First Lord of the Treasury 1679–84; Lord President of the Council 1684–5, 1710–11; Lord Treasurer 1685–7; Lord-Lieut. of Ireland 1700–3; High Steward of Oxford Univ. 1709–11.

ST JOHN, Henry, see BOLINGBROKE, Viscount.

SANDFORD, Sir Richard (1675–1723), 3rd Bt of Howgill Castle, Westmld.; MP for Westmld. 1695–1700, 1701–2, Morpeth 1701, 1705–13, Appleby 1713–23; Warden of the Mint 1714–17. Sedgwick, ii, 406.

SCARBROUGH, Richard Lumley (1650–1721), 1st Earl (1690) of; Lord-Lieut. of Durham 1690–1712, 1715–21; Commissioner for Union 1706; Chancellor of Duchy of Lancaster 1716–17; Vice-Treasurer [I] 1717.

SCHOMBERG, Mainhard (1641–1719), 3rd Duke (1693) of; also 1st Duke of Leinster [I] (1691); C.-in-C. of all the forces in Portugal 1703 (replaced by Galway 1704), he returned to England 1705.

SHARP, John (1645–1714), Rector of St Giles-in-the-Fields 1675; Dean of Norwich 1681, of Canterbury 1689; Archbishop of York 1691–1714. A. T. Hart, *The Life and Times of John Sharp, Archbishop of York* (1949).

SHARP, John (1678–1727), eldest son of Archbishop Sharp; MP for Ripon 1701–14; Commissioner of the Revenue [I] 1712; Commissioner for Trade 1713–14.

SHREWSBURY, Charles Talbot (1660–1718), 12th Earl (1668), and 1st Duke (1694) of; Secretary of State South 1689–90, 1695–8, North 1694–5; Lord Chamberlain of the Household 1699–1700, 1710–15; abroad mainly in Italy 1700–7; Lord-Lieut. of Ireland 1713–14; Lord Treasurer 1714; Groom of the Stole and Keeper of the Privy Purse 1714–18; m. Adelhida, daughter of Marquess Palleotti 1705. D. H. Somerville, *The King of Hearts, Charles Talbot, Duke of Shrewsbury* (1962).

SMALRIDGE, George (1663–1719); Preb. of Lichfield 1693; Deputy Regius Professor of Divinity, Oxford, 1700–6; Lecturer at St Dunstan's-in-the-West 1708–11; Dean of Carlisle 1711–13, of Christ Church, Oxford, 1713–19; Bishop of Bristol 1714–19; Lord Almoner 1714–15.

SMITH, John (?1655–1723), MP for Ludgershall 1679, 1681, 1689–90, Beer Alston 1691–5, Andover 1695–1713, East Looe 1715–23; Commissioner for Union 1706; Speaker of House of Commons 1705–8; Chancellor of the Exchequer 1699–1701, 1708–10; a Teller of the Exchequer 1710–12, 1715–23.

SMITH, John (1659–1715); Preb. of Durham 1696; Treasurer 1699; Rector of Gateshead 1696–1704, of Bishops Wearmouth 1704–15; compiler of the *Works of Bede* (1722); brother of Joseph Smith, Provost of Queen's College, Oxford.

SOMERS, John (1651–1716), 1st Baron (1697); Treasurer Middle Temple 1690–1; Solicitor-General 1689–92; Attorney-General 1692–3; Lord Keeper 1693–7; Lord Chancellor 1697–1700; President of Royal Society 1698–1703; Lord President of the Council 1708–10; one of the five Junto Lords. W. L. Sachse, *Lord Somers: a political portrait* (Manchester, 1975).

SOMERSET, Charles Seymour (1662–1748), 6th Duke (1678) of; Chancellor of Cambridge Univ. 1689–1748; Lord President of the Council 1702; Master of the Horse 1702–12, 1714–15; m. Elizabeth Percy (1682), Groom of the Stole 1711–14.

SOUTHAMPTON, Duke of, *see* CLEVELAND, Duke of.

SPRAT, Thomas (1635–1713), Bishop of Rochester 1684–1713; Dean of Westminster 1683–1713.

STAMFORD, Thomas Grey (c.1653–1720) 2nd Earl (1673) of; First Lord of Trade and Plantations 1699–1702, 1707–11; Chancellor of the Duchy of Lancaster 1697–1702.

STANHOPE, George (1660–1728), Royal Chaplain 1694–1728; Dean of Canterbury 1704–28.

STANHOPE, James (1673–1721), soldier and diplomat; MP for Newport (I.o.W.) 1702, 1707, Cockermouth 1702–13, 1715–17, Wendover 1714–15; second in command to Peterborough at the siege of Barcelona 1705; Envoy Extraordinary to 'Charles III' of Spain 1706–7, 1708–10; C.-in-C. of the British troops in Spain 1708–10, captured at Brihuega (1710) and a prisoner until 1712; Secretary of State South 1714–16, North 1716–17, 1718–21; First Lord of the Treasury and Chancellor of the Exchequer 1717–18; cr. Viscount (1717) and Earl Stanhope (1718). B. Williams, *Stanhope: A Study in eighteenth-century War and Diplomacy* (Oxford, 1932).

STANWIX, Thomas (c.1670–1725); MP for Carlisle 1702–21, Newport (I.o.W.) 1721–2, Yarmouth (I.o.W.) 1722–5; Colonel 1705; Lieut.-Governor of Carlisle 1705–25; served in Portugal 1709, Brig.-General 1710; Governor of Gibraltar 1710–15; Mayor of Carlisle 1715; politically a follower of Lord Carlisle. Sedgwick, ii, 440–1.

STRAFFORD, Thomas Wentworth (1672–1739), 1st Earl (1711) of, also Baron Raby (1695); Envoy Extraordinary 1703–5, Ambassador Extraordinary, Berlin, 1705–11, to The Hague 1711–14; Ambassador Plenipotentiary at Utrecht 1711; First Lord of the Admiralty 1712–14; impeached Sept. 1715 but no further action after June 1716.

STRATFORD, Nicholas (1633–1707); Warden of the Collegiate Church, Manchester, 1667–84; Dean of St Asaph 1674–89; Rector of Wigan, and Bishop of Chester 1689–1707.

STRICKLAND, William (c.1686–1735), of Boynton, Yorks.; MP for Malton 1708–15, Carlisle 1715–22, Scarborough 1722–35; brought in by Lord Carlisle for Carlisle in 1715; Commissioner of the Revenue [I] 1709–11, 1714–25. Sedgwick, ii, 452–3.

SUNDERLAND, Charles Spencer (1674–1722), 3rd Earl (1702) of; MP for Tiverton 1695–1702; Envoy Extraordinary to Vienna 1705; Secretary of State South 1706–10; Lord-Lieut. of Ireland 1714; Lord Privy Seal 1715–16; Joint Vice-Treasurer [I] 1716–17; Secretary of State North 1717–18; Lord President of the Council 1718–19; First Lord of the Treasury 1718–21; one of the five lords of the Junto.

TALBOT, William (?1659–1730), cousin of the Duke of Shrewsbury; Dean of Worcester 1691–1715; Bishop of Oxford 1699–1715, of Salisbury 1715–21, and of Durham 1721–30.

TENISON, Thomas (1636–1715); Rector of St Martin-in-the-Fields 1680–92, of St James's, Piccadilly 1686–92; Archdeacon of London 1689–91; Bishop of Lincoln 1691–4; Archbishop of Canterbury 1694–1715. E. F. Carpenter, *Thomas Tenison* (1948).

THANET, Thomas Tufton (1644–1729), 6th Earl (1684) of; MP for Appleby 1668–79; Lord-Lieut. of Cumb. and Westmld. 1685–7, 1712–14; PC 1703–7, 1711–14; Hereditary Sheriff of Westmld.

TODD, Hugh (?1658–1728), Preb. of Carlisle 1685; Vicar of Stanwix 1685–99, of Penrith 1699–1728.

TOWNSHEND, Charles (1675–1738), 2nd Viscount (1687); Lord-Lieut. of Norfolk 1701–13, 1714–30; Joint Ambassador Extraordinary to The Hague Conference 1709–11; Secretary of State North 1714–16, 1721–30; Lord-Lieut. of Ireland 1717.

TRELAWNEY, Sir Jonathan (1650–1721), 3rd Bt; Bishop of Bristol 1685–8, of Exeter 1689–1707, and of Winchester 1707–21; friend and supporter of Atterbury.

TRIMNELL, Charles (1663–1723), Preb. of Norwich 1691–1707; tutor to 3rd Earl of Sunderland; Archdeacon of Norfolk 1698–1708; Royal Chaplain 1700–8; Rector of St James's, Westminster, 1706–8; Bishop of Norwich 1708–21, of Winchester 1721–3; Clerk of the Closet 1714–23.

TULLIE, Thomas (c.1656–1727), Vicar of Newburn, Northumb., 1683; Preb. of Carlisle 1684; Chancellor 1685; Vicar of Crosthwaite, Cumb., 1710; Dean of Carlisle 1716–27.

TYLER, John (d. 1724); Preb. of Hereford 1688; Dean of Hereford 1690; Bishop of Llandaff 1706–24.

WAKE, William (1657–1737), Canon of Christ Church, Oxford, 1689–1702; Rector of St James's, Westminster, 1693–1706; Dean of Exeter 1703–5; Bishop of Lincoln 1705–16; Archbishop of Canterbury 1716–37. N. Sykes, *William Wake, Archbishop of Canterbury* (2 vols., Cambridge, 1957).

WAUGH, John (1655–1734), of Appleby, Westmld.; Fellow of Queen's College,

Oxford, 1688; Rector of St Peter's, Cornhill, 1704–34; Preb. of Lincoln 1718; Dean of Gloucester 1720; Bishop of Carlisle 1723–34.

WEYMOUTH, Thomas Thynne (1640–1714), 1st Viscount (1682); First Lord of Trade and Plantations 1702–7; PC 1702–7, 1712; Warden of the Forest of Dean 1712.

WHARTON, Thomas (1648–1715), 5th Baron (1696), 1st Earl (1706), and 1st Marquess (1715) of; also 1st Marquess of Catherlough [I] (1715); Comptroller of the Household 1689–1702; Lord-Lieut. of Oxon. 1697–1702, Bucks. 1702; Lord-Lieut. of Ireland 1708–10; Lord Privy Seal 1714–15; one of the five Lords of the Junto. J. Carswell, *The Old Cause; three biographical studies in Whiggism* (1954).

WILLIAMS, John (?1636–1709), Preb. of St Paul's 1683–96, of Canterbury 1692–6; Bishop of Chichester 1696–1709.

WILSON, Daniel (1680–1754), of Dallam Tower, Westmld.; MP for Westmld. 1708–22, 1727–47; nephew of Sir William and Michael Fleming, q.v., whose support he had for his election in 1708 and 1710. Sedgwick, ii, 548.

WINCHESTER, Charles Paulet (1685–1754), courtesy title Marquess of (1699–1722), later 3rd Duke of Bolton (1722); MP for Lymington 1705–8, Hants. 1708–10, Carmarthenshire 1715–17; cr. Baron Pawlet of Basing (1717).

WINCHILSEA, Charles Finch (1672–1712), 4th Earl (1689) of; Lieut.-Governor of Dover Castle and Deputy Warden of the Cinque Ports 1702–5; Envoy Extraordinary to Hanover 1702–3; Lord-Lieut. of Kent 1704–5; First Lord of Trade and Plantations 1711–12.

WOODSTOCK, Viscount, *see* PORTLAND, 2nd Earl of.

WRIGHT, Sir Nathan (1654–1721), Serjeant-at-law 1692; King's Serjeant and Kt 1697; Lord Keeper 1700–5.

WYNNE, John (1667–1743), Chaplain to Earl of Pembroke; Lady Margaret Professor of Divinity, Oxford, 1705–15; Principal of Jesus College, Oxford, 1712–20; Bishop of St Asaph 1715–27, of Bath and Wells, 1727–43.

YOUNGER, John (d. 1728), Preb. of St Paul's 1693–1728; 2nd Keeper of the Bodleian Library; Deputy Clerk of the Closet to Queen Anne and to King George I; Preb. of Salisbury 1680, of Canterbury 1685–92; Dean of Salisbury 1705–28; related by marriage to the Grahme family, q.v.

Appendix B

Nicolson's 'Note Book' of antiquarian visits,
4 January–12 February 1712

Bodl. MS Gen. Top. c.27/1 (Bishop Nicolson's Manuscript Collections), ff. 4–6,
8–11.

1711–12.

Jan[uary] 4.
Friday. Paying a Visit this morning (among others) to the Honourable Mr Archibald Campbel, he shewed me, in his most numerous collection of Scottish writers, the following Rarities:

1. *Conaeus de Duplici statu*, &c. which, in all the Copies he ever saw (save one) wants two Leaves, from p. 146 to 151. These he lately got transcribed at Edinburgh; so fine, as hardly to be distinguished from the print. He gave me a Transcript; which is in my Book.

2. The like want, he saies, is in David Chambre's Life of Queen Mary: But he has not that book. Qu[ery?]

3. *The Printed Acts of the Parliament of Scotland* (mostly rescinded by O. Cromwell, &c.) from 1633 to 1649 inclusive. Fol.

4. *Descrettione del Regno di Scotia*, &c. di Petruccio Ubaldini Cittadin Florentino. Fol. Anvers. 1588.

5. The two Editions of H. Boethius, both at Paris, 1520. 1574. The latter has the Preface to James 5 and the 18th and 19th Books; which are wanting in the former.

6. G. Buchanan's *History*. 1st Edition. Fol. Edinburgh (by Arburthnet, a fair Character) 1582.

7. *Altare Damascenum*, by D. Claderwood. 4°. 1623 with his Recantation, 4°. London 1622. The latter was the late Earl of Lauderdale's; who gave it to him, with Assurance that the Altare was really printed (by the Presbyterian Faction) a year after the Recantation.

8. Sir David Lindesay's *Satyre of the thrie Estaits*. 4°. Edinburgh 1602. 'Twas penned before the Reformation, to which it is said to have much contributed; being handed about in MS. and severely lashing the Vices of the Popish Clergy.

9. Jo. Wemius de Craigtoune, *de Regis Suprematu*. 4°. Edinburgh 1623. Much commended by my friend.

10. Nicol Burn's *Disputation against the Kirk*. i. the Reformers. Scottish. 8°. Par[is] 1581. Some of Beza's lewd poems are translated in such a manner, as to double the Charge (of Sodomy, &c.) which others have picked out of the Original.

This learned and curious Gentleman shewed me also his rich Cabines of Scotch Coins; wherein were Duplicates of (what Lord Pembroke wants) the Gold of Ja[mes] 2. He has more of Ja[mes] 3 and wants the One-Drop-Bonnet (in the Bishop of Sarum's hand) of Ja[mes] 5. Never saw the Square-Armed Crownpiece of Ja[mes] 6 after his Accession to England; but has the Half Crown, which I want.

Returning home, I met with Mr Robert Sanderson; who brought me a Note of Pro Dec. et Cap. Karliol. Pat. 33. Hen. 8. p. 9 m. 17. (May, 8) et Ibid. m. 34 (May, 6) Qu[ery?]. He also gave me a brass Medal of Severus, with the Style of Brittannicus; but the Reverse is different from that which we had in the late learned Dr Batteley's *Antiqq[uitates] Rutup[inae]*.

January 17. 1711/12.
On Appointment, I accompanyed the Bishop of Litchfield to Dr Sloan's; where the most noble library and Museum (of Books and Matters relating to Natural History) that I ever saw. Some Thousands of Serpents, Lizards, Insects, Plants, &c. of a finer sort are preserved in Spirits of Wine, or set in Frames covered with Glasses. The collection indeed, since the Accession of the whole Stores of the late Mr Charlton's Rarities of all kinds and Mr Dendridge's Insects, Dr Plukenets' dryed Plants, &c. is wonderful. What, in a Transient View of four large Rooms crammed with so much variety, I took notice of was:
1. Earths, of many different Colours and Consistencies; Amongst which a Sureing Green Sand from China, of the like grain with the Black sent from Virginia.
2. Metals, from all the Mines of England, and Foreign Countreys, in great plenty. Here I saw—1. A red Iron-Ore from Gloucestershire; which resembled what Dr W[oodward] once gave me for Native Cinnaber. 2. Several branches of a sort of stringy Copper-Ore; which some Naturalists will have to be Native-Copper, as they call it.
3. Formed and Precious Stones, in many large Cabinets; which are of different Richness, according to the different value of their several Contents. As, 1. Cups and other small Vessels of the finest Chrystals, Agates, Blood-stones, Cornelians and the like. 2. Varieties of all these, unpolished and in their Original State; as a Lump of Chrystal of betwixt seven and eight pounds weight, another with a bunch of Grass embodyed in it, a Round Agate of Twelve or Fourteen Inches in Circumference, a Blood-stone of the same Figure and not much less in Bulk, &c. 3. Great variety of Fossil-Coral: To which Tribe belongs the Brainstone of Jamaica, which grows up from seed; (as appears from a Specimen encircling a Spanish piece of eight;) as also the Stalamites, from Iron-Mines, dropping into a Corallin form 4 Two Bottles grown over with White Coral; haveing laid some time in the Sea, in the mouth of the Harbour of Port-Royal in Jamaica. 5. The Siliquastru . . . of Mr E Lhuyd; plainly proved to be a Splinter of the Tongue of a Pastinaca Marina.
4. Insects. Besides the vast number of Butterflies, from all Countries, curiously preserved by Mr Charlton, the Dr has infinite stores of that and other kinds as neatly secured by Mr Dendridge; as Beetles, Spiders, Flyes, Grasshoppers, &c. as well Foreign as British. 2. He also shewed me the Nest of Ants in Jamaica and the neighbouring Islands, which resemble those of our Bumble-Bees; but are built in Trees, to avoid the Floods which are usual at the time of their Breeding.
5. Plants and Fruits. Besides his own vast Collection of Dryed plants, he has all the stock of Dr Plukenet lately deceased. Several tender ones, and those of greatest Rarity, are bottled up in fair Christal-glasses; filled with Spirit of Wine. Together with Samples of all Common Drugs, he has a large Cabinet of those of China; whence he has also procured a Specimen of Father Le Compte's strange plant of that Countrey, which bears seed on the utmost extremities of its Leaves. [This should be the 4th Title; before that of Insects]
6. Serpents. All the kinds of these, from the Rattle-snake to the smallest

Sloe-worm, are preserved in Spirit of Wine; as are likewise very great varieties of Lizards, Salamanders, Frogs and Toads. Amongst the last, the most Considerable is the Bufo Dorsifera; which bears its young in small Kirnels (or Tubera) on its back, that drop off as they ripen and are able to shift for themselves. The Winged Salamander, which occasioned the Legendary Stories we have of Dragons, is of several sorts.

7. Quadrupedes. Whatever is most remarkable in the rarest kinds of these; As, Horns of all Sorts of Deer, from that of the Bufflar to the Dwarf-kind of Guinnea; A Hoof of the Sus Solidungulus of Pliny, bought in St James's market, whither it comes from Essex, where there is still a Breed of 'em; the Paw of the monstrous Sea-Bear; plenty of Land and Sea-Tortoises; Skins of wild Beasts; &c.

8. Marine Bodies, innumerable. Among which—1. The true shell of the Bucardites, with a doubly prominent head and globular body. 2. The Concha Anomia; which appeared to me to be rather a River-shell than the Product of the Sea, being thin and transparent. 3. Reading-Oysters, unpetrifyed; in a Bed, at the depth of 30 foot. 4. The Orbis Muricatus; with upper and Nether Milstone, in its Jawes, for grinding (its ordinary Food) small crabs and other Shell-fish. 5. Vastly large Turbinated Shells, Concha Veneris, &c.

9. Fowl; with their finest parts, in the Colour of their Feathers, shape of their Beaks, Extraordinary length or shortness of their Legs, and the like. The Red-Bird of the East Indies, with the Tail-feathers whereof the Greatest princes adorn their Helmets, is both stuffed and preserved in Sp[irit] of Wine. Two Cornish Choughs (with their Red, crooked, Bills) were feeding in a Cage: But these my Companion and worthy Brother (the Bishop of Litchfield) would not allow to be Rarities, affirming that they breed in the Walls of the Church and Castle at Windsor.

In his Library there are 110 large Folio-Volumes of dryed plants; Severn (of the like) of paints in water colours of plants, Beasts, Fishes, Habits of men and women, &c. the most exact and to the Life; Five (one in Folio the rest in 4°.) of, the Great Sorbon-Dr, W. Postel's MS. work, bought by O. Cromwel for 100 *l.* and by Dr S[loan] for 5 Guinneas.

February 5. 1711–12.
By appointment, I waited on (my worthy friend) Archibald Campbell Esqr. who shewed me a choice set of Teapots, Dishes, Sugar-Cask (with Skrews) and plates, of the German Serpentine Stone; and kindly presented me with a pair of Salts of Scotch Marble of almost the very same colour with his Tea-Dishes. He accompanyed me to Mr Kemp's in his Neighbourhood; where (for about three hours) I was most supprizingly entertained with the View of a Collection of Statues, Altars, Inscriptions, Medals, &c. too valuable for a Subject to keep, in his own private possession. What, in so little time and so great Variety, was most especially observed by me, was—

1. Two large and entire Mummies probably guessed (by the figures on their Antique Cases) to be of a Man and Woman; with their Teeth fair, the Bandishes on the Female very fair and (on that of the Male) some Hieroglyphicks. Mr Green, in his *History of Enbalming*, had given the Draughts of these [p. 294. 295.]

2. Amongst his Innumerable Collection of Roman, Greek, Jewish, and Egyptian, Lamps, Vessels, Urns, Lares, &c. (the Spoils of the late famous Musea of Dr Spon, Lord Carteret, Earl of Peterborough, &c). I took notice of—1. The owner's fancy in inscribeing his chief Repository with this Motto: *Sic sitis*

Laribus laetor: Vyeing with the — *Sic Siti laetantur Lares* of the Duke of Buckingham; who attempted the purchase of these same Lares, but was out bid by Mr Kemp. 2. A brazon Osiris, with Horns (on a Human Visage) with a Whip in one hand, &c. 3. The Goddess Isis, with her Son Ormus in her Lap, of the same metal. 4. Jupiter of several kinds, Mars, Mercury, Hercules, &c. of the like. 5. A naked woman lying prostrate, giving suck to one Child and looking over her sholder at another (behind her) crying and picking a Thorn out of its great Toe; a piece, for its inimitable variety of postures, much admired by the Statuaries. 6. An old Saxon in Armour; with an Helmet, haveing its Crown raised Tapering and ending in the Shape of a Hawk's head; a Fashion probably supposed to have given Original to the Use of Crests in Armory.

3. Amongst his Roman Busts of several Emperours and Empresses, with other statues in fine Marble: 1. A priapus, with the penis erect: very different from— 2. Baal. Peor, who is cutting off his own Pudenda; but has a Bunch of a dozen penes growing out of his Side and hanging on his left Shoulder; all circumcised. For this, the Duke of Bucks offered the Owner 100 *l.* 3. On a Sepulcharal Monument for a Child dyeing at three years of Age, 'tis said *Frumentum accepit die* X°. Qu[ery?]. 4. One of his Greek Inscriptions is in memory of Antinous's priest. 5. Another (by the smalnes of the [illegible] in the middle of several words, all cut in large Unical Letters) supposed to be older than the Time of Alexander the Great. 6. Many other Remarkable Heads of Cicero, Aristotle, Harpocrates (with his finger on his lips) Philip of Macedon, Alexander, &c.

4. In his Cabinet of Urns, Lachrymatories, &c.—1. Several, of both these, in Glass. 2. A large Family-Urn of Lead. 3. An Iron-Helmet; very Thin, with fair figures of the very same kind with those on Dr Woodward's Shield. Mr Kemp is of Opinion (with me) that neither of these are Roman; it being unconceiveable how any thing of this Metal, so slender, should have been preserved for so many Ages; either in the Earth, or open Air. He convinced me that the whole was wrought with the Hammer, and not Cast in a Mould; there being a Ring of Wire round the Outer Rim, over which the Helmet was plated, and the Substance more tough than any Cast-Metals (Iron especially) can ever be wrougt. 4. Roman Ballances; whereof the Just ones fine and nice, but the false had one End of the Beam longer than the other. 5. Multitudes of antient Fibulae, Seals and Rings; amongst which several Wedding-Rings of the Romans, with Keys and the Posies; Severus's Bull, of the like Shape with those of the Modern Popes; Egyptian Seals (I rather think 'em Amulets) with Coptic Inscriptions, cut on short cylindrical Bloodstones or Haematites. 6. The Talisman of a Mouse, found in a Roman Lamp; which Mr K[emp] thinks a sure proof of their putting out their Lamps before the Oil was quite spent: The Design of throwing in this Supertitious Figure being to preserve the Remaining Oil from being eaten up by Mice.

5. A curious Cabinet for a Lady's Dressing-Room, richly adorned with Topasses and other Gemms on the Drawers made in the same round Figure with Sir Samual Morland's Moveing Cylinder shewn me by my Lord of Canterbury: And, in one of its Valves, haveing the figure of a Nun in Amber, which (in several perspectives of looking-glass) is surprizeingly multiplyed.

6. His first Silver-Medals are in twenty Cards; each whereof carries 35 pieces, in all 700. These are all Roman; and the first Card has onely such whose Reverses have the Portraitures of their various Deities. The second begins at Pompey, Julius Caesar, &c. and the rest continue to succession of the Emperours down to Heraclius; of each whereof he has as many Reverses (to the Number of 14 or 15 in some) as are most Rare or Curious. I particularly took notice of—

1. That of Augustus Caesar and Marcus Antonius: face to face. 2. Severus Brit. and on the Reverse Victoria Brit. 3. Commodus Brit. with several Reverses. 4. Varieties of Tetrici, Victorini and Posthumi; all silvered over. 5. Several of Carausius's pieces and Allectus's of the like kind with the last mentioned; some of the former pure silver, but none of the latter. 6. A consecration-piece of the Constantine the Great.

7. Another Set of silver-coins, of the same size (that of Denarius) with the former, consisting of Ten Cards; each of which carries 24 pieces. Here we have the fairest coins and finest faces (Roman, Carthaginian, &c.) from Romulus to Heraclius; amongst which are about 240 of the nicest portaictures of Heads and Faces that are to be seen on Metal. An Attyla R. Goth. In Silver; purchased at the price of four Guinnees: a Carthaginian, with AΘPΘ very valuable: &c.

8. Twenty Cards of the antient Brass Medals; majoris et medij moduli. In Each of these there are 35 pieces. Amongst the Larger, were — 1. One of Julius Caesar; which haveing a △ upon it was supposed (by Col. Finch) to intimate that this Emperour had entered on his fourth year, before he was stabbed: But Mr Wanley rightly observed that Julius, haveing here the Title of *Divus*, must have been dead before this Medal was struck; and he therefore rather believed that the △ betokened its being struck (in memory of him) by Augustus; in the 4th year of his Reign. 2. A Paduam Otho; no true one, of this size, being ever met with: But, of the Middle Size, Mr Kemp has a Genuine brazen Otho (much fairer than Lord Pembroke's) and Col. Finch another. The larger Egyptian Otho, in Brass, is reckoned no great Rarity. 3. A very fair Commodus Brit. with Victoria Brit. on the Reverse. 4. One of Caracalla, and another of his brother Geta, with Brit. on the Face-side; and Victoria Brit. on the Reverse. 5. Four Gordians. 6. Series of Heads down to Postumus Junior. 7. A most fair Vitellius. 8. Another (most valuable) of Titiana ΣEB.

9. In other Drawers he shewed us the Roman As, with all its parts; the Egyptian and Jewish Shekel [which, saies the Bishop of Peterborough, signifies a Stone; as Selah is a rock] with several Species of Parthian, Phoenician, Persian and Turkish money (antient) in Brass; amongst which one of Mahomet the First, and another of Saladine, very rare.

10. Two Sets of Nur Mahal's Twelve Zodiac Medals (in Gold and Silver) mentioned by Tavernier in his *Travels*. Par. 2. p. 11.

11. Other large medalions is Silver; of Marcus Anthonius, Cambyses another other Great Princes of the old Greek and Romans.

On a Second View of Dr Sloan's Museum (on *Tuesday*, Feb. 12. with Mr Morton) I was much pleased with—1. The Nautilites of all sizes, some as big as the largest Nautilus (and of the very same shape) that are brought from the East Indies: All on 'em haveing rich politures of the Mother of Pearl, and one being of the Umbilicated kind. These were lately found in the Gravel-pits near Richmond in Surrey. The Dr gave me a Nucleus of one of them. 2. A small (Flat and Dusky-coloured) Cornu Ammonis; one Specimen whereof was also presented to me. 3. Great Varieties of the Tellinae, or Rasor-Fish, from the East. 4. Nephritic Stones, from the same, of Various kinds finely polished; but Greasy to the Touch. 5. Florentine Marbles, Flat and well polished, with fair Representations of Towers, Towns, Churches, &c. 6. Escara Marina; a Mass of Sea-Tubera, somewhat like the Conchae Auriculares of Dr Plott. 7. An Indian Birds-nest; made by a Convolution of a Single (Conical) Palm-Leafe, the Edges of the Leaf (at the bottome of the Nest) being closed by some glutinous Matter. 8. Eggs, of Birds and other Oviparous Animals; amongst which, that of the Crocodile

Cylingdrical and of the Tortoise exactly Globular, the Cassowars of a dark Green colour, &c. 9. The Armadilla, or Sea-Urchin of the Indies, with fine (and most beautiful) clasps of Armour, all over its body and sharp-pointed tail, with Helmet on its Head, and the like Furniture Cap-a-pee. 10. Opercula of various kinds of Sea Snails. A small one given me. 11. Buccina Heterostropha, both Marine and Fossil. A Specimen of the former given me by the Dr as, of the Latter, heretofore by Mr Morton. 12. The Gowries, or bunch-backed Conchae Veneris, current money in many Countries on the African Coast. 13. A pair of Oyster-shells of 90 *l*. weight, from the Coast of China; fellows to those in the King of Denmark's Museum. 14. Bracelets, Amulets, Elf-Arrows of Flint and Agats, &c. of diverse nations. 15. A Cabinet of Chinese Utensils, of several sorts; As, paper of many kinds, Ink Red and Black, Clue of Cotton-Yarn, &c. 16. One of the first Books printed at Harlem. 'Tis in Low-Dutch; and bears the Title of *Het Spiegel unsere behoudenes*. Each half is made up of two, pasted together; the Art of printing on both sides, of the same, being not then discovered.

Lord Chancellor Cowper's Notes on his meeting
with the bishops on 23 March 1717

Hertfordshire RO Panshanger MS D/EP. F131, f. 11.
Note: This document has been damaged by a large blot which has rendered parts of it illegible. Passages partly or totally obscured are enclosed in angle brackets ⟨ ⟩.

(1)

Lincoln	Saru[m]
Carlisle	Bangor
Exeter	
St Asaph	
Gloc[este]r	

C[hancello]r—that not having same oportunitys to come to their Bench, &c. or visit them, as oth[ers] of the Min[istry] had, He coveted this opor[tunity] of conferring with 'em on a Sub[ject] in which the Church think themselves p[ar]tic[ularl]y concerned.

—that for his own part He alwais opposed the B[ill] ag[ains]t Occ[asional] Conf[ormity] Exc[ep]t when it passed, with others He acquisced, solely fro[m] necessity bec[ause] it would certainly have passed, though opposed, and by not opposing it 2 good clauses wer got into it, &c . . .

—that if it came to voting; He would ther[fore to be] consist[en]t with his Constant opin[ion] giv[e] his vote for the Repeal. But as to the prud[ent] point, if *now* to be brought into Parl[iament]; He thought it turned on the *good* B[isho]ps being united or Divided.

—that He was glad to fine *ev[er]y one* he[?] had spok[e] to, of op[inion] that if the greater p[ar]t of the Honest B[ishop]s wer[e] ag[ains]t it, it would not be adviseable to bring it in.

2

—that as He bef[ore] hinted He *knew* nothing of the B[ishop]s opin[ion]: But *now* found it admitted by those who wer[e] *for* as well as *thos* ag[ains]t the Bill that the great number of the Bish[ops] would oppose it.

—that He had heard and bel[ieve]d that the K[ing] had set his heart on passing it; but Since He could not Speak to the K[ing] with so much freedo[m], as others on Subj[ects] of any nicety; their L[ordshi]ps would hav[e] that on bett[er] auth[orit]y fro[m] other; if they had not it allready. Things being in this Scit[uation] He thought it natural in the next place to consid[er] *if no exped[ien]t* could be found, to atteyn the same good end the K[ing] proposed to him self (*viz*) the uniting and strengthning the Prot[estant] interest, &c. and the making some publ[ic] acknowl[edgemen]t to the Dissent[er]s who had been faithfull to the K[ing] to a man.

—that He had this morn[ing] heard fro[m] good Hands (and bel[ieve]d the B[ishop] of S[arum] had too) that his M[ajesty] *most earnestly hoped* ev[er]y one of their ⟨Lordships⟩ would ⟨seriously apply them ⟩ to find ⟨such equivalents which they⟩ could ⟨agree in⟩. (He ⟨could not ⟩ be sure ⟨thes⟩ wer just his

M[ajesty]'s words; bec[ause] He was attending the busin[ess] of the Hous[e],
when told to him, but was sure they wer⟨ ⟩thir stronger words)

3

—that it did not become Him to propose any thing to their L[ordshi]ps, but
hoped some of the[m] would mention somthing of that kind to be considered
and spoke to at that time—

That he beleived if [the] s[ai]d Bill or an Equiv[alen]t was passed, it would
help the Parl[iamen]t—Elec[tion]s—but hoped it would not solely be relyed
on (Here he pr[odu]cd a short digression concerning the Corp[oration] Bill).

But then He desired to call back their thoughts to the Subj[ec]t in hand,
which was to consider of an Equiv[alent] in which they might beter agree.

Th[a]t He could not prop[er]ly leave this Subj[ect] till he had menti[o]ned
what they all no doubt, had heard that ther ⟨had⟩ been a meetin[g] of ⟨some
memb[ers] of⟩ that H[ouse] of Com[mons] on ⟨this subj[ect] an account⟩ of
which ⟨something

⟩ agreed ⟨

[five lines obliterated]

maner ⟨ ⟩ they ⟨thoug⟩ht fit.

4

of the H[ouse] of Com[mons]: to consid[er] if should be brought in.

that tho' the acc[oun]ts of *this* meeting a little differed, yet agreed in this
that much great part wer zealous for it.

that the Min[istr]y he Supposed, did not choose this Method; But that if the
Gentl[eme]n did ther was no hindring 'em.

that tho' this at one View might seem to postpone the cons[ideratio]n of an
Equiv[alent] till the success of the next meeting seen, yet in anoth[er] View, it
hastned, the consid[eratio]n of an Equiv[alent] since if one found, it might
taking air stop the proceeding to bring in the other Bill; which probably would
be the issue if no Equiv[alent] found.

5

The B[ishop] of S[arum] asked, How it appeared the greater part of the
B[ishop]s wer ag[ains]t the Bill, if any meeting, &c. [?]

The Chanc[ello]r interupted fro[m] answering by the Bish[op] beginning to
argue for[thrig]ht on the Subj[ect] of the intended Bill, &c.

On the whole Divided in opin[ion] as in the begin[nin]g of this paper—and
as to equiv[alen]t that the abrogating the Sacr[amental] Test had as to Religion
fewer or no obj[ectors] Doubtfull if could susteyn it.

St Asaph s[ai]d noth[ing].

Lincoln—should be restreyned.

Extracts from Nicolson's Account Book for 1706

Tullie House Library, Carlisle.

(1) Money received by my own hand since Jan. 1. 1705/6

		£	s.	d.
Jan. 26	From P. Gibson on Brother John's Bill	100	0	0
28	Brother Joseph the Remainder of Lincoln-shire Fines	25	0	0
Feb. 14	Lease of Newburn	90	0	0
Mar. 18	Mr Whitingdale's Institution to Sowerby	1	6	0
Apr. 3	Linstock Farmers	29	10	0
8	Thomas Head's Winterage	0	15	0
11	Sir R. Musgrave's Fines	40	0	0
12	Mr Thomlinson rep[ai]d	20	0	0
May 16	Ed[ward] Nicolson of Emont-Bridge	4	0	0
Jul. 5	Thomas Dalton of Brunstock, p[ar]t of Linstock	4	10	0
Aug. 6	Fine for Stockdale Q[arte]r of Ry-Parks Lives	20	0	0
8	Farmers of Linstock (Tho. Dalton behind)	30	10	0
Sep. 10	Ned, for 12 Crocks	1	10	0
Oct. 7	Thomas Gibson, Nine Hides	5	2	0
11	Mr Chanc[ello]r's Pension	6	0	0
	J. Nicols's old Horse	0	14	0
15	J. XXman for Skins	2	8	0
16	Wid[ow] Harrison, Hides	2	5	0
	Brother John's Welton-Rent	1	0	0
	Widow Porter's Fine	2	0	0
28	W. Wood's Customary Fine, at Aspatrick	1	13	6
Nov. 4	Mr Patteson's House	5	0	0
	Mr Green's two Leases	19	0	0
14	Archdeacon Pearson's Ballance of Brother John's account paid by me	9	15	0
Dec. 7	On Mr Ireland's Bill upon Mr Lee	30	0	0
		451	8	6

[recte 451 18 6]

APPENDIX D

(2) Hay, 1706.

First-Flatt (10 Acres, and this year 20 good Dayes work) richly manured the last Michaelmas, brought (instead of last years 32) 96 large Cart-loads of excellent Hay.

Stony-Holm (9 Days work) had 36 for last year's 21.

Kiln-Meadow (24 D[ays] work) had 68 for last year's 59.

Short-Lands (24 D[ays] W[ork]) had 77 for last year's 38.

Broad-Meadow (12 D[ays] W[ork]) 33 for 28 [least Difference being a Spungy Ground.] [1]

Cart-Loads in all

This year	280
Last	177
Difference	103

	£	s.	d.
280 at 5s. per Load make	70	00	00
Ded[uct] Costs more than value of Fogg	10	00	00
Qu[it] Loads — 310 infra	60	00	00

[1] Nicolson's brackets.

(3) Cattle at Rose, Nov. 6 1706.

1.	Two Bulls and 17 Cowes	19
2.	Old Oxen	3
3.	Twinter-stots	2
4.	Yearling-stots	3
5.	Twinter-whyes	5
6.	— Yearlings	2
7.	Fatling, two bought the last year, and six this, in all	8
8.	Calves, bred this year	18
	In all	60

Sheep	
Old Stock, with product of this year	106
Fat Weathers	18
Bought at Appleby 72 of which eleven are dead	61
	185

Mem[orandum] Greyson owes for an old Cow and 25 Crocks.

(4) My wife's Weekly Bills for half year beg[inning] with October 1705 and ending with March 1706.

		£	s.	d.
Oct. 5		1	8	10
12		3	11	2
19		1	19	3
26		0	15	5
Nov. 2	(£1 2s. wear)	2	14	11
9		3	3	10
16		1	10	9
23		1	6	7
30		0	9	7
Dec. 7		2	16	8
14		3	2	7
21		1	0	8
28		1	2	8
Jan. 4		1	18	1
11		1	3	1
18	(malt, £4)	4	11	10
25		3	11	10
Feb. 1		2	4	7
8		0	17	0
15	(Shoes, £2 4s.)	3	18	7
22		1	7	3
Mar. 1		1	16	7
8	(malt £4)	5	9	7
15		1	1	8
22	(mercer £3)	4	16	9
29		4	4	2
		64	3	8

NB. The Bills of these 6 months are near £15 higher than those in my absence the winter before; the Extraordinaries being in Duties on malt, mercer's Goods and Coals.

(5) My Brother Joseph's Accounts for March 25 1707.

	£	s.	d.
Rents received by him in London are usually	199	00	00
Add, An Odd half year's Rent then due from Mr Hewer	046	05	00
In all	245	05	00
Deduct			
Tenths and Fees	160	18	02
Allowed to himself	005	00	00
Dyer's Letter	004	12	00
Duke of Beaufort's and Mr Coke's present Taxes	017	04	00
makes	187	14	02

Rests, for Extraordinaries either on Account
    or to be returned to Oxford, &c.   057 10 10

March 4 1705/6. On stateing private Accounts
    with my brother Joseph, I stood then in
    debted to him   43 02 01

From which deduct the Ballance of his last
    Account sent May 4 1706   17 04 00

                           Rests   25 18 01

Memorandum. he charges the said Ballance in his
Accounts of July 28 1707 so that the whole   £43 02 01
still due to him.
Saveing his present Ballance of   18 09 04

                         Rests   24 12 09

(6) Hay, 1706

	£	s.	d.
Loads 310 at 5s. per Load makes	77	10	00
Deduct Costs more than Fogg.	10	0	0
Rests	67	10	0
Bad year, Loads 177 at 5s.	44	5	0
Deduct as above	10	0	0
Rests	34	5	5
Middle	50	17	6

(7) Coach-Hire in London this winter 1705/6.

	£	s.	d.
October	1	0	0
November	2	18	0
December	2	14	6
January	2	9	0
February	2	11	6
March	0	18	6
	12	11	6

Less than the foregoing 1 8 6.

(8) [Expenditure for 1706.]

January 1705/6.

1.	Coach, 3s. 6d. Brother's 3s.	0	6	6
	Su[san] Orfeur and Jo[seph] Rothery	0	15	0
2.	Coach, 5s. 6d. Mr Grand[orge] ½ [Crown?]	0	8	0
3.	Coach, 1s. Oars, 6d.	0	1	6
	Burnet's Memoirs, &c.	0	8	6
	Mrs Hallet's maid, New Year's Gift	0	2	6
4.	S. Boyes, of the Queen's Chapple	0	5	0
	Post-man's New Year's Gift	0	2	0
5.	Waterman, to and from Lambeth	0	1	6
6.	Coach, 1s. 6d. St Bride's, 2s. 6d.	0	4	0
7.	Mr King, Bookseller, for Cardinal Wolsey's Mem[oirs] and Nelson's Justice	0	10	0
	Coach to and from the Tower	0	5	0
	With Mr Madox, Holms and Dale	0	6	0
	Pamphlets	0	1	6
8.	With Mr Grascome, Mr Bell and Brother Joseph	0	4	6
	Coach, onely from Salisbury Court	0	1	6
9.	Mr King; for *Orygia*, Lives of King James and William Beaumont's Spirits	1	3	0
	James's weekly Bill	1	7	0
10.	Treating Dr Gibson	0	9	[0]
	To him, for	0	10	0
11.	Coach, 2s. 6d. Jet[ ] my Brother's	0	5	0
	pair of Garters presented	0	2	6
14.	Coach, 2s. 6d. pamphlets, 2s.	0	4	6
15.	Mr King, Art of Dying	0	4	0
	Binding	0	3	0
16.	At my Brother's (without Coach)	0	2	6
17.	Coffee, &c. with Mr G. Holmes	0	1	0
18.	Poor master Glaisters, mad	0	2	0
	Mrs Hallet, a month's Lodge[ings]	3	4	0
19.	Waterman, to and from Lambeth	0	1	6
20.	Coach to and from the Savoy	0	2	0
21.	Treating Mr Grandorge	0	8	0
	James's two weeks, Bills	2	8	0
	Coach, Dr Hicke's and Bishop of H[ereford's]	0	4	0
22.	Coach, to and from Lord Thanet's	0	3	0
23.	Rudbeckius's Essay	0	4	0
	Coach, 1s. 6d. Mr Bell, 3s. 6d.	0	5	0
24.	Treating Dr Waugh, Dinner	0	6	0
25.	Coach, 2s. 6d. Brother Joseph's 2s. 6d.	0	5	0
26.	Pamphlets	0	1	6
27.	Coach (Hire and procurer)	0	2	0
28.	James's weekly Bill	1	8	0
	Mr King, for Books	0	19	3
	Mr Willymot's Criticisms	0	3	8
	Coach, 2s. 6d. Brother Joseph's 1s. 6d.	0	4	0

29.	Coach, to Mr C. Musgrave and St James's	0	1	6
	Brown's Entries to Mr King	0	4	0
30.	Westminster-Boyes	0	5	0
	Coach, to and from Mr C. Musgrave	0	2	6
	Barber, in this month	0	4	0
31.	Coach, 4s. 6d. Pamphlets	0	5	0
	In all	20	9	5
	[recte	20	7	5]

February

1.	Treating (at Dinner) Dr G[ibson]	0	6	6
	Coach, 2s. 6d. Dr Hutton, Mr Dale, Mr Hare, and It[ ]	0	5	0
2.	Lambeth, vijs et modis	0	5	0
	Joseph Rothery, for Oxford	2	0	0
	Coach, 3s. Brothers 1s.	0	4	0
3.	Coach (Aldgate, &c.)	0	4	6
	Boyes at Christ's Hospital	0	5	6
4.	James's weekly Bill	1	5	0
	Globe, with Mr Hutchinson and Mr Bell	0	5	0
	Coach to and from Holburn	0	3	0
5.	Mr Buchanan, for the Prince's l[ette]r	3	4	6
	Books, bought at Moorfields	0	13	0
	Coach-Hire	0	4	6
6.	Yesternight's Treat	1	7	0
	Porter at Privy-Garden	0	1	0
7.	Mr King, for Monsieur Dungan	0	4	0
	Dean Graham's servants	0	3	6
	Coach-Hire	0	1	6
8.	Treat to Col. Nicolson and Dr K[ennett]	0	9	6
	Coach from Salisbury-Court	0	1	6
9.	Coach, 1s. J. Nicols, 10s.	0	11	6
10.	Coach, from Covent-Garden	0	1	0
11.	Young Mr Buch[anan] for J. Nicols	0	17	6
	Coach	0	2	6
	Dr Younger's servants	0	2	6
	Mr Davis, Singing-man	0	2	6
12.	James's last week's Bill	1	7	0
	Treating Dr Gibson	0	5	0
	A pamphlet	0	1	0
13.	Pontac's and Gresham-College	0	6	0
	Coach, 1s. 6d. Brother Joseph's 1s.	0	2	6
14.	Susan Orfeur, a 2d supply	1	0	0
	Mr King, for Books	1	1	6
15.	Jack Nicols	0	11	6
	Coach, 2s. Boat, 1s. 6d.	0	3	6
	Mr Le Neve's servant	0	2	6
16.	One month's Lodgeing	3	4	0
	Gloves and Buckles	0	7	6
17.	Taylor's Bill	2	7	0

17.	Mr C. M[usgrave]'s servants	0	5	0
18.	Taylor's Bill	2	7	0
	Coach, 2s. 6d. Sir W. B[owes?], &c. 3s.	0	5	6
19.	Coach-Hire	0	2	6
	Mr Madox's servants, &c.	0	3	0
20.	James's Bill and wayes	1	2	0
	Barber, Head and Beard	0	2	0
	Coach, 3s. Mr Gr[ascome] and Bell, 3s. 6d.	0	6	6
	Mr Bell, for Books	4	11	0
21.	Dinner, with Dr Gibson	0	5	0
22.	Dineing with Mr Lawson, &c.	0	3	6
	Coach to and from S[alisbury] Court	0	2	6
23.	Capt. Garret's New-year's Gift	0	5	0
	Coach, 3s. 6d. Mr Buttle, 2s. 6d.	0	6	0
	James's Weekly Bill	1	11	0
24.	Ja[mes]'s Bill for J. Nicols	8	6	6
	J. Nicols himself, at p[ar]ting	5	4	6
	Coach, to and from Colmanstreet	0	3	6
25.	Mr King, a Bill of	2	4	0
	Sir A. F[ountaine] for Mediobarbas	2	0	0
	Treating Mr Dale	0	8	0
	Coach, 2s. 6d. Brother's the like	0	5	0
26.	Condoleance with Mr L[owther]'s Agent	0	7	0
27.	Mr C. M[usgrave]'s Account and Inter[es]t	85	0	0
	Coach, to and from Swallowstreet	0	2	0
	Watermen, 1s. 6d. Coach, 1s.	0	2	6
	Sir W. Bowes and Philip Tullie	0	1	6
28.	Shoes and Slippers, £1 7s. 6d. ⎤			
	Spatter-dashes, 9s. 6d. Coffee, ⎥	3	15	9
	11s. 9d. Two Trunks, £1 6s. ⎦			
	Paper and Pocket-Book	0	7	6
	Porter and Messenger	0	1	6
		141	11	3
	[recte	142	9	9]

March

1.	Mal. Rothery	0	10	9
	Two pamphlets	0	2	0
	Scatter to Lambeth	0	0	6
	Coach, Charter-House, &c.	0	4	6
	Brother Joseph's Treat to Ladies	0	6	6
2.	J. Blamire's Horse	6	0	0
	Two more Trunks	1	2	0
	Saddle and other Furniture	4	3	0
3.	Brother Joseph's servants at parting	0	7	6
	Coach (Mr C. M[usgrave]'s 5s.)	0	6	6
4.	James's weekly Bill	2	8	0
	Mr Hallet, 3 weeks Lodgeing	2	8	0

	Coach, 5s 6d. Waterman, 2s. ⎤			
	Servants at Lambeth, 7s. 6d. ⎦	0	15	0
	Brother Joseph's Wine and Oysters	0	2	6
5.	Bills paid off, for Candles, 13s. 2d. ⎤			
	Washing, 11s. 1½d.	3	2	9
	Coals, £1 18s. 6d. ⎦			
	For the Horses, Feeding, Shoeing and Geer	2	14	6
	Mr King for Books	0	18	0
	Sent to Dr Gibson for Mr Lee	1	3	6
	Servants, &c. at takeing Horse	0	7	6
	Highgate with Brother Joseph and R. N[icolson]	0	5	0
	J. Blamire and Sleddale	0	10	0
[Nicolson left London on 5 March]				
6.	Dunstable	0	19	0
	Mr Wotton's servants	0	4	0
7.	Newport-Pagnel	1	10	6
	Brixworth, S. Bray, &c.	0	2	6
	Oxenden, Mr Morton's servant	0	1	0
8.	Harborough (6 Horses)	1	7	6
	Mount-Sorrel	0	2	6
	Glass-work at Nottingham	0	10	9
9.	Nottingham	1	3	6
	Clown	0	3	6
10.	To the Sexton, &c. at Rotheram	0	5	0
11.	Rotheram	2	10	6
	Mr Gill's servants at Carhouse	0	3	6
	Wakefield	0	6	0
12.	Leeds	1	14	0
	Hood and three Fanns	1	1	6
	Kirkby-Overblows, &c.	0	2	0
13.	Burrow-Bridge	1	11	0
	Salutation	0	10	6
14.	Greta-Bridge	1	2	0
	Burgh	0	8	6
15.	Appelby, Mr Bains's	1	7	6
	Mr Banks, for the Boyes	5	7	6
	Ringers, prisoners, Musick	0	10	0
	Servants Barber, &c.	0	4	6
	Servants, &c. in the road home	0	5	0
	Woodside	0	1	6
[Nicolson reached Rose on 15 March]				
16.	Carriage of two Trunks	2	5	6
	Newcastle for wine	1	5	6
	Mrs Miller's servants	0	1	0
	Carriage of the wine	0	1	6
21.	Haines, the Barber	0	2	6
22.	Good-friday, at Carlisle	0	11	6
23.	Carriage of 2 Trunks more	1	14	0
24.	Easter-day	0	5	6
26.	Mr Benson's Augmentation	2	0	0
	Jane Atkinson, from Crosby	0	1	0

27.	Bills and Hats for my Sons	5	5	0
28.	Scotch Mr Moor	0	2	0
29.	Rose XXman's Scholars	0	8	0
30.	Two Vagrants	0	1	6
		65	17	9

[April	Total of	20	14	2]
[May	non-London accounts.	30	8	0]
[June		26	0	6]
[July		16	5	3]
[August		33	16	1]
[September		6	3	0]
[October		10	18	10]

November

1.	R. Halton, dressing pistols	0	2	0
3.	Dr Law, a Fee for my self	1	3	6
6.	Brother John's, &c. congee	0	4	0
[Nicolson left for London on 7 November]				
7.	Rose and Salkeld	1	2	0
	Mr Banks, for the boyes	5	7	6
8.	Appleby, Boyes, servants Ringers, prisoners, Waites, &c.]	1	5	0
	Reckoning, to Mrs Baines	2	6	0
	Burrow-Bridge, Shott	0	15	0
	To my two Sons, left	0	10	0
10.	Ringers at Kendale	1	0	0
	Serjeants, poor and Servants	0	12	6
11.	Kendale-Waits in the morning	0	10	0
	Visits in the Afternoon	0	7	0
12.	Dr Archer's servants	1	2	6
	Sleddale, for Horses, &c.	0	5	0
	Kap-Knaves, Clapham and Settle	0	7	0
13.	Long-Preston	0	15	0
	Bingley, 4. Guides, 6s.	0	10	0
14.	Wakefield (6 Men and Horses)	1	7	6
15.	Blithe	0	15	0
	On the Road and Glassmen	0	2	6
16.	Nottingham	1	2	6
	Guide and Pilot	0	10	0
17.	Mr Mayor of L[eicester]'s Serjeant	0	2	6
18.	Leicester, Reckoning	2	3	6
	Harborough	0	2	6
19.	Northampton	1	16	0
	Stony-Stratford (Mr Wotton)	0	8	6

	Dunstable, Musick	0	3	0
20.	Reckoning at Dunstable	1	16	0
	Barnet, 6s. Fetter-lane, 4.	0	10	0
	Coach to Manchester-Court	0	1	6
[Nicolson arrived in London on 20 November]				
21.	Coach and water	0	3	6
	Paper, pens and Ink	0	5	0
	pair of Gloves	0	1	6
22.	Coach, 4s. Boat, 6d.	0	4	6
	Wine and Oysters at S[alisbury] C[ourt]	0	3	0
23.	To the Barber, Head shaved	0	2	0
	Boat, to and from Lambeth	0	1	6
	Coach, Kensington, &c.	0	6	0
24.	Mr C. M[usgrave]'s servants	0	2	6
	Coach	0	1	6
25.	John's Bill for Horses, &c.	2	3	6
	His week's Board-wages	0	7	0
	For his Charges home	2	3	0
	Mr G. Holmes, for Dalston-Rec[or]ds	1	5	6
	Coach, 2s. 6d. Mr Davis, the like	0	5	0
26.	Coach, to St Paul's	0	1	6
	Clergy-Feast	1	6	6
	Two pamphlets	0	1	0
27.	Mr Hallet's Maid	0	2	6
	Boat, to and from Lambeth	0	1	6
	Printed papers, &c.	0	1	0
28.	Coach, To and from the Tower	0	5	0
	Treating Mr Dale and Mr Holmes	0	11	0
	Messenger to Lambeth	0	0	6
29.	James's 2 several Bills	1	8	0
	printed-papers, &c.	0	1	0
	Pulvil for Teeth	0	1	0
	Oysters at S[alisbury] C[ourt] 1s. Coach, 1s. 6d.	0	2	6
30.	To the Barber	0	1	0
	Scotch Speeches, &c.	0	0	6
	In all	41	4	6

December

1.	Lambeth	0	4	6
2.	Almanack, Penknife, &c.	0	2	6
	Coach from Mr Musgrave's	0	1	0
3.	Barber	0	1	0
	Treating Mr Archdeacon Rogers	0	6	6
4.	Two printed papers	0	0	6
5.	To Dr Harris, Subscription	1	0	0
	Door-Keepers for last year and this	3	4	6
	Rachel, for Wood and Coals	1	12	6

6.	Mr Dale's Ordinary	0	8	0
	Oysters at S[alisbury] C[ourt]	0	1	0
	Coach, to and from	0	3	0
	James's weekly Bill	0	18	0
7.	Treating Dr Gibson and Mr Buttle	0	10	0
	To the Barber	0	1	0
8.	Coach, to and from S[alisbury] C[ourt]	0	2	6
	Sister Rothery, Arrears from wife	0	2	0
9.	Treating Mr Grandorge	0	7	0
10.	Mr Hanbury's Clerk at Entrance into Cotton-Library	0	5	0
11.	Watermen, to Dr Waugh's	0	1	0
	Prints	0	0	6
12.	Mr Elphinston, with a MS	0	2	6
	Coach, to and From Lord Thanet's	0	2	0
	Fleetwood's *Chron[icon] preciosu[m]*	0	3	6
13.	Dean of Salisbury's servant	0	2	6
	Coach to and from St Paul's	0	3	0
	James's weekly Bill	1	7	0
14.	Water, to the Bridge	0	1	0
	Coach, from Salisbury-C[ourt]	0	1	6
	Wine there, prints, &c.	0	2	6
15.	Coach	0	1	6
16.	Wine, at Salisbury-Court	0	1	6
	Coach, home	0	1	6
17.	Prints, &c.	0	2	6
18.	Given to S. Orfeur	0	10	0
	Treating Mr Hutchinson	0	6	0
19.	Lord of York's footman	0	2	6
	Soft wax, prints, &c.	0	1	0
	Mr Hallet, a month's Lodging	3	4	0
20.	Oysters and wine at S[alisbury] C[ourt]	0	2	6
	Coach home	0	1	6
21.	Treating Dr Gibson	0	5	6
	Pamphlets	0	1	6
22.		0	0	0
23.	James's last week's Bill	1	12	6
24.	Fr[ank] Briscoe, for J. Grainger	0	10	0
25.	Christmas-Boxes	0	6	0
	W. Tullie's servant	0	2	6
	Coach, to and from Red-L[ion] st.	0	2	0
26.	Lord of Canterbury's servants	0	12	6
27.	Cousin Richard Briscoe	0	5	0
	At my brother's	0	6	0
	Coach, to and from S[alisbury] Court	0	2	6
28.	Mr P. Tullie's servants	0	4	6
	With Mrs Bell and Buttle	0	5	0
	Coach, to and from Hatton-Garden	0	3	6
29.	Dr Lancaster's servant	0	2	6
30.	Coach, Bow-Church, &c.	0	5	0
	Mr C. M[usgrave]'s servant	0	2	6
	Pamphlets	0	1	6

31.	To the Bishop and Dean of St Asaph's servants	0	5	0
	Other Gifts	0	2	0
	Mrs Hancock, L[awn] Sleeves	3	18	0
		26	7	6

Index

Anne, Princess (*cont.*):
of Wales, elder sister of Princess
Caroline, 651, 653, ?658, 662, 679,
680
Anne, Queen, 38, 47, 48, 76, 80, 84,
86, 92, 98, 112, 118, 120, 123,
125, 126, 128–30, 132, 140, 142,
145, 147, 150, 153, 155, 156, 159,
161–4, 167, 169, 173, 176, 198,
200–3, 206–8, 210, 211, 214, 215,
221–3, 226, 227, 233, 238, 239,
244, 249, 250, 252–6, 262, 263,
267, 277, 281–8, 290, 292–4, 296,
298, 301–5, 307–17, 320, 324,
325, 328, 331–3, 338, 345, 355–7,
367, 373, 375, 379, 380, 382, 386–
90, 392, 394–7, 400–4, 406, 413–15,
417, 419, 420, 423, 424, 426, 429,
431, 434, 442, 448, 452, 454, 455,
458–64, 466, 469, 473, 482, 490,
500, 501, 506, 509–13, 516, 518,
519, 521, 523, 524, 527–32, 537,
542, 543, 545, 546, 548, 552, 554,
556–9, 562, 565, 566, 568, 573,
575, 578, 585, 587, 604, 607–9,
614
— courtiers of, 86
— ladies-in-waiting of, 86
Annesley, Catherine, 'a child', 579
Annesley, Francis, 423
Annesley, Maurice, appellant, 671, 676
Annesley, *see also* Anglesey, Countess of,
Earls of
Anstis (Ainstis), John, MP, 226, 537
Antiquaries, Society (College, Club) of,
480, 481, 548
Appian (Apianus), 318
Appleby, Westmld., 389, 430, 464,
470, 481, 508, 635, 707, 713,
714
— parliamentary borough, by-election,
420
Aragon (Arragon), 530
Archer, Dr, servants of, 714
Archer, John, brother-in-law of Diarist,
9, 14
Arches, Dean of, *see* Bettesworth,
John
Argyll (Argyl, Argyle), John Campbell,
2nd Duke [S] of, 50, 66, 73, 96–
97, 103, 316–17, 369, 454, 487,
488, 530, 531, 533, 536, 549, 550,
557, 566, 627, 647, 658, 671, 674,
685
Arlington, Henry Bennet, Earl of, 225,
375
Armagh, Archbishop of, *see* Boulter,

Hugh; Lindsay, Thomas; Ussher,
James
Arundel Library, 346
Arundell (Arundel), ?Francis, MP, 316,
340, 536
Arundell, ?Isabella (Wentworth), wife of
Francis, 316
Ascue, Mr, 633
Asgill (Asgil), John, 372
Ash, Simon, 647
Ashe (Ash), St George, Bishop of
Clogher, of Derry (1717), 619, 621,
646
Ashton, Charles, Dr, 183
Ashurst (Ashhurst), Sir Henry, 1st Bt,
301
Ashurst, Mr, 611
Aspatria (Aspatrick), Cumb., 706
Asheton (Ashton), Sir Ralph, 2nd Bt,
148
Association (Associations), 337
Atherton, John, Bishop of Waterford
and Lismore, 546
Atholl, John Murray, Duke [S] of
(1703), Earl of Tullibardine [S],
2nd Marquess [S] of (1703), 74,
98, 562, 685
Atkinson, Arthur, 424, 442–3, 534,
539
Atkinson, Jane, 713
Atkinson, John, Prebend of Carlisle, 428,
466
Atterbury, Bedingfield, nephew of Francis,
258
Atterbury, Francis, Dr, Dean of Carlisle (1704–11), Prolocutor of the
Lower House of the Convocation
of Canterbury (1710–13), Dean
of Christ Church, Oxford (1711–
13), Bishop of Rochester (1713),
'Pilot of Chelsea' 20, 21, 25, 26,
40, 46, 48, 67, 111, 117, 121,
128, 208, 210, 213, 214, 217,
219, 220, 222, 225, 230, 240, 242,
243, 258, 272, 274–7, 282, 293, 294,
302–4, 306, 307, 325, 328, 330, 331,
347, 348, 350, 357, 362, 364, 367–
8, 373, 389, 400, 401, 403, 404, 407,
409, 413, 422, 424, 428, 429–32,
437, 443, 445, 451, 455, 456, 458,
461, 465, 466, 468, 470, 479, 480,
483, 485, 499, 503, 505, 509, 510,
523, 535, 536, ?544, 547, 549, 550,
557, 564, 568, 588, 603, 606, 608,
612, 622, 627, 642, 676, 678, 681,
685
—friends of, 275

INDEX

Bell, ?Robert, Customer of Newcastle-upon-Tyne, Northumb., 117, 118, 136–7
Bell, Thomas, ?333, 371, 386, 397, 409, 488, 493, 523, 531, 536, 555, 564, 593, 597, 608, 610, ?611, ?620, 628, 711, 712, 716
Bellingham, Mrs, 665
Belwood, Mrs, 443
Bendish, Sarah, see Nicolson, Sarah
Benlowes, Mrs, 598
— young son of, 598
Bennet, Thomas, Dr, 649
Bennet, see also Arlington, Earl of
Benson, 'Brother' of Diarist, 626–30, 632–4, 639, 672
Benson, George, Captain, Major (1706), Lieutenant-Colonel (1706), 385, 402, 598, 625, 626, 628, 632, 633
Benson, Mary (Nicolson), daughter of Diarist, wife of Thomas, 9, 55, 604, 605
Benson, Mr, 628
Benson, Thomas, DD (1716), son-in-law of Diarist, 9, 16, 55, 56, 437–40, 444, 445, 447–9, 451, 454–6, 458, 460–2, 464, 466, 467, 477, 479, 482, 492, 604, 672, 713
Benson, William, Surveyor-General of Works, 77
Bentley (Bently), Richard, Dr, 17, 19, 198, 199, 298, 301, 420, 446, 459, 476, 499, 502, 549, 587
Bergavenny, Lord, see Abergavenny, Lord
Bergen op Zoom, 358
Berkeley (Berkley), Elizabeth (Noel) Berkeley, Countess of, wife of 2nd Earl, 501
Berkeley of Stratton, William Berkeley, 4th Lord, 181, 193, 445, 467, 685
Berkshire, Archdeacon of, see West, Richard
Berkshire, Henry Bowes Howard, 4th Earl of, 678, 686
Bernard, Charles, 414
Bernard, Francis, Dr, 199
Bernstorff or Bernsdorff, Andreas Gottlieb von, 641, 651
Bertie, Charles, MP, 241, 257
Bertie, see also Ancaster and Kesteven, Duke of
Berwick upon Tweed, Northumb., 255
Bethel, Slingsby, 295
Bettesworth (Beckwith, Betsworth), John, Dr, Dean of the Arches, 522, 533, 537, 540, 544, 546, 581, 587, 588, 612, 622
— wife of, 581, 588
Beveridge, William, Bishop of St Asaph (1704), uncle of Dean Stanley of St

Asaph, 30, 121, 208, 220, 221, 253, 260, 367, 404, 406, 415, 422, 423, 436, 437, 460, 686
— servants of, 717
Beverley, Robert, 373
Bewcastle, Cumb., 13
Bewley, Thomas, Minor (Petty) Canon of Carlisle, 240
Beza, Theodore, 698
Bideford (Biddiford), Devon, 596
Biggleswade (Bigglesworth), Beds., 117, 430, 503
Binckes (Binks), William, Dean of Lichfield, Prolocutor of the Lower House of the Convocation of Canterbury (1705–10), 45, 293, 299, 323, 372, 381, 426, 686
Bindon, Henry Howard, Earl of, Deputy Earl Marshal (1706–18), 398, 405, 406, 445, 448, 686
Bingley, Yorks., 714
Birch, Mrs, 613
Birch, Peter, Dr, 164, 483
Bircherod (Bircherodius), Johannes, 648, 649
Bircherod, Thomas Broder, 648
Bircherode, Mr, a Danish gentleman, 647–8
Bird, Os[ ], 266
Birkbeck, Catterick, 380, 384, 386
Bisse, Philip, Bishop of St David's, of Hereford (1713), 526, 565, 592, 593, 595, 597, 608, 610, 612
Bisset, Colonel, 'Spanish Officer', 448
Bisset, William, 547
Black, Mr, 417
Blackall (Blackhall), Offspring, Dr, Bishop of Exeter (1708), 301, 431, 440, 449, 478, 486, 488, 489, 525, 526, 543, 560, 595, 612, 640, 686
Blackburne (Blackburn), Lancelot, Dean of Exeter (1705–17), Bishop of (1717), 19, 35, 222, 437, 566, 567, 583, 652, 655, 656, 660, 664, 686, 704
Blackmore, Sir Richard, 221, 224
Black Rod, see Mitchell, Sir David; Oldes, Sir William
— room of, see Westminster, Palace of
Bladen, Martin, Colonel, MP, 646
Blair (Blaire), James, 330, 375
Blake, Henry, 675
Blamire, J., 712, 713
Bland, Sir John, MP, 402
Blecow, Mr, 494
Blencow, Cumb., school lands of, 241
Blencow, Mr, 617, 619, 620
Blencow, Mrs, 617
Blencowe (Blencoe), Sir John, Justice of

722